Ee Aye Addio - We've Won The Cup!

Liverpool in the F.A. Cup 1892 - 1993

BRIAN PEAD

with illustrations by Neil Cowland

Published by Champion Press

© Brian Pead (Text) 1993

© Neil Cowland (Pictures) 1993

ISBN 1-898058-00-8

Printed by Butler & Tanner, London and Frome

Distributed by Champion Press,
P.O. Box 284, Sidcup, Kent DA15 8JY
Telephone: 081-302-6446

CHAMPION PRESS

*This book is dedicated to the memory of those who lost
their lives as a result of the Hillsborough disaster
on April 15, 1989*

Ee Aye Addio - We've Won The Cup

Contents

ACKNOWLEDGEMENTS

I would like to thank several people who have been involved in the production of this book. In no particular order, my thanks go to:

Neil Cowland, a fellow Liverpool supporter, who has painstakingly produced the line drawings which form part of this book over a period of some two or three years, much of which has involved a great deal of research and study of original photographs. He has captured an accurate representation of the players in his magnificent drawings, which add to the historical emphasis of the book. He has gained several commissions as a result of his work on *Ee Aye Addio*.

Christopher Wood, another Liverpool supporter, has helped enormously with research, proof-reading, advertising and generally encouraging. His attention to detail has been much appreciated.

Ian Roberts, a Millwall fan, has been a source of great inspiration. His knowledge of typesetting, book layout, and the publishing world has been valued beyond words. A member of Sidcup Round Table, Ian has worked prodigiously on *Ee Aye Addio* over a long period, and at a time when he was busy on several other projects. My thanks go to him for all his help, knowledge and skills, but above all his friendship.

Ian Walker, a past Chairman of Sidcup Round Table, has been the brains behind the computer side of the production of *Ee Aye Addio*. His knowledge of computer systems never ceases to amaze me. This book would not have been possible without his enormous help which, again, goes beyond words. He has been a major light in the production of *Ee Aye Addio*. A good friend indeed.

Ray Spiller, Chairman of the Association of Football Statisticians (0268-416020), has been extremely helpful in a variety of ways. His cheerful co-operation and hospitality have been most welcome.

Mark Golledge, a Liverpool supporter, has been a great help throughout the production of this book. He has cajoled, offered advice, given practical help, and encouraged both the author and the artist for many months. His knowledge of the business world, as well as of Liverpool FC, has been invaluable.

Torbjørn Flatin, a fanatical Liverpool supporter from Kongsberg in Norway, has helped in advertising this book throughout Scandinavia. His help and friendship are greatly valued by the author.

Pål Møller, the Chairman of the Scandinavian branch of the Liverpool FC supporters' club, has also been marvellous in providing assistance in distributing this book.

Peter Macey, a Portsmouth fan, has assisted greatly in a variety of ways, including research, financial support, and general encouragement.

Sorrel Pead, for her help and encouragement throughout the production of this book.

Tommy Smith, M.B.E., for his kind introduction.

The staff of the Liverpool Daily Post and Echo, particularly Ken Rogers, for help and co-operation during the production of this book.

John Richardson, for his general contribution to the production of the book, and for his support throughout.

Alan Robinson, for his postscript and general help, and for his willingness to assist in every way possible.

Colin Cameron, a fellow author; thanks go to him for his cheerful willingness to aid the research of this book, and for his help and advice throughout its production.

Gerry Packman, for help with some of the printing, and *Colin Mason* for help with photocopying.

Nick Leesam and *Shaun Garvey* of Butler & Tanner for their generosity in sharing their expertise.

AUTHOR'S NOTE

I have attempted throughout this book to bring to life the unique magic of the FA Cup, and its special place in the lives of Liverpool supporters everywhere. The book has taken more than four years to bear fruit, and has involved much painstaking research in an attempt to produce the most comprehensive and accurate record ever written about Liverpool's FA Cup history throughout their 100 year involvement in the competition. However, despite the depth of research undertaken by a team of dedicated statisticians, it would be unlikely, given the timescale of the book, that it is without some error, and I would appreciate any discrepancies being brought to my attention via the publishers, together with details of sources of information. I hope you enjoy the book and that it revives many happy memories for you.

Brian Pead
August, 1993

Introduction
by
Tommy Smith, M.B.E.

THE F. A. Cup is the greatest knockout competition in the world. I have been lucky enough to play in four finals, winning against Leeds in 1965 and Newcastle in 1974. I was devastated in defeat against Arsenal in 1971 and Manchester United in 1977.

To give you an example of the importance of the competition to players and fans alike, I was physically sick when we lost to the Gunners in that 1971 Wembley final. It was a mixture of things. It was a very hot day, but I'd played in intense heat before.

Looking back, my response after that Arsenal game was all down to the heartache and personal anguish of missing out on a winners' medal. That's how much the competition means to all players.

Of course, I had the honour and pleasure of being in the first Liverpool side to win this most famous of trophies in 1965. It was a day that had everything. We were a very good side and the opposition, Leeds United, were also top class.

It was the legendary day when Gerry Byrne broke his collar bone and carried on, highlighting the character and determination of a wonderful side. The match itself had all the thrills and spills of a truly great final. We went one up in extra time through Roger Hunt, they equalised soon afterwards and Ian St.John scored a sensational flying header to win it.

We played 120 minutes of non-stop football and it felt as if we had endured a full season of action and emotion in just one afternoon.

This is the magic of the Cup. I treasure all of my medals, but I have a particular affection for that 1965 winners' medal. I will never forget my involvement in that historic day with Liverpool at the start of a very special era.

Tommy Smith, M.B.E.

The Early Years

1892- 1915

October 15, 1892

Nantwich (0) 0

Liverpool (0) 4
Wyllie 70, Miller (3)

LIVERPOOL began their involvement in the Football Association Cup on a day of vile weather. A perfect deluge of rain fell throughout the duration of the game. The weather affected all of the players considerably, but more especially the home team, the heavy ground telling on them, whilst their burly opponents were less affected.

Owing to the late arrival of the referee, the match did not commence until after 3.30. The toss was won by Liverpool, who immediately began operations on their left wing and a lively tussle took place in the home quarter, until Shenton by a masterly move out-manoeuvred them. Then Hope got hold of the ball, and carried it up smartly, but his career was short, and the homesters had to try back. They were just a bit behind, and it is not too much to say that Champion saved the goal.

The game was a good one, neither team getting any advantage until twenty minutes from the call of time, when Liverpool scored four goals in quick succession. Wyllie scored the first goal, and Miller hit the second after 75 minutes and went on to claim a hat-trick as Liverpool completely overwhelmed their opponents. Ross, in goal, only touched the ball once in the second half, such was Liverpool's dominance. The home defence was splendid. Champion played a sterling game at goal, some of his saves being exceedingly clever. Shenton and Keay at full-back were as safe as could be desired, frequently repulsing the onslaughts of Miller and his men of the front rank. The half-backs were in grand form. It would be hard to single out the best, Crawford proving too many for Messrs. Smith and Wyllie on many occasions. Of the forwards, Cartwright, Hollowood and Bull played a good game. Hope at times made a good run and centred well, but Garnett played rather shy against his heavy opponents. Of course the best team won, but had the day been dry the Liverpudlians would have had all their work cut out to have brought the game off.

One local newspaper remarked: "Should think it is nearly time the Wychers put some kind of shelter up on their ground. For a good rate club to have absolutely no provision for the Press is surely not quite the thing."

The matter of protection for the press was overshadowed by the matter of protection for the referee in the FA Cup tie between Crewe and Stourbridge. The *Athletic News* of Monday, October 17, 1892 commented:

The referee gave great dissatisfaction, and would assuredly have been mobbed had he not been taken under the protection of a couple of constables. The crowd was extremely demonstrative, but no one was hurt. During the match the play was stopped some time by a bull terrier running from the ring, getting the ball, and taking it to his master.

For the record, the referee in question, Mr Cooknell, Secretary of the Birmingham League, disallowed a goal for off-side early in the game, displeasing the 3,000 fans. Stourbridge won 2-1.

Another controversial decision was that of the Vicar of Middlewich, Francis Minton, who suggested to a local farmer that it would be appropriate for him to harvest his corn on a Sunday. The corn was apparently liable to disease due to the appalling wet weather prevailing at the time. Another kind of disease - that of smallpox - was found to be present in the Macclesfield Workhouse, being brought in by a tramp. The tramp came from Chapel-en-le-Frith, and when admitted he complained of shivering. He was ordered into the hospital, and in a few days developed a rash which the doctor pronounced to be chicken-pox. He was isolated completely, and ultimately it was found that the symptoms were those of small-pox. The case was progressing favourably. Liverpool's progress in the FA Cup was favourable, too.

John Miller's Liverpool Cup winner's medal

Nantwich: Champion; Shenton, Keay; Critchley, Hitchen, Crawford; Bull, Garnett, Cartwright, Hollowood, Hope.
Liverpool: Ross; Hannah, McLean; Cameron, McQue, McBride; Wyllie, McVean, Miller, Smith, Kelvin.
Referee: Mr J. Taylor (Wrexham)　**Attendance**: 700

October 29, 1892

Liverpool (4) 9

Wyllie (3), McVean (2), McCartney,
H.McQueen, Cameron, Townsend (og)

Newtown (0) 0

THE ground at Anfield was in capital condition, and there was a good crowd of spectators present when Worthington kicked off for the Welshmen, who showed capital form. Thomas attempted a shot on the Liverpool goal, but Ross was equal to it. The Liverpool left wing combined well but were repelled by the visitors. Two corners fell to Liverpool in quick succession, both taken by Wyllie. The first flag-kick was scrimmaged clear, while the second was kicked by Miller. A goalmouth mêlée developed in front of Edwards, but Cameron kicked over the bar.

The Welshmen made a rare attacking foray into the Liverpool half before Miller shot over. Taylor and Townsend played a capital back game for Newtown, and got their side out of difficulties on numerous occasions. A further fruitless corner fell to Liverpool and then the Welshmen were penalised for hands, but the free-kick brought no positive result. McLean and Hannah cleared the danger as the visitors pressed forward. Liverpool attacked and Wyllie dribbled past all opposition before slipping the ball to McVean, who shot in. Edwards cleared, but McCartney met the ball, and cleverly lobbed the ball into goal.

The Liverpool forwards indulged in a display of some excellent passing which resulted in a further corner, but it was cleared by the Welshmen. Worthington went smartly down the middle, but was brought up by McLean.

Liverpool again attacked, most of the front division having a shie at Edwards, but Edwards, Taylor, and Townsend played exceedingly well, and kept their opponents at bay for a considerable time.

Wyllie at length found an opening and he made good use of it, Edwards being defeated for the second time. Liverpool continued to attack at will and the visitors successfully cleared another corner. The homesters were now having by far the best of the game, and the third goal was scored for them by Townsend, the Newtown back. Scarcely another minute had elapsed before McVean carried the Welsh fortress again, amid rounds of applause. Two more corners fell to Liverpool, both being cleared, although with some difficulty. Half-time arrived with the scoreline 4-0 in Liverpool's favour.

When the second half got underway, the crowd had risen to about 4,000 spectators. Each side made strong attacks in the first few minutes, Newtown forcing a corner at the one end, and Liverpool doing the same at the other. Neither of the corners brought a positive result.

Even play was followed by a concerted attack on the Welsh goal, which had some incredible escapes. After twenty minutes' play, McVean scored a beauty, which brought great applause from the crowd. Another regular fusillade took place in front of Edwards. Wyllie scored a sixth goal with a flying shot. H. McQueen scored a very clever goal a minute later to make the score 7-0. The visitors were stung into retaliation, and Morgan and Pryce-Jones initiated raids to the other end, only to find the Liverpool defence too strong for them. Wyllie scored the eighth goal, and Cameron piled on the ninth goal. Liverpool were loudly cheered when they left the field. Everton were involved in a First Division match, losing 4-1 to Bolton Wanderers, despite having scored first.

Tom Wyllie *scores a magnificent goal*

Liverpool: Ross; Hannah, McLean; McCartney, M.McQueen, McBride; Wyllie, Cameron, Miller, McVean, H.McQueen.

Newtown: Edwards; Taylor, Townsend; Tucker, Chapman, Read; Pryce-Jones, Evans, Worthington, Thomas, Morgan.

Referee: Unknown

Attendance: 4,000

November 19, 1892

Northwich Victoria (2) 2
Fecitt (2)

Liverpool (1) 1
Wyllie 10

THE weather was miserable, rain falling during the greater portion of the game. The ground was very greasy, and before commencement Liverpool protested against its condition.

Hannah won the toss for the visitors. Hands in front of the Liverpool goal was taken by Crozier, but the ball passed through without being touched. Wyllie and Smith made a splendid run, but Scanlan brought the former to a stand-still very neatly. He, however, returned to the onslaught, and Scanlan, missing his kick, things looked very dangerous. Postles was in evidence, and cleared with a demon kick, and Fecitt gave Hannah some work to do. The visitors secured a corner, which was placed outside. A foul was given against the Victorians in dangerous proximity to Gow. McLean took it in fine style, and for some minutes the leather hovered around the goal-mouth, the defence being all there. An unusually smart kick would have sent the sphere outside had not Stanley headed it back. Then Wyllie, with lightning-like rapidity, fired sideways into the net. It was a well-earned goal, and one which no custodian could have prevented. A beautiful rush was made by the home forwards, Finnerhan crossing effectively to Fecitt, who missed a very easy chance of scoring. Again the Salt lads dashed down the field, and Stanley gave Fecitt an opening which he failed to turn to advantage. But the blood of the locals seemed to be up, and Crozier, having broken through the combination of Kelvin and Miller, got it down. He cleared himself of Hannah's attentions, and passed to the right wing. Hargreaves was there, and he made a fine centre, which was partially spoiled by McLean. Fecitt, however, converted it into a goal amid loud cheering. Like giants refreshed, Northwich pounced upon the burly Liverpudlian backs, and for some time gave them reason for great anxiety. At last they were repulsed, and the visiting forwards dashed through the mud with dire intent.

Gow saved a very hot shot from Wyllie, and McVean followed it up with several attempts to send the ball over the houses outside the field. Scanlan was not as sure as is his wont, the ball apparently eluding him on account of its greasiness; but Postles played a splendid game. The halves played with the utmost dash and most effectually routed the Liverpool forwards. Hargreaves and Finnerhan put on a fine spurt; but the latter being tripped, it looked as if the advantage was lost. Fecitt, however, stole from Hannah, and had it past Ross in a twinkling. Another goal was scored by the same man within the first half, though it was ruled offside.

The home team opened the second portion with pressure and Ross was repeatedly called upon to save. The same scene was soon afterwards enacted at the other end, and Gow won golden opinions from the Victorian supporters for the intrepidity he displayed in defending his charge. The play became more even for a while, Northwich having slightly the better of the argument.

Twenty minutes from the close the little salt representatives completely overpowered the stalwart city men, who appeared jaded. Ross's citadel was bombarded, the forwards getting round the backs trickily. Their efforts were futile from a scoring point of view, and the most exciting game played on the Drill Field this season ended in favour of Northwich by two goals to one.

Northwich Victoria - 7-0 winners at home to Flint in the Second Qualifying round - were drawn away against Loughborough in the First Round proper, winning 2-1. Their Cup run came to an end in the Second Round Proper when they lost 4-1 away to Blackburn Rovers, eventual semi-finalists.

J. Lewis of Blackburn was the referee in the 1894-95, 1896-97 and 1897-98 finals, all at the Crystal Palace.

Northwich Victoria: Gow; Scanlan, Postles; Ramsay, Crozier, Stanley; Finnerhan, Hargreaves, Bradshaw, Macbeth, Fecitt.

Liverpool: Ross; Hannah, McLean; McCartney, McQue, McBride; Wyllie, Smith, Miller, McVean, Kelvin.

Referee: Mr J. Lewis (Blackburn)

Attendance: 1,000

S.W. Widdowson, the former Nottingham Forest and international player, brought out and registered shinguards in 1874. He refereed the Cup-tie between Liverpool and Grimsby in 1894.

January 27, 1894

Liverpool (2) 3
Bradshaw (2), McQue

Grimsby Town (0) 0

A heavy gale prevailed as Hannah won the toss, and McCairns kicked off towards the Oakfield Road goal at half past two.

Liverpool: McOwen; Hannah, McLean; M.McQueen, McQue, McBride; Gordon, McVean, Henderson, Bradshaw, Stott.

Grimsby Town: Whitehouse; Lundie, Frith; Higgins, Graham, Russell; Ackroyd, Groves, McCairns, Riddock, Jones.

Referee: Mr S. W. Widdowson (Nottingham)

Attendance: 8,000

The visitors made little headway against the wind, which also spoilt the good approach work of the home forwards. Following a series of futile attacks, during which good defence was shown by Lundie and Frith, Liverpool were awarded a free kick close in. Matt McQueen had difficulty in placing the ball for the kick, which came to nothing. The Grimsby left-wing pair broke away and Jones dribbled away on his own before being denied by the home defence. On their previous visit to Anfield, the Ancient Mariners showed an inclination towards the rough style of play, but the Anfielders were equal to the task. Whitehouse proved to be a master

***Harry Bradshaw**, the scorer of two goals*

between the posts, repelling the Liverpool forwards on numerous occasions early on. McQueen and Henderson were both penalised for the use of hands, but the free kicks amounted to nothing. Shortly afterwards, Liverpool returned to the offensive and Malcolm McVean shot narrowly wide. Soon after, Jones broke away and gained a corner for the visitors, but the kick was well cleared.

Liverpool subsequently experienced a period of domination and several well-directed shots were carried wide of the target by the heavy cross-wind. Following a goalmouth mêlée in front of Whitehouse, Russell put Jones in possession, and the former Bootle player went on a fine run before crossing at the right moment for McCairns to blast a shot towards the Liverpool goal, where McOwen saved brilliantly. The game developed into an end-to-end affair, and Bradshaw skimmed the crossbar with a fierce shot. With 35 minutes gone, the game still lacked a goal, mainly due to the wind.

Finally, from a throw-in by McQueen, Bradshaw drew first blood for Liverpool. Further pressure was now put on by the home forwards and Whitehouse continued to save gallantly. However, after several narrow escapes, the Grimsby goal fell once again, this time to Joe McQue.

On resuming, a drizzling rain was falling, and many of the spectators, who objected to being soaked, sought the shelter of the covered stand. McOwen was called upon to make a save early in the second half and it was soon apparent that Liverpool would have to work extremely hard if they were to win the tie. Stott and Henderson combined well for the home side, and Ackroyd replied well for Grimsby. Skipper Hannah made a fine clearance at the back for Liverpool, and the home side enjoyed a period of sustained pressure.

A Grimsby move down the left led to a fierce shot on goal which McOwen saved well before excellent teamwork involving McQue, Stott, and Bradshaw almost led to another goal. Bradshaw received some particularly nasty treatment from the opposing back. The free-kick was of no advantage to Liverpool, and the Fishermen attacked strongly but were unable to pierce the Liverpool defence. Play at this juncture was extremely rough and Riddock and Hannah almost came to blows on the field. The referee cautioned both players, but the visitors showed no inclination to moderate their tactics. From an excellent centre by Gordon, Bradshaw gained possession and scored a brilliant goal for the home side. The play continued to be rough up to the final whistle.

Grimsby, who were initially drawn at home, received a solatium of £100 and half of the gate receipts. Liverpool, safe in the knowledge that Everton were drawn away to Stoke, were pleased to play at Anfield, although it was felt that they would lose about £15. Grimsby Town paid their own private expenses.

February 10, 1894

Liverpool (2) 3
Henderson (2), McVean

Preston North End (1) 2
Becton, Sharpe

THOUSANDS were unable to gain admittance and there were 18,000 people present a quarter of an hour before the kick-off. Hannah won the toss and elected to attack the Anfield Road goal, Ross kicking off for Preston. McQue gained possession and sent Gordon away down the right before Drummond cleared for the visitors. Shortly afterwards Gordon got in a marvellous shot, but it was Henderson who made the first breakthrough after a neat pass from Bradshaw, scoring after only four minutes.

Preston threatened to equalise, but the home halves were too quick to the ball, and on one occasion Ross was superbly tackled by McBride. A period of interesting midfield play ensued, but McBride and McQue were always too clever for the opposing forwards. After Trainer saved well from shots from both wings, Ross was placed in possession by Sanders and the Preston centre-forward enjoyed a good run on goal before McQueen conceded a corner, which was fruitless in its result. Liverpool continued to attack with venom and Holmes and Drummond defended well. Following a fine attacking burst and a flying shot by the Preston Gordon - which narrowly missed the mark - the barricades at the Oakfield Road end of the ground were forced down, and the crowd broke on to the field, and a long delay ensued before it was possible to resume operations.

Mr Lewis was eventually satisfied that play could continue and Gordon went close for Liverpool, before Preston briefly visited the home goal. A few moments later, a second goal ensued from the toe of McVean. From the centre, North End attacked strongly and Becton reduced the deficit. Liverpool replied swiftly and Henderson sent in a fine shot which Trainer did well to clear.

Henderson restarted for Liverpool, but it was Preston who carried the game to the home side and for a long spell the Anfield defence was severely tested. The home side attempted to attack, but Grier and Sanders were in splendid form, beating back the Liverpool forward line. The visitors counter-attacked strongly, and Sharpe equalised. Liverpool, however, were not to be denied, and the Preston left wing defence was beaten when McVean passed to Henderson, who scored a brilliant goal for the home side. With the score 3-2 in favour of the local club, their supporters were raised to a great pitch of enthusiasm, but the North Enders were determined to play to the final whistle, every inch of ground being stubbornly contested, and both sides producing good football. End-to-end play ensued in the manner of a cup-tie and a great attack by Preston ended with Becton shooting wide. From a throw-in, Preston had a good chance of working clear, but Henderson and McBride were too strong for the North Enders. Matt McQueen tried a long drive which brought Trainer yards out from his goal. Liverpool resolutely held on

to win a thrilling encounter against their more illustrious opponents.

Liverpool: McOwen; Hannah, McLean; M.McQueen, McQue, McBride; Gordon, McVean, Henderson, Bradshaw, H.McQueen.

Preston North End: Trainer; Holmes, Drummond; Grier, Sanders, Sharpe; Gordon, Cunningham, Ross, Becton, Cowan.

Referee: Mr J. Lewis (Blackburn)

Attendance: 18,000

Receipts: £460

John McBride, who had an outstanding game

February 24, 1894

Bolton Wanderers (2) 3   Liverpool (0) 0
Bentley 5, Willocks 25, Cassidy 77

THE approaches to the Pike's Lane ground gave every indication of a huge attendance, and every available inch of standing room was occupied half an hour before the kick-off, such was the enormous interest in this match. The weather was brilliantly fine, and the ground, despite the heavy rain which fell on Friday, appeared in good condition. At the last moment the Liverpool executive found that they would have to do without the services of McBride and Henderson, McCartney being called upon to fill the half-back position, while Stott undertook the duties of centre-forward.

A strong wind was blowing from goal to goal as the teams took to the field, and it was evident that a great deal would depend upon the winning of the toss. While waiting for the three o'clock kick-off, the crowd increased by leaps and bounds until there could not have been fewer than 16,000 spectators on the ground, with every indication that this number would considerably increase. Liverpool were first to take the field and were well received, but the Wanderers met with an extremely warm reception. Hannah won the toss and the Liverpool captain naturally took advantage of the wind. Cassidy started the game, and the Wanderers worked down on the left, but a free-kick gave the visitors a chance of encroaching on the home quarters, but Hugh McQueen was pulled up for offside. Somerville and Jones attacked with guile, but were repressed by the strong visiting defence, in which McLean shone. From a free-kick, Hugh McQueen went close to beating Sutcliffe, but Bolton broke away, only to be easily repelled. Bradshaw headed just over the bar from a Gordon centre. Once again Bolton went on to the offensive, and after a scrimmage, Bentley drew first blood by beating McOwen after five minutes' play.

Liverpool responded well and Stott missed a good chance before Matt McQueen shot wide. At this stage of the game, the wind was a more of a hindrance to the visitors than the home side. The ground also cut up badly, and the Liverpool players were all at sea in the mud. McLean pulled up Tannahill, and the linesman intervened, with the result that the referee awarded a free-kick to Bolton. McOwen was brought to his knees in saving from Cassidy. Bradshaw and Hugh McQueen made some headway in their opponents' half, but after 25 minutes, Willocks increased Bolton's lead. From the centre, Liverpool attacked from the right and had two free-kicks which went close, Jones heading to safety on one occasion. Soon afterwards, Bradshaw narrowly missed the goal with a tremendous shot.

After a somewhat long interval, Stott restarted for Liverpool, the attendance being close on 20,000 by this time. The first attack of the second period belonged to Liverpool, and Sutcliffe was penalised for carrying the ball. The free-kick was accounted for by Jones. Hannah repelled a

Bolton attack, and Liverpool countered, with a corner being won. It was a fruitless kick. Bradshaw at this point replaced Stott at centre, who had had a poor game so far.

Bolton began to dominate proceedings, and Liverpool were on the defensive for a long period, with Hannah outstanding at the back, and on one occasion he headed out of danger. Liverpool gained two free-kicks in quick succession, and McVean shot narrowly wide of a post as Liverpool fought desperately for a goal. In reply, Cassidy shot over the crossbar with McOwen beaten. A collision between Hannah and McQue led to McOwen conceding a corner, from which Cassidy scored a third point for the home side. Liverpool continued to play with determination to the final whistle. The captain of the Liverpool team lodged a protest against the temporary condition of the Bolton Wanderers ground. A portion of the field was on the heavy side, but no more so than to be expected after the frost and rain. However, the Liverpool committee decided not to proceed with the objection and sent the following wire to the Wanderers: *"Protest not confirmed by committee. We congratulate you on your victory."*

James Cassidy

Bolton Wanderers: Sutcliffe; Somerville, Jones; Paton, Hughes, Turner; Tannahill, Willocks, Cassidy, Bentley, Dickenson.

Liverpool: McOwen; Hannah, McLean; McCartney, McQue, M.McQueen; Gordon, McVean, Stott, Bradshaw, H.McQueen.

Referee: Mr J. Lewis (Blackburn)

Linesmen: Mr R. Birtwistle (Blackburn); Mr A. Scragg (Crewe)

Attendance: 20,000   **Receipts**: £480

February 2, 1895

Barnsley St.Peter's (0) 1   Liverpool (1) 2 aet
Cutts 80   *McVean 35, Ross 114*

THE draw for the first round of the English Cup ties resulted in the above-named clubs being brought together, the Yorkshiremen having the luck to come out first. An effort by Liverpool to bring about a change of venue fell through on a purely technical point, the Association authorities deciding that Liverpool had failed to comply with the rule by not lodging their protest against the ground, which has not the best of reputations, within the stipulated three days after the draw. Thanks to the enthusiasm of the Reverend J.T. Preedy and Mr J. Raley, association football had made great strides in the Barnsley district during the past few years, and it only required the visit of a First Division League club to give a final fillip to the game among South Yorkshire miners and glass bottle hands, of whom the population was mainly composed. Barnsley St. Peter's were quite unknown to fame, but the fact that the team survived the preliminary stage of the competition warned Liverpool that they could not afford to hold the Saints too cheaply, and the strongest available eleven were selected to do battle for the Liverpool club.

The Liverpool team left the Central Station at a quarter to nine on the morning of the match, and during the journey to Barnsley snow was noticed lying thickly on the fields. Barnsley was reached in good time, and an inspection of the ground showed that the Barnsley club officials had looked after the ground well, for although the adjacent fields were a foot thick under snow, the field of play was quite clear of the undesirable quantity, sawdust and ashes having been put down. At two o'clock sleet was falling, but despite this a large crowd assembled, the match evidently being a great event in the Yorkshire town.

Hail was falling heavily when the teams faced each other, before about 4,000 spectators, special provision of an additional stand proving extremely useful. Barnsley, who were the first on the field, were found to have made one change in their selected eleven, Vost taking the place of Smith. Referee Roberts, of Derby, made a careful inspection of the boots of the players on each side.

An immediate start was made by Bradshaw, the Liverpool captain having lost the toss to Black. A pass to the right gave McVean a chance of a good run, but an ineffectual shot followed. One lusty supporter implored the Barnsley team to "Get t' ball i'th' goal hoil."

Play was even until Liverpool scored a fortunate goal off the toe of McVean. Greaves kicked it with his foot, but the instep struck it too far underneath, and it rolled into the net. The visitors continued to press forward, but met with resilient defence. The Liverpool forwards played a fine game, their passing, quick, cool, and calculated, sorely trying the "Saints". A foul by Vost gave a chance but nothing resulted,

and a good burst off from Nixon was put into goal by Bairstow, but it was ruled off-side.

Play was restarted before a considerably increased attendance and Liverpool renewed their attack, but were kept at a respectable distance from Greaves by the excellent play of the home back division. Drummond got an off-side goal for Liverpool a quarter-of-an-hour after crossing over, and then the referee was knocked down in a struggle following a corner kick to the Peters. A breakaway by Barnsley called forth the best efforts of both McLeans. McQueen's goal was subjected to a fierce assault, and the Liverpool custodian met a well-directed shot by Boston. Then from Hay, Partridge got away finely and shot across goal, but Cutts failed to reach. From a foul near the centre-line, Black sent in a beautiful pass which Cutts again just missed, and a fine effort from Vost was just missed by Cutts once more.

Liverpool retaliated and Ross shot through, but offside nullified the goal. McVean and Davy Hannah then missed the target by inches. Liverpool worked harder than the home side in the field, but their scoring efforts were always cleverly dealt with.

With ten minutes remaining Cutts equalised for the home side following a free-kick and there were scenes of excitement never before previously witnessed at Barnsley. Both sides struggle for supremacy up to the final whistle, and the game went into extra time without a break being taken. The Saints wanted to finish and re-play another day, but the referee ordered extra time of fifteen minutes each way. Playing downhill once more, Liverpool attacked, but they were inclined to be rough in their tactics. Six minutes from the end of extra time, Ross was allowed to steady himself before taking his shot and he scored a fine goal.

The best work of the Barnsley team was performed by their backs and half-backs, who played a really fine game, although the forwards were rather weak.

Tom Nixon was head and shoulders above any other man on the ground, so far as defence was concerned. The Liverpool men admired him exceedingly, and many a time he repulsed the attacks of the opposing wing, and rendered service in all directions. Nixon is surely good enough for any First Division team.

Barnsley St.Peters: J.G.Greaves; F.Coupe, T.Nixon; W.Keech, S.Hay, A.Black; H.Partridge, G.Thompson, W.Bairstow, E.Cutts, T.Vost.

Liverpool: M.McQueen; Curran, D.McLean; McCartney, McQue, J.McLean; McVean, Ross, Bradshaw, D.Hannah, Drummond.

Referee: Mr T.M. Roberts (Derby)

Linesmen: Mr J. Lowles (Derby);
Mr E. Hickington (Derby)

Attendance: 4,000

THE
SUNDAY CHRONICLE

1d }   CONTAINS THE   { 1d

LARGEST NUMBER OF FOOTBALL RESULTS

The Saints had objected to play the extra time, and Mr Jos Raley was told by the referee to leave the field and object afterwards. Accordingly the Saints did object afterwards, serving a written objection upon the referee at his hotel, the Shakespeare. The objection was laid under Rule 17, which provided that extra time could only be played with the consent of both teams. Mr. Roberts acknowledged that he had heard the objection on the field, and the Liverpool representative being sent for, acknowledged also that he had heard the objection. The referee was of the opinion that the match would have to be re-played, and the Wednesday following the game was suggested by Liverpool as a likely date. The referee stated that the result of the match, with the particulars relating to the objection, would be laid before the committee of the English Association in due course, and for the time being the matter ended, both sides expecting that the match would be re-played.

The roar which greeted the Barnsley goal was reported to have been heard up to a mile away, and it was also later reported that when Ross fouled Black, it was due to the fact the players were old schoolfellows, and that the feud was an old one.

There was no difficulty about the protest when it went before the English Association. It was the first business taken. The match was ordered to count as a draw, the tie to be replayed at Liverpool on Monday, February 11, unless by mutual agreement they should meet on a different date. The officials were to be the same as before.

***Jimmy Ross**, who hit the extra-time winner against Barnsley St.Peters, although it was not to count*

LIVERPOOL -- Secretary: John McKenna, 28, Nuttall Street, Liverpool. Colours: Blue and white shirts (quarters), Royal navy knickers. Ground: Anfield Road. Dressing rooms on ground.

February 11, 1895

Liverpool (3) 4

*Bradshaw 15, Drummond 40,
McVean 42, H.McQueen 60*

Barnsley St.Peter's (0) 0

THE day was exceedingly cold, but fine. The visitors played the same team as in the original tie, but Liverpool were short of several of their usual players, Davy Hannah being missing due to an injury to the small of his back he sustained against Blackburn Rovers.

Ross, who acted as captain, won the toss, and the ground was extremely hard as Vost kicked off for St. Peter's shortly after half past two, before about 2,000 spectators. Joe McLean attempted to make an advance on the opposition goal, but he was thwarted by Cutts, who sent the leather back up the field. Bradshaw crossed to the right, and Ross took up possession before shooting at goal. His toe, however, got underneath the ball, which topped the crossbar by a yard or so. Before the tension was eliminated, several assaults were made on the Barnsley goal without result. On one occasion McCartney shot over the bar when well placed.

With fifteen minutes' play gone, Ross passed to Bradshaw, who drew first blood after a sustained period of Liverpool pressure, although Greaves partially cleared. The home side continued to dominate, but the shooting of the forwards was too erratic.

The St. Peter's left came close to scoring on one occasion, but Matt McQueen cleared the danger and set Liverpool on to the counter attack with a huge clearance from an effort by Cutts. The visitors looked rather amateurish in comparison with Liverpool, but in defence they looked less clumsy. A great move between Ross and Bradshaw ended with the centre-forward shooting wide of the post by inches. Joe McLean went on a brilliant solo run but was unable to find the net.

A free-kick to St. Peter's in front of the Liverpool goal was allowed to sail onto the crossbar before the defence shaped to clear. The ball afterwards struck the foot of the upright before being cleared along the right wing. This opened up another attack on the Barnsley goal with the homesters pressing strongly. Ross was twice fouled by Hay, but nothing came of the free-kick awarded for the second offence.

Shortly afterwards, however, Drummond registered a second point for Liverpool, a good shot glancing off Coupe's legs and into the net. Two minutes later Malcolm McVean added a third with a great shot. During the remainder of the first half the Liverpool custodian was a spectator, so well had Curran and Matt McQueen weighed up their opponents.

When the teams reappeared before about 4,000 spectators, Ross took up the outside position, owing to a slight injury to his ankle, but this did not affect Liverpool's supremacy.

Liverpool: McCann; Curran, M.McQueen; McCartney, McQue, J.McLean; McVean, Ross, Bradshaw, Drummond, H.McQueen.

Barnsley St.Peters: J.G.Greaves; F.Coupe, T.Nixon; W.Keech, S.Hay, A.Black; E.Cutts, W.Bairstow, T.Vost, G.Thompson, H.Partridge.

Referee: Mr T. M. Roberts (Derby)

Linesmen: Mr J. Lowles (Derby);
Mr E. Hickington (Derby)

Attendance: 4,000

Receipts: £80

Drummond and Hugh McQueen took the ball right up to the Barnsley goalmouth, but the attack was cleared with a huge kick upfield. The ball fell to Greaves, who blasted his shot high and wide. Moments later, McVean emulated the Barnsley goal attempt.

After a quarter of an hour's play, in succession to some fine forward exchanges, Hugh McQueen, from the extreme left, drove in a terrific grounder which completely beat the Saints' defence. The Liverpool side went in for a great deal of "diddling" with their opponents, seeming to prefer this to the scoring of goals. In one Barnsley attack the visitors were rewarded for some determined work, and McCann was called upon to handle smartly, and his clearance was effected under great difficulty.

Tom Nixon, Barnsley's left-back, gave another brilliant display and after the match he was invited by a member of the committee to write offering his services to the Anfield Road club. No offer was made as to terms. He has been similarly approached by Derby County and Bury. He formerly played for the now defunct Lockwood Brothers' team, and confessed that he would rather play for one of the Sheffield teams, preferring to remain at his home in Barnsley, except for matches and training. Nixon and Tom Hirst failed to reach the train in time for the return journey.

A strong appeal was made that the ball had crossed the line first, but the referee, who had been in an excellent position to adjudge the situation, did not uphold the appeal. Shortly afterwards the Yorkshire team created another opening through Vost and Cutts, and from a long pass a slashing shot was attempted by Partridge, but the ball flew a few inches over the bar. Ross had two opportunities presented to him, but he preferred someone else to take the honour of scoring a point, but nobody took advantage. Just before the end, the game was stopped due to an injury sustained by a Barnsley player, and on resuming, Hugh McQueen netted the ball once more, but it was disallowed for off-side.

The Saints were beaten, but not disgraced. One earnest Barnsley supporter as he left the game said, "Peter's would lick 'em every day i'th' week if t'Liverpool chaps he'd nobbut to wark like ah'r lads 'em. Them's fower quid a week chaps 'at does now't else but lake fooitball," and he added that Partridge had been working in the pit all Sunday night and had never been in bed at all; whilst Thompson had had a four miles walk from his home to catch the train in the early morning.

The Saints were further handicapped in the matter of footgear. They were shod in the usual hard leather, but their opponents had made a wiser arrangement, and bars of India-rubber underfoot gave them a wonderful advantage on the hard dry ground. Anybody who has tried the two will be able to understand the worth of the rubber in such cases.

Mutton chops and toast before the match, ham and eggs for tea after it, and the Barnsley players were ready for the evening, which most of them spent at the Prince's Theatre, where *Babes In The Wood* was being played.

Matt McQueen, *who had two good games against Barnsley St.Peter's*

February 16, 1895

Liverpool (0) 0   Nottingham Forest (2) 2

Stewart 15, McInnes 40

DESPITE the continuance of the frost, the Liverpool authorities were able to announce yesterday (Friday) that the Anfield ground was in "good condition", a statement borne out by its appearance this afternoon, although it could easily be seen that too close an acquaintance with the 'turf' would be highly undesirable. The Foresters had a long journey in the first round, having to travel to Southampton, where they vanquished St. Mary's by 4-1, the Southerners being no match for the Reds.

The draw for the second round went against the Notts Leaguers, who had again to make a journey and play on foreign soil - where, by the way, they have never been blessed with much luck, their first game with Liverpool at Anfield a season ago having resulted in defeat by 3-0, while on January 12 this year they had to submit to a 5-0 beating in the League competition, where, however, with 26 points from 23 games, they occupy a much better position than Liverpool, who have just 17 points. The Liverpool men have had a few days' quiet preparation, and the recent much-improved form shown gave their followers every hope of a successful issue to today's encounter. An unfortunate accident last Saturday to Davy Hannah meant a change in the team.

At the kick off, the frosty air was tempered by warm sunshine. The visiting team arrived in Liverpool on Friday night from Nottingham, where they had been training quietly. Several alterations were necessitated on the home side, James McLean and Davy Hannah being unable to take their accustomed places, Matt McQueen playing left half-back and Geordie Drummond inside-left, McCann again appearing in goal.

The Reds were first out, being received by a hearty cheer from the five thousand spectators on the ground, a much warmer reception awaiting the home players, who immediately followed. McLean won the toss, the visitors having to face the sun at the start.

Rose kicked off prompt to time. McQue, McQueen and McCartney in turn tackled well, but the Forest right wing succeeded in evading McQueen, the leather, however, travelling harmlessly over the line. A foul throw and a free kick in Liverpool's favour enabled McVean to get close to McCracken, who made a beautiful clearance, placing well for Rose, who raced off, and he was in the process of scoring when Duncan McLean rushed in and caused the Notts centre to send high over the bar. Hands against McVean and Matt McQueen in turn nullified some good work by Ross, the result being another visit to the home quarters, where McQue was penalised, Stewart taking the free kick and scoring the first goal for the Reds. At this period Notts were playing a much better forward game and came near to increasing their lead on several occasions, while Allsop was hardly called

upon to effect a save. With just five minutes of the first half remaining, Forest scored a second goal through McInnes. Shortly afterwards Ross was fouled by McCracken. McCartney took the free kick and scored, but the referee, after consultation with the linesman, decided that it had passed through untouched.

Bradshaw restarted, the three inside forwards trying to play the same close game which succeeded so well last Saturday but McPherson and McCracken were successful in breaking up the effort at short passing. A pattern of play evolved whereby both teams had numerous attempts on goal, but without success.

The Forest players were throughout quicker on the ball, and more accurate in their passing, and would frequently have defeated McCann only for the close attentions of Matt McQueen, who proved a glutton for work.

Liverpool: McCann; Curran, D.McLean; McCartney, McQue, M.McQueen; McVean, Ross, Bradshaw, Drummond, H.McQueen.

Nottingham Forest: Allsop; Ritchie, Scott; Stewart, McPherson, McCracken; Pike, Carnelly, Rose, Forman, McInnes.

Referee: Mr J.B. Brodie (Wolverhampton)

Linesmen: Mr J. Cooper (Blackburn);
            Mr S. Ormerod (Accrington)

Attendance: 5,000

Receipts: £108 2s 3d

(REUTER'S TELEGRAM.)
Madrid, Saturday.

The young King of Spain is said to be suffering from a severe cold.

February 1, 1896

Liverpool (2) 4
Ross 20, Becton, Allan, Bradshaw

Millwall Athletic (1) 1
Geddes

LIVERPOOL rarely entertain Southern teams, and Millwall attracted only 3,000 by two o'clock. Millwall Athletic have done better in their engagements this season than ever before, and have recently been strangers to defeat. To be drawn against the leaders of the Second Division of the League, and away from home, put a task on the Millwall team which few expected they would come through with success, but every effort was made by the management to get the team fit, and having journeyed to Liverpool on Friday, the visitors were in splendid condition. Liverpool had a strong team on duty.

Ross lost the toss, and Allan started towards the Oakfield Road goal, before about 6,000 on-lookers. The opening stages were rather tame, and then some intelligent work by the Millwall left resulted in the visitors securing a foothold in the Liverpool half. McCartney relieved, and this led to several onslaughts on the Londoners' goal. Geary, Goldie and Ross were all foiled when attempting to shoot. At this stage, the play was generally in favour of Liverpool, but their passing was not at its best, and several opportunities of scoring were lost.

A sudden rush by the visitors resulted in a corner to them. Whelan placed the ball in a splendid position, and Storer fisted away brilliantly.

With 20 minutes of the match gone, Becton fed Ross, whose low shot put the home side into the lead. The Londoners responded with some heavy tackling, and from one free-kick Goldie found Ross, whose delicate pass to Becton resulted in the inside-left blasting the ball home for Liverpool's second goal. This second reversal roused the Athletic to greater effort and in a goalmouth mêlée, Geddes shot through to reduce the arrears. After the usual five minutes' interval, Geddes re-commenced by kicking off towards the Oakfield Road goal. Both teams showed greater enthusiasm during the second period. Law was twice called upon to save from Bradshaw, before the outside-left passed to Allan, who, with a magnificent shot, scored Liverpool's third goal amidst a perfect storm of applause. Goldie was winded in a collision, but this only caused a brief stoppage, play proceeding at an accelerated pace until an accident to J. Matthews caused another stoppage, the Millwall centre-half having to leave the field for a time. On resuming, Liverpool renewed their pressure, but their shooting was inept. Eventually Ross fed Geary, who sped upfield and crossed to Bradshaw. The left-winger banged the leather past Law for the best goal of the afternoon.

The last ten minutes saw some wild kicking by the visitors, who were outplayed in every department, and they proved no match for their more illustrious opponents, though Geddes put in some neat football, only to be foiled by Goldie, who was ready for every attack.

Other results in the First Round Proper:

Everton	2	Nottingham Forest	0
Grimsby Town	2	Darwen	0
Derby County	4	Aston Villa	2
Stoke City	5	Tottenham Hotspur	0
West Bromwich	2	Blackburn Rovers	1
Blackpool	4	Burton Swifts	1
Burnley	6	Woolwich Arsenal	1
Newcastle United	4	Chesterfield	0
Bury	4	Small Heath	1
Sunderland	4	Preston North End	1
Wolves	2	Notts County	2
Sheffield Wed.	3	Southampton	2
Bolton Wanderers	4	Crewe Alexandra	0
Burton Wanderers	1	Sheffield United	1
Newton Heath	2	Kettering	1

OFFICIAL REFEREES 1895 - 1896
Adams, J., Enderley, City Road, Birmingham

Liverpool: Storer; Goldie, Wilkie; McCartney, McQue, Holmes; Geary, Ross, Allan, Becton, Bradshaw.

Millwall Athletic: Law; Graham, Davies; King, J.Matthews, H.Matthews; Whelan, Leatherbarrow, Gittins, Mallock, Geddes.

Referee: Mr J. Adams (Birmingham)

Attendance: 10,000

Receipts: £283

February 15, 1896

Wolverhampton W. (2) 2   Liverpool (0) 0
Woods, Owen (pen)

WITH the idea that Liverpool had a good chance of proceeding into the next round, the players were dispatched to Droitwich last Wednesday, arriving in Wolverhampton early on Saturday morning, evidently in fine condition. With the exception that Rose was unable to take his place in goal due to a bad attack of rheumatism, the Wolves were fully represented, and the match had aroused such interest in the Midland town that crowds rolled up to the ground an hour before kick-off. The weather was spring-like in its mildness, and the ground proved to be in excellent condition, the turf bearing little evidence of the wear and tear of five months' play. The Wolves, whether holding the match too cheaply or not it is impossible to say, did not deem it necessary to go into special training, and the team remained at home during the week.

Promptly to time, Ross and Harry Woods met to arrange the preliminaries and, the former winning, Liverpool took up their defence at the Town goal. The former Burslem centre, Beats, kicked off at 3.15pm towards the terrace end, and the ball travelled to the Liverpool right, where Bradshaw sent it to Allan, who was, however, robbed by Malpass, and the home left advanced in attacking order.

For a spell Wilkie and Holmes were kept busy, and then the former got the ball away. Ross and Allan then advanced towards the Waterloo Road end and Bradshaw had a shot at goal. Gradually, however, the home side re-asserted themselves and they went close on several occasions.

Liverpool found it a very difficult matter to shake off the Wolves, who were most persistent in their attack, and who showed more method than their opponents. At length Wilkie was beaten by Malpass and in endeavouring to remedy the mistake, Holmes conceded a corner, this leading to a prolonged attack on the Liverpool goal. A couple of free-kicks were awarded to the Wolves at close range, but in each case Storer had the luck to escape, the ball on the second occasion going into the net without touching another player. From a throw-in the ball was floated into the area, and after a hot bully Woods shot against the cross-bar, and Storer was charged through before he could handle the ball. Liverpool appealed strongly against the point, but Mr Kingscott, after appealing to both linesmen, granted the goal amid tremendous cheering on the part of the home supporters. From the kick-off Liverpool advanced swiftly into their opponents' area and a long-range shot from Becton narrowly missed the target. Unfortunately, the ex-Prestonian wrenched his leg in the effort, and he appeared to be useless for some time afterwards.

Play was then of an even character, the Liverpool defence being very capable whenever the Wolves got at close quarters. At length the Wanderers attacked with an irresistible rush, and in endeavouring to stop it, the Liverpool backs were very much at fault, and a free-kick resulted. A further bad foul by Wilkie led to the awarding of a penalty kick from which Owen scored a second goal.

The Liverpool forwards, who up to this period had made a poor show against the back division, now gave a glimpse of their usual form, but they were most unfortunate in their shooting, and they were again compelled to beat a retreat. McCartney, who was playing excellently, broke up a fine attack by Black and Woods, before moving upfield and shooting strongly at goal. As the whistle blew for half-time, Becton shot over the bar.

With a two-goal lead, and with Liverpool playing below par, the Wanderers merely had to keep the visitors out, and they managed this effectively. On occasions, Geary, Ross, Allan, and Becton promised good things, but over-anxiety rendered their efforts abortive. Allan had a fine opportunity but the lightning ground shot he sent in skimmed across the face of the goal and passed outside, and Ross headed a trifle over when a little more discretion would have beaten the custodian.

The Wanderers were known as an erratic team, but that the home training was more beneficial to them than going away was proved beyond doubt. Tennant was a capable substitute for Rose, and though he was not fully extended, he performed excellently. He was the only amateur playing for the Wanderers, and though originally a Rugbyite, he had done a lot of service for local junior Association football. Baugh and Dunn were sterling defenders, though they were inclined to stray too far away from goal. Owen was a thorn in the side of Geary and Ross, and Malpass and Griffiths were excellent.

Wolverhampton Wanderers: Tennant; Baugh, Dunn; Griffiths, Malpass, Owen; Tonks, Henderson, Beats, Woods, Black.

Liverpool: Storer; Goldie, Wilkie; McCartney, McQue, Holmes; Geary, Ross, Allan, Becton, Bradshaw.

Referee: Mr A.G. Kingscott (Derby)

Linesmen: Mr A.G. Hines (Nottingham); Mr A. Hall (Derby)

Attendance: 13,500

Receipts: £402

January 30, 1897

Liverpool (2) 4
Hannah 5, Allan 19, Cleghorn 70, Ross 89

Burton Swifts (2) 3
Dewey 15, Wyllie 25, Evans 55

HAVING fought their way successfully through the preliminary stages of the English Cup ties, Burton Swifts had the luck to be drawn against Liverpool for the first round proper, and after their experience of the seasiders a couple of seasons ago in the Second Division, the Brewery men well knew they had a heavy task in front of them. Liverpool annexed four points and made a very considerable improvement in their goal average at the expense of the Swifts. In season 1895-96 Liverpool twice heavily defeated Burton Swifts, winning 7-0 away (still their record victory on foreign soil) on 29 February 1896, and 6-1 at home on March 21, 1896. The 13-1 aggregate is not, however, a record, that being the 15-1 scored against Rotherham in the same season (Liverpool winning 5-0 away and 10-1 at home.) As might have been expected, the severe weather recently experienced left the Anfield enclosure in a sorry plight, and there appeared some doubt as to whether it would be considered fit for a Cup tie. Sand had been freely used in front of the goals, but pools of water were to be found all over the ground. The composition of the Liverpool team had been a matter for doubt during the week, but they fielded a strong side.

The Swifts started, and at once went away with a terrific rush on the left, the inside man shooting wide. From the goal kick the visitors came back, and a stiff bully in front of goal looked ominous for Liverpool until Allan gained possession and raced upfield. Minutes later, Allan was fouled. The free kick was well placed in the area and Hannah headed in from a loose ball after five minutes' play.

The terrible condition of the ground rendered accurate play

Joe McQue

impossible, and the players at times floundered about painfully. After this success the home players were encouraged strongly and for a time the Swifts were kept strictly on the defensive. Some excellent work by the home forwards culminated in a grand shot from Becton, which went just over the crossbar. Yardley and Evans now showed for the visitors a bit of form, whose forwards played the correct game on the heavy frozen ground, there being no attempts at short passing, though several long shots came very near the mark. Dewey sent in a raking shot which Donnelly had difficulty in steering clear of the danger. The next movement came from the Liverpool right wing, Allan and Michael giving an acrobatic display in the slush. The visitors then moved away, on the right, and the linesman, in endeavouring to follow the play, came to grief in one of the numerous pools on the touch line.

From some midfield work Allan received a nice pass, when he fell prone in a puddle, and he created great amusement by picking up the ball and throwing it forward. The referee, of course, declined to allow this bit of Rugby play, and from the free-kick the Swifts attacked strongly, Dewey shooting into the corner of the net.

Having put themselves on equal terms, the Swifts played up strongly, and for a time the home defence was kept busy. A free kick gave Liverpool a slight advantage, but the forwards were unable to make progress through the mud. McQue served up for Hannah, who by an overhead kick let in Allan, an oblique shot placing the leather in the corner of the net entirely out of the reach of Gray.

Other results in the FA Cup:

Aston Villa	5	Newcastle United	0
Notts County	2	Small Heath	1
West Bromwich A.	1	Luton	0
Wolverhampton W.	2	Millwall	1
Blackburn Rovers	2	Sheffield United	1
Stoke	5	Glossop North End	2
Everton	5	Burton Wanderers	2
Derby County	8	Barnsley St. Peter's	1
Preston North End	6	Manchester City	0
Stockton	0	Bury	0
Nottingham Forest	1	Sheffield Wednesday	0
Sunderland	1	Burnley	0

The following play was somewhat in favour of the Swifts, who equalised through Wyllie. Liverpool then played well, and displayed better tactics, but found scoring difficult. Michael missed a ridiculously easy opportunity of giving the home side the lead. McCartney took a free kick, and though another player appeared to have touched the ball on its way into the net, the point was disallowed. Ross created an opening for Michael, whose low shot was brilliantly saved by Gray. Following a spell of midfield work, the leather was sent across to Hannah, who had an open goal before him when he missed his kick. After a sprint by Yardley and Evans, easily repelled by Goldie, the home forwards advanced smartly, and from a free kick Michael headed narrowly over the bar. For a team with a weekly wages bill of only £14, it must be stated that the Swifts had given an excellent account of themselves during the first period, and it was recognised that the final result would depend upon stamina and a slice of fortune.

Allan restarted before 4,000 spectators, Hannah securing possession and progressing at speed upfield. He was robbed of the ball by the attentive Lawrence. Then Hannah, with a clear course, sent the ball to Michael, who overran the ball.

The Burton left wing responded with some neat combination, and McKenzie sent in a magnificent shot, which Donnelly fisted out, but Evans dashed up at full speed and crashed the ball into the net. This forced Liverpool to retaliate, but Leigh was again nearly through when McQue grassed him as the Swift was about to shoot, and the game became very interesting.

Cleghorn initiated a strong attack in which Allan tested Gray with a fast ground shot, and a corner finely placed by Ross proved wasteful. After a period of sustained pressure, Cleghorn beat Gray with a magnificent shot. The visitors determined to battle for the result, and Liverpool were forced to show improved form. After Michael had headed into the goalkeeper's hands, another foul against Ashby almost led to Liverpool regaining the lead. A bad miss by Wilkie let in Evans, and after a severe spell of pressure by the visitors, the ball was driven down the field in a huge clearance. Just before the final whistle, Allan gained possession and passed to Ross, who threaded his way past the backs and defeated Gray with a fine shot.

Liverpool: Donnelly; Goldie, Wilkie; McCartney, McQue, Cleghorn; Michael, Ross, Allan, Becton, Hannah.

Burton Swifts: Gray; Lawrence, Ashby; Ray, Wyllie, Chadwick; McKenzie, Dewey, Leigh, Yardley, Evans.

Referee: Mr J.H. Strawson (Lincoln)

Attendance: 4,000

Official Referees 1896 - 97

Strawson, J.H., Altham Terrace, Lincoln

The current League Tables:

Division One

	Pl	W	L	D	F	A	Pts
Aston Villa	20	12	4	4	43	29	28
Liverpool	**24**	**11**	**7**	**6**	**30**	**23**	**28**
Derby County	22	12	7	3	54	37	27
Everton	20	11	6	3	42	29	25
Sheffield United	20	8	4	8	32	19	24
Preston North End	19	8	4	7	40	26	23
West Bromwich A.	23	9	9	5	25	36	23
Bolton Wanderers	19	9	6	4	29	22	22
Sheffield Wednesday	21	7	7	7	30	28	21
Nottingham Forest	22	7	10	5	33	38	19
Blackburn Rovers	22	8	11	3	24	47	19
Bury	18	4	6	8	23	31	16
Wolverhampton W.	21	6	11	4	30	29	16
Stoke	21	6	12	3	31	48	15
Burnley	19	4	9	6	27	38	14
Sunderland	23	4	13	6	23	40	14

Division Two

	Pl	W	L	D	F	A	Pts
Notts County	21	16	3	2	71	30	34
Grimsby Town	23	13	7	3	52	36	29
Newcastle United	20	12	7	1	41	34	26
Newton Heath	20	10	7	3	34	26	23
Manchester City	20	8	7	5	41	35	21
Darwen	19	10	9	0	51	37	20
Leicester Fosse	17	10	7	0	39	34	20
Woolwich Arsenal	19	8	8	3	47	50	19
Small Heath	19	7	8	4	30	32	18
Gainsborough T.	18	6	7	5	26	29	17
Walsall	20	7	10	3	38	58	17
Burton Swifts	**18**	**6**	**8**	**4**	**30**	**39**	**16**
Blackpool	17	6	8	3	32	35	15
Burton Wanderers	19	7	12	0	19	38	14
Loughborough	19	6	13	0	32	44	12
Lincoln City	17	3	14	0	19	51	6

Thomas Cleghorn,
who beat Gray with a magnificent shot

February 13, 1897

West Bromwich Albion (0) 1   Liverpool (2) 2
Watson   *McVean 5, Neill 24*

LIVERPOOL were set a harder task in the second round than they appeared to have in the first round of the English Cup competition, and against the Albion at Stoney Lane they appeared to have little chance of success after their ignominious defeat at Stoke a week ago in which Liverpool were defeated 1-6. It was their heaviest defeat to date in League football. Determined to leave nothing to chance, however, the Liverpool directorate decided to give the players a week's training at Holt Fleet where, within easy distance of the brine baths at Droitwich, it was hoped the men would be so much improved that they would be able to give a better account of themselves.

Past experience prepared the supporters of each side for a close game, but with neither team at full strength, neither club felt very confident as to the result. Fred Geary displaced Michael, while Bassett was an absentee from the home ranks. A fair number of excursionists journeyed from Liverpool, and the ground was filled by a crowd numbering 16,000. Jimmy Ross won the toss, and Cameron started the match. McVean gave away an early free-kick, but Cleghorn cut out the danger. A timely header from Allan set Liverpool on their way down the right. The ball was moved across to the opposite flank and the visitors won their first corner of the game. Flewitt kicked the ball away for another corner, but the danger passed.

An optimistic shot by Richards was turned for a corner by Donnelly, but the Albion kick was unproductive. Good work by Cleghorn and Neill kept the visitors' left wing well on the attack, and presently Geary cleverly tricked Evans, and shot across the goalmouth, McVean getting his cranium to the ball and scoring the first goal after only five minutes.

From the centre Liverpool soon again went on to the attack, but Williams cleared the danger. Richards and Watson attacked with style before Goldie repelled their offensive inclinations. The repulse was only temporary, however, as the Albion, playing with dash, went at it in regular Cup tie style, and it was fortunate for Liverpool that Wilkie was in such fine form.

The game then settled into a period of midfield dominance before the Liverpool left advanced again and Becton sent in a long shot which just topped the crossbar. From the goal kick Perry served his forwards well but McCartney rushed across, and the ball once more rifled towards Reader. A throw-in by Cleghorn was headed to the right wing by Allan, but McVean failed to pass Williams. The home left wing advanced in grand style and several centres were put in but none near enough to trouble Donnelly.

Allan was badly fouled by Higgins, and the free-kick led to a corner which was particularly well-placed from the right wing, and Neill headed a second goal after 24 minutes' play. This inevitably dispirited the Albion and Cleghorn shot over the bar after fine work by Becton and Geary.

Presently a free-kick fell to the home side, but Williams' effort was met strongly by Neill, and the Liverpool forwards went off in grand style. Ross shot well and a corner resulted. This came to nothing, and Flewitt advanced strongly before Neill - who was having a fine game - cut out the danger. Then Watson made the best effort of the day for the Albion, his shot just shaving the post.

For a time the Liverpool defenders were kept very busy, Flewitt making a fine effort, and Williams having a free-kick, which was thrown away by Donnelly. The referee evidently had an inclination to penalise McCartney for his style of throwing in. However, no advantage occurred to the Albion. Eventually a free-kick from Williams resulted in the ball landing on top of the net. Liverpool's reply was swift as they moved on to the attack, but the referee's whistle blew for the interval.

The second half commenced in spirited fashion, the Liverpool men being first in evidence, but being repulsed by Williams, away went the home forwards and they were awarded a free-kick, which was splendidly placed, Donnelly saving well from a header at the expense of a corner. The free-kick was removed, but the home men returned to the attack. The ball was run from end to end rapidly, and there was not much brilliance about the movement or good combination to be observed. There was much excitement in the game, however.

Derby County v. Bolton Wanderers

At Derby, in fine weather, and before 15,000 spectators. Derby were without Leiper, whom the committee have suspended for insubordination. The visitors were short of Thompson and Nichol, who were injured on Thursday at Sheffield. Bloomer scored for Derby after ten minutes' play, and ten minutes later Fisher scored again from a centre by John Goodall. At the interval Derby led by 2 goals to nil. The visitors commenced the second half in better form, and in 15 minutes Brown scored for them from a pass by the left wing. Ten minutes later Bloomer ran round the Bolton backs, and scored the third for Derby by himself. The same player also scored the fourth.

Result - Derby County **4** goals; Bolton Wanderers **1**.

Thomas Wilkie,
*who was
in fine form
for Liverpool*

Geary and Becton worked the ball away, and Ross shot narrowly wide, whilst a moment later Becton's great shot flew inches over the bar. The Throstles moved down and gained a free-kick right in the goalmouth, but this was safely taken and following the relief, Geary ran along in grand style, Becton finishing with a fine effort which was just slightly off target. The Liverpool defence often came under pressure but Becton then tested Reader with a fierce shot which the goalkeeper just reached with his foot and coolly kicked away. The home side responded with greater determination and Richards placed Flewitt's centre on the wrong side of the posts, and Dean also shot over the bar after a fine piece of play by Higgins and Flewitt.

However, the visitors' left wing again relieved, and from Geary's centre Becton beat Reader, but the goal was disallowed for a previous foul.

The home right eventually got down, and Flewitt beat Wilkie before sending in a cross which gave Watson the easiest possible chance of scoring. Amidst the encouraging cheers of their supporters, the home team strained every nerve to equalise, but the Liverpool defence stood firm.

West Bromwich Albion: Reader; Williams, Evans; Banes, Higgins, Perry; Watson, Richards, Cameron, Flewitt, Dean.

Liverpool: Donnelly; Goldie, Wilkie; McCartney, Neill, Cleghorn; McVean, Ross, Allan, Becton, Geary.

Referee: Mr J. Fox (Sheffield)

Linesmen: Mr J.E. Carpenter (Leicester);
Mr A. Lovell (Leicester)

Attendance: 16,000

Aston Villa v. Notts County

At Perry Barr, before 18,000 spectators. The Villa kicked off, and the County were first to break away. Seven minutes from the start Prescott shot, and the County scored by the ball going in off Murphy. Fifteen minutes had been played when Wheldon equalised. Ten minutes later Bramley collided with Crabtree, and was carried off the field. The Villa gradually asserted their superiority, but failed to get ahead, and at half-time the score was equal - a goal each. After the interval, the game became more exciting than ever, a good order of play ruling. For a time the County had a fair share of aggression, but the Villa at length maintained a perfect fusillade, but were unable to get through the glorious defence. Then, about ten minutes from time, Campbell, off Athersmith, scored for the Villa. Notts failed to recover from this reverse. Result - Aston Villa **2** goals; Notts County **1**.

Preston North End v. Stoke

At Preston. The ground was very heavy, rain falling all the morning. Stoke started grandly, and pressed for the first few minutes, but the Preston defence were equal to the occasion. Stoke were playing the best game, and scored three minutes from the interval, crossing over with a goal to their credit. In the second half the game opened very fast, and after Stoke having the best of the game for a time Preston worked the ball down and scored from a scrimmage. Tom Smith had a grand run down, and after dodging the Stoke backs scored a grand goal for Preston. Stoke were pretty well worn out, but played better again at the finish. Result - Preston **2** goals; Stoke **1**.

Sunderland v. Nottingham Forest

This tie at Sunderland attracted an enormous crowd. The Forest won the toss, and within eight minutes scored from a corner, McInnes putting the ball through. Directly afterwards Richards beat Doig, but was ruled offside. After this play was fast and furious, and at length McInnes scored a second point for Notts, a little later Harvie putting through a fine goal for Sunderland. Half-time score - Notts Forest 2 goals, Sunderland 1. On restarting, Sunderland pressed severely at times, but the visitors adopted kicking-out tactics, Fred Forman and McInnes twice or thrice bothering Doig. Sunderland tried hard to equalise, and were extremely dangerous at times. The Forest once broke away, and from a scrimmage Fred Forman put the leather past Doig. The game was hotly contested to the finish, but the homesters were outplayed, and at the end the score stood - Notts Forest **3** goals; Sunderland **1**.

Blackburn Rovers v. Wolverhampton W.

At Blackburn, before 8,000 spectators, in wretched weather, rain falling and fog enveloping the ground. The Rovers were first to get dangerous, and after the Wolves had returned the compliment Wilkie scored for the home team. During a scrimmage the ball went through the net, and the Wolves claimed against the goal, but the referee allowed the point. Beats equalised for the visitors five minutes later. Nothing further was done up to the interval, when the score was 1 goal each. The second half opened in uninteresting fashion, neither side being able to claim any material advantage. Each goal was attacked, but there was little sting about the shots, and they were generally wide of the mark. The players showed signs of distress as the result of the heavy ground and wretched weather. Dewar scored for the Rovers five minutes from the finish. Result - Blackburn Rovers **2** goals; Wolverhampton Wanderers **1**.

Southampton St. Mary's v. Newton Heath

This match was commenced in the presence of 9,000 spectators. The teams were at their full strength, but the ground, in consequence of recent rains, considerably hampered play. Newton Heath playing with the slope in their favour pressed at the outset of the game, but hostilities were afterwards principally confined to the visitors' half. Just before the interval, however, the Heathens broke through, and Donaldson scored. Excitement was intensified on the resumption, as the home team pressed but the game opened after a while, the defence of both sides being put to a stiff test. The Saints, however, at length laid heavy siege to the visitors' goal, and Boyd fouling Naughton equalised with a header on the mouth of goal from a free kick. The Heathens pressed to the close, but were unable to score further, and the game ended in a draw of **1** goal each.

February 27, 1897

Liverpool (1) 1
Becton 30

Nottingham Forest (1) 1
McInnes 16

THE weather turned out brilliantly as both Liverpool and Everton entertained teams in the Third Round of the English Cup. With the ground at Anfield in the very best condition, there seemed every prospect that the supporters of Liverpool would witness a high-class game, the Liverpool v. Nottingham Forest tie being generally regarded as likely to produce as keen a struggle as any in the round. Only once have the Foresters been able to claim a victory over Liverpool at Anfield, that being in an English Cup tie a couple of seasons ago, when the Reds, who a few weeks previously had sustained a heavy defeat on the same ground in a League battle, relieved their foes of today from the necessity of taking further part in the competition. While Liverpool have reached their present position by a victory at home over Burton Swifts and by defeating the Throstles at West Bromwich, the men of Nottingham on each occasion have achieved their laurels on foreign soil, and after two years of no success away from home, such victories as they gained at Sheffield and Sunderland point to them as one of the most improved teams in the country.

No effort had been spared by either the Liverpool or Nottingham Forest executives to get their men fit for this afternoon's game, and the players arrived in Liverpool from their respective training quarters in splendid trim. Ross was dropped to let in Michael as inside-right, the former Hearts' player being expected to give a much better display as partner than he could on the left. Bradshaw was included in the home ranks instead of Geary, while the Foresters had their full cup team.

There were about 12,000 people on the ground when Liverpool took to the field, and the Reds received a very warm greeting when they stepped on the field a minute or two later, there evidently being a large contingent of "Lambs" present. The Forest captain won the toss, and Allan started prompt to time, the home players facing the sun.

Bradshaw and Allan were soon engaged hotly with Iremonger and Frank Forman, the Notts right-back eventually clearing the danger. Goldie then finely repelled an advance by the visiting left wing, and a free-kick for a foul gave the home side a good chance of opening their account. Allsop, however, was on the alert, and Liverpool were once more driven back. At this stage, McCartney and Neill were proving much too intelligent and skilful for the visitors' left wing and centre. Liverpool attacked down the right and Michael gave Allsop a difficult shot to save, but the Forest custodian handled the situation well. McVean and Becton both tried to score, but both shot wide. At this point in the game, the home forwards were working grandly together, their crisp and true passing

being frequently applauded. However, it was not all one-way traffic, McInnes and Arthur Capes gave McCartney and Goldie as much as they could manage, while the right-wing pair were also going strongly.

A rush by the Forest left brought Storer from his goal, but several players managed to get in each other's way and Storer got back to his goal before the visitors could improve their chance. Moments later Allan and Becton featured prominently in a raid which created great anxiety in the Forest defence, and it appeared that Bradshaw would open the scoring, but the left-winger missed his mark by a couple of inches.

A free-kick by Iremonger was beautifully placed, and McInnes steadied himself for a tremendous shot which flew into the net after just sixteen minutes.

Liverpool made strenuous efforts to equalise, Allan working most unselfishly in support of both wings, but the Forest defence seemed to be the best seen at Anfield this or any other season. Iremonger was giving a fine exhibition against Becton and Bradshaw, while McInnes proved a thorn in McCartney's side, and it took all of Goldie's speed to match the pace of the Notts' left-winger, who proved a glutton for work.

The game became a midfield battle until Adrian Capes tested Storer with a rasping shot. This had been cleared before the home goalkeeper was charged. The free-kick opened up the play, but a promising attack by Liverpool was nullified when Allan placed his hand on an opponent's shoulder. Liverpool began to attack with ferocity, and Becton shot wide after good work from Bradshaw, and Allan just topped the crossbar. The goal kick was followed by an attack on Storer's charge, but Wilkie and Goldie, well supported by the three half-backs, kept the visitors at a safe distance.

"Play up Liverpool" was responded to in fine style, the whole quintet taking part in a forward advance, and an irresistible attack on Allsop's goal, which, in spite of herculean efforts by the Notts' defenders, fell to a slow shot from Becton after half an hour's play.

This success put new life into the Liverpool team, and some brilliant attacks were made by the home left, while McVean and Michael gave Scott and Wragg no peace.

The attendance had greatly increased during the interval, there being 16,000 spectators who gave a good reception to the players of each side when they again took to the field. McPherson restarted towards the Oakfield Road goal. Michael and Allan immediately went on the attack and

Bradshaw broke away at top speed before being tackled by Iremonger. The Forest right and centre then made tracks, but were somewhat easily repulsed. Free kicks were now awarded to and against Liverpool in quick succession, both being fruitless. After a show of attack by the home front ranks, the Foresters pulled themselves together for a supreme effort, but their finest efforts were met by the home backs in masterly style, and Storer was seldom seriously threatened. Finely led by Bradshaw, the home front rank retaliated, and Becton and Allan each went close to winning the game for Liverpool. A free-kick by Goldie was placed right into the goalmouth and it seemed likely that the home side would score a second goal, but the Forest cleared to safety. After a pulsating game played in the true spirit of an English Cup tie, it was decided to replay the match at Nottingham.

Liverpool: Storer; Goldie, Wilkie; McCartney, Neill, Cleghorn; McVean, Michael, Allan, Becton, Bradshaw.

Nottingham Forest: Allsop; Iremonger, Scott; Frank Forman, McPherson, Wragg; Fred Forman, Adrian Capes, Richards, Arthur Capes, McInnes.

Referee: Mr J.B. Brodie (Wolverhampton)

Attendance: 15,000

Official Referees 1896 - 97

Brodie, J.B., Schoolhouse, Brewood, near Stafford

Frank Becton, who scored Liverpool's equalising goal after half-an-hour's play

March 3, 1897

Nottingham Forest (0) 0

Liverpool (0) 1

Allan

EARLY yesterday morning the Liverpool team travelled into the Midlands in order to meet Nottingham Forest in the replayed tie for the English Cup. The match, as only to be expected, attracted an enormous interest, and a number of excursions were run into the lace capital.

The weather, though fine, was terribly windy, but this did not prevent the spectators attending, and when the teams lined up there were over 10,000 people present.

Liverpool had two changes from the previous match, Dunlop coming in for his Cup début in place of Wilkie and Geary in place of McVean. The Notts team underwent only one alteration, Shaw taking the place of Fred Forman.

Nottingham Forest: Allsop; Iremonger, Scott; Frank Forman, McPherson, Wragg; Shaw, Adrian Capes, Richards, Arthur Capes, McInnes.

Liverpool: Storer; Goldie, Dunlop; McCartney, Neill, Cleghorn; Geary, Michael, Allan, Becton, Bradshaw.

Referee: Mr A.G. Kingscott (Derby)

Attendance: 10,000

Liverpool won the toss, and started with the strong wind in their favour. This availed them little at the start, for the home team at once made off in the most determined fashion, and a minute from the start Adrian Capes sent in one that gave Storer a good deal of trouble. With the aid of the wind Liverpool made a little headway, but they were soon pulled up, and the Forest forwards moved off in splendid fashion. In spite of the wind their progress was steady, and McInnes twice sent in good shots that gave the Liverpool defence trouble.

The visitors attacked strongly down the left, and from a great pass by Becton, Bradshaw shot over the goal-line. From the goal-kick the Forest attempted to make headway, but Neill pulled them up, and the Liverpool left wing again made for the Forest citadel, but Iremonger robbed Bradshaw when he was within shooting distance. The home side then moved off in fine combination, and Frank Forman shot twice in rapid succession, but Storer each time proved fully equal to the occasion.

Although Liverpool had all the advantage of the wind, the Foresters at this point had much the better of the game, their passing being distinctly better than that of the visitors, and a strong shot from the left was only saved by the alertness of Dunlop. A moment later Geary and Mr Kingscott, the referee, had a heated argument, which was followed by an advance on the Liverpool right.

A throw-in gave the visitors a further advantage, and from this Allan caused Allsop to run out. The return was well taken by Michael, and a short bombardment of the home goal followed, but nothing came of it.

The visitors continued to press, and Geary sent in a beautiful shot which Allan should have scored with, but he was too slow, and Iremonger jumped in and relieved the pressure.

Liverpool again raced away on the right, Geary and Michael taking the ball along, and the latter had a great opportunity which he spoiled by shooting wide.

Eventually Forest moved on to the attack, and the Liverpool defence was kept fully engaged, but the wind helped them, and they succeeded in keeping out the invaders.

A breakaway on the Liverpool left was interrupted by the referee being requested to examine Bradshaw's boots. These were found to be in order, and the game proceeded by Liverpool attacking on the right, Michael sending in a nice shot which Neill spoiled by sending right over the bar.

Bradshaw, Becton and Allan were involved in a beautiful piece of combination, but the movement broke down when the ball went behind.

The home side responded with an attack of their own, but Goldie repelled McInnes. Liverpool again took up the attack and a free-kick close in gave them a chance, but McCartney shot over, and this was followed by Geary sending in a shot which struck the post.

Liverpool kept the ball well within the home half, but their attack in front of goal was distinctly weak, and half a dozen chances were missed by the forwards not showing more composure in front of goal. Just before the interval, McPherson shot over the bar as Forest pressed for the opening goal.

On crossing over, the Forest men had the wind in their favour and they attacked strongly. Adrian Capes had a fine chance, but he shot over the bar, and a few moments later he had a second opening, but the ball went out of play. Liverpool then countered, with Bradshaw the architect of several promising openings.

After a breakaway by the home team, the visitors once more attacked with venom, and Allan gained possession from Michael before rifling a shot into the net past the Forest goalkeeper, who had no chance of saving. Following this goal, Liverpool played strongly, but although they tried hard, they failed to add to their score. However, Liverpool had reached the semi-finals for the first time, and were drawn to meet Aston Villa, 6-2 winners against Nottingham Forest.

March 20, 1897

Aston Villa (1) 3

John Cowan 40, 55,
Athersmith

Liverpool (0) 0

LAST week, these two teams fought out a goalless draw at Perry Barr, and on Christmas Day the result was a 3-3 draw at Anfield, so there was every indication that this would be a close encounter. The executives of both clubs made the greatest efforts to get their players into the best condition, the Villans sojourning at Buxton, while the Liverpool players returned to Freshfield on Saturday night, a good week's work having been put in under trainer Dodds, who took his men to Liverpool this morning in splendid condition. On each side there was a single change made from last week, Liverpool strengthening their front rank by the inclusion of Becton, while Crabtree's place in the Villa team was filled by Griffiths, the international not having quite recovered from the effects of the unfortunate slip at Perry Barr last Saturday.

The Liverpool team left from the Central Station at half-past ten, and were in Sheffield shortly before one o'clock. Fortunately the weather was beautifully fine in the cutlery town, and the large crowds of the excursionists who travelled from the homes of the contesting teams had the best provision made for their reception that the Bramall Lane enclosure is capable of. Three quarters of an hour before the start there were almost twenty thousand people on the ground, and the appearance of the approach roads indicated that this number could well be doubled.

The Sheffield authorities had got the ground in good condition, and there was every appearance of a fast game, both teams being reported in the best of condition. A skilled band had been engaged to fill up the waiting time, and as four o'clock approached every inch of space was packed, nine trainloads from Liverpool and eight from Birmingham providing an enthusiastic band of supporters for the teams, while, of course, there was a large contingent of Sheffielders, who would not miss a Cup tie. Referee Scragg and his assistant officials made their appearance on the ground about ten minutes before the start, and immediately afterwards the Liverpool players took the field, being shortly followed by the Birmingham cracks, each team being well received.

McCartney beat Devey in the choice of ends, and Whitehouse had to defend the Bramall Lane goal. Immediately on Campbell kicking off, the ball went to Reynolds, whose strong centre caught Becton full in the face, and causing his nose to bleed. After a short delay, the referee threw up the ball, and the Villa forward line secured possession and attacked strongly down the right wing. Cleghorn and Dunlop proved too strong for Athersmith, however, and a good piece of individual skill by Neill allowed Liverpool to counter attack, and Allan netted the ball, only for the strike to be disallowed for offside. Neill was having an excellent game, and he intercepted a free-kick, which enabled the Liverpool left to advance in a promising fashion, but Reynolds broke up the movement, and Liverpool were again called upon to defend, but Devey was caught offside. Presently Bradshaw and Allan got to work, but the only result of a fine movement was a fruitless corner.

Following the free-kick the Liverpool left wing advanced again, and Becton and Bradshaw exchanged passes neatly before the Liverpool centre-forward shot a couple of feet wide of the post. The Birmingham side countered with some fine offensive moves of their own and it took all the skill of Goldie and the Liverpool halves to keep out the Villans. The game flowed from end to end, and Allan, from a shot by McCartney, shot at goal, with Whitehead fisting clear. A free-kick fell to Liverpool without advantage, and the Villans forced a corner after a free-kick of their own.

Dunlop cleared, and Bradshaw then raced off at top speed, before being fouled on the touch line. Michael was cautioned by the referee before Reynolds crossed the ball to his left wing. Goldie, however, repelled the Villans gallantly. Dunlop robbed Athersmith and set his side going again, Whitehouse nearly succumbing to a long drive by the Liverpool left-back. Campbell dribbled clear but shot weakly, and Storer had no difficulty in picking up and punting clear.

From a throw-in, Liverpool gained the advantage and Michael shot in towards Whitehouse, but the ball went over the bar. The Villans then had their best chance of the match to open their scoring account with some effective passing between the left wing and centre, resulting in Campbell having a great opportunity. Storer, however, rushed out of his goal and fell on the ball, and, recovering himself quickly, he threw clear. For a brief spell the Villans maintained a persistent attack, but the Liverpool defenders played a cool game. For a time the Aston men could not be driven off, but at last Becton got an opening and raced off, a pass to Allan resulting in the Liverpool centre being pulled up for offside. The next attempt by the Liverpool forwards ended in similar fashion, but the Villa were no more successful in their forays. The game had now been in progress half an hour, and fouls had been as frequent as is generally expected in cup ties. One of these was given against Liverpool just outside the eighteen yard line and from this Reynolds nearly scored; Dunlop, however, keeping an opponent offside while Storer cleared his lines. Foul play by Reynolds against Allan gave Liverpool another free-kick, Becton working the leather close to Whitehouse before passing to Allan, who shot a few inches wide of the mark. At this point in the game Liverpool were having the better of the argument, but against the run of play, the Villans scored with a breakaway down the left wing. A foul against Liverpool was well placed by Spencer, and Athersmith sent the ball across to John Cowan, who cleverly hooked the ball into the net from long range, Storer being completely beaten.

Bradshaw and Devey both missed great chances of scoring, and a fine run by the Liverpool man was checked by Evans.

The second half opened in favour of Liverpool, and Neill shot strongly before an accurate centre from Geary went right across the face of the goal, but it was just too high for Bradshaw to reach. Liverpool pressed strongly, and Geary forced a corner. The ball bobbed about near Whitehouse before Becton seized on it and shot inches over the bar. Storer was then forced to handle a fine shot by Devey, who then hit the upright with a fierce shot.

The referee unaccountably awarded a corner and John Cowan headed a second goal with ten minutes of the second half gone.

Liverpool looked a beaten side, but Storer saved well from Campbell, whilst from a free-kick, Bradshaw got possession and passed it to Allan, but the chance was lost. A desperate attempt was made to score, and Whitehouse was injured, but he soon resumed. Though Dunlop repeatedly beat the Villa right-winger, Athersmith eventually got past him and, racing in at full speed, scored a magnificent goal.

In the last five minutes Bradshaw made two excellent runs, whilst Cleghorn put through from a free-kick, but the ball did not touch another player *en route* to the net, and the goal was disallowed.

John Cowan, *the Aston Villa skipper and two-goal destroyer of Liverpool in the semi-final*

Aston Villa: Whitehouse; Spencer, Evans; Reynolds, James Cowan, Griffiths; Athersmith, Devey, Campbell, Wheldon, John Cowan.

Liverpool: Storer; Goldie, Dunlop; McCartney, Neill, Cleghorn; Geary, Michael, Allan, Becton, Bradshaw.

Referee: Mr A. Scragg (Crewe)

Linesmen: Mr J.E. Carpenter (Leicester);
　　　　　　Mr J.T. Howcroft (Bolton)

Attendance: 30,000 (at Bramall Lane)

FATAL PRIZE FIGHT

Philadelphia, Saturday. - A fight between two pugilists, named Edward Gibbons and John Perry, took place last night during an entertainment at a club, and had a fatal termination. During the third round Perry gave Gibbons a straight blow with his left arm just below the heart. The blow was exactly similar to that by which Corbett was knocked out by Fitzsimmons on Wednesday last. Gibbons remained at the club for an hour, feeling none the worse, when he suddenly began to spit blood and became very sick. The physician who was sent for found that the pugilist had been internally injured. Gibbons became comatose, and was removed to hospital, where he died at midnight. Perry has been arrested. - Dalziel.

January 29, 1898

Liverpool (0) 2   Hucknall St.John's (0) 0
Becton,   McQue

OWING to the great counter-attraction at Goodison Park, where Everton were entertaining Blackburn Rovers (Everton beat Blackburn Rovers 1-0 with a second-half header from Williams before a crowd of 25,000, paying £700) there was only a mere handful of spectators at Anfield Road to witness this English Cup tie.

The Liverpudlians were distinctly fortunate in being drawn against such an unknown quantity as Hucknall St.John's - unknown, that is, so far as Merseyside was concerned. In the Sherwood Forest district, however, they had made a name for themselves, inasmuch as they were top of the Notts League, having lost only one game.

Liverpool: Storer; Goldie, Dunlop; McCartney, McQue, Cleghorn; Marshall, McCowie, Hartley, Becton, Bradshaw.

Hucknall St.John's: Lockyer; Mitchell, Woolley; Speirs, Jones, Baker; Chappell, Weston, Richardson, Emmerson, Palin.

Referee: Mr G.H. Dale (Manchester)

Attendance: 8,000

The weather was favourable, although rather hazy. McCartney lost the toss, and Hartley kicked off, a movement being at once made into Hucknall territory, and after one tackle had been administered by Mitchell, the home team advanced to the front and maintained a continued attack until a shot from McCowie gained a corner, which was not improved upon.

Owing to the unseemly behaviour of one of the few spectators, Mr Dale put a stop to the game while he went and interviewed the noisy individual, who at once subsided into extreme quietness.

Upon resuming, the visitors broke through on the left, but Emmerson's run was speedily checked when Storer cantered out and gathered the ball before clearing. Then the homesters made a further prolonged attack, which was at last broken up by Jones, and Weston galloped away, only to be pulled up in an offside position. Emmerson shot over the Liverpool crossbar, and Becton, at the other end, skied the leather over the Hucknall goal.

After a short period of stalemate in midfield, the visitors gained a corner on the right, which was easily accounted for. This was followed by a smart run on the part of Bradshaw, who was at the finish beaten by Mitchell, a scrimmage in front of the visitors' goal being finished by a wide shot from Hartley. The entire Hucknall forward line moved over the half-way line, but their progress was checked and Liverpool attacked again before Lockyer punched away an overhead kick from Becton.

McCowie gained a corner, and then forced Lockyer to save, but the display of both teams was disappointing in footballing terms. The visitors were distinctly awkward in their movements with the exception of the goalkeeper; but the "play" of the Liverpudlians left a lot to be desired. Goldie was hurt and had to leave the field, and when he returned he had his head bandaged.

The home side began to dominate the play and Becton had two great efforts saved well by the goalkeeper. The Hucknall right wing then attacked, but Chappell was pulled up for offside, and just afterwards the Notts men gave away a corner on the left which they managed to clear. Palin was cautioned for rough play, and then Dunlop tackled fiercely, but the visitors returned to the attack and Richardson shot inches over the bar. The interval arrived without any score.

Richardson restarted for the visitors, but it was immediately apparent that Liverpool had decided during the break to attack Hucknall from the first whistle and they monopolised the play for a lengthy period before Mitchell fisted out a shot inside the twelve yards line.

The inevitable penalty kick followed and Becton put the ball in the net, but one of the visitors had stepped over the prescribed line and Mr Dale ordered the kick to be re-taken. Becton was again trusted with the kick and Lockyer blocked the progress of the ball, but Becton dashed forward and, before the Hucknall goalkeeper could clear, the Liverpool forward scored the first goal.

Two corners followed to the home side and Hartley netted, only for the point to be disallowed for offside. Lockyer was under severe pressure, and he brought off several fine saves before he was beaten by a long shot from McQue. Liverpool continued to attack but they were beaten back time after time by a resolute defence.

February 12, 1898

Newton Heath (0) 0

Liverpool (0) 0

AFTER a week's hard training at St. Anne's-on-Sea, the Liverpool team left the healthy resort this morning for Manchester in order to meet their engagement with Newton Heath, who had trained locally. The teams met at Bank Lane, Clayton and the atmosphere in Cottonopolis was in striking contrast to that of the seaside, and at Newton Heath the surroundings were even more dismal, the cluster of chemical works sending clouds of odoriferous smoke across the ground.

The Liverpool team had one noticeable change from last week, Bradshaw being left out, and Lumsden coming in. The players were reported to be fully fit. The Heathens were without Stafford, still unable to play because of an injured leg, and Dunn resumed his position in the forward line and played with great skill until close to the finish when he was again hurt and had to retire from the field. McCartney skippered the Liverpool team.

Newton Heath: Barrett; H.Errentz, F.Errentz; Draycott, McNaught, Cartwright; Bryant, Collinson, Boyd, Cassidy, Dunn.

Liverpool: Storer; Goldie, Dunlop; McCartney, McQue, Cleghorn; Cunliffe, Becton, Hartley, McCowie, Lumsden.

Referee: Mr A.J. Barker (Newcastle-under-Lyme)

Linesmen: Messrs. J. Nicholson (Sheffield), J. Tillotson (Birmingham)

Attendance: 12,000

Receipts: £289

The Newton Heath captain, F. Errentz, won the toss, and played his team so as to have all the advantage of a pretty stiff breeze. Hartley kicked off in the presence of about 12,000 spectators. Cassidy at once made a race down to the Liverpool goal and passed out to Dunn, whose centre was well met by Boyd, but the centre-forward shot over the bar. Liverpool's only attacking move of the opening period ended with Hartley shooting into Barrett's hands. F.Errentz cleared the ball and Second Division Newton Heath (lying in sixth place) subjected First Division Liverpool (lying in twelfth position) to a period of sustained attack. McQue gave Liverpool some respite, but Collinson sent in a terrific shot which Storer just managed to kick away. A brilliant piece of dribbling by Becton gave the visitors another opportunity of showing what they could do in front of goal and McCowie finished the move with a powerful drive which went well wide of the target.

Becton made a similar mistake, and Lumsden, with an open goal at his mercy, failed to score as Liverpool gradually got into the game. Good centre-half play from McQue repelled Newton Heath, but after a while Goldie was bothered by Dunn and Cassidy, and the difficulty was averted when Cleghorn moved across the field and rendered valuable assistance to McCartney, who had been fouled.

Collinson and Bryant moved menacingly down the right, and the Liverpool defence was soon in danger as Boyd shot powerfully towards the goal. Only the referee, who stood in the way of the shot, prevented a certain goal.

The visitors' defence, however, failed to stave off the Heathens' attack, another shot from Collinson being swept away by Storer, and another drive by Bryant went wide of the post. Dunlop brought off a marvellous save almost on the goal-line as the home side pressed forward their advantage. Cartwright and Dunn initiated a further move and Cassidy took up the running. Collinson met the centre, but Dunlop saved Liverpool from falling behind.

Following a foul on McCowie, Liverpool were awarded a free-kick, but a flying kick by F. Errentz nullified the move. Boyd seized possession of the ball and sent in a shot from long range which Storer had no difficulty in saving, but the Newton Heath forwards sent the Liverpool goalkeeper tumbling head over heels. The referee had no hesitation in awarding a free-kick, and Liverpool advanced, but despite great effort they failed to score.

Shortly afterwards, Mr Barker stopped the game and administered a severe caution to Dunn, who had been on several occasions guilty of backing. The free-kick was of no advantage to the visiting team. Just before the interval, Storer saved well from a lob by Dunn.

Boyd restarted and although Liverpool had the wind in their favour, Newton Heath in the first few minutes made a vigorous attack on the visitors' goal. Cassidy shot in, but Storer cleared, and then Collinson almost gained the desired goal with a fast low shot which, however, Storer turned out by falling full length on the ground.

At length the Liverpool defence prevailed and Newton Heath were forced back, Becton having little fortune in not scoring, the ball striking one of the posts and bouncing over the home line. McNaught got away and centred well to Collinson, who shot wide. Shortly afterwards Dunn sent in a great shot which Storer saved by knocking the ball over the bar. Dunn had to leave the field due to an injury, but when the game resumed Liverpool attacked strongly. Hartley and Becton got close to goal, but Barrett safely dealt with their shots.

February 16, 1898

Liverpool (0) 2
Dunlop, Cunliffe 85

Newton Heath (1) 1
Collinson 35

WITH both Everton and Liverpool being involved in Cup replays, the Liverpool team decided to take the Wednesday, while Everton entertained Stoke on the Thursday. After the game at Clayton, Liverpool immediately returned to St. Anne's-on-the-Sea, from where they arrived in time for the match and all of the players appeared to be in the finest condition. The game kicked off at 3pm.

Liverpool: Storer; Wilkie, Dunlop; McCartney, McQue, Cleghorn; Cunliffe, Finnerhan, Hartley, Becton, Lumsden.

Newton Heath: Barrett; H.Errentz, F.Errentz; Draycott, McNaught, Cartwright; Bryant, Collinson, Boyd, Cassidy, Gillespie.

Referee: Mr A.J. Barker (Newcastle-under-Lyme)

Attendance: 6,000

The Heathens, who had undergone special training at Lytham, were strongly represented, but in the Liverpool line-up Wilkie took the place of Goldie, due to Goldie having buried his child the day before the match. The forward line was also re-arranged, McCowie being dropped in favour of Finnerhan, and Becton being transferred to his old position on the left wing. The only change in the visiting team was the substitution of Gillespie for Dunn. There was a strong wind blowing and the visitors took full advantage of the elements, gaining possession and embarking on prominent raids in the Liverpool half. Dunlop was over employed, but it was left to the half-backs to make an effective clearance, with Cleghorn shining in that role. Becton then took up the running and Hartley got into a good position before the custodian pounced on him. At the opposite end Wilkie was beaten, and Collinson tested Storer with a brilliant shot which was cleverly cleared. Cunliffe replied for Liverpool, shooting in hard and low, but Barrett was in fine form. Moments later Becton and Hartley combined well, when the centre-forward was ruled offside.

A beautiful shot from Cassidy forced Storer to effect a magnificent save, and Liverpool retaliated when Cunliffe shot across the face of the goal, but both Becton and Lumsden failed to get their foot to the ball. Two corner kicks in quick succession were taken at the Newton Heath end, but nothing resulted. Liverpool returned to the attack, and an exciting scrimmage flowed close in the goal, which was saved by the visiting backs. A free-kick enabled the Heathens to advance, and Storer was twice tested with difficult shots. An effort from Gillespie rebounded from an upright, and for several moments, the home goal had several narrow escapes. At length the visiting forwards were rewarded for their persistence when Collinson drove the ball into the net.

Upon resuming, Liverpool had the advantage of the wind, but the Heathens had more of the possession and Storer had several anxious moments in goal. Eventually the Liverpool forwards found their form and the play was immediately in front of Barrett, who was capably covered by his backs.

From a free-kick close in Dunlop drove the ball with great force and gliding off a player's legs, found its way into the net, much to the delight of the home supporters.

The Heathens would not be denied and they had as much possession as Liverpool. Storer was tested by Draycott, and Collinson also put in a fine effort. Becton, with an immaculate pass across the field, caused great consternation in the Heathen ranks. A prolonged spell of Liverpool pressure was negated through the ineffectiveness of the forwards to put the ball in the net.

Some fierce tackles followed, but no further scoring took place, although Becton had a good shot which grazed the crossbar. A further spell of Liverpool pressure followed, during which the ball was repeatedly headed out of the Newton goal and it ended with Cunliffe getting his cranium to the leather and depositing it in the net five minutes from the close of play.

Daniel Cunliffe

February 26, 1898

Derby County (0) 1
Stevenson

Liverpool (0) 1
Bradshaw

THIS morning a number of Liverpool supporters left the Central Station for Derby, and were joined at Marple by the team, who had been recuperating at St.Anne's-on-the-Sea during the week, and were reported by Mr Watson to be in the best condition. The Liverpool party arrived at noon. Derby had undertaken special training at Matlock Bridge. The weather had undergone a complete change: in the morning the sun shone brilliantly, but the snow-clad hills of Derbyshire bore testament to the recent severe weather. The wind was rather high across the ground, but was not sufficiently rough to interfere seriously with play. Almost at the last moment Methven was stated to be indisposed, being taken ill during the night with influenza, and his position was taken by Staley. The popular Steve Bloomer was also an absentee. Fryer reappeared for Derby. In the Liverpool ranks room was made for Bradshaw, who partnered Becton, the latter resuming his old position. In the Derby ranks was a former Liverpool player, Hugh McQueen. During the time the crowd were filling the ground the spectators were entertained by a marvellous brass band, and when the teams tripped gaily on to the enclosure, there were about 12,000 people present. The Derby men were accorded a hearty reception as they took to the field on the heels of John Goodall, and the crowd were vociferous in their welcome to the Liverpool team.

Derby County: Fryer; Staley, Leiper; Cox, A.Goodall, Turner; Leonard, J.Goodall, McConnachie, Stevenson, H.McQueen.

Liverpool: Storer; Goldie, Dunlop; McCartney, McQue, Cleghorn; Cunliffe, Finnerhan, Hartley, Becton, Bradshaw.

Referee: Mr J. Fox (Sheffield)

Attendance: 12,699
Receipts: £528

John Goodall won the toss and Hartley kicked off prompt to time. The first move was checked by Leiper, and then John Goodall quickly sprinted away and passed to his left. McQueen centred the ball and forced a corner which was brilliantly saved by Storer. Wilkie checked the progress of the homesters, but Derby continued to cluster around the Liverpool goal, and McConnachie sent in a great shot. Shortly afterwards, the visitors moved forward and Cunliffe was responsible for good work on the right, but at the last moment he slipped. Becton came to his rescue, although he failed at goal. John Goodall again rushed forward and passed out to his left, where Hugh McQueen again put in a lovely centre, and

after the leather had been drifting about in front of goal for several seconds, Storer at last ran along the goal line and kicked out of danger. End to end play ensued, during which Cunliffe missed an easy goalscoring opportunity, and at the other end Goldie cleared. Another fine centre from McQueen was met by Goodall, who headed at goal, Storer effecting a magnificent save. Liverpool made little use of their opportunities, whilst Derby were hard-working and skilful in reply. However, the Liverpool defence fulfilled every expectation. One shot from McQueen went close to the mark, and drew an audible sigh from the Liverpool officials who were keenly following play. The evergreen Johnny Goodall sent in a brilliant shot which flew over the bar, and a similar disappointment met a shot from McQue at the opposite end. Archie Goodall was instrumental in checking a bright move on the part of the Liverpudlians, but he himself was just afterwards well beaten by McQue, who easily beat Johnny Goodall before the Derby defence averted the danger. Shortly afterwards, McConnachie shot over the bar as play continued to move from end to end. Close on half-time, Derby instigated a tremendous onslaught and Johnny Goodall and Leonard sent in excellent shots which were magnificently cleared by Goldie and Storer.

Upon resumption the visitors had the advantage of the wind and sun. From a foul against Cox, Fryer effected a wonderful save. Then, from a centre by Cunliffe, Staley lost sight of the ball which went to McCartney, who sent it right across the goalmouth to Bradshaw, who slipped it past Fryer and scored for Liverpool from three yards out. Derby fought hard, but the Liverpool defence was splendid, and Fryer was forced to clear again. Hartley fouled Goodall, and Turner tripped Cunliffe as the game degenerated into an over-physical one. Fryer elicited enthusiastic cheers with a magnificent save from a free-kick at close quarters. The game became more fiercely contested than ever, the County eventually putting forth every effort, but the Liverpool defence was very determined. McConnachie hit the crossbar with a magnificent shot, and Storer saved six times in quick succession. At length Liverpool broke away and Bradshaw put in a tremendous shot which Fryer dropped, and Hartley had an open goal, but struck the goalkeeper's legs. Finally Stevenson got his head to a fine centre from Leonard and equalised. Derby surged onto the attack and Goodall missed scoring through a misunderstanding with Leonard. Hartley shot over the bar for Liverpool, and Stevenson had a wild shot at the target as the game flowed from end to end. Liverpool gained a corner near the end but Derby cleared easily. Stevenson missed a fine opening for the County through dallying. The closing stages of the game were intensely exciting. In the last minute Hartley was injured.

March 2, 1898

Liverpool (1) 1
Becton 44 (pen)

Derby County (2) 5
Boag (3), Bloomer (2)

THE weather was bright, though windy, and the latter helped to dry the ground which was rather on the soft side. Crowds of people began to flock to the enclosure before two o'clock, an hour and a half before kicking off time, and by half-past three the place was pretty well crowded.

Steve Bloomer and Boag took the places of Leonard and McConnachie in the Derby ranks. Owing to an objection against McConnachie for playing in the close season, Boag appeared at centre-forward. Methven was excluded owing to a sudden attack of influenza, while Liverpool were fully represented.

Liverpool won the toss, and for a time play was even. Bloomer shot wide, and Derby failed to take advantage of a corner. Liverpool then pressed severely, but the visitors' defence was excellent. The home side continued to have the better of the game and following a corner, Fryer expertly saved a header from Becton. After 30 minutes, from Stevenson's centre, Boag shot a goal for Derby, the Liverpool players protesting strongly on the grounds of offside. Liverpool pressed without scoring, and from a breakaway, Bloomer scored again. Becton scored for Liverpool from the penalty spot just before the interval.

There was an increased attendance when the game re-started. The County, who had the benefit of the wind and the sun, attacked strongly, and Stevenson shot over the bar. Boag, from right under the goal added a third for the visitors. Cunliffe missed from a splendid centre from Bradshaw, and the game was fast and fairly even, both goalkeepers being forced to save.

After Fryer had saved several times, Johnny Goodall initiated another attacking movement, from which Bloomer put on the fourth goal. Shortly afterwards, the Liverpool goal had a narrow escape, the County playing a magnificent game.

At times Liverpool performed admirably, but spoiled their approach work by weakness in front of goal. Boag scored a fifth goal for Derby.

At a meeting of the Health Committee of the Darlington Corporation the day before this game, a letter was read from a prominent medical gentleman calling attention to the selection of Darlington for the semi-final tie of the Amateur Football Cup between Middlesbrough and Thornaby.

Much indignation was expressed at the arrangement, considering the smallpox epidemic at Middlesbrough, and it was decided to communicate with the chairman of the Darlington directors regarding the letting of the ground. The match was ordered to be played at Darlington by the English Football Association on March 12.

THE FOOTBALL LEAGUE

List of Players Open to Transfer for Season 1897 - 98

FIRST DIVISION

LIVERPOOL

	£ s d
Cameron, J	10 0 0
Drummond, J	20 0 0
Givens, J	10 0 0
Hannah, D	35 0 0
Hannah, A.B.	50 0 0
Henderson, H	30 0 0
Henderson, D	15 0 0
Hughes, A	15 0 0
McLean, J	50 0 0
McLean, J	25 0 0
McCann, W	20 0 0
McLean, D	50 0 0

DERBY COUNTY

Buchanan, P	25 0 0
Hemstock, J	10 0 0

Liverpool: Storer; Goldie, Dunlop; McCartney, McQue, Cleghorn; Cunliffe, Finnerhan, Hartley, Becton, Bradshaw.

Derby County: Fryer; Staley, Leiper; Cox, A.Goodall, Turner; J.Goodall, Bloomer, Boag, Stevenson, H.McQueen.

Referee: Mr J. Fox (Sheffield)

Attendance: 15,000

January 28, 1899

Liverpool (1) 2

Cox,   Allan 87

Blackburn Rovers (0) 0

BOTH teams underwent special training for this fixture, such was the importance of the tie. For the first time this season, football enthusiasts received a shock in the shape of King Frost, which made the ground extremely hard and skating took away thousands of devotees. Fortunately, both committees were enabled to put their best men on the field. Liverpool relied on the identical eleven which defeated Everton, whilst Blackburn had out their strongest team.

The Rovers brought with them a large contingent of supporters, and both teams were heartily cheered as they took to the field. Jackson kicked off in front of 12,000 spectators.

It became apparent at once that the players would have difficulty in keeping their feet. However, Liverpool quickly assumed the upper hand, and during the first few minutes they maintained a fierce attack on Carter, but though two good shots were sent in, both failed to reach their target. A beautiful piece of inter-passing by the Rovers' front rank carried them well within their opponents' quarters, where Howell - making his Cup début - conceded a free kick, the ball being sent behind. Considering the adverse conditions under which the teams were contending, they exercised wonderful control of the ball, this being especially the case with the Blackburnians. Jackson and Halse dashed forward and a score seemed imminent when Raisbeck - also making his Cup début - repelled the visitors.

The home side exerted themselves with the aid of some excellent half-back work and Morgan and Allan each went close with good efforts. The game was proving to be an exciting contest at this stage with each goal receiving equal pressure. Clever work on the part of Morgan and Robertson put Liverpool onto the attack, and Morgan's final shot gave Carter a lot of problems. Crompton appeared unnecessarily rough in tackling Cox, and though the Reds were beaten back they soon returned and a fine bit of work by Howell pulled up the opposing left wing. Liverpool made a further onslaught on the Blackburn goal and Robertson sent in a powerful shot which Carter cleared. For some time, midfield play ruled. The Rovers made rapid progress up the centre, Jackson having a glorious opportunity of opening the scoring. The hard ground, however, sent the ball flying high in the air, and the visiting centre-forward scooped it down with his hands, thus nullifying the opportunity, much to the relief of the Liverpool supporters. For several minutes, the Rovers attacked incessantly and forced a corner from which Anderson almost scored. Jackson attempted a move towards goal and Raisbeck was unable to check his progress. Dunlop, however, rushed to the rescue of his side, though the relief was short-lived and the Rovers continued to press forward. Fortunately the

Liverpool defence was firm. Raisbeck, with a tremendous kick, again put Liverpool in an aggressive position. From a free-kick the ball was sent well into the goalmouth, before being cleared. It was returned, and fell to Cox, who met it and scored with a tremendous shot. This goal naturally spurred on Liverpool and for the next few minutes the home side severely tested the visitors.

Blackburn, however, were not to be denied, and they themselves were involved in several exciting episodes in front of the Liverpool goal.

When Allan re-started, the attendance increased to about 14,000. The Reds made progress, but Brandon, Booth and Crompton defied being beaten and kept their head cool and their goal intact. From a free-kick, the Liverpool goal had a very narrow escape, the ball being shot in and kept out on two occasions. The Rovers were not disconcerted by repeated failures, and for some time they maintained a heavy bombardment of the Liverpool goal, but for all their effort they could not break down the solid home defence. For the next ten minutes, Blackburn made strenuous efforts to draw level, and their persistence almost resulted in a goal, but time and time again the Liverpool defence denied them. After a brief move by Carter, who was practically a spectator of the game, the Rovers again paid a visit to Storer, Booth and Halse being inches away from the target. The display by the visitors during the second half was simply magnificent and they literally ran Liverpool off their feet. However, with three minutes remaining, Allan scored the conclusive goal.

Official Referees 1898 - 99

Scragg, A., 249, Walthall Street, Crewe

Liverpool: Storer; A.Goldie, Dunlop; Howell, Raisbeck, W.Goldie; Cox, Walker, Allan, Morgan, Robertson.

Blackburn Rovers: Carter; Brandon, Crompton; Booth, Howarth, Houlker; Briercliffe, Halse, Jackson, Anderson, Hirst.

Referee: Mr A. Scragg (Crewe)

Attendance: 14,000

February 11, 1899

Liverpool (1) 3
Morgan 5,   Raisbeck 50,
Higgins (og)

Newcastle United (0) 1
Peddie 78

LIVERPOOL, currently occupying second position in the League, entertained second-from-bottom Newcastle United at Anfield. In striking contrast to the previous week, the weather was almost balmy in its nature, and although a stiff breeze was blowing the wind was relatively mild. It was fine overhead, and the conditions altogether were of the best. The Liverpool team had been in their training headquarters at Fairhaven all week, while the "canny men" from Newcastle had taken their "breathing" in the neighbourhood of Carlisle, and came to town on the morning of the game from Lancaster, all being reported in the best of health.

In the Liverpool team there was one change from last week, Morgan coming back in place of McCowie. The visitors played the identical eleven which played "ducks and drakes" with Burnley in the League match at Newcastle. Nearly 500 spectators came from Newcastle, so that the North countrymen did not lack support.

The attendance, however, was generally disappointing, the counter-attraction at Goodison Park (where a 25,000 crowd were witnessing the Cup tie against Nottingham Forest, which the visitors won with a goal from Fred Foreman) taking the majority of the footballing public there.

Stott, the United captain, won the toss and Allan started towards the Anfield Road goal before about 7,000 spectators. Walker was the first away and he gave the ball to Cox, who sped away only to see Stott kick the ball to safety. From the throw-in Allan put the ball across the goalmouth, where Morgan dashed in and shot narrowly wide.

From the goal-kick the United advanced, but they were beaten back by Goldie. Aitken and Wardrope combined well and Archie Goldie and Howell were well beaten. From Wardrope's centre Peddie had a chance, but Howell dashed in and took the ball from his toes.

Shortly afterwards Allan had a clear run on goal with only Higgins and the goalkeeper in front of him, but in the excitement, the Liverpool centre fouled Higgins, and a free-kick followed.

Liverpool moved menacingly on to the attack and a magnificent shot by Allan was tipped over the bar by Kingsley. The corner was not cleared, and Lindsay conceded another, which was dealt with safely.

Lindsay was guilty of questionable play and a foul was given against him, which was taken by Dunlop who kicked strongly against a post. As quick as a flash Morgan pounced upon it, and succeeded in scoring the first goal for Liverpool amidst tremendous cheering five minutes from the start.

Coming almost straight back from the centre, Cox made for goal and missed by inches. Then Allan hit a perfect pass to Walker, who similarly missed only by inches. Afterwards, Newcastle attacked strongly. Peddie proved much too slow,

and he missed a great chance, but Rogers was swift in attack before Archie Goldie moved across from the opposite wing and blocked his progress. Peddie was tripped just outside the twelve yards' line, and from the free-kick Stott shot over the crossbar. Relief came from the goal-kick, the Reds rushing right up to Kingsley's charge, where Lindsay halted Liverpool's progress with a powerful clearance. At this point in the game, the play was typical of a cup tie, with each end being visited in quick succession, and play being fast and open.

Newcastle attacked through Wardrope, who passed to the centre from the left wing. Peddie hooked the ball over to Rogers, who continued the move and at the finish Stevenson shot strongly, but Storer had no difficulty in saving. For fully five minutes after this foray, the visitors, who were remarkably quick on the ball, kept pegging away, but the home defence was far too strong, with Dunlop, in particular, kicking accurately away.

Eventually Liverpool got away on the left and Allan was left with an easy chance. Seeing what was likely to be the outcome, Kingsley left his goal, no doubt thinking that he would have a better opportunity of clearing, and with almost an open goal, Allan sent the ball rolling slowly across the goalmouth, but Cox was just too late to score another point. Shortly afterwards, Cox shot straight into Kingsley's hands just as the whistle sounded for offside. At this stage in the game, there was little doubt about the superiority of the home side. However, Aitken and Wardrope showed occasional flashes of brilliance on the left, but Howell frequently cleared. At length the visitors got a corner off Dunlop, but Morgan cleared Rogers' kick.

Peddie restarted, and play opened in midfield but two minutes into the half Stott came into collision with Allan and the game was suspended for a few moments until the Newcastle captain recovered. A free-kick to the visitors was the outcome of the charge against Stott, and Rogers drove the ball against the angle between upright and crossbar. Kingsley made two saves in quick succession from Robertson and Walker but he was unable to prevent a long drive from Raisbeck registering another goal for the home side. Liverpool continued to dominate, and Robertson got in a fine centre which Higgins, in trying to head away, put through his own goal, Kingsley having no possible chance of saving. The United team were then forced back time after time and carried themselves like a beaten team. Twelve minutes from the end Rogers raced along the right and centred almost from the touchline. Peddie met the ball and shot at goal, and a regular scrimmage ensued right on the goal line. Raisbeck made a fine attempt to get the ball clear, but Peddie got to the ball again and literally put the ball into the net, registering the first point for United.

Liverpool: Storer; A.Goldie, Dunlop; Howell, Raisbeck, W.Goldie; Cox, Walker, Allan, Morgan, Robertson.

Newcastle United: Kingsley; Lindsay, Higgins; Ghee, Ostler, Stott; Rogers, Stevenson, Peddie, Aitken, Wardrope.

Referee: Mr A. Scragg (Crewe)

Attendance: 7,000

| FOOTBALL BAG. | 12in. 2/11 | 14in. 3/6 | 16in. 3/11 | 18in. 4/11 |

Peddie, of Newcastle, who scored against Liverpool

February 26, 1899

West Bromwich Albion (0) 0   Liverpool (0) 2

Morgan 49, Robertson

IN the League this season, Liverpool have attained a higher position (second) than their redoubtable cup opponents (seventh), but that is not much to go by when the fight for the coveted national trophy is concerned, and immediately after their victory over Burnley last week (Liverpool defeated Burnley 2-0 at Anfield before a crowd of 12,000, Allan and Robertson scoring the goals as the Reds extended their unbeaten run in the League and Cup to 13 matches) the Anfielders were sent back to their training quarters at Fairhaven, a pretty little spot situated between Lytham and St. Anne's-on-Sea. Here they underwent an excellent course of preparation, and yesterday they travelled to the town of Wolverhampton, where they spent the night, and proceeded to West Bromwich on the morning of the game. The Throstles had also been preparing for the fray, having a course of training at home, and both elevens were reported to be as fit as so many fiddles.

As indicative of the keen interest in this game, the excursions leaving Liverpool for the Midlands were densely crowded. Both the North-Western and Great Western specials were packed with enthusiastic passengers. The weather was beautifully fine, and this, coupled with the important nature of the match, induced a tremendous crowd to put in an appearance at the Stoney Lane enclosure, and large contingents arrived from Wolverhampton and Birmingham. Liverpool relied upon the same team as appeared last week, and the Throstles were fully represented.

The enclosure was packed to overflowing when West Bromwich eventually lost the toss, and started with their faces to the sun. They attacked immediately, but Dunlop repelled their advances, and Liverpool moved down the left, Robertson and Morgan taking the ball past the twelve yards line when it went out of play. Allan, Morgan and Robertson combined well but Williams cleared the danger. Jones fed his forwards well and Bassett raced away and looked dangerous before Dunlop again cleared. By a series of intricate passing, Liverpool advanced on the right before Williams negated their attack. The visitors kept up the pressure and Robertson sent in a magnificent shot which just skimmed the bar.

From the goal kick, the Albion advanced on the right with Bassett and Simmonds being prominent with fine work, but the Liverpool defence was as solid as a rock. The home side continued to attack and McKenzie sent in a low shot which was fortunately intercepted by the foot of Wilkie. For a period, Storer's goal was subjected to an unceasing bombardment and McKenzie and Richards sent in shots, but Dunlop and Wilkie both came to the rescue of their captain, and after exciting struggles the Throstles were eventually

driven back. The relief was short-lived, however, and Perry sent in a magnificent shot which Storer just succeeded in clearing. Following this, Robertson dashed away and passed both Perry and Cave. He had the goal at his mercy when he shot, but the ball went in an oblique direction across the goalmouth and, with no-one following up, the chance was lost.

End-to-end play ensued but eventually Liverpool made play on the right and Walker and Cox put in effective work which was nullified by the brilliance of Williams. Perry initiated a forward movement and a swift shot from Richards was cleared by the intervention of Raisbeck, who passed to Allan. The centre-forward sped away with Robertson alongside, but once again, Williams cleared the dangerous looking movement. Play was of an exceedingly fast and exciting nature, with both teams straining every nerve, and there was little difference between the teams at this stage, though the Throstles had the advantage of the sun and slope. Play was halted for a minute due to an injury to Cox, but it soon resumed and Robertson sent in a fine centre which Williams cleared. Shortly afterwards, Allan found the impressive Robertson, who centred to Walker and the inside-right's header was saved comfortably by Reader. The Reds continued with their onslaught and a screw shot from Walker just passed over the bar. Following this the Anfielders forced a corner off Dunn, but this came to nothing. Liverpool now had the better of the exchanges, and both Allan and Morgan had shots which, however, proved to be unsuccessful. At length, the Albion proceeded down the left as Perry relieved. Garfield sent in a lightning shot which Storer threw away. McKenzie met the return, and it looked as though he would score, but the ball passed over the bar. Liverpool then enjoyed another lengthy period of complete domination and it was only the superb defence of the home side which kept the game goalless. A free-kick close in gave the visitors a fine opening, but Allán's shot went wide.

The game was being so keenly contested that several of the players came to loggerheads, and the referee stopped play for some moments and ordered Allan, Jones and Morgan to settle their differences and continue with the game.

A free-kick against Allan let the Albion in, and Richards gave Storer some anxiety, but the Liverpool custodian was equal to the occasion.

After a period of midfield play, Robertson sent in a magnificent centre which Allan was about to meet when he was grassed by Williams. Morgan sent in another pin-point centre, but it was intercepted by Cave and the Throstles made play on the left. The ball was sent across to Bassett, but before he could shoot, half-time arrived. A jaunt round the ground during the interval showed that every nook and corner was occupied. The gate had been closed immediately after the start, and it was with extreme difficulty that Press messengers were able to leave and re-enter the enclosure.

From the re-start Liverpool at once broke away on the left. The ball went harmlessly over the line, and from the kick out the home team made progress on the left with Garfield and McKenzie, whose centre found Richards. The home centre-forward tested Storer with a shot, but the Liverpool custodian cleared with ease. Moments later, Goldie let in McKenzie and he skimmed the crossbar as Albion sought the opening goal.

A foul by Perry close in gave Liverpool a great opportunity. The free-kick found Morgan, who sent the ball flying into the net after just four minutes of the second half.

This reverse stirred the Albion to make strenuous efforts to get on level terms, and the ball was sent by Simmonds into Storer's hands. Liverpool, however, soon returned to the attack and Allan sent in a stinging shot which Reader cleared in magnificent fashion. Albion countered swiftly and from exciting play in front of goal the leather was headed just outside, greatly to the relief of the Liverpool spectators. At the other end, Walker sent in a powerful ground shot which Reader just stopped with his foot. Garfield then raced upfield and, beating Goldie, he centred but there was no-one near him and Raisbeck cleared comfortably. Robertson scored towards the finish to put Liverpool into the semi-finals for the second time in three seasons.

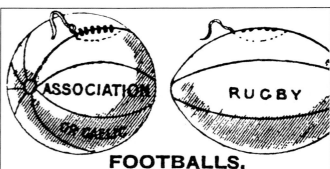

Other F.A. Cup ties

In the other quarter-final ties, Stoke beat Tottenham Hotspur 4-1 at home; while Sheffield United and Derby County both won away from home, United beating Nottingham Forest 1-0 in front of 30,000, and Derby beating Southampton 2-1 after being a goal down at the interval in front of 25,000 spectators.

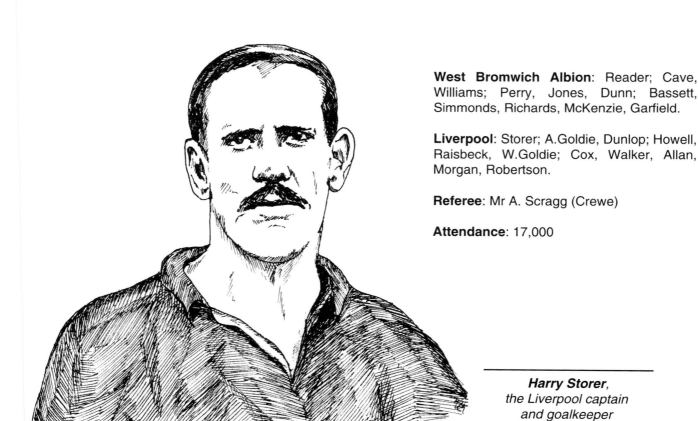

West Bromwich Albion: Reader; Cave, Williams; Perry, Jones, Dunn; Bassett, Simmonds, Richards, McKenzie, Garfield.

Liverpool: Storer; A.Goldie, Dunlop; Howell, Raisbeck, W.Goldie; Cox, Walker, Allan, Morgan, Robertson.

Referee: Mr A. Scragg (Crewe)

Attendance: 17,000

Harry Storer,
the Liverpool captain
and goalkeeper

March 18, 1899

Liverpool (2) 2
Allan 14, Morgan 30

Sheffield United (1) 2
Hedley 10, 70

THIS game generally attracted the keenest interest largely due to the doughty exploits of the Liverpool team, who were greatly in contention for a League and Cup double. Currently lying in second place in the League behind Aston Villa, who had the same number of points but a far superior goal average, and in the semi-finals of the cup, Liverpool are experiencing one of their best seasons, and their deeds have captured the imagination of all devotees of the winter pastime throughout the land. Sheffield United, for their part, created a mild sensation by beating Nottingham Forest - at the time Cup favourites - in the previous round and on Forest's own ground. It was little wonder that this engagement was voted the *pièce de résistance* of the day's contests. The executives of both elevens had left no stone unturned in preparing their men for the game, and had the players in the best possible condition, indeed, both teams have been practically under a course of special training since the middle of January, and with just one or two exceptions, have made their headquarters within three miles of each other - Liverpool at St. Anne's and United at Lytham. Naturally enough, when Liverpool learned that they were called upon to play on a ground where their opponents had been for two consecutive weeks, somewhat harsh words were used, but they soon cooled down and accepted the inevitable. Apart from the quarter-final tie, Sheffield United also played Forest in Nottingham on March 4, with Forest winning 2-1. Liverpool eventually finished the League season as runners-up to Aston Villa by two points, while Sheffield United finished third from bottom, avoiding relegation (which became automatic for the first time this season) by four points. In the League, Liverpool beat United 2-1 at Anfield and 2-0 away.

The railway companies catered for a tremendous crowd of people since, in addition to a large number of packed specials from Liverpool and Sheffield, Nottingham was besieged by a tremendous influx of visitors from the surrounding districts, the motley crowd of excited enthusiasts completely capturing the lace capital on a temporary basis. The brilliant ties of Liverpool's supporters were visible everywhere. Liverpool left their training quarters on Friday afternoon for Derby, where they remained the night, travelling on to the scene of the action for luncheon on the Saturday of the game.

The weather proved fine, though a high wind prevailed and ominous clouds hung overhead. The Forest Committee had made excellent arrangements to cater for the comfort of the visitors, whilst their new pitch - laid last year - looked at its best. Since Sheffield United triumphed there three weeks ago, additional accommodation had been made for the popular patrons, and the Forest Secretary, Mr Radford, stated that fully thirty-five thousand people could be comfortably accommodated. A band played whilst the spectators assembled on the ground, and the crowd whiled away the time in boisterous fashion, singing and shouting with some force, but nothing in the nature of a disturbance occurred. A strong police presence surrounded the ground, with several mounted police assisting.

Liverpool were able to field their strongest side, but United were without the services of Almond, the inside-left being a victim of injury. Field took his place. There was some doubt about Foulkes before the game, but he was pronounced fit.

About half an hour prior to the start, the sun shone forth brilliantly. Every vantage point was rapidly filled, and arrivals by the later trains had great difficulty in being allowed admission. The game was witnessed by the Mayor and the Sheriff of Nottingham, and the Football Association was also largely represented.

Each side received a tremendous ovation upon stepping into the arena. The band left the pitch, and the rival captains

Ernest Needham

advanced to toss for choice of ends amid almost breathless silence from the great concourse. A huge cheer went up from the Liverpool contingent when it was seen that Storer had won the toss, thus giving his side the advantage of a very powerful breeze.

Liverpool immediately took advantage of this with Robertson moving along the left, but he shot wide. Both sides appeared to be affected by nerves, and Archie Goldie and Howell made mistakes, which let in the United, and for a couple of minutes the Liverpool defence had to deal with a massive onslaught, shots coming in from both flanks. Dunlop, however, ultimately cleared out of danger and Cox took up the running for Liverpool. The ball moved to Robertson and then on to Morgan, whose brilliant shot was fisted away by Foulkes. Shortly afterwards Robertson centred, but no-one followed up and Boyle cleared. The United responded with a speedy move down the left wing and Priest shot towards Storer, who cleared rather weakly to Hedley, who in a flash had the ball in the Liverpool net amid loud cheers. Liverpool were not dispirited by this reversal, and they moved straight onto the attack. After a couple of shots had been repulsed by Foulkes, Raisbeck slipped the ball to Allan, who smashed a shot past Foulkes after fourteen minutes. With the teams level the tension became greater than ever, and for a time the United attack was completely baffled. To the intense delight of the Liverpool excursionists, Allan began to turn on the style, and Walker and Morgan received a lot of work from him, and it appeared that Liverpool would score with every attack. It required all of Needham's energy and leadership to stem the Red tide. The Sheffielders were not too concerned about their methods of stopping Liverpool and Morgan was twice tripped as Liverpool attacked incessantly. Walker sent in a long shot which Allan seized upon just by the foot of a post, but he was unable to net the ball. Eventually Sheffield United broke away and Beers put the ball over the bar.

With the wind and sun in their favour, Liverpool were expected to play with great effort and after twenty-nine minutes from the start Dunlop bullied in. Several players rushed towards Foulkes, but Morgan was the first to the ball and he deftly put the ball into the furthest corner of the net. The leading goal for Liverpool received hearty cheers, and it was generally felt that Liverpool were now safe. Almost from the re-start, Robertson put in a brilliant centre from which Cox should have scored, but his attempt was weak. At this stage, the Blades were in a sorry state.

They had begun like a rocket, but they now resembled a damp squib. Beers was the only Sheffield forward who could make any headway, and on one occasion he went on a solo run towards Storer, but fortunately for Liverpool, Dunlop successfully tackled and cleared the danger.

Liverpool, without showing any of the scientific methods which have characterised their play this season, maintained a steady attack and they tried desperately hard to score a third goal.

As the interval approached, the faces of the Liverpool supporters fell considerably when Dunlop fell to the ground, writhing in agony after a challenge from Bennett. He soon recovered, however, and continued to play.

When the teams reappeared, Dunlop was seen to be limping and this looked ominous for Liverpool, who now had to contend with the wind and the sun. After five minutes of the second half there was a scrimmage in front of Storer, and Bennett centred the ball precisely to Hedley, who was fouled inside the penalty line.

The Blades appealed strongly for a penalty kick, but to the joy of the Anfielders, an ordinary free-kick was given two yards from goal. The ball lay entangled between a mass of legs, and a goal seemed imminent, but, amidst a great roar, the ball was cleared, and the Liverpool supporters breathed easily again.

For a long period, Liverpool were on the defensive, the tide having turned completely in favour of the Sheffielders. Dunlop, with his injured leg, was little more than a passenger, but the plucky fellow still kept hard at work to help his side out of a tight corner.

Twenty-five minutes into the second half, Needham found Hedley with one of his characteristic long passes, and he broke through and beat Storer with a fast, low shot. As in the case of the first goal, Storer made little or no attempt to save his charge, and Needham was congratulated by his team-mates.

During the last fifteen minutes Liverpool were outplayed, and it was miraculous that they withstood the heavy pressure. Dunlop was nothing short of heroic as he fought gallantly for the Liverpool cause. Needham's men fought magnificently in the final minutes, and the end came as a positive relief to the Liverpool supporters.

The Liverpool team left Nottingham by the 6.50 express train for Liverpool.

OFFICIAL REFEREES 1898 - 99

Kingscott, A.G., Accountancy Department, Midland Railway Company, Derby

---

Liverpool: Storer; A.Goldie, Dunlop; Howell, Raisbeck, W.Goldie; Cox, Walker, Allan, Morgan, Robertson.

Sheffield United: Foulkes; Thickett, Boyle; Johnson, Morren, Needham; Bennett, Beers, Hedley, Field, Priest.

Referee: Mr A.G. Kingscott (Derby)

Attendance: 35,000 (at Nottingham)

March 23, 1899

Liverpool (1) 4
Walker 20, Allan 50,
Boyle 70(og), Cox 72

Sheffield United (0) 4
Beers 54, Bennett 65, Priest 84, 85

FOLLOWING last Saturday's memorable draw at Nottingham, interest was redoubled in the meeting of these semi-finalists, and during the week the encounter of the two clubs concerned at Bolton had been eagerly discussed. During the past few days, both teams had been in their training quarters at St. Anne's, and though the weather was somewhat severe, healthy exercise was indulged in. The weather at Bolton on the morning of the tie was bleak and wintry in the extreme and showers of snow alternated with snatches of sunshine. The ground had been well sanded, and though hard and lumpy in parts, it was in fairly good condition.

An hour before kick-off a steady stream of spectators moved towards the ground. Several excursions were run from Liverpool, and a large contingent journeyed from Sheffield, while from most of the Lancashire football centres crowds poured into the town. The weather became gradually worse, and at half-past three the outlook was ominous. The Liverpool team left Fairhaven at noon, and arriving at Bolton made straight for the ground. They played the same team as on the Saturday, but Sheffield United replaced Field with Almond. Towards four o'clock the crowd increased perceptibly, and the sun came out with considerable strength, but its rays were not sufficient to clear the heavy snow, while there was a sharp wind.

The Liverpool side in their bright red were first out and received a great reception. This was at five minutes to four, and they were followed three minutes later by the United, who had apparently not as big a following as their opponents. Three snap shot artists were unrelenting in their work whilst the referee and his linesmen dressed, having reached the ground late, and the merry gambols of these artists from end to end afforded the crowd not a little amusement.

Owing to the late arrival of the referee and his linesmen, who had only just reached the ground as the teams came out, it was seven minutes late when play was started, Liverpool winning the toss, and having the benefit of the sun, which, though giving no heat, was bright, and the benefit of the wind, which blew straight down the field.

Good work by Needham was the first feature, but soon Thickett had to clear from the Liverpool left, and on the dry ground the chances of a very fast game were evident. Again Needham cleared in great style as Cox tried to get away, and Thickett and Boyle each had to clear swiftly. Liverpool had the better of the opening exchanges. A fine cross by Cox was followed by Morgan, who sent in a rasping shot which was just wide. The kick out saw Foulkes clear the half-way line, and Bennett put the ball across well, though Raisbeck cleared

in the middle of the park. A beautiful dropping shot by Howell made Foulkes save under the bar, and then Priest and Almond got away, a foul against Almond pulling the effort up in midfield. A timely clearance by Dunlop robbed Bennett, and he repeated the clearance the next instant, whilst Raisbeck, with a huge kick, sent the ball harmlessly over the line. Foulkes got in a splendid goal-kick, but Bill Goldie returned the ball, after which Priest, well fed by Hedley, nearly got the better of Archie Goldie.

Near the line at the other end, Allan was kept well off the ball by Thickett until Foulkes had cleared, whilst the same back, rushing out, got rid of an attack by Morgan when it was growing dangerous. The wind blew in the manner of a hurricane down the field, and the United defence struggled on several occasions. Liverpool gained a corner, to which the United men loudly protested, but Johnson cleared. At the other end Beers outwitted Dunlop cleverly, but finished with a poor centre, after which Raisbeck set Liverpool on to the attack once more.

Thickett, after being badly tackled on the ground, cleared splendidly when Allan looked like getting through. A free kick to the Seaporters near to the United goal saw Morren head away well, and Storer was left with a long, slow, rolling shot to throw away. Liverpool gained a corner on their left, and from this Foulkes, in saving well under the bar, was impeded, and Liverpool had to fall back.

Throw-ins followed to both sides on the stand side of the ground, and United made poor use of a free-kick which followed on the same side. Bill Goldie was penalised for fouling Bennett in the back, but the Liverpool defence was solid, and a long shot by Cox rolled harmlessly over Foulkes' goal-line. Then Allan, working round, took a pass from Robertson, and gave Foulkes a teasing shot to clear, which the goalkeeper did in clever fashion. A fine hook by Cox was a yard wide, judging his effort from the flag. Liverpool had by far the greater share of the play at this stage of the contest, as was to be expected under the prevailing conditions.

A brilliant burst by the United followed, in which the ball was passed along from wing to wing in glorious fashion, and Priest hooked the ball past Storer, though from Raisbeck the ball cannoned back, and a loud appeal for a goal was negatived by the referee. Everyone at that end of the ground was confident that when Raisbeck saved Priest's shot, the ball was over the line a good foot.

Liverpool responded by attacking at the other end. Allan, when Walker had fastened on the ball, got Needham round the neck, and so prevented his interference. In the meantime Walker went on and scored with a fast shot, the ball travelling through Foulkes' legs into the net with twenty minutes gone. Walker raced through in the next moment, but he was penalised for trying to rush Boyle at the end. Allan was then penalised for jumping at Boyle in United's half, and Bennett hooked the ball across, but Dunlop cleared. Hedley raced up after Almond had failed with a great scoring chance, and gave Storer such a scorcher to stop that the Liverpool custodian could only clear at the third attempt. Bennett and Hedley were wide with their final shots as the Sheffield side gained the initiative. Then Liverpool attacked and Cox, Walker and Howell combined effectively, and the gypsy Howell hooked the ball in. Needham cleared right in front of Foulkes, whilst Thickett and Morren also cleared well.

A magnificent long shot by Morgan right into the goal-mouth brought Foulkes to his knees, but he saved excellently. A palpable case of hands in midfield against Raisbeck was not seen by the referee, though Hedley appealed strongly, and as Cox ran down and centred, both Thickett and Morren stood firm. A race half the length of the field between Dunlop and Bennett ended in favour of the Liverpool man, though both men fell over at the finish. Boyle was then hard pressed and he conceded a corner. From this Allan got in a bit of extraordinary clever manipulation of the ball, but he was unable to find an opening. Hedley pushed the ball well out to the right, but Bennett was robbed in fine style by Dunlop, who had the better of his opponent.

Poor kicking by both the Liverpool backs in turn followed, but this was only a momentary lapse and from yet another fine effort by Cox, Foulkes had to react quickly, just reaching and clearing as the ball got on to the line. In the next instant Robertson sent in a low drive which Foulkes dealt with admirably. Offside pulled up the Liverpool right when in full cry for goal. Just on the interval, United gained a corner through Bennett's shot, but the whistle went before the ball reached the goal.

In the second half Liverpool made the first advance, but this was repelled. With the wind at their backs it was fully expected that the Sheffielders would make the pace warm for their opponents, and so it proved, for Bennett was quickly rushing along his line, only to place the ball wide. He then put in a fine centre, but Hedley was foiled by Bill Goldie before he could shoot, and a free-kick to United in midfield saw Boyle place the ball right into the goalmouth, where a determined though fruitless effort was made to force it through. This was followed by a further advance, Thickett forcing Dunlop to twice head away, and the Sheffielders could not break through, though pinning Liverpool back into their own half.

With Thickett well beaten, Allan dashed for goal with the ball at his feet, when Boyle overhauled him, and bowled him over. The charge took place a couple of yards outside the penalty line, and from the free-kick Allan scored with a grand long drive, the ball passing just inside the post and out of the reach of Foulkes. This was the first time Liverpool had been over the half-way line in the second half, and the goal arrived after five minutes' play.

United were stung into retaliation and they pressed on their right, and from a free-kick on the same wing, the ball was put into the net by Beers, thus adding renewed interest in the game. The Sheffielders pressed forward again in this remarkably fast game, and they were forced back. A clever clearance by Morren robbed Robertson, and United were forced to defend for a considerable period. With a quarter of an hour gone, United took up the pressure again, though the power of the wind had abated.

The pace of the game was as great as ever, and both defences worked prodigiously, though the work of the forwards lacked combination. Robertson sent in a shot which Foulkes saved under the bar and cleared, avoiding Walker's challenge in a clever manner. Then Walker was penalised for an ugly challenge on Needham in midfield, and a brilliant centre by Bennett was well kept out by Raisbeck - still safe and excellent in defence.

Hedley gave Storer an easy shot to stop, and he had another the next moment, whilst United gained a free-kick for a push well inside the twelve yards line, and from this Bennett, taking Needham's touch beautifully, scored a second goal with a shot which first of all hit the bar and glanced inside.

Liverpool made a terrific effort but Thickett hooked the ball away in international form, and sent the attackers back. The pace was still fast and furious, and at the other end Storer saved well from Bennett under the bar. Storer impetuously rushed out and was fortunate to clear the ball. Storer then saved a long shot by Needham, and the Sheffielders pressed as strongly at this stage as Liverpool had done in the first half. In a breakaway a long shot from Liverpool went wide. A good clearance by Boyle robbed the Liverpool right and Bennett, taking a fine pass by Beers, was unable to get through.

Then Robertson hooked the ball across and Allan headed in brilliantly, only for Foulkes to parry splendidly. The ball fell to Boyle, after Foulkes had run out, and the defender kicked the ball against the far post, where it rebounded into his own net after 70 minutes.

United attacked with vigour and gained a fruitless corner, from which Bennett hooked the ball over the bar. Two minutes later Morren brought Cox down in full cry for goal, and the referee awarded a penalty without hesitation. This was taken by Allan, and though Foulkes saved a lightning shot in great style, Cox raced up, took the ball as it rebounded from Foulkes' hands, and banged it into the net. This appeared to settle matters, but United sped down the other end and Bennett, from a well-placed free-kick, hooked the ball over Storer's bar. Robertson got the ball in the net again, but the whistle had gone·for offside. Foulkes made no effort to stop the progress of the ball. The Sheffielders appeared to slacken a little at this stage, though their defence was still sound. Then Thickett took the ball to the left and Priest scored a third goal with a long shot into the corner of the goal. This was with six minutes left.

Just a minute later Storer saved poorly from the right and Priest rushed up and added the equaliser with a fast shot at an open goal. In the ensuing struggle Bennett was brought down in midfield, and the game had to be stopped, his leg being badly hurt. He resumed and again forced Storer to save, whilst United gained a free-kick near goal. With only a minute left, the free-kick was cleared by Raisbeck right in front of Storer. Foulkes then had to save, which he did in a cool manner, whilst Walker, who played a dirty game, was penalised for a foul charge. A fine save by Storer from the

United left followed, and a long centre by Bennett passed a yard wide. Then Howell cleared in front of his goal, whilst another United attack saw Bennett narrowly miss the target. The resulting corner was fruitless. The whole of the United men played good, hard football. Without an over-reliance on science, they played the real cup-tie game, and had their clever opponents demoralised in the final ten minutes or so. The halves were a treat to watch, whilst Priest's shooting was great.

On the Liverpool side, Storer was woefully weak as the game drew to a close. Dunlop was again a great back, whilst Raisbeck was the pick of the halves, and played fine football. Walker, of the front line, marred his work by a lot of unnecessary roughness. Robertson was the star of the line, his shooting and dribbling being splendid.

It was subsequently decided to replay the match at Fallowfield, Manchester, on Monday next.

George Allan,
Liverpool's Scottish international, who died at the age of 24 from consumption

In New York, representatives of Jim Jeffries and Bob Fitzsimmons had come to an agreement for a 25-round contest, to take place between the two pugilists on May 26, at the Coney Island Athletic Club, for a purse of 20,000 dollars, and the cinematographic rights.

In Nice, the motor car race was won by M. Lemaitre, who covered one mile in 1min. 36sec., and one kilometre in 57 seconds - a rate equivalent to over 63 kilometres per hour.

Official Referees 1898 -99

Hines, A.G., 129, Norton Street, Radford, Nottingham

Proctor, W., Woodbrough Road, Nottingham

Liverpool: Storer; A.Goldie, Dunlop; Howell, Raisbeck, W. Goldie; Cox, Walker, Allan, Morgan, Robertson.

Sheffield United: Foulkes; Thickett, Boyle; Johnson, Morren, Needham; Bennett, Beers, Hedley, Almond, Priest.

Referee: Mr A.G. Kingscott (Derby)

Linesmen: Mr A.G. Hines (Nottingham) ; Mr W. Proctor (Nottingham Association)

Attendance: 20,000 (at Burnden Park)   **Receipts**: £740

March 27, 1899

Liverpool (1) 1
Allan 6

Sheffield United (0) 0

Match abandoned

LONG before this abandoned game commenced, and while people were still pouring into the ground, there was always the fear that the mass of spectators would break through the boundary and flood the field of play. It is clear that the management - those who had the arrangements in hand for the match - showed their weakness and ineptitude for the task undertaken. If - with the knowledge and experience of what happened five years ago on this same ground when Everton and Wolverhampton Wanderers met in the final for the same Cup - the management had despatched even at that critical time a message to the police headquarters in Manchester for reinforcements to the handful of constables on the ground, or asking for half a dozen mounted officers, the disgraceful scenes would never have happened.

A mass of people was kept back by a thin strand of wire fence, and those people, only two or three in the rear, were unable to see the players' heads, let alone the field of play. The spectators said after the game that they had gone to see the game and not the backs of the heads of the supporters who were only marginally better off than themselves. They said that they had cheerfully paid the admission fee asked, and they thought they were entitled to get their money's worth. After the crowd on the popular part of the enclosure had broken through, those spectators who had paid high prices for their seats were the worst off, and it was the latter as much as the spectator paying 6d who was to blame for what happened.

Once the crowd got possession of the field, everything had to go as they wished. Police and officials were powerless to hold them in check, and it was not until every chance of a Cup tie taking place had vanished that a few more policemen put in an appearance and persuaded the crowd - always good tempered - to fall back. They, however, only gave way a little, for after they had once got loose, the people never backed beyond the touchline.

It was generally believed that the only reason the teams were put on the field again to make a pretence of playing was because the officials were afraid that the gate money would be seized. If such a thing had entered the minds of the 25,000 mass, the pavilion in which the cash was stored and counted would have stood little chance of surviving an attack. The crowd, however, wanted to see the football match, and if the majority could not do so, they were evidently determined that those in a better position should not. Ransacking the money "coffers" was not in the crowd's mind, but when the gate money had been removed to a place of safety, then the officials did not care so much what the crowd did.

Some strange tales were also told about the admission of the crowd at the various entrances, and if everything was true that was alleged, then the gate money did not get into the hands of the proper authorities by several hundred pounds. When the crush was greatest at the entrances of admission, many little peculiarities were said to have taken place. Anything was used for a "pass in" check. Bits of blank paper were torn up and sold for a shilling each by alleged custodians and checkers. The prestigious *Pall Mall Gazette* castigated the large crowd for encroaching upon the field of play but asked: "... Was it not also wrong to let so many thousands in, of course with a view to gate money?..."

There was an hour's delay because of the crowd invasion and Liverpool were anxious to get the game started again. They were a goal ahead, and United were reduced to nine men and a passenger - Morren was off the field, and a painful rap had been sustained by Thickett. But Mr Kingscott had already decided that so far as he was concerned the Cup tie proper finished when the crowd broke in twenty-eight minutes after the start. The play, which continued for another quarter of an hour or so, was merely something with which to occupy the attention of the crowd while the treasury chests, containing bullion to the amount of £1,066 were removed to a place of safety. The money ought to have been more, but either several thousand people forgot to take tickets, or those taking the gate money misappropriated the funds.

The majority of supporters moved off in orderly fashion except for a few hundred who waited in front of the pavilion to howl at Foulkes. The giant goalkeeper and George Allan had a disagreement in the match. It appeared that both were to blame, but the less weighty of the pair came off the worst, for Allan was lifted outwards, upwards and then dropped downwards rather heavily. The people who only saw the latter half of the incident yelled "Shame!" but Allan appeared to have desired a confrontation with Foulkes all along. Much of the sympathy shown towards Allan evaporated when the Scot executed a "royal crowner" on the back of Boyle.

The game itself was played in weather for the most part fine, though during the first few minutes rain fell heavily and afterwards, though the rain ceased, the sun came out, shining right into the faces of the Sheffielders to the interval. There was a tremendous crowd, both Sheffield and Liverpool sending thousands to the ground, and in addition, Manchester itself contributed a large quota.

On the United side Bennett was out, said to be suffering from an injured knee, whilst Johnson was taken with a bad cold, and in the place of these two men were played Whelan and Howard. On the Liverpool side, Archie Goldie was replaced by Stevenson, and Storer was left out, Matt McQueen taking his place. United lost the toss, and promptly had to defend, but it was not long before they attacked the Liverpool goal and Howard, Whelan and Morren each got in splendid cross-shots, whilst McQueen had to force himself to save on more than one occasion.

After three minutes Needham took a free-kick beautifully, and the ball was forced into the net, though the goal was disallowed for the goalkeeper being impeded. Another free-kick availed United nothing, and the Liverpool men went away at full speed with a storm of rain at their backs, which blew right into the faces of the Sheffield men.

Allan received the ball from Raisbeck and scored the first goal of the game after six minutes.

The United made another excellent onslaught and Morren put the ball well across to Whelan, whose accurate centre was headed over the bar by Priest. After some fine work by Almond, Priest shot through, but the point was again disallowed because McQueen had been impeded. Priest was then tripped and his side gained ground from the free-kick. A fine pass by Raisbeck to Robertson was not accepted, and with the rain falling heavily, the United front men fared badly. Their backs played well, and the halves worked prodigiously. Dunlop cleared a long and ragged rush by the Sheffield forwards.

At this stage of the game - fifteen minutes had elapsed - the crowd encroached onto the touchlines, and the referee had to stop the game until the spectators drew back. This interval lasted just under five minutes, at the end of which United again pressed forward, but Dunlop and Stevenson each cleared well.

Walker and Cox raced away but Cox's shot was too high and poorly directed. For a short period the rain ceased and United were forced to defend, Boyle heading out a good shot in the goalmouth, whilst Thickett cleverly outwitted Robertson. Good work by Raisbeck prevented Hedley breaking away as he more than once looked likely to do.

In United's goalmouth Boyle effected a grand clearance when it looked certain that Allan would score, and with the sun shining brightly into the eyes of the Sheffielders, their troubles were again accentuated. The crowd at the United end had now encroached on the field fully thirty feet, and again the game was stopped; whilst at the other end only the indefatigable efforts of the police kept the people back. This was after 24 minutes had elapsed.

A long wait ensued, whilst the officials did everything in their power to get the people to their proper limits again. In the meantime, the spectators in front of the Press seats had seized upon all sorts of hurdles and boxes, and had erected points of vantage for themselves which blocked the view of the reporters with the exception of half the field.

After a wait of seven minutes, the players left the field and a big effort was made to get the crowd back. The pitch was overrun by people at the United end, and thousands of supporters made the task of the officials, association and local, a very arduous one indeed.

After about twenty minutes the police made a combined effort to get the ground clear, having been largely reinforced. This was to some extent successful, though it looked beyond the bounds of probability that the playing surface could be cleared in time to restart the game.

Just on five o'clock, or after a wait of almost half-an-hour, the players took to the field again, the police manoeuvre having been brilliantly engineered, and successfully. Liverpool appeared first, the weather being fine and the sun shining as brilliantly as ever. All this time, the spectators still ringed the playing surface. After Liverpool had been on the ground some ten minutes, they were called off. However, both teams came out at 5.18 and, after having been stopped close on 50 minutes, the game was proceeded with.

The ball was thrown up in midfield and United pressed. A foul against Whelan for pushing sent them back and Howard, who had changed places with Needham, pulled up his wing very cleverly. Morren was absent with an injury, and Beers acted as right half, bringing off a great save from Cox's centre in the first minute. The presumption gradually gained ground that the Cup tie had been abandoned, though at this stage nothing was definitely known.

A fine save by Foulkes from Robertson followed, and a fierce attack on the other goal was seen, in which the light-haired Raisbeck cleared with great judgment. Cox gave Foulkes a teaser to deal with. The goalkeeper misjudged it, and the ball passed obliquely over the bar rather fortunately. It was difficult for the Pressmen to view the game. Cox was busy on his wing and repeatedly outstripped Howard and Boyle. Good work by Needham, who played centre half, was followed by Thickett clearing well in front of Foulkes, and at the other end Almond got through and forced McQueen to make a low save. A great hook by Raisbeck kept Hedley off the ball in front of the Liverpool goal, whilst Stevenson repulsed Priest a moment later.

With United pressing warmly, Dunlop headed the ball away right in front of his net, and then his forwards took it to the other end, where Foulkes had an easy task to stop a long low shot. Then Allan, rushing at Foulkes long before the arrival of the ball, repeated the offence when the United custodian got the ball, and was lamed by Foulkes as a result. The referee gave a free-kick against United close to the goal-post, and after this a tremendous struggle was cleared. Up to the interval United pressed more than their opponents, half-time arriving with the score in Liverpool's favour. The game came to an abrupt termination at this point and was to be replayed in its entirety on Thursday next at Derby, the kick-off time being 4.30.

Thickett was so severely kicked in the groin that, though he pluckily kept on the field to the finish of play, he fainted at its close as soon as he reached the pavilion. Then Morren, who for some weeks had been playing with a badly sprained thigh similar in its nature to the injuries from which Priest and Spiksley had been suffering, found in the course of play the injury became so much worse that, as he himself expressed it on the homeward journey, he had "done playing for the season". Beers also suffered at the end of the game from a kick on the body, but he hoped to be all right for Thursday. Thickett was seen by Mr Allison, the well-known "accident doctor", of Manchester, at whose establishment he was staying. Mr Allison expressed the opinion that Thickett would be right again sooner than the player himself thought. Needham was due to travel to Glasgow on the Friday to take part against the Scottish League the following day.

Keen disappointment was expressed in Glasgow on the evening of the game when it became known that the directors of the Liverpool Football Club had, on account of the undecided semi-final tie, and in view of other important engagements, considered it advisable to withdraw their players from the Scottish trial match, which was to take place the day after the Cup-tie at Cathkin Park, Glasgow. The decision meant that Dunlop (left-back), Raisbeck (centre-half), Robertson and Morgan (left-wing), and Allan (centre-forward) would have to relinquish the opportunity of displaying their powers before the Scottish selectors, and probably, in the case of the three first-named players, the prohibition would mean the loss of international honours.

Liverpool: M.McQueen; Stevenson, Dunlop; Howell, Raisbeck, W.Goldie, Cox, Walker, Allan, Morgan, Robertson.

Sheffield United: Foulkes; Thickett, Boyle; Howard, Morren, Needham; Whelan, Beers, Hedley, Almond, Priest.

Referee: Mr A.G. Kingscott (Derby)

Attendance: 30,000 (at Fallowfield, Manchester)

The Sheffield Daily Telegraph

~~~~~

There are no ropes or rails at all on the Fallowfield ground, and that in consequence it is the easiest thing in the world for a crowd to get over the touchlines. Add to this the further fact that there is little or no banking, apart from that of the cycle track, and it will be readily understood how easy it was for the crowd of people who could not see, and there were thousands in this unhappy predicament, to force those in front of them over the touchlines in the effort to get themselves closer to what was going on.

Yesterday's experience of Fallowfield was but a similar one to that of some years ago, when the final of the cup was played there, and when the reporters were swept away in an avalanche of humanity, and their seats and desks were crushed to matchwood. It has been proved now, surely well enough, that the ground is not fitted for the reception of a really excited crowd of any size, and the fiasco of yesterday was a sad reflection on the wisdom of the Association who sent the teams to play there. Those who had any knowledge of the ground trembled for the issue of the game from the very announcement of its selection, and their fears have been well borne out by what took place yesterday.

Billy Foulkes, the Sheffield United goalkeeper, who has up-ended *George Allan* after a confrontation

March 30, 1899

Liverpool (0) 0

Sheffield United (0) 1
Beers 85

THE selection of the Derby County ground as the venue of the fourth meeting of Sheffield United and Liverpool in the semi-final could scarcely have given satisfaction to all parties but at the same time, under the circumstances, it would have been rather difficult to find a better situated ground. Birmingham would have had the strongest claim, but the fact that the great International match was down for Villa Park extinguished Birmingham's chances of witnessing a semi-final this season. Though the day was about the most inconvenient possible for the getting together of a big crowd, supporters of both teams turned up very well, whilst the locals also showed their appreciation of the honour. Probably never in the history of the English Cup had the interest in a semi-final tie been maintained so well as in the United-Liverpool encounters. Certainly the Fallowfield fiasco caused many supporters to stay away, but when it was considered that Thursday was the eve of a rather long holiday, the attendance was rather a good one. Due to Morren's injuries, Howard took his place, with Needham going in the middle of the half-back line. Liverpool were able to play exactly the same team as that which did duty at Fallowfield, the only change from their usual and strongest eleven being that Stevenson played full-back in place of Archie Goldie, whilst Storer appeared to have been permanently dropped. The weather was fair and all in favour of a fast game, though a steady, useful wind blew from goal to goal. The Liverpool men were the first to make their appearance, and met with a good reception, but when the United appeared it was soon evident which side had the sympathies of the crowd. Liverpool won the toss and naturally chose to play with the wind at their backs.

Hedley started the game, and Howard cleverly robbed Howell. Liverpool made the first dangerous attack, Thickett clearing, the ball being immediately sent behind. Raisbeck and Needham were prominent for their respective sides in midfield, following which a free-kick to Liverpool was badly placed by Dunlop. A free-kick for hands against Liverpool saw Hedley shoot outside from long range. United were fully holding their own, and from a free-kick for fouling Bennett, Needham shot over the crossbar. Free-kicks were rather numerous, Liverpool being the chief offenders.

A brilliant piece of work by Howard, Priest and Almond looked dangerous, but the ball was run over the line. A combined attack by the United caused trouble to the Liverpool defence, and Beers was deliberately fouled by Dunlop. McQueen saved what looked like a certain goal, whilst a minute later Robertson tested Foulkes with a good shot. Then from a rebound from Thickett's kick Allan got on the ball, but Foulkes cleared his shot in fine style. Liverpool began to have more of the play, but could not get near Foulkes, although the United goalkeeper was forced to fist away a long, slow shot. A long, fast shot by Needham was intercepted by Howell, who dribbled down, and a corner to Liverpool followed, but Foulkes was impeded. Clever work by Robertson and Allan caused a struggle in the United goalmouth, but eventually Raisbeck kicked over the bar. Another corner to Liverpool was cleared, and Priest and Almond relieved the pressure, but Howell and Stevenson cleared the United danger, whilst Priest was only just too late to head in a fine shot by Hedley.

A further determined attack by United saw Beers nearly get through, but he was stopped just as he was about to shoot. Bennett placed United's first corner outside, obtained after good work by Hedley. The game was very fast, but United were often dangerous, and they made a powerful and sustained attack on the Liverpool goal. McQueen saved a dangerous shot from Beers, and another immediately after, just as it was sailing under the bar. Hedley got the better of Dunlop in a tackle, and centred across the goalmouth, the ball going out before Priest could get to it.

Then Liverpool attacked and took three corners in quick succession. Priest got the third away, but a fourth followed, and from this Needham headed away in fine style, though at the expense of yet another corner.

From the goal-kick United broke free, but Dunlop handled 20 yards from goal. The free-kick was not fruitful. Then Howard was slightly injured, but he resumed immediately. Liverpool then attacked in determined fashion, and from a corner Foulkes twice had to save, Howell missing a good opening. The free-kick to the United proved of little value. Robertson broke clear and passed cleverly to Allan, who looked like getting through until Boyle came across and dropped him heavily, a free-kick being awarded against the United full-back. .

On resuming, United made the first advances, and one of the Liverpool defenders headed towards his own goal, McQueen just saving a corner. Then Robertson broke clear, and though the linesman appealed for off-side, he was allowed to make progress, but Foulkes saved his shot. Play was fast and furious and extremely exciting. United gained a corner. This was cleared, but immediately Priest shot inches over the bar. Then Raisbeck was seen to great advantage in some fine defensive work. At the other end Foulkes cleared well from Robertson after Boyle had spoiled Allan. A most determined attack was now made on the Liverpool goal, but the United shooting was rather wild.

Some pretty play by Allan and his right wing gained ground, but Foulkes twice saved cleverly. The United men now played with great determination, and some smart crossing by Priest, Bennett and Almond saw the latter nearly get through. He was brought down just outside the penalty line.

From an attack by Liverpool, Allan was given off-side. When play had been in progress about 15 minutes, Beers and Hedley collided, and Beers was slightly injured. From a United corner Beers kicked high over the bar; whilst a long centre from Beers went outside. The United attacked dangerously and McQueen saved well from Almond, before the same attacker shot directly over the bar. Dunlop and Raisbeck stopped the United right wing in clever fashion, but a minute later Bennett got in a fine centre, which McQueen cleared. Hedley skimmed the crossbar as the United side attacked relentlessly. From a goal-kick to Liverpool, their forwards broke away, but Boyle robbed Allan at the expense of a corner. This was cleared, and Bennett got the better of Dunlop before putting in a fine shot which took McQueen a long time to clear.

From a breakaway, Foulkes had to fist away, and a corner was conceded. The Sheffield custodian easily cleared, and then Bennett was almost through when he was tripped by Stevenson outside the penalty line. The free-kick was put to no good use, and a similar one a moment later brought no reward. A long shot by Liverpool was dealt with comfortably by Foulkes and again the United took up the attack, but Dunlop, Stevenson and Raisbeck defended well.

Five minutes before time another good attack by United brought about the long-awaited goal. The United forwards had been swinging the ball about in dangerous fashion, and following a great attack the ball came out to the left wing, and Priest dashed up at top speed and sent the ball back towards goal. Almond helped it forward, and Beers put the finishing touch to some great attacking play. Just previously to the United goal, it was thought that one of the Liverpool defenders had deliberately handled the ball near goal, but this escaped the referee's attentions. The remaining few minutes of the game were desperately fought out. The Sheffielders had a narrow escape when Liverpool gained a corner, Howard eventually clearing. At the other end, the Sheffielders twice came very near scoring, McQueen having all his work cut out to save.

The Liverpool forwards played a very clever game, but on several occasions were beaten by their own cleverness. Often they brought the ball into United territory in first-class style, only to be robbed at the last moment. On the other hand, the United front rank were always dangerous and seldom lost an opportunity for a shot on goal. The Sheffielders were a "never-say-die" team, and displayed more cleverness in all departments.

In the final, Sheffield United beat Derby County 4-1 at the Crystal Palace, with goals from Bennett, Priest, Beers and Almond before a crowd of 73,833 on 15 April.

Liverpool: M.McQueen; Stevenson, Dunlop; Howell, Raisbeck, W.Goldie; Cox, Walker, Allan, Morgan, Robertson.

Sheffield United: Foulkes; Thickett, Boyle; Johnson, Needham, Howard; Bennett, Beers, Hedley, Almond, Priest.

Referee: Mr A.G. Kingscott (Derby)

Linesmen: Mr A.G. Hines (Nottingham);
Mr W. Proctor (Nottingham Association)

Attendance: 9,957 (at Derby)

Receipts: £503 13s 5d

***Beers**, whose goal five minutes from time robbed Liverpool of their first appearance in the Final*

January 27, 1900

Stoke (0) 0

Liverpool (0) 0

BOTH elevens underwent special training for this tie - Liverpool at Fairhaven and Stoke at Matlock. Both sides suffered from absenteeism, Maxwell and Johnson not having sufficiently recovered from their recent injuries to take part in the game, whilst Raybould and Satterthwaite were both ineligible on account of having assisted New Brighton and Workington respectively in the competition. Rain and snow fell in the morning and affected the condition of the pitch. Jack Cox played at outside-left for Liverpool, a position he was accustomed to occupy whilst playing for Blackpool. When the teams took to the field, the snow had ceased. There were no more than 8,000 present at the kick-off, despite a crowded excursion train from Liverpool.

Liverpool won the toss for choice of ends, Higginson giving the initial impetus to the sphere. The home centre-forward bore down on the visitors' goal, only to be denied by Dunlop.

Stoke

Wilkes

J.T.Robertson   Eccles

Capewell   Woods   Bradley

Parsons   Kennedy   Higginson   Jones   Turner

o

Cox   Morgan   Hunter   Walker   T.Robertson

Howell   Raisbeck   W.Goldie

Dunlop   A. Goldie

Perkins

Liverpool

Referee: Mr T. Helme (Farnworth)

Attendance: 8,000

Some excellent passing on the Stoke left wing enabled Kennedy to test Perkins - making his Cup début in Liverpool's goal - who had little difficulty in clearing. The Reds gained two corners in quick succession, but the only outcome was a shot from Raisbeck which passed narrowly wide.

The game, considering the slippery nature of the turf, was extremely fast, but several times it became a matter of great difficulty for the players to keep their feet. Jones beat Archie Goldie before sending in a cracking shot which Perkins did well to save. Hunter, Walker and Morgan each in turn tested Wilkes, but were unable to find the netting. Liverpool played with tremendous spirit, and from a free-kick the ball beat Wilkes, but without a second player touching it in flight. Eccles initiated a superb move which resulted in Turner and Jones making considerable progress before being pulled up by Goldie. Shortly afterwards Howell received a kick which compelled him to be led off the field. The interval arrived with no score.

Upon restarting, Howell was present in the Liverpool ranks. Hunter kicked off and the opening stages of this half were contested in midfield. Stoke gained an early corner on the right wing, but this was sent behind. Liverpool replied through Robertson on the right, but Eccles cleared his lines easily. A free-kick to the visitors was nullified by Morgan being offside. Cox and Morgan effected an opening for Raisbeck, whose tremendous shot was cleared with difficulty by Wilkes.

Liverpool maintained a strong attack on the Potters' goal, but the home defence held firm. For some time afterwards the game was evenly contested, but the heavy ground prevented accurate passing, and Liverpool committed the great mistake of trying to exhibit too much finesse under the adverse conditions.

As time drew near, however, the visitors altered their tactics, indulging in long kicking and rushing the game at every available opportunity and consequently they applied great pressure to the Stoke goal which was frequently threatened.

Ten minutes from the end, Hunter dashed along and eluded all opposition, but instead of shooting straight for goal he passed to Cox, who placed the ball in the net. The referee, however, after consulting one of the linesmen, ruled Cox offside, though it was later admitted that prior to Cox scoring the ball had rebounded off one of the Stoke backs. The end came without a legitimate point being registered.

The officials of both clubs met together after the match and decided to replay the tie at Anfield on the following Thursday. Liverpool were anxious for the game to be played on the Wednesday, but Stoke refused to agree to this, hoping that a day longer would enable them to get Johnson ready for the game.

February 1, 1900

Liverpool (1) 1

Hunter 2

Stoke (0) 0

THE weather was glorious as both teams took to the field. The elevens of both sides left their respective training quarters on the Thursday morning, arriving at the ground shortly before the kick-off. Liverpool were unable to field their strongest side with Howell and Morgan both suffering from Saturday's contest at Stoke, and Wilson and Kyle deputised. Stoke, on the other hand, were fortunate in being able to place their crack forward, Johnson, in the field, allowing Parsons to go to half-back, with Capewell standing down. The early hour of the start militated against a large attendance, and there were no more than 4,000 present when the teams appeared led by the Stoke captain, followed a moment later by Liverpool, who were arrayed in white.

Stoke won the toss, and a large contingent of the Potters' supporters cheered this early success. Hunter started operations, Raisbeck administering the first check to the visitors, but Stoke continued to make progress until Dunlop repulsed them. A free-kick to Liverpool enabled Robertson to swing the ball across, and Parsons cleared. Raisbeck, with a great header, caused Wilkes to make a difficult save. Shortly afterwards Johnson sped down the left wing before crossing to Kennedy, who missed the goal. Liverpool forced a corner on the right. Robertson took the kick with unerring precision, enabling Hunter to get his cranium underneath and place the sphere in the net, Wilkes having no chance of saving.

After the goal, play was even for some time and it was generally contested near the dividing line. A beautiful move by Hunter gave a fine opportunity to Cox, but he allowed Robertson to dispossess him. Gradually the visitors began to get into the game, and twice the Liverpool goal was subjected to a hot bombardment, but Dunlop and Archie Goldie averted all possible danger with their cool defensive play. A few moments later Kennedy tested Perkins with a fine, swift shot, but the Liverpool custodian saved well. From a free-kick Dunlop placed the ball so well that a second goal seemed inevitable, but Hunter's shot just topped the net.

The game continued to be evenly contested, with both goals visited in quick succession. Kennedy raced away at tremendous speed, only being brought down just outside the penalty line. The free-kick almost brought about Perkins' downfall, the home custodian fortunately planting his foot where the ball was placed.

A sustained onslaught by Liverpool ended in a brilliant attempt by Kyle, whose shot just missed scoring. After a spell of equal exchanges, Turner dashed along the Stoke left, but Goldie pulled him up before he could get his shot in. Stoke now had the best of the argument, Turner and Wood subjecting Perkins to a heavy bombardment, but the Liverpool custodian did not appear to be the slightest disconcerted, and cleared with cool indifference. Towards the interval a clever bit of play from Robertson gave Cox an opportunity to increase Liverpool's lead, but he failed to utilise it.

When the teams reappeared, it was noticed that Walker, who had retired just prior to the interval, did not accompany his comrades, and Liverpool continued with ten men.

Higginson restarted, and the opening exchanges were equally contested, but with Walker back again after five minutes, the home side pressed forward and twice Cox centred without anyone being able to take advantage. Play became very exciting with Liverpool attacking almost constantly. Cox almost scored, and a moment later the outside left sent the ball across the goalmouth. Robertson just managed to get a foot to the sphere, but as it was rolling over the line, the Stoke custodian cleared brilliantly.

During the final ten minutes, the game developed into a rough affair and Robertson was badly fouled by an opponent, but he was quickly brought round and he resumed. Raisbeck was the next to suffer by the close attention of the Potters. The quality of the football quickly deteriorated and free-kicks in favour of Liverpool were awarded with great frequency. The referee warned the Stoke players for their foul play. Towards the close Stoke made desperate efforts to pierce the Liverpool defence, but it remained impregnable.

Referee: Mr T. Helme (Farnworth)

Attendance: 10,000

Liverpool

Perkins

A.Goldie   Dunlop

Wilson   Raisbeck   W.Goldie

T.Robertson   Walker   Hunter   Kyle   Cox

'Sailor' Hunter
got his cranium underneath and placed the sphere in the net, Wilkes having no chance of saving.

Turner   Jones   Higginson   Kennedy   Johnson

Bradley   Woods   Parsons

Eccles   J.T.Robertson

Wilkes

Stoke

February 17, 1900

Liverpool (1) 1   West Bromwich Albion (0) 1
Cox 12   *Simmonds*

THE weather changed dramatically for this Cup tie, and the pitch had been entirely cleared of its wintry visitation, not a vestige of snow was visible. The teams had been in training all week, Liverpool at their favourite resort, St. Anne's, and West Bromwich at Holt Fleet, which they left on the morning of the match. Liverpool partook of luncheon at the Alexandra Hotel previous to reaching the Anfield enclosure. A week's rest had enabled the Liverpool directorate to get their injured men into condition, which resulted in Howell and Morgan being included in the eleven; whilst West Bromwich were at full strength. The ground was in the best possible condition and captain Perry won the toss, Hunter kicking off towards the Oakfield Road end. The home side pressed forward incessantly from the kick-off, and Raisbeck almost secured the vital first goal, but Reader saved brilliantly. Soon afterwards Howell kicked into the Throstles' goalmouth, Robertson secured possession and enticed Reader to leave his goal, with the result that the ball was driven across the goalmouth to Cox, who had no difficulty in scoring Liverpool's first goal after just twelve minutes' play.

Jack Cox

From the restart, West Bromwich attacked strongly, and Williams strained himself and limped off the field, Perry going in his place. After an absence of about five minutes, the international came back smiling, and took up his customary position. Bill Goldie set Cox on his way, but he was given offside, and this, coupled with a free-kick awarded the wrong way, led to Dunlop remonstrating with the referee.

The official appeared to take umbrage at this interference, and he stopped the game to talk seriously to the Liverpool skipper, evidently asserting his authority to the utmost. Mr Fox kept a very watchful eye on the players, and he found Raisbeck guilty of pushing. From the free-kick the visitors sent in a shot which Perkins just saved at the foot of a post.

Simmonds restarted operations, and Williams let in the home front rank, and a couple of shots by Robertson went wide of the mark. A shot by Raisbeck almost proved successful, and a throw-in saw Robertson making rapid tracks for Reader, but just as he shot in, Williams evaded disaster at the expense of a corner, which proved abortive. Following this Williams and Robertson came into conflict with the referee, who suspended the game for a moment in order to lecture the players.

Suddenly the Albion broke away and Roberts sent the ball in to the centre, Simmonds at once netting the leather. Doubt was expressed as to whether the goal was a legitimate one, but Mr Fox, after consulting the linesmen, allowed the point and West Bromwich were on equal terms.

With the sides level, the game became fast and furious. One excellent attempt by Perry almost ended in disaster to the Liverpool goal. His shot, however, just tipped the crossbar, and from the goal-kick, Liverpool made progress on the right wing, but the only advantage they gained was a couple of fruitless corners.

The game fluctuated considerably and each goal was the scene of exciting episodes. One incident occurred that called for an alteration of the rules. Hunter was speeding away, and had eluded all opposition, but just as he seemed certain to score, Walker was deliberately kicked near midfield, Mr Fox having no option but to pull up Hunter and deprive Liverpool of a certain goal in order to penalise the offender. The free-kick saw Liverpool literally all over West Bromwich, but they failed to find a winning goal.

The match was scheduled to be replayed on the following Wednesday with a 3.15 kick-off.

Liverpool: Perkins; A.Goldie, Dunlop; Howell, Raisbeck, W.Goldie; T.Robertson, Walker, Hunter, Morgan, Cox.

West Bromwich Albion:Reader; Adams, Williams; Dunn, Jones, Hadley; Chadburn, Perry, Simmonds, Richards, Roberts.

Referee: Mr J. Fox (Sheffield)

Attendance: 15,000

February 21, 1900

West Bromwich Albion (0) 2   Liverpool (0) 1
Dunn, Chadburn   *Robertson 46*

THE Liverpool team appeared at the Stoney Lane ground in order to meet their inveterate opponents, the Throstles, in the replayed Cup tie. Since the previous Sunday, the team had been staying at Matlock, journeying to West Bromwich at noon on the day of the game.

The atmosphere and the special training at the famous health resort had a beneficial effect on the Liverpool team, and all were in the pink of condition. There was only one change in the team, Wilson appearing in the place of Howell, who was not quite fit.

The Throstles were fully represented, and there were nearly 12,000 people present as the kick-off neared. Liverpool lost the toss, and Hunter started uphill in beautiful weather.

West Bromwich Albion: Reader; Adams, Williams; Dunn, Jones, Hadley; Chadburn, Perry, Simmonds, Richards, Roberts.

Liverpool: Perkins; A.Goldie, Dunlop; Wilson, Raisbeck, W.Goldie; Robertson, Walker, Hunter, Morgan, Cox.

Referee: Mr J. Fox (Sheffield)

Attendance: 13,000

After the opening exchanges, the Albion ran down dangerously, but Perry ran the ball over the line. From the goal kick Robertson and Morgan raced away, but Williams brought the latter up, and for some time play ruled in midfield.

The turf at the bottom goal proved to be on the soft side, and a rather prolonged attack on the part of the homesters gave the Anfield defence considerable trouble. Goldie on one occasion quite misjudged a shot. The invaders, however, were beaten back by Raisbeck. West Bromwich attacked with some venom and Chadburn shot wide.

A breakaway by Cox and Robertson ended in Cox sending in a rasping shot which Reader saved at the expense of a corner. This was cleared, but the Liverpool forwards returned to the attack, and for some time they were extremely dangerous. Morgan, on one occasion, sent in a shot which just passed outside. Liverpool were now playing a really splendid game, and their combination in the forward line was exceptionally good, though it lacked potency.

The Throstles countered with some fierce attacks and a warm bombardment ended with Richards missing a splendid chance of scoring. Keeping up the pressure, Richards again tried his luck, the ball passing two inches outside the post. At this stage in the game, the Albion were having much the better of the argument, but the Anfield defence remained solid. Raisbeck, getting hold of the ball in midfield, shot at long range into Reader's hands.

More midfield work was followed by an attack by Cox and Morgan, and the outside-left looked like getting through when Williams rushed across and cleared. Play became largely contested in West Bromwich territory, and although the Liverpool forwards worked with great cleverness their shooting lacked steam, and several chances were missed.

A fine movement by Walker and Robertson ended in the latter shooting strongly, and Williams saved only at the expense of a corner, from which nothing resulted. Some splendid work on the part of Morgan set the whole Liverpool line going, the ball being passed from left to right in clever fashion, and though Robertson tried hard to give the finishing touch, he was hampered by Williams, and missed his mark.

Still the Anfielders kept pegging away, and Robertson, with practically an open goal, missed, to the great joy of the crowd. There was no mistaking the great superiority of the visitors, so far as cleverness was concerned, and it was only the sterling defence of Williams and Adams which averted disaster.

The Throstles gradually worked their way down and a terrific kick by Williams sent the leather sailing over the bar. The homesters still pressed, and Perkins saved splendidly from Perry, who sent in a stinging shot. Still they kept at it, and for a minute the Liverpool goal was in great danger and a regular scrimmage in front of the custodian was cleared by Goldie.

From the restart, Liverpool got away in fine style on the right. Walker passed to Robertson, who ran along at top speed, and sent in a shot quite out of Reader's reach. This success came within the first minute, and naturally gave the visitors great delight, several of the men shaking hands with Robertson.

A free-kick to West Bromwich enabled Roberts to shoot just outside. From another free-kick Dunn shot into the net. The whole eleven claimed for a goal, and Mr Fox, after consultation with the linesmen, allowed the point.

The Liverpool team appeared by no means satisfied, and for some minutes a lively squabble ensued, the players congregating in midfield and arguing with the referee. At length the game was restarted and it was evident that both sides were out of temper and some rough play followed. Chadburn scored another goal for the Albion amid great excitement.

January 5, 1901

West Ham United (0) 0

Liverpool (0) 1
Raybould 60

WEST Ham United, members of the Southern League, were drawn at home for the intermediate round of the Football Association Cup. The game was played at Canning Town, before an enthusiastic crowd of approximately 6,000 spectators. One shilling, double the usual charge for admission, was thought to have reduced the size of the crowd. After a foggy, threatening morning, the sun broke through, and the match began in cold, crisp weather. Both sides were at full strength, the teams being:

West Ham United: Monteith; King, Craig; Dobe, Killy, McEachrane; Hunt, Grassam, Reid, J.Ratcliffe, Kaye.

Liverpool: Perkins; J.T.Robertson, Dunlop; Wilson, Raisbeck, W.Goldie; T.Robertson, McGuigan, Raybould, Hunter, Cox.

Referee: Mr A. Green (West Bromwich)

Attendance: 6,000

Raybould kicked off for Liverpool sharp to time. The first incident was a foul by Dobe against Cox, and Liverpool attacked, but Raybould shot high over the bar. The opening exchanges were rather scrambling, but Liverpool had the better of the Southerners. Some excellent passing by the Liverpool forwards followed, and a great low fast shot from Hunter was well saved by Monteith. A fine run by Kaye and a fierce shot almost secured the first goal for the "Hammers", but Perkins brought off a magnificent save. The home side were spurred on by this effort, and a moment later the Liverpool goal had a fortunate escape when Hunt sent in an oblique shot which touched Perkins' hands along the bar, and then rebounded into play. Perkins then made a grand save from a corner. The thawing frost rendered the surface extremely slippery.

Upon re-starting, play opened in a rather scrambling manner. A free-kick against Liverpool for a foul throw-in looked dangerous, but the ball was well returned, and Cox forced a corner. Another fierce attack was made on the West Ham goal, but a foul against the Reds sent the ball to the other end, where, from short range Ratcliffe sent in a hot shot which hit the bar and rebounded into play. Liverpool then initiated a fine attack, and Monteith made a marvellous save with a crowd of players around him. The former Bristol City man rolled over and over before he emerged triumphant from beneath a ruck of players with the ball, which he kicked upfield, only to see it returned almost immediately. A moment later he saved expertly on the line from Robertson. Play continued to be played at a fast and furious pace, and West

Ham attacked fiercely, the Liverpool goal having a narrow escape through Robertson miskicking and Perkins was forced to get rid of the ball by conceding a corner.

The flag-kick was cleared, and then Cox gained possession, as the crowd shouted "Offside!" The referee's whistle remained silent, and the outside-left went off on his run. Just as he shot he was charged by Craig, and the ball was deflected slightly, but Raybould dashed in and scored. In the collision between Cox and Craig, the West Ham man was injured, and the game was halted for some time. Craig went off the field, and during his absence, the London side were forced to play the one-back game. Eventually the left-back left the field again and for the remainder of the game West Ham played with only ten men.

Monteith made two marvellous saves from short-range shots. Robertson then went on a fine run before narrowly missing the target with a great shot. The home side attacked strongly, and the Liverpool backs were forced to kick out on several occasions. Continuing to advance, Kaye missed with a good effort.

THE LIVERPOOL COURIER

League matches are today interfered with to a certain extent by the introduction of the new preliminary round in connection with the English Cup competition which was rendered necessary by the failure of certain clubs to apply for exemption from the qualifying stages. One of the most important victims in this connection is Liverpool, who have to sacrifice a Saturday, which might well be devoted to a League match, to laying off a "preliminary", as it happens, with West Ham United. There was talk of the Southerners being seen at Anfield Road, but evidently the attraction offered was not great enough. Anyhow, the Liverpool players left the city on Thursday to prepare for this tie with the West Ham people.

THE ATHLETIC NEWS
[BY THE DOCKER]

Monteith had more to do than Perkins and did it better; the Liverpool backs were a bit more polished than King and Craig, but were no surer than they; the half-back play on each side was a worry, with Raisbeck and McEachrane as the pick of the six, while Liverpool had the cleverer forward line. The West Ham line ought not to have tried the short passing game against Raisbeck and company. The crowd might cheer their men a bit more.

February 9, 1901

Notts County (1) 2
Morris (2)

Liverpool (0) 0

LIVERPOOL arrived in Nottingham overnight. As time for the start drew near, the crowd gradually thickened, and augmented by the late excursions from Liverpool, the attendance when hostilities commenced was not far short of 15,000. The pitch was on the heavy side, and sawdust was scattered in the vicinity of the goals. Raisbeck won the toss, and Ross set the ball in motion. The slight breeze favoured the visitors.

County played well down the left before Hadley was pulled up for offside. Cox and Walker advanced for Liverpool but the outside-left was penalised for an infringement. The free-kick placed Hadley in possession, the home outside-right centred grandly, but Robertson repelled him in gallant style. At this stage, the game was typical of a Cup tie in its nature, and many mistakes were made by both sides due to over-eagerness. Raybould had a great opportunity, but Lewis cleared and set up an attack in which Morris featured prominently. He seemed certain to score when Raisbeck tackled him in gallant style. Two corners followed to Liverpool which proved abortive, but the visitors appeared to gain the upper hand. Relief came at last to the home ranks, and they themselves forced two corners which were brilliantly cleared, but the attackers could not be beaten back, and for fully five minutes Liverpool were under severe pressure, but Raisbeck, Dunlop, Robertson and Perkins rendered magnificent defensive work.

Cox was penalised for foul charging, and again County gave Liverpool a taste of their aggressive quality, but ultimately Warner shot wide, much to the relief of the visiting support. Play became contained in midfield, and Bull, who had retired a few minutes earlier, rejoined the fray amid a hearty cheer. A sudden rush by the County now ensued. Ross and Warner each failed to secure possession, whilst Raisbeck, the two backs, and Perkins each made frantic efforts to remove the danger, but Morris dashed up and planted the ball in the net after 22 minutes' play.

This reverse spurred on Liverpool who made a concerted effort to equalise, but their next attack brought no reward. The Reds were not disconcerted, however, and during the next few minutes, they kept the County busy in defending their charge. Notts advanced down the left wing at a tremendous pace failing, however, to get the better of Raisbeck, who was rendering a great account of himself. Robertson and McGuigan initiated an attack, but Walker's effort came to nothing. A tremendous effort by Gee brought a brilliant save from Perkins.

An onslaught on Pennington's goal resulted in an abortive corner. A few moments later the Liverpool goal had an extremely narrow escape, Walker dashing along and centring the ball across goal, but in their eagerness Ross and Morris missed an easy opportunity. As the interval drew near, the County men redoubled their efforts and some excellent work was displayed both by the halves and forwards. From a free kick the ball was headed into Perkins, who fisted away.

In the second half, Liverpool re-arranged their forward line, Walker and Robertson changing positions. Raybould re-started operations, but the home defence cleared. Raybould got possession and passed to McGuigan, who dribbled past all opposition before shooting fiercely at goal. The ball, however, struck an upright and was cleared.

Play became somewhat rough and both sides indulged in man-play. Gee and Morris were prominent for the County, and Morris and Ross missed chances of increasing the score in County's favour. Morris and Robertson came into conflict, and the referee deemed it his duty to send the Liverpool full back off the field.

With a man short the seaport team made desperate attempts to score, but the Nottingham defence could not be penetrated. Another attack by Liverpool ought to have produced a goal, but Cox's fine centre was not met by a colleague. Liverpool bore up manfully to their task, but with Walker breaking down completely, all chance of averting defeat was lost. Gee tested Perkins unsuccessfully, but ultimately Morris put on a second goal. In the last few minutes Liverpool forced a corner which proved of no account. In the end Notts County retired victorious and they thoroughly deserved the verdict on the day's play.

Liverpool only occasionally gave spasmodic evidence of their proper form, and were quite outclassed. Much sympathy was expressed after the game towards Robertson, as his behaviour since joining Liverpool, both on and off the field, had been exemplary.

Notts County: Pennington; Lewis, Prescott; Ball, Bull, McDonald; Hadley, Warner, Ross, Morris, Gee.

Liverpool: Perkins; J.T.Robertson, Dunlop; Wilson, Raisbeck, W.Goldie; T.Robertson, McGuigan, Raybould, Cox, Walker.

Referee: Mr F.H. King (London)

Linesmen: Mr J.E. Carpenter (Leicester); Mr A. Milward (London)

Attendance: 15,000

January 25, 1902

Liverpool (1) 2
T.Robertson 44, Hunter

Everton (0) 2
Taylor, Sharp

NATURALLY enough this fixture aroused great interest and, despite the sloppy roadways and threatened further snowfall there was a huge attendance for the tie. Two weeks previously Everton had resoundingly beaten Liverpool 4-0 at Goodison, but the reigning League champions felt that fortune would turn their way. Three-quarters of an hour before the kick-off every vantage point was filled and contemporary opinion was that it would have been wiser had the executives of both clubs chosen a larger venue for this tie. It was quite evident that the ground could not accommodate the surging stream who were travelling towards the enclosure anxious to witness the contest.

Both teams went into training nearly a fortnight previous to the game, Liverpool going to Lytham and Everton taking up their quarters at Southport. Everton were forced to fulfil their League encounter with Newcastle United during their Cup preparations, but they returned to their headquarters with a 1-1 draw. Liverpool were without the services of Raybould and Satterthwaite, and Fleming was drafted into the front line in place of Satterthwaite, while McGuigan played at centre-forward, Hunter at inside-right, and Wilson filled the vacant half-back position. Everton had their full team except for Settle, the champion goalscorer, who wrenched his leg on Saturday last, and his place was taken by Bowman. The snow which fell on the night before this tie and during the early hours of the morning had been cleared away, but the pitch was very heavy, and gave every promise of a game which would test the stamina of the players to the utmost. Among the spectators was Toman, the Everton player who fractured his leg in the first match of the season, and when he limped on to the ground on crutches he was given a hearty cheer.

Raisbeck led his men on to the field of play and they were immediately followed by Booth and his team. Booth and Raisbeck settled the matter of the toss for choice of positions at the third time of asking, the advantage lying with the Everton skipper, who placed his opponents to face the stiff breeze which was blowing. McGuigan started the game and the Evertonians immediately advanced on the right, but Cox gained possession and, after a short sprint, passed to the centre, where McGuigan dashed away before being fouled. Liverpool pressed forward persistently and Cox passed to Hunter whose stinging shot was fisted away by Kitchen. The Liverpool forwards continued to swarm around Kitchen and Fleming sent in another hard drive which the Everton custodian saved. Liverpool's quintet kept up the pressure with all their old skill, Cox particularly delighting the crowd, but, to the intense chagrin of everybody, he came into collision with Balmer, and slipped on the treacherous ground, twisting his knee so badly that he had to be assisted off the pitch and treated by a doctor. Fortunately he returned a few minutes

later, but he was much the worse for his accident. Sharp took the ball into Liverpool territory, but Dunlop prevailed and Fleming set Liverpool on their way before being repelled by Wolstenholme. Brilliant play by Wilson staved off a further Everton attack and then Cox, despite his injury, put in a good run before putting the ball outside. A second dash by Cox resulted in a fine centre, which Fleming seized upon before shooting at goal, where Kitchen saved at the expense of a corner. This proved fruitless, but another corner shortly afterwards pressurised Everton before Hunter allowed the ball to run outside. Goldie's pass to Fleming almost created a goal, but Kitchen anticipated the move and left his charge to clear the danger.

The Blues took up the attack on their left, and Bowman sent in a powerful shot which Perkins caught in magnificent fashion before distributing the leather and setting up a Reds attack. Perkins' goal had a narrow escape when Taylor missed the target by a foot or so. This was Everton's best effort of the game to date, Liverpool tending to dominate. A pass from Booth set his left wingers on the attack, and Bell shot at goal, but Robertson filled the breach. However, he made only a weak clearance and Young immediately jumped to the front and shot straight at Perkins who had his work cut out to save. A free-kick against Sharp led to an attack on the Everton goal, and when close in McGuigan drove for goal, Kitchen effected a miraculous save, being cheered heartily by the crowd. A move involving Young, Bowman and Bell culminated in Everton winning their first corner, which was well placed and Bowman shot over the bar. In response, Cox got away like a hare, and he finally put in an excellent centre which met Hunter, who darted up, but the sailor boy headed just outside the upright.

As the interval approached, Cox rushed down the left wing and shot over the crossbar. A throw-in just inside the penalty line found Young, who was standing behind Raisbeck. The position did not seem particularly dangerous when Raisbeck was pushed in the back. Immediately there was an appeal for a penalty, which was taken up by the crowd. The eagle eye of Mr Lewis had not missed the transgression and the penalty was awarded, being entrusted to Tommy Robertson. Kitchen pulled off a brilliant save, but he fell, and the ball ran loose which enabled Robertson to follow up and smash the ball into the net amidst frantic shouts from the vast crowd.

Young restarted, and the opening stages of the second half were decidedly in favour of Everton. Liverpool tried to break away on several occasions but were always checked by Balmer. Soon after the resumption, the Blues equalised with one of the finest attacking movements seen on the ground.

Wilson kicked out a dangerous effort, and from the throw-in the ball went to the Everton front rank. Raisbeck robbed Bowman, but he was in turn robbed by Young. Then Taylor and Sharp received the ball after a spell of intricate passing and Robertson left Perkins uncovered in an effort to rob Young, who had received the ball, but the leather went immediately to Taylor, who drove the ball past the hapless Perkins. End-to-end play ensued before Everton attacked down both wings. Bell dashed down and centred for Sharp who shot straight into Perkins' hands. Shortly afterwards the home contingent worked their way in after Dunlop had tricked Sharp and Cox, receiving Dunlop's pass, appeared to shoot for goal from the quarter line, but Hunter seized upon the ball and shot into the top corner of the net. At this stage the Liverpool forwards were enjoying a period of great domination as their skilful play deserved.

At three-quarter time Perkins brought off a brilliant save from Taylor. A sudden dash by Liverpool ended in Fleming forcing a corner, following which Raisbeck shot hard for goal, only to find Balmer in the way, and Dunlop finished up by lunging over the goal-line. The Liverpudlians further pressed their opponents, but eventually they were cleared out owing to a foul, and a short stoppage was necessary due to Fleming being injured. Moments later, a free-kick was awarded against the home side which ended with Sharp scoring a beautiful goal. After this equalising goal, Bowman took the centre-forward position, but despite several promising attempts Everton could not force a third goal.

Liverpool: Perkins; J.T.Robertson, Dunlop; Wilson, Raisbeck, W.Goldie; T.Robertson, Hunter, McGuigan, Fleming, Cox.

Everton: Kitchen; Balmer, Eccles; Wolstenholme, Booth, Abbott; J. Sharp, Taylor, Young, Bowman, Bell.

Referee: Mr J. Lewis (Blackburn)

Attendance: 30,000

Jack Taylor, who scored Everton's first equaliser

January 30, 1902

Everton (0) 0

Liverpool (1) 2
Raisbeck 40,   Hunter 53

THE sun shone brightly in a brilliant blue sky overlooking a pitch in splendid condition. There were two changes from the previous Saturday's game: B.Sharp took the place of Eccles at left-back in the Everton team, while Davies substituted for Fleming as inside-left on the Liverpool team. Before the kick-off there was a vast crowd of spectators. The stands were packed and the popular parts of the ground were well patronised. Booth won the toss and McGuigan kicked off in face of the sun. The Liverpool centre at once ran through his field, and was deliberately tripped by Balmer in front of goal. Raisbeck took the kick, which was cleared. Play transferred to the Liverpool end after a clearance by B.Sharp, and his brother and Taylor took the leather at top speed, before Dunlop cleared with a huge kick. The ball passed to the Liverpool right and Robertson rushed away at top speed and banged the ball right across the goalmouth, the leather passing only a few inches outside. Play now opened out considerably, and the Liverpool forwards showed beautiful combination and troubled the Evertonians. After a brief spell of midfield play McGuigan managed to get in a long shot which Kitchen cleared, this being the first occasion on which either of the custodians were called upon to handle. A Dunlop free-kick went across to the Liverpool right, but Kitchen cleared as a goal seemed imminent. A moment later Everton were given a free-kick close in but Bell sent the ball over the bar. The home forwards asserted themselves strongly, and some brisk work by Young and C. Bowman gave Perkins very grave anxiety, the Liverpool custodian only just fisting out the swift shot sent in by the Everton centre-forward. Shortly afterwards, Kitchen was tested by a shot from McGuigan. The pace began to quicken and the referee had his work cut out to watch the lightning-like movements on the field. Bell and Bowman forced the first corner of the game, which led to a hot bully in front of Perkins. Abbott sent in a good shot which Robertson intercepted, but the ball fell to B. Sharp who shot over the bar.

Liverpool took up the attack, and "Sailor" Hunter passed to Robertson who sent in a "clinker" which passed just outside. The visitors maintained the attack for some time, and McGuigan sent in a telling shot which just hit the wrong side of the upright. Everton responded when J.Sharp forced a corner, which led to another exciting scene in front of Perkins' goal, Abbott shooting over the bar. A foul gave the home side another chance down the left, but Robertson's defence was magnificent, and it was not long before the "Reds" were on the move towards Kitchen. Davies passed to Cox, and the Liverpool flier was just about to shoot when the whistle went for offside. A foul against Bowman let in the Anfielders, and as a consequence they forced a couple of impotent corners. Jack Sharp burst off with one of his famous sprints, and Dunlop, in trying to check him, was brought down by the

Lancashire cricketer, and for a spell the Liverpool back had to undergo the usual rubbing process. When play resumed Mr Lewis threw up the ball close to the Liverpool goal, where a free-kick had been given against McGuigan.

Just prior to the interval Bell shot over the crossbar when two yards out. Liverpool pressed forward and B. Sharp proved himself unnecessarily aggressive. From the free-kick which Raisbeck took, the ball went in the centre of the goal. Balmer, in attempting to head away, sent the ball in the wrong direction, the result being that Kitchen was unsighted, and the ball rolled into the net. From the re-start Liverpool nearly snatched a second goal, McGuigan toeing the leather over the crossbar. After this Balmer, in making a clearance, sent the ball right over the grandstand. To avoid loss of time another ball was obtained, but Mr Lewis refused permission for its use, and it was only after waiting several minutes that the game proceeded.

A rather prolonged interval ensued and Young restarted. Some beautiful passing by Davies, McGuigan and Cox ended in the outside-left swinging the ball into the goalmouth where Kitchen cleared cleverly. Taylor and Jack Sharp tried desperately hard to force their way through, but they were so closely watched by Goldie and Raisbeck that they were never allowed to get within shooting range.

As the Liverpool forwards were getting off from the centre of the field, Wolstenholme deliberately handled, and from the free-kick "Sailor" Hunter glided through the field, and sent in a beautiful long shot, which Kitchen failed to negotiate, and a tremendous roar went up when Liverpool registered their second goal eight minutes from the restart. The home side tried desperately to get back into the game, and a corner off Robertson was sent over the bar by Wolstenholme.

Both teams were still in the best of condition and the pace had not relented at all. The Liverpool forwards played a great game and their combination and methods of working the ball were infinitely superior to the tactics of the opposition. A mishap to Taylor caused another short stoppage, after which Liverpool forced another corner which Kitchen cleared. Through some lax play on the part of Balmer, Robertson gained possession and with an oblique shot he narrowly missed a third goal. From a free-kick by Raisbeck the ball went to McGuigan, whose shot struck an upright before rebounding into play. Gradually the pace slackened as it appeared that Everton had lost heart. The Anfielders took advantage of this by maintaining the pressure, and Kitchen jeopardised his charge with an awful clearance. Robertson took a long kick at an unguarded goal, but Kitchen just managed to effect a save. At this stage, Liverpool were completely the masters.

As the game progressed, Everton bore down on the visitors' goal and a Booth shot was saved by Perkins at the second attempt. Towards the finish Kitchen saved at his knees and Perkins brought off a miraculous save from the Everton left.

The gate money amounted to about £800, which, with the receipts at Anfield on the previous Saturday, left about £1,600 to be divided.

Everton: Kitchen; Balmer, B.Sharp; Wolstenholme, Booth, Abbott; J.Sharp, Taylor, Young, Bowman, Bell.

Liverpool: Perkins; J.T.Robertson, Dunlop; Wilson, Raisbeck, W.Goldie; T.Robertson, Hunter, McGuigan, Davies, Cox.

Referee: Mr J. Lewis (Blackburn)

Attendance: 20,000

Alexander Raisbeck, *who opened the scoring for Liverpool in the fortieth minute. Raisbeck scored only two goals for Liverpool in the FA Cup, his first goal coming against Newcastle United almost three years earlier.*

February 8, 1902

Southampton (2) 4
Chadwick (2), Lee 25, Joe Turner

Liverpool (0) 1
Fleming

LIVERPOOL's battle in the Second Round of the English Cup was invested with extraordinary interest when it was known that they had to journey to Southampton. The Southern Leaguers are notable and redoubtable opponents on their own ground, and, in view of the seriousness of the contest, the Anfielders took precautions to preserve their training. After enjoying the bracing atmosphere at Lytham for a week, the team left Liverpool on the Thursday for Winchester, in which ancient capital the time was quietly and pleasantly spent until the morning of the match, when the train was taken to Southampton. In the southern seaport the match had created great excitement and was the topic of conversation on everyone's lips. The weather was cold but fair, and showers in the morning had given way to springlike sunshine at twelve o'clock. The Liverpool team was, of course, accompanied by Mr Tom Watson and several directors, who paid assiduous attention to the needs of the players. An hour before the kick-off the neighbourhood of the ground became heavily congested, and it was evident that there would be a huge attendance. There was one change in the Liverpool ranks from the previous match, Fleming (now recovered) coming in to partner Cox. The home eleven put out their best team. At the time the men appeared the ground, which was rather on the small side, was packed, and the tedium of waiting for the game was relieved by some excellent music from a brass band. Just as the players appeared in the arena, the sky clouded over and rain began to fall, much to the discomfort of those spectators without shelter. Liverpool won the toss and Raisbeck elected to play against the sun and a slight breeze.

The start was almost sensational as the home side raced down at great speed and a foul against Fleming let in Southampton, Perkins clearing splendidly from a shot by Wood. Again the home side attacked and Dunlop was hopelessly beaten when Raisbeck jumped in to save the day. A minute later the Southampton forwards swarmed round Perkins and Turner shot just over the bar. Gradually play opened out somewhat, and Liverpool made ground but the home defence and half-back play was exceptional.

At length Liverpool broke away down the right, and some excellent passing characterised their work, but Fry came to the rescue and an attack by Turner and Wood was halted by Robertson. The home side, however, subjected the Liverpool goal to a tremendous bombardment which was only relieved when Perkins fisted clear a shot from Wood.

Still Southampton maintained the pressure, and after fourteen minutes a breakaway down the left ended with Chadwick scoring a fine goal. This success by the former Evertonian was met with great applause.

This spurred the home side on to greater efforts, but at length Liverpool got within shooting range, although Fleming missed a good opportunity of scoring.

With 25 minutes gone, Lee scored with a tremendous long range shot which gave Perkins no chance of saving. At this stage the Anfielders appeared quite disorganised and the half-backs appeared quite unable to settle down.

A good run by Cox looked promising for the visitors, but his centre was wasted by Robertson, who missed a great chance of scoring. A long, low drive by Arthur Turner was well saved by Perkins. Liverpool replied down the left and Cox twice outpaced Fry before being tackled by Robinson. Following this the Saints advanced in fine, combined order and, after shots by Arthur Turner and Chadwick, a corner was forced off Dunlop, Perkins saving at the expense of a further corner. The place kick was accurate and Brown shot in, but Perkins cleared and the danger was only averted when Bowman shot over the bar. Liverpool were literally penned in their own territory. Raisbeck did two men's work in trying to alter the situation, but the forwards could not get going, except for the spasmodic and fruitless dashes of Cox along the wing. Towards the interval Joe Turner sent in a fine shot which just passed outside. The Saints had all their own way and the supporters gave vent to their delight in continuous shouts in the broadest Hampshire dialect.

The band continued to delight the crowd while the players rested, but upon resuming Southampton immediately attacked and Edgar Chadwick sent in a low shot which Perkins just managed to save. After a period of sustained pressure from the home side, Liverpool broke away and Robertson shot just over the crossbar. Play was more even, but the Liverpool forwards had little change from the great defensive work of Fry and Molyneux. The visitors were reduced to trying long range shots, and one from Cox went flying over the bar. Liverpool then attacked persistently, only to encounter a stone-wall defence, and with a less-experienced goalkeeper against them than Robinson, Liverpool would surely have scored. The Saints custodian judged some excellent dropping centres from Cox with rare ability. On another occasion, Robertson beat Lee and Molyneux, and from short range drove in a terrific shot which the home custodian fisted out. Robertson again got hold of the ball but sent his shot over the bar. Only the slowness of the inside men in taking some magnificent passes from Cox kept Liverpool scoreless. There were fears that Southampton would have their lead reduced for they were ragged at this stage of the game. Fry and Molyneux maintained a solid front, and the Liverpool onslaughts achieved no tangible result. Encouraged by the success of their rearguard, the home forwards attacked with determination and Joe Turner succeeded in scoring a third goal for the Saints. From a rush by the left wing Fleming scored for Liverpool, but Chadwick responded with another lovely goal.

Liverpool's display was much below expectations. In the first half their form was worse than that shown by some of the weakest teams in the Southern League. The home attack was particularly efficient, but the visiting backs would have encountered such attackers in the League, yet on this occasion they succumbed with little resistance. Raisbeck was the only man in the defence who showed any ability to cope with the Southampton forwards, but his Herculean efforts were simply wasted. Neither Dunlop nor Robertson kicked with any power or accuracy, so that Perkins had an unenviable task. He could not have prevented any of the shots that went past him; in fact, he was responsible for keeping the scoreline down, and three shots which went past him rebounded off the crossbar.

The Liverpool defenders exhibited considerable improvement in the second half, tackling and kicking superbly, and the half-backs nursed the front-line well, though that improvement came too late. The only possible explanation for Liverpool's defensive frailties was that they met an attack which was not conducted on the recognised lines, and therefore they could not readily adapt themselves to it. The two Turners especially caused them trouble.

Neither were the Liverpool forwards a success. The only one who maintained his reputation was Cox, and the left winger was in brilliant form. Meston could do nothing with him. Fry held his own with Cox by reason of his tremendous speed, but there was little to choose between the two in a short sprint. Some of the centres that Cox put in presented great openings to the other forwards, but they were squandered. Cox made one blunder which cost Liverpool a goal. Robertson, after a smart run, whipped the ball across the goalmouth to the Liverpool flyer, who was close in, and had only Robinson to beat. It seemed likely that he would score, but he missed the ball altogether. McGuigan did not justify his sponsors who decided upon playing him at centre-forward. There was no spirit in his movements. He was a novice against the nippy Bowman. Fleming had the distinction of scoring, but beyond that he did nothing of note. It was doubtful that Fleming was fit to play. His inclusion was decided upon at the eleventh hour. Hunter was off colour, and so, too, was Robertson, until the game was approaching the conclusion, when he made some smart runs. Against the inglorious Liverpool performance, the excellent exhibition by Southampton stood out in bold contrast. It was the forwards who secured victory. The Merseysiders caught the home team at the top of their form and never looked like winning.

The Saints lost no time at the opening, and their early success had a wonderfully stimulating effect upon the players, while it seemed to dishearten the visitors. Every one of the forwards obeyed the advice to shoot quickly and often when there was the slightest opportunity of doing so. The most conspicuous player of the front line was Chadwick. The former Evertonian was as frisky as a kitten. His transfers were beautifully timed and well directed, and his marksmanship was first-class. Before this game, he had not worked successfully with Joe Turner, but the pair showed great understanding. Turner had a great advantage over Robertson in terms of speed, and was very dangerous in front of goal. Brown, the centre-forward, was uneven. He started splendidly, but went off after the interval, and the light-haired Raisbeck was his master. Wood improved with age, and played well this season. On this occasion he was very clever in providing openings for Arthur Turner, who was roughly handled by Dunlop towards the end. Bowman, the former Aston Villa player, was the shining light among the half-backs. He was an additional forward, and in defence he rendered C.B. Fry and Molyneux invaluable assistance. On the day's form, he was more prominent than Raisbeck, and had he but the Liverpool player's physique he would be a formidable rival to the Liverpool centre-half for international honours. Lee, who had been chosen for the South, always had the Liverpool right wing under control. His tackling was above reproach, and his headwork very clever. Meston did some good work, despite the fact that Cox was too much of a handful for him. The home backs, Fry and Molyneux overshadowed the Liverpool backs. The famous amateur was brilliant, whilst his partner, though less showy, was equally effective. Robinson deserved nothing but praise, as he effected two marvellous clearances, and he negotiated every shot in a manner that stamped him as one of the most brilliant custodians of the day.

THE WAR

~~~~~~

GENERAL BADEN-POWELL BUSY

Since his return to South Africa, says the *Pall Mall Gazette*, General Baden-Powell has been busy perfecting his police force. Having arranged matters at headquarters, he visited his principal posts, and made preparations for the further development of his plans. His men received him with extreme enthusiasm. The general is in the pink of condition, and has completely shaken off the last trace of the indisposition that necessitated his rest in England.

TROOPS FOR THE FRONT

A scene of much enthusiasm was witnessed at Shorncliffe Camp this morning when nearly 400 veterans of the Imperial Yeomanry left for South Africa under the command of Colonel Younghusband.

Southampton: Robinson; C.B.Fry, Molyneux; Meston, Bowman, Lee; A.Turner, Wood, Brown, Chadwick, J.Turner.

Liverpool: Perkins; J.T.Robertson, Dunlop; Wilson, Raisbeck, W.Goldie; T.Robertson, Hunter, McGuigan, Fleming, Cox.

Referee: Mr T. Kirkham (Stoke)

Attendance: 20,000

February 7, 1903

Manchester United (2) 2
Peddie 25, 40

Liverpool (0) 1
Raybould

LIVERPOOL appeared first to a rousing cheer as they trotted on to the heavily-sanded pitch. The ground was situated in the middle of chemical factories, and there was not a semblance of a blade of grass to be seen. Liverpool won the toss, and the United started against a strong wind. The visitors went down the right and Rodwell had considerable difficulty in clearing from Goddard, one of five Liverpool players making their Cup debuts for the Reds. Raybould gained possession of the loose ball and sent in a shot which Birchenough cleared. Chadwick got the return and shot strongly, but the home custodian intercepted it with his legs, and then Cox had a shot which was cleared. All this action had taken place in the first minute of the game, and it was followed by further heavy Liverpool pressure, and Chadwick sent a shot high over the bar. From the goal kick Peddie raced away, but the heavy ground impeded his progress and Glover was able to clear easily.

Raybould was dispossessed by Stafford when in a dangerous position, and this was followed by Raisbeck shooting over the bar. Moments later Livingstone ran right through and sent in a clinking shot which the home custodian dealt with in masterly style. After twenty minutes the Manchester goal remained intact, despite the game being a one-horse show for Liverpool.

Eventually United, whom Liverpool last played as Newton Heath in the Cup in 1898, winning 2-1, asserted themselves strongly and Peddie sent in a low shot from long range which troubled Perkins. Two unsuccessful corners to Liverpool were followed by a goal to United, for whom Peddie scored with a terrific shot after 25 minutes.

At this point the weather cleared and the crowd increased greatly. Restarting Liverpool made desperate attempts to equalise and Chadwick, Raybould, and Livingstone all had shots without success.

A breakaway by Smith and Hurst almost brought a second goal, but the Anfielders responded with an attack of their own and Livingstone missed a golden opportunity of netting the ball. Soon afterwards Chadwick - who had helped Southampton to beat Liverpool in the previous season's Cup competition - shot tamely from close range. The visiting left wing attempted to force the issue, but the home goalkeeper threw clear from an effort by Cox. A minute later a rasping shot from Raybould was saved in excellent fashion by Birchenough. As the half drew to a close, the United had the better of the exchanges and from a neat pass by Griffiths Peddie slipped through both backs and scored a second goal five minutes from the interval.

When the game was resumed the wind was still blowing hard, and Liverpool, with such a big task in front of them, at once commenced to play the one back game. As a result, the United were twice pulled up for offside, but Stafford adopted a similar course, and Liverpool were also placed at a disadvantage. On one occasion, Stafford, in clearing, fell to the ground, and one of the Liverpool players was cautioned for kicking him. The United made several efforts to break clear, and twice in as many minutes they got within shooting distance, but on each occasion offside spoiled their attacking movements. Rothwell took up his accustomed place again, and the Liverpool men made a determined effort to get through, but it was unavailing. Liverpool continued to play in an unsportsmanlike manner of only having one back, but the United forced a corner. Glover cleared, only to see Stafford return the ball well up the field.

Liverpool broke away again, and Raybould met a brilliant centre to reduce the arrears. Stafford then adopted the one-back game, and free-kicks to both sides became frequent. Much of the interest was subsequently removed from the encounter.

Liverpool rather spoiled the game in the second half by playing one back. They continued to play the same game even after Stafford had been ordered off. This drastic step which the referee took with regard to Stafford was to be regretted for there were certainly many worse incidents during the game. When he was cautioned there was an element of doubt as to whether the foul was intentional, and as far as could be seen when the incident arose which led to his receiving marching orders, Stafford was badly kicked on the ankle and retaliated by simply raising his fist. Previous to this, the home captain had been deliberately kicked whilst lying on the ground, but for this the offender was let off with a caution.

Referee: Mr A. Milward (Essex)

Attendance: 15,000

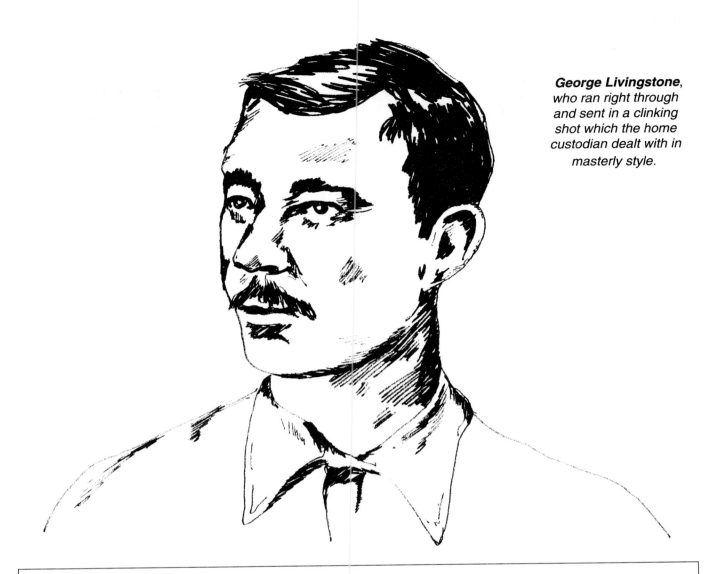

George Livingstone, *who ran right through and sent in a clinking shot which the home custodian dealt with in masterly style.*

Manchester United

Birchenough

Stafford   Rodwell

Downey   Griffiths   Cartwright

Street   Pegg   Peddie   Smith   Hurst

O

Cox   Chadwick   Raybould   Livingstone   Goddard

W.Goldie   Raisbeck   Parry

Dunlop   Glover

Perkins

Liverpool

February 6, 1904

Blackburn Rovers (2) 3
Watson, Dewhurst (2)

Liverpool (1) 1
Raybould 14

SO feebly had Liverpool fared in the League (they were currently at the bottom of the table) that Blackburn Rovers (in ninth position) were deemed automatic winners at Ewood Park. Under the care of Tom Watson, the players had been in strict training at Fairhaven, and they arrived at Blackburn from the health resort on the morning of the match. Three changes were decided upon from the previous week's game, Dunlop resuming in place of Hoare, Parry displacing Fleming and Chadwick returning after a lengthy absence to partner Cox. With the front line thus strengthened it was hoped that Liverpool would overcome their League deficiencies. A heavy drizzle fell during the morning of the match and at two o'clock the outlook was dull, drab and dispiriting. In spite of this, a large crowd turned out. Rovers were without three of their regular men, the most noticeable absentee being Pentland, a victim of scarlet fever. Liverpool won the toss, but there was little to be gained from this as there was no discernible breeze.

Blackburn Rovers: Evans; Crompton, Eastham; Smith, McClure, Bradshaw; Whittaker, Bowman, Dewhurst, Watson, Blackburn.

Liverpool: Platt; West, Dunlop; Parry, Raisbeck, Hughes; Goddard, Morris, Raybould, Chadwick, Cox.

Referee: Mr F.H. Dennis (North Ormsby)

Attendance: 10,000

Upon opening Raisbeck neatly dispossessed Dewhurst, but Chadwick was unable to pass Smith, who met the ball and punted strongly to his left wing. Blackburn attempted to get through and West was penalised but the ensuing free-kick came to nothing, though a similar concession looked likely to produce a goal until Raisbeck's astute judgment saved the day for Liverpool. The visiting forward line moved upfield in fine style and in order to prevent Goddard scoring, Eastham gave away a corner, which proved fruitless. Goddard and Morris put in some excellent work, and it was only the merest chance that Crompton charged down a brilliant low drive from Chadwick. At this stage in the game the Anfielders were all over their opponents, and a splendid series of attacks terminated in Hughes just skimming the bar.

Following a cross shot by the player Blackburn, the Liverpool goal seemed certain of capture until Dunlop got his foot to the ball just at the appropriate moment. The Rovers began to assert themselves, and Blackburn and Watson played well, but were unable to beat West. A Dewhurst shot was narrowly wide of the mark as the home side attacked.

Meanwhile Raisbeck was in the thick of the action, and he eventually put his forwards in possession. Play reached the Rovers' quarters and a brilliant effort on the part of Chadwick just missed the corner of the net. End-to-end play ensued in the manner typical of a Cup tie.

Eventually, in one of the many fine movements of the Anfielders, the evergreen Chadwick, finding himself hampered, back-heeled the ball to Raybould, who, surrounded by players red, white and blue, and without attempting to trap the ball, sent in an irresistible, low ball which never swerved from its purpose and which gave the home custodian no chance of saving. This goal came after 14 minutes' play and it had a stimulating effect upon the Anfielders.

Cox twice defeated Crompton with the greatest ease, and had Raybould not missed his footing on the heavy turf, he must have converted the winger's centre without too much trouble.

A sudden breakaway by the Rovers changed the complexion of the game. The Anfield quarters were reached and Raisbeck challenged Whittaker. The ball was about to pass over the line when Parry raced across and, for some unaccountable reason, placed the ball towards his own goal, with the result that Watson dashed up and netted the ball without any difficulty. Though the bulk of the spectators were now drenched with the rain which was falling heavily, there was great excitement around the ground now that the teams were on equal terms. Shortly afterwards Dewhurst, from fully twenty yards, drove the ball into the net. Another attack caused great concern to Liverpool and the resourceful Raisbeck had to concede a corner to prevent Whittaker from getting in his centre. The score scarcely represented the general run of play, but the Rovers tried to capitalise upon their lead, and only the fine work of Raisbeck and his defenders prevented the home side from increasing their advantage. One excellent run by Whittaker, and the former Evertonian, Bowman, found Dunlop in a somewhat helpless position, and following upon a cross shot to the left wing the ball was well placed into the goalmouth, where Parry obviously handled and the referee duly awarded a penalty kick. This was taken by Crompton and not the usual penalty-taker, Whittaker, but the home back shot straight at Platt, and West cleared. Before a minute had elapsed Hughes skimmed the crossbar from a corner kick and further good work by Morris placed the Anfielders in a very promising position, but after a short spell of attack the visitors were repulsed. The Rovers again took up the running and a low shot from long range by McClure troubled Platt.

Sam Raybould, *the scorer of Liverpool's goal against Blackburn*

Hughes, Raybould and Goddard were involved in a fine piece of combination which resulted in the outside-right having his effort charged down by Crompton. As the interval approached, Platt pulled off a brilliant save from Bradshaw. The Rovers initiated a fierce onslaught upon the Liverpool goal and a free-kick against the visitors endangered Platt's goal. The goalkeeper, who was limping badly from a kick, gave away a corner, and it was apparent from his movements that he would have some difficulty in getting off the mark should the occasion arise.

The game slowed down for a period after the change of ends. Following a splendid clearance by Eastham, Watson caused some anxiety to the Liverpool defence as he beat both backs, but Dunlop pulled himself together and retrieved the situation. A free-kick was awarded to the visitors, and they looked like scoring. As the ball flew across the goalmouth, Goddard rushed forward to put it into the net, but he failed to connect. An extraordinary incident was witnessed when the Rovers scored their third point. A pass by Bowman in the direction of the Liverpool goal saw Dewhurst dart past the back and take possession of the sphere before dribbling to within the penalty area and shooting. The ball flew high towards the goal and appeared to strike the corner edge of the inside of the bar or the top of the net before bouncing on the floor. Those who saw the shot were certain it was a goal, and Mr Dennis, the referee, also considered it was, for he turned his back to the charge as if to walk to the centre of the field. Then he heard a commotion, and glancing round, saw the Liverpool backs dribbling the leather away from their goal. Immediately he blew his whistle, again pointed to the centre of the field, and then commenced to walk there himself. In a second he was surrounded by the Liverpool men, one of whom excitedly clutched his jacket sleeve, claiming that the

ball had never entered the net. The referee was bewildered, and instead of waving the players aside, appeared to listen to their arguments. They remained in conversation for two or three minutes, and finally he rushed from the midst of the exponents towards Mr T. Armitt, one of the linesmen. Mr Armitt agreed with the Rovers that it was a legitimate point. Mr Dennis once more pointed to the centre of the field, but was again surrounded by the excited Liverpool players. He did not have the strength of mind to disregard their complaints, and darted across the field to Mr C. Sutcliffe, of Rowenstall, the other linesman, who also assured him that the point was just. The whole scene was caused by the referee not knowing his own mind on the subject.

The Rovers' defence performed superbly, while the forwards showed marked improvement. Evans and Crompton were in the best of humour. Crompton gave a mediocre display in the previous week's match, but against Liverpool he was brilliant. Eastham, who played instead of Riley, exceeded expectations, although he would have been more effective had he made fewer mad rushes. The half-backs were courageous. McClure, the father of the line, was happy to be in the thick of the fray and made his presence felt to all who got in his way. Bradshaw was an artist, both in robbing and shooting. Smith, who was developing into a classy half, was no longer a forward, but he had a rosy future in the half-back line ahead of him. Of the forwards, Dewhurst led his line well. Whittaker sprinted down the wing and dribbled excellently. He wasted no time, but banged the ball either at the goal or to the foot of a comrade. He played to the top of his form. His partner, Bowman, plied the little man with numerous passes. It was essential, however, that Bowman's marksmanship should improve. Watson was off colour, while Blackburn was a polished exponent, and, along with Whittaker, was the class man of the line.

Liverpool were in poor form; Platt, the Rishton cricketer, played well despite limping almost throughout the game. Raisbeck, Goddard, and Raybould were the three other players worthy of praise. Hughes did his fair share against the excellent Whittaker, but Parry was off his game. Parry did not appear to be fully fit to last the ninety minutes. West was the better back, doing some good work against great odds.

February 4, 1905

Liverpool (1) 1
Parkinson 27

Everton (0) 1
Makepeace (pen) 80

LIVERPOOL were unbeaten at home this season, and had beaten Everton 4-1 in a Liverpool Cup game in January. On that occasion, Booth, Settle, and Sharp were absentees, and Roose was not in goal. At half-past two several of the gates were closed, and at three the spectators were packed well nigh to suffocation. The large body of police kept them within the bounds of reasonable behaviour. Karno's band relieved the tedium of the wait with a selection of mostly rag-time tunes. In the Liverpool directors' box sat several well-known figures in the football world, Councillor Edwin Berry chairman of the club, acting as host to Mr C.J. Hughes, Mr J.J. Bentley, Mr A. Scragg, the referee, and others. Shortly after three o'clock Raisbeck led his men on to the field, accompanied by a huge roar from almost 27,000 throats. Everton were without Booth and Walter Balmer, whose places were taken by Makepeace and Robert Balmer. Raisbeck and Jack Taylor went to the centre to spin the coin, and "honest Jock" won and took advantage of the fair breeze.

Parkinson set the leather rolling towards the Oakfield Road goal and Raybould, Parkinson, Raisbeck and Goddard combined well in an early attacking move. An advance by Hardman was checked by West, but the Blue right wing took up the running before losing out near the corner flag. At this stage of the game, Everton were in command and there was indecision in the Liverpool defence. Sharp contrived to force an opening on his wing, but Dunlop stuck to him like glue and forced him over the line. The goal-kick did not bring Liverpool much relief, and Everton forced matters in home territory. Parkinson made several attempts to break clear, but Taylor proved too much for him. West was the most composed man on the Liverpool side, and he cleared splendidly on several occasions.

Taylor rushed across into the centre, but Raisbeck prevented a transfer to the opposite wing, and after some scrambling play, Taylor shot high over the bar with a long drive. Some excellent work followed by the Everton right-wingers, but when McDermott had his front opponents beaten, Raisbeck dashed across and cleared. Balmer cleared a raid by the Liverpool centre and right, and then Everton attacked strongly. Young's shot hit the side-netting and he followed this with a shot from long range which Doig saved easily.

Following a further Evertonian attack, Raisbeck cleared in front of goal, and the Liverpool skipper displayed peerless defence in keeping out Young and McDermott in turn. Raisbeck played particular attention to Young, and dispossessed him time after time. McDermott fouled Dunlop, but Liverpool were unable to use the free-kick to their advantage.

Raisbeck gained possession and he passed to Cox, who sped down his wing despite being closely attended, but his final pass went astray, and Makepeace secured the ball. Raybould then made off in a very promising manner, but he was dispossessed by Makepeace. Sharp then took up the running for Everton, but the veteran Fleming forced the cricketer off to make a faulty pass. Cox beat Sharp in a race for a loose ball, and this was the start of a promising Liverpool attack. Parkinson manoeuvred his way into the Everton box and headed for goal, but Balmer robbed the Liverpool man. Cox gained possession and shot at goal, but Roose saved at the expense of a corner. The ball was sent outside by Robinson.

Young and Settle moved swiftly down the centre with a clear opening, but Young was checked by Fleming. Settle had a clear course and a goal seemed imminent until Doig summed up the situation and rushed out of his goal to dispossess Settle at the critical moment. It was a fine example of cool, unnerving judgment.

Play was now more of an even character, and after 27 minutes, Liverpool opened the scoring. Cox initiated the move with a fine centre which was met by Robinson and Parkinson scored an easy goal, putting the ball into the far corner of the net out of the reach of Roose.

From the re-start, the Evertonians put on a spell of intense pressure. Sharp was repeatedly beaten on his wing and no headway was made down that side. Taylor worked like a trojan, and put his centre and left on the run. An exciting bully in front of the Liverpool goal ended in favour of the defenders. Everton displayed the superior finesse, but Liverpool created opportunities and sought to benefit from them. A fine clearance by Raisbeck opened up the play for Cox, and the flyer passed to Parkinson, but the Anfield centre-forward overran the leather. Taylor broke free, and aided by McDermott and Sharp, the Everton trio looked

---

Liverpool: Doig; West, Dunlop; Parry, Raisbeck, Fleming; Goddard, Robinson, Parkinson, Raybould, Cox.

Everton: Roose; R.Balmer, Crelly; Makepeace, Taylor, Abbott; Sharp, McDermott, Young, Settle, Hardman.

Referee: Mr J. Lewis (Blackburn)

Attendance: 28,000

Receipts: £1,070

---

dangerous until Raisbeck cleared magnificently. A foul was awarded to Liverpool, but it was neutralised by the ubiquitous Taylor, who put Sharp away. Raisbeck broke up Everton attacks initiated by McDermott, Young, and Sharp. Raybould was put in possession by Fleming, but Sammy finished with a dreadful shot. Goddard then forced a corner off Crelley and Parkinson shot into Roose's hands.

Everton made a sweeping movement up the right but Sharp shot too soon and Doig handled safely. Hardman took a throw-in, from which Abbott tested Doig with a well-directed shot from long range.

During the first half there had been a good deal of reckless and scrambling play, and a tendency to roughness on occasions. On the Anfield side the forwards' play was inferior, but Raisbeck played a brilliant game and made Young's efforts look poor. The Liverpool skipper was ably supported by West, who extricated his side from many difficult situations with his cool and judicious clearances.

Upon re-starting, Everton attacked fiercely, but did not make any headway. A number of free-kicks were awarded to Everton, but these simply meant further pressure and no score. At the opposite end, Cox and Parkinson dwelt too long on the ball and missed a fine opportunity to score. A further corner to Liverpool was headed away by Balmer. Parkinson was put in possession by Fleming, and the centre-forward avoided all opposition and fired wide with an open goal at his mercy.

With time running out, Everton pressed hard for an equaliser. Dunlop stopped Sharp with a brilliant header, and soon afterwards Raisbeck came to Liverpool's rescue. A free-kick to Everton resulted in Doig fisting away a goal-bound effort. The attacks of the Blues became more concentrated, and only ceased when Parry grassed Settle, the little winger receiving attention at the side of the enclosure.

A good deal of rough play ensued, and Young was the main sufferer. Ten minutes from the end, Young almost got through, when Raisbeck brought him down just outside the goal, and Mr Lewis immediately awarded the penalty, from which Makepeace brought equality. Makepeace feinted once, but he equalised although the ball just grazed the underside of the cross-bar in its flight.

Doig still had a sharp eye and a cunning hand for a veteran, while Dunlop and West generally obtained the ball when they advanced. In the half-back line Fleming worked extremely hard and with great enthusiasm. Raisbeck was the master strategist in the positions that he took up. However, he ought to have ordered his comrades to depart from their dubious methods which eventually brought retribution and cost them the game. With his long legs, Parry covered the entire pitch.

In the front line, neither Cox nor Goddard was spirited. The latter was slow in taking a pass, while the former Blackpool flyer was prone to dallying on the ball and to doubling back with the object of beating his man a second time, which was a waste of energy and skill, and gave the opposition every chance to re-form in defence. Robinson was a worker, while Parkinson was a young man who was keen to do well, not being afraid of foraging and making his own openings. When he was on the ball he was tenacious and difficult to dispossess. In midfield he dribbled dexterously and passed out to his wings with a thrilling enthusiasm. Generally, Everton's forward play was weak. Sharp and Hardman were

no more convincing than Goddard and Cox, and the inside forwards were not so thrusting and penetrative as those of Liverpool. Young and Settle were mediocre. The cleverest was McDermott, but even he failed to create enough openings for his men, for he was often hovering about between Sharp and Makepeace in a kind of hybrid position. Of the middle men, Taylor alone reached the standard of his best League form. His play was vigorous, occasionally too much so, but he performed well. Makepeace had given finer exhibitions, while Abbott was not quite himself.

On the following Monday morning, the Everton players left for Stafford to undergo a course of brine baths, and returned on the morning of the replay.

The other results:

F.A. CUP - FIRST ROUND

Bury	1	Notts County	0
Nottingham Forest	2	Sheffield United	0
Bolton Wanderers	1	Bristol Rovers	1
Newcastle United	1	Plymouth Argyle	1
Sunderland	1	Wolverhampton W.	1
Woolwich Arsenal	0	Bristol City	0
Blackburn Rovers	1	Sheffield Wednesday	2
Middlesbrough	1	Tottenham Hotspur	1
Lincoln City	1	Manchester City	2
Aston Villa	5	Leicester Fosse	1
Small Heath	0	Portsmouth	2
Stoke	2	Grimsby	0
Fulham	0	Reading	0
Derby County	0	Preston North End	2
Southampton	3	Millwall Athletic	1

Replays

Bristol Rovers	0	Bolton Wanderers	3
Plymouth Argyle	1	Newcastle United	1
Wolverhampton W.	1	Sunderland	0
Bristol City	1	Woolwich Arsenal	0
Tottenham Hotspur	1	Middlesbrough	0
Reading	0	Fulham	0

Second replays

Newcastle United	2	Plymouth Argyle	0
Fulham	1	Reading	0

February 8, 1905

Everton (1) 2
McDermott 3, Hardman 85

Liverpool (0) 1
Goddard 48

THE failure of the Anfielders to win outright on the previous Saturday required a great deal of understanding in view of the palpable advantages they had and, although the balance of Cup-tie form lay with Liverpool, there was a general feeling that Everton would administer a knock-out blow to their rivals. Even the Anfield supporters had to admit that defeat would have its advantages, especially in leaving the Reds free to devote their energies to regaining their lost place in First Division company. That there was no abatement of the previous Saturday's enthusiasm was shown by the great crowd which early on streamed towards Everton's ground long before kick-off. "Cabby" did rare business, and "growlers" and hansoms rolled up in endless streams. At the start there were at least 25,000 present. There was only one change from Saturday's programme, Carlin displacing Robinson, who had been seriously injured at Leicester, the fear being that internal problems would ensue. The weather was almost spring-like and was just sufficiently exhilarating for a game of football.

Taylor won the toss and Goddard and Carlin were the first to advance, and a centre looked dangerous, when Abbott cleared. The Everton right got away and Sharp brought Young into the game, who smartly returned to the cricketer and, aided by McDermott, the two worked their way in until Doig was left uncovered and McDermott placed the leather in the net after only three minutes.

Both sides attacked in turn and the game was played at a frantic pace. The Liverpool men had the edge and displayed what was colloquially known as "regular Cup-tie football", but their methods in front of goal lacked decision and, as a result, the Everton backs, young Balmer and Crelly were invariably allowed to clear. Liverpool dominated throughout the last twenty minutes of the first half, but they were unable to profit from their attacking strength.

Liverpool swarmed onto the attack again upon the resumption and Goddard, the former Glossop player, took a pass from Dunlop and netted the ball from long range. The spectators were treated to an exhibition of great skill as both sides strove for the lead. Raisbeck rushed through and sent the ball high into the crowd before sending the leather spinning over the cross-bar moments later. At this stage of the game, Everton are penned in their own half, and the Anfield supporters cheered frantically as shot after shot rained in on the Everton goal. The Liverpool forwards dallied far too long on the ball and numerous openings were spoiled. In one of the attacks, Cox was hurt, but the Blackpool flyer soon recovered under the trainer's attention. After this, both sides had spells of attacking play, but without result. Sharp almost got through, but was hampered at the vital moment. Then Roose ran out of his charge and saved splendidly from Parkinson. The pace of the game never slackened, and extra time appeared inevitable when Sharp broke away and passed across to Hardman. The little Blackpool amateur took the pass with great dexterity, and, running in, he netted the leather out of the reach of Doig.

The Liverpool men were undeniably the stronger side. Both backs were sound, and though West occasionally took a risk, he played a good game. The half-back line was exceptional. Raisbeck was out and out the best player on the field. The forward line was persistent and determined, but weak when in front of goal. Parkinson was the best of the quintet. He did not possess the high science of the game, but he had a great deal of enthusiasm and an indomitable spirit. The principal figure in the Everton ranks was Roose, who never played a better game. The Welsh international had often been charged with rashness in running out from "between the sticks". He never did so to better purpose than against Liverpool in this game. On two occasions he literally sprang forward and picked the ball off Parkinson's toes, and saved a certain goal. Crelly was the cleverer of the full-backs, although young Balmer further enhanced his growing reputation as a cool and confident tackler. The half-backs did not perform as brilliantly as Liverpool's, but Taylor was almost as good as Raisbeck, and once more proved himself an extraordinary fine footballer. The forwards were clever and showy, but they lacked that element of sterner stuff in front of goal. There was no roughness in the game, and fouls were few.

In other replays, Wolverhampton Wanderers beat Sunderland 1-0 at Molineux before a crowd of 18,000, Smith scoring. At Bristol, Bolton Wanderers beat the Rovers 3-0 before 6,000 spectators. Pudan scored an own goal, and Stokes added a second before the interval, and a third in the second period. Bristol City beat Woolwich Arsenal 1-0 at Bristol before 7,000 spectators. Dean scored the only game of the game ten minutes into the second half. At Plymouth, Newcastle United scored through Orr, before McLuckie drew level for the home side. In the second half, before 20,000 excited spectators, the United played the better football, but the game went into extra-time, and no further scoring took place. Reading and Fulham also went into extra-time, and no goals were scored in front of 12,000 spectators in perfect weather.

Hardman, Harold Payne; born April 4, 1882, at Kirkmanshulme, Manchester; ht 5ft 6½; wt 10st 11lbs; amateur. Played for Blackpool 1900-03. Resides at Blackpool; a solicitor.

Everton: Roose; R.Balmer, Crelly; Makepeace, Taylor, Abbott; Sharp, McDermott, Young, Settle, Hardman.

Liverpool: Doig; West, Dunlop; Parry, Raisbeck, Fleming; Goddard, Carlin, Parkinson, Raybould, Cox.

Referee: Mr J. Lewis (Blackburn)

Attendance: 40,000

Receipts: £1,020

Sharp, J., born 1879 at Hereford; ht, 5ft 7ins; professional. Is the well-known Lancashire County cricketer who made his name in football with Aston Villa, joining them in 1897, after serving with Hereford Thistle, first appearing in the reserve. Transferred to Everton in 1889. Assisted England against Ireland in 1903, and against Scotland in 1905. Considered one of best forwards in his position in the kingdom. Dashing forward with a true centre.

Settle, J., (inside-left); ht 5ft 6ins; Secured international honours five years ago and has since been the envy of football managers, but Everton's substantial offer has been enough to keep him in Liverpool. Born in 1876 at Millom. From Bolton Reserves he went to Halliwell Rovers in 1895, and attracted so much attention that Bury secured his transfer in 1897. Dribbles well, and shoots with deadly aim. Joined Everton in 1900. Represented England against Scotland 1899, 1902; against Wales 1899; and against Ireland 1899-1903.

Jack Parkinson, who was denied by the Everton goalkeeper on several occasions

January 13, 1906

Liverpool (1) 2
Raybould 7, Goddard 48

Leicester Fosse (0) 1
Moody 46

ROBINSON was unable to turn out, being injured, and Raybould was not completely fit to play. Carlin, who was a very dashing player at his best, was brought into the front line. Liverpool wore brand new jerseys. The weather was fine, and the pitch in excellent condition. The well-built Fosse side had been extremely successful of late and were on the top of their form in the Second Division. When the teams appeared the crowd was not above one thousand.

Moody led off for the Fossils, and Parry was the first to be troubled. Bradley then conceded a corner, which was placed behind. The Leicester halves then served up to their forwards in a very clever manner, and Moody put out to Blessington, who was brought low by Dunlop when within a few yards of the Liverpool lines. Parry gave away a corner, and a moment later Leicester forced another corner. Both were safely negotiated by Hardy. A misunderstanding by Parry let in Hodgkinson, and he put in a marvellous effort which finished a few inches wide of the posts.

The Reds then attacked, and Bradley gained a corner. Goddard took Bradley's corner kick, and Smith made a poor effort to repel the ball. A scramble followed in which Cox and Raybould were prominent, and the inside-left ultimately netted with his head, the point being allowed despite loud protestations from the visitors. It was a fortunate goal.

Upon re-starting, the game was confined to midfield for a lengthy period, until Bradley made an effort to feed his left, but Ashby proved too smart for Raybould. Then Smith rushed out to clear an accurate centre from Cox. From a long kick by the visitors, West was deceived by the spin on the ball, and Dunlop came to his colleague's assistance. Dunlop kicked the ball against Moody, and the leather rebounded in the direction of the Reds' goal. Dunlop, in his desire to keep Moody from the ball, was penalised for elbowing and a penalty was awarded to the Fossils. Bannister was entrusted with the kick, and the Leicester man shot hard enough, but missed the goal completely as the ball flew wide to the left when the kicker slipped and fell.

Roused by their fortune, Liverpool invaded the Leicester half, and Goddard tested Smith with a fierce shot. Cox carried the ball right across to the opposite wing, and winded up his movement by kicking the ball on to Bannister, and lost it. Goddard chipped the ball in quickly, but Morgan cleared. Shortly afterwards Raisbeck went on a solo run in an effort to beat Smith, and Carlin just failed to net the ball. West then took a free-kick and Cox sent a beautiful drive across the face of the goal.

The Fosse left then slipped away, but Raisbeck cleverly intercepted Hodgkinson's pass intended for Hubbard. Then a sensational incident followed. A fine centre by Cox was handled by Oakes within the penalty area and Mr Dennis had no hesitation in awarding the spot-kick. West took the kick, but shot straight at Smith, who saved admirably. Parry tired a long-range effort which Smith easily dealt with, before a miskick by Oakes caused trouble for the Fossils' defence. Cox failed to reach the leather before it went over the line. A magnificent flowing movement ended with Bradshaw putting in a long drive, which Smith did well to save. West saved from Hodgkinson, and then Parry, Raisbeck, Carlin, Hewitt, and Cox were concerned in a clever forward movement, which brought no tangible result. Another fine effort by Raisbeck, Raybould, Carlin and Goddard was brought to an end by Oakes. The Fosse attacked down the right and through the middle but Dunlop forced his opponents to carry the ball over the line. Parry then initiated an attack in which Hewitt and Goddard distinguished themselves, but the Fosse defence was solid, and Raybould was clearly offside.

Parry gained ground and a free-kick, but Goddard put the ball high over the bar. Carlin forced another corner, but though Dunlop, Raisbeck, and Raybould all made great efforts, they could not force the ball home. Goddard was at the top of his form, initiating several of Liverpool's most dangerous attacks. After an abortive effort to score by Parry, Smith conceded a corner to Hewitt by tipping the ball over the bar. The visiting defence was not artistic, but it was stubborn.

When the teams re-appeared the attendance had reached 12,000. Hewitt commenced for the Reds, and the first to break was the Fosse left wing, Hodgkinson being pulled up for offside. Moody attempted a long-range drive, and although Hardy flung himself at the leather, the ball entered the corner of the net. Immediately on re-starting, the Livers swept down the field in brilliant combination, and a great chance opened up for Goddard, who scored. Liverpool attacked relentlessly, and a second penalty was awarded to the home side. West took the kick, but he shot straight at Smith and the Fosse custodian saved his side. In their anxiety to score, both sides committed errors. Parry, with some intricate footwork, carried play into the Leicester half, and after outwitting several opponents he sent the leather in the direction of Cox, who was beaten for possession by Morgan. Both sets of defenders were forced to kick into touch when threatened with danger. Durrant went straight for goal, and succeeded in passing Dunlop, but West raced across and brilliantly dispossessed the Leicester man before serving up for his forwards. The Fossils attacked bravely in the final five minutes, and twice tested Hardy.

Liverpool looked like a team entirely new to each other's play, and though Hardy was seldom tested, it was due more to the ineptitude of the Fosse forwards than to the superior excellence of their opponents. In the front rank Liverpool were seen at their worst, and the left wing was virtually useless. When the second half had been in progress some little time, Raybould dropped back to the intermediate line, and Cox roamed all over the field, without being effective. The half-backs got through a tremendous amount of work, but they were not supported by their forwards, and much of their excellence was nullified by the ineptitude of the forwards. West and Dunlop performed well at full back.

West played at his peak, and his tackling was of the highest order. Hardy had little to do.

The Fosse worked hard, but their line was easily held in check. Morgan and Pollock did well at half-back, though they were more efficient in defence than initiating attacks on the home goal. Ashby kicked sturdily, and Smith gave a creditable display in goal, for he saved two penalty kicks, and proved equal to the Liverpool forwards.

Liverpool: Hardy; West, Dunlop; Parry, Raisbeck, Bradley; Goddard, Carlin, Hewitt, Raybould, Cox.

Leicester Fosse: Smith; Ashby, Oakes; Morgan, Bannister, Pollock; Durrant, Blessington, Moody, Hubbard, Hodgkinson.

Referee: Mr F.H. Dennis (Middlesbrough)

Linesmen: Mr B. Creswick (Sheffield);
Mr H. Pollitt (Manchester)

Attendance: 12,000

Arthur Goddard,
who scored the
second-half winner
against Leicester
Fosse

February 3, 1906

Liverpool (1) 1
West 20

Barnsley (0) 0

LIVERPOOL were at full strength, with Cox and Raybould again constituting the left wing, while Barnsley were also at full strength. The Anfielders were drawn away, but the tie was switched to Merseyside by arrangement with the Yorkshire club. Liverpool won the toss, and the Reds had the great advantage of a strong wind blowing diagonally towards the Oakfield Road goal. Taking full advantage of the breeze, the Reds attacked strongly, and a mêlée ensued in front of the Barnsley goal in which Robinson was badly hurt about the face when he collided with Thorpe after heading against the post. He was carried off the field, and Liverpool continued with only ten men.

In spite of their disadvantage, Liverpool dominated the play with only the occasional foray by Barnsley. The home side gained corner after corner and eventually Raisbeck struck the crossbar with a great shot. From the rebound, West, a former Barnsley player, beat the goalkeeper with a long drive which flew into goal.

Alfred West

Barnsley responded with a breakaway by Wilkinson, who missed with a fine effort, and then Hellewell created a magnificent chance but Beech wasted the opportunity.

Soon afterwards, Robinson returned, going to the outside-right position, and Liverpool looked dangerous again. Cox moved into the penalty area and shot, but a Barnsley defender knocked the ball down with his hand, though the referee refused the loud Liverpool appeals.

Wall went on a fine solo run and sent in a great centre, but Owen missed the cross and Hardy cleared. Towards the interval, Liverpool gained six corners in quick succession, but failed to utilise them to good effect.

Barnsley had the breeze in their favour after the change of ends, but the early stages of the second half were all in favour of the home side, although the defence of Hay and Stacey was excellent. The Anfielders' attack contained all the trickery and artistic touches of which the home side were masters, and shot after shot was sent in fast and furiously, and from every angle, but Thorpe and the strong wind denied Liverpool further goals.

The Barnsley defence gained praise from the spectators, but the visiting forwards lacked quality. The wingmen played well, however, running strongly and passing accurately, and frequently beating Parry and Bradley; but the attack invariably petered out in this area of the pitch as Raisbeck dropped back, and the visitors looked puny beside the Scottish international and his backs.

One of the Liverpool players punted the ball into the bedroom of one of the houses at the back of the small stand. Wall was always a source of danger when in possession, but his centres were not utilised. The home forwards were completely ineffective in front of goal and they deteriorated as the game wore on. Hewitt played feebly, but Raybould was even less effective, and the left wing pair failed to do themselves credit. Robinson was unfortunate to get an injury so early in the game, and it was only Goddard who played to his full potential, as he had done for several weeks. Raisbeck worked hard, and rarely allowed the visiting forwards any room, while Parry also played well. Bradley was less prominent, but West and Dunlop performed capably, and their powerful return kicks were the chief feature of their defensive work.

Hellewell in the centre and Wall on the left wing gave good exhibitions. The left-winger possessed a fine turn of speed, and believed in making for goal directly. Wilkinson was the pick of the half-backs, though Donagher was often in evidence.

Liverpool: Hardy; West, Dunlop; Parry, Raisbeck, Bradley; Goddard, Robinson, Hewitt, Raybould, Cox.

Barnsley: Thorpe; Hay, Stacey; Donagher, Wilkinson, Oxspring; Birtles, Owen, Hellewell, Beech, Wall.

Referee: Mr A.G. Hines (Nottingham)

Linesmen: Mr W. Rollins (Walsall);
Mr A.W. Dunton (Wolverhampton)

Attendance: 10,000   **Receipts**: £305

February 24, 1906

Liverpool (1) 2
Hewitt 35, Goddard 65

Brentford (0) 0

THE Southern League side from London were experiencing a successful season, but they faced Liverpool at the top of the First Division. Since September 9, the leaders had not lost a match at Anfield, and with a goal average of 35-8. The visitors had acclimatised at Southport during the week, while Liverpool went to Blackpool. There was a great deal of fog hanging around at the start of the game, that it was felt that the game might not be completed.

Liverpool were without the services of skipper Raisbeck, who was absent with a thigh strain, and Latham was brought into the side. Bradley was able to play. Shanks had recovered in the week's training at Southport, and the Bees were therefore at full strength. Several hundred supporters travelled from the Middlesex town to see the game.

Liverpool: Hardy; West, Dunlop; Parry, Latham, Bradley; Goddard, Robinson, Hewitt, Raybould, Cox.

Brentford: Whittaker; Watson, Riley; Jay, Parsonage, Robotham; Hartley, Shanks, Corbett, Hobson, Underwood.

Referee: Mr F.H. Dennis (Middlesbrough)

Linesmen: Mr J.A. MacGregor (Morecambe)
Mr G.W. Walker (Luton)

Attendance: 15,000

Receipts: £422

In dull weather and poor light, Hewitt started the match against a slight breeze. Goddard forced Whittaker to save in the opening minutes, and Liverpool dominated the early exchanges. The visiting backs, especially Riley, kicked well, and Brentford soon settled down. Watson's trick of slipping forward and placing the Liverpool attack offside was not appreciated by the crowd. West was none too safe at this stage of the game, allowing the opposing left to make progress, but he was well covered. After thirty-five minutes, Cox sent over a magnificent flag-kick, and Hewitt headed into the net. The ball was kicked out, but it had crossed the line, and the referee had no hesitation in awarding a goal.

Brentford began the second half in determined mood, and with more guile in front of goal, they might have equalised, though the Liverpool defence was solid. Feeling crept into the game, and fouls became frequent. Mr Dennis spoke to Jay, the visiting right-half. Hardy saved several shots in fine fashion, but after 65 minutes, Robinson tipped the ball from the goal-line to Goddard, who was waiting for it, and the winger

steered it past Whittaker. Brentford were reduced to solitary raids in the second period, and Liverpool toyed with their opponents, penning them into their own half. The Reds gained numerous corners, and just before the final whistle, Robinson netted from a Cox pass, but the referee ruled offside.

Brentford were a heavy, bustling team, and they fought hard to win. Liverpool played the ball with skill, while Brentford played the man, seeking to make up for their inferior skill with foul play. Finding themselves outclassed, they kicked into touch and back to the goalkeeper on many occasions.

Walter Whittaker, the goalkeeper, kept out many shots which looked likely to score. Watson, a robustly built man, did not stand on ceremony, and he kicked out too much. He also relied too heavily on the one-back game, and he kicked ball back to Whittaker at times when he should have driven the ball forward. Jay and Parsonage (formerly with Accrington Stanley), were the best of the half-backs, and were not afraid to use their weight. The forwards were workers rather than artists. Underwood was the fastest man on the field. He was not merely an athlete, having a command of the ball and sending in crosses in the manner of Cox.

Hardy played well, and was sure to improve. Dunlop was the safer of the two backs, and he kicked splendidly. Bradley was the best of the half-backs, and assisted Cox and Raybould admirably. Parry was in a fitful mood. He sent in some fine shots, tackled effectively against the best forwards of the opposition, and yet on other occasions he appeared to be indifferent whether he got the ball or not. Latham did well as Raisbeck's substitute.

Joe Hewitt

March 10, 1906

Liverpool (2) 3
Raybould 20, 30, 84

Southampton (0) 0

THE two elevens took to the field at the peak of fitness. The Reds had spent the last three weeks at Blackpool, while the Saints prepared at home, although since the previous Thursday, they had stayed at a hydro at West Kirby. Both teams were at full strength. Raisbeck lost the toss, and Hewitt set the ball rolling against the slightest of breezes.

Liverpool attacked strongly in the opening minutes, but then Raisbeck misdirected a headed clearance and Mouncher went off at full speed, and Parry was forced to drop on his knee and with his long leg propel the ball over the line for a corner-kick, which was headed out by Robinson. The Saints began well and some of their long crosses from left to right and back again caused Liverpool several problems in front of goal.

Tomlinson narrowly missed with a ferocious angled drive and then Bradley, instead of feeding his wing, dribbled through on his own initiative and wound up with a swift drive into goal, which Clawley saved.

With 20 minutes gone, Goddard flew down the wing, beat Hartshorne, and sent in a perfect centre which Robinson flicked on to Raybould. The inside man tapped it into the net with ease. Roars of cheering greeted this success, and the Saints protested that the point was offside, but the referee denied their claims.

Cox became more prominent and he sent across to Goddard who tumbled over, got up again, recovered the ball and put Raybould in possession, but he shot high over the bar. The Saints rallied, and from a pass by Lee, Brown ran on to the moving ball and drove in a surprise shot which Hardy saved.

Then Hewitt moved to the right wing and sent in a fine cross but Clarke tried to head the ball when he should have kicked it clear, and Raybould, with speed of thought and swiftness of foot, outmanoeuvred the back completely, and he scored the second goal after half-an-hour's play.

The Saints persevered and a miskick by West and an error by Bradley gave chances which Hedley and Harrison failed to capitalise upon. Lee was the Saints' most dangerous marksman, and he skimmed the crossbar.

At the other end Clawley had to clear a centre from Goddard and field a ball off the head of Hewitt, while Raybould once tricked both Lee and Clarke, and looked like scoring but Clawley turned the ball round the post.

Liverpool did not maintain their superiority in the second half. They practised long dribbles, and displayed too much finesse for a Cup-tie. Mouncher shot over the bar from long range, while centres from both wings gave Liverpool numerous problems. The home defence packed their goal, and danger was averted. Robinson dropped back among the halves, and Liverpool used only four forwards. The game deteriorated, and there were numerous fouls. Cox sent in several fine centres, although the winger indulged himself in playing to the gallery. In a further Liverpool attack, Raybould netted from a Goddard centre, but the point was nullified for offside. Six minutes from time, Goddard forced a corner-kick, and from this Raybould headed the third goal.

The Saints pressed strongly towards the close, but were repelled, and Raybould was chaired by some enthusiastic spectators, and carried shoulder high to the dressing room in recognition of his splendid feat in scoring three goals.

Liverpool: Hardy; West, Dunlop; Parry, Raisbeck, Bradley; Goddard, Robinson, Hewitt, Raybould, Cox.

Southampton: Clawley; Clarke, Hartshorne; Hogg, Lee, Houlker; Tomlinson, Harrison, Hedley, Brown, Mouncher.

Referee: Mr A.J. Barker (Hanley)

Linesmen: Mr J.T. Lingham (Northfleet); Mr A. Shawcross (Leek)

Attendance: 20,000

Receipts: £685

Liverpool deserved victory because they were a well-balanced team and strong in all departments, while the Saints, although clever forward, were weak in defence.

The feature of the match as far as Liverpool were concerned was the improvement in the front line over the display against Manchester City on the previous Saturday when City won 1-0 at Anfield. Raybould was the star of the forward line. He was alert and threatening and penetrative in front of goal. Goddard was also in fine form, though he sometimes delayed his crosses. Hewitt did not shoot as well as he can, but he distributed the ball with judgment and opened out the game in rare style. The whole front line was cohesive and polished. However, Cox was guilty of long dribbles without any specific purpose. At half-back, Raisbeck stood head and shoulders above everybody as a despoiler. The famous Scot was much faster on his feet than he appeared to be.

Bradley had not maintained his autumn form, and Parry was only moderate. He strained his left thigh and was not happy on the soft, treacherous turf. In the second half Robinson worked prodigiously on the left wing in assisting Bradley. Hardy was well protected and had little to do. West, in his calm manner, and Dunlop, with his dashing lunges, were a splendid pair of backs insofar as keeping the ball away, though they did not display much discrimination expected from players of their stature.

Southampton were an uneven team. The forwards on occasions showed glimpses of the form which beat Middlesbrough 6-1 in the previous round, but they were not clever enough to combat the guile of the home halves, while the backs were unreliable.

Division One
(Top six)
as at March 10, 1906

	Pl	W	L	D	F	A	Pts
Liverpool	**28**	**17**	**8**	**3**	**58**	**35**	**37**
Preston North End	28	12	5	11	41	29	35
Manchester City	27	15	8	4	53	31	34
Aston Villa	30	14	11	5	56	43	33
Sheffield Wednesday	28	13	8	7	44	34	33
Bolton Wanderers	28	13	9	6	66	45	32

Southern League
(Top six)
as at March 10, 1906

	Pl	W	L	D	F	A	Pts
Fulham	27	14	3	10	36	14	38
Tottenham Hotspur	24	13	6	5	34	17	31
Luton	26	13	8	5	50	32	31
Southampton	**24**	**13**	**6**	**5**	**40**	**30**	**31**
Portsmouth	26	12	8	6	43	27	30
Bristol Rovers	25	12	9	4	48	37	28

Alfred West, born December 15, 1882 at Nottingham; married; height 5ft 8in; weight 11st. 9lb; professional. Previously assisted Ilkeston and Barnsley; captained Rest of Midland League against Barnsley in 1901-2; scored the only goal for Liverpool in the English Cup tie against Barnsley. Resides in Nottingham.

Hardy, Samuel, born Dec. 1883 at Newbold, nr. Chesterfield; professional. Commenced his football career as a centre-forward at school. When 16 joined Newbold White Star as custodian. Two years later Chesterfield engaged him, but he never had the opportunity of figuring in an important match till he appeared against Woolwich on April 10, 1903. In 1903-4 he kept his place between the posts by sheer merit, and he gave such a display against Liverpool when they were in the Second Division that in May 1905 the Anfielders secured his services, and he superseded Doig, his club winning the League Championship and reaching the semi-final stage of the English Cup. Keen in anticipation, quick across goal, sure in his fielding and punting, and daring in desperate situations, he is acknowledged as one of finest custodians of the day.

Raisbeck, A.G., born at Larkhall; professional. Playing centre half-back for Liverpool, previous to which played for a club called Royal Albert. Has captained Liverpool for several seasons. Is particularly good at heading and placing to his forwards. Played for Scotland against England in 1900, 1902, and 1903; and against Wales in 1903.

Bradley, James Edwin, a fine consistent player. Possessing a fine turn of speed, he tackles with excellent judgment and places the ball to his forwards to an inch. Born at Goldenhill in 1881, he learnt his football in the village team, Goldenhill Wanderers. Whilst in his teens he was given a trial by Stoke, and he played for them on 195 occasions, scoring 4 goals, before joining Liverpool early in the 1905-06 season.

Robinson, Robert S., known as "Whitey". Born 1880. A native of Sunderland, played football as a boy at the Thomas Street Board School, before joining Sunderland 'A', and later South Hylton. Next went to Sunderland Royal Reserves, before joining Sunderland. Joined Liverpool before the start of the 1904-05 season.

Hewitt, Joe, very clever indeed both in combination and trickiness. Shoots well, and scored the highest number of goals for Sunderland in 1902-03, before his transfer to Liverpool.

Cox, John, born November 21, 1878 at Liverpool; single, professional. Made début for Blackpool in October 1897, and remained with the club until February 1898, when transferred to Liverpool, which club he has served with distinction ever since, occasionally having had the honour to captain the side. Both an inter-leaguer and international; played inter-league for England against Ireland 1900-1, and against Scotland 1902 and 1904; represented internationally England against Ireland 1900-1, and against Scotland 1902 and 1903; also assisted North against South 1900-1. A good runner and has won a number of prizes in sprint handicaps. Resides in Blackpool.

March 31, 1906

Everton (0) 2
Abbott 65, Hardman 66

Liverpool (0) 0

THE gates were opened at one o'clock and there were thousands waiting to gain admission. For three hours the iron frames of the turnstiles switched round and round, and the checkers were kept extremely busy. Among the notable spectators were Messrs. McGregor, Wall, Radford, Hart, Charnley, Rinder, and directors of both clubs, though Mr Edwin Berry, chairman of Liverpool FC, was unable to be present. The London and North-Western, and Great Western Railway Companies had made special arrangements and at half-past seven the first excursion train left Liverpool and from then onwards there was a continual exodus of trains on both railways bound for the Midland capital. Although several hundred supporters were disembarked at New Street and Snow Hill, several thousands were conveyed from Stafford, via Walsall and Perry Barr, to Witton. Some 15,000 Lancashire people were transported to London. In addition, there were excursion trains running from London and other places. Liverpool stayed overnight in Tamworth, while Everton, after a morning train journey from Merseyside, arrived in time for lunch at the Grand Hotel. The crowd was an enormous one, and Everton took to the field first.

Everton: Scott; Crelley, R.Balmer; Makepeace, Taylor, Abbott; Sharp, Bolton, Young, Settle, Hardman.

Liverpool: Hardy; West, Dunlop; Parry, Raisbeck, Bradley; Goddard, Robinson, Parkinson, Carlin, Hewitt.

Referee: Mr F.H. Dennis (Middlesbrough)

Linesmen: Mr E. Case (Birkenhead);
           Mr N. Whittaker (London)

Attendance: 37,000 (at Villa Park)

Receipts: £1,701

Cox was incapacitated, having been kicked on the leg at Preston, and Raybould had strained the muscles of his right thigh. Raybould was willing to don his jersey, but his team-mates feared that he would break down if he was touched on his injury. Hewitt replaced Cox, and was taken from centre-forward, where he had played since the second Saturday in September, and placed at outside-left, while Parkinson, who had not been in the centre since he broke his arm at Woolwich, resumed his old position, while Carlin was drafted into the side in place of Raybould.

Everton made three changes from the side which beat Sunderland 3-1 at Goodison in the previous week. Robert Balmer replaced his older brother Walter at right-back,

Makepeace replaced Tom Booth at right-half, and Harold Hardman replaced Joe Donnachie at outside-left.

During the season the Everton players had suffered greatly from injuries, and their comparatively humble position in the League was due to this fact. They were at full strength for the Cup-tie, however. Mr Cuff, the Secretary said before the match, "No team out of Liverpool can beat 'em."

After a season's play, the turf was firm and comparatively rich with grass, while there was an absence of breeze and a clouded sky. Parkinson kicked off and Liverpool settled early on, and Hewitt sent in three excellent centres, which reminded observers that he had played on the wing against Sunderland. Eventually Everton began to assert themselves, and Sharp ran on to a loose ball before moving in on goal. Parry was forced to go across to assist Dunlop in breaking down the move. Soon afterwards, Hardy was forced to field a shot from Taylor. The blues played well, and Hardy was called upon on three more occasions to prevent a goal, before Makepeace ended the immense Everton pressure by shooting wide of the posts. The Liverpool left-wing and centre were cheered for their excellent manoeuvring, but Abbott broke down their combination. Scott was almost deceived by a ball from Robinson, but it swerved over the bar. A fine centre from Hewitt forced Scott to save, before Bolton opened out the game, by putting Young in possession. The centre-forward was crowded out, and passed to Abbott whose powerful drive was erratic.

Liverpool were inspired by their captain, Raisbeck, but when Goddard and then Hewitt beat the backs, the exciting combination broke down when the ball seemed to be centred merely to be passed back to the wing again. Everton responded, and West was forced to concede the first corner of the match to prevent Young from lowering Hardy's colours. Bradley headed out from the flag-kick. Taylor then sent in a powerful drive which Hardy got both hands to.

Following a throw-in, Parkinson put Goddard in possession. The right-winger tricked Abbott and transferred the ball to the centre. Carlin looked likely to score when Scott rushed out and gathered safely. Everton retaliated, and Hardman forced Raisbeck to concede another corner. Young went close with a header from the corner-kick. The interval arrived with no score on either side.

Everton were quicker to the ball when the second half got underway. Bolton got right through to the penalty area, and, being hampered, he could only lift the ball a few yards, and Hardy cleared with ease. Liverpool then took up the running, and after Crelley had cleared, Carlin had a clear opening and Makepeace sprang into action to clear the danger. Crelley was then temporarily knocked out. Robinson sent in a stinging shot before Everton scored the first goal. Sharp ran after the ball, which was in the proximity of the corner flag. Bradley apparently thought the ball would not cross the line, though it would have done so if he had kept the right-winger off, and so he kept it in play, dribbled past Sharp, and in endeavouring to drive ahead, sent the ball over the side line. Makepeace threw the ball in, and it was swung over by Sharp to Abbott, whose powerful shot flew towards goal. Dunlop was on the goal-line, to the left of Hardy. He attempted to lift it out, but saw the ball curl over the top of his right boot. The goal was credited to Abbott, however.

Within a minute, Sharp, who had not been prominent, was the initiator of a second goal. He accurately sent the ball over, and Hardman, who was drawn in almost to centre-forward, deftly placed the ball in the net, the ball striking the foot of a post and glancing in.

Liverpool became too excited, when they should have been more methodical. From a centre by Goddard, Parkinson had a great chance, but Balmer conceded a corner, and from this Scott made two splendid saves, the first at the expense of another corner, and the second from a tight scrimmage right on the goal-line, where there was a little heated argument, Parry being apparently the cause of the discussion. Everton rallied again, and Bradley was on hand to prevent Hardman from scoring.

EXPERT OPINION
by
WILLIAM McGREGOR
(Founder of the Football League)

The match may safely be described as a fine game. Everton won because they took their opportunities. The best football was witnessed in the first half, in which, however, there were some miskicks on both sides. Liverpool were upset in the second half by the goal which Dunlop unfortunately put through his own goal. This upset his comrades, and they never seemed afterwards to pull themselves together. This was particularly marked in goal. They never seemed to get the better of Everton, while their opponents played a very much improved game. The victory was well deserved and popular. Perhaps the feature of the game, so far as individual play was concerned, was the wonderful form of Raisbeck, who was worth any two men on the field. Dunlop was the better of the backs on the defeated side, his long kicking being another feature of the game. Parry was a powerful half-back, but was not discreet in his methods. I thought Robinson was the best of the forwards, while Parkinson was not quick enough, the opposing backs frequently getting free-kicks. Scott performed splendidly in goal, although some of his saves were risky. The backs played superb football, especially in the second half of the game. The half-backs improved immensely in the second half, and Makepeace was the best of the bunch. Taylor was very useful, and Abbott, one was pleased to notice, had not lost his propensities for pot-shooting.

LIVERPOOL
Player by Player

Hardy: Did his best. Some of his thumps were worthy of Foulke, and no blame could be attached to him for either of the goals.

West: A fine exhibition; perhaps not quite so noticeable on account of his partner's excessive ability.

Dunlop: Best back on the field; and yet one lapse by him and the game was settled. It was his only error, but the price of it was enormous. His volleying was wonderful, and when the ball was in his vicinity he made certain of its appearance in the Everton quarters. The best of backs, and the best of all Scots' defenders.

Parry: Was responsible for the little ill-feeling which crept into the match, being too fond of shady tricks.

Raisbeck: Alexander the Great! The best footballer on the field. McGregor said he was worthy of any two men. He holds the key to the cupboard in which the League championship trophy is stored.

Bradley: A trifle weak at opening and afterwards prominent by reason of getting the better of the famous blue right wing.

Goddard: Should have scored the first goal. Scott was out of his goal, and he hooked the ball in altogether too near the Irishman, who caught the ball. A little to the left and a goal would have resulted. He gave his co-forwards the benefit of some very fine centres, and one which was made while on the run will never be forgotten by those who witnessed it.

Robinson: Missed an open goal, too. In his attempt to make certain that Scott should not reach the leather, he diverted the ball at too great an angle. The miss, and his inability to make any headway, were disappointing.

Parkinson: Did his best under the circumstances. He was short of pace, but his intentions and enthusiasm were good; but it was unrealistic to expect him to step onto the field after months of absence and expect him to play as of old.

Carlin: The most noticeable point in his play was the speed at which he bore down on goal, though he finished weakly. He filled Raybould's position with great credit, and apart from his inability to shoot more accurately, he was, along with Goddard, Liverpool's best forward.

Hewitt: Did exceptionally well playing out of position as the deputy for Cox, particularly in the first half. He would have been more valuable in the centre.

Late selection

Liverpool did not name their team until an hour before the kick-off, and the directors actually changed the line-up three times before deciding on the final eleven. Cox and Raybould had spent the week at their homes at Birmingham. The endeavour to strengthen the outside-left position led to two weakening forces - centre and outside-left.

EVERTON	Weight		Height			LIVERPOOL	Weight		Height	
	st.	lbs.	ft.	ins.			st.	lbs.	ft.	ins.
W. Scott	11	4	5	11		S. Hardy	12	0	5	9½
J. Crelley	12	0	5	9½		W. Dunlop	12	0	5	9½
R. Balmer	10	2	5	7		A. West	11	9	5	7
H. Makepeace	10	7	5	7		M. Parry	13	0	5	11
J. Taylor	10	12	5	9		A. Raisbeck	13	0	5	10
W. Abbott	12	2	5	9½		J. Bradley	11	10	5	9½
J. Sharp	11	13	5	7		A. Goddard	11	8	5	9½
H. Bolton	10	7	5	6½		R.S. Robinson	12	5	5	9
A. Young	11	2	5	8½		J. Parkinson	12	0	5	9
J. Settle	11	3	5	6½		J. Carlin	10	11	5	7½
H.P. Hardman	10	2	5	6		J. Hewitt	11	8	5	9

THE ATHLETIC NEWS

THE WEAK POINT OF LIVERPOOL
by Tityrus

Liverpool failed because they were not equal in all departments, for they were feeble forward, and Robinson, Parkinson, and Carlin were not in a deadly mood by any means. They frittered their away opportunities, and their supporters must have sighed for Hewitt in his accustomed place and for Raybould by his side. When we remember the part that Raybould played against Southampton, and the three goals that he took, we can understand his loss.

On the wing, Hewitt was a decided success, but if Tom Chorlton had been there and the Chester youth had been in the centre, I am obstinate enough to think that we should not have seen so many chances go begging. That is merely my idea.

Goddard was in form, but it is depressing to wing men when all the world seems at sixes and sevens and the ball appears to be ravelled in their opponents' legs.

The Liverpool half-backs were a fine body, and I should unhesitatingly say that Raisbeck was the most commanding figure on the field. What a game he played!

Here, there, everywhere, Raisbeck was always on the ball. Great in defence, I thought that he helped his forwards far more than on many occasions, and some of his touches were masterpieces.

There is, after all, only one Raisbeck, but even such a man cannot make a team.

Maurice Parry was a potent factor, Bradley being the weakest man in the line.

THE DASHING DUNLOP

If the Scottish selectors wanted to see Dunlop in his most dashing and impetuous vein they were gratified.

I doubt if Dunlop always knows where he is putting the ball, as a class back should, but he is a most valiant defender, and was well seconded by West, who is, by comparison, as pacific as a Quaker.

I have only pleasant thoughts of Hardy, who had nothing to reproach himself for.

Monday, April 2, 1906

The Football Who's Who 1905-06

Taylor, J.D., (inside-right), has had an extended stay at Everton, to which he came in 1895 from St. Mirren, where he had only been part of a season. He played originally for Dumbarton, the team connected with the town of his birth. Sound, strong all-round man who has some good work in him yet. Aged 31.

Young, A., Everton (centre-forward). A tenacious player, with an excellent conception of the duties of a centre.

HINTS TO REFEREES
by
W. Pickford

A Belfast correspondent "Arcadian", has suggested that a player who deliberately fouled an opponent inside the penalty area should be ordered off for, say, ten minutes, for a first offence (in addition to the penalty kick), and on a repetition be sent off permanently and reported. He says that it is not an uncommon thing in Ireland, when a man gets through, for an opponent to trip him up, preferring a penalty kick to a certain goal, and he adds, to my regret, that an official of a senior club in Belfast has been praising a man for doing such a dirty action.

January 12, 1907

Liverpool (1) 2
Raybould 15, 67

Birmingham (0) 1
Green (pen)

BEFORE this Cup-tie, Liverpool failed to score in their previous five League matches, of which they lost four. Their opponents, Birmingham, had found the net only once in their previous five League outings, so it was thought that goals would be scarce at Anfield. Parkinson occupied the centre-forward position whilst Hewitt was an absentee, due to the serious indisposition of his wife. The Birmingham eleven was practically the same in composition as that which defeated the Anfielders at Coventry Road by 2-1 on September 22, 1906. Though fine, the weather was gloomy, with a slight suggestion of haze. The spectators rolled up in good numbers, and there were 12,000 people present when the teams appeared.

The Birmingham skipper was fortunate enough to win the toss, and Parkinson set the ball in motion against a stiffish breeze towards the Oakfield Road goal. The opening exchanges showed the determination of both teams, and this was exemplified when Raisbeck, from long range, put in a swift ground shot which passed outside the goal. The Anfielders went about their work with great enthusiasm, and Bradley put the ball out to Cox, whose fine centre was met by Parkinson, who headed the ball into the goalmouth, where it was rather fortunately cleared.

Smart play from Beer and Glover put the visiting right wing in possession, but it failed to pass Dunlop, and further clever work by the Anfield half-backs put the home forwards again in possession. Raybould threaded his way through and looked very like drawing first blood when he was knocked off the ball by Stokes. Moments later Stokes intercepted a pass from Goddard as Liverpool attacked with inspiring dash and vigour. The Birmingham right wing, in response, excellently served by Beer, forced matters so that Dunlop was called upon. The incursion produced no profitable result as the ball rolled harmlessly outside from Harper's final efforts. Another forward rush by the Birmingham vanguard was only cleared by the Liverpool forwards falling back, and McPherson cleared with a fine punt upfield to Cox, whose fine centre was put outside.

The game now opened out and Goddard put in a glorious centre which Parkinson narrowly headed away from the target. By a series of flowing passes, the visitors made ground for the first time in the game, and the Liverpool half-backs were all at sea as Jones sent in a terrific shot which Hardy dealt with in his grandest manner. Shortly afterwards the Anfielders again asserted themselves, on the right Goddard distinguished himself with a run along the touchline and an excellent centre, but Parkinson once more failed to guide the leather into the net. The home side were not to be denied, however, and Goddard was responsible for a corner being forced, from which Bradley put over the bar. At this stage of the game, Liverpool dominated, and after Robinson had cleverly saved from Raybould, Raisbeck put in a tremendous drive which deserved a goal.

Following this near miss, the bombardment of the Birmingham goal became more intense than ever, and magnificent footwork on the part of the home forwards kept the ball in the visitors' territory, and a beautiful bit of work led to McPherson striking the upright with a long range drive. The ball rebounded into play and came to the foot of Raybould, who scored from close range, while on the ground, after fifteen minutes.

Liverpool maintained their position of complete dominance, and the ball was passed down the centre to Parkinson, who cleverly passed out to Goddard. The right-winger got in a beautiful centre which travelled right across the Birmingham goalmouth, where Cox sent it just outside. A fine breakaway from the Brums followed, and Mountenay, beating Saul - making his Cup début - sent over to Harper, who immediately drove in a splendid shot which Hardy fielded in brilliant fashion. The game became more even in character, and the visitors enjoyed a considerable amount of pressure on the right, but though Dunlop was occasionally in difficulties, he was superbly assisted by Bradley. An advance by the Birmingham left looked promising for the visitors, but Anderson's shot was dealt with easily. Mutual exchanges followed, and both goals were visited in turn without defeat, though Liverpool were always the more dangerous when within range. Parkinson brought Robinson to his knees with a swift drive. Both Raisbeck and Raybould tried their luck, only to fail by inches. Towards the interval the pace slowed down considerably, and the easing up by the Anfielders led to the visitors becoming extremely dangerous. Jones, after one shot which narrowly missed its mark, sent in another excellent effort which Hardy met and threw clear. The Midlanders occupied home territory with persistence, but they were opposed by a trio of half-backs which repeatedly broke up all their efforts of combination. Birmingham kept pegging away, and Parkinson was a little more vigorous than necessary in breaking up a dangerous move. From the ensuing free-kick the Anfield defence had to cope with two stinging shots from Jones and Green. A few minutes before half-time, Cox raced away and forced a corner which was well placed by Bradley, only to be cleared by the visiting defence. A few seconds later Goddard forced another corner, and from this Bradley sent the ball just over the crossbar.

During the interval the attendance increased considerably and there were fully 20,000 people present when the game resumed. Parkinson led off, but Bradley, Raybould and Cox

Liverpool: Hardy; Saul, Dunlop; Robinson, Raisbeck, Bradley; Goddard, McPherson, Parkinson, Raybould, Cox.

Birmingham: Robinson; Glover, Stokes; Beer, Wigmore, Dougherty; Harper, Green, Jones, Mounteney, Anderson.

Referee: Mr J.T. Ibbotson (Derby)

Attendance: 20,000

Alex Raisbeck, a giant in defence for Liverpool

were concerned in a movement which resulted in Cox putting in a glorious shot which Robinson cleverly fielded. Unlike their opponents, Liverpool were quick to take advantage of the wind, with the result that the Midlanders were practically penned in their own half for a sustained period. Once Robinson tried his luck with a fine long drive which just passed outside, while a few seconds later McPherson - also making his Cup début - grazed the wrong side of the post.

When the Midlanders next attacked, Dunlop, with one of his well-timed punts, removed the danger. From midfield Goddard got in a centre which caused Robinson to handle, and a moment later another opening forced by the home right allowed Parkinson to finish with a shot along the ground which went narrowly outside the goal. The home pivot had plenty of time to steady himself, and he certainly threw away a golden chance of improving the score.

For at least fifteen minutes the Anfielders dominated, but a rare breakaway by Anderson and Mountenay was smartly accounted for by Saul. The home players were imbued with confidence and when Jones led his wings to the attack, Raisbeck - a giant in defence - helped the backs to stop their advance. However, the work of the Liverpool forwards became less effective than formerly, and the three inside men let several chances go astray. On one occasion Bradley tried to put on a second goal when waltzing round Wigmore, but his shot went just wide. During one of their infrequent breakaways, the Midlanders came close to scoring through the laxity of Saul, who failed to intercept a shot by Green, which struck an upright. This escape spurred the Anfielders to the sense of their responsibility, and they made a determined rush down the left which resulted in a fruitless corner. This served as an incentive for further effort and Parkinson and McPherson dribbled right between the Birmingham backs, the

Scotsman giving to Raybould who, without any hesitation, let fly with tremendous force, the ball passing into the net without giving Robinson a chance of saving.

This second reverse moved Birmingham to greater efforts and the forward line looked very dangerous when Dunlop charged Jones inside the penalty area. The referee awarded a penalty without any hesitation, and the kick was converted by Green.

The tension now increased as the visitors sought an equaliser while Liverpool attempted to keep their lines intact. Fouls became rather frequent as the pressure mounted. In the closing stages the Liverpool forwards attacked strenuously, and Cox was twice fouled near the penalty area. The free-kicks, however, brought no profitable result to the Reds. In the last minute Anderson sent right across the Liverpool goalmouth, but the Birmingham forwards did not move fast enough and the opportunity was lost.

The gate receipts were approximately £500. The sensation of the round was a 1-0 home defeat for Newcastle, twice semi-finalists in two years - by Crystal Palace. Some contemporary observers described it as the sensation of the whole FA Cup competition since its inauguration.

Everton beat Sheffield United 1-0 at Goodison, while the biggest win of the day was Burslem Port Vale's 7-1 home win over Irthlinborough Town. Vale led 4-0 at the interval. The largest crowd of the day was at Fulham, where the home side drew 0-0 with Stockport County.

Seven hundred and four players were engaged in the opening round. Four First Division teams had to retire from the competition at the first time of asking.

Thirteen games were drawn, and fifteen home teams won. Of the drawn games six were with the score of 1-1 and five were without a goal. There were four away victories.

February 2, 1907

Oldham Athletic (0) 0

Liverpool (0) 1
McPherson 65

THIS Cup-tie had established a firm grip on the Oldham people, and little else was talked about. Excited groups of enthusiasts could be seen discussing the event. It was the first occasion on which the Oldham people had had an opportunity of seeing a first-class organisation on their own ground, and enthusiasm was at a high level. Elaborate arrangements had been made at Boundary Park to deal with a great crowd, and all previous records were expected to be broken.

The overnight frost had rendered the pitch extremely hard, but there was little fear of the game being interfered with. The home team had trained at Blackpool, and arrived in the cotton town looking fit and well. The weather in Oldham on the morning of the match was delightfully fine, and as the time for hostilities drew near, the approaches to the ground presented an animated appearance. In the previous week, Liverpool Reserves beat Oldham Athletic 2-1 at Boundary Park in the Lancashire Combination series.

League form, however, was no guide to Cup contests, and Liverpool were aware that they could not take Oldham lightly, especially in view of the fact that the visitors had casualties within their ranks. Goddard returned to the ranks in place of McKenna the amateur, while Raisbeck had been a doubtful starter all week owing to an attack of lumbago. Otherwise the men were the same which beat Birmingham 2-0 in the League and drew 5-5 with Sunderland. Oldham made no change in their team, but many changes in the ground, the accommodation in which had been greatly increased.

In the first round Liverpool had beaten Birmingham 2-1, whilst Oldham beat Kidderminster 5-0. Raisbeck's problems increased, and he was left out of the team due to a heavy cold, and Saul was an absentee for the same reason. Gorman and Chorlton took their places, both players making their Cup débuts for Liverpool. Half an hour before the game commenced 10,000 people were present.

The weather was remarkably fine, but the surface of the ground was sticky, and plenty of sand was used. The ground was very uneven, and seemed likely to trouble the immaculate passing game of the "Livers". The teams appeared at 2.52, and the Oldhamites were accorded a hearty greeting. At the start, the crowd numbered close on 20,000.

The home skipper won the toss, and Parkinson led off for the Reds and they looked like making headway until Wilson effected a temporary check, but Goddard put across a fine ball and Cox drove towards goal, but missed the target. A free-kick awarded to Liverpool brought no tangible reward, while a moment later a similar kick enabled the home side to move into Liverpool territory, but Chorlton returned the leather. Liverpool made little headway due to the uneven surface of the pitch. The Oldham left wing forced their way

ahead, and Chorlton and Robinson, failing to steady themselves on the bumpy turf, allowed Brunton to provide Hancock with a pass. The inside-left defeated Hardy amidst tremendous excitement which died down instantly when the crowd realised that it was a false alarm. The "Stripes" continued to press in ominous fashion, and the Livers' defence was distinctly hard-pressed on Hardy's right, where Ramsay took the ball out.

Liverpool countered with a fine run by Goddard who parted to Raybould. Cox received the ball, but the Blackpool flyer shot badly. The Athletic resumed their aggressiveness, but the "Reds" were much cooler at this point and they managed to hold their vivacious opponents at bay. The Livers were prominent again when Cox forced a corner, but Raybould was a yard wide of the mark. Oldham continued to make loose ominous rushes, with little attempt at combination.

The Livers forced another corner from which Daw was forced to concede yet another, and Raybould made a creditable effort to head into the net. The visitors had the best of the matter but were unable to combine effectively on the difficult ground. "Robbie" put in a fine shot on his own, the leather striking the inside of the upright and coming into play again. Immediately following this, Oldham showed their best form by advancing in capital order, and breaking down the Livers' defence, forced a corner, the ball being headed away by Robinson. Parkinson failed to maintain an advantageous opening on the right, and Wilson was enabled to set the Oldham left going, and some pressure resulted in a fine long shot from Walders. The Athletic half shaved the crossbar.

Excellent work followed from the Liverpool left wing, but fancy work was clearly useless on this ground. The defence on both sides was very steady, though Liverpool had so far forced the better openings, and Parkinson, in particular, looked dangerous when near goal. Another kick and rush by the Athletic proved successful and Dunlop brought J. Walders down very heavily. For some minutes the Liverpool defence had to deal with several disconcerting Oldham openings. Raybould gave Parkinson a good forward pass, and the Liver's centre was well placed, but Mr Whittaker ruled him offside. During a stiff Oldham attack Hardy emerged from his citadel, but the referee penalised him for overcarrying the ball. Walders shot high over the bar from the free-kick.

Brunton commenced after the interval, and the Athletic were the first to become dangerous. They forced a corner from a good attempt by Ramsay but, as in the initial half, their attack was more vigorous than scientific. Chorlton was weak in defence and again let in Ramsay, who hesitated before he shot so that Hardy was prepared for the effort and caught the sphere in his best style. The home forwards on the move were always a source of danger and had their attack been followed up with good shooting, Hardy might well have been beaten. As it was, they either lost the ball or hesitated and allowed the Livers' defence to anticipate their intention. Up to this point in the half the Oldham custodian had not been tested because the Liverpool forwards failed to get into their stride. Goddard was the first player to test the home goalkeeper, but his weak dropping shot was easily dealt with. Shortly afterwards Cox sent in a magnificent shot across the goalmouth which caused Daw to fall full-length in order to save.

A long kick and a tip by Ramsay took him past Chorlton, but the Oldhamite finished with a centre, which was not taken up. At this stage it was patently obvious that the bulk of the attack came from Oldham, and Liverpool's defence was severely tested on several occasions.

At length the pressure on the visiting goal was relieved and Parkinson dribbled round all opposition before being brought down when about to shoot. The ball was driven across from the left wing for McPherson to score. Following this reversal, the homesters stuck to their task with great persistency and Hardy's charge was under even greater threat than before. However, the newly-chosen international was in his best humour and he gave a masterly display.

Bradley was conspicuous with clever work, and he supplied Cox with a glorious opening, but the leather was sent across the goal to McPherson, who shot wide. In the closing stages Liverpool maintained the advantage which they had shown after McPherson's goal, and Oldham rarely looked like robbing them of victory.

Of the sixteen ties, only two were away wins - Liverpool and Everton (2-1 against West Ham). The biggest score of the round was Bristol Rovers' 3-0 win over Millwall. Five of the ties were drawn. Everton and Liverpool reserve teams drew a crowd of 20,000 at Goodison Park in the Lancashire Combination. The result was 1-1.

Tom Chorlton

Oldham Athletic: Daw; Hodson, Slater; Fay, D.Walders, Wilson; J.Walders, Shadbolt, Brunton, Hancock, Ramsay.

Liverpool: Hardy; Chorlton, Dunlop; Robinson, Gorman, Bradley; Goddard, McPherson, Parkinson, Raybould, Cox.

Referee: Mr N. Whittaker (London)

Attendance: 21,500

COMMENTS ON THE GAME
~~~~~~~~~~~~~~~~~~

In Oldham the idea of a runaway victory for Liverpool was utterly scouted, and victory over the League champions was hoped for. When the home supporters, by devious and winding pathways, found the ground and took its bearings, they at once recognised that its character was all against the classy play of the Livers. So it proved on the moment "Parky" set the ball a-rolling.

The home lot hopped over the mounds and ruts and crevices surefooted, as was clear, while the Livers struggled ineffectively to get into that sort of combination and understanding. But as the minutes went by the general cup-tie character of the game became more and more pronounced.

The Oldham forwards were a lively lot, and went ahead for all they were worth, but the ground they made was usually lost adjacent to goal, owing to their having little control of the ball.

Still, the Oldham lot shot, though more often than not very wildly. The Livers struggled on, trying to command the mischievous leather, but the passing and combination was extremely poor. During the first ten minutes the home left were seen to advantage, and did a lot of the pressing. Their style was very loose, but it upset the Liverpool defence sadly. The latter recovered themselves admirably, and Hardy was all there when wanted. At last Hancock netted and the crowd went frantic.

The preliminary work did the Athletic great credit, but Hancock was clearly off-side. Cox and Raybould were the best of the Liverpool forwards, but Parkinson was erratic.

McPherson did not like the going at all. The Reds improved as the game proceeded, and they accommodated themselves more, but on both sides the attack was scraggy and erratic, and was easily held by the defence. It was not surprising there was no score at the interval.

The first half dismissed the idea of an easy victory for Liverpool.

Commencing the second half, Oldham were seen in a most determined mood, and easily rushed the Anfielders off their feet, Hardy having to handle three times. Parkinson adopted the home tactics, but he failed to fluster either of the Oldham backs.

The Livers backed considerably, and as the second half progressed their superior footwork told the tale on the home defence. Nevertheless, the Oldham rushes came off against every one of the Liverpool defenders in turn excepting Hardy, who kept his charge in glorious fashion. "Go on, Ram! Use thee weight" was oft the cry.

After twenty minutes' hard game the chance of a Liverpool victory seemed remote until Parkinson was brought down when going clear for the goal. It served the purpose, however, for the Reds, resuming, tricked their opponents at every point, and McPherson found the net cleverly when everyone had anticipated a replay at Anfield.

To be perfectly fair to the Athletic, their rushing tactics succeeded admirably, and only the superb vigilance of Hardy thwarted the designs of the vigorous Oldham forwards.

After "Mac" scored, the steam of the home attack evaporated considerably. Their non-success when so often near scoring evidently disheartened them.

February 23, 1907

Liverpool (1) 1
Cox 40

Bradford City (0) 0

BRADFORD City of the Second Division had beaten Reading (2-0) and Accrington (1-0) in earlier rounds and hoped to make further progress against their First Division opponents. Liverpool had Robinson back again after he missed the previous week's League game against Sheffield Wednesday (the Reds won 3-2) and Gorman again filled Raisbeck's place. There were probably 15,000 spectators present when the teams made their appearance, and the toss went in favour of the Bradford captain, who forced the home players to face the sun.

The visitors at the start promised to be rather troublesome, but a free-kick against them put the home team on the attack and, well-served by Gorman and Saul, they made a brisk, though futile, attack. Mainly through the efforts of McLean, the Yorkshiremen again forced their way into the Liverpool half, and although twice repulsed by Saul and Bradley, they came again, and Smith put in the first shot of the game, a well-judged effort which proved to be unsuccessful. Following the goal kick, the Reds attacked strongly but it was some time before they could find an opening, Cox then driving in with great force, and Wise bringing off a fine save.

Penman beat off further Liverpool efforts, and attempted to set his forwards going, but Dunlop proved too much for them. Gradually Bradford made slight inroads on their right, McLean's free-kick being well followed up, and Clarke had a chance of running in and shooting, but the Liverpool skipper successfully tackled him, and the home left wing soon pressed their opponents very hard. McLean bore the brunt of the pressure in splendid fashion, and at last succeeded in relieving his line. The Yorkshire Robinson served up the ball to his front rank, and Newton made off in great style, only to be finely beaten by Saul. Liverpool advanced in fine style right up to the Bradford goalmouth, where a severe tussle took place and only a foul against Liverpool saved the Yorkshiremen's goal from defeat. A moment later McLean beat off an attack and Bradford took up the running. Handley made a fine sprint down the Bradford left and got in a clean centre, on which Bartlett at once fastened, but before he could get going for goal, Gorman beat him off.

The visitors recovered their composure and swarmed in front of the home goal but Robinson shot narrowly wide. At this point, Hardy was injured and when he retired behind the touchline for repairs, Dunlop filled the breach. Goddard put across an excellent centre which Raybould failed to convert, and after further pressure on the Bradford goal, the visitors rushed their opponents' line, and Dunlop saved from Smith. Then Hardy resumed to the accompaniment of rousing cheers. Goddard made a fine run and centre though Wise collected the ball before he was seriously troubled. Liverpool continued to attack but they were looked after by McLean and Wise.

The visitors' right wing broke away, and finally Clarke put in a fine shot which Hardy just managed to save. A corner was conceded, but this gave the defenders no trouble.

Soon afterwards Liverpool were rewarded for their efforts with a goal from the foot of Cox, who took the ball down the field from the half-way line, and shot from close to the touchline, the goalkeeper touching the ball with one hand, but it bounced on to the crossbar and then dropped into the net.

Upon resuming, the first attack by the Whites was met by a peculiar header from Dunlop, but the Yorkshiremen returned and rushed the ball over the goal-line, after which Clarke shot on the outside of the rigging. For some time the visitors had the better of the exchanges and a corner led to no tangible result. Liverpool retaliated by forcing a corner on the right, but failed to gain any advantage from it, and then another rush came from the visitors' right for which the Liverpool skipper accounted.

Almost immediately, however, the same wing claimed a corner, and on the ball being headed away from in front of goal, it was passed out to Cox, who dashed away, then halted, and finally spoiled his work by dancing about to no purpose, the result being that he quickly had a couple of opponents attending to him, and he was well beaten.

A halt was called because of an injury to Parkinson, but on resuming Saul beat off the visitors' left. Clarke started down his wing and Saul ran across to check, but fell, and the Bradford man crossed the ball beautifully, but Smith was unfortunate in not scoring.

At the other end the forwards closed in on Wise, who coolly picked the ball up, but he did not get it away without a struggle, and directly afterwards Cox made a great drive at the goal but failed to score. Again Cox and Raybould made play close to the penalty line, but Farran came to his side's rescue. Then Bradford attacked, and during a goalmouth mêlée, Hardy was laid out. When he recovered Cox made one of his characteristic dashes, but was pulled up for a previous foul. Just before time, Clarke caused the Liverpool defence a lot of trouble, but he failed to receive support from his colleagues. Clarke had been a brilliant forward throughout the game, running rings around Dunlop, something which few players managed to achieve.

The gate receipts were £500, and the attendance was reported in some quarters as being near 20,000 due to the overspill from Goodison Park, where Everton entertained Bolton Wanderers (0-0) before an estimated 56,000. Of the eight ties, three were drawn. Only Brentford, of the away teams, scored a goal. The biggest victory was the 4-0 Notts County win over Tottenham Hotspur.

Liverpool

Hardy

Saul   Dunlop

Robinson   Gorman   Bradley

Goddard   McPherson   Parkinson   Raybould   Cox

Billy Dunlop

Clarke   Bartlett   Newton   Smith   Handley

Robinson   Penman   Millar

McLean   Farran

Wise

Bradford City

Referee: Mr F.H. Dennis (Middlesbrough)   **Attendance**: 18,000

March 9, 1907

Sheffield Wednesday (0) 1   Liverpool (0) 0
Chapman 49

THE weather in Liverpool on the morning of this match was dull, dismal and dirty. The train passengers who passed through the dales and delightful Peak district witnessed the extraordinary sight of snow on the hills on the left, but on the opposite side of the carriage not a sign of the wintry element existed. Liverpool had not previously aroused the enthusiasm which leads to their supporters following them any great distance. Today was an exception. The Lancashire men had already bearded the Yorkshire lion in his den, winning 3-2 on February 16. It was naturally felt that what Liverpool achieved in the previous month, they could repeat this month. There were no alterations to the Liverpool ranks.

Owlerton was regarded as a compact little spot, surrounded by factories, smoke, and many trees, where rooks nested. There was a large stand which ran right round one wing of the ground. Alec Raisbeck and West were hailed with great applause when they were spotted in the grandstand. The captain was well muffled. Mr Tom Watson was rattled and cheered. Dunlop won the toss before 30,000 spectators.

Wilson led off with a pass-out to V. Simpson, but Dunlop anticipated the move and cleared the danger. From a throw-in Brittleton endeavoured to supply Simpson again. but once more the effort failed. The home side attacked immediately and Wilson dashed in, but Dunlop tackled him and Hardy picked up the ball and cleared. The opening exchanges were completely dominated by Wednesday and Liverpool's defence was hard-pressed, though it remained firm.

At last the Liverpool attack got underway, and Parkinson, Raybould and Cox moved up in a fine combination, with Cox dropping the ball right into the Wednesday goalmouth where Lyall fisted out valiantly. The Reds were not to be denied and Cox and Raybould looked like getting through with grand work. Burton got across two or three times to anticipate an extremely dangerous close pass from Cox to Sammy. Cox soon went away again, but he manoeuvred too long, and was ultimately grassed by Brittleton. Another home rush looked bad for Liverpool with Saul miskicking, but Dunlop got across and came to the rescue. Wednesday went close two or three times before Liverpool made progress. Cox gained possession and worked a throw-in, from which Parkinson headed over. The Sheffield warder soon got another scare from "Mac" who worked down marvellously to the corner flag, and would have netted had not Lyall got both fists to the leather.

A spasmodic rush by Wednesday enabled Wilson to attack, but he was ruled offside. A lovely centre by George Simpson was dealt with superbly by Hardy. Further pressure came from the home side and, running out to clear, Hardy was pushed over the line and conceded a corner, which was smartly negotiated. Cox, Raybould and Bradley featured in a fine attacking move, but Layton dispelled the danger. Soon afterwards Cox initiated another move, and "Mac" joined in, but the move broke down in front of the Wednesday goal. "Robbie" was next on the scene and he fed his right wing neatly, but Burton was not to be outwitted. Liverpool could do everything but score at this stage in the game, and it would have been better had they shot hard and often and dispensed with so much finesse which proved profitless.

A Bradley shot at goal which went wide was followed by a strong Sheffield attack which almost brought disaster to Liverpool. After Robinson and Gorman were both tricked, Saul miskicked, and then Hardy fell over Wilson and the Liverpool goal was empty, but just when all seemed lost, Gorman appeared upon the scene and brought salvation. Minutes before the interval, the home side had further openings, but weak shooting saved Liverpool.

Upon restarting, it was noticeable that the ground was in a heavy condition and well churned up. Raybould soon gained possession and he cleverly crossed to Goddard who fed Robinson, but the half-back's shot went wide. The game went from end to end and soon a smart move on the left was checked momentarily by Hardy. The ball was quickly passed back a couple of yards to Chapman, who took aim at very short range immediately and gave Hardy no chance. A huge roar followed the goal.

Parkinson might have equalised when he got through, but no-one followed up and the danger passed. Robinson made an opening for McPherson with some nimble footwork, and the inside-right tested Lyall with a rasping shot. McPherson and Goddard took up the Livers' attack energetically, but although the Sheffield defence was subjected to a rare gruelling, nothing tangible resulted to the Reds, though Cox and Raybould put in several goalward drives. Liverpool were determined not to go home defeated. Lyall was kept very busy, and one shot from "Parky" particularly shook the Wednesday warden up.

Shortly afterwards, the Wednesday landed in force in front of Hardy, who was very hard pressed, but he behaved heroically. "Villy" Simpson next rounded Dunlop in midfield, but instead of going right on he tried a long shot which failed. A glorious Chapman drive brought out an equally fine save from Hardy. Liverpool created several fine chances, but the Wednesday defence held firm, and Liverpool were out of the Cup.

Of the four ties, one was drawn (Everton 1-1 against Crystal Palace in London). West Bromwich Albion beat Notts County 3-1 at home, while Woolwich Arsenal beat Barnsley 2-1 away. In the Rugby Union international at Cardiff, Wales beat Ireland 29-0 after leading by six points at the interval. Of the previous twenty-one contests Wales had won twelve, Ireland eight, and one match was drawn.

Sheffield Wednesday: Lyall; Layton, Burton; Brittleton, Crawshaw, Bartlett; V.S.Simpson, Chapman, Wilson, Stewart, G.Simpson.

Liverpool: Hardy; Saul, Dunlop; Robinson, Gorman, Bradley; Goddard, McPherson, Parkinson, Raybould, Cox.

Referee: Mr N. Whittaker (London)

Attendance: 30,000

WEST BROMWICH ALBION v. NOTTS COUNTY

At the Hawthorns in wet weather, before 20,000 spectators. Notts won the toss, and Jordan kicked off. After three minutes Buck scored for the Albion. The Albion attacked, but Henderson disposed of Haywood. Notts forced their way in, but Pennington beat Matthews. A corner was well worked for, and Iremonger fisted away a header from Burton. Humphreys scored for Notts. Parker put in a good centre, from which Burton tested Iremonger. Burton put the Albion ahead.

HALF-TIME SCORE
West Bromwich Albion..........2
Notts County...........................1

Resuming the Throstles attacked, and Buck nearly scored with a brilliant effort. Albion forced a corner, and Jordan headed their third goal.

The Football Who's Who 1906-07

Wilson, David, born 1884 at Sheffield; height 5ft 9ins; weight 11st 7lb; professional. Playing centre-forward for the Wednesday. Distinguished himself in Sheffield Licensed Victuallers' League. Received overtures from a southern organisation, but terms were not sufficient to tempt him to leave native town. Was transferred to Wednesday 1906-7, and made his first appearance in Midland League match at Owlerton, when had satisfaction of scoring goal which gave his side victory. Resides at Sheffield.

Simpson, George, headed the winning goal when Wednesday beat Everton 2-1 in the 1907 Cup final. Came from Jarrow in 1902 and went to West Bromwich Albion along with Burton in 1909.

The Football Who's Who 1906-07

Lyall, John, joined Wednesday from Jarrow in 1901 and was regular first-team choice for eight seasons before moving to Manchester City. Born Dundee. Capped for Scotland against England 1905.

Layton, W., Sheffield Wednesday (right-back); born Blackwell, Derbyshire. Height 5ft 7ins; weight 11st. 7lbs. Tenth season with present team, previously with Chesterfield.

Burton, Horace, a local discovery signed from Attercliffe in 1903. Transferred to West Bromwich Albion during 1908-09. Cup-winners' medal in 1907.

Crawshaw, Thomas, born at Sheffield. Height 5ft 10½, weight 11st 7lb; playing centre half-back for Sheffield Wednesday. An international for England against Scotland, Ireland and Wales. Has been the mainstay of the Wednesday club for many seasons. His height gives him an advantage in heading, at which branch of the game he is a past-master. Has captained the team several years and held that honour when Sheffield Wednesday won the English Cup 1906-07, when they beat Everton at Crystal Palace. Was previously with Attercliffe and Heywood Central.

Simpson, Vivian S., amateur. Playing forward for Sheffield Wednesday. Making his reputation first as centre-forward, has played both inside-left and inside-right for the Wednesday; was very clever at the game as a boy, distinguishing himself among his comrades at the Wesley College, Sheffield. It was, however, with the Sheffield Club that he attracted notice by his skill as a forward and as a getter of goals. In March 1902, Sheffield Wednesday looked very much like falling into the Second Division, when the committee boldly tried an experiment in dropping several of their usual forwards, trying reserves in their places, and giving young Simpson, then a youth of 19, an opportunity at centre-forward of showing what he could do in first-class football. The experiment was made at Manchester on March 28, 1902, Wednesday beating the City team by three clear goals, and commencing a series of successes away from home which averted downfall into the Second Division. Although thoroughly loyal to Wednesday, does not play for the professional club when the Sheffield amateurs have an Amateur Cup tie. Very tricky, speedy and clever with the ball, indeed is one of smartest young amateurs of the day. Resides at Sheffield and is a solicitor. Also a member of the Sheffield Wycliffe club.

Chapman, Harry, brother of Herbert. Won two championship medals in 1903 and 1904 and a Cup-winners' medal in 1907.

---

84   *The Early Years 1892 - 1915*

January 11, 1908

Liverpool (1) 4
Cox, Gorman,
Bradley, Parkinson

Derby County (1) 2
Bentley (pen), Bevan

LIVERPOOL and Derby travelled to town on the morning of the game from Blackpool where they had been in special training, and both teams were in excellent trim. The home team was not definitely chosen until just previous to the kick-off. It was fully recognised that the Anfielders had no easy task on their hands, for though a Second Division side, the County were playing consistently. Their Cup record also marked them as tough opponents. A quarter of an hour before the start spectators dribbled into the Anfield ground, and there was little prospect of a decent gate. The weather was all that could be desired, and the playing surface appeared to be excellent. Several excursionists arrived from Derby in order to encourage the Rams. The Reds appeared on the pitch at 2.25.

The Derby skipper won the toss and Parkinson kicked-off. McPherson sent the ball deeper into Derby territory but Morris responded with a great clearance. The ball reached Saul, who punted it powerfully upfield. Cox was sent on his way, but his centre was awkward for Parkinson to capitalise upon. From a Derby attack, Saul distinguishes himself once again. Long and Davis made headway with some excellent footwork, and neither Bradley nor Rogers could hold them in check. Davis succeeded in passing the ball across the goalmouth, and Hardy was in difficulties. Davis got the ball but failed to net it, and an exciting scramble in front of goal ensued, the ball was put back to Richards, who got in a great shot from close quarters. Hardy pleased the crowd with a brilliant save. The Reds had showed no superiority so far, and Bradley appeared to be performing very gingerly on the half turn. After a piece of finesse from Goddard which proved abortive, the winger attacked again. He was challenged by Morris, but the Anfielder thoroughly outwitted the Derby back and succeeded in getting in a lovely centre which Cox headed into the net.

For five minutes after this the struggle was continued in midfield without either side looking particularly dangerous. Following a goal-kick Cox gained possession but found the Derby halves too cute for him. The ball was proving very lively on the hard ground, and accurate passing was evidently difficult, while some of the players were uneasy underfoot. A free-kick against Saul led to a corner which proved costly to Liverpool. The corner kick was nicely placed, but it appeared to be safely negotiated until Gorman, forgetting he was in the penalty area, gave away a penalty. Bentley easily defeated Hardy, and the visitors were on equal terms. The worst feature on the home side was that several members of the defence were suffering from the difficulty presented by the frost, and on both sides a considerable amount of anxiety was present. Goddard, however, was in good form and one excellent centre was met by Hewitt, who caused Maskrey to

emerge from his citadel to punch away. Following this a header from Parkinson was well managed by Maskrey.

The attack was taken up by the Rams, and Rogers let in Davis, who centred well. Saul cleared with difficulty, but Rogers made amends by coming to the rescue with a fine clearance. The game was held up when Hughes was injured, but play commenced shortly afterwards. Restarting, Bradley manoeuvred craftily and placed the leather comfortably for Hewitt, but Joe made too much of his fear on the surface, and instead of forging ahead he tried conclusions with the half back and came off worse. This was soon followed, however, by one of the spiciest bits of passing so far in the game. All the home forwards took part in it with credit and skill, and it culminated in Goddard trying to find the net with a glorious drive. Maskrey was fortunate in deflecting the ball, which travelled swiftly into the side netting. Cox took the kick, but the ball did not fall advantageously for the Reds, though Goddard got in a drive which proved fruitless. At this stage of the proceedings, the Rams were not particular in their methods, and the Liverpool players duly suffered. A contemporary reporter stated that "Mr Kirkham's eyesight was not very keen."

On the home side everything in the first period depended on Saul, for Rogers had left it to his colleagues too often. Saul played a great game in the first period. Gorman, too, had shown good judgment in all things except the penalty awarded against him. Bradley had a tricky wing to contend with, but the ex-Trotter was not over-confident on the hard ground and consequently that side of the home defence appeared weak.

From the restart, the Derby left was immediately busy before the ball went out of play. Ultimately Goddard beat Morris and centred to McPherson, who headed to Gorman, and the centre half, finding himself well placed, took aim immediately. The ball travelled at great speed and flew into the net. A well-sustained attack on the home left-wing brought about a corner and the ball was well placed, putting the entire Derby defence in great difficulty. None of the visitors controlled the ball, which bobbled about ominously near Maskrey until Bradley scored a third goal for Liverpool. Bentley, after a superb run, tested the Liverpool custodian and Hardy pulled off a sensational save. Immediately afterwards, McPherson finished some excellent passing with a powerful shot. Maskrey flung himself at the speeding ball and intercepted it, but he rolled over several times with the impetus he had obtained. The game thus witnessed two sensational saves in quick succession.

Five minutes later Cox had what was described by an onlooker as "the chance of his lifetime" but he failed to increase Liverpool's lead.

Liverpool: Hardy; Saul, Rogers; Hughes, Gorman, Bradley; Goddard, McPherson, Parkinson, J.Hewitt, Cox.

Derby County: Maskrey; Nicholas, Morris; Warren, Hall, Richards; J.Davis, Long, Bevan, Bentley, G.Davis.

Referee: Mr T. Kirkham (Burslem)

Attendance: 15,000

The Rams made several ineffectual attempts to get their front line going. Eventually a slip by Goddard led to a somewhat half-hearted attack by the visitors and Bentley sent in a weak shot. Almost from the goal-kick the Livers made a strong attack and with a great drive Parkinson put on goal number four. Just before the finish, after Liverpool had made a succession of futile onslaughts, the Derby men broke away, and from a centre by Davis, Bevan scored a second goal for the Rams.

Of the 32 ties, eight were drawn. There were five away victories, the most notable of which was the Fulham win at Luton by 8-3, after leading 5-2 at the interval. Chelsea recorded the day's biggest win, 9-1 against Worksop, after leading 4-1 at half-time.

The Liverpool gate money amounted to £295.

Sam Hardy, who was in inspired form against Derby County, making several fine saves

February 1, 1908

Liverpool (0) 1 Brighton & Hove Albion (1) 1
Cox 81   *Hall (pen) 43*

LIVERPOOL entertained Brighton who, at the third attempt, beat Preston North End. Both sides had been in special training for this important match, and the Liverpool men, who had been at Blackpool, fully realised what tough opponents they had to meet. The visitors travelled from Birkdale on the morning of the game, and relied on the same side which carried them through the first round, with the exception of Ronaldson, who was substituted for Joyne at the last moment. On the Liverpool side, Raisbeck reappeared at centre-half, and Parkinson at centre-forward, thus allowing McPherson to partner Goddard, while Joe Hewitt played alongside Cox. Ten minutes before the start, the crowd was over 20,000, and the spectators poured into the ground from every direction. The turf appeared to be in excellent condition, and the sun shone brightly, though a nasty crosswind blew. Captain Raisbeck won the toss and set Brighton with their faces to the sun. Hall was the first to make a move, but the wind took the ball out near the corner flag. From a throw-in, Parry fed Hewitt and Cox but the Liverpool attack broke down when Cox was impeded by Archer. Raisbeck began a promising move and the ball carried to Cox, but the winger was tackled in fine style by Kent. The Reds were not to be denied, and they maintained their attack and MacDonald was forced to come out and fist the ball away. The home side continued to press but Hewitt failed to make contact when a favourable opportunity occurred. The shooting of the home forwards was very reckless, though a corner accrued. MacDonald was called upon to fist out from the Anfield skipper. A second corner followed, and from this Cox worked in a lovely shot which shaved the bar. At this stage in the game, the visitors had been well held by their hosts, and a most pleasing feature from the home point of view was the judicious and effective work of Alec Raisbeck.

Rather slack work by Parry and West let in the Brighton left, and Hardy was forced to punch clear from a Wombwell goal attempt. Liverpool's shooting was woefully weak, though their passing was good enough to puzzle the Brighton halves, who were not accurate in their placing.

Parkinson began a smart move when he wormed his way between the half-backs, MacDonald and Morris; but Arthur Goddard failed to accept his pass, though the attack was taken up by Parkinson, Hewitt and Cox. The winger's shot was extremely weak and disappointing, though the fact that Liverpool were shooting into the wind may have accounted for this. A fine movement by Goddard, McPherson and Hewitt resulted in the Brighton custodian conceding a corner, which the referee allowed only after consulting his lineman. The kick was badly taken, however. The return to form of Raisbeck was a feature of the game, and he was ably assisted by Parry and Bradley. Indeed, Bradley held the opposing

wing extremely cleverly. A sudden rush by the Brightonians led to Saul conceding a corner against Ronaldson and the visitors forced four consecutive corners before Hardy was able to clear the danger. The Reds moved straight on to the offensive and Cox forced an abortive corner. Goddard next put in some dainty work and centred accurately, but the Brighton custodian anticipated the danger and left his goal to fist away. After Goddard had twice been disappointed, Liverpool gained a corner and Cox dropped the ball brilliantly in front of the goal, but it was scraped out in miraculous fashion. Then free-kicks were awarded to both sides, and from one, Raisbeck made a dash forward and shot over the bar. Shortly afterwards, Goddard collected a pass and sent in a powerful shot which MacDonald saved well. As the interval approached the Brighton men put on some pressure and a succession of throws-in ensued. Goddard broke away and centred square, but Parkinson was not up in time and the opportunity went begging.

Two minutes before half-time, Anthony threatened Parry within the penalty area. Maurice had plenty of room to clear, but he dallied too long, and finally in a most inexcusable and unnecessary way, he handled the ball. Hall took the kick and put the leather safely in the net amidst great cheering from their fans.

The game had not been nearly so difficult as imagined due to the gentlemanly tactics of the Brighton team who had declined to use their big weight unduly.

The second half opened with a promising movement from the left wing, but when Cox middled the ball, Parkinson lost the leather. Brighton were awarded a throw-in and performed cleverly in midfield which enabled Wombwell to get in a great shot which Hardy dealt with under difficult circumstances. The wind continued to be a factor in the game, sending several passes astray. A prolonged visit to Brighton territory was unproductive, but soon afterwards McPherson treated the crowd to some neat footwork which culminated in a tremendous shot. The home attack tightened, and the Hove defence looked more and more shaky. Goddard, Hewitt and Cox all went close for Liverpool as the home side increased the pressure, and the Brighton men were warned by the referee for time-wasting. The midfield work of the Anfielders was excellent, but there was too much fancy footwork in attack when a more direct approach would have been beneficial. McPherson, Parry and Goddard featured in a great move, with Parry heading against the bar. The ball rebounded into play, but only a corner resulted. At this stage, the visitors were outplayed in every department, and Liverpool did everything but score.   From an excellent cross by Cox,

Parkinson headed miles wide of the intended target. McDonald kept out a fierce shot by Raisbeck, and at the other end Hardy saved well from Hall. As Liverpool maintained the pressure, Joe Hewitt shot a foot wide of the post. McPherson, Cox and Bradley combined well but failed to produce a goal. With thirty-five minutes of the second period gone, Cox headed wide from a cross by Goddard. Immediately afterwards, Cox got in a header from a corner kick, and the ball struck the upright before curling into the net. The cheering was deafening as Liverpool went straight onto the attack, but McDonald incurred the wrath of the crowd when he hurt Parkinson, who writhed in agony on the ground. Upon resuming, Brighton took up the attack and claimed a goal straight from a corner kick, but the referee denied the visitors' claims.

Of the sixteen ties, five were drawn, including Everton's goalless game away to Oldham Athletic. The only away win was Crystal Palace's 3-2 victory over Plymouth Argyle. The biggest score of the day was at Grimsby Town, who beat Carlisle United 6-2.

The replayed tie was set for the following Wednesday, which was a half-holiday in Brighton.

Liverpool: Hardy; West, Saul; Parry, Raisbeck, Bradley; Goddard, McPherson, Parkinson, J.Hewitt, Cox.

Brighton & Hove Albion: H.McDonald; Archer, Turner; Kent, Morris, W.McDonald; Ronaldson, Burnett, Hall, Wombwell, Anthony.

Referee: Mr J.T. Ibbotson (Derby)

Attendance: 36,000

James Bradley held the opposing wing extremely cleverly, and he added to his fine performance with two goals in the replay.

February 5, 1908

Brighton & Hove Albion (0) 0   Liverpool (1) 3
Bradley 25, 80, Cox 82

LIVERPOOL made some forward changes in their team, Robinson coming in to partner Goddard, while Joe Hewitt took up the centre position, Bowyer - making his Cup début for Liverpool - replacing him at inside-left. McPherson and Parkinson were dropped. The men had stayed at Worthing, close to Brighton, since the Sunday. The wisdom of the Albion directors in making the replay a six-penny gate was amply shown when over eight thousand persons patronised the popular part of the ground. There was enormous local interest in the tie, due to Brighton's marvellous moral victory at Anfield, and their 1-0 defeat of Preston North End at Deepdale in a replay in the previous round. Joynes was still unable to play for the home side due to a strained leg, and the team, which had been training at Seaford, was the same as that which did service at Liverpool. The teams lined up under ideal conditions and the game started before 10,000 spectators. Raisbeck won the toss against Kent, and elected to play from the southern goal with the sun behind his men.

Brighton kicked off with the wind at their backs. Liverpool advanced on the right, Robinson sent the ball out to Cox, who raced off, but Archer put the ball outside. From the throw-in, Brighton made tracks for Hardy, and after Saul had administered a temporary check, Burnett sent in a tremendous shot which Hardy cleared.

The Southerners, who were playing with great determination, again moved along the right, and Hardy saved well. Cox and Bowyer completely tricked Archer, and when scoring seemed imminent Turner rushed across and punted the ball upfield to clear the danger.

Liverpool showed the crowd their true form and for some time Brighton were outplayed. Cox and Hewitt tested McDonald, but Hewitt's effort went inches over the bar. After a brief delay owing to an injury to Goddard, Liverpool again took up the offensive, and McDonald was forced to leave his charge in saving from Bowyer. Keeping up the pressure, Liverpool had another opportunity of drawing first blood, but McDonald cleared a great shot from Cox.

The ball travelled from end to end with great regularity and speed at this point in the game. Hall beat Raisbeck and swung the ball out to Ronaldson who raced off at top speed and sent in a terrific drive which Saul cleverly met and kicked clear.

Soon afterwards, Bradley was completely beaten by Burnett, who raced round the Liverpool half and sent in a beauty which went just wide. Liverpool then took up the attack on the right. The ball was sent over to Cox, who was right in the goalmouth, but McDonald made a magnificent save from the outside left, a feat which drew tremendous applause. It was Hardy's turn next to show off his defensive abilities, and his save from Hall matched that of McDonald. Liverpool were often disorganised by the bustling tactics of their opponents, but there was no mistaking their superiority, their pretty passing bringing forth many cheers from the spectators who were almost entirely Brightonians. Brilliant combination between Hall and Wombwell looked promising for Brighton, but Morris's shot struck an opponent.

After midfield exchanges the Liverpool outside-right gained possession, and broke through all opposition before forcing a corner off Turner. Goddard took the kick and placed the ball right in the goalmouth, enabling Bradley to steer the ball through the mass of legs, easily beating McDonald, who appeared to have no idea that the ball had reached the net.

Liverpool attacked with renewed vigour, but the Southern backs were steady and resourceful. In response to cries of *"Play up, Brighton!"* the Southerners moved off in combined order, and Anthony and Wombwell danced round Parry, and although West rushed to his assistance, Anthony was able to get in a swift, low shot, which Hardy just managed to save. The Brighton left wing gave Parry and West a hard time, their short passing being smart and pretty. Towards the interval Liverpool had all the best of matters, and a splendid shot by Bowyer, who had been playing most consistently throughout, would have scored had not McDonald rushed out and cleared. The visitors were attacking strongly when the whistle blew for half-time.

On their play in the first half, it was felt that Liverpool deserved the lead, their scientific combination being in striking contrast to the rushing methods of their opponents.

There was a largely increased attendance when play resumed. Brighton at once made ground and in the first minute forced a corner, but it was so badly placed that Liverpool cleared with ease. Brighton's shooting was very erratic, but when Hall had the ball at his toe, and was just about to shoot, Hardy rushed out and threw himself on to the ground in order to divert the ball outside the target.

A moment later the Brightonians swarmed around the Liverpool goal. Ronaldson received from McDonald and sent in a beauty which would have beaten any ordinary goalkeeper, but Hardy coolly fisted clear. Liverpool then attacked, and a sequence of passing involving Hewitt, Bowyer and Cox ended in Hewitt sending into McDonald's hands. Brighton again invaded their opponents' territory and it needed extreme vigilance on the part of the Liverpool defence to prevent a score. West relieved the pressure and Goddard raced away at top speed on the right, and was just outside the penalty area when Turner deliberately tripped him. The referee promptly allowed a foul, but the ball was sent outside.

Goddard gained possession and shot, but McDonald made a timely clearance. A mistake by Morris let in Hewitt, who sent out to Cox, and the speedy left-winger had a glorious opportunity of increasing Liverpool's lead when he overran the ball and enabled Archer to clear. For a time all the play was on the eastern side of the ground, Anthony and Wombwell being almost starved of the ball, though Liverpool fed Cox, who was playing down the hill. A brilliant piece of dribbling by Raisbeck produced a corner that led to a mêlée right under the Brighton bar, but the home side escaped, though McDonald was badly shaken up in the scrimmage.

Brighton now seemed a beaten team and Cox electrified the spectators with a characteristic run along the wing and, beating Kent and Archer, tipped the ball back to Raisbeck, whose tremendous drive was turned outside by the home goalkeeper. From the corner, Raisbeck had another shot, but Morris blocked the ball and kicked clear. Bowyer tricked Archer and, breaking free, sent in a fast, low drive which McDonald managed to fling himself at and divert for a corner. Bradley scored with a well-judged shot from an unmarked position with just ten minutes left.

The Albion played up desperately, and Ronaldson shot clean across the goal. Liverpool could do whatever they liked with their opponents at this stage and Cox, receiving in midfield, tricked Morris before taking the ball to within a yard of McDonald, whom he beat easily. At this point, Archer had left the field through injury. In a last despairing effort Hall sent a shot from long range wide of the posts and Liverpool looked like adding to their lead when Goddard sped past Turner and drew McDonald before shooting wide. The gate constituted a record for the ground. No fewer than 11,800 people paid for admission, the taking totalling £568. As an instance of the popularity of the sixpenny portion of the gate, close on eight thousand people realised £198.

On the same day, Everton beat Oldham 6-1 at Goodison in a replay.

At the Brighton Hippodrome, Yukio Tani, described as the greatest of ju-jitsu wrestlers and lightweight catch-as-catch can champion of the world, offered £100 to the man who could defeat him, and £20 to anyone lasting fifteen minutes with him. Any amateur lasting that long would be presented with a silver cup to the value of £40. As a special inducement to local wrestlers, the Japanese wrestler would give a solid gold medal to the amateur who made the best show against him.

At the Grand Theatre "*Dick Whittington*" entered its last fortnight. Members of the principal cycling clubs in the district made up almost the entire audience on the Monday before the Cup-tie.

At the Court Theatre, Mrs Barrasford's "*The Babes In The Wood*" pantomime entered its last week. On the Monday evening another large audience expressed itself unanimous as to the excellence of the pantomime, a great favourite with them being Miss Nora H. Brocklebank, who had made herself very popular as Maid Marion. She was possessed of a beautiful voice, and was warmly applauded for her rendering of "*Love me and the world is mine*". The attraction at the Court Theatre in the week following the Cup-tie was to be "*A Marriage of Convenience*".

There were contemporary reports of an English Court of Justice trial in which some of the most eminent Analytical Chemists in England had made sworn statements that a cup of beef tea made from a one-penny tablet of Ju-Vis contained double the nutriment contained in a cup of Beef Tea made of best known makes of Extract of Meat, according to the directions given. Ju-Vis was guaranteed to be made solely from Extract of Beef and Gelatine, with valuable vegetable properties added, the vegetable much improving the flavour.

The Selection Committee of the Football Association met at High Holborn on the Monday before the tie between Brighton and Liverpool, and chose the following to play against Ireland in Belfast on February 15:

Maskrey (Derby County)
Crompton (Blackburn Rovers)
Pennington (West Bromwich Albion)
Warren (Derby County)
Wedlock (Bristol City)
E.H. Lintott (Queen's Park Rangers)
Rutherford (Newcastle United)
V.J. Woodward (Tottenham Hotspur, captain)
Hilsdon (Chelsea)
Windridge (Chelsea)
Wall (Manchester United)

Reserve: Ducat (Woolwich Arsenal)

Mr R.P. Gregson was to be in charge of the team. For the record, the team lined up as printed, with England winning 3-1. Hilsdon scored twice, and Woodward once. Four months later on June 8 in Vienna, England beat Austria 11-1, Woodward hitting four. There were four changes from the team which beat Ireland.

In a South-Eastern League match at Tunbridge Wells, the local Rangers were beaten 2-1 by Clapton Orient Reserves. In the closing stages the game was very rough, and Thair had to be carried off the field, whilst there was an ugly scene at the close, the Orient linesman being struck by a spectator.

The Secretary of the Football Association stated that the Association did all it could to discourage Sunday football. One of the rules, he pointed out, provided as follows: "Matches shall not be played on Sundays within the jurisdiction of the Association. A player shall not be compelled to play any match on Good Friday or Christmas Day." If a member of a club which was under the jurisdiction of the Association, took part in Sunday football in England, he would at once be suspended, probably for a long period, from taking part in the game.

Brighton & Hove Albion: H.McDonald; Archer, Turner; Kent, Morris, W.McDonald; Ronaldson, Burnett, Hall, Wombwell, Anthony.

Liverpool: Hardy; West, Saul; Parry, Raisbeck, Bradley; Goddard, Robinson, J.Hewitt, Bowyer, Cox.

Referee: Mr J.T. Ibbotson (Derby)

Attendance: 11,800

Receipts: £568

February 22, 1908

Newcastle United (0) 3
Appleyard 49, Speedie 66, Rutherford 68

Liverpool (1) 1
Saul 23

THE League form of two months ago when Liverpool were beaten 1-5 at Anfield was an indication of the outcome of this tie, with Newcastle in second position two points behind the leaders Manchester United, and Liverpool just two points off relegation in thirteenth place. However, Liverpool had rallied in the League, losing only one of their previous nine games, and the Cup competition was a great leveller. Liverpool had been to Blackpool to prepare for the tie, while Newcastle had a prolonged sojourn at Rhyl, broken only at the weekends in order to fulfil various obligations.

Both teams arrived on Tyneside the night before the game, the Novocastrians after a long journey. Every player was fit, thereby posing a selection problem for the Newcastle directors. Liverpool chose the "old firm", with McPherson coming in. The weather was unreliable, but a large attendance turned out. Both sides turned out as expected. Quite unexpectedly, a gale sprang up in the surrounding district, and it was found that communication was almost impossible with wires down all over the North Country, rendering telegraph and telephone services virtually inoperable. Raisbeck won the toss and took advantage of the wind.

For a short time, play was of an even character, the Newcastle right wing being in evidence early on. West and Saul were busy, and were forced to clear the danger. Robinson forced an early corner off McCracken, and the flag-kick was well-placed, the ex-Wearsider making a crafty attempt to backheel the ball beyond Lawrence. The United custodian was too sharp to be beaten in that manner, and he punted the ball to midfield, where there was an exchange between Parry and Wilson, the Newcastle man limping away with a damaged knee. Wilson recovered quickly and joined Speedie in a fine piece of play, and when the ball was centred, a shot by Howie was followed by an abortive corner.

Then Liverpool went on to the offensive, and Hewitt was prominent, but when he appeared to be making progress, McCracken cleared in excellent fashion. The Reds were

Newcastle United: Lawrence; McCracken, Pudan; Gardner, Veitch, McWilliam; Rutherford, Howie, Appleyard, Speedie, Wilson.

Liverpool: Hardy; West, Saul; Parry, Raisbeck, Bradley; Goddard, Robinson, J.Hewitt, McPherson, Cox.

Referee: Mr T. Kirkham (Burslem)

Attendance: 45,987

adamant and Veitch and his colleagues had their work cut out to keep the Liverpool forwards at bay. Then the Novos combined well with clever footwork, but Parry was alert to the situation, and twice he served up nicely to Goddard. With twenty minutes gone, McPherson appeared certain to score after a brilliant dribble by Goddard, but his shot from six yards was miraculously saved by Lawrence, who dived full-length to turn the ball round the posts.

Three corners ensued and during an exciting scrimmage in the goalmouth, Saul headed on to the crossbar from where the ball rebounded on the back of either Pudan or Wilson, and went into the net while Lawrence was bustled by Robinson.

Newcastle responded immediately, and the Tynesiders came close to equalising. Rutherford slipped past all opposition and Appleyard centred to Speedie, who was standing unmarked within the penalty area. He failed to trap the ball, and subsequently Liverpool attacked the United goal in a period of sustained pressure.

The game re-started before an increased attendance. The Liverpool players were in good spirits, and they had played as well as the Novocastrians.

There was a distinct change in fortunes the moment Newcastle played with the wind, which continued to sweep across the ground with hurricane force. Four minutes after the interval Rutherford tapped the ball to Howie, who pushed it forward to Appleyard. The home centre screwed the ball through Hardy's legs for the equalising point. From this stage of the game onwards, the Novocastrian forwards maintained a period of intense pressure involving great skills far exceeding those of Liverpool in manoeuvring the wind-swept ball.

After 66 minutes McWilliam threaded a path through the Liverpool defence and then passed to Speedie, who volleyed the ball into the net with a magnificent diagonal shot. Two minutes later, Rutherford effectively sealed Liverpool's fate with a glorious solo effort. Saul failed to intercept a pass from Veitch and Rutherford broke free at speed and cleverly shouldered off the attentions of three opponents who came at him in turn before scoring a goal which brought roars from the thrilled crowd. Liverpool were a beaten team, faced with better players and a raging storm.

Newcastle achieved their victory by their greater resources and adaptability. The Liverpool forwards were nearly always outmanoeuvred by the United half-backs, Goddard and McPherson being the most conspicuous attackers in an erratic forward line. Raisbeck, Parry, and Bradley all played well in an attempt to restore the balance in the team. West and Saul played well with the wind behind them, but they were unreliable in timing the ball against the wind. Hardy allowed an easy shot from Appleyard to beat him, but he had no chance of saving the other two goals.

Rutherford and Howie worked well together, and Wilson and Speedie were a progressive pair, whilst Appleyard always went promptly for the main chance, his shooting being particularly good. McWilliam displayed sparkling form, and Veitch and Gardner deserved unqualified praise for their brilliantly-conceived tactics as interveners. McCracken and Pudan played an elusive ball with praiseworthy power and accuracy, while Lawrence's judgment as a custodian was a telling factor in the Novocastrians' victory.

In the Fourth Round, Newcastle beat Grimsby Town 5-1 at home, and in the semi-final they beat Fulham 6-0. In the final they lost 1-3 against Wolverhampton Wanderers at the Crystal Palace on 25 April before 74,967 spectators. The Newcastle United goalscorer was Howie. The referee was Mr T.P. Campbell of Blackburn.

The Football Who's Who 1907-08

McCracken, William, born Jan. 29, 1883, at Belfast; single; height 5ft 10 in; weight 12st 6lb; professional. Playing half-back with Newcastle United; made début for Belfast Distillery on December 25, 1900, and in 1903 transferred to Newcastle United; is many times an Irish international and has assisted his country against England, Scotland, and Wales from 1901-7. Resides at Belfast. Employment: a joiner. Hobby: bowling.

OTHER CUP RESULTS

Bolton Wanderers	3	Everton	3	Grimsby 1	Crystal Palace 0
Aston Villa	0	Man Utd	2		
Manchester City	1	Fulham	1	replays	
Portsmouth	0	Stoke	1		
Southampton	2	Bristol R.	0	Everton 3	Bolton Wanderers 1
Wolverhampton W.	2	Swindon	0	Fulham 3	Manchester City 1

*Three corners ensued and during an exciting scrimmage in the goalmouth, **Saul** headed on to the crossbar from where the ball rebounded on the back of either Pudan or Wilson, and went into the net while Lawrence was bustled by Robinson.*

January 16, 1909

Liverpool (3) 5

Orr (3), Hewitt,
Parkinson 47

Lincoln City (1) 1

Morris

IT was generally felt that Liverpool had a great chance of moving into the second round of the English Cup when they were drawn against the leaders of the Midland League. The Reds had to make changes, Robinson being injured. The enthusiastic forward had strained the muscles of his leg, and Parkinson, who had been down with pleurisy, was now recovered, and took Robinson's place. Lincoln had a good following, who made their presence felt when the teams took to the field.

During the morning of the match, lightning, thunder and hail prevailed, but by two o'clock the outlook cleared and, though the wind was bitterly keen, the conditions were generally much better. The ground had suffered through the storm, and just before the players came out it was little better than a quagmire. A liberal quantity of sawdust was thrown over the middle parts of the playing patch, but the surface was both hard and treacherous when play began. All these considerations had an adverse effect on the attendance, which numbered about 5,000 people when Dunlop and the Lincoln skipper tossed for choice of position. "Old Father William" won the deal, and set the visitors to face a hurricane-like breeze. The Liverpool team included Ronald Orr, the former Newcastle player. Harrop also made his FA Cup début for the home side. The strength of the wind hampered Liverpool's early threat as their passes went astray, and the Lincoln backs cleared the danger. The Lincoln forwards advanced down the left, but first Parry and then Chorlton checked, and for some time after this the men literally foundered in the mud. It was soon apparent that the home side was more at home on the heavy going than their opponents, for Hewitt again went ploughing through, only to finish with a shot that passed just outside. A corner was conceded a moment later, but though this was well placed, the danger was eventually cleared.

After Bradley and Cox had failed to make headway, the ball was punted into the centre of the field, where Morris had gained possession and, being nicely placed between the Liverpool backs, he ran on towards the Anfielders' goal. Dunlop was too far upfield to cope with the Lincoln men and Chorlton, who made a rather feeble attempt, was beaten by Morris, so that the centre-forward had a clear course towards Hardy. The Liverpool custodian awaited the shot, which he just failed to stop, the ball just entering the corner of the net high up.

This reverse stimulated the Liverpool attack, and for some time the Anfielders kept up a fierce attack on the Lincoln goal, Parkinson sending wide from a pass by Orr. Then Orr was tripped just outside the penalty area, but the free-kick brought no tangible result. Still the Liverpool men kept up the

pressure, and Saunders saved smartly from Cox, while a moment later Harrop and Hewitt both had shots charged down. At this stage Liverpool were outplaying their opponents, and Bradley sent in a strong shot which was repulsed, but the half-back again caught the leather and drove in another shot, but Saunders just caught the ball as it was rolling over the line. With a temporary lull in the gale, play opened out somewhat, and Lincoln made ground on the right and then on the opposite wing, but the home backs were safe. Then Hewitt made a great attempt to place his side on equal terms when he brushed aside all opposition and nipped between the backs before putting in a high shot which the Lincoln goalkeeper managed to save.

At this point, Bradley was kicked on the leg and had to leave the field. A promising rush by the visiting left wing was cleverly stopped by Chorlton. Parkinson persistently took up the attack on the Liverpool right, and swinging the ball into the centre, the visitors' custodian stumbled in saving a close range shot. Orr was on the scene in a flash, and easily placed his side on level terms.

After a spell of midfield play, Hewitt increased Liverpool's lead from a general mêlée in front of Saunders' goal. The Anfielders proceeded to pen Lincoln in their own half, and shots from Orr and Hewitt were wonderfully saved by Saunders, who was the outstanding player on the Lincoln side. A brilliant run by Goddard was overdone, and a swift ground shot from Hewitt was intercepted by Hood. Bradley, who had not been absent long, initiated a good move, and Cox was enabled to put in a timely centre from which Parkinson, who had now changed places with Hewitt, put in a glorious shot along the ground which finished just wide of the goal. Then Cox sent in a characteristically long dropping shot which Saunders cleverly saved, and in the next minute Dunlop stopped the Lincoln forwards and removed play with a glorious punt. Liverpool forced a corner, which was neatly and accurately placed by Cox for Parkinson to head just outside. Still enjoying the bulk of the play, Liverpool attacked and Cox was again to the fore with a brilliant centre, which gave Hewitt a splendid opportunity of scoring, but he shot just over the corner of the bar. Just before the interval, Liverpool increased their lead. The ball was nicely placed into the centre by Dunlop, and the whole of the home forwards were concerned in the movement which enabled Orr, who took up the attack from Hewitt, to score with a rather long shot, which entered the net near the upright.

Liverpool were the first away after the interval, and Parkinson passed to Hewitt who had a good chance of scoring when Wilson missed his kicked, but Goddard gained possession and he had his shot charged down. The home forwards pounded away at the Lincoln goal and it was fortunate on more than one occasion. After some amusement had been caused by Parry's heroic and eventually successful attempt to extricate the ball from a sea of mud, the Anfielders again took up the attack, and Parkinson, going through in characteristic fashion, passed the Lincoln backs and sailed full speed for Saunders' charge. The Lincoln custodian came out to meet Parkinson, and attempted to take the ball from the home centre's feet, but he was unsuccessful and Parkinson easily netted the leather. This was really the first mistake the goalkeeper had been guilty of, his previous work bearing the hallmark of excellence. Liverpool had the full measure of their opponents, and Cox and Orr walked the ball into the net for the fifth time. Lincoln did not altogether give up hope and for a short spell they were dangerous, but Dunlop and Chorlton allowed no liberties. The Lincoln backs, however, were repeatedly beaten with the result that Saunders was peppered with all sorts of shots. Two express deliveries from Orr and Parry were saved in fine style by Saunders, who dived full-length in glorious fashion.

Liverpool: Hardy; Chorlton, Dunlop; Parry, Harrop, Bradley; Goddard, Parkinson, J.Hewitt, Orr, Cox.

Lincoln City: Saunders; Hood, Wilson; Fraser, Ormiston, Nisbett; Foster, Watson, Morris, McCann, Grundy.

Referee: Mr A. Adams (Nottingham)

Attendance: 8,000

CUP TIE-CLIPS

COMMENTS ON LOCAL AND OTHER GAMES

Some great and some moderate games were seen today. Sixty-four clubs were directly interested in this season's FA Cup competition.

The number of drawn games last season in the opening round was quite unusual. Sixteen clubs meet again.

Up to this morning there were five teams surviving which have had to pass through the whole of the qualifying competition, viz: Workington, Wrexham, Kettering, Hastings and St.Leonard's, and Exeter City.

Wrexham's presence exposes the inaccuracy of those who insist on the title "English Cup."

London fared badly in the draw, only three of the eleven being drawn at home, and two of these having to face other metropolitans.

Norwich City's enclosure not being suitable, it was mutually arranged to play the match at the Chelsea FC enclosure at Stamford Bridge, instead of at either Elm Park, Reading, or one of the other enclosures at Norwich.

Fulham, after much negotiation, secured the presence of Carlisle United at Craven Cottage, granting half the gate, plus £220.

There were five fixtures in "town", three of them in West London. The increase was unfavourably viewed both at Brentford and Park Royal.

Strange, was it not, that last season's winners, the Wolves, were visited by Crystal Palace?

Wolves played the exact team which won them the Cup.

The draw favoured Lancashire clubs (seven home). Bury induced their opponents to change the venue.

In all the cities where there are two clubs both were drawn at home.

Ronald Orr, who hit a hat-trick against Lincoln

February 6, 1909

Liverpool (0) 2
Cox, Robinson 85

Norwich City (1) 3
Allsopp (pen) 35, Tomlinson, Smith 90

NORWICH City, who had been given the unique nickname of "The Canaries", and who wear a no less unique uniform, were an unknown quantity at Anfield prior to this game. Nevertheless, the Reds did not intend to take them lightly, for last season Norwich disposed of Sheffield Wednesday in the first round. Liverpool had never got past the semi-final stage of the Cup, but "The Honourable Sons of Watson" made no secret of the fact that they wanted to make the final this season.

The weather was fine and the fixture attracted a crowd verging on 30,000. The Livers were the first on the field, but when the Canaries appeared their supporters gave them a glorious reception. This was repeated when their skipper won the toss, and set his opponents with their backs to the sun.

At once, Cox advanced on Roney until he was brought down by French at the expense of a corner. The visitors safely negotiated this and forged ahead. Saul headed away from their right wing, and soon afterwards, on the opposite side, Allsopp was going strongly when Parry was penalised for hands. It was a doubtful decision, and Flanagan tried a long shot which Hardy collected with ease.

Saul and Long had a rare race for possession, but the burly back won. After Bradley and Raisbeck had partially checked the onrush of the yellow shirts, Parry travelled across and operations were changed to Norwich quarters. Cox centred, but French anticipated the ball. The performance of the Anfielders at this stage was extremely disappointing, for their work was clumsy and their manner was over-anxious.

Ten minutes after starting, the Canaries missed a fine chance of opening the scoring with the Liverpool defence in tatters, especially to the left of Hardy. Tomlinson put the ball out to his left wing, and had the pass been taken up there was only Hardy to beat, but the Norwich men delayed and Hardy was eventually well covered.

At the other end, Bradley won a corner, which proved unproductive. The Canaries emerged from the pressure and Long appeared in a dangerous position until he was tackled by Saul. The Norwich man had his revenge when he beat Saul and put the ball behind.

So far there had been little attempt at shooting and the respective goalkeepers had been idle for long periods. At length Hewitt tested Roney, but there was little power in his shot.

Orr had long seemed anxious to distinguish himself, but he was an energetic rather than a clever craftsman. On the other wing, Allsopp was always safely kept in check by Parry, and the Welshman's efforts were greatly appreciated by the crowd. Although the Anfielders frequently operated in Norwich territory, they did not seem able to obtain a firm footing. One of the best attacking moves was started by Saul

and involved Orr, Cox, Hewitt and Goddard, but the attack was held up at the finish when Newlands relieved.

The Canaries drew first blood after 35 minutes. A miskick by Chorlton led to a corner, and in negotiating this, the ball was kicked against Saul's hands. Mr Lewis promptly decided that it was a penalty kick, which appeared to be a drastic decision considering the circumstanes. Allsopp took the kick with unerring aim and Hardy was beaten.

Upon resuming, Goddard made several fine efforts to bring about the equalising goal. Cox forced a corner, but there was no luck in it for the Reds. Soon after Bradley tested Roney from a distance.

Five minutes from the interval the Reds looked like gaining equality. Hewitt and Cox worked the ball upfield, but though Robinson and Goddard were in the goalmouth they could not score. The Reds increased the pressure, but a goal was denied them and Roney kept a beautiful shot out of the corner of the net from Cox.

After the interval, the Anfielders attacked strongly, and a corner was forced. The ball was so beautifully placed by Goddard that the equaliser seemed certain, but Orr headed over the bar. At the other end Flanagan wound up an attacking move by shooting a little wide, but the Livers were quick to respond and only a vigorous shoulder prevented Cox from being dangerous.

Saul put the ball forward to Hewitt, who hesitated a moment and was lost; then Cox received and put the ball into the centre where a sharp rally took place before Robinson obtained possession and nearly scored with a tremendous drive. Shortly afterwards, Raisbeck grazed the crossbar with a terrific shot. Goddard then raced down and from his centre Cox headed out. This was followed by a perfect bombardment of the Norwich goal, but although shots were rained in from every angle, not a single effort reached the target and the climax came when Goddard received a pass in front of goal. He was unmarked, and Roney was obviously unprepared. A goal looked a perfect gift for them, but Goddard missed.

After several misses, Hewitt passed to Cox, whose shot struck the crossbar and rebounded into the net. Hardly had the cheers died down when Norwich moved swiftly down the left, and Tomlinson received a fine pass to put his side in front.

The home defence, including Hardy, was terrible. Chorlton saved the ball from going out and returned it with a long punt to Robinson, who wormed his way through several opponents before equalising with five minutes remaining. Just on time, Hardy was at fault and Smith won the game for the Canaries. The game proved to be Jack Cox's last FA Cup tie for Liverpool. He featured in 33 Cup games, a Liverpool record at the time, scoring 8 goals.

Liverpool: Hardy; Chorlton, Saul; Parry, Raisbeck, Bradley; Goddard, Robinson, Hewitt, Orr, Cox.

Norwich City: Roney; French, Gray; Newlands, Wagstaffe, Whiteman; Long, Flanagan, Tomlinson, Smith, Allsopp.

Referee: Mr H.P. Lewis (Rotherham)

Attendance: 30,000

COMMENTS

Hewitt, Robbie and Goddard made some beautiful points which never quite came off. Liverpool may have been bad up to the interval but what lucky little Canaries they were to be awarded a penalty for such a little offence.

Norwich showed the Livers that they were not going to have all the smart work to themselves.

Robbie was only a foot wide with a beauty, and Captain Raisbeck shaved the bar with an express. The Reds put the ball about with a vengeance, but their finishing was weak.

Jack Cox, who established a contemporary Liverpool record of 33 FA Cup appearances

January 15, 1910

Bristol City (1) 2
Burton 30, Ripon 50

Liverpool (0) 0

ON the Friday before the game the weather in Bristol was excellent, but overnight there was a change for the worse, and during the whole morning on the day of the game, there was a heavy and depressing rain which had its affect upon the pitch. Both teams did their training close by at health giving resorts and arrived in the pink of condition. Orr and Bradley were absentees, but Bowyer and McConnell - making his Liverpool cup début - had done so well that the change gave no cause for concern. The game brought a great excitement to the city, and the Reds were heartily greeted. A section of the crowd sang "Aye, aye, Stewart scored a goal" (referring to his hat-trick a week previously in a 5-1 home win against Chelsea) and the Liverpool skipper won the toss.

Rogers and Robinson were the first to make an advance in the centre, when a free-kick let in the Bristol right, but the home side's Hardy over-finessed and the chance was lost. Chorlton responded to a dangerous centre from Hardy by neatly heading away, and this relieved the early pressure. Gradually the Reds worked their way into Bristol territory where McDonald was prominent, but Clegg handled. Bristol - out to make amends for their 1-0 home defeat in the League against Liverpool back in October - would not be denied, and Gilligan crossed to the opposite wing in an effort to get his side going, but Robinson was aware of the danger and cleared. At this stage of the game it was apparent that both sides were nervous. Harrop failed to check Hardy and Gilligan - soon to become a Liverpool player - and the ball was transferred to the goalmouth. Hardy was out of his goal and missed his footing, and Ripon was on the point of scoring with an open goal at his mercy when Rogers came to the rescue. Liverpool had not settled as well as their opponents, and there was further cause for concern when Ripon forced his way in and Chorlton was beaten. The City forward got to the ball and returned almost into goal when Hardy got down to a very dangerous shot from Gilligan. The condition of the pitch militated against Liverpool's passing game, but they finally put together an aggressive move when McConnell passed to Stewart, but the Livers were unable to control the ball and posed no threat to Clegg. Wedlock was the chief cause of trouble to the Liverpool forward line as he continually nipped in and prevented any real cohesion. At last, Bowyer forced his way past Wedlock, and managed to outmanoeuvre Cottle. Just when it seemed that he would produce a powerful drive towards Clegg, Bowyer shot weakly.

Ripon and his right wing made an advance which neither Chorlton nor Rogers made much effort to check, and Hardy rushed out to anticipate Ripon, but he badly misjudged before Harrop dashed across to clear at the expense of a corner. When the kick was taken, no one effected a clearance. Ripon

John McConnell

was the first to measure up and got his head to the ball. It seemed a certain goal, but instead of entering the net, the ball struck an upright and, though Hardy was well beaten, it rebounded into play before Robinson cleared the danger.

Eventually Liverpool forced a corner through Rogers and the ball kept bobbing about in front of goal before being cleared. The Liverpool defence was always rocky and unreliable. Ripon led another attack and with Chorlton and Harrop well beaten, the City forwards were in a fine position close to Hardy when Rogers failed to check Burton, who let fly from close quarters and brought about the downfall of Hardy after thirty minutes' play.

The reverse stimulated the Reds and they settled down to produce some fine combination despite the conditions and ultimately Bowyer had Clegg well beaten with a rousing shot, the ball striking the underside of the crossbar and bouncing out again. McConnell appeared on the scene and dashed the leather across the goalmouth, but the opportunity passed by. Just before the interval Ripon should have scored again for the home side.

During the first half, Harrop, usually so sure and certain, made numerous mistakes, and even Hardy, who was so often the imperturbable, was as nervous as the proverbial kitten. On the other hand, the Bristol wings were a constant source of danger, with Shearman and Gilligan producing a sequence of several fine centres. They moved over the hard ground twice as fast as the Reds, and this fact alone accounted for their superiority. Ripon was far better than Parkinson.

Upon resuming Liverpool were soon on the offensive and a neat pass from Harrop opened the way to Parkinson who, wedged in between Annan and Cottle, looked likely to score until Clegg came out and robbed him. Although the Reds had opened promisingly, disaster was in store. Taking advantage of a long pass, Shearman raced along his wing, winding up with a grand centre. Chorlton was hard pressed, but he should have cleared, and, missing the ball altogether, he allowed Ripon to dodge past him and collect the leather to increase the score after just five minutes play in the second period. The City men became more and more aggressive and the Liverpool defence made blunder after blunder. Ultimately Chorlton let in Ripon who had an open goal at his mercy but the ball did not find the net. However, as the game progressed, the Liverpool forward line gave a better account of themselves, with Bowyer, Stewart and Goddard in particular producing some good football. The Reds' defenders, however, were never happy when danger threatened, for the Bristol men were far too speedy for them at all points.

Robinson produced several long-range efforts which hardly troubled Clegg, but Liverpool's extreme weakness was never more apparent than when Ripon in turn defeated Chorlton, Rogers, Robinson, and McConnell in a magnificent solo run which drew admiration from the crowd.

Bristol were full value for their win and for three-quarters of the game Clegg did not have a shot to save. Parkinson was overshadowed by Wedlock, and McConnell was rarely employed. Bowyer hit the post but was generally over anxious. The Anfield backs let the side down. They miskicked time after time and Ripon was a source of trouble in an aggressive team which found its form, while Liverpool suddenly lost theirs.

Bristol City: Clegg; Annan, Cottle; Marr, Wedlock, Spear; Hardy, Gilligan, Ripon, Burton, Shearman.

Liverpool: Hardy; Rogers, Chorlton; Robinson, Harrop, McConnell; Goddard, Stewart, Parkinson, Bowyer, McDonald.

Referee: Mr A. McQue (London)

Attendance: 10,000

James Stewart

January 14, 1911

Liverpool (2) 3
Bowyer 8, 10, Goddard 60

Gainsborough Trinity (1) 2
Coulbeck 40, Pattinson 85

IN the unfortunate absence of Longworth, the Reds called upon Alfred West, who was the only change in the team. Crawford made his Cup début for Liverpool. Gainsborough, languishing near the foot of the Second Division, were hardly expected to provide Liverpool with much opposition. Both teams received an encouraging reception and the Trinitarians looked strong and well.

The goalkeeper, Robinson, however appeared to be of rather small stature. Coulbeck led off, but was promptly checked by Harrop. Crawford and Harrop both failed to break up a Gainsborough rush, but "Robbie" was more successful. Goddard soon got away, but his centre went behind the post, and for some time the visitors were penned in their own half, their custodian ultimately having to rush out to deal with a centre from the left.

The efforts of the visitors were rather crude in the opening stages. The ground was soft and likely to become more difficult as the game progressed. Bowyer initiated a fine move which was taken up by Parkinson, Orr and Goddard and the right-winger gained a corner which was twice taken. The Reds' work was much the more stylish, in fact, most observers suggested that it was too stylish for Cup tie warfare.

Parkinson soon led an attack which puzzled Betts and Webster, and the Anfield skipper was well placed to receive but shot high over the bar, and an easy chance was gone.

After just eight minutes, West brought Parkinson into play. He put Bowyer in possession with a precision pass and the inside-left easily outmanoeuvred the backs to score rather easily past Robinson. From the restart the Reds forged ahead again with tricky footwork, Bowyer and Parkinson outwitting Jenkinson very comfortably. Betts and Webster presented timid opposition and Parkinson, in the manner of the first goal, threaded a pass through to Bowyer who, running in, deposited the ball in the net.

Robinson had a reputation as a useful custodian, but he made little effort to deal with the two shots which beat him. Liverpool, two goals to the good, indulged in unnecessary fancy footwork, taking liberties with the Gainsborough defence. The visiting attack was woefully weak and during the first fifteen minutes there was not a decent piece of combination or a solo effort. The Anfielders gave their opponents every opportunity, but the Trinity allowed themselves to be dispossessed with ridiculous ease.

Bowyer was venturesome in his methods and on one occasion he threaded his way through all opposition before giving Orr a great chance of scoring, but the inside-right fell at the vital moment. The "cat and mouse" tactics of the Anfielders nearly brought disaster when Masterman, making a sudden burst, shot beautifully, the ball glancing off the crossbar. As the game progressed, Webster showed more of his true form, and often put the bridle on McDonald and Bowyer. A corner fell to the visitors, but Harrop headed away comfortably. The heavy ground made things more difficult for the Reds and Trinity took more part in the game and Pattinson nearly beat Hardy with a glorious long drive.

The Trinity attack was always disjointed and unfinished, and against the polished and artful Anfielders the visitors appeared like a team of schoolboys. In justice to Pattinson, however, his shooting was the best on the field, though Hardy had no difficulty in timing them.

After 40 minutes, the visitors drew Crawford and Harrop, so that when the ball went to Coulbeck, he was unmarked with a clear line of fire. The centre-forward shot hard and true and reduced the arrears.

When the teams reappeared, Goddard led off with a fine movement, in which Orr and Parkinson joined. Bowyer was well placed for a shot at Robinson, but Parkinson's pass was too fierce. At this point a cheer went up from the crowd as Everton's successful score at the Crystal Palace appeared on the board. (Everton beat Crystal Palace 4-0 in Sydenham before about 15,000 spectators. Alex "Sandy" Young opened the scoring, while Magner, Gourlay and Robert Young completed the rout.)

West showed great hesitancy in his clearances. The Reds were able to attack with ease, but their finishing was woefully weak. Pattinson evaded all opposition in brilliant style, took the ball to the corner flag and passed in smartly to Tummon. The former Sheffield Wednesday man had a great chance of equalising but he skied the ball. This gave the Reds a fright, and they returned to the attack with vigour, responding with a series of raids which culminated in Goddard dropping the ball onto the crossbar. The Blues played better at this stage, and moved over the heavy ground as if they relished it. A corner kick was splendidly taken by Pattinson, and Hardy was compelled to give another in clearing.

The battle continued to be waged on even terms until McConnell, dribbling ahead, put a forward pass through to Parkinson, who similarly obliged Orr, but the little man stumbled as he tried to shoot. Harrop half-volleyed to Parkinson, who was robbed just in time by Webster. Goddard took up the back's return and, sprinting ahead like a racehorse, shot at ten yards range, beating Robinson with a glorious shot on the hour.

Two minutes later the Anfield captain made another startling venture. McDonald took his pass cleanly, but with a yawning goal, he headed wide. The Reds' third goal gave them an insatiable thirst for more goals, and for fully ten minutes they gave their opponents no quarter. The battle raged fiercely around Robinson's citadel, but Bowyer and Goddard were unfortunate in not being able to increase the score.

Five minutes from the finish Parker and Masterman attacked. West, Robinson and Harrop offered temporary respite until Masterman swung the ball out to the right wing, where Pattinson was lying unmarked. Hardy appeared to accept his fate and put up no opposition as the ball went speeding into the net.

Liverpool: Hardy; West, Crawford; Robinson, Harrop, McConnell; Goddard, Orr, Parkinson, Bowyer, McDonald.

Gainsborough Trinity.: Robinson; Webster, Betts; Tellum, Jenkinson, Lowe, Pattinson, Tummon, Coulbeck, Masterman, Parker.

Referee: Mr J.H. Pearson (Crewe)

Attendance: 15,000

Sam Bowyer, *who scored twice in the first ten minutes against Gainsborough*

February 4, 1911

Everton (0) 2
A. Young 51, 77

Liverpool (1) 1
Parkinson 23

ON the way to Goodison Park it was noted by contemporary reporters that there had been an alarming growth of taxi-cabs and motor cars. They had become a positive epidemic, suggested the reporter, who added that the cars kept up an infernal hubbub with their hooting and shrieking. The crowd was colossal, but the police arrangements, under the direction of Superintendent Tomlinson, meant that there was no undue crushing, and the ground was quietly and steadily filled. The crowd was in a particularly jubilant mood, and there was much harmless frolicking among them. In splendid contrast were the statuesque figures of four mounted police surrounded by a sea of excited faces.

The men stayed at Blackpool in the week before this game and returned on the morning of the match. Everton met at 1.30 at the Exchange Hotel and settled their team, which was without the services of Arthur Berry, who had sprained his ankle. Liverpool met on the ground. Goddard won the toss and Magner started at three o'clock. Alex 'Sandy' Young craftily wormed his way through several opponents and passed to Beare, who looked like being stopped by Robinson. The turf must have been greasy, for the half-back slipped and Beare got in a lovely centre which Crawford eventually cleared. From a Parkinson cross, Uren shot straight at Scott, but the ever-alert custodian saved comfortably. The going was indeed treacherous and Maconnachie once slipped near the goalmouth. Longworth's services were requisitioned on several occasions, and the doughty back - making his Cup début for Liverpool - seemed sound after his bad accident. Lacey and Gourlay played a forcing game on the right wing and drew Crawford well afield, so that Hardy was forced to come out of his goal on several occasions. The first time Longworth headed the ball he nearly beat Hardy who had to perform acrobatically. A Robinson free-kick for hands went directly to Scott, who handed the ball down. There was a sequence of interesting bouts between the Anfield skipper and Maconnachie, and the blue came off worst. Alex Young was the most dangerous forward on the field, but Robinson glued himself to Beare, and "Sandy's" passes were cleverly neutralised. From one of McConnell's passes, Orr put the ball over the bar. Stevenson dashed across to neutralise a forward pass from Orr, and following this McConnell shot into the "upper decker". Goddard repeated this feat after receiving a pass from Stewart. Accurate placing and shooting were difficult on the tricky turf. With the game 18 minutes old, the first deadly shot of the game arrived when Alex Young sent in a fierce drive which Hardy just managed to catch under the crossbar. Two minutes later the Reds were awarded a free-kick on the penalty line. At the first time of asking Mr Mason disallowed the kick. It was taken again by the Anfield skipper, and this time it puzzled the home defenders, who

were immediately in difficulties. The ball was kicked on to Makepeace, and Parkinson, obtaining from Stewart, hooked it in easy-going fashion into the net, Scott standing on his left leg.

This reverse infused plenty of vim into the Toffees, and they set to work in keen fashion in order to obtain an equaliser. They attacked vigorously from left and right, and followed up centres with fierce onslaughts in front of goal so that it appeared that Hardy's citadel must fall. During these charges, Hardy and Crawford were magnificent in defence. One straight drive from Gourlay appeared to have restored equality, but Mr Mason thought otherwise.

The luckless Blues did everything but score. Ten minutes before the cessation of hostilities, Harrop provided his captain in midfield, but Makepeace intervened and robbed. As the interval approached, the game quietened down, although the Blues continued to manipulate dangerously.

Upon resuming in a growing mist, Uren beat Stevenson cleverly, but was promptly tackled by Maconnachie. Crawford let in Lacey as Everton replied, and the Blues' outside-right centred for Beare and Young, who were both well-placed in the goalmouth, but they failed to take advantage of a glorious opportunity, although a corner accrued from which Magner tested Hardy.

Young gained another soon afterwards with some intricate footwork, and Hardy dashed into the fray to fist the ball away. A third corner was awarded to the Blues, and a mighty roar went up when Beare placed beautifully for Alex Young to head past Hardy and equalise. It was a well-deserved goal, for since Parkinson's simple effort, the Toffees had made strenuous efforts to redeem themselves. After the equaliser the feelings of the partisans became heated and intensified, and the slightest liberty taken by any player was heartily booed.

Longworth had not been so dashing as in the past, and up to the equaliser he had only headed the ball twice. Harrop, however, was always a great strategist, and dovetailed himself when occasion required between his two backs. A dangerous centre of Gourlay's was neutralised by Robinson and Crawford. Young was thwarted by McConnell at the expense of another corner and Hardy fisted out gallantly at the finish. The tactics pursued by both sides were to attack with great speed, and in the second half the Blues were excellent up front, while the Reds were resolute in defence. On one occasion, when Crawford made a bad mistake in the goalmouth, Magner and Gourlay had a great opportunity of scoring, but over-anxiety spoiled the chance. From a smart throw-in by Uren the Reds should have gained the lead, for

McConnell served up to Parkinson, who transferred to Stewart. The little man was unmarked, but spoiled a good chance by shooting wide. After 75 minutes Scott saved magnificently from Orr as the result of a clever move in which Stewart, Uren, and Parkinson all featured. After this McConnell and Crawford were well beaten, but Everton squandered the chance of taking the lead. The Toffees, however, held their ground, and "Sandy" Young sent in a wonderfully-deceptive shot which proved too speedy for Hardy. A minute later Gourlay struck the crossbar, and Everton attacked incessantly to the finish.

Over £1,000 was taken at the gates and probably another £800 resulted from the ticket sales.

Billy Dunlop said after the game, "I thought that in the first half we were good value for our goal. Although the free-kick was taken twice, it was an Everton player's encroachment that caused the ball to be placed a second time. Our men got into their work quite early, and Parkinson and Uren made some very fine efforts. I think that one of Hardy's best saves was off Longworth's head when the back misfielded the ball. It did not look much, but I am sure it was a good save. Then there was his great clearance from a ruck of players, and he thoroughly deserved the praise he received. "Sandy" Young was quite the outstanding figure on the field, and he was a hard nut to crack. Fortunately our men stood up nobly in defence, and the forwards, strengthened by the return of the captain, Stewart, and Uren, made some really solid efforts for goal. As

long as they kept hammering away they were relieving the defence, and there was no doubt that all of them were in fit condition. They played very much better than they have done for some weeks. Maconnachie, too, played a good steady game, but our half-backs and backs were not to be bested in the first half of the game at any rate. They were frequently tried, and were not found wanting. The referee and the play was good, and no one could grumble at the fare provided. I was delighted that we got the first stab in, because that means so much. Sandy Young was in great form throughout the game. Everton played better football in the second half, and they were very hard to hold. Parkinson was baulked frequently by offside ruling, but Stewart had a great chance of becoming famous, but he shot inches wide of the post. We had a hard nut to crack in Bob Young. Unfortunately for us, too, Scott was in grand order, and his save from Ronald Orr was a great piece of work. It was a low, awkward shot, but he cleared it quite cleverly. Sandy Young's leading goal came through a swift shot which Hardy did well to touch, although he could not prevent it passing over the line. Stevenson played particularly well in the second half, and my summing up of the matter is this: Everton were a shade the better team. They got the goals, and lasted better than our men. Well, the Reds played well, and deserve every praise, and I only hope now they will go strong in the League and rise from next Saturday onwards. One more word, "Good luck to Everton in the Cup fight."

The former Everton captain, Jack Sharp, stated that "Hardy made a save that would have beaten any goalkeeper of less ability. How he got the ball away was astonishing."

Ephraim Longworth

Everton: W.Scott; Stevenson, Maconnachie; Harris, R.Young, Makepeace; Lacey, Gourlay, Magner, A.Young, Beare.

Liverpool: Hardy; Longworth, Crawford; Robinson, Harrop, McConnell; Goddard, Stewart, Parkinson, Orr, Uren.

Referee: Mr J. Mason (Burslem)

Attendance: 50,000

January 13, 1912

Liverpool (1) 1
Parkinson 20

Leyton (0) 0

LIVERPOOL were unchanged from the team which beat Manchester City 3-2 away the previous week. Leyton were without the services of their left-half, Grey, and King took his place. The Londoners were at the bottom of the Southern League, having won just two games out of twenty played. They had drawn five, and lost thirteen games, scoring 13 goals, while conceding 42. They had just nine points, and were two points adrift at the foot of the table behind New Brompton. Goddard led the Reds on to the field, followed immediately afterwards by the Reverend Kenneth Hunt at the visitors' head. The visitors won the toss and elected to defend the Spion Kop end in the first half.

An abortive rush down into the Leyton area by Liverpool was followed by a sprint to the other end by Burrell. Lowe forced the ball into touch. For some minutes, the play was of an even character. Uren made several attempts to break clear, but each time his progress was impeded by the burly forms of either the Reverend Hunt or Leslie. Then Liverpool bombarded the Leyton goal without managing to find a way through. A rush by the visiting left wing was halted by the former Leyton player, Longworth. Stewart centred to Parkinson, who headed goalwards, and the goalkeeper fumbled the ball before finally scrambling it clear. A moment later Whitbourne safely dealt with a long-range effort from Harrop.

The Leyton forwards were applauded for some intricate passing which took the attack well into Liverpool's quarters. Busby, taking a pass from Coxon, looked like scoring until Harrop cleared at the last moment. During the first ten minutes, the visitors were largely employed in defence, only rarely troubling the Liverpool side. Following one of their attacks, Burrell gave Hardy a low shot to save.

Goddard centred as Liverpool responded and Parkinson sent over the bar with his head. The Leyton backs were stubborn in their tactics. There was a cry of disappointment from the crowd when, after good work by Bovill, first Parkinson and then Stewart failed to shoot when in a glorious position to score.

Liverpool drew first blood after 20 minutes when a breakaway by Goddard ended in Parkinson getting clean through between two defenders and flashing the ball into the net. Jack Whitbourne came out, and was within an ace of preventing a goal, but the ball grazed him as he finally flung himself at it and the Liverpool forward. The goal changed the complexion of a drab encounter as both sides redoubled their efforts.

Leyton came near to equalising with long swinging passes, and they worked themselves into a dangerous position. A great centre by Coxon enabled Burrell to run in and send in a powerful drive which Hardy did well to save. As the visitors fought hard and determinedly for an equalising point, Buchan hit the crossbar with a fine shot. Coxon's centres were particularly dangerous, and from one of these, Hardy was forced to make a fine save from a Buchan shot. The spirited display of the visitors won the sympathy of the crowd, who cheered them on heartily. After the Reverend Hunt had tested Hardy with a long shot, Burrell got in a neat sprint and Harrop intercepted his centre at the expense of a corner. Liverpool were playing poorly at this stage of the game. Hardy had to dart across the goal to keep out a close-range shot from Burrell. Uren carried play to the other end, and from his centre, Parkinson had a genuine goalscoring opportunity. His shot was weak, and Whitbourne kept the ball out with his fist. Another chance slipped by when a pass from Parkinson to Stewart saw the Liverpool inside man hesitate and finally fail to find the net. Moments later Parkinson sent in a high shot which the Leyton custodian diverted over the bar. At this point in the game, Liverpool created several opportunities, but their finishing was inept. Lowe earned ringing applause for a wonderful drive which struck the crossbar.

Early in the second half, great centres from both Liverpool wings were squandered. Whitbourne saved from Uren at the expense of a corner. The Leyton goal was almost breached moments later when Parkinson struck the goalkeeper with a shot from close range after a fine centre from the left. From the rebound Parkinson struck the foot of the post.

A stoppage occurred when Harrop was injured. He remained on the field, but he limped badly. Hardy saved a dangerous shot from Moles after good work on the Leyton right. Uren centred well and Parkinson again failed to score. Harrop then left the field, and Stewart fell back into the intermediate line.

Burrell, after showing Lowe a clean pair of heels, drove the ball into the side netting. A period of slack play followed, during which the spectators were not slow to show their disapproval. Harrop then re-appeared, but he continued to limp badly, and was not able to take his usual position in the play. The Leyton players were more hard-working and forced the Liverpool players into making numerous mistakes. Another fine centre by Uren saw all three inside men fail to connect with the ball. Parkinson made one of his spirited runs until he came into violent contact with Leslie, and turned somersault. The Reverend Hunt put in some excellent work, both in defence and attack, and on one occasion he brought Hardy to his knees with a powerful drive. Both teams indulged in some robust charging. In the next Liverpool attack, Parkinson sent in a strong shot which Whitbourne dealt with competently. Lowe then sent in a shot from long range, which was only inches wide. There was a further stoppage when Harrop was temporarily put out of action. There were cries of "Rouse yourselves!" from the home supporters, but the Liverpool side failed to respond to them. Uren then attempted a solo run, but after dribbling brilliantly, he finally placed his shot wide of the goal. A minute later Bovill drove over the bar. The visitors were largely occupied in defence, but from occasional breakaways they looked dangerous. Uren, having become disappointed with the number of his centres which had been wasted, now shot whenever he got the chance, and on one occasion Whitbourne only just saved in time one of the left wingman's shots.

Up to the last kick of the match, the Liverpool management were firmly of the opinion that a visit to Leyton would be necessary. One prominent official could not view the match at all; he paced up and down the corridors beneath the stand with his usually ruddy features wearing a strangely ashen hue. The Official Programme had foretold the result as a win for Liverpool with a margin of about four goals, but the prophecy was belied.

Whitbourne made a number of very creditable saves and acquitted himself in a manner which he had rarely excelled. It was thought that if he were able to reproduce the Cup-tie form in the Southern League, Leyton would not be at the foot of the table. At the start of the second half, he received a warm ovation from the crowd upon his re-entry to the field. Longworth was the best back on the field, but Newton was more subtle in his movements, and his old trick of flinging out his leg and hooking the ball away when it was apparently passing him by a yard, clearly outwitted his opponents. His speed was an asset, and allied to his cunning, he played a game of absolute brilliance. Leslie was an able partner, and the pair worked together with commendable understanding. At times Leslie was regarded as slow in his movements, tall and heavy players were often regarded as slow, but against Liverpool he was superb and his clean and clear movements were equal to Pursell's - the great Scottish capture, over whose signature one of their directors was suspended and the club fined £250.

The Reverend Hunt departed from his usual tactic of watching the outside man only. He was justly applauded for many splendid achievements by the sporting crowd. Mark Bell's play was uniformly good, as it had been throughout the season for the visitors. King began in disappointing fashion for the first ten minutes, but then he atoned for his poor display and was a worrier and a terrier to Liverpool. Both Busby and Coxon received excellent assistance from his forward passes.

Burrell, at outside-right, was the outstanding forward, and he caught the eye for his speed and courage and that instinct which all good forwards possessed. Buchan partnered him, and was a little more confident than usual and he took some considerable risks in view of his injured knee. Moles fed his wings splendidly, but had the problem of moving in semi-circles with the ball instead of making straight for goal. Coxon, although speedy and forceful at times, was too easily dispossessed. The Leyton defeat, even with the share of the £806 gate (which was almost the same as in Leyton's game against Chelsea), meant the loss of approximately £300 revenue compared with the previous season's total receipts from the Cup. Everton were drawn away against Clapton Orient, winning 2-1 with goals from Beare and Browell.

Liverpool: Hardy; Longworth, Pursell; Robinson, Harrop, Lowe; Goddard, Bovill, Parkinson, Stewart, Uren.

Leyton: Whitbourne; Leslie, Newton; Rev. K.R.G. Hunt, Bell, King; Burrell, Buchan, Moles, Busby, Coxon.

Referee: Mr W. Archer (Nottingham)

Attendance: 33,000

Receipts: £806

The wedding was solemnised at the Chapel Royal, Savoy, London, on the day of the game of Mr Victor D. Duval, the secretary of the Men's Political Union for Women's Suffrage, and Miss Una Stratford Dugdale, daughter of Commander Edward Stratford Dugdale, R.N., and niece of Viscount Peel. The bride was a prominent suffragist, and the parties had agreed that the amended form of the marriage service, in which the word "obey" was omitted, should have ben used. Before the commencement of the service, however, the Reverend Hugh Chapman, who officiated made a dramatic statement which went: "Before the commencement of the service I wish to state that, owing to the publicity given to it by the press, I have been compelled at the last moment to take advice as to the legality of a wedding with the omission of certain words which may not commend themselves to those concerned. Having been informed that the omission of these words is sufficient to render its validity at least doubtful, more especially in a Royal chapel which belongs to the King, we have agreed among ourselves to read the service throughout as an act of loyalty to his Majesty, while we sincerely hope that before long there may be an amended form of service which shall render it possible for Christian people to receive the blessings of the Church without hurt to their susceptibilities, and as we believe in the true spirit of the gospel of Christ." The marriage was then solemnised in the prayer book form.

February 3, 1912

Fulham (1) 3
Coleman 15, 66,
Pearce 50

Liverpool (0) 0

THE Liverpool team, accompanied by their chairman, Mr John McKenna and several directors, made the journey to London on the Friday afternoon before the game and were entertained in the evening at one of the halls. The players, all of whom reported fit and well, were out early in the morning, and they were hopeful of doing well against Fulham. During the night there was 20 degrees of frost on the grass, but under the influence of the sun, it had been reduced to eight degrees. The Craven Cottage pitch had been cleared of snow, and though all was done to reduce difficulties to a minimum, the going was somewhat dangerous. After several hours of sunshine, an inspection at two o'clock revealed that the top surface was lumpy and rather treacherous as the result of the playing pitch not having been rolled during the week. The central portion, from goal to goal, was liberally sprinkled with sand. The holding capacity of the enclosure was 52,000, and when the players took up their positions, there were close on 30,000 spectators present, and others were still filing into the ground.

There was a stiff breeze from end to end, and Longworth was fortunate in naming the coin correctly, though the sun was slightly against his side. Fulham went onto the attack first, but the forwards were at fault and Longworth cleared the danger. Lowe dispossessed Coleman, but Harrop fouled the ex-Evertonian and Pursell was forced to head out of goal. Fulham's right wing pair advanced and beat Pursell, sending in a cross to Brown, who, from just a few yards headed into the Liverpool goalmouth, but Hardy accurately anticipated the movement and safely gathered. From Hardy's clearance, Parkinson ran through and shot, but his effort hit the post.

Parkinson sped through the middle and put McDonald in possession, before taking a return pass and shooting at goal. Reynolds easily dealt with Parkinson's effort. Uren employed some neat little touches, but he had a strong opponent in Marshall. From a breakaway, Brown was well placed to test Hardy, but the lively ball beat him, and Longworth cleared. A fine tackle by Harrop prevented the next Fulham attack.

A fine sprint by McDonald concluded when he lost control of the ball and he could only drive the ball over the bar.

Pursell blundered over a high kick by Mavin, and before a recovery could be effected, Coleman broke clear for Fulham and took a fine pass from Pearce. He forced his way between the backs and Hardy, after hesitating to leave his line, was beaten after fifteen minutes when the ball entered the corner of the net.

The home side went straight back onto the attack, but the Liverpool backs displayed fine judgment and covered Hardy well. Liverpool's right wing was the most dangerous, but the close attention of both Sharp and Charlton prevented Reynolds from being tested. Bovill sent in a shot which was extremely wide, and the same fate befell a long-range effort from Lowe. Stewart and Uren advanced with great skill, but Bovill hung on to the ball too long and Liverpool lost a good chance of equalising.

The Anfielders changed their tactics. Having kept the play somewhat close, they opened it out by means of long swinging passes to the wing and they frequently presented problems for the home defenders.

The forwards' weakness was ineptitude in the final shot. Recognising that McDonald posed a great threat, he was closely shadowed by White and Sharp. Parkinson broke clear and beat Sharp before Mavin, the centre-half, out-paced him and pulled him up in the penalty area, where a strong appeal for a spot-kick was turned down. Bovill tried a shot from long range, but the ball passed over the bar.

A foolish handball by Bovill enabled Fulham to attack, but the danger was quickly cleared and Parkinson took up the attack only to fall short with his pass to McDonald. Harrop sent the ball well forward, but the Fulham custodian was first in the race for possession, and following his clearance, the game was halted for a minute or so through injury to Walker, who had slipped heavily on the hard ground.

Shortly afterwards Stewart shot from long range and Reynolds cleared with ease. From another breakaway, Coleman fastened onto a weak return from Longworth, and sent in a powerful shot which Hardy prevented from going in under the bar.

Upon resuming, the Fulham forwards threatened danger and for a long period the Liverpool goal looked certain of capture. Longworth relieved the pressure, and McDonald broke away to force a corner, which was cleared by Sharp. Fulham threatened down the left and Longworth challenged Walker and conceded a corner. This was superbly aimed, and the ball hit the front of the crossbar before Pearce - completely unmarked - headed into the net after only five minutes.

A further good movement by Brown and Walker caused Longworth a good deal of trouble, but the back stuck gamely to his work and repeatedly covered Hardy with sound judgment. Good work by McDonald provided an abortive corner and Walker, after a fine sprint, swung the ball across to Coleman, who went close with a header. Shortly afterwards, Coleman missed an open goal, but the clever little insider atoned for his mistake when, with the spectators leaving the ground in their hundreds, he took a great pass from Brown and scored with a fast ground shot which gave Hardy no chance of saving. The goal was timed at 66 minutes. The concluding stages of the game became almost uninteresting, and Liverpool were comprehensively beaten.

The Daily Chronicle
~~~~~~~~~

Corinthian writes: A fully inflated ball on a ground as hard as rock can only be controlled by the scientific mind and the agile foot. Such minds and such feet were more numerous in the Fulham team than in the Liverpool side, and that is why the Second Leaguers (in ninth place) not merely scored a deserved win, but quite outplayed the First leaguers. It is to the credit of Fulham that they made Liverpool look like one of the worst teams ever seen at Craven Cottage, where the home players performed as if they had made up their minds to play as fast as the ball. From about the third pass of the match Smith, the Fulham outside-right, allowed the quick-travelling ball to go beneath his upraised foot. That incident suggested many difficulties for the players in attempts to control the ball. The suggestion stopped at that stage, however, and Coleman, Brown, and Pearce gave a display of accurate short passing that would have done great credit to any three inside forwards on any sort of ground. The understanding between these three was so good that only Harrop, the Liverpool centre-half, could fathom their intentions. In every way the victory was splendidly won, and towards the end of the game the Liverpool players were as cold as the atmosphere.

The Daily News
~~~~~~~~~~~

D.D. writes: At Craven Cottage I had the almost unique experience of witnessing a winning team - Fulham - play always good and often brilliant football, and a losing team - Liverpool - give an incredibly poor display. Partisan crowds are deluded into believing that a home eleven have played well whenever they have won easily, whereas, of course, the less a team is extended, the fewer opportunities they have of displaying their capabilities. In this game, however, the Fulham players deluded themselves into believing that they were opposing a powerful First Division side, and so played at full stretch until their third goal came along. This spoof played upon themselves by the Fulham players was the finest tonic imaginable. Had Liverpool played up to their reputation a great game would have been witnessed. As it was the spectators merely saw an agreeably one-sided exhibition.

Fulham won simply because they were the better side, and had Smith been in top form at outside-right, Liverpool might have lost more decisively. Smith made several mistakes with his centres, and evidently preferred softer ground. Charlton and Sharp made superb full backs, and the halves maintained sterling form right up to the end of the game. Marshall was an able understudy for Collins, and in the centre Mavin kept the dangerous Parkinson under subjection. The Liverpool centre suffered considerably by comparison with Pearce, who received admirable support from both Coleman and Brown, while during the second half, Walker accomplished a number of brilliant movements on the extreme home left.

Fulham had beaten Burnley 2-1 in the First Round, and went on to beat Northampton by the same score in the Third Round, before losing 3-0 against West Bromwich Albion - the eventual finalists - at the Hawthorns.

The highest score of the round was Everton's 6-0 defeat of Bury in a Goodison Park replay. The original tie had also taken place at Everton's home ground.

Cricket
~~~~~

In Melbourne, the MCC were all out for 467 against Victoria. Hearne hit 143 and the Middlesex player's contribution was compiled in three hours and forty-eight minutes, and included twenty fours. He played admirable cricket throughout. J.W.H.T. Douglas's score then was 82, and he was finally out for 140, which occupied five hours and twenty-seven minutes. He hit fourteen fours. Stumps were drawn for the day with Victoria on 84 for the loss of six wickets.

The temperature in Melbourne was over 100 degrees for the fourth day in succession.

Weather
~~~~~

In the North-west of England the report was as follows: "South-easterly to Easterly winds, increasing strong to gale force in places; squally; changeable; snow; fair intervals; cold and frosty."

Fulham: Reynolds; Charlton, Sharp; Marshall, Mavin, White; Smith, Coleman, Pearce, Brown, Walker.

Liverpool: Hardy; Longworth, Pursell; Robinson, Harrop, Lowe; McDonald, Bovill, Parkinson, Stewart, Uren.

Referee: Mr R. Pook (Portsmouth)

Linesmen: Mr H. Thompson, Mr F.V. Winton

Attendance: 37,200

Receipts: £890

From a corner the ball hit the front of the crossbar before
Pearce *- completely unmarked - headed into the net after*
only five minutes of the second half.

January 15, 1913

Liverpool (2) 3
Goddard (pen) 27,
Peake 43, Lacey 90

Bristol City (0) 0

THE weather was fine and mild. Prior to the start, men were engaged prodding the ground with pitchforks in an endeavour to drain off some of the water. The pitch was waterlogged and quite sloppy, making conditions against good football, but both sides served up an exhibition of great excitement and interest throughout the whole ninety minutes. The middle of the ground was in a terrible condition, but along the touch-lines the surface was much firmer and the extreme wingers on both sides naturally derived great benefit from this advantage. The Liverpool forwards overcame a disposition to indulge in the short-passing game, and opened the game out to their advantage, securing a deserved victory against Bristol City. Under better conditions, the home side might have doubled their score, for it was the greasy condition of the ball which prevented accurate shooting. The young Bristol goalkeeper distinguished himself by a number of wonderful saves, and he was not responsible for any of the goals. In one fifteen-minute spell, nearly all the Liverpool forwards in turn tested him, Lacey with a centre, Miller with two tremendous drives from close range, and Metcalfe with a thrilling thrust. Liverpool were the better side in every department, and the West Country men were beaten by a team superior in skill and knowledge.

There were about 10,000 present when play began, but before the close the attendance numbered 15,000. Liverpool began brightly, adjusting to the conditions better than their opponents. They pressurised the visiting goal on numerous occasions, and Bristol were fortunate not to concede an early goal. The home side gained several corners, but these proved unproductive. Then Bowyer broke away and was beaten by Pursell before Moss finished by shooting a foot wide.

At the other end, Lacey broke clear and sent in a fine centre. Metcalfe met the ball, but he was fouled inside the penalty area by Nicholson. The referee swiftly acknowledged Liverpool's appeals for a spot-kick. Goddard took the kick and the Liverpool captain had the satisfaction of driving the ball into the corner of the net, just out of the reach of Ware.

Shortly before the interval, Harris made a solo run and beat both Lowe and Pursell before striking the foot of an upright with a powerful shot. Then the three inside forwards of Liverpool all had unsuccessful tries, the greasy ball accounting for inaccuracies in shooting. The home forwards indulged in some excellent footwork. For the first time in the game, the Bristol right wing got away, and the leather was swung about in masterly fashion before a cross was whipped in, from which Harris sent in a beautiful shot, the ball passing inches wide of the intended target. Then City came away in a fine combination and, after Campbell had cleared from Owers, Crawford cleared the danger.

Liverpool responded by moving down the left, and Peake steadied himself before scoring with a fast low shot which gave Ware no chance of saving.

In the second half Bristol fought valiantly to reduce the deficit, and the left-wing pair were dangerous on several occasions. Liverpool maintained their superiority, however, and their defence and attack worked skilfully and with great determination.

There were numerous genuine opportunities for Liverpool to have increased their lead, but it was not until the last minute that Lacey found some reward for his former attempts by scoring Liverpool's third goal with a swift shot which deceived the goalkeeper.

Collectively, Liverpool performed exceedingly well under difficult conditions. The forwards played well to a man, while the half-backs successfully broke up the Bristol attacks. Crawford and Pursell both performed well, and Campbell kept a clean sheet. Ware was brilliant in the Bristol goal, and he stopped the game from becoming a rout. The Westerners were a sturdy, hard-working side, but they were always out-classed by the home side.

In the other ties, Everton beat Stockport County 5-1; Aston Villa beat Derby County 3-1 away; Bury beat Southampton 2-1 at home; Woolwich Arsenal, playing with ten men in the

---

Liverpool: Campbell; Pursell, Crawford; Lowe, Peake, Ferguson; Goddard, Metcalfe, Parkinson, Miller, Lacey.

Bristol City: Ware; Kearns, Banfield; Young, Moss, Nicholson; Broad, Marrison, Owers, Bowyer, Harris.

Referee: Mr C.T. Lutwyche (Birmingham)

Linesmen: Mr E.J.B. Yeates (Chester);
　　　　　　Mr J.H. Alderson (Earlestown)

Attendance: 15,000

Receipts: £357 7s 6d

second half - McEachrane received an injury to his knee five minutes before the interval - beat Croydon Common 2-1 at Plumstead; Leeds City were beaten 2-3 at home to Burnley; Middlesbrough beat Millwall Athletic 4-1 at home in front of 10,000 spectators; Portsmouth lost against Brighton 1-2 at Fratton Park; Bradford and Barrow drew 1-1 in Yorkshire; and Huddersfield (at home) beat Sheffield United 3-1.

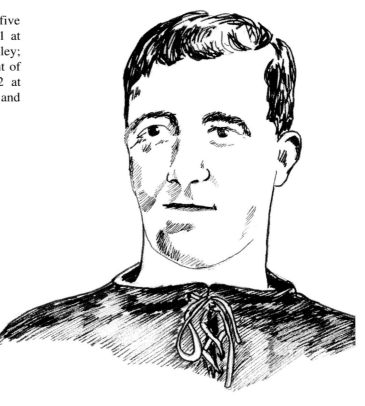

Ernest Peake

A SPOIL-SPORT PENALTY

ENRAGED CROWD AT ANFIELD

The spoil-sport penalty given against Bristol City against Liverpool at Anfield Road, yesterday ruined what would have been a splendid Cup-tie - probably the best of the round; and many of the Liverpool supporters were as much enraged as the City crowd.

For the first half-hour the game was a grand Cup fight, full of thrills, daring play, and characterised by tremendous energy and pluck, so that the spectators wanted nothing better than a straight fight to a finish and the best team to win. All their airy castles were rudely swept away by that disastrous spoil-sport penalty, which reduced a buoyant and exhilarating game to a red-tape anachronism. Football will die if it is to be fettered by such rigid rule reading which yesterday converted a fair, even fight into a deadening handicap of one team in a supposedly equal contest. I will go so far as to say that Nicholson, in charging Metcalfe, undoubtedly swung out his elbow, but that was all that was apparent, and having regard to the slippery ground, the excitement prevailing, and the fact that Metcalfe had not an open goal to shoot at, the referee might have issued a caution, and nothing more. The referee might reply that he had no option but to award a penalty, and that he could not have given a free-kick, while if he had failed to interfere the game would have got out of hand. In view of Metcalfe's position at the time, the whole matter could have been over-looked and nobody would have grumbled, for the unstable turf would have been a sufficient explanation to all and sundry. There were many queer tumbles and contortions during yesterday's game.

As a case in point, Lacey once jumped at the ball and Kearns got in the way, so that he was turned over on to the mud. The linesman signalled for a foul, and the crowd laughed. A man who jumps with opponents near him usually finds trouble, and does not expect to get a free-kick by so doing. But the crowd, too, were a little erratic, and after laughing at the penalty given against the City, clamoured for a similar decision for a lusty shoulder-charge and then applauded when Nicholson was also knocked over somewhat hurriedly...

But right through the game there were signs that the City had weighed up possibilities, and were using all their experience and craft to secure a favourable verdict...

I am glad to say the City gave Liverpool people a splendid impression, and they will be long remembered at Anfield Road. A comment by one of the spectators will convey the correct impression. It was, "What a game! ... Bristol all out to win ... Liverpool might have been in the cart, but for the penalty." Oh, that penalty!

ATTENDANCES AND RECEIPTS
~~~~~~~~~

	Spectators	Receipts
Derby County v Aston Villa	15,000	£658
Portsmouth v Brighton & Hove A.	16,000	605
Leeds City v Burnley	13,109	463
Middlesbrough v Millwall	13,000	458
Liverpool v Bristol City	15,000	357
Everton v Stockport County	10,000	277
Huddersfield v Sheffield United	8,187	250
Bradford v Barrow	8,500	248
Woolwich A. v Croydon Common	8,000	243
Bury v Southampton	6,666	226

STADIUM

TOMORROW (THURSDAY) AT 8
Great International Light-Weight Contest, 20 Rounds
PRIVATE BASHAM
(Newport), The Fistic Machine, Coming Light-Weight Champion)
v.
JACK LANGDON
(America). One of the toughest 10-stone men in the world. Was unluckily disqualified against Basham a few months ago after a rousing contest.

15 Rounds Contest: NAT WILLIAMS (Liverpool) v. KID LEWIS (Aldgate)
10 Rounds Contest: BILLY GERKIN (Hanley) v. FRANK BAKER (Liverpool)
Admission 1/- to 5/- Tel: Royal 647

February 1, 1913

Woolwich Arsenal (0) 1

Lewis 57

Liverpool (2) 4

Metcalfe 25, 66, 82,
Lacey 41

ARSENAL were having a particularly lean time and there was every hope that Liverpool would do well at Plumstead. The visitors were at full strength, while the home side were troubled over their team selection. The big gate did not materialise, probably due to the fact that Woolwich was difficult to get to. Seven thousand sixpenny tickets were sold prior to the Friday to Arsenal supporters, and the gate realised about £380, the ticket sales being a guarantee of £200. The ground was incredibly soft, though both teams declared that they liked the soft going better. The Arsenal were given a hearty cheer, while Liverpool's little band of supporters rallied the Reds. The Woolwich team were in white with red bands for the day. Liverpool won the toss.

There were approximately six thousand spectators present as Arsenal showed their style. They swung the ball about and hastened towards goal, only for offside to halt their progress. Parkinson and Miller produced some good football in the rain, but Miller fell in the mud as the attack was looking good. Liverpool broke down the opening burst of the Arsenal and got on top of them. Lacey went through smartly until the amateur Evans checked him. Shortly afterwards, Lacey got clear and centred, and though Metcalfe shot wide, the Reds attacked vigorously and Goddard, Metcalfe (twice), and Parkinson all had efforts saved. Liverpool had totally outplayed the home side in the first ten minutes, and Miller shot inches wide as the visitors kept up the pressure. Peake got a clump of mud in his eye and after he recovered, Burrell gave Campbell a really awkward shot which the Scot fielded in his usual crisp manner.

With 25 minutes gone, the Reds took a deserved lead. Goddard began the move, Parkinson shot hard, and the rebound was easily converted by Metcalfe.

A Goddard shot went for a corner, though corners had ceased to be as dangerous as in the past. Miller and Parkinson combined well up front, though at times there was too much close passing by the inside forwards. Crawford made a bold attempt to clear and wrenched his muscles. He was able to continue and helped to prevent Graham getting in a shot. Graham and Peake engaged in a little duel, and the referee had to call attention to their infringement of the rules.

With four minutes to go to the interval, Goddard produced a fine centre which caused the goalkeeper trouble. The ball went out to Longworth, who was placed well up the field, and he transferred to Lacey. The Irishman stumbled, but recovered just in time to get in a shot which McDonald tried to smother, but failed.

Lacey's goal was received with delight by the little band of Reds' supporters, and Arsenal's hopes of victory diminished. Just before the whistle, a Peake drive troubled McDonald.

Arsenal began the second half in the same manner as they had the first, and Campbell was called upon to produce a fine save. Goddard threatened to go through on his own when he was tripped up, and soon afterwards he went on a solo run but there was no-one to support him. Metcalfe drove the ball through Shaw's legs, but McDonald punched away the fast shot of the former Newcastle man. Liverpool were far superior, and Ferguson, Parkinson, and Miller all went close. Their combined efforts pulverised the Arsenal defence.

Eventually Campbell was called upon to fist away one shot and kick away another. One fine Liverpool movement involved Metcalfe, Goddard, Lowe, and Peake, and Metcalfe, beating a back, advanced on goal, only to screw the ball at too great an angle. Shot followed shot, and Lacey's fierce shot gave McDonald some anxiety.

Against the run of play, Arsenal scored twelve minutes into the second period. Burrell centred and Lewis headed powerfully into the net. Arsenal had to play Thompson at half-back due to his being injured, but the goal spurred them on to greater effort and twice Campbell had to save.

Gradually Liverpool re-asserted themselves, and an excellent move by the Reds brought a third goal. Parkinson, Goddard and Metcalfe combined well before Goddard was put in possession. He worked neatly for a better position, and answered Metcalfe's call for a pass.

Woolwich Arsenal: McDonald; R.Evans, Shaw; King, Sands, Thompson; Greenaway, Lewis, Graham, Flanagan, Burrell.

Liverpool: Campbell; Longworth, Crawford; Lowe, Peake, Ferguson; Goddard, Metcalfe, Parkinson, Miller, Lacey.

Referee: Mr R.W. Bussey (Northwich)

Linesmen: Mr H.G. White (Marlow);
Mr J.V. Lloyd (Hitchin)

Attendance: 8,653

Receipts: £343 10s 6d (7,000 tickets at 6d sold in advance)

Arthur Metcalfe, who hit a hat-trick against Woolwich Arsenal

The two sailors who had come to see Liverpool win gave the Woolwich spectators no peace, and the Reds gave the sailors a good chance to shine.

These jolly tars, with players, police, and cinematograph operators, had good fun, and the Arsenal were soon in the dumps and wanted some life.

Their forwards were weak, and their defence could not withstand the Reds' attack, which was cleverly conceived even if there were times when the ball should have been flung about instead of held so close. All the Reds played well in the first half, and Campbell was not given opportunity to show his work.

Liverpool had never won at Plumstead, but at half-time today the odds were on them achieving this feat.

The Reds' backs were in capital trim, and the half-backs, too, kept a level standard.

The Reds' forwards were keen on goals, and their unselfish combination and capitally-balanced football deserved more emphatic praise.

Metcalfe's three points were good ones but all the forwards contributed their share.

The Liverpool inside-right took the pass first time and slammed the ball well out of McDonald's reach. Liverpool were happier now that they had regained a two-goal lead. Arsenal fought on desperately in the hope of creating another opening, but Campbell's agility denied them. Three of the home side were semi-passengers due to injury, but there was no denying Liverpool's superiority. Eight minutes from time, Metcalfe scored his third goal.

THE PRICE OF PETROL

The latest rise in the price of petrol is accompanied by a mitigating statement to the effect that the combined oil companies intend to supply an article of better quality. This need not blind the eyes of the public to the fact that there is no note of finality about the present advance.

The world is being searched high and low for new oilfields, and wells, good, bad, and indifferent, come into the market daily; but still the demand grows apace faster than the supply.

As pointed out in this column a couple of days ago, oil is increasing in popularity as fuel for ocean-going steamers.

This is a comparatively new market, and it is a rapidly enlarging one. Motor traction also continues to expand all over the world, and so long as petrol remains the chief driving power relied upon, here is another source of demand which is always rising by leaps and bounds.

Artificial means, legislative or otherwise, to keep down the price of petrol must inevitably fail. They are apparently only resorted to in regions where the old belief is entertained that high prices are due to trusts and combines, and that these are illicit and ought to be smashed.

Whatever combines and rings may have accomplished in the past as affecting market prices, they are of little appreciable weight now as compared with the irresistible strain imposed by the law of supply and demand.

It is pointed out that the immediate effect of the present rise in the price of petrol has been to check forward business. There is a considerable future market, and contracts are well placed over the present year, owing to which fact it is that the spurt in price is immaterial in effect upon the protracted taxi-cab strike in London.

The companies owning the vehicles whose drivers are "out", have bought or contracted for the whole of their petrol for the present year.

A rise in present prices is, therefore, not an immediate factor in the situation, though it is not a negligible point by any means.

Every rise in price brings us nearer and nearer to the long-threatened period of famine, when some substitute will have to be found to relieve the world's want.

The contracts now being made for supplies for the year 1914 will, of course, be negotiated on the new terms.

February 22, 1913

Liverpool (1) 1
Lacey 14

Newcastle United (0) 1
Shepherd 52

A great game was expected at Anfield, for the meetings of Liverpool and Newcastle had always provided rousing displays. The clubs had met twice before in Cup warfare, with each team winning 3-1 on home territory. Gracie played instead of Parkinson, who was unable to play. Newcastle made a surprising move in bringing in Shepherd and Hibbert in the forward line.

The weather was excellent and the Liverpool club's arrangements were splendid, with 30,000 spectators being accommodated without a hitch forty-five minutes before the start. The megaphone man amused the crowd, who packed closer with good humour. A Territorial band whiled away the tedium of the wait, and were supported by hundreds who tinkled all kinds of strange instruments.

Liverpool: Campbell; Longworth, Crawford; Lowe, Peake, Ferguson; Goddard, Metcalfe, Gracie, Miller, Lacey.

Newcastle United: Lawrence; McCracken, Hudspeth; Hay, Low, Jobey; Rutherford, Hibbert, Shepherd, Wilson, McDonald.

Referee: Mr J.E. Hall (Olton)

Attendance: 40,000

When the teams appeared roars of greetings went up from 35,000 throats. At this time the gates had been closed, although there were a couple of thousand people outside, for the directors evidently had decided not to run any risks. It transpired that the International Board was present at the match. McCracken won the toss, and the game commenced at 3.19. Lowe and Goddard took the attack into Newcastle territory, but the referee's whistle twice checked the progress of the home side. From McCracken's free-kick, McDonald attempted to centre, but Peake headed away and a minute later Longworth ballooned the ball, which went out near the corner flag. Metcalfe relieved the tension, and Gracie dashed ahead, only to be anticipated by McCracken. Jobey put the sphere behind the goal as the Geordies were the first to get into their stride and it seemed as if the billiard board surface of the pitch suited their game.

An enthusiastic roar met Metcalfe, whose pass to Goddard was returned, and the inside-right found Ferguson, who drove goalwards. The Novocastrians continued to attack with persistence, but they were stoutly opposed by Longworth and Crawford. At length Miller was prominent, but before Lacey could receive his pass, McCracken got in a deadly tackle. Generally at this stage, the visitors were inclined to play a

dainty game, while Liverpool were determined to adopt bustling tactics. Newcastle played pretty football and most of their passes were neat and artistic. Still the crowd waited for Rutherford to disclose his genius. Low, always a dominant figure on the Newcastle side, stalked majestically and effectively and, backing up his forwards with dainty touches, he dominated the game at this point. The first corner fell to Newcastle, with Hibbert heading over.

Liverpool's three inside men, by artful play, nonplussed Hudspeth and McCracken, who were drawn out, leaving Lacey free. When the left-winger received he judged his shot carefully before firing, but Lawrence should certainly have saved it, instead of which he fumbled the ball, which appeared not to be goalbound. Lacey seemed fascinated as he watched the fate of his shot, but went frantic with joy when he saw it ultimately roll behind the goalpost.

For some minutes after this the game fluctuated, and there was a sequence of raids on both sides, but the only item of importance was a shot from McDonald which troubled Campbell. The Reds continued to play well within themselves until Peake got a kick on the nose. Goddard was also absent for a few minutes. Throughout the game so far, Rutherford was subdued. Ferguson's excellent pass found Miller, but before he could deliver to Lacey, the clever Hay got between the pair. Disaster nearly followed. McDonald, racing away, drew Crawford across, and Peake, falling back, evidently flurried, almost scored for Newcastle but for the alertness of Campbell. Ferguson played a magnificent game at this stage, and his craft and confidence bottled up Hibbert and Rutherford, who did not seem in fighting humour. A beautiful header from Peake broke up a stout Newcastle attack.

After 30 minutes, Liverpool were awarded a penalty kick, Low handling in the goalmouth when Lacey and Metcalfe were attacking strongly. Goddard took the kick and sent the ball straight at Lawrence, who saved easily. This was immediately followed by a sensational incident at the other end. Rutherford got clean away from Crawford, and looked certain to score but Campbell excelled himself with a dexterous save at close quarters. Rutherford had missed his chance and seemed incapable of doing anything brilliant in this game. Ten minutes from the interval, the Geordies attacked strenuously, but Peake was in outstanding form.

During the interval a loud cheer greeted Everton's success at Bristol, where the Toffees beat Rovers 4-0 with goals from Jefferis, Fleetwood, Harris and Browell. When the Reds restarted, they were encouraged by a din of hundreds of buzzing rattles and tinkling bells. Rutherford at once opened out strongly, thus showing a determination to improve upon his dismal first half display. McDonald beat Lowe and centred dangerously before Crawford headed away.

A minute later Hibbert shot high over the bar. The visitors attacked with vengeance and Liverpool had little response at this point. Fortunately for Liverpool, the Newcastle shooting was inaccurate. Lacey gained a corner and Lawrence ventured out to save, but immediately afterwards Ferguson shot at the goalkeeper.

Newcastle again took up the attack and gained a free-kick when Wilson was impeded. Crawford saved in the first instance, but the attack developed and Campbell was almost overpowered and consequently forced to carry the ball, for which he was penalised. Mr Hall gave a kick to the visitors which was taken by Shepherd from two yards. It seemed impossible to pilot the ball through the crowded goal, but Shepherd succeeded in doing the trick and placed his side on equal terms.

Following a raid on the Anfield goal, McDonald pulled Campbell to earth, and Mr Hall had to caution the former Liverpool player. The Spion Koppers, with one voice, expressed their disapproval of such Rugby tactics. Wilson was the mastermind of the Newcastle attack, and was always keenly alive to any chances that came his way, and he fought with all the tenacity of a half-back, but his subtle passes were sometimes too clever even for his own men.

During this period the Reds were confined to their own quarters and seemed unable to make a successful sortie. Gracie had not proved a forte in the centre and it was seldom that the Anfield attacks carried any real threat. However, a great pass from Lacey was missed by all the inside forwards when a goal seemed imminent. Soon after, Gracie - who had not been very prominent - tested Lawrence with a strong shot.

Longworth failed badly to stop the flying McDonald, who tested Campbell with a lovely shot. With half an hour gone, the home goal had a miraculous escape, for both backs let in Rutherford, who had a clear passage in the centre. Disaster seemed certain, when Campbell came out and flung himself at the feet of the Novocastrian.

The ball was blocked and the goal was saved, but Campbell lay inanimate, while Rutherford regained possession but he failed to find the net. Several Newcastle players joined in the fray, but were too excited to gather the ball and net it. Ultimately the referee saved Liverpool. The Reds were disorganised at this point, and Rutherford was a real powerhouse this half, and had something to do with most of the Newcastle attacking moves.

Aston Villa, with Sam Hardy in goal, beat Crystal Palace 5-0 at Villa Park.

Billy Lacey,
seemed fascinated as he watched the fate of his shot, but went frantic with joy when he saw it ultimately roll behind the goalpost.

February 26, 1913

Newcastle United (1) 1
Hudspeth (pen) 33

Liverpool (0) 0

IT was early closing day both in Newcastle and the surrounding districts and there were numerous excursions from towns far and near. There was a good muster of Sunderland supporters all intent on seeing the struggle which was to furnish the eleven to visit Roker Park in the next round. The excursion train from Liverpool was over an hour late, but still the enthusiasts from Merseyside, numbering several hundreds, arrived at the ground in ample time to witness the start. They were an enthusiastic band, most of them freely sporting the colours of the Reds, and being well provided with rattles, penny whistles, and, above all, lusty lungs. The spectators also included the Everton players, who were to appear at St.James's Park on Saturday.

The day opened dull, but the mist of the morning disappeared by noon, while the state of the ground was acceptable. Parkinson did not make the journey, and at the last moment the Liverpool directors decided to re-arrange their forward line to the exclusion of Gracie. Miller was given the centre-forward position, Lacey taking the inside-left berth, and McKinlay being introduced at outside-left. No change was made in the rear division. The only alteration made in the Newcastle team was at half-back, Jobey being deposed in favour of Hewson, with Hay crossing over to the left half-back position. This was Hewson's début in the Cup.

No increase was made in the admission charges, and there were about 40,000 present when the game began. Liverpool won the toss and Newcastle started the game with the advantage of a slight breeze.

Liverpool began well and a forward pass by Ferguson led to Lacey darting forward, and a corner followed, which was without result. Liverpool were attacking strongly when Metcalfe and Wilson banged their heads together and the game was held up for a few minutes. Upon resuming, Newcastle attacked and dangerous work by McDonald and Wilson threatened the Liverpool goal, but the dependable Longworth nipped in and cleared. After a fine run, Goddard put over a great cross but the inside men were too slow to react and the opportunity passed. Moments later, Goddard was limping, and it was evident that he felt the effects of a back injury sustained on the Saturday. Both sets of forwards were not playing well. A fine run by McDonald was wasted when Shepherd was too slow to accept his pass, and Peake cleared the danger.

At the opposite end, Metcalfe broke free and passed to Lacey, but the Irishman failed to receive the ball inside the area. There was little to choose between the teams at this point, and the Liverpool halves broke up the Newcastle forward-line's attempts in a resolute manner. Then Liverpool attacked through Metcalfe dribbling cleverly, but his final pass out to the left led to McKinlay being stopped for off-side. For the next few minutes, Liverpool attacked relentlessly but lacked penetration. Metcalfe had a fine chance, but he chose to send the ball out to the left instead of shooting for goal. On another occasion, Hudspeth was too quick for Miller.

A free-kick against Liverpool enabled Hibbert and Shepherd, who were only a yard or two from goal, to receive the ball, but Crawford realised the danger and cleared with a magnificent overhead kick. The home side attacked once more, and Crawford found himself in difficulties. He kicked the ball back to his goalkeeper, and Campbell fielded well. Shepherd then cleverly tricked Longworth and shot at goal with great power. The ball struck Crawford and was directed across to the left side of the goal, but Campbell sprung across and saved brilliantly. Crawford had the wind knocked out of him, and the game was stopped while he recovered.

Rutherford, who had been comparatively idle up to this point in the game, ended a fine run with an excellent centre from which McDonald headed over the bar. Hibbert was put in the clear, and as he was tackled by Crawford, Campbell sprung forward and turned the ball round the posts with his finger-tips. As Newcastle continued to attack, Wilson brought Campbell to his knees with a stinging drive. Rutherford dribbled cleverly past all opposition before passing to Hibbert, who grazed the near post with a powerful drive. With Goddard already injured and scarcely being able to run, Crawford was injured. McKinlay was forced to fill in at left-back, with Crawford going outside-left. Soon afterwards, Shepherd broke free but shot wide.

During a period of intense Newcastle pressure, Lowe, the Liverpool half, knocked the ball down with his elbow inside the penalty area from a centre by Hibbert. Hudspeth was entrusted with the kick, and he banged the ball into the net with a fierce strike which gave Campbell no chance of saving. Crawford left the field soon afterwards, and at this stage, Liverpool were completely demoralised.

Shepherd missed numerous openings, and the crowd howled its disappointment. He was well within shooting range when he preferred to dribble, and Longworth frequently dispossessed him. Rutherford shot wide as Newcastle continued to maintain their dominance. Crawford returned to the fray in the left-back position, and Liverpool resumed the attack. Metcalfe, after a fine run, passed to Miller, who was unmarked, but the centre-forward shot yards wide after steadying himself for a shot. Metcalfe showed his displeasure towards Miller for missing a genuine chance to equalise.

Twice McKinlay allowed McCracken to put him in an off-side position, but after some fine combination, Liverpool attacked but Miller wasted the chance. One exciting incident in front of the Newcastle goal ended with Peake having a great shot charged down.

Liverpool began the second half with McKinlay at left-back and Crawford at outside-left. The Reds were handicapped in having two passengers on the extreme wings. A long kick upfield by Hudspeth put McDonald in possession, and Longworth was forced to concede a corner. The kick, taken by McDonald, was well placed, and Shepherd headed towards goal, but Campbell effected a fine save. A breakaway found Crawford in possession, and he put in a low centre, but Lawrence rushed out and kicked clear.

In the next Newcastle attack, Liverpool almost conceded a second penalty for the use of hands, but the referee ruled otherwise. McDonald hit the side-netting as the home side pressurised the visitors.

Miller and Lacey changed places in an attempt to inspire Liverpool, but Newcastle had the better of the exchanges. Goddard, Metcalfe, Lacey and Crawford combined well before Crawford put too much screw on his shot, and Lawrence dashed out to save. Shepherd twice failed to beat Campbell when he was immediately in front of goal, and on one occasion he was presented with an opening when Longworth miskicked. Throughout the second period, Longworth dispossessed Rutherford and Shepherd on numerous occasions in a brilliant defensive display.

With twenty minutes to go Miller hit the underside of the Newcastle bar, and Lawrence deflected the ball for a corner, which Liverpool failed to capitalise upon.

Newcastle United: Lawrence; McCracken, Hudspeth; Hewson, Low, Hay; Rutherford, Hibbert, Shepherd, Wilson, McDonald.

Liverpool: Campbell; Longworth, Crawford; Lowe, Peake, Ferguson; Goddard, Metcalfe, Miller, Lacey, McKinlay.

Referee: Mr C.T. Lutwyche (Birmingham)

Attendance: 45,000

CENTRAL LEAGUE

Liverpool defeated Blackburn Rovers in a Central League match, at Anfield, by one goal. There were 5,000 spectators. Football of a very moderate character was served up, the forwards on both sides exhibiting a most elementary idea of scoring. In the first half Thompson scored for Liverpool, and a scrambling game ended in Liverpool's favour.

THE GREATEST BARITONE

Sir Charles Santley, who was undoubtedly the greatest baritone of the Victorian age, celebrates his 79th birthday tomorrow. He was born in Liverpool on February 28, 1834. His first London appearance was in 1857. He was knighted in 1907.

THE DAILY DISPATCH

It was an almost funereal affair in the second half; in fact, one might have thought the teams were playing a friendly game but for the amount of instructions disseminated among the rival forces by McCracken on the one side and Longworth on the other. It was really a fine talking match, but the football generally would not have done credit to many minor organisations. Newcastle were at their best in defence, where Lawrence, although he had practically nothing to do, brought off the great save which retained Newcastle's lead, and McCracken played with extraordinary effect and coolness, although throughout the game his voice was heard.

Hudspeth was sound and placed well, and at half-back the solitary change which Newcastle made was clearly one for good, as Hewison, who was at right half-back, was the best worker of the day, and the initiator of many of Newcastle's most dangerous efforts. Low was as steady as ever at centre half-back, and Hay accomplished fine service against Liverpool's best wing forward. However, Newcastle were a curious and disappointing mixture.

Although Shepherd managed a couple of great shots in the early stages of the game, he missed at least three scoring chances. The best work in the line was accomplished by the wingers, Rutherford and McDonald, both of whom, however, tapered off into mediocrity in the second stage. Wilson, the victim of an early accident, was always below par, and though Hibbert did many clever things, it could not be said that there was a good understanding between the ex-Bury forward and Shepherd. Shepherd was slow in movement and lacking in what used to be his strongest point, marksmanship.

Liverpool perhaps did not do so badly considering their handicap, for both Crawford and Goddard were practically crocks. Goddard, however, was always an effective fighting force. Campbell and Longworth were the best of the defence, and Lowe and Ferguson impressed more than did Peake at half, while in a handicapped attack Metcalfe and Miller were easily the most useful men, though the line as a whole was dominated by Newcastle's defence.

Newcastle were the better of two poor sides, but cannot hope to extend Sunderland on such unconvincing form.

THE LIVERPOOL ECHO

Newcastle won by a penalty goal. Apart from that shot Campbell was seriously troubled once during the ninety minutes, and that was when Shepherd got in a fine drive that would have just skipped over the bar. Campbell, however, took no risks, and edged the shot over the bar. Goals are the essence of the game, and Newcastle looked like scoring a dozen times, and failed wretchedly. Lawrence was busy attending to shots from all ranges. The other day we were told that a referee had said that Liverpool's players were never any trouble to a referee, as they took the decisions with good grace, and were sports. They showed what little trouble they are to the ruling officials. I think Lowe was about the only man who protested that he had not handled the ball. Some players protest too much, but in a case like this, with a vital issue, I think a vigorous protest from the players would have made the referee call in the aid of the linesman.

January 10, 1914

Liverpool (1) 1
Lacey 39

Barnsley (0) 1
T ravers 70

BARNSLEY visited Anfield for the third time in Cup ties, and Liverpool hoped to complete the "hat-trick". When the players turned out, the weather was extremely misty and it was felt that the game might not be concluded. The surface of the ground was well sanded, in spite of which it promised to prove treacherous. Liverpool started aggressively, rapidly forcing progress on their left wing, when the ball was swung into the centre and Wigmore nervously kicked over the goalline, deciding to concede a corner. It came to nothing, McKinlay being given offside. Barnsley retaliated with a scrambling attack into home territory.

The opening stages promised a rough and tumble type of game. Following a free-kick, Bratley shot for goal, but Pursell headed away strongly. The Reds made headway through Sheldon until he was pulled up for offside before being unceremoniously grassed by Bethune. On the other wing, Barson indulged in some dangerous high kicking. With ten minutes gone, the game developed sensationally as the home defence broke down with Fairfoul slipping and letting in Halliwell, who shot dangerously. Campbell effected a brilliant save to deny the visitors. Barnsley's rough and ready methods proved disconcerting to the home defence. Sheldon initiated a fine attacking movement involving most of the home forwards, but the route to goal was blocked. Barnsley were persistent and swung the ball about well and indulged in long passing which created problems for Liverpool. At length a beautiful shot by Dawson was saved by Cooper.

The Yorkshiremen did not waste time with fancy passing, but played so vigorously that it was a question of time whether their stamina would hold out. Moore was of an enterprising turn of mind, and effected several useful centres and he also shot well. A long shot from Lacey went wide as the home side attacked without real conviction. Lowe was a rare policeman in the centre, frequently dribbling the ball and gaining many yards on his opponents. With twenty minutes gone, the visitors continued to prove awkward opponents, and their lusty methods suggested that injuries would play a part in the game. Indeed, McKinlay was the first to suffer from the uncompromising methods of the visitors, who seemed experts at high kicking, and made free play with their legs. A Barnsley rush originated from a centre by Moore, and the ball was followed up with such over-zealousness by the visitors that a hand-to-hand encounter took place, and the referee had to speak with several players before play could resume.

Dawson was particularly useful on his wing, beating Barson repeatedly. Two of his centres should have brought goals, but both Lacey and Parkinson headed over. At the other end Halliwell eluded Longworth and shot low and hard at Campbell, who saved on his knees. After this attempt by the visitors, Liverpool took up the attack and a fine concerted move in full line terminated with a great shot from Lacey, which Cooper timed accurately. For fully ten minutes the home side had asserted themselves, but as the interval approached Barnsley delivered several severe onslaughts and Campbell came out to a great shot from Bartrop and also on the right wing he staved off Moore and Tufnell. McKinlay was weak in the home half-back line, and Pursell consequently was handicapped.

Six minutes before the half-time whistle, Sheldon allowed the ball to go out, but from the throw-in the Reds took a grip in midfield. Sheldon, Lacey and Parkinson made progress together and Lacey caught Cooper napping with a long drive which had just enough room to pass between the goalkeeper and the upright. It was hoped that, having gained the lead, the Reds would develop more confidence in themselves which had been their chief drawback, as there was no doubt that they were much cleverer than the visitors.

Restarting, the Reds raced clean through the opposition and a rasping shot from Parkinson sent the ball skimming over the bar. Lacey, Miller and Dawson combined effectively but Miller's shot was tame. Liverpool's goal had clearly motivated them and they attacked with more venom. Barnsley, however, were not to be denied. Bartrop was a fine, clean-limbed fellow, and his long legs were a continual source of anxiety and perplexity to McKinlay. Barnsley gained a corner and Bartrop manipulated the ball smartly causing Campbell to punch downfield with both fists. Downs' grand back game was a feature of the game, and his energy and resource seemed inexhaustible. Downs dribbled the ball right into the Anfield goal area before he passed it to his forwards.

Sheldon had not played as well as could, and he was always well marked by Wigmore and Bethune. Lacey, on the other hand, caused Down and Bethune more trouble than all the other forwards put together.

Barnsley were always threatening in their methods, and invariably came off well in struggles for possession. Their long passes were always teeming with possibilities, and from one of them the equaliser eventually arrived. Moore swung the ball across and Travers, running in, shot hard between the Anfield backs. Unfortunately for Campbell, the ball first struck the underneath of the crossbar, and the goalkeeper failed to locate it. Travers was warmly hugged by half a dozen of his colleagues in celebration of his success.

Miller, Parkinson and Lacey featured in an excellent attacking move and Parkinson would have scored had not Cooper tipped the ball over for a corner. From a corner kick in the last minute Campbell made a miraculous save.

Liverpool

Campbell

Longworth Pursell

Fairfoul Lowe McKinlay

Sheldon Lacey Parkinson Miller Dawson

James Dawson was particularly
useful on his wing

Moore Tufnell Halliwell Travers Bartrop

Wigmore Bratley Barson

Bethune Downs

Cooper

Barnsley

Referee: Mr H.S. Bamlett (Gateshead) **Linesmen:** Mr A. Roberts (Wigan); Mr E. Connor (Southport)

Attendance: 33,000

January 15, 1914

Barnsley (0) 0

Liverpool (0) 1
Lacey 89

THE weather was fine, and the excursion trains brought big crowds from Sheffield and the environs, whilst the special train from Liverpool carried 800 people, and it seemed likely that the gate would constitute a record one. Liverpool played McKinlay at outside-left, Dawson being unfit. Ferguson re-appeared in the half-back line and his inclusion was in the hope that he would add strength to the side. Barnsley had given itself up to the occasion. The shops were closed, and the ground, which was perched on the shoulder of a hill just outside the town, was well-filled three-quarters of an hour before the start. The pitch, though on the soft side, presented fairly good going. There were two changes in the home team, Royston appearing for Wigmore and Griffin for Moore. There were 20,000 spectators present when the rival captains tossed for choice of ends. The Liverpool players wore the colours of Newcastle United, which seemed to make them more robust than ever. The Barnsley men, in their brilliant red shirts, looked extremely fit as Parkinson kicked off.

There was little advantage in winning the toss as there was only the merest suggestion of a breeze. Lacey passed out to the left wing, and from a short pass by Parkinson, McKinlay was ruled offside. Liverpool immediately returned to the attack, and from a forward pass by Lowe, Parkinson was pulled up for offside. After a period of midfield play, Barnsley moved down the right and Travers headed wide. The home forwards settled down strongly on the right, but Pursell offered stubborn resistance.

Lacey put Sheldon in possession, but the latter shot tamely over the line. Soon afterwards, Lacey tried a daisy-cutter, but Cooper had no difficulty in saving it. Barnsley retaliated and became busy down the right, Pursell miskicked and Liverpool conceded a corner. This led to a tremendous mêlée in front of Campbell and only a huge punt upfield by Lacey relieved the pressure. Both sets of forwards looked over-anxious. At length Tufnell got clean away at top speed, and he was sailing straight for goal when he was pulled down unceremoniously by Longworth. Nothing resulted from the free-kick. Then Bratley beat three opponents before firing wide. A series of miskicks let in Liverpool, but Parkinson had a tendency to keep getting caught offside, and he was penalised on three occasions. An excellent tackle by Halliwell was loudly cheered, but Pursell turned the tables and Liverpool enjoyed a period of heavy onslaught on the home goal. Parkinson headed wide and Miller missed an opening. They kept the Barnsley backs fully employed and Lacey ought to have scored from a Sheldon lob. The interval arrived without a score.

For twenty minutes after the interval Barnsley dominated the game and the Liverpool defence was under severe pressure. It was generally felt that Liverpool would not win if the game went to extra-time because the Barnsley men were strong and in the best of condition, but trainer Connell had got the Liverpool eleven extremely fit and in fact, it was the home side which tired, and Liverpool looked stronger in the final twenty minutes.

Liverpool's defence throughout the game was rock-like; there was some doubt, however, as to whether they could score. Barnsley gave Liverpool a lesson in shooting as often and as hard as possible. Nevertheless, five minutes from time Parkinson received the ball from McKinlay and screwed the ball outside when scoring seemed easier. Travers then dashed forward and shot and it seemed that he would turn Parkinson's miss into a tragedy until he, too, failed to score. Lowe injured himself in trying to score and then Lacey attempted a shot which was too weak and lacking in direction to trouble Cooper.

The relentless pace continued and with just one minute remaining Liverpool attacked down the left wing. Parkinson gained possession before passing along the ground towards the opposite wing. It seemed that Lacey would not reach the ball since he was near the centre-forward but he strode out in his own peculiar manner and put the ball to Cooper's right, the goalkeeper covering his left-hand side. Liverpool had won the tie, and Lacey had worked like a tiger. He was the only forward who looked like scoring. If ever a forward deserved to score for his general contribution and tireless devotion to the cause, it was Lacey. There was little wonder that the crowd of Liverpudlians transposed the song of "*1906*" and made it "*Aye, Aye, Lacey Scored the Goals.*"

In general the Liverpool forwards had been disappointing. They were up against do-or-die backs and tough half-backs, but the extreme wing work was abysmal.

Bethune, in particular of the Barnsley players, was an especially strong back who cut in rather dangerously at times, and doubtless his tactics made Sheldon a trifle anxious for his limbs, though the Manchester man is full of pluck. Sheldon showed up well in the final minutes, but he did not perform well in the cloggy going.

McKinlay was good in parts but his centres too often hit a defender, whilst he and Parkinson had offside called against them far too frequently. Parkinson was unable to do more than pass the ball out to his wings. He was well held by Bratley and Downs; in fact, Downs was so impressed by his easy task that he began to take abnormal risks, and his dribbling and dallying in front of his own goal contributed to his side's downfall.

There were three occasions when Downs courted and found defeat, so the famed back blotted his copybook. The

Liverpool forwards must overcome their shyness in front of goal and their increasing determination to pit-pat the ball until it is in a perfect position for a shot. The ball was too frequently made "dead" before a shot.

Campbell was brilliant. His pick-up was clean, his kick was long, and the way in which he positioned himself for shots was excellent.

The ball generally went head high, and Campbell took it like a first-class wicket-keeper. It was a great exhibition of goalkeeping from the Cambuslang player, who was regarded as one of the greatest custodians in the world.

In front of him were two resolute backs of infinite strength and grim determination and a knowledge of how and when to cut in. Pursell had most of the work to do at the start, but things evened out and Longworth did some things which only Longworth would attempt.

Fairfoul, Lowe and Ferguson were an excellent half-back line. Fairfoul never wasted a ball. He passed along the ground and gave his men every chance to push for goal. Lowe's captaincy was as useful as his dogged play. He dominated the game with his tremendous heading, his breaking up, and his passes to the right wing.

Ferguson's return meant a strong link in the half-back line. The club have another man, in Ferguson, who passes along the ground and gets his forwards going.

Miller, while not shining brilliantly, did some useful work and he had the misfortune to be pushed in the back by Bratley without receiving a penalty.

Barnsley's backs were sturdy. Bratley was like Bob Clifford. In the forward line, the inside three were best. Tufnell was artistic, Halliwell fiery, and Travers possessed a powerful shot. Royston, a local player, was useful, being built on the right lines.

Former Liverpool players were present in George Fleming, Charlie Wilson, Bobbie Robinson, Joe Hewitt, and Mike Griffin (who played on the left against Liverpool).

Bob Ferguson, the Liverpool half-back, had lost his dog. A reward was offered to anyone who found the Airedale terrier, which answered to the name of "Nancy". Ferguson asked to be informed at 162 Stanley Park Avenue.

Before the game, the Anfield men received a telegram from the charming and popular Miss Nora Delaney, of the Shakespeare Theatre, wishing them luck.

Barnsley: Cooper; Downs, Bethune; Barson, Bratley, Royston; Bartrop, Travers, Halliwell, Tufnell, Griffin.

Liverpool: Campbell; Longworth, Pursell; Fairfoul, Lowe, Ferguson; Sheldon, Lacey, Parkinson, Miller, McKinlay.

Referee: Mr H.S. Bamlett (Gateshead)

Attendance: 23,999

Kenneth Campbell, was regarded as one of the greatest custodians in the world.

January 31, 1914

Liverpool (0) 2
Lacey 81, Ferguson 83

Gillingham (0) 0

LIVERPOOL played Sam Speakman in place of Longworth, who was ill, and McKinlay for Nicholl, who was ineligible. Gillingham were at full strength, and brought a number of excursionists with them. There was a genuine crush at Anfield, and the Kemlyn Road stand was closed long before the start.

Some of the visitors' supporters appeared to have a grievance, but they did not seem used to finding their way about in a large crowd. There were gloomy clouds overhead which threatened rain, but the squally wind of the early morning had subsided somewhat.

McDougall kicked off but Lee, the Gillingham pivot, did not shape too well in replying to Liverpool's challenge, although he recovered himself and the Southerns became aggressive. Speakman - making his Cup début, along with McDougall - kicked away three times, but Pinkney gained the ball and had a shot at Campbell.

In winning the toss Gillingham had secured the wind, and Liverpool's best policy was to keep the ball low and so avoid having it returned into their own goalmouth. At length Pinkney gained a corner, from which Hafekost headed over. Seven minutes had elapsed, and Liverpool had showed no sign of their attacking flair. Lacey, McDougall and Miller were involved in a move which ended with McDougall being grassed by Mosley as he was about to shoot.

With ten minutes gone, the Reds went within an ace of opening the scoring, as they appeared to have sized up their opponents, and they operated more freely and with more confidence. Lacey swung the ball over to Miller, who set McKinlay on the run. The winger cut in towards goal and passed to Lacey, who promptly headed into the gap between Bailey and the post. It looked like a goal until Mosley appeared from nowhere to clear the danger.

Corners came easily to the visitors, mainly because the Reds persisted in ballooning the ball, which was very difficult to control accurately, especially in the air. Liverpool attempted the short-passing game, which was wiser given the climatic conditions.

Yet another corner was awarded to the visitors, but Hafekost banged the ball into Campbell and the Southerners gained another corner. Fortunately for the Reds, the visitors were not experts at taking corners.

Lee was a massive player, and he used his weight occasionally to advantage. The visitors' methods of moving goalwards were of the crudest description, and they had evidently not used much of their spare time in studying the nice points of the game.

Nor had they the dour determination and tremendous vigour which characterised Barnsley. The Reds were lying low, and not wasting their energy against the stubborn wind, but due to the patient game, nine-tenths of the game had been played in the Liverpool half. At length Miller initiated a move which proved troublesome, and McKinlay twice centred well.

Soon after, the Gillingham left raided Anfield territory, and Tatton crossed the sphere to Pinkney, who had an open goal, and tapped the ball lightly without allowing for the wind, which curled it round the post.

A marvellous forward movement involving Lacey, McDougall, Miller and McKinlay ended when the winger was ruled offside after delivering a fine cross. Five minutes from the interval Gilligan and Hafekost shot over the bar. Just before the half-time whistle, McDougall missed a good chance after a pass from Miller.

Restarting, Sheldon and Lacey were prominent and a corner soon resulted. There were shouts of "Goal!" as the ball was headed a foot wide of the mark. The Reds still insisted on an over-indulgence in pattern-making instead of making direct for goal, and many of Liverpool's insidious meanderings were ingloriously cut short.

Gillingham seemed to have learnt from their first half experience, and they forced two corners in quick succession which nearly brought disaster to Campbell when Gilligan shot hard at the custodian. The Reds continued to be affected by nerves and they were unable to take advantage of the favourable wind.

However, they gained a sequence of successive corners which provided no reward. Frequently the Liverpool forwards gained good shooting positions without testing Bailey. One Red after another failed dismally, and the spectators frequently showed their anxiety. The home side simply did not force the pace enough, and allowed their more cumbersome opponents plenty of time to recover themselves.

It was remarkable that a team of Liverpool's calibre could not make a greater impression on their crude visitors. Liverpool were always stylish, but strangely ineffective. At length Miller shot hard from long-range, and then McKinlay forced a corner. Clever manoeuvring by Fairfoul and Sheldon enabled Lacey to have a shot at Bailey, but there was no power behind it.

Liverpool's chances were further improved when Mosley left the field. Their best efforts were a high shot from Miller and a sledge-hammer one from Lacey which went into the side netting. Later on, a brilliant cross from Lacey enabled McDougall to force an attempt on goal, but Bailey was alert and cleared the danger. The Reds swarmed around the Gillingham goal like so many wasps, but they failed to sting.

With time running out, and an inexplicable draw looking certain, Liverpool struck. McDougall, Lacey and Sheldon sprinted ahead through the opposing defence without a tackle being given. McDougall swung the ball over to Sheldon, who returned it into the goalmouth, and Lacey, running in, netted with a first-time drive to the obvious delight of the crowd. The goal inspired the Reds, who swamped Gillingham until a second goal was recorded by Ferguson.

Liverpool: Campbell; S.Speakman, Pursell; Fairfoul, Lowe, Ferguson; Sheldon, Lacey, McDougall, Miller, McKinlay.

Gillingham: Bailey; Mosley, Leslie; Mahon, Lee, Johnson; Pinkney, Gilligan, Glen, Hafekost, Tatton.

Referee: Mr J.W. Bailey (Leicester)

Linesmen: Mr J. Mottishead (Macclesfield); Mr R.T. Bradshaw (Leicester)

Attendance: 42,045

Below: **Thomas Fairfoul**, *who had a good game against Gillingham*

February 21, 1914

West Ham United (0) 1
Puddefoot 60

Liverpool (0) 1
Miller 47

HEAVY rain fell during the night preceding the game and the pitch had only a few patches of green turf around the corner flags. The rest of the field was a quagmire. Liverpool arrived in London on the Friday night, and were followed at midnight by a fairly large crowd of supporters. The team was fit and fairly confident of success against a team which ended Chesterfield's and Crystal Palace's Cup hopes. The Hammers made a late change, Rothwell - who used to play for South Liverpool - had a knee problem, and found himself unable to play. Burton therefore dropped from half-back to full-back, and the veteran Randall became left-half. The attendance was not as large as expected due to the inclement weather. It was, nevertheless, a shilling gate, and the receipts were relatively large. A new, large stand had recently been built and it was well patronised. Liverpool had a mascot in the shape of a young boy with a red-coloured top hat. The backs of the goal, usually so popular a viewing point, were sparsely filled, and the crowd was near 15,000 when the teams made their appearance on to the enclosure. The walling in of the ground must have been a novelty to the followers of Liverpool, who wondered how a fast forward would fare if he ran on at any pace when making an advance for goal. Liverpool, who appeared in black and white striped jerseys, were accorded a very hearty reception. The West Ham colours were the same as those of Villa, though the official description is "Red, white, and blue". The game was started a few minutes before time. Lowe won the toss.

The first pass by a West Ham player showed the policy the Hammers adopted. The ball was swung well across to the left, but shot off the turf quickly. For some time the home side showed signs of anxiety, while Liverpool enjoyed three excellent raids, each of which brought a corner. Miller and Metcalfe tried hard to score from them, but the ball was blocked each time. West Ham's goalkeeper had to handle, and a curiosity was seen as a linesman signalled for a case of hands, but the referee adjudged him wrong. At this stage in the game, Liverpool were the masters and played some good football. West Ham, though, attacked through a solo run by Leafe, who was said to be slow, but he was certainly fast enough to chase forward and shoot at Campbell, who brought off a magnificent save at the foot of a post. Randall made a bad blunder and let in Sheldon, but Metcalfe could not turn the shot into a goal. This was followed by a fine centre from Lacey, who had gone to outside-left, but Miller fell and the opportunity passed. No penalty was awarded when Miller was pushed in the back by Burton as he was about to shoot. Captain Lowe pushed the ball to Metcalfe, who slipped it to Miller, and the centre-forward's hard drive swerved away from the goal.

West Ham did not shoot often, but they were not afraid to let fly, and twice Puddefoot drove in tremendous shots. Campbell saved one cleverly, and the other passed wide. In defence for the Hammers, Brandon's mud-slides amused the crowd, but more valuable was his solid defence. During the final ten minutes of the first half, West Ham outplayed their visitors, and the Liverpool defence struggled to keep their goal intact, particularly with the powerful shooting of Puddefoot. Leafe, the former Sheffield player, was of great assistance to his centre-forward. The Liverpool forwards played better than in previous Cup-ties, but Lowe, while full of energy, was not as successful as usual and found the going awkward round the middle of the field.

The second half started at 4.12, and within two minutes Miller scored. The goal came as the result of some brilliant approach-work by Nicholl and Lacey, who got the ball out to his partner, and Nicholl, despite a trip, turned towards goal. Miller took a fraction of a second to size up the opportunity and his shot found its mark amidst great cheering from the Liverpool throng. Within a minute, Nicholl almost increased the lead.

At the other end, Puddefoot beat all opponents and shot powerfully at goal, but Campbell made a wonderful save by throwing himself at the ball and managing to edge it out. Leafe had a long drive at goal which Campbell saved and then Puddefoot's shot hit an upright and cannoned to Campbell. Nicholl's determination to score deserved a goal, and Lacey's powerful drive was unfortunate. Pursell and Woodards saved certain goals for their respective sides, and Pursell was the best back on the field. West Ham gradually gained control of the game and Askew, in midfield, passed forward to Puddefoot who scored with a great shot on the hour which sent the crowd ecstatic.

The Hammers brought all their forces forward in an attempt to gain the lead and the lame Casey drew a daring save from Campbell. In the closing minutes a goal by Miller was ruled offside.

West Ham United: Hughes; Brandon, Burton; Woodards, Askew, Randall; Ashton, Bailey, Puddefoot, Leafe, Casey.

Liverpool: Campbell; Longworth, Pursell; Fairfoul, Lowe, Ferguson; Sheldon, Metcalfe, Miller, Lacey, Nicholl.

Referee: Mr A. Warner (Nottingham)

Linesmen: Mr F.W. Hammond (Birmingham);
    Mr. E.B. Friend (Ipswich)
Attendance: 15,000

February 25, 1914

Liverpool (4) 5
Lacey 7, 34, Miller 16, 45,
Metcalfe 62

West Ham United (1) 1
Puddefoot 13

THE incentive of a Fourth Round tie against Queen's Park Rangers was tremendous to both teams as it was likely that it would mean almost automatic inclusion in the Semi-final of the English Cup. West Ham stayed in Southport for a couple of days before the game, moving on to Liverpool on the day of the match, while Liverpool made an important alteration in their ranks. The club captain, Lowe, had been troubled with a bad muscle and he should not have played on the previous Saturday. Ferguson was moved to centre to try to hold Puddefoot, and McKinlay, the utility man, became the newcomer to the side. West Ham had beaten Chesterfield 8-0 and Crystal Palace in previous rounds. They could not expect much vocal support. Those who "stole the afternoon" agreed that the risk entailed was worth it for, after a gloomy morning, suggesting a foggy afternoon, the sun broke through, and the day became beautifully bright. The ground was in good condition, and the attendance was enormous. From one o'clock onwards the stream of enthusiasts to Anfield made a fine spectacle. There was a crowd of about 35,000 when the game started and the turnstiles continued to click away merrily. The gates were eventually closed. West Ham were not at full strength. The Old Xaverian, Casey, was unable to take his place at outside-left and Randall, the veteran half-back, was pressed into service as a wing forward. Rothwell was able to play, and the crowd had the novelty of seeing two ex-South Liverpool players at full-back in the opposing team. The Kemlyn Road stand was full an hour before kick-off. The crowd was rather slow in filling the space behind each goal, while the new stand was well filled. There was no band to while away the time, and the crowd only had the various mascots to keep them amused. One of the striking effects of the day was created through a huge red flag being waved by someone on top of the Spion Kop. Ferguson acted as Liverpool's captain. West Ham changed their colours, and turned out in blue jerseys. The Everton element present smiled when they saw the colour chosen, because the colour was supposed to be a death colour to Liverpool. The game started at one minute to three o'clock.

After Miller kicked off he was involved in a collision and hurt his right thigh. The game was suspended for a while, but he was able to continue. Liverpool soon worried the West Ham defence, and when Leafe handled Lacey shot high over the bar from the free-kick. In another incident, Sheldon was unable to get on the end of Lacey's strong cross and the ball went for a goal-kick. A splendid McKinlay centre to Sheldon forced the goalkeeper to take a risk, but he succeeded with a flying kick to clear the danger. With just seven minutes gone, Lacey scored. He had scored in every round, with the exception of the previous Saturday's game. Play had gone down the right wing, and Metcalfe passed the ball square to Lacey, who had just sufficient time to steady himself for a shot. It was a fast shot which had the goalkeeper well beaten.

Another shot was passed by, and then a sensational incident occurred. Pursell, who had been playing well, blundered in front of his own goalkeeper and the ball turned to Campbell's left and made his position hopeless. Pursell should have left it to the goalkeeper. Puddefoot was given the credit for the goal. Three minutes later, however, Miller had re-gained the lead. A West Ham defender, in trying to clear, turned the ball towards his own goal. Miller, with a deft touch, hooked the ball over his instep. As he had his back to the goal when he received the ball, his idea was a good one.

Soon afterwards Puddefoot seemed to waste a shot that went high in the air, but the spin on the ball was so great that it kept in play and dropped onto the angle of the goal. Miller, provided with excellent forward passes from Ferguson, made a splendid solo run and beat two men, but his way to goal was blocked.

The veteran Randall made a useful contribution at outside-left and he provided some laughter when he and Sheldon got mixed up and fell to the ground together. Later on he forced a corner off Longworth and Campbell had to save smartly. With 34 minutes gone, Ferguson and Lacey dovetailed well and they made good ground. The ball went to Nicholl, and Lacey screamed for a return pass. The pass was given, and Lacey, without any hesitation, made a left-foot drive from 20 yards which flew past Hughes.

Despite being well marshalled by Ferguson, Puddefoot drove a tremendous strike at goal from fully 30 yards which Campbell cleverly saved. Longworth and Ferguson later miskicked, and Randall shot hard against the side netting. The West Ham defence was kept at full stretch as Miller was in splendid form, and the forward line was incisive. Although the right wing worked hard, it was not dominating, though Sheldon began the move which brought a fourth goal. He tried a shot which proved unsuccessful. The ball went out to Metcalfe, whose close range shot hit the goalkeeper, passed on to the upright, and cannoned out to Miller, who scored from an easy position.

With 62 minutes gone, Metcalfe increased Liverpool's score. The changes the visitors made did not work out for them. From being an excellent back on the Saturday, Burton became a half-back of no great merit, while Randall, at outside-left, was a veteran who lasted well and was not tied to one particular spot, although he usually played at half-back. But Randall was slow and a handicap to his side, and with Leafe cumbersome, the wing was not a difficult proposition for Liverpool. Liverpool's team changes won them the game.

Ferguson, without being stuck to Puddefoot, kept the young centre in hand perfectly. Lowe was not able to perform at his best on the Saturday due to injury. McKinlay was useful against a small-built wing and he was a man who could drop to full-back when pressure was heavy and who could relieve with any number of full-length punts. Furthermore, he can score goals too. West Ham were a team of plucky players who came up against a team full of confidence and on its best form. It had been at forward that Liverpool had been lacking in the League, but now that the forward line consisted of five very good players, it was hoped that Liverpool's League position would improve.

Puddefoot gave the crowd two examples of his tremendous shooting power, and £2,200 had been refused for his transfer.

The gate receipts totalled £1,429 1s 3d, and the furore over a winning side in Liverpool had been demonstrated again. The city was fond of football and each year showed a tremendous increase in football followers. The schoolboy was not *au fait* if he did not have a complete knowledge of football matters. The city's grounds were big and compact, yet they were tested severely on occasions.

West Ham's fall was witnessed by a big crowd, yet thousands were turned away from the ground. There was room for a few thousand in the ground, but the officials wisely decided that they could not take any risks, and therefore the gates were closed before the ground was packed. The trouble was that the Anfield spectators would not pack. Spectators arrived early, took up their positions, and refused to "move up" or "move down". The result was that the Spion Kop was crowded in parts, and in other parts sparsely populated. Ground improvements and other big items of expenditure had cost Liverpool a large sum, and for some years there had been a millstone around the neck of the club. This was being steadily reduced, and the Cup assistance of last season and the present campaign had reduced the bill. In fact, the change from poverty to comfort was welcomed by the Liverpool board who had dug deep into their own pockets and risked losing a lot of money. At present the club was without a chairman. Mr John McKenna's resignation had been followed by the resignation of his successor, Mr Will Briggs, who was fully recovered from a severe illness. Mr J. Astbury was acting chairman.

Other receipts included £876 at home to Barnsley, £820 away. Against Gillingham the gate money was £1,317, while away to the Hammers it was £392.

Liverpool: Campbell; Longworth, Pursell; Fairfoul, Ferguson, McKinlay; Sheldon, Metcalfe, Miller, Lacey, Nicholl.

West Ham United: Hughes; Brandon, Rothwell; Woodards, Askew, Burton; Ashton, Bailey, Puddefoot, Leafe, Randall.

Referee: Mr A. Warner (Nottingham)

Attendance: 43,729

THE DISPATCH

by VETERAN

In every way the display of Liverpool was a satisfactory one, but especially was this the case with the forwards, where previously the greatest trouble had existed. If there is a finer inside-man playing football at the present time than Lacey, I do not know him, for Lacey is right at the top of his form, and Everton must be sorry they parted with him.

Not only is he shooting with tremendous power and pace, but he is playing good football in every way, and is making Nicholl into a very useful winger. The pair seem to understand each other thoroughly, and they are a dangerous wing.

Billy Lacey

PICKPOCKETS CAUGHT

LIVERPOOL DETECTIVES COMPLIMENTED

Four men were charged at the Liverpool City Police Court today with loitering with intent to pick pockets at the tram terminus near the Liverpool Football Club ground yesterday.

Detective-sergeants McCoy and Kinley deposed to seeing the accused put their hands into the hip pockets of male passengers who were waiting for the cars. When spoken to by the detectives they replied that they had just come to Liverpool. They now pleaded guilty.

Inquiries showed that two of the men were awaiting trial at Sheffield Quarter Sessions.

In passing sentence of three months' imprisonment on all the prisoners the stipendiary remarked:

"I must compliment the Liverpool police upon their smartness in apprehending these four men as soon as they arrived in the city."

March 7, 1914

Liverpool (2) 2   Queen's Park Rangers (0) 1

Sheldon 6, Miller 20   *Mitchell (pen) 66*

QUEEN'S Park Rangers made their first visit to Anfield and a tremendous crowd attended, despite the rumours of a boycott through the admission prices being raised. Liverpool selected their team at mid-day, and Queen's Park Rangers arrived from Southport on the morning of the match. The Southerners announced a strong side, despite the fact that Higgins did not play. The band of the 4th Artillery kept the waiting crowd in good humour. The weather was fine, and the pitch was in a fair condition.

The Spion Kop was patronised very early and when 18,000 were accommodated the gates were wisely closed at 2.20. There were several "guys" on the ground who got a somewhat mixed reception, if oranges and similar missiles counted for anything. At 3.30 the ground did not appear so densely packed as at the West Ham game last Wednesday week, and everyone appeared to be accommodated quite comfortably. A most unusual coincidence lay in the fact that both centre-forwards bore the same name. The Reds appeared at 3.25 and received a tumultuous reception.

Liverpool: Campbell; Longworth, Pursell; Fairfoul, Ferguson, McKinlay; Sheldon, Metcalfe, Miller, Lacey, Nicholl.

Q.P.R.: Nicholls; Ovens, Pullen; Whyman, Mitchell, Wake; Thompson, Birch, Miller, Gregory, Fortune.

Referee: Mr G.H. Moody (Bilston)

Linesmen: Mr J.W. Wright (Wolverhampton); Mr C.H. Norton (Birmingham)

Attendance: 43,000

The Liverpool Miller started and Pullen kicked out. Thompson set off on a great run until he was stopped by Ferguson, and soon after Birch was allowed a free passage but he shot wildly over the goal-line. Fairfoul and Ferguson both made mistakes to let the Rangers' centre in, but he moved into an offside position. The vigour and enthusiasm of the visitors perplexed the Anfielders, but after six minutes the home side took the lead. The Reds attacked in strong formation, and Pullen and Wake were soon in difficulties. The home right verged goalwards and the strength of the Anfield attack overwhelmed the Rangers' defence. Sheldon, Metcalfe and Miller secured the ball and Sheldon beat Nicholls with a great shot from close range.

Undismayed by this reverse, the visitors attacked resolutely, and Campbell, after gathering a ground shot from Thompson, dropped the ball, but with great presence of mind he booted it away. McKinlay found Birch and Thompson a crafty couple to beat and on one occasion, when Pursell had covered the half-back by blocking the ball, Birch forged ahead again and let fly with a shot which curled round the upright.

The visitors were inclined to be somewhat over-physical and were penalised on several occasions. McKinlay was spoken to by the referee for nudging Thompson. Although a goal ahead, the home defence lacked their usual resolve, mainly due to the strong breeze which militated against accurate judgment.

The visitors' footwork was not at all subtle or intricate, but they kept on the move and they swung the ball about so vigorously that the situation frequently looked ominous for the Anfielders. The Rangers had a fatal weakness, however, as they did not combine well. If the inside trio had performed as a unit, they might well have caused Liverpool some serious problems.

With twenty minutes gone, Ferguson swung the ball out to the right and Sheldon, Metcalfe and Miller dribbled the ball skilfully through the Rangers' half-back line. Pullen seemed to lose his head momentarily and Miller put the ball into the net. In view of the threatening tactics of the Southerners, Liverpool were fortunate to be two goals ahead. Fortune and Gregory could not get the better of the artful Fairfoul, who was a real "bag of tricks".

The Rangers' methods of stopping their opponents were extremely tough, and the "Spion Koppers" became furious when Sheldon got a Rangers' knee in the stomach and was badly winded. A hearty cheer greeted his recovery.

Fortune dribbled into the area and centred accurately to Birch, who was well-placed to score but shot erratically. At the other end Nicholls made a splendid save from Ferguson who was having an excellent game at pivot.

After the resumption the Rangers adopted the same crude tactics; they were full of enthusiasm but they seemed incapable of working out an intelligent plan. Following a throw-in, Ferguson fouled Gregory inside the penalty area and Mr Moody awarded the ultimate penalty of the law. Birch managed to get too much elevation to his kick and the vast crowd cheered loudly when the ball sailed high over the bar.

Soon after this incident Gregory and Miller broke through and were almost in the goalmouth when they were beaten off the ball by Fairfoul. The referee turned down the Rangers' penalty appeal.

From close range the Southerners always appeared dangerous, and Campbell skilfully patted down a shot by Birch. With a lead of two goals, the Reds appeared to become somewhat complacent, and the defence was lax, though the Rangers' inability to score was a telling factor. An example of the Rangers' wild shooting came when Birch once ignored the whistle and, determined to have the satisfaction of netting the leather, he shot, but even that missed to the great delight of the crowd. Some sparkling individual play by Sheldon earned a corner which proved unsuccessful.

A mêlée in front of Campbell occurred and although no foul was apparent, Fairfoul and Longworth seemed concerned and there was a general surprise when the referee awarded another penalty, which Miller converted. The Reds were at fault for easing off too soon. The reverse steadied the Reds and improved a rather insipid game. The Rangers continually lofted the ball into the goalmouth which created great anxiety for Campbell. During this period of intense pressure, Ferguson was a remarkable asset to his side, as he had been throughout. The Rangers strove manfully in the final ten minutes to gain equality, but Liverpool were equally determined to score again and Nicholls was kept on the alert. Although Longworth's play was of a high standard throughout, it became even better during the closing stages.

Liverpool thus reached the semi-finals of the Cup for the fourth time, having lost on all three previous occasions. Manchester City drew 0-0 with Sheffield United, and Sunderland and Burnley also fought out a goalless draw. Sheffield Wednesday were beaten 0-1 at home to Aston Villa, for whom Sam Hardy excelled in goal.

THE LIVERPOOL FOOTBALL ECHO

BEE SUMS UP

Fielding the side that thrashed West Ham at Anfield, last Wednesday week, Liverpool beat Queen's Park Rangers today and thus the club enters the semi-final stage for the fourth time in their history. These are their previous "concluding" ties:

1897 - Beaten by the Villa 3-0
1899 - Beaten by Sheffield United 1-0
(After four games)
1906 - Beaten by Everton 2-0

Today they had little to beat, as Queen's Park Rangers were poor opponents in attack and defence. Readers may judge this truth from the fact that Liverpool scored twice in the first two visits to the Queen's Park Rangers goal, and the visitors were attacking against unsettled full-backs for the first ten minutes of the game, and never looked like converting their chances. Further, Queen's Park Rangers had the benefit of a stiff breeze at their backs, and sometimes the sun troubled Liverpool in the opening half.

Queen's Park Rangers have never previously played before so big a crowd, and may be they lost their heads sometimes. At any rate, their defence was very insipid, and Miller and Sheldon scored goals with ease. The crowd was about 43,000 strong, and the gate should be about £1,600.

Things went Liverpool's way when Birch ballooned the ball with a penalty kick. Liverpool had been toying with their opponents, but this incident served to waken them up somewhat, and make them realise that the South would fight to the finish.

Queen's Park Rangers' best forward was Thompson, and their best half was Mitchell.

The best thing Rangers did was to pass prettily.

Misses by Metcalfe were followed by another penalty (Mitchell converted), and Liverpool were then worrying because they had but one goal lead.

SHEFFIELD WEDNESDAY v. ASTON VILLA

HARD STRUGGLE

VILLA IN SPARKLING TRIM

The Sheffield Wednesday's ground was hardly big enough to hold all the people who wanted to see the game today, for half-an-hour from the kick-off over 45,000 people were inside the ground, and thousands lined up at the turnstiles. Sovereigns for seats were refused. The weather was delightful, and the ground in lovely condition. The Wednesday team was the same as last Saturday, and Villa were at full strength.

Teams:

Sheffield Wednesday: Davison; Worrall, Spoors; Brittleton, McSkimming, Campbell; Kirkman, Glennon, McLean, Wilson, Gill.
Aston Villa: Hardy; Lyon, Weston; Barber, Harrop, Leach; Wallace, Stephenson, Hampton, Bache, Edgeley.
Referee: Mr H.N. Taylor (Haslingdon)

Wednesday won the toss, and Villa kicked off against wind and sun, both fairly strong. Villa immediately attacked on the right, but the ball went into touch, and when the visitors came back again Brittleton cleared beautifully from Bache. In making a characteristic dash on McSkimming, Hampton was injured, but soon came round, and was quickly giving the home defence trouble.

Villa were making light of the fact that the wind was against them, and once the greatness of Brittleton saved the home side, who went straight away from the capital clearance. The home left made a grand run and Hardy had to come right out to kick away, while in the next minute Hardy again

SAVED A FINE SHOT.

A terrific drive followed by McLean which missed by inches. Wednesday were

STORMING THE VILLA GOAL

now, and Hardy got his fist to a long shot from Campbell just as Gill rushed at him. Having found the way to the Villa's goal, the Sheffielders kept in that neighbourhood for a fairly long time.

They were playing typical Cup-tie football, the forwards going at a tremendous pace, while the halves were passing perfectly. The Villa's defence stood up to the rush wonderfully well, and they were lucky when Gill put the ball weakly to a defender when three of the Wednesday's forwards were waiting to make a goal of it.

Hampton was always dangerous, however, for he lay well up on the Wednesday's backs ready to dash through. When the Villa did get going the home

GOAL HAD A NARROW ESCAPE,

Davison had to come out to punch away. Before he could get back Bache tried a shot which struck a defender.

The rebound went to Edgeley, whose shot was well stopped by Davison, and in the next minute Gill gave Hardy

A CURIOUS SHOT TO STOP.

Glennon missed a fine chance when he shot behind from a free-kick twenty yards out. McLean put the ball over the bar.

Kirkman dribbled right into goal, and when he might have scored he stumbled, and the ball went behind. The Villa had hardly been seen in the first twenty minutes, and as a rule, when they did attempt an invasion either Spoors or Brittleton drove them back. Full time: Villa won 1-0.

March 28, 1914

Liverpool (1) 2
Nicholl (2)

Aston Villa (0) 0

ACCORDING to the London Press the Villa were hot favourites to win this tie, probably due to the fact that Villa's Cup record was far better than Liverpool's and their respective League positions also suggested that Villa would be victorious. The press had little good to say about Liverpool, but the players ignored this when they arrived in Chingford they looked extremely fit and stated that they believed they could win the tie despite the fact of the severity of their task. The directors met on the morning of the game and announced that the team would be what had become known as the usual team, which meant that Lowe was at centre-half and Metcalfe at inside-right. Aston Villa were at full strength, and the day was similar to that of the Grand National. The sun shone brilliantly, and the spectators had a glorious afternoon's outing. There were not many spectators from Liverpool on account of the fact that the match was being boycotted due to the unfair selection of venue by the F.A. The linesmen were Mr A.H. Manning and Mr G.O. Miller.

In the Strand, and other main arteries of the Metropolis, it became obvious at noon that there was a provincial invasion of football supporters. The Aston Villa contingent were the more numerous, but some Liverpool supporters could be seen - workers who had made the long journey overnight. The well-equipped enclosure at White Hart Lane was well filled at two o'clock and an hour later almost every place was filled. The tedium of waiting for the commencement of the game was pleasantly passed by an excellent programme of music and a notable incident was the announcement that Cambridge had won the Boat Race. The victory of the Light Blues seemed to find popular favour. The playing pitch, though on the fast side, was in excellent condition except for a strip down the middle which was barren of grass. The Liverpool team received several telegrams from friends, one of which was from Miss Nora H. Delaney and read: *"Good Luck To The Boys. Another win, please! And then the Cup!"* Tom Browell, who played at Chelsea, sent a wire to the Liverpool players wishing them luck. The players returned the compliment.

Bache, the Villa captain, led his men on to the field amid ringing cheers which were repeated when the Anfielders appeared. There had been some talk of the clashing of colours, but Liverpool sported a very light red jersey which compared well against the Villa's claret. Lowe lost the toss and Liverpool started against a slight breeze.

From the kick-off Liverpool attacked down the left, and Lyons punted away a long shot from Nicholl. The Livers returned immediately on the same wing, and Miller, taking the pass, almost broke through, but Weston saved the situation. Aston Villa broke away and Longworth was forced to grant a corner. This was satisfactorily negotiated, but the Villa attacked again and Pursell intercepted a flying shot from Hampton. Villa burst down the left and Edgeley put in a perfect centre which Bache tried to convert, but failed. Hampton, in his usual impetuous manner, sent in a stinging shot which struck the upright before Campbell cleared. At this stage of the game, the Villa left wing was in great form and presented Longworth with several difficulties.

Liverpool attacked through Sheldon, who rounded Weston and sent in a square pass which Lacey directed straight to Hardy, who picked it up without difficulty. Play was of an even nature, though the Villa forwards looked the more potent. Edgeley put in a glorious centre which Hampton sent over the bar. The pace of the game increased at this point, and Miller was almost through when Lyons cleared the pressure.

Lacey put all his strength into a cracking drive which struck the crossbar and rebounded into touch. From long range Barber shot high over the bar. Bache caused Campbell to save a goal while lying prone. The Midlanders continued to peg away, and a Hampton free-kick glanced off Lowe's head for a corner, which amounted to nothing.

Soon after, a long dropping shot from Wallace caused Campbell some trouble. Then Liverpool broke away in the most astonishing fashion. The whole forward line moved along with precision, and so troubled Hardy that he conceded a corner. This was perfectly placed by Sheldon and Nicholl headed the leather into the net amidst tremendous excitement after 30 minutes. It was a great goal which made amends for a shocking miss which the outside-left had made. The goal was well received at Anfield where Liverpool Reserves were playing Huddersfield Reserves in the Central League [Liverpool Reserves won 2-1 with goals from Peake (first half) and Terriss (63 minutes)] and both players and spectators gave vent to their feelings when the scoreboard indicated that Liverpool were leading. Liverpool's goal was also well applauded at Goodison Park, where Everton were drawing 1-1 with Tottenham Hotspur in a First Division encounter.

Sheldon then sent in a cross which might well have beaten even a greater custodian than Hardy. Aston Villa responded with some excellent half-back play. Bache tried desperately to rush the ball through and Stephenson was stopped from causing too much damage. Hampton had a shot which passed over the bar as Villa sought to get on equal terms. At this stage, a spectator aged about fifty dropped down dead, apparently with a heart attack. (A spectator died in the Chelsea v Liverpool match on 9 September 1912 when Lacey scored a last-minute goal in the Reds' 2-1 victory.) As the tension mounted, Nicholl and Lacey attacked. Nicholl centred magnificently and Sheldon, trapping the ball, sent in a shot which missed the mark by inches. The Villa pressed hard and Bache was slightly injured in trying to force his way past Lowe and Longworth. Wallace then tried a shot which Campbell dealt with in masterly fashion, and another shot from Stephenson was equally well dealt with.

There was electricity in the air when Hampton dashed away and put the leather well wide of the mark. The Anfielders replied with venom. They moved off strongly on the left and after some excellent footwork, Nicholl took a pass from Lacey before putting in a rising shot which struck the inside of the upright and bounced back to Hardy, who seemed to be over his line when he cleared. There were strong claims from the Liverpool players for a goal and the referee seemed to have some doubt about the matter and so he consulted with a linesman before deciding that the claim be disallowed and a free-kick awarded. The Anfielders appeared extremely irate at the decision, but proceeded to play even better.

The Villa defence was troubled as Nicholl, then Lacey and Sheldon all had shots. A slight relaxing on the part of the Liverpool halves let in the Villa forwards and Pursell handled the ball just outside the area. The Villains claimed emphatically for a penalty kick, but Mr Bamlett merely gave a free-kick, which was cleared.

A fierce daisy-cutter from Hampton tested Campbell. Metcalfe played well to rob Bache of the ball as he was about to shoot. A promising movement by Nicholl was spoiled through Miller lying offside.

The Liverpool left forced a corner and Metcalfe shot wide from this. The Villa right caused tremendous problems for Campbell until Fairfoul headed clear. Liverpool then shot away at top speed and Nicholl could have walked the ball, but instead shot tamely into Hardy's hands. Presumably he thought he was offside.

At the other end a shot from Wallace hit Campbell full in the face. The Liverpool 'keeper was stunned momentarily, but he quickly recovered. The Anfielders then attacked and a fine shot from Metcalfe struck the bar.

The leather rebounded into play, and Nicholl pounced on it before netting from close range, giving Hardy no chance of saving. In the closing stages, Liverpool were more than a match for Villa, and Lacey just missed the mark with a tremendous drive. Hampton hurt his head in the last minute of the game.

In the other semi-final, Burnley drew 0-0 with Sheffield United at Old Trafford before 56,000 spectators. Burnley won the replay 1-0 with a goal from Boyle.

BURNLEY v. SHEFFIELD UNITED

Burnley: Dawson; Bamford, Taylor; Halley, Boyle, Watson; Nesbitt, Lindley, Freeman, Hodgson, Mosscrop.

Sheffield United: Gough; Cook, English; Sturgess, Brelsford, Utley; Simmons, Gillespie, Kitchen, Fazackerley, Revill.

Sam Hardy, the brilliant former custodian of Liverpool

LIVERPOOL'S FIGHT FOR FIRST FINAL HONOUR

GOOD WINNERS OF A GOOD GAME

BRAVO, REDS!

Liverpool: Campbell; Longworth, Pursell; Fairfoul, Lowe, Ferguson; Sheldon, Metcalfe, Miller, Lacey, Nicholl.

Aston Villa: Hardy; Lyons, Weston; Barber, Harrop, Leach; Wallace, Stephenson, Hampton, Bache, Edgeley.

Referee: Mr H.S. Bamlett (Gateshead)

Linesmen: Mr A.H. Manning (Kent); Mr C.L. Miller (Norfolk)

Attendance: 27,474 (at White Hart Lane)

LIVERPOOL LOSE FINAL TO FREEMAN GOAL

KING IN ATTENDANCE

Liverpool (0) 0

Burnley (0) 1
Freeman 58

SOMETHING like 20,000 excited, shouting people left Liverpool for London on the Friday evening, and the enthusiasm bubbled over into the morning of the match, and filled one of the biggest trains on record, for the early football "special" which left Lime Street at 7.40 in the morning carried over 1,200 people.

Coaches

Eighteen and a half coaches had to be used to transfer the population of a "village" from Liverpool to London in one swoop. The travelling village from Merseyside was very happy. Liverpool had reached the Final for the first time in their history. They did not seem to mind the crush, although in places they were packed like cigars in a box. However, that was largely their own fault.

They came in parties and refused to be separated; so if fifteen or sixteen people came together they crammed into one compartment, preferring to suffer the discomfort of standing or sitting on one another's knees to the cruel alternative of splitting up and being unable to discuss the possibilities of the match together. Many of the early folk had been working nearly all night, but enthusiasm buoyed them up, and they added their sleepy cheers to those of their fresher comrades.

Ribbons

It was a train of streamers. Every carriage blazed with red and white ribbons and rosettes. Portraits of the Liverpool team were stuck on the windows, and Liverpool Echo badges bearing football Battle cries were worn in nearly every hat or button-hole.

A young fellow with a bowler hat of red and white kept things merry as he leaned out of a window and chastised the porters, breaking off every now and then with erratic suddenness to cheer the favourites.

Song

Some of the enthusiasts were moved to song, and they sang "*You made me love you*", while others chanted Burnley's Swan song, a doggerel setting forth how Liverpool trounced their opponents and carried off the Cup.

It went like this:

*The Burnley men came like the wolves on the fold,
And their faces gleamed bright as the Klondyke gold;
To the football field they all wended their way,
To see their old foes at football to play.
But alas and alack, when they got on the field
And saw their opponents, they knew they'd to yield;
For they rushed them and pushed them until all were sore,
And beat them all hollow, as they'd oft done before.*

Cup

Some of the supporters took the Cup up to London with them. They had it pinned on to their coats - a little facsimile of the trophy worked on a medal, and they seemed confident that they worked on a medal, and they seemed confident that they would see a victory. There had been little time for breakfast, and some of the travellers took a little extra on the train. All had come well provided with provisions. Many pockets bulged with sandwiches, and room was also found for several well-filled bottles.

Loyalty

To show their loyalty, some of the enthusiasts had even packed the sandwiches in red and white paper. It was a remarkably merry crowd. Among the excursionists were many lady supporters of the club who took a leading part in the display of enthusiasm. The train was half full by a quarter-past seven, and it went out on time twenty-five minutes later, packed with people. As the train puffed slowly out of the station they opened their lungs and showed what they could do.

Enthusiasm

In view of the visit of the King there was an extraordinary number of people on duty in and around the playing ground. The supporters of Burnley were apparently in the majority, although Liverpool men, if in smaller numbers, seemed to excel in enthusiasm. Motor conveyances appeared to be more popular than ever, and it was estimated that there were something like 200 motor-buses employed in bringing sightseers to the Palace during the day, and these made a formidable "park" as they were drawn up alongside the principal entrances. The new arrangements which had been made by the Football Association for the comfort of the visitors proved most

acceptable, and amongst the tremendous crowd which assembled to witness the match there was hardly one person who did not have a fairly clear view. At the entrance to the pavilion, his Majesty was met by Lord Derby, Lord Kinnaird, Mr Cramp, and Mr Clegg, and was conducted to the Royal Box.

Arrival

The King's arrival was heralded by great cheering by the enormous crowd meanwhile the brass band of the Irish Guards and the Liverpool Regiment and the Fifes of the latter regiment played the National Anthem. It was a great scene, and the King was palpably moved by it. Every head in the crowd was uncovered and everybody appeared to be shouting at once; and as the cheers died down, those in the neighbourhood of the pavilion sang the concluding lines of the National Anthem to the accompaniment of the band, and the idea caught on with the great assembly. His Majesty wore a dark grey lounge suit and bowler hat.

Cheering

A tremendous volley of cheering was sent up by the crowd all round the pitch as His Majesty walked to his reserved seat. The King passed down the gangway to his place while the National Anthem was played, and then took his seat, with Lord Derby on his right and Lord Kinnaird on his left. There was still a further scene before play actually began. The two teams trooped out from the pavilion, lined up in front of His Majesty, and at the call of one of the captains gave three ringing cheers. Then they turned and ran to the centre of the field, and

the kick-off followed immediately.

The scene presented from the Royal pavilion was a remarkable one, the football ground lying below and all around it was a sea of white faces crowned by dark headgear.

Most of those announced as having accepted invitations to attend as the guests of the Football Association were present, and there were also a number of well-known gentlemen present including Mr Will Crooks, M.P.; Mr A. Smith, M.P. (Clitheroe); Mr J. Hodge, M.P. (Gorton); and Mr S. Roberts, the Member of Parliament for Eccleshall.

His Majesty

The King followed the game with the keenest interest. At exciting moments he watched intently, and did not miss a single point in the game. At other times he kept up a running comment with the Earl of Derby. When the players left the field for the interval, the bandsmen took it again and played selections of music during half-time, one very striking performance being a stately march to music from goal to goal by the men of the Liverpool Regiment. Mr Wall, on behalf of the Association, invited His Majesty to have tea in the pavilion during the interval but the King elected to retain his seat until the resumption of play.

Risks

Lowe, the Liverpool captain, could not play. A late change in the team recalled the Final of 1907 when Hugh Bolton unexpectedly came into the Everton team which lost 1-2 to Sheffield Wednesday. Lowe said, "I am going to try

my leg on Saturday morning, and if there is any sign of its failing me, I shall not play. It would not be fair to the 'boys' on our side if I took any risks." It was a great blow to Lowe that he was unable to play especially as his father hoped to see him play for the first time, and illness at home prevented Mrs Lowe joining the party in London, and, altogether, the Liverpool captain had had an unfortunate week.

Masseur

He attended the masseur on the morning of the Final, but when he got back to Chingford he gave the injured leg a trial and found he was in pain. He decided immediately that he would not play. Donald McKinlay, the utility man of the team, was therefore included in the half-back line, Ferguson moving from left-half to centre-half.

Overcast

At noon, when some 300 spectators had already taken up their positions on the ground at the Palace, the weather was fine but rather overcast. A slight breeze was blowing up the ground towards the Rosary end, and the playing pitch appeared to be a trifle hard, but otherwise was in excellent condition. The special seats for His Majesty and his suite had been fitted up in the centre of the grand-stand, and the surroundings were tastefully decorated with flags and flowers.

Burnley - the Cup favourites - had been training at Lytham, and arrived in London on the Friday night. Their full team was engaged. The Liverpool team went by taxis from Chingford to the Palace, and the Forest Hotel friends gave them a send-off.

Bert Freeman scores the only goal of the game

The honour conferred upon the game and the clubs was highly appreciated by all football folk and there was a distinguished air about the grandstand, the equal of which a Final tie had never known before.

Distinguished

Among those present, apart from the King, were the Earl of Portsmouth, Earl Howe, Lord Desborough, Lords Faber and Porchester, the Lord Mayor of London, the Hon. Arthur Stanley, the Mayor and Sheriff of Chester, the Mayor of Burnley, Mr F.E. Smith, M.P.; Colonel R.G. Chaloner, M.P.; and Mr P. Morel, M.P.

The King

The King motored to Sydenham, and was received by the Earl of Derby , Lord Kinnaird, Mr F.J. Wall, secretary of the Football Association, and others. There was a sense of tremendous enthusiasm

when the teams turned out and the captains tossed for choice of ends.

Welcome

Each side received a great welcome and Ferguson, who acted as captain in Lowe's absence, and Boyle met in the centre circle. Liverpool lost the toss and the Burnley skipper elected to face the fitful sunshine.

Over-anxiousness

The opening exchanges were tinged with much over-anxiousness, but Burnley speedily settled down to work and Lindsay, making his way between Pursell and Longworth, got in a powerful shot which passed over the bar. Liverpool responded when Sheldon took an inside position and broke clear before passing to Miller who was lying offside. The game developed into a situation of cat-and-mouse, but then Burnley gained a

corner off Ferguson, although nothing came of it. The North Lancashire club were now more vigorous in attack than their rivals. McKinlay was penalised for being over-physical in the tackle, but the free-kick was safely negotiated.

True form

Liverpool once more attacked through Sheldon, who slipped the ball expertly through to Miller, but once again he was lying in an offside position. The Liverpool men now began to show their true form and good work by the halves gave Sheldon possession.

Fierce

The auburn-haired youth passed to Miller, who passed out to Lacey, but the Irishman missed the ball, although Nicholl got it and drove a fierce shot at goal. Fortunately for Burnley Taylor was in the way and he deflected the ball over the touchline.

The game was held up while the Burnley player recovered his wind, and then the game continued at the same frenetic pace as before. The wearers of the claret and blue attacked again, and the burly Bert Freeman, taking the ball in its flight, headed for goal, but Campbell raced out of his goal and cleared. Liverpool attacked with determination and Nicholl and Lacey made ground before passing to Metcalfe, who was about to shoot when he was questionably ruled offside.

Daisy-cutter

The game had been even up to now and, although Burnley had enjoyed the bulk of the attack they had not seriously shaken the Liverpool defence. Taking a pass from Miller, Lacey sent in a real "daisy-cutter" which brought Sewell to his knees.

Miskicked

The crowd cheered the popular Irish international for his solo effort. In response, Mosscrop put in a glorious centre which was well cleared, and then Liverpool had yet another attempt to gain the lead. Miller, having got behind the Burnley halves, had the ball at his toes when he miskicked and spurned a glorious opportunity of scoring. Burnley were busy at the other end where Boyle put in a few judicious touches, enabling Lindley to test Campbell's famed custodianship. A sprint along the wing by Nicholl, in which he showed a clean pair of heels to both Halley and Bamford, culminated in a shot which went wide of the goal.

Dangerous work by the Burnley left wing looked ominous, but Longworth cleared with a clever bit of headwork.

Lacey went through and passed to Nicholl, but he was ruled offside again when he received the ball and the move broke down.

Cinematographer

A throw-in near a cinematographer gave McKinlay an opportunity for a special film.

With half-an-hour gone, the eagerness of both sides remained unabated. The Burnley right wing looked dangerous as Nesbitt closed in, but Ferguson ran across and kicked into touch. Towards the interval, Burnley were awarded a free-kick within fairly easy range, but Boyle sent the leather just outside the upright.

Dangerous

The most dangerous attack of the afternoon so far occurred when Miller sped away and passed to Nicholl, who centred well. Metcalfe, however, was unable to get to the ball, and so a great chance of gaining the lead went begging. Just before the interval, Liverpool were busy on the left and a foul awarded against Halley gave them one more chance of scoring but the free-kick was intercepted by Bamford.

Affected

Both sides had been adversely affected by the importance of the occasion, and the presence of the King and his suite lent added dignity to the gathering.

The main feature of the Liverpool attack had been the intelligent work of Lacey, who was evidently a popular idol.

The opening stages of the second period - which began at 4.26 - were sensational. McKinlay led the way with a long drive which was blocked by Taylor, and at the other end Freeman put a shot over the bar.

Weakness

The Anfielders made themselves felt but there was still a certain amount of weakness about their finishing, although, in general, their forward work was much more convincing than that of Burnley. Sheldon raced away and passed to Miller, but he failed to take the opportunity.

Play opened out, and Mosscrop went on a solo run which culminated in a wild shot.

Spectators used every available vantage point in their efforts to watch the game

Suddenly Burnley attacked with speed. Boyle, who had played a masterly game, put the leather nicely forward to Hodgson, who, nursing it well, placed it to Freeman, and the ex-Evertonian shot strongly into the net after 58 minutes without any hesitation.

Goal

It was a good goal, and Campbell could not be blamed for failing to stop the ball in its flight. This setback was a severe blow to Liverpool, but they played with commendable spirit, and Taylor was injured in stopping a dangerous rush by Metcalfe and Sheldon. Goddard was said to have interested Stockport.

Improved

Chingford had been used by the Everton team in 1906 and 1907. Since last year, the Palace had been improved somewhat.

Risk

The trees were well "birded" with spectators who would risk anything. The unroofed stand looked bad, and rather out of place by the side of the King's box. For some thirty or forty people the scenic railway provided a good view of the match. The King received warm applause from the tremendous crowd and after the players had been photographed they cheered the King. Captains Boyle and Ferguson were presented to the Duke of Lancaster who wore a red rose in his coat.

Goodwill

The telegraph boys and postmen had been going backwards and forwards to the Liverpool hotel all day with messages of goodwill from all over the globe, and one arrived from a big firm in Church Street, and the names on the telegram numbered about thirty, including that of Mr G.D. Niven, the old Scottish footballer.

Rush

There was a wild rush to get the best possible position to witness the presentation of the Cup to the leader of the winning side. The cheering of the throng was long and loud, and the greatest enthusiasm prevailed.

Presentation

The presence of King George caused most of the spectators to stay to witness the presentation and the crowd was very much larger than at other presentations. A race to the Cup Final had been revealed in the *Liverpool Football Echo* on the day of the game. John Gibson, a plasterer of Samson Street, Everton, was charged with being drunk on the railway the night before the game. He was travelling to the Final and as a result of his uncivilised behaviour between Liverpool and Crewe, two ladies pulled the communication cord and stopped the train.

Prisoner

The prisoner then quietened down, but before Crewe was reached the train was again stopped, and he was put in the guard's van. The accused, who wore a huge rosette, pleaded to be dealt with as early as possible as he wanted to see Liverpool win the Cup. If he were allowed to go, he said, he could just catch the London express and arrive at the Palace after half-time.

Apologised

He hoped Liverpool would draw, so that he could see more of the game, since this was the first season that extra-time had been introduced in the final. He apologised for drinking the health of his team so vigorously, and was allowed to go on payment of five shillings. He left the court hurriedly to catch his train.

Before the game, the referee had been presented with a silver whistle to be used in the Final.

*Captains **Ferguson** and **Boyle** are presented to the King before the historic game*

Liverpool: Campbell; Longworth, Pursell; Fairfoul, Ferguson, McKinlay; Sheldon, Metcalfe, Miller, Lacey, Nicholl.

Burnley: Sewell; Bamford, Taylor; Halley, Boyle, Watson; Nesbitt, Lindley, Freeman, Hodgson, Mosscrop.

Referee: Mr H.S. Bamlett (Gateshead)

Linesmen: Mr J. Talks (Lincoln); Mr R.O. Rogers (London)

Attendance: 72,778 (at the Crystal Palace)

Receipts: £6,687

January 9, 1915

Liverpool (3) 3
Pagnam (2), Metcalfe 25

Stockport County (0) 0

LIVERPOOL, after their 1-3 defeat at Notts County on the previous Saturday, decided to drop Ferguson and Lacey due to poor form. Metcalfe and McKinlay entered the side, for whom Elisha Scott and Fred Pagnam made their Cup débuts. Stockport County had beaten Leeds United 3-1 away in the Second Division.

The attendance at the start was distinctly disappointing. The Spion Kop presented a very dreary spectacle, though it was rapidly being filled as the match progressed. The weather was cold, windy and threatening, and the ground, albeit on the soft side, appeared to be in very good condition.

A fair sprinkling of Stockport supporters gave the County a ringing cheer on their entrance into the arena. There were about 5,000 spectators present when the game started. Stockport were put to face the wind.

The visitors were the first to make any headway and Rodger, getting down the right, put in a tame shot. A minute later Kenyon passed to the same player, who again failed. Pursell then headed away an almost certain goal from Lloyd. Soon afterwards Liverpool attacked for the first time through Sheldon, who sent in a lovely, dropping centre, which Evans saved at the cost of a corner. This was well placed and Pagnam just failed with a header. Liverpool now found their rhythm, and a long drive from Fairfoul went just over the bar. As the home side attacked relentlessly, Sheldon advanced and passed to Pagnam, who scored a beautiful goal.

A foul against Liverpool just outside the penalty line gave Stockport an opening, and after a free-kick had been intercepted, Mitton shot into Scott's hands. The Stockport left wing got busy and Scott cleared from Wood. Play became more vigorous, and Stockport often attacked, but did not show any great skill or penetration. Play was stopped for a few minutes when Kenyon was temporarily knocked out.

The constant feeding of the Liverpool right wing enabled Sheldon to drop in a great centre and the Liverpool players appealed for a penalty against Mitton, but the appeal was summarily dismissed by the referee. Following good work by Nicholl and Miller, Pagnam got through before being fouled. Lowe took the free-kick and the ball deflected to the right. Metcalfe closed in and scored from short range after 25 minutes.

Stung by this reverse, Stockport livened up and first Wood and then Lloyd put in shots which went wide, while Rodger tested Scott with a powerful shot which went along the ground. From a centre by Sheldon, Pagnam shot over. Liverpool began to ease off and Stockport had a greater share of the attack, and Rodger put in a glorious shot, which almost beat Scott, who just saved at the expense of a corner. After good work by the half-backs, Pagnam shook off Goodwin to beat Evans with a fine shot which went into the far corner of

the net. A free-kick for Stockport close in gave them a chance and Scott was injured in saving his charge, the game being momentarily suspended. Miller, Nicholl and Pagnam were involved in a clever piece of inter-passing, and the Liverpool centre finished by shooting a yard wide. Evans rushed out to meet a centre by Sheldon, and fisted it away, only for Miller to rush in and shoot high over the bar. Nicholl centred accurately, and Miller was unfortunate in failing to score. Just before the interval, Pagnam sustained damage to his knee, and the game was again stopped for a time. For the last twenty minutes or so of the first period Stockport had done very little and Scott had an easy time. Liverpool tried hard to score a fourth goal before the change of ends, but Evans kept goal well.

The first half had all been in favour of the Reds. The work of the Anfield halves and forwards was of their best and, having once gained a substantial lead, they literally played with their opponents. To the credit of Stockport they continued to fight gamely and on at least two occasions they might have scored. The attendance increased steadily to 10,000 before hostilities resumed.

The County exerted great pressure and Scott was forced to save from Kenyon, while Metcalfe went close with a header. Stockport attacked down the left, and from a centre by Lloyd, Scott saved well from Rodger. Liverpool bombarded the Stockport goal and Metcalfe was unfortunate to have a stinging shot blocked by a defender. As the half wore on, Stockport gained a penalty for hands against Pursell. Rodger was entrusted with the kick, but in his excitement he missed the target by a yard. The failure was greeted by enormous cheers from the now well-filled Spion Kop.

A foul against Fairfoul gave Stockport a chance, but, with five forwards standing near the goalmouth, they failed to score. Pagnam gave Metcalfe a glorious chance, but the greasy ball twisted off his boot to go wide. Metcalfe was again unlucky after good work by Lowe.

Liverpool continued to be the superior side, although on occasions the defence was hard pressed to stop the vigorous, if unskilled, Stockport forwards. The visitors improved and seemed to have a better understanding than they had in the first half, however. McKinlay came to the rescue when the visiting advance guards came down in combined order. Sheldon was questionably ruled offside as he closed in on goal. In the last few minutes of the game Liverpool became very careless, and once the ball was almost dribbled through, but Scott saved his charge. A solo effort by Pagnam was spoilt when he pushed the ball too far forward, allowing Evans to pick up easily. Then Metcalfe was ruled offside, a decision which upset the home supporters. Mitton, the Stockport centre-half, defended well and fed his forwards with great skill, and on several occasions he stemmed dangerous onslaughts by the Liverpool forwards.

The receipts amounted to £250. The highest score of the round was Middlesbrough's 9-3 home win against Goole. Carr, Elliott, and Tinsley all scored hat-tricks, while Ford, Morley and Spavin scored for Goole, who trailed 1-5 at the interval. The shock of the round was Blackburn Rovers' 1-0 defeat away to non-League Swansea Town, Beynon scoring a spectacular goal. Rovers were without Shea, Dawson and Simpson, but they still fielded five internationals, and Swansea fought out the second half with only nine men, due to injuries. The Rovers had tried to get Swansea to sell their ground right, but the Welsh club refused. Hewitt, the former South Liverpool player, was in the home ranks. The Cup-holders, Burnley, beat Huddersfield 3-1 at home, with goals coming from Freeman (after 22 minutes), Thorpe and Kelly before 15,000 spectators. Millwall and Orient, like Everton and Barnsley, had players sent off for fighting.

Liverpool: Scott; Longworth, Pursell; Fairfoul, Lowe, McKinlay; Sheldon, Metcalfe, Pagnam, Miller, Nicholl.

Stockport County: Evans; Goodwin, Fagan; Davies, Mitton, Graham; Proctor, Kenyon, Rodger, Wood, Lloyd.

Referee: Mr D.H. Asson (West Bromwich)

Attendance: 10,000

GREECE PREPARES?

REPORT SAYS MOBILISATION HAS BEGUN

An Athens message to the *New York Herald* emphasises the increasing sentiment throughout Greece in favour of the Allies, and asserts that mobilisation is actually, though not officially, in preparation. The correspondent believes that Greece intends to enter the war at the close of the winter, if nothing meanwhile occurs to hasten her mobilisation.

In the real fight, the Germans claimed to have taken 2,000 prisoners on 7 January and seven machine guns on the Eastern Front. On the Western Front there had been very heavy rains and thunder had been heard all that day. The Lys had overflowed its banks in some parts. The French claimed to have gained possession of 400 metres of the enemy's trenches between hill 200 and the village of Perthes. In addition they re-captured the village. It was reported that Greece were set to join the war on the side of the Allies. Back in England, there was a huge operation in effect which was attempting to stem the floods in Norfolk. Rivers had overflowed the protective works, and the pumping stations were unable to check the rising floods. Between Southery and Littleport, many farms were submerged in a lake fifteen miles long and seven miles wide.

Fred Pagnam shook off Goodwin to beat Evans with a fine shot which went into the far corner of the net for Liverpool's third goal.

January 30, 1915

Sheffield United (0) 1
Davies 89

Liverpool (0) 0

IT was many years since Liverpool last met United in the Cup, and on that occasion the United made progress into the Final by disposing of Liverpool after four games. All of the city of Sheffield was agog with Cup fever as Wednesday were also at home - to Wolverhampton Wanderers. The home side won 2-0. The tie was a repeat of the previous season's tie, when the Wednesday drew at Wolves and the replay was sensational in that a wall collapsed, injuring many people. The Wolves protested against Wednesday's victory on the grounds that the game should not have been continued due to the fact that Peers, their goalkeeper, had fainted and was unable to continue in the final ten minutes. However, Peers was in goal in this game, and the Wednesday won with first-half goals from Robertson and Glennon before a crowd of 20,000.

Liverpool arrived at Bramall Lane in good time. The popularity of Liverpool meant that several hundred people made the journey to Sheffield and there were 20,000 spectators present when the game opened. United lost the toss, and started with their faces to the sun, although there was practically no wind.

The home right wing were the first to make ground, but the movement came to nothing, for Liverpool replied with an advance on the left. Miller lost possession, however, and the ball travelled to the right, where it was lobbed into the goalmouth. Cook cleared with a fine kick, and the Sheffield left were off again at top speed. Evans rounded Longworth and shot fiercely, but Pursell dashed across and saved the situation. Davies led a dangerous move in the direction of Scott until he was brought up in time, while at the other end Pagnam seized the ball and was clean through when he was ruled offside. Then the Liverpool goal was subjected to further bombardment. The three Sheffield inside forwards were closing in dangerously when Lacey came to the rescue, and when a few moments later Kitchen tried to make ground on the right he put the ball out.

Lacey, playing out of position, was having a great game. The visitors made progress on the left through McKinlay and Miller until Sturgess broke up the promising move. Then, for the first time in the game, the Liverpool right attacked but Sheldon's progress was impeded by English. Lacey and Lowe broke up a combined move by Davies and company and a little later Lowe shot wide of the target from long range. Both teams played a long passing game, but Sheffield showed more skill than their opponents and when Kitchen swung the ball right across the goalmouth, Masterman missed it by a hair-breadth. The pace of the game increased, and the balance of the attack lay with the home side. In their anxiety, however, they missed many genuine opportunities, and the first direct shot came from Davies, whose rasping shot was coolly saved by Scott. Liverpool made several attempts to break down the home defence, but their efforts were rather disjointed and when at length Sheldon broke clear he was pulled up for offside. Miller fouled Brelsford which almost cost Liverpool a goal, but Davies put the leather just outside the post. Another effort by the home centre was only a couple of feet outside the range, and a fierce shot from Kitchen passed just outside the upright as the home side attacked with venom.

Liverpool did not seem to be able to get into their proper stride, but at last Pagnam, Metcalfe and Sheldon advanced with clock-like precision and Pagnam looked like forging his way through when Cook stopped him.

The home side continued to enjoy the greater part of the attack, and Pursell got in the way of a dangerous free-kick, but moments later Simmons failed with a snap shot. Metcalfe tried to inspire his forwards with a solo effort, but his shot lacked power, and the home side's right wing again tested Scott's resourcefulness. Liverpool's response came through Pagnam, who was knocked off the ball, and Nicholl, who was ruled offside.

A breakaway by the home ranks led to Simmons and Pursell almost coming to blows, but other players intervened and prevented fighting. Kitchen's perfect centre was put over the bar by Davies, who was well positioned. Kitchen then attempted a solo effort, but his shot was weak. An oblique shot from Evans was headed away by Pursell, and Longworth immediately afterwards cleared the defence with a timely interception. A few moments before the interval, Sheffield redoubled their efforts to score, but their shooting lacked precision. The first half had been typical of a Cup-tie. Neither side had shown much skill, but the home side undoubtedly enjoyed the greater attacking moves.

Sheffield began the second period with a concerted series of attacks, but Longworth featured well in defence. Miller and Pagnam were thwarted by Utley and Brelsford before the Cutlers attacked through Masterman, who missed the target by inches. As the game progressed, the tension mounted and first Evans shot a foot wide of the goal and then Lowe put over the bar. A temporary lull followed some pretty, but ineffective, play in midfield. A shot from Kitchen, who was completely unmarked, went wide. The Anfield left-wing pair then became prominent and they gave Cook and Gough a torrid time until the ball was put into touch. Then the game developed into one of long-passing which led to haphazard shots at both ends. English was hurt in a collision and had to be carried off. Liverpool, who pressed strongly, ought to have scored through Miller who missed an open goal. After being absent for some time, English returned to the fray, but he was obviously lame. Just before time, Sheffield forced two corners, and from one, Scott was forced to tip the ball over the bar. The following corner led to a tremendous volley from which Davies scored the only goal of the game. Liverpool's fine attacking moves had evoked admiration from the crowd during the second half, but they lacked penetration and were put out of the Cup.

Burnley continued their run, winning 6-0 at home to Southend. For the first time in the history of the game, Cup ties were to carry an extra half-hour if the game was drawn after ninety minutes. The idea grew from a suggestion that people should not give up their work in midweek, particularly those people involved in the war effort. One major surprise was that not a single club sold its ground-right, and it was reported that this was the right direction for the Cup competition to move in. A curiosity of the first halves, was that not a single game had witnessed a score of more than 2 goals. Everton beat Bristol City 4-0 at Goodison. The draw for the Third Round of the Cup was to take place in London on Monday week, 8 February.

Sheffield United: Gough; Cook, English; Sturgess, Brelsford, Utley;   Kitchen, Simmons, Davies, Masterman, Evans.

Liverpool: Scott; Longworth, Pursell; Lacey, Lowe, McKinlay; Sheldon, Metcalfe, Pagnam, Miller, Nicholl.

Referee: Mr G. Richardson (Nottingham)

Attendance: 25,000

The military authorities at Rhyl have issued orders prohibiting soldiers being on licensed premises after 9p.m. This is reverting to the original order, which was revoked a few weeks ago in favour of a ten o'clock rule.

Elisha Scott

Between The Wars

1919 - 1939

January 10, 1920

South Shields (0) 1
J.Woods

Liverpool (0) 1
Lewis 75

SOUTH Shields, who had never entered the Second Round of the Cup, rather fancied their chances against Liverpool for, although Lillycrop was an important absentee, Cresswell and his pals had made such an effect on Second Division sides that their form stood scrutiny, and Liverpool had to acknowledge their task was a difficult one. The Anfield boys had been preparing for the game at Whitley Bay and the doubtful starters, Longworth and Walter Wadsworth, were chosen because by the middle of the week they had improved so much. The game created enormous interest around South Shields.

The morning opened with storms of rain and sleet which subsequently developed into a raging blizzard of snow. At one o'clock the ground presented an Arctic appearance, yet a great crowd collected outside, waiting for the gates to open. Unfortunately, the referee was late in arriving, and the question as to whether the game could be started or not was unsettled until two o'clock. By this time the snow had ceased and, although the playing pitch was covered, the touchlines were soon swept clean. The Liverpool players left Whitley Bay on the morning of the game and arrived in good time.

South Shields kicked off on the slippery, snow-clad surface. They immediately attacked down the right, and then on the left, but both shots were weak and Campbell - in his first FA Cup tie for six years - was not seriously troubled. Liverpool were quick to respond with a sprint on the wing by Sheldon, but the speedy little man was unable to control the ball and his effort was wasted.

The Shields forwards attacked aggressively and made a dangerous attempt on Campbell's goal and J. Smith, in particular, gave the Liverpool goalkeeper a hard time. Considering the conditions, the game was fast and exciting. Accurate passing was obviously out of the question, and the players improvised with long-range drives aimed at the respective keepers.

Longworth came through a ruck of players on a solo run and finished with a tremendous drive that passed only a foot wide. A storming attack by the Liverpool forwards sent the crowd almost frantic with excitement, and after Lewis had been intercepted, Lacey rushed along and put the leather high over the bar. A spell of long-range kicking proved of no advantage to either side, but at length the Shields forwards made progress on the left and forced a corner which was well placed by A. Smith and J. Smith sent in a swift shot which was marvellously cleared by Campbell.

The visitors took up the running and on the right Sheldon and Lacey weaved a pattern with their footmarks in the snow. They were well held by Maitland, and soon afterwards Lewis shot wide after a dazzling run. Lacey, who was evidently out to take full advantage of every opportunity that offered itself, wriggled his way through the home defence and sent in another drive which gave Walker some trouble. For a considerable period after this the bulk of the pressure lay with the visitors, who were clearly the better side. The conditions, however, militated against flowing football and were rather more reminiscent of snowballing than of footballing. An accurate pass or any degree of precision could not be expected when the ground was a mixture of mud and frozen water. However, as the game progressed, the pace became faster, and the contest resolved itself into a typical rough-and-ready Cup tie.

Liverpool attacked down the right and from a mêlée in front of Walker, Miller put the ball over the bar. A. Smith had a shot which deserved better than missing the mark by inches. There was still a lack of precision about the play, but it was all sportsmanlike and vigorous. Both the Liverpool wings attacked strongly in turn, only to find that Maitland and Cresswell thoroughly understood their particular business. Some of Maitland's clearances were remarkably good, and the crowd laughed loudly when he and Lacey came to grief on the slippery surface.

Towards the interval, South Shields looked dangerous, and A. Smith forced Campbell to save on his knees. The Liverpool 'keeper cleared well, but the other Smith almost scored with a shot that struck the woodwork. Bamber was injured just before the change of ends, but did not leave the field. Billy Lacey showed wonderful forcefulness and initiative during the first period.

There was a largely increased attendance when the players reappeared after a rather lengthy interval, during which the crowd kept itself warm with a sort of restricted dancing as an accompaniment to the band that discoursed popular pantomime tunes.

South Shields imitated their opening performance by rushing down in great style and from a pass by Woods, A.Smith had a magnificent opening which he put wide. After a temporary check administered by the Liverpool halves, Shields again pressed on the left, but they unable to make any impression upon the watchful and imperturbable Longworth. At length Woods raced clean through and sent in a lovely shot which passed a foot the wrong side of a post. The playing pitch, although churned up, was now rather easier, and as a consequence the shooting on both sides was much more accurate. Shields kept up a regular bombardment for a time and it looked as though they would open the scoring through Charlton, but his shot was cleared. The home side were thoroughly wound up and there was a tremendous scene when from a corner kick by Charlton, Woods scored with a fast drive from close range. A scene of unrestrained cheering greeted the goal, and it was re-echoed when Walker staved off a combined movement on the part of the Liverpool inside-forwards. It was not long, however, before Woods and his wings were pressing for further goals, but their approach work was ruined by over-anxiety. With just fifteen minutes remaining, Lewis equalised to earn Liverpool a well-deserved replay.

South Shields: Walker; Cresswell, Maitland; Frith, Hopkins, Dreyer; Charlton, J.W.Smith, J.Woods, Oxberry, A.Smith.

Liverpool: Campbell; Longworth, McKinlay; Bamber, W.Wadsworth, Bromilow; Sheldon, Lacey, T.Miller, Lewis, Pearson.

Referee: Mr J. Cable (Yorkshire West Riding)

Attendance: 10,000

*With just fifteen minutes remaining, **Henry Lewis** equalised to earn Liverpool a well-deserved replay.*

RESERVES' DAY

LIVERPOOL v. EVERTON AT ANFIELD

Liverpool: Armstrong; Lucas, Penman; Checkland, Butler, Barlow; Newman, Forshaw, Miller, Matthews, Dagnall.
Everton: Mitchell; Thompson, Evans; Peacock, Lievesley, J.Robinson; Jones, A.Robinson, Sharpe, Mayson, Donnachie.

With the seniors being drawn to play their English Cup tie away from home, much interest was today centred upon the first meeting of the Reserves in a Central League fixture.

Everton placed a strong team in the field, including their latest capture, Brewster, at centre-half. Liverpool also were strongly represented, and played two new men in Armstrong and Butler.

At the last minute Brewster stood down owing to a cold, and Lievesley took his place at centre-half. When the game started there were fully 10,000 spectators.

Everton lost the toss, and the first advance came through Liverpool, who made play on the right, but Thompson intervened and punted clear.

Everton were next busy on the right, and Jones sent in a centre which was badly placed by Sharpe to Donnachie. The game looked like being fast, as both sides were putting all they knew into it.

Liverpool were now giving the Blues' defence some trouble, and Mitchell had to run out to clear from Miller. Jones, receiving from Peacock, was making tracks for goal when he was nicely pulled up by Barlow.

Robinson and Jones were combining well on the right, which ended in the latter sending in a great centre for Sharpe to be only just wide with a header. Miller was next pulled up for offside when a goal looked certain.

Matthews and Dagnall were next in evidence, and carried play to the Everton goal, only to find Thompson was able to clear before Matthews could get in his final shot. Up to this point there was little to choose between the teams, and it was quite a typical local Derby.

Liverpool at last opened the scoring, Matthews shot in hard, and the ball being only partially saved by Mitchell, Miller shot into the net before the custodian could recover himself.

This only spurred on the Everton team, who gave Lucas and Penman some trouble, and one great effort by Robinson almost brought about the equaliser. The game was fast and free from fouls. Everton next gained a free-kick near goal through a foul on Mayson, and Robinson grazed the bar with a splendid effort.

Two minutes from the interval Sharpe equalised for Everton Reserves.

Half-time: Liverpool Reserves 1, Everton Reserves 1.

When the game re-started, Jones went centre forward for Everton, Sharpe going outside right. The early stages of the opening play went slightly in favour of the Blues, who attacked strongly.

Miller then had a glorious chance for Liverpool to take the lead, but Evans saved the situation.

Three-quarter time: Liverpool Reserves 1, Everton Reserves 1.

Final: Liverpool Reserves 1, Everton Reserves 1.

January 14, 1920

Liverpool (2) 2
Lewis 40, Sheldon 42

South Shields (0) 0

THE game was played in ideal weather, despite the fact that the previous night's storms blew at speeds of up to 60 miles per hour, although this was a reduction on the preceding night, when the storms reached up to 70 miles per hour. Liverpool were doubtful about Longworth, and South Shields also had doubts about their full-backs. The tie promised to be keen and exciting, and when the players lined up there was a crowd of large dimension, the half-holiday numbers being added to by the regular Anfield-goers.

South Shields sport a most uncommon attire - green jerseys with a red collar and cuffs. They looked more like racing colours than football colours. The ground looked in perfect trim, but as soon as Liverpool had won the toss and play had started, the top turf was seen to be very unreliable.

Liverpool started well and mainly on their left wing. Pearson gained a corner, and from Bromilow's kick, Wadsworth was a matter of inches wide with a header. Pearson screwed in an almost impossible angular centre, but Dreyer dribbled out of defence.

For a time, Liverpool looked to have an easy passage into the next round, but South Shields eventually got going through Woods, whose shot against the wind went close. There was then a short stoppage for an injury to Frith's head. Cresswell soon showed his ability at full-back, and his length of kick and his judgment were excellent. In the early stages, Pearson's work was noteworthy, and he put in several dangerous centres from acute angles, one of which Walker deflected for a corner.

Young Ted Charlton sent across to the left wing where Smith fumbled and never got his shot in. The visitors broke dangerously until they were prevented from scoring by Longworth. Liverpool continued to attack, and from the half-way line McKinlay sent in a lob which hit the crossbar before going over. Walker, nevertheless, was perfectly placed to save.

Sheldon forced Walker to concede a corner, and the goalkeeper damaged his leg slightly when he was charged against the goalpost. Pearson's corner kick entered the goal without a second player touching the ball so that the goal did not count. The standard of defence on both sides was high, and though Liverpool showed the superior skills in combination, the visitors made up for their lack of prowess with great determination.

A Pearson centre was nodded sideways by Lacey instead of forwards and the ball travelled wide of the post. Play had been clean and free-flowing and there had been hardly a stoppage for a trip in 25 minutes. In this period, Campbell had not been troubled by any kind of shot and Walker had not

been much busier as both sets of forwards were weak. The big pivot, Hopkins, held a tight rein on Miller, and equally Wadsworth - playing much above his usual game - refused to let Young in.

After a period of sustained pressure Lewis scored, and two minutes later Sheldon increased the score. Lewis's goal was the result of some excellent combination, the ball in turn being played by Sheldon, Lacey, Miller and Lewis. Probably Miller earned much credit for allowing the ball to pass on to Lewis, and certainly the scorer deserved credit for his clean, swift shot. Sheldon got his goal from easy range and he was helped by the fact that Maitland tripped up at a critical moment. The goalkeeper did not cover the space and Sheldon's goal was well received. Just before the whistle, Lacey, who had played excellent football throughout, put in a swerving shot, but Walker judged it right, and Miller sent in a high shot which went over the bar. Liverpool were well worth their interval lead as they had played good, sharp football. As a sportsmanlike exhibition, the game was remarkable in that there were only three free-kicks in the first period.

The teams were quickly out for the second half due to the fact that a mist was descending upon the ground. Campbell was immediately called upon to make a catch. Dwyer was injured and Cresswell's job became more difficult. Although they were two goals behind, the visitors battled on courageously, but without result against the brilliance of McKinlay, Longworth and the half-backs. Woods, the ex-Norwich forward, was the only reliable attacker, and the visitors' left wing was idle throughout the game. Cresswell thought it advisable to play a semblance of the one-back game, and for a while Shields took a lot of stopping, Oxberry shooting hard, but wide. Cresswell, in falling, let in Miller, who again turned the ball to Lewis, just as he had done with the first goal, but Hopkins rushed in and prevented the shot.

It was natural that a lead of two goals should kill off the interest in the game to some extent, but the crowd became enthusiastic when Lacey, in trapping the ball cleverly and in dribbling and passing, made great strides. Further applause came when Walker flung himself at Miller's shot and turned it outside the goal area.

A dog invaded the pitch and was a big nuisance to the referee and the players, but a source of great amusement to the crowd. Liverpool should have scored a third goal, but Lewis could not clinch the opening so beautifully created for him by Bromilow. Bromilow then tried a shot on his own which was well saved by Walker, who was plainly a formidable custodian. Woods shot against the angle of the bar in a vain effort to score.

There was only one team in the game, and the referee never had a simpler task to govern a game. The players, in effect, refereed the game themselves. Liverpool were drawn against Luton Town, who had overcome Coventry in the previous round.

Liverpool: Campbell; Longworth, McKinlay; Bamber, W.Wadsworth, Bromilow; Sheldon, Lacey, T.Miller, Lewis, Pearson.

South Shields: Walker; Cresswell, Maitland; Frith, Hopkins, Dreyer; Charlton, J.Woods, Young, Oxberry, A.Smith.

Referee: Mr J. Cable (Yorkshire West Riding)

Attendance: 40,000

Jackie Sheldon, who scored after 42 minutes from close range

January 31, 1920

Luton Town (0) 0

Liverpool (1) 2
Lacey 10, 68

LIVERPOOL fought their way into the Third Round of the Cup on a day when the Rugby Union players of Wigan went on strike for more money, when Liverpool Schoolboys beat Bradford Schoolboys 5-0, when England beat France by 8 points to 3 at Twickenham, when Everton's friendly with Hull City was called off due to Everton being held up at Guide Bridge owing to a collision on the line, when the price of imported beef was reduced by twopence a pound as from Monday, February 2nd, and the price of imported pork was increased by a penny a pound to correspond with the recent price increases in the sale of pigs, and when suits at five guineas each sold like wildfire from the Bradford Municipal Stores, and when the prices charged at some football grounds was as much as ten shillings and sixpence (52½p). Attendances and receipts at most grounds broke all records. In previous rounds the appalling weather had hindered large crowds, but, although the preceding days had threatened otherwise and had ruined the telegraph wires and telephone lines, many attendances were so great that the gates had to be shut early.

A record 450 clubs had already affiliated themselves to the Liverpool County F.A. as the population recovered from the Great War. Jimmy Wilde (7st 10lbs) knocked out Mike Ertle (8st 3lbs) in the third round in Milwaukee as Liverpool attempted to reach the third round of the Cup. Three Irish members of parliament were arrested in Dublin. One of them had escaped from Mountjoy Prison in the previous summer. A motor-scooter to carry two people or one person and two hundredweight of luggage was being developed.

Luton had a pretty ground with a Pressbox more like a Royal Box than a Pressbox. It was in direct touch and view with the play and players. The pitch looked better than it actually was, and it had a clay subsoil that was very sticky. The pitch looked to have a pronounced dip, whereas, in fact, it was absolutely level. But for the soft nature of the turf, it would have been one of the best-drained surfaces in the country.

Luton had a band that played *"Chu Chin Chow"* like a theatre orchestra. Many people walked from London to Luton to watch the game. *En route*, the Liverpool team travelled down Liverpool Road - a happy omen. Liverpool had a fine rest in Chingford and were fit and well. One paper announced that Chambers would be playing, but there was never any doubt about Lacey. Luton found that Rutherford could play, and both sides were at full strength. There was a lot of fraternising between the players because Lacey and Bookman were in Ireland together, and Parker, Summers and Sheldon all came from the same town, and a Luton reserve player, Tomlinson, had played behind Pearson and Lewis. The game kicked off with the weather squally and wet. The ground was full just after two o'clock. The time was passed most pleasantly due to a red and blue attired supporter dancing very expertly in full view of the crowd. His journey and his incidentals must have cost him the best part of ten pounds, and in view of his "star turn" Luton or Liverpool might have made the amount good to him, for it was uncommonly good dancing for a "Cartwright". The home side won the toss, which meant no discernible advantage because there was little wind, and Liverpool kicked off. Lacey showed up well early on, beating three men in four yards' space, but the really sensational opening was provided by McKinlay trying to kick clear and the ball cannoned right in front of goal, where Longworth made a lovely and timely interception. Bamber was injured in a collision with an opponent's boot, and then Dunn charged Lacey so hard that the Irishman was seated on his pants. Liverpool settled down reasonably well, but Luton had the first dangerous chance which Campbell cleared. Dunn was cautioned for a third foul.

Lacey scored after ten minutes from a debatable corner, taken by Sheldon. It was a clean, penetrating goal, and soon afterwards Liverpool might have scored again when Miller's pass to Lewis enabled the inside man to shoot fiercely against the crossbar. It would not have counted, since the referee adjudged Lewis offside. Luton tried hard to make headway, but Longworth and McKinlay were in excellent form. Liverpool's forward line played like the whole team - cute, steady, and capable. One remarkable instance was the way McKinlay, after seeming beaten, outstretched his leg behind him and made the ball come back. It was a football trick and it came off, although it involved a lot of luck. At this point a cloud came over the proceedings, and threatened a deluge. Parker produced some fine headed clearances. Longworth put one safety kick over the stand and on to the roof of some houses.

A Roe header sent Campbell the wrong way, but he recovered in time. This encouraged Luton, and for three or four minutes, they remained encamped in the Liverpool area. Lacey, however, withdrew to full-back, and although there were words about his involvement, the ball was cleared. Rutherford wasted several opportunities after he had worked hard to create them. Roe was unmarked when he took Dodd's centre, and he headed it well, though Campbell timed his fall nicely. Hoare scored direct from a corner and brilliant sunshine had made Campbell and company shade their eyes. Campbell attempted to save, but there was some doubt as to whether he had touched the ball. The referee ruled that no other player had touched the ball as it sailed into goal. The home supporters were extremely disappointed and booed the referee for some time. With sixty-eight minutes gone, Liverpool scored again through Lacey.

Luton Town: Summers; Elvey, Dunn; Urwin, Rutherford, Parker; Hoare, Roe, Simms, Dodd, Bookman.

Liverpool: Campbell; Longworth, McKinlay; Bamber, W.Wadsworth, Bromilow; Sheldon, Lacey, T.Miller, Lewis, Pearson.

Referee: Mr Robinson (Wembley)

Attendance: 12,640

A PIG IN A POKE

IMPORTED BEEF DOWN TWOPENCE; PORK UP A PENNY

The Food Controller has made orders reducing the maximum price of imported beef by 2d per lb. wholesale and retail as from Monday next, February 2nd.

The retail price of imported pork is raised by 1d per lb, to correspond with the recent increase in the controlled price of pigs. The maximum wholesale meat prices in Ireland are revoked as from the same date.

*One remarkable instance was the way **Donald McKinlay**, after seeming beaten, outstretched his leg behind him and made the ball come back.*

February 21, 1920

Liverpool (1) 2

Sheldon 4,   T.Miller 62

Birmingham (0) 0

THE cup brought fine weather and record attendances and receipts yet again. The Birmingham trains were packed, and many of those who made the journey could not get inside the ground. Early birds from the Midlands took the wise precaution of making sure by queuing up outside the Spion Kop as early as eight o'clock on the morning of the game. It was the best weather that the Cup had encountered this season. All around the country the story was the same: full grounds and lively scenes.

The Liverpool players left Blackpool on the morning of the game and at midday had a hearty welcome from those who saw them at Exchange Station. It was a curious fact that the former Chairman of Liverpool F.C., Mr Edwin Berry, went to Blackpool by the same train on the previous Monday and stayed at the same hotel, but he did not know until he checked in that the players were staying there.

The day was brilliantly fine and the air nippy; there was a wind, but not a spoiling wind, and the turf was in excellent condition. On the previous Thursday, Ephraim Longworth, the skipper, had an injured thigh and it looked as though he would miss this tie, but trainer Charlie Wilson attended to the leg and Longworth made a remarkable recovery.

The Spion Kop was like a miniature Hampden Park and it was filled more quickly than any other part of the ground. In fact, one hour before the kick off, the youngsters were allowed over on to the playing slope. There was one casualty. The stands filled slowly because they were reserved seats and people could take their time. As time wore on, there were further casualties from the Kop, but in general the crowd was very orderly and the arrangements excellent. The young fellows of the band played their part, and the mascot, attended by three or four others, was bedecked in red. The mascots did something more than amuse, as they took up a collection for the band, which happened to be in need of funds, and there were coppers in blue in plenty, and the band gained financial recompense for its work as coppers rained down heavily from the Kop.

A remarkable feature in the city was that the streets were almost empty an hour before the game started, everybody having taken the wise precaution of being early. There was one uncommon case of juggling - one little fellow being handed down from the middle of the Kop right on to the playing pitch - a distance of some thirty yards. There was no risk in this practice, but there was a risk when supporters climbed onto the girders. One grey-haired adventurer climbed half-way up, and then found his hat knocked off by an orange. He did not try to go over the top again.

The noise from the pent-up spectators when the teams turned out, was amazing. The side winning the toss gained a useful advantage, the sun being the chief factor. Birmingham won the toss and Liverpool were set to face the sun. Longworth made play at once and Tremelling left his goal. Miller was unaware that the goal was empty since he did not try a shot when in position. Longworth, in trying to clear, put the ball to an opponent, and this was followed by Lewis's powerful shot being blocked.

Wadsworth gave away a free-kick early on, and another should have been awarded in the next minute because the referee made an error of judgment when he allowed Sheldon to go ahead from an offside position and score. The linesman had signalled offside by vigorously waving his handkerchief, and at least three Liverpool players were offside, including Sheldon. Mr Fowler would not listen to the appeals of the Birmingham men and the home side were fortunate to be in the lead.

For a time the Midlanders were upset by their reversal. However, Hampton created some danger by a nice swinging pass to the outside-left, and only a free-kick against Wadsworth stopped the danger.

Roulson was admonished by the referee for a nasty offence on Pearson, and there was another stoppage when Gibson was knocked out temporarily. McKinlay did not kick true at the start, but it was only a question of time before he began to put power and precision into his punts.

Liverpool gained a corner kick and there was a hum of excitement as Bromilow went across to take it, for the player was so adept at taking these place kicks. He put the ball so accurately that Lacey was able to head it, and Bamber and Miller went near to converting it. Whitehouse badly fouled Wadsworth and he was severely cautioned by the referee. Ball, at this time, was virtually a passenger, yet Birmingham worked some useful openings and Whitehouse's tremendous shot flew towards Campbell, who pulled off a spectacular one-handed save.

Hampton, as in days of old, charged the goalkeeper immediately, but the Liverpool players took offence at the charge, so much so that McKinlay threatened to take an abnormal risk. Up went Hampton's knee and there was a mêlée in front of goal. Eventually calm was restored.

Ball ruined any chance he had of staying on for the rest of the half when he cleared upfield with a long punt, and he left the pitch after 25 minutes. Birmingham were outplayed for a long spell and Tremelling caught a beautiful first-time shot from Miller, and when Lacey headed back into goal, the little custodian effected another fine save.

After an absence of five minutes, Ball returned. The game was marred with little accidents and Miller, Womack and McClure had problems. The game developed into one of fouls and impetuosity as both sides were guilty of playing the man and not the ball.

During the first period, Campbell had had just one shot to deal with, and the home backs and half-backs had done their work thoroughly. The forward line had not performed as well as they should have done despite beating the man easily enough. The final pass lacked real penetration. Lacey did not predominate in the manner he did against Luton and South Shields. On the Birmingham side, only Womack approached true form. The half-backs were not strong and the forwards could not cope with Liverpool's resolute defence.

Ball turned out in the second half, despite limping badly. Birmingham tried to rush the ball through early in the second half, but their naivety was in evidence when they won a free-kick early on. The ball was not placed and no one was set for business when the ball was sent on its way. Pearson put in a nice run and attempted centre and at the opposite end Hampton was tackled by McKinlay as he advanced.

The standard of wing play was abysmal throughout the second half and Morgan was completely starved of the ball. However, the dirty play had ceased and the only stoppages now were for the ball finding touch. Longworth injured his side and this let in the visitors until McKinlay, cutting across from the opposite side, cleared.

Campbell was forced to save from a visiting forward and Hampton attempted a charge and failed. Miller scored a splendid second goal for Liverpool after 62 minutes. McClure kicked Lacey as the rough play began again, but the referee failed to stamp his authority on the game. Birmingham were reduced to eight men when Morgan was sent off, Ball left the field through injury and McClure also went off through injury.

Lewis nearly scooped the ball into an empty goal and Hampton, one of three forwards, scooped the ball over the bar. Bromilow made one fierce drive which suggested that he was a forward, not a half-back. Roulson committed an extraordinarily bad foul on Pearson, and Lacey was at fault for trying to get his own back.

It was difficult to imagine that these players were brothers in a union and were all playing the game as a means of livelihood. Bromilow was added to the list of those injured. Liverpool were due to return to Blackpool on the Monday after the game, the day of the Cup draw.

Liverpool trainer, **Charlie Wilson**

THE KING AN ONLOOKER

CHELSEA v. LEICESTER TIE HONOURED

The King arrived at Stamford Bridge shortly before 3pm to see the Cup-tie between Chelsea and Leicester City. He received an extraordinary enthusiastic welcome from the huge crowd of spectators, and then went into the field, where he shook hands with the players on each side.

His Majesty then spoke to numbers of wounded and blinded soldiers who were accommodated with seats on the ground.

Leicester brought a big following down in three special trains, and at the start there were 60,000 people on the ground. Many people also came from the Midlands in motor-charabancs.

OTHER THIRD ROUND RESULTS

Chelsea	3	Leicester City	0
Aston Villa	1	Sunderland	0
Tottenham H.	3	West Ham	0
Bristol City	2	Cardiff	1
Bradford	4	Notts County	3
Bradford City	3	Preston North End	0
Huddersfield T.	3	Plymouth A.	1

Liverpool: Campbell; Longworth, McKinlay; Bamber, W.Wadsworth, Bromilow; Sheldon, Lacey, T.Miller, Lewis, Pearson.

Birmingham: Tremelling; Ball, Womack; Roulson, McClure, Barton; Burkenshaw, Gibson, Hampton, Whitehouse, Morgan.

Referee: Mr J.W.D. Fowler (Sunderland)

Attendance: 50,000

March 6, 1920

Huddersfield Town (0) 2

Swann 60, Taylor

Liverpool (0) 1

T.Miller 49

HUDDERSFIELD - going well near the top of the Second Division (they eventually finished runners-up to Tottenham and gained automatic promotion) - deserved some success for the way they had fought a life and death struggle in the boardroom and in the banking department. This latest victory enabled the Yorkshire club to become much more sound financially. The club had entertained the idea of moving to share with Leeds, but with victories over Newcastle and Liverpool, they forgot all about a move. In fact the Yorkshire club reached the Final, only losing to Aston Villa 1-0 after extra time. Huddersfield was not altogether a pleasant location as many of the excursionists from Liverpool found.

A number of Liverpool men made their abode in Huddersfield the previous night, although many had difficulty in getting accommodation. However half a dozen or so were given accommodation in the lounge of an hotel, where the porter made a fire and the party made themselves comfortable in the easy chairs. The ground was surrounded by typical Yorkshire buildings, drab and dreary, and the situation of it is about a quarter of an hour's walk from the station.

In spite of the circumstances whereby Liverpool supporters were practically barred from getting tickets, there was quite a good measure of support for the Reds, as was made evident when Sheldon, McKinlay, Campbell and Bamber, and the referee who controlled the Everton-Newcastle final in 1906, Mr Fred Kirkham of Preston, made their appearance on the field three-quarters of an hour before the game to inspect the pitch. Sheldon was very anxious about the state of the ground because of his doubt about playing. Judging by the way he went off the field, he had decided that he would take the risk.

The ground resembles Liverpool's, except for the massiveness of the Spion Kop. However, if Huddersfield developed on the right lines, it was possible for them to have Kops on three sides of the ground. The main stand - the only stand - was a well-constructed affair, and its only fault was its acute angle, which gave it a moderate view because spectators were so far away from play. There was little grass on the pitch, although it was level and the markings were unmistakable. Liverpool travelled from Blackpool, and Huddersfield from Whitley Bay, and before they made their appearance on the field, the mascots did good work in collecting.

The familiar firm of Cartwright and Company appeared in navy togs which created a great deal of amusement for the Yorkshire men. The Huddersfield colours, blue and white stripes, were very prominent. Before the start the crowd in one part had to be lifted down on to the track around the pitch. Fortunately the people were in good humour, and

helped greatly. The sun was brilliant after a few showers in the morning. The huge crowd of spectators threatened to break in at one end of the ground, but the surplus onlookers were banded down on to the track that surrounds the playing pitch. The kinema operators and the photographers made the most of this incident.

There was an emphatic protest against the allocation of the bulk of the high-priced stands to Liverpool supporters, who paid ten shillings (50p) a ticket. The Liverpool Football Club promised that they would take definite action on behalf of their supporters. Ambulance men were out in huge numbers. Liverpool were out first, and Sheldon came with them. There was great applause and cheering when Longworth led his men on to the field. Huddersfield won the toss, and as the teams lined up, the home men looked the bigger players.

Liverpool kicked off, Lacey tried to put the ball out to the left, but the ball skidded off the turf. Play was ragged at the start and the players did not settle down speedily. Liverpool found the sun in their eyes something of a hindrance, but the visiting backs held out sternly against the rushing tactics employed by Huddersfield.

At length Liverpool began to work with machine-like action. Miller made a superb pass across the field and Lewis and Bromilow joined the attack which came to nothing. Further evidence that the wind was in favour of Huddersfield was produced by a goal-kick from Mutch, the ball travelling three-quarters the length of the field and going for a throw-in.

For a long time the left-half, Watson, had been quiet and unemployed, and a move on his part led to him falling and handling the ball as he fell. The cry went up for a penalty, but the referee refused to allow it on the grounds that Watson had accidentally handled the ball. The play was fast though uncohesive, and gradually Liverpool, with swinging passes, got the ball out to their wings, and if Pearson had not played League instead of Cup-tie style, some good might have resulted.

There was great excitement when Sheldon had a race for the ball and pulled it towards the centre, when the linesman signalled that the ball had passed outside. After this, Huddersfield had their greatest chance, which Smith centred across, and Richardson could have done better than shoot tamely outside. The outside-right was well placed and close in. Huddersfield tended to over-pitch their forwards, for the ball was sent too far ahead on several occasions. Twenty-five minutes had elapsed, and the Liverpool rearguard had had plenty of work to do. However, the home side had not looked incisive in their finishing. Miller got involved in a little minor trouble with the home goalkeeper. A free-kick changed the situation and Lacey, in spite of having his back to the goal, knocked the ball in. Mutch made a wonderful one-handed punch for a clearance. The game had been without much incident and with little work from the Liverpool right wing. However, Cup-tie football was to blame, for it was all excitement and little result, since combination was out of the question in the race for semi-final honours. Campbell made a great save from Taylor, while McKinlay was too busy appealing for offside. The ball travelled to Campbell's left-hand side and was gathered in perfect manner. At this stage of the game, Longworth's defence was stupendous. Liverpool eventually realised their offensive responsibilities. After Sheldon got in front of goal he screwed the ball wide. Pearson, running in on goal, was stopped by Mutch. Liverpool resumed their tactics of slinging the ball about with some effect and both sides were inclined to force the forwards to keep one eye on position and one eye on the ball. Just before the half-time whistle, Wadsworth headed back into his goalmouth with the defence spreadeagled, but the danger passed.

The ground had churned up due to the rain and was sticky on top. Huddersfield opened the second half, and immediately created problems for the visitors until Bamber cleared. Liverpool responded through Wadsworth, who sent in a powerful drive, and Sheldon, who went wide with a low shot. Huddersfield continued as they had finished the first half with strong swinging passes, and Liverpool had to shake themselves to become aware of their responsibilities, with the result that Lewis and Miller dove-tailed nicely and Miller's shot missed by inches. Immediately afterwards, Miller scored a most uncommon goal. Lewis tossed the ball high and strong, and Mutch came out of goal, and it seemed odds against Miller touching the ball. However, he reached it at the critical moment and turned it high into the gaping space. The ball only just managed to find the net, and it was curious how it took so long for the ball to reach the target in the thick mud. Miller and Lewis almost scored a second goal, and Huddersfield adopted, to all intents and purposes, the one-back game. Lacey was wide with a shot and Mutch saw Lewis's low shot crawl inches wide of the post.

The Yorkshire club went for the spoils with both hands, and used the offside theory.

An equaliser came on the hour, Swann scoring after Campbell had handed out twice with punches. It was a good, clean goal which originated from Smith's dainty centre.

Huddersfield were now a new team. This was their second goal in eleven matches against Liverpool. Sheldon began to play some fiery football as Liverpool were stung into retaliation. Smith was fed as though he owned the team as Huddersfield sought the winner. Taylor, with a terrific shot, hit an upright, which was fortunate for Liverpool since Campbell could not possibly have saved. Eventually Taylor gave Huddersfield the lead with a perfect header.

The home supporters went mad and the Second Division side's combination had been better than Liverpool's. Smith - who cost the club nothing - created further openings for the home side. He was the cleanest attired man on the field, yet he had created the most damage. Near the end, McKinlay drew a brilliant save from Mutch, low down, which was described as one of the finest saves ever seen on the ground. In the last few minutes, McKinlay went to inside-left, but the home side hung on for victory.

Smith *was fed as though he owned the team as Huddersfield sought the winner.*

Huddersfield Town: Mutch; Wood, Bullock; Slade, Wilson, Watson; Richardson, Mann, Taylor, Swann, Smith.

Liverpool: Campbell; Longworth, McKinlay; Bamber, W.Wadsworth, Bromilow; Sheldon, Lacey, T.Miller, Lewis, Pearson.

Referee: Mr H. Rylance (Earlestown)

Attendance: 44,248

January 8, 1921

Liverpool (1) 1
Chambers 33

Manchester United (1) 1
T. Miller

IN 1902-03 Liverpool went to Manchester United in the first round of the Cup and lost 2-1, and they therefore had an old score to settle. The Mersey men had been to Blackpool for the week, and the team was not chosen till very late on. Unfortunately the weather at the seaside town was not at its best. Like Liverpool, Manchester were uncertain about the composition of their team owing to Moore being absent, and the doubt between Barlow and Hofton. Mew and Silcock were able to play.

The Lord Mayor and Lord Derby graced the proceedings with their presence. The stands were full, but the Spion Kop, with careful packing, could have held many more, but the club took no risk in the matter of crowd safety.

Tom Miller - one of the members of the infamous result-fixing group of players in the Liverpool v Manchester United match in 1915 when Liverpool missed a penalty and deliberately lost 2-0 - won the toss against his former colleagues and elected to kick towards the Anfield Road end. United were forced to change their colours to blue and white stripes in view of the clash of the colour red.

Liverpool broke away as though they were determined to win the game in the first minute. Chambers waited too long before shooting, but a corner won by Pearson and taken beautifully by Bromilow began a sequence of movements upon Mew and company. A second corner was headed over by Walter Wadsworth. Chambers forced Mew to fall full length to save, and just prior to that Johnson performed a tricky dribble without being able to get the ball under way for a shot. Harrison was wasteful with a wild shot and Johnson came again, only to be robbed by Mew.

The game was fast and entertaining and Pearson dribbled beyond two men in only a yard of space. Bromilow, too, took the eye and so did Harrison when he revealed his former speed, the ball, when centred, spinning off Bromilow into touch. Silcock's defence was solidity itself. He showed intuition by passing to his outside-right. The visitors took up the running and Miller hurt his foot when he kicked over the ball, while Lewis, at the other end, broke through and would have scored if the ball had not bumped unevenly when he was about to shoot. While Silcock was in fine form, Barlow was not too sure, and if Chambers had not tried to plough his way through he would have fared better.

Wadsworth was in the thick of the fray and the mud, and he gave Johnson a snap chance that might easily have been a goal. Liverpool were clearly the better side in terms of ball control and artistry, but that was of little use if there was a lack of accuracy in shooting. Lewis, for example, beat three men and shot wide. United, on the other hand, scored when

Miller beat Scott with just his second shot of the game. Here a Liverpool cast-off scored against his former comrades. Bisset feinted to pass to Harrison, but turned the ball forward. Miller waited for each of the backs in turn to approach him, and by pushing the ball forward and rounding his men, he created a great opening. He shot instantly, and scored. Liverpool had a habit of playing better when a goal in arrears than when on level terms, and soon the home side had equalised.

Lewis was barred by Silcock, but the United could not get Bromilow's corner kick away quite so easily, and while Mew could get to a cross-header from Chambers he could not see the way the player's scoring shot went, when Chambers got a rather fortunate break through the ball coming off Silcock's body, the full back attempting to smother a ballooning shot made by Wadsworth. Chambers had never hit a ball so hard, and twice within as many minutes he might have added to his goal. Pearson beat the defence and Mew turned round to kick the ball out of the net. The ball struck the foot of the inside of a post and rebounded diagonally into play. Johnson headed a corner-kick over the crossbar, with Mew stranded. Liverpool had dominated the first half.

When the game restarted, the Liverpool defence allowed Partridge to move dangerously into the box unmarked, but his shot went outside. Bisset then drove a fierce shot at Scott, which was the goalkeeper's first serious test since Miller's goal. At the other end, the first stoppage of the day occurred when Johnson injured his knee. From a free-kick, Chambers produced a deceptive shot which Mew turned for a corner with his right hand. Bromilow was, as usual, inch-perfect with the place kick, but there was not a single forward who could take advantage of the kick.

Liverpool's defence allowed United no licence, and Harrison was particularly quiet. Bamber went close, but otherwise there was no work for "idle Jack" Mew. Liverpool had the wind to help them, and Chambers became a sort of acting centre-forward due to the injury to Johnson. By degrees McKinlay and Harrison began to talk to each other - no doubt reviving old memories of old-time football and war-time struggles.

Liverpool lost their grip on the game, and for a time were penned in their own half, and Miller slipped just as he shot. Partridge was tackled brilliantly by Walter Wadsworth when a goal was imminent. An injury to Foster's side broke the Manchester momentum, and Liverpool were pleased with the respite. Except for the first few minutes when Pearson did so well, none of the four wingers lived up to their reputation, although Lucas and Silcock showed flashes of brilliance. Lewis had half a chance when Pearson centred from the corner flag, but the inside-left handled the ball. From a goal-kick, Hopkin - soon to be transferred to Liverpool for a fee of £2,800 - made for goal, with Sheldon trailing in his wake. Hopkin crossed the ball and Miller lifted it high over the bar when a judicious pass to the in-running Harrison would have secured a second goal.

Chambers hit an enormous shot which cracked against the crossbar and rebounded towards Anfield Road. Darkness crept on, and Liverpool's continued pressure did not make any impression. McKinlay was not as dominating as Lucas, but he performed his task of watching Harrison with diligence. Ten minutes from time, Partridge looked likely to score when Wadsworth blocked his way. In spite of the defender's tackle, it looked odds on a goal but Scott made a marvellous save and was injured in the process. Again Scott saved in masterly fashion from another Manchester attack, and Harrison crashed into an upright in an attempt to score. For the last few minutes of the game, Johnson went to outside-right.

Tom Miller

Liverpool: Scott; Lucas, McKinlay; Bamber, W.Wadsworth, Bromilow; Sheldon, Chambers, Johnson, Lewis, Pearson.

Manchester United: Mew; Barlow, Silcock; Harris, Grimwood, Forster; Harrison, Bissett, T.Miller, Partridge, Hopkin.

Referee: Mr A. Scholey (Sheffield)

Attendance: 35,000

Receipts: £2,700

F.A. CUP TIES AT THE INTERVAL
~~~~

Liverpool **1** Manchester United **1**
Everton **1** Stockport **0**
Tottenham H. **4** Bristol Rovers **0**
Burnley **3** Leicester City **1**
Notts Forest **1** Newcastle United **0**
Cardiff City **1** Sunderland **0**
Swansea **1** Bury **0**
Reading **0** Chelsea **0**
Southend **3** Eccles United **1**
Watford **1** Exeter **0**
Brentford **1** Huddersfield **1**
Lincoln **1** Millwall **0**
Hull City **3** Bath City **0**
Aston Villa **2** Bristol City **0**
Notts County **2** West Bromwich A. **0**
Bradford City **2** Barnsley **1**
Northampton **0** Southampton **0**
Derby County **1** Middlesbrough **0**
Blackburn Rovers **1** Fulham **1**
Brighton **3** Oldham **0**
Crystal Palace **0** Manchester City **0**
Q.P.R. **0** Arsenal **0**
Luton **1** Birmingham **0**
Darlington **1** Blackpool **0**
Sheffield Wednesday **1** West Ham **0**
Plymouth **0** Rochdale **0**
Swindon **1** Sheffield United **0**
Wolves **2** Stoke **0**
South Shields **1** Portsmouth **0**
Bradford **1** Clapton Orient **0**
Grimsby **0** Norwich City **0**
Preston **0** Bolton Wanderers **0**

FULL-TIME RESULTS
~~~~

Liverpool **1** Manchester United **1**
Everton **1** Stockport **0**
Tottenham H. **6** Bristol Rovers **2**
Burnley **7** Leicester City **3**
Notts Forest **1** Newcastle United **1**
Cardiff **1** Sunderland **0**
Swansea **3** Bury **0**
Reading **0** Chelsea **0**
Southend **5** Eccles United **1**
Watford **3** Exeter **0**
Brentford **1** Huddersfield **2**
Lincoln **3** Millwall **0**
Hull City **3** Bath City **0**
Aston Villa **2** Bristol City **0**
Notts County **3** West Bromwich A. **0**
Bradford City **3** Barnsley **1**
Northampton **0** Southampton **0**
Derby County **2** Middlesbrough **0**
Blackburn Rovers **1** Fulham **1**
Brighton **4** Oldham **1**
Crystal Palace **2** Manchester City **0**
Q.P.R. **2** Arsenal **0**
Luton **2** Birmingham **1**
Darlington **2** Blackpool **2**
Sheffield Wednesday **1** West Ham **0**
Plymouth **2** Rochdale **0**
Swindon **1** Sheffield United **0**
Wolves **3** Stoke **2**
South Shields **3** Portsmouth **0**
Bradford **1** Clapton Orient **0**
Grimsby **1** Norwich City **0**
Preston **2** Bolton Wanderers **0**

January 12, 1921

Manchester United (1) 1
Partridge 20

Liverpool (0) 2
Lacey 55, Chambers 63

ON a day when the M.C.C. named their team for the third Test Match against Australia in Adelaide on Friday January 14th, and New South Wales amassed a world record 770 for the third innings in the game against South Australia, Liverpool beat Manchester United 2-1 at Old Trafford and were the only side to win away from home in the five Cup replays, and that after being a goal down at the interval. The torrential rain that swept the city in the morning left the ground almost under water. The conditions were deplorable, so much so that not only was scientific play impossible, but the players were often disgusted with their own futile efforts to dislodge the ball from its surroundings of mud and water. It was a gruelling contest which contained great excitement. The United had the better of the game in the first half and were well worth their lead at the interval. The forwards showed greater skill in adapting themselves to the conditions, for they controlled the ball well, and for some time the Liverpool halves were outplayed. The Liverpool backs were also overwhelmed by the vigorous rushes of the United forwards.

The Anfielders were a different side after the interval, and after drawing level they improved beyond recognition and won, and thoroughly deserved to do so. The visitors were as strong in the second half as they were weak in the first. The forwards shot with greater regularity, and this alone won them the match. Both Scott and Mew performed heroically. Lucas and McKinlay were very uncertain early on, but after the interval, they tackled and cleared with great success, while the half-backs reproduced their best form, Bamber being especially prominent. As on the previous Saturday, Chambers was the outstanding figure in the attack. He was a strong leader, and the way he ploughed through the mud and water was a revelation to the United defenders. Lacey added weight to the attack, and if he had a lean first half, he revelled in the heavy going afterwards. Sheldon had a few opportunities, but he did not respond well to the service he was given. Pearson and Lewis played well, with Lewis ever on the alert for a scoring chance.

Partridge was the best of the United forwards, for he was able to control the ball when his colleagues found the task impossible. Partridge generally opened out the game, and it was from his work that most of Liverpool's problems originated.

In spite of the terrible conditions, the game opened, with United playing towards the Stretford End, at a tremendous pace, and Chambers sent the ball into the goalmouth in the first minute, but Mew held on to it, despite being surrounded by several Liverpool forwards. A swerving run by Miller gave Harrison a fine chance, but his shot went wide. Lucas slipped as Partridge was bearing down on goal, and although Wadsworth tried to cover the mistake, Partridge got in a tremendous shot and Scott brought off a wonderful save. A first-time drive by Chambers from Sheldon's centre went over the bar, and when Chambers put Lewis in possession, the inside man was well placed and although Lewis shot accurately, Mew was well placed and handled safely. After Scott had made a double save from Partridge, the inside-left attacked again and, beating Lewis, finished a clever run with a brilliant left-foot shot from eight yards that Scott could not reach despite having moved to that side of the goal.

At this point in the game, the United forwards were extremely dangerous. They swung the ball about in lively fashion, and the Liverpool halves could not hold them. A fine individual effort by Miller completely deceived Lucas, but Scott saved Miller's shot, the ball almost entering the net near the upright. So far the Liverpool forwards had been operating on the most treacherous part of the ground, but in the second half, the United forwards fared no better at the "deep end". Chambers was much more influential, and with his particular patch not so holding, he was a difficult man to keep under control. He first headed into Mew's hands, and then caused Mew to put the ball behind in saving a shot. After Scott had kicked out a long ball from Hopkin, and Grimwood had sent an effort very wide with a fine chance, Lacey equalised at 55 minutes. Bromilow placed a corner kick with excellent judgment, and Lacey nodded the ball into the back of the net. Liverpool continued to improve, but Harrison went near when he sent the ball across the Liverpool goal, and both defenders and attackers failed to reach it. Then Mew held the ball at the second attempt for Lacey, and he was bundled over the line by Pearson and Chambers, but the point was disallowed for pushing. A moment later, however, Chambers got the winning goal. He went through on his own and, with a side tap, evaded the opposition to finish with a shot that completely beat Mew. A swerving shot by Lewis went near, and in the last few minutes Miller threw away a glorious chance. He was right in front of goal and shot, but Scott was well placed and easily held the ball.

The receipts were £2,706 and some compensation to a United side which was forced to include Hofton and for whom Harrison did not live up to expectations. Liverpool, on the other hand, probably benefited from the absence of their regular centre-forward. Johnson was only light, and the moving of Chambers to centre provided room for Lacey who had plenty of weight and experience. These two played a major part in securing Liverpool's victory.

McKinlay was excellent, while Lucas was better than Hofton, so that on the whole Liverpool had a slight advantage at full-back. Bamber, Wadsworth, and Bromilow made up a line not only sound and clever, but remarkably level in merit,

Manchester United: Mew; Hofton, Silcock; Harris, Grimwood, Albinson; Harrison, Bissett, T.Miller, Partridge, Hopkin.

Liverpool: Scott; Lucas, McKinlay; Bamber, W.Wadsworth, Bromilow; Sheldon, Lacey, Chambers, Lewis, Pearson.

Referee: Mr A. Scholey (Sheffield)

Attendance: 29,189

Receipts: £2,706 11s 6d

whereas Albinson was not so good as Grimwood and Harris, the former of whom did particularly well. On a day made for heavy-weights, it was remarkable to find Partridge, the most lightly-built man on the field, the best forward of all in the first half. His ball control was delightful; he moved fast and freely and he placed well. Straight for goal did he go, too, when opportunity presented itself. Partridge was a gem.

The whole United line did finely in the first half, but, in the second, Harrison attempted to accomplish the impossible on the worst part of the turf.

Miller seemed slow, and Bisset was rather patchy. Hopkin played well.

Chambers was a dashing, tenacious centre, with Lacey an earnest worker. Lewis was smart, and Pearson and Sheldon swift raiders. They worked desperately hard for victory.

Partridge was the best of the United forwards, for he was able to control the ball when his colleagues found the task impossible.

REPLAYS
~~~~~

Newcastle United v. Nottingham Forest
~~~~~~~

Newcastle United made no mistake in their replayed tie with Nottingham Forest, and won by two goals to nil, scored by Harris and Seymour.

Their superiority was marked. The weather was wet and misty, and the ground churned up until anything approaching good football was out of the question. Players as well as the ball stuck in the mud, and the second half was a poor affair.

The home team had their two goals before the interval, and that they did not add to the lead was due in part to their inside forwards attempting to indulge in close passing under hopeless conditions. Harris also missed a penalty for hands.

The Newcastle defence was never seriously tested, but Curry, returning to the side for the first time since August, played finely at half-back, his leg standing the strain.

Forward, the wing men, and particularly Seymour, were about the best, the inside trio being too concerned with indulging in tricky short passing of a rather stereo-typed character. Harris shot badly, and there was more than a suggestion of selfishness.

For Forest, Bennett did well in goal, and Jones was a great back. Parker was strong at centre-half, but the forwards lacked cohesion, and their play generally was ragged.

Chelsea v. Reading
~~~~~~~~~

After a remarkable game, Chelsea and Reading drew at Stamford Bridge and will replay on Monday on the same ground.

Though Chelsea twice had the lead, they were lucky to save the game, for Reading were too fast for them, and at least as clever.

Cock headed a goal in little more than a minute, but Maving, with a penalty, equalised before the interval.

The second half was poor, but ten minutes from the end Croal gave the Londoners the lead, only for Bailey to equalise with the last kick of the match.

There was nothing of note in the extra time save an offside goal.

Southampton v. Northampton
~~~~~~~

At Southampton in fine weather, and on a heavy ground, before 12,000 spectators. The visitors took the lead through Lockett after five minutes, but the home team were always having the better of the game, and after 25 minutes Dominy equalised. The game was contested at a fast pace. Thorpe made a brilliant save for the visitors. In the second half the home team had practically all the play, but were constantly thrown off-side by the visiting backs. However, Rawlings obtained the lead for the Saints, and Dominy added a third. Rawlings notched a fourth just before time, the visitors being run to a standstill.

Blackpool v. Darlington
~~~~~~~

There was no scoring in the first half. Eight minutes into the second half Travis scored for the visitors. Ginn equalised three minutes later, and Ratcliffe got the winner ten minutes from time for Blackpool.

January 29, 1921

Newcastle United (0) 1
Harris

Liverpool (0) 0

THE home side were at full strength, and Liverpool's was virtually at full strength, with only the exclusion of Johnson preventing them from naming their strongest side. At half-past ten on the morning of the game, there was a queue of some 400 youngsters lined up outside the enclosure, and at noon the assembly had assumed the dimensions of an army of occupation. From all the outlying districts, trains brought in trippers at full fare, and there was a considerable following from Liverpool. The Liverpool players did not leave Whitley Bay until after an early lunch, and reached Newcastle about 1.30, proceeding at once to the ground. The weather, though a little windy, was beautifully fine, and the closely-packed ground presented an animated appearance when the teams took to the field. The time of waiting had elapsed with the strident singing of choruses and the playing of a brass band. There was the usual number of trumpets and rattles, which made the air hideous, and some of these enthusiasts had gone so far as to array themselves in fancy dress in the colours of their respective sides. The home captain won the toss and elected to play uphill with the wind behind them. The St. James's Park pitch was in excellent condition, though a little on the soft side.

Newcastle United: Lawrence; McCracken, Hudspeth; Curry, W.Low, Finlay; Aitkin, Ward, Harris, Smailes, Seymour.

Liverpool: Scott; Lucas, McKinlay; Bamber, W.Wadsworth, Bromilow; Sheldon, Lacey, Chambers, Lewis, Pearson.

Referee: Mr F.A. Freemantle (Retford)

Attendance: 61,400

Receipts: £4,479 0s 9d

The home right wing pair immediately attacked, but they were finally checked by McKinlay. Bromilow gave his forwards possession but Hudspeth intervened and the Newcastle left wing looked dangerous until blocked by Bamber, who passed to Chambers, and the forward waltzed through the defence with great agility and finished with a low shot which Lawrence gathered in his usual clever manner. Seymour and Smailes showed an almost perfect understanding, and Smailes shot a foot outside the post. For some time Newcastle maintained the attack, and two corners were forced in quick succession, relief only coming when Lucas kicked away from Harris. The game was exceedingly fast, and Liverpool shared the honours. Lewis once got through in a solo effort until he was stopped by McCracken, and when he attacked on another occasion, the ball was intercepted by Hudspeth. With a quarter of an hour gone, the pace was still furious.

Smailes, running across to the opposite wing, tested Scott with a difficult oblique shot, which he just succeeded in saving, at the expense of a corner. The place kick led to a second corner, and this was ultimately cleared. Liverpool then made their most dangerous attack to date. Moving down on the left, Lewis put in a hard drive, which was well saved by Lawrence, and a few seconds later the goalkeeper cleared another tremendous effort from Chambers.

At the other end, Newcastle were very busy on the right, where another couple of corners had to be conceded. Both of these led to exciting mêlées in front of Scott, and the Liverpool custodian had only cleared his lines when Harris nipped in and put the ball against the foot of a post, where it glanced over the line, with Scott struggling to save. There were loud cries for a goal, and the referee rightly ruled that the United centre-forward was offside when he shot. The Liverpool forwards changed the scene of action through a breakaway on the part of Sheldon and Lacey, but the outside man's final cross fell just short of Chambers' head and so a likely opportunity was lost.

The Newcastle vanguard produced some clever combined play. The three inside men were at times wonderfully clever with their exchanges, and it said much for the skill of the Liverpool backs that they were kept at bay. From a centre by Aitken the three inside-forwards in turn missed a glorious chance of finding the net.

The visitors attacked next, and Sheldon ran down before passing inside to Chambers who shot just wide of the far upright. With half an hour gone, the game slackened slightly in pace, and Liverpool began to assert themselves. Their more calculated method proved extremely dangerous, and before many minutes the United goal was in jeopardy. Lewis went on a solo run and finished with a fierce shot which Lawrence saved just in time. Sheldon then tried a lob which was well saved, and the bombardment came to a close when Lacey sent the ball over the bar. The home side enjoyed some luck in not conceding a goal for after Chambers had put across a fine centre, Lewis miskicked in front of goal and a sigh of relief went up from the crowd.

The first half had proved to be extremely fast and free from fouls. In fact, the game had all the strenuous warfare of a Cup-tie, coupled with some of the prettiest touches of a League game. In the opening quarter, Newcastle were rather the better side; being quicker on the ball and more nippy in their movements, but as the half wore on the Anfielders developed their style admirably.

The ground was absolutely packed when the struggle was renewed. The weather had clouded somewhat, but this did not affect the high spirits of the crowd. Newcastle attacked down the left but they were held up well, and Liverpool became busy in the same position. McKinlay put the ball over the goal-line with a huge kick, and it was soon evident that no quarter would be asked or given on either side.

Newcastle, having the slope in their favour, proceeded to bombard Scott, but he continued to be well supported by his backs and good work by the Liverpool halves enabled the visitors to attack with venom. Lacey worked his way through and passed to Chambers, who sent in a slow shot, which was easily gathered by Lawrence.

The Newcastle side aroused themselves to some purpose. Seymour and Smailes raced away at top speed, and the inside man looked very like sailing through when Lucas cleared with a timely interception. Ward put in a tremendous drive which Scott jumped to like a cat and saved at the cost of a corner. This was followed by further exciting incidents in which the home forwards tried to force the ball through and

Scott seemed to lead a charmed life when he kept out another great drive from Ward. Newcastle now showed their considerable attacking prowess, and for a considerable time Liverpool were kept on the defensive.

The Anfield rearguard proved equal to the demands made upon them and after sterling half-back play, the visiting forwards moved on to the offensive. A shot from Sheldon was headed away by Hudspeth and when Lewis attacked, he was repelled by McCracken.

With time running out, little Sheldon was roughly grassed by Low, but the Liverpool winger took it in good part. Bromilow was conspicuous with some clever work, but the United continued their attacking forays and after some time they were rewarded with a well-deserved goal.

The ball was taken down the right, where McKinlay appeared to hesitate, and Harris nipped in to put the ball over Scott's shoulder into the net. It was in some ways a rather fortunate goal, but it was received with frantic cheers. Liverpool made desperate attempts to equalise, but the home side held on for victory.

Neil Harris nipped in to put the ball over Scott's shoulder into the net.

January 7, 1922

Sunderland (0) 1
Stannard 70

Liverpool (1) 1
Forshaw 25

ALTHOUGH the going was heavy and treacherous - it had rained heavily all morning - the pace was quite fast throughout the game, and in the last few minutes it became furious and the issue hung in the balance until the final whistle. Some of the referee's decisions on the offside rule were debatable and he raised the ire of the home supporters and on more than one occasion he was booed loudly by the miners who crowded the enclosure. Liverpool were the better balanced side, though they had to go all the way to keep out the spasmodic attacks of the Sunderland forwards, who were well looked after by the half-backs. The home side was not fully represented. Parker and Milton were victims of influenza and were unable to turn out, while Martin was also absent. Their places were filled by Hunter, Stannard and Ellis, all of whom acquitted themselves well. The Liverpool directors did not definitely decide upon the team until a couple of hours before the kick-off, when they rearranged the forward line by putting Chambers in the centre and bringing Lewis in to partner Hopkin. The arrangement worked quite smoothly, and with a little luck Chambers might have put the issue beyond doubt. On the other hand, Buchan might have secured a Second Round place when he tried to "walk the ball" into the net.

There was an attendance of almost 30,000 people when the match began. Liverpool led off in thrusting style, and in the first few minutes corners were forced at either end. One of these might have been converted by the Liverpool centre, but he was just too late to beat Dempster. At the other end first Buchan and than Stannard were at fault. Worry tactics on the part of Wadsworth kept the Liverpool forwards in frequent possession and Hopkin was conspicuous with one or two fine screw centres which were allowed to pass over the line. Buchan was a constant source of danger, but he was well marshalled by Bromilow and McKinlay, who showed skill and coolness in tackling. For 25 minutes there was little to choose between the teams, and then the visitors took the lead. From a mêlée in front of the Sunderland goal, Chambers dashed in and passed the leather to Forshaw who scored from close range. The ball struck Dempster, but he was unable to stop it, and it glanced off the upright and went over the line. It was immediately booted away by the backs, but the referee adjudged that the ball had crossed the line. From this point up to the interval Sunderland enjoyed the bulk of the attack, and it was in one of these powerful thrusts that Buchan missed the opportunity to score. Ellis and Hawes tried to equalise with long-range shots, but they were wide of the target and so Liverpool held their lead at the half-way point.

Crossing over, the Wearsiders developed their attack in most determined fashion, with Buchan a recurring figure throughout the home side's efforts to gain equality. Liverpool

tried to score a second through Lewis and Chambers, and the centre-forward shot frequently with great force, but always at the 'keeper. Twenty minutes from the end the Wearsiders secured the equaliser when Hawes got down the wing at top speed and, beating McNab, put Stannard in possession, who steered the ball into the net. In the closing minutes both sides might have scored.

Chambers performed well in his new position; he was fast, sturdy, and never hesitated to make for goal. Lewis, too, did well, and the work of the outside men was effective. Wadsworth dominated the half-back line, with Bromilow and McNab, in their own way, rendering good service. The full backs both did splendidly, and Scott was once again as elusive as an eel. For Sunderland, Ellis was especially good, as was Best on the opposite wing. Buchan, though clever, was scarcely himself.

Everton were beaten 0-6 at home to Crystal Palace.

EVERTON 0, CRYSTAL PALACE 6

Everton: Fern; McDonald, Livingstone; Brown, Fleetwood, Peacock; Chedgzoy, Fazackerley, Irvine, Wall, Harrison.
Crystal Palace: Alderson; Little, Rhodes; McCracken, Jones, Feebury; Bateman, Connor, Menlove, Wood, Whibley.

Goals:

Whibley 5 minutes
Menlove 25
Connor 70
Menlove 80
Wood 81
Connor 88

Sunderland: Dempster; Hobson, England; Hunter, Kasher, Poole; Best, Buchan, Stannard, Hawes, Ellis.

Liverpool: Scott; Lucas, McKinlay; McNab, W.Wadsworth, Bromilow; Lacey, Forshaw, Chambers, Lewis, Hopkin.

Referee: Mr A. Coward (Bradford)

Attendance: 30,000

January 11, 1922

Liverpool (1) 5
Forshaw (2), Chambers (2),
W.Wadsworth

Sunderland (0) 0

LIVERPOOL won the toss and had a gale of a wind behind them. It was astonishing that a much depleted Sunderland side - several players were the victims of influenza - was only one goal in arrears at the interval. However, the direction of the wind changed completely round in the second half, and with the aid of the elements, Liverpool added greatly to their score.

Apart from the goal and McKinlay's hard drive against an upright, Liverpool's attacking strength in the first period was poor, and Dempster had little to do. Liverpool were at the top of the League and had to be judged by those high standards. However, Liverpudlians knew that the Liverpool club had always played to the strength or weakness of the opposition. When the task was severe, Liverpool played well. When the task was seemingly easy, they eased off. Except for one shot by Hunter, taken at a most unexpected time, and a lob by Buchan, to which Scott had to go back a distance, Sunderland's forward line was inept. Buchan had lost his artistry, inclining to pass out quickly rather than face the consequences of a dribble, and he had lost that personal touch which meant so much to the young Sunderland side. Hawes played very well, and he kept Ellis going along with nice passes; but the centre and right-wing were very weak. Stephenson did not justify himself as a right-winger, and Mitton, lamed twice, could not bring the line into action. The visitors' half-backs were sturdy and severe in the tackle, but the wily ways of Chambers, the intricate movements of Forshaw, the surety of Lacey and the virile attitude of Lewis were too good for Ferguson, deputising for Kasher, who, like Stannard, was ill with the 'flu. Poole was Sunderland's best half, and Hawes the best forward; and while the boy Gibson, acting for Hobson, played well late on, he was too inexperienced to figure in such a game. He was a boy who needed encouraging, for his kicking was sure and of good length.

McKinlay played his best game for a month, and Lucas, apart from one error - a very severe one that might have cost a goal - was successful. Bromilow was peerless; Wadsworth tackled remorselessly and McNab, after a shaky start, gathered confidence and some sense of touch with his wing adversaries. In the forward line, every man worked well with the others. Hopkin was hardly as forceful as of old, but Forshaw was best because of his deadliness and his willingness to shoot when the chance arrived. Sunderland played clean football but Liverpool had to learn to win without warnings from the referee. Burnley, the League champions, were beaten 3-2 by Huddersfield before a crowd of 30,000. Stephenson (11), Mann, and Stephenson again scored for Huddersfield, while Kelly (30) and Boyle (79) scored for Burnley.

***Dick Forshaw**, the scorer of two goals against Sunderland in the replay*

Liverpool: Scott; Lucas, McKinlay; McNab, W.Wadsworth, Bromilow; Lacey, Forshaw, Chambers, Lewis, Hopkin.

Sunderland: Dempster; Gibson, England; Hunter, Ferguson, Poole; Stephenson, Buchan, Mitton, Hawes, Ellis.

Referee: Mr A. Coward (Bradford)

Attendance: 46,000

January 28, 1922

Liverpool (0) 0   West Bromwich Albion (1) 1
Davies 7

LIVERPOOL were one of five clubs beaten at home in the Second Round of the F.A. Cup. The only goal of the game came after seven minutes and was scored by Davies for the Albion. It was Liverpool's first home defeat of the season. As anticipated, the meeting drew a big crowd and the ground was filled half an hour before the game commenced. The spectators saw little that was brilliant, but they had plenty of thrills and excitement in a contest that was always strenuous and contained many of the features of a typical Cup-tie.

Liverpool: Scott; Lucas, McKinlay; McNab, W.Wadsworth, Bromilow; Lacey, Forshaw, Chambers, Lewis, Hopkin.

West Bromwich Albion: Pearson; Smith, Pennington; Richardson, Reed, Bowser; Magee, Blagden, Davies, Morris, Crisp.

Referee: Mr C. Austin (Kidderminster)

Attendance: 50,000

Receipts: £3,050

The Albion faced the sun in the first half, but this did not prevent them from initiating an early attack, and Scott caught the short-length centre from Morris. Liverpool responded, but Hopkin was slow to take in a situation that had several possibilities. Then the only goal of the game arrived. The Albion left wing was put in possession by Bowser, and McKinlay got the ball away when Crisp put in his centre. Reed, however, passed the ball forward to Davies, who was fully thirty yards from goal. The Albion centre steadied the ball with his left foot and with his right sent in a tremendous drive that no custodian could have saved.

Pearson did not hesitate to leave his goal when there was a possibility of effecting a clearance. In doing so he took risks, and more than once he was almost beaten when out of his goal.

Richardson dashed up just as Lewis was preparing to shoot, and Chambers could not hit the ball squarely when Lewis had dispossessed Pearson. Liverpool rallied splendidly, and the Albion defence was well hammered, but Pearson revelled in his work, and he made several thrilling saves from shots by Chambers. He fell in making one save from Chambers who drove in a long ground shot, while in the next minute Pearson fisted out a fine centre from Lacey. Then Chambers headed against the crossbar with Pearson out of his goal. The Albion custodian certainly played a big part in keeping out the Liverpool forwards. His daring methods proved successful, and he did not hesitate to throw the ball for a corner when in danger.

The Albion came near to increasing their lead just before the interval, when Blagden got the ball from a partial clearance by

Scott, but the inside man in his eagerness to score sent the ball over the bar. The visitors made their most dangerous attack of the second half immediately after the interval, when Lucas failed to check Crisp. Then Liverpool put more determination into their work, and Lewis made a desperate attempt to score. Good shots came from Lacey and Forshaw. Scott was never troubled, but Pearson was in great demand. Liverpool's efforts, however, were futile against Pearson's excellent custodianship.   *Below: **Pearson***

In the early stages the Albion produced their best work. They were confident and methodical, but Liverpool were never outplayed, in fact, the reverse was the case, especially in the second half, when the visitors rarely crossed the centre line. Pearson, the goalkeeper, played a magnificent game, and with Pennington and Smith made a defence that was almost faultless.

Chambers was the only forward who showed anything like his true form. He shot often, but his ideas rarely materialised because he was poorly supported. Forshaw and Lewis were weak, and it was only in the second half that Hopkin and Lacey did anything effective. The halfbacks played an uneven game. Their energies and efforts were almost wholly employed in destroying the Albion attack, and in this they were generally successful, but when it came to assisting their own forwards their deficiencies became obvious. McNab was very poor, and he frequently let in the opposing forwards. While Lucas and McKinlay did good work, they were not as reliable as usual. They miskicked and their passes were often erratic. Smith was the best defender. He never missed a ball, and Pennington showed wise judgment. Richardson was a clever halfback, and Reed a splendid worker. The Albion forwards were well held after the early stages. The left wing was the more dangerous, but Davies did little after the goal.

January 13, 1923

Liverpool (0) 0

Arsenal (0) 0

THE Arsenal side had been rebuilt along youthful lines and they deservedly drew 0-0 at Anfield. Liverpool's ripe experience and excellent past record counted for little in the grim struggle that resulted in a goalless draw. The home side could not complain of a lack of chances; their failure lay in not making the most of the chances that came their way. Arsenal realised that their only hope of success lay in preventing the Anfielders utilising their skill and in this they were successful, for the standard of play never rose above mediocre. It was a typical Cup-tie which contained many thrilling incidents, but Liverpool made the mistake of allowing Arsenal to call the tune. The Anfielders' best plans were shattered by the tireless Arsenal defenders. Scott had little to do, but Robson, in the Arsenal goal, played a great game; he handled long, straight drives by McKinlay with the sureness of an expert fielder, and he made daring saves at close quarters. He certainly played a big part in keeping the Liverpool forwards at bay. The backs on both sides were excellent. Longworth and McKinlay were the more polished, but for quickness in decision and accurate anticipation, the Arsenal pair were the superior. The work of the half-backs was mainly defensive, although Bromilow was always in touch with his forwards, and Butler, especially in the first half, passed the ball very effectively. The Liverpool forwards were disappointing. They kept the play too close, which allowed the Arsenal defenders to cut in and many times the merest touch was sufficient to discount a clever movement. The work was unevenly distributed; Hopkin and Chambers had the biggest share, which was not always to Liverpool's advantage, for John, the opposing half-back, was far more effective than Milne, yet Forshaw and Lacey were not offered the same chances. Liverpool's left wing was their best and Hopkin made some clever runs, but the openings he made were frequently neglected through lack of co-operation. Chambers was erratic with his shooting, and Johnson, although he played hard, was rarely successful. The right wing received little support because McNab was too busy with defence, and Forshaw was quite unable to keep Lacey employed. Baker was Arsenal's best forward, and in the first half he passed the ball with great accuracy. Blyth and Turnbull added vigour to the attack, but the line as a whole was deficient in shooting power.

Liverpool led off in their most approved style, but Chambers failed to find the net in the first few minutes with two excellent chances. Hopkin was very forceful, but the best Chambers could do was to send a fast drive into the side netting. Arsenal gradually gained in confidence and Butler gave his forwards several good openings and the visitors forced the first corner. A clever pass by Turnbull, however, gave Arsenal their best chance and Baker sent a beautiful ball across the Liverpool goal. It was a trifle wide, although Scott had the ball well covered. The game increased in endeavour and both sides fought grimly. Science played a small part in the game. Once Robson lost the ball after saving a shot from Wadsworth, but he recovered possession by falling on it and managed to push the ball behind. Johnson failed to time a pass by Chambers near the Arsenal goal, and Bromilow sent a fine drive over the bar. The Liverpool forwards, in spite of their numerous chances, were very unsteady when they came to apply the finishing touch to their work. Robson was very safe, and he held fine drives from Chambers and McKinlay. He was fortunate, however, to push the ball away when McNab shot hard, and although Liverpool redoubled their efforts near the interval, the Arsenal defenders maintained an unbroken front.

There was no slackening of effort in the second half; in fact the contest was waged with even greater intensity. Johnson neglected another fine chance, and Hopkin finished a clever run with a weak shot. Liverpool were unable to lift themselves above their opponents' tactics, and their superior skill was of little use. Chambers had one of the best openings of the game, but when he shot Mackie had taken the speed off the ball and Robson had little difficulty in saving. Later on, Longworth, by throwing himself into the breach, saved what seemed a certain goal, as Turnbull was splendidly placed for a shot. It was a triumph of defence over attack.

Twelve of the thirty-two matches necessitated a replay; nine away teams proved successful; and Bristol City's 5-1 home defeat of Wrexham was the biggest score of the day. The gates were not quite as large as twelve months ago, but there were crowds of over 40,000 at Sunderland, Cardiff, and Birmingham while the two games on Merseyside attracted about 60,000 spectators. Perhaps the two biggest surprises of the day were provided by Worksop (a Midland League club, who forced the Spurs to a goalless draw at White Hart Lane) and Charlton Athletic's defeat of Manchester City at Hyde Road by 2-1.

In Scotland, Falkirk hit ten against Breadalbane without reply, while St. Bernard's beat Dalbeattie Star 8-1, and East Fife beat Berwick away by 7-1. Four other teams hit six as goals were the order of the day north of the border.

Liverpool: Scott; Longworth, McKinlay; McNab, W.Wadsworth, Bromilow; Lacey, Forshaw, Johnson, Chambers, Hopkin.

Arsenal: Robson; Mackie, Kennedy; Milne, Butler, John; Baker, Blyth, Turnbull, R.Boreham, Dr.Paterson.

Referee: Mr G.M. Pardoe (Kidderminster)

Attendance: 37,000   **Receipts**: £2,416

January 17, 1923

Arsenal (1) 1

Turnbull 44

Liverpool (1) 4

Chambers 7, 48, Johnson,
McKinlay (pen) 80

SIX of the nine replays attracted four-figure receipts, but the largest crowd of the day was at Highbury, where 39,000 paid £2,627 to see the League leaders and last season's champions. Not since the war had Liverpool scored a goal at Highbury, but in this game they equalled the score they registered when they won at Plumstead - the old home of Woolwich Arsenal - in 1913 in the last Cup-tie played on the old ground. Since then the Arsenal have become recognised as good Cup fighters, and their draw on the previous Saturday at Anfield was a performance of real merit. It was a disappointment at Highbury that the home side could not play Blyth or Butler, who gave a good display at Anfield, and Voysey and Townrow proved poor substitutes. However, there were other reasons why the Arsenal did not win, the chief being the concentration on Turnbull, whose fame led him to be seriously watched by Wadsworth. The Arsenal lacked the balance of Liverpool in the second half, and showed incompetency in front of goal, while Liverpool - mainly through Chambers - were in a lively mood, and once their defence had overcome the first half barrage of the Arsenal forwards, the game was won by the bigger and more scientific side.

Arsenal: Robson; Mackie, Kennedy; Milne, Voysey, John; Baker, Townrow, Turnbull, R.Boreham, Dr.Paterson.

Liverpool: Scott; Longworth, McKinlay; McNab, W.Wadsworth, Bromilow; Lacey, Forshaw, Johnson, Chambers, Hopkin.

Referee: Mr G.M. Pardoe (Kidderminster)

Attendance: 39,000

Receipts: £2,627

As a Cup-tie it was a little below the standards as regards quality, and a little above in terms of determination and hard work. In fact, with two penalty kicks and some temper, the referee had a lively time, but he performed his work very well. There was no doubt that Liverpool's weight would not move in the mud of Anfield, and the improved conditions were all in favour of the League leaders at Highbury. An early goal was a great help to them. Yet nearly 40,000 spectators expected the equaliser long before it came after 44 minutes. Liverpool's defence had suffered a trial in the first half, and the home team had been very energetic, so much so that they were worth their draw at the interval, even if the equaliser came from a free-kick against Scott for carrying the

ball beyond the requisite number of steps. An early goal in the second half upset the Arsenal's calm confidence. This was the turning point in a game of fluctuations. The Arsenal had seen Chambers score twice; they had lost Boreham for a time through a collision, and they had lost hope in all except their central figure Turnbull - a revived centre-forward who had long been a full-back.

The first goal came after seven minutes through Chambers. The shot was a curious one in that Chambers did not apply his customary force or "slice" to the ball, and Robson in goal might have made a better effort at saving, according to Londoners, who did not know what peculiar shots Chambers could, and did, make. Turnbull equalised a minute from the interval from a free-kick against Scott, who with his backs, had had an anxious time for the greater part of the first half - so much so that the crowd inquired "Is this the championship side?" Turnbull did not know how he had scored, the goal coming from a mêlée. Three minutes after the interval, Chambers headed the third goal of the match. He divined Lacey's corner kick - a corner made by Forshaw, his best effort in the match - and, rushing through, Chambers headed a great goal, and, carrying on his run, he was temporarily stunned. The Arsenal were even more stunned. They had begun to row with the tide, and no sooner taken their seats than the boat capsized.

The fourth goal was recorded by Johnson, after Chambers had caused Robson to field the ball. The lead was now 3-1, and Liverpool played more convincing football. The sensations of the day were not nearly over, however. Turnbull's penalty shot was magnificently saved by Scott, and the fifth goal went to McKinlay with a penalty kick after 80 minutes, through Kennedy fouling Hopkin.

The game was desperately hard and during the opening stages Liverpool could not cope with a trying ball that seemed to have far too much life in it. Liverpool were below their best form, and the secret of it was that they were tired, and the forwards were not convincing. When the left wing got moving, and goals did not count so much to them as time, they played their best football. Prior to that there had been a hesitancy on the right wing, and some mistiming of the ball among the half-backs. Perhaps the ground was firm beneath its soft covering, giving rise to the miskicks and misplaced passes. The Liverpool side must be judged on two separate planes - in the first half all defence, and in the second half a quick goal, confidence restored, and much greater penetration, which produced some holes in the Gunners' armour - and at full-back and at centre half-back.

Scott deserved praise for his penalty save, and for other sure catches and clearances. He was only out of judgment with the ball once, and out of rules, the referee declared, when he caught Turnbull in the small of the back, thus producing a penalty kick. McKinlay and Longworth were hard-worked, but they did many fine things. There was a time when McKinlay faltered in heading - generally his sure point - but in the end he toyed with Baker in the same manner that Bromilow toyed with the right wing in the second half. Wadsworth was the winner's best half-back because, he did so well against that live wire with the electric burst - Turnbull. Dr. Paterson was held firm in the second half, and McNab found touch too readily in the opening half, yet he tried to remedy his own wing forwards by racing through at times. In the attack Forshaw was pretty in his footwork if not successful, Johnson worked hard all the time, and the left wing was the jewel in the crown of victory. The Arsenal did not have a wing, and Voysey did some foolish things. The young backs started well and finished tired and uncertain. Liverpool should find Wolverhampton Wanderers - with two former Everton players in Fazackerley and Brewster - much easier prey than the Arsenal.

Ephraim Longworth, who worked hard against Arsenal and showed many fine touches

February 3, 1923

Wolverhampton W. (0) 0   Liverpool (1) 2
Johnson 23, Forshaw 57

WITH ideal weather conditions prevailing, the sixteen games in the second round of the English Cup attracted nearly 600,000 spectators and the record attendance for the competition - outside of the final - established at Bolton last season, was broken at Stamford Bridge, where 67,106 people witnessed Chelsea and Southampton play out a goalless draw. Just a few people less - 65,911 - saw Wednesday and Barnsley fight it out at Hillsborough, where the receipts were £4,911. The lowest gate of the day in terms of money was at Wigan, the receipts being £1,246. Even this was a record for the club, and several thousands broke into the ground after the game had started.

As in the First Round, Charlton Athletic provided the big surprise of the day by defeating Preston North End, last year's finalists, by two clear goals. The young London club accounted for Manchester City away in the previous round, and the team accomplished a great performance in dismissing two First Division sides from the competition. Exactly half of the sixteen home sides proved successful, and the proportion of drawn games - five out of sixteen - was about the same as in the first round. Millwall put up a splendid fight against the Cupholders, Huddersfield, at New Cross and forced a goalless draw, before a record crowd of 39,700 paying £2,550. Tottenham Hotspur overwhelmed Manchester United at White Hart Lane by four clear goals, all scored after the interval.

Wolverhampton Wanderers were beaten by two clear goals, and they deserved a heavier defeat. That they did not lose by more goals was due to the policy of the First Division leaders who were content to hold on to a two-goal lead. It was ample, as it turned out, because there was practically no sign of life in the Wolves attack until a decision was made to play Edmonds in his old place at centre-forward, and bring Fazackerley to the left-wing. Even then Edmonds worked on his own, his wing men being weak. Hargreaves and McMillan were poor.

Only one period of play suggested that Liverpool had any cause for concern. It occurred soon after the second half had begun. Wolves were then a goal in arrears, and they suddenly found confidence and inspiration from an unknown source. They extended the Liverpool defence, and then Scott mis-timed a ball that came from a corner with spin on it. Then came the crucial point as far as the Liverpool defence was concerned.

When the attack had been cleared, Liverpool played more confidently. Forshaw's goal enabled them to bring out their best methods of attack and constructive game, so that the spectators had value for money. The match did not previously arouse much enthusiasm, and the football was generally colourless through the incompetency of the home side. Scott had two strong shots to handle, but otherwise he was rarely called upon.

Liverpool would have increased their margin of victory had they stuck to their first half tactics of shooting on sight. They missed very narrowly on occasions in the first period, but they played the right game and cannot be faulted for that against their Second Division opponents. There is always the fear that a surprise will accrue, and Liverpool were out to see that it did not occur. To do this, they could not afford to trifle with openings, and not only did they twice hit the woodwork, but the Liverpool forwards were within inches of scoring six goals. They scored twice, hit the bar twice, and George was a fortunate man in goal. It was his good fortune to get off so lightly. His display was a poor one; he lacked judgment and surety in throw. His backs, however, were fortunately very strong against a persistent attack and therefore saved George much work. George was young, and should outlive his impetuosity; Gregory, usually a half-back, went to full-back with Marshall, both Cup final heroes of two years ago (Wolves lost the 1921 Cup final against Tottenham Hotspur to a Dimmock goal at Stamford Bridge before 72,805 spectators on 23 April. The team that day was: **George; Woodward, Marshall; Gregory, Hodnett, Riley; Lea, Burrill, Edmonds, Potts, Brooks**) and they merited praise for their good work. At half-back, Edmonds, a former centre forward, was the best, for he made excellent passes, and played in real Cup-tie style.

Brewster against Johnson fared fairly well with his sure heading, but he did not bring any tangible result when he got the ball; while Hodnett ran foul of everybody on the left wing, and was lucky not to have an order from the referee. It was Hodnett who was rough on Johnson, the latter retaliating; while Hopkin, too, had some bouts with the half-back, and both did things which they should not have indulged in. In attack, the Wolves' forwards were inept. Bissett hit one shot from too far out, and McMillan made one solitary run of worth, while the rest were not worth considering.

Liverpool won through teamwork. The backs started in strange fashion. The turf in the first few minutes seemed to upset McKinlay, who slipped and could not get the right force and direction to the ball. Both played well, however, but without that certainty of touch that usually stamps their work. At half-back, there was uniform strength and judgment. Wadsworth simply would not let Fazackerley go, and Edmonds made no deeper impression on him. In the forward line, Chambers was the best schemer, and he merited goals, too. His work was of outstanding merit, but Hopkin never really got over his early knock-out blow. Johnson was cool and quick, and Forshaw did better than for many a past week; while Lacey, if only for his following up, was worth his inclusion in the honours list.

The first goal was due to a finely-judged pass from Chambers to Johnson, who dribbled forward and shot in spite of his being kicked at from behind. It was not a particularly good shot, but it counted. The second goal came after Wolves' only real threat. Hopkin centred so far across goal that the ball seemed likely to travel out near Lacey's wing. Lacey kept the ball in play, and passed to Forshaw, who hit a splendid ball out of the reach of George. It was generally an easy victory for Liverpool.

Wolverhampton Wanderers: George; Gregory, Marshall; Hodnett, Brewster, Edmonds; McMillan, Bissett, Fazackerley, Burrell, Hargreaves.

Liverpool: Scott; Longworth, McKinlay; McNab, W.Wadsworth, Bromilow; Lacey, Forshaw, Johnson, Chambers, Hopkin.

Referee: Mr G.D. Nunnerley (Ellesmere)

Attendance: 40,079   **Receipts**: £2,511

Dick Johnson, who dribbled forward and shot in spite of his being kicked at from behind.

February 24, 1923

Liverpool (1) 1
Chambers 10

Sheffield United (1) 2
Gillespie 28, Waugh 74

ONCE again Charlton Athletic provided the shock of the round in defeating West Bromwich Albion by a single goal in London, but fifth-placed Sheffield United caused a surprise in beating League leaders Liverpool at Anfield. A decision was reached in six of the eight third round ties. The success of the Spurs at Cardiff was an outstanding feature before a crowd of 54,000 paying receipts of £4,200. Generally the crowds were down: 287,000 against 495,000 the previous season, and the decision of the Bury directors in doubling the prices of admission to the ordinary spectator did not prove popular and there was a partial boycott of the game. Prior to the game, Liverpool, who had been beaten only once at home this season, were strong favourites for the Cup, and although their record entitled them to be classed as the best side in the country, they were beaten by a superior side on the day.

The game started at a terrific pace, and Liverpool seemed very sure of themselves. They applied stern pressure and forced three corners, and Blackwell made three early saves. His best was to a fine effort by Forshaw, and he was indeed fortunate to escape defeat.

Liverpool took the lead after ten minutes and Chambers was the scorer. It was the culmination of a fine individual effort, for when Lacey centred the Liverpool forwards were too near the United goal to utilise the opportunity. Waugh, however, was beaten, and Chambers went through with a clever dribble and finished by driving the ball into the net. Liverpool played excellent football, and their superiority at this stage was obvious.

Forshaw and Lacey seemed to have the measure of Milton, and the work of Hopkin and Chambers was almost perfect. Scott had little to do in the first twenty minutes, for the United rarely got a chance to invade Liverpool's territory. Scott's first shot was a long one from Mercer, and then Gillespie headed into Scott's hands.

At twenty-eight minutes, however, Scott was beaten with a header from Gillespie. Johnson pushed the ball out to Mercer, who centred so accurately that Gillespie had only to nod the ball into the net. Sheffield's equalising goal was all against the balance of play, for the Liverpool defence had held the United attack so easily that the home forwards had applied almost continuous pressure. The goal, however, acted as a powerful stimulant, and Sampy and Mercer gave a glimpse of their best work. Wadsworth was just in time to prevent Sampy from shooting at point blank range, and Scott cleared with difficulty from Johnson's header.

When the game resumed after the interval, both Forshaw and Johnson failed in the goalmouth, and the subsequent play veered strongly in favour of the visitors, and they worked with great determination. Liverpool's Johnson hit the crossbar, and his namesake almost headed through from Sampy's centre. Shortly afterwards the Sheffield centre missed one of the best chances of the day when he lifted the ball over the bar from a fine position engineered by Mercer. Chambers attempted to put life into the Liverpool attack and he got in a brilliant run, but he left his final shot a little too late, and Blackwell was able to narrow the angle of the shooter so that he met the shot with a wonderful punch.

After 74 minutes, the winning goal arrived. There was a mêlée in the Liverpool goalmouth, and with the defenders huddled together, most of them on the ground, Waugh had ample time to drive the ball into the net at the corner furthest from the Liverpool players.

Liverpool strove hard to get on terms with their opponents, and the excitement was intense when Hopkin sped goalwards at top speed. He lifted the ball into the centre but it was cleared, and Scott had anxious moments when Johnson dashed into the goal in a futile effort to convert Tunstall's centre.

Gillespie, *who equalised for Sheffield United after 28 minutes*

OTHER CUP RESULTS

~~~~~~~~~~~~

Huddersfield Town **1** Bolton Wanderers **1**
Charlton Athletic **1** West Bromwich Albion **0**
Queen's Park Rangers **3** South Shields **0**
Bury **0** Southampton **0**
West Ham United **2** Plymouth Argyle **0**
Derby County **1** Sheffield Wednesday **0**
Cardiff City **2** Tottenham Hotspur **3**

Replays

Bolton Wanderers **1** Huddersfield Town **0**
Southampton **1** Bury **0**

THE LIVERPOOL FOOTBALL ECHO

The game was regarded as the best of the Cup-ties, but the result was a great disappointment to the Liverpool supporters but, taking the game as a whole, there was no doubt that the visitors were the better side.

Thus history repeated itself, and for the third time in succession the United put an end to Liverpool's aspirations in the Cup.

The main cause of Liverpool's defeat was their failure to play the right type of game - the game best suited to a Cup-tie struggle.

The close, short-passing game has its good points, but, as was in evidence, the long, swinging passes of the United side were far more effective, and not so tiring.

In addition, the United were quicker on the ball, and the equalising goal had the effect of restoring their shattered morale to such an extent that from that point Liverpool were fighting a hopeless battle. At the same time, nothing could have been better than Liverpool's work in the opening half-hour, and with a goal by Chambers they looked to be well set for victory.

The whole side played with wonderful cohesion, and the United custodian was almost beaten several times.

However, there came a remarkable change, and the tide of success turned much in favour of the visitors.

Once having established themselves, they dominated the game with fine confidence, and Liverpool never regained the initiative they lost so easily.

No blame for defeat could be attributed to Scott, for he made some clever saves.

He had little to do in the early stages, because the United were so well held, and were mainly on the defence; but afterwards he was very often called upon to show his skill.

Both Longworth and McKinlay played a steady game, and Longworth never lost his coolness, but McKinlay was inclined to be erratic, and, against Sheffield's best wing, he had much trying work. The half-backs held the key position and failed to carry out their mission. They did well in the first half, and McNab and Bromilow had a fine understanding with the forwards.

Afterwards, however, they had as much as they could do to reduce the effectiveness of the Sheffield forwards, and in this they were not successful.

In fact, Bromilow had rarely been seen in such an unfavourable light. Without the support of the half-backs, the Liverpool attack went to pieces in the second half.

Hopkin and Chambers produced wonderful football in the first half. Clean, crisp, clever footwork that kept the Sheffield defenders continually on the stretch, and the right wing was very little inferior, but everything changed dramatically after the interval. All the sparkle and buoyancy had evaporated and only at rare intervals did the Liverpool forwards reveal their true form.

Sheffield's methods were far more effective.

Sampy was the mastermind of the attack, and he inspired his colleagues by the way he opened up fine scoring chances.

He not only provided his partner Mercer with intelligent passes, but he swung the ball across to the extreme wing with telling effect, Johnson was a superb leader and infused plenty of speed into his work, while Tunstall and Gillespie were a fine wing.

The half-backs made a strong line with Waugh a thrustful pivot. The backs kicked weakly at the start, but they improved considerably and never wavered afterwards.

Blackwell was sound in all he did, especially in the early stages when he had some very difficult shots to field from close range.

January 12, 1924

Liverpool (1) 2
Chambers 41, 87

Bradford City (1) 1
Logan 15

DUE to the Everton game at Goodison against Preston North End - which the Blues won 3-1 - and the dull day, the attendance at Anfield was only moderate. Bradford City made several changes from the previous week. The ground was in fine condition and promised an excellent Cup-tie.

Liverpool: Scott; Lucas, McKinlay; Bromilow, W.Wadsworth, Forshaw; Lacey, Shone, Walsh, Chambers, Hopkin.

Bradford City: McLaren; Hargreaves, Cheetham; Duckett, Storer, Lloyd; McKinnay, Logan, Donaghy, Chalmers, Winn.

Referee: Mr T. Crew (Leicester)

Linesmen: Mr D.R. Proctor (Leicester);
Mr J. Pennington (Bury)

Attendance: 25,000

Receipts: £1,420

Liverpool kicked off and advanced down the Bradford right. The immediate danger was cleared, but the ball went out to Hopkin who was pulled up for offside after a fine run. Shortly afterwards, Shone was flagged offside as Liverpool attacked with determination. The visitors weathered the early storm and set about their job in workmanlike fashion. Donaghy was provided with a good opportunity, but Lucas prevented him in getting through. Liverpool responded with an attack of their own and they gained a throw-in on the right near the corner flag. This amounted to nothing, and for a period play was confined to midfield. Lacey initiated a marvellous attacking movement as he tricked his marker and passed inside to Walsh, who fired in a shot which flew inches over the bar.

Bradford advanced down the right, their most dangerous wing so far in the game, and after several passes the ball went to Logan, who fired in a cross which hit the inside of the post and bounced into the net after 15 minutes. Scott had no chance of saving. It was an excellent goal, but it forced Liverpool into retaliation.

On two occasions Chambers made use of his brilliant dribbling skills and tried to create an equaliser. The first time, he was tripped, but he recovered and the referee blew for a free-kick. Liverpool gained two successive corners without result. Walsh tricked Hargreaves but finished excellent approach work with a weak shot. Hopkin raced down the

wing, but his centres were too low and his colleagues failed to reach them. On the opposite wing, Lacey centred in beautifully, and Walsh headed the ball into the path of Chambers, who failed to reach it by inches. Liverpool attacked relentlessly, and a Lacey drive was deflected for a corner off a full-back's knee. Walsh then directed a powerful header towards goal, and it struck the bar. As it came out, the goalkeeper could only push it into the path of Shone, but McLaren recovered and parried Shone's shot. The ball went to Lacey, but his shot was turned away by a defender. As the Reds maintained their momentum, a powerful drive from Chambers passed a foot wide. Then Walsh was pulled down a few yards outside the penalty area, but McKinlay drove the free-kick wide.

Chambers was having a marvellous game, getting through an amazing amount of work. On two occasions he raced through into the clear and passed to Walsh, but the Liverpool centre could not get the ball under control and the opportunities were lost. Storer, the veteran City half-back, was in excellent form, and he was largely responsible for breaking down most of Liverpool's attacks. From a Hopkin centre, McLaren punched the ball into the air and an exciting goalmouth mêlée ensued before the Bradford defence cleared. Danny Shone was injured in a collision, and he had to receive attention to a cut forehead behind the line. The visitors attacked while Shone was off the field and forced a corner, but Storer shot outside.

Shone returned with a plaster on his head, and the little man was undeterred by his injury. Liverpool equalised just before the interval.

A fine movement on the right finished with Lacey passing to Walsh, who brought Chambers into the game, and the Liverpool man sidefooted the ball into the net. The goal was loudly cheered.

At the other end Scott saved a Donaghy shot. Just before the whistle sounded McLaren scooped out a header from Chambers in fine style.

McKinnay was brought down in a tackle by Forshaw, and he lost the leg of his pants. The crowd assumed he was badly injured, but the trainer returned with another pair of pants, which McKinnay quickly donned over his other pants.

Liverpool began the second half with the same attacking flair as they had shown in the first half. McLaren did well to collect a Hopkin centre, and then Chambers shot wide. Liverpool were superior in their attacking ideas and they continued to have the bulk of the play, but their finishing was weak. A fine lob from Hopkin was saved brilliantly by McLaren. Then from a Lacey centre, Chambers was left in front of goal, and he attempted to place the ball wide of the goalkeeper, but McLaren pounced on the ball like a cat and received the applause of the crowd for his coolness.

At the opposite end Chalmers broke clear and had only Scott to beat, but the keeper came out to narrow the angle, and the forward shot straight at the Irishman, who collected the ball safely.

McLaren stood between Liverpool and further goals, his judgment being superb. As the game drew to a close, Bradford gained a corner, which was cleared. Three minutes from time, Chambers struck the winner. At the final whistle the visiting goalkeeper received a standing ovation.

HULL CITY v. BOLTON WANDERERS
~~~~~~~~~~~~~~~

At Hull; fine weather. Twenty-five thousand spectators; ground wet and slippery. Rollo took place of Butler in the visiting team.

Martin scored for Hull after twelve minutes, and it was not until one minute before the interval that J.R. Smith secured the equalising point.

Half-time: Hull City 1, Bolton Wanderers 1.

Final result: Hull City **2**, Bolton Wanderers **2**.

McLaren stood between Liverpool and further goals, his judgment being superb.

Other results in the First Round:

West Ham United	5	Aberdare	0
Newcastle United	4	Portsmouth	2
Blackpool	1	Sheffield United	0
Manchester City	2	Nottingham Forest	0
Derby County	2	Bury	1
Accrington Stanley	0	Charlton Athletic	0
Hull City	2	Bolton Wanderers	2
Huddersfield	1	Birmingham	0
Swindon Town	4	Bradford	0
Manchester United	1	Plymouth Argyle	0
Burnley	3	South Shields	2
Notts County	2	Queens Park Rangers	1
Barnsley	0	Brighton & Hove A.	0
Wolverhampton W.	3	Darlington	1
Corinthians	1	Blackburn Rovers	0
West Bromwich A.	1	Millwall	0
Arsenal	4	Luton	1
Oldham Athletic	2	Sunderland	1

Replays

Charlton Athletic	1	Accrington Stanley	0
Bolton Wanderers	4	Hull City	0
Brighton & Hove A.	1	Barnsley	0

February 2, 1924

Bolton Wanderers (1) 1
J.R. Smith 2

Liverpool (1) 4
Walsh 3, 88, 89,
Chambers 50

SIX excursion trains, all crowded with 28 in a carriage, were run from Exchange Station in a mass of colour. In addition, several parties who had completed their arrangements during the strike, made the journey by road and charabancs with streamers and bunting gaily flying. The Bolton supporters were confident that their team - as Cupholders - would secure victory. The respective sets of supporters displayed their colours lavishly, the blue and white of Bolton contrasting vividly with the more lurid red and white of their rivals, and the sea of faces completed an inspiring picture. The Liverpool team travelled to Manchester, where they had lunch, and then proceeded to Bolton, the players walking to the ground. The gates were opened at 12.30 and the turnstiles began to click immediately, many supporters having queued for hours to secure prominent positions.

Despite the fact that he had a bad cold, J.R. Smith turned out, and the teams were as follows:

Bolton Wanderers: Pym; Howarth, Finney; Longworth, Seddon, Jennings; Butler, D.Jack, J.R.Smith, J.Smith, Vizard.

Liverpool: Scott; Lucas, McKinlay; McNab, W.Wadsworth, Bromilow; Hopkin, Forshaw, Walsh, Chambers, Lawson.

Referee: Mr T. Tomlinson (Sheffield)

Linesmen: Mr A. Freemantle (Sturton-le-Steeple)
Mr W. Leuty (Leeds)

Attendance: 51,596   **Receipts**: £4,126

Both sides were accorded a warm welcome as they took to the field. Many supporters found places on the roof of the stand. McKinlay won the toss, and the Reds played with a slight breeze behind them. The early exchanges were even, and a foul throw against McNab led to a Bolton attack, but Butler swung the ball over the bar.

The home side swung the ball about in brilliant fashion and within two minutes the Wanderers were a goal up. After a splendid passing movement, Butler sent in a square pass across the face of the goalmouth, and J.R. Smith dashed in and scored from close range.

Within a minute, Liverpool were on equal terms. The Reds attacked down the left, and the winger passed inside to Chambers, who beat his man with ease, and dropped the ball

right in front of goal for Walsh, who wheeled round and put the ball past Pym with a slow shot. The Liverpool centre received the ball under difficulties, but he made excellent use of it. Pym dived, but he was too late. It was thrilling football, and the crowd were roused to a pitch of great excitement.

The Wanderers attacked again and forced two corners. The right wing proved extremely troublesome, while Liverpool attacked mainly down the left flank. Howarth missed his kick, and Walsh dashed in, but he was beaten in a race for possession by Pym. Walsh tried to get the ball off the goalkeeper, and was whistled for a foul. Several offside decisions upset the Merseyside supporters, but Liverpool continued to make a real game of it. Howarth made several mistakes as Liverpool attacked dangerously, but Pym was alert. Several players, including Seddon and Chambers, were hurt, and some feeling appeared to be creeping into the game. The Reds' first-time touch was excellent.

From Vizard's centre Scott pulled off a great save, and the winger worked his way close in and placed the ball across the face of the goal, but Scott pushed it out to the right, and Jack turned the ball behind. Liverpool responded with an attack of their own, and Wadsworth drove a ball wide of the post. For a time, free kicks were frequent, and the referee worked hard to hold the balance between the sides. The Wanderers, nearing the interval, increased the pressure, and Vizard and Butler were extremely dangerous, but McKinlay and his colleagues denied them. Hefty shoulder charges were given and taken, but Liverpool at last worked their way up, gaining a free-kick 30 yards out. McKinlay shot wide of the upright. Following clever play by Forshaw and Hopkin, Pym was forced to clear. Several players received hard knocks, and Chambers had a nasty scar right across his chest.

Upon resuming, play was as fast and furious as in the first period. After just five minutes, a long forward pass was sent through. Chambers followed, and Pym came off his line, but the Liverpool inside-left cleverly tricked the goalkeeper, and simply dribbled the ball into the net.

The Liverpool contingent went wild with delight. It appeared that the movement had stemmed from a back pass by Jennings. Seddon retired injured at this point, and the Wanderers played on with ten men.

Following this reverse, the home side attacked dangerously and sent in several shots. Jack charged Lucas heavily, and the players nearly came to blows, but the referee intervened. Moments later, Jack broke clear and when it seemed that he must score, he shot over the bar. The home side performed well despite Seddon's absence. Joe Smith went into the half-back line, with Jennings in the centre, and Bolton relied on four forwards. Bolton forced two corners on the right, and McKinlay managed to turn a shot behind. Chambers had a fine chance but Pym was fortunate to scrape the ball away from Hopkin. Joe Smith charged into Scott, and the goalkeeper fell against the upright, injuring his back, but he resumed. The home side enjoyed a spell of immense pressure, and Liverpool were unable to lay siege on the Bolton goal for more than a brief spell. With twenty minutes of the second half gone, Pym had not touched the ball once. Walter Wadsworth stemmed the tide which threatened to engulf the Liverpool defence, and he hooked away a fine shot from J.R. Smith. The first real attack by Liverpool for some time ended when Chambers drew his man and then slipped the ball to Lawson, who centred admirably, but no-one was on hand to put the ball into the net. In a Bolton attack, Scott was injured, and moments later Wadsworth was laid out through heading a ball for a corner. He soon recovered to assist his defence. Butler shot towards goal, and there was no doubt that the ball struck McKinlay's hand, but the referee decided, after consultation with the linesmen, that it was not a penalty. Captain McKinlay had words with his vice-captain, Wadsworth, when he kicked into touch squarely. The captain pointed forward as if to say, "Make progress, Walter, if you have to do that."

Two minutes from the end, Walsh put the issue beyond doubt. Hopkin returned a pass, and Walsh hit it first time into the back of the net. A minute later Walsh added a fourth goal in a game that had opened and closed in a sensational manner. The Liverpool players were absolutely mobbed as they left the field. The victory went some way towards relieving Mr Matt McQueen's stubborn break of the leg.

Jimmy Walsh

	Pl	W	L	D	F	A	Pts
Cardiff City	27	16	3	8	48	24	40
Bolton Wanderers	**29**	**12**	**5**	**12**	**49**	**23**	**36**
Sunderland	27	14	6	7	49	35	35
Huddersfield	26	15	7	4	40	22	34
Aston Villa	29	11	7	11	33	25	33
Newcastle	28	13	9	6	45	32	32
Blackburn Rovers	27	13	8	6	42	30	32
Sheffield United	27	10	7	10	39	33	30
Everton	28	11	9	8	38	38	30
Tottenham Hotspur	27	10	8	9	31	27	29
West Ham United	27	9	9	9	22	23	27
Notts County	27	7	9	11	24	33	25
Manchester City	26	9	10	7	30	42	23
Burnley	26	8	10	8	38	37	24
Liverpool	**27**	**9**	**13**	**5**	**30**	**32**	**23**
West Bromwich Albion	26	7	11	8	32	47	22
Nottingham Forest	27	7	13	7	31	44	21
Birmingham	27	5	11	11	23	37	21
Arsenal	26	7	12	7	22	40	21
Preston North End	27	7	14	6	35	47	20
Chelsea	28	5	14	9	16	34	19
Middlesbrough	27	6	16	5	24	34	17

Brighton & Hove A.	5	Everton	2
Manchester United	0	Huddersfield	3
Southampton	3	Blackpool	1
Swansea	0	Aston Villa	2
Sheffield Wednesday	1	Bristol City	1
Bristol City	2	Sheffield Wednesday	0
Swindon	2	Oldham Athletic	0
Derby County	2	Newcastle United	2
Newcastle United	5	Derby County	3
West Bromwich A.	5	Corinthians	0
Exeter City	0	Watford	0
Watford	1	Exeter City	0
Crystal Palace	0	Notts County	0
Notts County	1	Crystal Palace	2
Manchester City	2	Halifax Town	2
Halifax Town	0	Manchester City	3
West Ham United	1	Leeds United	1
Leeds United	1	West Ham United	0
Burnley	0	Fulham	0
Fulham	0	Burnley	1
Charlton Athletic	0	Wolverhampton W.	0
Wolverhampton W.	1	Charlton Athletic	0
Cardiff City	1	Arsenal	0

February 23, 1924

Southampton (0) 0

Liverpool (0) 0

THERE was a nip in the air when the Liverpool party arrived in Winchester on Friday afternoon. The players enjoyed a stroll about the old-world town before tea, and after a quiet evening the boys were early to bed and up in good time for breakfast. There were several wires conveying good wishes, and charms and mascots were numerous. As the train pulled out of Rock Ferry on the journey south, one railway enthusiast threw a doll dressed as a demon into the saloon car, with the request to give it to McNab. The label on the doll read: "Wishing the Devil's own luck." Mr Jack Hayes (M.P. for Edge Hill) and Davie Ashworth, the former Liverpool manager, were among those who sent their wishes to the captain. Jack Hayes' telegram to Donald McKinlay read, *"May good luck attend your boys. We have set our minds on having the Cup this year."* There were further telegrams from Ted Parry, the Liverpool reserve full-back, and one from Billy Matchett.

Mr R.W. Williams (chairman), Mr J. Astbury (vice-chairman), Mr John McKenna (English League president), Mr Edwin Berry (former chairman of Liverpool) and his grandson, together with a number of other directors and officials from Liverpool, left Winchester at mid-day on the day of the game.

Saturday morning was fine and cold, and after lunch the players journeyed on to Southampton by motor. The town was aglow with red, since both teams sport that colour, although the Saints have a dash of white stripes in their colour scheme. The gates were opened at one o'clock, and immediately the long queues outside the ground filed in through the turnstiles. The first view of the playing pitch was curious. The whole ground, hollowed out, was good for the spectator because it had no interruptions of view. The most awkward corner from the players' point of view was the notorious padded wall. The players were pleased with the condition of the pitch. The small ground was packed before the kick-off, with spectators ringing the touch-line.

The Southampton manager, Mr McIntyre, pointed out before the game that Southampton had not lost at home since October 15; whilst another feature of their side was that they did not have a single Scotsman, Irishman, or Welshman in either their first or second team. Mr Harry Webb and Mr Patterson went to the ground at ten o'clock on the morning of the game, and there was a ring around the ground of about one thousand people. The Liverpool supporters stared in amazement at the little red house up the hill, which butts right on to the touchline, and is padded so that the players would come to no harm should they bump into it. In attendance was a press man from Cologne. He was chartered by thousands of troops in occupation to come over to report the game for them. There were thousands of men in khaki looking on,

arriving in an incessant flow of charabancs from Aldershot and Salisbury. Portsmouth is less than twenty miles away, and several Liverpool supporters came from there. Further colour was lent to the proceedings by a number of R.A.F. men from Flowerdown Camp. The crowd had a lot of fun through a Liverpool supporter hanging some red balloons on to one of the standards. The spectators took turns to try to burst them by throwing oranges at them. Alf Milward, Fred Geary and Edgar Chadwick's brother were in attendance. The teams were at full strength and lined up in this order:

Southampton: Allen; Parker, Titmuss; Shelley, Campbell, Turner; Henderson, Dominy, Rawlings, Price, Carr.

Liverpool: Scott; Lucas, McKinlay; McNab, W.Wadsworth, Bromilow; Hopkin, Forshaw, Walsh, Chambers, Lawson.

Referee: Mr H.J. Webster (London)

Linesmen: Mr J.C. O'Neil (Essex);
Mr J. Martin (London)

Attendance: 16,671

Receipts: £1,790

The Reds received a loud cheer from their supporters, many of whom were exiled dock workers, and soldiers or sailors. Dominy won the toss, and the home side had the sun at their backs. The sun shone into the faces of the visitors.

Henderson ran through and centred, but McNab was on hand to clear the danger. Bromilow's trickiness and his pass to Hopkin produced a corner, which led Allen to make a fine catch from Forshaw's header. Play swung from end to end, and Lucas intervened to prevent Rawlings going through after a great pass from Campbell. Then Lawson won a corner which Bromilow took, and Walsh headed inches over the bar. There was a mix-up in the Southampton defence when Parker and Shelley attempted to clear, and Parker appeared to lose his temper with his colleague. Dominy had a shot which passed inches wide, while Hopkin lost two chances to make ground. As the crowd were lined on the touchline, it was natural that the ball went out of play frequently, because players could not go through with their runs.

A Liverpool defender tried to kick out from a foot out, and failed, and when the ball was returned to the corner of the goal, Scott picked it up as if he had a perfect view of it all the time, although he was unsighted. Rawlings was the key man

Tom Bromilow

in the Saints' attacks, and initiated several fine movements. Price hit a powerful drive which went inches over the bar. Near half-time, Scott was forced to punch away. Liverpool had looked the more stylish side, but the Saints were better in front of goal. Bromilow had never played better for Liverpool in this current season. The Saints, with four or five tall men, had been relentless in their forward play. Liverpool had disappointed in the forward line, mainly because there was a lack of combination. The ball had constantly been sent high in the air towards Walsh, but he had been faced by the giant Campbell.

The sun had gone down when the teams reappeared. In the first attack, McKinlay half stopped the rush, but McNab sent the ball out for a corner. Shelley injured his jaw and shoulders in a tussle with Lawson. The referee missed a foul on Wadsworth, and spoke to Wadsworth for retaliation. From the free-kick, Rawlings shot hard and drove the ball too high.

Forshaw sent in a cross shot that swung out of Allen's reach and beyond the far post. The Liverpool forwards were weak, and Bromilow led the way with his fine display of dribbling and feinting. He went on one solo run which saw the ball flash inches over the bar with Allen beaten. Hopkin then broke through and shot wide, before beating an opponent and putting in a centre which Chambers handled.

This was a match in which the defences triumphed, mainly due to the ineffectiveness of the forwards. Chambers was speedy and strong in his dribbles, but he was marked too well to allow him to get within shooting range.

With thirteen minutes to go, Liverpool increased the pressure, and Chambers got too much screw on a ball that swung outside. With only a few minutes to go, Dominy sent in a great shot which Scott pushed over the bar. Immediately after this the Saints claimed a penalty, but the referee dismissed the appeal. The home side forced a corner in the last minute which was cleared after a protracted tussle.

ENGLAND ENTERTAIN FRANCE

HONOURED BY THE KING

The King was present this afternoon at the rugby football match between England and France at Twickenham. His Majesty arrived about ten minutes before the start of the game and had a most enthusiastic reception. He walked on to the field of play and shook hands with each of the players. The gate numbered nearly forty thousand.

The French XV came to Twickenham today with the avowed intention of beating England for the first time. There had been thirteen previous meetings between the two countries, of which England had won all but the game at Twickenham in 1922, which was drawn with 11 points each.

There was a huge crowd present, a constant stream of visitors being admitted from the time the gates were opened at one o'clock. The air was cold, and it was inclined to be frosty, but the ground was in fine condition, having been covered by straw during the night. There were close upon 40,000 spectators when play started.

Before that the scene had been set for the arrival of the King, who received a tremendous reception. The players of both teams were presented to the King.

Cassayet, the forward, captained France in the absence of Crabos, but faulty handling by their backs saw England get up to their 25, and Catcheside was well placed but Corbett's pass was not a good one. England pressed now and Myers and Locke were in good form. England came out of the two scrums in fine style, but again a pass to Catcheside was faulty. Pardo, the French back, was brilliant in fielding, and he stemmed some great rushes.

England were bound to score, by the way they pressed, and in fifteen minutes they took the lead, Jacob going over. Luddington failed with the kick, which was a difficult one. Bequet had previously given France a good chance, but the three-quarter fumbled the ball.

The score after 26 minutes was England 6 points, France nil.

Jacobs scored a second try for England and Luddington failed again. The degree of passing among the England backs was consistent. The visitors got but few chances.

With Pardoe going for his legs, Catcheside made a four foot jump and romped over for one of the best tries seen at Twickenham. So far as initiative in tight corners, and the ability to improve on mistakes, England had much the better of it. The forwards had rare fight, and England showed more virility.

Half-time: England 9pts, France 0

Behouteguy dropped a goal for France after 55 minutes, making the score England 9pts, France 4. Jacobs scored another try after 60 minutes. Conway took the kick and converted.

Then Young scored after 68 minutes with a fine try, and Conway converted. The score after 70 minutes was: England 19 pts, France 4pts.

Ballarin scored a try for France after 78 minutes.

The final score was:

England 19pts (2 goals, 3 tries)
France 7pts (1 dropped goal, 1 try)

February 27, 1924

Liverpool (0) 2
Chambers 46, Forshaw 84

Southampton (0) 0

Liverpool: Scott; . Lucas, McKinlay; McNab, W.Wadsworth, Bromilow; Hopkin, Forshaw, Walsh, Chambers, Lawson.

Southampton: Allen; Parker, Titmuss; Shelley, Campbell, Turner; Henderson, Dominy, Rawlings, Price, Carr.

Referee: Mr H.J. Webster (London)

Linesmen: Mr J. Mellor (Stockport); Mr F. Leigh (Hanley)

Attendance: 49,000

Receipts: £3,145

THE game was by no means a classic, both sides being afraid to make a mistake. Chambers played well in the first period, and Forshaw distinguished himself in the last ten minutes with some fine play, but it was never going to be a brilliant game when Titmuss - surely a player of international standard - caught a drive from Chambers full in the eye, and he had to leave the field within seven minutes. He was taken to the Eye and Ear Hospital, and found to be suffering from haemorrhage of the eye, and was unable to continue the game. There were several incidents which led to serious consequences. Wadsworth, the big-hearted Liverpool player, re-opened a wound he sustained at Luton two or three years previously, and he had one eye closed when he reappeared after a lengthy absence. Then Walsh, early in the game, was stunned by a blow that affected him badly. Parker was knocked out, and Bromilow was injured when Campbell fell on him in a catalogue of injuries in a game which was never dirty.

Liverpool won the game because they were quicker to the ball and more solid in defence. Scott enhanced his reputation by collecting a fine cross-ball from Shelley, the half-back, whose shot appeared to be going away from Scott's right hand. In spite of that, the agile goalkeeper managed to catch the ball with both hands. Allen was far busier in this match than the one on Saturday, and Chambers and McNab tested him with powerful drives.

A minute into the second period Lawson, appearing at inside-left, suddenly dribbled closely and eventually passed to Chambers, who scored with ease. The Saints fought back with great fire, and twice came close to equalising.

Then Forshaw feinted, turned, passed, received the return pass, and drove the ball into the net in a magnificent piece of football. To the final whistle, Liverpool played in their own inimitable style, with Forshaw constantly dribbling through a dispirited Saints' defence, and finding Allen blocking his way.

Chambers approached his old-time form and Forshaw made inroads into the defence. Chambers, by sharp shooting, virile movements, changing position, and taking with him two or three defenders, did much towards the Liverpool victory. All the half-backs played so well that the Southampton forwards were never really in the game. Dominy was an exceptional forward, and Rawlings, was able to make the defence suffer at times. The Saints rallied for ten minutes near the close, but to no avail. After the game Dominy went to McKinlay and wished him luck to Wembley and thanked him for a fine tussle. McKinlay offered his thanks, expressed his sorrow at the ill-luck that had befallen the opposition, and Mr W.R. Williams, chairman of the Liverpool club, went to the Saints' players and commiserated with them also.

Dick Forshaw

March 8, 1924

Newcastle United (1) 1

McDonald 19

Liverpool (0) 0

THE Liverpool party left Saltburn on the morning of the match and left behind them some ice and snow. In the party were Bill Lacey, Longworth, trainer Connell, and McDevitt, as well as Charles Wilson. McDevitt left at Newcastle to go on and play for the reserve side at Sheffield.

The Newcastle ground had one big, long stand, and the rest of the ground was uncovered and was, in effect, a Spion Kop with three sides. Beyond one goal there was a park, and beyond the broad side there were houses with people at every window. Some had climbed through the skylights, and sat on the roof. There were a number of ambulance cases before the game, though of a minor nature. The spectators here, as in Scotland, hoist a white handkerchief to signal distress. The playing surface was fine, though it was a little firm in consequence of the icy weather which had prevailed on Tyneside in the past week. Gibson was unable to play and neither could Cowan, the clever ball player. Cowan had a thigh strain, and Gibson had not recovered from the blow to the knee he received in the Cup-tie at Watford. Liverpool played what had become known as their Cup team.

Hudspeth captained the home side and when the game started the gates had not been closed. Newcastle won the toss, and took advantage of the little wind which was blowing. McDonald sent in a great shot which Scott caught without trouble. Newcastle gained a free-kick when Wadsworth and Harris became embroiled in a disagreement. Harris showed signs of fight and retaliation, and a moment later was caught getting his own back.

Forshaw, with good ball control and dribbling, gained ground, and passed up the middle, where Walsh turned the ball to Hopkin. The winger advanced, and, after seeming to have lost the ball, made a fine centre which hit the angle of the post. In the next incident, the crowd booed McNab and the referee did not witness Harris hacking. The ball went to Seymour, who made a centre which put Harris in a fine position three yards from goal, but the header from Harris was brilliantly saved by Scott.

With 19 minutes of the game gone, McDonald scored. Play was initiated down the right, and when the ball was centred, McDonald headed downwards. Scott prepared himself to catch the ball, but it seemed to spin at a tangent away from his left hand. The ball had undoubtedly taken the wrong turning, and when it entered the right-hand side of the net high up, Scott, realising his error, tried a left-handed punch without success.

Newcastle were spurred on by this success, and for a lengthy period, the Liverpool defence was hard-pressed. Harris shot over the bar, and on one occasion Lucas put the ball to Scott,

and the goalkeeper was forced to stretch his foot out to prevent a goal. Then McNab passed back in wayward fashion and Bromilow, in the penalty area, had to make an excellent clearance in order to prevent a second goal.

Liverpool had had a poor twenty minutes, but when they broke away in a rare attack, Hampson miskicked badly, and had a Liverpool forward been closer to the ball, they would have scored. Walsh, in lively form, forced Hampson to spoon the ball and Mutch could reach it with only one hand by a superb effort. Then Harris broke down the middle and beat Wadsworth and McKinlay with ease, before Bromilow fell back and cleared the danger. Newcastle netted from the corner, but referee Ike Baker had blown for a foul. Five minutes before the interval, Chambers had to have his shooting foot attended to, after it had caught a divot. Hudspeth and Hampson showed signs of age and were relatively weak, but the Liverpool forwards were unable to capitalise.

Immediately after the second half began, McNab attempted a back-pass, but he under-hit it and Scott was forced to run out and throw clear. Harris was in exceptional form, being full of determination and swift of brain. The crowd booed McNab for his attentions towards Seymour, and the referee intervened by speaking with the Liverpool player. McNab complained of the crowd throwing cinders at him, but the referee and linesmen were at first disinclined to agree with him, but at length he ran to the referee, who spoke with the crowd.

Eventually Bromilow shot from long-range, but his shot sailed high over the bar. The Liverpool left-wing did not touch the ball for a period of some fifteen minutes. The Liverpool forwards were extremely ragged, without wings and purpose. The game degenerated though Newcastle's reluctance to attack, and the more Liverpool went on the offensive, the more they displayed their weakness. In the course of 85 minutes, Mutch had saved only from a member of his own side. Harris back-handed Lucas in the face, but the referee missed the infringement.

OTHER MATCHES

Central League

Half-time:
Sheffield Wednesday Reserves **0**   Liverpool Reserves **0**

Full-time:
Sheffield Wednesday Reserves **2**   Liverpool Reserves **0**

Newcastle United: Mutch; Hampson, Hudspeth; Curry, Spencer, Mooney; Low, Aitken, Harris, McDonald, Seymour.

Liverpool: Scott; Lucas, McKinlay; McNab, W.Wadsworth, Bromilow; Hopkin, Forshaw, Walsh, Chambers, Lawson.

Referee: Mr I. Baker (Crewe)

Attendance: 56,595

Receipts: £3,926

MEN FAINT WHILE WAITING FOR GAME TO START

Shortly before the start matters became worse than ever so far as the crowd was concerned, and several men had to be carried away on stretchers in a complete state of collapse.

They were apparently ex-soldiers, for whom the excitement and pressure had been too much.

One thing very noticeable was the absence of mascots. So far as could be seen from the Press box, there were only black and white umbrellas visible.

Donald McKinlay, the Liverpool skipper, had a number of messages of goodwill from various parts of the country, but the one that heartened the officials best of all came from Jack McNab. Just before the train reached its destination, he went into the saloon and, in his own inimitable style, said: "Mr Chairman and gentlemen, on behalf of the players, I have to say we are all fit and well."

It was said in a joking way, of course, but it indicated the spirit of the side - just the kind needed before such an important game.

The United were the first to come out five minutes before the start and they were given a hearty reception, but it was no greater than that accorded to the visitors.

Mr Baker, the referee in charge, promptly went to the middle and whistled for the captains, and an army of photographers snapped the spinning of the coin, which Hudspeth won.

F.A. CUP ---- FOURTH ROUND

Aston Villa 2, West Bromwich Albion 0

Manchester City 0, Cardiff City 0

Swindon Town 1, Burnley 1

Newcastle United 1, Liverpool 0

The Score Board
~~~~
Today's Results At A Glance

___

FIRST LEAGUE

	P	W	L	D	F	A	Pts
Sunderland	32	18	6	8	55	36	44
Cardiff City	30	17	4	9	51	27	43
Sheffield United	33	15	7	11	58	39	41
Huddersfield Town	30	17	7	6	45	24	40
Bolton Wanderers	33	13	7	13	54	27	39
Blackburn Rovers	33	15	11	7	48	40	37
Everton	33	13	9	11	45	42	37
Aston Villa	33	12	10	11	35	31	35
Newcastle United	32	13	11	8	48	36	34
Tottenham Hotspur	31	10	10	11	35	36	31
Birmingham	33	10	12	11	32	41	31
Manchester City	30	11	11	8	38	50	30
Burnley	30	8	12	10	42	43	26
Liverpool	30	10	14	6	34	36	26
West Bromwich A.	29	8	12	9	36	51	25
Nottingham Forest	33	9	17	7	37	54	25
Preston North End	32	9	16	7	39	52	25
Arsenal	30	8	15	7	27	48	23
Chelsea	33	5	16	12	19	45	22
Middlesbrough	33	7	21	5	29	43	19

(The above includes today's matches)

Notts County	31	9	9	13	32	34	31
West Ham United	30	9	9	12	24	27	30

MIDDLESBROUGH 2	BLACKBURN ROVERS 0
NOTTINGHAM FOREST 1	SUNDERLAND 2
PRESTON NORTH END 1	BIRMINGHAM 0
SHEFFIELD UNITED 6	TOTTENHAM HOTSPUR 2
WEST HAM UNITED 1	NOTTS COUNTY 1

SECOND LEAGUE

MANCHESTER UNITED 0	NELSON 1
BURY 1	HULL CITY 0
LEEDS UNITED 3	SOUTHAMPTON 0
LEICESTER CITY 5	BRISTOL CITY 1
STOCKPORT 1	SHEFFIELD WEDNESDAY 0

January 10, 1925

Liverpool (1) 3
Shone 32, 50, Hopkin 82

Leeds United (0) 0

THE game was blessed with fine weather. Leeds, who had been to Cheveleys, were hopeful of a draw. The tram arrangements at Victoria Street were extremely busy. Top-hatted enthusiasts with a sense of humour and a fantastic back-heel kick gave great pleasure, and a new note was struck when a monkey, attired in a red jersey, took his place in goal. McNab went down with lumbago and Bromilow was drafted in. In the Leeds side, Richmond and Duffield were absent, and Armand and Speak - the former Preston man - were included.

Liverpool lost the toss, but nearly scored in half a minute through Shone, who headed on to the iron bar which supported the net. The Leeds backs made several mistakes, and after Hopkin was ruled offside, Rawlings had an opportunity to enhance his goalscoring record in the Cup. Forshaw began the move, Shone passed it on to the unmarked Rawlings, who hit a sharp shot and saw the goalkeeper fist out before a defender kicked away for a corner.

Walter Wadsworth went close with a fierce drive, before sending a pass through the middle which Forshaw anticipated, but the home centre was forced out by the Leeds defence. Twice Swann made hasty first-time efforts, then Whipp broke through but found Longworth capable of good defence as he dribbled his way clear. Hopkin then went off for a spell with a cut eye. Scott then made two surprise saves at the foot of the post from Armand.

Hopkin returned and initiated a move in which Shone headed a goal when Menzies tried to head clear, and actually succeeded in ensuring it went into the net. Liverpool then enjoyed a five-minute period of intense pressure. Rawlings should have scored, but spent too long on dribbling his way through. Down, the Leeds goalkeeper, saved well from Chambers and Shone, and Forshaw, with a great solo dribble and shot, went close.

Shone, the chubby little Garston fellow, finished a Rawlings run with an instantaneous left-foot shot that swung the ball to the left upright, and the only danger about the shot was that the ball would cannon out from the woodwork.

Pratt had two drives at goal, and Chambers was narrowly forced out while in the process of breaking clear. Leeds were outplayed at this stage of the game, and Menzies, standing on the goal-line, saved a goal by heading out a Forshaw effort. The brightest note about Liverpool's display was their determination to continue struggling, and taking nothing for granted. Forshaw's shot was caught by the goalkeeper, before a second shot was smothered by a full-back. Lucas then went off the field after heading the hard ball. The full-back returned to see Forshaw break through from the half-way line.

Shone missed a hat-trick chance when his fierce drive crashed against the crossbar. Then Forshaw went through and from a few yards out shot straight at Down, who took the ball and fell over the goal-line, but he retained his grip and saved the goal. He was injured in the process, but resumed after receiving attention from the trainer. Hopkin was in full flight for goal with two players closing in, when his shot went inches wide.

With 82 minutes gone, Liverpool added a third goal. The ball came across from the Liverpool right wing, and Hopkin, having closed in to virtually the centre-forward position, drove the ball high into the net.

Danny Shone

Liverpool: Scott; Lucas, Longworth; Bromilow, W.Wadsworth, Pratt; Rawlings, Shone, Forshaw, Chambers, Hopkin.

Leeds United: Down; Speak, Menzies; Sherwin, Hart, Smith; Robson, Armand, Whipp, Swan, Harris.

Referee: Mr E. Pinkston (Birmingham)

Attendance: 39,000   **Receipts**: £2,400

January 31, 1925

Bristol City (0) 0

Liverpool (0) 1
Rawlings 75

THE Liverpool party left Penarth on the morning of the match in dull weather, but bright spirits. The Bristol manager, Alec Raisbeck, the former Liverpool stalwart, urged the crowd to pack together in an effort to ensure a record crowd, but there was an opposition game in the town. The Liverpool mascot, top-hatted and with an umbrella, who made good fun in the first round, tickled about 30,000 spectators with his hop, skip and jazz. The pitch was bad in the middle. There were a good number of Liverpool people present, including the former chairman, Mr McKenna and Mr Edwin Berry. The Liverpool chairman, Mr Martindale, was unable to attend, but sent his ambassador. A former Liverpool star, Fred Geary, was also present, as was another Liverpool mascot, Mr Jack Hayes, M.P. Liverpool played as selected, and Dick Johnson's inclusion indicated that Walsh was a doubtful starter.

There were two or three ambulance cases before the game began, and a lot of youngsters were hoisted over the railings to a position round the ground. Bristol City's ground, which was overlooked by Cabot Tower, was lacking in stand accommodation. There was one good stand and one extremely small stand, and the rest of the spectators were in the open. The pitch was fine in the corners, but it was sticky in the middle. Just before the teams appeared, it began to rain. Hawley won the toss for the home side.

Hawley created a good opening, which Sutherland tried to convert, but only slid along in the mud. Liverpool were unable to get going, and when Wadsworth let Walsh in it looked ominous. McNab, however, fell back and headed out from under the bar, but Pocock returned it, and Longworth saved in front of goal. Liverpool were playing terribly, and Paul hit the post before the intense pressure was relieved through a free-kick. Hughes was hurt in a collision with Rawlings, but returned after receiving attention.

The ball played many tricks, especially in the centre, where the strongest drive failed to shift it more than a yard.

Walsh worked hard to get the ball out to the Reds' wings, but on each occasion Hawley and Smailes were fierce in the tackle and Vallis was not troubled. The home side proved to be the better side in the conditions, but Liverpool, playing in white, defended resolutely. On the first occasion Liverpool really threatened, Rawlings got the ball across but it was too high for Walsh and Chambers. The ball went over to Hopkin, who sent it back to the inside-left. Chambers got under the ball and it passed over the bar.

Pratt conceded a corner which Scott miscalculated. The ball dropped at the foot of the post, but Longworth scooped it out for Scott to complete a clearance. Chambers continually put the ball too far forward for Hopkin, and the ball ran into touch

on four consecutive occasions. The winger then sent in a great centre which Rawlings took in the middle, only to be grassed as he shot, and the ball sailed over. Both sides were soaked in mud, and mistakes were numerous, but the crowd admired the wholehearted endeavour shown by the players. Rawlings got to within shooting distance of Vallis when he was knocked off the ball which passed outside for a goal-kick.

The rain was heavy when the players resumed. Liverpool stopped a raid by Worlock and then Vallis saved three times in as many minutes. The third save was brilliant. Rawlings had closed in and then Chambers was inches wide with a storming shot. Longworth then stopped a drive from Walsh, and then when the centre-forward broke clear again, McNab conceded a corner, which proved fruitless. Shone, with a great double kick, sent Rawlings away, but Vallis fielded the winger's shot like a cricket ball for an excellent save. There was a howl when Longworth kicked the ball across the goalmouth, and the City players claimed a penalty, alleging that McNab had handled. A few seconds later, Walsh was brought down a few inches from the line, but the referee ruled that the offence had occurred outside the area.

The game was open until Hawley conceded an unnecessary corner, from which Liverpool scored. The City saved the corner, but could not clear the danger, and Hopkin raced ahead before swinging over a ball that Hughes and Dyer missed. The ball went to Rawlings, and the winger screwed it into the net.

The home side strove hard for an equaliser, and Scott twice fisted out from under the bar. McNab annoyed the crowd by kicking the ball over their heads and into the waste ground behind the stand.

The Liverpool backs had been a study in solidity. They had been worked incessantly, but Scott did not have a great deal of work to do because of their magnificent display. Bristol City's backs had been their weak link, and apart from T.Walsh, the Bristol forwards had not much idea of combination. The receipts were £2,025.

Bristol City: Vallis; Hughes, Dyer; Neesam, Hawley, Smailes; Warlock, Paul, T.Walsh, Sutherland, Pocock.

Liverpool: Scott; Lucas, Longworth; McNab, W.Wadsworth, Pratt; Rawlings, Shone, J.Walsh, Chambers, Hopkin.

Referee: Mr H.E. Gray (London) **Attendance**: 29,362

February 21, 1925

Liverpool (1) 2
Rawlings 14, Shone 73

Birmingham (1) 1
Briggs 17

THE promise of a bright spring morning was not maintained, and drizzling rain fell when the crowds of spectators made their way to Anfield via packed tramcars and taxis from twelve o'clock onwards. Birmingham had a good quota of supporters with two full trainloads arriving soon after one o'clock, and they made themselves heard with their loud cries of "One, two, three, four, five!" The scene at the ground was lively, with red and blue balloons flying about in large numbers, while a couple of home supporters, dressed in red and white suits, amused the crowd with their antics. Birmingham solved their forward problem by playing Briggs in the centre and Bradford at inside-right. The teams lined up as follows:

LIVERPOOL
Scott

Lucas   McKinlay

McNab   W. Wadsworth   Pratt

Rawlings   Shone   Forshaw   Chambers   Hopkin

o

Linlay   Islip   Briggs   Bradford   Hawes

Dale   Cringan   Liddell

Jones   Womack

Tremelling

BIRMINGHAM

Referee: Mr R. Bowie (Northampton)

Attendance: 44,000   **Receipts**: £3,360

A number of spectators fainted and had to receive the attentions of the ambulance men. Birmingham won the toss, and the first incident of note was a free-kick against Shone five or six yards outside the penalty line. The kick did not, however, cause any real danger. The pitch was slippery on top and mistakes were frequent. Hopkin received a fine pass, and he was all out on his own. His centre was blocked by Womack, and the ball went back to Hopkin, whose shot was safely caught by Tremelling. The visitors were the more methodical in their methods, and they forced a corner on the left, from which Scott punched out as Briggs tried to charge him.

Jones was then injured, and he retired behind the goal line for a few minutes. During this time the ball was swung out to Hopkin, and as the winger closed in, the goalkeeper went out to meet him. Hopkin, seeing this, lobbed the ball over in an attempt to score. Amid great excitement, the ball dropped on the top of the crossbar and rebounded into play. A mêlée

ensued and a corner resulted, but eventually the danger was cleared. As Liverpool pressed, Forshaw headed into Tremelling's hands, and Shone shot a foot wide.

After 14 minutes, Liverpool scored. A free-kick had been awarded for a foul on Shone, and from this the ball was placed nicely in front of goal, and Rawlings, running in, deceived the backs and smashed the ball into the net. The Birmingham players protested vigorously, and Womack followed the referee up the field, but the official waved him off and pointed to the centre.

Three minutes later, Birmingham advanced down the right, and Bradford, after a neat dribble down the wing, centred excellently, and Briggs threw himself forward and landed the ball into the net completely out of the reach of Scott. The football was fast and forceful, and there was little to choose between the teams. Jones, the visiting left-back, was prominent with some brilliant play, and he spoiled Rawlings when the Liverpool man was in possession. Then clever work by Rawlings gave Forshaw a chance and the centre dribbled round Womack before firing in a shot which Tremelling saved at full length. Moments later, Chambers thrilled the crowd with one of his old-time shots, which Tremelling saved.

One of McKinlay's specials from a free-kick was also stopped by the Birmingham goalkeeper. At the other end, Scott ran out to make a flying clearance. Rawlings brought down both Islip and Wadsworth in trying to get at the ball, and the winger also executed a wonderful acrobatic feat by standing on his hands and kicking the ball with his heels. Just before the interval, Womack was injured and carried off the field.

Womack did not resume with the other players, but a few minutes afterwards, he turned out and played in the outside-right berth. He was limping badly as the result of an injury to his thigh. Birmingham were unfortunate not to score when a Linlay centre flashed across the face of the goal. Three visiting forwards attempted to make contact, but failed, as did Scott, and the ball curled outside the post. Islip and Bradford were strong and elusive, ploughing through the mud in characteristic fashion.

Rawlings ran down the right and centred. The ball went to Forshaw who missed the chance, but Shone closed in and drove the ball into the net after 73 minutes to give Liverpool the lead.

Liverpool missed several chances, McNab once dribbling right through, and the goalkeeper stopped his shot. Chambers then missed a great opening. Forshaw netted again, but was ruled offside. The game was gruelling, but Liverpool lasted better than their opponents, and deservedly went into the next round.

Left: **Archie Rawlings**, running in, deceived the backs and smashed the ball into the net after 14 minutes
(see report opposite)

THE TWO RAWLINGS

Archie of Liverpool;
William Ernest (Bill) of Southampton

Right: **Bill Rawlings** of Southampton, the scorer of the only goal of the game
(see report over page)

March 7, 1925

Southampton (0) 1

Rawlings 85

Liverpool (0) 0

THE Liverpool players and officials, accompanied by their mascot, Mr John McKenna, Mr Jack Hayes, M.P., sporting a black swan gollywog, and Freddie Geary, made the journey from Winchester in good time and arrived at two o'clock. They took Longworth and Walsh as reserves. They were welcomed at Southampton by a large number of followers. The man with the umbrella, top hat and black coat, met his Southampton rival comedians, and there were roars of laughter as they tossed for ends and proceeded to shoot goals. The ground was rather bare of grass, but otherwise in good condition. Just before the teams made their appearance drizzling rain began to fall. Liverpool were without their two regular half-backs.

The crowd included men perched on the roof, hoardings and embankment. Three men from Liverpool were seen asleep on the grass slopes outside the ground, and an inspector of police declared they had been there since 8 o'clock. The referee was one of the world's best; he refereed the final last year.

The gates were closed about 2.30 by order of the police. The toss was won by Southampton, but there was no advantage to be gained as the slight breeze blew across the ground.

Shone began in lively manner and play went down the home left, and when Rawlings headed across goal, the ball hit the crossbar and rebounded to Campbell, whose powerful drive passed inches outside. The Saints were excellent in defence, and Parker and Titmuss just prevented Chambers and Hopkin. Bradford hooked out a corner ball which looked as though it was going to Shone. Pratt found a bouncing ball from Campbell beat him, and Henderson raced along the wing and dropped across a brilliant centre which Harkus got his head to, but it crashed against the bar.

Southampton, who had set a great pace gave evidence of tiring, and Lucas and McKinlay ventured forward into the attack. The captain turned the ball out to the right, where Titmuss was just in time to stop Rawlings. The Reds attacked again, and Forshaw, Chambers, and Shone opened out play with some excellent judgment, and Titmuss was beaten by Rawlings for pace. The winger cut into goal and turned back a great pass, but Shone was not up with play and a fine opportunity was lost. Just before the interval Scott side-stepped Henderson and collected the winger's poor shot.

The second half was opened by Rawlings attempting a long kick. He caught Lucas in two minds and, while the back kicked, the ball went straight to Harkus, who was taken by surprise and his shot went well wide. Hopkin broke clear but was brought down by Shelley. The Liverpool winger was hurt, but recovered.

McKinlay made his first mistake when he mistimed a shot from Dominy, but the Reds' goal escaped when Pratt dropped back and cleared.

The second half had been in progress some twenty minutes when Parker, who had never been comfortable after hurting his leg, was forced to retire. Pratt forced his way through but was brought down by Shelley. McKinlay took the kick, but put too much spin on the ball, and it curled past the upright. Cockburn was spoken to for a foul on Dominy, and this led to heavy pressure on the Reds' goal. McKinney worked prodigiously, and twice stemmed the Saints' advances. Twice Forshaw was inches wide of the goal.

Five minutes from time, McKinlay was penalised for tripping Rawlings, and although he protested his innocence, the referee was adamant. The defence gave Liverpool the dummy. One player pretended to take the kick, but stepped over the ball, and Rawlings rushed up to blast the ball into the far left corner of the net. It was a cleverly worked goal.

Liverpool piled on the pressure in the closing minutes, but time was against them, and Scott had his hat in his hands in the last minute, realising the hopelessness of the situation. There were tremendous scenes at the finish, the crowd invading the field and chairing Rawlings, who was also given musical honours. It was a most dramatic finish, and the game was won in the last gasp through one of the oldest of tricks with a free-kick.

SOUTHAMPTON

Allen

Parker   Titmuss

Kelly   Campbell   Bradford

Henderson   Dominy   Rawlings   Harkus   Carr

o

Hopkin   Chambers   Forshaw   Shone   Rawlings

Pratt   Cockburn   Bromilow

McKinlay   Lucas

Scott

LIVERPOOL

Referee: Mr A.E. Russell (Swindon)

Attendance: 21,501   **Receipts:** £1,963 6d

January 9, 1926

Southampton (0) 0   Liverpool (0) 0

LIVERPOOL met Southampton for the third time in three seasons, and there was a clamouring for tickets because of the 24,000 limit on the ground. The Saints played Keeping and Woodhouse, the only changes from the previous meeting, while Liverpool kept their selection until the last possible moment on the day of the match. Richard Forshaw received news of the new arrival of a son as he got to the ground. Liverpool played Longworth, as Lucas might have broken down during the game, and Bromilow returned in place of Pratt. Mr Secretary Patterson was not present, having left for another port of call, where he was doing some angling. Two people amongst the crowd, Mr Jack Hayes, M.P., and Mr Joe Beckett, were at the previous two meetings, which seems to be developing into an annual affair. The Liverpool mascot was present doing his customary dancing and jigging. Liverpool brought fourteen players, Baron, Pratt and Lucas being in the number. The ground was in good condition, considering that it was flooded on Thursday. In certain parts it was ankle deep in soft mud. Mr John McKenna, the English League president, and former Chairman of Liverpool F.C., had three important calls this week-end - the first the match at the Dell, the next an F.A. committee meeting with the liquidators of Wembley, and on Monday the Cup draw.

John McKenna

The winning of the toss meant that Southampton had a little wind at their backs, and the left and centre flanks of the Liverpool defence had the sun in their eyes. Cockburn - making his Cup début for the visitors along with Oxley, Jackson and McMullan - soon started a movement which showed Keeping was not sure in his clearance. He sliced the ball and Bromilow soon worked away on the left in neat fashion. His centre went too far, and when play had gone a moment, Jackson was a sheer delight in his close dribbling. A long ball went towards goal, and Scott, coming forward, cleared when his feet were over the penalty box. Carr pushed across a perfect centre which Dominy took first time, but the shot was easily smothered by Scott.

Henderson missed a golden chance by centring weakly, and later in a sudden break the Liverpool defence were surprised, and a chance goal looked well on the cards, but the danger was covered. This was an unnerving experience, and confidence was restored when Chambers - playing in his 20th consecutive Cup tie - made a run and strong drive, which Allen fielded well.

Southampton played in demon fashion in the early stages, and when Rawlings got a lucky cannon he was left with a good shooting chance, but he fired wide. Woodhouse passed back to the goalkeeper in dangerous manner, and Keeping saved when Oxley looked to be going right through. It was little wonder that Keeping prevented Titmuss from playing in the first team. In an inspired breakaway, Henderson was smothered out by McKinlay and Scott. Southampton adopted the sensible way, that of taking the most direct route to goal, by lobbing centres and the open game.

Liverpool's defence got some relief when Jackson put the ball up for Forshaw, but unfortunately it was a shade too far from the centre to make it a gift goal. Allen was able to run out and kick away. There were miskicks made by Longworth and Bromilow, which was due to the uncertain nature of the pitch. Oxley lobbed instead of shooting for goal, and Allen had no difficulty in catching. McMullan made a beautiful hook and let in Forshaw, who collided with Allen and Parker. The game was stopped for quite a long time while the goalkeeper got his breath back. This incident might easily have brought a goal, but when the goal was empty Oxley could not quite reach the ball in time. Allen went off the field, and Campbell decided to put Harkus in goal, but eventually Bradford was prevailed upon to go in goal. Liverpool attacked in an attempt to secure a point, but McMullan's long drive went outside. Bradford kicked a good length in his new position. Campbell was not the dominating force he had been a year ago, having become slower. Allen looked very ill as he went towards the dressing-rooms. Longworth did so well in one move that McNab patted him, and at the other end Forshaw made a vicious attempt to drive, but entirely missed the ball. The first half had been a succession of defensive successes, with few shots at goal, even though Harkus, from half-back, made one useful effort that was two yards wide. Near the interval, the Liverpool forwards got going and when the left-wing centred, and Bradford punched away to prevent Oxley scoring, the crowd showed their delight. Cockburn came through a ruck of defenders after a rousing raid and opened the way out for McMullan. Bradford cut it short by racing out and clearing. Throughout the first half, the four backs had worked like Trojans. Right on the whistle, Scott saved from Dominy off a free-kick for hands against McNab.

Allen was found to be suffering from damaged ribs and he did not turn out in the second half. A longer interval than usual was taken. Forshaw headed in from close range and then delivered a charge on Parker, who complained to the referee that his shins had been hit. Southampton were not taking their difficult position lying down. Carr was a lively winger and the best forward on view. His centre led to Campbell kicking over the ball. As he was in the penalty area, there was great consternation. At last Liverpool began to have the ascendancy. Jackson was unfortunate to have a rasping shot charged down. The visitors tried a set plan of pushing the ball up the middle to Forshaw, who always found a collection of opponents covering him. Forshaw went right over to the right wing in order to find some space. Scott dived at the ball when Rawlings broke through. The Anfield forwards made little headway against Keeping and Parker, the youngster Keeping playing admirably. At the other end, Longworth twice saved the goal with solid heading. Bradford made his first blunder in picking up, but in the next minute he tapped out in a critical moment. The game now became almost exclusively punt and run, and either side might have won the game. Cockburn made a brilliant solo run, but nothing materialised. When Harkus went off for a time, Parker lost his temper and attacked McMullan, and Henderson fouled Bromilow, but Liverpool got nothing from a sleepy lineman.

Bromilow crossed the ball sweetly for Oxley to rush in and breast the ball, but he handled it at the same time and the chance was lost. Towards the end, Forshaw shot into the side netting.

Sunderland were not so shy in front of goal, beating Boston 8-1 on Wearside. The eventual finalists started well, Newcastle beating Aberdare Athletic 4-1 at home, and Aston Villa winning 3-0 away to Hull City.

Southampton: Allen; Parker, Keeping; Bradford, Campbell, Woodhouse; Henderson, Dominy, Rawlings, Harkus, Carr.

Liverpool: Scott; Longworth, McKinlay; McNab, Cockburn, Bromilow; Oxley, Jackson, Forshaw, Chambers, McMullan.

Referee: Mr R.G. Rudd (London)

Attendance: 18,931

Receipts: £1,725 2s

EVERTON'S HOME TIE WITH FULHAM

FIRST APPEARANCE OF LONDON CLUB AT GOODISON AND A TILT AT THE CUP

DIXIE'S GOAL OFFSET - TO MEET AGAIN

Goodison Park had the city to itself today and a great crowd attended to see Fulham's first appearance here.

Everton: Hardy; Raitt, McDonald; Peacock, Bain, Virr; Chedgzoy, Irvine, Dean, O'Donnell, Troup.

Fulham: Beecham; Dyer, Chaplin; Oliver, McNabb, Barrett; Harris, Craig, Pape, Prouse, Penn.

Fulham brought quite a good following. There was a nasty wind and it was in Everton's favour that they had its assistance in the first half.

What play there was in the first few moments undoubtedly went in favour of Everton, although it was easy to be seen that the Fulham defence wasted no time in their tackling, and it was this fact which put out two promising Everton attacks.

Then Troup kicked the ball on to his own chin and followed with a perfect pass to O'Donnell, who in turn hooked with the defence and made such a sensible inward pass that everybody believed that an Everton goal was in the making. The Fulham goal, however, still remained intact despite all Everton's advances.

Fulham got in a raid and won the first corner of the day. Fortunately for Everton, it came to nothing. The schemings of Irvine are often hard to understand, but everybody, the boys in the gallery included, understood his action when he allowed a long pass to go between his legs and on to Chedgzoy, who was running in.

Chedgzoy, however, was unable to get a true kick at the ball through the attentions of Chaplin; but nevertheless Beecham had to go down low to prevent a goal.

The speedy and keen half-back play by Oliver, McNab and Barrett meant that Everton failed to score despite their dominance.

Then Irvine sent in a great shot and the ball rose at a terrific speed and was travelling just underneath the angle of the upright when Beecham made his jump and turned it aside. It was a great shot, and an equally great save.

Penn, who was one of Fulham's most dangerous forwards, put a ball across the Everton goalmouth just as Craig, Pape, and Prouse were crowding down upon the Everton citadel. Hardy shot out his hand to make a startling save.

Chedgzoy and Irvine followed instructions and gave it to Dixie. He was at the right-hand side of the goal when Irvine passed it, but turning swiftly he dashed it into the net, but not before Beecham had touched the ball. This happened at the fortieth minute.

Half-time: Everton 1, Fulham 0

Dean, cleverly lobbing the ball over the head of the remaining back, dribbled onwards. Beecham advanced and pounced upon Dean's shot and turned it away from goal.

Dean and the two full-backs went after the ball, and Dean was accidentally tripped, but he retaliated and brought a warning to himself and others. Fouls had been very frequent.

A free-kick was awarded to Fulham. Harris placed the ball into the goalmouth where McDonald headed out, but he had not headed out far enough and Craig fastened on to the ball and steered it into the net through a ruck of players after 70 minutes.

Final score: Everton 1, Fulham 1

January 13, 1926

Liverpool (0) 1

Forshaw 65

Southampton (0) 0

James 'Parson' Jackson,
*who showed consistent form
against Southampton*

Liverpool: Scott; Longworth, McKinlay; McNab, Cockburn, Bromilow; Oxley, Jackson, Forshaw, Chambers, McMullan.

Southampton: Hill; Parker, Keeping; Bradford, Campbell, Woodhouse; Henderson, Dominy, Rawlings, Hough, Carr.

Referee: Mr R.G. Rudd (London)

Attendance: 42,000

Receipts: £2,670

LIVERPOOL'S victory was not a worthy victory. They beat precious little because Southampton were not a powerful side anywhere except in the full-back division. Hill was the deputy goalkeeper, and Hough was named in place of Harkus. The players produced a hard, fast game operating on turf which was frozen. Liverpool's attacking strength was vastly superior to that at the Dell but the fact remains that at the moment Liverpool's forward line had lost touch with itself; they had no considered plan of campaign, and much that was haphazard was allowed to go on. Oxley seemed impressed - as were the crowd - by the work of Keeping, who was regarded as the best young back playing football in his day, and well worth international honours. Keeping dominated this game in the same way that Crompton of Blackburn Rovers used to take charge of international games. He was an aviator. His partner, Parker, was overworked and none too steady under pressure, and his length suffered. Hill, the deputy goalkeeper, saved well from early shots of worth that were put in by Forshaw and Jackson. They were really good drives, yet Hill, with the left hand, edged them over for corner kicks. They were surprising saves which brought a torrent of applause from the home spectators, even though the saves went against their club. Hill made a gallant attempt to stop Forshaw's header from going into the net, and in doing so he pulled a muscle and hit a part of the goalpost. It was some time before he returned to his work. Forshaw's goal came through Chambers and McMullan, and one goal was always likely to secure a tie between clubs who had only scored four goals in five meetings.

Forshaw took a lot of watching, even though he did not attain his former brilliance, and he made Campbell slow up long before the end. Dominy and Hough were slow, too, and Hough eventually went to his normal place as full-back, and Parker went to centre to shake up his delinquent forwards. His mission was to no avail, for Henderson and Carr were at fault where centres were concerned, and Rawlings had little chance against the towering Cockburn. Southampton were at their best just before the interval, and Dominy lashed out in fury and the ball beat nearly everyone, but Longworth sent it for a corner. Oxley and McMullan were moderate in attack, and only Jackson and Chambers showed form such as one associated with a side that had recently won the league championship twice in succession.

The football was not good, but it was rousing and rushing, and at least Liverpool played Southampton at their own game. Their style on the previous Saturday had been all wrong. The great barrier to the victory over Southampton was the fact that it was gained against a poor side which had its resources stretched by injuries. There was little fault with the Liverpool defence, and the half-back line was of a steady level character, all sharing in the work and the honours. On the visiting side, only Woodhouse did well at left half-back. He challenged comparison with Bromilow, and Keeping had no contestant in the matter of being the most outstanding player on the field.

January 30, 1926

Fulham (2) 3
Pape 4, 65, Penn 41

Liverpool (1) 1
Forshaw 30

THE players saw the Coliseum show on the night before the match, and there was a clean bill for Trainer Connell to report when the team that beat Arsenal was ready to take up the cudgels with the southern foe. In successive weeks Liverpool had beaten West Ham 2-1 away and Arsenal 3-0 at Anfield and they believed the third and best win of all would be associated with the first meeting in senior football of the brothers McNab - one a Liverpool player, and the other a Fulham man. It was announced before the game that Pape would play and the man who troubled Everton in the previous round, Edmonds, would be absent. Among those present were Mr Jack Hayes M.P., Mr John McKenna, the mother and father of the ex-Darlington player, Tom Scott, and the Liverpool mascot, who had never before been seen on a London ground, and caused quite a stir among the Cockneys. Around 3,000 people arrived from Liverpool, and two other McNab brothers arrived from Scotland to witness the game. Donald McKinlay announced that he was to definitely give up the game of baseball, at which he was a more than effective player. When Everton lost 0-1 at this ground the snow fell fast and darkness covered the earth. Although it was not a bright day, the scene of the day's tie was much more pleasant. It was a perfect day for visibility, and the ground was nicely soft, due to the early morning rain. There was little wind, but there was much rattle from partisans. Around the touchline the youngsters soon took up their positions, and the hospital blue made a contrast to the red-hatted Liverpool followers. Probert acted as Fulham's captain in Chaplin's absence. The Liverpool team were greeted with a thunderous reception. Young Beecham, looking like Sam Hardy in face and figure, seemed to be the most confident man on the field. The home side won the toss.

Scott was the first to handle after a long shot by Prouse. Bromilow stopped Penn, and the ball was put to Forshaw, who, with Tom Scott, easily beat the opposition, and had Forshaw shot first time he might have opened the scoring, but he delayed, made one move too many, and Scott shot outside.

With just four minutes gone, Oliver surprised everyone with a good piece of heading, and the ball was crossed from the right wing. McKinlay miskicked, as did Craig, and Pape was left with an easy chance five yards out. He clumped the ball to the right-hand side of the goal.

For a time Fulham played an open game which suggested that they were not satisfied with one goal, but the Liverpool forwards passed the half-backs with such ease that it looked equally likely that the Reds would secure an equaliser. Tom Scott performed better than most in the forward line, and Jock McNab had a good show against a lively left wing. Forshaw

broke through and after he determined to shoot, he let the ball move on to Tom Scott, who was bowled over unceremoniously. Prouse, who was the real brain of the home attack, was half-stunned through a bang on the back of the neck. Bromilow not only timed the ball brilliantly, but he also lifted it up to the middle to give Forshaw a chance. The right wing did not often come into prominence, but when it did, it was extremely useful. From a Harris centre, Pape headed the ball against the crossbar. Scott saved a long drive from Prouse, and as Fulham attacked in earnest, the ground began to cut up. Elisha Scott left his goal but missed his punch, and Bromilow tidied up at the back, enabling Scott to gather at the second attempt.

Forshaw hit a perfect drive which looked a goal all the way until Beecham flung himself at the ball and saved miraculously. McMullan was unable to squeeze in the rebound, and Cockburn, with a powerful drive, missed the target by inches.

With 30 minutes gone, Donald McKinlay moved up towards centre-half, and Forshaw had a great chance with an up-the-middle pass. He made four attempts to put the ball out to Oxley. It looked as though a golden chance had passed by, but Probert, in trying to clear, kicked the ball on to Barrett, and Forshaw, waiting for such a chance, nipped in to equalise. Before he shot he was tripped, but the ball entered the net.

After 37 minutes Dyer went off the field, looking rather ill with a knee injury. McKinlay rolled up his sleeves and ran up to take a free-kick which went over the bar. Barrett went to full-back, and made a terrible misss, with the result that Forshaw was gifted another chance, but he smashed the ball against the crossbar. Dyer returned to the fray. With 41 minutes gone, Liverpool suffered another blow. Penn headed through in simple fashion and Scott missed his punch and actually helped the ball into the net. Immediately afterwards, Liverpool netted without getting the verdict, and the referee failed to see Chambers charged in the middle of the back in the penalty area. Right on time Fulham nearly scored again through a forward diving after the ball.

The previous week, Scott had performed heroically in the 3-0 win over Arsenal, but his goalkeeping display was rather poor in this match. Dyer came back on to the field late, and shortly afterwards the first offside of the game occurred. Forshaw went on a solo run, but Fulham's McNab covered well. Dyer was spoken to by the referee for a nasty bump on McMullan. Jock McNab tried a long shot, which Beecham fielded well, and Tom Scott, with a pretty hook, opened the way for Forshaw to make an intense drive, to which Beecham fell at the right moment to effect a brilliant save. Penn and Oliver were both nippy and Chambers had little chance. McMullan broke away and, producing his best work so far, centred for Forshaw to try another shot at goal and, although Beecham appeared to tip the ball over, the referee did not award a corner.

A free-kick against McKinlay for a foul on Harris led to Fulham scoring again. McKinlay protested that it was not a foul, and Pape, stood beside Scott while the free-kick was taken practically on the touchline. Pape changed his position and left Scott some two yards space. As the ball came to the middle of the goal, a number of heads went towards it, and Pape nodded it through, only to receive a crack on the head as he scored.

From a free-kick, McKinlay tried to reduce the arrears, but Beecham twisted the ball over the bar again. Then the goalkeeper pulled off an amazing save. Forshaw broke through and shot at goal. The ball was travelling away from Beecham, yet with both hands, he gripped the ball as though he was used to catching cannon balls. Craig was another Fulham hero, playing a fine half-back game. Oxley had little chance to show his paces, and Tom Scott had become slow. Liverpool had become disheartened. Fulham had gained the initiative by sharp, short raids and runs and sureness in front of goal. Jock McNab headed away in fine fashion to prevent a further goal.

Bromilow continued to be Liverpool's star half-back. As the game reached its final few minutes, Chambers seemed to have scored with the ball a good half-yard over the line, and the referee was nearly pulled to pieces by the Liverpool players when he would not allow the goal. With trouble he reached a linesman, whom he consulted, but the goal still did not stand. Beecham had been dispossessed for once and lost the ball, which Chambers hooked into goal.

The next incident in this sensational match was a linesman reporting the spectators for throwing, and then followed a verbal exchange between Cockburn and Prouse. With 15 minutes remaining, McKinlay joined the forward line as a last resort. McMullan became effective, and Tom Scott shot wide. Pape was hurt and left the field, and with the minutes running out, Prouse hit the crossbar.

As after the Everton match, Ernie Beecham was chaired by his admirers to the cottage at the other end of the field.

Liverpool lost because of rare mistakes by Elisha Scott, and McKinlay revealed a slowness which proved fatal to his side. He played well in timing his tackles, but he did not have the scope which Lucas and McNab possessed. Bromilow had no superior at half-back; he was an artist and yet efficient. Cockburn was below par, and Tom Scott laboured heavily late on as though he was not fully recovered from an operation for appendicitis.

Fulham: Beecham; Dyer, Probert; Oliver, McNab, Barrett; Harris, Craig, Pape, Prouse, Penn.

Liverpool: E.Scott; Lucas, McKinlay; McNab, Cockburn, Bromilow; Oxley, T.Scott, Forshaw, Chambers, McMullan.

Referee: Mr A.E. Caseley (Wolverhampton)

Attendance: 36,381

Receipts: £2,427

In Sportive Memory

of

TWO MERSEY FOOTBALL CLUBS

whose Rudders were interred at
Craven Cottage by

THE FULHAM FOOTBALL CLUB.

COME, COME, NO INQUESTS!

January 8, 1927

Bournemouth (0) 1
Taylor 52

Liverpool (0) 1
Hodgson 86

LIVERPOOL had two main fears about this tie - firstly, that Lucas would not be able to play, and secondly that the cramped state of the Boscombe ground would prevent them showing their best form. Bournemouth was bathed in sunshine and the air was summer-like, and the kiddies filled their buckets and pushed their boats down the ready-made rivers of the parks. Lucas was tried on the ground just before dinner-time and his calf muscles stood the test. As a result there were no changes in either side. The turf at Boscombe was really good but the accommodation was naturally primitive. The ground had just one stand. Most of the spectators sported the red and white colours of the home team, which, strangely enough, are identical to those of Liverpool's old-time Cup rivals, Southampton. Four years in succession Liverpool have visited Winchester *en route* for a Cup-tie, and they had never scored in Hampshire. A draw looked the likeliest result. Outside the ground there were thousands of cycles, and they were parked in a manner that was awkward and inconvenient. Also astonishing was the large number of motor-cycles. The Mayor of Bournemouth and Mr Jack Hayes, M.P., who never misses the Liverpool side when they are anywhere down south were present. In view of a recent announcement, a jocular wag called Mr Hayes a "Bootlegger". Mr Tom Crompton, chairman of the Liverpool Club, attended with other officials, and a confident and merry party was made up of people interested in Liverpool Football Club. The Anfield club took no risks and sent down four reserves, Cockburn, Oxley, Done, and Generalissimo McMullan. The Liverpool officials had some doubts about the ground and its accommodation, which they feared would not cope with the demand. People swarmed over the scoreboard planks. A new temporary covered stand at the back of the goal with its white cover would probably have made the task of the shooter none too easy, for seeing the white of the covering he would not think it anything other than a target. However, it was the same for both sides. The fact that Bournemouth had their ground on a yearly lease had prevented them from spreading their wings in the park. Naturally the locals thought they had a good chance on the form they showed last year against Bolton Wanderers, the eventual Cup winners. Liverpool knew that they had a difficult task on their hands. The home team, known as "The Cherries" had a fat boy of Peckham type of mascot, who, with the aid of his bell, kept the rather silent crowd from going to sleep. There was no community singing and though there was a band present the limited size of the crowd prevented a mass roar. There were early indications of the fears of the Liverpool officials of the breaking in of the crowd if it touched record figures when workmen were sent round the popular side to hammer in some staves to ensure that the

boards surrounding the touch line did not fall in. However, at the start there did not seem to be any danger from the crowd which had got to its stands and seats early to avoid crushing. The real danger lay behind the goals where any semblance of swaying would lead to the very flimsy sort of boards being snapped to matchwood. Blair had not lost a hair since he left Cardiff and Sheffield, and when Referee Lines got the men lined up everything was in order for a stout contest. Bournemouth were certainly a big side; in fact, there were only three small members. Liverpool turned out in white with red armlets. The visitors lost the toss, and as there was no wind there was nothing in that fact. The game started with Liverpool moving up on the left through Hopkin and Bromilow. Bromilow threw the ball so well that Chambers was able to move up and shoot in his very best fashion. It was a flying high ball and when Robson got it, he was sternly challenged by Forshaw, and when the goalkeeper went down to earth, most people expected a free-kick, but play was allowed to go on. Robson had a severe blow when Edmed centred and Forshaw charged the goalkeeper over the line. The home side were slow to settle and rather nervous. Chambers, who had been using his right foot more than usual in shooting, ran into Miles, who hurt himself and delayed the game for some time, before he was led off the field. The Liverpool left wing was the great source of trouble and Hopkin once walked his way through and beyond three men and centred a ball that was going away from Chambers. The shooter made the shot go towards the corner flag and a golden opportunity went begging.

The injured pivot returned, and for some reason took exception to Liverpool's tactics, which had been clean and fair. Scott had his first employment just under the half-hour. Boscombe's left wing had done little due to McNab's defence and improved passing. Hodgson - making his Cup début along with Dick Edmed - was a willing worker and a good controller of the ball, and his partner had bad luck in a good run after which a free-kick for a foul on Forshaw brought much trouble, Blair heading out of the goalmouth and Bromilow making a surprise daisycutter which passed a yard wide. Forshaw followed up with an excellent first-time drive which Robson saved as he fell to earth. Hodgson, who had played superb football, engineered a combination which ended with a tame shot from Forshaw to Robson's hands.

Early in the second half Taylor had his leg damaged and this formed the second stoppage of the game. Bromilow twice stopped the opposition walking through, but within seven minutes the Liverpool goal had fallen, Scott being beaten by a header from Taylor, who with Eyre, went to head the ball at the same time, Scott being crowded out. The goal had come from a Buchanan centre which everyone thought was passing outside. Spectators were agreed that the ball was going outside, but Thomson had other ideas, and when he caught the ball almost on the parallel line, he centred awkwardly to the Liverpool defence, and the goal resulted.

As Liverpool struggled to get on equal terms with their opponents, Forshaw headed outside. Pratt and McNab played a more forward game and their help in attack was most welcome. Bournemouth concentrated on defence and packed their goal. Robson effected a useful catch from Forshaw after an Edmed cross. Fifteen minutes remained, and Liverpool were still in arrears.

Even corner kicks became of great importance. Lucas and McKinlay continued to press back the youthful side, and Chambers lofted one outside. Ten minutes to go. Pratt became a centre-forward, but it was Forshaw who failed with a header. Five minutes to go. Edmed took a corner; the ball was headed against the crossbar, Robson was nowhere near, and it looked like a goal, because Bromilow was in a good position, but Hayward took the ball away from him. At the other end, Scott saved Liverpool before the Hodgson goal.

Gordon Hodgson

The South African was close in when he took a pass from Chambers four minutes from time and equalised. With a minute to go, Scott made a catch from a corner that could easily have been a goal.

The replay was scheduled for the next Wednesday, kick off at 2.15. Tickets were to be issued for the centre portion of the new stand and centre portion of Kemlyn Road stand only. Numbered and reserved 3s 6d each. Application had to be made to the office, Anfield Road, by post, enclosing cash (no cheques) with stamped addressed envelope for reply. Shareholders and members would have first preference up to Tuesday noon, and envelopes had to be endorsed "Shareholder" or "Member". The charges for admission to the remainder of the ground were to be the same as in League matches: Ground 1s, boys 4d; Kemlyn Road Stand (ends) 2s; New Stand (centre portions) 3s 6d; Ends 2s; Paddock 2s. All to pay at the turnstiles.

Bournemouth: Robson; Hayward, Blair; Halliwell, Miles, Smith; Buchanan, Taylor, Eyre, Stringfellow, Thomson.

Liverpool: Scott; Lucas, McKinlay; McNab, Pratt, Bromilow; Edmed, Hodgson, Forshaw, Chambers, Hopkin.

Referee: Mr C.E. Lines (Birmingham)

Attendance: 13,243

Receipts: £1,668 11s 6d

January 12, 1927

Liverpool (2) 4

Hopkin 5,
Chambers 22, 60, 65

Bournemouth (0) 1

Eyre 70

THE value of playing in one's customary jersey and in front of home supporters was shown in Liverpool's decisive victory. Bournemouth, playing in white, had their chances, especially when Lucas tried to back-heel the ball and did not move it a foot, which gave the visitors a great opportunity of scoring, but the chance was spurned.

After Liverpool had missed splendid opportunities, Hopkin scored, aided by centre-half-back Miles, who turned the ball out of his goalkeeper's reach. As if this was not sufficient, Blair re-headed a Chambers' header and turned it into goal at a merry pace; in fact, had Blair been a forward he could not have headed the ball more perfectly out of the goalkeeper's reach. Bournemouth looked an ever-dangerous side with their stockily-built players and their ever-practical measures which sent them up and onward at a fast pace. The visitors always looked good for one goal, the trouble was it arrived too late for them to make a contest of the match. Eyre got the goal, and it was reward for his persistence which was in stark contrast to the feeble display given by Thomson at outside-left, who was no better than in the game played at Bournemouth. Liverpool won because of their superior skill; and they asserted themselves with their devious dribbling methods, and while Bromilow and Lucas fell a trifle short of their own exacting standards, others came to the fore and Edmed played sparkling football, showing a capacity for centring and juggling with the ball that made him the best forward on view. Taylor, Chambers, and Stringfellow were also fine forwards on the day, while Hopkin's response to his partner's cuddling passes was of much help. Hodgson was not unduly prominent, but contrived to make one run half the length of the field that worked the crowd into a high state of excitement. They urged him to part with the ball, but he hung on to the end, and having beaten three men he squared the ball to Forshaw, who shot outside. Pratt played good football, and McKinlay bore the defence-work with his customary safety, while McNab had never before dominated a winger so completely. The weather broke down at midday and kept many people from the game. Bournemouth played below normal and were unduly impressed by the occasion, the crowd, and the spaciousness of the ground, as compared to their close contact with their supporters.

The outstanding player in the game was Pratt, the centre half-back. The Scot appeared to have recovered his best form, and his play in the two games against Bournemouth had shown him to be not only a good defensive pivot, but a constructive player who used his brains. Pratt, in fact, made his name as a centre-half but he did not show his best form with Bradford City. He had played many fine games as a wing half for Liverpool, but rarely had he shown up so well in the pivotal position as he did in this game.

Hopkin had rarely figured on the scoring sheet, but his goal, the first of the match, gave his colleagues confidence. It was recalled that Hopkin's first goal for Liverpool was scored against Bolton Wanderers, and that day was marked by a fire on the stand. In this tie, a water pipe burst on the stand at the Anfield Road end after Hopkin had scored.

David Pratt, who had a good game as pivot against Bournemouth

Liverpool: Scott; Lucas, McKinlay; McNab, Pratt, Bromilow; Edmed, Hodgson, Forshaw, Chambers, Hopkin.

Bournemouth: Robson; Hayward, Blair; Halliwell, Miles, Smith; Buchanan, Taylor, Eyre, Stringfellow, Thomson.

Referee: Mr C.E. Lines (Birmingham)

Attendance: 36,800

Receipts: £2,430

January 29, 1927

Liverpool (1) 3
Hodgson 13, Chambers 50, Edmed 88

Southport (0) 1
White 90

IN the week that Lon Chaney was appearing in *The Road To Mandalay*, Liverpool took a step further along the road to Cup glory. The sun shone brilliantly, and although there was a high wind the Anfield ground was so well sheltered that little of its effect was felt. Southport were well represented and they took a hand in the community singing, while the rival mascot waltzed to the tune of the band. A Southport correspondent wrote: "Southport comes to Liverpool! "Marshside will be there - the boys with their peak caps and blue jerseys and the girls (up to seventy) with their poke bonnets or lace caps, customs which are relics of their Flemish forbears. They have a lingo of their own and manners of their own, too. If a Marshside lad wears a cloth cap, he wears it with the peak hanging down his neck-hole! If he says his team is "Playin' oop whaare" he means that they are playing against the wind. They are all known by nicknames: "Bill-o'-Jacks", "Derham", "Bluey", "Fewer", "Dickerty", "Cotty's Bill", "Ginger", "Burglar", "Dubby" and thousands of others. A football official once went for a player to play in a representative team. "I asked for Will Johnson for two solid hours," he said. "Then I told one chap that I wanted the goalkeeper of a certain team. "Ah, tha meuns 'Bunger'," was the reply. And for two hours I hadn't been fifty yards from where he lived. But nobody knew Will Johnson, while even the cocks and hens knew 'Bunger'."

The only change was that of George Jones, the former Everton winger, for Parker. While Liverpool received a good reception, the Southport boys were welcomed with greater acclaim, which was evidence that Southport were well supported. Liverpool won the toss and Southport faced the wind.

In the very first moment Halsall was brought to his knees with a shot from Hodgson, who hit a hat-trick last week against Derby County in 22 first-half minutes. Good work down the Liverpool right saw Edmed's centre headed on by Forshaw to Chambers who spurned the chance high over the bar. Southport's first attack came from their right wing, a Jones header creating anxious moments for Scott and McKinlay, but they eventually cleared their lines. A Hopkin centre enabled Forshaw to test Halsall, but the goalkeeper punched away. The ball fell to Hopkin near the corner flag, and he sent over another cross which would have resulted in a goal but for the timely intervention of Glover, the former Everton full-back, who kicked the ball off the line. From a half-hearted shot from Hodgson, Halsall scrambled the ball around the post. The home side dominated at this stage, but Southport were working against a strong sun. However, there was never the craft about their movements as there was in the Liverpool side, but their defence was brave in the face of the enormous pressure which Liverpool put it under.

Dick Edmed, *who scored a fine goal after a great piece of combination with Gordon Hodgson*

The Third Division side fell behind after 13 minutes. Edmed created the goal by dashing in and taking a Hopkin centre on his head and turned it into the goalmouth. It was a certain goal, for Edmed had Halsall beaten all the way, but Hodgson made sure. The Southport players were keen enough when they got the opportunity, but with McNab, Bromilow, and Pratt, they found many of their hopes shattered to fragments; and even if they did overcome this trio, there were always McKinlay and Lucas. Liverpool eased up, and the visitors made several well-defined moves in midfield, and made some progress, but such was the solidity of the Liverpool defence that Scott was not tested for nearly half-an-hour. On the other hand, Halsall was constantly called upon, but he should never have been allowed to get in the way of a Forshaw shot when the Liverpool centre was offered a sitter by Hodgson and had time and space and almost the whole of the goal to shoot at. Forshaw's drive went straight to Halsall's hand, and the goalkeeper held it safely. A second goal appeared to be on the cards when Chambers crashed in a great left-footed drive which struck the crossbar and rebounded over into the spectators' enclosure. This was followed by a Hodgson header which just went outside, and a Forshaw header which did the same. Southport's earnestness prevented Liverpool from adding to their tally. Simpson was ruthless in his tackles, but at the same time quite fair. It was the usual sort of tackling one saw in the Third Division. During the first 35 minutes play, Scott had handled the ball just once, and that was from a long distance shot, or perhaps a pass, by one of the visiting half-backs.

The Anfielders tried hard to increase their lead, and it was not due to the brilliance of Halsall in goal, but due to the fact that the home forwards were inept in their marksmanship. The nearest the visitors came to equalising was when Jones was able to collect a ball through Bromilow slipping as he made a header. Jones tried a lob into the Liverpool goal and Scott did not get as clean a punch at the ball as he desired with the result that Marshall got a chance to shoot. Although his shot was of great power, Scott had fully recovered and patted it down; but even if the ball had entered the net it would have been disallowed because the referee had blown for an infringement.

This incident gave Southport more heart and for a short spell they clustered round the Liverpool goal, before the home side cleared and essayed an attack in their own right. However, the visitors played like fiends, and Sapsford, with a push-through pass, offered Marshall a chance, but unfortunately for the inside-right, Bradley, his colleague at centre-forward, was obviously offside. Just on the interval, Halsall had to catch and clear from Hopkin.

In Scotland, the Hamilton-Celtic Division One match was abandoned owing to a severe storm four minutes before the interval with the visitors leading 2-1, but at Anfield the sun continued to shine, the crowd working up a thirst for Higson's "Trojan" at 8d a pint.

Southport resumed with an attack and Scott had to hand out a bouncing ball, which did not trouble him unduly. Liverpool's response was swift, and they increased their lead after 50 minutes with a goal which came through as pretty a movement as it was possible to see. Edmed began the move, and, seeing that he could not have middled the ball to the liking of his inside man, he decided to send it back to Pratt, who pushed the ball forward to Chambers and the inside-left drove in a shot that sped into the net, giving Halsall no chance of saving.

Liverpool might have scored a third goal when Hopkin made another of his dragging centres, for the ball travelled right across Halsall's goalmouth. Hodgson made a brave effort to rush it into the net, and received an injury as his reward. Southport retaliated down their left wing and it looked ominous for Scott until Lucas broke down the attack. Minutes later Bradley missed an easy chance nine yards from

goal. Hopkin charged Halsall but he found the Southport 'keeper as solid as a rock, and the crowd were amused to see Hoppy brought to earth.

Liverpool realised that it would be as well to play their left wing now that Hodgson was limping, and Hopkin and Chambers led the visiting defence a merry dance with their inter-passing. Hodgson headed in from Hopkin's centre, and a section of the crowd believed that the home side had scored, adjudging that Halsall was standing well inside his goal when he caught the ball, but in fact, the goalkeeper had his hands stretched out in front of him.

Halsall twice saved from Chambers as the home side continued to dominate. At this point, there was great cheering all round when it became known that Everton had equalised at Hull through Virr. (The game finished 1-1.)

With 88 minutes gone, Edmed scored a goal from a wonderful movement. Edmed and Hodgson, through changing places when on the move, puzzled the Southport defence, and when Hodgson made his centre Edmed ran through and placed the ball into the net. Liverpool should have had a fourth for Forshaw practically had the ball on the goal-line, but could not push it into the net. With one minute remaining, White, who had run into the centre, took a forward pass by Simpson and beat Scott, who seemed to throw himself at the ball a shade too late.

Liverpool: Scott; Lucas, McKinlay; McNab, Pratt, Bromilow; Edmed, Hodgson, Forshaw, Chambers, Hopkin.

Southport: Halsall; Allan, Glover; Sinclair, Newnes, Simpson; Jones, Marshall, Bradley, Sapsford, White.

Referee: Mr A.J. Caseley (Wolverhampton)

Attendance: 51,600

Receipts: £3,200

February 19, 1927

Arsenal (2) 2

Brain, Buchan

Liverpool (0) 0

IN the week that Fay Weldon was starring at the Palais de Luxe in the most intimate of stage life stories called "*London Love*", Liverpool found no love in London and were soundly beaten by a much better side on the day. An hour before the kick-off there were 20,000 spectators present, and others were arriving whistling "*Let's all go to Highbury's House*". In the big party which included mascots, the directors' wives, the member for Edge Hill, Mr Jack Hayes, also the member from the music hall department, "Billie" Matchett, the chairman, Mr Tom Crompton, his co-directors, the secretary, manager, and players, all expressed a confidence which was catching.

Liverpool had already applied to the Football Association for the release of Bromilow, who had been selected to play against the Shropshire Association at Shrewsbury in mid-week, but Liverpool felt they may well have needed him in the games at Leeds in the week after this tie, if the Cup result went in favour of the Reds. (Liverpool did, in fact, play Leeds on the 23rd, drawing 0-0. Bromilow played at number six.)

Another item of special interest was the fact that a famous Third Division club had asked headquarters to quote them a price for insurance against their famous left wing depreciating in value in the next five years. They value the pair at £10,000. This was in addition to the freak business that football was suffering since Buchan's goals were priced at £100 each.

Harper, the Scottish international, was brought back in place of Lewis, the Welsh international, who had played so well at Anfield and Wrexham. The situation created a dilemma for the Arsenal directorate, though they were fortunate to have two goalkeepers of international repute. On the Friday night, the Liverpool side arrived in London near bedtime, but another party of officials left by the midday train. There were nearly 3,000 excursionists present.

There was a real crush at Lime Street for the 7.30 excursion, and a large number came at midnight or by the 8 o'clock train. Jack Cock, Forbes, and other Plymouth players stayed at the same hotel en route to their Third Division South game at Coventry (Plymouth drew 3-3). The Swansea club chairman, Mr Morris, called in to the hotel to offer his best wishes. Before the game, Charlie Buchan revealed that Swansea had knocked Arsenal out of the competition in sensational fashion the previous season, (Swansea Town beat Arsenal 2-1 at home in the quarter-finals) adding "I've been waiting for seventeen years for a final-tie show," to which Donald McKinlay replied, "Same here, lad." (Arsenal progressed through to the final at Wembley, losing 1-0 against Cardiff City through a Ferguson goal after 73 minutes on 23 April before a crowd of 91,206. The Cup went out of England for

the first time, and Arsenal had further cause to rue the Welsh clubs. Of the Arsenal team, apparently only Buchan lived up to his reputation, but he never gained a winner's medal.)

The turf was well sprinkled with sand and the fog lifted as the kick-off approached. Alderman Austin Harford and former Liverpool player Frank Checkland were present in the crowd. Liverpool lost the toss and the game started three minutes before time, Bromilow bringing in his famous swerve three times before he gained his desire. Brain and Blyth were responsible for Arsenal's first attack, and Buchan made a blind pass to where Hoar should have been. He later tried a shot and jarred his leg. Reid - making his Cup début for the visitors - began with a first-class first-time pass, and Hodgson made Harper pick up close in.

The culmination of a move involving Hopkin, Hodgson, Edmed, and Reid was that the débutant hooked the ball over his head and wide of the goal. After Edmed had headed outside, Harper once more showed the length of his kick. Liverpool, who played in white, found Arsenal inclined to over-dribble, but the Liverpool forwards were very useful on the move. John, the Arsenal half-back played the best game of the lot. A free-kick against Hodgson brought the first thrilling shot of the day. Buchan was the marksman, and the ball soared over the bar. Then came a second foul against Hodgson. Cope's first free-kick had been smothered by a wall of defenders.

The second free-kick was fatal. It was closer in, and when the ball went to the right wing, Hulme headed towards goal, and Brain rushing in at full pace, scored from no more than two yards' range to the extreme right hand corner of the goal. Scott, who had a minute or two before picked up a ground drive, was near to hand but he had no chance of saving.

This goal spurred on the visitors. McNab became an extra forward and concluded his dribble by feeding his forwards. Hodgson could not get the ball under way for a shot, and therefore offered Reid a low pass. The Liverpool centre shot in a beauty which spun no more than half a yard out. Reid followed this with a strong run, and Harper left his goal and missed his objective. Davie Pratt, racing in, blazed away at a goal guarded by Parker, the full back, and the ball went high over.

A second goal arrived from another free-kick, awarded against McNab. Buchan used his height to nod the ball over the line at the identical spot at which Brain had been successful. Buchan made Scott catch in electric fashion to prevent a third goal, and Reid, aided by Hodgson, should have done better than shoot outside from close range. Lucas smothered Hulme two yards out, and Baker shot over the bar.

Hopkin nearly scored direct from a corner as the game swung from end to end.

The second half opened with a spell of good work by McNab and a flashing shot by Edmed. Chambers shot from thirty yards but the ball veered off to the right. Blyth continued to carry the ball in masterly fashion, and his failure arose from an offside trap set by the Liverpool captain. One ball was crossed from the right and Reid and Chambers got in each other's way. Arsenal seemed content to sit on their lead. Their half-backs were very strong, while the Liverpool full-backs were overworked by a nippy forward line that got over the ground in double quick time and with sleekness of movement.

One of the funniest incidents in a game which lacked humour was when Scott left his goal to push the ball forward, and as he ran backwards towards his goal he fell over the prostrate figure of Brain.

A forty-yard drive by Baker threatened the Liverpool goal, but Scott was in fine form. Buchan was having an inspired game. From a throw-in on the extreme left-hand side, he ran from inside-right to inside-left and made a first-class surprise shot, and in the next moment he sauntered around, at outside-right, created a corner and a lot of work for Pratt and Lucas.

As Reid broke through, Harper raced out and covered him. Liverpool had the better of the second half without really looking able to pull the game out of the fire. Hoar broke free of McNab and put Blyth in possession, but the Scot blasted the ball over the bar. Chambers moved to the centre-forward position and shot brilliantly. With fifteen minutes to go, all Liverpool's hope vanished, with Parker and Cope in such fine form. The Arsenal players had been half-a-yard sharper than their opponents all afternoon. Brain netted on time for the home side, but it was disallowed for offside.

Charlie Buchan *used his height to nod the ball over the line at the identical spot at which Brain had been successful*

Arsenal: Harper; Parker, Cope; Baker, Butler, John; Hulme, Buchan, Brain, Blyth, Hoar.

Liverpool: Scott; Lucas, McKinlay; McNab, Pratt, Bromilow;   Edmed, Hodgson, Reid, Chambers, Hopkin.

Referee: Mr Strouther (Nottingham)

Attendance: 43,000

Receipts: £2,871 12s

RATES OF INCOME TAX FOR SINGLE PERSONS

Income wholly earned	Tax		
£	£	s	d
163		2	0
175	1	2	0
180	1	10	0
190	2	6	0
200	3	4	0
210	4	0	0
225	5	4	0
250	7	6	0
270	9	0	0
285	10	4	0
300	11	10	0
350	15	14	0
400	19	16	0
450	25	10	0
500	33	18	0
550	42	2	0
600	50	10	0
650	58	18	0
700	67	2	0
800	83	18	0
900	100	10	0
1,000	117	6	0
1,150	142	3	4
1,200	150	10	0
1,500	200	10	0
2,000	300	10	0

January 14, 1928

Liverpool (0) 1
Chambers 60

Darlington (0) 0

LON Chaney appeared in *Tell It To The Marines* and was said to "put ginger into their step and fear into their hearts", but it was Third Division Darlington who fought like heroes to frustrate the Anfielders and cause the home side to fear for their Cup lives.

The Spion Kop's new covering was a boon to the large number of spectators which had gathered there. Darlington won the toss, though there was little wind.

The first attack of note arrived when Edmed went inside and flicked the ball forward to Walsh, who forced a corner. Edmed placed a perfect lob to Chambers, but the inside-left man's header was not powerful enough. It was the beginning of an anxious spell for the visitors, but they cleared their lines with an up-the-middle movement which brought Ruddy face to face with Riley. The South African goalkeeper won the ball.

McGiffin broke clear down his wing and Lees tested Riley with a low swerving effort. Darlington's short bursts were rather scrappy in nature, but always dangerous. The lanky McGiffin sent across another ball which was just too high for Lees. Cochrane got away and although Riley punched away, Waugh followed up and shot, but Riley had recovered the situation and patted the ball down.

Moments later Ruddy attacked from close range, but he was blocked out by McKinlay and Jackson.

At this point Liverpool had done all the attacking, and they got to close quarters and Edmed, who took a corner, gave Reid a fine opportunity with his head, but Archibald smothered the ball and eventually turned it round the post.

McGiffin was injured in a collision and he went off the field, but the visitors still caused Liverpool many problems. Jackson, with a marathon run, managed to turn the ball away for a throw-in instead of a corner, and McKinlay, kneeling on the ground, got the ball away when there was real danger. Darlington were playing exceptionally well, while Liverpool struggled to find any rhythm. A drive from Chambers beat Archibald but struck the upright and rebounded to safety. Jackson defended well, but he had never been so lacking in constructive work.

Edmed went near to scoring with an intended centre which flashed across the face of the goal and then Cochrane, who had done little, got the better of Bromilow and put in a nice cross which was not capitalised upon. Just before the interval, McGiffin re-appeared bandaged. In making a great full-length save from Walsh, Archibald was temporarily injured.

Darlington stood on no ceremony in the second half and Liverpool were penned in their own half for long periods. Hopkin, however, went on a fine solo run which culminated in a shot which went inches wide. The light became worse

and when Chambers shot after close range work by Edmed, it was difficult to see whether the ball had entered the net.

Just on the hour, Liverpool attacked with venom and Archibald was finally beaten. From a ruck in front of goal, it seemed that Chambers put the ball through.

Darlington still fought like tigers, and for a period of at least four minutes, Liverpool were outplayed. Lucas saved the equaliser by kicking off the line as the visitors took the game to their more illustrious opponents. Darlington made strong appeals for a penalty when McMullan was caught by McGiffin's centre. Darlington's close passing was a revelation at this period of the game, but they could not manage to score.

The Cup-holders, Cardiff City, beat Southampton 2-1 in Wales. The highest score of the round was Manchester United's 7-1 thrashing of Brentford, while Stoke City hit six against Gillingham. However, in Scotland, Rangers beat Airdrie 7-2 away, while Celtic beat Dunfermline 9-0.

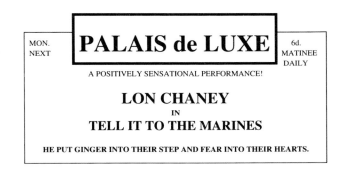

Liverpool: Riley; Lucas, McKinlay; McMullan, Jackson, Bromilow; Edmed, Walsh, Reid, Chambers, Hopkin.

Darlington: Archibald; Brookes, Mellon; Dickson, Waugh, McKinnell; Cochrane, Gregg, Ruddy, Lees, McGiffin.

Referee: Mr A.J. Weaver (Grimsby)

Attendance: 28,500

Receipts: £1,810

January 28, 1928

Cardiff City (1) 2
McLachlan 35,
Nelson 68

Liverpool (1) 1
Edmed (pen) 32

SHARP'S Tromboneers, the original combination from the Alhambra, London, were playing in the Palais de Luxe, while Joan Crawford and Owen Moore appeared in the film *The Taxi Dancer*, but the Cup-holders Cardiff hit the right note to send Liverpool back along the road to Anfield. Only two Liverpool directors accompanied the team to Cardiff, the others travelling near and far in the search for new talent. Messrs Cartwright and Harvey Webb were the two officials concerned, while several of their colleagues were in Scotland negotiating for new players. Mr W.R. Williams, the former Liverpool chairman, was to undergo an operation for throat trouble the following week. Mr E. Bainbridge was in the Northern Hospital, Mr Astbury was not well, and Matt McQueen was not fit to travel. Gordon Hodgson saw his pals off; he expected to start light training in a few weeks' time. Mr Jack Hayes, M.P., joined the party at Penarth on the morning of the match. Friday was an excellent day for weather, but on the morning of the game there was heavy rain, which continued right up to kick-off time.

Cardiff's ground was not one of the best, and the slightest suggestion of rain turned it into a swamp, so that conditions at Ninian Park were atrocious. A dozen men were busily engaged forking the centre piece, which was covered by a sheet of water, only the wings being free of rain. Fifteen minutes before the kick-off, men resumed probing the goalmouths, which resembled a miniature lake. There were not many excursion trains due to the bad weather. Cardiff won the toss and started before about 10,000 spectators.

Liverpool opened with a flank attack by their left wing, to which the Cup-holders replied with a movement down the centre of the field, which was brought to a conclusion when three Liverpool men tackled Ferguson successfully. It soon became apparent that football would be a difficult proposition, and that the side able to stay the distance would be better. Hardy showed early on his wisdom when he drifted the ball out to Thirlaway, only to find his colleague in an offside position. Hopkin forced Nelson to kick into touch, and then the Liverpool defence had a gruelling few minutes, during which Davies shot over when well placed. Gaining a corner, Cardiff launched an attack which looked likely to produce success, for McLachlan's kick was well placed, but neither Ferguson nor Irving, who both went out to meet it, could gain contact, so a great opportunity went by. A ground pass was practically useless, for the ball would not travel much more than half-a-dozen yards. However, Reid cleverly side-stepped Nelson, and, rather than let the ground beat him, he transferred to Hopkin, who was able to work on a more solid foundation. The Liverpool winger was aware of the advantage of a first-time effort, and the only thing wrong with his shot was direction, the ball sailing over the crossbar. Both sides had chances, but Cardiff had the best shot up to the sixteenth minute, Ferguson hitting a rare drive that passed only a matter of inches over the crossbar. Hardy shot through a ruck of players and Riley appeared to be unsighted, but he dived across his goal just in time to get his hands to the ball and force it on to the face of the upright. The danger even then was not cleared, for Ferguson and Irving went up in an effort to dispossess the goalkeeper, but Riley saw that they did no damage.

Little had been seen of the Liverpool right wing; most of the play taking place on the far side of the field where Hopkin was highly successful. He gave Reid an opportunity, but the best the Liverpool centre could do was to slam the ball on to Nelson, who stood bang in front of him to stop the ball going across to the unattended Edmed. Keenor had a shot, Bromilow conceded a corner, but nothing came from it. For some time poor football was witnessed, the rival defences being well able to hold the opposition.

McKinlay stopped a powerful centre from Thirlaway with his back and was put out of action for a minute or two, but he recovered to continue to play a strong game. Attempts to tip-tap on such a surface were bad judgment, and Cardiff paid the penalty. Watson attempted a back pass to his goalkeeper, but the ball did not run, and Reid nipped in to gain possession. He pulled to the right and shot, but Watson impeded the progress of the ball by the use of his hands. Edmed was entrusted with the penalty kick, and he sent the ball flying high into the net after 32 minutes.

Liverpool did not hold their lead for long, and three minutes later McLachlan defeated Riley with a great shot. This equalising shot had a great effect upon the Welshmen, who ran rampant for a time. Prior to the Cardiff goal, Riley had saved spectacularly from Ferguson, and a spectator ran onto the pitch to shake him by the hand.

The players resumed in new kit, and the rain had ceased as the teams restarted. McKinlay stopped Ferguson, and from his clearance, Reid and Hopkin paired off, a manoeuvre which ended in Chambers shooting narrowly wide of the wide with a lob. For some time the game was quiet, and it fell to the home right wing to enliven matters, but they could not find a way through the Liverpool defence. Gradually Liverpool asserted themselves, and then Reid let in Edmed, who tricked Watson and left him standing. Edmed continued his run and created a perfect centre for Hopkin, but the ball tricked the winger before he could line it up for a shot. Liverpool concentrated on defence, but this proved their downfall because these tactics made Cardiff look a better team than they were, and gave the home side self-belief where little had previously existed. Cardiff continued to have the better part of the attack, but Reid sent in a glorious shot which went inches wide of the upright. The home side stormed back onto the attack, and when McNab went over to help Jackson stem the tide, he accidentally handled the ball just outside the penalty area. Liverpool built a wall, and when Nelson was called out to take the free-kick, the full-back found the only hole in it, and piloted the ball into the net with almost half-an-hour remaining. Edmed, running to inside-right, delivered a shot which brought Farquharson to his knees, and he only saved at the second attempt. Liverpool realised the folly of their previous defensive tactics, and Edmed, in particular, was a menace to the Cardiff defenders. Towards the end both Hopkin and Reid limped. Reid hooked the ball over the bar by a fraction of an inch. Cardiff went through, but were beaten 2-1 by Nottingham Forest on Trentside in the next round.

Cardiff City: Farquharson; Nelson, Watson; Wake, Keenor, Hardy; Thirlaway, Irving, Ferguson, L.Davies, McLachlan.

Liverpool: Riley; Lucas, McKinlay; McNab, Jackson, Bromilow; Edmed, Walsh, Reid, Chambers, Hopkin.

Referee: Mr W.J. Paisley (Wolverhampton)

Attendance: 20,000

Receipts: £1,666

*The game against Cardiff marked the end of **Harry 'Smiler' Chambers'** magnificent run of 28 consecutive FA Cup appearances. It was also Chambers' last appearance in the Cup, in which he scored 16 goals.*

January 12, 1929

Bristol City (0) 0

Liverpool (0) 2
Salisbury 50, Hodgson 75

DAVIE Pratt, of Bury, went to see his old Liverpool team off to Bristol, and on the morning of the match there was a train load of enthusiasts from Liverpool to Bristol, all gathering at Ashton Gate to see the third meeting in thirty years between these two sides. Four years ago there was a deluge of rain. Today it was frozen, but the midday sunshine helped to melt some of the frost. The playing conditions were admirable, except for a portion where the sun had been unable to pierce through owing to a stand at the back of the goal. That particular goal was something of a novelty because of its arched crossbar, while the turf near the posts rose four or fives inches, which presented difficulties to the visitors and there were suggestions that the crossbar was not lawful. The Liverpool party resumed acquaintances with Tom Scott, Cyril Gillespie, and David Bain, as well as Manager Alex Raisbeck, who superintended what he believed would be a record crowd. However, there was a big rugby attraction in the town, and the City's League form was not conducive to a large crowd. The home side played Bertie Williams in place of Tom Scott, who, like McBain, was a doubtful starter, and the five home forwards had been able to score only four goals between them in seventy-two appearances. Gillespie - who had grown considerably since leaving Liverpool - nursed a strained groin muscle, while Tom Scott was also declared unfit to play. Liverpool lined up against Bristol - rather a small team - in white jerseys, while Jackson took a fatherly interest in the five-year-old mascot. Bristol won the toss, and had the wind and sun at their backs, but neither was particularly strong.

Liverpool went straight onto the attack with Reid and Done, though no-one did better than McDougall in the early stages. He went on a splendid solo dribble before getting the ball out to Edmed on the wing. Bristol appeared as though they were intimidated by the opposition, and when Clarke either miskicked or skidded, Edmed went away and his centre caused concern for the home backs, but Salisbury was a shade too slow to take advantage. Shortly afterwards Hodgson broke through the middle and forced Glenn to concede a corner. Bristol responded by packing their goal in a nervous manner. Eventually the home side made progress on the right where Foster was clever and practical. Jackson, Reid, and McDougall scrambled the ball away from the forward line which had not shown a shot. David Bain was the instigator of Bristol's main attack, in which B.Williams made an emphatic shot, which Riley gathered confidently. This was the encouragement the home side wanted, for Paul began a further attack which was spoiled by Hick giving away a foolish foul. Foster chased round Done, who fell, and centred, and Paul, the old man of the side, shot magnificently. The ball struck the left upright. Riley had little trouble from forwards who generally shot from long distances. Bain proved once again to be the rock upon which Bristol began their attacks, and Paul screwed the ball to the right when a goal was gaping at him.

The Liverpool players were strangely unsettled, and the miskicks by Jackson and Davidson in turn did not get the forwards going easily. Bain tried a long shot which hit the side netting, and Done then needed the trainer's help. Bristol were not impressive, and neither were Liverpool. The home side had more genuine goalscoring opportunities. Liverpool eventually netted through Clarke, but Hodgson charged the goalkeeper a fraction too late for the goal to count. The crowd reacted angrily at this behaviour by Hodgson and booed him for several minutes. The spectators cried "First Division!" in scornful tones when Edmed, through slipping, made the ball go out in tame fashion. Bain and Foster were thorns in the Liverpool side, and Riley had to jump out and punch out a centre when he fell to the ground.

Perhaps playing in white as against the red of Bristol had an effect on the Liverpool team, for they had made little show in the first half against a very ordinary side; the forwards had not revealed any signs of combination, though now and then Clarke had shots charged down. When Liverpool wobbled, Riley stood firm and resolute.

Liverpool were more lively in the second half. A shot by Edmed hit the top netting as the visitors took the game to Bristol.

With 50 minutes gone, Liverpool scored a really soft goal. The home backs got themselves in trouble and Hodgson and Salisbury were together just beyond the centre of the field. Salisbury was, therefore, well out of position. He elected to take the ball up the middle of the pitch, but when he shot he hit the side of it, and it bounced his way beyond the goalkeeper, who was at fault in not saving such a tame shot. Hodgson rushed up to complete the ball's travel. Salisbury's effort touched the upright and crossed to the left, so that Hodgson was wise to make sure the goal was completed, though the goal was distinctly Salisbury's.

In spite of the arched goal, Hick failed to score when he was nearly under the bar.

The home side responded by going on the attack, and Liverpool still did play to their true form. The half-backs did not play well, and Clarke took on the role of roaming half-back. The football was very poor at this stage. There was no shooting and the goalkeeper had a gala afternoon. After 68 minutes, a second goal arrived which effectively killed off the game. Salisbury, instead of centring, pushed the ball upwards, and Hodgson, having got the goalkeeper out, drove in with his left foot, the ball entering the net at the extreme right-hand side. Edmed should have scored a third with ease, but this was not one of Liverpool's better days. Reid went close with a shot late on.

Huddersfield - losing finalists in 1928 - hit seven away to Chesterfield, while Aston Villa smashed six past Cardiff City - winners in 1927. Luton Town and Crystal Palace drew 0-0, only for Palace to win the replay 7-0. The Corinthians beat Norwich City 5-0 at Carrow Road. Bolton Wanderers - who were to go on and win the Cup against Portsmouth - beat Oldham Athletic 2-0 at home, while Portsmouth beat Charlton Athletic 2-1.

Bristol City: Coggins; Walsh, Glenn; Bain, Sleman, Taylor; Foster, Williams, Hick, Paul, Johnson.

Liverpool: Riley; Jackson, Done; Morrison, Davidson, McDougall; Edmed, Clarke, Hodgson, Reid, Salisbury.

Referee: Mr T.G. Gould (London)

Attendance: 28,544

Salisbury elected to take the ball up the middle of the pitch, but when he shot he hit the side of it, and it bounced way beyond the goalkeeper, who was at fault in not saving such a tame shot.

January 26, 1929

Liverpool (0) 0   Bolton Wanderers (0) 0

LIVERPOOL and Bolton Wanderers met on turf that was rather firm. The Wanderers won the Cup in 1923 and 1926 and would go on to win it again this season. The day was excellent, and the game drew thousands by road and rail from Bolton and there were many from surrounding towns. Ted Vizard, the former Bolton player, was seen in the crowd. Mr Charles Foweraker, the Bolton secretary, told of Finney's injuries. Finney was carried off last week, and by Wednesday was fit, but by the Thursday found he could not play, so that Greenhalgh took his place, otherwise the team today was that which won the Cup on 27 April before 92,576 spectators at Wembley, Butler and Blackmore scoring for Bolton in a 2-0 win. Liverpool were equally troubled about the team sheet, and Salisbury was unable to play. He tested his knee, on which were two boils, at eleven o'clock, but he had to give up the idea of playing and Lindsay, of Rhyl, had his first baptism of cup-tie work with Liverpool FC.

A family party drove up to the ground after two o'clock, and the party consisted of Mr and Mrs Bromilow, young Bromilow and friends. This was a strange contrast to the old days when players walked to the ground and hero-worshippers carried their bags so that they could get free admission.

There was a very orderly crowd, but a quarter of an hour before the start there was an awkward occurrence underneath the number board. There was not a big crowd there, but the space was small, and every ambulance man was summoned immediately to the assistance of the men, who were lifted over the concrete barrier. For some minutes the wafting of clothes suggested that there was a boxing match. There were about twenty fainting cases, and the police and ambulance, under Superintendent Hughes, told the spectators in the affected area to move towards the boys' pen, and this relieved the tension and the trouble. There was a slight haze over the magnificent Spion Kop structure, otherwise the picture would have been a beautiful one. The people who received attention from the ambulance men were soon accommodated with fresh positions in the ground. The police closed the paddock entrance early on, and in front of the Press Box was a row of spectators who could not hope to see any part of the game unless the people in front of them moved down. Youngsters were bundled out, and, in addition, the little mascot, Glazebrook, fought shy of his task and would not cross the touchline when Bromilow led his men out to the accompanying cheer of a crowd of over 50,000. Seddon had an equally hearty reception, and won the toss. The early play showed that both teams would struggle due to the condition of the pitch Liverpool moved off down the left and Hodgson, by

back-heeling the ball to inside-right, did the only thing possible in the circumstances. From this move came a free-kick taken by Done, the ball travelling a yard outside the mark. Done was very clever with a dead ball, but on this particular day spot-kicking was difficult. It needed Howarth's best work to prevent Hodgson's header going into goal, and Clarke and Edmed, at their first wing pairing, threatened to go through as a consequence of Nuttall's rather fanciful back-heeler. The main trouble early on was produced by Seddon with strong heading and fine passing. Bromilow's "dummy" led to Lindsay heading forward and Hodgson passing square, Nuttall conceding a fruitless corner. Seddon carried Bolton in the first quarter of an hour, and when he kicked away furiously, the ball was returned, and Edmed, from eight yards, shot to make fisherman Pym clutch the ball.

Liverpool roused themselves and McDougall's cleverness led to Davidson shooting over the bar. Hodgson passed to Edmed, whose cross was not met by Lindsay and McDougall, who flew in like greyhounds and just failed to connect with their heads.

The first stoppage came when Howarth, kicking clear, knocked his own captain on the head. Seddon was down for a few moments, and the first thing he did when he resumed was to give McDougall a bump that sent him to the ground and damaged his elbow. McDougall's answer was a fine pass to Lindsay, and the brilliant young left-winger drove in a beautiful shot which Pym managed to catch. Moments later Clarke found himself in front of an open goal but was too slow to snatch the opportunity. Jackson went to the aid of Done, and Morrison made an overhead clearance to turn the course of the game at a critical moment. Bromilow followed with a back-header from the mouth of the goal which enlivened Liverpool.

For half-an-hour, Bolton had taken a lot of punishment, and the crack Bolton forwards were completely out of the picture. Gibson headed into the hands of Riley, but this came as the result of a linesman deciding to act as referee and giving a free-kick against Morrison. Considering the state of the pitch, the display was excellent.

Lindsay played brilliantly and gave Kean a lot of trouble, but Bolton at last produced a thrilling attack. Butler started the move and tried to complete it with a high, brilliant drive that Riley punched up with one hand. The ball came to earth with Riley awkwardly placed because he could sense the players coming at him with a charge when he made a second save and thus kept Bolton at bay. In reply, Lindsay made another beautiful hook centre that Hodgson could not quite reach, and Edmed slipped as he was about to convert. Bolton had another thrilling effort started by a long dribble by McClelland and ended when Jackson narrowly failed to reach a ball that led to Blackmore closing to the right-hand side of the post and lashing out a shot that possibly hit Riley, but at any rate, was cleared as a consequence of Riley's positioning himself in such a way that Blackmore could not squeeze the ball through. Bolton had little of the attack, but when they got near goal their shooting had been stronger than that of the home side. Near half-time Edmed was hurt in a collision with Pym, both being dazed in an incident which occurred through a succession of heads in front of the Bolton goal. For the third time in the match, Lindsay opened out in fiery fashion and Pym saved a fierce drive from the Liverpool youngster. Gibson, kicking into touch, knocked a spectator's hat off - the spectator was James Jackson's brother, the Tranmere player. The first half had been a triumph for nearly all the Liverpool side, and for Jackson, Lindsay and Riley in particular, while on the Bolton side only Seddon gave a good account of himself.

All the gates had been closed five minutes before the kick off, and the crowd had seen a first half which belonged almost exclusively to Liverpool. The value of a good throw-in was shown when Nuttall brought off a brilliant throw for the benefit of McClelland, who produced danger, which was cleared. The slippery turf caused the pace to drop, though there was no reduction in the number of incidents. Butler's hook shot was punched away with one hand by Riley, and Clarke - who had had a poor first half - broke into a dribble down the middle, and a Bolton defender passed the ball back to the empty goal. The crowd watched a race between Greenhalgh and the travelling ball. The Bolton full-back kicked the ball off the line. Hodgson was cautioned by the referee for his sixth foul of the game. Throughout the game, Done's defence had been superb. The Bolton forwards played with greater determination and there was a loud claim for a penalty against Davidson for hands, but the referee was on the spot and turned the appeal down. Edmed went through on goal and Hodgson and Clarke were on the line, but were unable to score from a mêlée. The defences dominated, and there was no more effective half-back than Bromilow. Jackson used his head on numerous occasions to foil Bolton's thrusts, and Riley saved brilliantly from Cook's shot. Pym, in contrast, was not so good, saving from McDougall in fumbling fashion. With only eight minutes left Riley saved the home side when Bolton appeared likely to score.

Cook left all his best work for the last quarter-of-an-hour, when he was very lively. It had been a thrilling ending to a goalless cup tie, but Bournemouth and Watford certainly went goal crazy, Bournemouth winning 6-4. Burnley, 1-3 down to Swindon at the interval, forced a draw with two second-half goals.

John Lindsay

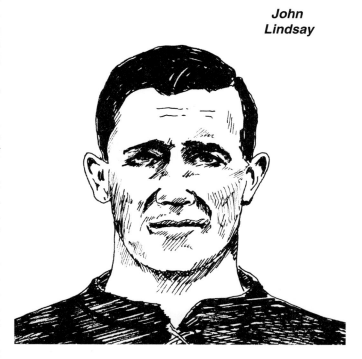

L.M.S.

F. A. CUP ----- 4th Round Replay

LIVERPOOL v. BOLTON WANDERERS

SPECIAL EXCURSIONS
TO
BOLTON
WEDNESDAY, JANUARY 30th

	pm	pm	Return Fare
Liverpool (Exchange) ..... dep.	12.20	12.45	
Kirkdale .... dep.	--	12.51	
Preston Road.. dep.	--	12.57	**2/6**
Bolton (Trinity Street) arr.	1.05	1.31	

Return at 4.28 pm for Liverpool only, and at 4.48 pm for all stations. In the event of Extra Time being played the Special Trains will leave at 5.07 pm for Liverpool only, and at 5.25 pm for all Stations.

See bills   (7394)

Liverpool: Riley; Jackson, Done; Morrison, Davidson, Bromilow; Edmed, Clarke, Hodgson, McDougall, Lindsay.

Bolton Wanderers: Pym; Howarth, Greenhalgh; Kean, Seddon, Nuttall; Butler, McClelland, Blackmore, Gibson, W.Cook.

Referee: Mr A. Josephs (South Shields)

Attendance: 55,055

January 30, 1929

Bolton Wanderers (2) 5

*Blackmore (2), Butler,
McClelland, Gibson*

Liverpool (1) 2 aet

Lindsay 33, Hodgson 70

GOALS flowed in the replays; Swindon beat Burnley 3-2 after trailing by two goals, Aston Villa trounced Clapton Orient 8-0 away; Crystal Palace beat Millwall 5-3, Blackburn Rovers beat Derby County 3-0 away, and Bolton Wanderers overcame a resilient Liverpool side to win 5-2 after extra time with exactly the same side which went on to win the Cup.

After three-and-a-half hours of football, Liverpool went out of the Cup, but the result gave no idea of the gallantry of the side against odds and fate, for the score was no indication of how the game went. Liverpool began by Morrison striking the crossbar, and from that moment the course of the game from Liverpool's point of view did not run smoothly. Changes in the positions of the eleven were necessitated by injuries. Hodgson struggled on at centre-forward to the interval, but afterwards he turned out at outside-left, where he produced some excellent centres and scored the vital equalising goal. Then he took up the centre-forward position again, but finally he and McClelland were out of place. Added to Hodgson's severe blow to the thigh, wrenched muscles, and a damaged ankle, was the thigh injury to Clarke, and a minor injury to Salisbury. These incidents did not deter the team from gallant efforts to save the game, which started in their favour. Lindsay scored with a shot that was helped through by Pym. Having the initial goal might ordinarily have secured victory, but this was no ordinary game. The heavy turf, cut up by the players, who slid when they made tackles, made any attempt to work the ball difficult. It was natural that there should be mistakes, and these were largely produced by the Bolton half-backs, who were surprisingly beaten by the sheer determination of the Liverpool forward line. Bolton had four chances in the first half and took two, while Liverpool had six chances and took just one. They lost the game because they tried too hard to make up for their inadequacies. It was a game of numerous thrills; it was the embodiment of all that is best in football, and the continuous endeavour of all the Liverpool men to carry the banner to success was worthy of the highest honours.

Lindsay scored after 33 minutes, Pym being at fault and letting the ball slip behind his hands. Three minutes later McClelland scored from close range, and three minutes after the equaliser, Gibson scored from what looked like an offside position. Hodgson left a few minutes before the interval and reappeared a few minutes after the break, and ten minutes later he went to outside-left, Lindsay becoming centre-forward.

Riley made his first save at the hour, and Hodgson equalised for Liverpool after 70 minutes, after McDougall had taken the ball forward. Haworth troubled McDougall, whose shot was eventually netted by Hodgson with ease, and extra time was necessary, but not before Gibson had missed the easiest

chance of the match and Pym had fallen to stop Edmed scoring.

After 96 minutes, Blackmore scored from Butler's centre. Hodgson resumed at centre-forward, but Butler scored direct from a corner, the ball escaping all the men gathered in the goalmouth, and entering the net at the far side, touching the goalkeeper before it passed over the line. Finally, with Hodgson at outside-left once more, McClelland broke away and centred, for Blackmore to score with ease.

Bolton were fortunate in that they had to contend for a large part of the game with only nine fit men. Lindsay was remarkably consistent; Morrison used the ball brilliantly; Davidson was steady and wise in his passing; Bromilow displayed his usual leadership; and Riley and Jackson and Done performed heroically. The full-backs covered much ground, had a fine understanding, and did monumental work that led the home crowd to give them a special cheer. Never was there such defence, even though five goals were conceded. This was, indeed, honour in defeat.

F.A. CUP RESULTS
(Fourth Round Replays)

Clapton Orient	0	Aston Villa	8
Crystal Palace	5	Millwall	3
Swindon Town	3	Burnley	2
Derby County	0	Blackburn R.	3
League Division 1			
Manchester City	6	Bury	4

Bolton Wanderers: Pym; Howarth, Finney; Kean, Seddon, Nuttall; Butler, McClelland, Blackmore, Gibson, W.Cook.

Liverpool: Riley; Jackson, Done; Morrison, Davidson, Bromilow; Edmed, Clarke, Hodgson, McDougall, Lindsay.

Referee: Mr A. Josephs (South Shields)

Attendance: 41,808

Receipts: £3,458

January 11, 1930

Liverpool (1) 1
McPherson 19

Cardiff City (1) 2
Len Davies 44, 80

IN the Palais de Luxe - "The Home of Golden Silence" - Colleen Moore starred in the great musical comedy success "*Oh Kay*", but at Anfield Road Liverpool fans were silenced as Cardiff delivered a Cup k.o. Among the large crowd were the former Everton players Jack Page and George Beare, later with Cardiff. All around the country there were Arctic conditions, but Liverpool was blessed with fine weather, a cold air, and a dry ground - abnormally dry considering the deluge which occurred earlier in the week. Cardiff won the toss, and kicked off towards the Stanley Park end.

Liverpool: Riley; Jackson, Lucas; Morrison, Davidson, McDougall; Edmed, Hodgson, Smith, McPherson, Hopkin.

Cardiff City: Farquharson; Jennings, Roberts; Wake, Keenor, Blackburn; Thirlaway, Len Davies, Munro, Robinson, McGrath.

Referee: Mr E. Pinkston (Birmingham)

Attendance: 50,141

At once Morrison made a delightful move towards the right wing but Keenor slammed in and covered the position, which opened the way for the big Munro at centre-forward. He, like his captain, was far too strong in his kick up the field and the chance was lost. However, Cardiff attempted three more attacks from which they might have scored had they shot more quickly. They were inclined to move the ball a yard before shooting, and Blackburn once kicked round the ball in attempting to shoot it.

Riley was busy four times in the first quarter of an hour, though Farquharson had the more difficult work to do. Edmed shot so well that the Irish goalkeeper did well to pick up the ball. Riley saved with clean catches, except in the case of Wake and a corner kick, Wake making a long drive and Riley needed to be smart on four occasions. Yet of all the efforts, none had the sting of Edmed's, who got his chance through Hopkin, playing his first FA Cup tie for two years, when Liverpool lost 2-1 in Cardiff.

Liverpool realised that the Second Division side were playing as though they were still in the First Division, and Farquharson, in one of Liverpool's rallies, found himself in the back of the net, and the ball hung for an appreciable time. Smith - making his Liverpool Cup début - was out to snap up anything, and on one occasion he looked to be offside owing to his speed, whereas he was actually well onside. He was beaten, however, near the corner flag. The best solo effort came from Jennings, who was not only daring but competent

in carrying the ball with his head and making a shot. Neither side settled down early on, and the customary Cup-tie fear pervaded the atmosphere, except in the case of Jackson and Morrison. McPherson made a dribble and shot, and Edmed should have shot instead of squaring the ball.

Len Davies shot from long range which was not his usual form, and Riley edged the ball away with an outstretched hand in a period when Cardiff enjoyed themselves with corners, and McGrath sent in an excellent centre, but no colleagues were up to meet it. Cardiff had their chances when Len Davies and Thirlaway found the Liverpool defence in a generous mood. Liverpool were more definite in their first-time passes, and the left wing was the ruling factor.

With 19 minutes gone, Liverpool took the lead. Smith appeared to be offside when he went ahead and forced a corner. Hopkin took it in his own perfect manner, and Farquharson punched it away only a short distance. Even so, the save seemed to have been made when Roberts, the Cardiff back, got to the ball. The former Glasgow Ranger, McPherson, had scored some valuable goals in his time, but none was as important as this one which gave his side the lead. He stood in the centre-forward position and knocked the ball into the net with a sweep of his right foot.

Cardiff's sorrow was magnified when Munro beat the defence, heading the ball onto the goalline, and getting no reward for his effort. There was a series of bumping matches between Jackson and Munro, and a couple of fouls by Morrison, only one of which was seen, but it entailed a talk from the Birmingham referee, who had a lower jaw like Carnera.

Cardiff went through a series of passes of the highest quality, but there was no reward for all their effort. When Liverpool did get away at rare intervals, they showed Cardiff how deadly they could be. James Smith made a perfect ankle-hook to the left-hand side of the goal.

Farquharson dived at the ball, and was thankful for the resulting corner kick until Hopkin applied his consummate skill to the ball and made it drop on the line. Munro found a way down the middle, but never really got the ball to his left foot, so that his shot went well wide of the goal. Edmed's effort from the inside-right position was struck firmly and true, but Farquharson managed to tip it over the bar. Morrison, in stretching out for a ball, fell to the ground and Munro very coolly moved the ball to his right, and Len Davies, breaking all rules of angles, used his left foot and drove a terrific shot into the right-hand corner of the goal. The few hundred excursionists who came with the Welsh side cheered enthusiastically.

Thirlaway began the second half by handling and shooting in the minute after the whistle was sounded for an obvious foul. Liverpool looked like going ahead after a long period of Cardiff attacking pressure when a race developed between Smith and Farquharson. The odds favoured the home centre, but the goalkeeper picked up in an amazing manner. It was the thrill of the game. There were accidents to Wake and Smith, but the referee wisely played on in spite of calls from the crowd, many of whom did not realise the law on the point. Smith looked for his customary goal and a long range effort held the crowd in suspense before it went out of play, the goalkeeper being out of touch with the position of the ball. The Liverpool centre also made a glancing header, and in a solo test with the goalkeeper, pushed the ball about a yard too far to the right. Cardiff responded in an electrifying manner, Thirlaway curled the ball at a fierce angle and at great pace, and if Jackson had not got in the way of a shot by Robinson, the visitors would have taken the lead. They went closer still when Thirlaway sent in another curling centre far to the left post. Smith began to play Cardiff on his own. He made a fine drifting shot, instantly from Morrison, that Farquharson stopped, and Smith, perseverance personified, headed twice to try and force a victory.

For the first time in history a referee took exception to a player carrying the ball to his position before throwing it to the man waiting anxiously to throw in. Wake was the half-back and it was felt that the referee drove attention to a fine point.

A cracking shot from Smith hit the goalkeeper, and the danger was cleared. While Keenor was lying knocked out, Munro, on his own, with the goalkeeper to beat, drove the ball to the right-hand side of the goal. This was the miss of the game, and with just a quarter-of-an-hour from the finish, it appeared to prove costly. Smith deserved a goal when he headed with perfect precision after Hopkin and McPherson had made the running. There were few thrills in what was essentially a grim battle.

Ten minutes from the end, Cardiff secured victory. Thirlaway received the ball from Len Davies, escaped the long throw of Lucas's left leg, and then hesitated before making his centre. He took an abnormally long time, but when he centred, the ball seemed to carry no power. It appeared that Riley grabbed at the ball which was passing out in case it struck the post and went in. Riley's action, however, had the opposite effect. The ball turned from his right hand just over the line, so that Len Davies had scored both goals. Jackson, the Liverpool skipper, called his forces together for one last, supreme effort. He turned on full steam in an effort to save the game, and at one point he was found under the Cardiff goalpost charging the goalkeeper.

Hodgson tried to reduce the deficit with a shot which went for a corner.
Five minutes to go. Then four; Len Davies was limping. Three minutes. Cardiff attacked; Munro chased the impossible. One minute to go; Hopkin and McDougall and Smith tried a combined effort, but to no avail - the Second Division side had won through to the next round. The Cup respected no team.

Leeds United beat Crystal Palace 8-1; the eventual Cup-winners, Arsenal, beat Chelsea 2-0 at home; while the runners-up, Huddersfield Town, drew 0-0 with Bury, before winning the replay 3-1.

Len Davies, who scored both the goals for Second Division Cardiff in their shock 2-1 win at Anfield

January 10, 1931

Liverpool (0) 0

Birmingham (0) 2
Curtis 64, Bradford 90

LIVERPOOL had some difficulty as to the composition of their side. Everything had been done to get McDougall fit, and although at one point there was every likelihood of his donning the red jersey, a trial on the morning of the match did not prove satisfactory, and the club took the wisest course and brought in Thompson at left-half. This boy played magnificently in the "fog match" a week ago.

Liverpool adopted a new measure in respect of the sale of tickets, for outside the grandstand a taxicab stood with placards on its sides denoting "tickets for sale", and quite a good business was done.

The ground was well sanded and looked in excellent condition. There was some doubt as to how it would play, since the softness of its surface belied the firmness beneath. The young mascot, Glazebrook, who was early on the ground, had visited Edmed in the nursing home on the morning of the game. Mr Jack Hayes, M.P., was present.

Liverpool opened proceedings through their right wing, but their progress was soon held up, and the Birmingham left-wing linked up for an inter-passing movement which brought trouble to the Liverpool defence. A terrific shot from Briggs hit the foot of a post, although Riley appeared to have the shot covered. Morrison received a stunning blow from the ball on his face, and he went down like a log, but a few minutes with the sponge worked a miracle, and he was soon able to continue. The Birmingham left-wing was in great form, and Bradford in particular was desperately keen to shoot at every opportunity. In turn, Bradshaw tried a long-range shot which travelled wide of the mark. When put in a great position, Horsman slammed the ball across the face of the goal. Half a minute later he crashed the ball into the side netting. Then there was a fracas. Hibbs dashed out of his goal to make a magnificent save, for, as he picked up the ball, two Liverpool players were very close at hand, and the slightest suggestion of a fumble would have proved fatal. Gunson, the Liverpool left-winger, came running in and apparently tried to kick the ball away from the goalkeeper, which seemed a rather dangerous manoeuvre. There was a rush of players and trouble looked ominous until better counsels prevailed. The Liverpool half-backs, while good in their defensive methods, did not get the ball to their forwards as often as they would have liked, and this was one of the reasons why the Liverpool attack was not nearly so successful as that of their opponents', who received every support from the men behind them.

When Hodgson found the ball coming back to him, he went for a chance shot but the ball went wide, and when Gunson came up he shot into the crowd. This spurred Liverpool on, and when Lucas dropped a free-kick close into the goalmouth there were prospects of a goal, but Hodgson was too well watched, and Scott was out-manoeuvred by Liddell, so that Hibbs was able to come out of his goal, pick up and clear. Thompson showed good form, and McPherson was in rare dribbling mood; but up to this point in the game, Scott had received very little, and the Birmingham defenders were fierce in the tackle. Neither side had stamped their authority on the game, but when Hodgson collected a forward pass from Morrison, there was hope for the home side. He tried a shot which was deflected to Alan Scott, but before the Liverpool leader could make any use of it, Liddell, Barkas, and Morrall were on to him immediately. Hibbs later took a back header by Hodgson in a safe way, but as he did so Scott charged him over the line, the goalkeeper throwing the ball round the post as he fell.

Birmingham played above themselves in the first period, and had they had a shooter they would have scored goals. After Crosbie cleverly edged a centre by Briggs over the Liverpool crossbar, the home side enjoyed a period of sustained pressure. Barkas, Liddell and Morrall kicked anywhere in an attempt to stem the Liverpool tide. Hibbs had to make a smart catch from a McPherson shot, and later on he had to be very sure in his punch when dealing with a Hopkin effort and at the same time steer clear of a Hodgson charge.

Having overcome Liverpool's bombardment, Birmingham took the lead after 64 minutes. It was a curious goal in that touches were made by the Liverpool man, Lucas. Horsman made a centre, Bradford nodded the ball on as Riley left his goal in an effort to prevent Bradford from making a connection. Curtis, however, who had closed in in anticipation, saw the ball come to him, and without hesitation he nodded it towards the empty goal. There was no pace behind the header, and there was doubt as to whether the ball was over the line when Lucas dashed in to effect a clearance, but in doing so took the ball into the net.

Liverpool were not done with, and Hibbs had to make yet another of his clever saves. Hibbs had a great deal to do with Liverpool's failure to score. Curtis, having scented the glorious effect of a goal, sought another, and his shot was deflected past the post by not more than a foot. Liverpool attacked with great effort, but Hibbs and his fellow defenders erected a successful barrier to all of the home side's efforts. Gunson should have scored from close range as the Liverpool pressure mounted. Another Birmingham attack nearly produced a second goal. A ball flung up the centre of the field was chased by Bradford. Jackson was in attendance, and Riley also advanced to meet the oncoming Birmingham centre. Bradford shot and the ball cannoned away towards the Liverpool goal and was slowly trickling on its way when Thompson came tearing across to kick it away a yard or two from the goal-line. Despite their incessant pressure, Liverpool could not find a way through. Just before the end, Bradford got through and scored what proved to be an offside goal. Right on time Birmingham scored a second goal through Bradford, who turned a corner taken by Curtis beyond Riley. The gate receipts of £2,655 were little consolation for such an early departure from the competition.

Birmingham went on to the final, where they were defeated 1-2 by West Bromwich Albion on 25 April before 92,406 spectators, Bradford scoring their goal. The Albion had two drawn games with Charlton Athletic before winning the second replay 3-1. The highest score of the round was Wolverhampton Wanderers' 9-1 thrashing of Wrexham. The Wolves led 3-1 at the interval. Jimmy Dunn broke his collar-bone for Everton in their 2-0 away win over Plymouth Argyle.

In the Scottish League, Celtic beat East Fife 9-1.

Liverpool: Riley; Jackson, Lucas; Morrison, Bradshaw, Thompson; Hopkin, Hodgson, A.Scott, McPherson, Gunson.

Birmingham: Hibbs; Liddell, Barkas; Cringan, Morrall, Leslie; Horsman, Crosbie, Bradford, Briggs, Curtis.

Referee: Mr A. Josephs (South Shields)

Attendance: 40,500

A spectator in the Kop was taken to hospital immediately after the match suffering with an injury to his head as a result of being pushed over on the Spion Kop. His name was understood to be J. Lyon, of Adlam Road.

THE TEN-MEN ATTACK

BY DICK PYM, THE GOALKEEPER

During this season we have been hearing every week about the "eight-man defence". I want to say something about the "ten-man attack".

The eight-man defence has the merit of being a tactful formation that you can bring to perfection and work persistently until somebody finds the way to counter it. The ten-man attack is a move brought into action to save a losing side, or force a win from a position of stalemate.

After nearly ten years with Bolton Wanderers, I can say that this is a move that the goalkeeper must always guard against.

Football enthusiasts will all have seen matches won in the last few minutes - just as people are getting up to go home.

The last few minutes, in fact, are a testing time.

If a team have the energy left they can bring the ten-man attack to bear at this critical moment. Defence is flung to the winds. The whole team except the goalkeeper concentrate for a few frenzied minutes in endeavouring to force the ball through.

You can imagine the effect of such an attack on a jaded defence - or a "nervy" goalkeeper.

The perfect situation for a ten-man attack is when you are a goal down.

The adversaries, after a long tussle, have won the advantage of a goal. If it is a vital match, that may seem to them a treasure almost too good to believe. Their one fear will be that their lead will be snatched away in the last minute of the game.

Victories have so often been dashed away in this manner, that footballers are wary about deciding that they have won until the final whistle. Stamina tells.

I am convinced that the team that can fling the last ounce of energy into a ten-man attack in the last minutes of the game will often turn the scale.

That, in fact, is the reason why surprises so often occur in vital matches.

IN THE MUD

You probably have a clever team working hard at their ball control, perhaps in heavy mud. They have had most of the game, and earned a goal; but their efforts begin to tell towards the end. Much as they may not wish to do so, they cannot help slowing down a bit.

Then, if the less skilful team are better trained, they may come on with a rush.

January 9, 1932

Everton (1) 1
Dean 1

Liverpool (1) 2
Gunson 38,   Hodgson 75

EVERY precaution had been taken by the Goodison Park management to ensure that there was no repetition of the New Year's Day occurrence when thousands of people were left outside. It appeared that some people in the shilling and one-and-sixpence portion of the ground fought shy of the difficulties of seeing the game. Instead of the estimated 65,000 spectators being present, there was room for thousands more in the cheaper portions. Superintendent Hughes declared at one o'clock that there were 25,000 people in the ground. Mr McIntosh - the Everton secretary - said that the orderliness and the early arrival of the crowd had been such that by two o'clock there was no-one entering the ground. It was a fine, cold, winter's day, and the ground had much improved since its day of deluge in the middle of the week. The game aroused more talk than any other previous encounter between these two adversaries. There were two ambulance cases, and one of these took real objection to leaving the ground, insisting that he had not waited for a couple of hours to be taken off the ground at the last minute. In addition to the policeman on the terrace patrolling a tin shed by the result board, there was a remembrance of Wembley and the grey mare, except that in this case at Goodison Park, it was one of the famous Liverpool police horses, chestnut-coloured, which kept watch over the flock that might have fought their way between the goal-decker and the paddock. Near to this mounted policeman was a giant horse-shoe, with blue ribbon attached, hanging from the stand. Colour was also lent to the proceedings by the appearance of a red and a blue follower standing shoulder to shoulder, rattle-to-rattle, on one of the crush barriers. Toy balloons floated across the ground, but for the first time in history a mascot was not allowed on the ground.

The sporting Lord Mayor of Liverpool - Alderman James Conrad Cross - and his good lady, together with the Mayor and Mayoress of Bootle - Mr and Mrs Hankey - had a royal welcome. The music of the band was practically drowned by the hum of conversation. Cresswell acted as steward in the Press stand. There were no sensations about the teams, although there had been rumours about Bradshaw not playing. On the morning of the game, Liverpool FC announced that not only Bradshaw but Wright would play, so that the Liverpool side was in perfect trim. Everton had the chance to play Bocking or Lowe at left-back, so soon as Cresswell had found both ankles unfit. They elected to bank on age and experience and chose Bocking instead of the more youthful Lowe, formerly of Southport. Dean's return was Everton's cause for joy, and the only regret in this third-round tie between the two teams drawn out last of all the clubs just before Christmas Day, was that Cresswell could not play. The teams ran onto the pitch two by two, and in half a minute

Bradshaw and Dean tossed up and welcomed each other. Dean won the toss and, having sized up the elements at midday, elected to kick towards the Aintree goal.

Immediately the game opened it was plain to see the nervous tension in some quarters. Jock Thompson hesitated whether he should swing round with the ball at his foot or pass back, and his slight delay caused thousands of hearts to beat abnormally fast. The ball was lobbed high in the air by Sagar, and Morrison and Bradshaw between them could have cleared. Each was in the other's way, and the crowd gasped as to what the effect might be. Bradshaw, like Thompson, delayed his killing of the ball, with the result that it went out to Dean. Fear entered the hearts of the Liverpool defence. A blunder, or even half-blunder, on the part of two men had opened up a way for the crack scorer of the game. Dean, in a flash, offered a body swerve to the defenders suggestive that he was going one way whereas he was going the other. He sprinted forward with a deadly eye for goal, and everyone could see a chance of a goal. The only question was one of balance and control, and Dean with his left, seemed to shoot to the wrong end of the goal, according to all theories, but it actually paid off because Scott went down late, and the ball escaped the Irishman's right hand and entered the net after slightly touching the left upright. Dean leapt into the air, and the new red jerseys of the Liverpool side seemed to wear a wan appearance.

A free-kick against Clark for a trip on David Wright was ominous until McRorie kicked round the ball and sent it wide. A free-kick against Hodgson, which led Johnson to double in his midriff, led to a surprise and debate. The free-kick led the ball into the goalmouth, where Scott punched away at the moment Dean elected to time his charge on the Irishman, who fell backwards and near the post. The ball had been cleared.

Two tackles by Bradshaw on Dean were good enough to prevent the possibility of goals. In addition, Bradshaw found Jackson raced by "Springer" Critchley, and the captain went to the Parson's aid and stopped the sprint down the right wing.

Hodgson's towering figure enabled him to get behind two players and Liverpool became busy down the left, where Gunson was deadly and enthusiastic. He had the Cup spirit, and when Hodgson, McRorie, and Barton introduced a fine sense of open combination, Barton made his first appearance of note with a shot that skimmed the crossbar. Liverpool began to attack with some resolve, and McRorie's shot forced Sagar to fall to the ground to make a magnificent full-length save which was the prelude to some excellent goalkeeping. Scott prevented Dean from scoring a second goal with a perfectly-timed runout, even though Dean drew his right sole

William Ralph 'Dixie' Dean, who scored a first minute goal against Liverpool

somersault as he punched the ball away. Then McRorie sent the ball over to the left of an empty goal. The ball seemed to hang in the air for an appreciable length of time, and nearly 60,000 eager spectators looked on, wondering whether Gunson could stretch his neck to a ball that was always travelling away from him. Although he had the energy and the enterprise to go after the half-chance, he failed to connect. After Stein had made a shot that hung for some time, Bradshaw failed to trap the ball and Dean shot. Scott saved. Dean followed with a header from a Williams pass, and Scott, with his keen eyes, never relaxed his look at the ball, and recaptured the sphere. Clark made a header of some strength, and Dean made an astonishing left-foot hook intensely earnest and strong, but the ball sped two yards too far to the left. Dean went through practically on his own and was cleverly baulked by Steel, the ball bouncing back to Dean, who was rather wild in his shot.

Bocking swept McRorie's feet from under him. It was an ordinary free-kick with no suggestion of a goal until Jock Thomson failed to get the ball away, and it fell to Gunson, who shot from the left flank out of Sagar's reach, and brought a superb equaliser for the Reds after 38 minutes.

Hodgson went on a rare solo run in which Gee, with arms akimbo, missed his mark, but did not create a foul. The last breath of a pulsating first period was a gem. Gunson trapped and pushed the ball along every four yards in fine style, and when everyone expected him to make a centre he stabbed the ball backwards to Wright, who knew what to expect. If Wright had shot instantly, he would have given Liverpool the lead. Instead, he moved the ball on a yard or two, and Gee, without further ceremony, went into the tackle and Wright went down. Three red jerseys consulted with Referee Harper with the view to obtaining a penalty, but the referee declined. The finger declared "Goal-kick", and it was taken.

At the half-way period at Highbury, the Arsenal were already 8-0 up on luckless Darwen, who eventually succumbed 11-1. Leicester City were 3-0 up on Crook Town, who eventually lost 7-0.

The teams re-appeared rather quickly, suggestive of their desire to get on with the game. Johnson began with his patented opening pass. Critchley got a throw-in from it. Dean almost scored in the first minute of the second half, as he had done so in the first period. Later on Clark tried a hook shot which went over the bar. Hodgson gained possession through a piece of fortune and went on a run, his progress only being impeded by Williams, and Sagar completing the defence of the Everton goal. David Wright went on a sinuous dribble typical of the man and a tribute to his power of control and command.

The wind got stronger and more irregular as the game progressed, and the pace of the game faltered to a degree. Dean gained possession from a Johnson pass and elected to go on a dribble, but Jackson cleared the danger resolutely. Bradshaw indulged in some pretty football reminiscent of a friendly match, and eventually Stein broke loose and his centre was headed away by Jackson, who jumped high in the air to save a dangerous situation. Jackson again tackled with a deadliness that was all-compelling. No one quite equalled David Wright in his skill and collating ideas, bringing his team-mates into the game. The game was played from end to end and became more of a compelling drama as each minute

across his left heel with the thought of catching the ball in the most novel way of all. Scott earned a pat on the back from his skipper, Bradshaw, for a further fine save, and then Sagar went down to grip with unerring accuracy a truly ferocious ball shot in by Gunson, who had an attempt at anything and everything. There had been a great deal of incident in the opening twenty minutes.

Liverpool almost equalised when Sagar left his goal to try and catch a centre from the right wing, but Ben Williams, the Swansea boxer and footballer, raised his big thigh and kicked the ball away. Liverpool had had six shots to Everton's one. They had been on the attack more than their rivals, but they did not have anything to show for all their efforts.

After McDougall had been hurt, the game continued just as fast and full of commitment as before. Critchley found it easy to exploit his pace, and he got across centres which might well have been headed into goal by Dean, but Bradshaw and Steel between them kept the ball from Dean. Johnson was noticeable for some hardworking, close dribbles, in which he always found the man who was unmarked. It was anybody's game at this stage. Bocking showed his forte by full-length drives of unusual length. McRorie put across a fine centre which caused Sagar, bothered by his full-back, to turn a ticked by. Gee, Thomson, and the Everton forwards played some delightful football with the ball on the ground - and the possibilities endless - but Scott stood his ground with his hands on his hips with complete calm assurance and the knowledge that a shot would not arrive.

The biggest difference between the sides was that Liverpool were extremely dangerous in front of goal, whilst Everton were not quick up front. Clark produced a thirty-five yard drive which spun outside the target. Free-kicks became more frequent, and there was a gale of a wind at this point, together with a drop of rain which made the conditions awkward. Everton should have scored when, from a foul against McDougall, Dean headed the ball nicely for Stein that a shot, not a square pass, should have taken place.

Jackson earned the respect of his colleagues by his superb marshalling of the irrepressible Dean. Onlookers began to wonder what would happen in the event of a draw because Jackson was due to go back to Cambridge on the following Monday and would therefore be unable to play. With 75 minutes gone, thoughts of a replay receded into the background. Gunson and Wright were the key men in the goal. Hodgson had two men in attendance on him at the moment that he stung the Cup record.

Five minutes of intense Everton pressure followed, which was a joy to behold to the passionate crowd. The saving grace of this impressive spell was Scott's fourfold save, most noticeably an anticipation of a header by Dean which was full of goal prospects. Scott advanced a couple of yards out of his goal, realising what the home centre would do, and a catlike catch prevented an equaliser. The noise of the crowd was incessant, and Everton's endeavour equalled it.

With two minutes left, Everton were awarded a free-kick against Steel. Scott could not see through the crowd of players as Stein struck the ball. The sphere hit Scott's body. In the final minute, Stein put the corner kick outside. In the dying seconds Sagar saved from three attackers. Liverpool had achieved a famous victory.

Everton: Sagar; Williams, Bocking; Clark, Gee, Thomson; Critchley, White, Dean, Johnson, Stein.

Liverpool: Scott; Steel, Jackson; Morrison, Bradshaw, McDougall; McRorie, Hodgson, Barton, Wright, Gunson.

Referee: Mr F.P. Harper (Stourbridge)

Attendance: 57,090

Receipts: £5,047 3s 8d

Jimmy McDougall, *who was injured in the game against Everton, but managed to play on*

Liverpool took 49 throws-in against Everton's 50; 1 corner against 4; 13 free-kicks against 16; 16 shots on goal against 21; and 26 goal-kicks against 15. But whatever the statistics showed, it was Liverpool who won through to the next round.

January 23, 1932

Chesterfield (0) 2
Abel, Ruddy 80

Liverpool (3) 4
Barton (4)

IN 1927 the Football Association increased the Geographical Divisions from 24 to 26, and the Fifth and Sixth Qualifying Rounds became rounds one and two in the competition proper, with the number of exempted clubs rising from 24 in the Fifth Qualifying Round to 43 (mainly Third Division clubs) in the First Round proper, and 47 clubs being exempted until the Third Round of the competition (mainly First and Second Division clubs.) With this re-organisation, the fairy-tale history of the cup became further strengthened as more and more clubs from the lower divisions and beyond fought their way through to the competition proper. The romance continued.

The Chesterfield ground had a reputation for being as crooked as the spire, but £1,500 had been spent on it and Liverpool were delighted when they saw the state of the ground and its billiard-like levelness. There were thousands of spectators from Liverpool and they got some idea of the comforts of Anfield and the discomfort of Third Division spectators, Chesterfield having been newly-promoted at the end of the previous season with a scoring record of 102 goals.

The Second Division club looked upon this as their gala day. The weather was fine, the locals turned out in full force to create a record attendance, the previous having been 21,000 against Nottingham Forest a fortnight ago, a game which the home side won by five goals to two. There was one small stand and a slight covering along the length of the pitch.

Liverpool stayed in a Sheffield hotel overnight, where the proprietor, Mr Dixon, formerly the chairman of Dundee United, met Archie McPherson, a fellow Scot. The hotel proprietor and the player found to their amazement that they had been next-door neighbours and worked in the same office in years gone by. With the Liverpool club were directors W.H. Cartwright, W.H. Webb, S.R. Williams, together with the manager, Mr George Patterson, and his assistant, Mr Rouse.

The only doubt in the minds of the Liverpool selectors was the question of inside-left. Wright had been hobbling about since the Villa *débâcle* - where Liverpool lost 1-6 on January 16, Barton scoring Liverpool's only goal after 62 minutes - and trainer Charles Wilson worked on him with rare vigour and a happy result. On the other hand, the operation for appendicitis on Wass unfortunately left Chesterfield wondering what to do about the full-back position, and eventually Hamilton and Wright became the pair, Wright being on the left flank. The Liverpool directors took the opportunity on the morning of the match of visiting Johnny Cuthbert at his training home, not to wish him success, of course, in his meeting with Dom Volante, but rather to pay graceful tribute to a good sport who was remembered for his Stadium and Anfield appearances.

Half-an-hour before the start Mr Teddy Davidson, the former international goalkeeper, and present manager of Chesterfield, assured the Press that the ground record had been broken and that there were 25,000 people present. James Jackson travelled from Cambridge last night, arriving an hour after the team from Liverpool had landed, and he was due to return to Cambridge immediately after the match. He was the only man marked absent from the pantomime overnight, so that the Liverpool side was identical to that which beat Everton.

A quiet, orderly crowd, more concerned with the blare of trumpets than the rattle of partisans, revelled in the elements, the wind being very slight, and the air just right for football. The sun was such that it would not trouble the players. Only two portions of the ground were sanded. The sporting Lord Mayor of Liverpool, Alderman J.E. Cross, was present to lend his civic authority to the Liverpool players.

The packing of the ground was the greatest difficulty on the day. At certain points behind the goal, it was possible to walk about, but outside the ground there was talk of the breaking down of gates. Judged from the Press Box, everybody inside, whether seated on the advertisement hoardings or on the forked staves that supported the stand, would have a perfect view of the game. There were one or two fainting cases, but nothing of real importance. A concrete wall around the ground saved the situation, but, as usual, immediately one young man decided to scale the wall and sit around the touchline thousands followed suit and became an army of squatters.

The gate attendance and receipts were both a record for the Chesterfield club.

Chesterfield: Ashmore; Hamilton, Wright; McIntyre, Froggat, Halliwell; Austin, Pynegar, Abel, Ruddy, Lee.

Liverpool: Scott; Steel, Jackson; Morrison, Bradshaw, McDougall; McRorie, Hodgson, Barton, Wright, Gunson.

Referee: Mr H.E. Gray (London)

Attendance: 28,393

Receipts: £1,757 17s

The Lady Mayoress of Liverpool sported three carnations showing the rosy red of Liverpool, and a spectator in the paddock called for three hearty cheers for the Lord Mayor of Liverpool and the Mayor of Chesterfield, who sat side by side.

Chesterfield, in their blue and white stripes, looked more like Sheffield Wednesday, the stripes had the effect of making them look bigger and taller than they really were. Liverpool were given a splendid reception, and three mascots, one young Bracegirdle, the five-year-old boy, who, by the side of the 6ft 4in Bradshaw, was but a dwarf. Bradshaw, having won the toss, patted some of his players on the back.

The game got off to a flying start until the boot of Morrison hooked the ball to safety. McDougall responded with a close dribble and Wright failed to capitalise upon the move through slipping over. Barton twice showed intricate footwork, but Wright, the full-back, covered for the home side. There was great excitement when Hodgson broke through to shoot outside from an offside position. From the free-kick, Wright slewed the ball badly and Barton had only Hamilton to beat and the goalkeeper. He successfully engineered the ball slightly to the left flank and a goal was begging, but Barton shot straight into the hands of Ashmore.

Barton took his revenge in a very certain manner. As he went on, following good work by Hodgson and McDougall, and some fine punting by Jackson and Steel, Barton found himself nicely placed for a run in. It had to be a quick body swerve and a solo effort. A back crossed his path, and he stumbled, not sufficiently to suggest a penalty kick, however. Barton continued in his solo effort, and, still stumbling, he poked the ball into the extreme left-hand corner beyond Ashmore's right hand. Barton fell full length on his face as the ball entered the net. It appeared that the funeral vans Liverpool had encountered on the road to Chesterfield were not to be a bad omen.

Austin and Lee had been fêted for their skill before the game, but these extreme wingers were out of gear for a long time in the match until Austin made one of his sprints as if flying from Manchester, and McDougall, who had been outstanding, produced a sliding tackle of great power and precision. Pynegar and the rousing Abel rolled up their sleeves in an effort to drag Chesterfield back into the game, but Bradshaw's height and speed counted against them. It was Bradshaw who headed away a free-kick awarded when the referee indicated a foul against McDougall for a tackle on Austin. James Jackson was in superb form.

It was clear that one goal would not be enough to beat this side, Austin being their main anchor and Pynegar offering a powerful shot which missed the goal. Barton hooked a ball after a free-kick from Morrison which set Gunson in full flight, and the Wrexham man, who scored against Everton, ran far forward and, having closed in, sent in such a powerful shot that the ball crossed along the goal-line and carried on towards the far corner flag.

With 21 minutes gone, Barton scored a second goal. Barton drew a Chesterfield defender and finally passed the ball to Gunson, whose centre caused the Chesterfield backs to get in each other's way. McRorie looked likely to score as he tried to force the ball over the line, but it was cleared by the Chesterfield backs, but only to Barton, who scored with consummate ease. Chesterfield rallied, but Scott had only to touch the ball on two occasions, and on both there was no real difficulty or danger in the movement.

Twenty-year-old Barton, in only his second year in the First Division side, completed his hat-trick when McDougall, who had played so well, slung the ball up the field a considerable distance, and Barton at once showed great marksmanship with a powerful shot. Ashmore advanced fully twelve yards out of his goalmouth, apparently too far, and certainly without confidence of being able to stem young Barton, whose left-foot drive found the target and was the prelude to Barton having his hand wrung as token of his fine individual effort. The daring young man from Blackpool was not recognised at Liverpool as a first-class outside-right. Then, at Sheffield in particular, and then at Birmingham, he showed great promise as a centre-forward, not because of his goalscoring, but because of his able command of the ball and almost old-fashioned work when surrounded by defenders. He had ability to work the ball when in close confines, and the only flaw in his makeup was the possibility of his being seriously injured. In less than half-an-hour, Liverpool had secured a three-goal margin.

The visitors were infinitely superior, and Hodgson, who had replaced Done as the taker of free-kicks, struck a dead ball so hard that had the whiting of the concrete wall not come away with the ball, everyone in the ground would have believed that a goal had been scored. Too late, Chesterfield decided to employ the offside trap, which was extremely defensive. Froggatt and Pynegar tried to stem the tide, but Liverpool played in supreme fashion. After Scott had made his first real save of the match, Austin shot to the foot of the post, Abel stood so close in that he could not help but score just as easily as Barton had done for his second goal. Chesterfield jumped for joy, and then rose in their anger. The referee disallowed the goal for offside. The home side argued that the ball had come into play from the foot of a post, but the question of the post did not enter into the argument at all. The question was "Where was Abel when the ball was last played?" and the referee adjudged that Abel was offside. Chesterfield protested long and hard, but the decision remained. The home side had lost their way through the inside-forwards and their half-backs being unable to hold Liverpool, and at the same time provide passes for their own attacking men. Towards the interval came the finest solo run of the match when Austin, recapturing his Manchester flair, made a fine dodging run which ended with a brilliant shot slightly over the bar. As the teams left the field, the referee was subjected to some loud boos.

Barton had made his goals through his ability to be quick in his stride and quick thinking and acting. Barton had proved the judgment of the former Liverpool players, Jack Cox, who with Peter Quinn, had nursed this butcher boy in the cause of Liverpool FC.

Chesterfield turned from a striving team into an inspired side when they broke their goalscoring duck. Pynegar began the move, placing the ball out to Lee, who had Steel to beat. The winger beat his man, and could have shot or centred. He elected to centre the ball and slipped as he delivered a cross. Abel saw his chance and scored. The battle was re-opened. Wright, the home full-back, had improved and the Second Division side improved also. For a while, Liverpool lost touch, but they recovered some of their confidence when

Hodgson made a delightful dribble and a pass out to McRorie, whose centre was nearly converted by Gunson, following which Wright ambled nonchalantly through the Chesterfield defence before falling to the ground in the hope of a penalty. Chesterfield began to rattle the visitors, and Jackson won a bout with Austin that ended with the referee wagging a finger of scorn at the home player. Again Jackson crossed the path of Austin, but the crowd craned their necks to see the best goalkeeper in the world in action. A free-kick near the corner flag led to Abel heading in swiftly and from close range. Scott was on the ball like a cat. Scott also fielded the ball from the same Neston player when he hooked a shot over his head. Steel was not so secure as usual, making rash kicks at the ball. Chesterfield gained three corners in three minutes, which were all taken with deadly accuracy, though nothing tangible came from them.

The home side continued to attack almost at will as Liverpool's Cup dream began to fade. Jackson looked the fittest man on the field as the other Liverpool players appeared as though they would be happy to hear the final whistle. Bradshaw continued to do some fine work for the visitors.

When the Chesterfield defence slipped up, Barton looked likely to add to his tally of goals, but Ashmore, after going the wrong way to the ball, recovered his balance and stuck out his right hand to make a fine save.

A first-time pass by Morrison went beyond the centre circle and Barton snapped up the opportunity, racing through like a greyhound and shouldering off two players as he scampered away with the ball at his toe. He could have taken the goal in a dozen different ways. He chose to go right up to the goal and slide the ball out of the reach of Ashmore. It was a brilliant goal, and stung Chesterfield at a time when they were dominating the match.

Ruddy scored for Chesterfield after 80 minutes with a close-range shot which Steel could not quite catch before it passed over the line, the full-back running in to save. It was a gallant gesture, which ultimately proved to be futile.

Sheffield Wednesday beat Bournemouth 7-0, while finalists-elect Arsenal beat Plymouth Argyle 4-2. Newcastle United drew 1-1 with Southport, from the Third Division North. In the replay, the 1-1 scoreline was repeated. In the second replay, the half-time score was 0-0. Forty-five minutes later, the score was 9-0 in Newcastle's favour.

Liverpool's next opponents, Grimsby Town, beat Birmingham 2-1 at home.

***Harold Barton**, the first Liverpool player to score four goals in an FA Cup tie*

February 13, 1932

Liverpool (0) 1

Gunson 60

Grimsby Town (0) 0

THE crowd was very quiet until the Edge Hill band struck up "*For he's a jolly good fellow*" when the Lord Mayor of Liverpool appeared. The only streak of red and enthusiasm prior to the game was young Glazebrook, 2ft 3in tall, with a ball bigger than his head but nothing quite so big as his heart. He was the official mascot of the team, and he ran his heart out before the start of the game. Grimsby were in the throes of relegation, yet had beaten Liverpool 5-1 in the week before this game.

Both teams were at full-strength. Liverpool had feared trouble to Morrison, but the X-ray was positive. The air was a little nippy, but there was no snow and ice, as in other parts of the country. The ground was nicely filled, but there was room for more in the paddock. Liverpool lost the toss and kicked off towards the Aintree end.

Grimsby started in a manner which belied their League position until Wilson's error allowed McPherson - the only one of the twenty-two players who had his sleeves rolled up - got in some strong work. Buck was a stern challenger, and he forced play on the left, where Cooper's cross was met by Fielding, who turned it on to Bestall. A little fellow like Bestall was not easily reached by a tall half-back, and when the diminutive man from Grimsby got a free-kick from a leap by McDougall, there was trouble for Liverpool. The visitors should have scored with ease when Coleman and Bestall were two yards from goal. A swinging shot from the Grimsby centre followed by a much faster shot which went just over the bar, showed Grimsby's determination and they should have scored, such was the power of their play.

Wright turned the ball towards Gunson whose shot hit the side netting with Hodgson and Barton appealing for the ball. Hodgson tried a low shot which missed the mark. With ten minutes gone, Wilson hurt his thigh and the game was halted. Steel and Jackson had been given a torrid time as the visitors had played above themselves. Bestall, whose right shoulder hurt him, brought the ball down with a beautiful hook of the toe, no mean performance on the part of a man who was 5ft in height, and the little man's pass to the left wing led to perfect combination amongst the Grimsby forwards, ending with Coleman shooting hard, and all too neat to be comfortable for Elisha Scott. Hall, the red-haired half-back, conceded a corner which might easily have been an own goal after a back-heel by Wright to Barton caught out the defence. Wright was clever enough to realise that he must be offside, and ran out of the playing area. The game was at its fiercest as the ambulance men carried out a working man who had apparently been affected by the excitement of the day. The game had been very exciting up to this point. Bradshaw began

to play with his usual calmness and influence, while Bestall buzzed around him like a busy bee. Nobody worked harder than Priestley, the captain of Grimsby. James Jackson at last found his best form, in spite of a limp of the right foot, and he covered Fielding when the former Stockport player suggested goalscoring possibilities. Bradshaw then prevented Coleman from scoring a certain goal with a tackle of power and precision, and he dribbled his way out of trouble under the shadow of the Kop. Moments later McDougall dribbled out before passing to Hodgson. Goalkeeper Read ran out of his goal, and the ball fell to Barton, whose first-time shot sailed high over the bar. Marshall and Coleman attempted to lower Liverpool's colours, but the ball went to Coleman at his back. Bestall bundled all his tricks together like a music-hall artiste, and was rarely caught out, with the result that Grimsby were inspired by his tricks and attacks. Scott was tested to the full. Only a Scott would have known what to expect and where to stand when Fielding, who has good height to help him, tried to head into the right-hand corner of the goal. Scott stood in that position, the identical position, and saved a certain goal. Scott was not so convincing a moment later when he gathered the ball at the other end of the goal and fumbled his save. From this save Wright not only delivered a hefty charge, but chased a ball which played a trick in striking the corner flag and coming back into play.

Grimsby had been not only clever, but also much sharper on the ball than the Anfielders, and little opportunity had fallen the way of Gunson or Barton. The second stoppage of the game came when Wright suffered an accidental knock from a Grimsby full-back. Wright was dazed and had to leave the field on the arm of trainer Charles Wilson. Gunson was perhaps the most successful of the Liverpool forwards because he could always anticipate the robust tackle of Hall, and could easily escape the sliding foot.

The crowd looked upon Bestall as a provider, not the possessor of a cannon-ball shot, but he indulged in the liberty of a beautiful shot which Scott saved with a magnificent leap to a ball that was so fast that it threatened to spin out of his grip. If Grimsby had been stronger at outside-right they would have created even more trouble for a bewildered Liverpool team. Gunson went on a run half the length of the field with Fielding in close attendance, yet the Grimsby man was unable to make a challenge, and it needed one sweeping decisive tackle by Wilson to put an end to Gunson's solo run.

Coleman began the second half with a sharp dribble before being crowded out and then Gunson tried to shoulder-charge the goalkeeper and the ball into the net, but Read was too big and strong. Then there was a stoppage because Wilson and

Hodgson had collided, Hodgson going off the field with a bump on his forehead, which led the trainer to call for assistance from the doctor. Hodgson had cut his forehead, but it did not look likely that he would be off the field for too long. Grimsby continued to dominate the game, but Bradshaw relieved the pressure with a strong solo run and a shot which caused Read to dive to the ground to make a save of urgent need. There was a further stoppage when Morrison accidentally "stabbed" Cooper on the thigh, and Hodgson returned at this point, his head well bandaged.

Liverpool's greatest effort came from a combined move on the part of McPherson, who set Hodgson and Gunson going, and the centre was shot outside. The Grimsby captain rolled his arms and hands in the manner of a racing tic-tac artist, indicating that he wanted his men to come to his aid. It was, indeed, necessary because in one minute Liverpool had gone from a mood of lethargy to one of fieriness and fury, and on the hour Gunson scored.

David Wright made the goal. He was out of position through finding himself cramped for room in the centre berth, and he drifted towards the right before finally delivering a centre which was just right for the incoming Gunson, whose header smashed into the net, and he along with it.

The goal signalled a period of intense work for the ambulance men because the crowd on the Kop fell headlong down the steps and were crushed. For fifty minutes Liverpool had been weak and indecisive; now they were a transformed side.

Coleman, eight yards from goal, sent in a splendid drive which Scott, leaping high, managed to save. Bestall was not so prominent at this stage of the game, but he took up the inside-left position and narrowly misjudged a ball that the team had given up. Liverpool regained the initiative, and Gunson shot fiercely, only for Read to effect a brilliant save. James Jackson began to inspire with his well-judged tackles and enthusiasm for work at a time when Grimsby crowded all their best work into a period of intense dominance. From a corner kick, Priestley shot high over the bar as Grimsby strove for an equaliser.

The players left the field shaking hands with each other, and Grimsby wishing Liverpool the best of luck. Arsenal beat Portsmouth 2-0 away, while Newcastle beat Leicester City 3-1 at home.

In Scotland there was crowd violence at Fir Park as the home side, Motherwell, beat Celtic 2-0. The ground held about 30,000 and so great was the crush that half-an-hour before the match started the crowd invaded the field. Disorder was made worse when a free fight occurred at one end of the ground. Scores of people ran across the field, and the disturbance broke out afresh. Policemen used their batons, but the trouble broke out again when rival factions came to grips. Belts and other weapons were used, and the police were forced to make another baton attack. Numerous arrests were made, and ambulances were busily occupied removing the injured. Women were among the casualties. The two teams contested the 1931 Scottish Cup final, Celtic winning 4-2 in a replay.

In Belfast, England beat Ireland 11-8 in the Rugby Union match, having led 6-3 at the interval.

Liverpool: Scott; Steel, Jackson; Morrison, Bradshaw, McDougall; Barton, Hodgson, Wright, McPherson, Gunson.

Grimsby Town: Read; Wilson, Jacobson; Hall, Priestley, Buck; Fielding, Bestall, Coleman, Cooper, Marshall.

Referee: Mr T. Thompson (Leamington-on-Tyne)

Attendance: 49,479

Receipts: £3,650

Gordon Gunson, whose header after 60 minutes smashed into the net to secure victory over Grimsby Town

February 27, 1932

Liverpool (0) 0

Chelsea (1) 2
Gallacher 44, Pearson 90

ON a day of perfect weather, the crowd were in distress at certain points of the Spion Kop, where ominous-looking rushes in waves of humanity carried the people into a crush barrier and hurt them. The St. John ambulance people came to the forefront.

As Richard Arlen and Fay Wray starred at The Futurist in "*The Conquering Horde*", Chelsea came to Anfield and conquered their hosts in a thrilling match full of Cup-tie excitement and drama.

Liverpool entertained fears overnight that Gunson would not be able to play owing to a cold. Chelsea had a fear about Mills, the man who made such a brilliant finish to the replayed tie against Sheffield Wednesday at Stamford Bridge, which the Londoners won 2-0. Mills suffered from boils as well as an injury, but he was declared fit and both teams were at full strength. It was not often that a player made his début at home for a new club in so late a stage as the Sixth Round of the Cup, yet this experience befell Leslie Bruton, the Blackburn forward, who played so well in the previous week against West Ham, when he made his first team début in Liverpool colours. Last week Liverpool played in white; there was no clash in this Cup-tie, Liverpool in their customary red and Chelsea in their usual blue and white. The Edge Hill Band kept the crowd in good humour, and there was a man on the touchline acting the part of a "rooter", which was an American feature introduced for forcing the spectators to join together to create a unanimous noise. He operated just about as long as a Hyde Park orator, and once a shower of coppers fell upon him there was an additional copper in blue, and this meant the end for the orator. The Lord Mayor was greeted with musical honours, and accepted a red emblem from a spectator.

Young Dave Glazebrook was present to give his mascotry a further chance, and among the number of telegrams to the Liverpool captain, Tom Bradshaw, wishing him success, was one to Director Ronnie Williams from Sir Hugo Rutherford, M.P., which said, "*I regret I cannot be with you this afternoon owing to serious illness. Please convey to all members of the Liverpool team my heartfelt wishes for a thumping victory over Chelsea.*"

The Chelsea goalkeeper wore white knickers and a white jersey, whereas Elisha Scott wore his country's colours, green. There was very little wind, the middle of the field was bare, but the wingers and the wing half-backs had everything in their favour. This was the first game missed by James Jackson, who was reported to be fit, but Lucas was seen in action at West Ham and the directors chose the little man. Bradshaw and Jackson tossed for the honour, which, after a

first coin had got stuck in the mud, went to Liverpool, who started with the advantage of the sun on their backs. The Anfielders kicked towards the Stanley Park goal, Chelsea kicking off, and Mills at once started to go through on his own with his own particular type of dribble, namely a swerve and a long stride, but he was crowded out by Bradshaw and the referee then gave a free-kick, which amounted to nothing. Alec Jackson failed to time a fast flowing ball that went far too quickly.

The referee gave another free-kick which surprised both players and spectators, after which Bradshaw and McDougall displayed their excellence. Chelsea's front line attacked by means of good footwork, and O'Dowd not only got his pass away on the ground, but he also leapt out of the way of a strong tackle. Miller, in spite of his lack of inches, was an engaging personality, although his lightness proved his undoing to the staunchness of Steel's two-footed tackles.

Bruton made his first pass on this ground for his new club with precision, Barton getting the ball and centring for Bruton to head over. Gunson tried an angular shot which passed wide of the mark. Chelsea's skipper, Jackson, took throws-in very quickly in order to set up surprise attacks, and Mills shot towards Scott's right hand, but the ball went wide. Chelsea were clever in the way they made neat dribbles, and unmistakably the reappearance of Hughie Gallacher must have inspired Jackson, who played infinitely better than he had done against Sheffield Wednesday at Stamford Bridge. A fine volley by Steel went over, and Hodgson slipped the ball to Barton, who also shot over. A Barton centre was so dangerous that Russell was content to ankle the ball outside for a corner. From this corner came the sparkling eyes of Gallacher glued on the ball, but the enormous frame of Bradshaw denied the Chelsea forward, despite the wee man's juggling.

Chelsea had the easiest chance of scoring when Lucas was beaten and Gallacher, slightly to the right of the goal, kicked round the ball rather than upon its face, so that Scott was able to pick up. Scott had, in fact, escaped with some fortune after Jackson had centred from the corner flag with perfection. Scott was nearly charged through the goal by Mills, and the Irishman took umbrage at his treatment and raced out in a threatening attitude towards Mills. Then Alec Jackson found the sharp tackle of McDougall troublesome, because Jackson did not work with sufficient speed to gather the ball to his liking. However, a kind of peace was restored to the game when David Wright and Alec Jackson bumped together strenuously and found time to smile over their collision.

The thrill of the first half occurred when Hughie Gallacher ran out to a point near the left corner-flag and, racing Scott for speed, caught the Irishman in the throes of a grave error.

Scott had run out and had not connected with the ball. As he lashed out his foot, it failed to connect, and Gallacher centred to an empty goal. The centre was rather strong, and though Jackson leapt high into the air, he fell flat on his back and failed to convert the opportunity.

Liverpool were not comfortable although when a free-kick was taken by Gunson, Hodgson made a first-time shot of rare power which narrowly missed the target. Barber, the Chelsea back, played delightfully steady football and the crowd admired the way he accepted an accident when Gunson, with his foot up to the tall man's shoulder, ripped Barber's jersey.

There was a stoppage as the interval approached when Miller ran in riotously, damaging his heel rather badly. The Liverpool forwards stood for long periods watching the progress of the game and yearning for a chance. After Gallacher had cleverly tried to anticipate Scott shielding a ball that was going for a goal kick, Gallacher a second time weaved his way through and centred so well that Miller made a grand shot that had Scott in despair. The ball struck underneath the crossbar, and Chelsea deliberated that the ball had crossed over the line. It had not, and the referee adjudged that it had not. In forty minutes, the Chelsea goalkeeper had not handled the ball except to take the goal kicks.

A goal arrived after 44 minutes. The Chelsea forward line had gone through at will against a harassed and overworked defence. Mills was quite an unusual player and did a lot of unexpected things which led to the goal. He was in the penalty box, and the crowd expected him to go forward, instead of which he trod on the ball to bring it back to Jackson. The captain's centre went over to the left wing, where Miller and Bradshaw collided. Bradshaw held his head in his hands, while play went on, but the referee's duty was plain. He had no cause or rule to stop the flow of the game unless it was a serious injury. The ball turned to Pearson, and his centre left the unmarked Gallacher the merest of tap-ins.

When Gunson, Morrison, and McDougall started the second half with abandon, the crowd set up one of its famous Anfield roars. It began with a buzzing on Spion Kop, and developed into the roar that made Liverpool beat Grimsby after the visitors had enjoyed so much of the play. Bradshaw did not seem too sound with a plaster across his eye, and Chelsea were left to dribble in and out of the defence at will. Neither of the Liverpool wingmen had anything to do, and so little was seen of the home inside-forwards that the game looked lost to Liverpool so early in the second period. However, Liverpool netted the ball through Gunson, and in the Third Round of the Cup Tranmere Rovers believed that they had scored a legitimate goal against Chelsea. Liverpool believed that they, too, had scored legally, but the referee declared the goal offside. The ball spun off Barber, and turned in towards Gunson, who, by the collection, could not have been offside. A linesman flagged from the earliest moment, and apparently he insisted that it was not a goal, because the referee, after consulting him, re-affirmed his previous firm decision. Despite this cruel blow, the crowd shouted Liverpool on towards an equaliser in the Spion Kop goal. Millington's first save in practically an hour came from a first-class drive by Bruton. Barber received an accidental kick on the chest from Hodgson, but he remained implacable. Hodgson tried to score with a free-kick but only a corner resulted, which Barton wasted. Wright gained a free-kick parallel to the goal two

yards beyond the penalty area. Again the kick was wasted by Barton.

With twenty minutes remaining, Liverpool swept down to any centre from the right wing. The football was pure defiance, and no attempt was made at finery, although Gallacher on one occasion troubled the Liverpool defence with his usual box of tricks. Chelsea determined to battle on the retreat, which was a dangerous tactic in view of Liverpool's enthusiasm and spirit. However, the visitors showed how easily they could score if the ball ran well for them when Gallacher netted the ball with a ferocious shot, but found himself offside.

The crowd's roar, which had died down, was aroused again when Scott, Morrison and Bradshaw tried to revive Liverpool's flagging hopes. An injury to Mills provided an interlude in the play; Pearson, in an attempted clearance, gave Mills a knockout blow on the chin. Trainer Whitley, who used to keep goal for Everton, trotted on to the field and offered his services. The game was full of the usual cup-tie excitement, but from a footballing perspective, it had lost its art. Liverpool forced the pace throughout the second period and Chelsea's forward work was minimal. In the last minute Pearson beat Scott with a fine drive to the right-hand side of the goal. Scott got his hands to it, but was unable to stop the ball from entering the net.

In the other quarter-finals, Manchester City beat Bury 4-3 away, Arsenal beat Huddersfield 1-0 away, and Newcastle thrashed Watford 5-0 at home.

The St. John's Ambulance authorities reported that there were over fifteen ambulance cases at Anfield, two of which had to go to hospital.

Liverpool: Scott; Steel, Lucas; Morrison, Bradshaw, McDougall; Barton, Hodgson, Bruton, Wright, Gunson.

Chelsea: Millington; Barber, Law; Russell, O'Dowd, Ferguson; Jackson, Mills, Gallacher, Miller, Pearson.

Referee: Mr R. Bowie (Northumberland)

Attendance: 57,804

Receipts: £4,179 9s 0d

January 14, 1933

West Bromwich Albion (1) 2   Liverpool (0) 0
Wood 24,   W.G. Richardson 60

THE city of Birmingham was itself clear of fog, but near the Hawthorns it became thicker and there was doubt expressed as to whether the game would start. However, as 2.30 drew near, visibility became distinctly good. The Albion had one change from their Cup-winning team of two years ago, Murphy taking the place of Magee. (West Bromwich Albion beat Birmingham 2-1 with two goals from W.G. Richardson). Liverpool were at full strength. They opened well, but the Albion were soon on the attack, and it was the right wing which was the cause of Liverpool's trouble. Two centres by Glidden were disposed of only with great difficulty. From another dangerous move by Glidden, Bradshaw conceded a corner. Eventually Wright forced Pearson to a save, and for some minutes the Anfielders threatened the home side, and Pearson was fully employed, but he was able to cope. Bruton was unquestionably offside when he shot against the goalkeeper's legs. At this stage, Liverpool were fighting with great spirit.

Sandford charged Scott as the Irishman gathered a shot from Glidden, and although the goalkeeper was sent back a yard or two, the ball had been cast away by Scott. Hodgson's pass to Barton put the right-winger in a favourable position, and he used the ball well by centring into the goalmouth, but the Albion defence stood firm and cleared the danger before Pearson was threatened.

With 24 minutes gone, the home side took the lead. The goal originated from a throw-in by Carter. The ball went to W.G. Richardson, who swept it over to Wood, who travelled at a great pace to take the pass and smash the ball into the net. Liverpool, although mainly on the defensive, effected occasional raids into Albion territory, and Barton put in a great centre that Bruton deliberately headed away from Pearson, but the ball swung away outside the upright.

Scott saved a low shot at the foot of a post, and shortly after he turned another shot round the post for a corner. Some of Liverpool's attacking plans were excellently executed and Barton, in particular, was well fed. He was generally the master of Edwards, but when he centred, Shaw and Trentham gave little away and only feeble shots found their way to Pearson. Glidden and Shaw tried to spread-eagle the Liverpool defence by wide passing, and but for the intervention of Bradshaw, Scott would have been over-worked. Hodgson, Wright, and Bruton kept the ball too close which was an error against Trentham and Shaw.

A centre by Wood flashed across the face of Liverpool's goal, and Carter went hurtling into the back of the net without the ball. Steel made two perfect tackles on the touchline.

The home side went further ahead on the hour. Sandford found the Liverpool backs wide open and he promptly sent the ball through the opening, and W.G. Richardson took it up and beat Scott with ease.

From a free-kick, Morrison shot half a yard wide of the upright. Hodgson cleverly tricked two men and then passed to Barton, who hit the post. There was an appeal for a corner which was not granted. At this stage in the game, there was a tremendous cheer from the crowd when it became known that Walsall were leading Arsenal - last season's finalists - by a goal. (Third Division Walsall beat Arsenal 2-0 with goals from Alsop [60 minutes] and Sheppard from the penalty spot. Arsenal were top of the First Division.) Scott caught one effort from Glidden with ease, and a few moments later a great header from the outside-right was saved by the Irishman. Bradshaw was magnificent in defence, heading away several dangerous centres.

Everton - the eventual Cup-winners - beat Leicester City 3-2 away, while beaten finalists Manchester City drew 1-1 at Gateshead, before winning the replay 9-0.

W.G. Richardson

West Bromwich A.:
Pearson; Shaw, Trentham; Murphy, W.Richardson, Edwards; Glidden, Carter, W.G.Richardson, Sandford,   Wood.

Liverpool: Scott; Steel, Done; Morrison, Bradshaw, McDougall; Barton, Hodgson, Bruton, Wright, Gunson.

Referee: Mr T. Crew (Leicester)

Attendance: 29,170

Receipts: £1,685

January 13, 1934

Liverpool (1) 1
Hodgson 22

Fulham (1) 1
Lambert

THE day was perfect for the tie and the crowd was much larger than had been anticipated. Liverpool kicked towards the Spion Kop in the first half. Sir Hugo Rutherford, M.P. for Edge Hill, was a spectator.

Liverpool fielded their strongest team, but a murmur went round the field when the crowd saw the height and weight of the Fulham side, who were a powerfully-built team, though they soon showed that this was not their only asset. They possessed a great deal of ability in both their attack and defence, and their right wing was particularly active. During the time that McDougall was off the field with an injury, they produced a lot of trouble for the Liverpool defenders. Finch had run close in before sweeping the ball along the ground right across the face of the goal. Arnold was a shade too late to steer the ball into the net, and it flew past an upright. A minute later Lambert got the ball into the Liverpool net, but was adjudged offside by Mr Pinkston, who seemed to have trouble with his whistle. He went to the touchline and asked a spectator for a pin to clean it out.

Lambert and Wood queried the referee's decision, but they received no satisfaction from the strong man among referees. Fulham were renowned for their defence, but they were distinctly fortunate when Tootill ran too far out to catch a lob, threw the ball down, and then lost it.

With 22 minutes gone, Nieuwenhuys adroitly dragged the ball back for Hodgson, and he shot into the net without a second's delay, the ball travelling just under the crossbar, giving Tootill no chance. This was the first goal scored by Hodgson for a matter of ten weeks. He had his last success against Birmingham on November 4. Tootill effected a good one-handed save from Nieuwenhuys, while Finch spoiled good work by Lambert when he elected to shoot from long range when he could have gone in some yards closer to the goal.

Morrison sent out some great passes and on one occasion he was seen over on the left holding down a forward movement by Wood and Finch. Liverpool might have been awarded a penalty when Gibbons appeared to have charged English in the back when he was just about to shoot. There was no great appeal for a penalty although English was observed beckoning to a colleague that he had been pushed in the back. Considering the height of the Fulham forwards, they were not dangerous when in front of goal. The Liverpool defence always managed to get a man to head away the troublesome centres. The value of the cross-pass from wing to wing was in evidence when Arnold swept the ball right over to Finch. The ball beat McDougall, who jumped up to intercept, but it went on to Finch, who quickly got it under control and centred.

Lambert had stationed himself at the far side of the goal, and all he had to do was put the side of his boot to it to make an equaliser.

Scott made a fine save from Wood, who almost put his foot into Scott's chest, so that a free-kick was awarded for dangerous play. Keeping cut out a Hanson centre which was bound for English, Hodgson and Nieuwenhuys, all of whom might have scored.

In the first period Fulham had proved themselves to be a strong, fighting team, while Liverpool had been below their best in a very ordinary game. With 51 minutes gone, Liverpool created a superb interpassing movement by English and Hodgson, who passed the ball from one to the other three times before English struck the ball hard and true and a goal seemed certain. Tootill, however, patted the ball away, and a tussle between four Liverpool players and four visitors ensued. Tootill eventually cleared, and English had to be carried off with an injury. He was absent from the field for four minutes.

The home side began to exert more pressure and for quite a long time penned Fulham in their own half but without really calling upon the services of Tootill. Finch, on the Fulham right, was one of the more dangerous members of his side, but the remainder of the line did not provide ample support. Lambert had a few opportunities to show his shooting ability, but his leadership could not be disputed, for he made some rare openings with his astute passing. Arnold missed scoring a goal when his header passed narrowly outside.

Liverpool altered their forward line, which read: Nieuwenhuys, Wright, Hodgson, Hanson and English, but it was Fulham who began to dictate matters, forcing Scott to make a number of saves, while several other shots were blocked. Liverpool's defensive plan was often hard pressed to check the onrushing visiting forwards. Lambert was a fine leader. He opened the way in every conceivable manner.

Fulham began to play for the draw, playing only three forwards up the field, and employing the others in a defensive capacity. This meant that the Londoners had to rely upon quick breaks, and from one of them Lambert headed over Finch. Near the end, Fulham nearly snatched victory, and would have done so had Elisha Scott not possessed the agility of a cat. Wood had shot, and everyone expected a goal until Scott sprang up and turned the ball away for a corner. When the final whistle sounded, the Fulham players clapped their hands with delight, and the police had to take charge of the two Fulham mascots who wanted to invade the field.

The London and Midland Railway were running a sixteen shilling (80p) excursion to London for the replay on the Wednesday after the game. The train was due to leave Lime Street at 11.50 pm on Tuesday, January 16.

The most notable victims of the Third Round were the Cup-holders, Everton, who crashed 3-0 at White Hart Lane to Tottenham Hotspur. The eventual Cup-winners, Manchester City, beat Blackburn Rovers 3-1 at home, while beaten finalists Portsmouth, drew 1-1 with Manchester United, before winning the replay at Fratton Park by 4-1.

At the Olympia and Prince of Wales cinemas from the Monday after the game was a film strictly for adults only entitled *Damaged Lives,* which was billed as a "... fearless exposure of humanity's greatest scourge!..." Shown under the auspices of the British Social Hygiene Council, the film - 61 minutes, with a 29 minute lecture - was one of a rival pair of moral tales which had trouble from the censors on subject matter alone. The black-and-white film was an American import which told the story of a young man infecting his wife with syphilis. It had been based on an earlier silent version in 1914.

Liverpool: Scott; Steel, Done; Morrison, Bradshaw, McDougall; Nieuwenhuys, Hodgson, English, Wright, Hanson.

Fulham: Tootill; Birch, Keeping; Oliver, Gibbons, Barrett; Finch, Wood, Lambert, Hammond, Arnold.

Referee: Mr E. Pinkston (Birmingham)

Attendance: 45,619

Receipts: £2,641 (approximate)

With 22 minutes gone, Berry Nieuwenhuys adroitly dragged the ball back for **Gordon Hodgson,** *and he shot into the net without a second's delay, the ball travelling just under the crossbar, giving Tootill no chance. This was the first goal scored by Hodgson for a matter of ten weeks.*

January 17, 1934

Fulham (1) 2
Hammond, Arnold 51

Liverpool (0) 3 aet
Hanson 60, Bradshaw 88,
Roberts 116

LIVERPOOL had been known all their football life for the way they did the most extraordinary things. The simple victory for them was made a task of enormous character. The difficult task was one in which they revelled. They beat Fulham 3-2 after a struggle which lasted for two hours. They had been amateurish in the tie at Anfield, and, but for Scott's agility, would have been dumped unceremoniously out of the Cup. Liverpool had not won in League and Cup for twelve games, losing eight of those matches. The manner of this victory was remarkable, for Liverpool were two goals down, not playing at all well, and with deputies for Hodgson and English. Rain had fallen heavily, and there was a doubt about the size of the forward line and the officials wondered if the heavy going would be too much for their smaller players. However, the Fulham turf was in excellent condition. Bradshaw won the toss and got the benefit of a very strong wind behind his team. Scott produced a master save against Fulham at Anfield and he now produced one for the benefit of the Londoners. The incident began with Wright finding Gibbons too sharp for him as well as too heavy. Arnold received the ball and centred to the far post, where Lambert made a placed header that everyone thought had scored. Scott stretched out his left hand, and by some miraculous means turned the ball away only a few inches, but prevented it from crossing the line. Bradshaw conceded a corner as Fulham attacked, but the Liverpool skipper cleared his lines. Hammond, at inside-left, was neat and skilful and Liverpool's attack was essentially too light for the task. Neither side, however, were good finishers, and after Scott had kicked away in his own individual manner, Bradshaw finished one of his attacking movements with a tame punt.

Fulham opened their account through a perfect piece of work by the limping Finch, who crossed to Hammond, a 6ft 2in tall forward whose header beat Scott. He headed into the left-hand corner, and before the ball had come to rest over the line, he rushed across the field to shake hands with his wingman.

There was no change in Fulham's style and they succeeded through combination. Tootill punched away a centre from Nieuwenhuys, while Hanson sent in a first-class centre which Wright tried hard to steer into the back of the net. Liverpool had a spell of attack near half-time in which Wright was stern and Roberts was unfortunate to find a strong shot strike a defender when nothing could have saved the goalkeeper. A Nieuwenhuys header across goal was seized upon by the inrushing Hanson, whose fierce shot went to the left of the goalkeeper and struck the right hand side of the upright before returning into play. The wind changed course at the interval

and favoured Liverpool once more, who scored through Nieuwenhuys early into the second period, but the goal was ruled offside.

With six minutes gone, Fulham increased their lead. Hammond began the goal by traversing from inside-left to the right touch line. He slipped the ball forward to Finch, who paired off with Lambert near the bye-line, and when the ball was centred fast and low, Arnold closed in and, although falling to the ground, got the ball into the net with some speed. Liverpool dared not face Tranmere manager Bert Cooke and captain Barton, here taking notes for the future game if they did not make a supreme effort.

Liverpool appeared apparently afraid to take a shot, yet, the wind was quite fierce. It was in Liverpool's favour for the first half, and that made it inexplicable that Liverpool did not try any telling long-range shots.

The visitors had the wind at their backs in the second half, and with the Fulham defenders undecided as to which way to go, Hanson scored on the hour. This was the signal for Liverpool's change in fortune. They rained in numerous shots on goal and unsettled the previously steady Fulham defence. The forwards were closed down by Bradshaw and Steel. There was a magnificent, dour struggle as Liverpool sought to equalise before the final whistle. However, a pre-arranged plan of campaign bore fruit. The plan was that at a point near the finish, if Liverpool were losing, the whole team should move up *en masse* for a solid and unflinching attack. This was carried out. Bradshaw led the way and Fulham wilted. Shots poured in and Tootill pulled off many fine saves. Finally the Liverpool captain, who had borne the brunt of the work, saw a chance. Roberts was about to take the shot, but Bradshaw "took the honour" and waved his hand to indicate he wanted the task. Bradshaw was about 25 yards from goal, but, taking the ball as it came to him, he drove in a beautiful shot to equalise and force extra time. Nieuwenhuys nearly scored a winner in normal time, and Wright and full-back Steel almost settled the game.

Extra time meant a test of stamina rather than football skill and Liverpool played Fulham to a standstill, showing much more power and resource than the London side, whose big men had little left to offer. Liverpool tested the strength of the wind against them for the first time in the whole match. They endured fifteen minutes of headwind and they came through it with skill and judgment. With the wind at their backs in the final fifteen minutes, people talked of the Villa ground as the likeliest place for a third meeting scheduled for Monday next, but Roberts scored neatly after Done had made a long punt that seemed to carry too much leeway in the wind. Wright brought the ball to earth by using his body, and he passed to Roberts, who drove home the winner.

Elisha Scott produced a master save against Fulham at Anfield and he now produced one for the benefit of the Londoners. He stretched out his left hand, and by some miraculous means turned the ball away only a few inches, but prevented it from crossing the line.

At noon on the day of the replay (Wednesday), Southport encountered the highest tides of the year. The strong winds and rain which swept the country helped the 31-foot tide to flood the Marine Drive, which ran at the back of Prince's Park. The Peter Pan fairground, on the site of the old bathing pool at the side of Marine Drive, was flooded in parts to a depth of several feet. The municipal golf links were partly flooded, and the Marine Lake, on the north side of the pier, had disappeared under the sea. Mountainous waves, helped by a strong south-west wind, broke over the lower promenade on the north side of the pier near the Floral Hall, and at one time there seemed a danger of the gardens being flooded. On the south side of the pier the sea ran through on to the tennis courts, which were soon several inches under water.

The inclement weather coincided with the visit of the Duke of Gloucester to the Corporation tenements at Dingle during his tour of boys' clubs in Liverpool.

A thirty-foot tide and a sixty miles an hour wind combined at Blackpool and were so menacing along the promenade from Manchester Square to Squires Gate, that the tram service had to be suspended. At North Shore there were clouds of spray over 100 feet high.

Fulham: Tootill; Birch, Hindson; Oliver, Gibbons, Barrett; Finch, Wood, Lambert, Hammond, Arnold.

Liverpool: Scott; Steel, Done; Morrison, Bradshaw, McDougall; Nieuwenhuys, Taylor, Wright, Roberts, Hanson.

Referee: Mr E. Pinkston (Birmingham)

Attendance: 28,319   **Receipts**: £1,907 4s 6d

January 27, 1934

Liverpool (2) 3
English 17, 85,
Nieuwenhuys 33

Tranmere Rovers (1) 1
Meacock 23

CUP-TIE scenes, the like of which had not been seen for several years, were witnessed at Anfield when Tranmere Rovers visited Liverpool by arrangement after the Cup draw had been made with the Rovers at home. The queues were enormous and a perfect summer's day added to the atmosphere, though it was unfortunate that two members of the cloth should see fit to help spectators from the paddock into the five-shilling seats, which was grossly unfair to the ticket-holders. Casualties at the corner of the ground at the angle of Kemlyn Road and the Kop were numerous. The police allowed spectators to form up in orderly fashion around the touch-line. The boy mascot performed his customary greetings and both sides had a tremendous welcome. The Liverpool team was playing together for the first time. At the Pavilion, Sandy Powell was presenting for the first time in Liverpool *My New Show*. At Anfield Liverpool and Tranmere prepared to put on a show of their own for the record crowd. Liverpool won the toss and had the sunshine at their backs. They kicked off towards the Park end, and within one minute had nearly scored a goal and lost English, the leader of their forward line. Morrison initiated the movement, and Hanson and English continued it, the centre-forward attempting to make a draft pass for the benefit of Hodgson's shot, which was so close that Gray was content to turn the ball round the corner. It was a fine save on the part of Gray, but English was found to be so lame that he had to leave the field. Tranmere responded down the right, and young Hunt centred with the steadiness of a Meredith. After Done cleared to stop Barton, there was an intensive campaign on the part of Liverpool's forward line which resulted in Gray saving excellent shots from Hanson, Hodgson, and Syd Roberts, the best of all being the save from Hodgson's masterly ground shot. Gray, the Welsh international, was a tall goalkeeper who knew his angles well. Another attempt by Roberts was thwarted by the Tranmere defence. Bell found Bradshaw head and shoulders above him, and the surprise of the day was the calm, collected way in which Hunt had shaped when he ambled up the right wing with his quaint gait. Tranmere had several openings, but the forwards did not receive the ball to their liking, and "Ginger" Lewis inclined to go to the half-back position and suffered the glare of the sunshine. English had not been prevented by his earlier injury from dribbling or showing his pace.

English and Hodgson bore down on the visitors' goal in tandem, both with the chance of scoring, but it was Hodgson who elected to shoot, but he missed his shot and the ball went back to English, who pushed it up to the top of the almost empty net to open the scoring. Tranmere were not dispirited by this reverse, and Woodward forced Scott to produce a fine save with a square low ball directed right and driven hard.

Although Scott had done his best, the ball was not totally cleared and Meacock, unmarked, was able to stride forward and shoot a goal from five yards out after 23 minutes. Liverpool were completely surprised; Tranmere were overjoyed, and the game was finely balanced once again.

Eventually Liverpool gained the ascendancy once more and Gray tipped an English header over the bar. McDougall effected a shot, and Liverpool gained four corners in five minutes. Nieuwenhuys placed his corner kicks well, but his other work was not so polished. Nieuwenhuys gave Roberts a splendid chance, but he put the ball on to the top of the shed at the back of the goal.

With 33 minutes gone, Liverpool went ahead through a typical "Nivvy" run in which he pranced beyond his opponents, and finally shot with his left foot. The ball passed through Gray's legs. McDougall and "Nivvy" made further strong efforts and it appeared that the visitors had run themselves out in their brilliant first-half display. Lewis, the bundle of ceaseless energy, saved a certain goal. Hodgson made two thrilling back-headers which amounted to nothing.

The second half began with a fine solo run by English and a simple fall by Roberts, who had to leave the field for attention, and finally resumed at outside-left. Bell had few chances for the visitors. Barton produced some neat touches in another Tranmere revival, and Liverpool, although in front, were not content with their narrow margin, and Bradshaw's excellent headwork proved to be a powerful barrier to the Rovers.

Liverpool continued to play good combination football, and "Nivvy" bewildered the defence and sent in several dangerous crosses. English, Nieuwenhuys and Hodgson had chances of scoring, but they tried to walk the ball through in Austrian fashion. Both goalkeepers were injured, Scott's problem arising through a breakaway by Urmson, who had received little assistance for an hour. The game was stopped while Gray had his leg bandaged.

Scott had to make his famous cat crawl to scoop the ball over the line from Urmson, and was prepared for a second save when the ball passed out. McDougall was a consistent shooter, and on three occasions he was inches off the target. Roberts dropped to the ground without a player near him and it was a recurrence of his former injury which required him to be stretchered off. Hanson was charged into the Spion Kop area and fell headlong among the people, requiring to be dug out and attended by the ambulance men. Bradshaw showed his intense anger, and in the next minute Scott was nearly carried over the line with the ball through the attentions of Bell. Liverpool had nine men and an extremely difficult task, as Tranmere were on top. Hanson recovered after five minutes rest and attention. Nieuwenhuys rounded his man and centred so that it looked as though Liverpool might extend their lead, but English struck the crossbar with the Tranmere goalkeeper in a helpless position. Liverpool were reduced to nine men again when Nieuwenhuys was off for a time. Hodgson forced his way to within four yards of goal but shot a foot outside with the goal gaping at him. Lewis committed a further dangerous foul on Nieuwenhuys. Five minutes from the end the issue was clinched with a goal scored by English after Hodgson had gone to the near inside-left position.

Tranmere were disposed of by Liverpool on the day when the French Government had decided to resign. Arsenal beat Crystal Palace 7-0 at Highbury, while Aston Villa thrashed Sunderland 7-2 at Villa Park. Leicester City beat Millwall 6-3 at the Den.

Right: **Berry Nieuwenhuys**

Liverpool: Scott; Steel, Done; Morrison, Bradshaw, McDougall; Nieuwenhuys, Hodgson, English, S.Roberts, Hanson.

Tranmere Rovers: Gray; Dawson, Lewis; Barton, Fishwick, R.Spencer; Hunt, Meacock, Bell, Woodward, Urmson.

Referee: Mr Cartlidge (Burslem)

Attendance: 61,036 (a record)

Receipts: £4,007 2s 6d

F.A. CUP - 4th Round

Arsenal	7	Crystal Palace	0
Aston Villa	7	Sunderland	2
Birmingham	1	Charlton A.	0
Brighton & H.	1	Bolton W.	1
Bury	1	Swansea Town	1
Chelsea	1	Nottingham F.	1
Derby County	3	Wolves	0
Huddersfield	0	Northampton	2
Hull City	2	Manchester City	2
Millwall	3	Leicester City	6
Oldham Athletic	1	Sheffield Wed.	1
Portsmouth	2	Grimsby Town	0
Stoke City	3	Blackpool	0
Tottenham H.	4	West Ham	1
Workington	1	Preston N.E,	2

Replays

Bolton W.	6	Brighton & H.	1
Nottingham F.	0	Chelsea	3
Manchester City	4	Hull City	1
Sheffield Wed.	6	Oldham Ath.	1
Swansea Town	3	Bury	0

February 17, 1934

Liverpool (0) 0

Bolton Wanderers (1) 3
Milsom, G.T. Taylor 65, Westwood

THE weather was reminiscent of a perfect summer's day; the League attraction at Goodison Park, where Everton drew 1-1 with Middlesbrough, eased the congestion around Anfield; there was no pre-match excitement, although there was a good band; young Glazebrook, the mascot, was present, and a stray dog was removed from the field. Finney and Bradshaw were the rival captains, the Liverpool skipper won the toss. Barton was on trial at outside-left, and Eastham, at 20, was making his début in the Cup for Bolton. Referee Gibb was the smallest referee in the game.

Liverpool: Scott; Tennant, Done; Morrison, Bradshaw, McDougall; Nieuwenhuys, Hodgson, English, Taylor, Barton.

Bolton Wanderers: Jones; Smith, Finney; Gosling, Atkinson, G.Taylor; G.T.Taylor, Eastham, Milsom, Westwood, Cook.

Referee: Mr Gibb (Reading)

Attendance: 54,912

Receipts: £3,842

Liverpool began in strong fashion on the left and the right, McDougall feeding the right wing after Tennant had opened with a brilliant piece of play and a telling pass. Nieuwenhuys' centre was headed away, and Hodgson, on the half-turn, let out a smashing shot just as he had done in the first moment of the tie versus Tranmere. Barton's first effort was a squared centre after Eastham had been as putty in the hands of Bradshaw. Barton's centre crossed beyond English and passed on to Hodgson, whose shot was diverted for a corner. Bolton eventually attacked through the cleverness of young Eastham.

Nieuwenhuys meandered through the opposing defence and a bout of passing concluded with the ball in the back of the Bolton net through Taylor's efforts. The little referee with the enormous power ruled that it was offside. In a breakaway, Milsom shot well wide of the target.

Liverpool began to over-complicate matters with their intricate passing movements which brought no tangible results. Bolton broke with speed through Cook transferring his affections from outside-left to near outside-right. He beat McDougall and Done, and when Bradshaw threw himself full-length on the ground to arrest the pass he was out of line with the idea. When Done was beaten through his leaping in the air, Milsom was full of danger until he committed a foul on Scott. After the former Everton goalkeeper, Jones, had made a good catch, Scott made a thrilling save from Cook,

not knowing that Cook had been rightly given offside. At this stage, Bolton were very impressive, rather cute in their movements and helped by the forward display of Goslin and an equally tall half-back in Atkinson. The first stoppage occurred when G.Taylor was injured in the Liverpool penalty area which was at the Kop end.

Liverpool suffered the shock of a reverse when Milsom had a long ball delivered to him down the middle, and when he had brushed beyond Tennant he had to face Scott, who was so often the master of close-range efforts. Scott made a dive for the ball, but could only see the ball travel into the right-hand corner of the net.

The reply from Hodgson was without fortune; his first shot, of great power, struck a defender, and the second was a perfect drive, to which Jones leapt and swept the ball out of the way in a thrilling incident. Tennant took the place of Done as a free-kick specialist on the right wing without getting any better direction than Done had obtained. Bolton went forward through Woodward, whose shot towards goal was brilliantly turned over the bar by Scott.

The visitors played well, and their numerous attacks were chiefly broken up by the heading ability of Bradshaw. Atkinson and Finney were stalwarts, while Liverpool's rhythm had almost completely broken down, notably at left-back and centre-forward. Scott effected a double-handed punch away from one Cook effort. Liverpool were too fond of ballooning the ball considering the height of Bolton's half-backs. Just before the interval, Barton injured his back and Westwood made a run as thrilling as Milsom's, but his shot went outside.

Nieuwenhuys headed away from a corner taken by Barton, and Milsom failed by inches to reach a Cook centre as Bolton maintained their superiority. The Kop roared its head off to encourage their heroes.

Liverpool changed their forward line in an effort to draw level, Barton becoming centre-forward and English inside-left, with Taylor on the wing. Finney prevented this re-arranged attack from scoring with a well-timed tackle. Morrison and Nieuwenhuys combined well to create a chance for Barton, but he screwed his shot wide. Finney was steadfast and rock-like as Liverpool pressed forward in an attempt to salvage something from the game. From a long punt by Scott, "Nivvy" tried to redeem the match by making a strong shot which struck a defender and the rebound went for a corner, from which Jones pulled off a great save at the foot of a post.

The danger had not passed because Hodgson produced an excellent shot when goalkeeper Jones was unsighted, yet Jones got his hands to the ball and patted it away for the save of the match.

Just as Liverpool appeared to have a genuine chance of saving the match, Bolton scored a second goal. Bradshaw had gone forward to help the good work when English, standing at inside-right, passed back beyond Bradshaw's reach. Westwood took up the ball and sped towards the Liverpool goal, dribbling in and out of the home defence before passing to G.T. Taylor, who netted after 65 minutes.

Bolton nearly scored a third when the ball struck Tennant's back. Taylor was unlucky not to convert a sharp run and centre by Barton. Jones saved a header from Barton as Liverpool sought a goal. Moments later Hodgson backheaded the ball against the crossbar with Jones well beaten. Westwood completed the scoring with a goal after a solo run. It was an all-round triumph for Bolton, with Milsom, Cook, Westwood, Finney and Jones in outstanding form. Bolton lost 0-3 at home to the eventual beaten-finalists, Portsmouth, in the Sixth Round.

The other Fifth Round results were:

Arsenal	1	Derby County	0
Preston North End	4	Northampton Town	0
Stoke City	3	Chelsea	1
Tottenham Hotspur	0	Aston Villa	1
Birmingham	1	Leicester City	2
Sheffield Wednesday	2	Manchester City	2
Swansea Town	0	Portsmouth	1

Replay

Manchester City	2	Sheffield Wednesday	0

DIVISION ONE

Everton	1	Middlesbrough	1
West Bromwich	2	Wolverhampton	0

DIVISION TWO

Bradford	4	Plymouth Argyle	1
Burnley	3	Brentford	1
Bury	1	Southampton	0
Grimsby Town	1	West Ham United	1
Hull City	0	Fulham	0
Lincoln City	2	Blackpool	2
Millwall	1	Bradford City	1
Notts County	1	Nottingham Forest	0

In the Swansea - Portsmouth tie a broken barrier caused many casualties, several of whom were taken away to hospital. In the Third Division North, Tranmere lost 0-1 at New Brighton. Bell had the ball in the net, but the goal was ruled out for being offside. New Brighton fully deserved their victory for their endeavour.

Eighteen Blackshirts were arrested and charged in court with conspiring together to effect a public mischief by obstructing the removal of cattle and pigs unlawfully impounded under distress for tithe. They were remanded in custody until Monday week, February 26. Bail was refused.

The King and Queen returned to London on the day of the game from Sandringham, where they had been since before Christmas.

January 12, 1935

Yeovil & Petters United (1) 2   Liverpool (1) 6

McNeil 4, 79

Nieuwenhuys 26, Wright 46,
Hodgson 56, 65,
Roberts 57, 90

BRAVE Yeovil and Petters United, who had beaten Crystal Palace 3-0 in the First Round and Exeter City 4-1 in the Second Round, finally succumbed to mighty Liverpool's stern challenge, though not without the joy of taking a sensational fourth-minute lead through McNeil, a former Liverpool player. Yeovil - the smallest town in England with a professional team, played well and with much spirit, but Liverpool's class eventually told. Bridgwater greeted Liverpool as if they were a royal party. The party visited the battle place of the last war raged in England. The weather was so good that there was never any doubt that there would be a record gate, despite price increases of up to 12s 6d (52½p). Louis Page had to have his neck muscles massaged a moment before the start, but with only twelve professionals, he had little choice but to play. The ground sloped from touchline to touchline, but there was plenty of grass on it. The Yeovil players bathed at Beer on the Thursday. Liverpool sent a telegram to Everton wishing them good fortune, and it seemed to work, for the Toffeemen beat Grimsby Town 6-3 at Goodison Park, both Merseyside clubs registering the highest score of the day in the Cup. There were eighty excursionists from Liverpool, and the time was passed with community singing. People were perched on noticeboards, such was the interest in the game. Jack Page, the former Everton and Cardiff City player, was present to cheer on his brother. Riley was in white, while Yeovil wore green. Liverpool won the toss, and Hanson made the first run and centre and Liverpool opened with a degree of ease, but Riley had to make the first run out to kick away a dangerous ball. Parle made his famous down-slope pass for Page's benefit, but offside halted the play. Tennant's first plunge-in startled the natives who had not seen such a lengthy drive before. Tennant followed with a kick into touch so hard that it passed over the heads of the spectators.

With just four minutes on the clock, the home side scored. The goal came from a corner kick and a natural safety move by Bradshaw. The corner was taken by Holbeach. Parle seemed to touch it to McNeil, and the former Liverpool and Colwyn Bay Scot shot immediately into the back of the net out of the reach of Riley. The crowd had covered the corner area so densely that Holbeach had to get them back for his fatal corner kick. A sensation looked imminent.

Liverpool responded immediately, and Hodgson tried a charge on the goalkeeper, winning a corner, which "Nivvy" tried to head through. Hanson went to centre-forward to meet an opportunity, but Lynch saved Hanson's straight drive. The visitors, though naturally troubled by the reverse, did not lose control, preferring to play steadily in order to mount a

worthwhile assault. Lynch made another great catch, and took a ball sky-high, pitching on his head, turning a somersault, and getting up as if nothing had happened. He came from Barnsley, where Cup-fighters are produced by the score. Liverpool had half a gale at their backs, and Lynch became the hero of the day. McDougall centred so well that Hodgson was able to head in. The ball headed towards the top corner of the net, but Lynch leapt up and just touched the ball. He fell headlong against the foot of the post, but got up as if he had done nothing.

Parle and Taylor combined well, but Holbeach shot outside. Hanson was the star of the Liverpool forward line, but Horatius Lynch was in defiant mood. Bradshaw tried two shots which were both blocked.

Roberts went close with an effort, and after 26 minutes, Liverpool got on level terms. Hodgson headed towards goal in customary fashion, and although Lynch saw the goal scoring opportunity of the effort he was surrounded by a group of players in the goalmouth who impeded his vision, and Nieuwenhuys nipped in to score from six yards, though the ball appeared to touch a Yeovil defender, Price, before entering the net. Roberts twice almost put the visitors ahead, but first he was wide, and then he drove the ball a little too high.

McDougall, showing rare pace, got beyond Smith, who was injured in the process. A very narrow offside decision stopped Hodgson, who went on to net the ball. Parle worked like a Trojan and forced Savage to pay for a slow back-pass. Riley came out to meet the centre, fell to the ground, lost possession, and a goal looked likely. Wright was unfortunate in beating the goalkeeper, only to see his goalbound effort hit a defender, and moments later he went inches wide. Three balls had been used this half, and Wright was once more inches away from scoring the leading goal. As the half-time whistle approached, Taylor broke clean through and had only Riley to beat, but he made a shocking miss.

One minute into the second period, Liverpool took the lead. Wright, standing close in through his own effort, was able to make a left-foot drive into the left-hand corner of the goal. McNeil tried to equalise, but the ball struck Tennant. McDougall, who scored a hat-trick here in a friendly match, went through in solo fashion and gave Roberts a chance, Lynch making a brilliant save. Yeovil attacked and Taylor made his second glaring miss of the game. Hanson swept right through and his shot struck Lynch's body as the game flowed from end to end. A free-kick was drifted by Nieuwenhuys to Hodgson, who headed with supreme ease into the goal after 56 minutes. One minute later, Liverpool increased their lead. Hanson shot and the half-save left Roberts with a gift.

The home side, although plucky and quite clever, were no match for Liverpool. There was a skirmish in Yeovil's goalmouth and Wright was seen in fistic action. With 65 minutes gone, Hodgson scored from the left flank after a fine run-up by Tennant.

Yeovil never ceased their endeavour, and McNeil reduced the arrears with a fine header from a Holbeach centre. McDougall was then injured, and Nieuwenhuys slipped up as he was on the point of scoring a sixth goal. In the last minute of the game, Roberts scored a sixth goal.

In the Wigan Athletic - Millwall Cup tie, a spectator, Richard Ward, dropped dead. Mr Ward, a miner, of Lyon Street, Wigan, died while the game was in progress. Millwall won the game 4-1. The Cupholders, Manchester City, lost 0-1 against Tottenham in London, while Portsmouth drew 1-1 with Huddersfield at Fratton Park, before winning the replay 3-2. The eventual Cup-winners, Sheffield Wednesday, beat Oldham Athletic 3-1 with goals from Palethorpe, Rimmer and Surtees, while the beaten finalists, West Bromwich Albion, beat Port Vale 2-1 at home.

In Scotland, Hearts beat Airdrieonians 7-4 away, while in Rugby League, Sullivan brought his total of tries for the season to 103 as Wigan overwhelmed Barrow 44-8 to remain top of the table.

Yeovil & Petters: Lynch; Wood, Birks; Smith, Price, Parkin; Holbeach, Parle, Taylor, McNeil, Page.

Liverpool: Riley; Cooper, Tennant; Savage, Bradshaw, McDougall; Nieuwenhuys, Hodgson, E.V.Wright, Roberts, Hanson.

Referee: Mr H.E. Gould (London)

Attendance: 13,000

Receipts: £900 (approximate)

SPURS' LONE GOAL

~~~~~

Puts Manchester City, Cupholders, Out

~~~

For the second year in succession Tottenham have defeated the Cupholders. Last year it was Everton; today 55,000 people saw them put an end to Manchester City's hopes. The Spurs played streets above their recent form, and were full value for a goal by W. Evans in 21 minutes. The Spurs' halves checked the City forwards continually, though Brook missed one sitter.

City reversed their "pretty" methods after the interval, and by swinging the ball about more strengthened their chance of saving the game, but all their efforts could not break down Spurs' excellent defence, and the Londoners won after a hard game.

F.A. CUP
THIRD ROUND

Everton	6	Grimsby	3
Aldershot Town	0	Reading	0
Aston Villa	1	Bradford City	3
Birmingham	5	Coventry City	1
Brentford	0	Plymouth Argyle	1
Brighton & Hove A.	0	Arsenal	2
Bristol City	1	Bury	1
Bristol Rovers	1	Manchester United	3
Burnley	4	Mansfield Town	2
Chelsea	1	Luton Town	1
Chester	0	Nottingham Forest	4
Hull City	1	Newcastle United	5
Leeds United	4	Bradford	1
Leicester City	2	Blackpool	1
Middlesbrough	1	Blackburn Rovers	1
Northampton Town	0	Bolton Wanderers	2
Norwich City	2	Bath City	0
Portsmouth	1	Huddersfield Town	1
Preston North End	0	Barnsley	0
Sheffield Wed.	3	Oldham Athletic	1
Southend United	0	Sheffield United	4
Sunderland	3	Fulham	2
Swansea Town	4	Stoke City	1
Swindon Town	2	Chesterfield	1
Tottenham Hotspur	1	Manchester City	0
Walsall	1	Southampton	2
West Bromwich A.	2	Port Vale	1
West Ham United	1	Stockport County	1
Wigan Athletic	1	Millwall	4
Wolverhampton W.	4	Notts County	0
York City	0	Derby County	1

Replays

Reading	3	Aldershot Town	1
Bury	2	Bristol City	2
Luton Town	2	Chelsea	0
Blackburn Rovers	1	Middlesbrough	0
Huddersfield Town	2	Portsmouth	3
Barnsley	0	Preston North End	1
Stockport County	1	West Ham United	0

Second Replay

Bristol City	2	Bury	1

(at Villa Park)

January 26, 1935

Blackburn Rovers (0) 1   Liverpool (0) 0
Milne 53

THERE was little sunshine and icy blasts to greet the record number of trekkers from Liverpool. Nudist colonies were closed because of the weather, though the ground was packed and the turf in excellent condition. Hughes played in goal for the Rovers. Five trains had been booked for Liverpool supporters by the Wednesday before the game. Three more trains were added. Charabancs and motor-cars wended their way along and the scene at the ground was just like good old Blackburn days. The wind howled and the spectators followed suit in trying to get warm. There were loud cheers for both sides. McDougall named the call correctly and Blackburn kicked off.

Tennant caused the first attack on the left which was deemed offside, and Nieuwenhuys's first centre curled menacingly towards goal, though it went just over the bar. Bradshaw stopped Blackburn's raid on the cornerline and kicked clear, whereas Cooper's first effort was a miss followed by a clearance.

Nivvy's speed and football skill carried him beyond the Blackburn backs and the centre was a possible chance for Wright or Hanson. Wright was covered a little, and pushed the ball out. Hanson drove at once without his usual fierce power, and the ball went wide of the goalkeeper but touched a defender, before going out for a corner. Liverpool's early raids had caused Blackburn to become nervous in the same way that they had done against Middlesbrough in the Third Round replay at Ewood Park.

Then came a dramatic moment. First Tennant performed one dribble too many, then Savage kicked far towards his own goalkeeper. Riley went forward with confidence, bold and cool. He kicked the ball away but it hit Milne's leg, and although Milne was outside the penalty area Riley could not pick up the ball because of this. The ball travelled on and on towards the Liverpool goal. A score seemed certain. It seemed an age as it went on its fateful journey. Riley gave chase and no Blackburn player challenged him. By degrees Riley's stride carried him to his goalmouth, and he made his kick away just in time to prevent a goal.

Hughes made two catches, one from his own full-back, the ball swirling into the arms of the 'keeper. Bradshaw had done much heroic work in the first quarter and followed this with a great piece of intricate dribbling work when Tennant, blinded by the sun, had not been able to hold Bruton. Moments later Bradshaw assisted Tennant again, when the Liverpool left-back was in danger from Beattie.

The players experienced great difficulty in timing a pass or shot or clearance kick in the stern wind. Blackburn's inside forwards played with menace and great skill. Bruton was in

form and one centre from him was missed by Thompson. A foul against Nieuwenhuys had been signalled a split second before Hodgson netted. Savage tried a long shot which passed narrowly outside, but it was a welcome effort. Gorman went great guns against Liverpool's left flank, but McDougall became a forward and was fouled by the former Liverpool lad. Vic Wright charged Hughes and the ball so hard that it looked as though a goal had been scored, but the charge had not quite carried the ball over the line.

Hampson had scored in a similar way for England against Scotland. Wright, a clever schemer, tried to back-heel the ball when it was thrown away by Hughes. Hughes made another great save from Hodgson's back-header. Again Wright charged the goalkeeper. The first real straight shot was saved by Riley from Milne.

The second half opened with great excitement as Gorman miskicked and at the other end Bradshaw kicked way and found the ball strike one of his own players. McLean grafted away at half-back, but there was no-one to support his efforts. Savage went on a mazy run which allowed Hodgson his first real shooting chance of the game. The drive was fierce but struck an opponent.

With eight minutes of the second period gone, Blackburn scored. Wright had joined the defence, which was unusual for a centre-forward. Bradshaw did not get the ball clear, and Whiteside, the half-back, gave chase among his forwards. Thompson received and shot across the goal. The ball looked to be going out when Milne, the outside-left, closed in and shot from close range.

Liverpool fought desperately to stem the tide, and Hodgson shot hard but without fortune and Hughes mishandled a ball in another attack, but again, fortune did not favour the visitors. Some of the Liverpool players had difficulty in staying the course and playing against the strong wind. Liverpool were not as sharp as Blackburn in attack, who were much quicker on the ball. Beattie hit the crossbar with a cross-shot, although Riley was well-placed for the effort. McLean changed his shorts, but Liverpool failed to change their tactics.

Christie could hardly walk through an injury, yet Liverpool continued to hold the ball too long and get trapped by a rugged Blackburn side. Whiteside, the smallest man on the field, was the most captivating half-back on view. Roberts at last broke away, but Hughes took the centre with panache.

At Fulham last season, Liverpool equalised when everyone went onto the attack in the final five minutes, but this tactic was not employed and Liverpool were dumped out of the Cup. Tennant kicked off the line to save a second goal as the seconds ticked away. Hanson had the best chance to equalise, but he shot against a post from two yards.

In Scotland, goals were the order of the day in the First Round of the Scottish Cup. Greenock Morton beat Boness 9-0; Albion Rovers beat Paisley Academicals 7-0; Forfar beat Chrinside United 7-1; Dundee United beat Fraserburgh 6-2 away; Dumbarton beat Vale of Ocaba 6-2 away; Hearts beat Solway Star 7-0; and Third Lanark beat Creetown 6-2.

In Rugby League, Wigan got back to winning ways with a 34-6 defeat of Halifax. Swinton, 7-0 victors over Dewsbury, led the table by two points.

Blackburn Rovers: Hughes; Gorman, Crook; Whiteside, Christie, Pryde; Bruton, Beattie, Thompson, McLean, Milne.

Liverpool: Riley; Cooper, Tennant; Savage, Bradshaw, McDougall; Nieuwenhuys, Hodgson, E.V.Wright, Roberts, Hanson.

Referee: Mr A. Noble (Sheffield)

Attendance: 49,546

FOURTH ROUND

Bradford City	0	Stockport County	0
Burnley	3	Luton Town	1
Derby County	3	Swansea Town	0
Leicester City	0	Arsenal	1
Norwich City	3	Leeds United	3
Nottingham Forest	0	Manchester United	0
Plymouth Argyle	1	Bolton Wanderers	4
Portsmouth	0	Bristol City	0
Reading	1	Millwall	0
Southampton	0	Birmingham	3
Sunderland	1	Everton	1
Swindon Town	0	Preston North End	2
Tottenham Hotspur	2	Newcastle United	0
Wolverhampton W.	1	Sheffield Wednesday	2
West Bromwich A.	7	Sheffield United	1

Replays

Stockport County	3	Bradford City	2
Leeds United	1	Norwich City	2
Manchester United	0	Nottingham Forest	3
Bristol City	2	Portsmouth	0
Everton	6	Sunderland	4

FIFTH ROUND

Norwich City	0	Sheffield Wednesday	1
Reading	0	Arsenal	1
Birmingham	2	Blackburn Rovers	1
Nottingham Forest	0	Burnley	0
Tottenham Hotspur	1	Bolton Wanderers	1
Everton	3	Derby County	1
Bristol City	0	Preston North End	0
West Bromwich A.	5	Stockport County	0

Replays

Burnley	3	Nottingham Forest	0
Bolton Wanderers	1	Tottenham Hotspur	1
Preston North End	5	Bristol City	0

Second Replay

Bolton Wanderers	2	Tottenham Hotspur	0
(at Villa Park)			

SIXTH ROUND

Sheffield Wednesday	2	Arsenal	1
Burnley	3	Birmingham	2
Everton	1	Bolton Wanderers	2
West Bromwich A.	1	Preston North End	0

SEMI-FINALS

Sheffield Wednesday	3	Burnley	0
(at Villa Park)			
Bolton Wanderers	1	West Bromwich A.	1
(at Leeds)			

Replay

Bolton Wanderers	0	West Bromwich A.	2
(at Stoke)			

FINAL

Sheffield Wednesday	4	West Bromwich A.	2

January 11, 1936

Liverpool (1) 1

Wright 17

Swansea Town (0) 0

THE well-known Liverpool comedian was seen inside the ground as a follower of the Liverpool club. The wind had died down and conditions were excellent for a Cup tie. Riley, the groundsman, had done his best, with the result that the ground looked to be splendid condition. There was a good sprinkling of Welshmen, two trains having been requisitioned. The sides appeared to be very evenly matched as regards height and weight, though Swansea from the Second Division were expected to be lacking in skill. The Welsh side won the toss and played with their backs to the Kop. McDougall broke through first, but finished by sending the ball wide of the goal. Swansea responded through the efforts of Brain, but he was also wide with his shot.

McDougall sent a long ball down the centre for Howe, but the forward was tackled as he was about to shoot. The visitors put in some telling work and Liverpool were hard-pressed against their opponents. A long cross by Pears sent the ball out to Lewis, who was beaten near the corner by Dabbs. Then came a sparkling move by Johnson and Carr. When Carr centred Moore brought off a clever catch. There was little in it, but a great shot by Johnson was blocked before it could cause any real damage. Milne, in the Swansea defence, was performing heroics and a one-handed punch by Moore stopped a very dangerous looking centre from Carr. Liverpool played a typical third-back game, but not much was seen of Bradshaw.

An overhead kick by Brain surprised Riley, but the ball passed narrowly outside. The Second Division side were quicker on the ball than their more famous opponents. A free-kick taken just outside the penalty area saw Carr lift the ball into the Swansea goalmouth. Moore rushed out, missed his punch, and Wright headed the ball into the net. It was a bad mistake by Moore.

The spectators from the Kop chanted for Hodgson. Wright forced his way through and the goalkeeper missed the ball, which went for a corner. Excitement reigned round the Swansea goal, with Moore so unsure, but nothing came from the kick. Carr was just a yard offside following a great piece of combination with Johnson. Three overhead kicks found Riley prepared, and then Brain had a splendid chance, but he shot rather weakly and the ball went outside. Carr was Liverpool's finest forward, and he got across some excellent centres. Liverpool's right wing was in poor form.

The whistle went for a foul on Howe, but the centre-forward carried on and the referee pulled him up and spoke to him. The free-kick was taken by Bradshaw, who lifted the ball high into the Swansea goalmouth, where Moore caught it before being heavily charged. Swansea's best scoring effort

came when Brain shot powerfully, but Riley was equal to the effort. Lewis dropped a centre on top of the Liverpool net. Then followed a clever move by Johnson, who put Nieuwenhuys in possession, and from the winger's centre Carr shot, but he was wide of the target. Riley saved as Pears drove in from a corner. The game had not produced the real Cup-tie excitement expected, but there was some hard, keen play from both sides. Liverpool appeared to be leaving too much space in midfield through their third back play. It meant that the forwards were not getting the support of their half-backs, which they needed in a game such as this. Howe tried frequently but he could not connect with the ball.

The second half opened with a beautiful shot by Brain which Riley tipped over the bar for a corner. Both sides appeared to be putting more steel into their game, and Nieuwenhuys got a corner when Howe centred from the goal-line, the ball going off one of the Swansea defenders. Moore was still unsafe, and he displayed over-anxiousness when he ran out a long way and lost the ball. Fortunately for him nothing came from his blunder. Swansea kept the play down Liverpool's flanks which created some consternation for the home side. Lewis and Brain were the best Swansea forwards and were responsible for the Swansea attacks. Milne, the Swansea left-back, was a stalwart in defence. Carr was injured in a tackle as he tried to back-heel the ball, and he was taken to the touchline to receive attention.

The match offered a contrast in the styles of play; Swansea kept the ball on the wings, while Liverpool favoured going down the middle. Firth sent in a screaming shot which Riley saved just as Carr returned to the field. Swansea fought desperately for an equaliser, and the Liverpool forwards were harassed due to the failure of their half-backs to back up. A corner to Liverpool brought great excitement, but Moore caught the ball cleanly with both hands, and made an excellent clearance. Little had been seen of Bradshaw because he was playing behind his full-back on occasions and the Liverpool attack did not get their usual support. The Welsh side continued to work hard and they maintained a degree of superiority. Lewis centred, and Pears headed into the Liverpool goal, but Riley took the ball with both hands.

During the last quarter of an hour, Swansea played their best football of the season with their open style of play. Lloyd, the left-back, was a promising young player. Liverpool were continually foiled by the offside tactics of their opponents.

With the minutes ticking away, Brain and Lewis again forced their way through, but Brain finished the move by sending the ball wide of the posts. The best shot of the day came from Johnson - a real McKinlay type effort - which Moore saved well. Wright headed and then shot into the hands of Moore. Swansea continued to attack desperately, and

Vic Wright, who headed the goal against Swansea after just seventeen minutes

it was only their lack of steadiness in front of goal, coupled with the superb defence of Cooper and Riley, which prevented a deserved equaliser. In the closing minutes Johnson's shot struck the foot of an upright. Riley did well to tip the ball over the bar for a corner as Brain dashed in to convert a centre from Frith.

Everton lost 1-3 at home to a Preston North End side which included Bill Shankly at right-half. Sheffield Wednesday, the Cup-holders, drew 1-1 at Crewe before winning the replay 3-1. Arsenal, who went on to win the Cup this season, were a goal down to Bristol Rovers at the interval, but won 5-1 after a superb second-half display. Sheffield United, who lost the Final 0-1, drew 0-0 with Burnley, before winning the replay 2-1.

Liverpool: Riley; Cooper, Dabbs; Savage, Bradshaw, McDougall; Nieuwenhuys, Wright, Howe, Johnson, Carr.

Swansea Town: Moore; Lawrence, Milne; Warner, Hanford, Lloyd; I.Lewis, Firth, Brain, Olsen, Pears.

Referee: Mr E. Pinkston (Birmingham)

Attendance: 33,494

Receipts: £1,800

HALF TIME	CUP-LINES		FULL TIME
Sunderland	0	Port Vale	1
Bristol Rovers	1	Arsenal	0
Blackpool	0	Margate	1
Bradford	0	Workington	2
Sunderland	2	Port Vale	2
Bristol Rovers	1	Arsenal	5
Blackpool	3	Margate	1
Bradford	3	Workington	2

DIVISION 3 (NORTH)

Accrington	2	Halifax Town	0
Chesterfield	5	Rotherham United	0
New Brighton	1	Mansfield Town	0
Chester	4	Gateshead	0
York City	2	Carlisle United	0
Southport	1	Oldham Athletic	1

January 25, 1936

Liverpool (0) 0

Arsenal (1) 2
Bowden, Hulme 75

THE Arsenal played James and Bowden in the forward line, and Hulme and Bastin on the wing. After a week of winter and ice came a rather foggy atmosphere, although the turf was in good condition. The increased admission prices meant that the gate receipts were expected to be above £4,000.

The gates were closed twenty-five minutes before the kick-off, and when all was set, an impressive ceremony of homage and silence was paid to the late King, George V. A verse of "*Abide With Me*" and a silence which could be felt were the arrangements which heralded the tie. The Liverpool manager was not present; he was in the Sunderland area concerning himself with the possible signing of Patsy Gallacher. As the teams came out *en bloc* Hapgood stumbled on the top step of the subway. The impressiveness of the singing of the National Anthem after the silence was reminiscent of Wembley scenes at which the late King was so regularly a spectator.

Liverpool won the toss, and Tom Cooper chose to kick towards the Spion Kop end, and, possibly because of the inspiration of the Kopites, Eddie Hapgood began by giving himself the "dummy" when bothered by Nieuwenhuys. The game opened with a great ferocity of purpose and organised endeavour. When Carr forced a corner-kick, Tom Johnson - revived for the purposes of Cup-ties - made a telling header from the left side of the goal, the ball escaping the vigilance of Moss, but passing out slightly beyond the upright.

Nivvy played as he had played in the opening phases of the first game of the season against Chelsea. He was in sparkling form, sprightly and sweeping in his measures, but when he was beaten Copping and Bastin began to use the ball with excellent discretion, and it went out to Bowden, whose shot was punched away by Riley.

Arsenal, with their red hoops, looked just as strange as Liverpool, but the art of James stood out as he dribbled his way through the opposing defence before passing to Drake. The crack centre-forward was superbly marshalled by Bradshaw, who never left the Arsenal man's side. Johnson went over to the right and combined well with Savage and Wright to unsettle the rather nervous Arsenal defence. Hulme sailed through when the faithful Dabbs closed him out.

Then James revived memories of old with his use of the body swerve and the control which he exercised over the middle of the field. The crowd stared in astonishment at the pace produced by James over five yards, but the most important feature in the creation of the opening goal was the way in which James opened out the Liverpool defence, which expected a pass from the unselfish James, but a shot came instead.

The ball was never thoroughly cleared from the Anfield goal area, and Bowden received the ball before cracking a low shot into the back of the net. He fell in the process of scoring, but upon rising he received the congratulations of his team-mates. The Arsenal manager, Mr George Allinson, had not named James and Bowden in his team until the last possible moment.

Hulme almost added a second goal with a shot which went close. Sidey, who had played only three first-team games this season, and all against Liverpool, began to stretch his neck like a stork over the top of Freddie Howe's head. The Liverpool forwards had not played as well as this for more than six weeks; they were a revelation, but there was doubt as to whether they would be able to maintain their confident tone and resolve.

Some idea of Drake's unquenchable endeavour for his club was in evidence when the centre-forward was found on the right wing one moment and the next second was found challenging Cooper on the half-way line on Drake's left flank. McDougall saved a certain goal by falling in the way of Drake. Eventually Moss had a save to make when he handled a fiery centre from Carr. Bastin, who moved to the inside-right position on a run, forced Riley to tip over the bar. The Arsenal were able to change positions at will, and this naturally disturbed the Liverpool defence. One result of this was a most spectacular back-heel shot by James, which Dabbs saved for his goalkeeper. Liverpool began to show signs of fatigue and low morale, and Bowden dribbled through with ease. Riley saved at the foot of a post from Hulme. Cooper was in excellent form as the Arsenal swept all before them. Tom Johnson tried to revive Liverpool's hopes by making his way to the outside-right berth, and Savage did the same. Moss had to punch away the centre from the right-half and watch with keenness the long lob by McDougall. Bastin, in front of the directors' box, showed the beauty of the dribble on a sixpenny piece. A small plank of wood was thrown on to the field by someone on the Kop, and the referee held up play until the police had advanced to the affected spot. Wright shot outside, and Arsenal once more proved themselves to be the best team of headers in any division. The best save of the first period came when Riley leapt high and caught Drake's fierce shot.

In the opening seconds of the second half, Drake came near to heading a second goal, but Riley anticipated well. A slight fog hung over the ground throughout the game, but the possibility of an abandonment was not great. Joe Hulme, despite his veteran status, ran nearly as fast as ever, and one individual run and dribble enabled Bastin to have the chance of a lifetime, but to the winger's horror, he shot well to the left of the goal. Bradshaw dashed forward and tried to force the issue, but he was injured in the process. The first free-kick of the half was awarded to Arsenal against Dabbs. The visitors did not use it in their normal manner, and Bastin, swinging his way in and out of his rivals, gave an opportunity to Bowden, whose shot passed over the bar. Sidey, the only member of the Arsenal team without an international cap, had played his part manfully. Liverpool's defence was under constant severe pressure, and the only relief arrived when Cooper was attended to by the trainer. Cooper went to outside-right because of his damaged thigh, Savage going to right-back, and Vic Wright took up the right-half berth. Howe, becoming desperate for an opportunity, moved to his favourite flank on the left, and sent in a fierce shot which was kicked away by Male. Liverpool were briefly revived by Johnson who came close to scoring after a poor back pass by the Arsenal defence. The good turf became a morass of mud and water. Nieuwenhuys wandered to outside-left and saw his captain force a corner from the right wing. Moss saved. Liverpool's determined effort was not matched by their football craft or shooting ability, but the crowd urged them on.

Fifteen minutes from the finish, Bowden, on the extreme left, sent in a beautiful length centre and Hulme, closing in, caught the ball on the half-volley and smashed home the winner.

Sheffield United drew 0-0 with Preston, but won the replay 2-0 at Bramall Lane. The highest score of the Fourth Round was Leicester City's 6-3 home win over Watford. One of the ties - Leeds United versus Bury - was abandoned after 75 minutes with Leeds 2-1 ahead. Three ties were postponed, whereas in Scotland fifteen ties were postponed due to the poor weather.

Liverpool: Riley; Cooper, Dabbs; Savage, Bradshaw, McDougall; Nieuwenhuys, Wright, Howe, Johnson, Carr.

Arsenal: Moss; Male, Hapgood; Crayston, Sidey, Copping; Hulme, Bowden, Drake, James, Bastin.

Referee: Mr C.E. Lines (Birmingham)

Attendance: 53,720

Receipts: £4,157

PROCLAMATION SCENE

~~~~~~~~

CROWD BREAK RAILINGS; FIVE INJURED

~~~~~~~~

Screams and shouts from hundreds of people interrupted a prayer by the Bishop of Bristol during the proclamation ceremony there to-day.

Railings skirting a church gave way, owing to the press of the crowd, and two men, two women, and a girl were pushed over the edge of the churchyard wall and fell twenty feet.

They were taken to hospital suffering from head injuries and shock.

FOOTBALL'S PATRON

As a mark of respect for the late Sovereign, King George V., football crowds all over the country to-day observed a period of silence before the matches began, with the teams lined up in the centre of the field.

ROUND REGENT'S PARK

~~~~~~~~

BLIND MAN WINS WALKING RACE

~~~~~~~~

Mr T. ap Rhys, Bangor, won the nine-mile walking race round Regent's Park, London, in the record time for this race (which is organised by St. Dunstan's) of 85 minutes and 18 seconds. He also won the first prize in the handicap.

Mr ap Rhys, who was blinded in the war, was formerly Labour candidate for the Caernavon Boroughs.

January 16, 1937

Norwich City (2) 3   # Liverpool (0) 0
Vinall 1, 6,
Scott

NORWICH set out to conquer a foe they last beat 26 years ago at Anfield. The Second Division side achieved their ambition with ease. Vinall scored against Liverpool in less than a minute. Five minutes later Vinall scored again and the game was all but over. On this occasion Vinall beat three men without assistance and on the right flank he drove in a high ball which appeared to be floating high over the left-hand corner of the goal. It curled into the far corner of the net, giving Hobson no chance of saving. Some criticised Hobson for the goal, but his out-stretched right hand was never going to stop such a shot.

The contrast between the two sides was remarkable. Norwich, without undue flurry, and with great endeavour, went into their work with the knowledge that Liverpool could be stampeded if they applied constant pressure by means of the instant pass, and the raid made up of practical means. Not for them the holding of the ball, not for them the personal outrageous long run; not for them a delay of any sort. They got into the business side of the game instantly, they were determined to win the game and they therefore adopted a professional approach which enabled them to do just that. Liverpool continued to play in their colourful manner; their flicks and taps were of the daintiest character; when the ball could be passed onward to make ground the ball was held a split second too long; the shooting was weak; there was a lack of spirit, but the losers could learn a great deal from this defeat if they were prepared to learn. Earlier in the season, the same players had been heralded as internationals, and the youngest and best forward line the club has ever had. It was proven to be an unfounded exaggeration. On dry ground the forward line would still look good. In this game, on a slightly heavy turf, Eastham and the improved Nieuwenhuys did some really good work for long spells, but the other forwards were inept. Matt Busby was the one man who did something to suggest First Division standards. His urging of the right wing pair was of fine character, a model of priceless half-back arts - the use of the ball, the control and collection of the ball; the upward tendency to force a poor line of attackers to have some belief in themselves. It was of little use; the team was poor, and even Captain Cooper had a bad game.

Hobson blundered with the third goal, a simple headed goal from Scott, the most rugged man on the field, landing at the goalkeeper's feet and even a fingered attempt to pick up the ball failed, and Hobson saw the ball pass on with snail-like pace over the line.

Although the goalkeeper was definitely at fault, the error did not cost Liverpool the game. A general inability to score had done that. Nieuwenhuys, Eastham and Busby kept finding holes in the Norwich defence, but Bowen, the former Villa back, was not a young man but he has his manager's aptitude

for standing firm. As long as he stood firm Norwich held up. In three minutes there was sufficient work on the right flank to show the ease with which Bowen could be beaten, and also his half-back, Burke, a boy who used to play for Liverpool 'A' team. Norwich were worthy of their victory.

The eventual Cup-winners, Sunderland, beat Southampton 3-2 at the Dell, while runners-up Preston North End - Bill Shankly and all - beat Newcastle United 2-0 at home. The Cup-holders, Arsenal, beat Chesterfield 5-1 away. Everton defeated Bournemouth 5-0 at Goodison Park.

Norwich City: Hall; Halliday, Bowen; Burke, Scott, Proctor; O'Reilly, Manders, Vinall, Burley, Madden.

Liverpool: Hobson; Cooper, Harley; Busby, Savage, McDougall; Nieuwenhuys, Eastham, Howe, Balmer, Hanson.

Referee: Mr A.J. Jewell (London)

Attendance: 26,800

Receipts: £1,769

E. Vinall, scorer of two goals in the first six minutes

January 8, 1938

Crystal Palace (0) 0   Liverpool (0) 0

THE Liverpool players were taken to Shirley Hall in mid-Surrey during the morning to take the air and create an innovation, and when they arrived at the ground they were met by several excursionists who had left Lime Street at 7.30 on the morning of the match. Among those who welcomed the visiting party was Tom Bromilow and his wife; Dick Edmed, the former Liverpool player, now in business at Gillingham, and many others with a Liverpool angle to their name. London's six other Cup-ties helped to keep a really big crowd from the natural amphitheatre at the ground, but it was easy to see that with very little change Selhurst could be converted into another Wembley. This was Shafto's first visit to town, and for others in the Liverpool side - Rogers and Fagan - it was the start of their first big Cup campaign. Dawes, one of the Crystal Palace players, could not appear due to injury, and he was carried into a stand seat to watch the game. Palace were more than dispirited over the absence of two of their regulars, Owen and Dawes, full-backs who had made the side earlier in the season. It was a splendid day for football, and the pitch was in perfect condition. Palace started with great vigour, and Pritchard curled in a dangerous centre before being given offside. Liverpool struggled to get down to their work in the opening five minutes, so busy were the Palace forwards. Liverpool's first real opportunity came when a high ball down the centre led to a defensive miskick, Shafto nodding the ball over to Hanson, whose shot was so well placed that it caused Chesters difficulty. In the next minute, Riley missed his attempted punch away and Pritchard hooked the ball back into the goalmouth, but without any great danger to the visitors. Shafto put a shot over the bar. Nieuwenhuys, with a characteristic run, evaded a tackle and swung the ball over at the last second, travelling at full speed, but Hanson failed to connect with the ball.

Rogers tackled severely and surely, and saved his side on several occasions. Nieuwenhuys was put through by Shafto in an effort to use the South African's great speed, but he deliberated over his shot and Chesters saved well. Riley was the busier of the two keepers, and he had to withstand some severe charges when he ventured from his goal to make his pickups. Palace continued to dominate the game, mainly through the use of both wingers, who caused Liverpool a great deal of trouble. Hanson was kept quiet by the quick tackling of Lievesley, and in addition to lacking his usual fire, Hanson had several centres blocked. A foul given against Rogers caused him to be booed by the crowd, and the free-kick nearly led to the demise of Riley, who lost the ball in a ruck and had to rely upon Busby for a hook-away to safety. Shafto centred the ball from the outside-right position and Chesters made a good save at the angle of post and crossbar. Taylor missed the best chance of the match when

Chesters punched away Nieuwenhuys's corner kick and a point-blank opportunity was offered, but Taylor's shot went yards wide.

Taylor almost burst through in the first minute of the second half, but at the critical moment he lost his feet and the chance. Lievesley, the half-back, uprooted Hanson in the penalty area but there was no response from the referee. Hanson was fouled in the next minute, and Nieuwenhuys headed the ball inside to Fagan from the free-kick, but Fagan slipped up and Palace were relieved. The home side were desperate defenders and they never allowed the opposition a moment's rest when they were in possession of the ball. They played ferociously and their tenacious policy unsettled Liverpool. Hanson maintained his enthusiasm in spite of several stern challenges, and when he put the ball across squarely Collins could only put the ball over his own bar. From the corner Bush stole up to deliver a surprise shot which almost found the mark. Liverpool looked attractive when they punched the ball about, though they were still inclined to dwell too long on the ball before releasing it.

Liverpool looked a beaten side when Horton fired in a ball that was blocked out within inches of the goal-line by Rogers,

Fred Rogers

but it was not until the ball had come out and Horton had returned a shot which skimmed the crossbar that the danger was over. Palace overwhelmed the visitors in the closing minutes and Riley made a full-length save from Waldron as the home side sought outright victory.

The replay was scheduled for Anfield on the following Wednesday at 2.15. Ordinary League prices would apply. Numbered and reserved seats in the grandstand and Kemlyn Road stand were to go on sale at the club offices.

Undoubtedly the tie of the round was Bradford's 7-4 victory over Newport County. The Cup-holders, Sunderland, beat Watford 1-0 at Roker Park, while this season's winners, Preston North End, beat West Ham United 3-0 at Deepdale. The runners-up, Huddersfield, beat Hull City 3-1 at home. Everton beat Chelsea 1-0 at Stamford Bridge.

Crystal Palace: Chesters; Turton, Booth; Lievesley, Walker, Collins; Pritchard, Gillespie, Palethorpe, Waldron, Horton.

Liverpool: Riley; Cooper, Harley; Busby, Rogers, Bush; Nieuwenhuys, Taylor, Shafto, Fagan, Hanson.

Referee: Mr S. Hedley (Leicestershire)

Attendance: 33,000

EVERTON IN
FOURTH ROUND

~~~~~

Stevenson's Point
Decides

~~~~~

SHOUT MEANT A SCORE

~~~~~

The score does not tell of Everton's superiority. The score should have been 3-1. Chelsea's attack fell down to Everton's quick tackling defence.

Chelsea: Woodley; Barkas, Barber; Allum, Griffiths, Weaver; Buchanan, Gregg, Mills, Burgess, Chitty.
Everton: Morton; Cook, J.F.Jones; Britton, T.G.Jones, Mercer; Geldard, Cunliffe, Lawton, Stevenson, Gillick.
Referee: Mr E. Woods (Sheffield)
Attendance: 41,946
Receipts: £2,689

Everton had the escape of their lives with 30 minutes gone. J.Jones had headed away from Chitty, and with Morton out of goal, Gregg took a shot which was labelled goal until Britton dropped from the clouds and kicked off the line.

STEVENSON DOES IT

Almost immediately afterwards Everton attacked with great determination and Geldard supplied a centre which provided a goal after 43 minutes. It appeared that the chance was going to be lost, but **STEVENSON** shouted. Lawton left it to him and from Stevenson's header the ball flew into the net well wide of Woodley.

Half-time: Chelsea 0, Everton 1
Full-time: Chelsea 0, Everton 1

F.A. CUP - THIRD ROUND

Aldershot Town	1	Notts County	3
Arsenal	3	Bolton Wanderers	1
Birmingham	0	Blackpool	1
Bradford	7	Newport County	4
Bradford City	1	Chesterfield	1
Brentford	3	Fulham	1
Bury	2	Brighton & Hove A.	0
Charlton Athletic	5	Cardiff City	0
Chelsea	0	Everton	1
Derby County	1	Stoke City	2
Doncaster Rovers	0	Sheffield United	2
Grimsby Town	1	Swindon Town	1
Huddersfield Town	3	Hull City	1
Leeds United	3	Chester	1
Manchester U.	3	Yeovil & Petters	0
Mansfield Town	1	Leicester City	2
Middlesbrough	2	Stockport County	0
Millwall	2	Manchester City	2
New Brighton	1	Plymouth Argyle	0
Nottingham Forest	3	Southampton	1
Norwich City	2	Aston Villa	3
Preston North End	3	West Ham United	0
Scarborough	1	Luton Town	1
Sheffield Wed.	1	Burnley	1
Southend United	2	Barnsley	2
Sunderland	1	Watford	0
Swansea Town	0	Wolverhampton W.	4
Tottenham Hotspur	3	Blackburn Rovers	2
Tranmere Rovers	1	Portsmouth	2
West Bromwich A.	1	Newcastle United	0
York City	3	Coventry City	2

Replays

Chesterfield	1	Bradford City	1
Swindon Town	2	Grimsby Town	1
Manchester City	3	Millwall	1
Luton Town	5	Scarborough	1

Second Replay

Bradford City	0	Chesterfield	2

(at Bramall Lane, Sheffield)

January 12, 1938

Liverpool (0) 3

Shafto, Collins (o.g.),
Fagan 115 (pen)

Crystal Palace (0) 1 aet

Waldron 53

LIVERPOOL'S first real attack began with a beautifully-judged pass from Fagan to Hanson, who got the ball across in spite of apparently taking it too far towards the line. The centre was close to the goalmouth, and Chesters pulled the ball down confidently. Immediately afterwards the referee waved Palethorpe on when there was a doubt of his being offside, and the centre-forward went clean through but his shot veered to the right side of the post.

Liverpool responded through Hanson, who burst through and won a corner off Walker. Hanson's flag kick was within inches of being converted into a goal. Both sides showed signs of nerves, and Palace looked dangerous when on the attack, but their finishing was as poor as in the first game. Shafto burst down the right and closed in on goal but lifted the ball over the bar.

Turton made two mistakes after 29 minutes. He let in Hanson, and then handled Hanson's centre. The referee immediately awarded a penalty. Hanson took the spot kick and pulled the ball wide, to the dismay of the crowd.

Hanson tried to atone for his error with a header from a Taylor centre, but got under the ball too much. The London side continued to threaten, and only an offence by Palethorpe as he and Riley went up for the ball relieved the pressure after Pritchard's centre. Shafto flicked the ball to Fagan, and a defender, in attempting to clear, banged the ball against Fagan's body so hard that it rebounded to Chesters, who magnificently saved the unexpected ball.

A long-range effort from Waldron was easily dealt with by Riley, and then Chesters again tipped the ball over the bar with Shafto charging in to try and connect with Walker's mis-header. Liverpool then enjoyed a piece of good fortune. Horton centred and Riley was forced to scoop the ball out. With the goalkeeper lying on the ground and the goal open, Gillespie shot against Rogers when his back was turned, and the centre-half knew little about his save.

Liverpool were still inclined to hold the ball, while Palace harassed the man in possession. The home side gave away too many free-kicks for their own safety, and when Bush conceded one, Walker lobbed the ball into the goal area where Rogers, attempting to head it away, found it travel on towards goal. Waldron nodded the ball over the head of the advancing Riley. If Rogers had not played Waldron on, the goal would not have counted.

Liverpool lacked urgency, but a pre-arranged plan which saw Nieuwenhuys move inside and Shafto go to outside-right brought immediate results. Bush became a forward and swung the ball over, Shafto scoring the equaliser with a header. Palace appealed that the ball had been handled. Liverpool almost made it two when Shafto slashed the ball wide after Busby had a shot blocked.

Both sides seemed to be feeling the stress of the pace and the nervous tension, and the Palace defence, which had begun so well, began to show signs of wilting. Chesters saved on the line from a downward header by Fagan. The Palace goalkeeper then made an even better save from Shafto, who was clean through and shot from an oblique angle. As the game approached its conclusion, Palace found a new source of inspiration, and they were on the ball quickly, and never stopped trying. With the score at 1-1, the game moved into extra time.

It was unusual that before the start of the extra time the referee and the captains "shook on it" again. The light was none too good, and although the lemons came on to the field, there was not time for the usual refresher.

Liverpool kicked the same way as they had been kicking during the second half, and the first incident of note was the referee over-ruling a linesman's decision of a corner in Liverpool's favour. Hanson, who had taken a knock on the face which seemed to have unsettled him, was not playing at his best, and he received some attention from the trainer. Although it was a simple sort of injury, it proved to be an unusually lengthy stoppage.

When Fagan had a shot blocked, Shafto closed in and centred. Collins, in attempting to kick away, only succeeded in deflecting the ball past his own goalkeeper. Before Liverpool had a chance to congratulate Shafto for his part in the goal, Hanson collapsed with his shoulder injury when no-one was standing nearby, and he had to be assisted off the field.

There was some danger of the match being abandoned because of the poor light. Hanson resumed, and this quelled Palace's endeavour as they sought to gain an advantage with the player off the field. Then Shafto was injured, and he had to leave the field. Rogers conceded a corner and Palethorpe almost scored with a good left-foot volley from the corner-kick.

Shafto returned for the second half of extra-time. Then Walker went down after Nieuwenhuys caught his knee. Cooper became an outside-right and Taylor dropped back to right full-back, and Shafto went to inside-right. With five minutes remaining, Nieuwenhuys was uprooted in the penalty area, and Fagan scored.

Liverpool

Riley

Cooper   Harley

Busby   Rogers   Bush

Nieuwenhuys   Taylor   Shafto   Fagan   Hanson

John Shafto

Horton   Waldron   Palethorpe   Gillespie   Pritchard

Collins   Walker   Lievesley

Booth   Turton

Chesters

Crystal Palace

Referee: Mr T. Smith (Birmingham)   **Attendance**: 35,919   **Receipts**: £2,180

January 22, 1938

Sheffield United (0) 1
Dodds 84

Liverpool (1) 1
Hanson 15

LIVERPOOL'S hopes depended largely on Harley at Sheffield. He had been suffering from bronchitis all through the week and right up to within an hour of the kick-off, he was not sure whether he would play. He was tried out, with Manager George Kay donning togs again, at the Wednesday ground, but it was not until the club held an official board meeting with the player consulted at the hotel that it was decided to go through with the risk. There were well over 40,000 spectators five minutes before the game began. The pitch was sanded in parts and was very heavy.

Sheffield United: Smith; Hooper, Cox; Jackson, Johnson, Jessop; Barton, Richardson, Dodds, Pickering, Leyfield.

Liverpool: Riley; Cooper, Harley; Busby, Rogers, Bush; Nieuwenhuys, Taylor, Shafto, Fagan, Hanson.

Referee: Flight-Sergeant S. McKenzie (R.A.F.)

Attendance: 50,264

Richardson should definitely have scored when Pickering put him clean through, but instead of getting the ball down, Richardson headed in very weakly, and Riley was able to make a catch. In the same minute, Pickering nodded a free-kick on to the bar, and Harley collected the rebound and nodded away. Liverpool then had two men injured. Rogers got a smack on the nose which bled profusely, and then when Pickering got clean through, Riley made a good pushaway and followed with a one-handed punch away from the corner. After this, Riley was hurt, and while he received attention from Charlie Wilson, Duggie Livingstone, the former Tranmere and Everton player, who currently trained Sheffield United, gave attention to Rogers, who had gone to the outside-left position. During this period of intense pressure, Sheffield United could have had the match won beyond all doubt, but their finishing was weak, and Dodds twice finished badly when Riley seemed almost certain to be beaten. United were excellent up to the edge of the box, where their courage seemed to desert them.

With 15 minutes gone, Liverpool scored with only their second shot of the game. Hanson slewed the ball across the face of the goal and took a return pass from Shafto and left Smith with little chance.

Fagan tried a shot on the run and Smith had to get down very quickly to save at the foot of the post. Rogers was still on the wing, and Fagan combined duties in the centre of the field. Cooper slipped the ball away from Pickering as he scrambled through, and Barton - the former Anfield player - drove in a great shot which Riley pushed away. Rogers had to go off, but he soon returned. He wanted to return to his centre-half position, but found that instructions from the field were to the effect that he should go outside-left. It was possible to hear Rogers shout to the touch-line: "I want to go back but they won't let me." Eventually, after he had gone back to centre-half, he was recalled to outside-left again.

Rogers and Shafto almost snatched a goal between them, but Rogers was not quite quick enough to get in his shot first in a race against the goalkeeper for a through-pass. Throughout the game, Bush had used his great height to good advantage at centre-half, with Fagan working extremely hard at left-half and linking up with the forwards whenever possible.

Liverpool continued to be put under a lot of pressure, but Riley, Cooper, and Harley were playing brilliantly, and when Pickering curled the ball in from a ready-made shooting chance, Riley made the save of the match with a full-length fling of his body. Busby applauded the effort spontaneously. Shafto went to outside-right in a good movement which ended with him centring too close to Smith.

The second half continued to be played with great passion and fierce commitment. Riley saved a Richardson header and a Barton shot in quick succession and he dealt with a great deal of work in a confident manner. The Liverpool attack was Busby, Nieuwenhuys, Shafto, Hanson and Rogers. Busby sustained a thigh injury which meant that he moved across to the right wing. Dodds was not playing with his usual deadliness and he put one shot over the bar. Bush continued to fight gallantly at centre-half. This was regarded as his best match for the club, and his most successful game so far as positioning and anticipation were concerned. He was the giant in more ways than one.

Although Liverpool were being overwhelmed, they did break through in one glorious movement which should have brought them a goal. Nieuwenhuys burst through and angled a pass for Hanson, whose instant shot swung wide of the mark at a tremendous pace. Bush then chased back to a shot by Dodds, and just as the ball was about to cross the line, Bush hooked it away to safety. There was a tremendous outcry that it was a goal, but the referee was adamant that the ball had not crossed the line.

Barton and Leyfield changed positions, and then the home side lay siege to the Liverpool goal. Hanson kicked away desperately; Taylor headed over his own bar; Richardson shot inches wide. Then Riley lost the ball, but did not concede a goal. Six minutes from the end Dodds took a loose ball and, closing in, evaded Cooper and slipped the ball past Riley. The crowd went frantic, and Sheffield United increased the pressure as Barton skimmed the bar with a splendid hook-shot in the closing minutes. The replay was scheduled for the following Wednesday at 2.15.

Tom Bush

DIVISION THREE (NORTH)

Barrow	2	Oldham Athletic	1
Crewe Alexandra	2	Darlington	2
Halifax Town	0	Carlisle United	0
Lincoln City	2	Hull City	1
Bradford City	3	Rotherham United	2
Port Vale	1	Doncaster Rovers	1
Southport	2	Rochdale	0
Tranmere Rovers	5	Accrington Stanley	0
Wrexham	0	Gateshead	0

DIVISION THREE (NORTH) top fourteen

	Pl	W	L	D	F	A	Pts
Tranmere Rovers	24	14	6	4	48	21	32
Hull City	24	13	5	6	54	25	32
Gateshead	23	13	4	6	49	30	32
Rotherham United	25	14	7	4	49	37	32
Oldham Athletic	23	10	3	10	39	23	30
Doncaster Rovers	23	12	5	6	42	27	30
Carlisle United	24	12	8	4	41	35	28
Lincoln City	22	11	6	5	41	20	27
Chester City	23	8	6	9	44	37	25
Rochdale	25	10	10	5	41	43	25
Port Vale	25	8	9	8	39	44	24
Wrexham	24	9	9	6	33	43	24
York City	22	9	8	5	40	40	23
Halifax Town	23	7	9	7	28	35	21

F.A. CUP   4th ROUND

Aston Villa	4	Blackpool	0
Barnsley	2	Manchester United	2
Bradford	1	Stoke City	1
Brentford	2	Portsmouth	1
Charlton Athletic	2	Leeds United	1
Chesterfield	3	Burnley	2
Everton	0	Sunderland	1
Huddersfield Town	1	Notts County	0
Luton Town	2	Swindon Town	1
Manchester City	3	Bury	1
New Brighton	0	Tottenham Hotspur	0
Nottingham Forest	1	Middlesbrough	3
Preston North End	2	Leicester City	0
Wolverhampton W.	1	Arsenal	2
York City	3	West Bromwich A.	2

Replays

Manchester United	1	Barnsley	0
Stoke City	1	Bradford	2
Tottenham Hotspur	5	New Brighton	2

DIVISION ONE

Bolton Wanderers	0	Derby County	2
Birmingham	1	Chelsea	1

DIVISION TWO

Fulham	8	Swansea Town	1
Coventry City	2	Southampton	0
Sheffield Wednesday	1	Norwich City	0
West Ham United	1	Stockport County	0

DIVISION THREE (SOUTH)

Aldershot Town	5	Newport County	0
Bournemouth	0	Brighton & Hove A.	0
Reading	3	Crystal Palace	2
Cardiff City	2	Queen's Park Rangers	2
Northampton Town	2	Clapton Orient	0
Walsall	1	Southend United	5
Bristol Rovers	2	Torquay United	0
Exeter City	1	Watford	2
Gillingham	0	Mansfield Town	0

January 26, 1938

Liverpool (0) 1
Johnson (o.g.) 53

Sheffield United (0) 0

LIVERPOOL had to play an almost purely defensive game after the first five minutes of a particularly stormy match, in which Eastham had a knee broken and other players were injured. At one stage both sides were two men short. Eastham's knee had been reset, and he left the hospital for his home on the day of the match.

The first incident was when the referee spoke to Nieuwenhuys after he had argued the point for a Liverpool throw-in when the linesman had other ideas. Hanson cleverly kept the ball in play as Liverpool attacked, and Howe chased up his lob to force a corner against Johnson, but the kick was unproductive. Dodds and Barton interchanged positions and the centre-forward curled in a centre which swerved and became a shot for Riley. Liverpool responded through "Nivvy", who came from his wing right across the field and tenaciously held the ball before making a left-foot centre from which Hanson shot rather hurriedly, and the ball went wide. Ramsden - making his Cup début for Liverpool - displayed plenty of spirit at left-half and from one of his clearances Howe went on from an offside position to put the ball in the net.

The game was fought at a tremendous pace, with no quarter given, and Jessop's throw of Eastham caused a furore, with all the players congregated in one place and arguing furiously. Eastham had to leave the field. He was attended to by both ambulance men and trainer Charlie Wilson. The injury was diagnosed as being a dislocated knee and he was transferred to hospital. A Sheffield United defender's long punt from the half-way line was well caught by Riley, who had to side-step quickly to evade the charge of Dodds. Pickering's swerving shot went inches wide of the post. Cooper and Dodds came into heavy collision, and both trainers were called on. Both players were taken off with eye injuries. Ramsden went to right-back and Fagan became a half-back as a result of Liverpool's re-shuffling.

Leyfield stood alongside Ramsden, who was unaware that the Sheffield man was near, and in trying to turn round with the ball, Ramsden let in Leyfield, whose shot trickled towards the goal before passing the post. There was another stoppage when Jackson was knocked out by the ball, and when he went off the field it meant that both sides were down to nine men. The referee had policemen patrolling the front of the Spion Kop where there was a barrage of fruit being thrown.

Cooper went to outside-right with Nieuwenhuys as his partner. Dodds played brilliantly and Liverpool struggled to keep him from scoring. Just on half-time Barton put in a good centre for which Riley came out a couple of yards to make a confident catch.

The second half had not been going more than three or four minutes when Riley allowed Barton's cross to pass into the net. The referee decided that Riley had been impeded as he went to collect the ball. Liverpool took the lead after eight minutes of the second half through the mistake of a defender. Hanson took the ball when Hooper misjudged its flight, and centred, and Johnson inexplicably turned the ball into his own net. Ramsden put in a timely intervention when Dodds burst through in an effort to equalise. When Howe and Johnson both chased through in a challenge for possession, there was the possibility of Johnson scoring a second own goal, but he was spared that indignity. United almost equalised when full-back Hooper drove the ball in and a slight deflection upwards caused the ball to swing just over the bar.

Hanson missed an easy opportunity with a left-foot shot that curled outside after he had sped through to a perfect scoring position six yards from goal. Liverpool had to withstand some intense pressure. While Cooper had plaster administered to his head, Barton and Leyfield switched over on their wings as they had done at Sheffield. Leyfield sent in a curling shot which Riley tipped over the bar. Howe twice went near scoring. Dodds hit Riley almost from point-blank range with a minute to go, and Hooper shot wide by inches as the final whistle sounded.

Liverpool: Riley; Cooper, Harley; Taylor, Bush, Ramsden; Nieuwenhuys, Eastham, Howe, Fagan, Hanson.

Sheffield United: Smith; Hooper, Cox; Jackson, Johnson, Jessop; Barton, Richardson, Dodds, Pickering, Leyfield.

Referee: Flight-Sergeant S. McKenzie (R.A.F.)

Attendance: 48,297

Receipts: £3,260 (approximate)

THE HUDDERSFIELD TIE

No personal applications will be considered for tickets for the Huddersfield match. The centre portion of the two main stands will be priced 5s, and the end portions 3s 6d. Tickets will be issued on Monday, and applicants should enclose stamped addressed envelopes and remittance.

February 12, 1938

Liverpool (0) 0

Huddersfield Town (0) 1

Barclay 69

THE current League table (bottom six):

	Pl	W	L	D	F	A	Pts
Grimsby Town	28	6	10	12	33	43	24
Huddersfield Town	**27**	**10**	**13**	**4**	**32**	**43**	**24**
Birmingham	27	5	9	13	32	37	23
Liverpool	**26**	**7**	**11**	**8**	**36**	**46**	**22**
Portsmouth	28	6	13	9	38	53	21
Blackpool	29	7	15	7	33	48	21

Some of the gates at Anfield were closed half an hour before the start, but five minutes before the kick-off the crowd was not nearly so large as when Tranmere were at Anfield four years ago. The weather was gloriously clear, but the gusty wind caused problems. While the back of the goal opposite Spion Kop was comparatively free from crowding, the corner underneath the scoreboard swayed badly, and so did another Kop corner. Again spectators had to be rolled down over the heads of other spectators, yet other parts of the ground were comparatively comfortable. Cooper won the toss against Willingham, and Liverpool played with the sun in their favour.

A Beasley dribble was full of promise until the referee gave a decision against him and in favour of Balmer. Liverpool hearts missed a beat when the ball was curled up for McFadyen, and with the wind holding it back, he was able to get his head to the ball. Riley smothered away the effort.

There was some extremely keen and quick tackling in the opening minutes, and Huddersfield played the better constructive football. The game was only a few minutes old when Hanson was off the field with an ankle injury sustained in a tackle near his line. The visitors remained persistent, and Bush and Harley were kept busy cutting out danger at the last moment. Hanson resumed while Huddersfield were attacking with force, and the Spion Kop was disgorging its quota of casualties.

Liverpool had an escape when Weinard found himself about 12 yards out and banged in a lovely shot which a Liverpool defender deflected over the bar. The wind prevented both sides from playing to their full potential. Balmer moved into the outside-right position and took the ball along the line before closing in and shooting into Hesford's hands. Liverpool survived another period of intense pressure when Cooper eventually headed the ball away after three shots had been blocked. Hanson left the field to have his injury properly attended to.

A strange sight appeared on the Kop when nine or ten holes big enough to accommodate twenty or thirty people each were seen. Apparently injured spectators lay on the ground in these places.

Hanson re-appeared, and took the throw-ins, while seemingly reluctant to be tackled which suggested that his injury still troubled him. McFadyen almost rounded Bush from Willingham's pass, and in the scrimmage for possession between Bush and McFadyen, Riley eventually had to go down to field the ball close to the post. McFadyen sportingly jumped over the goalkeeper in order to save injuring him. Nieuwenhuys went on a brilliant solo run in which he always had the ball under perfect control before finishing with a full-strength shot which soared high over the bar. Every time there was any excitement in front of the Kop goal, waves of spectators were pushed down the terraces, and one of the worst incidents came when McFadyen, profiting from a mistake by Bush, went on to drive the ball against the concrete surround.

Nieuwenhuys had his name taken when he questioned a decision, but Boots' strong free-kick met the usual wall of defenders. Liverpool's inside-forwards played indifferently, although Balmer's positioning was excellent, and he ran into the right place for many passes. Huddersfield's defence was rock-like.

Boot handled the ball to prevent Nieuwenhuys taking a pass early in the second period when it was apparent that Hanson was still little more than a passenger. Howe initiated an excellent move when he put the ball out to Nieuwenhuys. The South African made certain of his shot and drove the ball in fiercely, but Hesford pulled off a brilliant save. He also saved a moment later a deflected shot from Rogers. Nieuwenhuys and Cooper both received great roars from the crowd, "Nivvy" with a grand tackle against Beasley, and the full-back with some enlivening moments on the right wing.

Taylor - probably Liverpool's best player - initiated a move which ended with Balmer testing Hesford. The goalkeeper saved at the second attempt. Balmer forced a corner from Fagan's best move of the game, a through pass, and from this Hesford punched away one-handed a lovely header by Balmer. With 69 minutes gone, Huddersfield scored. Beasley began the move by going to inside-left and making a good pass to Weinard. The South African made a good length centre to the far post, where Cooper and McFadyen stood. Cooper was unable to get up to the ball first and McFadyen nodded it across to Barclay, who got little power to his shot which bounced before it crossed the line. Hanson left the field after the goal had been scored, because he had been unable to contribute much to the game. Weinard struck the side-netting as the visitors maintained their control of the game.

Liverpool were awarded a free-kick when Rogers was fouled on the angle of the penalty area. Fagan took the kick and Balmer headed in, but Hesford again got the ball. The visitors hung on to the final whistle.

Preston North End beat Arsenal 1-0 at Highbury with a goal from Dougal after 62 minutes before 72,121 spectators paying £7,214. Goals were relatively scarce in England in both the League and the Cup, but in Scotland Raith Rovers beat Edinburgh City 9-2 in the Second Round of the Cup, and Airdrie beat Brechin City 10-0 in the Second Division.

The Huddersfield side which represented them in the Cup Final was: Hesford; Craig, Mountford; Willingham, Young, Boot; Hulme, Isaac, McFadyen, Barclay, Beasley.

Liverpool: Riley; Cooper, Harley; Taylor, Bush, Rogers; Nieuwenhuys, Balmer, Howe, Fagan, Hanson.

Huddersfield Town: Hesford; Craig, Mountford; Willingham, Brown, Boot; Weinard, Barclay, McFadyen, Chivers, Beasley.

Referee: Mr H.T. Wright (Macclesfield)

Attendance: 57,682

Receipts: £4,107

Phil Taylor - probably Liverpool's best player - initiated a move which ended with Balmer testing Hesford.

January 7, 1939

Liverpool (0) 3
Balmer 54, 89,
Paterson 83

Luton Town (0) 0

THE match took place in spite of the threat of frost and fog which had gripped the country and led to the postponement of dozens of matches in England and Scotland. In Liverpool, however, the weather became mild and only the hard end of the pitch in front of the Spion Kop remained doubtful. Both sides were unchanged. Liverpool went direct to Anfield from Cleeleys. The directors of both clubs toasted the King at a pre-match function in which the loving cups presented by Sir Francis Joseph to Football League clubs were used for the first time. There were not more than 30,000 in the ground at the start, but outside the spectators were numerous.

Luton opened brightly, but it was Balmer's long pass to Nieuwenhuys which opened up the play, but "Nivvy" mis-timed his intended centre on the watery surface. The ground at Anfield had not been seen in such a poor condition for a long time.

Fagan looked promising in a characteristic run, but he slipped up at the vital moment. Paterson - playing in his first Cup-tie for Liverpool - chased after a useful Taylor pass, but the winger ended up in the piled snow. Billington headed towards Stephenson, but the ball went over the head of the outside-left who landed in the mud and snow. All four wingers had misjudged the ball in the early minutes. Billington crashed in a shot which Kemp dived full-length to turn round a post for a brilliant save. Redfern, the former Marine, shot a foot wide of the goal as Luton attacked.

Coen handed away a good corner from Paterson as the crowd increased to around 40,000. Stephenson showed an unexpected burst of speed against Harley and went on, confidently expecting to have left Harley behind, but by the time Stephenson had steadied himself, the Liverpool player had recovered and got his foot to the ball to turn it for a corner. Just before the interval, Balmer pulled the ball across the face of the goal, but no Liverpool player was in position to convert.

The second half began with a tremendous drive from Paterson which crashed against the foot of a post. Clark's shrewd pass to Billington brought a good shot from the one Luton player born in the visiting ranks, but Kemp had taken up a good position and took the ball to his body confidently and with good judgment.

Nieuwenhuys was injured in collision with Dunsmore and trainer Wilson was called on. Dunsmore pulled his shirt from inside his slacks and wiped the mud out of his eye. With Nieuwenhuys limping, Billington sent in a fourth dangerous shot and Kemp had to be at his best to push the ball away with a full-length dive and he grasped the ball at the second attempt. Balmer tackled five players on his own and still got

in his pass to Fagan, but a foul against the centre-forward brought snowballs from the Kop, issuing their protest against the Luton defence.

From the free-kick which followed, Liverpool scored. Nieuwenhuys dug up the kick, and despite the fact that Fagan went up in front of him, Balmer's head connected with the ball, which sped into the net.

But for the ball bouncing awkwardly, Billington would have scored a few moments later. This was undoubtedly Kemp's best game for Liverpool, because apart from his magnificent saves from Billington, he came out and bravely risked injury at vital moments. Bush played magnificently, too, his head getting in the way of numerous Luton attacks. The game was stopped for an injury to his hand. Balmer cleverly kept the ball in play with a back-heel which allowed Taylor to get in a shot and the goalkeeper, Coen, was forced to dive full-length to save.

Jack Balmer

Liverpool were now well on top, and the visitors rarely ventured out of their half. Nieuwenhuys continued to hobble, and Busby became an outside-right and curled in a left foot lob which Coen scooped round the post after diving late. Nieuwenhuys' lameness left him when Fagan put through a nice forward pass. The South African raced through and looked a likely scorer until he pulled his shot in the heavy mud. Kemp held a screw shot from Billington in a rare Luton attacking move.

Gradually the visitors became more dangerous and Liverpool lost their grip on the game which they had in the early part of the second half. Clark got down to within a foot of the ground to head a ball, but the passer of the ball was offside. Connelly tried a speculative shot which Kemp punched away two-handed.

Phil Taylor's approach work and his lofted centre, which passed over Coen's outstretched arms and on to Paterson, brought the second goal. Paterson took his chance well and scored after 83 minutes to finally quell any lingering Luton enthusiasm. The other Cup-tie débutant, Kemp, went from success to success and when he eased away Stephenson's low shot, Billington made his one serious mistake by putting the ball over the bar from five yards.

Dunsmore played magnificently at full-back, putting in some sterling work, but one minute from the final whistle Balmer scored again with one of the most spectacular goals of his career. Nieuwenhuys took up Busby's perfection pass and slung the ball over, and Balmer, running in at full speed, smashed the ball in the net.

The highest score of the day was Tottenham's 7-1 victory over Watford, while Fulham hit six against Bury. The Cup-holders, Preston, beat Runcorn 4-2 away. Portsmouth beat Lincoln City 4-0, while Wolves beat Bradford 3-1. In South Africa, thousands of miles away from the severe wintry conditions in England and Scotland, the M.C.C. were 237 for 1 at the close of play. Len Hutton was 152 not out, and Paynter was 27 not out.

TRANMERE PLAY
ON TUESDAY

~~~~~

Grimsby Ground
Unplayable

~~~~~

POOLS ON FROZEN PITCH

~~~~~

The Cup-tie match between Grimsby Town and Tranmere Rovers was postponed until Tuesday, at 2.30pm, owing to the ground being unplayable.

Recent keen frost had made the ground as hard as iron, and the heavy rain which fell in the early hours of this morning had formed huge pools all over the ground.

REFEREE'S DECISION

The ground staff had worked hard in a vain endeavour to get the water away, but the frozen ground would not take it.

The pitch was inspected by the referee, Mr Nixon, of Prestwich, about 1pm., and he unhesitatingly declared the match off.

During this afternoon, the groundsmen were trying to pump the water off with hand pumps. At the time of phoning the sun was shining and there is every indication of the weather becoming warmer.

Liverpool: Kemp; Harley, Ramsden; Busby, Bush, McInnes; Nieuwenhuys, Taylor, Fagan, Balmer, Paterson.

Luton: Coen; King, Dunsmore; Finlayson, Dreyer, Roberts; Clark, Redfern, Billington, Connelly, Stephenson.

Referee: Mr M.J.A. Tucker (Nottingham)

Attendance: 40,431

Receipts: £2,300 (approximate)

Derby County	0	Everton	1
Aston Villa	1	Ipswich Town	1
Barnsley	1	Stockport County	2
Birmingham	2	Halifax Town	0
Blackburn Rovers	2	Swansea Town	0
Blackpool	1	Sheffield United	2
Brentford	0	Newcastle United	2
Cardiff City	1	Charlton Athletic	0
Chelmsford City	4	Southampton	1
Chelsea	2	Arsenal	1
Chester	1	Coventry City	0
Chesterfield	1	Southend United	1
(match abandoned)			
Fulham	6	Bury	0
Leicester City	1	Stoke City	1
Middlesbrough	0	Bolton Wanderers	0
Newport County	0	Walsall	2
Notts County	3	Burnley	1
Portsmouth	4	Lincoln City	0
Queen's Park Rangers	1	West Ham United	2
Runcorn	2	Preston North End	4
Sheffield Wednesday	1	Yeovil & Petters	1
Sunderland	3	Plymouth Argyle	0
Tottenham	7	Watford	1
West Bromwich A.	0	Manchester United	0
Wolverhampton W.	3	Bradford	1
Matches Postponed			
York City	v.	Millwall	
Huddersfield Town	v.	Nottingham Forest	
Norwich City	v.	Manchester City	
Leeds United	v.	Bournemouth & B.A.	
Southport	v.	Doncaster Rovers	

January 21, 1939

Liverpool (4) 5

Nieuwenhuys 6, 41
Eastham 29,
Balmer 35, 51

Stockport County (1) 1

Reid (pen) 26

LIVERPOOL received a good welcome from a crowd which numbered about 40,000 on a day of bad light. The ground was heavy, but not in the same poor condition as in the Luton game. Six minutes had elapsed and referee Mortimer had given free-kicks liberally in order to control the game when Nieuwenhuys scored. From a free-kick on the right, Busby put in a good lob and Nieuwenhuys and Bowles went up for the ball together. The goalkeeper got the ball away to the right-hand post and when Fagan turned it into goal with his head it looked as though the ball was outside, over the line, but Nieuwenhuys promptly flicked it into goal with his head. After a moment of indecision, the Liverpool players were awarded a goal.

Stockport - of the Third Division North - retaliated when Sargeant drove in a tremendous shot which sailed over the bar. Liverpool began to command the game and they were allowed to do as they pleased, though the Stockport defence stood up to their job. There was an unusual incident when a free-kick had been given for a foul on Harley. Although the ball was dead, Fagan went on and Bowles, coming out to pick up, grasped the ball, and his speed caused him to stand on his head for an appreciable time out at the edge of his penalty area. Liverpool were not ruthless enough despite dominating the game, and they played the ball too close in front of goal. These tactics meant that Stockport were always likely to produce an equaliser. The light was so bad that it was possible that spectators at the Kop end had no idea that a penalty had been awarded after 26 minutes. Kemp had got the ball away, but Reid was fouled near the post. After receiving some attention, Reid himself took the penalty and comfortably scored.

Just three minutes later, Liverpool scored a second goal. Balmer's inter-passing with Nieuwenhuys was the start of the goal, and a back-heel pass from Balmer to the outside-right led to a half-blocked shot which spun across goal and became a perfect chance for Eastham, who was running in. It was Eastham's first goal for the club in League and Cup.

The light deteriorated more and more, and the possibility of the match being abandoned grew appreciably. It was so dark that the lights of hundreds of matches on the Kop and elsewhere were picked out just as easily as they were on an Anfield boxing night.

With 35 minutes gone, Balmer made it 3-1. A characteristic over-head flick and wheeling round led to the third goal. In the next minute Balmer rocketed a shot against a defender. Still tried a long-range shot which went extremely close.

Four minutes before the interval, Nieuwenhuys nodded home a centre from the left. Moments later he mis-connected with a Balmer centre. At the interval, Liverpool led by 4-1. Over at Goodison Park, Everton led Doncaster Rovers 3-0, but in the second half they ran riot, beating their Third Division North opponents 8-0, with Tommy Lawton scoring four goals.

Liverpool battered Stockport unmercifully and after 51 minutes Balmer, after failing to time a header correctly, picked up the ball again and shot it home for his side's fifth goal.

Liverpool began to ease off, feeling that the game was safely won, and coupled with Bowles in splendid form, no further goals came. As an exhibition Liverpool played superlatively. Every forward move promised a goal, and even playing in a practice match with no opponents, some of the Liverpool moves would have looked exceptional.

Fagan was given offside when he had the ball in the net for a sixth time. An injury to Nieuwenhuys meant that he had to leave the field for a period of time. A foul against Fagan led to a Liverpool penalty, but before Fagan took the spot-kick a Stockport defender went up to the goalkeeper and exchanged words. It was advice of the right kind, because Bowles made a brilliant save from a hard drive by the centre-forward.

Birmingham beat Chelmsford 6-0 and Wolverhampton Wanderers beat Leicester 5-1, while Portsmouth could only manage two goals without reply against West Bromwich Albion.

In Scotland, the goals flowed like Borden's Malted Milk, available in grocers, chemists and other stores at 1/9 and 3/-. Celtic beat Burntisland Amateurs 8-3 away; Hearts beat Penicuik 14-2; Huntley lost 1-8 at home to Motherwell; King's Park shared ten goals with Babcock and Wilcox; Nithsdale Wanderers drew 5-5 with Buckie Thistle; Queen of the South beat Arbroath 5-4; St Mirren beat East Stirling 7-0 and Third Lanark beat Clacknacuddin 8-2.

Liverpool: Kemp; Harley, Ramsden; Busby, Rogers, McInnes; Nieuwenhuys, Taylor, Fagan, Balmer, Eastham.

Stockport County: Bowles; Smith, Owens; Reid, Titterington, Still; Bagley, Essex, Law, Harker, Sargeant.

Referee: Mr R.A. Mortimer (Huddersfield)

Attendance: 39,407

Receipts: £2,200

February 11, 1939

Wolverhampton W. (2) 4
Burton 8, Westcott 23,
McIntosh 72, Dorsett 80

Liverpool (0) 1
Fagan (pen) 54

IT was a perfect day at Wolverhampton but for a slight breeze. Matt Busby led his side out to a great reception, and Liverpool's mascots - official and unofficial - rather hampered the customary shooting-in. Police eventually saved Liverpool from their friends. The crowd was approximately 55,000 when Busby went up for the toss. He won the honour, and with it the right to make the Wolves face the strong sunshine in the first half. It was a firm surface which was likely to produce a fast game.

With the war-clouds hovering menacingly across Europe, the Wolves declared their war-like intentions with a goal after only eight minutes. Maguire pulled back a nice centre. Kemp came out and handed it away, but before he could regain his composure, Burton had wheeled round like lightning and had the ball in the net. A despairing effort by Ramsden to intercept the shot made no difference to the outcome.

***Jack Balmer** broke through and shot and although the*
effort beat Scott, the ball passed outside by inches.

Liverpool played without conviction, and Ramsden had to get his head down low when Westcott had beaten Bush in order to cause more trouble for the visitors. Ramsden gave away a corner in a mis-judged back-pass to Kemp. Burton made a great header from a Maguire centre and Kemp tipped the ball over the bar in fine style. Burton and Maguire set up a constant stream of excellent centres as the home side sought a second goal. Busby tried to prompt his colleagues and for a short spell Liverpool looked useful, but they could not compare with the solid superiority of the Wolves.

With 23 minutes gone, Maguire began a second goal in much the same way as the first. Kemp was at fault when he tenderly handed away the centre, and Westcott was ready to pounce as he headed the ball into the net without opposition.

From this point on, the game was an uphill struggle, and Liverpool continued to play without a real desire to win. A quickly-taken left-foot shot by Balmer swung across goal, but Scott collected with ease. McInnes moved upfield with great determination, but the Wolves were soon back on the offensive with a cross-shot by Maguire which went close.

DIVISION ONE

	Pl	W	D	L	W	D	L	F	A	Pts
Everton	27	12	1	1	6	1	6	55	28	38
Derby Co.	29	10	2	2	6	4	5	53	36	38
Wolves	**27**	**7**	**5**	**1**	**6**	**3**	**5**	**48**	**21**	**34**
Charlton A.	28	10	2	2	5	2	7	52	38	34
Middlesbro.	29	8	5	2	4	2	8	60	48	31
Stoke City	28	8	4	2	4	3	7	51	49	31
Liverpool	**28**	**9**	**3**	**2**	**2**	**5**	**7**	**46**	**44**	**30**
Arsenal	27	8	3	3	2	6	5	32	24	29
Bolton W.	27	6	3	4	4	6	4	48	39	29
Aston Villa	27	6	1	6	5	4	5	46	41	27
Leeds Utd.	27	6	3	4	4	7	3	43	47	27
Grimsby	27	7	3	3	3	7	4	39	46	27
Man. Utd.	28	5	4	5	3	6	5	39	43	26
Sunderland	27	3	5	5	6	5	3	34	40	26
Preston N.E.	26	7	1	5	2	9	2	38	40	25
Blackpool	27	5	3	6	2	8	3	33	46	23
Brentford	27	6	6	1	2	7	5	38	57	22
Leicester C.	28	6	3	5	1	10	3	34	54	22
Huddersfield	27	8	5	2	0	9	3	37	42	21
Chelsea	26	7	3	3	1	10	2	46	55	21
Portsmouth	26	6	2	6	0	9	3	24	44	21
Birmingham	27	7	5	1	0	11	3	44	58	18

Balmer broke through and shot and although the effort beat Scott, the ball passed outside by inches. Liverpool's main fault appeared to be one of keeping the ball too close when it would have been wiser to bang the ball upfield. Burton left the field two minutes before the interval, having earlier been injured in a tackle with Ramsden. The outside-right did not immediately re-appear after the break.

Liverpool became far more aggressive in the early stages of the second half, with Harley fouling Maguire badly, and Dorsett being dangerously charged by Bush.

The visitors appeared to have lost the game, and their tempers, and there seemed little chance of a goal until Fagan tried to round Cullis with no apparent danger and the Wolves' centre-half used his elbows. Fagan scored with a low shot from the penalty spot.

Wolves almost got a goal before the referee consulted a linesman, who gave Maguire offside as he centred the ball. The home side's best spell had been in the eight minutes prior to the Liverpool goal, and Cullis and his colleagues were in excellent form. Busby, who had performed with great style, became annoyed with some of his forward's failings. Then Fagan went to outside-right and got in a good centre which Scott fumbled. The ball went away to the right, and Nieuwenhuys had it in the net to the delight of the Liverpool followers. The goal was disallowed.

With 18 minutes remaining, Burton put across a centre which Kemp went up for, but lost. McIntosh and Westcott bundled the ball into the net, the decisive touch being awarded to McIntosh. Busby continued to try to inspire his side, and he went on a fifty yard run with the ball before shooting weakly. The game continued to be marred by fouls. When Bush and Kemp both chased Westcott, the Wallasey boy hooked the ball over his head from a position to the right of the goal and Dorsett had only to walk the ball into the net. Liverpool tried in vain to reduce the deficit, and Eastham centred onto a post. Liverpool lost because they were simply not good enough on the day.

DIVISION ONE

Charlton Athletic	7	Manchester United	1
Derby County	1	Brentford	2
Leeds United	0	Middlesbrough	1

Wolverhampton Wanderers: Scott; Morris, Taylor; Galley, Cullis, Gardiner; Burton, McIntosh, Westcott, Dorsett, Maguire.

Liverpool: Kemp; Harley, Ramsden; Busby, Bush, McInnes; Nieuwenhuys, Taylor, Fagan, Balmer, Eastham.

Referee: Mr R.W. Blake (North Riding)

Attendance: 61,315

Post-War
To
Shankly

1946 -
1959

January 5, 1946

Chester City (0) 0

Liverpool (1) 2
Liddell 30, Fagan 86

THE drizzling rain had its effect upon the gate and at the start the attendance was no more than 12,000. There was no alteration to either side, although Billy Liddell only arrived at the ground twenty minutes before the kick-off. The ground was soft. Liverpool began well and almost scored in the first minute. Fagan initiated a movement which sent Nieuwenhuys through, and a goal seemed likely. The inside-left put great force into his drive, but the ball swung outside.

After Nickson had picked up a back-pass by Harley, Priday was sent on a raid, but he was flagged offside. The home side hit back through Yates, but his shot cannoned off a Liverpool defender. The turf was extremely treacherous and several players slipped over. Liddell tried a thunderbolt drive, but he was off the mark.

Chester attacked through Turner and his oblique shot dropped in the mud, causing Nickson difficulty in picking up. In the next minute the Liverpool goalkeeper handled well a fine header from Yates. As Chester threw everything into the attack, a long shot by Marsh went outside. A long ball down the middle from Liverpool went straight into the hands of Shortt. With twenty minutes gone, the crowd bayed for a goal. In the Chester goal area, Baron dallied and Lee made a back-pass which might have caused problems, but the Liverpool forwards could not capitalise on it.

The main danger to Liverpool came from Yates, and the centre-forward sent in a sparkling header which forced Nickson to rush out of his goal to catch. The home side continued to pressurise the Liverpool defence, and Nickson had to punch away three times inside a minute. Nickson turned away a shot by Hamilton, stumbling as he did so. Then Burden tried another shot and Nickson leapt to his feet to make another fine save. Then Marsh, trying to find an empty net, saw Nickson spring forward and punch clear again. Nickson's work saved Liverpool.

After 30 minutes, a fine piece of combination involving Fagan, Nieuwenhuys, and Priday culminated in a goal. Priday sent in a centre and the ball appeared to strike Nieuwenhuys and run to Liddell, who had stolen into the penalty area to simply tap the ball home. McNeill had temporarily left Liddell unmarked, and Chester paid the penalty. Hughes denied Astbury as Chester attacked, but then the Liverpool player was injured and went to the outside-left position, Nieuwenhuys taking over the centre-half berth. After a minute or two on the left wing, Hughes went off the field to return shortly afterwards at outside-right, with Liddell going centre-forward. A header from Yates flashed over the crossbar.

Liverpool were back in their original formation when the second half began. Hamilton headed a Chester centre into the goalmouth and Astbury attempted to hit the back of the net, but he got under the ball and his header passed over the bar. Turner found Paisley and Lambert a difficult proposition, because both Liverpool men tackled with power and determination. Shortt saved a pile-driver from Liddell, before Nickson saved well from Astbury. A moment later Astbury headed wide. Nieuwenhuys created an opening for Liddell, and Shortt was injured in saving. On one occasion, the Liverpool defence was ragged, but the three inside men were unable to convert the chance. Shortt displayed a magnificent piece of goalkeeping when he produced a one-handed save from a Priday drive. Yates then received an injury, and Chester's attacking prowess diminished. Four minutes from the finish, Liddell and Fagan linked up to outwit the Chester defence, Fagan running through to crack an oblique shot past Shortt.

The award of gold medals to FA Cup finalists, a prized peace-time honour, is unlikely to be resumed this season. The Football Association have not yet made a decision, but it is expected that the war-time practice of presenting Saving Certificates will be continued.

Price of an FA Cup winner's medal, which is the size of half a crown, was about £7 pre-war. With the present 100 % luxury tax and increase in labour and material costs, a similar medal would now cost in the region of £20. The runners-up medal is slightly smaller.

Preston: Fairbrother; Beattie, Scott; Shankly, Williams, Hamilton; Dougal, Mutch, Livesey, Wharton, McIntosh.
Everton: Burnett; Jackson, Greenhalgh; Bentham, Humphreys, Mercer; Rawlings, Elliott, Catterick, Fielding, Boyes.
Result: Preston 2 goals, Everton 1.

Chester City: Shortt; Stubbs, McNeill; Marsh, Lee, Cole; Turner, Burden, Yates, Astbury, Hamilton.

Liverpool: Nickson; Harley, Lambert; Finney, Hughes, Paisley; Liddell, Baron, Fagan, Nieuwenhuys, Priday.

Referee: Capt. F.T. Green (Wolverhampton)

Attendance: 12,000

January 9, 1946

Liverpool (2) 2
Fagan 3, 40

Chester City (0) 1
Astbury 86

THE counter-attraction of Preston's visit to Goodison Park and Liverpool holding a two-goal lead had its effect upon the attendance, and there were no more than 8,000 when the game started. At Goodison, Preston, leading 2-1 from the first leg, drew 2-2 after extra time. Bill Shankly, at number four, inspired his side to a draw after being behind at the interval.

Liverpool played the team advertised (Liddell was missing through the injury he received in the first leg), while Chester made two changes, Leakey made his début, and Mills deputised for Marsh.

The Liverpool players wore black armbands in token of respect for their former director, Mr Ted Bainbridge.

Liverpool supporters had the pleasure of seeing their side score in three minutes. The goal began on the left wing. Priday centred, and Lee failed to clear, the ball going to Nivvy, who was presented with an excellent opening. His shot, taken from close in, bore little strength, and Shortt was able to get the ball away. Before he had time to recover, Fagan shot home, to increase Liverpool's aggregate lead to three goals.

Liverpool looked as though they would add further goals and Fagan went close. Then Chester hit back, and Nickson had to drop on the ball with three Chester men in close proximity. The Liverpool goalkeeper then had to effect a good catch in order to prevent Chester from scoring. However, Liverpool were soon back on the attack, with Fagan hitting the side netting and then putting in a fast drive which Shortt turned outside at the second attempt. Nivvy was given a presentation goal but refused the gift by shooting outside.

Paisley took a free kick and shot behind. There was an infringement, however, and the kick had to be retaken. This time Paisley gave Shortt a fast, low shot which he dealt with ably. Nickson misjudged the flight of the ball as it came across his goal, and it was fortunate that the ball swung outside, otherwise it would have been a goal.

Whenever Chester did stage an attack, their promise was not fulfilled. Nickson and Hughes once let the Chester left wing through due to a misunderstanding, but finishing power was not one of the Cestrians' strong points. The visitors never gave up trying. Their midfield play was of good quality, but the Liverpool defence kept a really tight hold. The Anfielders seemed to be at half pressure, but still had too many moves up their sleeves for the Chester defence. Fagan simply revelled in his work, providing passes here, openings there, and was ready to take the shot when there was one to be had. Five minutes from the interval, Nivvy made a perfect opening, sweeping the ball right across field to Fagan, who

'killed' it dead and then shot hard into the Chester goal to mark up goal number two.

Nickson punched away a nasty-looking cross before the half-time whistle.

After the resumption, Nivvy tried a left-foot shot which sped outside, and Harley, from just over the half-way line, gave Shortt a long drive to field. Nickson turned one shot over his bar, and then followed with a one-handed save to send Cole's drive sailing over the bar and among the crowd.

The play was so one-sided that it lost some of its interest. Turner broke through the Liverpool defence, and there seemed a possibility of a Chester goal but Nickson came out, threw himself at the feet of the Chester man, collected the ball and cleared.

Baron shot from a bad angle and Shortt had to save at the foot of the post. For a few minutes, Liverpool allowed Chester the initiative, and during those moments Nickson was seen diving at the feet of Hamilton and stopping a ball from Astbury, but the danger was only slight. Turner was wasteful after beating Lambert.

Nickson made another excellent one-handed save from Hamilton, sending the ball spinning over the bar. Chester, fighting back for the first time in the game with any real conviction, were a thorough menace. Four minutes from the end, Chester got their due reward for their gallant fightback, Astbury scoring with a long dropping shot.

OTHER THIRD ROUND F.A. CUP TIES

Wolverhampton Wanderers beat Lovell's Athletic 8-1 (12-3 on aggregate), and Middlesbrough beat Leeds United 7-2 (11-6 on aggregate).

The eventual winners, Derby County, beat Luton Town 9-0 on aggregate, while the beaten finalists, Charlton Athletic, beat Fulham 4-3 on aggregate.

Liverpool: Nickson; Harley, Lambert; Finney, Hughes, Paisley; Nieuwenhuys, Baron, Fagan, Taylor, Priday.

Chester City: Shortt; Stubbs, McNeil; Mills, Lee, Cole; Turner, Leakey, Yates, Astbury, Hamilton.

Referee: Capt. F.C. Green (Wolverhampton)

Attendance: 11,207

January 26, 1946

Bolton Wanderers (3) 5   Liverpool (0) 0

Lofthouse 20, 40,
Westwood 43, 55, 60

IN spite of the thaw and heavy rain, the ground looked in reasonable condition, though there were worn patches in several places. Liverpool had Hobson in goal, and Balmer was the ultimate choice as partner to Liddell at inside-right. Liverpool had a good following in the crowd, for when Fagan led his men out Liverpool received a great cheer. The visitors began in confident mood and Bolton were hard-pressed. Balmer, Fagan, and Liddell combined well up to the edge of the area, but the final pass was always absent. Nieuwenhuys then sent Balmer on his way, and Fagan added his contribution with a back-heel pass which left Balmer unmarked sixteen yards from goal. His shot was weak, and passed wide of the post. Kaye then had a long-range effort which passed wide of the post.

Bolton then attacked for the first time in the game, and Geldard produced a pinpoint centre which Lofthouse got his head to, but Hobson saved comfortably.

Liverpool enjoyed the greater share of possession and the Bolton defence was over-worked to deny the wiles of Fagan and the swift thrusts of Liddell. Fagan took a free-kick just on the edge of the area, and his powerful shot was brilliantly saved by Hanson just below the angle of upright and crossbar. From a Liverpool corner, Hanson was forced to save from Fagan's header. Balmer was robbed by Hamlett, who set Bolton on to the attack, but Hughes cleared the danger in great style.

At the other end, Balmer was sent on his way with an inimitable pass from Fagan, but he elected to shoot instead of passing to Priday, in an unmarked position, and Balmer sliced his shot.

Bolton then produced a spell of attacking football and took the lead through Lofthouse. The ball had come up from a Bolton clearance after Balmer's miss, and there did not appear to be any danger until Howe cleverly headed the ball over the head of Hughes, who tried desperately to retrieve the situation, but Lofthouse was too quick, and the Bolton centre dashed in to head down towards the foot of the post. Hobson managed to get to it, but could not grasp it properly and it trickled over the line with 20 minutes gone.

From the kick-off Hanson stopped a shot from Fagan on the line, and Hamlett kicked away to safety before a Liverpool player could tap the ball home. Fagan and Liddell spearheaded the Liverpool attack, but ineffectiveness in front of goal proved their downfall.

Hamlett was injured following a tackle on Priday, with whom the referee had a word. With 40 minutes gone, Lofthouse increased the score for Bolton. Woodward began the move on the left and passed to Westwood, and after rounding Harley, the inside man offered Lofthouse an easy opening, from which the Bolton forward made no mistake.

Moments later Geldard shot outside as he was challenged by Balmer. With 43 minutes gone, Westwood picked up a pass from Lofthouse and beat Hobson with a fine effort. Liverpool's defence began to show signs of nerves, while the attack lost all its former fire and understanding.

Liverpool began the second half in command, and they stretched the Bolton defence for several moments. Hamlett was laid out when he was struck by a powerful shot from Nieuwenhuys. Hamlett was forced to leave the pitch for treatment, and he looked groggy when he resumed. A cross from Woodward was headed down by Geldard to the feet of Lofthouse, and a well-timed tackle by Hughes denied the Bolton centre. Bolton progressed with long passes, the ideal method on the heavy ground, and Liddell and Fagan attempted to inject some virility into the Liverpool forward line.

With 55 minutes gone, Lofthouse let the ball run between his legs from a Geldard pass to Westwood, and the Bolton inside-left scored. After 60 minutes, Westwood beat Hughes to connect with a Geldard cross.

Liverpool looked tired and dejected and Bolton eased off the pressure. Balmer was put through by Fagan, and when Hanson came out Balmer ran round him and had an open goal to aim at, but he took a fraction too long to net the ball, and Hanson recovered to take the ball off the forward's toes. Lofthouse shot over the bar as he was challenged by Hughes.

The crowd laughed when Woodward, who had sent a message for tape to tie up his shorts, made a run along the wing, holding them up with one hand.

Bolton re-arranged their attack near the end, following an injury to Hurst.

Bolton Wanderers: Hanson; Threlfall, Hubbick; Hurst, Hamlett, Murphy; Geldard, Howe, Lofthouse, Westwood, Woodward.

Liverpool: Hobson; Harley, Lambert; Kaye, Hughes, Paisley; Liddell, Balmer, Fagan, Nieuwenhuys, Priday.

Referee: Mr H. Nattrass (Sunderland)

Attendance: 39,692

January 30, 1946

Liverpool (1) 2

Balmer 5, Nieuwenhuys 75

Bolton Wanderers (0) 0

LIVERPOOL had further changes in addition to those already announced owing to Liddell's absence. Ramsden came in at full back in place of Harley, Lambert crossing to the right flank; Bush took the place of Hughes at centre half, with Paisley at right half instead of Kaye, and Spicer came in at left half.

After Geldard had made two sparkling runs on the Bolton right, and Nickson had two attempts to pick up a back-pass by Bush, Liverpool got an early goal to encourage them in their uphill task of saving the tie on aggregate.

Balmer was the scorer, and he got his chance when, after some miskicking in the Bolton penalty area, Murphy finally sliced the ball on to the foot of Baron. The inside man transferred the ball to Balmer who side-stepped a challenge by Atkinson and then directed his shot out of the reach of Hanson into the net. This was just what the crowd had been waiting for, and whenever Liverpool, who were kicking into the Kop end, attacked, the spectators gave them terrific encouragement. Balmer had another attempt, but a Bolton defender interposed his body before the ball could reach Hanson. It was evident early on that Bolton meant to hold on to their advantage, if necessary by putting the ball out of play whenever danger threatened. However, they were a lively and virile side in attack, and Geldard and Woodward, by their speed and accurate centring, more than once brought a threat to the home goal. Nickson made two excellent saves, a one-handed turn round the post for a corner from Woodward, and an equally brilliant save from Geldard.

Liverpool threw everything they had into the game and Bolton were awarded three fouls within a few minutes - none of them 'vicious', but only the outcome of Liverpool's determination and eagerness. Bolton's defence became unsettled under Liverpool's heavy pressure, but Hanson was implacable in goal. Just as in the first leg, Liverpool had the greater part of the game territorially, with Bolton confined to spasmodic breakaways. The home side did not produce enough shots, however, mainly because of the split-time tackling of Bolton, who did not allow their opponents a fraction of a moment to settle on the ball.

Geldard served up one electrifying run three-parts the length of the field, finishing with a shot-cum-centre which Nickson double-fisted out. Fortunately for Liverpool, there was no Bolton forward to meet the rebound. Liverpool soon returned to the attack, but Ramsden and Paisley had no more luck with their shooting than the home side's forwards. Bolton had another of their breakaways - which were becoming a little

more frequent - and Nickson effected a brilliant full-length save from Lofthouse. Liverpool switched Fagan and Balmer for a spell, and Balmer just failed to get properly hold of the ball, otherwise Hanson would have had a difficult shot to save instead of a simple clearance. Liverpool held the ball too close, making the work much easier for Bolton, who many times had eight defenders in their own penalty area.

Liverpool continued their onslaught, and they were unfortunate not to reduce Bolton's lead still further when Hanson was beaten to the ball by a Fagan header from a corner. Hubbick had sized up the position, and kicked away off the goal-line. It was a let-off for Bolton, whose defence had had a gruelling time.

The second half started with Ramsden kicking away after Nickson had failed to gather a ball from Howe. Again Liverpool moved onto the attack, only to see Priday fire well behind from close range with only Hanson to beat.

Nickson nipped in and gathered the ball smartly when Westwood looked dangerous from a Geldard pass. Ramsden, too, robbed the Bolton inside-left as he was running through at top speed. Westwood had a great chance of equalising the score on the day's play, but slipped at a crucial moment, leaving Lambert an easy clearance.

Baron thrilled the crowd with a sinuous dribble which took him from inside-right nearly to outside-left, but Priday could not take full benefit from his final pass. Geldard, too, electrified the crowd with two brilliant touch-line dribbles. Nickson was very unorthodox in a lot of his work, but it was serving its purpose. He was winded stopping a shot from Howe, and had to receive the trainer's attention.

Shortly afterwards, a hailstorm swept over the ground for a second time and conditions underfoot - which had been bad throughout - became more treacherous.

Fagan was brought down four yards outside the Bolton penalty area, the free kick being held up while he drew the referee's attention to the fact that the Bolton players were nearer than the permitted ten yards. Referee Nattrass moved them back. Fagan, shaping as though to deliver a shot, tapped the ball instead to Nieuwenhuys, who hit a curling drive which deceived Hanson and thus put Liverpool two up on the day and reduced the deficit on the aggregate to three.

It had been a hard, dour typical cup struggle throughout. The football had not been as good as at Bolton, for the visitors were content mainly to act in the role of stoppers and packed their penalty area as a counter to Liverpool's aggression.

A Shankly penalty against Manchester United was struck straight at Crompton, but the Preston wing-half scored from

A **Bill Shankly** penalty against Manchester United was struck straight at Crompton, but the Preston wing-half scored from the rebound to give his side the lead.

the rebound to give his side the lead. Preston won 3-1 after extra-time. The round's biggest score was Aston Villa's 9-1 defeat of Millwall, but the best comeback of the round was by Bradford, who had lost 1-3 at home to Manchester City, only to win the away leg 8-2, six of the goals coming in the second period.

Liverpool: Nickson; Lambert, Ramsden; Paisley, Bush, Spicer; Nieuwenhuys, Baron, Fagan, Balmer, Priday.

Bolton Wanderers: Hanson; Threlfall, Hubbick, Hamlett, Atkinson, Murphy, Geldard, Howe, Lofthouse, Westwood, Woodward.

Referee: Mr H. Nattrass (Sunderland)

Attendance: 35,247

Kevin Baron thrilled the crowd with a sinuous dribble which took him from inside-right nearly to outside-left

January 11, 1947

Walsall (2) 2
Kelly 4, Wilshaw 22

Liverpool (3) 5
Foulkes (og) 6, Done 31,
Liddell 32, Balmer 48, 63

BILL Jones found that an injury sustained in training on the Thursday before the game caused him concern, and there was the possibility that he would miss the game, and as a consequence he and trainer Shelley went on from Bridgnorth ahead of the main party so that Jones could be tested for fitness. It was found that the player was satisfactory, and Jim Harley was not required. When Liverpool arrived the gates had been closed for the portion in front of the stand. George Kay, who was quite ill, inspected the heavily-sanded pitch. The ground was similar to that at Rake Lane. The public address system reminded the crowd of Arsenal's fate here in the 1930s. Liverpool were forced to change their colour, the referee fearing a clash of claret and red. Liverpool were in white and Walsall in blue. The light improved considerably before the game. There were a few pools in some parts of the pitch. Liverpool won the toss and chose the slope.

Alsop almost scored with the first attack. A through ball to Lishman ended with a first-time shot which Sidlow caught high up. Walsall had the better of the opening exchanges, and Hughes had to make a good tackle against Wilshaw after a marvellous cross-field movement. The winger was injured and had to be taken off the field for several minutes. From the corner kick which Hughes conceded, Kelly scored after four minutes.

Lishman did a Sheffield United corner-kick trick, and sent a short ball to Newman, whose centre produced a mêlée from which Kelly stabbed the ball home.

Liverpool were soon level. Foulkes, in trying to head clear, only deflected an Eastham centre and Lewis, taken by surprise, could only knock it on to the underside of the bar, from where it rebounded downwards and over the line, as Done came in to apply the finishing touch.

Walsall's tackling was fierce and competitive, although Liverpool gradually got on top.

After 22 minutes, Walsall restored their lead when Wilshaw found himself in the clear when the ball came across from the right and eluded everybody near the penalty spot. Wilshaw cut inside and scored with ease. The goal was greeted with huge cheers.

Phil Taylor and other players claimed that it should not have been allowed, but the referee waved away their claims. Paisley and Liddell were involved in a movement which ended with Paisley moving inside the box and shooting into the arms of Lewis. The home side's tackling was fierce but fair. Kelly was so fast that Hughes was kept at full stretch.

With 31 minutes gone, Liverpool equalised. Done, at least two yards offside, went on and wisely finished off by putting the ball into the net. The referee allowed the goal. Just one minute later, Liddell cut in to shoot brilliantly into goal. Lewis dived full-length to deny Liverpool a fourth goal.

The game had been resumed only three minutes when Liddell cut in and flicked the ball out to Balmer, who smashed the ball into goal. Liverpool, with a two-goal lead, had the time and renewed confidence to show their ability. Sidlow saved twice in succession from Talbot. Lambert, Hughes, and Jones did well to contain the lively Walsall forwards. Stubbins broke free and sent in a lob which passed wide.

Liddell and his right-wing colleagues were allowed a lot of time in which to perpetrate their skilful deeds, and with 63 minutes gone Balmer scored with a first-time shot from Taylor's pulled-back centre.

Alsop and Kelly changed places, but the tactical initiative arrived too late for effect. Lewis saved well from Liddell when Taylor started a move which led to Eastham cutting in on his own. Towards the finish, Paisley was spoken to for a tackle, and Taylor missed an open goal.

Jack Balmer

Walsall: Lewis; Methley, Skidmore; Crutchley, Foulkes, Newman; Alsop, Talbot, Kelly, Lishman, Wilshaw.

Liverpool: Sidlow; Jones, Lambert; Taylor, Hughes, Paisley; Eastham, Balmer, Stubbins, Done, Liddell.

Referee: Mr G. Clarke (London)
Attendance: 17,700

January 25, 1947

Liverpool (1) 2
Stubbins 22, Done 53

Grimsby Town (0) 0

A quarter of an hour before the start of the game spectators on the Kop were able to move to fresh vantage points. In no league match this season had the ground been so empty so near to the time of kick-off. The most crowded of the enclosures was the paddock. Liverpool arrived from Birkdale, and Grimsby, who were without Betmead and Vincent and other regulars, arrived at Anfield in a resigned frame of mind. Chairman Will McConnell, who had a temperature of 102 last week, said, "Nothing will keep me from this game." Despite the cold, he was in his place.

With a mild thaw the ground did not appear to be hard, but inevitably it would be firm under foot. Cup-tie rattles were not prominent and there appeared little enthusiasm for the tie, the gates being open right up to kick-off time. During the kick-in before the game, Stubbins tried a shot and slipped and fell heavily on his back.

Liverpool: Sidlow; Lambert, Ramsden; Taylor, Jones, Paisley; Eastham, Balmer, Stubbins, Done, Liddell.

Grimsby Town: Tweedy; Mouncer, Fisher; Hall, R.E.Taylor, Blenkinsop; Wallbanks, Clifton, Cairns, Keeble, Wardle.

Referee: Mr T.S. Norcott (Gloucester)

Attendance: 45,256

Jones, filling in at centre-half, sent a confident back pass to Sidlow after Wallbanks had swung in a high centre. The players found the surface difficult and all were careful to run and turn. As the game progressed, strong sunshine bothered the Grimsby defence.

Mouncer stopped Liddell in his tracks before Jones slipped up and lost the ball to Keeble. A pass by Stubbins was anticipated by Liddell, who ran on, but conditions caused him to mistime his shot and Tweedy collected safely. Jones out-headed Cairns in a goalmouth duel, and then Paisley cleared the danger completely with a magnificent headed pass. Stubbins back-heeled the ball to Liddell, who shot hard and wide.

The first stoppage was for an injury to Grimsby's Taylor, who wrenched an ankle in trying to stop Done on the left wing. The centre-half resumed in great pain, and from Liddell's corner, which Tweedy punched away, Phil Taylor ballooned the ball in a half-volley on to the roof of the stand. The referee examined the ball before calling for another. Liverpool scored after 22 minutes. Liddell provided the centre from which Stubbins, unmarked, got under the ball with his head to plant the ball into the corner of the net. Tweedy

appeared to have had time to reach the ball, but stood rooted on his line.

Wallbanks and Cairns almost snatched an equaliser two minutes later, but Ramsden tailed Wallbanks all the way, forcing the winger to make only a weak shot which Sidlow collected easily.

Hall and Liddell continued to argue after an earlier tackle, and the Grimsby player openly showed his temper in front of the referee without warning. Although two yards offside, Wardle struck a shot from the edge of the penalty-box after the whistle had gone, and the drive struck the crossbar. The Grimsby attack promised much but was ineffective in front of goal. Liddell put the ball in the net with a fine shot from a headed pass by Done, who had been given offside.

Eastham began the second half with a dribble along the right wing and almost to the post, where he pulled the ball back for Balmer, whose low shot was deflected across to Liddell, but the flying Scot just failed to connect.

Blenkinsop disputed the decision which awarded a free-kick against him for handling, and Taylor, looking over to the left wing as though about to kick the ball there, did the opposite and pushed it low along the ground towards Done, who had anticipated the move. Tweedy came out, and a defender was with Done, but the Liverpool man turned the ball into the net.

Liddell almost scored a third goal, but Tweedy came out and got his hands to a fast moving shot which earned him great applause. A shot from Keeble screwed wide. The visitors attempted to make a breakthrough down the middle, their wingers having had little luck against the Liverpool full-backs. A shot by Stubbins was half-saved by the goalkeeper, but left-back Fisher breasted the ball down and cleared. Grimsby's tactic of playing football in conditions not suited to it was their downfall. Liverpool continued to dominate up to the final whistle, when Hall sportingly waited for Liddell and shook his hand as they walked off.

Liverpool, who go to Goodison Park on Wednesday for a rearranged League match, have no serious injuries, but the club is returning to Birkdale today (Monday) and will stay there until Wednesday morning. Stubbins' heavy fall in the pre-match shoot-in did no more than shake him, otherwise he might have been off the field before the match began. It would still have been possible for Liverpool to use a substitute.

Latest trainee at Anfield is Stan Hawthorne, the boxer, who has come to Liverpool to live, and who makes his next appearance at the Stadium on Thursday.

February 8, 1947

Liverpool (0) 1
Balmer 75

Derby County (0) 0

IN spite of the bitter wind almost 45,000 spectators turned up at least half an hour before the start. The pitch was hard underneath with a light covering of snow, the remainder having been brushed off. The most dangerous aspect of the pitch was that where a sure foothold was most needed, the snow had been completely swept away.

Both sides stayed overnight at Birkdale and the teams were as announced. Fagan was tried at outside-right, and Woodley came in to the Derby goal, while previously-injured Morrison and Stamps, returned. The ambulance men were not over-worked although some spectators collapsed through the cold. Referee Wort, of Liverpool, started to prepare to run the line when the official linesman appeared just twenty minutes before the start. A spectator invaded the pitch as the teams kicked in to wish the side well, and he attempted to assist Sidlow in making a save.

From the kick-off it was apparent that the players would find it difficult to stay on their feet, particularly the wingmen. The first casualty was Phil Taylor who, in going up to outhead Stamps, fell heavily, but he resumed after attention. Fagan did good work as a retriever of the ball, but when he got his first chance on the wing, he tended to be over-elaborate. Harley, in trying to head clear, put the ball in the path of Carter, whose powerful drive flew inches over the bar. A free-kick against Paisley created a fine opportunity for Carter, who took a long through-ball in his stride before pulling the ball wide of a post. Stamps, Morrison, and Carter had the better of the Liverpool defence at this stage of the game. A marvellous side flick of the foot by Mozley killed Fagan's long cross-field pass to Liddell. The Liverpool forwards did not work as a unit, and the Derby defence was able to cope with ease.

A well-timed shot by Stubbins caught Woodley by surprise, but the goalkeeper grabbed the ball with both hands above his head. From Harrison's corner, Broome was presented with a heading opportunity, but Sidlow's good positioning and a fine catch saved the danger. Balmer hurt an ankle in making a snap shot, and upon resuming he went to outside-right, Fagan going inside.

Harley and Lambert had both defended resolutely, and Jones was characteristically cool and unflustered. Harley was forced to use his Powderhall sprinting ability to match Stamps' speed when going for a pass down the middle.

Liverpool's first move of real class began with Taylor's pass to Liddell, and the Scot's centre created difficulty for Woodley. Moments later Woodley produced a glorious save from Stubbins, after Done's centre. These thrills caused the people on the packed terraces to sway dangerously. Fagan was having a magnificent match, while for Derby, Stamps, the former New Brighton player, worked prodigiously.

Liverpool combined well with Balmer, Fagan, Stubbins and Liddell involved, and it ended with Liddell's first time shot going wide to Stubbins, who was unable to take advantage. Then Fagan was robbed of the ball almost on the Derby goal-line, and Woodley made a brilliant save at point-blank range from Liddell. Liddell congratulated the goalkeeper as they left the field at the interval.

The second half began with a Stubbins shot which hit the underside of the bar before Mozley took it upfield. Within half a minute, after Sidlow had come out, and the ball had flashed across to Broome, Taylor got his body in front of the winger's shot which was aimed at an open goal. At the other end a Fagan header passed over the bar. Liverpool began to indulge in some fancy football which the situation did not demand, and they were spurred on by the Kop roaring almost continuous encouragement.

Jones, on the ground after a charge from Stamps, still managed to dispossess the Derby man. Liverpool then enjoyed a spell of supremacy with Taylor, Paisley and colleagues advancing to lend weight to an attack which did everything but score. Stubbins appeared to have centred the ball out of the reach of Woodley, but the goalkeeper managed to get his fingers to the ball and tip it round the post.

With 75 minutes gone, Liddell turned the ball goalwards from 30 yards out and Balmer, anticipating the flight of the ball, stepped in front of Woodley and glanced a magnificent header into the net.

Stubbins almost scored in the final moments, but Woodley edged away his shot. There was a last-minute scramble in front of Woodley, with manager George Kay on the touch-line urging his side to defend in case of a breakaway.

Liverpool: Sidlow; Harley, Lambert; Taylor, Jones, Paisley; Fagan, Balmer, Stubbins, Done, Liddell.

Derby County: Woodley; Mozley, Howe; Ward, Leuty, Musson; Harrison, Carter, Morrison, Stamps, Broome.

Referee: Mr J.M. Wiltshire (Sherborne)

Attendance: 44,493

Receipts: £4,400

March 1, 1947

Liverpool (1) 4
Stubbins 33, 57, 74
Balmer 64

Birmingham City (0) 1
Mitchell (pen) 56

THE arrangements at Anfield to handle the all-ticket crowd worked smoothly and the queues from one o'clock onwards were very orderly. Although crowds continued to arrive between two and three o'clock, latecomers were able to walk in without queueing. The strong sun had softened the half-inch layer of snow, and the goal and penalty areas had been marked out in blue as a precautionary measure. Four thousand Birmingham supporters with tickets were prevented from attending the match because of transport difficulties. Ten minutes before the start there were several ambulance cases, although nothing serious. Liverpool lost the toss, and kicked towards the Kop, facing the sun.

Liverpool opened with an advance down the right wing, but the ball was held up in the snow as Liddell threatened to break clear. From a Paisley throw-in, Taylor moved upfield to hit a shot from just outside the penalty area, but Merrick caught the ball with little difficulty. Birmingham attacked through Edwards down the left wing, but Harley used his speed and made a hard tackle to put the ball out of play. Mitchell cajoled the ball at will, although Birmingham showed little real threat. Balmer gained possession in the area, spun round and blasted a shot goalwards which struck the crossbar. Liddell, having beaten Duckhouse, was unfairly tackled and the incident led to a delay in the free-kick being taken, the referee having instructed the linesman to bring police supervision to a point in front of the Kop.

From a free-kick against Liddell, Mulraney sent in a centre from which Bodie headed over the bar. Harley headed for a corner, and Edwards' flag kick ran along the top of the crossbar for a few feet before finishing on top of the net.

Turner and Stubbins both went for the same ball, but the Liverpool man won possession and advanced on Merrick. Stubbins went on ten yards and hit a powerful swerving shot which flew into the net. The goal and subsequent reaction caused some swaying in the crowd, but no-one was injured.

The Liverpool left wing was particularly destructive and caused the visiting defence several problems, and it was only the wise positioning of the veteran Turner which stemmed the flow from Liddell. Paisley went over to the opposite wing to make a successful tackle, and he appeared to sustain a leg injury, but he insisted on playing on. Sidlow had not had a real shot to save, and his most dangerous work came from an almost continual supply of back-passes from Jones and other colleagues.

Dougall began the second half with a long dribble and a fine pass to Edwards, who looked like scoring, but the Liverpool defence remained solid, and Jones headed powerfully away. Birmingham attacked strongly in the first five minutes of the second period. Edwards forced a corner from which Sidlow made a fine catch, and the goalkeeper followed this by collecting safely a header from long range by Trigg. Liddell then dashed along the wing and beat three opponents before being dispossessed by Turner. The sun shone strongly in the faces of the Birmingham defence. Ten minutes after the game had resumed, Edwards took the ball through and passed to Trigg, who was twice beaten off the ball, but a mêlée arose in front of goal and Harley clearly tripped Mulraney. Liverpool appealed loudly against the penalty, but Mitchell - the County cricketer - after blowing on his hands, calmly slotted the ball home to the left of Sidlow.

Within a minute, Liverpool regained the lead. Liddell was fouled and the home side appealed for a penalty, but the referee decided that the offence had occurred outside the box, almost on the goal-line. Liddell put the ball low into the mass of players, and Balmer stuck out a foot to connect with the ball and turn it into the net.

Shortly afterwards, Paisley went up for a header but was challenged and fell awkwardly. He was carried off the field almost immediately with a suspected head injury. Fagan went to left half-back.

Then came one of the best goals ever seen at Anfield. Done gained a free-kick in the vicinity of the corner of the penalty box, and Liddell attempted a shot which flew towards the far post and appeared to be going out of play. Stubbins dived full-length to power the ball home with a magnificent header. The goal was warmly applauded.

As Birmingham lined up for the restart, Paisley was back at outside-right, with a confirmed head injury. After a spell at outside-right, Paisley moved back to his original position. Fagan caused Merrick to concede a corner with a useful shot. From the flag-kick, Fagan dropped the ball beyond the far post, where Stubbins met it and headed into goal. Liddell made some excellent runs on the left, but Liverpool were content to sit on their lead and safeguard their passage into the semi-finals.

F.A. CUP - 6th ROUND

Charlton Athletic	**2**	Preston North End	**1**
Middlesbrough	**1**	Burnley	**1**
Sheffield United	**0**	Newcastle United	**2**
Replay - Burnley	**1**	Middlesbrough	**0**

Albert Stubbins *dived full-length to power the ball home with a magnificent header*

Liverpool Football Echo

As The Clock Ticked

~~~~~~~~~~~

Anfield Cup-Tie Time-Table

2.58   Turner wins toss for Birmingham.

3.00   Liverpool kick into Spion Kop goal.

3.08   **Botheration**: Balmer bangs it against the bar.

3.10   Liverpool have had four shots and two corners without reply from Birmingham. Sidlow unemployed.

3.15   Police called to spot near Spion Kop following foul on Liddell.

3.24   **Acclamation**: Great run by Liddell followed by fierce shot which hits side netting.

3.25   **Vexation**: Crowd boos visiting defender for unceremonious upending of Liddell.

3.33   **Jubilation**: STUBBINS seizes on slip by Turner and puts Liverpool in front with fine angled shot. Roar must have been heard at Pier Hotel.

3.42   Sidlow punches away centre by Bodie, when situation looks ominous.

3.45   **Half-time**: Home supporters jubilant.

4.05   **Mortification**: Penalty against Harley. MITCHELL scores from the spot.

4.06   **Jubilation**: BALMER puts Liverpool in lead from Liddell's free-kick.

4.11   Paisley carried off by ambulance men but returns five minutes later.

4.15   **Intoxication**: STUBBINS makes it 3-1 with miraculous header from Liddell's pass.

4.18   Sidlow has anything but friendly words with Mulraney, and too much "bite" was now apparent in the play, which was scrappy.

4.25   **Exhilaration**: STUBBINS gets Liverpool's fourth and repays his transfer fee.

4.25   Stubbins nearly gets another, but shot strikes defender.

4.31   Birmingham put up gallant fight, but the rest is anti-climax. Liverpool defence is solid.

4.41   **Final whistle**. Liverpool supporters depart jubilantly to indulge in rosy dreams of Wembley.

Birmingham contingent dispirited, but not downhearted.

by

RANGER

Liverpool: Sidlow; Harley, Lambert; Taylor, Jones, Paisley; Fagan, Balmer, Stubbins, Done, Liddell.

Birmingham City: Merrick; Duckhouse, Jennings; Harris, Turner, Mitchell; Mulraney, Dougall, Trigg, Bodie, Edwards.

Referee: Mr G. Tedds (Nottingham)

Attendance: 51,911   **Receipts**: £5,420

March 29, 1947

Burnley (0) 0

Liverpool (0) 0 aet

JUST before the kick-off rain fells in torrents and the crowd were forced to use handkerchiefs, newspapers, and other items in order to protect themselves from the elements. An hour before the game, the ground was seething with noise and excitement from the vociferous crowd. Liverpool arrived from Clitheroe, their training headquarters. Owing to a problem with tickets, an officious gatekeeper refused to allow them admission at first. After a long explanation, the team was allowed through, but the reserves and the skips had difficulty in gaining admission. The crowd was reminiscent of a Test match crowd such was the wealth of headgear. Brown spun the coin and lost the toss, Fagan decided to kick with the slight wind in his favour.

Lambert made two beautifully-timed headers to prevent Burnley danger from through the middle and down the right wing. Liddell glanced a header towards Stubbins, but Brown tackled Stubbins with ease. Harrison ran on to a through-ball, but Harley was on hand to effect a firm tackle and prevent the threat. So great was Burnley's team-work that when Fagan gained possession from Taylor's pass, he was surrounded by five men in white. Fagan managed to get in a centre, but Strong left his line and evaded the incoming Done to collect.

At this stage in the game, the crowd encroached onto the pitch, and created problems for Chew, who was about to take a corner. He was so eager to get on with the job that he pushed aside ambulance men before sending in a cross which Lambert headed out for another corner, which came to nothing. Liverpool's tackling was good, but Burnley had the greater share of possession. Liddell was the star of the Liverpool attack, but when the Reds advanced on goal, the opposition got all their men behind the ball.

Kippax gained possession, swivelled and drove a left-foot shot inches over the bar. Burnley's right-wing pair combined well and caused Jones and Lambert enormous problems, though Jones was at his best. Liverpool's first shot of any consequence was from Stubbins at long range, but the ball passed well wide. During the game the crowd were permitted to move from crowded parts to less dangerous parts of the terracing. Burnley's half-backs were in supreme command of the game. Without the game being stopped, Jones ran off the field and doused his neck in cold water, and was back on the field of play before a throw-in was taken. Lambert appeared to receive a facial injury when he attempted to head the ball in a duel with Chew, and although dazed, he carried on after smelling salts were administered. Just before the interval, Liddell outpaced Woodruff but failed to get in his cross.

Liverpool gave away numerous free-kicks in an attempt to contain the lively Kippax. A free-kick by Liddell was charged down, but the ball went to Fagan, who got in an angled shot which Strong saved at the foot of a post. Liddell moved across to the right wing in an effort to add a greater threat, but the Burnley players were faster to the ball and more determined in the tackle. Taylor moved to left-half and Fagan and Balmer combined well to show some understanding to produce the pass from which Liddell shot wide. The Burnley left-back was injured, and the game held up. A corner taken by Fagan led to Liddell shooting wide. Liverpool maintained their fierce approach to Kippax, who curled the ball over the angle from a free-kick. Burnley were unhurried in their approach and always prepared to play the ball on the ground. Making progress with passes tapped from the inside of the boot, the Burnley left wing broke free and Kippax flashed a shot across the face of the goal. The game moved into extra-time.

Balmer and Taylor and others sucked on a sponge and lemons, and Liverpool played the first period of extra time in the same direction as they had finished the ninety minutes. Manager George Kay set a good deal on the stamina of his side. A Liddell centre flashed across the goal, but no Liverpool player could make contact. Brown hooked away a volley from Stubbins. Liverpool began to increase the pressure, and a back-header by Stubbins was tipped over the bar by Strong. Minutes later Harrison was injured in a sliding tackle. Liddell then forced a corner, but put the kick behind and Liverpool were on top for the first time in the game. The teams turned round immediately and Liddell created an opening for Stubbins, but the ball bounced awkwardly and Mather cleared. There were numerous mistakes on both sides due to exhaustion. Jones conceded a corner to stop Harrison, and from the flag-kick Chew headed into Sidlow's hands. Just before the final whistle, Stubbins shot over the bar from long range.

F.A. CUP - SEMI-FINAL

Charlton Athletic (3) 4   **Newcastle United (0) 0**
Dawson 18, Welsh 39, 43, Hurst 52

Burnley: Strong; Woodruff, Mather; Attwell, Brown, Bray; Chew, Morris, Harrison, Potts, F.P.Kippax.

Liverpool: Sidlow; Harley, Lambert; Taylor, Jones, Paisley; Fagan, Balmer, Stubbins, Done, Liddell.

Referee: Mr F.S. Milner (Wolverhampton)

Attendance: 53,000 (at Ewood Park)

April 12, 1947

Burnley (0) 1   Liverpool (0) 0
Harrison 77

BURNLEY won the toss and chose to kick towards the City end into the slight breeze. Liddell began raiding down the left and Paisley took a long throw-in, which Brown headed away. The game was held up for a brief spell when Brown twisted his leg in clearing. Paisley burst through but was brought down by Stubbins in his eagerness to get the ball to Liddell. Burnley's defence remained calm and resisted the strong Liverpool attacks, especially on the left wing. Done struggled against Attwell, while Harrison was a constant threat. Paisley caught Harrison's boot behind the ear and the game was held up while Paisley received attention before resuming. Kippax was in fine form, trapping the ball brilliantly and making threatening passes. He was hampered by the cut on his nose. Liddell attempted a long-range shot which went well wide.

Burnley began to attack, but Jones was in brilliant form, making excellent interventions and using the ball constructively in combination with his half-backs and inside forwards. Mather marshalled Fagan well, and the Liverpool man was kept quiet. Strong performed capably in goal, and dashed off his line to beat Stubbins to the ball. Stubbins tried to beat Strong and Brown for possession in the air but he was knocked out. Liddell then drove in a powerful shot from twenty yards which Strong tipped over the bar. Liddell swung the ball over and it landed on top of the netting, while the fans at the opposite end celebrated what they imagined was a goal. Harley was booed for a foul on Harrison just before the interval.

The second half opened with Kippax tackling Taylor, who fell awkwardly. Balmer protested to the referee, but was waved away before Kippax was cautioned. Kippax was forced to beat Fagan when in possession, due to the Liverpool man always dropping back to cover the danger. Lambert was at the top of his form as Burnley began to take control of the second half. Billingham turned and shot all in one movement as Burnley increased the pressure. Paisley and Taylor were the main thrusts of the Liverpool attack, creating and cajoling throughout. Brown called the attention of the referee to photographers sitting behind the goal-line, and at least ten yards from the nearest post, and a line was made between them in order that Strong could take his goal-kick.

Jones dallied with danger by dribbling in front of his goal, and on one occasion he gave away an unnecessary corner. Fagan drove a powerful shot from 30 yards towards goal but Strong handled with perfect judgment. Then the goalkeeper punched away a Liddell corner, and the ball fell to Taylor, who blasted the ball high over the bar. The Second Division side began to gain the initiative, but they lacked the finish to their approach work. Taylor handled the ball in trying to prevent it from reaching Kippax, but the referee waved play on and the centre found Harrison and Billingham in the clear.

The outside-right did not put in a good centre and Jones breasted the ball down in fine style. The Burnley trainer attended to Brown, who had been injured in a tackle with Liddell. The referee spoke to both players before resuming.

From a corner conceded by Sidlow, the ball hung dangerously in the air until Harrison seized upon it after one shot had been blocked, and he spun round and smashed the ball into the back of the net after 77 minutes.

Strong dived full-length to save from Stubbins, but the whistle had already gone for offside. Liverpool lacked the guile to unlock the solid Burnley defence. Liverpool were informed that they had just five minutes left, but Burnley threatened again and wasted a lot of time by kicking into touch. Lambert prevented Harrison from scoring with a fine tackle.

With two minutes left, Liverpool threw everybody except Sidlow forward in an attempt to equalise.

Burnley: Strong; Woodruff, Mather; Attwell, Brown, Bray; Billingham, Morris, Harrison, Potts, F.P.Kippax.

Liverpool: Sidlow; Harley, Lambert; Taylor, Jones, Paisley; Fagan, Balmer, Stubbins, Done, Liddell.

Referee: Mr F.S. Milner (Wolverhampton)

Attendance: 72,000 (at Maine Road)

GREAT RECOVERY BY ENGLAND
Equaliser After Scots Set Pace

ENGLAND: Swift (Manchester City); Scott (Arsenal), Hardwick (capt. Middlesbrough); Wright (Wolves), Franklin (Stoke City), Johnston (Blackpool); Matthews (Stoke City), Carter (Derby County), Lawton (Chelsea), Mannion (Middlesbrough), Mullen (Wolves).

SCOTLAND: Miller (Celtic); Young (Rangers), J.Shaw (capt. Rangers); Macaulay (Brentford), Woodburn (Rangers), Forbes (Sheffield United); Smith (Hibernian), McLaren (Preston North End), Delaney (Manchester United), Steel (Morton), Pearson (Newcastle United).

Referee: M.C. de la Salle (France)
Attendance: 99,000
Receipts: £34,200
Scorers: McLaren (Scotland) 15 mins; Carter (England) 65 mins.

January 10, 1948

Liverpool (1) 4
Priday 15, Stubbins 78, 87,
Liddell 82

Nottingham Forest (0) 1
Wilkins 48

TAYLOR - captain for the day - became inside-right in place of Jack Balmer, whose stomach trouble persisted; Done came in at inside-left. The Forest goalkeeper, Walker, was fit, but it was felt wiser not to trust his groin injury on such heavy going. The Lord Mayor and Lady Mayoress of Liverpool gave a civic touch to a match which had few cup-tie trimmings in the way of rattles and favours. Forest brought about 2,000 fans with them. The visitors played in white with a thin red band ringing the lower part of the workmanlike shirts, which were of the sleeveless variety.

Liverpool began brightly on the right wing, and a big Paisley throw-in almost reached the goalmouth, where centre-half McCall made a calm clearance immediately after the whistle had blown for an infringement.

Forest were inclined to be rather nervous in the opening period, but McCall and Edwards were full of confidence and left-back Hutchinson did well against the Liddell menace. Liverpool got a goal through Priday in 15 minutes. It came from a Paisley throw-in - a long distance one which Taylor and Liddell between them succeeded in getting into the goalmouth. Stubbins tried one of his famous overhead kicks and the ball ran on to Priday, who came running in at top speed to deliver his strongest shot and give his side the lead.

Liddell, from well outside the penalty area, struck a free-kick which was so truly hit and at such pace that the ball, hitting the concrete surround of the Kop on its rounded portion, rebounded almost to the Kop roof.

Wilkins took advantage of Lambert's slipping on the greasy turf and dummied his way through to a shooting opening, but Minshull punched the ball away. There was a succession of three Nottingham shots blocked away before the dangerous attack fizzled out. The wily Wilkins usually did the right thing when in possession, and he was certainly the most dangerous of his line's five.

Lee missed a golden opportunity when Jones failed to connect with a through pass. It was only Minshull's speed in getting out of his goal which saved the day. Lee's shot struck the goalkeeper on the legs.

Taylor lay injured for a long time before the referee realised his plight, in spite of the fact that the crowd roared to him to stop the game. The Forest trainer, the old half-back, Tom Graham, very decently came on to the field to ask trainer Albert Shelley if he needed help. When the game was resumed Taylor went to outside-right with Liddell as his partner.

Just before the interval, Minshull, who had saved two almost certain goals, nearly dropped the ball before he cleared it when faced by Johnston.

Liverpool started the second half in sensational fashion with a Taylor-Done move which all but led to Priday scoring a second goal. It appeared that Platts eased Priday's shot round the post, but the referee did not award a corner.

Shortly afterwards, Lee, standing far out, delivered a ball into the goalmouth where Wilkins guided it home for the equaliser.

Wilkins, of portly build, may have been inclined to slowness, but he always appeared to know what he was doing, and when he came through in another dangerous dribble, the ball remained with him as though tied by strings. Liverpool were glad to see the end of his control of the ball finish a few yards in front of Minshull. Some of the Forest forward play at this time was first class, and Liverpool had a period of desperate defence and indecision.

Taylor and Liddell resumed their normal positions as the Forest onslaught eased. Here was an occasion when the mind of a Busby would have gone a long way to calming Liverpool's fears and enabling them to resume a more even tenor.

Hughes went upfield to hit a shot which, like Liddell's earlier one, struck the concrete surround and bounded high into the air. Then Paisley received a knock on the head, but he resumed after attention.

Forest's forward play along the floor was of the highest standard, and they belied their lowly Second Division status. The visitors began to believe in themselves, and caused the home side innumerable problems. The game, however, became even more ragged than the first half, but it was always a do-or-die cup tie in an atmosphere of failing light, which would have become a problem if extra time were needed.

Liverpool went into the lead at 78 minutes when Stubbins angled a beautiful pass to Done, who then placed a model pass in front of Priday. The South African's centre came quite fast and low to where McCall and Stubbins stood, and it appeared as though McCall turned the ball into his own goal and Stubbins went on to make doubly sure. There was a momentous pause while the referee. on the appeal of Forest, consulted a linesman, but having done so, there was a second great cheer as the referee indicated that the goal would stand.

With only eight minutes remaining, Liddell made it 3-1. He beat Hutchinson in a race for a pass from Stubbins, and Platts, who had come out of the goal was beaten by a cross-shot from the winger. It was little wonder that McCall retrieved the ball from the net and with some venom kicked it towards the touchline. His side did not deserve to be 3-1 down on the state of play, and his own part in the game had been dauntless. With three minutes to go, Stubbins made it 4-1, getting clean through after a free-kick given against Wilkins for a foul charge. Stubbins might have had another goal, but for pushing the ball too far ahead on the heavy mud, and giving Platts a chance to reach it first.

The tie of the round was undoubtedly Manchester United's 6-4 away victory against Aston Villa. The cup-holders, Charlton Athletic eased into the next round with a 2-1 home win over Newcastle United.

Liverpool: Minshull; Jones, Lambert; Paisley, Hughes, Spicer; Liddell, Taylor, Stubbins, Done, Priday.

Nottingham Forest: Platts; Thomas, Hutchinson; Barks, McCall, Knight; Scott, Wilkins, Johnston, Edwards, Lee.

Referee: Mr A.W. Leuty (Leeds)

Attendance: 48,569

Receipts: £4,619

Albert Stubbins, *two-goal hero against Forest*

January 24, 1948

Manchester United (3) 3   Liverpool (0) 0
Rowley 30, Morris 34, Mitten 36

IT was a raw day, but half an hour before the game the terraces were packed and swaying. It took the people with rattles all their time to get their hands above their heads to produce the inevitable Cup-tie pre-match sound. With Old Trafford out of commission due to the damage sustained by the Luftwaffe, the game was played at Goodison Park (Everton being drawn away to Wolves), and there was a strong wind blowing into the Stanley Park end of the ground. Casualties became more frequent, and people were rolled over the heads of the crowd to St. John's Ambulance men waiting to receive them below. Twenty minutes before the kick-off Goodison Road entrances were closed, and there was a crowd estimated at about 12,000 in Bullens Road. The pitch looked good, but it was not until one of the mascots dribbled a ball to the centre spot that its softness could be gauged, and it then appeared to be very soft. There was a great cheer for Carey as United came out first. Liverpool, led by Balmer, appeared in startling white with very new black numbers. It needed a second toss before United called correctly and decided to face the wind.

Liverpool were bright and good in the early minutes, and a Priday centre led to Balmer poking his foot rather tentatively at the ball for a low shot which Crompton watched safely round the post. From very early on, it appeared that United had a solid defence and were rather lethal in attack. Rowley, going to outside-left, won a corner at the expense of Lambert, and when Liddell lost possession to Aston, the full-back's lobbing kick into the goalmouth provided further problems for Minshull, who got up well above the ruck to make his second well-judged punch away.

All the time ambulance men were busy dealing with crowd casualties, several of whom were stretcher cases. Though Liverpool had almost as much of the game as their opponents, they got their reward through sheer will-power and enthusiasm, whereas United's skill shone out like a beacon. It was a shrewd tactical ploy of United's that when Mitten became a half-back, Cockburn went forward in a most versatile way.

Liverpool went close to a goal when Done, from the inside-right position, and standing only ten yards out, shot past the onrushing Crompton, the ball missing the far post by a matter of inches.

There appeared to be no particular danger when Mitten and Rowley won a clinch for the ball. Mitten's pass left Rowley a fine angled chance which he took with a shot which wanted an awful lot of stopping. Liverpool lost some of their earlier zest, and became somewhat ragged. The United attack was so good that it made beating a good defence like Liverpool's appear absurdly easy. A free-kick for a handling offence by Lambert in midfield was headed away, and little Morris -

standing 12 yards out - hit it without delay past an astonished Minshull.

Worse was soon to follow. Mitten, being alive to a through pass, drifted the ball beyond Minshull as he came off his line. The interval arrived with the game palpably lost.

Liverpool began the second half in improved style, but still not convincingly enough to warrant much hope. Priday tried to conjure his way past Carey, but when he passed the ball there was little accuracy in his direction.

Mitten was brilliant at outside-left, and United simply toyed with Liverpool. Most of the United passes were on the floor, and left nothing for the receiver to do save run on to the ball unchallenged. Liverpool, for their part, enjoyed no luck when Balmer hit a glorious shot which Crompton pushed away in a superb save. Priday's return centre led to Done striking the post, and the ball cannoned out of play.

Minshull - who used to play full-back for Army teams in Rome - effected two brilliant saves from Pearson and Mitten. Liverpool, in trying so hard to improve, only succeeded in playing nervously and in staccato fashion. They possessed a great deal of fighting spirit, but their ideas were ineffective against such a strong side as United. Jones saved a fourth goal by kicking a header from the line as United overran the visitors. The second half was simply a duel between the United attack and the Liverpool defence.

Stanley Matthews shone in a 4-0 win for Blackpool against Chester, playing one of his best games since joining Blackpool. Shimwell scored after 8 minutes, and a second goal was scored by Mortensen after 25 minutes. With 65 minutes gone, Mortensen added a third goal, and Johnston completed the scoring with just five minutes remaining.

In the next round United went on to beat the Cup-holders, Charlton Athletic, by two goals to nil, and eventually won the Cup by 4-2 against Blackpool.

Manchester United: Crompton; Carey, Aston; Anderson, Chilton, Cockburn; Delaney, Morris, Rowley, Pearson, Mitten.

Liverpool: Minshull; Jones, Lambert; Taylor, Hughes, Paisley; Liddell, Balmer, Stubbins, Done, Priday.

Referee: Mr J.M. Wiltshire (Dorset)

Attendance: 74,721 (at Goodison Park)

Receipts: £8,810

January 8, 1949

Nottingham Forest (2) 2
Jones (og) 24, Scott 37

Liverpool (0) 2 aet
Fagan 78, Done 89

FOREST - languishing in the depths of the Second Division - almost figured as giant-killers, and would have won this Third Round tie but for a late, dramatic equaliser from Done. Forest's first real attack got the Liverpool defence in a tangle, and beside punching away from the head of Hullett, Minshull had to look on while some desperate defence kept the Forest forwards from surging through. The home side so dominated play in the first ten minutes with left-wing centres coming across with great frequency, that sooner or later it seemed likely that Hullett would make connection and open up the scoring.

Walker's one-handed touch deflected Liddell's left-foot shot beyond the goal angle when the Liverpool supporters were ready to acclaim a goal. But with 24 minutes gone, Liverpool suffered a crushing blow. There was little danger about a scrambling movement when the ball was pushed through and Jones, catching it with his heel, spun it up and into his own goal, with Minshull apparently petrified and unable to move to it.

Liverpool conceded several corners, and although it had been reported that the Forest forwards were their weakest link, left-winger Lee and others played some first-rate football.
Gager revelled in his job, and Forest were enthusiastic and confident. Liverpool plodded hard and earnestly, but it was Forest who played inspired football, and they grew more confident as every minute passed.

After 37 minutes, Wilkins, who made the ball do his work in the style of a James, kicked it out to Scott, who went on and on, and when expected to duly make his centre, elected to take the ball on another three yards and then deliver a first-rate cross-shot to score the second goal. The crowd roared deliriously, and soon afterwards Forest almost went three goals ahead when Minshull saved from point-blank range against Hullett, and with the goalkeeper on the ground, Hullett slashed the ball yards over the top from not more than five yards out. Everything - including the weather - seemed to be conspiring against Liverpool.

The second half began with them facing a freshening wind and a heavy drizzle. Hullett got the better of Lambert by flicking the ball over his head and then centred strongly. Minshull was on the post to cut it out. Apart from a Paisley free-kick which swerved over the ruck and caused Walker a little concern, Liverpool did little of note.
With fifteen minutes of the second half gone, Liverpool roared into life, and for the first time in the game they were right on top. Liddell made one long run when challenged all the way, but he was not able to keep his centre in play. There was a nasty scene when a Liddell centre found Taylor, whose shot was deflected so that Walker had to come out and fall at the feet as the winger Brierley shot. The goalkeeper was hurt in this piece of gallantry, and although the game continued, Brierley bent down and tried to draw the referee's attention to the injury. Matters were not improved when Brierley was twice pushed away by a Forest defender. There was a lengthy hold-up while Walker was attended to as he lay on the field. Trainer Shelley, of Liverpool, went on to see if he could help and a policeman's cape was put round Walker while his head was attended to. Eventually the jersey was taken off Walker, and Johnson took his place in goal. Walker was assisted to the dressing-room - it was learned later that he was suffering from concussion - but even with ten men the Forest forwards found a trick too many for a Liverpool defence which seemed strangely uncertain and lacking in confidence. Lee, with a shot which scraped the top of the bar, was near to scoring a third goal for the Second Division side. At this point in the contest, Liverpool had lost their rhythm and looked a beaten side.

With 78 minutes gone, Liddell hit across a good centre and Fagan beat Johnson and the other Forest defenders in the air to head through. This was just the impetus that Liverpool needed, and they set about Forest with a much greater conviction. A Liddell shot which Johnson seemed to push on to the post provided a sensational incident. The goalkeeper could not collect the ball and it bobbed about for several seconds before Done finally put it in the net. The referee signalled a goal, but was persuaded to consult a linesman, and after doing so, he disallowed the goal. In the 89th minute, Done scored a genuine goal in a similar mêlée, and no sooner had the game been restarted than the final whistle sounded, which signalled the commencement of extra-time.

Forest won the toss for the extra-time, for which Hullett went into goal. Balmer opened up with a glancing header of no special power and directed the ball a few yards wide of goal. Done got the ball in the net after Hullett and Gager had indulged in the ruse by which the goalkeeper touched the ball outside the penalty box and had it returned to him so that he could make a pick up.
The referee disallowed this goal which appeared to be perfectly legitimate, and soon Liverpool battled away against a tired and much slower Forest defence. The stars of this game were Ottewell, a rugged Paisley type of half-back, Gager and Wilkins, who held the ball and used it to good advantage.

Cyril Sidlow, who was in goal for the replay against Forest, and managed to keep a clean sheet

From a Scott free-kick, the Liverpool defence was all at sea. The second goalkeeper casualty was Minshull, whose right knee caused him to hobble, and again the game was stopped, though he was able to resume after attention.

Nottingham Forest: Walker; Thomas, Clarke; Ottewell, Gager, Burkitt; Scott, Wilkins, Hullett, Johnston, Lee.

Liverpool: Minshull; Shepherd, Lambert; Taylor, Jones, Paisley; Liddell, Fagan, Done, Balmer, Brierley.

Referee: Mr A.W. Leuty (Leeds)

Attendance: 35,000

Everton In Cup With Last Minute Goal

~~~~~

HIGGINS WAS HERO WITH STEVENSON AS PROVIDER

~~~~~

Gallant Ten Held City After Hedley Was Sent Off

~~~~~

TWO "GOALS" DISALLOWED

With one minute to go Higgins scored for Everton. It was Stevenson with his little tricks and fancies that produced this goal. He jinked with the ball before he finally gave it to Fielding, who returned it upfield, and Stevenson, who had moved forward, scooped the ball into the City goalmouth, and Higgins got his head to it to beat Swift.

Final score: Everton **1**, Manchester City **0**

January 15, 1949

Liverpool (1) 4

Payne 28, Balmer 68, 89,
Stubbins 76

Nottingham Forest (0) 0

ALTHOUGH the weather was atrocious - the rain overnight had persisted all through the morning, and the pitch was covered with shallow pools of water - the attendance was good as Liverpool kicked off at two o'clock into the Stanley Park end. Payne, Stubbins and Sidlow were newcomers to this tie, and they received a big reception. It was cut and thrust Cup-tie stuff in the first five minutes, and the way the ball hung in the sticky turf was disconcerting to everyone.

Liverpool showed early signs that they would play better football than at Nottingham, but their policy of keeping the ball on the ground down the centre of the pitch was an expensive method of progress. A long left-wing centre by Cyril Done passed right across goal and out to Payne, who, instead of shooting promptly, beat his full back, and then centred rather too strongly to be of value.

Liverpool scored through Payne at 28 minutes. It was a tragedy for Forest in that it all arose through right-back Thomas trying to play Liddell offside from a pass by Balmer. Gager had Liddell well onside, and the Scot was able to go forward and make a shot which escaped Balmer and was partly deflected by Thomas, though at this stage it seemed unlikely to produce a goal. However, everyone had reckoned without the speed of Payne, and he appeared as if from nowhere to nonchalantly send the ball home and get his first cup goal in his first big tie. Forest fought back desperately, although for a small team on the heavy going it was a desperately stern business.

Forest's tackling in the second half was enthusiastic, but was so severe that it bordered on the questionable. One could understand their eagerness, however, to wipe out Liverpool's lead and to do all in their power to see that it did not become greater. For the first time in the game, they failed to find Hullett, and Liverpool enjoyed a period of great supremacy. Stubbins played well, and he and the persistent Payne got together in a very determined inter-passing movement which needed equally determined tackling to stem it. Done, who was now playing with his right-hand bandaged after a first-half challenge, played as well as any Liverpool forward.

Forest too often tried to move the ball along the carpet - a dismal policy when the carpet was so unresponsive to the lighter touches. On one occasion, Gager was indecisive when opposed to Stubbins, and the centre-forward nipped in and went ahead all alone in the mud to shoot against the body of the gallant Walker, and lose yet another excellent chance of putting the match safe. Gager soon afterwards kicked the ball high over his own bar for a corner to get rid of a menacing Liddell centre, and from Payne's corner Paisley shot high into the Kop. The corner was taken to the accompaniment of the constant roar of the Kop, a disturbing influence on the surest of defences.

With 68 minutes gone, Balmer scored a second goal. Payne, with a lovely inside pass to Balmer, got his partner on the move. Clarke appeared to take the ball, but then presented it back to Balmer, who had only a foot or two between the post and the outcoming Walker to shoot through. He side-tapped the ball into goal to a tremendous roar, and one would never have thought that the scorer had his critics.

Trainer Albert Shelley was kept busy supplying everyone with tape for their shorts, the mud and the general sliding about having caused these to go to half-mast.

Seventy-six minutes had gone when Stubbins scored the third goal. Thomas, in trying to slip the ball back to his own goalkeeper through the mud, only succeeded in placing it in the precise spot which made it impossible for Walker to reach it. Stubbins strode in to collect and the match was safe.

By this time, Gager's light hair was black with mud, but he still stood out in the heroic Nottingham defence, which refused to be beaten.

Forest won a penalty in rather mysterious circumstances, and when the referee went to consult a linesman, and Hullett had placed the ball on the penalty spot, Shepherd threw it away as though to say, "There's going to be no penalty here." On the contrary there was, the linesman having confirmed what the referee saw. Wilkins hit a nice shot from the spot, but Sidlow not only pushed it away, but was ready to save a second shot from Johnston. With a minute remaining, Balmer slashed the ball for goal number four off a ruck of players standing just outside the goal-line.

Liverpool's next cup opponents, Notts County, led by Tommy Lawton, beat Newport County 11-1 in a Third Division South League game. Tickets for the game were sold at five shillings each.

Liverpool: Sidlow; Shepherd, Lambert; Taylor, Jones, Paisley; Payne, Balmer, Stubbins, Done, Liddell.

Nottingham Forest: Walker; Thomas, Clarke; Ottewell, Gager, Burkitt; Scott, Wilkins, Hullett, Johnston, Lee.

Referee: Mr A.W. Leuty (Leeds)

Attendance: 52,218

January 29, 1949

Liverpool (0) 1
Liddell 58

Notts County (0) 0

THE attendance was just 33 below Liverpool's record against Tranmere, also in the Fourth Round, in 1934. Receipts were £5,419. The weather was perfect for the game, with the sun shining brightly. The ground was full about an hour before the start.

Tommy Lawton

Tommy Lawton received a great reception, but Liverpool's was an even greater roar. Balmer spun the coin, Lawton won the toss, and set Liverpool to play against the sun, into the Kop goal.

Liverpool opened strongly, and Payne and Liddell went close. A foul on Done by Baxter produced a free-kick from which Liddell walked back three or four paces and then hit a glorious shot which appeared to be a goal until the balding Smith reached up an arm and put it round the post. He also made a good catch high up from Liddell's corner. Payne, who got a pat on the back from a boy who was on the way out to avoid the crush, put across the corner from which Liddell's hook shot caused Smith some anxiety. It was going away from him, but he got up well, and made a two-handed punch away.

Paisley's tackling was extremely good, even for a player of his quality and determination. County came nearest to a goal when Lawton caught Jones napping, and after Lambert had moved across to stop a Johnston shot.

The Balmer-Payne-Stubbins-Done sequence which followed came as near to a goal as anything, and was the best move of the match. Stubbins merely flicked the ball up, and Done went on to make a nice shot against which Smith brought off a wonderful save. Within seconds, Sidlow had to perform as equally as well, but in his case Johnston's header was saved via the inside of the crossbar.

Early in the second half the Liverpool contingent in the crowd became silent when Lawton worried Sidlow into a punchaway, which went straight to Sewell, who lashed the ball wide when well placed.

Liverpool won an indirect free-kick in the penalty area when Stubbins was obstructed, and the taking of this became quite a lengthy procedure. Taylor paced out the distance between the ball and the opposition when the referee commanded him to desist. When all was set, Done merely tapped the ball two feet, and Liddell smashed it straight through with a terrific shot. The excitement had hardly died down when Hold was straight through and hit his shot against Sidlow - a remarkable escape for Liverpool when it appeared that County would equalise.

So far in the game, Lawton had played as the 'general', but when a through ball came sweetly to him he took it on a few yards and then delivered an excellent low shot that Sidlow half stopped, the ball travelling quite slowly a few yards wide of the outside post.

With time running out, and County making a last-ditch effort, Paisley sustained an injury to his left leg, and he signalled that he would play at outside-left, with Liddell in his place. County went all up for a last minute corner won by the sweat of Adamson's brow, but it was a Liverpool head which nodded the ball away.

ENGLAND v. AUSTRALIA

Britain won the first two tests and the destiny of the Ashes had already been decided, but there was still a crowd of 43,500 to welcome the teams.

Half-time: Great Britain 5pts, Australia 6pts.
Full-time: Great Britain 23pts, Australia 9pts.

Liverpool: Sidlow; Shepherd, Lambert; Taylor, Jones, Paisley; Payne, Balmer, Stubbins, Done, Liddell.

Notts County: Smith; Southwell, Purvis; Gannon, Baxter, Adamson; Houghton, Sewell, Lawton, Hold, Johnston.

Referee: Mr G. Salmon (Stoke-on-Trent)

Attendance: 61,003

February 12, 1949

Wolverhampton W. (1) 3
Dunn 45, Smyth 73, Mullen 79

Liverpool (0) 1
Stubbins 62

BOTH sides were unchanged. Payne suffered from a stye on his left eye, but it was not a serious problem. Liverpool came on from Bridgnorth, and found the ground well filled with people wearing red an hour before the kick-off. The weather then was perfect, but 15 minutes before the start there was a hailstorm.

The attendance had been limited to 55,000 and consequently there was little crushing, and everything was orderly. The silence before the toss up was disturbed by people at the right hand corner of the Molineux "Kop" - the only seriously-crowded portion. Wolves won the toss, and Liverpool had the sun in their eyes as they kicked towards the town.

The home side started strongly. A Pye through-pass to Mullen finished in a low centre which Jones breasted down, and then put away to safety. Within the next minute, Mullen was in the danger zone again, and he struck a half-hit shot which Sidlow allowed to pass wide of the post. Sidlow went full length to another Mullen shot which seemed to be just finding the target, and Lambert was responsible for a fine tackle which prevented Hancocks picking up an easy chance to centre.

A brilliant tackle by Paisley on Hancocks, after Lambert had failed against the same player, was another example of Liverpool's sterling defensive work.

Eventually Liverpool won a corner through the efforts of Payne and Stubbins, though the home defence cleared with ease. Liverpool's tackling was first-class. The sun bothered all the defence, and, coupled with some surging left-wing moves by Mullen, the visitors were kept busy. However, the forward line fought harder than usual for the ball.

Midway through the first period Liverpool suffered their biggest moment of anxiety. With Sidlow out of goal, Paisley skied away off the line from Dunn, and followed up by deflecting Mullen's shot inches wide of the post - it was regarded by contemporary reporters as Paisley's most valuable piece of retrieving in a great career.

The contest grew in excitement. Mullen went close for the home side, and Sidlow caught a header directed downwards by Pye from a Mullen centre.

Balmer hit a shot on the turn which caused Williams great consternation. From a Liddell free-kick, Balmer drove the ball narrowly over the bar. Shorthouse put the ball to safety from a Balmer shot with Williams on the ground. Balmer, with an immaculate pass, got Liddell going just on the interval. He took the ball towards the home goal, turned it in, and then hit a glorious shot. Williams jack-knifed his body and managed to turn the ball over the bar.

With the game approaching its half-time cessation, Dunn scored for Wolves. The goal came from a Mullen centre, which was only half headed away. The chance was for a volley quickly taken, and Dunn scored through a ruck. The pitch had begun to churn up a lot, making things difficult for both sides.

The second half started with a Wolves appeal for a penalty decision against Shepherd, and was followed by a head injury to Liddell, who resumed after a minute or two. Payne hooked a ball over to Stubbins, who advanced goalwards and delivered a shot which careered right across the face of the goal. The visitors were so much on top at this point that Taylor kept moving up into attack to make a sixth forward. The sun was less troubling to the Wolves as it began its ascendancy.

At 62 minutes Liverpool scored a deserved equaliser. Liddell cut inside and hesitated before slipping the ball through to Done who had advanced swiftly up the field. Done tried to wriggle away from Shorthouse, who timed his tackle for possession as the ball came through. Both players fell to the muddy floor in a heap, but Done was up first and advanced goalwards. Williams came out, and defenders closed in, but Done kept his head and slipped the ball towards the post. It was about to cross the line when Stubbins applied the final touch.

Wolves almost made it 2-1 but Sidlow made a point-blank save from Smyth, who was covered by the goalkeeper's body when standing not more than five yards out. Liddell left the field momentarily to get a refreshing wipe of the trainer's sponge, and before he returned Balmer netted, but was offside.

Twenty-eight minutes of the second half had elapsed when Sidlow caught, but just failed to keep close to his body, a header by Mullen. Like a flash, Smyth dragged the ball out of the goalkeeper's grasp and into the net. The applause was deafening.

Mullen finished off Liverpool's interest in the Cup for this season with a goal 11 minutes from time. Balmer chased back half the length of the field in an effort to cut into the Wolves' left-wing move, but he failed to achieve his objective, and when the Liverpool defence had been torn open, Mullen scored almost at his leisure to guarantee his side a place in the

Wolverhampton Wanderers: Williams; Kelly, Pritchard; W.Crook, Shorthouse, Wright; Hancocks, Smyth, Pye, Dunn, Mullen.

Liverpool: Sidlow; Shepherd, Lambert; Taylor, Jones, Paisley; Payne, Balmer, Stubbins, Done, Liddell.

Referee: Mr C.W. Fletcher (Northwich)

Attendance: 54,983

Sixth Round. Two first-half hat-tricks provided highlights of the day's Cup ties. Gallant Yeovil ran up against a masterful Manchester United at Maine Road, and inside-left Rowley registered a hat-trick in 22 minutes, Burke adding a fourth before the interval. United eventually won 8-0. The lead changed hands several times at Luton, where Lee, the Leicester centre-forward, scored three times to give his side a 3-2 half-time lead. The game ended 5-5, and Leicester won the replay 5-3.

Manchester United were eventually beaten in a semi-final replay against Wolves by a goal to nil, while Leicester City reached the Final by beating Portsmouth 3-1.

In the Final, the Wanderers beat Leicester 3-1 at Wembley.

Right: **Bob Paisley**

January 7, 1950

Blackburn Rovers (0) 0   Liverpool (0) 0

SECOND Division Blackburn Rovers gave Liverpool an unrelenting battle in the Third Round of the cup on a quagmire of a pitch. If the ground had not dried a little overnight there was every chance that the tie would have been postponed. Blackburn usually received a good deal of rain, and a river which ran close to the ground was a hindrance, and on the Friday the pitch was under water in parts. Even after forking, it was merely a sheet of mud, and manager George Kay, and trainer Albert Shelley, after having inspected it, declared that football "could well become farcical when it becomes churned up."

Liverpool brought with them their American follower, Mr Shennan, who had never seen them lose, and a greater contingent of followers than they had in the Cup semi-final at this ground two years ago.

An hour before the match, Ewood Park was a mass of red and white favours, and the noise from rattles and bells and bugles was unceasing, almost deafening.

Westcott captained Blackburn, while Liverpool's general was Phil Taylor, and the ground was almost full as the two teams came out to a tumultuous welcome. Patterson, the Blackburn goalkeeper, played in white gloves. Liverpool won the toss, and kicked into the Blackburn goal.

As soon as play began, the players' heels threw up mud in large chunks. The home side began with a straggling, but persistent, attack, in which Liverpool remained calm, if a little disconcerted by the way the ball hung in the thick, cloying mud.

Liverpool's first attack was magnificent. Jones put Liddell in possession and the flying Scot left Gray floundering in the mud before dummying his way beyond Holt, who had gone across. Liddell then delivered a square ball which Stubbins just failed to reach, and Baron fired a high shot wide of the goal.

Priday - formerly of Liverpool - almost set Blackburn on their way with a centre which proved to be too square in its execution.

McCaig went closest to scoring when he picked up a pass from Graham, and hit a swerving shot across goal, and Sidlow had to go full length to put the ball away for a corner. Graham produced a good save from Sidlow with another powerful header. Soon afterwards Liddell caught the full force of the ball off a Holt clearance. He revived after attention, but it was a heavy blow with the ball so weighty.

The flying Scot celebrated his recovery with an excellent shot just off target from a Stubbins centre from the left. Spicer and Jones had a tough time against the Blackburn right wing terrors, of whom Graham was by far the best. The smaller men nipped about with zest, and to good effect, and on such a sticky surface trapping the ball was unnecessary because it fell dead as it hit the ground. The interval arrived with no score.

Even play ensued throughout the second period. Priday returned with a knee support and continued to limp, although he was far from fit. Graham went on a fine run, but he finished weakly.

Then Liddell broke free in his inimitable style against a flat-footed defence, and went on towards goal before pulling the ball wide with a right-foot shot.

At this stage of the game Spicer robbed Westcott, who had been rather quiet throughout. Stubbins was seen at his best with a meandering run which ended with a fine shot, but Patterson pulled the ball down with consummate ease. Hughes twice tackled Horton after Westcott had produced a testing through-ball.

Lambert miskicked the ball and presented Westcott with an opportunity for a goal, but the forward shot from an impossible range to gain a corner. From the flag-kick little McCaig was unable to control the ball to his liking for an angled shot and Westcott rose high, but Sidlow punched the ball away. Horton then put Westcott in possession with a magnificent ball which split the Liverpool defence and enabled the centre-forward to run in on goal, but he squandered a good opportunity.

Despite the attentions of the Blackburn defence, Liddell hit the side-netting as the goal loomed large. Payne nodded the ball over the top acrobatically after a Liddell corner had been half-cleared, but Blackburn were on top as the game came to a close. Sidlow single-handedly punched away from McCaig to keep Liverpool in the cup. Receipts were £5,000. Newcastle United registered the highest score of the Third Round by beating Oldham Athletic 7-2 away. Arsenal, who went on to reach the final, beat Sheffield Wednesday 1-0 at Highbury.

Blackburn Rovers: Patterson; Gray, Eckersley; Campbell, Holt, Bell; McCaig, Graham, Westcott, Horton, Priday.

Liverpool: Sidlow; Lambert, Spicer; Taylor, Hughes, Jones; Payne, Baron, Stubbins, Fagan, Liddell.

Referee: Mr R.A. Mortimer (Huddersfield)

Attendance: 52,000

January 11, 1950

Liverpool (1) 2
Payne 32, Fagan 52

Blackburn Rovers (1) 1
Edds 21

FIVE minutes before the game started, people were being led off the field, not being able to stand the pushing and crushing in the paddocks. Blackburn Rovers had the honour of kicking-off, and they opened the game facing the Kop goal.

Liverpool: Sidlow; Lambert, Spicer; Taylor, Hughes, Paisley; Payne, Baron, Stubbins, Fagan, Liddell.

Blackburn Rovers: Patterson; Gray, Eckersley; Campbell, Holt, Bell; McCaig, Graham, Westcott, Horton, Edds.

Referee: Mr R.A. Mortimer (Huddersfield)

Attendance: 52,221

The home side opened brightly in front of their partisan supporters, but after enjoying 20 minutes of almost incessant pressure, Liverpool had to accept a blow one minute later. Liverpool had refused at least three scoring chances. Blackburn accepted the only one they had up to this point. Westcott began the move when he swept the ball out to McCaig, who carried it forward a few strides before he centred across the Liverpool goal to Edds, who came up and without a second's hesitation hit the ball to the back of the net at lightning speed.

This resulted in Blackburn becoming electrified, and they swarmed onto the attack, whereas they had previously been purely defensive. For several minutes Blackburn rode the crest of the wave, but eventually Liverpool tightened up their belts and hit back with great determination.

Payne left his post on the wing to pick up a ball almost in the centre of the field and delivered it to Stubbins, who tried a shot which got him nowhere.

In the next minute the Rovers' goal fell to a great shot by Payne, who left Patterson with an onlooker's view of the ball as it sped to the back of the net after 32 minutes. There was a great roar from the Liverpool crowd.

At times Liverpool simply clustered round the Rovers' goalmouth, but no further damage was suffered by Patterson. In fact, the next action took place in the Liverpool penalty area. Westcott tried to get the ball down to his liking, but while he did it he lost those fractional seconds which proved to be costly.

Liverpool played towards their favourite end in the second half, and soon tested the Rovers' defence, but only temporarily. Blackburn replied with a good attack, but Sidlow saved the situation for Liverpool. The home side soon went ahead. The Liverpool attack soon moved swiftly into formation and Baron hit the underside of the crossbar. The ball came out and Fagan promptly cracked it back into the net. It appeared that all the Liverpool forwards were offside, and the Rovers' defenders also thought so, for they appealed against the goal to the referee who, however, stood firm in his decision.

Westcott almost levelled matters again when he tried a surprise shot while on the half turn, and Sidlow had to go scrambling across his goal line to keep the ball out. The Rovers' goal was equally fortunate after Payne had popped the ball into the middle, and Stubbins' shot went just outside of the upright.

Fifteen minutes after the interval Gray had to be taken off the field with an injury. During his absence, Payne tried to improve Liverpool's lead, but did not get a true hit at the ball, which slewed outside. Gray was off the field only a matter of moments, just in time to see Stubbins head over. He also saw Westcott beat the Liverpool defence with a good pass to McCaig but the Rovers winger did not make the best use of the opening. The Liverpool defence was not too confident, which was unusual because Liverpool's defence had been their backbone in a season in which they had gone undefeated in the First Division in their first nineteen games.

Stubbins hooked a throw-in from Payne over his head and into the goalmouth where it landed at the feet of Fagan. The inside-forward dribbled his way through, but was dispossessed and the ball ran away for a corner. Shortly afterwards, Patterson turned a header from Fagan over the bar.

Blackburn fought hard to get on to level terms and they were awarded a free-kick just outside the penalty area, though it appeared that a handling offence had taken place inside the area.

Sidlow made a fine save when he pushed his foot out to prevent a shot by Horton entering the net. Liverpool were confined to defence at this stage of the game as the Rovers fought desperately hard and with great skill.

With the game in its dying seconds, Blackburn were awarded a free-kick. This was taken by Edds, and he hit the Liverpool upright with a shot that swerved. Another inch and all would have been equal.

Stubbins put Liddell in possession, and the Scot sent in a drive towards the near post, but Patterson scrambled across his goalmouth and managed to turn the ball round the post to safety.

January 28, 1950

Liverpool (1) 3
Baron 45, Fagan 82,
Payne 88

Exeter City (0) 1
Smart 83

THERE were two surprises before the fourth round cup tie between Liverpool and Exeter at Anfield. Firstly, both teams changed colours, Liverpool playing in white and Exeter in blue. Secondly, although the first spectator had arrived as early as 9am on the morning of the match, the ground, when the teams came out, was far from full. No doubt the icy coldness which was emphasised by a fair breeze, caused many to stay away.

Exeter were first out, led by Goddard, their centre-half, and some of the legs in those light blue stockings of theirs looked puny by comparison with those of Liverpool.

Taylor won the toss and kicked away from the 'Kop' goal. Inside-left Greenwood and inside-right Kevin Baron exchanged greetings, and the game commenced on a pitch which showed itself to be phenomenally hard and full of treachery. Exeter began by employing an offside trap, but it failed miserably in the opening minutes so that Payne from the inside-right position was left with a clear shooting chance but he shot over the bar.

The opening minutes were tentative in many ways and lacking in the usual drama of cup ties and the crowd's intense excitement. In attack, Exeter - from the Third Division South - were very orthodox and not very convincing, but the ball behaved strangely and Liverpool themselves found it difficult on such a treacherous pitch. The freak ground brought the teams to a level.

Exeter had their best chance of scoring just before the interval when Smart took too long to position himself for an angled shot and pulled the ball back very square for the limping Regan to try his luck, but his shot passed right across the goal. Right from this incident, Liverpool went into a scrambling type of attack, Stubbins providing the chance for Baron to guide the ball with the side of his right foot just inside the post prior to the half-time whistle.

The diminutive Regan made a magnificent burst to open up the second half, and Exeter went through the Liverpool defence in a concerted move, which went on and on and finished only when Regan was crowded out near the post. City never stopped playing good football, even though the odds were stacked against them, and they did not present Liverpool with a greater danger because of their inability to fire in the lethal shots.

Stubbins did extraordinarily well to attempt to convert a ball deflected to him in a sharp half-volley as the ball came to him on the iron turf. The ball passed over the crossbar. Exeter were unlucky once again not to score when Hutchings shot across the goal face, and Sidlow turned to see the ball wobbling a few inches away from the post. Hutchings was injured in the process, but resumed soon afterwards. Walker was damaged in a heavy collision with Lambert, and Smart was injured for a second time when falling heavily after attempting to make a header, and there were too many injuries at this juncture to be conducive to flowing football.

When Fagan scored after 82 minutes he was falling as he shot from a pass by Stubbins, and the ball merely trickled over the line. Exeter appealed for an offside verdict, but received no reprieve from the official. Goddard was spoken to sharply by the referee for his loquaciousness.

Within a minute, it was 2-1. A free-kick against Baron appeared to be going out of play, but Hutchings headed it back on the goalline, and Smart added the final touch with his head. The Liverpool defence looked at one another aghast that they could be so lax as to allow such an occurrence.

Before another minute had elapsed, Payne had headed Liverpool's third goal and Exeter were virtually out, although they fought bravely.

The receipts were £4,383. Arsenal beat Swansea Town 2-1 at Highbury.

Willie Fagan

Liverpool: Sidlow; Lambert, Spicer; Taylor, Hughes, Paisley; Payne, Baron, Stubbins, Fagan, Liddell.

Exeter City: Singleton; Johnstone, Clark; Fallon, Goddard, Davey; Hutchings, Smart, Walker, Greenwood, Regan.

Referee: Mr C. Warburton (Scunthorpe)

Attendance: 45,209

February 11, 1950

Stockport County (0) 1
Herd 90

Liverpool (0) 2
Fagan 57, Stubbins 70

IT was a case of full house at Edgeley Park and the official receipts were £4,300. There were probably more spectators in the ground than the official attendance figures of 27,833 because some people had climbed a wall into the ground, and so got in "on the nod". The Liverpool team was as announced during the week, but right up to lunchtime there was a doubt about Payne who had been taken off training for a couple of days owing to a cold on the chest. However, he reported perfectly fit on the day of the match, so that Liverpool were unchanged, with the exception, of course, that Taylor was at right half.

Stockport were represented by the same team which did such a fine job of work in the fourth round against Hull City (they won 2-0 in a replay). It was a glorious day, the sun shone brilliantly, and the ground, considering the rain which had fallen in the district, was in excellent condition.

Stockport County: Bowles; Staniforth, Sanaghan; McCulloch, Glover, Patterson; McGuigan, Herd, Cocker, Swinscoe, Reid.

Liverpool: Sidlow; Lambert, Spicer; Taylor, Hughes, Paisley; Payne, Baron, Stubbins, Fagan, Liddell.

Referee: Mr R. Wood (Sunderland)

Attendance: 27,833

The County won the toss, and set Liverpool to kick off against the bright sunlight. This proved to be somewhat of a handicap as County were determined to strike an early blow. For the first five minutes they attacked incessantly and Liverpool had to concentrate their defence to beat them back. Even early on, County showed themselves to be a side above the expectations of a usual Third Division side. Herd spread the ball about wisely, and Swinscoe and Reid indulged themselves in a series of inter-passing that often had Liverpool struggling to win the ball.

Gradually Liverpool went onto the offensive, and a fierce Liddell shot tested Bowles. Shortly afterwards, a section of wooden fencing collapsed and about fifty spectators were thrown to the ground, but none was hurt. Afterwards they had to stand close to the touchline. The visitors had to put their whole attention into the matter of defence, for Stockport were not only a lively side, but one which was full of imagination. Sidlow released one ball as McGuigan bore down on him, and then Herd had a shot blocked out.

Liverpool were forced back into defence time and time again, and Sidlow then had to effect a save from Swinscoe. The County took full advantage of the wind in the first half to add to Liverpool's problems. The visitors' appreciation of the County's attack was evident when Hughes decided to give away a corner rather than take any risks. Sidlow punched the corner kick away, but it fell to Swinscoe, whose fierce shot flew marginally wide. After Liverpool had produced a solitary raid on the Stockport defence in the first minute of the second half, the home side returned to the attack, and were almost as dominating as they had been in the first period. However, there were few chances for either goalkeeper to show his worth. Stockport had an appeal for a penalty turned down after Herd - the former Manchester City player - was definitely brought down from behind by Taylor. The referee refused to listen to the appeals, which brought forth a cacophony of boos and jeers.

With 57 minutes gone, Liverpool scrambled a goal. Liddell pushed the ball into the Stockport goalmouth, which was busy with players, and Paisley tapped the ball closer in, when Fagan came running in to put the ball over the line.

For a while the Anfielders attacked strongly, but the home side had no intention of lying down and giving the game to their more illustrious opponents, and they went onto the offensive. First, Sidlow had to push the ball out, and then Hughes got his head to one effort to turn it away. The County refused to acknowledge Liverpool's superiority, and Hughes and his colleagues had to work hard to stay ahead. Reid, with a free-kick, smashed the ball against the side netting, and McGuigan, from well out, gave Sidlow a difficult shot to deal with, the Welsh goalkeeper having to use his knuckles in the old-fashioned punch-away to clear the danger.

The ground, owing to the rain, had turned into a quagmire, and made ball control extremely difficult. Stubbins picked up the ball near the half-way line, dashed between the two backs and, as the goalkeeper came out, shot. The 'keeper, however, was right in the line of fire and the ball struck him, only to come out right to Stubbins' foot again. This time, the Liverpool centre-forward made no mistake at the 70th minute. Shortly afterwards Baron shot and caused Bowles to fly across his goal and turn the ball round the posts. The second goal had taken the heart out of the County and during the next few minutes, Liverpool were dominant.

The home side refused to be beaten by the current leaders of the First Division, and just on time Swinscoe caused Sidlow to tip a shot over the bar. As a result of this corner, Stockport scored a well-deserved consolation goal. Reid took the corner kick and Herd jumped up high to get his head to the ball to steer it well out of Sidlow's reach. Everton beat Tottenham 1-0 at Goodison before a crowd of 72,921, while Arsenal beat Burnley 2-0 at Highbury.

March 4, 1950

Liverpool (1) 2
Fagan 19, Liddell 81

Blackpool (1) 1
Mortensen (pen) 23

THE weather was ideal, and there was almost as much tangerine inside Anfield as there was red. Not only did Blackpool supporters bring a live duck - appropriately dyed yellow - with them, they also brought a pail of water to refresh the bird. Harry Johnston and Phil Taylor, rivals for the England right-half position, were the captains, and when red-haired Mr Griffiths spun the coin, it was Blackpool who won the toss and elected to defend the Kop goal.

Payne and Baron began with a sharp right-wing thrust, but the tall amateur, Slater, not only extricated his side, but did it with a magnificent sixpenny-piece dribble. There were few genuine chances in the opening quarter. Johnston, like Paisley, threw the ball vast distances, but Blackpool had thus far been too ineffective in their passing and Mortensen ought to have shot at goal himself rather than pass the ball to McIntosh.

Farm, from a tentative shot by Stubbins, finger-tipped the ball to safety. This great save led to a Liddell corner and was the beginning of Liverpool's leading goal. Farm tried to punch away, but failed to, and Stubbins, heading into a goal without its 'keeper, found Wright heading away on the line. The ball hung a few yards from goal when Fagan fastened on to it, and with a cute and most deliberate right-foot effort, placed it where it would do most damage.

Just four minutes later came a dramatic equaliser. Hughes - in trying to stop the flying Mortensen, who appeared to have jockeyed Hughes from the ball - unmistakably handled, and the penalty decision was immediate. Mortensen took it, and hit a very solid shot to Sidlow's left. The Welsh international stretched out his left hand and made solid contact, and it appeared that he might turn it wide of the post, but the ball sped on just inside the upright.

Blackpool's defence looked unsettled on most occasions when Liverpool attacked. However, the half-backs in midfield did well, and the forwards had moments of sheer inspiration. The visitors' shots out-numbered Liverpool's by about ten to one. Liverpool were shocked by the swiftness of Blackpool's equaliser, and their football became somewhat ragged. Laurie Hughes, nevertheless, remained calm and sure, and he linked up his defensive units with aplomb.

Liddell had hardly been seen, while Blackpool grew in confidence as the minutes ticked by. An odd sight was to see Johnston explain to little Kevin Baron as they walked off, that when he had shouted a minute or two before the interval, he had not been angry with the Liverpool player, but with his own inside-forwards.

The early minutes in the second half were evenly contested. There were opportunities at both ends, and some fierce tackling, which was well marshalled by referee Griffiths.

As time progressed, a Liddell corner caused Blackpool some problems. Farm was unable to reach the ball and Stubbins, nodded it towards the goal, but Wright half-stopped it on the line. Shimwell completed the job when all seemed lost. Within seconds, the ball was at the other end and Lambert just held off Mortensen to allow the ball to go over the dead-ball line. Shortly afterwards, Slater drifted into the centre and shot almost casually, but he imparted terrific spin on the ball, and Sidlow did well to knock it up and catch it at the second attempt.

The tackling on both sides was unrelenting, and Blackpool covered up like a boxer on the ropes. The only clear-cut scoring chance came when Baron did magnificently to attempt to glance the ball off his head. Liddell and Payne then changed places.

With 81 minutes gone, the Liverpool section of the crowd erupted when Liddell scored. Payne jigged up the left wing, attended by a retinue of three Blackpool defenders. Just when it seemed that Payne would shoot, he passed the ball a few yards to his right to where Liddell slewed it with his right foot beyond the dismayed Farm. Mortensen almost earned undying fame for his daring flying header to try to get the equaliser when it seemed likely that he would collide with the post and end up in hospital. Blackpool ran out of time, and Liverpool had reached the semi-finals.

Everton beat Derby County 2-1 at the Baseball Ground, while Chelsea beat Manchester United 2-0 at home. Arsenal beat Leeds United with a 53rd-minute Lewis goal. Leslie Compton required two stitches in a head wound sustained in the first half against Second Division opponents.

Liverpool: Sidlow; Lambert, Spicer; Taylor, Hughes, Paisley; Payne, Baron, Stubbins, Fagan, Liddell.

Blackpool: Farm; Shimwell, Wright; Johnston, Crosland, Kelly; Hobson, McIntosh, Mortensen, Slater, Wardle.

Referee: Mr B.M. Griffiths (Newport)

Attendance: 53,973

March 25, 1950

Everton (0) 0

Liverpool (1) 2
Paisley 29, Liddell 62

MAINE Road looked a picture in the bright sunshine, with red and blue colours dotted about in such profusion that the terraces looked almost like a herbaceous border. With the crowd fixed at 72,000 - compared with a record attendance of 84,000 - the terrace spectators did not appear to be unduly crushed, though in one or two corners they were perhaps a little too tightly packed. The official receipts were £13,497.

The first incident of note was a rather poor back pass by Moore which saw Stubbins dashing in quickly in the hope of picking it up before it reached Burnett, but the goalkeeper got to the ball first. Straight from this, Everton dashed away on the right and Spicer was guilty of a half-hearted back pass. Instead of putting the ball to Sidlow, Spicer presented Everton with a corner. Buckle pulled the corner back to Farrell, who slipped it forward to Fielding. The inside-left hooked the ball just over the bar. Everton looked strong again after some dangerous work by Eglington, but Catterick put the ball behind from a long range shot.

Everton's attack in the early stages was more forceful than Liverpool's, and a well-judged Fielding pass saw Wainwright fire in a cannon-ball effort which went narrowly wide of the post. The stiff wind appeared to assist Everton in their attacking forays.

Liverpool responded, however, with a piece of footballing magic. From a throw-in Stubbins back-headed the ball to Baron, who swivelled round and knocked it on to Payne. The right-winger, in almost the centre-forward position, eluded Hedley and fired in a grand right-foot shot from about ten yards which Burnett saved in brilliant fashion, at the expense of an unproductive corner. Moments later, Payne again called Burnett into action with a long effort from 20 yards which the Everton 'keeper hugged to his chest in a careful manner.

The Everton defence endured a period of anxiety, and the crowd witnessed the unusual sight of Eglington tackling Liddell - who had gone to outside-right - on the line near the corner flag.

At the 24th minute there came an incident which was debated by fans of both sides. Fagan chased quickly to a ball which seemed to be going out, screwed back a centre which Stubbins bent down to and headed out of Burnett's reach. Moore stood behind the goalkeeper on the line, and cannoned the ball out a couple of yards where Burnett, on his hands and knees, regained possession and booted it upfield. Several Liverpool players immediately appealed for a goal on the grounds that the ball had actually crossed the line, but Referee Fletcher waved them away and beckoned play on.

Five minutes elapsed, and the Reds went ahead. The movement was started by an upward pass by Taylor to Baron,

just inside the Everton half. Baron slipped it back to Taylor, Taylor on to Payne, who beat Hedley, cut in and centred with his left-foot for Burnett to punch away to Paisley. The half-back lobbed the ball goalwards high in the air, where Liddell, boring in at top speed, jumped for it at the same time as Burnett and two Everton defenders. It looked as though Liddell might have connected, but he did not, and Paisley was the scorer.

The half-back's freebooter was an ominous sign for Everton - Mrs L. Brotherton's Freebooter (the joint-favourite) was an ominous sign for the other horses in the Grand National as it romped home to victory.

Everton responded with an attack of their own, and Eglington - in acres of space - found himself with an unimpeded shot from 12 yards, but he sliced his effort wide. Liverpool's reply was to attack Everton at every opportunity. Payne and Baron gave the Blues' defenders a torrid time, and on the opposite flank, the referee wagged an admonishing finger at Moore, who brought down Liddell. Just on half-time, Payne forced Liverpool's fourth corner of the half, from which Liddell headed the ball downwards to Baron without the latter being able to get in a shot. It had been a grim and hard-fought first period, characterised by tenacious tackling and sheer determination, rather than any outstanding classic touches, though Payne was often prominent. Liverpool's front line dovetailed more impressively than Everton's.

The second half opened with Everton, for a few minutes, providing some of the most entrancing combinations that the game had seen, and it took the combined efforts of Lambert, Jones and Spicer to hold them at bay. A Liddell run thrilled the Liverpool supporters as he dashed down the middle to beat both Falder and Moore, but he was unable to control a return pass from Stubbins and Burnett collected safely.

Paisley had to receive attention after effecting a headed clearance from an Eglington shot, but the tough little Anfielder shook himself a couple of times and dashed back into the fray.

Liverpool had the benefit of the sun and wind, and after Everton's early exuberance wore off, the Reds attacked constantly, though with little effect. Burnett made a spectacular save when he tipped a high dropping shot from Baron over the bar at the last split second, when a goal seemed certain.

Liverpool were fortunate to score their second goal, despite a period of intense pressure. In his anxiety to save a flag-kick, Farrell pulled the ball back right to Liddell's feet. Although angled, Liddell shot hard and true, and managed to squeeze it into the goal, just inside the far post to put Liverpool into a commanding position. It appeared, however, that the ball had been over the dead-ball line before it had gone to Liddell. A couple of minutes later Burnett saved brilliantly from Stubbins, and Liddell fired into the side-netting as the Reds held the advantage. Liddell then went head-over-heels over a group of photographers crowded near the dead-ball line. The referee moved them further back.

In the first twenty minutes of this half, Liverpool had forced four corners, three of them through Liddell's persistence. Everton, however, refused to lie down and accept defeat unquestioningly, and a determined piece of work by Fielding, Wainwright and Catterick carried the ball into the Liverpool penalty area, where Jones, who had played calmly and confidently throughout, stood firm between Catterick and Sidlow. Everton's only possible course of action was to throw caution to the winds, and attack Liverpool at every possible opportunity. But Liverpool's defence was in command, and the Reds counter-attacked with speed and accuracy.

With 15 minutes to go, Liddell again forced a corner, the twelfth which Liverpool had gained so far, to Everton's three, nine of which had come from Liddell's flank. With his twelfth one, Liddell tried an in-swinger which curved appreciably and struck the near post. Baron continued to do some excellent foraging work, and he had never played better.

As the minutes ticked by, Wainwright shot into the side netting. Catterick won Everton's first corner of the second half off Paisley, the result being a Falder lob into Sidlow's hands. Everton won another corner with only three minutes to go, but they were unable to turn it to their advantage.

Arsenal - by virtue of their 1-0 replay victory over Chelsea - also won through to the Final. A colour clash meant that both sides would have to change shirts. This was Liverpool's second Final, and Arsenal's third.

Everton: Burnett; Moore, Hedley; Grant, Falder, Farrell; Buckle, Wainwright, Catterick, Fielding, Eglington.

Liverpool: Sidlow; Lambert, Spicer; Taylor, Jones, Paisley; Payne, Baron, Stubbins, Fagan, Liddell.

Referee: Mr C. Fletcher (Northwich)

Attendance: 72,000

---

*Below: **Bob Paisley's** lob beats the Everton defence*

LIVERPOOL LOSE TO LEWIS DOUBLE STRIKE

PLAYERS INTRODUCED TO KING GEORGE VI

Arsenal (1) 2   Liverpool (0) 0

Lewis 17, 62

WEMBLEY did not look the cheery picture that it had done so for many years. The crowd in the uncovered portions, protected against the weather to the extent, in some hundreds of cases, by umbrellas - which obviously would have had to be closed when the game started - looked more drab than usual.

Uncovered

In some cases wives and relatives of the Liverpool players had elected to take uncovered seats in order to be nearer the play. Had the weather been fine, they would have backed a winner, but as it was, one could only hope that they were adequately prepared for the heavy showers. The pitch, tended by a Liverpool man, Mr Percy Young, head groundsman, looked immaculate, as usual, despite the fact that snow had fallen earlier in the week!

Whatever effect the rain may have had, the pitch was as true as a billiard table, and the ball did not go off at unexpected angles.

Fell ill

Prompt at 2.55, the teams appeared in the arena, with Arsenal's Old Gold shirts looking more like canary yellow. Liverpool were dressed in white with black shorts. The party was led out by Mr Whitty, an F.A. official, followed by the managers, Mr George Kay - who fell ill on the morning of the match - and Mr Tom Whittaker. They lined up on the field with Liverpool on the right, and Arsenal on the left.

Sartorial

There was a sartorial fashion note for trainers in the attire of Albert Shelley, for the Liverpool trainer was dressed in red trousers, a cream linen jacket and beneath it a red shirt. The respective captains were presented to His Majesty the King by Mr A. Brook Hirst, chairman of the F.A., and they in turn presented to his Majesty their own players.

Talking point

The major talking point among Liverpool fans was the omission from the team of Bob Paisley. Laurie Hughes was fit again after breaking a toe, and he was an almost automatic selection at centre-half, but Bill Jones had done so well as his deputy, and was so experienced in other positions, that his place in the side was almost as strongly guaranteed. With Taylor an essential midfield link, the one to be left out of the four possible half-back choices was Paisley, who was heartbroken when told of the decision.

Omen

After Phil Taylor and Joe Mercer - soon to be elected Footballer of the Year - had shaken hands, Taylor set a good omen by winning the toss for Liverpool.

Arsenal came through after the kick-off in somewhat leisurely fashion for Forbes to try a shot from long distance which was some yards off the mark. A long clearance by Lambert developed into a race between Stubbins and Leslie Compton, won just in the nick of time by the Arsenal player, and finished off by him with a pass back to Swindin, to give the goalkeeper an early feel of the ball. The treacherous nature of the top surface was seen when Fagan slid two or three yards and left a clear mark on the virgin turf. Arsenal had shown some neat touches up to this point, but their efforts lacked real power.

Corner

Taylor put the ball up to Liddell just inside the Arsenal half. Liddell took it upwards before passing forward to Stubbins, who had veered out to the outside-left position, just a few yards in front of Liddell. Stubbins found himself badly angled as he was tackled by Compton, and tried to pull the ball back, only to see it bounce off Barnes for a corner, which proved of no value. A particularly hard tackle by Forbes on Liddell, well inside the Arsenal half, resulted in both players falling flat out and requiring the attention of their respective trainers. The resultant free-kick to Liverpool was taken by Jones. The ball was headed forward by Baron, but eventually cleared by Compton.

Cox picked up a through-ball from Lewis and lobbed in a peach of a centre which Lambert was glad to head away for a corner. This was well placed by Compton, but headed away by Taylor.

Goal

It was picked up and slipped out by Denis Compton to Logie, who quickly put across an ideal centre right into an open space on the edge of the Liverpool penalty area. Lewis, quick off the mark, ran forward with no one to hinder his progress, and slipped the ball from about ten yards' range well out of Sidlow's reach.

Liverpool's fifth corner followed immediately and Liddell's strong cross went to Taylor on the far side of the field, though again without producing any positive result.

Pile-driver

The best scoring effort of the first half came from Forbes, who worked the ball through beautifully with little Logie, right from his own half, and then unleashed a pile-driver from the edge of the penalty area which passed narrowly outside.

The Arsenal had a real escape when Liddell beat Scott and put over a centre which at first looked as though it was out of Payne's reach. The winger, however, managed to screw it back, and as it dropped a foot in front of the crossbar, Swindin, in trying to tip it over, actually knocked it

King George meets the players and shakes hands with **Billy Liddell**

Reg Lewis, *number 10, scores the first of his two goals*

against the bar and then caught the rebound. A few inches lower and Liverpool would have equalised.

Precise

For the first half-hour Liverpool had had more of the play territorially, but they had not been as precise or methodical as the Arsenal side in their approach work. An upward pass from Fagan saw Stubbins beat Leslie Compton with a delightful piece of ball control and then fire in a strong shot which cannoned away from an Arsenal defender.

Accurately

The ball was slipped over quickly to the left where Liddell centred accurately and Stubbins, throwing himself headlong at the ball, only missed connecting by a fraction of an inch. Had he done so, there was no possible doubt of Liverpool getting on equal terms, for Swindin was hopelessly

placed to effect a save. There was loud booing from behind the Arsenal goal when Scott swept Liddell's legs right from under him as the winger was boring through. Liddell took the free-kick himself, and put it to Stubbins' head, only for the Liverpool leader to nod it outside.

Efficiently

Little had been seen of Jimmy Payne. He did not receive the usual service of passes from his right flank colleagues, and when he did find himself in possession, Mercer was there to tackle efficiently and clinically. Mercer brought down Baron about five yards outside the penalty area after 35 minutes.

Keen

It was the tenth free-kick given against Arsenal in those opening 35 minutes. The game was not, however, over-physical or vicious, but the Arsenal tackling was

keen and strong. Liverpool started off the second half in encouraging fashion, and for the first few minutes they had the Arsenal penned in their own half, and then the Arsenal goal had another fortunate escape. Liddell, after a prolonged tussle with Forbes, got the better of the Arsenal half-back and put over a beautiful centre which Swindin, coming out, failed to gather, and the ball went to Payne.

Miraculous

Payne threw himself forward and headed goalwards, only to see Swindin make a miraculous recovery and fall on the ball right on the goal line. Liddell bored his way through with one of his characteristic efforts in which he beat three men brilliantly, but he was unable to get in a shot.

Victim

Then Payne, although upended by Compton, got to

his feet, recovered the ball, and beat two men before falling victim to a tackle by Mercer.

Fighting qualities

Liverpool displayed all the fighting qualities which had seen them reach the final and go unbeaten in the League for their opening nineteen matches.

Superiority

At this stage of Liverpool superiority, even Lambert attempted a shot, but the ball finished up on the touchline side of the corner flag. A marvellous bit of work in the Liverpool attack saw Taylor, Baron, Payne, Liddell, and Fagan take part in a machine-like movement which only broke down at the last moment when a Fagan pass to Stubbins was ankled away by Compton.

Arsenal's reply to Liverpool's pressure was swift and decisive. Cox, on the wing, found himself unmarked and he slipped the ball through to Lewis, who was in the inside-right position. Lewis, swivelling round quickly, again placed the ball with a powerful shot in a position where Sidlow had no chance.

Pride

From this point on, the Cup was Arsenal's, though Liverpool's fighting spirit and pride would not allow them to admit the fact.

When Compton pulled the ball down preparatory for a clearance, Stubbins was too quick for him and Liverpool's leader shot at goal, but it was blocked by Arsenal's resistance in defence. An excellent run by Stubbins was finished off with a through-pass which Baron just failed to reach before Swindin got there. A goal to Liverpool at this stage would have given them vital inspiration.

Switched

With time running out, Liverpool switched their wingers and the first result was a run and shot by Liddell, the shot ending up in the side netting. Thirteen minutes from the end Liverpool suffered another blow when Phil Taylor collided with Lewis, was also struck by the ball, and had to be assisted off the field by trainer Shelley and reserve centre-forward Cyril Done.

Attention

After a few minutes attention on the touchline, Taylor returned to the field and immediately signalled it with a brilliant run, in which he beat four men in succession, passed to Fagan, who in turn gave Stubbins a glorious chance from eight yards out. Stubbins, from a difficult angle, pulled the ball past the far post. The Arsenal goal had an even narrower escape when Jones headed onto the crossbar from a corner. Spicer tested Swindin from long range as Liverpool threw everything into attack.

Determination

Although Liverpool fought with grim determination, the final whistle signified an Arsenal victory.

Liverpool's attack was short of ideas and not good enough to overcome a resolute Arsenal defence.

Kevin Baron shoots at goal. Barnes, of Arsenal, is in attendance

Arsenal: Swindin; Scott, Barnes; Forbes, L.Compton, Mercer; Cox, Logie, Goring, Lewis, D.Compton.

Liverpool: Sidlow; Lambert, Spicer; Taylor, Hughes, Jones; Payne, Baron, Stubbins, Fagan, Liddell.

Referee: Mr A. Pearce (Bedfordshire)

Attendance: 100,000

Receipts: £39,296

January 6, 1951

Norwich City (0) 3
Docherty 63, 80, Kinsey 76

Liverpool (0) 1
Balmer 87

THE Liverpool players sought tonic air along the sea-front at Great Yarmouth on the morning of the game as a preliminary refresher to the cup-tie with Norwich City at Carrow Road. Because of the influenza epidemic, an eve-of-the-match theatre visit was cancelled. An additional incentive to lower the colours of Norwich - unchanged in the last 17 matches, and unbeaten in 22 successive games, and currently leading the Third Division South - was the knowledge that Liverpool had an old score to settle: a 3-0 defeat in 1937 at this ground.

To ensure no delay in the Norwich traffic, the coach with the Liverpool party was met by a police patrol at the city boundary and escorted to the ground.

Albert Stubbins returned to lead the Liverpool attack after an absence of five weeks, and Done, the deputy leader, was at inside-left. Otherwise, the team was that which had done service in recent weeks. Crossley and Heydon were making their Cup débuts.

The Norwich groundstaff broke ice on the pitch as late as the night before the game. With heavy rain on the morning of the match, it was thought that the surface would be heavy, but in bright sunshine at the kick-off the turf looked good. The compact ground, with high terracing, appeared to be packed to capacity an hour before the kick-off. There were few supporters wearing the red of Liverpool.

Liverpool kicked off against a strong sun and early on Jones had to make a sliding tackle to deprive Hollis of a likely opening. It was soon apparent that Norwich were to stand on no ceremony as they kicked the ball first time up-the-middle. Nor did Norwich hesitate in the tackle, or shooting on sight. Twice Crossley saved point-blank efforts from Hollis and Eyre. Norwich played with verve and imagination, and Liverpool looked like the Third Division side. Liverpool's defence was slow and cumbersome in comparison to the slick movements of the opposition. No matter how much effort Liverpool expended, there appeared to be a Norwich player wherever the ball went. The do-or-die interception of Heydon brought relief to Liverpool as Norwich swarmed all over the visitors.

Stubbins was brought down a few yards outside the penalty area, but Done's free-kick went wide of the goal.

The manner in which the Norwich wing-halves supported their forwards was delightful to witness. When Hollis - tall, with the speed of a greyhound - again threatened, Heydon nipped in to push the ball back to Crossley. Norwich were given a great ovation as they left the field for half-time.

Early in the second half, Done almost scored for Liverpool. At the vital moment he just failed to connect properly and Nethercott managed to scramble the ball away. From this point, Norwich went onto the attack and Heydon was knocked out when he got in the way of a shot by Hollis. Play continued around the Liverpool goal area and it was Heydon who, rising from the prone position, eventually cleared the danger. Norwich were demons for work, and they harassed Liverpool at every possible opportunity. A corner for the home side brought the first goal. Gavin placed the ball low and hard and after it had come out from a crowd of players, Docherty shot first time into the net. Further goals appeared to be inevitable as their fast movements simply riddled the Liverpool defence. Two shots in quick succession by Hollis and Eyre just missed the mark.

With 76 minutes gone, Norwich scored a second goal which their effort deserved. Kinsey barged his way through the Liverpool defence to find the net with a shot that was partially blocked. Within a minute, Norwich were again attacking viciously. Their inter-passing and positioning were too hot for Liverpool, and Eyre, with a magnificent shot, struck the upright after Crossley had failed to get at a ball which was beyond his reach.

Four minutes later, Docherty scored a third goal. It was a magnificent effort from about twenty yards which gave Crossley no chance at all of saving.

In the gathering dusk, Liverpool had a final rally, and Balmer scored a consolation goal after 87 minutes, with a fine piece of opportunism. However, Liverpool were beaten by a superior all-round team which reached the Fifth Round before losing to Sunderland 3-1 at Roker Park.

Norwich City: Nethercott; Duffy, Lewis; Pickwick, Foulkes, Ashman; Gavin, Kinsey, Hollis, Eyre, Docherty.

Liverpool: Crossley; Lambert, Spicer; Heydon, Jones, Paisley; Payne, Balmer, Stubbins, Done, Liddell.

Referee: Mr A.W. Smith (Aldershot)

Attendance: 34,641

Receipts: £3,000

January 12, 1952

Liverpool (0) 1
Payne 76

Workington Town (0) 0

GALLANT newcomers to the League, Workington Town, almost held Liverpool to a goalless draw and, although they had more shots than Liverpool, they fell to a Jimmy Payne goal in the last quarter of an hour.

Although Workington could hardly have been regarded as attractive opposition, there were thousands of people outside the ground five minutes before the start and the paddock had to be closed. Liverpool played in their first change - white shirts with red facings and black shorts. Workington were in a blue which was even darker than that worn by Everton.

Liverpool played with their backs to the sun - away from the Kop. Baron set Liverpool going with a dribble and an upfield pass to Smith, who helped the ball on towards Liddell. The Scottish international sliced the ball away from his objective so that it soared into the crowd nearer the corner flag than the goal. It was a portent of Liddell's ineffectiveness.

Payne drove through and Ford failed to catch his shot. Payne, full length on the ground, made a gallant effort to hook the ball in from the rebound. McAlone kicked the ball off the line from a Smith shot with Ford hopelessly beaten, and a moment later Smith almost headed in from the corner.

The Workington players were a big, strapping lot in certain positions, while even their shorter players were thick-set. The visitors' tackling was extremely keen, and Liddell, in particular was superbly marshalled by Wallace. Payne, who had been Liverpool's most dangerous forward also attracted careful attention.

The most exciting individual run was contributed by Mullen - the younger brother of the Wolves' player - who took the ball half the length of the field beating all opposition until he was challenged by Taylor and ran the ball behind. Liverpool, however, were continually afflicted by an epidemic of mis-passing.

Maxfield, who had gone off with blood streaming down his face following a collision right on the interval, came back with a plaster over the wound. Liverpool began in determined fashion, but their approach work was somewhat too fanciful when they needed to take the shortest route to goal. The ball was frequently passed and repassed a matter of only a few yards which meant not only that the ground gained was infinitesimal, but also that Workington were able to close their ranks down the centre avenue.

When Liddell and Jackson changed places the Workington backs did likewise, so that Wallace who all through had played a great game against the mercurial Scot, was still shoulder to shoulder with him. The longer the game progressed the more unsettled Liverpool - and their loyal supporters - became, and the more confident Workington

grew. It took a courageous dive by Crossley at the feet of Dick to deny Workington. Ten seconds later, Liddell, with a terrific drive from six yards off a Jackson pass, hit Ford on the legs and the ball rebounded out of the penalty area with Ford knowing nothing about it.

Jimmy Payne

After 76 minutes Liverpool took the lead through Payne. The move originally began way out on the left through good work by Paisley, whose centre was cleared to Taylor. The captain slipped it out to Liddell, and the Scot's centre, after Baron had missed it, was slipped into the net from three yards by Payne with Ford helpless. Workington hardly deserved to be behind. They had had as much of the play as Liverpool and certainly more scoring opportunities.

Baron should have added a second goal three minutes from time after a cross from Liddell, but he screwed the ball wide.

The official receipts were £5,408. Newcastle United - the Cup-holders and eventual winners again in a 1-0 victory over Arsenal - beat Aston Villa 4-2 at home, while Arsenal beat Norwich 5-0 at Carrow Road in the Third Round's biggest score.

Liverpool: Crossley; Jones, Lambert; Taylor, Hughes, Paisley; Jackson, Baron, Smith, Payne, Liddell.

Workington Town: Ford; Wallace, Hainsworth; Cushin, McAlone, Hardy; Maxfield, McDowall, Simmonds, Dick, Mullen.

Referee: Mr L.N. Peake (Rotherham)

Attendance: 52,581

February 2, 1952

Liverpool (2) 2
Paisley 5,   Done 9

Wolverhampton W. (0) 1
Mullen 72

LIVERPOOL had a tactical plan to beat the Billy Wright plan of the Wolves to blot out Liddell. The Anfield plan won the day and saw Liverpool safely into the next round, though not before they had many anxious moments in the second half. The Reds played Liddell at centre-forward for the first hour, and Done at outside-left. The result was that before Wolves had settled down, they were two goals in arrears, through Paisley and Done. For the last half hour, Liddell and Done took up the positions they were given in the programme. At the 72nd minute a bad mistake by Crossley gave Mullen a gift goal and meant that Liverpool, after seemingly having the game well won, had to struggle hard to hang on to their slender lead. Done was excellent in the first half at outside-left, with Liddell not as prominent as usual in his new position. Balmer opened the game out splendidly during Liverpool's first-half ascendancy, and all through Taylor, Jones, and Lambert were excellent in defence. Heydon also did well. Wolves might have made a draw of it if they had swung the ball about more in the first half instead of indulging in close passing.

The Lord Mayor and Lady Mayoress of Liverpool (Alderman and Mrs Vere E. Cotton) and the Town Clerk attended the game and were accompanied by the Mayor and Town Clerk of Wolverhampton. The usual colours and mascots were much in evidence with Liverpool's crippled mascot doing his stuff, in fancy dress as usual. Some of the gates were closed before the start and people in the Kop who had overflowed on to the cinder path were escorted out of the ground. Taylor won the toss and elected to defend the Spion Kop end in the first half. There was a lapse before the ball was kicked, because the Wolves inside-forwards lined up facing the wrong way.

The game opened up in a very lively manner, with Liverpool surging down on the Wolves' goal, first through Williams, whose low cross was cleared by Wright and then by means of a Done centre from the outside-left position. Liverpool gained an important psychological blow when they scored through Paisley as early as the fifth minute. When Williams centred to Liddell in the inside-right position, there appeared to be little danger, but Liddell headed the ball a good 12 yards back towards the incoming Paisley, who hit a strong shot through a ruck of players to put his side a goal up.

Just four minutes later and Liverpool had scored again. A long cross-field pass by Balmer opened up play beautifully. The high ball passed over the head of Shorthouse and Done, cutting in like a flash, fired home a fierce first-time effort which Parsons was unable to reach. Done played brilliantly at outside-left. He delivered another strong effort which had

Parsons in trouble, and then followed two corners which might have brought further success.

In the Wolves' first attack for many minutes, Wright came through with the ball at his feet and hit a shot from 30 yards which Crossley caught very confidently. An unusual overhead kick from Paisley brought an equally unusual clearance from Parsons, who elected to kick the ball clear, rather than save it in the usual manner. The Liddell-Done switch was not the only tactical move employed by Liverpool, for Balmer moved to outside-left, Done to inside-left and Payne inside-right as Liverpool did not allow the Wolves' defence to become accustomed to any settled formation.

Paisley appeared to pull a thigh muscle, and went off to have an elastic bandage put on it, returning after a minute and going outside-right, with Williams taking over at left-half. A bit of ill-feeling crept into the game when Swinbourne nudged Taylor, and the Liverpool skipper went down. Referee Ellis had a word to say about it, but the problem did not become serious.

Following a free-kick for a foul against Williams, Broadbent picked up Wright's pass, and, turning round quickly, hit a nice shot which Crossley caught confidently. Liverpool were strong and resolute in their tackling, putting more into their game than of late.

Wolves started the second half with fire, similar to that which Liverpool had shown earlier and for a few minutes they looked particularly dangerous. A great header by Pye was brilliantly saved by Crossley, who leapt and plucked it out of the air in spectacular fashion.

Pye tested Crossley with a terrific drive, which the goalkeeper managed to knock against the bar, before its impetus carried it safely over.

A splendid dribble by Balmer preceded a fierce shot by Liddell, which brought out a full-length save by Parsons from the Scot's pile-driver.

On the hour, Done went to centre-forward and Liddell to outside-left as the programme proclaimed. Immediately on making the change, Liverpool nearly snatched a further goal, Done throwing himself at a Liddell centre to head narrowly over the bar.

The injured Paisley did his best under difficult circumstances, and he helped out in defence as often as possible.

At long last, Wolves got the goal that had seemed likely to come throughout the second half. A high shot by Mullen almost from the touchline saw Crossley misjudge the ball and the Wolves were now only one goal in arrears. This strike lifted the Wolves' spirits, and they swarmed on to the attack. A corner taken by Pye saw Broadbent leap a terrific height and head only inches over the bar. Within the space of a couple of minutes Taylor twice needed the attention of trainer Shelley, and Paisley required further attention to his injuries. Liverpool hung on to their lead desperately.

With only a few minutes to go, Pye shot just over the Liverpool bar, and at the other end, Liddell's fierce drive was turned behind by Parsons.

The record attendance - paying £6,607 - at Anfield had witnessed a brilliant encounter.

Newcastle United beat Tottenham Hotspur 3-0 (G. Robledo 14 and 65 minutes, Mitchell 28) at White Hart Lane, while a Lewis hat-trick in seven minutes for Arsenal against Barnsley saw the Londoners win 4-0 at home. After 27 minutes Lewis redeemed earlier lapses by giving Arsenal the lead with a glorious goal. He ran on to a through pass from Lishman, outpaced Mitchell, and from fully 20 yards crashed a left-foot drive past Hough. Three minutes later Lewis scored again from close range, and completed his hat-trick with a header in the 34th minute. The rout continued and after 39 minutes Lishman put Arsenal four goals ahead with a fine solo effort.

Liverpool: Crossley; Jones, Lambert; Heydon, Taylor, Paisley; Williams, Balmer, Done, Payne, Liddell.

Wolverhampton Wanderers: Parsons; Shorthouse, Gibbons; Wright, Chatham, Baxter; Hancocks, Broadbent, Swinbourne, Pye, Mullen.

Referee: Mr A.E. Ellis (Halifax)

Attendance: 61,905

Cyril Done, cutting in like a flash, fired home a fierce first-time effort which Parsons was unable to reach. Done, below, played brilliantly at outside-left

February 23, 1952

Burnley (2) 2
Morris 2, Shannon 45

Liverpool (0) 0

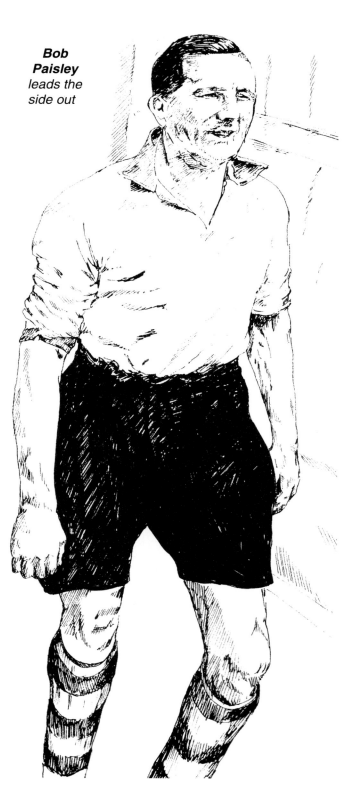

Bob Paisley *leads the side out*

THIS was Liverpool's third Cup encounter with Burnley (they lost 0-1 in the 1914 Final, and 0-1 in a Semi-Final replay in 1947) and, though they were hoping to gain victory, they fell to the better side on the strength of the ninety minutes' play. Bob Paisley was made captain.

Burnley were first to take to the field in blue shirts which were so dark that they looked almost black. Before the start the Liverpool chairman, Mr G.R. Richards, received a telegram of good wishes from the Lord Mayor and Lady Mayoress (Alderman and Mrs Vere E. Cotton).

Paisley lost the toss and Liverpool kicked off before a crowd of 53,000 in the formation stated in the programme. There was an early shock for Liverpool when Morris put them in front after two minutes. Aird put the ball over to Chew from a free-kick, and he centred quickly. Shannon and Cadden, going up for the ball together, resulted in it being turned away from goal towards the onrunning Morris, who hit a strong first-time drive through a ruck of players past Ashcroft, who appeared to be unsighted.

This was an encouraging start for the home side, but Liverpool fought back to such good purpose that the next few minutes Burnley were hemmed in their own quarters and Paisley had two efforts at scoring. The first, a header, was caught and cleared by Strong, and the second struck a defender and went for a corner. Liverpool maintained their attacking policy and twice centres by Liddell flashed across the Burnley goalmouth with nobody there to apply the finishing touch. After ten minutes, Liverpool switched Done and Liddell.

Williams came near to levelling matters when a long throw-in by Paisley was helped forward by Liddell and Williams, stooping low, headed narrowly outside. The first quarter of an hour had been typical cup-tie football with both sides tackling strongly, and Liverpool were the more dangerous and aggressive side.

Liddell was brought down unceremoniously by Adamson about three yards outside the penalty area. The free-kick was taken twice, first by a side-step from Paisley to Liddell which resulted in a blocked shot, and then by a Liddell lob which was close enough to the mark to cause Burnley anxiety. Liverpool went closer still soon afterwards. Done - still limping from a tackle by Cummings - fired in an excellent left-foot shot which Strong palmed away at full length and which was eventually cleared by a Cummings back-heel. The visitors continued to be the more aggressive side and Paisley again went near.

After 20 minutes, Shannon - the former Liverpool player - got the ball in the net after it had bobbed about in front of the Liverpool goal, but he was obviously in an offside position, and the referee had no hesitation in giving such a ruling. Soon afterwards, Ashcroft and Shannon collided, which resulted in the Liverpool goalkeeper requiring attention.

Liddell and Done soon afterwards resumed their positions according to the programme. A foul by Lambert on Chew produced danger to the Liverpool goal when the free-kick went out to Elliott, whose swerving shot was punched out by Ashcroft to the feet of Adamson. The Burnley half-back swung at the ball but missed it completely.

Liverpool continued to change their formation, and Liddell had a temporary spell at inside-right, with Payne moving to outside-left. A little of Liverpool's earlier fire had gone out of their play, and Burnley gained the initiative. The home side switched players of their own, and Elliott moved temporarily to the right wing.

Cadden, although playing only his fifth senior game, held his own well against the bustling Holden, while Paisley worked harder than ever in his role as skipper. The best concerted move of the first half was the magnificent Cadden-Jones-Williams-Heydon-Done-Balmer effort which took the ball three-quarters of the length of the field without a Burnley player touching it. Balmer applied the finishing touch, but it was yards off the target from a narrow angle. Liverpool gradually re-asserted themselves and Strong was forced to save twice in swift succession from Done and Payne. A few minutes before the interval Liddell and Done switched again. There had been several stoppages for injuries - none of them serious - and the first period ran over normal time, with Burnley securing a second goal. The goal arose when Paisley was penalised for a foul on Chew. The Burnley outside-right lobbed the ball just outside the six-yard area where Shannon, leaping high, found his effort parried by Ashcroft, but the former Anfielder followed up and hit the ball home. The goal was definitely against the run of play, but Burnley had taken both their chances.

Payne's persistence early in the second half almost reduced Burnley's lead, but he hooked the ball over the bar after Strong had only half-cleared his earlier effort. Liddell was back at centre-forward and ploughing a lonely furrow, with Cummings proving to be a stumbling block to Liddell's attacking ambitions. The visitors began to lose their attacking impetus, the main cause of the problem being their inability to link defence and attack effectively. Balmer, to his credit, did his best to open up play with long passes to either wing, and on one occasion he met the return by Payne and tried a gallant header which went close.

Burnley might have added a third goal when Ashcroft failed to cut out a high free-kick by Elliott, but Cadden headed away.

Ashcroft immediately atoned for his error when he dived full-length to make a magnificent save from Chew's strong shot from Elliott's centre.

Apart from very brief periods Burnley had been the more accomplished and stylish side since the break, and though Liverpool fought hard individually, they lacked the rhythm or balance in the front line necessary to get the better of Burnley's splendid defence.

Right on time, Done got the ball into the net from a Liddell pass, but a linesman had raised his flag and Done was given offside.

Burnley were defeated 3-1 in the quarter-finals at Blackburn. Newcastle beat Swansea 1-0 away, while Arsenal beat Leyton Orient 3-0 away.

Billy Liddell, *Liverpool's Scottish international*

Burnley: Strong; Aird, Mather; Adamson, Cummings, Attwell; Chew, Morris, Holden, Shannon, Elliott.

Liverpool: Ashcroft; Jones, Lambert; Heydon, Cadden, Paisley; Williams, Balmer, Done, Payne, Liddell.

Referee: Mr W. Ling (Cambridge)

Attendance: 53,000

January 10, 1953

Gateshead (0) 1
Winters 85

Liverpool (0) 0

THE game on Tyneside was farcical - the fog, which had not been too bad in the first half, came down like a thick blanket and at times it was impossible to see either goal from the Press box. The pitch was very heavy and, although the pools of water had disappeared, the full stretch from goal to goal had been well sanded down the middle.

Gateshead, from the Third Division North, generally outplayed their First Division opponents and deserved their progress into the Fourth Round, where they beat Second Division Hull City 2-1 away. In the Fifth Round, Gateshead beat Second Division Plymouth 1-0 away, before finally succumbing 0-1 at home to First Division Bolton Wanderers. In the light of these results and the atrocious weather conditions, which are always a great leveller, Liverpool's demise was not so great.

The game started in clear weather, but after a quarter of an hour a rather heavy mist descended which made it difficult to follow the ball on the far side of the ground. The home side began confidently and Saunders cleared a T. Callender free-kick, and Lambert cleared a corner soon afterwards. A half-hit shot from Liddell was easily saved by Gray.

Campbell sent over a strong centre which passed over everyone's head and was returned to the middle by Ingham, where Winters, who was well placed, shot wide from about ten yards.

In a goalmouth mêlée, the ball moved threateningly backwards and forwards until Lambert cleared the danger with a huge clearance upfield. Bill Jones was continually in the action, and he twice headed away from Wilbert, before getting his head to an Ingham centre.

Brown collected a loose ball and shot, but his effort was well wide of the mark and finished near the corner flag. Liverpool had been on the defensive for several minutes, but eventually broke free when Smith sent the ball up the middle for Baron to chase, but Gray was alert to the danger and raced off his line to clear.

The fog gradually thickened as the first half elapsed. Brian Williams required treatment after heading away an Ingham corner, but he soon resumed.

Saunders was playing well, and he showed tenacity and courage as he tackled with determination. Just before the interval Jones headed away a centre by Ingham.

The interval arrived with both sides having played with determination and vigour on a surface which was more a test of stamina than of skill.

When play resumed, a white ball was in use, which was a little improvement when it was within sight, but to a great extent play was farcical, for it became impossible to follow either the players or the flight of the ball over fully three-quarters of the field. Only the disappointed cries of the crowd behind the Liverpool goal gave a clue on two occasions to the fact that Gateshead had missed possible scoring opportunities. Here and there some white-shirted or red-shirted player came into view, bearing down on the opposition goal, but it was only by the actions of the players and the way they faced that the fans could gather the trend of the play.

With half-an-hour of the second half played, a congregation of players and a terrific roar following a free-kick by March seemed to indicate that Gateshead had scored. Spectators in the paddock were throwing their hats in the air, and those in the stand rose to their feet cheering wildly. It was, however, a false alarm. Just what happened only those near the goal would know, but play seemed to be held up while Gateshead claimed something and Liverpool protested. The only certain thing was that the players did not return to the middle to centre the ball.

Liddell made a run along the touchline and centred strongly, but the opportunity was not converted. Liddell then conceded a free-kick for a foul on March, and Crossley was pushed in his area as he went to save from the kick.

The home side had the territorial advantage throughout the second period and five minutes from the finish Gateshead scored following a corner. Campbell took the corner and Winters headed home through the fog to rousing cheers. The Liverpool players lined up around the centre circle as the roars from the crowd were still ringing, but the goal came too late for Liverpool to salvage something from the tie.

Manchester City beat Swindon 7-0 at home, and Tottenham beat Tranmere Rovers 9-1 in a White Hart Lane replay. Derby County and Chelsea shared eight goals at the Baseball Ground before the Blues won the replay 1-0.

The eventual Cup winners, Blackpool (4-3 against Bolton), beat Sheffield Wednesday 2-1 away, while Bolton beat Fulham 3-1.

Gateshead: Gray; Cairns, March; J.Callender, T.Callender, Brown; Ingham, K.Smith, Wilbert, Winters, Campbell.

Liverpool: Crossley; Lambert, Moran; Heydon, W.Jones, Saunders; J.M.Jones, Baron, J.Smith, Williams, Liddell.

Referee: Mr F.B. Coultas (Hull)

Attendance: 15,193

January 9, 1954

Bolton Wanderers (0) 1
Moir 46

Liverpool (0) 0

THE weather was ideal at the start and the ground, which was sanded in places, looked in good trim, and at least there was none of the frost which had been prevalent. The Anfielders had a good sprinkling of supporters with red balloons. Most of the fans congregated behind the railway goal. Young David Goodman, the five-year-old mascot recently out of hospital, came out with the Liverpool team which received almost as good a reception as the home side. Liverpool, with their "old guard" back in harness played well in the early stages, and Hanson was called upon three times before Crossley had handled the ball from a Taylor back-pass.

For the first quarter of an hour, Liverpool had the better of the argument. Wilkinson gained a cheer for a crafty back-heel which completely bamboozled Stevens. Taylor fell heavily when Lofthouse side-stepped an intended tackle, and the game was held up while he received attention.

The play became fast and furious with Bolton taking the upper hand, during which Crossley twice made splendid saves from Lofthouse pile-drivers. Only the sticky turf prevented Liverpool taking the lead just on the half hour when Liddell headed into the centre and Jones found the ball come to a sudden stop when he expected it to run on to him. In spite of this, he got in a shot, but it lacked power.

The recalled Anfielders, Hughes and Taylor in particular, did well, denying Lofthouse who wanted to shoot at every opportunity.

Evans kicked away on the goal line from Moir right on the resumption, but the corner which followed this save produced a goal to Bolton. Holden took the flag kick and dropped the ball close to the near post. Crossley, going up, only succeeded in pushing it against the upright, and it rebounded to Moir, who headed in to give Bolton the lead. Liverpool hit back vigorously and within a minute of the restart Evans hit the post from ten yards.

The visitors forced three corners in a minute as they sought an equaliser. Bolton broke away and Holden got the ball into the net. Fortunately for Liverpool the whistle had previously gone for a foul on Parry by Lambert. Liverpool kept plugging away without producing any work for Hanson beyond a long lob by Jackson. As Hanson hugged this to his chest, Liddell tried to charge him over the line without success.

Evans had a great chance to equalise, but although dribbling well and beating two men, he delayed his shot too long and Hanson dashed out and smothered the ball. Wilkinson continued to play exceptionally well for Liverpool and several times he got a cheer from the crowd for some classic touch or other, which showed mastery of both the ball and the conditions. Liverpool altered their forward formation, Liddell going in the middle, Jones inside-left, and Payne outside-left. The going was extremely tough, with the surface cutting up badly, but Liverpool stuck to their task and created several problems for Bolton, without managing to equalise.

The receipts were £6,290. West Bromwich Albion, who eventually won the cup by beating Preston North End, beat Chelsea 1-0 at home, while Preston beat Derby County 2-0 away. The highest score of the day was at Blundell Park, where Grimsby drew 5-5 with Fulham, only to lose 3-1 in a second replay.

Nat Lofthouse

Bolton Wanderers: Hanson; Ball, R.Banks; Wheeler, Barrass, Bell; Holden, Moir, Lofthouse, Stevens, Parry.

Liverpool: Crossley; Lambert, Lock; B.Wilkinson, Hughes, Taylor; Jackson, Evans, Jones, Payne, Liddell.

Referee: Mr A. Bond (Fulham)

Attendance: 45,341

January 8, 1955

Lincoln City (0) 1
Munro 83

Liverpool (1) 1
Evans 10

IT was something of a blow to Liverpool that Jackson was unable to play. It was not until Thursday that he noticed any trouble, but on Friday morning his leg had swollen badly. He had several penicillin injections, but it was impossible for him to take his place, and Payne deputised. Liverpool journeyed up from Woodhall Spa on the morning of the match, and the playing conditions looked good for football. Much to the dissatisfaction of the home club, the ground was far from full, although there was a big contingent from Liverpool.

Lincoln won the toss and Liverpool set their sail for the Lincoln goal, but their advance was cut short and Lincoln replied with an attack of their own until the united effort of Lambert and Saunders repelled them. Liverpool were awarded a free-kick for a foul by Emery on Liddell, but the miscreant headed away Liddell's powerful kick. Shortly afterwards, Rudham tipped a Garvie shot over the bar.

With ten minutes gone, Liverpool drew first blood. A brilliant cross-field pass from Saunders found Liddell, who headed down to Evans. The inside-left moved up a few yards and crashed his shot past Downie.

Lincoln fought back immediately, and Rudham had to make good saves from Garvie and Finch. At the other end, Graham had to kick the ball off the line from Bimpson, who had the better of a struggle with Emery. Evans played well, and some of his ball control was far too good for the opposition, but Lincoln fought like tigers. Saunders, despite a sore toe, tackled strongly whenever Lincoln attacked.

Emery and Liddell had several skirmishes, with the Lincoln player coming off best. Littler moved to the outside-right position when Middleton sent City attacking. The Liverpool defence was playing competently against a spirited Lincoln side which showed a good deal of scientific football. The Second Division side had played well up to the interval.

In the first minute of the second half, Liverpool were awarded a free-kick for a foul on Rudham, who tapped the ball to Hughes, for him to return the ball to the goalkeeper, but Rudham slipped and Littler nipped in. Fortunately for Liverpool, Littler held on too long and Lambert kicked off the line. Then Munro sent in a centre which was far too strong and it passed high over the bar. Lincoln then embarked upon a period of complete domination, and it was only the outstanding defensive contribution from Hughes which kept Liverpool in the game. Neal attempted a hook shot which Hughes breasted down and cleared. Bimpson tried a ferocious volley, but it lacked accuracy. Lincoln then claimed a penalty for hands, but the referee waved away their appeals. Liddell streamed down the wing but was pulled up when Bimpson

was adjudged to be offside. Littler had an opportunity when Munro centred, but his header lacked pace and Rudham collected with ease.

Dykes, who had moved over to right-half, put the ball over the bar, and Rudham punched away from Munro. The Liverpool defence remained resolutely impregnable, until seven minutes from time. Munro was fortunate to get a second chance after the ball had rebounded off Saunders. He made no mistake from fully 15 yards and the ball went into the net away from the helpless Rudham.

Just before the end, Liddell almost broke free from the fetters around him imposed by Emery, but his corner was unsuccessful.

Just prior to the final whistle, Evans was ordered off the field for arguing with the referee.

In other games, League champions Wolves came back from a 2-0 deficit to beat Grimsby 5-2 away, four of the goals coming in the last fifteen minutes. Cup-holders West Bromwich Albion successfully negotiated a 1-0 victory at Bournemouth. Newcastle United, who beat Manchester City 3-1 in the Final, won 1-0 away to Plymouth, while Manchester City beat Derby 3-1 at the Baseball Ground.

Lincoln City: Downie; Graham, Troops; Middleton, Emery, Neal; Munro, Garvie, Littler, Dykes, Finch.

Liverpool: Rudham; Lambert, Moran; Saunders, Hughes, Twentyman; Payne, Bimpson, Liddell, Evans, Arnell.

Referee: Mr R. Wood (Sunderland)

Attendance: 15,399

January 12, 1955

Liverpool (0) 1

Evans 100

Lincoln City (0) 0 aet

LIVERPOOL supporters had a shock when they learned that Hughes, although pronounced fit on the Friday, was not playing in the replay against Lincoln. The going was very hard where the sun had not got to the frozen pitch and in view of this Hughes decided it was unwise to take any risks with his knee. Alec South, the 22-year-old centre-half signed last December from Brighton for £5,000, made his senior début in place of Hughes. Anderson came in at inside-right. Lincoln included Birch in place of Dykes at inside-left. The pitch had a thin covering of snow, about half-an-inch, though at the Anfield Road end, which was under the influence of the sun, the pitch was quite green for a considerable distance in the area of the corner flags. In the absence of Hughes, Liddell captained Liverpool, who took to the field several minutes before Lincoln.

It was immediately apparent that the going was very hard and treacherous, and the players would obviously have their work cut out in keeping a firm footing. Lincoln had a narrow escape when Emery tried to put the ball back to Neal and Jackson nipped in like a flash to make a strong right-foot shot which was no more than six inches from the upright. When a misdirected pass by A'Court let in Garvie, South effected a lusty clearance.

The skating rink conditions were not conducive to good football. With 22 minutes gone, Liddell struck a fierce shot which Downie tipped over the bar. It was clearly better to shoot on sight rather than play neat, cultured football. The referee waved aside Lincoln's appeal for a penalty when Lambert tripped Finch just inside the penalty area, and then Neal wasted a chance by blasting the ball ten yards wide. South made two smart interceptions, and then he received a round of applause for the determination with which he stuck to two opponents and finally won possession. The biggest thrill of the first period was when Liddell darted down the middle and dribbled round Downie, who had advanced almost to the edge of the penalty area, but from an angled position, Liddell's final shot went into the side netting. Just before the interval, Liddell went close with a 20-yard drive.

The first notable incident on the resumption was a fine lofted shot from A'Court which Downie turned round the post. This followed a fine move involving four Liverpool players.

South again earned applause for the confident manner in which he dispossessed Garvie and took the ball up in an effort to start his forwards on the move. The sun retired behind the clouds and light snow began to fall as Lincoln temporarily gained the upper hand. Gibson robbed Evans not far outside Liverpool's penalty area and worked his way through to deliver a fierce shot a couple of yards over the bar. The home side lacked the determination of their visitors. Liverpool's

passing was erratic and their wing halves had problems in coping with the lively Lincoln attack. Sliced clearances became the norm on the awkward surface, and both South and Lambert put the ball to opponents, but were fortunate to see a colleague step in to redress the error. Lincoln looked certain to score when Munro raced onto a through ball, but Rudham bravely dived at the forward's feet. The South African's action undoubtedly saved the day, and the Kop gave him a cheer when he resumed following the trainer's attention. Just before the end of the ninety minutes, Liddell had a header saved by Downie.

Liverpool won the toss and defended the Spion Kop for the first portion of extra time. Rudham effected a brilliant save off Gibson following a corner, then Liverpool dashed away for Graham to head away a pile-driver by Twentyman.

After ten minutes of extra-time, Evans gave Liverpool the lead with a brilliant header off a corner on the left wing. Liddell swung the ball in with his right foot and Evans rose above two opponents to give Downie no chance. Just before the second interval, Rudham saved at the foot of the post from Munro.

OTHER CUP REPLAYS

Bishop Auckland	3	Ipswich Town	0
Bradford City	2	Brentford	2*
Torquay United	4	Leeds United	0
Manchester United	4	Reading	1
Stoke City	1	Bury	1*
Darlington	2	Hartlepools United	2*

* after extra time

Liverpool: Rudham; Lambert, Moran; Saunders, South, Twentyman; Jackson, Anderson, Liddell, Evans, A'Court.

Lincoln City: Downie; Graham, Troops; Middleton, Emery, Neal; Munro, Garvie, Gibson, Birch, Finch.

Referee: Mr R.J. Leafe (Woodthorpe)

Attendance: 32,179

Receipts: £3,840

January 29, 1955

Everton (0) 0

Liverpool (2) 4
Liddell 18, A'Court 29,
Evans 57, 75

LIVERPOOL were undoubtedly worthy winners, for after the first fifteen minutes, they were the better side and always looked the more dangerous side in front of goal. They eliminated all the fancy work and approached the tie with a view to working hard in order to make progress.

The Reds were two goals ahead at the interval through Liddell and A'Court, and though Everton staged a rally for ten minutes or so in the second period when the visiting goal had some narrow escapes, Liverpool stuck to their task and still got to the ball quicker than their opponents as the game wore on.

This was Liverpool's first away win since last Good Friday when they beat Middlesbrough 1-0 as both teams fought to stave off relegation, which neither managed to do. As Liverpool slipped into the Second Division for the first time since 1905, Everton were promoted after finishing runners-up to Leicester City.

Two goals to Evans in the second half put the issue beyond all doubt and Liverpool's victory was all the more meritorious in view of the fact that Hughes was injured six minutes after the resumption and had to go in the forward line, with Liddell moved to left-half, and Twentyman a resolute and brave deputy pivot. Liddell, though not captain, inspired his men in both attack and defence.

Half an hour before the kick-off the terraces were well filled and only the stands showed a few gaps which rapidly disappeared as the time of the start drew ever nearer. The two teams took to the field simultaneously, as is traditional in these derby affairs. The spectators were in good humour and everybody seemed to be indulging in lively and bantering remarks with those in the rival camp. There was a great display of rosettes, coloured favours and bedecked headgear.

Hughes won the toss for Liverpool and elected to defend the Gwladys Street end. The match kicked off at 2.45. A corner to Everton in the first minute brought no danger, but a long clearance by O'Neill dropped more than halfway inside the Liverpool half, where Lambert just failed to head away and Eglington quickly rounded him and shot into the side netting.

The first shot of real note was one by Fielding from just outside the penalty area which Rudham caught confidently, and then Potts hit a first-timer well over the bar as Everton established their superiority.

The Evertonians behind the Gwladys Street goal howled their derision when Hughes, out near the right touchline, saw Hickson - the "stormy petrel" - tearing upfield at top speed and decided that discretion was far better than trying to beat his opponent, so lofted the ball high into the crowd. Wainwright had a great chance in the 15th minute when, in

the centre-forward position, Hickson, from the right wing, crossed the ball to him beautifully. Wainwright hit it first time, but the ball swerved away outside the far post.

The most fervent Evertonians appealed for a penalty when Lambert and Eglington became entangled in a challenge and Eglington finished up on the ground. Referee Ellis, however, was right on the spot, and waved play on.

With just 18 minutes gone, Liverpool took a surprise lead through the auspices of the hardy Scot, Billy Liddell. There appeared to be little danger when Jackson received the ball 20 yards inside the Everton half, but when Jackson swung the ball over to Liddell, the "flying Scotsman" gained quick control, beat Jones in a dribble and challenge for possession, and then fired in with his left foot from a slightly angled position.

Almost directly from the restart, Fielding had an opportunity to test Rudham, but he shot well outside. Everton got the ball into the net in the 27th minute when Hickson placed it there with an acute shot off a pass by Potts, but the Everton leader was well offside and there were no protests from the home crowd or players when the referee gave a free-kick.

Liverpool began to turn on the power in the manner of their performance against Blackburn Rovers in the League last week. The forwards ran into position well, and the inside men did not fall so far back that when it came to an attack they were unable to give proper support.

With 29 minutes gone, Liverpool went two goals ahead. Liddell put the ball forward and both Evans and Anderson went for it. Evans completely missed his shot, and Anderson tapped the ball to A'Court, who, coming in at an angle on the left, scored from about eight yards.

The enormity of the psychological blow to Everton could not be underestimated as the Second Division side ran riot. Liverpool should even have had a third goal two minutes later when a square pass from Anderson found Liddell in space, but the Scot fell at the critical moment. For the second time, Everton got the ball in the net, Potts netting. The linesman's flag had already been raised when Potts ran on to Eglington's pass.

At half-time, Liverpool went off to a storm of cheers from all parts of the ground. After the first 15 minutes the Reds had proved themselves the better takers of chances and had surprised everyone by their spirit, ball control and refusal to concede ground without a desperate struggle.

Shortly after the resumption, Hughes was injured in a tackle with Hickson, but he was able to resume. The referee held up play for half a minute while he took a bottle which had been thrown on to the field to a police sergeant. This was the only incident of an unpleasant nature - the score apart.

Liverpool never made two moves when one would do, and after 57 minutes they scored a third goal. Jackson beat Rankin and fired a tremendously powerful oblique shot from 20 yards which O'Neill caught but could not hold and the inrushing Evans had the simplest of chances to score and maintain his record of having scored in all three of Liverpool's cup-ties this season.

***John Evans**, who scored two goals against Everton*

Lambert gave away a corner when harassed by Eglington and the ball bobbed about in the Liverpool area for some seconds before Potts tried an overhead kick which was only a yard or two off the mark. Hughes continued to show signs of discomfort following his injury, but Liddell, Twentyman, Saunders and all the red-shirted players pulled out a little bit extra to make up for their handicap.

Everton were unfortunate not to score when Rudham dashed off his line to clutch the ball from Hickson's head. When Hickson beat Twentyman and advanced on goal with only Rudham to beat, Liddell appeared from nowhere to take the ball off his toe. Liddell was certainly inspirational, leading by example, correcting his colleagues' disposition whenever necessary and all the time being in the centre of the action.

The Reds had another narrow escape when Potts crossed the ball from the outside-right position, but no Everton player could get a touch on the ball. Obviously, Liverpool were handicapped by the injury to Hughes, who went to outside-left, with Evans in the middle, and it was little surprise that Everton became superior. With half an hour gone

in the second half, they forced six corners, and the Liverpool goal enjoyed a rather charmed life.

With 75 minutes gone, the Reds put the issue beyond all doubt when, following a free-kick for a foul by Hickson on Saunders, Liverpool got away on the right, and a beautiful centre by Jackson was headed in by Evans to put the visitors 4-0 up. O'Neill was hurt in trying to save, but he soon resumed.

Everton had no hope beyond making the score a little more respectable, and Rudham was fortunate when a Hickson header, which he had misjudged, bounced into his hands as he turned round. Two minutes from time Lello sent Fielding away, but the inside man, who had had no luck all afternoon with his shooting, was again off target. Skipper Hughes was just remaining on the field in order to lead his lads off, for he had not touched the ball for some time. When the ball did go to him, all he could do was tap it into touch.

It was beyond the power of the police to do anything about the hundred or so eager Liverpool fans who swarmed on to the field as the final whistle went.

OTHER FOURTH ROUND TIES

Birmingham	2	Bolton Wanderers	1
Bishop Auckland	1	York City	3
Bristol Rovers	1	Chelsea	3
Doncaster Rovers	0	Aston Villa	0
Hartlepools United	1	Nottingham Forest	1
Manchester City	2	Manchester United	0
Newcastle United	3	Brentford	2
Preston North End	3	Sunderland	3
Rotherham United	1	Luton Town	5
Sheffield Wednesday	1	Notts County	1
Swansea Town	3	Stoke City	1
Torquay United	0	Huddersfield Town	1
Tottenham Hotspur	4	Port Vale	2
West Bromwich A.	2	Charlton Athletic	4
Wolverhampton W.	1	Arsenal	0

Everton: O'Neill; Moore, Rankin; Farrell, Jones, Lello; Wainwright, Fielding, Hickson, Potts, Eglington.

Liverpool: Rudham; Lambert, Moran; Saunders, Hughes, Twentyman; Jackson, Anderson, Liddell, Evans, A'Court.

Referee: Mr A.E. Ellis (Halifax)

Attendance: 72,000

Receipts: £10,715

February 19, 1955

Liverpool (0) 0   Huddersfield Town (0) 2

Hobson 50, Glazzard 83

THE gates at Anfield were shut an hour before the start, leaving thousands outside. The queues had started about six hours before the kick-off yet despite the bright sunshine of the early morning, it was a bitterly cold day. There was much good humour among both sets of rival supporters, and some lusty community singing. A great proportion of spectators sported coloured favours of one kind or another, ranging from modest button-holes to some as big as a soup plate. When Liverpool came out, a forest of gaily-painted rattles were held aloft on the Kop to give the Reds a tumultuous welcome. The ground had a light covering of snow, except at the Anfield Road corners, where the morning sun had dispersed the snow and allowed large triangular patches of grass to protrude. At the Kop end, beneath the shadow of the huge roof, the ground still appeared to be frozen hard. The Liverpool players were out four minutes before their opponents and spent the time shooting in with four balls. Staniforth won the toss for Huddersfield and decided to defend the Kop end as the teams kicked off at 3 o'clock.

Liverpool: Ashcroft; Lambert, Moran; Saunders, Hughes, Twentyman; Jackson, Anderson, Liddell, Evans, A'Court.

Huddersfield Town: Wheeler; Staniforth, Kelly; McGarry, Taylor, Quested; Hobson, Watson, Glazzard, Frear, Metcalfe.

Referee: Mr W. Clements (West Bromwich)

Attendance: 57,115

Receipts: £7,810

It was obvious early on that conditions underfoot were very bad in the Kop half of the goal, and the players had great difficulty in keeping a foothold. Once Liddell slid a couple of yards with his legs almost out of control.

Nearly twelve minutes had elapsed before Ashcroft had anything to do, and then it was only to pick up a slow mis-hit shot from Glazzard that was nowhere near the goal. While Liverpool endeavoured to make progress by long passing and lightning raids, Huddersfield worked the ball much more craftily and varied their tactics. Some of their spells of short passing were excellent considering the treacherous conditions. Metcalfe established a dangerous move when he crossed accurately into the centre, but Ashcroft flung himself forward and double-fisted the ball away from any possible danger. Both sides tackled quickly and incisively, and the game was fast and exciting, with play fluctuating quickly

from one goal to the other. Ashcroft palmed away another Metcalfe centre, but he did not clear the danger completely and Twentyman finished the job. Liddell, away out on his own, darted through at top speed but on the slippery surface he could not deliver one of his usual powerful efforts. His shot along the ground was not held by Wheeler, and it took a rescue act by Kelly to forestall Liddell as he carried through in anticipation of the rebound. Metcalfe sent Lambert the wrong way and unleashed a powerful right-foot shot which Ashcroft plucked out of the air with great aplomb. It was a brilliant shot and an equally good save. Little had been seen of A'Court, who was superbly marshalled by Staniforth, whose experience was too much for Liverpool's youthful winger. The interval arrived with no score. After Ashcroft had saved beneath the bar from Metcalfe, Liverpool attacked through Liddell, who was temporarily at outside-left, and when the Scot put over a high dropping ball Evans was only a yard or so over the bar with a header.

With just five minutes of the second period gone, Huddersfield scored. The move began on the left flank, where Glazzard put the ball into the middle and Hughes just failed to get to it. The ball ran on to Frear, who also partially lost his footing, but managed to divert it to Hobson. Even the right-winger lost his footing as he shot, and the ball curled and found the inside of the far post.

Moran showed the right idea when he took the ball half the length of the field before slipping it through to Evans, who was crowded out. Liverpool's main hope was to throw everything into the attack. Liddell worked with his usual non-stop energy, but he found that Ken Taylor - though a comparative novice in first-class football - was a most difficult man to beat.

Evans twice went near with headers as the home side attacked relentlessly. Controlling the ball still proved to be difficult on the awkward turf. Watson, dropping back to help his defence, elected to waste time by booting the ball into the stand. With ten minutes to go, Evans managed to win a corner and following the clearance of Jackson's flag-kick, he ran into the Huddersfield goal to avoid putting his team offside when the ball looked as if it would be returned to the Huddersfield goal. Time slowly ran out, and Huddersfield were quite content to let time go by with free-kicks or throw-ins.

After 83 minutes, Glazzard put the Yorkshire club two goals up. Frear, the young Huddersfield player who came into the side only a week ago, had a hand in the execution of the goal. He placed the ball nicely in front of Glazzard, who hit an angled shot which Ashcroft got his fingers to but was unable to save. Huddersfield were beaten in the Sixth Round by the eventual winners, Newcastle, 2-0 at St. James's Park, after a 1-1 draw in Yorkshire.

January 7, 1956

Liverpool (2) 2   Accrington Stanley (0) 0
Liddell 31, 32

LIVERPOOL took to the field first and wore yellow shirts with white shorts and their customary red and white stockings. Accrington wore white jerseys and black shorts with a bright red stripe down the seams. After the early morning fog, visibility was good though the pitch appeared to be on the soft side, especially in the centre. Jimmy Harrower won the toss and much to the delight of the Liverpool supporters elected to kick into the Kop goal.

Liverpool: Underwood; Molyneux, Moran; Saunders, Hughes, Twentyman; Payne, Bimpson, Liddell, Evans, A'Court.

Accrington Stanley: McQueen; Ashe, McCredie; Hunter, Harrower, Sneddon; Cocker, Wright, Stewart, Dick, Scott.

Referee: Mr R.J. Leafe (Nottingham)
Attendance: 48,385

Accrington - of the Third Division North - showed their keenness when Scott charged down a kick by John Molyneux, but Laurie Hughes cleared at the expense of a throw-in. Harrower and Norman McCredie used the ball well to start another raid, but Ronnie Moran rescued Liverpool. Roy Saunders came across to the left to hold up another Accrington assault before a quickly taken throw-in by Moran saw Liverpool on the offensive for the first time. John Evans and Alan A'Court combined but Louis Bimpson was challenged by two opponents and a back pass to Tom McQueen brought the raid to a finish. Some of Stanley's football was of a standard higher than their League status, and it took a determined tackle by Molyneux to end another thrust on the left. McCredie, with time to spare, misplaced a header so badly that the ball went out for the game's first corner after striking the flag. Evans headed in from Jimmy Payne's kick only for McQueen to save without difficulty and the goalkeeper's clearance brought the biggest thrill so far. Les Cocker put the ball up to George Stewart, who was the leading scorer in the Northern section, and the centre-forward's swerving drive from the corner of the penalty area was only inches high. When Payne was brought down, three successive Liverpool headers across the face of the goal yielded a fierce shot by Billy Liddell which was deflected for a corner, and this, in turn, brought a scramble until Accrington claimed relief with a goal kick. Liddell put one centre over the angle and McQueen gathered another from A'Court before the game was stopped for a back injury sustained by Cocker. Geoff Twentyman won a corner which McQueen failed to hold and Accrington had to respond quickly to get the ball away before Liddell or Bimpson could take advantage. Liverpool were coming into the game more and a run and centre by A'Court enabled Payne to make a short pass to Twentyman, whose fierce drive travelled narrowly over the top. Liddell moved into space to pick up a pass from Molyneux, and his centre left Evans with a reasonable chance of scoring, but the inside-left put the ball into the side netting from close range. McQueen saved well from the head of Evans as Liverpool stepped up the pace. A'Court then had a shot deflected and put the corner straight to Bimpson. Once again McQueen did well, taking the ball as he dived to his right. A free kick from Moran led to the first goal after 31 minutes. After two shots had been charged down, Liddell seized on a rebound and smashed it home via the underside of the cross-bar. Within a minute he had scored again. Harrower, whose defence had been outstanding, blundered with a through pass and Liddell, after making his challenge and winning possession, drove home another fierce shot to put Liverpool into a commanding position. With the crowd roaring its encouragement, Liverpool continued to attack relentlessly. McQueen made a fine one-handed save from Bimpson, only to find that the whistle had gone. The visitors' defence was now becoming confused and hesitant against Liverpool's attacking inventiveness. Liddell, moving over to the right, frequently found open space which he could exploit and use to his advantage.

The opening minutes of the second half were largely uninspiring, though two passes by Bimpson might have brought rewards but for the lethargy of his colleagues. The visitors were obviously going to fight to the last minute of the game, and Scott, who had been their liveliest forward, was not far out with a long-range drive, although Underwood was well sighted. Stewart lashed the ball over the bar, and Liverpool replied when A'Court forced a corner, but Evans' shot went wide. A bout of good Accrington passing which started deep in their own half brought a centre from Archie Wright which Underwood could not hold at first, but he recovered and made a safe clearance. Liverpool were faster to the ball, but many of their attacking moves faltered on the edge of the Stanley penalty area through poor passing. Wright's low shot, from a corner, was kicked away from the foot of a post by Moran. Liverpool were awarded a dubious free-kick, and McQueen effected a great one-handed save from Evans after a pass from Payne. Liverpool's best raid for some time brought centres from Payne and Saunders, but on each occasion Harrower proved equal to the task of preventing further danger. The Accrington captain must have been disappointed to see his forwards squander so many good chances. In the gathering gloom near the end, Bimpson beat McQueen with a long shot that dropped just over the bar.

January 28, 1956

Liverpool (1) 3
Liddell 32, 90, Payne 54

Scunthorpe United (1) 3
Gregory 22, Davies 75, 76

***Billy Liddell** leads the team out against Scunthorpe*

THE Anfield pitch, though on the soft side and liberally sanded in the middle and in the vicinity of the goals, was in far better condition than last week. Mervyn Jones and Jack Haigh were welcomed by their former Liverpool colleagues. Liddell won the toss, so that Liverpool defended the Kop half in the first period.

With fifteen minutes gone, the home side had made four good shooting efforts, whereas Scunthorpe - of the Third Division North - had only made one attempt, a wild effort by John Gregory which soared high over the bar.

Nevertheless, Liverpool did not have it all their own way. Scunthorpe showed a certain amount of enterprise and fought hard, but the positioning and anticipation of the home defence prevented the visitors from becoming too dangerous. Mervyn Jones, though the smallest man on the field, was not an easy proposition for Molyneux, who had to watch him closely and found him full of tricks. Liddell again set up Alan Arnell, whose drive struck Jack Brownsword.

With 22 minutes gone, the home supporters were shocked into silence when Scunthorpe took the lead through John Gregory. Haigh, picking up a Scunthorpe clearance ten yards inside the Liverpool half, lofted the ball over towards Gregory, in the inside-left position. Laurie Hughes tried to head away, but only succeeded in partly deflecting the ball, and Gregory, running on to it, delivered a left-foot drive which entered the net a yard inside the far post.

This goal brought the game to life and twice in the next eight minutes the ball was in the net, though without the effort counting on either occasion.

Gordon Brown netted for the visitors, but he was palpably offside. A similar decision nullified a shot by Liddell. In between these two efforts, the home goal had a couple of narrow escapes, the first when Underwood stuck out a leg to save from Gregory in very fortunate fashion, and then from the rebound, when Ronnie Moran kicked away from John Davies a few yards in front of goal.

When Liverpool finally broke away, John Hubbard saved Scunthorpe when he kicked away an effort by Evans following a corner, which would have been a goal but for the full-back's intervention. Excitement came thick and fast, and after 32 minutes, Payne sent Arnell away on a brilliant solo run which produced the equalising goal.

Liddell was the scorer, but his task was purely the nominal one of tapping the ball in after Arnell had done all the hard work. Peter Marshall managed to touch Liddell's effort but he could not keep the ball out.

Two more exciting incidents set the crowd buzzing. Hubbard was knocked unconscious when he was struck in the face with a terrific drive from Liddell. He fell like a stunned boxer, but he regained his senses after a minute or two. From one Scunthorpe attack, Davies delivered a splendid header from Brown's centre. It was fortunate for Liverpool that Underwood had positioned himself so well that he able to effect a marvellous catch.

Liddell covered a tremendous amount of ground, not only in his efforts to give his side the lead, but also to give the defence a hand in time of need. He came back well to dispossess Haigh well inside the Liverpool half, and then stepped into the breach for a quick throw-in.

After the interval, Scunthorpe pegged Liverpool in their own half for a full five minutes. Alan Bushby and Andy McGill gave strong support to the visitors' forwards and Bushby, after a clever dribble, put over a cross which looked as though it would produce a goal until Brown, unable to get to the ball, could not resist the temptation to use his hands.

Eventually Liverpool cleared their lines, and a free-kick to the home side when an attempt was made to sandwich Liddell brought a leading goal to the home side after 54 minutes. Liddell took the free kick about twenty-five yards from goal and lofted the ball over to Evans, in the inside-right position. Evans immediately returned it to the area of the far post where Payne gave Marshall no chance.

A few minutes later, Evans had a great chance to put Liverpool further ahead, but with only Marshall to beat, he shot so close to the Scunthorpe goalkeeper that Marshall was able to stretch out his hands and parry the effort.

Little had been seen of A'Court throughout the match, for the Scunthorpe manager's canny move in putting the experienced Hubbard at right-back to counter the menace of the Liverpool winger had paid dividends.

However, A'Court eventually turned his speed to advantage, left Hubbard trailing in his wake, and delivered a fierce drive which passed right across the goal and outside the far post, missing by inches. Moments later, A'Court tore down the left wing and put over a high ball which Arnell and Marshall both went for. The goalkeeper suffered a blow in the ribs, and required attention before he could resume. Arnell put Liddell through, and the Scot streaked down the middle before producing a pile-driver which Marshall managed to get his body in the way of.

Two goals in quick succession turned the game on its head. Liverpool were a goal ahead and kicking into the Kop goal. Scunthorpe had gone off the boil, while the home side were beginning to look more and more dangerous.

The first goal, scored by Davies, was the result of a speedy run by the right-winger in which he was allowed to go on fully thirty yards without being tackled. He delivered a strong left-foot drive which Underwood failed to reach. The referee had some doubt in his mind about the goal and he consulted a linesman before pointing to the middle.

A minute later, following a free-kick by Brownsword, Underwood came out of his goal, failed to take command of the ball, and Davies hooked it into the net to put the visitors ahead. It was a sensational course of events.

With only ten minutes left, Liverpool looked as though they were out of the competition. Liddell, clean through, was

foiled by Marshall, who again got his body behind the ball. Payne, from eight yards, scooped the ball high over the bar. Nothing was going right for the Reds.

Five minutes from the end, Scunthorpe almost increased their lead when Brown headed outside from Davies' centre.

With only a minute to go, Liverpool broke away, Payne centred the ball and Liddell equalised with a header. There was only just time to centre the ball before the referee blew his whistle.

F.A. CUP FOURTH ROUND

Arsenal	4	Aston Villa	1
Barnsley	0	Blackburn Rovers	1
Bolton Wanderers	1	Sheffield United	2
Bristol Rovers	1	Doncaster Rovers	1
Burnley	1	Chelsea	1
Charlton Athletic	2	Swindon Town	1
Fulham	4	Newcastle United	5
Leicester City	3	Stoke City	3
Leyton Orient	0	Birmingham	4
Port Vale	2	Everton	3
Southend United	0	Manchester City	1
Tottenham Hotspur	3	Middlesbrough	1
West Bromwich A.	2	Portsmouth	0
West Ham United	2	Cardiff City	1
York City	0	Sunderland	0

Replays

Doncaster Rovers	1	Bristol Rovers	0
Chelsea	1	Burnley	1
Stoke City	2	Leicester City	1
Sunderland	2	York City	1

Liverpool: Underwood; Molyneux, Moran; Saunders, Hughes, Twentyman; Payne, Arnell, Liddell, Evans, A'Court.

Scunthorpe United: Marshall; Hubbard, Brownsword; McGill, Heward, Bushby; Davies, Haigh, Gregory, Brown, Jones.

Referee: Mr K. Howley (Middlesbrough)

Attendance: 53,393

Receipts: £6,758

February 6, 1956

Scunthorpe United (0) 1
Davies 52

Liverpool (1) 2 aet
Liddell 19, Arnell 109

BOTH teams set off at a cracking pace, but the forwards were up against well-balanced and quick covering defenders who allowed them no time to settle, and were grimly determined to close every route to goal, so that there were few genuine opportunities. With nineteen minutes gone, Brown and Saunders collided in the Liverpool penalty area and fell to earth as Hughes nipped in to hook the ball away from the unprotected goal, Underwood having dashed out. Molyneux's clearance went upfield to Liddell, who ran through the spreadeagled home defence at top speed and beat the advancing Marshall after getting him to move the wrong way. Ten minutes later Scunthorpe were awarded a penalty after a centre by Jones had struck Molyneux on the arm. It was more a case of "ball to arm", since Molyneux was so close to Jones that he could not possibly get out of the way. Brownsword's tame shot was saved by Underwood diving to the right and making a one-handed save. The visitors continued to hold the advantage up to the interval, yet they were unable to break down Scunthorpe's gallant defence in which Heward, Bushby, McGill and Hubbard were outstanding.

Within seven minutes of the resumption, the home side equalised following a free-kick taken by Mervyn Jones, who placed the ball accurately for Davies to head well out of Underwood's reach. From this point on, it was a titanic struggle, a typical cup-tie involving end-to-end play. Scunthorpe enjoyed more of the possession, but were incapable of breaking down Liverpool's resolute defence. Jones missed a great chance to put the home side ahead when he shot behind with only Underwood to beat. In the last minute of normal time, Liddell almost repeated his rescue act of the Anfield encounter with another splendid header which was equally well saved by Marshall.

The first fifteen minutes of extra-time were all in favour of the home side, who relentlessly bombarded the Liverpool goal, while the visitors did not have a single shot on goal. During this period Underwood distinguished himself with excellent saves which foiled Haigh, Brown and Jones.

After 109 minutes of this hectic and fluctuating encounter, Arnell snatched victory. A'Court put over the centre which began the move. Liddell headed the ball on to Arnell, who cut in and beat the back before slotting it safely home despite the narrow angle.

In the last sixty seconds, Brown skied the ball high over the bar from eight yards. Just before this, there had been an unusual incident when the referee stopped the game while he received attention from both trainers for cramp. Immediately after the whistle had blown, an incident involving Saunders

and Brown ended with the Scunthorpe player on the ground. The referee did not see the incident, but it was reported to him by a linesman. In view of what he learned, he is reporting the matter to the F.A. Saunders said that he approached Brown with the intention of shaking hands, but was met instead by a threatening gesture, which drew from the Liverpool man a defensive move. Manager Bill Corkhill refused to let Brown speak to the press.

Scunthorpe: Marshall; Hubbard, Brownsword; McGill, Heward, Bushby; Davies, Haigh, Gregory, Brown, Jones.

Liverpool: Underwood; Molyneux, Moran; Saunders, Hughes, Twentyman; Payne, Arnell, Liddell, Evans, A'Court.

Referee: Mr K. Howley (Middlesbrough)

Attendance: 19,500

Roy Saunders

February 18, 1956

Manchester City (0) 0   Liverpool (0) 0

THE pitch had a half-inch covering of snow and was steel hard underneath. Two main talking points arose from the game which, considering the state of the pitch, was a keenly contested affair. Billy Liddell had a goal disallowed, but the Liverpool captain could not have been offside. Jimmy Payne, however, appeared to have been adjudged offside. The linesman, to his credit, flagged immediately Payne made his pass. The other main talking point was John Evans' miss after 69 minutes, but he could be forgiven for no-one could have anticipated a Roy Paul blunder as he attempted a back pass to Bert Trautmann. Evans had turned away when he saw Paul in possession and was the most amazed man on the field when he saw the ball coming over to him. He quickly wheeled about and ran on to shoot, but the ball passed wide of the intended mark.

First Division City created the better openings, but the Liverpool defence stood resolute. Roy Saunders, Laurie Hughes and Geoff Twentyman were the rock on which City's hopes were dashed. Behind them, John Molyneux, Ronnie Moran and Dave Underwood formed the link which kept the Liverpool goal unbreached.

The game was ten minutes old before Underwood was called upon to effect a save of any description when he plucked out of the air a corner by Bob Johnstone. He also saved a surprise flick by Jack Dyson, the Lancashire cricketer. Trautmann had little to do.

The Liverpool forwards were disappointing and never really threatened, although Alan A'Court made several fine runs just after the interval when Liverpool were at their most menacing. City tried to play football as if the pitch were lush turf instead of the uneven frozen surface that it was. Johnstone was at outside-left only on the team sheet - he was more at inside-forward than anywhere else and always doing good work. Don Revie was always closely marked. Trautmann's only real save of the match came from the foot of Payne, while Molyneux's sterling efforts were carried out with a broken nose which he sustained at Plymouth.

Manchester City: Trautmann; Leivers, Little; Barnes, Ewing, Paul; Spurdle, Hayes, Revie, Dyson, Johnstone.

Liverpool: Underwood; Molyneux, Moran; Saunders, Hughes, Twentyman; Payne, Arnell, Liddell, Evans, A'Court.

Referee: Mr B.M. Griffiths (Newport)

Attendance: 70,640

Receipts: £9,453

Laurie Hughes, was a rock upon which Liverpool's fine performance was built

February 22, 1956

Liverpool (0) 1
Arnell 52

Manchester City (0) 2
Dyson 64,   Hayes 89

A goal fifteen seconds after the final whistle by Billy Liddell was, quite naturally, disallowed by referee Griffiths, but it remained a talking point. Mr Griffiths blew for time but did not stop his watch, and let it run on until Liddell had shot. He stopped it then, and it showed fifteen seconds beyond the 45 minutes mark.

One Liverpool official, however, was adamant that only two seconds of stoppage time had been added on. Several Liverpool players did not hear the final whistle, though the referee blew twice.

Nevertheless, victory went to the better side. Liverpool put up a good performance, but City were the more stylish and cultured, mastered the tricky conditions better and played the more convincing football for the most part.

Liverpool: Underwood; Molyneux, Moran; Saunders, Hughes, Twentyman; Payne, Arnell, Liddell, Evans, A'Court.

Manchester City: Trautmann; Leivers, Little; Barnes, Ewing, Paul; Spurdle, Hayes, Johnstone, Dyson, Clarke.

Referee: Mr B.M. Griffiths (Newport)

Attendance: 57,528

Receipts: £6,978

The visitors had a touch of class about them which the home side lacked, despite their reliance on speed and sudden bursts rather than on methodical and accurate progression. There was a period in the first half, however, when City might have been trailing by two goals had they not led a charmed life.

The narrowest escape came when Bert Trautmann could not gather a back-pass by Little and the ball was twice kept out in the luckiest manner, Leivers finally heading it over the bar when he was standing almost beneath it.

Two excellent headers by John Evans followed, and at this point, Liverpool were well on top. Eventually City clawed their way back into the game and little by little asserted their superiority.

The hopes of the home supporters soared when Alan Arnell put Liverpool ahead after 52 minutes. He neatly side-footed a header from Evans out of Trautmann's reach following a freekick by Geoff Twentyman for a foul by Paul on Payne.

The joy of this lead was short-lived, however, for the equaliser came twelve minutes later from another free-kick. Molyneux was the offender, a dozen yards or more inside the City's half. Paul, who took the kick, got compensation for his own earlier slip by helping in the goal, scored by Dyson after a fine dribble by Johnstone. It was unfortunate for Molyneux that his feet went from under him as he attempted to tackle Clarke, who somersaulted over the prone body of the fullback.

Johnstone was the main architect of City's victory. Though the Scot was not always in the game as often as some of his colleagues, he did much excellent work in a quiet and unobtrusive manner, and he was also the instigator of City's second goal after 89 minutes, though Hayes added the vital finishing touch.

Underwood, the Liverpool custodian, could not be blamed for the goal, for had he stayed on his line he would probably have been beaten just the same. Liverpool's defence did well against a strong and virile City attack.

Laurie Hughes was once again outstanding, and John Molyneux had a good game against the best wing to visit Anfield this season, until he tired in the last fifteen minutes. He had more to do than usual, because Roy Saunders had the unenviable task of shadowing Johnstone, who wandered all over the pitch.

While Liverpool's attack offered little in the closing stages, this was due mainly to the fact that City had become so dangerous that Liddell and Arnell in particular were compelled to fall back to help their defence. The result was that when the home forwards got away they were invariably out-numbered.

Ewing and Paul marshalled Liverpool's skipper in superb fashion, and Liddell's chances were greatly reduced. Ewing was very severe in some of his tackling, and the crowd showed resentment at his treatment of their captain. The Mancunians' centre-half is not a polished player, but as a rugged stopper, there are not many to beat him.

Johnstone had taken on the Revie mantle of deep centre-forward in telling fashion, and with Hayes and Dyson acting as dual spearheads, and Johnstone occasionally having a dart through himself, City produced many awkward situations for the home defence.

Barnes was a much improved half-back on this form. He rarely wasted a ball, and compared favourably with his captain. City's backs always appeared cool and comfortable and the whole side just had that edge of class which Liverpool could not match.

January 5, 1957

Southend United (1) 2
Duthie 4, Thomson 82

Liverpool (0) 1
Wheeler 48

TOMMY Younger, Jimmy Wheeler and Jimmy Melia made their Cup débuts against Southend, who adapted to the conditions much better than Liverpool. Younger made some brilliant saves and the defence was tight, but there was little penetration by the front men. It was noticeable during the kick-in that the players would have problems because they were ankle deep in mud.

The visitors made the first attack when Alan Arnell slipped the ball out to Billy Liddell, whose centre finished up in the arms of Harry Threadgold. The United replied but did not get beyond the penalty line, while Liverpool were soon back on the offensive and a swirling shot by Alan A'Court curled outside.

With just four minutes gone, Southend took the lead. Jim Duthie wove his way through the middle and with his left foot he shot the ball well out of the reach of Younger. Gordon Barker's astute pass had given Duthie the goalscoring opportunity. For several minutes, the home side pegged Liverpool in their own half, and Jimmy Thomson shot narrowly wide as Southend pressed forward relentlessly.

Liverpool's answer was sporadic as they replied in staccato fashion. A good run by A'Court was nullified by the United defence, and soon afterwards a corner was easily disposed of. However, Wheeler had a shot saved well by the former Chester goalkeeper. Threadgold made a daring save at the feet of A'Court, but United attacked strongly and Ronnie Moran cleared a dangerous-looking situation in front of the Liverpool goal. The first half belonged almost entirely to Southend.

All the players were rekitted for the second half. Liverpool almost scored a sensational equaliser in the first minute when Jimmy Stirling miskicked and let in Melia, but he also miskicked when six yards out. Soon afterwards, however, Wheeler scored. John Molyneux thumped the ball into the goalmouth and it stuck in the mud. Threadgold came out, but Wheeler shot over the goalkeeper's head and just underneath the bar.

A centre by Arnell was palmed away by Threadgold, but the United menace was still apparent and John McGuigan twice had shots blocked and a corner followed on. Liverpool were resolute, however, and Roy Saunders fought like a tiger. At one stage Saunders called on trainer Albert Shelley to wipe the mud from his eye. Both sides were looking for the winning goal, but it looked ever more likely that the home side would win the game. Saunders went on to the wing limping, and Liddell went into the middle. A'Court had a shot at goal, but Threadgold had it covered all the way. Although Liverpool had slightly more of the play at this stage, their attacks lacked potency, whilst Southend always looked capable of scoring whenever they got into the opposition box.

With just eight minutes left, Southend took the lead. McGuigan slipped the ball across to Thomson, who was left in a glorious position and his shot passed through Younger's legs. With Guy Mitchell top of the UK charts with *Singing The Blues,* Liverpool had an apposite theme song.

A spectator collapsed and died at the game.

Southend United: Threadgold; Williamson, Anderson; Duthie, Stirling, Lawler; Barker, McCrory, Hollis, Thomson, McGuigan.

Liverpool: Younger; Molyneux, Moran; Saunders, Hughes, Twentyman; Liddell, Wheeler, Arnell, Melia, A'Court.

Referee: Mr B. Crawford (Doncaster)

Attendance: 18,253

***Tommy Younger,** who played brilliantly on his Cup début for Liverpool*

January 4, 1958

Liverpool (1) 1
Smith (og) 33

Southend United (0) 1
McGuigan 69

LIVERPOOL decided that Brian Jackson would take the place of the injured Tony McNamara at outside-right for today's Cup tie. An innovation was a Scottish pipers' band - a change from "canned" music. In spite of the cold, the ground looked in fairly good condition, with a sprinkling of sand in both goal areas and the centre circle. Liverpool made the first attack, a Liddell header passing well wide. Liverpool dominated the opening ten minutes, and Jimmy Melia accepted a centre by Jackson to bang in a terrific shot which went straight into the arms of Threadgold. A moment later the goalkeeper watched a fast rising drive by Wheeler pass high over the bar. Stirling kept a close watch on Liddell and on several occasions he stopped promising Liverpool attacks. Tony Rowley swung round at a centre from the left and hit the ball against Threadgold. Up to this point there had been genuine opportunities for either side. Jimmy Stirling, defending like a lion, was inclined to be somewhat over-vigorous at times, and a free-kick against him led to the opening goal. Wheeler took the kick and Rowley carried it on before pushing the ball across goal to Jackson, whose short-range shot struck Ray Smith and went into goal after 33 minutes. The Liverpool players shook hands with Jackson, but there was doubt that the ball would have entered the goal but for Smith's intervention.

Melia beat several opponents before putting Wheeler in possession, and Rowley just failed to reach Wheeler's lob. Then Crossan attempted a low shot, which Younger got down to and saved.

Towards the interval, Liddell raced through and was challenged near the goal-line. Such was the intensity of the tackle that Liddell finished up amongst the photographers, scattering cameras to all parts.

Liverpool almost increased their lead in the first minute of the second period when an A'Court-Liddell move saw Threadgold push Liddell's centre away to A'Court, whose header was kicked off the line by Smith. The ball came out to Wheeler, but his shot only produced a corner.

A fast raid by the Southend right wing appeared to be dangerous with Younger scrambling about in front of his goal, but the danger was cleared.

Rowley was grounded with play yards away from him, and then Liddell tried a header which Threadgold saved. Molyneux prevented Hollis from having a shot and then Melia sent in a swerving shot from just outside the penalty area.

Liddell failed to get in a shot and the ball ran to A'Court, who struck the ball fast and accurately, but Threadgold managed to get the ball away for a corner.

Corners came frequently, and Threadgold saved well from a Campbell header. The home side squandered several opportunities before the visitors equalised. Former Anfield star Kevin Baron back-heeled to Errol Crossan, whose centre went straight to McGuigan. His terrific drive left Younger helpless. Rowley missed a reasonable opening as Liverpool strove to get back on top, but Southend held the initiative up to the final whistle.

ON TELEVISION

The World Cup football
match Northern Ireland
v. Italy, at Belfast.
Will be on B.B.C. television
at 2.25p.m. next Wednesday.

SPORTS NOTICES

FOOTBALL LEAGUE MATCH

LIVERPOOL v. FULHAM, at Anfield.
Saturday, 11th inst; kick-off 3.15p.m.
Admission: Ground 2/-, Boys 9d.
Paddock 3/-, Stands 4/6 & 5/-.

Liverpool: Younger; Molyneux, Moran; Wheeler, White, Campbell; Jackson, Rowley, Liddell, Melia, A'Court.

Southend United: Threadgold; Williamson, Anderson; Duthie, Stirling, Smith; Crossan, McCrory, Hollis, Baron, McGuigan.

Referee: Mr J.G. Williams (Nottingham)

Attendance: 43,454

January 8, 1958

Southend (2) 2
Molyneux (og) 40, McCrory 44

Liverpool (1) 3
Molyneux 1, White 79,
Rowley 81

SIR Stanley Rous, secretary of the F.A., and a former referee, and Commander Beetham, of the F.A. Council, were spectators at the game, after Liverpool protested that the referee should have been changed after the first game.

Liverpool played Bimpson on the right wing and brought in Saunders at half-back for the first time this season. Molyneux shot the visitors into the lead in the first minute. Following a right-wing corner, he shot left-footed into the net. The home side performed well, and held the initiative throughout the first half. After a Hollis shot had hit a post, they equalised when Crossan's close-range shot struck the far upright after 40 minutes and rebounded across goal without crossing the line. Molyneux tried to turn the ball away but only succeeded in knocking the ball over the line. Just before the interval, the Liverpool defence was caught napping again and Hollis sent in a ball across the face of the goal, giving McCrory the simple task of slotting it home.

In the second period, Southend appeared to tire, though Hollis and Crossman had other opportunities to add to the score and put Liverpool out of the tie. However, the Southend forwards were weak in front of goal, and Younger had little to do, since he was not going to be beaten from long range.

Saunders, who was signed by George Kay at no fee after Hull City had not retained him as a boy, played well and fitted into the side comfortably.

Liverpool gained a corner with time running out. Bimpson, who had been preferred on the right to Jackson, took the flag-kick, and White advanced upfield to nod the ball into the back of the net. A defender went up to handle the ball as it crossed the line under the bar. The linesman signalled that the ball had been over the line and the referee acknowledged the goal. Southend hardly protested. Referee Williams said, "If the ball had not been over the line I should have awarded a penalty."

Two minutes later Rowley began and finished a fine move. He passed to A'Court, who had gone to inside-right, and he centred for Rowley to smash the ball home to avoid the necessity of extra-time.

Two players had their names taken, McGuigan and White. Billy Liddell, the Liverpool captain, walked off the field at the end of the game after receiving a punch in the face when he charged Threadgold.

Bob Paisley said after the game, "You have to scramble through cup-ties. That's the way things go."

At Goodison Park later the same day, Everton beat Sunderland 3-1.

John Molyneux, who scored in the first minute for Liverpool then put through his own goal after 40 minutes

Southend United: Threadgold; Williamson, Anderson; Duthie, Stirling, Smith; Crossan, McCrory, Hollis, Baron, McGuigan.

Liverpool: Younger; Molyneux, Moran; Wheeler, White, Saunders; Bimpson, Rowley, Liddell, Melia, A'Court.

Referee: Mr J.G. Williams (Nottingham)

Attendance: 20,000

January 25, 1958

Liverpool (1) 3
Liddell 28, Collins (og) 79, Bimpson 82

Northampton Town (1) 1
Hawkins 42

THE ground was covered with an inch or two of melting snow which had been cleared from the goal areas, in which sand had been placed. The pitch was only declared fit to play on at a quarter to one, after Mr Tirebuck, who had inspected it last night, had had another examination. However, it was obvious that it was going to be heavy and tricky going and that neither side would be able to play anything approaching stylish football. Louis Bimpson was a late choice in the Liverpool team in place of Jimmy Melia.

Liddell won the toss and as usual Liverpool defended the Kop end in the first half. After two quick Northampton raids had broken down, Liddell and A'Court paired off on the left, but as Liddell was forcing a way through following A'Court's low pass, he was brought down by Ron Patterson right on the edge of the box. He came to earth heavily inside the line, but the referee gave a free-kick outside the area.

The first few minutes provided an abundance of spills and thrills and players slid yards as they went into the tackle. Liverpool's goal was threatened when Jack English darted through, rounded Geoff Twentyman and then as he was tangling with Ronnie Moran, he appeared to catch the full-back in the face with his elbow. Moran went down like a log, and he required attention before he could resume.

Third Division Northampton were strong in their tackling, quick on to the ball and realised that the conditions put them in with a chance against their more illustrious opponents. Liverpool's best scoring effort was a great header by Tony Rowley, who was only inches off target following a corner by Alan A'Court. But this was not football at its best because of the appalling conditions. Anything could happen to the ball once it had been played, and those who tried to propel it along the ground had the greatest difficulty in moving it any distance.

Spectators were still being helped from the premises by the ambulance men, one going on a stretcher. Though the crowd was large, it did not look to be anywhere near a record. A fine pass by Tony McNamara almost sent Louis Bimpson away, Colin Gale just cut across in time to boot the ball off his toe.

Liverpool were somewhat inclined to be fanciful, trying to work the ball accurately along the ground in some instances. Under such conditions as these, the long punt upfield would have been the best tactic. Liverpool did most of the pressing, but Northampton's defence stood up to its work well.

With 28 minutes gone, Liverpool took the lead with a splendidly taken goal by Billy Liddell, following a corner. A'Court's flag kick was punched away, but Liddell's right foot volley while the ball was still a couple of feet off the ground, was in the net almost before Reg Elvy could move. Within the next three minutes the opposing goal had narrow escapes in turn from headers by Rowley and Bimpson, and a fierce drive by McNamara, which was blocked away by a defender. When the visitors eventually broke through the stranglehold which the Liverpool defence was gradually inflicting upon the game, Bob Tebbutt delayed his shot so that Johnny White was able to intercept.

The players continued to slide all over the pitch. The ball either stuck in the icy water or skidded violently off the surface, and the strong and icy wind only added to the difficulties. Referee Tirebuck waved aside appeals for a penalty when Liddell was brought down and Bimpson, finding himself in possession 12 yards from goal brought Elvy to a full length save, Gale completing the clearance.

The game was stopped while Tebbutt received attention after being struck in the midriff by a strong shot by Bimpson. Liverpool continued to hold the upper hand, and for some minutes, Northampton were unable to get out of their own half. When at last they got away, their attack was not long sustained, and following a free-kick to Liverpool, Rowley put Liddell through with only Elvy to beat from 16 yards. In trying to put the ball out of the tall goalkeeper's reach, Liddell screwed it beyond the far post.

Almost immediately, Northampton broke away and equalised three minutes from half-time. There appeared to be no real danger when Leek put the ball out to Tom Fowler, nor even when the outside-left centred it after eluding John Molyneux, but Peter Hawkins got his head to it, and his effort went into the net, low down, off the inside of a post.

This was a severe blow after such a long period of domination by the home side, but Northampton had not been outclassed despite their lack of possession. A minute before the interval, Tebbutt was carried off after he had apparently twisted his leg badly when falling.

During the break, four members of the ground staff forked the turf around the centre circle to let the surplus water away, while ambulance men were still busy taking spectators for treatment. One of the stretcher cases sat up and got off the canvas when he realised that he was being taken out of the ground, but he wisely decided to go off.

Tebbutt resumed when the teams reappeared. He had had a kick on the knee which had temporarily numbed his leg. The icy, swirling wind seemed to favour Northampton, who forced two quick corners in succession, though their efforts to convert them into goalscoring opportunities proved fruitless. Liddell was an inspiration. He took throw-ins and corners and appeared all over the park. One corner floated onto the head of Rowley, but his effort was wide of the mark.

Although the conditions prevailed against skilful football, both sides attempted to raise the level of the game above the farcical. A Northampton raid was repelled by White, whose enormous clearance enabled Rowley and Bimpson to take command. Both failed to get in a shot.

A charge in the back on Rowley by Ken Leek provided Liverpool with a free-kick six yards outside the penalty area. Molyneux placed it for the onrunning Rowley, but the inside-right's header was yards wide.

The visitors continued to press forward and the Liverpool goal escaped on several occasions, but in the 79th minute, tragedy came to Northampton. Liddell, on the edge of the penalty area, took an age to get the ball to his liking, but he finally switched it from his right foot to his left and put in a curling shot which had no particular danger about it until Ben Collins, trying to head behind, directed the ball beyond his own goalkeeper. Collins, obviously crestfallen, was patted on the shoulder by two of his colleagues to show that they absolved him from blame. The Northampton player had to do something, because Rowley was coming up behind.

Eight minutes from the end Liddell laid the foundation of another goal. After beating his man, he squared the ball for A'Court, who slipped it through for Bimpson to make it 3-1. Liverpool squandered three more genuine opportunities before the final whistle.

F.A. CUP FOURTH ROUND

Everton	1	Blackburn Rovers	2
Cardiff City	4	Leyton Orient	1
Newcastle United	1	Scunthorpe United	3
Wolverhampton W.	5	Portsmouth	1
Chelsea	3	Darlington	3
Stoke City	3	Middlesbrough	1
York City	0	Bolton Wanderers	0
Manchester United	2	Ipswich Town	0
Sheffield Wednesday	4	Hull City	3
West Bromwich A.	3	Nottingham Forest	3
Tottenham Hotspur	0	Sheffield United	3
Bristol Rovers	2	Burnley	2
Notts County	1	Bristol City	2
West Ham United	3	Stockport County	2
Fulham	1	Charlton Athletic	1

Replays

Darlington	4	Chelsea	1
Bolton Wanderers	3	York City	0
Nottingham Forest	1	West Bromwich A.	5
Burnley	2	Bristol Rovers	3
Charlton Athletic	0	Fulham	2

Louis Bimpson, *who scored with just eight minutes remaining after taking a through ball from Alan A'Court*

Liverpool

Younger

Molyneux   Moran

Wheeler   White   Twentyman

McNamara   Rowley   Liddell   Bimpson   A'Court

o

English   Tebbutt   Hawkins   Leek   Fowler

Yeoman   Gale   Mills

Collins   Patterson

Elvy

Northampton Town

Referee: Mr L.J. Tirebuck (Halifax)

Attendance: 56,939

February 15, 1958

Scunthorpe United (0) 0   Liverpool (0) 1

Murdoch 76

LIVERPOOL preferred Bimpson to Brian Jackson at outside-right for today's Cup-tie at Third Division Scunthorpe and retained Murdoch - making his Cup début - and Harrower in the inside positions. Twentyman had been troubled by a knee injury, but he reported fit.

Liverpool supporters were very prominent in the crowd and they gave Liddell and his colleagues a tremendous roar as they took to the field. Harrower gave supporters a nasty shock as he tripped on the cinder path when coming out of the tunnel and looked to have twisted an ankle. He crouched down on the touchline for a moment or so while testing out the injured foot.

Liddell won the toss and the kick-off had to be taken twice, for John Marriott had been caught in the Liverpool half on the first occasion. Marriott provided the first shot after Twentyman had misplaced a pass meant for Moran, but the winger's attempt was well off target. Ken Hardwick moved out quickly to take possession of a centre by Wheeler, but the goalkeeper misjudged a long effort by Molyneux and must have been relieved to find the ball dropping over the bar.

The home side began to pile on the pressure, and after one goalmouth scramble, Liverpool escaped with a corner, which Tommy Younger caught safely. As he came to earth, he crashed into Eric Davis and had to receive prolonged attention from trainer Albert Shelley, while the referee had a few words with the centre-forward.

Jack Haigh - the former Liverpool player - picked up almost every loose ball in the midfield and he was the mainspring of the Scunthorpe attack. Two corners were forced and Mervyn Jones - another former Liverpool player - taking a long pass in his stride and centring while still travelling at speed, forced Younger to make a catch. Dick White almost put the ball past his own goalkeeper and straight to the feet of Davis, but Younger moved quickly and was able to smother the ball.

Liddell was the man Scunthorpe obviously feared, and he appeared to be Liverpool's main hope. He left Barry Horstead standing and was within shooting range when John Hubbard saved the day with a glorious tackle from behind.

Shortly afterwards, Liddell showed his danger, beating two men and standing aside to let A'Court fire the ball across the face of the goal.

The tackling was tremendously hard and players were given little time to settle on the ball. Hardwick pulled down a long-range effort from Wheeler, but the Liverpool forwards were generally weak. Nevertheless, Hardwick fisted away a free-kick by Bimpson, and Twentyman, timing the dropping ball to perfection, volleyed it beyond the far angle - an effort which deserved better reward.

After a brave header by Bimpson, Liddell battled his way through and got beyond Hardwick, but his shot hit the side netting from the narrowest of angles.

During the interval, about two hundred Liverpool supporters left their places behind Hardwick's goal and ran down the pitch to join the crowd at the other end, presumably in the hope of having a better view of any goals. The bottom rungs of the two floodlighting pylons were also full of eager supporters.

The first thrill in the second period came when Murdoch dashed away down the right and Hardwick pushed his centre away to Harrower, who met the ball first time at the edge of the penalty area, only to hit it high over the vacant net.

Rain began to fall heavily and the pitch became more and more testing on the players' reserves of stamina. Liddell evaded Horstead and drove a left foot shot past the angle from ten yards. Again Liddell put Scunthorpe under pressure when he let fly with his left foot and the ball came back into play after striking an upright.

After all their incessant pressure, Liverpool almost fell behind when Jones caught the defence sleeping and ran through alone only to shoot wide with Younger to beat.

With the field becoming more of a morass, Liverpool's pressure was eventually rewarded when Murdoch put the visitors ahead. In the gloom on the far side of the field A'Court drew Hardwick towards him before slipping the ball back in front of goal, where Murdoch put a low shot into the net.

Scunthorpe struck back immediately and Younger had to save from Davis. Five minutes from time Horstead - who appeared to have mud in his eye - ran off the field in company with the trainer. Horstead returned just in time to chase Liddell as the Scot ran 40 yards through the mud before delivering a crashing shot towards Hardwick.

Scunthorpe United: Hardwick; Hubbard, Brownsword; Marshall, Horstead, Bushby; Marriott, Waldock, Davis, Haigh, Jones.

Liverpool: Younger; Molyneux, Moran; Wheeler, White, Twentyman; Bimpson, Murdoch, Liddell, Harrower, A'Court.

Referee: Mr K. Howley (Middlesbrough)

Attendance: 23,000

March 1, 1958

Blackburn Rovers (0) 2
Clayton 78, McLeod 81

Liverpool (1) 1
Murdoch 19

BLACKBURN Rovers enjoyed the majority of the play throughout the game, and although Liverpool took an early lead which they almost held on to, the superior class of the First Division team saw the home side through as they scored two goals in the last twelve minutes of the match.

Peter Dobing was upended by White six yards outside the penalty area, but Younger came out to take Bryan Douglas's free-kick. Hands against White - again six yards outside the box - saw Roy Vernon put the free kick to the head of Dobing, who flicked it only a foot over the bar. Another free-kick for an offence by Molyneux was fisted away by Younger as Blackburn took the play to their opponents.

Liverpool defended gallantly as the home side played with passion and skill. Play was stopped after 13 minutes when trainer Albert Shelley gave Harrower an elastic bandage for his right thigh. A couple of minutes later, Harrower pulled out a burst of speed, but he was obviously not right and he rubbed his leg on more than one occasion.

With 19 minutes gone, Moran, from the half way line, hit a terrific shot which Matt Woods headed into the air while standing in the penalty area. The ball went on to Jackson, who squared it for Murdoch to put Liverpool ahead from 12 yards, despite being challenged by Clayton and Woods. Murdoch immediately toppled over and did a somersault after releasing his shot.

Blackburn's response was to continue to play their own game of attacking, skilful football and for some minutes they penned Liverpool in their own half. However, despite all of Blackburn's territorial superiority, Younger had little to do other than collect high crosses and loose balls. The Liverpool goalkeeper not only dominated the six yard area, but almost half of the penalty box. His catching was immaculate.

Although limping slightly, Harrower's injury appeared to have receded at this stage of the game.

Despite constant attacking forays, Blackburn could not penetrate Liverpool's close-knit defence, which remained unbeaten up to the interval.

Midway through the first half, several policemen had been called to a corner of the ground where the crowd appeared very tightly packed and had been swaying. A broken crush barrier was taken away and four people were carried off on stretchers, while two or three others were assisted out of the ground.

During the interval two more people were taken off on stretchers from another part of the ground, and a fight took place on the far side from the Press box which necessitated police reinforcements. Three people wearing Liverpool colours were led away by police officers.

A low cross by Roy Stephenson was only partially saved by Younger and the ball was hooked away by White. Before the corner was taken, Younger received attention for an injury to his shoulder.

Liverpool had a narrow escape when a fierce low shot by Dobing was saved at full length by Younger at the foot of the post, and as he lay on the ground, Stephenson shot behind from three yards' range.

In terms of territorial advantage, Blackburn were in the ascendancy, but they had little fortune against a resolute Liverpool defence which refused to yield an inch against the superior skills of their opponents.

Harrower was little more than a passenger throughout this half, and the home side forced nine corners in 25 minutes as they sought an equaliser. The Blackburn captain, Clayton, played exceptionally well, despite an injury sustained in a tackle with Liddell.

With twelve minutes remaining, Blackburn scored. A foul against White - for hands - was taken by Vernon, who lobbed the ball forward and Clayton headed out of the reach of the diving Younger. Clayton had to throw himself forward in order to make proper contact with the ball. It was a brilliant goal.

Three minutes later, Blackburn went in front. Douglas beat two men and squared the ball for Ally McLeod, in the centre-forward position, to ram home a right foot drive.

As the home side pressed forward their advantage, Younger saved well from Vernon, Stephenson and McLeod.

After the game, an official stated that about five people had been treated, the worst injuries being broken ribs. No-one had been admitted to hospital.

Blackburn Rovers: Leyland; Taylor, Eckersley; R.Clayton, Woods, McGrath; Douglas, Stephenson, Dobing, Vernon, McLeod.

Liverpool: Younger; Molyneux, Moran; Wheeler, White, Twentyman; Jackson, Murdoch, Liddell, Harrower, A'Court.

Referee: Mr A.W. Leuty (Leeds)

Attendance: 51,000

Receipts: £7,688

January 15, 1959

Worcester City (1) 2
Skuse 9, White (og) 80

Liverpool (0) 1
Twentyman (pen) 83

WORCESTER City from the Southern League pulled off a sensational victory in beating Second Division Liverpool, who were without the services of Billy Liddell - relegated to twelfth man for this cup tie. There was not a blade of grass to be seen on the St. George's Lane pitch, apart from a few small patches in two corners. The surface was brown and bare, and was soft in parts. The condition of the pitch was greatly improved from that which caused referee Tirebuck to postpone the game on Saturday.

In the first two minutes, Liverpool were awarded two free-kicks, both of which were taken by Moran. From the second kick, Fred Morris - making his Cup début for the visitors - got in a hook shot which Kirkwood pulled down under the bar.

Worcester's tactics were to send the long ball through the middle, and in putting one away for a corner, Ronnie Moran fell heavily. From the kick, Eddie Follan's header was punched away by Tommy Younger.

The home side's spirit was remarkable, and in the ninth minute they took the lead. Gosling put a low ball into the goal area and John Molyneux, in trying to put it back to Younger, turned it away from the goalkeeper, and Skuse came in like a whippet to shoot low into the net.

Liverpool were finding the conditions difficult, and the home side's policy of booting the ball upfield as quickly as possible was making them the more dangerous. Worcester's tackling was strong and resolute, so that whenever Liverpool tried to keep the ball close they met with little success. The Reds were obviously the more skilful side in midfield, but their skill was negated by the home side's insistence on the long ball.

Whenever Worcester attacked, the Liverpool defence looked unhappy. Liverpool's failure to move the ball more quickly was their downfall, and Worcester's defence always looked the more composed, while Liverpool's attempts to use the short pass in their own half was leading to problems and causing the defence much unnecessary toil.

Soon after the interval, Alan A'Court was pulled down just outside the area. Geoff Twentyman's free-kick passed over everybody into the arms of Kirkwood. Liverpool made a concerted effort to equalise, but Jimmy Melia shot straight at the goalkeeper after being put through by A'Court. Worcester replied with a long punt down the field from Bryceland, which was only just out of the reach of Follan.

There were numerous free-kicks and Liverpool gained three in quick succession, but from the last of these Louis Bimpson and A'Court got in each other's way when the winger attempted to force a way through. After Gosling shot over the bar, Twentyman joined the attack to fire in a low drive which passed across the goal and out of play. The visitors began to show more urgency, and only a great diving save by Kirkwood prevented the equaliser from the head of A'Court. Liverpool's territorial advantage increased as the game wore on, but the Worcester defence kept the game simple and were happy to put the ball anywhere rather than take any risks.

Liverpool's task became more difficult when Twentyman had to go off for attention to his leg. He returned later in the game, but limped slightly. A mistake by John White nearly let in Knowles, but Molyneux cleared the danger when he covered swiftly. The home side kept a firm grip on the game; their determination to get to the ball first was paying dividends. Melia, however, had a great chance of scoring the goal Liverpool so desperately needed when the ball ran loose to him near the six-yard line, but in attempting to place it with the side of the foot, he put it well outside.

Shortly afterwards Worcester had a narrow escape when Twentyman hit a first-time volley against the bar. There were signs of desperation about Liverpool and their play became increasingly ragged. Neither Harrower nor Melia could find a way of splitting the dour Worcester defence, for which Paul was in outstanding form.

With just ten minutes remaining, a combination of errors saw the home side increase their lead. First Moran and then White failed to get the ball away, with the result that Knowles got away on the right and when his low centre came over, White, racing back, tried to put the ball outside, but it skied up off his foot and went over the advancing Younger.

Almost straight from the kick-off, Kirkwood saved from Morris in a scramble near the goal and the referee gave a penalty, apparently for an offence on Bimpson. Twentyman converted the kick. There was an amazing scene when the referee blew for offside against Bimpson, because hundreds of youngsters took it to be the final whistle and ran onto the pitch.

Worcester City: Kirkwood; Wilcox, Potts; Bryceland, Melville, Paul; Brown, Follan, Knowles, Gosling, Skuse.

Liverpool: Younger; Molyneux, Moran; Wheeler, White, Twentyman; Morris, Melia, Bimpson, Harrower, A'Court.

Referee: Mr L.J. Tirebuck (Halifax)

Attendance: 15,011

The Shankly Years

1960 - 1974

January 9, 1960

Liverpool (1) 2
Hunt 1, 90

Leyton Orient (0) 1
Foster 62

KEN Facey won the choice of ends and set Liverpool to kick into the Kop goal. The first cheer of the afternoon at Anfield was the one which greeted the news that Everton were a goal down at Bradford. The Reds opened brightly and Harrower and Hickson set A'Court going. His fast high centre came in so menacingly Dave Groombridge could only turn it round the post for a corner.

A'Court's kick came in perfectly for Hunt to nod the ball into the net with a fast, glancing header that completely beat the goalkeeper.

On two subsequent occasions, Groombridge mishandled the ball, but the Orient were fortunate in getting the ball away to safety. The goalkeeper then put on his white gloves in an attempt to get a better grip on the ball.

Gradually the London side clawed their way back into the game after such a devastating psychological blow and their steady progressive football gave them the initiative, although their final ball lacked real threat.

Liverpool played the offside trap against Leyton Orient with mercurial precision. Tom Johnston was always dangerous in the air, and Slater, despite his lack of height, did well to effect several fine catches in the face of numerous challenges by the former Blackburn leader. The game was stopped for a brief time while Molyneux received attention to his right knee. He was able to continue.

Johnston was the instigator of every Leyton attacking move, and the visitors enjoyed a period of successive corners which endangered the Liverpool defence. Alan A'Court was injured when he stopped a thundering shot in the stomach, but he continued after attention from trainer Bob Paisley. Just before the interval, young Terry McDonald centred close to the face of the goal before White headed for a corner.

Liverpool lacked a sense of urgency, whilst Orient played as though they were in the lead. Foster beat Wheeler and opened up the way for McDonald, but the Leyton winger shot high over the bar.

While Leyton vainly appealed for an offside decision, Dave Hickson - who, along with Slater, Leishman and Hunt, was making his cup début - picked up the through pass from Leishman and powered towards the goal with every likelihood of scoring. Groombridge, however, came swiftly off his line and covered the shot. It was a courageous move, and one which denied Liverpool at a crucial time.

A'Court beat several players in a long run which started deep in his own half, but he was eventually dispossessed. An excellent drive by A'Court was fisted away by the goalkeeper, and another shot by the tricky winger was deflected for a corner. A'Court's flag-kick was headed wide by Hunt.

Liverpool's left-winger was in brilliant form, and Groombridge pushed aside a low shot by A'Court before saving from Hickson, who raced onto the rebound.

At the other end, Slater pulled off a magnificent save from Johnston, whose header was both powerful and accurate. The Liverpool goalkeeper, however, could only knock the ball upwards, and Moran, standing almost on the line, hooked the ball for a corner. The corner kick from Phil White found the net at the far side of the goal, but referee Taylor awarded Liverpool a free-kick a few yards short of the goal line.

Inevitably, Leyton Orient's period of pressure brought about an equaliser. Johnston combined well with McDonald in a left wing movement and he delivered a cross shot which Slater could only palm away, with the result that Ron Foster, standing 12 yards outside the box, rammed the ball home.

Johnston's performance was remarkable. The big Scot from Kilmarnock had speed, guile and attacking punch.

Tommy Leishman's through balls were delightfully pleasing and one of them produced a marvellous chance for Hickson, whose clinch with Alan Eagles almost produced a penalty for the Reds, but the referee awarded a free-kick to Orient, despite Ronnie Moran being upfield ready to take the penalty while Eagles was receiving attention from the trainer.

With the seconds dying away, Dick White moved upfield for the first time in the match. He crossed the ball to Hickson, whose short pass found Hunt. The Liverpool inside-right shot weakly at the goal, but Groombridge went down late and the ball found its target. A moment later the whistle sounded for the cessation of hostilities.

F.A. CUP FINAL

May 7, 1960

WOLVERHAMPTON WANDERERS (1) 3   **BLACKBURN ROVERS** (0) 0
McGrath (og), Deeley (2)

Liverpool: Slater; Molyneux, Moran; Wheeler, White, Leishman; Melia, Hunt, Hickson, Harrower, A'Court.

Leyton Orient: Groombridge; Eagles, Charlton; Facey, Bishop, Sorrell; P.White, Brown, Johnston, Foster, McDonald.

Referee: Mr J.K. Taylor (Wolverhampton)

Attendance: 40,343

January 30, 1960

Liverpool (1) 1
Wheeler 36

Manchester United (2) 3
Charlton 13, 44, Bradley 69

ANFIELD was filled almost to capacity for this tie against First Division United. Rain fell incessantly but the pitch was in excellent condition. The Lord Mayor of Liverpool and the England team manager, Mr Walter Winterbottom, were present. United's Warren Bradley wore a large thigh support. The floodlights were on from the start, and Ronnie Moran, who won the toss, elected to defend the Kop goal.

Roger Hunt might have scored in the first minute when Shay Brennan blundered. Hunt seized on the ball as it came loose, and screwed in a shot which Maurice Setters prevented from crossing the line with goalkeeper Harry Gregg hopelessly placed. A moment later Jimmy Harrower chased a high through ball from Dave Hickson and he caused Gregg to lose possession, but referee Murdoch adjudged Harrower's challenge to be foul. Shortly afterwards, Hickson was put through by Hunt, but he was offside. It was a marvellous opening for the home side, but United struck back through Bradley after Melia let him through on the left. Bradley's shot went wide.

Bobby Charlton,
United's two-goal hero

Liverpool continued to move onto the offensive at every opportunity and Harrower beat his man before hitting a shot which just rose sufficiently to clear the bar. United began to settle down after the home side's excellent start, and Bobby Charlton tested Slater with a right foot shot which passed narrowly wide. With 13 minutes gone, United took the lead with a goal created out of nothing. Charlton took the ball through at inside-left and left Molyneux beaten for pace before hitting a left-foot shot which found the net just inside the far post. The goal gave United greater confidence, while it appeared to deflate Liverpool's early enthusiasm. Molyneux tried to make amends for being beaten by Charlton when he moved menacingly upfield before hitting a shot just past the far post. Left-half Brennan came in for some criticism after

his numerous clashes with Hunt. Charlton gained a corner for United, and from the cleared kick Liverpool advanced upfield, where Hunt sent in a dipping shot which Gregg turned over for a corner to Liverpool.

A free-kick by Moran led to Gregg only half-clearing the ball, and Wheeler, standing at the edge of the box, drew back his trusty right foot and hit a thundering shot into the roof of the net. United were stung out of their complacency, and Bradley's shot was crowded out as the visitors struck back. A moment later Charlton drove the ball just wide of the goal angle. Immediately prior to the interval, Bradley moved towards the goal-line before cutting a centre back very square, which left Charlton with the easy job of lashing the ball home for United's second goal.

Upon resuming, Wheeler presented Charlton with a gift of an opportunity to secure his hat-trick, but the United inside-left made nothing of it. Hunt responded with a fine header from a Melia centre which went inches too high. Bobby Charlton was having a magnificent game, and his distribution on such a treacherous surface was nothing short of brilliant. United were gaining the upper hand, and Moran headed away Albert Quixall's left-foot shot when standing on the goal-line and with Slater beaten. United's inter-passing was of a high calibre and when Quixall found Bradley in the clear on his wing, the little man cut the ball back and closed to make a left-foot shot which struck the underside of the bar on its way into the net. The visitors shut up shop, but Liverpool bravely attempted to reduce the deficit. Gregg produced a good save from Melia.

But for the sterling work of Molyneux, United would have torn Liverpool apart down their right wing. Hunt went to centre-forward in a last-ditch effort to salvage the game, but United held firm.

Liverpool: Slater; Molyneux, Moran; Wheeler, White, Leishman; Melia, Hunt, Hickson, Harrower, A'Court.

Manchester United: Gregg; Foulkes, Carolan; Setters, Cope, Brennan; Bradley, Quixall, Viollet, Charlton, Scanlon.

Referee: Mr A. Murdoch (Sheffield)

Attendance: 56,736

Receipts: £9,459

January 7, 1961

Liverpool (2) 3
Hunt 37, Lewis 40,
Harrower 61

Coventry City (0) 2
Straw 56, Myerscough 58

THE pitch had been sanded a little in the centre and the goalmouths, but it looked in excellent condition for this first-ever meeting between the two clubs. Both teams were wearing black arm bands as a mark of respect for the death of a Coventry director - and former chairman - yesterday.

Liverpool: Slater; Molyneux, Byrne; Wheeler, White, Leishman; Lewis, Hunt, Hickson, Harrower, A'Court.

Coventry City: Lightening; Kletzenbauer, Austin; Kearns, Curtis, Farmer; P.Hill, Straw, Myerscough, Hewitt, Imlach.

Referee: Mr L.J. Tirebuck (Halifax)

Attendance: 50,909

A mistake by Ron Farmer let Harrower through in the first minute, but the Liverpool player took his shot too quickly and it lacked direction, going straight to Lightening. The home side went all out for a swift opening goal and a 50 yard run by White ended with his shot being blocked. Harrower set up A'Court, and the winger's long, dropping centre completely deceived Arthur Lightening, who was relieved when the ball dropped just over the crossbar.

Coventry's first real attack came after 10 minutes, and both White and Slater hesitated in going for a long centre, but Straw's header went wide.

After Gerry Byrne - making his cup début along with Kevin Lewis - had been brought down in the penalty area, the referee played the advantage rule and allowed the ball to run on to Lewis, whose shot was so far off target that it almost struck the far corner flag.

For a period of time, Liverpool's passing became woefully inept, and with Coventry playing the offside trap to good effect, the home forwards did not trouble Lightening for some time. Hickson was well policed by George Curtis, a strong-tackling player, and this cancelled out Liverpool's wing-play.

A shot by Bill Myerscough cannoned off White's body and flew into the air, to bounce on the crossbar and come down for Byrne to cleverly turn it back to Slater, who completed the clearance and averted the danger. Liverpool were spared the ignominy of falling behind to middle-of-the-table Third Division Coventry when the referee awarded an indirect free-kick just inside the penalty area for obstruction on Hill after Wheeler had turned the ball into his own goal. Shortly afterwards, Stuart Imlach attempted a 25-yard shot which went wide. Hunt, who was struggling to find the form of last season, had done little in the game so far until he suddenly

burst through from a pass by Lewis and cleverly went past Curtis before firing a left-foot shot on the run inches over the bar.

A quickly taken free-kick by Lewis after 37 minutes led to Liverpool taking the lead with some fortune. Lewis slammed the ball upfield to Hickson who won possession in a duel with Curtis. The Liverpool centre-forward tried to beat the goalkeeper, but the ball ran off Lightening's body into the clear for Hunt to have the simple job of placing it delicately into the empty net.

Three minutes later Liverpool increased their lead. The ball was swung in from the right by Hunt and Lewis's header rebounded off Curtis out again to Hunt on the right. The inside man crossed it once again and with two or three Coventry defenders failing to make contact, Lewis rammed the ball into the net from one yard out.

Liverpool kicked into the Kop goal in the second period. With 56 minutes gone, Byrne was adjudged to have fouled Hill, and the visitors scored. Farmer lobbed the free-kick forward towards the far post and with both White and Molyneux hesitating to go for it, Straw nipped in between them to head a good goal.

Two minutes later, and the game was turned completely round when the visitors got on level terms. A superb pass by Myerscough to Hill enabled the Coventry winger to turn the ball low inside for the Coventry leader to turn on a sixpence and flash it past Slater from close range.

Liverpool were stung into retaliation and after 61 minutes they regained the lead. A'Court pulled the ball back to Harrower, who was standing two yards outside the penalty area. He hit a fine shot which beat Lightening's dive, struck the upright and turned into the net.

Harrower made the best pass of the match to set Hunt free on the left. The inside-right declined to cross the ball and elected to work his way inside for a shot but took too long and the defence covered back before Hunt shot wide.

Wheeler was off for a short time, receiving attention to his right knee, but he resumed in his usual position before moving into the forward line and swopping places with Harrower.

The game became somewhat over-physical, and Leishman and Farmer were involved in a scrimmage in the goalmouth. The referee called together the two captains in an effort to calm the proceedings down after Lewis had been fouled. Frank Kletzenbauer cleared off the line from Hunt with only two minutes to go.

January 28, 1961

Liverpool (0) 0

Sunderland (2) 2
Hooper 3, Lawther 14

SUNDERLAND came to Anfield fresh from their 2-1 Third Round victory over Arsenal and on the crest of an unbeaten fourteen-match run. Liverpool were without the services of Wheeler, who was recovering from a chill, and Milne deputised. The inclusion of Morrissey was reported in the local press as being an odd one because the player had threatened to quit soccer just a few weeks previously - a threat which had been repeated several times.

Liverpool had undergone a sequence of six games with only one victory, but they displayed great courage in their attempt to defeat the First Division side.

The Anfield pitch recovered from the morning's soaking. The referee inspected the pitch at 11am when there were pools of water caused by the torrential downpour, which abated at lunchtime. There was a crowd of about 40,000 at the start to see Liverpool's re-modelled forward line. The floodlights were on from the beginning of the game due to the grey skies. Liverpool skipper White won the toss and chose to defend the Kop goal in the first period.

Liverpool: Slater; Molyneux, Byrne; Milne, White, Leishman; A'Court, Lewis, Hickson, Melia, Morrissey.

Sunderland: Wakeham; Nelson, Ashurst; Anderson, Hurley, McNab; Hooper, Fogarty, Lawther, McPheat, Dillon.

Referee: Mr H.G. New (Havant)

Attendance: 46,185

Receipts: £7,440

The visitors attacked from the start and Hooper tested Byrne, but White cleverly anticipated a return ball and cleared the danger. Liverpool responded with an attack of their own, but the move broke down when Lewis fouled Ashurst near the corner flag.

With just three minutes gone, Sunderland took the lead through Hooper. The winger moved across field to the inside-left position to take a pass from Dillon, and his centre was misjudged by Slater. The ball dropped over his head into the far corner of the goal.

Liverpool responded immediately and Morrissey collected a rebound off Anderson before cutting into the middle and attempting a fine right-foot shot from 20 yards which flew past an upright with the goalkeeper beaten. Moments later Lewis weaved his way into a shooting position, but the

Sunderland goalkeeper saved at full stretch. The ball ran loose before Nelson cleared.

The brilliance of Hooper was evident as he meandered past Leishman to leave the Liverpool player in his wake, but White anticipated the pass to Fogarty and intercepted the danger. Liverpool appealed for a penalty when A'Court fell as he cut into the box, but Mr New declared that the winger had fallen over the foot of Ashurst.

With 14 minutes gone, Lawther tried a speculative shot from 20 yards which appeared to be in Slater's sight, but the goalkeeper was too slow to get across and the ball found the net. Liverpool then won three corners on the left wing in succession, but Sunderland withdrew their attack and the danger was cleared.

The Reds threw everything into the offensive, and Lewis was the most dangerous forward in a strange position at inside-right. The game became one of kick-and-rush, although Hooper's skill was the highlight of the half.

Lawther flicked the ball out to Hooper, and the winger cut inside and hit a tremendous shot which beat Slater and struck the crossbar. The ball rebounded to Dillon, but the winger was offside when he had a fine chance to score.

Just before the interval, Morrissey sent in a good centre which Wakeham fisted away. The ball fell to A'Court, who attempted a volley which flew inches over the bar.

Liverpool gained a throw-in close to the corner flag and the Kop roared its approval and encouragement. A'Court's centre was headed by Melia against the body of Hurley, but the ball rebounded to safety. From a long centre by Byrne, Hickson headed the ball across to Lewis. The inside-right flicked it forward neatly to Hickson, who tried another header, but the ball grazed an upright. Liverpool continued to attack, and Wakeham was forced to leave his line in order to catch a good centre from Morrissey.

As Sunderland went onto the attack, they displayed a level of skill which Liverpool were unable to match. Hooper left Byrne for dead and from his centre, White conceded a corner, which proved fruitless. Hurley effected a clearance with too little power and Morrissey seized upon the loose ball to blast a first-time effort inches over the bar.

The Sunderland fans sang *The Blaydon Races* as their team strode through the tie, and contented themselves with their lead. Some of Hurley's touches were first-class, and he initiated several excellent moves by Sunderland. Slater had little to do in the second period but there was no sign of the Sunderland defence cracking because Liverpool's second half territorial advantage was not utilised due to their forward line inadequacies.

January 6, 1962

Liverpool (4) 4
St.John 16, 41,
Hunt 28, A'Court 44

Chelsea (1) 3
Tambling 18, 67,
Bridges 76

THE pitch was in fine condition considering the snow of the previous week. The home side almost took a sensational lead in the opening seconds when Mel Scott turned back a centre from Callaghan - making his Cup début - and Melia took a first time shot which was heading for the corner of the net until Peter Bonetti made a superb flying save at the expense of a flag-kick. Liverpool started with tremendous drive and initiative, and Bonetti foiled A'Court from scoring the opening goal, after the winger had been put in the clear by Hunt. Melia next tested Bonetti, but it was far from a one-sided contest and both Chelsea wingers displayed excellent pace and skill. A fine move between St.John and Hunt almost broke clear through Chelsea's defence, but St.John's final pass was just a little too strong for Hunt. Immediately afterwards, a mistake at the other end by Byrne left Peter Brabrook in possession and he flashed the ball across to Bert Murray, whose shot was brilliantly saved by Slater.

With 16 minutes gone, St.John scored his first cup goal and his first goal for Liverpool in the Kop end of the ground. A superb pass from Hunt split Chelsea's defence down the middle and St.John pounced on it quickly to turn a shot past Bonetti from ten yards. It was a great effort in view of the fact that the ball was running away from the centre-forward as he just got his left foot to it. Within two minutes, Chelsea equalised. Frank Blunstone, who caused trouble to Liverpool every time he got the ball, sent across a fine centre for which Ron Yeats and Bobby Tambling challenged. The ball ran off Yeats's legs to the Chelsea inside-right who beat Slater with a swiftly-taken low drive.

In places, the pitch was a little sticky, but it did not prevent both teams from playing good, open attacking football. Liverpool maintained their edge, but Blunstone's form always created danger for the home side every time the ball moved down the left wing. With 28 minutes gone, Hunt put Liverpool ahead. The goal stemmed from a mistake by Alan Harris, who put the ball straight to the feet of Callaghan. The young winger's accurate cross in front of goal found Hunt, whose foot connected with the ball and he turned it high into the roof of the net from close range.

Liverpool might have gone 3-1 ahead when Hunt, standing in an offside position, went through to drive the ball past Bonetti via a post, but the referee disallowed the goal for offside, despite the fact that the ball had gone to Hunt via a re-bound from Tambling.

The home forwards moved with great power and skill which was exacerbated for Chelsea by the excellent wing play of both Milne and Leishman. Gradually, however, the weather deteriorated, and a mist crept in strongly to make visibility a problem on the far side of the ground.

The 18-year-old Bonetti was performing heroically in the Chelsea goal, denying numerous attempts by Liverpool, and one powerful drive from A'Court went straight to the goalkeeper through a crowd of players. Four minutes before half-time, Liverpool increased their lead with a magnificent header from St.John off an A'Court corner kick. Hunt went up first for the cross, missed the ball, but St.John was behind him to put the ball into the corner of the net with a bullet-like header.

It became 4-1 when Bonetti dropped a corner from the left-wing. The ball ran out to Melia, whose shot hit the upright with the goalkeeper stranded yards out of his goal, and A'Court ran in from the left wing to volley home St.John's cross.

The floodlights came on after the interval, and the mist had become so thick that it was difficult to see the far side of the ground from the main stand. Hundreds of schoolboys were shepherded around the pitch by police to the Kop corner because of overcrowding on the far side of the ground. A perfect cross from the left to Callaghan on the right wing ended with the winger's centre passing over the bar. Soon afterwards, Bonetti effected a full-length save as Hunt headed in from Callaghan's cross. The mist gradually lifted, and Bonetti saved at the foot of a post from St.John's header off a Callaghan centre. In a rare Chelsea attack, Tambling pulled his shot wide with only Slater to beat after having been put through with a superb pass by Andy Malcolm. With 67 minutes gone, Chelsea pulled a goal back. Tambling took advantage of some sloppy defensive work to go through after a pass from Barry Bridges to turn the ball past Slater.

Chelsea fought with renewed vigour, and it looked as though Liverpool had slackened off their control of the game too soon. Brabrook went through to beat the defence, but a fine interception by Yeats prevented Bridges from scoring. After 76 minutes, the London side drew nearer to Liverpool with a goal from Bridges. Murray's well-flighted ball beat the Liverpool defence, and the young inside-man got up well to head past Slater. Liverpool managed to hold on, however, to earn a Fourth Round tie against Oldham.

Liverpool: Slater; Molyneux, Byrne; Milne, Yeats, Leishman; Callaghan, Hunt, St.John, Melia, A'Court.

Chelsea: Bonetti; Shellito, Harris; Malcolm, Young, Scott; Brabrook, Tambling, Bridges, Murray, Blunstone.

Referee: Mr R.H. Windle (Chesterfield)

Attendance: 48,455

January 27, 1962

Oldham Athletic (0) 1
Colquhoun 83

Liverpool (0) 2
St.John 74, 80

OLDHAM had the first shot on target when John Colquhoun lobbed the ball across to Bob Johnstone standing on the edge of the penalty area. The Scot hit it first time and Slater saved at the foot of a post. Liverpool replied through Hunt, whose 20-yard shot sailed high over the bar. The football went from end to end, and Johnstone set up Jimmy Frizzell with a perfect through-ball. Frizzell flicked it to the unmarked Bert Lister, whose weak shot went safely to Slater's arms. The visitors almost went ahead when Hunt, after a fine individual run, turned the ball across the face of the goal, but St.John marginally failed to connect.

Liverpool gradually asserted their authority over Fourth Division Oldham and Melia, attempting to lob the ball over a crowd of players, succeeded only in putting the ball over the bar. At the other end, a Frizzell header went straight to Slater. Johnstone sent a stream of immaculate passes down the middle, but Yeats was in command in the air, and he cleared everything with an air of confidence.

Liverpool's inside-forwards held on to the ball too close, and their attacks broke down at the final pass in the Oldham penalty area.

A wild clearance by Leishman sent the ball high in the air. It dropped at the feet of Peter Phoenix, who sent in a magnificent volley which Slater saved at the foot of a post. As the interval arrived, Liverpool's authority grew less, and despite an enormous amount of running from St.John, the forward line was ineffective because of bunching in the middle. However, in one sweeping movement, the ball went from Milne to Melia and on to Hunt, whose shot, taken on the turn, went high and wide.

Oldham began to attack with increasing regularity and four times in less than a minute Yeats intercepted Oldham shots during the home side's finest spell of the game. Scott fed Johnstone, but a tremendous sliding tackle by White sent the ball for a corner. Both Yeats and White received attention from the trainer, and it was a full two minutes before the game resumed with White wearing a bandage below his right knee. On the stroke of half-time, Byrne headed off the line from a corner by Colquhoun.

The floodlights came on for the start of the second half and Liverpool played with the advantage of an appreciable slope. White limped noticeably at the commencement of the second period. From a free-kick, Johnstone lobbed the ball into the goalmouth where it was partially cleared to Brian Jarvis, who shot just over the bar. Liverpool earned numerous corners, but they made little of them, principally due to Ken Branagan's immaculate tackling.

The home side's offensive tactics were to use the left wing, where White was performing at about half-pace. Colquhoun beat White on one particular occasion and flashed the ball across the face of the goal. An unlucky bounce robbed Phoenix of a perfect shooting position, although the winger managed to centre the ball for Lister to head wide. At this stage of the contest, Liverpool were unable to string two passes together while Oldham attacked with skilful venom.

With 65 minutes gone, Lister, in an offside position, put the ball past Slater. Oldham assumed that the goal would stand, but the linesman had his flag up as Lister received the ball from Johnstone. From the free-kick, Liverpool broke away with Melia and St.John linking up and providing an opportunity for Hunt, whose gentle lob beat Rollo but hit the crossbar and bounced to safety.

After an Oldham corner, Liverpool cleared and went upfield to score through St.John after 74 minutes. Hunt and Melia got the ball through to the centre-forward, who beat Jimmy Rollo with a gentle shot which struck the crossbar and bounced down. It looked as though the ball had rebounded out of goal as Branagan kicked it away, but the referee, who was on the spot, immediately awarded a goal. Oldham protested, but the referee spoke to a linesman, who confirmed the decision.

At this point, two crush barriers collapsed. The crowd surged forward and at least half a dozen people were injured. Police and St.John's ambulance men rushed across and members of the crowd were brought out on to the running track around the pitch. The game continued, but the attention was focussed on the scene where people were taken away on stretchers.

Ten minutes from time A'Court swung the ball over from the left wing and St.John nipped in smartly to flick the ball high in the air past Rollo before following up to head it past the goalkeeper. The centre-forward missed a hat-trick when his shot from a brilliant Melia pass was saved by Rollo.

With just seven minutes remaining, Oldham pulled a goal back. Johnstone created a gap down the right for Lister to put the ball over to Phoenix, whose centre was tipped away by Slater. The ball fell at Colquhoun's feet and the winger drove it into the net from close range with Slater prostate.

Oldham Athletic: Rollo; Branagan, McCue; Scott, Williams, Jarvis; Phoenix, Johnstone, Lister, Frizzell, Colquhoun.

Liverpool: Slater; White, Byrne; Milne, Yeats, Leishman; Callaghan, Hunt, St.John, Melia, A'Court.

Referee: Mr K.R. Tuck (Chesterfield)

Attendance: 42,000   **Receipts**: £7,600

February 17, 1962

Liverpool (0) 0   Preston North End (0) 0

APART from a high wind, it was a perfect day for football between Liverpool and Preston, who met for the first time in the Cup for 68 years. Liverpool won the toss and defended the Kop goal.

There was a sensational start when Alex Dawson went to the left wing and beat Yeats before crossing the ball. Leishman nodded the ball away for a corner and collided with Slater. Preston might well have gained a fortunate own goal. Gordon Milne tried to make a dream come true by hitting a goal against his father's club, but the ball was intercepted.

Dawson, sensing the linesman's flag was down, went on to hit a left-foot shot into the net off the right post, only to find that the same linesman had decided that he was offside. The football from both sides was rather hurried and lacking in control, though Preston were extremely determined in the tackle. Liverpool were awarded a free-kick 30 yards out, and Yeats hit a glorious shot which Alan Kelly turned round the post in a brilliant save.

Liverpool struggled to find their true form and their best effort came when St.John fired over from an acute angle after a movement involving Callaghan and Yeats. Preston gave the home side little time to settle on the ball and no space in which to work.

Attempts on goal were extremely limited as both sides became engaged in a midfield battle. Soon after Dawson's disallowed goal, Kelly brought off a fine save from A'Court.

The game was contested roughly, and above all Yeats dominated. Kelly effected a good save at the post from Callaghan, and Alf Biggs - for the third time - missed the bar by inches after a pass from Dave Wilson. A'Court moved to outside-right, but he was unable to elude his shadow, Bill Cunningham. A Yeats header from a left-wing corner taken by Callaghan sailed inches over the bar in the dying moments. Dawson collected a crossfield pass from Biggs and drove it hard towards goal, but a deflection off Yeats turned the ball past a post.

Gordon Milne who tried to make a dream come true by hitting a goal against his father's club, but the ball was intercepted before reaching the target.

Liverpool: Slater; Byrne, Moran; Milne, Yeats, Leishman; Callaghan, Hunt, St.John, Melia, A'Court.

Preston North End: Kelly; Cunningham, Ross; Wylie, Singleton, Smith; Wilson, Biggs, Dawson, Spavin, Thompson.

Referee: Mr K.Howley (Middlesbrough)

Attendance: 54,967

Receipts: £10,480

CROWDS WAIT FOR A6 VERDICT

JURY OUT FIVE HOURS

A crowd of 500 milled outside the red brick Shire Hall at Bedford as the A6 jury considered their verdict today - the 21st day of Britain's longest murder trial.

The jury filed out at 11.22am, after Mr Justice Gorman had ended his 10-hour summing up, spread over three days.

More than five hours later the jury were still out.

James Hanratty, aged 25, has pleaded not guilty to the murder of Michael Gregsten, a 36-year-old physicist, in a lay-by off the A6 at Deadman's Hill, Clophill, Bedfordshire, on August 23 last year.

The prosecution has said that, after shooting Gregsten, Hanratty raped and shot Gregsten's companion, Miss Valerie Storie, aged 23.

February 20, 1962

Preston North End (0) 0   Liverpool (0) 0 aet

LIVERPOOL captain Dick White had recovered from the leg injury he sustained in the FA Cup fourth round tie at Oldham Athletic on January 27 and was fit and ready to play if manager Bill Shankly needed him. Mr Shankly named White and John Wheeler in thirteen players who were going to Deepdale and from whom the side would be chosen shortly before the kick-off.   Before his injury White was at right-back, although he had played most of his games for Liverpool at centre-half.

Liverpool arrived 25 minutes after the scheduled kick-off time due to a 15-mile head-to-tail traffic jam. They were unable to get to their skip in the boot, and were thus unable to change into their playing strip on the coach to save time. Thousands of Liverpool fans were locked out more than an hour before the scheduled kick-off at 7.30pm. Fans waited outside the ground throughout the entire ninety minutes of the game, and when the gates were opened to let people out, the waiting fans were able to walk into the ground and see extra time free of charge. Referee Howley conducted the "canned" music on the touchline before Liverpool - in spite of the help of their police escort from Aintree - could filter through to Deepdale and change in twenty minutes flat. The BBC commentator Bernard Taylor, missed his appointment on the radio for the first time in 25 years. Nonetheless, despite all this off-the-field drama, the main event provided enough thrills to last several cup-ties.

Preston survived due to the great goalkeeping efforts of Kelly, while Liverpool were still in the Cup because Moran kicked Dawson's shot off the line in extra time.

The standard of play was far superior to that in the match at Anfield. The North Enders maintained their tactical plan in marking man-to-man, allied to their incredible appetite for hard work. They harried and chased all night.

Kelly, whose safe hands and lightning reflexes kept Preston in the competition, was assisted by Cunningham, the old war-horse. Yeats, towering above the home forward line, nullified their efforts. The Liverpool skipper was the basis of the visitors' defence. In the first twenty minutes Dawson killed the ball with his body and spread passes across the park to both wings with great menace, but Yeats eventually got to grips with the Preston centre-forward.

Biggs, at outside-left, crossed the ball perfectly in the first minute, but Wilson got under it and ballooned his header over. A moment later an excellent pass by Milne to A'Court produced the centre from which Hunt, with a right-foot shot, tested Kelly, but the goalkeeper gave away a corner. Callaghan took the flag-kick, but St.John's volley flew wide.

Moments later Biggs expertly hooked a volley wide after Wylie had attempted a header from a corner on the right.

Preston North End: Kelly; Cunningham, Ross; Wylie, Singleton, Smith; Wilson, Biggs, Dawson, Spavin, Thompson.

Liverpool: Slater; Byrne, Moran; Milne, Yeats, Leishman; Callaghan, Hunt, St.John, Melia, A'Court.

Referee: Mr K. Howley (Middlesbrough)

Attendance: 37,831

Receipts: £5,714

February 26, 1962

Liverpool (0) 0

Preston North End (0) 1
Thompson 60

PRESTON won the toss and had the bitterly cold wind at their backs in the first period, but they scored the important goal in the second half, playing against the wind and snow. The conditions were not conducive to good football, but both teams served up a fine display. In the air, the varying wind made accurate judgment of a header almost impossible, while on the ground it was difficult to judge the height of the bounce of the ball.

Liverpool kicked off and after Kelly had collected the ball, he kicked it down-wind almost three-quarters the length of the field. It bounced over the head of Yeats and allowed Dawson a shot from close range which Slater turned round the post. Liverpool then embarked upon a period of unrelenting pressure, but their forwards were unable to capitalise on the openings created. St.John, Melia and Callaghan were all unable to control the awkwardly bouncing ball and the movement broke down. Right-half Wylie attempted a lob from about 45 yards out, and the ball shot up sharply off the ground before Slater saw the ball narrowly miss the angle of the goal.

Five minutes before the interval, Milne shot from the edge of the penalty area and, with goalkeeper Kelly in a poor position, the ball struck St.John on the back and rebounded to safety.

Shortly after the interval, Dawson beat Byrne and Slater and got in a header which passed inches wide of the goal.

On the hour, referee Howley overruled his linesman and gave Preston a throw-in near the corner flag. Right-half Wylie took the throw and fastened onto a return pass before beating Moran and getting in a centre. Yeats was impeded by Gerry Byrne as he tried to head clear, and the result was that Yeats only headed the ball as far as the edge of the penalty area. Thompson met it on the half-volley and crashed it past Slater.

Two minutes later St.John found himself about 12 yards from goal with only Kelly to beat, but the Liverpool forward shot straight at the goalkeeper as he came off his line to narrow the angle.

Liverpool increased their effort and Kelly raced out to deny Melia as he bore down on goal. Then A'Court took on four defenders in the penalty area, but was eventually crowded out. In the next minute Kelly made a brilliant save from A'Court and turned the shot round the post for a corner. In the final twenty minutes of the game, Kelly's performance was exceptional. He dived full-length to save a ground shot from Melia, and then cleverly took a shot from Melia with St.John in close attendance. Shortly afterwards, St.John headed over the bar from a beautifully-flighted Callaghan centre. Before the end, Kelly made fine saves from Milne and Hunt.

Preston's left-half Smith kept Hunt quiet for long spells. Left-back Ross and right-half Wylie also performed admirably, but centre-half Singleton, who treated St.John roughly, was not as outstanding as Yeats.

In the Liverpool defence, Moran had a good game, while Milne and Leishman, who was booked for a tackle on Wilson, tried hard to give the attack a sharper edge. The man-to-man marking of the Preston defence gave the Liverpool forwards little room in which to manoeuvre.

As the players changed after the match, Mr T.V. Williams, the Liverpool chairman, revealed that he had signed Jim Furnell, a 6ft 1in, 12 st. 12 lb goalkeeper from Burnley. Furnell, 24, was signed on the Friday and registered as a Liverpool player on the Saturday morning, but Mr Williams and Mr Bob Lord, the Burnley chairman, agreed not to release the news until after the game.

SPURS NOW 15-8

The FA Cup was called over at the Victoria Club last night an hour or so before Tottenham's European Cup-tie.

Would-be backers preferred to wait, although there were the usual requests for odds a fraction over what was offered.

The offer was 2-1 against Spurs, as against 7-4 at the last call-over, but most punters wanted 85-40.

15-8 Tottenham Hotspur
9-2 Burnley
5-1 Manchester United
8-1 Sheffield United
Blackburn Rovers
20-1 Aston Villa
25-1 Fulham
100-1 Preston North End

Liverpool: Slater; Byrne, Moran; Milne, Yeats, Leishman: Callaghan, Hunt, St.John, Melia, A'Court.

Preston North End: Kelly; Cunningham, Ross; Wylie, Singleton, Smith, Wilson, Biggs, Dawson, Spavin, Thompson.

Referee: Mr K. Howley (Middlesbrough)

Attendance: 43,944 (at Old Trafford, Manchester)

January 9, 1963

Wrexham (0) 0

Liverpool (1) 3
Hunt 18, Lewis 72, Melia 89

TOMMY Lawrence in goal and Willie Stevenson at left-half made their débuts for Liverpool on a pitch which was so sanded that it resembled a brown desert. The pitch had sufficient grip on top for the players to run freely, although there were times when men went down as they tried to back-pedal or turn quickly. Below the sand was a bone-hard surface on which the ball bounced unpredictably and both teams showed skill of the highest calibre in producing flowing football.

Roger Hunt opened the scoring after 18 minutes after Jimmy Melia had pushed the ball through the defence for the England international to tap it over the line. Wrexham's football perished because they had no adequate finisher. Without the incentive of an early goal, the home side gradually fell away, though Arfon Griffiths was at the centre of most of Wrexham's initiatives. The restless Melia wandered far and wide in his determination to keep the Liverpool attack moving, and Ken Barnes could never completely subdue him.

With 72 minutes gone, Kevin Lewis added a second goal. Ian Callaghan was fouled by Fox and Melia came over to take the free-kick. He floated the ball invitingly just outside the far post. Four players went up in an attempt to get their heads to it and Lewis, rising two feet above anyone else, nodded the ball superbly wide of the helpless Simpkins.

The referee was consulting his watch when Ian St.John took the ball from Gordon Milne and sent it wide out to Melia on the left wing. Melia darted forward, bore infield and surprised everyone with the power and accuracy of his shot.

Wrexham: Simpkins; P.Jones, McGowan; K.Barnes, Fox, T.Jones; R.Barnes, Griffiths, Phythian, Whitehouse, Colbridge.

Liverpool: Lawrence; Byrne, Moran; Milne, Yeats, Stevenson; Callaghan, Hunt, St.John, Melia, Lewis.

Referee: Mr H. Webb (Leeds)

Attendance: 29,992

Tommy Lawrence *saves on his Cup début*

January 26, 1963

Burnley (0) 1
Connelly 50

Liverpool (1) 1
Lewis 25

THREE hours before the kick-off Bill Shankly and his team inspected the pitch and found it in what Shankly described as "the most difficult conditions possible". The ground was concrete hard, but there was a very thin film on top which made the top surface very slippery. An hour before the kick-off, the Liverpool players tested three types of studs to wear in either leather or rubber boots. When the teams took to the field, the players were wearing black armbands as a mark of respect on the death of Mr Jack Robinson, chairman of the Lancashire F.A.

Burnley: Blacklaw; Angus, Elder; Adamson, Talbut, Miller; Connelly, Robson, Lochhead, McIlroy, Harris.

Liverpool: Lawrence; Byrne, Moran; Milne, Yeats, Stevenson; Callaghan, Hunt, St.John, Melia, Lewis.

Referee: Mr G. McCabe (Sheffield)

Attendance: 49,885

The first incident of note came when Connelly pushed across a centre from the left and the ball skidded off the turf and flashed past the far upright. Byrne was forced to give away a corner, and from McIlroy's kick, Yeats cleared well. Melia created Liverpool's first attack with some clever work on the left and when the ball was pushed inside, Lewis dispossessed Adamson and tried a shot which swung over the bar. When Miller handled the ball 15 yards outside the penalty area, Ronnie Moran came up to try one of his long-range power-shots, but this was intercepted by Talbut and cleared.

A brilliant burst of speed by Callaghan as he took the ball past Elder made the opening and he turned the ball back where it rebounded to Hunt, who smashed it towards the goal from 20 yards. It beat Blacklaw, only for Angus to stick out a foot and divert the ball high into the air. Although Blacklaw failed to catch the ball as it came down he was still able to complete a scrambled clearance as the Liverpool forwards moved in. Liverpool played with more determination than Burnley, who were inclined to misplace their passes.

The visitors took the lead after 25 minutes with a great goal by Lewis and hundreds of youngsters poured on to the pitch and held up play for a minute or so. The goal came via a Melia corner kick, with Angus going up to try to head clear, but seeing the ball skid off the top of his head out to Lewis, in the inside-right position. Lewis collected it cleverly and smashed a tremendous ground shot past Blacklaw from 12 yards. Lewis's goal was Liverpool's first Cup goal against Burnley - in four previous meetings they had never scored.

Liverpool's defensive cover was excellent. Only St.John stayed upfield whenever Burnley attacked. Gradually the home side asserted their authority, but they took too long to get in their shots. Liverpool's defence was able to re-group and cover up because the Burnley forwards tried one pass too many. Shortly before half-time, Connelly had the ball in the net but the score was disallowed because Lochhead had fouled Yeats a moment before.

During the interval, hundreds of young Liverpool supporters tried to move downfield to take up position behind the goal Liverpool were attacking. The police tried to stop them but there were too many on the move and when they reached the far end of the ground they were unable to climb on to the terraces and stood on the pitch surround for the second half.

Burnley equalised five minutes after half-time with a goal from Connelly made initially by a first-class run from Harris. The left-winger moved out to the right and crossed the ball from the goal line despite the challenge of Moran. Yeats got his head to the ball, which skidded away to the far side where Connelly, in the outside-left position now, hit it back instantly into the corner of the net.

The goal gave Burnley the confidence they had lacked before. Harris suddenly brought the game alight with some first-class wing play and he was very unlucky not to put Burnley into the lead. He was awarded a free-kick for obstruction by Byrne and when Elder took the kick the ball came out to the winger, who hit a curling ground shot through a crowd of players, the ball hitting the foot of the upright and bouncing back into the arms of Lawrence. From a Callaghan corner, a shot by Melia was blocked but the ball was never properly cleared and it was Lewis, playing the game of his life, who got in another effort which was blocked again. Milne swung the ball across to Melia, who headed it in to Hunt. The Liverpool inside-right put it high over the bar from 10 yards.

The heroes for Liverpool in this pulsating match were Lewis and Stevenson and the Scot got his side out of great trouble with a brilliant piece of cool defensive play by the corner flag. Lewis produced another flash of genius when he headed the ball down from a pass by Melia and he hit it with his right foot like a bullet, only for Blacklaw to produce the save of the match and fling himself across the goal to turn the ball away.

Hunt had a great chance to score when St.John back-headed the ball to him. Attempting to lob the ball over Blacklaw as the goalkeeper came out, Hunt put it yards wide, although he was challenged by Talbut as he was in the act of shooting. Burnley appealed for a penalty when Lochhead went down as Yeats headed clear, but Mr. McCabe denied the appeal.

February 20, 1963

Liverpool (1) 2
St.John 45, Moran (pen) 119

Burnley (1) 1 aet
Elder 25

BURNLEY began well and Elder was in magnificent form as the visitors had clearly come to win the game. Twenty-five minutes had gone when the visitors took the lead. Adamson sent the ball to Elder. Elder lobbed the ball forwards to Pointer, who moved to take it and completely obscured the view of Tommy Lawrence. The Burnley forward failed to take the ball at full stretch, but Elder's lob landed in the back of the net.

Liverpool responded with their usual attacking forays and the Burnley goal had several close attempts made upon it. Melia opened the way for Hunt with a magnificent through pass, but Hunt, with only Blacklaw to beat, had his shot charged down by the advancing goalkeeper and the opportunity was lost.

Almost on half-time, Byrne began a movement near the Liverpool goal. Melia carried it on and swept the ball out to Lewis on the wing, who saw Milne frantically signalling on the opposite wing, and he sent the ball across. Milne moved forward and feinted to drive a shot and turned the ball into the path of St.John, who controlled the ball in one movement and hit a shot past Blacklaw for the equaliser. There was no time to re-centre the ball.

The 45 minutes had actually elapsed and the referee had allowed injury time for the occasion when Byrne had to receive attention earlier in the half.

In the second period it appeared as though Burnley were content to play for a replay, but Liverpool fought to the end, and in the final ten minutes they monopolised the attack with unrelenting pressure.

With just thirty seconds of this pulsating Cup-tie remaining, Elder tapped the ball back to his goalkeeper as he had a dozen times before. Blacklaw, having denied Liverpool on his own time and time again, had only to pick the thing up and belt it to the three-quarter line as he had done a dozen times before. St.John went through the motions of embarrassing the kicker. He stood about eight yards away and not apparently in the line of flight. Blacklaw gave the ball a mighty kick. The crowd gasped as St.John's body rose and charged it down. It flew behind Blacklaw and slightly to the right. Before he could turn St.John was on it. All Blacklaw could do was fling his arms at St.John's thighs and hope to get away with it. A great roar went up as the referee was seen signalling for the obvious penalty.

Ronnie Moran placed the ball meticulously on the sanded spot. Blacklaw stood his ground on the line. Moran took a short run, and hammered a left-foot shot to the back of the net and Anfield erupted.

Melia was the man through whom most of Liverpool's attacks began, and he was well supported by the tireless Stevenson, who roamed prodigiously to ensure that Pointer was not given the time or space to do any damage. St.John was closely marked by Talbut, but the canny Scot was extremely effective nonetheless. Hunt and Lewis were almost marked out of the game, although both players managed shots which were hurried and failed to find the target. Yeats dominated Lochhead and the Burnley wingers Harris and Connelly were denied from playing an attacking role, leaving it to the scheming McIlroy to maintain Burnley's offensive responsibilities. On numerous occasions, the entire Burnley team were back in their own half in an attempt to present a formidable barrier to Liverpool's attacking thrusts.

Ian St.John

Liverpool: Lawrence; Byrne, Moran; Milne, Yeats, Stevenson; Callaghan, Hunt, St.John, Melia, Lewis.

Burnley: Blacklaw; Angus, Elder; Adamson, Talbut, Miller; Connelly, Pointer, Lochhead, McIlroy, Harris.

Referee: Mr J. Powell (Rotherham)

Attendance: 57,906   **Receipts**: £10,500

March 16, 1963

Arsenal (0) 1
Skirton 85

Liverpool (1) 2
Melia 33, Moran (pen) 65

LIVERPOOL, watched by Mr Andrew Hepburn, a Scottish F.A. selector, held their own in the early minutes and Ian Callaghan drew a save from McClelland with a fast, low centre. There was quick tackling on both sides, but Liverpool had the better of the exchanges, despite the lack of continuity. The swirling wind benefited Arsenal with Liverpool giving away three corners. The Liverpool inside forwards and the wingers always assisted in defence when needed. Eastham put Baker through with a brilliant pass but Yeats' tackle was successful and severe. Both men needed attention from the trainers before continuing. Stevenson had played well up to this point, and if Skirton had been sharper to Eastham's crosses, Liverpool would have been in real trouble.

A wall of Arsenal defenders kept out a strong shot from Melia after St.John had cleverly backheeled a pass to him and a moment later St.John had the ball in the net from a through pass but was palpably offside.

The pitch, which was liberally sanded and showing scarcely any grass was dry but played heavily and took its toll of players' stamina. A corner by Eastham caused Liverpool problems with Lawrence twice palming the ball one-handed before Barnwell hit a shot from 10 yards which sailed high and wide.

With 33 minutes gone, Liverpool took the lead. There appeared to be little danger as Brown moved to pick up a ball travelling slowly near the goal line. He contrived to lose control and Roger Hunt cut the ball back for Melia to run on to it and guide it with his left foot wide of McClelland's outstretched left hand.

Lawrence was injured when taking a high free-kick from Eastham. He caught the ball safely but Strong crossed him with his leg and the goalkeeper needed attention for a severe blow to the ribs.

Byrne, embarrassed by Skirton, handled on the goal line near the corner flag, but Eastham's free-kick found the head of Yeats, who cleared successfully. Macleod got the better of Moran as Arsenal pressed dangerously. McClelland brought off a wonderful save for a corner from a header by Lewis after St.John had sent the ball across with a clever overhead pass. Play on both sides became full of blunders.

With 65 minutes gone, Liverpool increased their lead. Lewis took a corner which appeared easy for Barnwell to head away, but the swirl of the wind baffled him and the ball dropped on his left hand. He appeared to jab it forward. Referee Howley gave the penalty, but although Barnwell and McCullough demanded of a linesman that he should give his version to the referee, the award stood and Moran scored with a low shot. Arsenal reduced the lead five minutes from the

end. Macleod crossed the ball so that it virtually dropped on the line at the far angle. Brown and Skirton both went in and Skirton's head signalled a rousing finale as Arsenal sought equality, but Liverpool held on for a famous and well-earned victory.

***Gerry Byrne**, who was dependable at right-back*

Arsenal: McClelland; Magill, McCullough; Barnwell, Brown, Sneddon; Macleod, Strong, Baker, Eastham, Skirton.

Liverpool: Lawrence; Byrne, Moran; Milne, Yeats, Stevenson; Callaghan, Hunt, St.John, Melia, Lewis.

Referee: Mr K. Howley (Middlesbrough)

Attendance: 55,245

March 30, 1963

Liverpool (0) 1
Hunt 81

West Ham United (0) 0

THE weather was dull and there was a crosswind from the west as Liverpool entertained the Hammers in the Sixth Round of the Cup. West Ham were first out, led by Bobby Moore. They played in a powder-blue strip including stockings and shorts, with two broad bands of claret around their chests. The noise at the commencement of the game was deafening. Yeats won the toss and elected to defend the Kop goal, giving his side the traditional second half task of scoring into the Kop end.

Liverpool began well and only an inaccurate pass by Milne helped to relieve the pressure on West Ham. The visitors retaliated but Kirkup's volley finished high among the Kopites.

Roger Hunt was obstructed when trying to plough his way through just outside the left-hand edge of the box. Lewis surprised everyone in the ground by hitting the free-kick with his right foot and driving it low right across the face of the goal. It passed outside the upright by a matter of inches.

Gradually the Hammers took charge of the game and both full backs in turn showed their finesse. On the half-hour Liverpool had a lucky escape. Brabrook, unchallenged on the right, floated a perfect centre over and Sealey, with a quick flick of the head had Lawrence clutching at air, as the ball dipped inches over the bar.

The second half began with Liverpool on top, but the visitors continued to move the ball about neatly and with fine effect.

With the game going into its closing minutes, Anfield erupted when Hunt scored. The goal was conceived in Liverpool's own half. Stevenson brought the ball twenty or thirty yards and looked likely to lose it before he recovered his grip on it and Melia took over from him. Melia made one quick assessment of the position, tapped the ball 10 yards forward with a through pass and Hunt, moving quickly to seize a difficult chance, turned the ball into an empty goal, Standen having started off his line to try to beat him.

Anfield went wild with delight and a few youngsters encroached on the field, but they were soon removed and within a moment Liverpool were defending desperately, against West Ham who all but got the equaliser from a scrambling movement in the six yard area. Byrne emerged with the ball, and the semi-finals beckoned.

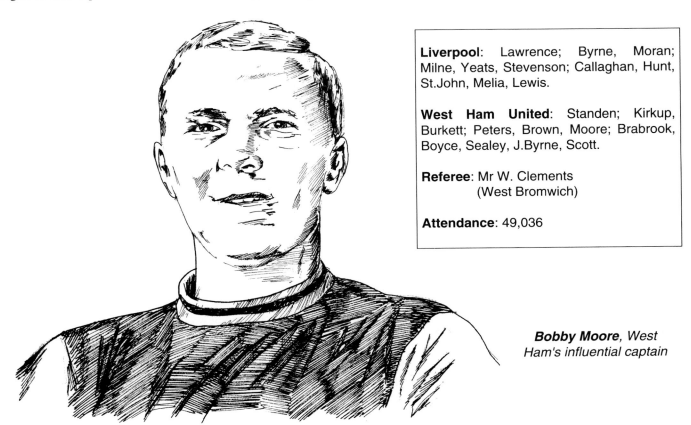

Liverpool: Lawrence; Byrne, Moran; Milne, Yeats, Stevenson; Callaghan, Hunt, St.John, Melia, Lewis.

West Ham United: Standen; Kirkup, Burkett; Peters, Brown, Moore; Brabrook, Boyce, Sealey, J.Byrne, Scott.

Referee: Mr W. Clements (West Bromwich)

Attendance: 49,036

Bobby Moore, West Ham's influential captain

April 27, 1963

Liverpool (0) 0

Leicester City (1) 1
Stringfellow 18

CHRIS Lawler made his FA Cup début in his third senior game. Leicester were first into their stride and McLintock's shot, through a crowded goalmouth after Yeats had headed the ball out, was only a foot wide. Callaghan earned two corners, for both of which Lawler moved into the goal area, but Leicester cleared the danger each time. Lewis put a clever lobbed pass near the penalty spot, and both Hunt and St.John almost made contact. At this stage of the contest, Liverpool had taken control of the game, although it was still punctuated by errors.

From another Callaghan corner, Liverpool nearly took the lead. The ball swerved, and with Hunt getting the slightest of deflections to it, the ball ran only inches wide, with Banks out of position. Liverpool, playing only four forwards, did well in attack early on.

Against the run of play, Leicester took the lead after 18 minutes with their second real attack of the game. It came from a free-kick awarded for hands by Moran and taken by Gibson. He floated the ball into the goalmouth and Stringfellow went up high and deflected it just inside the upright. Although Liverpool continued to attack far more than Leicester, they missed Melia's generalship. The rain fell heavier at this point and the players slipped on the greasy turf a great deal. Callaghan was the most consistent forward for Liverpool and after some clever work by the corner flag, he got across a good centre which St.John headed wide.

Liverpool continued to have more of the play, but the game was generally mediocre. Liverpool kept the ball a little too close on a pitch that became heavier every minute. With the tackling strong and instant, there was hardly any sustained play of note. Liverpool were reduced to a great deal of lateral passing, and the incisive pass, in the Melia manner, did not materialise.

Moran was spoken to by the referee when he fouled Gibson at the start of the second half. From the free-kick, Liverpool cleared comfortably and progressed downfield. Hunt got in his first shot of the match, which Banks saved well at full stretch. Hunt's shot, after 47 minutes, had been the only notable one of the game up to this point, indicating how poor and uninteresting the game had been. Hunt now came into the game more effectively. He fought his way down the middle, but was off balance when he shot and the ball went well wide.

Liverpool: Lawrence; Byrne, Moran; Milne, Yeats, Stevenson; Callaghan, Hunt, St.John, Lawler, Lewis.

Leicester City: Banks; Sjoberg, Norman; McLintock, King, Appleton; Riley, Cross, Keyworth, Gibson, Stringfellow.

Referee: Mr A. Holland (Barnsley)

Attendance: 65,000 (at Hillsborough)

Chris Lawler

Liverpool persisted with crossfield passes; no-one being able to take a straightforward route to goal. The spoiling tactics of the Leicester defence denied Liverpool on numerous occasions. Leicester produced almost nothing in attack and Liverpool began to dominate more than ever. Sjoberg had his name taken for an appalling foul on St.John, and some of City's tackling was more than rugged. Leicester cleared anywhere in the face of tremendous Liverpool pressure.

From one wild miskick by Sjoberg, the ball went high in the air, and Hunt made a fine shot which beat Banks, only to hit the bar. Callaghan shot wide from the rebound. A moment later St.John nodded down to Hunt, but his hooked shot went straight into Banks' arms. Leicester had ten men in defence and whenever they cleared the ball it invariably went to a Liverpool defender, who promptly put it back into the packed penalty area. Liverpool changed wingers and Yeats moved permanently into the forwards with Lawler at centre-half as Liverpool sought an equaliser. But City held on despite tremendous Liverpool pressure.

January 4, 1964

Liverpool (2) 5

Arrowsmith 23, 38, 73, 88
Hunt 63

Derby County (0) 0

WITH just eighteen minutes of this Cup-tie gone, Ian Callaghan turned the ball back towards his goalkeeper, Tommy Lawrence, who never had a hope of getting to it first. The Kop groaned as Derby's Williamson took it up and with Lawrence diving desperately, put it inches outside. A goal at this juncture might well have changed the complexion of this game.

Five minutes later, however, Alf Arrowsmith began his day of glory with the opening goal and the tie was effectively sealed.

Until Liverpool scored, Derby had played some neat football in mid-field and there were times when right-winger Hughes bore through threateningly, but there was no strength or finish.

Arrowsmith, on his Cup début, hit the first goal with his left foot after a Callaghan cross had been deflected to him and in 38 minutes he put the ball out to Peter Thompson before cracking the return past Matthews from 20 yards. Roger Hunt made it 3-0 after 63 minutes from Gordon Milne's pass and ten minutes later Arrowsmith fastened on to St.John's excellent through ball and took it forward a few yards before beating Matthews once more. The last goal came two minutes from time when Arrowsmith was on to Milne's low cross in a flash to hammer it into the net.

Arrowsmith scored four brilliantly taken goals and showed how menacing he could be, twenty yards out. He had no inhibitions about trying a shot and allied to this striking power was an intelligent grasp of a situation and the ability to make the quick, telling pass.

Alf Arrowsmith, *who hit four goals against Derby County*

Liverpool: Lawrence; Ferns, Moran; Milne, Yeats, Stevenson; Callaghan, Hunt, Arrowsmith, St.John, Thompson.

Derby County: Matthews; Barrowcliffe, Ferguson; Waller, Young, Parry; Hughes, Webster, Curry, Williamson, McCann.

Referee: Mr M.A. Fussey (Retford)

Attendance: 46,460

January 25, 1964

Liverpool (0) 0

Port Vale (0) 0

BOTH teams contributed to a marvellous exhibition of Cup-tie football. The power and skill of Liverpool were never really generated because Port Vale denied the home side the ability to generate it. The visitors were quick to the ball, strong in the challenge and kept trying to play football calmly and with great purpose. Their poise and composure allied to a tremendous defensive determination kept the Reds at bay. The mid-table position occupied by Vale in the Third Division belied their ability on this showing. Every Port Vale player gave his all. John Nicholson, who used to be at Anfield, was brilliant at centre-half and with his half-backs, Rawlings and Sproson, put a stranglehold on Liverpool's inside forwards for most of the match. Goalkeeper Hancock was fortunate to retrieve a fiery first half shot from Stevenson, but another save from St.John late in the game was equalled only by those Tommy Lawrence made from Steele and Mudie.

Liverpool lacked someone to hold the attack together. Thompson, for a while, appeared as though he might be the man to sink Port Vale, but the forwards never got together and in the defence it was Lawrence, Stevenson and Yeats who played near to their true form.

The most dramatic incident occurred in the second half when Nicholson emerged from a mêlée in his own goalmouth and advanced at speed upfield before passing to Rowland and racing for the return ball.

It went fast and low across the face of the goal and Nicholson was no more than inches away from connecting with the ball and scoring.

Near the end, Hunt missed a sitter when he shot straight at Hancock.

Liverpool: Lawrence; Thomson, Byrne; Milne, Yeats, Stevenson; Callaghan, Hunt, Arrowsmith, St.John, Thompson.

Port Vale: Hancock; Whalley, Wilson; Rawlings, Nicholson, Sproson; Rowland, Steele, Richards, Mudie, Smith.

Referee: Mr H.P. Hackney (Barnsley)

Attendance: 52,327

Receipts: £10,800

F.A. CUP - FOURTH ROUND

West Ham United	1	Leyton Orient	0
Aldershot	1	Swindon Town	2
Burnley	2	Newport County	1
Chelsea	1	Huddersfield Town	2
Sunderland	6	Bristol City	1
Leeds United	1	Everton	1
Barnsley	2	Bury	1
Manchester United	4	Bristol Rovers	1
Ipswich Town	1	Stoke City	1
Sheffield United	1	Swansea Town	1
West Bromwich A.	3	Arsenal	3
Oxford United	2	Brentford	2
Blackburn Rovers	2	Fulham	0
Bedford Town	0	Carlisle United	3
Bolton Wanderers	2	Preston North End	2

Replays

Leyton Orient	0	West Ham United	3
Everton	2	Leeds United	0
Stoke City	1	Ipswich Town	0
Swansea Town	4	Sheffield United	0
Arsenal	2	West Bromwich A.	0
Brentford	1	Oxford United	2
Preston North End	2	Bolton Wanderers	1

INDIA v. ENGLAND

In Bombay

INDIA: First Innings: 300 (A.S. Durani 90; C.G. Borde 84). Second Innings: 249 for eight declared (D.S. Bardesai 56, M.L. Jaisimha 66).
ENGLAND: First Innings: 233 (F.J. Titmus 84 not out). Second Innings: 206-3 (J.B. Bolus 57; I.G. Binks 55; M.J.K. Smith 31 not out; J.M. Parks 40 not out).

January 27, 1964

Port Vale (0) 1
Cheesebrough 79

Liverpool (1) 2 aet
Hunt 35, Thompson 118

BEFORE the game Stevenson said to Thompson: "We are due a goal from you tonight. You've not hit a good one since you knocked us out of the Cup. It's time you made amends."

The game was dying from the moment that Roger Hunt opened the scoring after 35 minutes. He fastened on a ball which Gerry Byrne put straight into the middle of the penalty area. As goalkeeper Hancock came out Hunt at full stretch guided the ball into goal with stunning accuracy.

Liverpool became somewhat complacent as they sauntered throughout the rest of the game and they paid the price for their casualness when, with only 11 minutes left, Rowland crossed the ball to Steele who pushed it to Cheesebrough. The man who came in as a last-minute substitute for the injured Jackie Mudie slammed the ball wide of Lawrence in goal. Vale, who had earlier looked like a team resigned to their fate, emerged as a team of footballers. They had much the better of the closing stages of the game without looking as though they would score against a competent Liverpool defence.

Peter Thompson grabbed only his third goal since joining Liverpool with just two minutes of the game remaining. Gordon Milne went up in a last desperate effort to avoid the necessity for a second replay and his well-hit shot cannoned off one of the many Vale defenders who were making the penalty area congested. The ball went straight to Thompson just inside the angle of the area. Without the slightest hesitation he hit a tremendous shot which soared into the corner of the goal.

The tactics of Port Vale when they were in arrears were difficult to understand because they packed their defence rather than seek out a goal. However, it appeared that their tactics may have been sensible once they equalised, for they dominated afterwards.

The return of Jimmy Melia helped Liverpool to function more smoothly, despite the fact that he was superbly marshalled by Rawlings, Vale's player of the match. The game highlighted Liverpool's attacking weaknesses. For all their strength and creativity, Liverpool lacked a finisher, though St.John worked prodigiously to elude the close-marking Nicholson.

Vale's tackling stifled Liverpool's creativity, and the Reds were closed down immediately they gained possession. Thompson was difficult to contain as he sought space for himself. Nicholson's height was the dominating factor in the Port Vale defence and several of Thompson's crosses were not improved upon. On the opposite wing Callaghan got past Wilson only on a few occasions, and even then Sproson covered for the full-back. It was a testing time for Liverpool's wingmen.

Scenes of great joy greeted Thompson's goal with fans chanting "When The Saints Go Marching In", followed by "Yeah, Yeah, Yeah". The pitch was covered with hundreds of excited fans as the final whistle sounded. After 210 minutes of battle, Liverpool had qualified for the fifth round of the FA Cup. Port Vale had been gallant opponents from the Third Division.

CALL-OVER

United are clear favourites

Cup holders Manchester United were installed as clear favourites, at 4 to 1, at the Victoria Club call-over, in London, last night.

Barnsley, who entertain Manchester United, in the Fifth Round, on February 15, were listed at 200 to 1.

Most support was for Sheffield United. The Yorkshire club were backed to win £5,000, and closed at 28 to 1.

Second Division Sunderland (22 to 1), and Blackburn Rovers (11 to 2), were also backed - both for £2,000.

THE PRICES

4-1 Manchester United
11-2 Blackburn Rovers
7-1 Burnley
9-1 Arsenal
12-1 Liverpool, West Ham
22-1 Sunderland
25-1 West Bromwich Albion
28-1 Sheffield United
33-1 Preston North End
35-1 Stoke City

Port Vale: Hancock; Whalley, Wilson; Rawlings, Nicholson, Sproson; Rowland, Steele, Richards, Cheesebrough, Smith.

Liverpool: Lawrence; Byrne, Moran; Milne, Yeats, Stevenson; Callaghan, Hunt, St.John, Melia, Thompson.

Referee: Mr H.P. Hackney (Barnsley)

Attendance: 42,179

February 15, 1964

Arsenal (0) 0

Liverpool (1) 1
St.John 15

ARSENAL set out to win the match with an all-out offensive in the first twenty minutes, but they met with a resilient Liverpool defence. The visitors took an early lead through Ian St.John. From Callaghan's quick throw-in Gordon Milne directed the ball over Ian Ure's head with measured calm. Groves stood still and Magill, not far from the bye-line, waited for the ball to reach him. St.John, running at top speed for ten or fifteen yards, leapt in the air and directed the ball just under the bar with a perfect header.

With 37 minutes gone, Liverpool skipper Ron Yeats and Arsenal centre-forward Joe Baker were dismissed. Yeats' mastery of Baker was so complete that when he beat the centre-forward to a ball it was just common-place. Then Baker clearly fouled the Scot and sent him tumbling on his back. Yeats rose to his feet and ran towards Baker. There was a clash of bodies, a flurry of fists and Yeats was kicked again as he went down. A cut opened above his left eye. Baker was first to be sent off. Then the referee forced his way through to where trainer Bob Paisley was trying to revive Yeats and he, in turn, received his marching orders, protesting vigorously as he went. Yeats said afterwards, "I have never struck a player in eight years and I never will."

With Yeats gone, Willie Stevenson took over at centre-half, and St.John filled in at left-half. The height of the skipper was missed, especially during corner kicks. Liverpool's most dangerous moment came in the first half when Byrne diverted a shot from Armstrong and Lawrence moved out before twisting backwards as the ball flew towards goal. Lawrence stretched out his left hand and miraculously deflected the ball to safety. In his one moment of near glory, Baker put the Liverpool goal under serious threat in 23 minutes when his shot beat Lawrence and was going in until Ronnie Moran headed out with athletic prowess. Arsenal protested long and loud that Moran had used his hand instead of his head, but the referee dismissed their appeals.

Liverpool were overwhelmingly committed to a defensive rôle after their leading goal but they might have scored on four or five occasions. Hunt drew Furnell from goal, and then pushed the ball no more than a foot wide with an angled shot. Alf Arrowsmith hit the ball narrowly wide in similar fashion after rounding Furnell, and then there was a last minute penalty awarded when only a Rugby tackle by Furnell on Arrowsmith denied a goal. Hunt failed from the spot. On another occasion, St.John was right through, faced only by Furnell, when he was upset from behind by McCullough. The referee waved aside appeals for a penalty.

Left: **Ron Yeats**, *who was dismissed after a fracas with Baker*

Arsenal: Furnell; Magill, McCullough; Groves, Ure, Snedden; Macleod, Strong, Baker, Eastham, Armstrong.

Liverpool: Lawrence; Byrne, Moran; Milne, Yeats, Stevenson; Callaghan, Hunt, St.John, Arrowsmith, Thompson.

Referee: Mr J.K. Taylor (Wolverhampton)

Attendance: 61,295

February 29, 1964

Liverpool (0) 1
Thompson 63

Swansea Town (2) 2
McLaughlin 37, Thomas 39

LIVERPOOL suffered a shock Cup defeat at the hands of Second Division Swansea, for whom goalkeeper Noel Dwyer was the hero. The Irishman Dwyer thwarted Liverpool on numerous occasions, and rarely had the home side created so many genuine opportunities. Indeed, thirteen minutes passed before Dwyer's counterpart, Tommy Lawrence, touched the ball.

With 37 minutes gone, McLaughlin snapped up his opportunity with a magnificent goal and just two minutes later, Thomas scored a second goal for the visitors. Liverpool hopes soared when Peter Thompson pulled a goal back from an intelligent Gerry Byrne pass. Three minutes later he tricked his way in from touch and hit a magnificent shot which struck the inside of the post and came out.

Ten minutes from time, Williams tripped Ian Callaghan and the Reds were awarded a penalty. Previously discarded in favour of Hunt as penalty-taker, Ronnie Moran eventually stepped forward to try to repeat from the same spot the feat which made him a hero and match winner against Burnley in the FA Cup last season. Not until the referee had waved away Thomas from his conversation with Dwyer was Moran able to take the shot. Acting on local knowledge, Thomas advised Dwyer that Moran would shoot high to the right. To make certain that Moran would choose that side, Dwyer stood a foot or so left of centre to create an inviting gap. Moran shot narrowly outside. Hunt had failed with a last-minute penalty at Arsenal in the last round, so no-one doubted the wisdom of recalling Moran, the most experienced player afield.

After the game, the Swansea manager, Trevor Morris said, "We had hardly dared to think in terms of more than a draw at the best. Here we are victorious. No wonder I am delighted. We have not had much luck in the Cup so far, but today we got it, just when we needed it most."

Liverpool: Lawrence; Byrne, Moran; Milne, Yeats, Stevenson; Callaghan, Hunt, St.John, Arrowsmith, Thompson.

Swansea Town: Dwyer; R.Evans, Hughes; Johnson, Purcell, Williams; Jones, Draper, Thomas, McLaughlin, B.Evans.

Referee: Mr G. McCabe (Sheffield)

Attendance: 52,608

F.A. CUP - SIXTH ROUND

West Ham United	3	Burnley	2
Manchester United	3	Sunderland	3
Oxford United	1	Preston North End	2

Replay

| Sunderland | 2 | Manchester United | 2 |

Second replay

| Manchester United | 5 | Sunderland | 1 |

RAMOS KEEPS TITLE

Cuban too tough for challenger

Sugar Ramos, of Cuba, retained his world featherweight title last night when he stopped his Japanese challenger, Mitsunori Seki, in the sixth round of their fifteen round contest in Tokio.

Seki retired after being down twice in the sixth round. His seconds threw in the towel mid-way through the round.

Seki did well up to the fifth round when he suffered a cut over his left eye. Soon after the start of the next round he went down from a right and another right to the chin dropped him a second time.

He staggered to his feet at eight, but his seconds threw in the towel and asked the referee to stop the fight.

The Japanese southpaw had delighted the big crowd in Tokio's Kuramae Stadium with some good leading and defensive footwork in the early rounds, but Ramos always looked threatening.

Stalking his dancing opponent, Ramos picked his punches and finally caught up with Seki in the fifth when he landed the punch which cut the left eye. After the bout, Ramos said he would like to meet world lightweight champion, Carlos Ortiz.

January 9, 1965

West Bromwich Albion (0) 1   Liverpool (1) 2

Astle 80

Hunt 44, St.John 63

LIVERPOOL arrived at the Hawthorns at 3 o'clock and the start of the match was put back to 3.15. Progress almost ground to a halt a few miles outside Wolverhampton due to road works and sheer weight of traffic. Liverpool supporters obligingly pulled over to the kerb to allow free passage for the team coach, but other drivers were not as considerate. Chairman Mr Sidney Reakes left the coach and sought the assistance of the police in the centre of Wolverhampton and this action helped to reduce the problem. Not until a police motor-cycle escort appeared did the first glimmer of hope arise. The police pilot met the coach at twelve minutes to three and the crowd were informed of the Liverpool team's plight. The Throstles were first out at 3.12 and Liverpool came out five minutes later. The game eventually started at 3.20.

West Bromwich Albion: Potter; Clam, G.Williams; Fraser, Jones, Simpson; Fenton, Fudge, Astle, Hope, Clark.

Liverpool: Lawrence; Lawler, Byrne; Milne, Yeats, Stevenson; Callaghan, Hunt, St.John, Smith, Thompson.

Referee: Mr. K. Howley (Billingham)

Attendance: 29,851

Liverpool showed no ill effects from the nervous strain they had endured and after Jones had been penalised for a foul on St.John, Liverpool attacked spiritedly. Stevenson sent the ball through to Hunt, who was caught a yard offside. The home side responded with some speedy attacking play, with Jeff Astle most prominent.

After 15 minutes, Thompson quickly brought Clam's overhead kick under control and with everybody expecting him to cross the ball, he cut in and hit a great shot only narrowly wide of the post, with Potter stranded. Liverpool began to take control. Tommy Smith, making his Cup début, raced up regularly to join the Liverpool attack.

It was a thrilling, absorbing cup encounter. Liverpool had a miraculous escape in 22 minutes when Cram's free-kick was headed by Jones. The ball struck Lawrence, who was on the line, and there was an uncomfortable sequence of events in front of Liverpool's goal before the danger was cleared.

Smith went close with a great shot which Potter saved magnificently. Within a minute Astle had a powerful header saved by Lawrence. Lack of accuracy reduced Liverpool's effectiveness and St.John resorted to taking a speculative shot from twenty-five yards out.

One minute from the interval, however, the balance of play swung Liverpool's way. St.John began the move and Gordon Milne raced up to continue the move. Milne pin-pointed a pass to Hunt right in front of goal, and the inside man methodically side-footed the ball past Potter.

Soon into the second half, Astle netted from an indirect free-kick, and the goal did not stand. After 55 minutes, Astle was left with the perfect opportunity in front of goal, but he shot weakly and Lawrence was able to collect with ease. A minute later Astle sought to make amends, but headed wide. Liverpool went further ahead after 63 minutes when Peter Thompson exploited Albion's tendency to move upfield. From a long ball, Hunt squared a pass across goal and St.John's shot went in off the underside of the crossbar.

The Liverpool goal had a narrow escape when Lawler intercepted a pass from Hope after a Yeats clearance had been charged down, and the home side began to look increasingly dangerous. Thirteen minutes from the end, Yeats, under the impression that the referee had awarded a foul against a West Bromwich player, picked up the ball in the penalty area. The referee immediately awarded a spot kick. There was jubilation throughout the Liverpool side when Cram hit the ball well wide.

In a furious attack, Astle shot past Lawrence to reduce the arrears ten minutes from time. In a thrilling finale, Liverpool held on to make further progress in the Cup.

Tommy Smith

January 30, 1965

Liverpool (0) 1
Milne 51

Stockport County (1) 1
White 18

LIVERPOOL attempted to go undefeated for their fifteenth successive game, and they achieved this despite a spirited display by Stockport, who currently lay in bottom place in the Fourth Division. The visitors included Len White, the former Newcastle player, in their line-up. Stockport kept Liverpool in their own half for nearly all the opening few minutes and the Liverpool defence, with the ball bouncing high and sometimes unpredictably, looked indefinite in their work.

Lawrence lost possession of Collins' free kick when challenged by centre-forward Sandiford, but Liverpool contrived to get the ball away. Stockport were giving Liverpool a lesson in effort and enthusiasm at this stage of the game.

Liverpool were awarded a free-kick and, after their usual ruse in which the identity of the taker was concealed, Smith hit a tremendous shot which Mulhearn appeared to move too late to, but which he eventually reached in a brilliant save at the far post.

With 18 minutes gone, the visitors took a shock lead. White sent Watt away and the winger effected a fierce cross-shot which Lawrence appeared to save, but in fact he turned the ball straight to the head of White, from which it travelled into the roof of the net. Lawrence was injured in this incident and he needed attention for some time before the game resumed. White was also knocked out, but he recovered comparatively quickly.

The visitors played the better football up to the interval. At 51 minutes, Liverpool equalised with a goal from Milne out of nothing. Milne gained possession just inside the penalty area and, faced with a wall of defenders, he swivelled and hit a low shot through the ruck to score a goal just off the inside of a post.

The traditional Liverpool onslaught ensued, but the Fourth Division held on gallantly to earn a deserved replay.

F.A. CUP - FOURTH ROUND

Preston North End	1	Bolton Wanderers	2
Leicester City	5	Plymouth Argyle	0
Charlton Athletic	1	Middlesbrough	1
West Ham United	0	Chelsea	1
Tottenham Hotspur	5	Ipswich town	0
Peterborough United	2	Arsenal	1
Swansea Town	1	Huddersfield Town	0
Wolverhampton W.	2	Rotherham United	2
Sheffield United	0	Aston Villa	2
Stoke City	0	Manchester United	0
Reading	1	Burnley	1
Southampton	1	Crystal Palace	2
Sunderland	1	Nottingham Forest	3
Millwall	1	Shrewsbury Town	2
Leeds United	1	Everton	1

Replays

Middlesbrough	2	Charlton Athletic	1
Rotherham United	0	Wolverhampton W.	3
Manchester United	1	Stoke City	0
Burnley	1	Reading	0
Everton	1	Leeds United	2

Liverpool: Lawrence; Lawler, Byrne; Milne, Yeats, Stevenson; Callaghan, Hunt, St.John, Smith, Thompson.

Stockport County: Mulhearn; Collins, Cuthbert; Eckersall, Parry, Porteous; Watt, White, Sandiford, Hodgkinson, Phoenix.

Referee: Mr P.G. Brandwood (Walsall)

Attendance: 51,851

SHANKLY MISSES CUP TIE

~~~~~

Bill Shankly missed the Cup tie against Stockport because he was on a scouting mission to Germany to watch FC Cologne, Liverpool's next opponents in the European Cup.

Shankly was back for the replay with Stockport, and in the European tie with FC Cologne, Liverpool won through to the semi-final after winning on the toss of a coin.

February 3, 1965

Stockport County (0) 0

Liverpool (1) 2
Hunt 39, 85

FOR five minutes at Edgeley Park, Stockport threatened to run Liverpool off their feet, and so unsettled the Liverpool defence that there were visions of another major upset. Then the bubble burst, and Stockport appeared to be just what they were - a mediocre Fourth Division side. A superb exhibition of goalkeeping by Mulhearn and some inept finishing by Liverpool's forward line kept the scoreline respectable. Had Liverpool's finishing been more precise, they might well have scored ten goals. They had the ball in the net on five occasions; two attempts were disallowed for offside, and one was debited for a handling offence by St.John.

Even if the match fell below expectations in entertainment value, the tension in the little ground packed to capacity made it a memorable occasion. The fun started when someone set fire to a goal net before the game, and with crowds of youngsters spilling over on to the surrounds of the pitch there was all the excitement and atmosphere of a country fair. It was a great night for Stockport fans and a fitting background to the end of a very gallant Cup run.

Each time a goal was scored thousands of wildly excited youngsters raced on to the pitch. When Hunt got the last goal, five minutes from the end, he drove the ball into the net and kept on running in a wide arc back to the centre circle - running for his life from the invading army who wanted to mob him. For the whole of the second half hundreds of people crowded close to the goal-line where Liverpool attacked. It was remarkable that Referee Stokes permitted play to continue, but perhaps he realised that it would have been impossible to get the crowds back on to the terraces. These crowd scenes became the highlight because Liverpool's domination had become monotonous long before the end. Stockport never looked like scoring apart from the brief opening spell and Lawrence did not have one save to make. Hunt and St.John had far too much class for Stockport.

Mulhearn stood out as the one Stockport player who excelled. In the first half hour he made three top-class saves from Hunt, St.John and Yeats before he was beaten by Hunt after 39 minutes. St.John brought the ball along the line before cutting it inside to Hunt and the side-footed push into the net was a formality.

Smith, scorning his usual defensive role, moved up into attack with Stevenson for most of the second half, but Mulhearn coped efficiently with everything.

The second goal was snapped up by Hunt when left-back Cuthbert misplaced a back pass. Cuthbert and Collins had played well in the face of intense pressure.

Roger Hunt

Stockport County: Mulhearn; Collins, Cuthbert; Eckersall, Parry, Porteous; Watt, White, Sandiford, Hodgkinson, Phoenix.

Liverpool: Lawrence; Lawler, Byrne; Milne, Yeats, Stevenson; Callaghan, Hunt, St.John, Smith, Thompson.

Referee: Mr K. Stokes (Newark)

Attendance: 24,080

February 20, 1965

Bolton Wanderers (0) 0   Liverpool (0) 1
Callaghan 85

THE pitch was in excellent condition with a fine covering of grass. A strong wind was in Liverpool's favour. From a free-kick in the opening seconds, Yeats headed the ball over the bar for a corner. Arrowsmith was the spearhead of the Liverpool attack, with St.John dropping back to fill the role usually played by Milne. Liverpool were awarded their first free-kick for a ferocious tackle by Hartle on Thompson, and from the kick taken by Byrne, the ball was eventually moved into the centre where Smith tried a 30-yard shot straight at Hopkinson.

Play was held up for a minute or two while Yeats received attention for a blow on his right knee. It had occurred in yet another goalmouth skirmish when Lee centred and Yeats had headed the ball away, where Bromley fired in a shot which was blocked. Yeats limped upfield and Lawler was pulled into the middle to mark Davies. Yeats played in no known position, drifting round on the left with Thompson in the middle. Smith took over Lawler's place at right back. A fine header by Davies slipped just over the crossbar. Shortly afterwards, Yeats seemed to have recovered and their usual formation was restored.

The tackling on both sides was fierce and intense. The first twenty minutes belonged to the home side, and Liverpool were often under intense pressure. Gradually, however, Liverpool began to find their rhythm. Thompson started a first-class move over on the right. He switched the ball inside to Stevenson, who made a fine pass for Arrowsmith to effect a good shot which Hopkinson saved at full stretch for a corner. Bolton believed in moving the ball about first time.

The second period continued in a similar vein to the first, with most of the football being played in midfield. Liverpool looked the classier side in terms of their approach work, but the final pass was missing. The visitors played better against the wind than they had with it, and for several minutes they pinned Bolton in their own half of the field. The Liverpool attack appeared to have greater stamina and with fifteen minutes left the Reds were well on top. St.John and Hunt penetrated deep into the Bolton penalty area to set up a chance for Thompson, but the winger put the shot high over the bar.

Five minutes from the end, Callaghan deservedly gave Liverpool victory with an easily headed goal after a St.John-Thompson move had cut the Bolton defence to shreds. Stevenson - by far the best player on the field - began the move with a pass to St.John out on the left. St.John moved it inside to Thompson, who pulled it back cleverly, sent it across the goalmouth and Callaghan was unmarked as he headed the ball into the net. The wooden railing behind the goal collapsed under the pressure of the crowd who had surged forward to greet Callaghan's goal. Police and ambulance men raced to the spot but the referee carried on with play. Liverpool dominated the closing exchanges.

Bolton Wanderers: Hopkinson; Hartle, Farrimond; Rimmer, Edwards, Hatton; Lee, Hill, Davies, Bromley, Taylor.

Liverpool: Lawrence; Lawler, Byrne; Smith, Yeats, Stevenson; Callaghan, Hunt, St.John, Arrowsmith, Thompson.

Referee: Mr T.W. Dawes (Norwich)

Attendance: 57,207

Willie Stevenson

March 6, 1965

Leicester City (0) 0

Liverpool (0) 0

YEATS won the toss and in the first half defended the goal where the pitch was at its worst. The first shot came from Milne, whose 35-yard drive was comfortably held by Banks. Callaghan missed an attempted volley and in the early stages Liverpool had more of the play, though Goodfellow was only a yard or so wide with a shot from 20 yards.

There was a nasty-looking accident when Smith and Goodfellow had a collision of heads in midfield and the referee stopped play for both players to receive attention.

Peter Thompson

While both trainers were on, Banks took the opportunity of changing his boots and the game resumed after two or three minutes' delay. The combination of Smith and Milne was working well at this stage of the game, and it gave Liverpool the edge over the home side. The referee spoke to Smith for a particularly vicious foul on Gibson. From the free kick Gibson tried to turn the ball back from the goal line and finished up among the photographers. The referee went over and moved them back from their position. Leicester were reduced to isolated bursts. From one of them, Stringfellow was fouled by Lawler just outside the penalty area and from the free-kick taken by Gibson, Stringfellow tried a hook shot which went high over the bar. Leicester gained their first corner after 28 minutes' play. From the flag kick, taken by

Gibson, Stringfellow beat Yeats in the air and headed the ball wide. Lawrence had his first shot to save on the half-hour. Stringfellow's shot was poorly angled and the Liverpool goalkeeper saved the ball comfortably. Goalmouth incidents were so rare that the crowd had gone very quiet as the teams slogged it out in midfield.

The first real excitement of the game came from a right wing corner for Liverpool. The ball moved over to the opposite wing and Banks - in trying to punch clear - fell over King and the ball ran to Yeats. Liverpool's skipper hit it back instantly, but the ball struck Banks on the head and bounced away. For Leicester, Cross got the ball in the net but he was yards offside and the Liverpool players had stopped. The interval arrived without a goal and with little for the crowd to enthuse about.

The second half began in similar fashion. Liverpool always showed more method than Leicester in midfield, but they were unable to get through the strong tackling home defence. While Liverpool were preparing to take a free-kick for a foul by Sjoberg on St.John, a paper container was thrown at Lawrence and landed in the penalty area. Lawrence retrieved it and handed it to a policeman.

Midway through the second period, Leicester became more purposeful in attack, and from a twice-taken free-kick Hodgson made a good shot which Stevenson headed away for a corner. From Hodgson's kick, Cross made a great hook shot which flashed only inches wide. Liverpool survived Leicester's burst of pressure and reasserted themselves as they had done in the first half. From a right wing corner, Lawler went up and was unlucky when his close range shot through a crowded goalmouth ended in the arms of Banks. Then Hunt made a fine drive down the middle but he put his shot 10 yards wide. As happened at Bolton, Liverpool's fitness and stamina gave them the edge over their opponents and Leicester began to look tired as they held off the constant Liverpool attacks.

Leicester City: Banks; Sjoberg, Norman; Roberts, King, Appleton; Hodgson, Cross, Goodfellow, Gibson, Stringfellow.

Liverpool: Lawrence; Lawler, Byrne; Milne, Yeats, Stevenson; Callaghan, Hunt, St.John, Smith, Thompson.

Referee: Mr A.W. Leuty (Leeds)

Attendance: 39,356

March 10, 1965

Liverpool (0) 1
Hunt 72

Leicester City (0) 0

THIS was a tremendous match in every respect - it was harder than the first tie, it produced football of a higher quality, and it always went more favourably Liverpool's way. The first two clear-cut shooting openings both came early to Callaghan. He hit the first one low with his left foot and Banks, a superb goalkeeper by any standards, saved spectacularly. The second shot Banks took confidently overhead. A long lob by Lawler had caused the goalkeeper greater embarrassment. When the 'keeper got to the ball first at the feet of Hunt who shaped to pick up a through pass, it looked ominous for Liverpool that this would be another of Banks' great days. For much of the game Liverpool were on top, with Leicester struggling. However, before the interval Stringfellow twice went close for the visitors.

Peter Thompson was the victim of much late tackling in the second half, and from one free-kick awarded by Referee McCabe, Hunt scored. Ian Callaghan on the other wing had brought yet one more great save from Banks off a hard-hit hooked shot before the almost innocuous free-kick had the ball switching from one angle to another in such a way that Banks scarcely had any chance of saving it from the moment the ball left Hunt's foot. Hunt's aim, just inside the far post, was perfect. The ball spun over the line in front of the noses of 20,000 Kopites. Rarely has Hunt shown such jubilation at scoring. Hundreds of the thousands who had been locked out from the terraces almost an hour before the game began were left in no doubt from the intensity of the noise that Liverpool were on their way to Villa Park and the semi-final against Chelsea.

George McCabe (Sheffield) took over from Arthur Leuty (Leeds) because Leuty stated that he preferred not to referee midweek matches.

Liverpool: Lawrence; Lawler, Byrne; Milne, Yeats, Stevenson; Callaghan, Hunt, St.John, Smith, Thompson.

Leicester City: Banks; Sjoberg, Norman; Roberts, King, Appleton; Hodgson, Cross, Goodfellow, Gibson, Stringfellow.

Referee: Mr G. McCabe (Sheffield)

Attendance: 53,324

Liverpool's confidence increased visibly from the moment they went ahead. The game toughened, too, and the referee, who did not believe in spoiling continuity by a succession of free-kicks, was lenient on several occasions. For Liverpool, the game was won with characteristic team effort; the gradual wearing down of tough, talented opponents who were themselves capable of scoring the first goal and holding on to that lead. Liverpool suffered from defensive indecision at times, but their passing, apart from one short spell early in the second half, was fast, accurate and usually along the ground.

Gordon Banks

March 27, 1965

Liverpool (0) 2
Thompson 63, Stevenson (pen) 79

Chelsea (0) 0

LIVERPOOL played in their familiar all-red strip, and Chelsea took to the field in dark blue shirts and shorts with white socks. Chelsea won the toss and played with a slight wind in their favour. Liverpool made the running from the start, and Hinton made a bad header in an attempted clearance, pushing the ball out to Milne, who passed to St.John, but the centre-forward's pass was too far forward and ran outside. The first shot of the match came from Milne after a good move involving Stevenson, Callaghan and St.John. From the edge of the area Milne put the ball a yard wide. St.John missed an excellent chance of putting Liverpool ahead after 12 minutes. Again the move stemmed from Stevenson, who put the ball in the middle for Thompson to hit a good shot which Bonetti fumbled and the ball bounced out to St.John, who side-footed it wide with all the goal at his mercy.

Lawler, who ventured upfield at every opportunity to join his attack, was heavily brought down by McCreadie three yards outside the Chelsea penalty area to give Liverpool their first free-kick of the game. Milne touched the kick to one side for Smith to run up and try a strong shot, but the ball hit a Chelsea defender and bounced away to safety. Stevenson, who had an excellent game, got St.John away down the middle after a fine piece of defensive work. The Scot tried to find Milne, but put the ball forward a little too far, and the ball bounced off Bonetti as the goalkeeper came out and Hinton cleared.

Hollins raced downfield for a long pass from Venables and badly fouled Yeats as he went for the ball. The Liverpool skipper turned on Hollins in anger, but quickly calmed down and Liverpool received a free-kick.

Venables was the mastermind of the few Chelsea attacks of the game and another long ball from him found Bridges, but Yeats went across and conceded a corner. Chelsea's best move of the first half was the long through pass at which Venables showed himself the master, and Liverpool would have done well to copy it instead of passing laterally across the face of the penalty area. The pitch began to cut up badly which was responsible for some misplaced passes. Generally the game was of a high standard considering the tension and the ultimate prize of a place in the final. Chelsea started to get on top as they began to open out the play and after 23 minutes they had a goal disallowed. Mortimore went up to an inswinging corner from Tambling, climbed higher than Lawrence and headed the ball in. The referee ruled, however, that he had elbowed Lawrence on the way up.

Liverpool continued to have the better of the exchanges after the interval, and Byrne produced the best shot of the game after 54 minutes. He brought the ball in from the left and with the Chelsea defenders holding off, he was able to go on and produce a shot which hit the outside of the upright and went away for a goal-kick. Chelsea were laborious. They showed none of the smooth teamwork which took them to the top of the table this season.

After 63 minutes, Liverpool took a deserved lead with a superb goal from Thompson. St.John put a great pass out to the winger, who took the ball inside, beat Hinton with a brilliant body swerve, steadied himself, and crashed the ball into the net from ten yards. Venables tried hard to rally his men, but the front runners made little headway against Liverpool's well-organised defence. Chelsea were reduced to long, hopeful passes down the middle of the park which rarely succeeded. St.John had his name taken for retaliation on Harris.

With 11 minutes to go, Liverpool clinched their place in the Final with a penalty from Stevenson. It was awarded for a foul by Harris on St.John. Stevenson went up to take the kick for the first time and he placed the ball high into the net past Bonetti's left hand. Apart from the excellent Venables, McCreadie and Mortimore, Chelsea were a disappointing side.

The Liverpool fans were delirious in their excitement and pleasure, and considering the midweek exertions of the team against Cologne in Europe, this was a fine performance. During the closing stages, Liverpool stroked the ball around with ease. After the final whistle, the Liverpool players were in more danger from their fans than they had been from the Chelsea team. Thousands of wildly excited supporters poured on to the pitch, mobbing every player and carrying Thompson off shoulder high. It was Thompson's goal which settled the match and he was surrounded by hundreds of fans and led off in triumph to the dressing room. The rest of the players had disappeared from view for minutes before Thompson, helped by a police escort, finally found safety in the dressing room.

Liverpool: Lawrence; Lawler, Byrne; Milne, Yeats, Stevenson; Callaghan, Hunt, St.John, Smith, Thompson.

Chelsea: Bonetti; Hinton, McCreadie; Hollins, Mortimore, Harris; Murray, Graham, Bridges, Venables, Tambling.

Referee: Mr D.W. Smith (Stonehouse, Gloucester)

Attendance: 67,686

LIVERPOOL WIN CUP FOR FIRST TIME

HUNT AND ST.JOHN SCORE GOALS

YEATS LIFTS CUP

EXTRA TIME NEEDED

Liverpool (0) **2**
Hunt 93, St.John 111

Leeds United (0) **1**
Bremner 101

THE Liverpool team left their Weybridge hotel at 12.30 and the Football Association had arranged that a police motor-cycle escort pick them up *en route* approximately ten miles from Wembley. The arrangements broke down and no police turned up.

Orders

On the orders of manager Bill Shankly, the coach carried on its route and encountered heavy traffic just outside Wembley. When it looked as though the team might be held up, a police motor-cyclist was noticed and trainer Bob Paisley left the coach and asked him to guide them on to the stadium.

Crawled

The coach crawled its way through dense traffic and the thousands of people pouring into the stadium, but it reached its destination at two o'clock. Within a few minutes the players walked across the pitch together with their manager and received a tremendous reception from their fans at the north end of the ground.

Crowd

When Bill Shankly strode out of the tunnel and walked to the goal behind which a Liverpool contingent was massed, he was cheered loudly. The inimitable manager stood on the penalty spot and raised his arms to the crowd.

One coach held up for a long time in the traffic held the 1950 Cup team. There were many Liverpudlians bedecked in huge rosettes.

An hour before the start the Kop choir was in fine voice.

They had tunes and chants ready for everything, and countered the martial music played by the white helmeted band of the Royal Marines.

Songs

The Liverpool supporters' various songs included *"Coming Round The Mountain"* and *"When The Saints Go Marching In"*, as well as their usual chant of *"Liv-er-pool!"* Considering their allocation of only

15,000 tickets, the Liverpool supporters created a tremendous volume of noise.

The sun failed to shine, but the Liverpool supporters brought colour and brightness to the Wembley scene.

Bed

The Liverpool players stayed in bed until 11am before taking a stroll in the hotel grounds and then having a meal at noon. This consisted of the usual pre-match lunch when the players could choose between steak or fish or eggs - but no potatoes or vegetables. Several reserve players, together with directors and club officials arrived in London on the Friday night with their wives to stay at various hotels in the city before going to the match and then meeting afterwards at the Grosvenor House Hotel, Park Lane, for the official club banquet.

Contact

They were to be joined there by the players who represented the club in the 1950 Cup Final and several former players that the club had been able to contact up and down the country.

Extra medal

Liverpool were to apply to the Football Association for an additional medal to be awarded to Gordon Milne, who had played in all the other rounds.

Last night's visit to the London Palladium to see the Ken Dodd Show was a great success. Before the show, the players went backstage to meet the Liverpool comedian, have their photographs taken with him, and receive a few tickling sticks.

Applauded

During the show Doddy told his audience that Liverpool's Cup team was there and called for the house lights to be put on. The players stood up and were applauded. During the return trip to Weybridge the players were in good spirits. They had adopted the Kop's famous tune of *"You'll Never Walk Alone"*, and they gave a marvellous rendering of this, to the considerable surprise of passers-by in Piccadilly Circus as the coach drove back.

Supper

When they reached Weybridge they had a light supper and were in bed shortly after 10pm.

Criticism

Bill Shankly commented on the incoming of Geoff Strong for the injured Gordon Milne. He said: "I have been annoyed for some time that people have been criticising us for spending almost £70,000 in the last year on Strong from Arsenal and Phil Chisnall from Manchester United. Where would we be today if we hadn't signed these players? I know they have not played very often in the first team, but our regular side was playing so well and keeping fit, so they just couldn't break into the first team. Strong and Chisnall were brought as insurance for the future, and Gordon Milne's injury at this time has given me the chance of being able to call on either player. The real strength of any club lies

in its reserves and that is why Strong, Chisnall and others are absolutely invaluable to me."

The Final

The Duke of Edinburgh spent a few minutes in conversation with Liverpool skipper Ron Yeats and manager Bill Shankly and the three match officials. The side which defended the dressing-room end had the advantage of playing with the wind in the first half. Yeats won the toss.

Strong began the game in the right-half position and immediately before the kick-off Billy Bremner left the field to hand a ring to manager Don Revie on the touchline.

Foul

The first foul was by Collins on St.John. Stevenson took the free-kick, but Hunter cleared the danger with a huge clearance. Then Collins found full-back Reaney moving speedily down the right and gave him an immaculate pass which ended with Reaney shooting at Lawrence.

Attention

Thompson moved into the centre circle to initiate Liverpool's first real attack, but the move broke down when Collins committed a heavy foul on Byrne, who needed attention from the trainer. At the same time, Hunter received attention for an injury to his left leg. On resuming, Bremner was sandwiched between Byrne and Smith and was brought down heavily just outside the penalty box. Bremner received attention. Charlton was dominant in the air but

he misheaded a long clearance kick from Lawrence, but his mistake did not allow Liverpool to gain the initiative.

Then Charlton headed a powerful right-foot shot by Strong for a corner. Liverpool's fault was that they were too inclined to play the ball across the field too often.

Hunt made the best run of the game to date when he exchanged passes with St.John before moving forward and sending his right-foot shot high over the bar.

Slow

Leeds were somewhat slow in their build-ups and Liverpool had the better of the opening exchanges. St.John went on a fine solo run and dribble before passing to Callaghan, whose powerful strike hit Charlton and went for a corner.

Caution

A bad foul by St.John on Johanneson, who was breaking down the left, led to the Liverpool player being cautioned by the referee. Leeds covered well in defence and began to play some fine constructive football, but Liverpool were equally good in defence. Bell won a corner for Leeds, and from the flag-kick taken by Collins, Peacock got his head too far under the ball and it passed high over the bar. Bremner then received attention from the trainer just as the rain began to fall.

Fluency

The Liverpool attack played with greater fluency than Leeds' attack, but the defence of the Yorkshire side was in great form.

Gradually, however, Leeds settled down and Giles moved to the left wing to link with Collins.

Then Sprake failed to hold a great centre by Callaghan, but Giles had dropped back and cleared the loose ball.

Danger

Collins found Peacock with a wonderful pass, and it took a tackle from Yeats to remove the danger.

The best shot of the game to date arrived when Smith powered in a ball which went just wide.

Then Hunt showed all his determination and brought cheers from the Liverpool fans with a magnificent long-range shot that Sprake did well to flick over the top. He then made an excellent catch from the corner kick.

A pass from St.John to Hunt almost brought a goal, but the ball was cleared for a corner. Then a shot from Strong was also deflected for a corner just before the interval.

Rain

The rain fell heavier as the second half began and Liverpool created a movement involving six passes but finished it still a long way from the Leeds' goal.

Lawler sent in a centre from the right wing which found the head of Hunt, but the forward's attempt on goal passed wide. Bremner's despairing left foot sent Thompson's centre for a corner, and it took the efforts of the entire Leeds defence to keep out Hunt. Moments later Callaghan's powerful strike from close in hit Charlton and went for a corner. Liverpool were on top at this stage, and appeared almost nonchalant, playing the game virtually at walking pace. The Leeds defence always stayed back in numbers to prevent any promising Liverpool move from breaching their goal.

Referee

Bremner was spoken to by the referee for kicking the ball from his hand into the crowd when Liverpool had been given a throw-in, and the Liverpool crowd made their feelings known. Callaghan struck the side netting with a left-foot shot as Liverpool sought the vital first goal. Byrne and Lawler kept the Leeds wingers on a tight rein, and Smith made an exceptional tackle on Hunter to turn defence into attack, but Callaghan's centre was cut out.

Glanced

Then Lawler sent in a cross which St.John glanced wide of the post with his head.

Jack Charlton collided with a photographer just off the pitch when he allowed the ball the ball to pass out of play and got to his feet rubbing his thigh. While this incident took place, winger Peter Thompson received attention from Paisley on the touchline.

Photographer

Moments later a wild shot by Storrie on the right wing hit a photographer seated at the other end of the ground. Sprake produced a thrilling save at full stretch from a shot by Thompson to turn the ball for a corner. Following the flag-kick, Sprake caught the ball before Yeats could reach it with his head. A great shot by Byrne rebounded to Strong, who returned it, but the Leeds goalkeeper was perfectly positioned to save the powerful strike.

Extra time

The game moved into extra time for the first time since 1947, when Charlton and Burnley met.

Three minutes into the first period of extra time, Hunt scored from a pass by Byrne.

Stevenson slipped the ball out to the full-back near the left wing corner flag and Byrne turned the ball into the goalmouth where Hunt stooped low to nod it over the line.

Wild

The Liverpool fans went wild with delight and one fan climbed the barrier and appeared on the pitch trying to congratulate the scorer before being removed by five policemen, but still waving his red and white scarf.

Equaliser

The equaliser came from a Leeds left-wing move with Charlton nodding the ball across to Bremner, just inside the penalty box and the Scot smashed the ball full on the volley to ram it into the top corner of the net.

Liverpool were then forced to start all over again and try to win the Cup for the first time in their history.

The game moved into the second period of extra time and Bremner controlled the ball and shot all in one movement on the half turn from a pass by Reaney. There was not sufficient force in the shot, and Lawrence saved easily.

Roger Hunt congratulates *Ian St.John*, the scorer of the winning goal

Strong shot from five yards outside the box, but Sprake dived full length to turn the ball away for a corner.

From the corner St.John hooked the ball on to the top of the netting.

Winning goal

Nine minutes from the end, Callaghan crossed the ball expertly and at great speed and St.John nodded the ball powerfully into the net.

Removed

Another Liverpool fan found his way onto the pitch and he was removed by the police.

A minute after the goal, Bremner looked like breaking clean through, but he was adjudged to be offside. Then Thompson

robbed Charlton as the Leeds player moved swiftly towards goal, and forced Sprake to another brilliant save at full length.

Victorious

The final whistle blew with Liverpool victorious by two goals to one and the Liverpool supporters sang raucously *"Ee Aye Addio, We've Won The Cup!"*

Liverpool: Lawrence; Lawler, Byrne; Strong, Yeats, Stevenson; Callaghan, Hunt, St.John, Smith, Thompson.

Leeds: Sprake; Reaney, Bell; Bremner, Charlton, Hunter; Giles, Storrie, Peacock, Collins, Johanneson.

Referee: Mr W. Clements (Birmingham)

Attendance: 100,000

Ron Yeats, *the Liverpool skipper, receives the FA Cup from **Her Majesty the Queen***

January 22, 1966

Liverpool (1) 1
Hunt 2

Chelsea (1) 2
Osgood 7, Tambling 67

LIVERPOOL had not been beaten in the Third Round of the Cup since their humiliating experience in 1959 at the hands of Worcester City, but there was some credit in this defeat, for Chelsea achieved their objective of victory with a display which required efficiency, polish and great determination. Forty-five minutes before the start, the Chelsea players were out in track suits testing the heavily-sanded pitch, which was slippery in the corners. The teams were:

Liverpool: Lawrence; Lawler, Byrne; Milne, Yeats, Stevenson; Callaghan, Hunt, St.John, Smith, Thompson.

Chelsea: Bonetti; Harris, McCreadie; Hollins, Hinton, Boyle; Bridges, Graham, Osgood, Venables, Tambling.

Referee: Mr J. Finney (Hereford)

Attendance: 54,097

Boyle fouled Hunt just outside the area, but Liverpool did not make good use of the free-kick and the ball went for a goal-kick. The Chelsea goalkeeper did not take this well and Liverpool took the lead after just two minutes. Hunt sent Thompson away on the left and the winger took the ball into the penalty area before crossing to the unmarked St.John on the far side of the goalmouth. The Scot headed the ball back into the middle, where Hunt volleyed it into the net from five yards.

Chelsea equalised with their first real attack after seven minutes play. They gained a corner on the right, which the home side disputed, believing that the ball had gone off Osgood. Bridges took the kick and Graham cleverly flicked the ball over his head towards Osgood, who rose above all others to steer the ball into the net with a classic header.

Chelsea employed a four-two-four system without an outside-right, and Bridges roamed midfield, with Osgood dropping back to help the defence. Tommy Smith was warned by the referee for a foul on Graham as the game flowed from end to end. The Liverpool defence looked flat when Graham headed the ball past Yeats for Bridges to run onto, but Bridges missed an easy opportunity after beating Lawrence and sending the ball wide of the open goal. Moments later Lawrence pulled off a magnificent save to prevent Bridges from giving the Blues the lead. A miskick by Yeats in front of goal almost let in Tambling, but the ball bounced to safety. A header by Hunt from Stevenson's cross was directed straight at Bonetti. Chelsea caused Liverpool enormous problems despite using only three forwards for most of the half. Tambling broke free after some neat combination with

Graham, but his shot was diverted off the boot of Lawrence high into the air, and Smith cleared. St.John and Callaghan were Liverpool's most dangerous forwards, and the Scot, in particular, caused Chelsea numerous problems. One header under pressure, after a cross from Thompson, went narrowly wide. Boyle pulled Hunt's shirt, and the crowd went wild, but the referee did not spot the offence. Towards the interval, Bridges missed another easy opportunity when he shot over the bar from 12 yards after he had drawn the goalkeeper out of position.

Liverpool were awarded a free-kick in the Chelsea penalty area after Boyle had obstructed Hunt, and the ball rebounded off the defensive wall to Yeats, whose shot was blocked. Harris saved Chelsea after Bonetti had been drawn out of position by Milne, whose centre went straight to the Chelsea full-back with four Liverpool players waiting to strike.

Liverpool attacked powerfully in the second half, and a shot from Milne hit an upright before going for a goal-kick. Then Hunt had the ball in the net, but he was clearly offside from Milne's pass. Liverpool adopted the tactic of playing first-time balls, which was sensible in these conditions. The referee spoke to Venables for a severe foul on Callaghan. From the free-kick, Lawler headed the ball down, where St.John flicked it on as he fell, but Bonetti dived full length to save on the line. Chelsea rarely ventured out of their half as Liverpool dominated. Both Thompson and Callaghan shot wide from outside the area, and only Bridges lay upfield for Chelsea as the Reds dominated. Bonetti pushed Lawler's header over the bar with nine Liverpool players in the penalty area. St.John's skill on the difficult ground was extraordinary.

With 67 minutes gone, Chelsea took the lead with a magnificent headed goal from Bobby Tambling. Chelsea broke quickly down the right, and Graham centred accurately into the box. Tambling rose high and directed a powerful header just under the bar.

Then Osgood brought the ball deep out of his own half in a brilliant 60-yard run which was halted when Yeats tackled him just outside the penalty area, enabling Lawrence to leave his line and safely collect the ball. Chelsea began to taunt Liverpool with their close passing moves, but St.John forced Bonetti to push the ball over the bar from a close-range hook.

MATCH OF THE DAY
B.B.C. 2 at 10.15 tonight
Liverpool v. Chelsea

January 28, 1967

Watford (0) 0

Liverpool (0) 0

THIS FA Cup tie was an all-ticket affair with 33,553 paying some £10,000. Heavy rain had left the ground soft on top and it was soon evident that the players would experience some difficulty in keeping their feet. Watford, who had conceded only five goals at home this season, soon set a defensive pattern by withdrawing every player except Melling whenever Liverpool threatened danger. St.John nearly created an early surprise when Slater took a short kick to Garvey. The fiery Scot leapt in for the return pass to the goalkeeper, but could only flick the ball against the former Liverpool goalkeeper's body. Watford withdrew Scullion to a defensive role and he required the assistance of Furphy when the winger threatened to break through. Occasionally Watford threatened themselves to break quickly, although they relied rather too heavily on their defensive tactics. Bond prodded forward to Melling, whose cross to Scullion opened up several possibilities until Smith's wholehearted tackle dispossessed the Watford winger. Callaghan floated across a fine centre beyond the far post. Slater went for the ball and missed, and when Hunt connected, the linesman flagged for a dead ball. Furphy had to jump high to cut out another cross from Callaghan with St.John challenging dangerously. From a Thompson corner, Yeats and Strong headed forward for St.John to nod the ball towards the post, where Slater made a desperate bid to save, although the referee had decided that St.John was offside. Liverpool had most of the possession, and they played the better football, but Watford - fourth in the Third Division - defended so tenaciously that genuine opportunities were scarce.

Yeats was forced to clear desperately when Scullion found Garbett in front of goal. Although the visitors continued to dominate, Watford hit their first real shot of the match through the former Everton player, Alec Farrell, whose shot was too wide to really trouble Lawrence. Instead of Watford attempting to force the pace early on and perhaps snatch an opening goal, they seemed more intent on a holding role, although from a free-kick Bond sent a fierce shot screaming over the crossbar. Watford gained success and growing confidence with their defensive plan against Liverpool, who found it impossible to breach the wall of yellow across the goal. Whenever Milne or St.John sought a path through the middle for Hunt, the ball was usually cut off before reaching its target.

Smith tackled Scullion superbly inside the penalty area, but the game lacked the real tension and high drama normally associated with the Cup. Encouraged by their ability to deal with Liverpool's attack, Watford switched five men to the attack, and Yeats cleared when Scullion tried to find support in the middle. Smith defended brilliantly and several of his tackles halted Watford in their dangerous stride. Seven

minutes before the interval Watford combined well with Bond, Melling and Farrell, which allowed Bond to hammer the ball wide of Lawrence and the post.

From an inswinging Thompson corner, Lawler sent the ball across goal but just missed the target. Right on the interval, Slater saved magnificently from a St.John header.

It was raining heavily when play resumed. Twice within a minute in the opening stages of the second half, Liverpool had scoring chances. First Hunt spent too long seeking out the perfect shooting position, and then a St.John header missed the unmarked Milne by no more than a yard. Liverpool attacked with great determination, and St.John opened up the way for a Hunt raid. He was brought down by Furphy five yards outside the area, though nothing came of the free-kick. Watford broke swiftly, and Yeats had to stretch out a leg to pass back to Lawrence as Bond raced in. With Callaghan and Thompson linking up cleverly on the right, Thompson beat off three tackles before pulling the ball back from the bye-line to Milne, who slipped it across to St.John, and from the six-yard line the Scot blazed the ball high over the bar. Thompson's ball control on a difficult surface was exceptionally good as he cut inside, beat two defenders, and hit a 25-yard drive which rebounded from Slater's body. The goalkeeper recovered before Hunt reached the ball. On the hour Thompson's corner-kick was cleared to Callaghan, who hit one of his "specials" from 25 yards. The ball was destined to find the net, but it struck Geoff Strong, standing a yard out, and he was penalised for being offside.

Watford became an eleven-man defence and they worked hard to cope with a Liverpool side which went all out to get the breakthrough they so desperately wanted. As Watford were subjected to a heavy Liverpool bombardment, their crowd responded magnificently and got behind them. A strong ground shot by Scullion rebounded from Lawrence's body and the goalkeeper had to recover quickly to smother the danger with Melling running in. Scullion cleared the crossbar with another shot and Melling forced Lawrence to save from a long-range drive. The Liverpool goalkeeper had to race right outside the area to kick clear from Scullion. Then Thompson hit the crossbar after the whistle had blown for offside. Slater was called into action to save well from Hunt's fierce shot. Furphy kicked clear from a St.John header and Watford continued to frustrate their more illustrious opponents. For a Thompson corner Watford pulled back all eleven men and the Third Division side held on gallantly for a draw.

The eventual Cup-winners, Tottenham Hotspur, drew 0-0 with Millwall at the Den, while the runners-up, Chelsea, beat Huddersfield 2-1 away. The highest score of the round was achieved by Peterborough United, who beat non-League

Bedford Town 6-2 away. The Cup-holders, Everton, drew 0-0 with Burnley, before winning the replay 2-1 at Goodison Park.

Watford: Slater; Furphy, Williams; Welbourne, Garvey, Eddy; Scullion, Bond, Garbett, Melling, Farrall.

Liverpool: Lawrence; Lawler, Milne; Smith, Yeats, Stevenson; Callaghan, Hunt, St.John, Strong, Thompson.

Referee: Mr E.T. Jennings (Stourbridge)

Attendance: 33,553

Receipts: £10,850

THIRD DIVISION
Final Table

	P	W	D	L	F	A	Pts
Queen's Park R.	46	26	15	5	103	38	67
Middlesbrough	46	23	9	14	87	64	55
Watford	**46**	**20**	**14**	**12**	**61**	**46**	**54**
Reading	46	22	9	15	76	57	53
Bristol Rovers	46	20	13	13	76	67	53
Shrewsbury	46	20	12	14	77	62	52
Torquay	46	21	9	16	73	54	51
Swindon	46	20	10	16	81	59	50
Mansfield	46	20	9	17	84	79	49
Oldham	46	19	10	17	80	63	48
Gillingham	46	15	16	15	58	62	46
Walsall	46	18	10	18	65	72	46
Colchester	46	17	10	19	76	73	44
Leyton Orient	46	13	18	15	58	68	44
Peterborough	46	14	15	17	66	71	43
Oxford	46	15	13	18	61	66	43
Grimsby	46	17	9	20	61	68	43
Scunthorpe	46	17	8	21	58	73	42
Brighton	46	13	15	18	61	71	41
Bournemouth	46	12	17	17	39	57	41
Swansea	46	12	15	19	85	89	39
Darlington	46	13	11	22	47	81	37
Doncaster	46	12	8	26	58	117	32
Workington	46	12	7	27	55	89	31

F.A. CUP - THIRD ROUND

Huddersfield Town	1	Chelsea	2
Aldershot	0	Brighton & Hove A.	0
Bradford Park Avenue	1	Fulham	3
Charlton Athletic	0	Sheffield United	1
Manchester United	2	Stoke City	0
Norwich City	3	Derby County	0
Sheffield Wednesday	3	Queen's Park Rangers	0
Mansfield Town	2	Middlesbrough	0
Sunderland	5	Brentford	2
Bedford Town	2	Peterborough United	6
Leeds United	3	Crystal Palace	0
Northampton Town	1	West Bromwich A.	3
Barnsley	1	Cardiff City	1
Manchester City	2	Leicester City	1
Ipswich Town	4	Shrewsbury Town	1
Blackburn Rovers	1	Carlisle United	2
Nuneaton Borough	1	Rotherham United	1
Birmingham City	2	Blackpool	1
Bolton Wanderers	1	Crewe Alexandra	0
Bristol Rovers	0	Arsenal	3
Millwall	0	Tottenham Hotspur	0
Hull City	1	Portsmouth	1
Halifax Town	1	Bristol City	1
Barrow	2	Southampton	2
Nottingham Forest	2	Plymouth Argyle	1
Coventry City	3	Newcastle United	4
West Ham United	3	Swindon Town	3
Bury	2	Walsall	0
Oldham Athletic	2	Wolverhampton W.	2
Burnley	0	Everton	0
Preston North End	0	Aston Villa	1

Replays

Brighton & Hove A.	3	Aldershot	1
Cardiff City	2	Barnsley	1
Rotherham United	1	Nuneaton Borough	0
Tottenham Hotspur	1	Millwall	0
Portsmouth	2	Hull City	2
Bristol City	4	Halifax Town	1
Southampton	3	Barrow	0
Swindon Town	3	West Ham United	1
Wolverhampton W.	4	Oldham Athletic	1
Everton	2	Burnley	1

Second Replay

Portsmouth	3	Hull City	1

February 1, 1967

Liverpool (2) 3
St.John 38, Hunt 41,
Lawler 67

Watford (0) 1
Melling 88

WATFORD came out early to a heart-warming reception from the crowd which increased in volume when they lined up in front of the Kop to greet the famous edifice, and at the same time, to receive the greetings of the Kop crowd. The visitors packed nine and ten men in defence and blocked and tackled superbly, with their half-backs, Welbourne, Garvey and Eddy, particularly good, while Slater flung himself around heroically. Liverpool waited patiently for the break and the right opening. Liverpool dominated the game, but Watford had moments when they played with splendid composure, moving the ball smoothly out of defence with slick passing. But they could not find a penetrating final pass against Liverpool's masterly defence which soaked up everything Watford were able to throw at them.

The first goal arrived after 38 minutes when Watford had tried an optimistic raid with full-back Furphy up near the Liverpool line when Milne stepped in to intercept. He passed quickly to Thompson, who went on a fast run down the middle before passing to St.John, who moved quickly inside with the Watford defence split for the first time, and the Liverpool centre-forward hit a magnificent shot past Slater from 20 yards. Much of the competitive edge went out of the game from the moment the ball hit the back of the net. Three minutes later Hunt scored with an impudent goal after taking a pass from St.John. He cleverly side-stepped the desperate outcoming dive of Slater and calmly chipped the ball over the goalkeeper's body into the far corner of the net. Watford's football up to this point had been as good as several First Division sides seen at Anfield this season, but the two-goal salvo took the heart out of them.

The second half was simply academic, with Liverpool pressurising Watford without really extending themselves. Lawler hit a third goal with a splendid shot from his left foot, and Watford's football began to lack the class of the first half,

The Watford defence was cut to ribbons by the speed and artistry of **Peter Thompson**

though they matched Liverpool in effort and a determination to work hard.

Liverpool crashed in shot after shot, and with Slater beaten, Eddy twice cleared off the line from a header by Hunt and a shot from Milne. Liverpool were able to indulge in a policy of freedom to attack at will, in the knowledge that Yeats, playing spectacularly, was able to cope with anything Watford were able to muster. The Watford defence was cut to ribbons by the speed and artistry of Thompson, the skill of St.John, and the directness and determination of Callaghan.

Although Watford reinforced the cover for Furphy on the right, Thompson excelled himself, and on this form it needed three or four men to hold him. An indication of the way the game flowed was in the fact that it was 65 minutes before Liverpool conceded a free-kick, and most of the eight free-kicks Watford conceded were for technical offences rather than malicious fouls.

Two minutes from the end, Melling scored and brought some respectability to a fine display from a side which rightly earned a great deal of respect and admiration from the crowd.

A former Liverpool player, Dave Hickson, was selected to play for the club where he began his career 21 years ago, Ellesmere Port. Hickson was in their line-up for the club's Cheshire League fixture against Witton Albion at York Road on the Saturday after the Cup replay. He was selected to play at centre-forward. Hickson was turning out for the club on an expenses-only basis in order to help the club in its financial plight, with flagging gates and moving down the League.

Liverpool: Lawrence; Lawler, Milne; Smith, Yeats, Stevenson; Callaghan, Hunt, St.John, Strong, Thompson.

Watford: Slater; Furphy, Williams; Welbourne, Garvey, Eddy; Scullion, Bond, Garbett, Melling, Farrall.

Referee: Mr E.T. Jennings (Stourbridge)

Attendance: 54,451

February 18, 1967

Liverpool (0) 1

St.John 77

Aston Villa (0) 0

WITH Roger Hunt still unfit, Liverpool fielded the same team which beat Aston Villa 1-0 in the League last Saturday. The visitors made two changes, leaving out Chatterley and Rudge and bringing in Deakin and MacLeod. It was the first meeting of these two clubs in the FA Cup since the semi-final of 1914, which Liverpool won 2-0. Liverpool defended the Kop goal in the first period.

The home side were soon on the attack and Thompson won a free-kick. From Stevenson's lob, Lawler got in a header which was kicked off the line. Aston Villa began with more determination than they had in the previous week's League encounter, and when Milne made a poor pass, Wright intercepted and sent the ball on to Anderson, whose awkward dipping shot was tipped over the bar by Lawrence.

Liverpool went within inches of taking the lead after five minutes when Callaghan made a brilliant run down the right and centred for St.John to put in a great diving header which Withers managed to push round the post with his fingertips. An incisive Villa movement split the Liverpool defence wide open and after Deakin's shot had rebounded off the body of Lawrence, Anderson hit the bar with Lawrence lying prostrate on the ground. Liverpool struck back immediately and Strong headed a right wing centre into the net before being ruled offside.

Aston Villa were not afraid to move the ball about and they surprised the big crowd with the quality of their play. A rebound put MacLeod through on the left and it took a fine tackle by Lawler to prevent a goal. A minute later Anderson had the ball taken off his toe in the goalmouth.

Thompson was closely marked and he featured little in the game up to this point, while his opposite number, MacLeod, made a quick dart through the middle to create great danger until a well-timed tackle by Yeats saved Liverpool. Strong blasted the ball wide when he appeared to be in a good scoring position, though the whistle had blown for a free-kick to Liverpool.

Withers dived at Thompson's feet after St.John had nodded the ball forward, and when it ran loose again the centre-forward fired a shot which would have entered the net but for a spectacular goal-line clearance by Aitken. The game flowed from end to end, and Broadbent hit a left-foot shot just over the bar. A quick flick inside by MacLeod caused danger for Liverpool, but Lawrence's speed prevented a goal. A foul on St.John won the home side a free-kick just outside the penalty area. Stevenson turned the ball quickly inside and Smith shot with great power only to see his effort rebound off a defender. A minute later Thompson broke free on the left, but he was repelled by a well-timed tackle, but moments later

he broke through again and hit a fierce low centre into the goalmouth which Strong blasted high over the bar. Liverpool's finishing continued to be erratic and when Callaghan put the ball across from the right, St.John nodded it in front of the in-coming Milne, who failed to control and shoot from five yards out. Then the ball ran loose in front of Strong, whose shot went high over the bar again.

Liverpool had more of the play without threatening to take complete control of the game. The majority of their attacking movements continued to break down near goal, and Villa's ability to counter remained a danger.

Yeats ventured upfield to add weight and height to the attack when Callaghan won a corner, and he sent in a strong header which Withers did well to hold underneath the bar. Moments later the Villa goalkeeper was again in action when he brilliantly kept out a point-blank shot from Stevenson. The Reds continued to pile on the pressure and Callaghan raced away on the inside in an effort to force a way through. He had two attempts on goal which met a wall of defenders. Just before the half-time whistle, Stevenson was brought down in the penalty area, but appeals for a spot-kick were rejected by the referee.

Liverpool began the second half in the same manner as they had concluded the first. Their football was pretty, but ineffective against a resolute side. Three attacks were cleared when it appeared as though no Liverpool player wanted to take on the responsibility of shooting. However, Villa almost presented Liverpool with a goal when two defenders got in each other's way and the ball rebounded to the feet of Strong, whose powerful close-range shot went into the side netting.

Callaghan aroused the crowd to fever pitch with a 50-yard run down the left wing and it took a wonderful flying header by Sleeuwenhoek to prevent Strong from scoring. The ball went out to Milne and was scrambled away. Milne missed a further opportunity to score when the ball went out to him following a heading duel in the goalmouth. Although he was at a poor angle, he was in a good position to score, but he sent the ball high into the Kop.

Play was held up briefly while the Villa trainer attended to Deakin, who was injured in one of Villa's rare forays into the Liverpool half. A minute later he was replaced by Rudge.

Chance after chance was squandered by Liverpool until they finally went into the lead after 77 minutes. The ball was worked down the left wing and Stevenson flicked it inside, where it was deflected in front of St.John, who dived full-length to direct it out of the reach of Withers.

A minute later, the Liverpool centre-forward almost scored again when he broke from the half-way line and went on a

40-yard run which culminated in a shot which Withers saved at full-length. With just ten minutes remaining, Withers saved from less than five yards from Milne, after St.John had run clean through the defence and pulled the ball back for him. Aston Villa were forced to abandon their defensive shell as they went in search of an equaliser, and after winning a corner, full-back Wright forced Lawrence to a brilliant save with a superb shot. Yeats was left flat-footed in another Villa raid, but the dependable Smith cleared the danger, and Liverpool made further Cup progress.

The shock of the round was Manchester United's 1-2 home reverse against Norwich City, while the highest score of the day was recorded by Sunderland, who beat Peterborough United 7-1 on Wearside. Everton drew 1-1 with Wolverhampton Wanderers, winning the Goodison Park replay 3-1.

F.A. CUP
FOURTH ROUND

Brighton & Hove A.	1	Chelsea	1
Fulham	1	Sheffield United	1
Manchester United	1	Norwich City	2
Sheffield Wednesday	4	Mansfield Town	0
Sunderland	7	Peterborough United	1
Leeds United	5	West Bromwich A.	0
Cardiff City	1	Manchester City	1
Ipswich Town	2	Carlisle United	0
Rotherham United	0	Birmingham City	0
Bolton Wanderers	0	Arsenal	0
Tottenham Hotspur	3	Portsmouth	1
Bristol City	1	Southampton	0
Nottingham Forest	3	Newcastle United	0
Swindon Town	2	Bury	1
Wolverhampton W.	1	Everton	1

Replays

Chelsea	4	Brighton & Hove A.	0
Sheffield United	3	Fulham	1
Manchester City	3	Cardiff City	1
Birmingham City	2	Rotherham United	1
Arsenal	3	Bolton Wanderers	0
Everton	3	Wolverhampton W.	1

FINAL LEAGUE TABLE
DIVISION ONE
1966 - 1967

	Pl	W	D	L	F	A	Pts
Manchester U.	42	24	12	6	84	45	60
Nottingham F.	42	23	10	9	64	41	56
Tottenham H.	42	24	8	10	71	48	56
Leeds United	42	22	11	9	62	42	55
Liverpool	**42**	**19**	**13**	**10**	**64**	**47**	**51**
Everton	42	19	10	13	65	46	48
Arsenal	42	16	14	12	58	47	46
Leicester C.	42	18	8	16	78	71	44
Chelsea	42	15	14	13	67	62	44
Sheffield U.	42	16	10	16	52	59	42
Sheffield W.	42	14	13	15	56	47	41
Stoke City	42	17	7	18	63	58	41
W.B.A.	42	16	7	19	77	73	39
Burnley	42	15	9	18	66	76	39
Manchester C.	42	12	15	15	43	52	39
West Ham U.	42	14	8	20	80	84	36
Sunderland	42	14	8	20	58	72	36
Fulham	42	11	12	19	71	83	34
Southampton	42	14	6	22	74	92	34
Newcastle U.	42	12	9	21	39	81	33
Aston Villa	**42**	**11**	**7**	**24**	**54**	**85**	**29**
Blackpool	42	6	9	27	41	76	21

March 11, 1967

Everton (1) 1

Ball 45

Liverpool (0) 0

GOODISON Park was packed more than half-an-hour before the kick-off. Everton brought back Derek Temple to centre-forward and Liverpool had Gordon Milne as the midfield link man after being rested the previous week. The ground had dried after the effects of a strong gusty wind, and - the wind apart - the conditions were good. The majority of the Liverpool supporters were grouped behind the goal at the Stanley Park end of the pitch and the crushing appeared bad in this section of the ground. Long before the players came out, ambulancemen were dealing with several casualties, and people were pulled out of the densely packed crowd at that end.

In the usual derby match tradition, the teams came out together to a cacophony of sound. Labone won the toss for Everton and elected to defend the Stanley Park goal in the first half. A fan ran onto the pitch while the players took their positions before the kick-off and shook hands with Alex Young.

St.John kicked off and Liverpool tried to make progress down the left where Wright made a good interception to turn the ball back to West as Thompson looked like breaking through.

Labone brought down St.John five yards outside the penalty area. Yeats went up for the free-kick and Smith aimed the ball in his direction, but the Liverpool captain collided with Morrissey and the ball ran harmlessly out of play.

Both teams appeared to be nervous in front of the crowd which maintained a tremendous roar. Liverpool did most of the attacking in the early minutes, and the Reds gained the first corner when Ball put the ball behind in a tackle on St.John. Although Yeats and Lawler both went up for the ball, it was eventually cleared by Hurst. In Everton's first attack, Young tried to find Temple with a through pass, but Temple was adjudged offside.

Everton were awarded a free-kick when Smith brought down Husband and though Morrissey sent Wilson down the wing the full-back's centre from the line went behind.

Milne's back-pass to Lawrence was too weak, and danger threatened when Morrissey moved in, but Stevenson came across and cleared. Ball set up a good Everton move down the right, and Temple passed to Young, but before the forward could shoot, Callaghan - operating as an extra defender - swept the ball off his toes.

The ball bounced awkwardly and beat Labone, and St.John slipped the ball across to Hunt, but Harvey made a wonderful interception. Morrissey was spoken to for a foul on Lawler, but Smith's free-kick swung away in the wind. The tackling was so fast and efficient that neither side could sustain a flowing movement. Thompson went on a jinking run down the left, but his centre was cleared by Hurst. Liverpool used

an offside trap to stop Temple from another long pass by Ball, after Wright had tackled Thompson deep in the Blues' half.

The first save of the game arrived after 15 minutes when a half-hit shot from Morrissey rolled to Lawrence. Then West came off his line to punch away a high dropping ball from Smith. He missed his punch and the ball bounced away to Hunt as the goalkeeper fell, but Hurst, performing brilliantly in defence, cleared the danger.

The game was halted for two or three minutes while Husband received attention to a leg injury when he went down heavily as Yeats moved in with a tackle. The referee re-started the game with a dropped ball.

Morrissey was spoken to for another foul on Lawler, and the Liverpool full-back had to receive attention. Liverpool gained a corner from a quickly taken throw-in by Milne. Before Callaghan could take the flag-kick, he had to move yards of toilet paper which swirled round the corner quadrant. Both teams were guilty of trying to play football at too great a speed.

Labone struggled to judge high passes down the middle, due to the swirling wind.

The referee missed a flare-up between St.John and Ball in which the Evertonian went headlong. Play continued until Young was flattened by Stevenson. The referee blew for the free-kick and Gordon West ran 30 yards out of his goal to run in among a group of players and push St.John. Yeats then ran up and pushed West away and after the man in black went across to speak with a linesman, he had a word with St.John before the game restarted with a free-kick to the Blues. The standard of football was extremely poor considering the quality and reputations of both teams.

Husband was brought down again with a double tackle by Stevenson and Byrne, but Everton did not utilise the free-kick to their advantage because Liverpool's defensive cover was excellent. The Blues' defence did not look as good as Liverpool's, but Hurst and Harvey were in brilliant form. The wind was troublesome, but the passing and inaccurate work of the players reduced the game to a midfield battle. When Hunt burst through from an offside position, he did not hear the referee's whistle. West came charging out of goal and collided with Hunt on the edge of the area. Before Everton took the free-kick for offside, the referee spoke to West and told him to calm down. Players began to argue with the referee after almost every decision he gave. From one free-kick awarded against Young for a foul on St.John, Smith tried a shot from 25 yards but the ball swung well wide of the target. It was only the second shot so far after 41 minutes' play.

When Morrissey - a former Liverpool player - beat Smith near the line, Smith chased back 20 yards to bring the Everton winger down for a free-kick but the referee did not penalise

Smith for his transgression. From the free-kick, Labone went up and there was confusion amongst a mass of bodies in which half a dozen men went down and Labone and Yeats tangled before the ball was cleared.

From this incident, Everton took the lead seconds before the interval. Milne tried to find Lawrence with a back pass but Husband pounced on the ball as it went past Yeats, and as Lawrence came out Husband and the Liverpool 'keeper collided. The ball bounced free and Ball, following up quickly, turned it into the net from the narrowest of angles.

The goal provided the highlight of a half which had provided only three shots and in which the defences, with ruthless first-time tackling, had held complete mastery and control. It was evident that the tackling was so fierce that the talent and artistry of the ball players on both sides was being obliterated.

A long high pass from Stevenson looked dangerous as St.John and Labone moved to it, but when the ball went out the referee gave a goal-kick, which angered St.John. The referee ran 50 yards to speak to Stevenson after he had tripped Husband when the Everton youngster had broken away down the right. A moment later the referee had to speak to St.John for fouling West as the goalkeeper went to pick up the ball, and it was clear that it required a strong referee making firm decisions to put a halt to the constant interruptions and free-kicks.

The Everton defence was almost breached when, from a long through pass by St.John which Hunt chased, West came out and Wilson tried to turn the ball back to him. Wilson almost put through his own goal, but the ball trickled wide of the post.

From a free-kick, Hurst cleared with an excellent header, and Liverpool played with their usual power as they sought an equaliser. Thompson found the weakness in the middle of Everton's defence by pushing the ball up fast for Hunt to chase and West had to come far out of goal and make a dramatic save in which he pushed the ball away. Hunt chased it, turned it back to Callaghan, but the Everton defence had recovered its composure and cleared the ball.

The game developed an interesting angle as Thompson began to show flashes of his real form which stimulated the Liverpool team. In an isolated Everton attack in the midst of the Liverpool dominance, Harvey went past three men and pushed the ball up to Temple, but Yeats turned the ball away for a corner. Hurst and Smith were the finest players on display. They had both covered up well in defence and at times the extra man behind the centre-half was urgently needed.

With 58 minutes gone, slackness in the Everton defence allowed Thompson to get the ball across and it fell nicely for St.John, who hit his shot quickly enough but West went down low and saved superbly. Moments later the referee had to speak to St.John for a foul on Labone. Alan Ball gradually came into the game more with a tremendous display of midfield urgency, but the Everton defence was at full stretch as the Reds turned on the pressure as they fought desperately for an equaliser. From a corner-kick, West raced out 10 yards to try to punch away, but only directed the ball to Thompson, who shot back quickly and West was fortunate to find the ball coming straight at him as he got to his feet. Liverpool dominated the exchanges so far in this half, and although the

tension was apparent because of the nature of Cup-ties, the quality of football was generally quite poor. The first save that Lawrence had to make came after 65 minutes. From a corner, Young turned the ball back to Morrissey, who tried to float the ball into the far corner, but Lawrence went up well and touched the ball over the bar. From the second corner Morrissey got in a brave header but sent the ball wide. Thompson swung the ball over and the Everton defence watched it pass, not realising that Hunt was moving in fast behind them and the Liverpool forward came within inches of collecting the ball before it ran out of play. Yeats went up for a corner which Thompson had to take three times in all, and when he finally got the ball across, West came out well and made a good catch. He ruined his good work by throwing the ball out to Stevenson, but the defence cleared the danger. The Reds looked faster and more aggressive than Everton in this second half, and the Blues' defence took a tremendous pounding as Liverpool displayed all their traditional power and attacking football. When Everton did get the ball out of defence they were far too hurried in trying to kick the ball upfield.

It appeared as though Husband had broken past Yeats for once, and Smith - who had had a great game - came across to turn the ball back to Lawrence. The referee had given Everton a free-kick for Yeats having pulled at Husband's jersey, and from the free-kick Ball touched the ball to one side for Hurst to try a long range shot, but he swung the ball wide of the goal.

Labone had a nightmare of a game, and it was only the work of his colleagues in defence which kept the Everton goal from falling. He once put the ball straight to Milne from the edge of the penalty area. In the mêlée which followed, the ball was not properly cleared and when Thompson hit the ball hard across the goalface, West made a desperate save as St.John ran in. The goalkeeper was hurt in the incident and Wright also had to have attention at the same time from the Liverpool trainer as he had been injured a few moments earlier.

With just under ten minutes remaining, Liverpool maintained their steady pressure and for the first time since the interval the Everton fans could be heard chanting "Ev-er-ton!" The Everton defence scrambled the ball away time after time as Liverpool's attack was relentless in its quest for equality. Several of the Everton forwards had rarely been in evidence, but Husband kept on working hard and effectively. He produced one of the best passes of the day to Temple, but the centre-forward completely mistimed his shot and it rolled wide.

From a free-kick taken by Stevenson, Hurst headed the ball away, but St.John returned it into the middle and Yeats headed magnificently as he fell, sending the ball just over the bar with West beaten. Lawrence had had little to do, but he produced a first-class save from a fine shot by Husband who turned on to a ball from Young's pass and cracked it goalwards. Everton came again with a strong attack, but Yeats robbed Temple brilliantly. With the minutes ticking away, every Liverpool player except Lawrence was in the Everton half and the excitement and tension were greater than at any other point in the game. Liverpool threw a wave of red shirts at the Everton defence, which managed to scramble the ball away time after time in the face of intense and persistent pressure. The game entered injury time and Liverpool, who had never given up the cause as a lost one, came again in the dying seconds with Smith swinging the ball in from 30 yards and West touching it over the bar. From the corner, West, who had been in brilliant form, made a fine save.

At the final whistle, scores of young fans ran on to the pitch to signal Everton's win which put them through to the quarter-final. The police quickly cleared the pitch and the vast Everton contingent on the terraces remained to cheer and chant a victory which had been extremely hard-earned. In the Sixth Round, Everton fell 3-2 away to Nottingham Forest.

Everton: West; Wright, Wilson; Hurst, Labone, Harvey; Young, Ball, Temple, Husband, Morrissey.

Liverpool: Lawrence; Lawler, Milne; Byrne, Yeats, Stevenson; Callaghan, Hunt, St.John, Smith, Thompson.

Referee: Mr K. Howley (Billingham)

Attendance: 64,851 (with a further 40,149 at Anfield)

Receipts: £25,800

Alan Ball, *the Everton goalscorer and influential midfielder*

January 27, 1968

Bournemouth (0) 0   Liverpool (0) 0

DEAN Court, the home of Third Division Bournemouth, was packed to capacity for the visit of Liverpool. The home side included at inside-right, Eddie Rowles, a 16-years-old apprentice with only three first team games behind him. Liverpool, who had Tony Hateley as substitute, were in white shirts because of a clash of colours.

As expected, the home side attacked from the start and East broke through and tried to deflect the ball past Lawrence, but the goalkeeper managed to palm it down and then fall on it on the line as Pound raced in. Callaghan found Thompson on two separate occasions with brilliant passes, but the moves came to nothing. Liverpool won a corner on the left, but Thompson's kick was headed to safety.

Bournemouth struck back quickly and Pound squared the ball across the edge of the penalty area, where Bolton was running in, but he was unable to control the ball and in a mêlée around the penalty spot, Byrne eventually came to Liverpool's rescue and kicked the ball for a corner.

Bolton appeared to have hurt his nose and was led off by both trainer and ambulance men with a sponge over his face. Hold replaced the winger. With 15 minutes gone, Liverpool had hardly made a worthwhile attack and all the honour went to Bournemouth.

East missed a great opportunity to put Bournemouth into a shock lead after 20 minutes when standing six yards out. A low cross reached him, but he poked it first time a few inches wide of the goal. In the next minute he drove wide from the edge of the penalty area.

St.John, who had been working hard to no avail, broke through and took the ball to the by-line before pulling it back into the middle, but Jones intercepted. Strong and Thompson tried to force an opening from a long cross by Byrne, but as Thompson tried to slip the ball through for his centre-forward, Strong fell over and the opportunity was lost. With a dazzling dribble down the left, Thompson laid the foundations for Liverpool's first shot after 25 minutes. From his centre, Hunt swivelled and hit a shot towards the far post, but Jones managed to gather at full stretch. Strong was fouled just inside the Bournemouth half, and after Hunt headed the kick across the home goalmouth, Stocks had to step in at the last moment to prevent Callaghan from scoring. From the ensuing corner, Lawler headed wide.

After 32 minutes East got the ball in the Liverpool net when he deflected a hard low cross by Hold, but referee Leo Callaghan disallowed the score for offside. Full-back Gulliver had his name taken two minutes before the interval after a foul on Thompson. He had been guilty of several fouls on the Liverpool winger after Thompson had shown early on that he had the beating of him.

Early in the second period Hunt was robbed and the Bournemouth move ended with Kevin White having a shot blocked. Pound managed to reach a ball that seemed to be going out of play and centred. Instead of allowing Lawrence to gather the ball, Yeats headed it behind for a corner, which Lawrence eventually cleared. A foul by Smith on East brought Bournemouth a free-kick 15 yards outside the penalty area. Gulliver tried a low drive into the goalmouth, but the ball was blocked and cleared. Both defences dominated, and Lawrence's handling had been impeccable.

The home side almost took the lead after 67 minutes when, from a right-wing corner, Lawrence was unable to hold the ball and centre-half Jimmy White, who had come up, tried an overhead shot which went narrowly wide. Liverpool looked certain to be awarded a penalty when Stocks appeared to handle, but referee Callaghan refused to award the kick. Six policemen removed a spectator from the field after the penalty appeal had been turned down.

After 73 minutes, the ball crossed a packed Bournemouth goalmouth to the unmarked Hunt, who shot, but Stocks managed to block the effort and a certain goal. The ball rebounded to St.John, whose shot was also blocked. As the minutes ticked by, Liverpool swept onto the attack in relentless waves which threatened to overcome the Third Division side, who held on gallantly for a draw and a deserved replay.

The Cup-holders, Tottenham, drew 2-2 with Manchester United at Old Trafford, before winning the replay 1-0. Everton - this season's runners-up - beat Southport 1-0 away, while West Bromwich Albion, the eventual Cup-winners, drew 1-1 with Colchester United, before winning the replay 4-0 at home.

Bournemouth: Jones; Gulliver, J.White; Naylor, Stocks, Bumstead; K.White, Rowles, East, Pound, Bolton(Hold,15).

Liverpool: Lawrence; Lawler, Byrne; Smith, Yeats, Hughes; Callaghan, Hunt, Strong, St.John, Thompson.

Referee: Mr L. Callaghan (Merthyr Tydfil)

Attendance: 24,388

January 30, 1968

Liverpool (2) 4
Hateley 33, Thompson 44,
Hunt 51, Lawler 73

Bournemouth (0) 1
Hughes (o.g.) 74

WITH Gerry Byrne injured, Liverpool manager Bill Shankly had the option of introducing young full-back Peter Wall in place of Byrne, but he shuffled his pack and introduced Tony Hateley at centre-forward. Hateley -who had been dubbed football's most expensive substitute, returned after being dropped after Christmas following a spell of only two League goals in 17 games.

Liverpool: Lawrence; Lawler, Hughes; Smith, Yeats, Strong; Callaghan, Hunt, Hateley, St.John, Thompson.

Bournemouth: Jones; Gulliver, J.White; Naylor, Stocks, Bumstead; K.White, Rowles, East, Pound, Hall.

Referee: Mr L. Callaghan (Merthyr Tydfil)

Attendance: 54,075

The centre-forward came back after a four-match absence to prove to the Kop what he is like at his best. His distribution was immaculate - especially to Callaghan - and his presence in and around the penalty area was such a menace to the Bournemouth defence that panic set in.

Hateley eventually opened up the Bournemouth defence after 123 minutes of this Third Round tie. The goal was created by Tommy Smith, who, from his own penalty area, worked the ball, with the help of St.John, to the right wing, where he floated a magnificent centre for Hateley to bullet a header past Jones.

With some of the pressure off, Liverpool began to stroke the ball around with a calm assurance, and but for some hesitancy by Hunt, Liverpool might well have scored more than the four goals they did. Still somewhat tired after Saturday's efforts, Bournemouth continued to hold Liverpool in full attack for half-an-hour. The visitors had their heroes in twin centre-halves Jimmy White and Tommy Naylor. Kevin White worked hard in midfield while Keith East and Ken Pound covered a lot of ground for little reward up front.

Liverpool's victory was gained on the wings. Ian Callaghan was back in the form which won him a place in the England side, and Peter Thompson had the beating of his full-back. Liverpool's biggest star, alongside of Hateley, was the implacable Tommy Smith, who gave a great display in defence and was a man of ideas in attack. Emlyn Hughes, back to his natural full-back role after playing as a midfield man all season, seemed more comfortable and played well apart from a blunder when he put the ball into his own net 16 minutes from time. Adding the final touches to the Liverpool

rearguard was Ron Yeats, who dominated East in the air. St.John and Strong sealed up the midfield area and Liverpool produced some of their best football of the season which culminated in a relentless wave of attacks.

Thompson smashed in a second goal a minute before the interval with a shot that Jones was unable to hold, and Hunt rapped in a third after a brilliant Callaghan run. Chris Lawler scored a fourth for Liverpool a minute before Hughes turned East's low cross past Lawrence for Bournemouth's consolation goal.

__Emlyn Hughes__, back to his natural full-back rôle after playing as a midfield man all season, seemed more comfortable and played well apart from a blunder when he put the ball into his own net 16 minutes from time.

February 17, 1968

Walsall (0) 0

Liverpool (0) 0

TWENTY minutes before the start of the game two crush barriers behind the goal at the covered end gave way and about 100 youngsters were taken from the section to other parts of the ground which was packed with 21,000 fans. Seven minutes before the scheduled kick-off, Fellows Park resembled the famous Wembley scene of 1923. Behind the goal at the covered end the wall suddenly collapsed and thousands of fans were rushed onto the pitch. A large number of Liverpool fans stood at that end. At least one child was carried away on a stretcher. Police gradually managed to pack the fans back on to the terracing. The three-foot wall was down for half the length of the ground behind one goal.

The sloping pitch was very heavy and muddy and had been sanded in one half. Where the crowd had trampled on it. there were deep footmarks. Liverpool retained an unchanged side, and Walsall brought in 17-year-old centre-forward Derek Clarke for only his fourth game, and his third Cup-tie. Five minutes after the scheduled kick-off time Liverpool appeared for the pre-match kick-about, closely followed by Walsall. The home side eventually kicked off ten minutes late. Liverpool won the toss and decided to kick down the slope in the first half. Heavy overnight rain had turned the pitch into a quagmire and players found turning and control difficult.

The visitors did all the attacking in the early minutes and Third Division Walsall believed that Thompson was the biggest threat to them, for whenever he touched the ball he had at least two men racing in to tackle. Callaghan and St.John both worked hard to get Liverpool moving, but their efforts came to little against a stout and stubborn Walsall defence. Watson was Walsall's liveliest player in the early stages, but he was well marshalled by Hughes. The winger was given a superb pass by Jackson, but he held on to the ball too long and allowed Hughes to concede a corner.

When St.John and Hunt put Callaghan in possession near the corner flag, the winger beat Harris and chipped a dangerous cross into the Walsall goalmouth, where Wesson made a good catch. Hunt robbed Simpson just inside the Walsall half and ran 20 yards towards goal before slipping the ball to Hateley, who was closely marked.

Jackson, the former Birmingham inside-forward, proved to be the power in midfield for the home side. He tried to chip the ball through the middle for Taylor, but the left-winger was fractionally offside. Centre-half Bennett was the strong man in the Walsall defence, keeping a tight rein on Hateley. Liverpool had the best chance of the match after 25 minutes when St.John laid on a great pass for Hunt. The Liverpool man beat Wesson to the ball, but as he tried to lob it past him it hit the goalkeeper and was scrambled away. In defence Walsall produced the resolve normally associated with potential giant-killers, but it was the mud which prevented Liverpool getting into their rhythm. Callaghan collected a Smith pass after 31 minutes and beat two men before cutting in towards goal. From 25 yards out, he tried a shot which went narrowly wide of the far post.

Walsall were awarded a free-kick on the left-hand edge of the Liverpool penalty area when Smith brought down Taylor. The winger took the kick and tried a shot which was off target. Yeats cleared as Clarke raced in again. Play was held up for a minute while, on the request of Wesson, the referee asked for a policeman to go behind the goal at the open end of the ground. Liverpool then won a free-kick just outside the penalty area when Hunt was brought down. Smith tried to find Thompson, but Harris gave away a corner. The Walsall defence missed the flag kick, but so did the Liverpool players. Gregg then conceded another corner and from the kick a Lawler header was scrambled off the line by Gregg.

Liverpool surged into the attack when they kicked off in the second half. St.John tried to open the way to the Walsall goal with a ball to Callaghan, but from the winger's low cross the ball bobbed around the penalty area, with Walsall desperately blocking Liverpool's efforts. Parts of the pitch were ankle-deep in mud. The Third Division side sensed that they were still in the game with a chance, and they pressed forward, but St.John and Strong combined well to relieve the pressure. The game degenerated into a battle in the mud as both sides fought grimly for the opening goal. There was little constructive football, but Liverpool carried themselves forward with their weight and power. With 57 minutes gone, Walsall substituted Trevor Meath for Baker.

After 58 minutes, Liverpool had a great chance engineered by Thompson. From Hughes the ball went via Smith and Callaghan to Thompson on the left. He beat three men and cut in towards goal before sliding the ball back along the ground. Callaghan, racing in, hammered it three yards wide. The move brought a great surge in the crowd at the damaged end of the ground and another crush barrier was broken.

St.John played his heart out in the Liverpool cause, and Tommy Smith had an excellent game. Only a fine save by Lawrence prevented Walsall from taking the lead after 68 minutes. Taylor broke on the left wing and chipped the ball over the Liverpool defence to Watson. The right-winger mis-hit his shot, but it was still going in the left-hand corner of the net until Lawrence fisted the ball for a corner. Moments later Lawrence raced off his line and threw himself at the feet of the substitute, Meath, and the ball went for a corner. The Liverpool goalkeeper dropped the flag-kick, and Jackson sent a magnificent opportunity over the bar.

Lawrence's goal-kick was weak and went straight to Meath, but he blasted the ball yards wide with an open goal beckoning, when a delicate chip would have brought about a goal.

In the dying minutes, Wesson tipped over a 25-yard drive by Callaghan.

Substitute: Meath for Baker (57 minutes), Walsall

Referee: Mr M.A. Fussey (Retford)

Attendance: 21,066

Walsall

Wesson

Gregg   G.Harris

Simpson   Bennett   Atthey

Watson   Baker   D.Clarke   Jackson   Taylor

O

Thompson   St.John   Hateley   Hunt   Callaghan

Strong   Yeats   Smith

Hughes   Lawler

Lawrence

Liverpool

February 19, 1968

Liverpool (3) 5

Hateley 24, 33, 64, 71,
Strong 34

Walsall (0) 2

Watson 76, 89

TONY Hateley joined Alf Arrowsmith (1964) and Harold Barton (1932) as the only Liverpool players to hit four goals in an FA Cup tie. He nodded Callaghan's chip past Wesson in the 24th minute and he continually laid the ball up with precision and constantly lurked near the Walsall goal in a demonstration befitting a £100,000 centre forward.

On the previous Saturday, Hateley had looked far from convincing and Walsall fell into the trap of believing that Roger Hunt was the man they would have to watch in the replay. Hunt was rarely seen, but it left Hateley able to move through the fog at will and wreak havoc amongst Walsall's defence. Nine minutes after the first goal he finished off a great movement by Tommy Smith for his second goal. Liverpool were in complete control and Geoff Strong scored an opportunist goal after 34 minutes.

Walsall might have had an early goal through slackness in the Liverpool defence, but generally the home side moved the ball around with a degree of arrogance which no Third Division side could hope to match.

The Liverpool forwards spent most of the game pumping shots at an overworked Bob Wesson in the visitors' goal. Walsall's man of the match was Tommy Watson, who scored twice and was a constant thorn in Liverpool's side. Alec Jackson had a good game for Walsall, who were generally never in the game.

After 64 minutes Hateley volleyed home from a Hughes cross, and a half volley from a Callaghan chip after 71 minutes put Liverpool into a commanding lead. Two late goals from Watson hardly detracted from Liverpool's superior performance. Liverpool's victory in the fog pin-pointed the need for fresh thinking on whether games should be played or not under such conditions. As the rule stood, if the referee was satisfied that he could see both linesmen operating down the lines, and also see the corner flags from the centre, then the game was playable because it could be controlled. However, there were suggestions that the law should be changed so that the spectators should be considered. Over 39,000 spectators paid a great deal of money to see shadows flitting through the fog. It was proposed that the game should not go ahead if spectators behind one goal could not see what was happening at the other end. There were times when the fog lifted so that it was just possible from the Press Box to see who scored at the Anfield Road end of the ground. It was impossible to see in detail, but the impression through the haze was sufficient to detect the scorer.

Just after half-time, when the referee called the players off for eight minutes, it did not look as though the game would continue. It lifted sufficiently for the game to restart, but near the end the fog became more dense and it was difficult for the spectators to see what was happening. The farce was saved by the inimitable humour from the Kop fans which kept everyone highly amused. If they were unable to see through the fog, they would sing through it. Their chanted question, *"Who scored?"* was answered from the Anfield Road end by *"Tony Hateley"*. This was a clear indication of how little the Kopites could see.

Liverpool: Lawrence; Lawler, Hughes; Smith, Yeats, Strong; Callaghan, Hunt, Hateley, St.John, Thompson.

Walsall: Wesson; Gregg, G.Harris; Simpson, Bennett, Atthey; Watson, Baker, D.Clarke, Jackson, Taylor.

Referee: Mr M.A. Fussey (Retford)

Attendance: 39,113

*Left: **Tony Hateley***

March 9, 1968

Tottenham Hotspur (0) 1

Greaves 52

Liverpool (0) 1

Hateley 54

HALF an hour before the kick-off several Merseyside fans were escorted out of the ground by police from behind one of the goals. Liverpool were at full-strength as they took on the Cup-holders, who beat Preston North End 3-1 in the Fourth Round.

Tottenham Hotspur: Jennings; Knowles, Want; Mullery, England, Mackay; Robertson(Jones,79), Greaves, Chivers, Gilzean, Beal.

Liverpool: Lawrence; Lawler, Strong; Smith, Yeats, Hughes; Callaghan, Hunt, Hateley, St.John, Thompson.

Referee: Mr K. Howley (Durham)

Attendance: 54,005

Liverpool worked a great opening after only three minutes when Smith broke up a Spurs' attack and slipped the ball to St.John, who pushed a through ball to Callaghan. From the edge of the penalty area, the winger put in a shot which Jennings could not hold but which was deflected wide of a post for a corner. From the kick, Hateley hooked the ball high over the bar. Although Strong wore the number 3 shirt, Hughes played as left-back. Spurs won a corner off Hughes, but Lawrence rose to catch the kick from Greaves.

There was some trouble behind one goal and hundreds of fans spilled over the wall to sit on the gravel track. It looked as though a crush barrier had given way. A Smith tackle on Chivers gave the home side a free-kick 10 yards outside the penalty area, but Lawrence was quick off his line to take Mackay's chip at the second attempt. Both sides played open, attacking football and Liverpool won a corner on the left, but Jennings was fouled as he went up for Thompson's kick.

Spurs began to move around well and danger threatened from a long cross by Robertson, but as Gilzean raced in Lawrence did well to take the cross. England and Beal kept a tight rein on the Liverpool attack, while Mackay was the lynchpin of the London side. Liverpool looked the more dangerous side and as Hunt broke through his shot was deflected into the air and Jennings took the ball on his line. Up to this point in the game, Spurs had not had a direct shot on goal.

After 30 minutes, Callaghan put Hateley away down the right wing, and the centre-forward slipped a low cross to Hunt, who side-footed the ball towards goal, but it bounced on top of the bar and went behind. Spurs retaliated when Robertson burst through the Liverpool defence. Lawrence raced out of his penalty area and stuck out a leg to bring the winger down. Hateley, back in defence, got the free-kick

clear. Almost on the stroke of half-time, Tottenham had another great chance which fell to Greaves as he went streaking on to a through ball, but Lawrence came out to dive and take the ball from his feet.

The second half began in the same attacking vein as the first, with Strong trying to burst his way through for Liverpool and Mackay volleying a shot yards wide at the other end. After 52 minutes Greaves scored one of his typically brilliant goals, coming from nowhere to seize the opportunity. Jennings collected a Beal back-pass and punted a long ball upfield. Gilzean rose unchallenged to flick the ball on with his head and Greaves burst between Lawler and Yeats to smash a shot from a corner of the penalty box over Lawrence's head and into the net.

Two minutes later Tony Hateley equalised for Liverpool with a brilliant header. St.John picked up a loose ball, swivelled and chipped it into the middle, where Hateley soared above England to put a superb header wide of Jennings. Tottenham almost scored a minute after the equaliser.

Greaves burst through and laid on a fine chance for Chivers, but the centre-forward failed to control the ball and pushed it back for Greaves. Tommy Lawrence dived at the feet of Greaves once again to deny the dazzling forward.

St.John's superbly-judged pass allowed Hunt to run on to it, but the Liverpool inside-right did not have the speed to beat Jennings to the ball and the goalkeeper had to kick wildly to clear. Greaves missed a wonderful opportunity to put Spurs back in front after 61 minutes when he nodded a Chivers cross wide with the goal gaping in front of him.

Thompson wriggled his way past Knowles and then, from the edge of the area, sent in a shot which beat Jennings but flashed a foot wide of the far post. Only a brilliant save by Jennings kept out a Hunt header after 65 minutes after Thompson had supplied the chance. Thompson headed the ball across the goal where Hunt connected and forced Jennings to palm it over the bar as he dived backwards. Callaghan robbed Want, and as the full-back raced to recover, he conceded a corner. Hateley rose to Callaghan's flag kick, but Gilzean intercepted to nod the ball to safety. At this stage of the game, Liverpool more of the possession.

With 79 minutes gone, Spurs substituted Jones for Robertson. Almost immediately Greaves hooked a shot from a Mackay header only inches wide.

As both teams tired towards the end, the punch was missing in attack and it looked as though both teams settled for a draw. Liverpool had done a magnificent job in holding the Cup-holders on their own ground, and Spurs did not relish the prospect of facing Liverpool at Anfield, where they had not won for 56 years.

March 12, 1968

Liverpool (1) 2
Hunt 23, Smith (pen) 78

Tottenham Hotspur (0) 1
Jones 88

LIVERPOOL were unchanged, while Tottenham replaced Robertson with Venables. Roger Hunt, who was rarely out of the clutches of the fair-haired Phil Beal, put Liverpool on their way to victory with a cracking right-foot volley from a Jennings punch out that sped into the net off the underside of the bar.

The home side tried to force their advantage as they powered forward, but they repeatedly got lost in a forest of white legs as Tottenham packed their penalty area. Spurs continually pulled back ten men to repel Liverpool and they rarely had more than Chivers and Greaves in attack. Greaves had the ball in the back of the net after 33 minutes only to be ruled offside. He had the ball in the net again in the second half, but was palpably offside. Liverpool played a dangerous game in playing for offside, for Yeats was not the commanding figure he had been in the first game.

Tommy Smith played his usual dynamic game, while Emlyn Hughes had one of his best games at full-back. St.John's midfield contribution was considerable. Both Thompson and Callaghan had the beating of their full-backs, Knowles and Want, but their advantage was not put to good use. Thompson had the annoying habit of speeding past Knowles on several occasions only to double back and beat him again. Apart from his goal, Hunt never escaped the shackles of Beal, and Hateley failed to reproduce his earlier Cup form. Jimmy Greaves produced one of his finest displays to send the Liverpool defence into panic as he advanced goalwards.

Mullery had another fine game, while England, Jennings and Mackay excelled in the Spurs' defence. Spurs introduced Cliff Jones towards the end and he scored for them after 88 minutes, but his introduction cost Tottenham the match. While he was trying to get on to the field Jennings hauled down Hateley as he burst into the penalty area. Jones came on as Tommy Smith was about to take the kick, but Mackay had not left the pitch. It was a blunder for Spurs, because Jennings brilliantly saved the penalty. Referee Kevin Howley spotted 12 white shirts on the field and ordered the kick to be retaken, and Smith made no mistake to put Liverpool two goals ahead.

The match had not been a classic, but the Reds were through to the last eight.

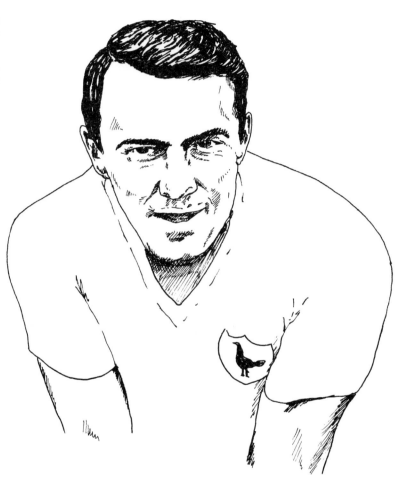

Jimmy Greaves, who produced one of his finest displays

Liverpool: Lawrence; Lawler, Strong; Smith, Yeats, Hughes; Callaghan, Hunt, Hateley, St.John, Thompson.

Tottenham Hotspur: Jennings; Knowles, Want; Mullery, England, Mackay(Jones,77); Venables, Greaves, Chivers, Gilzean, Beal.

Referee: Mr K. Howley (Billingham)

Attendance: 53,658

March 30, 1968

West Bromwich Albion (0) 0   Liverpool (0) 0

WITH his mind on next week's vital First Division battle with Manchester United at Old Trafford, Liverpool manager Bill Shankly took no risk when he named his side to meet West Bromwich Albion in the sixth round of the Cup at the Hawthorns. Tommy Smith and Tony Hateley were ruled out through injury and in their places, as last week, were Ian Ross and Alf Arrowsmith. Bobby Hope was ruled out of the Albion side, and in a reshuffle Dick Krzywicki came in on the right wing. Liverpool went on to beat Manchester United 2-1 with goals from Yeats (9) and Hunt (17) before a crowd of 63,050. Ross retained his place, but Arrowsmith was dropped in favour of Hateley. Ross and Arrowsmith played at 3 and 9 against Sheffield Wednesday at Hillsborough in a 2-1 win. Hunt gave Liverpool the lead after 27 minutes, and Arrowsmith gave the Reds a 2-1 victory with a goal two minutes from time.

West Bromwich Albion: Osborne; Colquhoun, Williams; Brown, Talbut, Fraser; Krzywicki, Kaye, Astle, Collard (Stephens,75), Clark.

Liverpool: Lawrence; Lawler, Hughes; Ross, Yeats, Strong; Callaghan, Hunt, Arrowsmith, St.John, Thompson.

Referee: Mr J.E. Carr (Sheffield)

Attendance: 53,062

Liverpool kicked off and tried to make progress down the left wing, but Albion hit back and were awarded a free-kick midway inside the Liverpool half when Hughes brought down Astle, but the Liverpool defence got the kick away easily. Then Clark gave Collard a chance but from the edge of the penalty box the inside-left shot across the face of the goal and inches wide. A promising Albion move was broken up when St.John robbed Astle, and in a quick break St.John tried to find Arrowsmith with a through ball, but Fraser was quick to cover. Both sides played some enterprising football and the early exchanges promised a fine match. Hughes lobbed a free-kick into the Albion penalty area and when Yeats went up with Osborne, the goalkeeper dropped the ball. A defender cleared the danger. Albion almost went ahead after 18 minutes when Brown found Collard on the right, but as the inside forward's low cross whipped into the goalmouth, Krzywicki was tackled by Ross as he was about to sidefoot the ball home.

Liverpool responded as Hunt put a shot well over the bar from the left-hand side of the penalty area. Then Brown picked up a clearance, and his shot from 20 yards spun a yard wide. Liverpool looked dangerous when Thompson slipped the ball through for Hunt to run on to, but Osborne was quick to save the danger as he left his line. The visitors had the greater share of the attacking play, but they found the Albion defence in resolute mood. A new ball was needed when the original one got stuck behind a hoarding on top of a stand. A long cross from Krzywicki looked dangerous with Astle lurking near the far post until Lawler stepped in to concede a corner, which proved fruitless.

Arrowsmith failed to connect with a cross from the left in the opening seconds of the second half, and Brown tried to burst through for West Bromwich, but Yeats managed to deflect his shot for a corner. The Albion gained a free-kick just outside the penalty area for obstruction by Yeats on Clark, but the kick was cleared with the whole of the Liverpool side back in their own penalty area. With 51 minutes gone, Arrowsmith squandered an easy opportunity. Talbut, attempting a clearance, kicked the ball against the centre-forward, and it rebounded to give Arrowsmith a clear run to goal. He raced away on his own but hit the ball straight at the advancing Osborne.

The home side had a chance when Krzywicki was put through, but the winger did not lift his shot high enough as Lawrence advanced and the 'keeper caught the ball above his head. Hunt dribbled in from the right, but he hesitated too long before shooting and an Albion defender stole in to tackle and concede a corner. From the flag-kick Strong hit a hard drive too high.

The Albion became too casual, and almost paid the ultimate penalty after 62 minutes when a throw-in by Lawler found Strong, who had acres of space just inside the Albion half. He collected the ball, moved forward, and from 30 yards sent a tremendous shot hammering against the Albion crossbar. Lawler tackled back well when Clark raced through after beating three Liverpool defenders. From the corner Talbut sent a header just over. After 75 minutes Albion substituted Stephens for Collard.

Liverpool confirmed their superiority as they surged into attack. Again the ball got stuck behind the hoarding on the roof of a stand, and the Albion provided another new one. Thompson forced Osborne to go full-length to save as Liverpool maintained their intense pressure.

SIXTH ROUND

Leeds United	1	Sheffield United	0
Leicester City	1	Everton	3
Birmingham City	1	Chelsea	0

*With 68 minutes gone, right-back Clarke sent Fraser away. The wing-half centred to Brown, whose left-foot cross found the head of **Astle** and the striker buried the ball in the net.*
(See report opposite)

__Ian Ross__, who deputised for Tommy Smith in the goalless draw against West Bromwich Albion
(See report over page)

April 8, 1968

Liverpool (1) 1   West Bromwich A. (0) 1 aet
Hateley 24   *Astle 68*

LIVERPOOL began as though they would tear Albion apart, a formula which had served them well in their current campaign, having been drawn away in every round, forcing a replay and then winning at Anfield. Tony Hateley banged in a goal after 24 minutes after Yeats had headed against the bar, and miskicked the rebound. Four minutes later Roger Hunt blazed a glorious opportunity a foot wide. The Albion, realising their impending salvation, stormed back into the game. Liverpool's powerful football evaporated under Albion's calm and precise response in the Anfield cauldron masterminded by Tony Brown, Doug Fraser, and Ian Collard. They tore into Liverpool and were worth their equaliser after 68 minutes when Jeff Astle leapt to put a perfectly-placed header wide of Lawrence from Brown's centre. It was Astle's 24th goal of the season. Then Brown just failed to convert a Fraser centre as the Albion attacked with relish, and Yeats had to race back to hook a Collard lob off the line as the visitors dominated the game.

Albion began intent on defending. Colquhoun marked Hateley and Talbut played as sweeper, while Clarke, Williams and Fraser maintained Albion's poise at the back. Liverpool displayed their traditional attacking policy early in the game, and with only four minutes gone St.John and Callaghan combined cleverly down the right and created an opportunity for Hateley to nod the ball forward, but Fraser headed the ball out of danger. Then Strong attempted a shot from outside the box which sailed inches over the bar before Thompson tried a shot which Osborne saved. Then the winger sent in a low drive which went across the face of the goal and passed narrowly wide of the post. Astle skimmed the crossbar for the Albion after 15 minutes, and Brown forced Lawrence to save a free-kick.

With 24 minutes gone, Liverpool went into the lead. Williams obstructed Thompson just outside the box, and St.John floated the free-kick across to Yeats, whose header struck the post. The centre-half miskicked as he tried to force the rebound home, but Osborne punched the ball away. Hateley, however, was in the right position to intercept and smash the ball home. The Kop erupted.

The Albion pressed diligently throughout the first half and Fraser netted the ball from a cross by Kaye, but the referee had blown for offside.

Soon in the second half, Thompson went on a magnificent run and shot wide. At the opposite end, Collard shot over the crossbar. Then Thompson drove a shot inches wide, before Hunt's shot flew wide of the angle. West Bromwich showed great determination and some flair, but they lacked the guile to break down the Liverpool defence. Fraser and Brown moved up with the strikers, and Liverpool were at full stretch to stem the tide as the visiting forwards constantly changed their positions, and the defenders overlapped down the wings.

With 68 minutes gone, right-back Clarke sent Fraser away. The wing-half centred to Brown, whose left-foot cross found Astle's head, and the striker buried the ball in the net.

In defence Talbut had a magnificent game as he kept Roger Hunt on a tight rein, and he also found the time to be in the right place when danger threatened from another source. In equally dominant mood beside him were Colquhoun, Clark and Williams.

Liverpool never found the rhythm which took them to a glorious victory at Old Trafford and at Anfield against Spurs in the previous round. They missed Tommy Smith, who would have taken the game by the scruff of its neck and put his team back on top as the game began to slip from their grasp. Ross, for all his genuine qualities, did not possess Smith's power to dominate a match, and with Yeats having a slow start, it was left to Hughes to star in defence.

After being troubled by Clive Clark early on, Chris Lawler gradually asserted himself and blotted the left-winger out after the interval and throughout extra-time. Standing alongside Hughes in the battle for honours in a game which tested the courage of men was Ian St.John, who supplied all of Liverpool's craft and guile until he limped off after 114 minutes with an attack of cramp and was substituted by Bobby Graham. The Liverpool forward line rarely found a way past a dominant Albion defence and the visitors had the better chances.

Liverpool: Lawrence; Lawler, Hughes; Ross, Yeats, Strong; Callaghan, Hunt, Hateley, St.John (Graham,114), Thompson.

West Bromwich Albion: Osborne; Clarke, Williams; Fraser, Talbut, Colquhoun; Kaye, Brown, Astle, Collard, Clark.

Referee: Mr J.E. Carr (Sheffield)

Attendance: 54,273

April 18, 1968

Liverpool (1) 1   West Bromwich Albion (1) 2
Hateley 39   *Astle 7, Clark 60*

THE East Lancashire Road was the scene of a huge traffic jam and many Liverpool supporters missed much of the game. Hundreds of fans arriving in coaches did not get in until an hour after the start, just in time to see Albion's winning goal. The Liverpool FC coach was guided expertly through the back-streets of the city of Manchester by reserve team coach Joe Fagan, on familiar territory, heading for the ground where he began his football career, but it still took two hours to arrive at Maine Road from Anfield.

The Albion were overall the more controlled and inventive side and they took their chances well to beat a Liverpool side which was strangely sterile in ideas and which panicked when they conceded the second goal on the hour. Any composure they possessed vanished and they relied too heavily on high balls pumped up the middle in the vain hope that someone might run on to the end of one of them. Liverpool were faced by a cool and extremely competent Albion defence in which Talbut, Williams, Fraser and Kaye stood out, but Albion's man-of-the-match was Bobby Hope. His deft control, precision passing and mental work-rate reminded the crowd of Bobby Collins.

The pass that laid on the opening goal from Jeff Astle after only seven minutes was a gem. It split the Liverpool defence and left Astle clear to send a finely placed shot into the narrow gap between Lawrence and the post. It was Albion's first attack, and the signal for Liverpool to unleash all their power and ferocity in attack. After the white-hot atmosphere engendered in the Anfield cauldron, these two fine sides continued to battle it out all the way.

Roger Hunt emerged as the man most likely to pierce the Albion defence. Osborne twice saved from Hunt's shots, and then Lawler headed off the line from Astle, who later headed straight into Lawrence's arms. Ian St.John was booked for a foul on Clark as Liverpool fought valiantly for an equaliser, which arrived after 39 minutes and followed a superb piece of refereeing from Jim Finney. He played the advantage rule after Callaghan had been fouled and the winger galloped on to float a centre on to Hateley's head while the Albion defence stood waiting for a foul to be given. Hateley calmly picked his spot and gave his side the position of equality their play deserved.

Hunt mis-kicked at a chance presented to him after St.John had shot across the face of the goal in the opening minute of the second half. A quarter of an hour later Clark settled the issue. After Dennis Clarke had had little success against Peter Thompson in the first half, he was substituted by Ken Stephens for the second half. Brown dropped back and kept the winger under control, denying Liverpool one source of attack. Thereafter the ball came either down the right or through the middle and Hateley rarely had a genuine opportunity.

Throughout the game Hope directed the proceedings like a conductor at an orchestra and Albion's calm assurance and threat of a surprise breakaway always threatened danger. While Hope continued to spray the ball around, Astle was always a potential menace to the overworked Liverpool defence which grew more fragile as the game unfolded. Helping to blunt Liverpool's desperate thrusts was John Kaye, playing as a second centre-half alongside Talbut in the absence of Colquhoun, with his head bandaged after a first half injury. Albion's more controlled football and poise was the way Liverpool used to play in their great years of success, power and determination added to make a mighty and formidable combination.

With only one victory to show for their last five matches in nine days, Liverpool had to travel to West Ham in the knowledge that only a victory would suffice. With their Cup ambitions shattered Liverpool had to go all out for the League title as their only opportunity to qualify for Europe.

West Bromwich Albion beat Birmingham City 2-0 in the semi-final, and eventually beat Everton 1-0 at Wembley with a goal from Jeff Astle in the first period of extra-time. Astle had scored in every round of the Cup. The Albion side that day was: Osborne; Fraser, Williams; Brown, Talbut, Kaye(Clarke); Lovett, Collard, Astle, Hope, Clark.

Liverpool: Lawrence; Lawler, Hughes; Smith, Yeats, Strong; Callaghan, Hunt, Hateley, St.John, Thompson.

West Bromwich Albion: Osborne; Clarke (Stephens,46), Williams; Fraser, Talbut, Kaye; Brown, Collard, Astle, Hope, Clark.

Referee: Mr J. Finney (Wellington, Hereford)

Linesmen: Mr S. Poulton (Red Flag);
           Mr R. Bassindale (Yellow Flag)

Attendance: 56,139 (at Maine Road)

January 4, 1969

Liverpool (0) 2

Hunt 70,
Callaghan 84

Doncaster Rovers (0) 0

DONCASTER made three positional forward changes, Jeffrey moving to the left wing with Webber crossing over to the right and Rabjohn moving inside. Alun Evans, the former Wolves teenager, made his Cup début for the Reds. Doncaster included John Ogston in goal, the Liverpool reserve goalkeeper. Doncaster were guided to Goodison Park by mistake before finding their way to Anfield, where they arrived in good time.

The game got off to a vigorous start with five fouls, four of them by the Fourth Division side, in the first two minutes. From the last by Robertson on Evans just outside the penalty area, St.John touched the free-kick to Smith who forced Ogston to a fine save.

Smith and Strong drove Liverpool forward and the majority of the play was in the Doncaster half. Liverpool won a corner when a Callaghan centre was deflected behind and another when a Lawler shot was deflected. From the flag-kick the ball came out to Evans, who tried a shot that Ogston turned magnificently over the bar.

Doncaster only left Webber upfield as Liverpool threw themselves into the attack. When Regan barged Strong over after only 13 minutes it was the Fourth Division side's eighth foul and it earned Regan a stern warning from referee Gow. After 16 minutes Callaghan chipped the ball back from the touch-line and Lawler headed a yard wide. A minute later the name of Doncaster's John Flowers went into the book after he had committed the tenth Doncaster foul by upending Hughes. The Fourth Division side seemed to be aware of the fact that they could not match the skill and pace of their First Division opponents and were therefore out to stop them by fair means or foul.

Ogston - on loan to Doncaster - had a fine game for the Rovers as Liverpool attacked relentlessly in a red tide. The visitors' first real attack arrived after 26 minutes when Webber, with a neat piece of play on the right wing, rounded Yeats and cut in on the Liverpool goal, but with the rest of the defence racing back he had to shoot from an oblique angle and Lawrence saved. The home side played all the football, which was pretty at times, but their opponents withdrew all their players into defence and Liverpool struggled to find a way through. Wilcockson, the full-back, was the next player to be booked after a foul on Thompson, who was kicked on his left thigh by Wilcockson as he went for the ball. The crowd became incensed at Doncaster's methods of survival and they slow-handclapped, jeered and chanted *"We want football"*. Liverpool refused to be drawn into retaliation and kept their minds on the job of beating Doncaster by playing football. Evans charged down a pass from Strong, swivelled

to beat three men and got in a shot which flew inches wide with Ogston diving in vain.

Smith was hurt in a tackle with Regan but he resumed after several minutes treatment. His left knee caused him problems. Strong fouled Rabjohn on the edge of the penalty area and it almost cost Liverpool a goal. Jeffrey took a hard, low curling free-kick and Hughes, who was positioned by the near post, headed the ball off the line. Seconds later Hunt hooked an overhead shot inches wide of a post from a Callaghan centre. The teams left the field at the interval amid a storm of protest and boos directed at the illegal and unnecessary tactics shown by Doncaster.

Liverpool attacked the Kop in the second half, but Doncaster maintained their reliance on the over-physical aspects of the game. In the first minute of the second half, Thompson and Callaghan went close. Thompson shot straight at Ogston and Callaghan shot narrowly wide. Regan and Yeats were involved in a continual battle throughout the game and whenever Yeats chose to move up in attack, Regan immediately followed him and there was a lot of pushing and shoving between the two players. Thompson revelled in the freedom afforded him down the left wing and his shot brought Ogston to his knees as he collected a low centre from the winger.

Hughes was Liverpool's director of play with his ceaseless running, capacity for hard work and with an eye for an opening. Evans, up front, had shown some delicate touches when he had been able to keep clear of some tough tackling by Robertson. Liverpool's offensive policy almost brought a goal as Evans pivoted a shot over the bar. Smith shot inches wide as Liverpool maintained their superiority. Hunt got the ball in the net after 66 minutes, but the referee disallowed the goal for the use of hands by Evans a moment earlier. Two minutes later a good run down the left by Hughes ended as he cut in along the touch-line and passed to Evans, whose shot was deflected by a defender on to the top of the bar and over. Seconds later a thunderous volley by Hunt from 20 yards whistled past the post.

Liverpool eventually took the lead after 70 minutes when the ball went between Thompson, Smith and Lawler before the full-back's shot rebounded from a defender to Hunt, who crashed the ball into the net from 10 yards. An incredible flying save by Ogston prevented Callaghan from putting Liverpool further ahead after 80 minutes when he turned the winger's shot for a corner.

Six minutes from time, Callaghan killed off Doncaster's lingering hopes of a draw with a magnificent right-foot drive which gave Ogston no chance of saving. Hughes initiated the goal with a high-speed burst through the middle and a pass to the left wing to Thompson, who slipped the ball along the edge of the penalty area, where Callaghan hit his shot. The Cup-holders, West Bromwich Albion, beat Norwich City 3-0 at the Hawthorns, while Manchester City, this season's Cup-winners, beat Luton Town 1-0 at Maine Road. Leicester City - beaten finalists - drew 1-1 with Barnsley, before winning 2-1 at Filbert Street. Everton beat Ipswich Town 2-1.

Liverpool: Lawrence; Lawler, Strong; Smith, Yeats, Hughes; Callaghan, Hunt, Evans, St.John, Thompson.

Doncaster Rovers: Ogston; Wilcockson, Clish; Flowers, Robertson, Haselden; Webber, Rabjohn, Regan, Johnson, Jeffrey.

Referee: Mr W.J. Gow (Swansea)

Attendance: 48,330

Roger Hunt, who crashed the ball into the net from ten yards for Liverpool's first goal

January 25, 1969

Liverpool (2) 2
Smith (pen) 13,
Hughes 23

Burnley (1) 1
Latcham 35

ROGER Hunt - who broke the Liverpool goalscoring record against Chelsea last week - received a hero's welcome. The rest of the Liverpool team ran out, lined up and then applauded Hunt as he came out. The fans also gave him a tremendous ovation in recognition of his record of 234 league goals which beat the previous highest set up by Gordon Hodgson in the 1930s. Sheila Cannon, 20, the Burnley fan from Todmorden, injured after the Boxing Day match when a brick smashed her coach window, arrived forty-five minutes before the kick-off as the guest of the Liverpool club and watched from a seat in the Directors' Box. There was some crowd trouble before the game when one fan was carried out from the corner of the Kop by four policemen after a scuffle.

Liverpool: Lawrence; Lawler, Strong; Smith, Yeats, Hughes; Callaghan, Hunt, Evans, St.John, Thompson.

Burnley: H.Thomson; W.Smith, Latcham; Bellamy (Kindon,65), Waldron, Blant; Thomas, Coates, Casper, Collins, J.Thomson.

Referee: Mr J. Finney (Wellington, Hereford)

Attendance: 53,677

Only a magnificent save by Tommy Lawrence after 11 minutes prevented Burnley from taking the lead. A Yeats clearance rebounded from Thomas, and the winger raced clear of the defence and on into the penalty area. Lawrence judged his dive brilliantly, and went down at the winger's feet to block his shot. This game was full of excitement and interest. Peter Thompson swung over a cross from the left and Hunt hit it low on the volley to Thomson's left. Seconds later Hunt rocketed in a shot which Thomson managed to palm away. Less than a minute later Hughes sent in a curling shot from 25 yards which soared towards the top right-hand corner and curled away from the goalkeeper. Full-back Wilf Smith was on hand to palm the ball to safety at the expense of a penalty.

Tommy Smith sent Thomson the wrong way with the spot-kick. Burnley tackled quickly and showed that they were capable of breaking out at speed and a fine move between Latcham and Coates ended with Thomas centring and Lawrence plucking the ball off the head of Casper.

A tremendous shot from Hughes put the Reds two up after 23 minutes. He picked up an intended clearance outside the penalty area, held off the tackle of Bellamy and crashed in a tremendous shot just under the bar.

Burnley retaliated and Yeats was forced to dive across his own penalty area to keep out a shot from Casper. With 27 minutes gone, Burnley were robbed of a goal after an amazing offside decision. Collins, working well on the right, moved goalwards and hit a hard, low cross which Latcham burst on to and slipped back for Casper to push into the net from close range. A linesman's flag was raised and referee Finney disallowed Burnley's claims for a goal. Collins, Coates and Thomas fought hard to unlock one of the meanest defences in the League. Collins inspired Burnley with a great display and Yeats got in the way of a powerful shot from the inside-forward. Lawrence then dived at the feet of Casper as the centre-forward almost reached a loose ball in the penalty area. The industrious Collins orchestrated a move which resulted in Burnley scoring. Collins put Coates away on the right wing and from the by-line, Coates pulled the ball back low for Latcham by the near post to flick the ball over Lawrence and into the net.

Thompson twisted his way past Burnley defenders to set up a chance for Evans, whose tremendous shot crashed inches over the bar. Collins sent Coates racing down the right again, but Yeats went across to concede a corner from which Blant shot wide. Liverpool were forced to defend desperately at times. Just before the interval, Thompson handled the ball and Burnley's free-kick was punched away to safety by Lawrence.

St.John laid on a chance for Evans to send a first time shot straight into the goalkeeper's arms as Liverpool moved onto the attack as the second half opened. Thomson was called upon again, flinging himself out of goal to intercept a cross from Hunt as Evans threatened danger. A great move involving Hunt, Thompson and Evans almost brought a goal, but from the edge of the penalty area Evans shot narrowly wide of the post.

Two basic errors by Burnley defenders almost brought two goals in a minute. Thomson dropped the ball almost on his goalline with no-one challenging, but he managed to grab the ball before it rolled over. Then a complete mis-kick by Waldron allowed Callaghan to move in for a clear shot from 15 yards, but he blazed his shot wide. Moments later a St.John lob from Thompson's chip had the Burnley goalkeeper cartwheeling backwards to flick the ball over the bar. From the corner, Lawler had a shot blocked by Blant. With 65 minutes gone, Burnley substituted Bellamy and brought on Kindon. Thomson was forced to concede a corner to prevent Hunt from scoring after a free-kick from Strong. Shortly afterwards Hughes had a shot blocked. After 74 minutes, Liverpool were fortunate not to concede a goal when a cunningly-placed free-kick by Thomas was headed against the bar by Casper. Towards the finish Yeats was injured but he carried on after treatment.

March 1, 1969

Leicester City (0) 0   Liverpool (0) 0

THE pitch was in a terrible condition with a covering of sand and the lines painted on it in blue. The sand covered a thick layer of mud which, as well as snow and ice had been the reason the tie had been delayed for three weeks and postponed six times.

Liverpool moved swiftly onto the attack with Hunt down the left, and his pass inside to Hughes allowed the midfielder to test Shilton with a 25-yard drive. Clarke then combined with Lochhead on the left, and the centre-forward swung over a centre which Roberts hit first time to bring a superb save from Lawrence, who parried the ball for Yeats to clear.

The Liverpool defence was in good form, and Leicester had no genuine opportunities. From a flag-kick Hughes shot high over the bar. With 13 minutes gone, Glover moved down the left, but his cross went over the heads of the lurking Lochhead and Fern. Nish then beat three defenders before unleashing a powerful 25-yard drive which rebounded off the chest of Lawrence, but he recovered to deny Clarke. Yeats rescued Liverpool when Glover moved inside to threaten Lawrence, and then Callaghan moved in from the right and chipped the ball forward, but Evans was unable to reach the ball, and Shilton collected.

Liverpool began to dominate the game but Glover forced Lawrence to produce a magnificent one-handed save while diving to his right. Glover then centred from the left and Lochhead beat Yeats in the air for the first time and his header was only inches wide. Liverpool hit back when Thompson sprinted down the left and centred hard and low, but although the ball reached Hunt, he was unable to control it. Five minutes before the interval, Callaghan crossed from the left, and with Hunt and Evans lurking, Shilton tried to punch clear, but the ball fell to St.John, whose lobbed header scraped the bar.

A foul by Rodrigues on the left gave Liverpool a free-kick. With Evans challenging strongly for the ball, Shilton palmed down Thompson's free-kick, and then dived on the ball as the predatory Hunt raced in. Hunt was then brought down just outside the penalty area, and Smith's free-kick rebounded off the defensive wall.

Liverpool maintained their attacking policy and a cross from Thompson found Evans, whose shot struck a defender and spun over the bar. With 66 minutes gone, Hunt had an opportunity to score. He worked his way into a shooting position inside the box, but angled his shot past Shilton and beyond the post.

Five minutes from the finish, Lochhead ran clear of the Liverpool defence, and Lawrence sprinted off his line to block the ball with his body.

With three minutes to go, Liverpool had shots by Hunt and Evans blocked. In a rousing finish, Hughes sent in two magnificent shots, one of which passed just wide, and the other which brought a great save from Shilton. Hunt shot over the bar from the loose ball. Shilton also saved from St.John as Liverpool fought desperately hard for the goal which would secure victory.

Peter Shilton, *who was in inspired form for Leicester*

Leicester City: Shilton; Rodrigues, Nish; Roberts, Sjoberg, Cross; Fern, Gibson, Lochhead, Clarke, Glover.

Liverpool: Lawrence; Lawler, Strong; Smith, Yeats, Hughes; Callaghan, Hunt, Evans, St.John, Thompson.

Referee: Mr B.J. Homewood (Sunbury-on-Thames)

Attendance: 42,002

March 3, 1969

Liverpool (0) 0

Leicester City (1) 1

Lochhead 34

THE talking point of this game was not Andy Lochhead's goal after 34 minutes, nor Tommy Smith's missed penalty after 39 minutes, but Roger Hunt's substitution after 72 minutes when he was replaced by Bobby Graham. Hunt was seen to take off his shirt and throw it down in disgust and anger as he disappeared down the tunnel. Hunt himself described the incident in his autobiography *Hunt For Goals*, Pelham Books, 1969, page 105 : "...We got a 0-0 draw, and I think everyone was pretty sure that we would be all right in the replay. But it didn't turn out like that. It turned out to be a nightmare ... because for the only time in my career I was taken out of a game. Midway through the second half, when we were trailing to a fine header by Andy Lochhead, I was told to come off. I could not believe what was happening, for although I had not been playing well, I knew that Bill Shankly has never made much use of substitutes. Unlike some managers, he does not go in for putting the 12th man on the field unless an injury makes it necessary. I was so worked up about the way the game was going, and so surprised, that for a moment or two I did not react. Then, when it sank in, I must admit that I lost my temper. I marched off, pulling my jersey over my head and throwing it down. Since then, of course, I have had time to think it over. The decision was the manager's, and I should have accepted it as such. I still do not think that Bill Shankly was right to bring me off, but he's the boss, and he's entitled to do what he thinks best, at any time. I am certain he was doing what he thought best at that moment, even though it was a terrible blow to me..."

Leicester took the lead after 34 minutes with a move of swift and simple brilliance. Gibson moved the ball rapidly out of his own half upfield to Fern, who slipped it to the left where Glover neatly beat Lawler to float the ball dangerously into the Liverpool goalmouth. Lochhead beat Yeats in a heading duel and placed a header out of Lawrence's reach. Leicester then fell back and relied on mass defence to protect their single-goal lead.

Shilton was in inspired form in the Leicester goal and he made two incredible saves from St.John and Thompson before Cross handled the ball and Liverpool were awarded a penalty. Smith angled the ball low and to the goalkeeper's left. On the morning of the match Shilton remembered being beaten by a Smith penalty in the League game at Anfield and had been practising saving penalties to his left in preparation for the Cup-tie. Shilton lunged to his left and, although the kick was hard and accurate, Shilton palmed it to safety and from that moment on, Liverpool were virtually out of the competition. Liverpool's football up to that point had been hurried and frantic and so frenetic that it contained little

method or direction; it was founded on the erroneous belief that goals were inevitable if they spent a great deal of time in their opponents' half. Leicester, for their part, were content to soak up all the pressure and protect their solitary lead. They had the players who were well-equipped to follow that plan. Liverpool lacked a general, an orchestrator who could slow them down to an even tempo before unleashing a destructive note. They hurled long, high balls into the Leicester penalty area and failed to create any genuine goalscoring opportunities. Leicester were brilliant in their exploitation of Liverpool's naivety. Cross missed little in the air, Nish marshalled his team well, and Roberts cut off innumerable balls with unnerving anticipation and excellent positioning. Shilton was brilliant between the posts, though the Liverpool forwards were too content to shoot from long-range, although his handling of the ball in the air was immaculate.

After his penalty miss, Smith's game deteriorated rapidly. He inexplicably lost the confidence which was the hallmark of his game and committed several errors. The responsibility of taking a game by the scruff of its neck fell upon Hughes, and although he tried hard and played well, he found little response from his team-mates. The forwards, apart from Evans, were sadly out of touch. Hunt's substitution was justified for he had rarely made any impression on the game and had been unable to get in a shot. Thompson, Callaghan and St.John had also been guilty of making no impression and Evans strove valiantly in an attempt to salvage the game for Liverpool. Evans was sharp and alert despite the fact that his shooting was off-target. Against men of the height of Cross and Sjoberg, the Liverpool centre-forward stood little chance of success, particularly in the air. It was largely a lone battle up front for Evans. Leicester might easily have increased their lead in the second half but for the excellence of Tommy Lawrence in goal. He flung himself fearlessly at opponents' feet as they were clear through on two occasions, once to repel Fern and then to deny Lochhead.

Liverpool: Lawrence; Lawler, Strong; Smith, Yeats, Hughes; Callaghan, Hunt(Graham,72), Evans, St.John, Thompson.

Leicester City: Shilton; Rodrigues, Nish; Roberts, Sjoberg, Cross; Fern, Gibson(Manley,86), Lochhead, Clarke, Glover.

Referee: Mr J.K. Taylor (Wolverhampton)

Attendance: 54,666

January 7, 1970

Coventry City (1) 1
Martin 27

Liverpool (1) 1
Graham 30

WREXHAM, the Fourth Division opponents waiting for the eventual winners of this tie, were watching both teams at Highfield Road as Liverpool fought back to earn a draw. Wrexham, winners in the First Round by 4-1 away to Spennymoor, beat Hartlepool United 1-0 away in the Second Round and Norwich City 2-1 away in the Third Round.

Coventry attempted to use their home advantage and the wintry conditions and continually lobbed high balls into the Liverpool goalmouth, hoping that the firm conditions would unsettle Liverpool's rearguard in the air. The visitors did have difficulty getting spring from the treacherous pitch, but the defence made up for that inadequacy with great determination. Apart from the long ball into the goalmouth, Coventry had few other attacking ideas and Ian Ross shadowed Willie Carr brilliantly, cutting off the home side's main threat and chief initiator of attacking movements. Carr rarely figured in Coventry's offensive tactics and their rhythm suffered as a result.

Liverpool had St.John and Callaghan at their best in midfield and they provided some delightful touches in the conditions. Callaghan made Liverpool's 30th minute equaliser for Bobby Graham after Martin had given the home side the lead just three minutes earlier. The irrepressible Callaghan nodded a perfect headed pass that split the Coventry defence and although they vainly appealed for offside, Graham took control. Clements, on the far side of the field, played Graham onside and with Barry recovering, Graham coolly swerved to his left and, as Glazier advanced, slipped his shot under the goalkeeper's body and into the net.

The visitors began to take command after a long, early spell of Coventry pressure, but the home side took the lead with a goal which stemmed from a foul by Lawler on Hunt. From the free-kick taken by Clements, the ball was lofted into the Liverpool goalmouth and Martin rose in front of the defence to glance a header down just inside the far post.

The quality of the play suffered in the second half, though a moment of high drama occurred when referee James denied Coventry a penalty when Martin went sprawling following Strong's challenge. Strong, however, was Liverpool's man-of-the-match. He had given great service in all the nine positions he had occupied in the team, but he was at his best as a defensive wing-half. He covered for any mistakes that his colleagues made. Callaghan also had a great game, as he worked ceaselessly and kept his balance as he broke up Coventry attacks and set Liverpool onto the attack.

St.John never stopped chipping away at the Coventry defence searching for openings which would have given the visitors the tie at the first time of asking.

In the second period, Hughes stormed through into the penalty area to meet Callaghan's cross. Glazier made a magnificent diving save to his left to keep the wing-half's header out.

The awkwardly bouncing ball in the conditions had both teams in trouble throughout the game, and Tommy Lawrence performed well to keep out a first-half overhead kick by Martin. He also parried another shot from the centre-forward, who was the best player on the home side. Despite the frozen surface, each trainer was called onto the pitch only once throughout the game, which was keenly fought.

Geoff Strong

Coventry City: Glazier; Coop, Clements; Machin, Barry, Blockley; Hunt, Carr, Martin, O'Rourke, Mortimer(Setters,77)

Liverpool: Lawrence; Lawler, Wall; Strong, Yeats, Hughes; Callaghan, Ross, Thompson, St.John, Graham.

Referee: Mr V. James (York)

Attendance: 33,688

January 12, 1970

Liverpool (1) 3

Ross 39, Thompson 54,
Graham 72

Coventry City (0) 0

LIVERPOOL - with Ian Callaghan surprisingly off form - produced a dazzling display which dispatched Coventry from the Cup and left Liverpool manager Bill Shankly proclaiming that his side would win the Cup. There was a blow for Coventry when they discovered they would have to play without 19-year-old left-half, Jeff Blockley, who had developed into one of the most reliable and consistent defenders in the country. Blockley was left out for the first time this season, when he reported yesterday that he was still troubled by a leg injury he received against Manchester City on the previous Saturday. Maurice Setters, who had not been on the losing side for the Sky Blues this season, was in the party, and manager Noel Cantwell named him as Blockley's replacement.

The Reds were at their brilliant best as they harnessed patience and composure to their undoubted skill and capacity for hard endeavour. The headlong dashes and streams of centres into a packed penalty area aimed at two front runners, were a thing of the past at Anfield. With Graham on the right and Thompson on the left stretching the opposing defence wide open, any number of players could exploit the huge gaps as they came through from behind. Once again Willie Carr was shackled by the immaculate Ian Ross, and St.John was enabled to utilise the space in midfield. The wily Scot used the space to the full, spraying passes around the entire pitch and splitting the visiting defence wide open on numerous occasions with inch-perfect passes which were brilliantly weighted. The drive and energy of Emlyn Hughes helped Liverpool to dominate the game, and the wing skills of Thompson and Graham added to Coventry's problems. The first goal arrived six minutes before the interval. Thompson dashed to the line, leaving Coop in his trail. Ross, temporarily leaving Carr behind, with a delicate flick of the head, sent the ball rifling into the bottom corner of the net. Coventry responded in a belligerent manner and their tackles up to the interval became reckless and dangerous. Clements was booked for a foul on Hughes and Barry was booked after he kicked the ball away in disgust.

Liverpool were firmly in control in the second period. Thompson cut in from the left and flashed a low, right-foot shot inside the near post after 54 minutes and Coventry's fate was sealed. The Reds began to play exhibition football, holding onto their lead and spraying passes all around the field. With 72 minutes gone, Graham scored the goal of the match to seal a fine individual performance. Strong's shot was blocked and the ball ricocheted out to Callaghan, who chipped to the far post where Hughes headed it back into the middle. Although the ball bounced awkwardly waist high behind Graham, he managed to pivot and hook an incredible shot into the goal in one elegant movement.

Ernie Hunt, Coventry's former Everton forward said after the game, "We should have beaten Liverpool at Coventry. That was our chance, and we didn't take it. Naturally I'm bitterly disappointed, more so because I used to be across the park and wanted to win here to-night. It's the first time we've been here and been really beaten."

John Neal, the Wrexham manager, said: "It was a very good performance by Liverpool. I was very impressed. I think we have a chance, but it is an honour and a privilege for the lads to come here and play at Anfield."

Liverpool manager, Bill Shankly said, "We played well. It was a fantastic performance. Don't forget, Coventry have lost only nine goals away from home this season and we put three past them to-night. We are now scoring as many goals as we ever scored at our peak. We are setting the pattern for the future if teams have the men to exploit it. When we had Hunt, he was always very closely marked and there was a jam up front. Now the opposition never know who is coming through next. And there is more space in midfield through Ross's work, and the result is being seen in St.John's play."

Bobby
Graham

Liverpool: Lawrence; Lawler, Wall; Strong, Yeats, Hughes; Callaghan, Ross, Thompson, St.John, Graham.

Coventry City: Glazier; Coop, Cattlin; Machin, Barry, Setters; Hunt, Carr, Martin, O'Rourke, Clements.

Referee: Mr V. James (York)

Attendance: 51,261

January 24, 1970

Liverpool (0) 3
Graham 51, 73,
St.John 59

Wrexham (1) 1
Smith 24

ANFIELD was packed for the return of Tommy Smith in the number 8 shirt, and for the Cup début of Ray Clemence in for the injured Tommy Lawrence. Liverpool's two boys pleased the crowd, and the Rolf Harris song, *Two Little Boys*, was still at number one in the UK charts after six weeks.

As Clemence took his place in the Kop goal for the kick-off, he was given a huge ovation. He was soon in action as the first shot came from Wrexham - a hard-hit low 25-yard shot from Griffiths as he cut in from the left, which Clemence took comfortably at the foot of the post. Wrexham carried the game to their hosts, but Liverpool soon forced their way into the game and they came within inches of being awarded a penalty after seven minutes when Wall's free-kick after Ingle had brought down Hughes was handled by centre-forward Ray Smith, who was back helping his defence. The referee awarded a free-kick inches outside the penalty area. With nine minutes gone Gaskell produced a daring save from Hughes, who began the move in midfield with a pass to St.John, who chipped it into the goalmouth for Graham to nod the ball down for the incoming Hughes.

The visitors attacked in rare moments and whenever Liverpool moved onto the offensive, the visitors often brought eight men behind the ball. The Welshmen survived a scare after 18 minutes. Following a free-kick and then a corner, Thompson, and then Yeats and Lawler, all had shots charged down. As the Liverpool team attacked relentlessly, Graham was unable to find space to get in a shot through a packed defence. Thompson then had a shot blocked before Smith drove high into the crowd.

With 23 minutes gone, Wrexham lost full-back Steve Ingle, the man with the task of keeping Thompson under control. Ingle limped off with an injured leg, and was substituted by Tinnion. A minute later the brave Fourth Division side took an unexpected lead through their centre-forward, Ray Smith. Bobby Park beat Hughes by the corner flag, and put over a fine centre which Ray Smith reached, towering above the Liverpool defence to head the ball into the corner of the net.

Liverpool's response was immediate, and Graham pivoted on to a Callaghan pass and hit a low shot straight at Gaskell. Wrexham's May did a magnificent job in the air and on the ground against the excellent Graham. Liverpool's search for an equalising goal was relentless and Wrexham hung on grimly. Ten minutes before the break Alan Bermingham's out-stretched leg prevented Hughes from equalising with a 25-yard shot. Davis then kicked off the line from Callaghan. With 38 minutes gone, Callaghan's 20-yard shot from Thompson's square pass thundered against the base of a post and rebounded into play before being frantically cleared.

The visitors went close to increasing their lead early in the second half. Tinnion beat Lawler and Strong's tackles but

pushed the ball too far ahead, allowing Clemence to come out to collect. The Reds once again turned to relentless attack as they sought an equalising goal. The inevitable goal arrived after 50 minutes. It stemmed from a free-kick five yards outside the penalty area. St.John's inch-perfect kick behind the Wrexham defence allowed Graham to run in and head into the corner of the net. Three minutes later Wrexham's Ian Moir was booked for a foul on Thompson.

The Welshmen used centre-forward Ray Smith alongside Eddie May in defence in an effort to stem the relentless Red tide. Smith cleared close to the line moments before Liverpool took the lead after 59 minutes. St.John combined with Graham before speeding forward and blasting a 20-yard shot past Gaskell. The Kop began to chant *"Easy"*, although it had been far from easy against such a gallant and courageous side in which May and Gaskell starred.

With 64 minutes gone, Liverpool substituted Ross for Thompson, the winger appearing to have pulled a hamstring muscle. Graham scored his second goal of the game after 73 minutes. The move began with a firm tackle on the half-way line on the left by Peter Wall. Tommy Smith's superb cross-field pass to Ian Callaghan kept the movement flowing and from close to the line near the corner flag, Callaghan beat Tinnion and crossed for Graham to out-jump the Wrexham defence and flick a header over Gaskell and under the bar. With the minutes ticking away, Clemence flung himself to his right to finger-tip away a fierce 20-yard shot from Bobby Park.

Chelsea - the eventual Cup-winners - drew 2-2 with Burnley, winning 3-1 in the replay. Leeds United beat non-League Sutton United 6-0 away.

Liverpool: Clemence; Lawler, Wall; Strong, Yeats, Hughes; Callaghan, Smith, Thompson(Ross,64), St.John, Graham.

Wrexham: Gaskell; Ingle(Tinnion,23), Bermingham; Davis, May, Mason; Moir, Park, R.Smith, Kinsey, Griffiths.

Referee: Mr G.C. Kew (Leeds)

Attendance: 54,096

February 7, 1970

Liverpool (0) 0

Leicester City (0) 0

PETER Thompson failed before the game to get his injured thigh fit and Ian Ross deputised in the number 9 shirt. Tommy Lawrence returned to the Liverpool goal after recovering from a calf injury and he received a tremendous reception from the Kop as he took to the pitch.

Liverpool: Lawrence; Lawler, Wall; Strong, Yeats, Hughes; Callaghan, Smith, Ross, St.John, Graham.

Leicester City: Shilton; Woollett, Nish; Roberts, Sjoberg, Cross; Farrington, Fern, Lochhead, Matthews, Glover.

Referee: Mr P. Partridge (Middlesbrough)

Attendance: 53,785

In the first minute a clearance from Cross hit Ross and spun high under the bar, but Shilton acrobatically leapt to palm the ball clear. Lawler prevented Glover from moving on to a loose ball in the penalty area in front of the Liverpool goal. St.John led the attack with Ross in midfield. Confusion between Cross and Nish let in St.John on the right of the penalty area, but his shot was too high. Ross kept a close watch on Glover, who operated in midfield for Leicester. The visitors attacked frequently and a Smith foul on Fern earned them a free-kick midway inside the Liverpool half. Roberts sent the ball low into the goalmouth where Lochhead met it on the volley from 15 yards, but he drove the ball straight at Lawrence.

With seven minutes gone Shilton dived full-length to keep out a header from St.John following Callaghan's cross. Roberts worked well in midfield for Leicester and a cross from Fern was sliced up into the air by Strong in front of his own goal. Lawrence was alert to the danger and collected the ball. Leicester took the initiative as the home side struggled to find their composure.

Lochhead went back into defence for a Liverpool free-kick, but he burst through with the ball and avoided several tackles before reaching the Liverpool half. A fine ball to Fern appeared to have the Liverpool defence in trouble, but the Leicester inside man could not keep the ball in play. Eventually Liverpool took control with Ross marshalling the midfield and Graham and St.John moving intelligently in attack.

The visitors tackled swiftly and incisively in an effort to destroy Liverpool's rhythm. The Reds almost took the lead after 24 minutes when Sjoberg's attempted clearance outside his own penalty area rebounded goalwards off St.John. The Scot and goalkeeper Shilton reached the ball together, but it rebounded off Shilton to Callaghan, whose lob goalwards was going wide of the far post until Hughes hooked it back into the middle. The ball went behind St.John and the Leicester defence cleared. Moments later Shilton was at his mercurial best as he palmed a Hughes cross off Graham's head. Seconds later Smith's angled 25-yard drive flashed inches wide of the Leicester goal. Liverpool attacked relentlessly at this stage, forcing two corners, one of which forced Cross to head away a goal-bound shot from Hughes. An excellent tackle by Fern on Smith gave Farrington a shooting chance, but he shot straight at Lawrence from 20 yards.

With 33 minutes gone, Graham moved on to a St.John pass and raced clear of the Leicester defence before Shilton blocked Graham's shot with his foot. Hughes, Smith and Ross forced Liverpool forward and, although they had the greater share of the attacking moves, their advances broke down due to the combined factors of Leicester's quick tackling and the slippery pitch. The visitors were not outplayed, however, and Woollett overlapped brilliantly before forcing Lawrence to a flying save from a low cross into the goalmouth. Although Lawler, Wall and Strong played well, Yeats was not at his commanding best, often appearing hesitant. Just before the half-time whistle, Farrington sent a powerful header only inches wide from a Glover corner.

The Reds attacked inexorably at the start of the second half, but Leicester were equal to the task, defending resolutely and counter-attacking with great speed and venom. After a foul on Ross, Yeats stormed in to tower above the Leicester defence to meet Callaghan's free-kick, but the Liverpool captain's header dipped fractionally over the bar. Lochhead, Fern and Farrington broke quickly and on numerous occasions they caught Liverpool defenders upfield. The home side were not at their best despite having the greater part of the game. Leicester, however, played a controlled game and Cross, Sjoberg and Woollett were outstanding in defence.

Graham beat Cross and went to the line before pulling the ball back low into the goalmouth. The ball went behind his forwards and a marvellous opportunity was spurned. With Roberts and Matthews working tirelessly in midfield, Leicester began to attack in numbers. Liverpool appeared to miss the silky skills and attacking wiles of Peter Thompson, for without him, the attack was disjointed.

Ten minutes from the end, Leicester might have won the game when Glover raced down the left and from the half-way line sent Lochhead through with a glorious pass, but Lawrence was quick off his line to fling himself at Lochhead's feet. Yeats also went in with a last-ditch tackle and the ball ran loose for Lawler to clear.

February 11, 1970

Leicester City (0) 0

Liverpool (0) 2
Evans 64, 90

ALUN Evans was Liverpool's man-of-the-match for a stirring display both in defence and attack and for his two goals which sent Leicester crashing out of the Cup. Evans started his Anfield career with several goals after his £100,000 transfer from Wolves, but he had faded into relative obscurity after losing his place to Bobby Graham on the opening day of the season due to suspension.

Peter Thompson's injured thigh lasted only 22 minutes and Evans was thrust into the thrilling action. Liverpool were the more controlled and disciplined team on the night, with Leicester a pale imitation of the side which drew at Anfield four days ago.

The home side threatened just before the interval and were aggressive either side of Liverpool's opening goal, but otherwise, the game belonged to the Merseyside club, for whom Geoff Strong and Ron Yeats were in marvellous form. Strong covered superbly, while Yeats marshalled the dangerous Andy Lochhead brilliantly.

Tommy Lawrence produced two magnificent saves after Liverpool had taken the lead. First he flung himself to his left to clutch a fierce 20-yard shot from Bobby Roberts and he later dived the other way to fist an effort from John Farrington for a corner.

Farrington was generally never allowed to utilise his pace, while Rodney Fern had a quiet game and Len Glover spent almost the entire game in midfield. Paul Matthews was assigned the task of marking the impish St.John, who prompted and provoked Liverpool's attacking designs.

Liverpool dominated the greater part of the first half and went close to scoring the opening goal before the interval when an astute pass from St.John allowed Hughes to round Sjoberg, but as he turned away in triumph, the ball struck the base of the left-hand post and rebounded into play. The game was played at a tremendous pace throughout on a pitch which was soft in one half but hard in the other because the shadow from the stand had prevented the sun from thawing the frost.

With 64 minutes gone, Evans side-footed the ball home from close range after Callaghan's centre had rounded off a move by Smith and Graham. In the final minute St.John set up the chance and Graham pushed the final pass through for Evans to race forward and clip an intelligent lob over Shilton's right shoulder.

*Above: **Alun Evans**, the teenager Bill Shankly bought from Wolves. On his League début, Evans scored in a 4-0 rout of Leicester, and a week later he netted two as Liverpool crushed his former club, Wolves, 6-0. The two goals against Leicester were his first in the FA Cup for Liverpool, in a Reds' career total of three.*

Leicester City: Shilton; Woollett, Nish; Roberts, Sjoberg, Cross; Farrington, Fern, Lochhead, Matthews, Glover.

Liverpool: Lawrence; Lawler, Wall; Strong, Yeats, Hughes; Callaghan, Smith, Thompson(Evans,22), St.John, Graham.

Referee: Mr P. Partridge (Middlesbrough)

Attendance: 42,100

Receipts: £ 12,881 19s 9d

February 21, 1970

Watford (0) 1
Endean 63

Liverpool (0) 0

LIVERPOOL were without the services of Tommy Smith, out with a groin strain, and Peter Thompson, still suffering from a thigh strain. Ian Ross and Alun Evans deputised. Watford were without their captain, Keith Eddy. Several Anfield fans went to Watford's rescue on the morning of the match, helping to clear straw from the pitch and fork away surface water so that the game could go ahead. They were rewarded with free tickets for the game. The pitch looked heavy underneath a huge diamond of sand stretching from goal to goal.

Watford: Walker; Welbourne, Williams; Lugg, Lees, Whalley; Scullion, Garbett, Endean, Packer, Owen.

Liverpool: Lawrence; Lawler, Wall; Strong, Yeats, Hughes; Callaghan, Ross, Evans, St.John, Graham.

Referee: Mr D. Smith (Stonehouse)

Attendance: 34,047

Watford - languishing near the bottom of the Second Division - almost scored in the second minute when Lugg sent Garbett through to the left of goal with a fine pass. Yeats challenged and Lawrence hesitated half-way out of his goal, as Garbett's shot hit the side netting. Liverpool began to settle down and after an excellent five-man move, Chris Lawler stole up to try a 25-yard shot that Walker saved low down.

St.John and Lawler were prominent as the visitors took the game to Watford, though the home side's swift counter-attacks caused Liverpool some problems. Owen broke down the left wing and Endean's shot struck the outcoming Lawrence's leg before going behind. Lees and Whalley performed well in the centre of Watford's defence and on three occasions they scrambled away dangerous crosses.

With 15 minutes gone Owen missed a marvellous opportunity to put Watford ahead when Lugg evaded a tackle by Yeats and chipped the ball to the far post. Lawrence was stranded, and, with an open goal to aim at, Owen headed a foot over the bar. At the other end Yeats headed over the bar from a Callaghan cross after the winger had been sent clear by Graham. Liverpool's best effort arrived after 24 minutes when Callaghan cut in from the right and hit a fierce volley that was deflected inches wide by a defender.

A fine piece of short inter-passing by Watford caused the Liverpool defence problems but Scullion's shot was inches wide. Four minutes from the interval a 15-yard shot from Endean passed inches wide of the goal. Conditions dictated play with the heavy mud in the middle militating against a free-flowing passing game and making it difficult to turn.

At the start of the second half the Liverpool defence appeared to be more composed, but in attack they were weak and inept and rarely threatened the grip that Whalley and Lees held in the Watford area.

Evans produced a 30-yard drive after 54 minutes which Walker managed to turn over the bar. From the corner Yeats led vociferous appeals for a penalty which the referee dismissed. The nearest Liverpool got to a goal came on the hour when St.John flicked a through pass to Graham, whose shot was finger-tipped away by Walker. As Hughes raced in, Welbourne cleared.

Three minutes later Watford took the lead. From a throw-in on the right Lugg lifted the ball high into the penalty area where Endean, racing in, sent in a header which Lawrence got his hands to, but failed to stop. The Second Division side deserved their lead and they were full of hard running and honest endeavour.

Liverpool fought back and Callaghan crossed high from the left before Lawler nodded the ball down for Graham to hook a shot just over the bar. After 73 minutes the referee spoke sternly to Yeats and Garbett after the Liverpool skipper had sent Garbett flying with a heavy tackle as he threatened to break clear. Garbett appeared to retaliate by throwing mud in the face of Yeats. The visitors battled for an equalising goal and Wall sent a long centre from the left which was inches away from the incoming Strong. Overall, the Liverpool performance was a poor one, and the home side deserved their victory, before losing 5-1 to Chelsea in the semi-final. Leeds beat Manchester United 1-0 after two goalless draws.

The official attendance was only 52 fewer than the ground record established last season in a Cup tie with Manchester United. The receipts of £17,084 were a new record, beating by £7,000 the previous record created when Liverpool last appeared on this ground three years ago.

Bill Shankly: "... I could see that some of the players were going a bit. When you have had success it can be a difficult job to motivate yourself ... Now it was obvious that while some players still had an appetite for success, others hadn't, and might do better elsewhere ..."

Shankly by Bill Shankly, Arthur Barker Ltd, 1976

January 2, 1971

Liverpool (1) 1
McLaughlin 28

Aldershot (0) 0

FORMER Liverpool star Jimmy Melia was accorded a tremendous reception when he led out the Aldershot team on to a fog-bound Anfield pitch. The new floodlights penetrated the murky afternoon. The Reds kept the team which drew with Stoke City on Boxing Day.

Jimmy Melia

Aldershot kicked off towards the Kop and advanced down the left before being resisted by the Liverpool defence. Toshack won Clemence's long kick in the air and nodded the ball down for Boersma to beat Giles and cross the ball low. Dixon cut out the centre. The Fourth Division side pressed forward again and Walden collected a pass on the right before centring for Howarth to rise above the Liverpool defence. His header lacked power and Clemence saved comfortably. Aldershot combined well down the right through Melia, Howarth and Brown before Callaghan fouled Howarth and the move broke down. The free-kick was easily cleared. With six minutes gone, Brown had a chance to put the visitors ahead. A centre from Walton caught out the Liverpool defence and Brown found himself with only Clemence to beat from 18 yards, but he shot hurriedly over the bar as Clemence left his goal.

Liverpool responded with attacking moves of their own and from a Callaghan cross Boersma won the ball in the air, but he was unable to get any power or direction behind his header. After 15 minutes a first-time shot by Toshack from the edge of the area beat Dixon but hit the bar and bounced over. As the game progressed, the mist became thicker. Aldershot played with an assurance which belied their lowly League position. Heighway weaved his way through the Aldershot defence before he was robbed by Giles.

Liverpool took the lead with an individual goal by the 18-year-old John McLaughlin. The youngster created and scored the goal himself with a calm assurance far beyond his years. He robbed Melia with a firm tackle just inside the Liverpool half and raced forward. A neat body swerve took him past Giles and as he reached the edge of the area, he curled a brilliant shot over Dixon and into the far corner of the net. Five minutes later Boersma almost scored a second goal when he rose to a cross from Hall and sent in a header which Dixon did well to save low. With Liverpool attacking in determined fashion, Aldershot were forced to pull every man back behind the ball. Dixon palmed away a shot from Toshack before Boersma shot inches over the bar from 20 yards after a Callaghan corner.

Aldershot lacked real penetration and Clemence had not had a real save to make until the visitors struck twice within minutes. Joslyn lobbed the ball forward and Howarth's flicked header was comfortably collected by Clemence, who had anticipated well, and then the young goalkeeper had to go down at the feet of Brown as the Aldershot man chased a through ball from Melia. Toshack's aerial threat, combined with the darting runs of Heighway and the pace of Boersma created numerous problems for Aldershot, but the visitors looked dangerous when Brown cleverly slipped a tackle by Smith and cut in to chip the ball across the goalmouth. Brodie, near the far post, failed to make contact.

With 57 minutes gone, Boersma collected a loose ball and sped forward to hit a low shot which beat Dixon but rebounded into play from the base of an upright. Despite Liverpool's attacking promise, Aldershot continued to contest every ball and they never allowed Liverpool to dominate the game completely.

After 71 minutes Liverpool had the ball in the net again, but Hall was adjudged to have been offside as he scored. Five minutes later Priscott went on for Walton. Giles and Dixon were responsible for keeping the score to a manageable level, and full-backs Walker and Walden had cut out the threat of several dangerous crosses aimed towards the aerial menace of Toshack.

Ten minutes from the finish Heighway cut in from the right and blasted a shot yards wide. The slippery surface had not helped Liverpool as they stumbled to victory.

Liverpool: Clemence; Lawler, Boersma; Smith, Lloyd, Hughes; Callaghan, McLaughlin, Heighway, Toshack, Hall.

Aldershot: Dixon; Walden, Walker; Joslyn, Dean, Giles; Walton(Priscott,76), Brown, Howarth, Melia, Brodie.

Referee: Mr G.C. Kew (Leeds)

Attendance: 45,500

January 23, 1971

Liverpool (0) 3

Toshack 53, St.John 85
Lawler 87

Swansea City (0) 0

IAN Callaghan was competing in his 50th consecutive FA Cup tie for Liverpool this afternoon against Swansea City, who beat Liverpool 2-1 in 1964 when they were known as Swansea Town.

With six first-team players on the injured list, Liverpool recalled Ron Yeats at left-back to make two members of the Liverpool side which saw defeat in 1964. Swansea's Herbie Williams was also a veteran of that game.

Liverpool attacked towards the Kop goal in the first half and Lawler drove the ball low and hard across the face of the goal, but neither Heighway nor Toshack was able to reach it. Swansea almost scored in their first attack through the 39-year-old Len Allchurch. A pass out of defence found Hole on the left touchline and his long centre was headed on by Gwyther for Allchurch to half-volley from 25 yards. Clemence was forced to fling himself to his left to turn the ball round a post for a corner.

With eight minutes gone, Heighway almost capitalised on some slack work by Slattery, but his shooting chance from the edge of the area passed narrowly wide. A foul by Tony Screen on Hall brought Liverpool a free-kick near the right corner flag, but Millington made a magnificent catch above Toshack's head from a kick by Hall.

Swansea often had seven or eight men defending against the enormous Liverpool pressure and captain Alan Williams performed well in the heart of their defence, while Millington's handling was superb. Swansea employed a man-to-man marking system with Slee marshalling Hall and Screen shadowing Heighway, with Nurse alert to the presence of Toshack. Hall, in particular, played well in attack for the Reds.

Heighway beat Slee on the right and bore down on goal, but the full-back was then penalised for a late tackle on the flying winger.

Then Lawler was brought down as he moved towards the penalty area, but the free-kick by Emlyn Hughes was blocked by the wall. Liverpool enjoyed the greater share of the play but genuine opportunities were rare against a solid Swansea defence.

Yeats attempted a 40-yard drive which flew inches over the bar. A header from Callaghan sent Heighway sprinting towards goal, but instead of shooting from 20 yards out with the goal beckoning, he elected to carry the ball further and was dispossessed.

In the first minute of the second half, Screen fouled Hall which brought a rebuke from the referee. From the free-kick a header by Lawler went wide of a post. Smith was so excellent in the heart of the Liverpool defence, halting any promising Swansea move as soon as it began, that Lawler was able to move forward at every opportunity as an auxiliary forward.

With 51 minutes gone, Lawler tried to clear his lines under pressure from Gwyther, but he only succeeded in slicing the ball over the head of Clemence, inches wide of the far post.

With 53 minutes gone Allchurch fouled Hughes midway inside the Swansea half. Smith touched the free-kick out to Yeats on the touchline, and his centre to the far post was met by the leaping Toshack, who left Millington with no chance of saving the well-directed header.

As Swansea fought desperately for the equaliser, they had two shots blocked by defenders in the penalty area, before winning a further corner and then a third when Yeats headed behind.

Millington punched clear a Hall cross after the winger had brilliantly beaten Screen with his trickery. Toshack was presented with a fine opportunity by McLaughlin, but the Welshman sliced his shot wide from 15 yards.

With 74 minutes gone, Liverpool sent on Ian St.John in place of Ian Callaghan. A fierce 25-yard shot from Hughes flashed across the goal, but the Reds increased their lead when Toshack and Heighway combined. The tall forward nodded a high ball to the winger, who dribbled forward and saw his shot deflected. St.John had the easy task of slipping the ball into the back of the net.

Seconds later, the Scot had the ball in the back of the net again after a headed pass by Toshack, but the effort was ruled offside.

Three minutes from the end, Lawler picked up a clearance, ran dazzlingly through the Swansea defence, and hammered a shot past Millington. Then Millington produced a wonderful save to deny St.John another goal as Liverpool produced their customary storming finale, with Toshack causing chaos in the penalty area.

Liverpool: Clemence; Lawler, Yeats; Smith, Lloyd, Hughes; Callaghan(St.John,74), McLaughlin, Heighway, Toshack, Hall.

Swansea City: Millington; Slee, T.Screen; A.Williams, Nurse, Hole; Allchurch, Thomas, H.Williams, Gwyther, Slattery.

Referee: Mr C. Howell (North Shields)

Attendance: 47,229

February 13, 1971

Liverpool (1) 1
Lawler 29

Southampton (0) 0

LIVERPOOL retained the side that had beaten both Arsenal and Leeds in their previous two games, while the Saints fielded the side which had beaten Tottenham Hotspur 3-1 in London a fortnight previously. Torrential rain fell an hour before the kick-off and left pools of water on the pitch and groundsmen forked away the water up to twenty minutes before the start.

Liverpool attacked towards the Kop in the first half, and were awarded a free-kick for a tackle from behind by Gabriel on McLaughlin, and the Kop chanted *"Alehouse! Alehouse!"* at the Saints.

The visitors drew Walker deep into defence to play alongside McGrath as Liverpool provided the early pressure. Boersma went on a good run and gained a corner when his shot was deflected by O'Neil. Saints had ten men back in their penalty area to clear the flag-kick. Good combination by McLaughlin and Hall brought the Reds a further corner which was headed behind from Hall's kick. From the next corner, Lloyd back-headed the ball into the goalmouth where Lawler had a shot blocked in the mass of players.

Hall worked prodigiously in midfield, and most of Liverpool's attacks stemmed from his efforts. Toshack won another corner and it almost led to the opening goal, as the Welshman met Hall's kick with his head, forcing Martin to produce a fine save.

With 18 minutes gone, the ball entered the Southampton net via Boersma, but the goal was disallowed, the referee ruling that Toshack had fouled McGrath to reach the ball.

Heighway seized on a poor pass by Fisher before streaking almost fifty yards and Martin did well to save at the feet of the winger. The Saints got men behind the ball at every opportunity, leaving only Channon and Davies up front.

With 29 minutes gone, Liverpool took the lead. Hall provided the final pass, but the move began further back. Hughes fed Heighway far out by the left-hand touchline and from his high centre, Lawler rose to head towards goal, but his header was deflected off the head of a defender. As the ball broke loose, Hall sent in a neat header for Lawler to nip forward and force the ball over the line.

Hall was in mercurial form, jinking this way and that and creating numerous chances for his colleagues. He wrong-footed Hollywood, before cutting inside and unleashing a shot which a defender headed behind.

The goal had given Liverpool the opportunity to relax a little and show their fine flowing football skills. Toshack performed magnificently against McGrath in the air.

Kirkup stopped a Lawler shot on the line as the Reds increased the pressure. Two minutes from the interval,

Liverpool broke free again. Boersma broke free and fed Toshack, who put Hughes in possession. The elegant Hughes went round McGrath and had a clear run on goal, but on the edge of the penalty area he elected to shoot instead of going further forward, and he shot straight at Martin.

The Saints switched tactics in the second half, sending Gabriel up into attack with Paine also playing further forward. A cross by Kirkup was misheaded by Smith and Davies was presented with an ideal opportunity, but the ball bounced awkwardly and he could only manage to tap the ball towards goal. Heighway put over a long centre to the far post, where Toshack headed it back across the goalmouth. Boersma was unable to reach it at the far post.

On the hour, Walker was booked after he had blatantly held Heighway as the Liverpool winger went forward. Moments later Boersma sent in a fine header from Hall's centre. Martin pushed it out of the angle and turned it round the post.

Southampton's best chance came when Gabriel rode a strong tackle by Smith and sent Davies clear. Clemence was forced to race off his line, but Davies pushed the ball past him and then appeared to be brought down. The referee waved play on.

Then Paine centred into the goalmouth, but Gabriel missed his header. At the other end, Heighway shot inches over the bar as the pace of the game quickened and play flowed from end to end. A foul by Yeats on Paine gave the Saints a free-kick and from Paine's cross, Davies leaped to nod the ball over Clemence towards the far corner. The goalkeeper somehow managed to leap and arch backwards to pluck the ball out of the air.

The Saints attacked strongly and a mistake by Lloyd almost let in Channon, but the ball bounced towards goal and Smith cleared the danger. Then Martin flung himself at the feet of Heighway as he burst through.

Liverpool: Clemence; Lawler, Yeats; Smith, Lloyd, Hughes; Boersma, McLaughlin, Heighway, Toshack, Hall.

Southampton: Martin; Kirkup, Hollywood; Fisher, McGrath, Gabriel; Paine, Channon, Davies, O'Neil, Walker.

Referee: Mr D.A. Corbett (Wolverhampton)

Attendance: 50,226

March 6, 1971

Liverpool (0) 0   Tottenham Hotspur (0) 0

CHRIS Lawler passed a late fitness test and made his 301st consecutive first team appearance. Alec Lindsay was fit again and replaced Ron Yeats at left-back. Tottenham brought in John Pratt for his second game of the season in place of Alan Gilzean.

Liverpool kicked off towards the Kop before a capacity crowd. The pitch was very soft in front of the main stand, but icy and covered in a layer of snow in front of the Kemlyn Road stand. The home side won an early corner when Boersma moved on to a flick by Toshack and, from just

Ray Clemence pulls off another fine save in a magnificent performance against Tottenham

outside the area, tried a shot which was deflected wide by a defender. Hall took the corner kick and Lloyd back-headed the ball into the goalmouth, where Lawler lobbed a header goalwards, but the ball passed inches over the bar. Perryman knocked Heighway off the ball midway inside the Tottenham half and Smith slipped the free-kick across the field to Lindsay. The full back chipped the ball into the penalty area, where Toshack out-jumped the visitors' defence before heading over the bar.

The Reds had asserted their authority early on and they forced Tottenham deep into their own half. Collins headed behind for another corner as Toshack challenged for a Lawler cross, and from the flag kick Neighbour got the ball clear after Jennings missed his punch. Tottenham were awarded a free-kick when Hughes fouled Mullery. In trying to find Chivers with a headed flick, Perryman sent the ball wide of the goal. With 14 minutes gone, a mistake by Chivers almost brought about the first goal. He tried a long-range back pass and put the ball at the feet of Boersma, running in from the right. Jennings left his line to narrow the angle, but Boersma's shot went behind.

Perryman fouled Heighway, and Toshack headed Smith's kick down to Lawler, whose shot was kicked behind for a corner by Knowles. The visitors won a corner on the right, and Pratt tried a shot from the edge of the area which was blocked by Liverpool defenders. Some excellent covering by Knowles prevented Heighway from racing clear of the Tottenham defence on to a chip from Brian Hall. Lindsay showed that he was back to his best form when he twice broke up Spurs' attacks when the visitors had broken through the rest of the defensive line.

Liverpool's football was of a high calibre, and Toshack caused numerous problems for Collins. From a foul on Boersma, Lindsay chipped the ball into the goalmouth and, as it broke loose, Toshack fired in a shot from 15 yards which rebounded from the body of Knowles.

After 35 minutes Kinnear caught Liverpool upfield and sent Chivers racing through on his own. Clemence raced out of his box and robbed Chivers with a fine tackle to avert an almost certain goal. Jennings saved from Boersma after Toshack nodded down a cross from Hall. A fine piece of play by McLaughlin in midfield sent Heighway racing through, and though Jennings was unable to hold the winger's fierce, low shot, the goalkeeper managed to recover and dived on top of the ball as Boersma raced in.

A minute before the interval Knowles slipped as he took a free-kick inside his own half, and the ball moved on to Boersma's feet. Boersma sped forward and crossed the ball. Beal raced across with his back to the referee and flung himself forward and palmed the ball for a corner. The referee was unsighted and turned down Liverpool's appeals for a penalty. Jennings produced a brilliant save from the corner to prevent Lawler from scoring after Toshack had risen above the Spurs' defence to nod forward Hall's corner. The Liverpool full-back nodded the ball down towards the corner of the net, but Jennings threw himself to his right to fall on the ball.

Liverpool began the second half in the same rich attacking vein as they had ended the first half. Jennings punched off the heads of Toshack and Lloyd as the Reds searched for the opening goal. Tottenham hit back and from a corner Pratt hit a magnificent volley on the edge of the area that dipped narrowly over the bar. From the goal-kick Clemence slipped and the ball went weakly to the feet of Chivers, who was robbed by the ever-alert Lloyd. With 53 minutes gone, Heighway's excellent pass found Toshack, whose angled shot to the left of goal was saved by Jennings. The Irish goalkeeper dived to turn the ball into the side netting as the Welsh forward attempted to squeeze it between him and the post. Tommy Smith hit a tremendous 30-yard drive narrowly wide as Liverpool maintained their relentless onslaught. Spurs broke away and Clemence fell to his right to save from a Pratt shot. Chivers was often beaten in the air by Larry Lloyd, and Spurs' main threat was neutralised.

After 68 minutes Hall crossed into the penalty area and Toshack shot towards goal but hit the prostrate figure of Boersma. From the rebound Hall saw his shot strike Knowles before being cleared. Two minutes later Liverpool brought on Alun Evans for John McLaughlin. It was Evans' first game for the seniors since he injured his cartilage four months previously in Bucharest.

A magnificent shot from 25 yards by Hughes passed inches over the bar and Lindsay shot wildly as the home side attacked inexorably. In a breakaway, Perryman gave Mullery a chance as he cut in from the right and Clemence fell on the shot to save. With ten minutes remaining Clemence pushed a shot from the unmarked Pratt away. Pratt chased a loose ball to near the by-line before chipping it back into the middle. The ball passed over the heads of Chivers and Peters and Lindsay turned it for a corner. Liverpool won a corner on the right and Heighway nodded Hall's kick into the middle, but Jennings managed to fist the ball away as the tall Liverpool defenders threatened.

With five minutes remaining Mullery centred from the right high over the defence to Pratt on the far side. Pratt attempted to chip over the Liverpool goalkeeper and inside the far post, but shot inches wide. Following this, Boersma netted but the referee had blown for a foul on Jennings. Just before the final whistle, Mullery broke down the right and crossed hard and low. Chivers flung himself forward and narrowly failed to turn the ball into goal. At the Tottenham end Boersma headed inches wide from a Lindsay cross.

Everton beat Colchester United 5-0, while Stoke beat Hull 3-2 away. Arsenal, the eventual finalists, drew 0-0 at Leicester, winning the replay 1-0.

Liverpool: Clemence; Lawler, Lindsay; Smith, Lloyd, Hughes; Boersma, McLaughlin(Evans,70), Heighway, Toshack, Hall.

Tottenham Hotspur: Jennings; Kinnear, Knowles; Mullery, Collins, Beal; Pratt, Perryman, Chivers, Peters, Neighbour.

Referee: Mr G.W. Hill (Leicester)

Attendance: 54,731

March 16, 1971

Tottenham Hotspur (0) 0   Liverpool (1) 1

Heighway 25

ON the night that 21-year-old Joe Bugner became a triple champion at the Empire Pool, Wembley, deposing 36-year-old Henry Cooper into retirement, Tottenham suffered their first Cup replay defeat for 60 years as Liverpool valiantly fought their way into the semi-finals of the FA Cup. Goalkeeper Ray Clemence was the hero in a masterful display by Liverpool's new young team, producing a string of magnificent saves as Spurs attacked with great force at the rock-like Liverpool defence.

Tottenham were in superb form but met Liverpool in inspired mood. The Reds employed four men forward and carried the game to their north-London opponents. A goal up, the team changed their tactics, and left only Alun Evans and Steve Heighway up front, John Toshack often using his height in defence.

The home side were full of international stars, Martin Chivers, Martin Peters, the inspirational Alan Mullery and the spirited Steve Perryman. With John Pratt using a shoot-on-sight policy, Tottenham were rampant and determined to win through to the semi-final. On at least six occasions Clemence produced world-class saves to deny Tottenham. The entire Liverpool defence was in brilliant form. Tommy Smith produced a masterful display, inspiring his team-mates forward at every opportunity. Chris Lawler was his usual calm and immaculate self.

Larry Lloyd marshalled the threat of Chivers superbly and dominated the penalty area in the air. Alec Lindsay was both cool and efficient, and he made wise use of his cultured left foot with inch-perfect passes out of defence. Emlyn Hughes worked tremendously hard and supported the attack in breakaways.

Brian Hall was indefatigable in midfield as he systematically destroyed Spurs' cultured build-up. In attack, Peter Thompson - playing in his first senior game for three months - tired after a long absence, though not before shining in Liverpool's offensive movements.

Far out on the left flank, Steve Heighway was fouled by Joe Kinnear. Alec Lindsay floated with his left foot an inch-perfect cross towards the head of Toshack in the penalty area. The Welshman outjumped Collins and, as his header sliced its way through into the goalmouth, Alun Evans failed to make contact, though his presence appeared to unsettle Jennings and Heighway ran in to stab the ball home. From this point on, Tottenham enjoyed greater possession, but Liverpool's grim determination enabled them to make further progress on the road to Wembley.

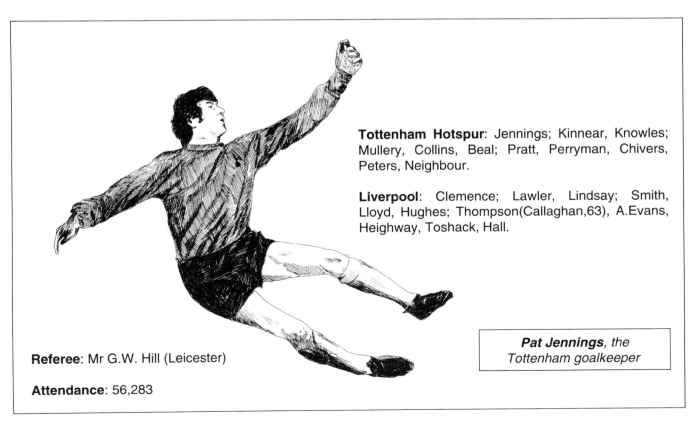

Tottenham Hotspur: Jennings; Kinnear, Knowles; Mullery, Collins, Beal; Pratt, Perryman, Chivers, Peters, Neighbour.

Liverpool: Clemence; Lawler, Lindsay; Smith, Lloyd, Hughes; Thompson(Callaghan,63), A.Evans, Heighway, Toshack, Hall.

Pat Jennings, the Tottenham goalkeeper

Referee: Mr G.W. Hill (Leicester)

Attendance: 56,283

March 27, 1971

Everton (1) 1
Ball 10

Liverpool (0) 2
Evans 59, Hall 72

THE Everton manager, Harry Catterick, was ill in bed with influenza and missed this epic confrontation between Merseyside's greatest rivals. The Blues fielded the team which played in Athens on the Wednesday before the game, which meant that Henry Newton and Jimmy Husband were still unfit. Liverpool brought back Heighway and Hall, who did not play in Munich in midweek. Ian Callaghan made his 51st full appearance in FA Cup ties. Tommy Smith won the toss and elected to defend the Stretford Road end, where the majority of Liverpool supporters were congregated.

From an early throw-in, Heighway slipped majestically past Newton, but Wright turned the ball away for corner. The tension ran high as both teams sought the first goal. But it was Everton who struck the decisive first blow. Excellent combined play between Harvey and Morrissey on the left led up to the goal. Morrissey's accurate centre forced Clemence to go up for the ball, but the goalkeeper missed and the ball went across to the far side of the goal where Ball ran in and scored from a narrow angle.

Within a minute, Callaghan had the ball in the back of the net, but the referee ruled that the Liverpool winger had handled. A shot by Lawler struck Rankin's body and the ball rebounded to Heighway, who smashed it into the goalmouth where it struck Labone. With Rankin still out of his goal, Hughes drove the ball high and wide. An excellent pass by Hall to Evans saw the former Wolves player slip past Labone before Hurst went back to cover. Kendall's calm assurance was an integral part of the Everton defence and it prevented them from committing too many errors. Royle beat Lloyd in the air and headed across to Whittle. With Ball unmarked on the left and well-placed for a centre, Whittle attempted a shot which went high over the bar.

Gradually Liverpool asserted themselves, and Everton often had nine or ten men back behind the ball. Liverpool's defence was the best in the League, and Smith was in tremendous form as Everton tried to break through. The Reds went close when Toshack rose high above Labone to meet Callaghan's corner kick, but the ball went wide. At this stage in the game, Liverpool were first to the ball and dominated midfield. The referee spoke to Lloyd for a foul on Royle and the Everton centre-forward required attention before he could continue.

Liverpool looked impressive on the attack, though their finishing was weak. From a free-kick by Smith, Lloyd's header went well over. Whittle received a warning from the referee for a foul on Lindsay, but the game was played in a good spirit. When Royle fouled Hughes, he received a warning from the referee, who handled the game well. Toshack's heading ability caused Everton problems, since he put in some excellent constructive headers. Five minutes before the interval Lloyd was booked for a nasty tackle on

Royle. There were some disturbances in the crowd, and the police dealt with fans who created the trouble. Whenever Lloyd touched the ball after this incident, he was booed loudly by the Everton fans. Everton attacked rarely and Harvey shot wide before he sent one shot straight at Clemence.

Labone strained a muscle in turning the ball away from Toshack as he moved in to take Evans' cross. Labone was forced to limp off after 50 minutes and was replaced by Brown. Following a Callaghan cross, a Lloyd header was headed away by Royle, standing under the bar. A scramble resulted in Morrissey receiving attention after a blow in the face.

Everton embarked on a period of sustained pressure and Morrissey won a corner which was cleared by Lloyd. The ball went to Morrissey in midfield and Smith brought down the Everton winger with a crunching tackle which earned the Blues a free-kick.

Liverpool withstood the pressure and asserted themselves and they equalised after 59 minutes when Heighway brought the ball in from the left and passed inside to Evans, who raced through a wide channel in the Everton defence and drove the ball past Rankin.

With 72 minutes gone, Hall put Liverpool ahead. Heighway centred from the left and Rankin left his goal in an attempt to cut off the ball as the dangerous Toshack closed in. The goalkeeper only managed to knock the ball down and Hall smashed it into the empty net.

Having surrendered the lead, Everton moved on to the offensive and Ball placed a free-kick into the heart of the Liverpool goalmouth where Clemence punched away off the head of Hurst. Ball exemplified the great spirit in which this game was fought when he raced back 40 yards to dispossess Evans. A third goal for Liverpool looked likely when Heighway broke clear on the right and crossed the ball towards Evans and Toshack. Wright burst between them and turned the ball over the bar. From the corner, Rankin saved magnificently from a Hughes drive.

After the game Bill Shankly said, "We have not got to Wembley just for the thrill of playing there. We intend to bring the Cup back. A lot of teams are happy just to appear at Wembley - not us. We've not come so far just for that; we mean to bring that Cup back to Anfield."

Brian Hall said afterwards, "It was my first goal for the first team and how's that for starters? I started running from the halfway line following the play down the left. The ball came across and Tosh touched the ball down. The ball landed, bounced perfectly and I just hit it."

Alun Evans said, "I was expecting someone to be on me and I didn't expect it to be open. When I got the ball, looked up and saw that it was just a matter of putting it in the net." Tommy Smith: "It's a great feeling to be captain of a team going to Wembley. I'm a mighty proud man tonight, proud of the lads - the way they've played not only today but throughout the season, and the way they have supported me. They've done a magnificent job. The crowd gave us great support, too."

In the other semi-final, Arsenal drew 2-2 with Stoke City, but the London side won the replay 2-0.

Everton: Rankin; Wright, K.Newton; Kendall, Labone (Brown,50), Harvey; Whittle, Ball, Royle, Hurst, Morrissey.

Liverpool: Clemence; Lawler, Lindsay; Smith, Lloyd, Hughes; Callaghan, A.Evans, Heighway, Toshack, Hall.

Referee: Mr K.H. Burns (Stourbridge)

Attendance: 62,144 (at Old Trafford)

Receipts: £75,000

Alun Evans has just scored the equalising goal against Everton

ARSENAL COMPLETE DOUBLE

FINAL GOES TO EXTRA TIME

HEIGHWAY'S OPENING GOAL

Arsenal (0) 2
Kelly 102, George 111

Liverpool (0) 1 aet
Heighway 92

LIVERPOOL kicked off with Tommy Smith finding Toshack with a high ball to the left hand side of the penalty area as Toshack rose above Rice to head into the centre. Simpson cleared for Arsenal, the league champions. Storey crudely brought down Heighway five yards outside the Arsenal penalty area and Lindsay's delicate free-kick found Hughes, but he shot behind the goal.

Scramble

Arsenal might have taken a fourth-minute lead when George got the ball clear after a scramble in the Arsenal half. George found Kennedy lurking onside with the Liverpool defence forward in support of the attack. Kennedy raced on with Lloyd in attendance, but the Arsenal man shot before he needed to and put his attempt wide of the far post.

Champions

The champions settled down to their rhythm and Storey and McNab combined well before Lloyd covered and cleared the danger. After 12 minutes Liverpool had their first shot on goal. Hughes cleverly dummied Graham and shot from just outside the area but the ball trickled through to Wilson. Graham sent Radford clear down the left wing, but Clemence left his goal to clear the danger by kicking the ball into the crowd. Storey banged Clemence as the goalkeeper was in mid-air taking a cross. Smith and Lloyd went to gesticulate with Storey, but the referee took control of the situation. Shortly afterwards Storey brought down Heighway as the Liverpool man was in full flow.

Dangerous

With 33 minutes gone an excellent Heighway cross cleared the head of Evans and went towards Toshack, running in behind. The defences dominated the game, though Arsenal looked the more dangerous side in attack. After another foul on Heighway by Storey, Hughes touched the free-kick to Heighway, whose lob into the goalmouth was met by Lawler. The full-back was unable to get above the ball and his header fell into the arms of Wilson.

Scorching

Charlie George hit a scorching shot from 30 yards narrowly over the crossbar. Two minutes before the interval Ray Clemence produced a world-class save from virtually point-blank range from a header by Armstrong. Clemence flung up his arms instinctively, parried the ball and then fell on it as it dropped at the feet of Armstrong.

Simpson fouled Evans just outside the penalty area and Smith touched the free-kick sideways to Lindsay, whose ferocious low drive towards the inside of the right-hand post was finger-tipped away by Wilson as he flung himself to his left.

With 51 minutes gone, Arsenal missed another great opportunity of opening the score. Radford pulled the ball past Lawler and then set up Kennedy who miskicked two yards out in front of an open goal.

As Kennedy swung at the ball it became entangled in his legs and it trickled forward before being cleared by Lindsay. Arsenal had created the better openings while Liverpool had come close to scoring on only two occasions.

Thunderbolt

After 56 minutes George struck a thunderbolt which was narrowly off target. After 62 minutes Arsenal brought on Kelly in place of Storey. Radford eluded Smith on the right wing, cut in towards goal and beat Lawler before unleashing an 18-yard shot straight at Clemence. The Liverpool defence only half-cleared a centre from the right and Armstrong pulled a weak shot well wide of the post.

Liverpool introduced Peter Thompson for Alun Evans and the flying winger collected a long crossfield pass before beating Rice and racing to the line before sending over a high centre which Toshack met at the far side of the penalty area.

Overhead kick

Toshack nodded it into the centre where only a brilliant overhead kick by Simpson prevented Heighway from getting to the ball. Thompson's introduction appeared to galvanize Liverpool into action and he was involved in a fine move which included Callaghan and Heighway. The move created an opportunity for Lindsay, but he sliced his 20-yard shot into the crowd.

Radford drifted to the right wing and created a chance for Kennedy lurking at the near post, who sidefooted the ball narrowly wide.

With 77 minutes gone, a long throw-in by Radford was met by Graham and Clemence pushed his header up on to the bar before Lawler got the ball away for a corner with an overhead kick.

Header

Armstrong's kick was met by Graham, who rose high above the defence to power in a header which was cleared by Lindsay.

Liverpool replied through Thompson, who raced to the line on the right and centred for Toshack, but Wilson's handling was impeccable and he averted the threat of danger.

Three minutes from time Radford split the Liverpool defence with a perfect through pass to Kennedy, 15 yards from goal. With only Clemence to beat, Kennedy blasted his shot wide of the far post.

The game moved into extra-time, and Liverpool broke the deadlock with a sensational goal from Heighway just two minutes into the first period. Thompson hit a pass to Heighway on the left. There was no Arsenal player within 20 yards of him and the high-kicking winger sped on towards goal, drawing Armstrong and Rice before dummying Wilson off the line and shooting left-footed between the advancing goalkeeper and the near post from an almost impossible angle.

Equalising goal

Nine minutes later the resilient Arsenal equalised. Radford sent the ball into the heart of the Liverpool goalmouth where Kelly challenged Lloyd and Smith. Graham appeared to help the ball on its way into the net,

Tommy Smith (far right) and Frank McLintock shake hands before the Final

but afterwards the goal was credited to Kelly.

Winning goal

Arsenal scored the winning goal nine minutes later. The inimitable Charlie George controlled Radford's pass and hit a powerful right-foot shot from 20 yards which Clemence was unable to get to. Arsenal had achieved the Double, and there was no doubt that on the day they were the better side.

Comments

From the dressing room after the game, Tommy Smith declared, "We'll be back here, you can bet on that. And next time we'll win 5-0."

Sitting alone and dejected, Larry Lloyd said, "I'm sick. But we'll be back."

Manager Bill Shankly said, "The Cup was there for the winning. I thought a break would win it - and Arsenal got a break for their equaliser.

One goal in extra time is enough to win any game. You don't give away goals like that equaliser. Ray Clemence was coming for the ball thinking that Tommy Smith was leaving it and Tommy deflected it past him. It hit Graham on the leg and bounced in."

Steve Heighway said, "In the last two years I've been on the losing end in semi-finals. Now I'm a loser in the Final."

Heighway's goal

He described his goal. "The ball fell right and the only thing I could do was hit it with my left foot. Nine times out of ten shots like that go anywhere. This was the tenth time."

Difficult

Ron Yeats, veteran skipper of the 1965 Cup victory over Leeds United said, "This side has got plenty of time to come back here a few times. They're going to be a very difficult side to beat."

Watches

Later at a banquet at London's Savoy Hotel, Yeats assisted his successor as captain, Tommy Smith, present watches, collected for by the players to some of the behind-the-scenes staff at Anfield, who had worked so hard to get Liverpool to Wembley.

Arsenal: Wilson; Rice, McNab; Storey(Kelly,62), McLintock, Simpson; Armstrong, Graham, Radford, Kennedy, George.

Liverpool: Clemence; Lawler, Lindsay; Smith, Lloyd, Hughes; Callaghan, Evans(Thompson,68), Heighway, Toshack, Hall.

Referee: Mr N.C.H. Burtenshaw (Gorleston)

Attendance: 100,000

Charlie George *after scoring the winning goal*

Steve Heighway *and* ***Peter Thompson*** *celebrate the opening goal in the Final*

January 15, 1972

Oxford United (0) 0

Liverpool (0) 3
Keegan 47, 81,
Lindsay 84

LIVERPOOL dropped Jack Whitham and Steve Heighway from the team and brought in Peter Thompson and Alun Evans. Hughes recovered from his knee injury to take his place in the side and Oxford's John Evanson was declared fit to play.

Liverpool won the toss and elected to play up the slope with the wind at their backs. The pitch had dried out well after the week's rain and the home side took advantage of the slope to initiate two swift raids which were broken up by Smith and then Ross. As Oxford created the early pressure, Clemence was forced to dive full-length to his right to collect a low 25-yard drive from Aylott. With seven minutes gone, Liverpool survived a moment of confusion between Smith and Clemence when the goalkeeper called for a back pass and as Smith turned to comply with the order, he was robbed. With Clemence yards out of his goal Derek Clarke put a great opportunity from 15 yards wide of the target.

Liverpool gradually asserted their authority over the Second Division side, though the bumpy pitch caused them some problems. On numerous occasions promising moves by Liverpool players ended with offside being ruled against them. Oxford operated a 4-4-2 system, with only Derek Clarke and Cassidy up front, while the visitors chose the more adventurous 4-3-3 formation. Most of the play was centred in the middle of the park.

With 19 minutes gone, Kearns dropped a high centre at the feet of Evans but he atoned for his error when he dropped at the Liverpool player's feet to block the shot, which was finally cleared by Way. Thompson's corner kick was flicked on at the near post by Keegan but Shuker cleared.

Following an Oxford corner, Hughes miskicked and presented Aylott with a clear shot on goal. Smith blocked the effort, but from the rebound Skeen's wayward shot was diverted towards the target by Derek Clarke, but with Clemence diving in desperation, the ball went inches wide. At the Oxford end Colin Clarke dived to head a Thompson cross for a corner as the dangerous Evans lurked nearby.

After 37 minutes an Oxford breakaway almost led to the opening goal as Cassidy hit a hard low centre across the face of the goal. The ball travelled to the far side where Skeen chipped it back onto the head of Derek Clarke, five yards out. Clemence was well-positioned to save. Three minutes before the interval Lawler almost scored from a Thompson corner as Kearns missed the ball.

Just two minutes into the second period Liverpool scored. The former Scunthorpe player, Keegan, collected the ball deep in the Oxford half and ran round the back of the defence before hitting an angled drive from 20 yards past Kearns and into the far corner of the net. It was Liverpool's first goal for five matches and more than 400 minutes of playing time. The home side responded immediately and a fine tackle by Smith prevented Cassidy from breaking free. A high centre by Aylott was nodded back by Cassidy, but Fleming sent the ball high over the bar.

The Second Division side fought desperately in an attempt to find an equaliser, and Evanson was the architect of several of their most incisive moves. Lindsay was equal to the task as Liverpool defended resolutely.

Keegan, Thompson and Hall were in lively mood and created several problems for Oxford. Thompson forced a great save from Kearns after 72 minutes with a magnificent 30-yard drive. Smithson's outstretched boot prevented Evans from scoring with thirteen minutes remaining. Liverpool were awarded a free-kick on the left-hand side of the penalty area and Lindsay's low, hard shot was destined for the inside of the near post when Kearns produced a tremendous diving save.

Nine minutes from time Keegan scored. A perfect pass by Lawler caught the Oxford defence flatfooted and the sprightly Keegan controlled the ball on the edge of the area before turning and hitting a fierce shot past the hapless Kearns.

Three minutes later Lindsay scored his first goal of the season after Evans had initiated the move, taking a pass down the left before moving forward and drawing the defence. He squared the ball back to Lindsay, who hit a low, 20-yard shot into the net.

The Cup-holders, Arsenal, beat Swindon 2-0 away, while the winners this season, Leeds United, beat Bristol Rovers 4-1 at Elland Road.

In the First Round Bournemouth beat Margate 11-0, with former Red reserve, Ted MacDougall, scoring nine of the goals.

Oxford United: Kearns; Way, Shuker; Smithson, C.Clarke, Evanson; Skeen, Fleming(Sloan,70), D.Clarke, Cassidy, Aylott.

Liverpool: Clemence; Lawler, Lindsay; Smith, Ross, Hughes; Keegan, Hall(Graham,70), Thompson, Evans, Callaghan.

Referee: Mr W.J. Gow (Swansea)

Attendance: 18,000

February 5, 1972

Liverpool (0) 0   Leeds United (0) 0

LIVERPOOL kept the side which beat Crystal Palace 4-1 the previous week, while Leeds were without the services of the former England centre-half, Jack Charlton, who was a victim of flu. Madeley switched to centre-half, with Reaney going in at right back. Bates took over from the injured Gray on the left wing. The gates were shut soon after 2.10 with thousands locked outside.

Liverpool: Clemence; Lawler, Lindsay; Smith, Lloyd, Hughes; Keegan, Ross, Heighway, Toshack, Callaghan.

Leeds United: Sprake; Reaney, Cooper; Bremner, Madeley, Hunter; Lorimer, Clarke, Jones, Giles, Bates.

Referee: Mr G.W. Hill (Leicester)

Attendance: 56,300

Leeds kicked off towards the Kop and Lorimer, from just inside his own half, attempted to beat Clemence with a huge kick down the park. Clemence was alert to the danger and palmed the ball down from under the bar before picking up and clearing it. Liverpool carried the game to Leeds in the early minutes and low crosses from Callaghan and Heighway threatened danger, but resulted in nothing positive. A Lindsay chip aimed for Toshack's head was cut out by Sprake. With seven minutes gone, Reaney was booked for a tackle from behind on Heighway, who needed attention.

In the opening quarter-of-an-hour neither side had created any real attempt on goal with both defences solid and yielding nothing. With 17 minutes gone, Bremner pounced on to a loose ball 25 yards out and drove a low shot straight at Clemence. A minute later Heighway squandered a marvellous opportunity to put Liverpool ahead. Out near the corner flag on the Leeds left, Bates attempted a clearance which was headed down by Lawler to Toshack. As Sprake left his goal, Toshack pulled the ball wide of him and towards the penalty spot, where Heighway was racing in. The speeding Heighway completely missed his kick. A long-range shot from Cooper was easily dealt with by Clemence. Liverpool looked to be the sharper, smoother side as Emlyn Hughes contested everything in midfield and Toshack leading purposefully up front.

After 23 minutes a lob sent Clarke through. The entire Liverpool defence stood still, waiting for the whistle for offside, but the referee waved play on and Clemence dived bravely at the feet of Clarke, whose moment of hesitation on expecting to hear the whistle cost a certain goal.

Toshack rose high to nod down a chip from Hughes to Ross, who moved on to a shot which was blocked by the Leeds defence. Then Lorimer centred from the right, Smith beat Jones in the air, but could only send his clearance towards Clarke, whose first-time shot went over the bar. As Liverpool countered, Keegan robbed Madeley and passed to Heighway who dribbled forward at a retreating defence before unleashing a shot from outside the area which was deflected for a corner. Larry Lloyd dominated in the air as the Liverpool defence was in commanding form along the line. Five minutes before the interval Bremner's deep run down the middle resulted in him slipping the ball to Lorimer, whose shot from a narrow angle on the right was well saved by Clemence.

The Cup-tie was typical of games between these teams over recent years - dour and lacking in exciting goalmouth action. Shortly after the re-start a Keegan back-header presented Toshack with an opportunity inside the Leeds penalty area, but the chance was lost as Toshack was crowded out before getting in a shot. Liverpool attacked the Kop in this second period, and Toshack robbed Hunter on the halfway line before slipping the ball to Keegan, whose darting run enabled him to elude Hunter and then Cooper before having his shot blocked.

With 55 minutes gone a short corner on the right from Heighway to Callaghan was centred towards Lawler, who nodded the ball down into the path of Lloyd, but the centre-half failed to connect. Jones narrowly avoided an accident when, in trying to prevent the ball from going out near the corner flag, he ran headlong into railings at the corner of the Anfield Road end and the main stand. He was able to continue.

During a Liverpool onslaught, the Reds won a succession of corners on the right. From one flag kick, Keegan flicked on to Toshack, whose volley was deflected for another corner. The Liverpool midfield of Callaghan, Ross and Hughes was in great form, dominating the play.

After 70 minutes Callaghan beat Bates and Cooper in a race to the line and chipped across a perfect centre which Toshack met and headed powerfully down before Sprake saved on the line. An excellent Keegan run down the left took him past three defenders along the touchline, but his attempt to flick the ball into the middle was blocked. As the game entered its last ten minutes, Leeds played possession football in an attempt to secure a replay.

The official attendance of 56,300 was the highest at Anfield since February 20, 1963 when 57,906 saw a Fourth Round replay against Burnley.

Stoke drew 2-2 at Prenton Park against Tranmere, for whom Ron Yeats scored the Rovers' first goal. Tommy Lawrence played in goal, while the home side contained another former Red in Chris Fagan. Fred Molyneux, a former junior at Anfield, was also in the Tranmere line-up.

February 9, 1972

Leeds United (1) 2
Clarke 22, 63

Liverpool (0) 0

LIVERPOOL proposed to strangle Leeds in midfield by employing a 4-4-2 formation, bringing in Graham in the fourth midfield role in place of Toshack. Liverpool's initial caution did not prevent them from creating some genuine goalscoring opportunities, and Keegan placed a header in the path of Heighway, who was unable to get in his shot. Up for a free-kick, Lloyd headed against a post.

Leeds took the lead after 22 minutes when Allan Clarke sent a lob into the top corner, out of the reach of Clemence, who dived in desperation. Bremner had created the opportunity with a flamboyant flick of the heel.

During the second period Liverpool cast aside their defensive shackles and relied on their attacking force. They began to dominate the game for long periods, but Leeds broke away and stole a second goal through Clarke. Giles side-stepped Smith's desperate tackle on the half-way line and slipped the ball up the left to Clarke, who moved inside before beating Lloyd and squeezing the ball under the advancing Clemence.

Liverpool's indomitable spirit did not allow them to concede the match. Phil Boersma substituted for Steve Heighway and skied a shot over the net from less than ten yards out. Lawler had a shot blocked almost on the line by Charlton and Sprake produced a magnificent save to palm off the line a Graham header which looked destined for the net. Throughout the game Keegan, Graham and Callaghan worked prodigiously, but Leeds were always in control once they opened the scoring. Once Liverpool had released their grip on the midfield as they sought an equaliser, Giles found more space in which to orchestrate affairs and reduce the game to the pace he desired.

Tranmere lost 0-2 in a replay against Stoke. Leeds United went on to win the Cup against Arsenal with a goal from Clarke after 53 minutes.

PROGRESS TO THE FINAL
~~~~~

Fifth Round:	Cardiff City **0** Leeds United **2**
Sixth Round:	Leeds United **2** Tottenham Hotspur **1**
Semi-Final:	Leeds United **3** Birmingham City **0**
Final:	Leeds United **1** Arsenal **0**

Leeds: Sprake; Reaney(Jordan,79), Cooper; Bremner, Charlton, Hunter; Lorimer, Clarke, Madeley, Giles, Gray.

Liverpool: Clemence; Lawler, Lindsay; Smith, Lloyd, Hughes; Keegan, Ross, Heighway (Boersma,64), Graham, Callaghan.

Referee: Mr G.W. Hill (Leicester)

Attendance: 45,821

Allan Clarke, the scorer of both of the goals which put Liverpool out of the Cup

January 13, 1973

Burnley (0) 0

Liverpool (0) 0

SECOND Division Burnley held Liverpool to a goalless draw in a tense, thrilling Cup tie at a mist-shrouded Turf Moor on a bitter, wintry day. Jimmy Adamson, Burnley's manager, had proclaimed two seasons previously that his side would be the team of the 70s. He had certainly built a fine, young side which did not hold their more illustrious opponents in awe.

Burnley went closest to scoring when the busy Ingham went on a long run and the ball was crossed for centre-half Waldron, whom Bill Shankly tried to sign as a teenager, to hammer a tremendous shot inches over the bar. Right-half Dobson also went close to registering the first goal, while Hughes hit a powerful drive which the brave and agile Stevenson tipped over. Then the Liverpool number six fired another drive narrowly wide of the angle between post and crossbar. Hughes then finally beat Stevenson with a third superb shot, but Nulty cleared off the line. Nulty's endeavour was prodigious. He combined dour defensive qualities with an open mind on attacking at every opportunity. Nulty pounced swiftly to chip an angled shot over the bar when Smith stumbled as he chased a ball back towards his own goal.

The Liverpool defence coped admirably with the tricky Leighton James, while Lloyd marshalled Fletcher superbly. Toshack's return was disappointing, while Keegan and Heighway flattered to deceive with their tricks which brought no positive reward.

The Cup-holders Leeds drew 1-1 with Norwich, and it eventually took a third game before they settled the tie with a 5-0 victory. Sunderland - the surprise Second Division winners this season - drew 1-1 away to Notts County, before triumphing in the replay 2-0.

Burnley: Stevenson; Docherty, Newton; Dobson, Waldron, Thomson; Nulty, Casper, Fletcher, Ingham, James.

Liverpool: Clemence; Lawler, Lindsay; Smith, Lloyd, Hughes; Keegan, Cormack, Heighway, Toshack, Callaghan.

Referee: Mr H. Williams (Sheffield)

Attendance: 35,730

F.A. CUP - THIRD ROUND

Arsenal	2,2	Leicester City	2,1
Bradford City	2	Blackpool	1
Brighton	0	Chelsea	2
Carlisle United	2,1	Huddersfield Town	2,0
Charlton Athletic	1,0	Bolton Wanderers	1,4
Chelmsford City	1	Ipswich Town	3
Crystal Palace	2	Southampton	0
Everton	3	Aston Villa	2
Grimsby Town	0,1	Preston North End	0,0
Luton Town	2	Crewe Alexandra	0
Manchester City	3	Stoke City	2
Margate	0	Tottenham Hotspur	6
Millwall	3	Newport County	0
Newcastle United	2	Bournemouth	0
Norwich City	1,1	Leeds United	1,1
Notts County	1,0	Sunderland	1,2
Orient	1	Coventry City	4
Peterborough United	0	Derby County	1
Plymouth Argyle	1	Middlesbrough	0
Portsmouth	1,1	Bristol City	1,4
Port Vale	0	West Ham United	1
Queen's Park Rangers	0,3	Barnet	0,0
Reading	2	Doncaster Rovers	0
Sheffield Wednesday	2	Fulham	0
Scunthorpe United	2	Cardiff City	3
Stockport County	0,0	Hull City	0,2
Swindon Town	2	Birmingham City	0
Watford	0	Sheffield United	1
West Bromwich A.	1,0	Nottingham Forest	1,0
Wolverhampton W.	1	Manchester United	0
York City	0	Oxford United	1

Second Replays

Leeds United	5	Norwich City	0
West Bromwich A.	3	Nottingham Forest	1

January 16, 1973

Liverpool (1) 3
Toshack 31, 49, Cormack 75

Burnley (0) 0

THE hero of this tie was not two-goal John Toshack, but 22-year-old Alan Stevenson, the Burnley goalkeeper who saved his side on numerous occasions and in the first half alone he produced five excellent saves which gave his team some hope on a night in which Liverpool's form would have destroyed many First Division sides. He received a standing ovation from the appreciative Anfield crowd and Clemence responded by clapping and thumping the young goalkeeper warmly on the back. He saved from Lindsay before flicking a Lawler shot wide of the posts. Then he produced a fine finger-tip save from Cormack's 30-yard drive. He excelled himself by reaching a Cormack shot.

But after 31 minutes he was beaten by a relatively simple move. Cormack's corner dropped invitingly for Toshack to head just inside the post. The young Burnley side displayed their resilience and they responded by moving onto the offensive themselves. Defensive confusion in front of the Liverpool goal left Dobson with a shooting opportunity and, with Clemence out of his goal, a score appeared likely until the hard-working Cormack - who made his Cup début in the first tie against Burnley - cleared the danger. Then Casper gave Fletcher an easy chance of scoring, but he sent the ball high over the bar.

Soon into the second period Toshack scored again. From a Smith free-kick Keegan nodded the ball across and Toshack's header rolled slowly over the line as the goalkeeper fumbled for the only time in the match. Toshack's position was under threat with the proposed transfer of Lou Macari. Still Burnley would not concede the game, and after a James shot had rebounded, Clemence dived desperately to gain possession. The referee booked Lindsay and then Heighway for the first time in the winger's career - much to the consternation of Heighway.

After 75 minutes Heighway's cross was headed by Toshack towards Cormack who glided the ball away from Stevenson for a magnificent goal which underlined Liverpool's superiority.

Five Liverpool players were called up for international duty. Ray Clemence, Emlyn Hughes, Larry Lloyd, and Kevin Keegan were included in Sir Alf Ramsey's England squad to face Wales at Wembley on January 24. In addition, Wales selected John Toshack. England were forced to win the game to send them into their games with Poland in the World Cup qualifying competition with optimsim. Of those selected for the squads, only Larry Lloyd failed to play in the 1-1 draw. Toshack scored for the Welsh.

***Alan Stevenson**, the 22-year-old Burnley goalkeeper, who saved his side on numerous occasions and kept the scoreline down to respectable proportions*

Liverpool: Clemence; Lawler, Lindsay; Smith, Lloyd, Hughes; Keegan, Cormack, Heighway, Toshack, Callaghan.

Burnley: Stevenson; Docherty, Newton; Dobson, Waldron, Thomson; Nulty, Casper, Fletcher, Collins (Ingham,81), James.

Referee: Mr H. Williams (Sheffield)

Attendance: 56,124

February 4, 1973

Liverpool (0) 0

Manchester City (0) 0

THE gates were closed half-an-hour before the start of this bruising, ill-tempered Cup-tie with more than three thousand fans locked outside. Manchester City were guilty of 37 fouls, while Liverpool were penalised for 12 fouls. The Reds were not blameless in their retaliation to the violence, but the Manchester City manager, Malcolm Allison, appeared to have cast aside his footballing principles for ones more related to boxing. Heighway, Keegan and Cormack seemed to receive the greater share of City's violence. Keegan contributed little to the game although Heighway, despite being the victim of some ruthless scything tackles, remained a minor problem for the visitors.

The referee had an opportunity to stamp his authority on the game from as early as the first minute when Towers recklessly fouled Cormack. The referee failed to book Towers and the game was lost as a spectacle. Bell fouled Cormack without warning from the referee. Tony Book became the first man to be cautioned after 30 minutes. With 58 minutes gone, Larry Lloyd also had his name taken.

In the second period football eventually shone through, but chances were at a premium throughout the game. Toshack shot straight at Corrigan when in the clear. A Toshack cross passed over Book's head to Keegan, who blasted the ball wide of the goal. Before that, Heighway shot wide when in a good position.

A Summerbee header beat Clemence and struck the bar, and Cormack kicked out of play when the Liverpool goal was unprotected after a Hughes back-pass to Clemence had been intercepted by Marsh.

In the Central League Liverpool Reserves beat Manchester United Reserves 2-0 at Old Trafford with goals from Jack Whitham after 53 minutes and Derek Brownbill seven minutes later. Both were headed goals. Earlier Hugh McAuley had a penalty saved by Jimmy Rimmer.

Emlyn Hughes was brilliant in Smith's normal role, although the Liverpool midfield was lacking in Hughes' aggressive qualities. Phil Thompson performed well on his Cup début, and illustrated why manager Bill Shankly predicted great things for the youth with the spindly legs.

In the Cup, Sunderland drew 1-1 with Reading, though they won the replay 3-1 at Elm Park, while Leeds beat Plymouth Argyle 2-1 at Elland Road.

Liverpool:
Clemence;
Lawler, Lindsay;
Thompson, Lloyd,
Hughes; Keegan,
Cormack,
Heighway,
Toshack,
Callaghan.

Manchester City:
Corrigan; Book,
Donachie; Doyle,
Booth, Jeffries;
Summerbee, Bell,
Marsh, Lee,
Towers.

Referee:
Mr P. Partridge
(Middlesbrough)

Attendance:
56,296

Emlyn Hughes

Fourth Round replay

February 7, 1973

Manchester City (1) 2
Bell 13, Booth 51

Liverpool (0) 0

LIVERPOOL were deservedly beaten by a controlled and incisive Manchester City at Maine Road. The Reds failed to command the midfield, while man-for-man marking reduced the threat of Toshack, Keegan and Heighway to ordinary proportions. The home side preferred to rely on their football in the replay, casting aside their more belligerent proclivities.

With five minutes gone, Thompson's pass was pushed into the area by Keegan who found Toshack. The tall Welshman was opposed only by Corrigan and he aimed wide of the goalkeeper, but the 6ft 5ins giant managed to get to the ball and push it clear.

A simple Cormack mistake led to City's first goal. Bell pounced on the ball and put Towers in possession. A pass wide to Donachie enabled the full-back to put Lee in possession with an excellent cross. Lee crashed a fierce 20-yard drive at Clemence, but the goalkeeper could only parry the shot and Bell took the opportunity of scoring into an open goal. Shortly afterwards Doyle was booked for a foul on Keegan. The visitors responded in their traditional manner and Toshack hit the foot of a post, but from an offside position. Marsh almost scored with a spectacular kick, and on the stroke of half-time Clemence saved brilliantly from a Booth header. Six minutes into the second period City sealed Liverpool's fate. A free-kick just outside the area saw the ball expertly chipped for Bell, who missed with a header. The ball fell at the feet of Booth, who scrambled it into the goal. A clash between Lloyd and Lee ended with the Liverpool player being booked for the second game in succession. Cormack, who had been injured earlier, was replaced by Boersma immediately after City increased their lead. Thompson dropped back into Hughes' position in the back four, and Liverpool became much more assertive as they fought for an opening. Lee charged into Lloyd and received a booking.

Sunderland scored after only 80 seconds through centre-half Watson, who was used as a striker by manager Bob Stokoe. The Wearsiders won 3-1. The game of the round was Derby's thrilling 5-3 victory at White Hart Lane. County were 3-1

down with eleven minutes to go. A goal from Roger Davies - to complete his hat-trick - and another from Kevin Hector in extra time completed a remarkable recovery.

In the Welsh Cup, Oswestry were beaten at Victoria Road by visitors Bangor City, who won 8-1.

Phil Thompson*, who dropped back into Emlyn Hughes' position in the back four*

Manchester City: Corrigan; Book, Donachie; Doyle, Booth, Jeffries; Summerbee, Bell, Marsh, Lee, Towers.

Liverpool: Clemence; Lawler, Lindsay; Thompson, Lloyd, Hughes; Keegan, Cormack(Boersma,52), Heighway, Toshack, Callaghan.

Referee: Mr P. Partridge (Middlesbrough)

Attendance: 49,572

Receipts: £26,035

January 5, 1974

Liverpool (1) 2
Keegan 3, 57

Doncaster Rovers (2) 2
Kitchen 6, O'Callaghan 18

DONCASTER Rovers, bottom of the Fourth Division, held Liverpool at Anfield after leading the home side until almost an hour of the game had elapsed. The injured Larry Lloyd was replaced by local product 19-year-old Dave Rylands, playing in his first senior game for the club. John Toshack, also out through injury, was replaced by Phil Boersma. The Rovers lost the toss and kicked towards the Kop goal in the first half.

Doncaster's Liverpool-born Wignall brought down Keegan with a scything tackle which earned him a lecture from the referee while Keegan received treatment for an injured ankle. The visitors went close to scoring when Murray hit a low centre across the goal with Elwiss and O'Callaghan narrowly failing to make contact.

Liverpool scored in their first attack. Thompson broke up a Doncaster attack and sent Heighway racing clear with a brilliant pass. The high-kicking winger put Boersma in possession, and then the ball travelled on to Callaghan, whose centre was met by Keegan, and his header found the top corner.

The Rovers responded almost immediately, winning a corner on the left. The Liverpool defence failed to clear the ball properly and Woods sent it back into the middle for Kitchen to toe-end a shot towards the net. Clemence appeared to have stopped the ball but it rolled out of his hands and into the net.

An excellent dribble by Keegan created a chance for Boersma, but Book's brave save deflected the ball away. The inspirational Keegan had a magnificent game against the team he supported as a boy. With 18 minutes gone, Doncaster produced another shock for Liverpool by going into the lead. Murray drove across a low centre and three Liverpool defenders watched it go past towards O'Callaghan. Standing behind them, O'Callaghan tucked his shot past Clemence.

The Rovers went close to increasing their lead as Storton failed to move quickly to the ball as Woods sent an overhead pass to the wing. Kitchen sidefooted the ball high and wide from a genuine opportunity. The Liverpool defence gave too much room to O'Callaghan and Elwiss, while Murray was performing well on the right wing. The Reds appeared nervous and disjointed and Hughes hit a dangerous back-pass towards Clemence, which the goalkeeper saved at full stretch. Just before the interval Thompson hit a rasping 25-yard drive which beat Book but struck the bar. Liverpool then forced three corners in quick succession before Callaghan's shot was deflected wide by Brooks.

In the second period, Boersma almost equalised when, from a Callaghan cross, Keegan turned the ball inside, but Boersma's delay enabled Book to come off his line and divert the shot wide. Shortly afterwards a great header by Keegan was well saved by Book.

After excellent work by Keegan, Cormack failed to get any pace on his shot and Book saved easily. Callaghan and Keegan were the driving force behind Liverpool's fight to stay in the Cup, but defensive errors caused some concern. Rylands almost presented Elwiss with a goal.

After 57 minutes, Keegan equalised, to the relief of the Kop. Callaghan sent in a cross and Keegan jumped high to direct his header past Book with tremendous pace. The Fourth Division side continued to play football, and a fine move involving several players ended with Irvine shooting narrowly wide from the edge of the area.

With 20 minutes remaining, Liverpool substituted Boersma and sent on Hall. At this point in the game Liverpool attacked relentlessly and Doncaster soaked up the pressure bravely. Clemence was a virtual spectator in this second period, although he had to remain alert since Doncaster looked dangerous in breakaways.

Hall's calm assurance helped settle Liverpool into their rhythm. Irvine cleared off the line from Cormack's shot while at the other end Wignall's header following a corner was cleared off the line by Lindsay. In the final minute Kitchen hit the crossbar following another breakaway.

Newcastle United - this season's losing finalists drew 1-1 at home to non-League Hendon, winning the replay 4-0. Sunderland, the Cup-holders, drew 0-0 with Carlisle United, but lost in the replay by the only goal of the game.

Liverpool: Clemence; Storton, Lindsay; Thompson, Rylands, Hughes; Keegan, Cormack, Heighway, Boersma(Hall,70), Callaghan.

Doncaster Rovers: Book; Ternent, Brooks; Irvine, Uzelac, Wignall; Murray, Woods, O'Callaghan, Elwiss, Kitchen.

Referee: Mr R. Capey (Cheshire)

Attendance: 31,483

January 8, 1974

Doncaster Rovers (0) 0

Liverpool (1) 2
Heighway 15, Cormack 60

LIVERPOOL progressed into the Fourth Round with a performance which was smooth and controlled and which emphasised the gap between these two teams. Liverpool's defensive mistakes at Anfield were eradicated with the re-introduction of Larry Lloyd, though he was not fully fit with his thigh strain. However, his presence strengthened the Liverpool defence and his aerial command gave Liverpool complete authority in the middle at the back. Hughes and Lindsay played to their usual form, while Phil Thompson was switched to right-back and played with calm assurance. Hall, brought into midfield, employed thoughtfulness and intelligence to the creative rôle. Peter Cormack was in sparkling form, while Ian Callaghan performed competently. Unable to pick Peter Woods, Rovers brought in teenager Terry Curry at number seven, switching Alan Murray to an inside position.

Heighway was excellent in attack and he put Liverpool into an early lead as he took a headed pass from Waddle - making his début - before bringing the ball swiftly to his right foot and striking a shot firmly past Book. Keegan was in subdued form, and he shot over from a pass by Cormack, who had taken the ball to the by-line in excellent fashion. Cormack laid on a chance for Heighway, who also shot over the top. A tremendous drive by Lindsay was well saved by Book as Liverpool sought to increase their lead.

Cormack's firm header from Lindsay's free-kick settled the tie without doubt. Doncaster Rovers played well on the day and performed heroically at Anfield, but class eventually told. Liverpool's opening goal was magnificent. Alan Waddle headed the ball down for Steve Heighway to give Kim Book

no chance with a powerful strike from 15-yards. A minute later only the finger tips of Ray Clemence prevented the home side from scoring a swift equaliser. Brendan O'Callaghan headed from point blank range, but Clemence atoned for his mistake with Kitchen's goal in the game on the previous Saturday by making an outstanding save.

The absence of Peter Woods, who missed the game because of gastro-enteritis, seemed to take some of the balanced look away from the Rovers side and, until the latter stages, Kitchen played deeper than usual in order to fill the gap. The enforced move robbed the frontline of the man most likely to seize on the half-chance. Kitchen tried desperately to work in midfield and apply potency up front. A late goal by 20-year-old striker Mike Elwiss was disallowed for offside, after he had side-footed a Murray cross past Clemence. Earlier, Brendan O'Callaghan played on and planted the ball in the net although he was well offside.

Peter Cormack *was in sparkling form*

Doncaster Rovers: Book; Ternent, Brooks; Irvine, Uzelac, Wignall; Curran, Murray, O'Callaghan, Elwiss, Kitchen.

Liverpool: Clemence; Thompson, Lindsay; Hall, Lloyd, Hughes; Keegan, Cormack, Heighway, Waddle, Callaghan.

Referee: Mr R. Capey (Cheshire)

Attendance: 22,499

Colours: Rovers: African Violet shirts, black shorts
Liverpool: Red shirts, white shorts

Weather: Rain

Ground: Good

January 26, 1974

Liverpool (0) 0   Carlisle United (0) 0

LIVERPOOL had Phil Boersma replacing Steve Heighway, with Brian Hall as substitute and John Toshack back in the side after having missed four games through injury. Second Division Carlisle opened brightly and beat Liverpool to the ball in midfield. Carlisle were aware of the threat of Keegan, Green and Balderstone bringing the impish striker down with fierce tackles which earned them words from the referee. A Smith free kick was met by Toshack, but his header went high into the air and Ross dealt with it easily. The visitors were skilful in building up swift attacks, though Liverpool's superiority was evident, mainly through the endeavour of Keegan.

Martin switched the ball inside with a delicate touch before Martin volleyed over the bar when challenged by Lloyd. Balderstone was Carlisle's most skilful and enterprising player and he was the lynchpin in a Carlisle defence which came under increasing pressure from the hosts. With 24 minutes gone, Toshack initiated the best move of the match. The Welshman dispossessed Gorman before heading for goal and driving a fine shot on target which Ross brilliantly turned round a post. Then Smith moved up to rob Laidlaw and slip the ball through to Thompson. An early pass found Toshack, but his shot, taken in his stride, went past the far post. As Liverpool attacked with urgency a shot by Cormack was deflected to Lloyd, who had moved upfield for a corner. Lloyd's shot struck the goalkeeper and ran away to safety. The home side were superior in technique and had the bulk of the possession, but their Second Division opponents defended competently. The gusting wind and incessant rain created problems for Liverpool, though their attacking ideas lacked real invention. An accurate Boersma cross found Toshack and the striker's header was stopped on the line by Green with the Carlisle goalkeeper well beaten. At the other end, Clemence had little to do, such was Liverpool's dominance.

The referee reduced the interval time to the minimum due to the deteriorating conditions and poor light. Keegan moved swiftly down the right and put an inch-perfect pass into the path of Toshack, but he overran the ball and missed it altogether. The visitors pulled nine men back in defence as Liverpool continued their policy of all-out attack. Thompson hit a shot which passed just over the bar and Lindsay's 35-yard drive went narrowly wide. Callaghan gave up his customary midfield role in favour of the old-fashioned outside-right position. He made several runs down the wing with Smith keeping him fed with a constant supply of the ball. With the rain falling in torrents, Ross caught the ball from a Boersma corner as Lloyd lent his menacing height to the attack.

Eventually Carlisle broke free, but with Clarke as a lone striker they were unable to threaten much. In a crowded goalmouth, Ross effected saves from Cormack and Toshack. The mercurial Callaghan laid on a further opportunity for Toshack, but Ross dived bravely at the Welshman's feet and turned the ball away for another corner. Callaghan continually took the ball to the line before crossing the ball with pinpoint accuracy in a wonderful display of the art of wing-play. Green and Balderstone were excellent in the air, and prevented Callaghan's crosses from being more potent.

Tommy Smith was booked two minutes before the end for a tackle on Martin.

In the other ties, Manchester United were beaten by a single goal at Old Trafford by Ipswich Town, while Newcastle drew 1-1 with Scunthorpe, before winning the replay 3-0.

Bill Shankly

Liverpool: Clemence; Smith, Lindsay; Thompson, Lloyd, Hughes; Keegan, Cormack, Toshack, Boersma, Callaghan.

Carlisle United: Ross; Carr, Gorman; O'Neill, Green, Balderstone; Martin, Train, Owen, Clarke, Laidlaw.

Referee: Mr J.K. Taylor (Wolverhampton)

Attendance: 47,211

January 29, 1974

Carlisle United (0) 0

Liverpool (0) 2
Boersma 50, Toshack 81

CARLISLE dominated the first half with their calm, cultured football played in an intelligent style. The Liverpool defence rocked under the constant pressure from Laidlaw, O'Neill and Martin. Hughes worked prodigiously in the middle of the defence, but Carlisle went close on several occasions. O'Neill almost scored when his shot was blocked by Clemence, who swiftly left his line to prevent a goal. Liverpool were impotent in attack with Balderstone directing operations with great composure.

Manager Bill Shankly told his players during the interval that they had been far too casual and that if they persisted with that mood, they would be beaten. The Reds rallied to his inspirational call and in the first five minutes of the second period they attacked with such relentless ferocity that a goal resulted.

Liverpool's pace and direct running at the opposition was finally too much for Carlisle and Boersma scored after 50 minutes. He turned and hammered the ball into the roof of the net after Toshack and Keegan had opened up the defence.

The Second Division side appeared to become dejected, and while they fought to regroup Liverpool went close on three occasions. Eventually the home side's spirit enabled them to get back into the game, though they could not find the composure which had been the hallmark of their earlier play.

Hughes cleared an O'Neill shot which Clemence turned on to a post, and then the goalkeeper pushed another O'Neill shot over the bar. Generally, however, the Boersma goal had given Liverpool a platform upon which they built victory by dictating the pace and displaying their skills.

Nine minutes from the finish Toshack settled the issue beyond doubt. Hall began the move by worming his way past three tackles before laying on the chance for the Welshman.

Carlisle were unfortunate in defeat. Only a magnificent display in midfield from Callaghan, with Hall in great supporting role, saved the day for the Reds. Hall replaced Cormack as the only change in the team since the previous game, and his tenacity and skill helped to provide a determined look to the midfield and, with Thompson's strength, this victory was achieved through the grip exercised by the men in the middle of the park.

Boersma was in inspired form after the break, while Keegan - ineffective in the first half - found his passion and determination later on. Hughes was the master in defence, though he was ably assisted by Tommy Smith, who, although being booked for a tackle on Laidlaw, was generally successful against the Carlisle midfielder.

Liverpool's reward for overcoming gallant Carlisle was a draw against First Division Ipswich Town, the tie to be played on February 16.

***Brian Hall**, who played a great supporting rôle to Ian Callaghan's brilliance in midfield against a determined and skilful Carlisle side*

Carlisle United: Ross; Carr, Gorman; O'Neill, Green, Balderstone; Martin, Train(Tiler,67), Owen, Clarke, Laidlaw.

Liverpool: Clemence; Smith, Lindsay; Thompson, Lloyd, Hughes; Keegan, Hall, Boersma, Toshack, Callaghan.

Referee: Mr J.K. Taylor (Wolverhampton)

Attendance: 21,262

February 16, 1974

Liverpool (1) 2
Hall 33, Keegan 55

Ipswich Town (0) 0

LIVERPOOL skipper Emlyn Hughes was declared fit before the game while Ipswich recalled their Irish international, Hunter, into defence for their only change. The rain-laden sky looked ominous as Liverpool moved swiftly onto the attack towards the Kop goal. The pitch was heavily sanded down the middle.

Although Lindsay was under pressure, he managed to get in a fine centre which was met by Waddle, who headed the ball across to Cormack, whose first-time effort went low into Sivell's arms. Shortly afterwards Lindsay robbed Burley on the line before turning the ball inside to Keegan, but Mills raced across to effect a fine interception. From the corner, Waddle's header was well saved by Sivell.

Ipswich won a corner from their first attack. Thompson pushed the ball away as Hamilton challenged, but Morris's kick was met by Waddle, who was fouled by Johnson. Whymark initiated a fine Ipswich move with a pass to Lambert, and when he got the return ball he hit a great shot on the turn which Clemence had covered. Lambert put a long pass out to Johnson, whose pace enabled him to collect, but Hughes anticipated the danger and relieved the threat of Johnson.

Smith was in sparkling form, repelling Ipswich with a series of firm tackles and precision passing. Ipswich moved with pace and commitment, but the Liverpool defence was resolute. The game ebbed and flowed in the traditional manner of a Cup-tie. A splendid run by Boersma, in which he turned the ball from the left to the right before Hunter turned it away for a corner was warmly applauded. Kevin Beattie, the Ipswich Town youngster, was in his usual immaculate form as he stamped his class and authority on the heart of the defence. Waddle limped slightly and his injury began to handicap Liverpool and Keegan carried the responsibility of the attack on his broad shoulders. Hall assisted the attack whenever his job allowed, and when he moved out of midfield to operate down the right he passed the ball inside to Callaghan, who drove a fine left-foot shot from 20 yards which Sivell turned round the post after a full-length dive.

Waddle headed the ball through to Boersma, who did well to get it under control in the penalty area. As Sivell advanced off his line, Boersma managed a shot which trickled just wide of the far post. Keegan was booked for an off-the-ball incident in which he retaliated against Morris after provocation.

Liverpool began to dominate, and with Callaghan doing his usual job of stemming the opposition flow and creating Liverpool attacks, the Reds took the lead after 33 minutes. Hall initiated the move and completed the task of scoring. The goal began with a pass to Callaghan, on the right, and the midfielder cut inside with pace and took the ball past Talbot, before slotting through a precision pass to Hall, who saw his chance and hit an accurate shot past Sivell, the ball hitting the inside of the far upright before entering the net. Hughes had attention from trainer Joe Fagan before the game restarted and soon afterwards Lindsay was also injured. Whymark went close to an equaliser when he headed the ball down from Morris's free-kick, but Clemence was equal to the task and saved well. As the interval approached Smith stormed through from defence and brushed aside tackles with an air of casual ease before pushing the ball through to Waddle, who was adjudged offside.

As the second half began Waddle was still limping. Liverpool controlled the game and restricted Ipswich to showing rare glimpse of their true ability. Smith hurt his arm and held it awkwardly by his side. The injury did not prevent him from pushing a pass up the line to Hall, though Beattie cleared the danger and conceded a corner. Both defences dominated.

Ten minutes after the interval Liverpool scored through Keegan. Waddle, who collected a loose ball 25 yards out, took it down the left before crossing low into the goalmouth. Boersma tried to shoot but miskicked, and the ball ran through to Keegan, who had the simple task of pushing it into the net.

The crowd rose *en masse* to Smith as he contemptuously took the ball upfield after several Ipswich tackles and sent in a fierce shot which Sivell had to turn round the post.

With 64 minutes gone Viljoen substituted for Lambert, who had had a poor game against Smith. The Reds continued to dominate the game and Sivell tipped the ball over the bar from a fine Waddle header. Liverpool lay siege to the Ipswich goal and Beattie took the ball off Waddle's toes after Keegan had presented the tall striker with a glorious opportunity. Then Boersma stormed through on an excellent run but he shot against Sivell's body.

Liverpool: Clemence; Smith, Lindsay; Thompson, Cormack, Hughes; Keegan, Hall, Boersma, Waddle, Callaghan.

Ipswich Town: Sivell; Burley, Mills; Morris, Hunter, Beattie; Hamilton, Talbot, Johnson, Whymark, Lambert (Viljoen,64).

Referee: Mr J. Hunting (Leicester)

Attendance: 45,340

March 9, 1974

Bristol City (0) 0

Liverpool (0) 1
Toshack 48

BILL Shankly named the team which won 1-0 at home in the previous week to Burnley with an 89th minute Toshack goal. Heighway made his first appearance since he dropped out of the team prior to the Cup-tie with Carlisle. Merrick, the City captain, lost his week-long struggle against fitness after an ankle injury. He was replaced by Rodgers.

Bristol City: Cashley; Sweeney, Drysdale; Gow, Collier, Rodgers; Tainton, Ritchie, Fear, Gillies, Hunt (Emmanuel,71).

Liverpool: Clemence; Smith, Lindsay; Thompson, Cormack, Hughes; Keegan, Hall, Heighway (Boersma,85), Toshack, Callaghan.

Referee: Mr D. Turner (Cannock)

Attendance: 37,671

The Liverpool defence was under pressure in City's first attack, but Hunt, the former Everton player, handled the ball before shooting. Hunt was made skipper in Merrick's absence. Keegan's headed pass sent Toshack down the right and when the impish Keegan received the ball back, Rodgers managed to push it for a corner.

Tainton robbed Cormack and sent in a fine cross which Smith nonchalantly nodded back to Clemence before Gillies could make contact. Toshack headed the ball into the goalmouth after a Lindsay free-kick. The ball was partially cleared, but it went out to Hall who returned it and Keegan's header was saved by Cashley as he dived.

The dual partnership of Toshack and Keegan caused City several problems and the Welshman headed down to Keegan, whose hook shot as he fell slipped wide of the post. A moment of indecision led Callaghan trying to turn the ball back to Thompson, but Fear anticipated and pushed it to the right for Tainton to hit across a fast, low centre which Clemence dived and held.

Excellent work by Hall put Heighway in possession and his centre was headed away by Gow for a corner with Toshack lurking dangerously nearby. City won their first flag-kick after 23 minutes. A swift, incisive pass by Fear to Gillies opened Liverpool's defence down the left. Hall went back to get a foot to the centre and turn it over the line.

Fear hit a strong 20-yard shot straight at Clemence. Liverpool dominated and allowed City few goalscoring opportunities. The Reds displayed greater technique and control, though both goalkeepers had been rarely troubled.

Three minutes after the interval Liverpool took the lead. The move started in their own penalty area as Thompson cleared

the ball down the line to Lindsay, who passed it on to Heighway. Keegan collected on the half-way line, beat Collier neatly and sped away down the left wing. From his cross Rodgers challenged Toshack, but the City player lost possession as he stumbled and the Welshman made no mistake from 10 yards.

The home side responded with a series of worthwhile attacks, but the Liverpool defence stood firm. Five minutes after the goal Smith went close with a brilliant shot. Cormack pushed the ball to him from a free-kick and Smith's fiercely-struck drive curled over the bar. The visitors produced some delightful touches in the middle of the park, but with Keegan having a poor game, several moves broke down without a shot on goal. With 71 minutes gone, City brought on Emmanuel for Hunt, who had made little impact on the game. A great pass from Fear opened up the Liverpool defence, but Tainton, after moving at speed down the left, shot hurriedly and missed the target.

John Toshack

After good approach work Callaghan's instinctive shot passed wide. From a free-kick just outside the City area, Cormack touched the ball to Lindsay, who caught it with his left foot, but the ball travelled straight to Cashley.

With just five minutes remaining, Liverpool sent on Boersma for Heighway, who was limping after a series of fierce tackles by Sweeney.

Leicester beat Queen's Park Rangers 2-0 in London, while Burnley beat Wrexham 1-0. Newcastle and Nottingham Forest fought out a thrilling seven-goal encounter, which Newcastle won 4-3.

The F.A. ordered a replay of the original tie, which finished goalless. Newcastle won the replay 1-0. Both replays were at Goodison Park.

March 30, 1974

Leicester City (0) 0   Liverpool (0) 0

LIVERPOOL kicked off attacking the Stretford Road end, and won an early free-kick for a foul by Worthington on Smith. Weller cleared the ball, but Liverpool responded immediately and went on the attack. A long pass from Smith was intended for Toshack, but it was intercepted by Cross.

A Cross foul on Keegan gave Liverpool a free-kick outside the penalty area, and Hall's kick went across the goal before being put behind for a corner. The kick was put behind by Lindsay. Liverpool won a further free-kick and Callaghan hit the ball high into the goalmouth but Shilton raced off his line to collect the ball as the ominous Toshack threatened. Liverpool maintained their pressure and Keegan headed on for Toshack, but Munro got to the ball first. Weller cleared the danger with a back pass to Shilton. Heighway sped past Whitworth and crossed into the middle where Toshack stabbed at the ball. There was little power behind Toshack's shot, and Shilton held the ball without trouble.

Clemence was called upon to make a serious save after 11 minutes. He raced off his line to hold the ball from Glover's left wing cross as Worthington moved in dangerously. A Thompson foul gave Leicester a free-kick 10 yards outside the Liverpool penalty area. The ball was charged down but Sammels had a second shot which he hit wide of the target. Keegan was brought down by Munro, and from the free-kick Lindsay chipped the ball over the defensive wall. Toshack rose above the Leicester defence but directed his header wide of Shilton's left-hand post.

Callaghan was busy in midfield and he cut in from the right before having a shot blocked. Heighway pounced on the rebound, but his right-foot shot was blocked and cleared. Waters and Whitworth combined well but Weller's foul on Lindsay brought the attacking move to an end. Lindsay then put Liverpool away again but Keegan headed straight at Shilton.

Leicester were awarded a free-kick when Cormack fouled Worthington and Earle headed over the bar from the free-kick. With 32 minutes gone, Liverpool almost took the lead. Heighway won a corner on the left and Keegan's header beat Shilton, but Rofe headed the ball off the line.

The game was held up for a lengthy spell while Keegan received treatment after clashing with Cross. Soon afterwards Callaghan was treated after being brought down by Weller. Keegan raced onto a ball from a first-time clearance by Smith, and crossed from the right, but the ball was intercepted by Cross before Toshack could reach it. Liverpool dominated the first half and won a further corner from which Shilton caught the ball diving at full stretch to catch the ball after

Heighway's flag-kick. With a minute to go to the interval, Munro was booked for bringing Keegan down from behind. From the free-kick, Hughes' powerful shot was blocked by the defensive wall.

Leicester attacked strongly from the restart and Glover went past Smith and Thompson before crossing into the middle, where Worthington hit a first-time left-foot shot past the post. A long pass down the middle by Sammels was intercepted by Hughes, who headed back to Clemence as Earle raced in behind. Liverpool responded with a back-heel from Keegan which opened up the Leicester defence to give Heighway room for a shot, but the ball went straight at Shilton.

With 51 minutes gone Lindsay almost scored when, from a Heighway cross from the left, Toshack headed the ball on to Lindsay, who ran through to lob the ball over the advancing Shilton, but just wide of the post. At this stage in the game, the Liverpool pressure was at its height.

After 54 minutes Toshack crossed from the right and the ball beat Shilton. Keegan got in a header, but brilliant covering by Cross enabled him to clear off the line. In the next minute Hall's left-foot shot passed narrowly wide of the post. Leicester broke away and Waters shot wide with a 20-yard drive. Heighway had to receive treatment after being brought down in a crunching tackle. From the free-kick, just outside the penalty area, Hughes shot wide. Liverpool's attacking strength continued and Toshack had a header saved by Shilton before the goalkeeper cut out a dangerous Keegan cross from the left-wing.

When Smith and Worthington clashed in the penalty area after 70 minutes Leicester appealed for a penalty, but the referee waved play on. Some great skill by Keegan took him past Rofe and into the penalty area before attempting a right-foot shot from a narrow angle which Shilton turned behind. Keegan then put Heighway clear on the left, and the Republic of Ireland international hit a perfect centre into the middle which Shilton caught at full stretch.

Nine minutes from the end a foul by Sammels on Callaghan earned Liverpool a free-kick. Smith tapped the ball sideways from the kick and Lindsay blasted it wide of the post. A minute from time Keegan beat Shilton with a header but the ball hit the post and bounced out.

In the other semi-final, Burnley, with Leighton James in brilliant form, dominated the first half against Newcastle at Hillsborough, but were unable to turn their smooth attacks into goals. Bobby Moncur was excellent in the heart of the Newcastle defence and his side went in front after 65 minutes through Malcolm Macdonald. Eleven minutes later Macdonald scored again and put Newcastle into the final.

Leicester City: Shilton; Whitworth, Rofe; Earle, Munro, Cross; Weller, Sammels, Worthington, Waters, Glover.

Liverpool: Clemence; Smith. Lindsay; Thompson, Cormack, Hughes; Keegan, Hall, Heighway, Toshack, Callaghan.

Referee: Mr K.H. Burns (Dudley)

Attendance: 60,000 (at Old Trafford)

Division One

	Pl	W	D	L	F	A	Pts
Leeds United	35	20	12	3	58	29	52
Liverpool	**33**	**20**	**8**	**5**	**41**	**23**	**48**
Derby County	35	14	13	8	45	33	41
Ipswich Town	36	15	10	11	59	52	40
Q.P.R.	33	12	14	7	50	41	38
Everton	35	14	10	11	43	38	38
Burnley	33	13	10	10	43	40	36
Leicester City	**34**	**11**	**13**	**10**	**41**	**34**	**35**

Peter Shilton, Leicester City's goalkeeper, who had a magnificent game in the semi-final

April 3, 1974

Leicester City (0) 1

Glover 48

Liverpool (0) 3

Hall 46, Keegan 62,
Toshack 86

THE first half was goalless and Leicester deserved to be level, forcing Clemence to work harder than Shilton. Sammels twice went close with efforts that passed over the bar and Clemence was twice in trouble, first with a cross by Weller that he dropped and then a shot by Stringfellow that he could not hold. On both occasions he recovered. For Liverpool, Keegan shot outside the near post after breaking free following a free-kick. The fleet-footed Liverpool man also went close with a header from a Heighway cross. Another Heighway centre was palmed away by Shilton, and then Hall went close with a magnificent drive. Just before the interval Toshack was put clear by Keegan, but the Welshman finished poorly.

The Reds scored within a minute of the resumption. Keegan passed to Heighway, whose cross was headed into the goal by Toshack. A mêlée developed and Hall forced the ball home. The adage that a team which has just scored is vulnerable to conceding a goal was justified when Leicester equalised within three minutes of the shock opening goal. The move was initiated by Worthington, and was continued by Earle in the box. Although the ball seemed to break loose with the Liverpool defence in disarray. Glover was on hand to slam the ball into the back of the net. It was the first goal Liverpool had conceded in nine matches.

With Sammels in the centre of the middle three, and Glover and Weller attacking from either flank, Liverpool were not allowed time to dwell on the ball.

Soon after the equalising goal, Stringfellow, who returned to the side in place of Waters and played well up front, worked a superb one-two with Weller. The number seven ran on and sent in a vicious left-foot shot. Clemence managed to knock it away brilliantly, and this appeared to be the turning point of the game.

With 62 minutes gone, Keegan volleyed home an unstoppable shot. The Reds went on to play magnificently and their possession football completely unsettled Leicester, who pushed Cross forward. With the defence stretched, Cormack slipped a perfect through-ball to Toshack, who ran on to score. Liverpool always had a man to pass to and their ability to turn defence into attack was remarkable. Whitworth had a good match in the Leicester defence and Cross was outstanding. In front of him, Sammels was sound and Weller showed some touches of brilliance. The Liverpool defence was superbly marshalled by Hughes, and presented a formidable barrier, although Thompson often miskicked.

After the game, manager Bill Shankly said, "Now we're ready for the assault on the League Championship. Semi-finals are usually so full of tension that they tend to be games of kick and rush. But this was a magnificent match with hardly a foul in it and was a credit to both teams. We

played as well as we have ever played. We played class football from the back, moving the ball around with skill and flair. It was marvellous to watch in such an electric atmosphere. Now perhaps these boys who have done so much for so many years will receive the credit they deserve. They all played well but Kevin Keegan was just brilliant. He is the finest player in England and why he doesn't play for England, I'll never understand. He scored a goal that only a brilliant player could score. It was a fantastic performance."

Keegan had been suffering from a stomach upset for three days before the replay. Assistant manager Bob Paisley said, "We were worried about Kevin since Monday. He didn't feel well but it must have just been nerves because everyone saw how he played. I have never seen any player turn on two consecutive performances of such class as he did against Leicester."

Kevin Keegan

Leicester City: Shilton; Whitworth, Rofe; Earle, Monro, Cross; Weller, Sammels, Worthington, Stringfellow, Glover.

Liverpool: Clemence; Smith, Lindsay; Thompson, Cormack, Hughes; Keegan, Hall, Heighway, Toshack, Callaghan.

Referee: Mr K.F. Burns (Stourbridge)

Attendance: 55,619 (at Villa Park)

SHANKLY'S FINAL TRIUMPH

KEEGAN'S DOUBLE STRIKE

LINDSAY'S DISALLOWED GOAL

Liverpool (0) 3 Newcastle United (0) 0

Keegan 57, 88
Heighway 75

LIVERPOOL prepared for the Final with two days in a small, quiet country hotel while Newcastle spent five days in a big hotel and became increasingly bored. They played golf as Liverpool rested. Manager Shankly's message was "Keep it simple and stick to the normal routine as much as possible."

Psychology

Apart from a chorus of *"We're on the way to Wembley"* and *"You'll Never Walk Alone"* on the coach ride from the hotel to Wembley, it was as though Liverpool were playing a League game in London rather than the FA Cup Final itself. A piece of the Shankly psychology.

The Liverpool manager was convinced that his team would win the Cup after the semi-final victory over Leicester City. His great determination and unswerving belief in victory over Newcastle was imparted to his players in his own inimitable style.

Banners

The weather conditions were perfect with an overcast sky, a cool day with little wind. The Liverpool supporters were in fine voice and they displayed several banners in red and white which flouted the Wembley bye-laws. Emlyn Hughes won the toss for Liverpool and chose to attack the goal where their fans were grouped. The Reds won two free-kicks within a minute. From the second, Lindsay sent the ball curling across the goalface but no Liverpool player was able to make contact.

Rhythm

Liverpool found their rhythm immediately and, winning the ball in midfield, they launched several strong attacks. From a Lindsay cross Howard mis-headed and the ball looped over to Keegan but Clark headed the ball over the bar for a corner. Hughes headed away a dangerous cross from Hibbitt as Tudor lurked near the Liverpool goal. Tommy Smith tackled McDermott fairly but heavily, and his authority was therefore soon established.

Soon afterwards Lindsay was spoken to by the referee for a heavy tackle on Jimmy Smith. Alan Kennedy raced 20 yards to bring down Keegan and the Reds were awarded another free-kick. McFaul went up to gather Tommy Smith's centre. Newcastle first troubled Liverpool when Macdonald backheaded the ball into the penalty area and Hughes and Thompson were involved in a scramble before Clemence dived among the players to grab the ball.

Fiercely

Heighway sped into the penalty area and crossed hard from the line. The ball went to Tommy Smith, who drove the ball back fiercely towards Hall, but the speed of the ball was too much for Hall to control.

As Newcastle attacked, Liverpool withdrew everybody into their area as Hibbitt took a free-kick 25 yards from goal. He chipped the ball goalwards but Toshack headed clear.

Collided

With 21 minutes gone, MacDonald's fierce shot struck Lindsay and went for a throw-in. Thompson and McDermott - both from Kirkby - clashed and the Newcastle midfielder had to receive attention.

Moncur and McFaul collided in going for a ball which the goalkeeper should have left to his captain.

Keegan sent in a fine shot, noticing that McFaul had left his line in anticipation of a centre. Keegan aimed at the gap behind him, but McFaul turned quickly and made a good save by the post.

Brilliant

Liverpool almost scored after some brilliant work by the mercurial Keegan, who raced down the left wing beating two tackles before crossing the ball into the goalmouth.

The Newcastle goalkeeper dropped the ball as Toshack went for the header, but McFaul recovered swiftly to dive on the ball before Toshack could reach it. Liverpool began to dominate with Keegan in sparkling form. The former Scunthorpe player's speed in chesting the ball down presented Toshack with an opportunity, but the shot was deflected for a corner by Howard. Hibbitt began to limp badly after injuring himself in turning quickly for the ball. The Reds

dominated the first half due to the immense grip their midfield had on the game.

A Keegan shot went high and wide before Thompson dispossessed MacDonald and won a free-kick when the Newcastle striker pushed Thompson.

Offside

Lindsay's magnificent left-foot shot from just outside the penalty area was held by McFaul. With seven minutes of the second half gone, Lindsay beat McFaul with a magnificent cross shot, but the flag had been raised against Keegan who had run into an offside position. Keegan raced on to a long pass from Smith but the linesman signalled that the ball had just run over the line before he crossed it.

Keegan's goal

With 57 minutes gone, Liverpool took a deserved lead. Hall dummied to let a right-wing cross go past him. Keegan controlled the ball at speed and from just inside the area he drove a right-foot shot past McFaul. The goal spurred Liverpool to even greater action. Hughes drove a free-kick narrowly over the bar as Liverpool attacked at will. Newcastle responded when McDermott flew past Lindsay and hit a low cross which went past the goalkeeper and eluded everybody. Heighway crowned a great Liverpool move with a strong left-foot shot which sailed narrowly past the post. Clemence handled the high balls with great aplomb, though he had little to do in the general run of play.

After 75 minutes Heighway scored in his second final.

Clemence hit a high ball up the middle and Toshack back-headed it to Heighway. The Eire international took it round Howard and hit a low shot past McFaul. It was Heighway's second goal in finals for Liverpool, having scored against Arsenal in 1971.

Substituted

Newcastle substituted Smith with Gibb before the game restarted. MacDonald pulled his shot wide and the menace of the much-vaunted Supermac had been completely eliminated by Liverpool's resolute defence. The Liverpool fans created a tremendous noise as their team put on an exhibition of great inter-passing and free flowing football. With two minutes of the match remaining, Smith laid on Liverpool's third when he raided down the right before hitting a low centre which Keegan drove into the net.

Shankly

After the game Bill Shankly was calm and reflective, saying: "What pleased me most was the way we won the Cup. It was done in style. I think now that this team can go on to become even better than the mid-sixties side. The prospects are endless. The old team won the League-Cup-League in successive years. We'll win the League next year." Tommy Smith and Ian Callaghan, who played in the 1965 Final against Leeds agreed that this was a much better occasion because of Liverpool's improved performance.

Skipper Hughes said: "How can we fail with a bunch of lads like this?"

Before the match Hughes introduced Callaghan to Princess Anne saying: "This is the lad who has won everything this year." The Princess replied: "Yes, I've read all about him." Emlyn responded with: "You'll have to watch out if he takes up horse riding as well!" The Princess laughed.

In a humorous vein, Chairman John Smith said that it was clear that the Royal party at the game were made confirmed Liverpool fans by the brilliance of the Reds' display.

Continuing, Mr Smith praised the Liverpool fans as the "best supporters in the country."

The banquet at the Savoy was a grand affair. The speeches were kept to a minimum. Mr Smith paid full tribute to Bill Shankly and his players and singled out Peter Robinson as the "best secretary in the game."

Sincerity

Bill Shankly thanked his players and his devoted staff. His words came from the heart and with complete conviction, mixing humour with absolute sincerity. Emlyn Hughes, cheered by his team-mates, thanked "the Boss and his wife, the chairman and the directors, the training staff, and our wives for their understanding in a time of stress."

Delirious

The Liverpool party was welcomed back home by hundreds of thousands of delirious supporters. The massacre of Newcastle United - who had never been beaten in a Wembley final - was complete.

Abba - the Swedish winners of the Eurovision Song Contest - were top of the UK charts with the song "Waterloo". Newcastle had certainly met theirs.

Worship

At the end of the one-sided contest, several Liverpool fans ran on to the pitch and knelt as if in worship at the feet of manager Bill Shankly.

The delighted fans were simply paying their respects to the manager, who had masterminded his team to a glorious victory against a very good Newcastle side.

Kevin Keegan is mobbed after scoring the first goal against Newcastle United

Liverpool: Clemence; Smith, Lindsay; Thompson, Cormack, Hughes; Keegan, Hall, Heighway, Toshack, Callaghan.

Newcastle United: McFaul; Clark, Kennedy; McDermott, Howard, Moncur; Smith(Gibb,76), Cassidy, MacDonald, Tudor, Hibbitt.

Referee: Mr G.C. Kew (Amersham)

Attendance: 100,000

Kevin Keegan and Alec Lindsay celebrate victory

From Paisley

To
The
Double

1975 - 1986

January 4, 1975

Liverpool (0) 2
Heighway 78,
Keegan 89

Stoke City (0) 0

BOTH teams lined up on the pitch as they came out of the tunnel to warmly applaud Ian Callaghan, who received the M.B.E. for his services to football in the New Year's Honours lists. Phil Neal made his Cup début for Liverpool, while this was Bob Paisley's first FA Cup game as manager, having taken over the reins upon Bill Shankly's retirement. Shilton, in the Kop goal, received a great ovation.

Stoke cleared an early Keegan free-kick and won two corners on the right. Salmons took the second of these and Smith rose high above the Liverpool defence to meet the kick and send a header narrowly over the bar. Stoke countered a Liverpool attack and Hudson forced another corner down the left. The ball was partially cleared to Pejic who shot over the bar with a powerful volley.

The visitors threatened dangerously early on, finding their composure more quickly than Liverpool. Hudson worked busily in midfield trying to create goalscoring opportunities and Salmons' long-range shot swung wide of the post. At this stage in the game Liverpool had not created a serious attack on the Stoke goal.

With ten minutes gone, Callaghan broke clear of the Stoke defence with a genuine chance of scoring, but he was pulled down with a clear rugby tackle by Smith, who was booked. Liverpool were awarded a free-kick seven yards outside the penalty area. The visiting defence stood still expecting an offside decision as the ball broke clear, but the referee waved play on and Neal raced goalwards unchallenged, but he overhit his centre and the ball ran to the far side of the ground.

Pejic was booked for dissent after a free-kick had been awarded against him for a foul on Heighway just outside the Stoke area. With 20 minutes gone, Callaghan took a free-kick after Keegan had been fouled and Toshack ran in to meet the ball on the volley, but Shilton's perfect positional sense enabled him to save with ease. Shortly afterwards Toshack headed the ball into the net, but the ball had run out of play before Hall got in his cross. Clemence left his line at great speed to effect an interception from a Greenhoff centre after Hughes had failed to cut out the danger with Hurst waiting to pounce.

Keegan broke clear of Dodd's illegal shirt-pulling and raced down the right before crossing for Toshack, but Shilton was alert and came out to catch at full stretch. Neal and Lindsay were in excellent form as they denied the visitors, whose smooth, ball-playing skills created several opportunities.

Keegan had his name taken when he threw the ball away in disgust and dissent after a linesman had signalled offside against him. Keegan's frustration was generated in the feeling that he was the only constant threat to Stoke, whose solid defensive wall was difficult to break down. Liverpool manager Bob Paisley leapt to his feet in anger near the touchline after a tackle by Hudson had felled Hall. Play went on and from Heighway's centre, Keegan's header was touched over the bar by Shilton. From the corner the ball went to Cormack, whose fiercely-hit shot knocked over Mahoney and while the ball travelled on for a further corner, the Liverpool players appealed that Mahoney had handled. From the second corner, Toshack headed the ball forward and from six yards Keegan hooked the ball over the bar as Shilton came out to challenge. As the interval approached, Liverpool found their rhythm and relentless pressure on the Stoke defence ceased only when the referee blew for the end of the half.

From a Hall free-kick Toshack rose high and headed goalwards, but Shilton stretched to turn the ball round the post. Then Toshack and Marsh collided, with both players requiring attention, though Marsh was the more seriously hurt. Toshack beat the Stoke defence in the air from Hall's corner kick, but he headed wide. Stoke pulled nine players back in defence as Liverpool produced their customary onslaught. Heighway broke clear down the left, took the ball past Marsh but shot straight at Shilton. Stoke attacked on rare occasions, and it was 15 minutes into the second period before their first shot arrived, a long-range shot from Mahoney, which cleared the bar. Keegan was in sparkling form, trying to produce a goal.

With 12 minutes remaining Shilton made his first mistake of the game. A right-wing cross by Hall found Toshack, who challenged Shilton. The goalkeeper appeared to mis-time his move for the ball and deflected it straight at Heighway, whose shot from 12 yards found the back of the net. The goal changed the nature of the game, with Stoke having to throw off their defensive shackles and formulate an attack. Hurst brought the ball down and Hughes and Clemence got in each other's way. The ball ran loose with Clemence yards out of his goal, but Conroy's centre was cut off.

Shortly afterwards Conroy broke up a Liverpool attack and brought the ball out on a long run into Liverpool territory, but the home defence remained solid. Hughes looked as though he still felt the effects of his midweek training injury, but he still held the defence together.

A minute from time Hall's excellent centre cut open the Stoke defence and found Keegan, who had a free header with Shilton yards out of position.

Last season's beaten finalists, Newcastle, beat Manchester City 2-0 at Maine Road, while this season's winners, West Ham (2-0 against Fulham) beat Southampton 2-1 at the Dell.

Second Division Fulham drew 1-1 with Hull at Craven Cottage, winning the second replay 1-0 after a 2-2 draw. There was a dearth of goals, Leeds being the only club to score more than three as they beat Cardiff 4-1 at Elland Road. In Scotland, however, Montrose beat the Vale of Leithen 12-0 away, having led by six goals at the interval.

Liverpool: Clemence; Neal, Lindsay, Thompson, Cormack, Hughes, Keegan, Hall, Heighway, Toshack, Callaghan.

Stoke City: Shilton; Marsh, Pejic, Mahoney, Smith, Dodd, Conroy, Greenhoff, Hurst, Hudson, Salmons.

Referee: Mr T.H.C. Reynolds (Swansea)

Attendance: 48,723

City doctors plan protest

More than 20 Liverpool doctors are expected to meet outside the main gate of Sefton General Hospital on Monday as part of a protest against the imprisonment in Russia of a Russian doctor, Dr. Mikhail Shtern.

They will be accompanied by members of the Liverpool 35 group, the Jewish women's organisation pledged to help Jews persecuted by the Soviet authorities.

Paraffin store hit by blaze

A hardware store containing 400 gallons of paraffin, was damaged by fire at Toxteth, Liverpool, to-day, but firemen were able to control the blaze before it reached the drums.

The paraffin was stored directly above a cellar at Jameson's store in Granby Street.

Ian Callaghan, M.B.E.

January 25, 1975

Ipswich Town (0) 1

Mills 87

Liverpool (0) 0

THE gates at Portman Road were closed almost an hour before the kick-off and several thousand fans were locked out. This was Ipswich's record crowd, though on 8 March the record was beaten when 38,010 saw Ipswich draw 0-0 with Leeds United. There was a strong, swirling wind and constant drizzle.

The match began at a frenetic pace and Liverpool cleared the home side's initial raid before moving onto the attack through Neal, whose cross just eluded Cormack. Johnson caused problems with his speed on the right. Lindsay conceded a free-kick but headed away when Viljoen crossed the ball. Both sides were full of attacking promise and an excellent run by Hall gained a corner in the eighth minute.

Toshack failed to clear Lambert's corner kick and Whymark had two shots blocked before the danger passed. With 16 minutes gone Callaghan robbed Collard and found Toshack, who held off Burley's challenge and chipped the ball over Sivell and against the bar. The ball bounced down and into Sivell's arms. Mills shot well over the bar from the second of two successive Ipswich corners.

After 24 minutes Keegan picked up a ball from Neal and his low shot went inches wide. Both teams adopted a policy of more deliberate build-up rather than the frantic quality of the opening minutes.

Lambert crossed from the left and Johnson's diving header cannoned off the legs of Clemence as Ipswich attacked strongly. Play was held up while Johnson received treatment and almost immediately Talbot required treatment after colliding with Cormack.

The home side went on to the offensive and when Lambert's kick was cleared, Collard's shot was cleanly held by Clemence. The rampant home side won a further corner after 37 minutes, and from the free-kick Hunter and then Beattie had shots blocked.

With Ipswich beginning to dominate, Liverpool often had to pull back their three midfield men into defensive positions in order to repel the Blues.

Talbot was forced to leave the field, apparently suffering from concussion after his collision with Cormack. The interval arrived with no score.

Ipswich began the second half without Talbot, Woods substituting. The rain eased off and the wind relented as Hughes cleared two dangerous Ipswich raids. Lambert took advantage of a rare slip by Neal and made ground to the bye-line before crossing into the goalmouth. However, there was no Ipswich player able to reach the ball. Heighway sped down the wing and earned a corner, which Keegan took. He bent the ball towards the near post but Sivell collected under pressure from Thompson. The game was fast, open and exciting, with both sides looking capable of snatching victory. Heighway switched to the right wing and Keegan moved across to the left to test Burley. With 54 minutes gone, Lambert headed on to Johnson who was standing in an apparent offside position. As Johnson raced into the penalty area, Clemence raced off his line to clear the danger. With Ipswich piling on the pressure, the home side won a corner through Lindsay. The ball was cleared, but Lambert returned it and Whymark's effort was cleared off the line by Hughes. Clemence made a good save from Johnson's overhead kick, and then Beattie had a shot blocked on the line. As Ipswich attacked relentlessly, Johnson headed Viljoen's free-kick wide. Liverpool responded when Callaghan put Keegan through for a run on goal, but Beattie cleared. Callaghan cut out several Ipswich attacks as he worked tirelessly in midfield.

Ipswich continued to put pressure on their opponents, and Hughes cleared one raid for a corner. Beattie's powerful header from Lambert's flag-kick was saved on the line by Neal. With ten minutes remaining, Liverpool pulled back nine men to resist the Ipswich attacking force.

With just three minutes left, the home side sealed the game. Beattie found Burley on the right, and his cross to the far post fell to Mills, who stabbed the ball over the line from close range.

Non-League Leatherhead took a 2-0 lead over Leicester City, having switched the tie to Filbert Street, but the home side won 3-2 with goals from Sammels after 53 minutes, Earle after 73 minutes and a winner from Weller. Peter McGillicuddy (13) and Chris Kelly (27) gave the home side a 2-0 interval lead. West Ham drew with Swindon 1-1, winning the replay 2-1 away. Fulham drew 0-0 with Nottingham Forest, winning the third replay 2-1.

Ipswich Town: Sivell; Burley, Mills, Talbot (Woods,46), Hunter, Beattie, Collard, Viljoen, Johnson, Whymark, Lambert.

Liverpool: Clemence; Neal, Lindsay, Thompson, Cormack, Hughes, Keegan, Hall, Heighway, Toshack, Callaghan.

Referee: Mr P. Partridge (Bishop Auckland)

Attendance: 34,709

January 3, 1976

West Ham United (0) 0

Liverpool (1) 2
Keegan 37, Toshack 82

WEST Ham suffered from the loss of Bonds, Taylor and Robson, bringing in former Sunderland defender Mick McGiven for his first senior game for two seasons, while Liverpool introduced Smith and Ray Kennedy, an able deputy for Peter Cormack. There were few Liverpool supporters in the ground at the start because hundreds of them had been delayed by train problems, and among the missing spectators were six Liverpool directors, including the chairman, John Smith. The gale force wind had dropped to a breeze and the pitch, despite the rain during the week, looked firm. The teams were:

West Ham United: Day; Coleman, Lampard; Holland, McGiven, Lock; Taylor, Paddon, Brooking, Jennings, Curbishley.

Liverpool: Clemence; Smith, Neal; Thompson, Kennedy, Hughes; Keegan, Case, Heighway, Toshack, Callaghan.

Referee: Mr P. Partridge (Bishop Auckland)

Attendance: 32,363

Liverpool gained an early corner and from the kick by Case, Keegan volleyed the ball two yards wide. The home side responded when Brooking intercepted a clearance by Smith, and took the ball on several yards before driving the ball over the bar from just outside the box. Liverpool attacked again, and in the early stages Heighway was prominent. On one occasion after a dribble his left-foot shot went close. West Ham, who paraded the cup on the pitch before the game as Cup-holders, gradually got into the game as Curbishley created from midfield. Jennings had a shot blocked, and Paddon looked dangerous down the right.

Keegan hit a swerving shot from 25 yards which almost deceived Day, who fumbled with the ball, but recovered to clear the danger. At the other end, Taylor showed flashes of the skill which had helped the Hammers win the cup last May, and he moved on to a perfect pass by Jennings to hit the ball on the run inches over the bar.

After about twenty minutes, some of the Liverpool fans arrived. Clemence made a fine save under pressure from Lampard's centre, and immediately set up a Liverpool attack. Keegan split the West Ham defence with an excellent crossfield pass to Smith, but the move broke down when Toshack fouled Day in going up for the centre.

Neal lost the ball to Taylor near the corner flag and the centre was well placed for Jennings, but Smith headed the ball over the bar. Then Day dived full-length to save a powerful free-kick taken by Case. A mistake by Smith let in Jennings, but Hughes intercepted to clear the danger.

Smith slipped the ball forward to Case, who hit an excellent centre into the penalty area, where Toshack headed it back down to Keegan, who took the ball past Lock before his right-foot shot hit the inside of the post and rebounded into the net.

Liverpool almost increased their lead, but McGiven got his body in the way of a left-foot volley from Case. Just before the interval, Heighway struck the goalkeeper with a shot from point blank range.

The Liverpool directors reached the ground during the half-time interval. Liverpool went back on the offensive and Heighway drove the ball at Day before mis-hitting a shot after bringing the ball inside the area. Then Day was forced to save a Toshack shot as the visitors maintained their superiority. Liverpool's authority stemmed from the positive influence of Kennedy and Callaghan in midfield. West Ham were made to look ordinary, though occasional flashes of skill from Brooking highlighted their game. The Hammers were guilty of passing inaccurately on numerous occasions. On the few instances that West Ham threatened, Hughes and Thompson were solid in defence, and Liverpool's display was one of authority and complete control. Keegan initiated a fine move from which Case thundered a shot towards goal which the young Day saved.

Then Keegan laid on the second goal. Heighway sent in an inch-perfect pass for Keegan's run down the right, and when he drew the defence towards him, he created space for Toshack to score into an open goal. A minute later Keegan delayed his shot and a third goal was lost.

John Toshack explains a point to Kevin Keegan

January 24, 1976

Derby County (0) 1
Davies 72

Liverpool (0) 0

THE pitch was in good condition and the overnight snowfall had been slight in the Derby area, though snow fell as the game kicked off. Liverpool gained an early corner, and Neal seized on the clearance to hit a 20-yard drive off target. Callaghan performed well down the left and Kennedy's fierce volley went wide. Derby responded when Powell pushed the ball down the middle to James, who was brought down by Kennedy, but the free-kick was cleared by Neal.

Liverpool showed the initiative in the early stages with Kennedy the master of midfield, and Toshack headed the ball across to Keegan, who played a one-two, allowing Toshack to shoot, but the ball went wide. Then a mistake by Powell allowed Toshack to run unchallenged on to the ball, but Moseley saw the danger early and rushed off his line to dive bravely at the Welshman's feet.

With twelve minutes gone, Derby gained their first corner, which Neal cleared with a powerful header. A minute later Lee and Rioch combined well, and Rioch's shot bounced off Hughes and went to Lee, whose first-time shot was saved by Clemence.

Keegan sent Neal down the left wing, and his centre was pushed across to Toshack by Case, but Nish intercepted with a well-timed tackle. With Gemmill increasingly prominent in midfield, Derby found their attacking rhythm. Derby based most of their attacks down the left in an effort to utilise the skills of James.

Heighway relieved the pressure when he took the ball on a meandering 60-yard run before being fouled by Nish. Then Case blasted the free-kick against the defensive wall. The game was evenly balanced, with McFarland marshalling the Derby defence, while Smith employed all his experience to control the threat from James. When James switched to the right wing, Neal was effective. A foul by McFarland on Keegan gave Liverpool a free-kick and Smith touched the ball to Hughes, who blasted it high over the bar from 25 yards. Then Gemmill was spoken to by the referee for a foul on Heighway, but it was the first sign of over-physical play in a match which displayed skill of the highest level by two first-class teams.

Just before the interval, Liverpool almost scored when, from a free-kick, Keegan pushed the ball out to Neal, whose centre was met perfectly by Toshack. The header fell straight to Keegan, who volleyed the ball straight at Moseley. Liverpool appealed for a penalty when Keegan went down under challenge from Powell, but the referee indicated that he thought Keegan had dived.

Nish surprised the Liverpool defence early in the second half when he shot instead of passing to James. His 20-yard shot went inches wide as Clemence dived. Then Hughes lost a ball to Lee, who had a clear run on goal, but Clemence raced off his line and blocked the shot. From a free-kick Kennedy saw Thompson moving into position and delivered a perfect pass, enabling Thompson to head the ball down, but just past the post.

The attendance was Derby's highest of the season, and spectators spilled out of the terraces to sit on the track around the pitch.

With the Derby defence in trouble, Moseley left his line to clear from the dangerous Heighway. Then Gemmill pushed the ball down the right to George, who centred to Lee, but his header was wide.

After 67 minutes, Derby introduced Davies in place of James, who had been superbly marshalled by the effective Tommy Smith. Then Heighway raced clear, only for Nish to make a clearance at the last moment.

With eighteen minutes left, Derby scored with a move initiated and concluded by substitute Davies, whose crossfield pass from right to left beat the outstretched foot of Smith. Rioch moved on to it unchallenged before sending in a powerful low centre which just missed Lee in the goalmouth, but Davies, who stood behind him, rammed the ball into the net from six yards.

Liverpool brought on Hall in place of Toshack, with Case moving out of midfield and into the attack, but it was a desperate gamble which failed to force a replay.

Palace shock Leeds United

Malcolm Allison's Third Division pacemakers Crystal Palace gave Leeds an early shock at Elland Road when David Swindlehurst headed the visitors into the lead after 24 minutes. Final score: Leeds **0**, Crystal Palace **1**.

Derby County: Moseley; Thomas, Nish, Rioch, McFarland, Todd, Powell, Gemmill, Lee, George, James(Davies,67).

Liverpool: Clemence; Smith, Neal, Thompson, Kennedy, Hughes, Keegan, Case, Heighway, Toshack(Hall,77), Callaghan.

Referee: Mr E. D. Wallace (Swindon)

Attendance: 38,200

Receipts: £47,810

January 8, 1977

Liverpool (0) 0

Crystal Palace (0) 0

LIVERPOOL omitted John Toshack, manager Bob Paisley feeling that the Welsh international had not fully recovered from his heavy cold which had cost him two days' training earlier in the week. David Johnson replaced Toshack, while Palace left out former Liverpool defender Peter Wall, but nevertheless leaned heavily on defence. Hammond had conceded just one goal in the last 889 minutes of football. Liverpool attacked the Kop goal in the first half.

Liverpool: Clemence; Neal, Jones, Thompson, Kennedy, Hughes, Keegan, McDermott (Fairclough,37), Heighway, Johnson, Callaghan.

Crystal Palace: Hammond; Hinshelwood, Sansom, Holder, Cannon, Evans, Chatterton, Graham, Perrin, Swindlehurst, Silkman.

Referee: Mr K. Burns (Wordsley)

Attendance: 44,730

Liverpool started the game against their Third Division opponents at a tremendous pace, but the Londoners gained the first corner. Silkman flicked the ball into the middle where Graham, the former Villa and Arsenal player, turned it on before Clemence saved well.

Heighway's skill down the left gained two corners in quick succession, and from the second of these, Johnson climbed well but his header just cleared the bar. With 15 minutes gone, McDermott went down, holding his right leg after an accidental collision with Sansom. He was helped off by coaches Fagan and Moran and a stretcher was brought, while Fairclough was off the bench and warming up. Paisley left the bench to look at McDermott's injury, and after further attention the stretcher was sent away, and the midfielder returned after an interval of about four minutes.

Palace's defensive cover was extreme, leaving only Swindlehurst up front for most of the game, and every time a Liverpool player was on the ball, there were three or four Palace players crowding him out. In an isolated Palace attack, Holder's 25-yard shot forced Clemence to dive full-length to save. Then Silkman ran 30 yards before shooting at Clemence, who made another fine save. Thompson mis-headed a clearance straight into the path of Graham, whose lob was turned over the bar by the Liverpool goalkeeper. The home side were not playing to their true form. With 20 minutes gone, Liverpool almost scored against the run of play. A centre by Neal was headed inside to Johnson, but the striker's shot was mis-hit, and Hammond saved with ease. Shortly afterwards, Liverpool replaced

McDermott with Fairclough. Keegan dropped back into midfield with Fairclough going up front. The flame-haired Liverpool youngster went an a 40-yard run before hitting a powerful shot which Hammond had covered.

Liverpool began the second half by attacking strongly, though their ideas were lacking in invention. Holder, the former Tottenham player, inspired the visitors with a wonderful display of midfield football, and the attacking threat of Palace carried more potency than that of Liverpool's. The Kop was silenced by the inept performance from the Champions. Keegan was injured, but he resumed despite limping as the result of a knock to his right ankle. Chatterton marshalled Keegan effectively, and Liverpool were subdued as a result.

Fairclough hit a left-foot shot over the bar but generally both goalkeepers were inactive in this period.

Towards the finish, the police moved into the paddock area to break up a fight. Hundreds of Palace supporters were in the paddock, and some of them were led away by the police.

Liverpool produced one final desperate attempt to secure victory but Hammond punched away from Kennedy's free-kick. The visitors thoroughly deserved a replay, such was the power of their display at Anfield. Liverpool manager, Bob Paisley, said before the game that he expected Palace to play the way they eventually did. They arrived at Anfield with the intention of preventing Liverpool from playing their normal game, and they achieved their objective with considerable ease.

Manchester United, the winners of the 1977 Cup final, beat Walsall 1-0 at Old Trafford. Southampton, last season's shock winners over Manchester United, drew 1-1 at home to Chelsea, winning the replay 3-0 at Stamford Bridge. Non-League Northwich Victoria beat Watford 3-2, despite trailing 1-2 at the interval.

Shankly campaign called off

The campaign to make Bill Shankly a director of Liverpool Football Club has been dropped, at the request of Mr. Shankly himself. But petition organiser Mr. Sam Leach is to continue collecting signatures, which he will present to the former Liverpool manager as a personal memento.

"I am confident we can reach the target of 250,000 signatures we originally aimed for," said Mr. Leach. "Mr. Shankly asked me to call the campaign off because he feels it may do Liverpool FC great harm and I appreciate his reasons. But at least we have made our point and asked the question which needed to be asked."

January 11, 1977

Crystal Palace (1) 2
Hinshelwood 17
Graham 88

Liverpool (1) 3
Keegan 20
Heighway 66, 72

Steve Heighway, scorer of two goals, skilfully taunted the opposition with his dribbling runs

Crystal Palace: Hammond; Hinshelwood, Sansom, Holder, Cannon, Evans, Chatterton, Graham, Perrin, Swindlehurst, Silkman(Harkouk,70).

Liverpool: Clemence; Neal, Jones, Thompson, Kennedy, Hughes, Keegan, Case, Heighway, Fairclough, Callaghan.

Referee: Mr J.K. Taylor (Wolverhampton)

Attendance: 42,664

LIVERPOOL'S calm authority and years of experience of competing at the highest level was the key factor in their progress into the Fourth Round. The Londoners were rampant in the opening quarter-of-an-hour, scoring through Hinshelwood, but Liverpool equalised swiftly and from that point onwards, the Reds controlled the match.

The visitors played Heighway and Fairclough up front and their pace caused Palace numerous problems, but the home side took the lead after Hinshelwood picked up a Keegan cross intended for Heighway. The Palace defender passed forward to Chatterton, took a short inside pass on the run and hit a drive over Clemence's head from 25 yards. The Palace fans bayed in expectation of a shock defeat, but Liverpool had other ideas.

Skipper Hughes led the assault on the Palace goal from a short free-kick. His cross low into the middle found Heighway and the winger, with great speed of thought and perception, noted that Keegan was in a better scoring position.

From Heighway's short tap Keegan placed the ball inside the post for a prompt reply to Palace's temerity. Fairclough failed with a header from close range as Liverpool took the game to their opponents.

It was not until the 66th minute that Liverpool finally got the goal their approach work deserved. Keegan took the ball into the penalty area and crossed to Heighway in front of goal. The Eire international calmly placed the ball wide of Hammond.

Just six minutes later Heighway, enjoying his skilful taunting of the opposition, drilled the ball home to secure victory after good work by Jimmy Case, whose power and strength helped Liverpool's cause.

Two minutes from the end Chatterton coasted clear on the right and Graham ran on to the cross to ram the ball past Clemence. The goal excited the crowd and provided an exciting finale, but the result was not in doubt.

January 29, 1977

Liverpool (2) 3
*Keegan 17, Toshack 34,
Heighway 69*

Carlisle United (0) 0

A week previously Carlisle - languishing in 20th place in the Second Division - lost 0-6 at home to Southampton, then in eighteenth place. The Cumbrians had been in the First Division in 1974-75, but were destined to be relegated at the end of this current season. In the previous round, Carlisle had beaten Matlock Town 5-1 at Brunton Park. In 1974 Carlisle visited Anfield and drew 0-0 before losing 0-2 in the replay as Liverpool went on towards Wembley and that magnificent final victory over Newcastle, for whom current Carlisle player-manager Bobby Moncur was playing. The omens loomed large.

Liverpool: Clemence; Neal, Jones, Thompson, Kennedy, Hughes, Keegan, Case, Heighway, Toshack, Callaghan.

Carlisle United: Burleigh; Hoolickin, Carr, Bonnyman, MacDonald, Moncur, O'Neill, Barry, Clarke, Rafferty, Martin.

Referee: Mr K.W. Baker (Rugby)

Attendance: 45,358

The conditions were treacherous and made turning and pulling up difficult, but Liverpool's England captain, Kevin Keegan, mastered the conditions admirably. He gave Liverpool the lead after only 17 minutes. A shot from Heighway was blocked and Toshack flicked the rebound into the middle, where the ball was turned for a corner. Phil Neal's cross was met by Keegan, who outjumped Carr to head over Burleigh into the net. Six minutes later Keegan was involved in an amusing incident with goalkeeper Martin Burleigh. The 'keeper raced out in a desperate attempt to prevent a corner and was at the corner flag before he could come to a slithering halt. Keegan, who spotted the opportunity to be exploited, grabbed the ball and began the race to see whether he could get to the flag and take the kick before Burleigh could get back between the posts. Burleigh narrowly won, but he could not prevent Toshack's powerful header which Hoolickin heroically headed off the line.

In 34 minutes Keegan put Toshack clear with a superb flick and Toshack held off a challenge from MacDonald to celebrate his return to the first team with a well-struck low shot.

In the second period, Ray Kennedy took a couple of strides to steady himself before shooting hard and low. Burleigh dived to save, and Keegan was ready to pounce for any mistake. Liverpool were rampant in the second half. Case had a magnificent drive saved, while some excellent moves

between Toshack, Keegan and Heighway ended with shots passing narrowly wide or high. Carlisle had no response, devoid of real attacking ideas. Liverpool's third goal arrived after 69 minutes. The move was initiated by Phil Thompson, who, along with Hughes, had performed with calm assurance. Thompson broke up a raid about ten yards inside his own half, and spotted Heighway just inside the Carlisle half. The pass was immaculate and the flying Irishman set off at full speed, going past MacDonald and Carr before unleashing a left-foot shot which gave Burleigh no chance.

Manchester United beat Queens Park Rangers 1-0 at Old Trafford.

*Kevin
Keegan*

February 26, 1977

Liverpool (2) 3
Keegan 21, Case 31,
Neal (pen) 73

Oldham Athletic (1) 1
Shaw 27

OLDHAM, in ninth place in the Second Division, drew the second largest crowd of the season at Anfield and put up a brave fight playing attractive football against Liverpool in top spot in the First Division. The Reds were below par but still good enough to go forward into the Sixth Round.

Liverpool: Clemence; Neal, Jones, Thompson, Kennedy, Hughes, Keegan, Case, Heighway, Toshack, Callaghan.

Oldham Athletic: Platt; Wood, Blair, Bell, Hicks, Hurst, Robins Shaw, Halom, Chapman, Groves.

Referee: Mr G.C. Kew (Middlesbrough)

Attendance: 52,455

John Hurst - the former Everton player, and consequently no stranger to Anfield - marshalled Keegan superbly and provided the main thrust of Oldham's inventiveness, but he was guilty of pushing Keegan in the back just outside the penalty area after 20 minutes. Keegan and Case caused confusion as they jockeyed behind the ball and Toshack joined the defensive wall. As Case rushed in with the intention of hammering the ball to his left, the wall tilted in that direction. Running in from the other direction, Keegan found himself with a gap to shoot through and his drive was tremendously powerful and accurate.

Groves passed perfectly inside the area for Shaw to equalise with a superb shot just inside Clemence's post after 27 minutes. Oldham were back in the game and played with greater confidence, but Liverpool regained the lead just minutes later. Toshack's path to goal was blocked, but he saw Case running up and let the ball go. Case hit a shot which was as true as an arrow in flight as it soared over the advancing Platt and under the bar. It was Case's first goal since last April. Although his career had developed in midfield, he had lost the scoring touch.

A debatable penalty decision sealed victory for the home side after 72 minutes. After the game Heighway said, "The decision seemed a bit harsh, but at the same time I couldn't keep my feet. Whether Wood touched me or not I cannot say." Heighway did not claim a penalty and immediately commiserated with Wood. Neal sent Platt diving to his right as the ball entered the net on the left.

Oldham manager, Jimmy Frizzell, said afterwards, "A bad penalty decision won them the game. We were the best team until they scored their first goal. We have come out of the game with a lot of pride and gave them a few frights. We had a go and did part of what we wanted to do."

F.A. CUP
FIFTH ROUND

Aston Villa	3	Port Vale	0
Cardiff City	1	Everton	2
Derby County	3	Blackburn Rovers	1
Leeds United	1	Manchester City	0
Middlesbrough	4	Arsenal	1
Southampton	2	Manchester United	2
Wolverhampton W.	1	Chester	1

Replay

Manchester United	2	Southampton	1

March 19, 1977

Liverpool (0) 2

Fairclough 55, Keegan 62

Middlesbrough (0) 0

JUST three days after one of the most magnificent victories in the history of Liverpool Football Club, when they defeated the French club, St. Etienne, 3-1 at Anfield on a night of high drama to win through to the semi-finals of the European Cup, the mighty Red machine ground out another victory, this time against Middlesbrough.

The north-eastern side had built a strong team based upon the defensive capabilities of Boam and Maddren and the midfield strength and creativity of Souness. In the first half, Middlesbrough had little difficulty in dealing with Liverpool's great pressure and the numerous high balls pumped into the box were cleared with ease. The brilliance of Clemence kept Liverpool in the game at a time when Middlesbrough looked dangerous.

Liverpool played without the services of Callaghan, and Terry McDermott replaced him. The second half was dominated by Liverpool and ten minutes after the interval the Reds took the lead. Smith pushed the ball out to Fairclough on the right wing, and a piece of Supersub magic followed.

Fairclough cut inside full-back Cooper and, still running, took note of the massed ranks of the Middlesbrough team between him and his objective. Still about 45 yards from goal, he accelerated once he had seen some space before unleashing a left-foot drive from at least 30 yards that Cuff could only grope at in desperation.

Fairclough said after the game, "I was thinking of crossing the ball, but then I saw some space, burst into it and then it was just a question of cracking it. They didn't give us any chance at all in the box."

Once in the lead, Liverpool kept the initiative with Heighway weaving his way round Craggs, Kennedy striding majestically around midfield providing the superb through ball, and with Tommy Smith tackling ferociously in defence and playing a constructive game, laying the ball off quickly and accurately. Smith was adamant that this was to be his last season in football. Joey Jones was also superb in defence for Liverpool, getting his body behind the ball and heading to safety on those occasions when Middlesbrough threatened.

Keegan scored the second. Fairclough sent over a cross from the left, Kennedy went up at the far post to head back into the middle and Keegan headed home unmarked. The visitors attempted to break down Liverpool's rearguard, and went close at times, but when Middlesbrough were forced to abandon their defensive mode, Liverpool went close through Keegan, Heighway and Case. Towards the final whistle Heighway hit the post. Both Case and Souness were booked.

Manchester United beat Aston Villa 2-1; Leeds United beat Wolverhampton Wanderers 1-0 at Molineux; and Everton beat Derby County 2-0.

*The mercurial **David Fairclough***

Liverpool: Clemence; Neal, Jones, Smith, Kennedy, Hughes, Keegan, Case, Heighway, Fairclough, McDermott.

Middlesbrough: Cuff; Craggs, Cooper, Souness, Boam, Maddren, McAndrew, Mills, Brine, Wood (Boersma,63), Armstrong.

Referee: Mr J.K. Taylor (Wolverhampton)

Attendance: 55,881

April 23, 1977

Everton (1) 2
McKenzie 33, Rioch 82

Liverpool (1) 2
McDermott 10, Case 73

LIVERPOOL failed to reach their normal form in conditions of wind and rain, while Everton, under new manager, Gordon Lee, played above themselves and almost won the match. In a few short weeks Gordon Lee had restored some pride into the Everton team, and hope where there was just despair. Living under Liverpool's shadow had not helped Everton's cause. Ten minutes into the game McDermott saw Lawson so far off his line that he chipped the ball over the goalkeeper's head and into the net. Liverpool fans began chanting "*We'll be running round Wembley with the Cup*", but their conviction was rather premature. Out on the touchline, Hughes scorned the simple thing by trapping the ball into touch or over the bye-line. Instead, he tried to beat Pearson as he had done throughout the opening half-an-hour, but he slipped on the turf and Pearson ran on before delivering a great cross. Dobson's shot rebounded to McKenzie, who stroked the ball home for an equalising goal.

Liverpool failed to gain a single corner in the first period. With 72 minutes gone, Liverpool substituted Fairclough, who had injured his back in the opening minute when failing to connect in front of goal, with David Johnson, the former Evertonian.

A minute later, Liverpool went into the lead. Darracott fouled Heighway, and the Reds were awarded a free-kick. Kennedy put the ball into the goalmouth and Lawson, under pressure from Keegan, punched clear, but only as far as Case, who assessed the situation carefully before sending his header into the net.

Everton continued to fight, and eight minutes from the end Pearson and McKenzie linked up and a cross beat Clemence and Rioch equalised for a second time. With the minutes ticking by, Goodlass centred, McKenzie headed on, and Hamilton put the ball into the net via his hip. Referee Clive Thomas ruled that Hamilton had handled, but television showed that he was inches offside. It was a reprieve that Liverpool hardly deserved, but one for which they were grateful. In the other semi-final, Manchester United beat Leeds United 2-1.

Everton: Lawson; Darracott, Pejic, Lyons, McNaught, Rioch, Buckley, Dobson(Hamilton,81), Pearson, McKenzie, Goodlass.

Liverpool: Clemence; Neal, Jones, Smith, Kennedy, Hughes, Keegan, Case, Heighway, Fairclough(Johnson,72), McDermott.

Referee:
Mr C. Thomas (Treorchy)

Attendance: 52,637
(at Maine Road)

Receipts: £140,000

*Referee **Clive Thomas**, waves away the protesting Everton players*

April 27, 1977

Everton (0) 0

Liverpool (1) 3
*Neal (pen) 31, Case 88,
Kennedy 89*

THE game began quietly with both teams in an edgy mood. It was nine minutes before the first piece of real action, which came when Case blasted a shot wide of the target. Case and Kennedy dominated the midfield as Liverpool played true to their usual form. With 20 minutes gone, Keegan sped down the right, skilfully stopped the ball dead in the penalty area and then laid it off to Johnson, who narrowly missed. The Reds increased the pressure and after 27 minutes Fairclough collected the ball in defence before working a fine one-two with Johnson and speeding down the left wing. His cross was, however, too quick for Case. Just after the half-hour, Liverpool took the lead. Pejic was adjudged to have pushed Johnson in the back as they rose to meet a Hughes free-kick. Everton protested vigorously, but Neal despatched the kick into the net past Lawson's despairing dive to his left for the opening goal. The goal enlivened the game and two minutes later the referee instructed both dug-outs to calm down after Kennedy had fouled Rioch. With Rioch and Buckley working hard in midfield, Everton created chances of their own. Jim Pearson worked prodigiously but was robbed of the ball on too many occasions. Duncan McKenzie showed flashes of his skill, but his passing was often astray.

The second period was a real battle. Everton pushed forward relentlessly in an attempt to salvage their Wembley dreams, but the Liverpool defence was resolute and Clemence was not unduly tested. Mick Lyons and Ken McNaught moved up into attack whenever they could, but they failed to capitalise upon the array of crosses. The ageless Tommy Smith performed heroically in midfield as Liverpool responded to Everton's dangerous thrusts. With 74 minutes gone, Buckley handled a Fairclough cross in the box, but the referee deemed that it was accidental.

Two minutes from time, Liverpool sealed victory. Fairclough was in possession on the left, and the ball went to Case, who side-stepped a defender and smashed the ball with his right foot from the edge of the box past Lawson. Then Ray Kennedy scored from close range at the second attempt from a Keegan free-kick on the right.

Scotland beat Sweden 3-1 with Kenny Dalglish scoring one of the goals.

*Left: **Tommy Smith***

Everton: Lawson; Darracott, Pejic, Lyons, McNaught, Rioch, Buckley, Dobson(King,66), Pearson, McKenzie, Goodlass.

Liverpool: Clemence; Neal, Jones, Smith, Kennedy, Hughes, Keegan, Case, Johnson, Fairclough, McDermott.

Referee: Mr C. Thomas (Treorchy)

Attendance: 52,579 (at Maine Road)

LIVERPOOL'S TREBLE DREAM OVER

UNITED WIN FINAL

THREE GOALS IN FIVE MINUTE SPELL

Liverpool (0) 1   Manchester Utd. (0) 2

Case 52   *Pearson 50, J.Greenhoff 55*

HAVING beaten Manchester United 1-0 at Anfield on May 3rd with a Keegan goal, Liverpool were marginal favourites to win the coveted League and Cup double. And with their first European Cup final beckoning on the Wednesday after this game, Liverpool were in contention for an historic treble. The triumph at Wembley belonged to Manchester United, while Liverpool's tragedy was that they given their all and failed to win the Cup.

Liverpool were the better side in the first half, but paid for their inability to translate their superiority into goals.

Early into the game Macari shot into the side netting, but Liverpool soon settled into a relaxed, confident rhythm which allowed them to display all their skills. They varied the emphasis of their attacks imaginatively and often, and caused United several problems.

With seven minutes gone, Liverpool had two successive shots blocked. Heighway, amazingly fast and adventurous, was involved in both.

After 16 minutes Clemence was forced to tip an awkward, swerving centre from Hill over the bar.

However, Liverpool continued to fail in front of goal - the malady which had marred their League campaign on the way to Wembley. David Johnson, unmarked six yards out with his back to goal, failed to turn on the ball and Keegan was equally unsuccessful in attempting to beat Albiston

to a magnificent through ball from Case.

Johnson and Jones also shot over the bar, and when Liverpool did create a genuine opportunity three minutes before half-time, Kennedy's far post header from Case's centre struck the foot of a post.

Five minutes into the second half, Jimmy Greenhoff sent Pearson away on the right with a neat flick of the head. Pearson sped down the wing, but was forced out to an unlikely angle. He struck

The two skippers, **Emlyn Hughes** and **Martin Buchan** (far left) shake hands before the kick-off

the ball with his right foot and the ball found its way into the net between Clemence and his near post.

Equaliser

Just two minutes later, Liverpool were level. Case was allowed time and space on the edge of the box and he drove a powerful right-foot shot past Stepney's left hand.

Only three minutes later Jimmy Greenhoff and Smith challenged for the ball, which broke off Smith to Macari on the right of the goal. The diminutive Scot, who had done little in the game, drove a cross shot which appeared to hit Greenhoff, before changing direction, and veering past Clemence into the net. With time running out, Liverpool sent on Callaghan in place

of Johnson, with Case pushing further forward.

Keegan fed Case who unleashed a powerful left-foot drive which Stepney was forced to save. Then McDermott provided a further opportunity, but Stepney managed to grasp the ball.

United sent on McCreery for Hill late on as they fought to hang on to their lead.

In the last minute Kennedy hit the bar with a thundering left-foot drive.

Paisley

Liverpool manager Bob Paisley said after the game: "We had more of the game, but Fortune was against us. They had just that little bit of luck with the finishing and we didn't. The lads' heads are down at the

moment, but they will rise by Wednesday. I have told them we have nothing to be ashamed of and they will bounce back in Rome.

We didn't have any injuries apart from Joey Jones who cut his head. But he should be fit for the Borussia match. The run in has been like the last ¼ mile of a mile race. If it had been a little cooler out there it might have helped us."

Docherty

United manager Tommy Docherty said, "Wonderful, marvellous. We were very patient and it worked. I thought it was a great game. When we scored our first, I thought that might be it, but Liverpool came back as they can. When we scored our second it was touch and go afterwards, hanging on."

Billy Liddell - the Liverpool legend, who played in the 1950 Final - said: "I thought Jimmy Case was outstanding.

The others seemed to tire later on and Jimmy was still chasing. The way he took his goal was marvellous."

Rome

On the same day that Liverpool had lost the final, Borussia Mönchengladbach, of West Germany, had won their third successive title after a 2-2 draw against Bayern in Munich. Borussia Mönchengladbach's defence was the best in the Bundesliga, but their attack was weak, having scored only 58 goals in 34 games.

Four days later, in Rome, Liverpool beat Borussia Mönchengladbach 3-1 in the European Cup Final.

Liverpool

Clemence

Neal　　　　Smith　　　　Hughes　　　　Jones

Case　　　　Kennedy　　　　McDermott

Keegan　　　　Johnson　　　　Heighway

0

Hill　　　J.Greenhoff　　　Pearson　　　Coppell

Macari　　　McIlroy

Albiston　　　Buchan　　　B.Greenhoff　　　Nicholl

Stepney

Manchester United

Referee: Mr R. Matthewson (Bolton)　　　**Attendance**: 100,000 (at Wembley)　　　**Receipts**: £420,000

Substitutes: McCreery (for Hill,82); Callaghan (for Johnson,63)

Jimmy Case scores the equalising goal with a powerful right-foot strike from the edge of the box

January 7, 1978

Chelsea (1) 4

Walker 15, 64
Finnieston 49,
Langley 51

Liverpool (0) 2

Johnson 60, Dalglish 81

DAVID Fairclough returned after injury and Alan Hansen was substitute for Liverpool, while Chelsea's side had several changes due to injury. The most notable absentees were Ray Wilkins and Mickey Droy. Liverpool began the game with Johnson operating in midfield.

Chelsea: Bonetti; G.Wilkins, Sparrow, Britton, Harris, Wicks, Garner, Lewington, Langley, Cooke (Finnieston,33), Walker.

Liverpool: Clemence; Neal, Jones(Hansen,72), Thompson, Kennedy, Hughes, Dalglish, Fairclough, Heighway, Johnson, Callaghan.

Referee: Mr P. Partridge (County Durham)

Attendance: 45,449

Dalglish led the attack, but dropped back quickly as Chelsea began in attacking mood. Garner failed to take advantage of a misplaced clearance by Hughes before Kennedy sent Fairclough away. The flame-haired youngster passed to Dalglish, who was crowded out. Operating down the left, Fairclough showed that he had the ability to open up the Chelsea defence. A late tackle by Harris on Fairclough earned the wrath of the referee. The opening exchanges were confined to the midfield. Walker swept past Jones before Thompson, who had settled down quickly, intercepted well and broke up a dangerous attack. Jones then mis-timed a pass to Thompson and Langley sped past him. Langley's low centre was heading for Garner until Hughes stuck out a leg and broke up the attack. The first shot of the game arrived after 13 minutes when a mistake by Harris enabled Dalglish to nod the ball down to Fairclough, whose quickly-taken shot was on target, but Bonetti dived full-length to turn the ball away.

Within a minute, Chelsea had a fine opportunity of taking the lead. From a harmless situation, Hughes failed to control the ball, and Langley blasted the ball over the bar from an ideal shooting opportunity.

With 15 minutes gone, Walker put Chelsea into the lead. He beat Jones on the flank before taking the ball inside and shooting from 25 yards. It appeared as though Clemence thought the ball was going wide, but it swerved at the last moment and just went in under the bar.

Within seconds, Chelsea might have added a second goal against a clearly suspect Liverpool defence. Cooke flicked the ball over the heads of the visiting defence from just inside

his own half of the field, and Walker raced on to beat Jones for speed. Clemence came out quickly, blocked Walker's shot with his legs, and the ball rebounded on to Jones and bounced away for a corner. The Liverpool defence was in disarray. Fairclough relieved the pressure with a dazzling run in which he left Wicks behind before turning the ball inside, but Heighway's sidefooted flick slipped inches wide.

Liverpool were able to unsettle the Chelsea defence at times, too, and Dalglish beat Harris before turning the ball inside to Fairclough, whose first-time shot went well over the top. A magnificent cross-field pass from Heighway sent Johnson clear down the right. Johnson brought the ball in but mistimed his left-foot shot and the ball travelled wide. Fairclough was revelling in the space he created with his dazzling skill, taking the ball past a bemused Harris before floating the ball beyond the far post and out of play. In Liverpool's next attack, Fairclough went up with Bonetti for a Heighway centre, but collided heavily with the goalkeeper and fell awkwardly. He needed attention off the pitch. Fairclough had hurt his right ankle but he returned after a few minutes in time for a Liverpool corner, which Chelsea cleared. Thompson had to receive attention after colliding with a Chelsea defender. Heighway beat Wilkins on the line and brilliantly put Kennedy in possession, but he shot wide. Finnieston substituted for the injured Cooke after 33 minutes.

As the game progressed, Liverpool began to put together some fine moves, but they lacked the decisive finish necessary. Hughes, who was below his usual form, allowed Langley to speed away and turn the ball inside to Finnieston, whose poor attempt was cleared by Thompson, who was playing in inspired form. Clemence then dived full length to hold a shot by Britton, and Bonetti repeated the action when he saved from Kennedy. The Chelsea goalkeeper failed to hold the ball and Dalglish ran in, fell over him, and the move broke down. Seconds before the interval, Dalglish, with a neat headed pass, gave Kennedy a shooting chance, but Kennedy's well-struck shot hit Bonetti on the knee and bounced away for a corner.

At the commencement of the second period, Dalglish and Johnson swapped places, with Johnson leading the attack. Jones was spoken to for a tackle on Walker, and from the free-kick Finnieston put Chelsea further ahead.

Liverpool's defence was exposed down the middle as Langley headed the ball across to Finnieston, whose well-placed shot, just inside the post from 15 yards, beat Clemence after 49 minutes.

Two minutes later, Chelsea struck again. A weak back-pass by Neal left Clemence stranded as he came out for the ball, and Langley beat him to it, to turn the ball into the empty net from a narrow angle.

In an attempt to retrieve something from such a dismal defensive performance, Liverpool pushed four men up in attack, with both full-backs ranging far upfield. After a Chelsea appeal for a penalty had been turned down following Thompson's tackle on Garner, Johnson showed his speed when collecting a headed pass from Dalglish. Johnson's angled shot narrowly went wide of the far post.

Chelsea refused to sit on their lead and they created numerous opportunities afforded them by Liverpool's defensive inadequacies. At the finish of another promising Chelsea attack, Clemence was forced to dive full-length to save from Finnieston.

On the hour Johnson gave Liverpool a shred of hope. Dalglish's persistence brought the ball past two attempted tackles by Harris and the Scot slipped it forward to Johnson, who side-stepped Wicks and beat Bonetti from six yards. Liverpool's attack suddenly found a new confidence and they began to pressurise the Chelsea defence.

Just four minutes later, however, the 20-year-old Walker scored Chelsea's fourth goal. Liverpool left themselves exposed at the back as they pushed forward and Neal failed to clear cleanly. Garner turned the ball inside to Walker, who had the simple task to drive it wide of Clemence.

The Chelsea attack, which had failed to score in two previous meetings with Liverpool this season (0-2 in the League and 0-2 in the League Cup - both at Anfield), carved open the Liverpool defence with consummate ease.

Britton, who worked prodigiously for Chelsea, almost scored number five when he shot just over the bar. With 72 minutes gone, Liverpool replaced Jones with Hansen, who took over at right back.

Liverpool never stopped fighting to get themselves back into the game, but their passing went astray and their rhythm was broken. The Liverpool defence, which had conceded only one goal in their previous six games, had now let in four in just the one match. Hansen gave the ball away to Langley, who failed to get pace onto his shot and Clemence saved with ease.

Nine minutes from time Dalglish scored following a corner. Thompson headed the ball on from Heighway's flag-kick, and Dalglish went up to head it past Bonetti. Liverpool refused to concede defeat, and for several minutes the Reds had only Thompson and Clemence in their own half of the field, with Chelsea hanging on desperately in defence.

The Cup-holders, Manchester United, drew 1-1 against Carlisle away, before winning the replay 4-2. This season's winners, Ipswich Town, beat Cardiff City 2-0 in Wales.

In cricket, Geoffrey Boycott scored an unbeaten 100 in steering England to a draw on the final day of the Second Test against Pakistan in Hyderabad. The Yorkshire skipper put on 185 for the first wicket with Mike Brearley, who was out for 74.

LIVERPOOL FOOTBALL ECHO
~~~~~~~~~~~~~

PRESTON RESERVES: Smith,A.; Pennell, Morris, Spavin, Davies, Uzelac, Doyle, Robinson, Campbell, Smith,J., Cochrane. Sub: Brown.

LIVERPOOL RESERVES: Ogrizovic; Ditchburn, Kettle, Irwin, Smith, Ainsworth, Kewley, Cribley, Birch, Toshack, Gayle. Sub: McCartney.

Referee: Mr J.J. Lydon (Warrington)

John Smith burst through for Preston but shot well over. Ditchburn tried a long range effort for Liverpool but screwed his effort just wide with Smith beaten.

North End, playing neat possession football, had the Liverpool defence on the hop and there were appeals for a penalty as Mick Robinson was brought down in the penalty box by Colin Irwin.

Smith and Campbell combined well and Irwin kicked off the line as Robinson rifled in a shot which caught Ogrizovic off his line.

Howard Gayle, who had been teasing the Preston defence was brought down in the area by David Pennell but North End survived when Kevin Kewley's penalty shot went wide.

But Alex Cribley shot Liverpool ahead after 30 minutes.

North End hit back and Jim Campbell headed home a fine equaliser after 36 minutes but one minute later Gayle put Liverpool ahead again, prodding home the ball from short range.

Half-time:
Preston North End Reserves 1, Liverpool Reserves 2.

Robinson scored for Preston at 60 minutes.
Toshack scored for Liverpool after 75 minutes.

Final:
Preston North End Reserves **2**, Liverpool Reserves **3**.

CUP SNIPS
~~~~~

Blyth Spartans	1	Enfield	0
Bristol City	4	Wrexham	4
Everton	4	Aston Villa	1
Leeds United	1	Manchester C.	2
Nottingham F.	4	Swindon Town	1
Peterborough	1	Newcastle U.	1
QPR	4	Wealdstone	0
Sheffield U.	0	Arsenal	5
Stoke City	4	Tilbury	0
Tottenham H.	2	Bolton W.	2
West Ham U.	1	Watford	0

January 10, 1979

Southend United (0) 0   Liverpool (0) 0

BOB Paisley declared during Liverpool's flight home after the match at Roots Hall that "This was no night for a football match. It may have been an exciting Cup-tie, but there is no way anyone could play football in those conditions. All you could do was try and play it tight, and not give away a soft goal by accident. We did that, and nobody was hurt, so I'm reasonably satisfied. I only hope we can play a game of football at Anfield, because in conditions like this, skill is cancelled out totally. This must be the only country in the world where you can have four seasons in one day. At 3 o'clock in the afternoon I was out on the pitch, the sun was shining, and conditions were perfect. Two hours later, after tea, we were in the middle of a blizzard and more than an inch of snow fell before the game. I wasn't going to ask for it to be postponed, but you could see for yourself it made football a farce. People talk about these great Continental stars - but I'd like to see them play in conditions like these. I wonder how Cruyff would look on a skidpan - and then on thick mud a day later." Southend manager, Dave Smith said, "The lads did us proud and deserved to win. I'm a bit disappointed we didn't snatch it at the last minute - and I still think we might manage to win at Anfield. The conditions handicapped us worse than them because we like to play a lot of short passes. But it was significant they committed more fouls than we did, because that tells you how hard they had to play."

Graeme Souness made his Cup début for Liverpool. Genuine goalscoring opportunities were rare, although Dalglish almost caught Southend cold in the first minute, while Hansen had two headers that troubled Cawston and Kennedy had a powerful shot well saved. At the opposite end Clemence came out speedily to prevent Parker and in the final minute or so, he dived brilliantly to hold a good shot from Morris. With 25 minutes gone, Gerry Fell put Derrick Parker away in a break and Clemence came out to dive at Parker's feet and block the shot. Just before the interval Case was booked for a foul on Fell.

The second half followed the pattern of the first with Southend unable to break down Liverpool's resolute rearguard. With 71 minutes gone, Hughes sent over a cross and Cawston only just reached it to push it over the bar. Liverpool's main problem was that the midfield failed to create sufficient clear opportunities for Fairclough and Dalglish in attack. The two strikers were well marshalled by Hadley and Moody. Paisley pulled off McDermott and introduced Heighway with 13 minutes left, but it was too late for Heighway to produce anything tangible for Liverpool.

Mervyn Cawston was watched by nine of his family, who had chartered a plane from Norwich. Cawston was brought back from American football the previous summer for £20,000 and the former Norwich and Gillingham 'keeper, who played for Chicago Stings in the North American League, had an outstanding game.

England beat Australia by 93 runs in Sydney to score a remarkable victory on the last day of the Fourth Test and retain the Ashes. The win, 65 minutes after tea, gave England an unbeatable 3-1 lead in the six-Test series, and was a tribute to the professionalism and fighting spirit of the side. England scored just 152 in their first innings, while Australia recorded 294. In their second innings, England scored 346, with Derek Randall hitting 150. England bowled the home side out for just 111, with Emburey claiming 4-46 in just 17.2 overs.

Graeme Souness

Southend United: Cawston; Stead, Yates, Laverick, Hadley, Moody, Morris, Pountney, Parker, Dudley, Fell.

Liverpool: Clemence; Neal, Hughes, Thompson, Kennedy, Hansen, Dalglish, Case, Fairclough, McDermott(Heighway,77), Souness.

Referee: Mr K.S. Hackett (Sheffield)

Attendance: 31,033   **Receipts**: £36,559 (a record)

January 17, 1979

Liverpool (1) 3
*Case 38, Dalglish 75,
R.Kennedy 85*

Southend United (0) 0

THIRD Division Southend provided determined opposition throughout the first period, but when Jimmy Case opened the scoring after 38 minutes, the game was effectively over. Kenny Dalglish hit the ball to the right to Case, who spotted David Fairclough on the left. Fairclough went on unchallenged but his shot was parried by goalkeeper Cawston and Case struck. Derek Parker missed two clear chances before Liverpool had scored. After 18 minutes he headed high over the bar from five yards when a Colin Morris corner kick was nodded on to him by Alan Moody. Twenty minutes later England defender Phil Thompson slipped and fell as Mervyn Cawston's long clearance came towards him and Parker was given a free run on goal. Clemence timed his run from goal with perfection before plunging at Parker's feet.

Southend ran tirelessly but rarely troubled Liverpool's defence. Hansen was immaculate, and Thompson was solid, while full-backs Neal and Hughes often joined in Liverpool attacks. The Liverpool and England skipper hammered two shots just wide, had another shot charged down and appealed strongly for a penalty after dribbling into the penalty area and falling full-length. Fairclough relished in the conditions, which were more conducive to football than those at Roots Hall. After a comparatively slow beginning, the flame-haired winger entertained the crowd with some spectacular running. Southend countered the threat of Fairclough by putting two or three players on him. He still created room for himself and put in several telling crosses.

With 75 minutes gone, Liverpool settled the issue beyond doubt. Hansen thumped a high clearance down the middle and Dalglish, bursting between Tony Hadley and Moody, lobbed the ball over Cawston. It was the Scottish international's first goal since October 21, when he scored against Chelsea. Dalglish had gone twelve games without a goal.

Five minutes from the end, Ray Kennedy scored Liverpool's third. Dalglish knocked a corner kick back to him and Kennedy hammered a right-foot shot into the net.

Case produced a fine all-round performance, tackling firmly and distributing the ball intelligently. He continually cut in from the right wing and posed a constant threat with his powerful shooting. Two players were booked in a hard game which never became dirty - Hadley after a tackle on Dalglish and Yates after a foul on Case.

At Filbert Street, Arsenal drew 3-3 with Sheffield Wednesday in a third replay.

*Kenny Dalglish,
who scored his
first goal after
twelve games
without scoring*

Liverpool: Clemence; Neal, Hughes, Thompson, R.Kennedy, Hansen, Dalglish, Case, Fairclough, McDermott, Souness.

Southend United: Cawston; Stead, Yates, Laverick, Hadley, Moody, Morris, Pountney, Parker, Dudley, Fell.

Referee: Mr K.S. Hackett (Sheffield)

Attendance: 37,797

January 30, 1979

Liverpool (0) 1
Dalglish 82

Blackburn Rovers (0) 0

SECOND Division Blackburn Rovers played defensively and almost secured a replay at Ewood Park until a late goal from Kenny Dalglish gave Liverpool their just reward after a relentless attacking performance. The pitch had been covered in places with tons of sand, and this reduced the game to a lottery, eliminating the skill factor, due to being treacherous and icy in part. The area in front of the Kemlyn Road stand was particularly bad, and as the night progressed, the pitch hardened. According to acting-manager John Pickering, Blackburn were prepared to go "hell for leather" at the Liverpool defence. Their tactics never materialised. But, with Butcher in brilliant form, and centre-backs Round and Fazackerley dour and resilient, they held out until near the end against a Liverpool side which won 17 corners as opposed to just one gained by the visitors.

Alan Kennedy made his Liverpool Cup début, but it was Alan Hansen who was in sparkling form for the Reds. Celebrating a call-up to the Scottish international squad, Hansen strode majestically across the park. Liberated by Liverpool's attacking policy, he rose high to head the ball inches over the bar. Five minutes from the end, Hansen's shot was turned over the bar by Butcher.

Heighway replaced McDermott after 65 minutes and Liverpool's fortunes began to change. Dalglish, taking the ball from Heighway, was flattened by Birchenall. Liverpool were awarded an indirect free-kick, and Dalglish was booked for protesting for a penalty. The Reds launched attack after attack, but they lacked the decisive finish. Nine minutes from the finish, a superb 30 yard pass from Hansen to the feet of Case initiated a goal. Case broke down the right and his centre found Dalglish, who timed his half-volley to perfection and netted. In the last minute Heighway created a chance for Neal, who smashed the ball against the post.

Scotland manager, Jock Stein, said of Hansen, "He is a ball-playing centre-half and although he is young he has experience at the highest level with his club." Of his selection, Hansen said, "I just couldn't be more delighted. I have been working and hoping for this ever since I gained a regular place with Liverpool. You look at the Liverpool side and they are nearly all internationals. It will be great if I can join them. Every time there are international matches, ten or eleven players are called up and it's pretty lonely when you are left behind. I don't like that. An empty dressing room with only a handful of players seems unreal. This is something to look forward to and I hope to be involved, especially with Kenny Dalglish and Graeme Souness in the side. I don't want to build up my hopes too high, but there's no harm in hoping. Just being in the squad is a big step, but I will be delighted if I am called on to play."

Liverpool: Clemence; Neal, Hughes, A.Kennedy, R.Kennedy, Hansen, Dalglish, Case, Fairclough, McDermott(Heighway,65), Souness.

Blackburn Rovers: Butcher; Fowler, Bailey, Metcalfe, Round, Fazackerley, Hird, Garner, Craig, Birchenall, Morris(Brotherston,73).

Referee: Mr P.G. Reeves (Leicester)

Attendance: 43,432

Alan Hansen, *who strode majestically across the park, liberated by Liverpool's attacking policy*

February 28, 1979

Liverpool (1) 3
Johnson 43, 61, Souness 59

Burnley (0) 0

SECOND Division Burnley held Liverpool for almost 45 minutes before succumbing to a goal from David Johnson. Burnley almost caused a shock after ten minutes when Ray Clemence was forced to make two magnificent saves to foil Peter Noble. Firstly, he tipped a 20-yard drive over the bar, and then from the resulting corner, he reached a close-range shot to make a save which even the Burnley skipper applauded. Clemence said," I was pleased with both of those saves. If Burnley had scored at that stage we could have been struggling."

In the opening minutes, Steve Kindon caused Thompson and Hughes several problems with his pace and Fletcher created trouble for Liverpool in the air. There was a glimmer of a Cup upset before Liverpool settled into their traditional rhythm.

A link-up between Dalglish and Heighway sent Ray Kennedy racing away down the left to supply a deep cross to the far post, where Johnson, moving in, powered a header into goal.

Burnley were close to an equaliser when a left-wing run by Steve Kindon led to a frantic scramble in the Liverpool penalty area. The ball eventually broke to Ingham, whose shot from ten yards was blocked.

Liverpool raced to the other end to score two goals in quick succession. Graeme Souness added the second goal with a vicious 18-yard drive after 59 minutes after Ray Kennedy had burst through the defence and laid the ball neatly in front of him. Just two minutes later Johnson completed the scoring after Heighway dribbled right into the goalmouth.

Heighway was in inspired form, giving Scott a terrible time, cutting past him on both sides at will. Johnson was particularly strong in the air. He was inches away from a hat-trick when a well-directed header passed inches over the bar, and he sent three other shots wide of the target. He was booked after 81 minutes for an unnecessary foul on Rodaway.

Kenny Dalglish was in excellent form, twisting and turning before delivering inch-perfect, beautifully-weighted passes.

Peter Noble said after the game, "I thought we did quite well in the circumstances. It was hard because Liverpool are such a great team. They remind me of the Leeds team of ten years ago. They don't mind whacking the opposition to stop them playing and when they get the ball they pass it around really well.

If we could have scored in the first half, it might have been a different story. But once we got behind it makes it so much harder to keep running and chasing. Yet we had to keep going

or we might have got a real drubbing. We were playing for our pride then and I was pleased with the way we stuck at it to the end. We didn't disgrace ourselves by any means.

Having to play four games in eight days, with the last one at Liverpool, was perhaps a bit unfair. But whether we would have done any better with a less hectic build-up is something we'll never know."

***Steve Heighway**, who was in inspired form for Liverpool*

Liverpool: Clemence; Neal, Hughes, A.Kennedy, R.Kennedy, Thompson, Dalglish, Johnson, Heighway, McDermott, Souness.

Burnley: Stevenson; Scott, Brennan, Noble, Thomson, Rodaway, Ingham, Hall, Fletcher, Kindon, James.

Referee: Mr B.J. Homewood (Sunbury)

Attendance: 47,161

March 10, 1979

Ipswich Town (0) 0

Liverpool (0) 1
Dalglish 52

IPSWICH failed to turn their first-half supremacy into goals, while Liverpool failed to capitalise on the benefit of a following wind. Liverpool's football did not flow as normal, and Souness - usually so precise - directed several passes astray. Manager Bob Paisley said after the game, "We would have liked to have come here and won by playing top quality football, but the swirling wind and the positive attitude of the Ipswich lads made it impossible. So we had to revert to what you might call ale-house football." Liverpool's physical and total commitment not only helped them weather Ipswich's brilliant attacking storm in the first-half, but it also won them the match against Bobby Robson's exciting and talented side.

After the interval, Liverpool slowly began to dominate and dictate the exchanges with teamwork above the norm. Phil Thompson tackled supremely, and assisted Alan Hansen in closing up the middle. Ipswich, the Cup-holders, did not capitulate readily, and Clive Woods tormented Emlyn Hughes all afternoon. Even with a recurrence of his thigh injury sustained against Chelsea, Hughes typified Liverpool's fighting spirit and refused to concede an inch. Liverpool rolled up their sleeves and got on with the job. The hallmark of a real champion is the ability to survive and then succeed when little is going right.

Liverpool grafted and produced the sort of football necessary to win the tie, not fans of pretty football. The Liverpool defence planted the ball into the stands or got their bodies behind the ball as Ipswich fought gallantly to remain in the Cup.

With 52 minutes gone, Jimmy Case initiated the move by winning possession in midfield. From Ray Kennedy, the ball went to David Johnson and a pass to Case preceded the centre to Dalglish, who breasted it down and took it away and wide of the goal. The 19-year-old Terry Butcher hovered menacingly, but Dalglish twisted past Butcher, drew back his left foot, and the ball hit the back of the net.

Arsenal drew 1-1 with Southampton, winning the replay 2-0, while Wolves and Shrewsbury drew 1-1, the Wolves winning the replay 3-1 away.

Manchester United and Spurs also drew 1-1, United winning 2-0 at Old Trafford.

Ipswich Town: Cooper; Burley, Mills, Thijssen, Osman, Butcher, Wark, Muhren, Mariner, Gates(Brazil,63), Woods.

Liverpool: Clemence; Neal, Hughes, Thompson, R.Kennedy, Hansen, Dalglish, Johnson, Case, McDermott, Souness.

Referee: Mr R. Challis (Tonbridge)

Attendance: 31,322

Emlyn Hughes, who was tormented by Clive Woods

March 31, 1979

Liverpool (1) 2
Dalglish 17,   Hansen 82

Manchester United (1) 2
Jordan 19,   B.Greenhoff 56

THE opening minutes of the game were based on destructive play rather than patient construction, with nerve-ends raw and frequent free-kicks. Liverpool opened the scoring when, receiving from Case just inside the penalty area, Dalglish twisted and turned in a packed penalty area past three men, including United goalkeeper Bailey before hitting a shot just inside the post. United struck back immediately through Jordan and dominated the play afterwards. They unsettled Liverpool, not allowing the Anfielders to play. United's directness, sharpness and powerful attacking reduced Liverpool's customary midfield dominance to a physical struggle for possession which the Merseysiders lost. United were more eager for the ball. Former Wrexham player Mickey Thomas worked prodigiously to motivate his side. Jordan was given a free header from a hopeful centre by Jimmy Greenhoff. Ray Clemence stood flat-footed on his line with Hansen's challenge virtually non-existent.

With the scores level, the staccato pattern of play continued, with numerous stoppages for fouls, but it was nevertheless an enthralling encounter. With 37 minutes gone, Terry McDermott missed a penalty, awarded after Buchan's challenge on Dalglish. McQueen was booked for protesting too strongly. McDermott's shot rebounded off an upright with the goalkeeper going the wrong way. The Liverpool midfielder said afterwards, "The post moved six inches." Almost immediately afterwards Buchan headed a thunderous shot from Souness to safety. The game continued to be fought with passion and commitment of the highest level.

Early in the second half, United took the lead when Brian Greenhoff clipped the ball past Clemence after Coppell beat Hughes. Liverpool were struggling, but they showed their determination, their mental strength and their courage. Goalmouth incidents occurred every two minutes or so. Heighway was sent on for Jimmy Case to provide more attacking width, and the move released Ray Kennedy from his defensive responsibilities. Liverpool then began to attack in full flow and they began to slowly dominate the game. Dalglish lobbed a ball over the bar, but then Clemence produced a magnificent save to deny Thomas from a free-kick. Coppell raced through before shooting wide. Bailey saved well at Kennedy's feet, and when he was beaten by a shot from Souness, Buchan - majestical at the heart of United's defence - cleared off the line. Thompson, who typified Liverpool's fighting spirit, drove forward into the area and centred low into the goalmouth. The ball spun off Bailey's arm and into the path of Hansen, who carefully sidefooted the ball home. Liverpool had further opportunities to score, but United battled valiantly to deny them. Manager Bob Paisley said after the game, "We gave them two soft goals. We should never have let them hit back so quickly after we had opened the scoring, or let them take the lead in the second-half when we were just starting to play some football." Liverpool's problems stemmed from the midfield's inadequacies, where the United trio of Greenhoff, McIlroy and Thomas were a yard quicker to the ball.

Hansen was awarded a radio after the game by the match sponsors as Liverpool's man-of-the-match. Hansen said, "I was the worst player in the team. Is that what they give awards for these days?" Certainly Hansen and Clemence remained uncertain at times throughout the match.

In the other semi-final, Arsenal beat Wolverhampton Wanderers 2-0.

Liverpool: Clemence; Neal, Hughes, Thompson, R.Kennedy, Hansen, Dalglish, Johnson, Case (Heighway,62), McDermott, Souness.

Manchester United: Bailey; Nicholl, Albiston, McIlroy, McQueen, Buchan, Coppell, J.Greenhoff, Jordan, B.Greenhoff, Thomas.

Referee: Mr D. Richardson (Great Harwood)

Attendance: 52,584 (at Maine Road)

Phil Thompson

April 4, 1979

Liverpool (0) 0   Manchester United (0) 1
J.Greenhoff 78

THE First Division table:

	Pl	W	D	L	F	A	Pts
Liverpool	**30**	**21**	**6**	**3**	**63**	**11**	**48**
West Bromwich Albion	29	19	6	4	61	27	44
Everton	34	15	14	5	46	32	44
Nottingham Forest	30	14	14	2	45	19	42
Arsenal	33	15	10	8	51	33	40
Leeds United	32	14	11	7	57	41	39
Coventry City	35	11	13	11	43	57	35
Manchester United	**30**	**13**	**8**	**9**	**49**	**50**	**34**

On a night when Nottingham Forest and West Bromwich Albion both won 4-0 at home to close the gap on Liverpool at the top of the First Division, Liverpool's dreams of a League and Cup double were shattered by United, just as the Manchester club had done back in 1977 when they defeated Liverpool at Wembley to rob them of a treble.

The game was not a classic, but it provided many incidents with both teams going close. At the interval, United were unfortunate not to be in the lead, but at the end of 90 minutes, Liverpool were the unfortunate team to lose to a solitary United effort from Jimmy Greenhoff.

Graeme Souness and Terry McDermott covered the entire pitch in a vain attempt to win the game for Liverpool. Ray Clemence stood firm in the face of intense United pressure to deny his opponents on numerous occasions. Souness struck a fine shot past Bailey which went narrowly wide.

Ray Kennedy crashed a free-kick against the crossbar and Dalglish dived low to get in a header which Bailey pulled down. Kennedy had a great opportunity but shot too high from a good position in front of goal, while McDermott laid on a perfect heading chance for Souness, but the ball went over.

Steve Heighway made some devastating runs down the left as Liverpool overran United in the second period. The Manchester side were pushed back into their own half for long spells, being restricted to breakaway attacks with only Jordan up the field. But Liverpool's attacking forays displayed more vigour than accuracy and more desperation than planning.

The first half belonged almost entirely to United. Clemence was forced to make three tremendous saves in the first ten minutes from Macari, Thomas and winger Coppell. Twice more inside the first half-hour the Liverpool goalkeeper was left for dead, when Jordan, an ever-present menace in the air, hit the bar once and saw the ball scraped off the line by right-back Neal. Centre-half Gordon McQueen hoisted another excellent opportunity high over the bar. United's spell of midfield control stemmed from Macari and McIlroy, who was at the heart of every move in the battle for possession. On occasions the game became over-physical and Macari, Jordan and Hughes were all booked.

Just twelve minutes from the end, United hit the goal which removed Liverpool from the competition. A Thomas cross from the touchline found Greenhoff in acres of space completely unmarked as he raced forward to head the ball past the advancing Clemence.

Arsenal won a thrilling Wembley final by 3-2. Trailing by two goals and with only five minutes remaining, United drew level, but lost to a last-minute goal from Alan Sunderland.

Liverpool: Clemence; Neal, Hughes, Thompson, R.Kennedy, Hansen, Dalglish, Johnson(Case,82), Heighway, McDermott, Souness.

Manchester United: Bailey; Nicholl, Albiston, McIlroy, McQueen, Buchan, Coppell, J.Greenhoff, Jordan, Macari (Ritchie,78), Thomas.

Referee: Mr D. Richardson (Great Harwood)

Attendance: 53,069 (at Goodison Park)

Receipts: £174,945 (ground record)

January 5, 1980

Liverpool (2) 5

Souness 19,
Johnson 42, 65, 74,   Case 87

Grimsby Town (0) 0

MORE than 8,000 Grimsby supporters added to the sense of occasion as their side lined up in Continental fashion to salute the crowd before the match. Grimsby, attacking the Kop goal, opened with a fast attack with Waters heading wide following poor marking in the Liverpool defence. The Reds, however, settled into their attacking rhythm, moving swiftly down the right flank. Case got in two penetrating crosses which troubled the Grimsby defence. After being on defence for several minutes, Grimsby broke free and with Liverpool expecting an offside decision, the ball travelled to the unmarked Drinkell. He laid it off to Kilmore, whose hastily-taken shot went well wide of the target. Grimsby's captain and Eire international, Waters, was always searching for space in midfield from which to build an attack. The Reds struggled to break down the visiting defence, in which Wigginton superbly marshalled Dalglish. With 15 minutes gone, Neal was booked for a foul on Cumming. Liverpool cleared the kick and the ball went swiftly upfield for Johnson to chase, but Batch ran 20 yards out of his goal to clear the danger with a tremendous kick.

After 19 minutes, Graeme Souness hit his first goal of the season. He combined well with Dalglish in a run through the midfield, broke clear of the Grimsby cover on the edge of the area and drove a left-foot shot just inside the post.

Grimsby fought back and Clemence saved well from Cumming. Liverpool responded and McDermott forced Batch to a full-length save. Liverpool increased the pressure, but their final pass lacked incisiveness and several promising moves broke down. The Mariners fought back determinedly, emphasising the quality of their play which had taken them to second place in the Third Division. Cumming posed a threat as he stole upfield from his midfield position, but a well-timed tackle from Hansen cleared the danger. From a long centre by Neal, Johnson beat Stone in the air, but his header went narrowly wide with Case unable to make contact as he went dashing in. From a corner, a McDermott volley was well saved by Batch, who dived late as the ball arrived through a crowd of players. Crombie was booked when he pulled Case down by the jersey as the Liverpool player raced clear down the right. From the free-kick, Batch made a tremendous save from Dalglish.

A fine attacking move involving several Grimsby passes caused problems for Liverpool and only a firm tackle by Thompson on Drinkell saved the situation. Neal and McDermott had shots blocked by Grimsby defenders as the Reds struggled to gain the initiative. In their isolated attacks, Grimsby stretched the Liverpool defence. Alan Kennedy had problems curtailing Brolly and Waters as they carved their

way through from midfield. Thompson held the defence together with a sterling performance. Stone was booked for a foul on Dalglish. Five minutes before the interval, Liverpool almost scored a second goal. Johnson turned the ball back to Dalglish, who let it run to Souness and he hit a tremendous shot from 20 yards which beat the goalkeeper but flew over the bar.

Three minutes before half-time, Johnson put the League champions two goals ahead. From a clearance, the ball bounced over the head of the Grimsby men to give Johnson a clear run and he took the ball just inside the area before hitting it wide of the goalkeeper. From a Grimsby corner, Wigginton's header was turned away one-handedly by Clemence.

The second period began with Liverpool moving the ball around in a series of intricate passing movements, but they lacked the killer instinct. A great move featuring Neal, Kennedy, Case, McDermott and back to Kennedy ended with Ray Kennedy's fierce drive missing the target by inches. Liverpool began to turn on the style. A move between Neal, Dalglish and McDermott, who back-heeled the ball into the path of Ray Kennedy, ended with the ball flashing wide. The instigator of most of Liverpool's attacking moves was the mercurial Dalglish, who skipped over despairing tackles as he put on a show involving all his trickery. Play was based permanently in the Grimsby penalty area and they replaced Kilmore with Ford on the hour. Case produced an exceptional 30-yard pass of precision to send Johnson away, but he delayed his shot a fraction too long and the opportunity was scorned.

With 65 minutes gone, Johnson scored again. Hansen took a free-kick quickly, spotting McDermott running into space down the middle. The ball landed perfectly for McDermott, who took it on and lobbed the ball over the advancing Batch. It was going wide until Johnson ran in from the left and steered it into the net with his head.

The flow was virtually in one direction as Liverpool bore down on the Kop goal. A magnificent pass by Dalglish sent Case streaming down the right and from the pass aimed for Dalglish, Waters almost directed the ball into his own net. From the corner the ball was worked across to Ray Kennedy, whose shot from the edge of the area hit the bar and bounced down for Johnson to drive it back into the roof of the net for his hat-trick. It was Johnson's 20th goal of the season. As Liverpool were rampant, Batch blocked a McDermott shot with his feet and Waters deflected a Ray Kennedy shot off the line. Case hit a swerving shot inches wide. Three minutes from the end Case hit Liverpool's fifth with an unstoppable shot past Batch. Everton beat Aldershot 4-1. Wrexham beat Charlton 6-0, while Bristol City defeated Derby County 6-2. Nottingham Forest won 4-1 at Leeds. The Cup-holders, Arsenal, drew 0-0 at Cardiff, winning the replay 2-1. West Ham United drew 1-1 at West Bromwich Albion, winning the replay 2-1 on their way to winning the Cup. The shock of the round was Fourth Division Halifax's 1-0 home victory over First Division Manchester City. Paul Hendrie scored after 75 minutes to send Malcolm Allison's men crashing out of the Cup. Fencing collapsed behind the goal half-an-hour before the start of Yeovil's tie against Norwich. Wire netting and advertising boards were forced over by the pressure of fans pushing forward.

Liverpool: Clemence; Neal, A.Kennedy, Thompson, R.Kennedy, Hansen, Dalglish, Case, Johnson, McDermott, Souness.

Grimsby Town: Batch; D.Moore, Crombie, Waters, Wigginton, Stone, Brolly, Kilmore(Ford,60), Drinkell, Mitchell, Cumming.

Referee: Mr K. Baker (Rugby)

Attendance: 49,706

David Johnson, *who hit a hat-trick against Grimsby*

January 26, 1980

Nottingham Forest (0) 0　　Liverpool (1) 2

Dalglish 31,
McDermott (pen) 71

THE pitch had dried considerably since the Tuesday prior to the game and the match began in bright sunshine. Liverpool began with a bout of neat passing in defence, but the first incident arrived when Bowyer kicked McDermott on the back of the ankle. McDermott retaliated in anger and was spoken to by the referee, who also spoke to Bowyer. From a move near Liverpool's right corner flag, Johnson took the ball inside and forced Shilton to a full-length save with a tremendous shot. A shot by Souness soon afterwards went just wide. Following a wild back-pass from Hansen, Alan Kennedy was forced to concede a corner and Clemence held a shot by O'Neill, the ball arriving through a crowd of players. Following their 0-1 Semi-final first leg League Cup defeat by Forest on the previous Tuesday, Liverpool were in determined mood.

Liverpool moved the ball around in a series of short passes, whilst Forest were always looking for the direct ball to set Birtles or Francis on a run at the Liverpool defence. Following a quickly-taken free-kick, Ray Kennedy headed towards goal. Shilton moved out but failed to collect the ball which appeared to have crossed the line, but Dalglish was penalised for a challenge on the goalkeeper. Johnson lost both boots as Lloyd prevented him jumping to reach the ball in the air. Johnson was forced to go to the touchline for repairs to his right boot, getting new laces as the game progressed without him. The Forest crowd chanted *"Liverpool are boring"* as the Reds relied on the same stifling tactics as they had employed in midweek.

After 20 minutes, the game flared up. Bowyer fouled Case, and McGovern became so incensed that he had to be restrained by Neal. The referee called McGovern and Case together, booking both players. The physical element of the game was just below the surface, and the game required firm handling by referee White.

A perfect pass from Dalglish to the unmarked Johnson almost brought Liverpool a goal. Johnson's powerful shot beat Shilton but hit the inside of a post and rebounded across the face of the goal before being put behind for a corner. Liverpool pushed Forest back consistently and a fine pass by Alan Kennedy to Dalglish enabled the Scot to turn the ball into the path of Ray Kennedy, whose right-foot shot lacked power and direction. A new right boot was brought out to Johnson, the original having been torn down the back by the challenge from Lloyd.

An elementary goalkeeping error from Shilton gave Liverpool a goal. He ventured out of his goal for a long centre by Neal and dropped the ball, which fell to Dalglish to slam it into the back of the net - his first goal against Forest and only

Liverpool's fourth in eleven meetings. Five minutes later Liverpool almost scored again. Souness broke up a Forest attack with a magnificent pass down the left to Johnson, who beat Needham and crossed the ball beyond the far post to Dalglish. Diving full-length, the Scot just failed to make contact. As Liverpool pressed forward in an irrepressible red tide, Lloyd was booked for a foul on Dalglish. A minute later Souness followed for a high tackle on McGovern - the fourth booking in under 40 minutes. Forest looked disorganised as Liverpool took complete control of the game. Three minutes before the interval Shilton flung himself to his left to turn away a powerful drive from Ray Kennedy. Just before half-time Case robbed the too-casual Gray and set off on an unchallenged 30-yard run. As Shilton advanced Case placed the ball wide of the goalkeeper but also wide of the far post.

As the first half moved into injury time, Thompson became the fifth player to be booked for a tackle on Birtles. During the interval Forest replaced Lloyd with Burns. The booking of Souness took his points total to 20, and he faced suspension by the F.A.

Forest began the second half with determination. O'Neill sent Birtles away and Thompson brilliantly challenged the Forest striker. The home side pushed O'Neill into the attack with Francis and Birtles into an attempt to score an equalising goal. A poorly directed back-pass by Alan Kennedy forced Clemence to dive full-length to prevent a corner. Bowyer's back-pass to Shilton was seized upon by Johnson but the Liverpool striker was crowded out. A moment of indecision by Neal gave Forest a glimmer of a chance and there was a huge scramble in the goalmouth before Alan Kennedy finally cleared. Forest increased the pressure and Liverpool's defence was now forced to work hard with their midfield making passing errors. Hansen was booked for a foul on Bowyer. He had brought the ball out of defence in his customary manner, lost it when he pushed it too far forward and carried on with his run as Bowyer collected the ball and fouled him.

Liverpool halted Forest's progress with a corner from which the ball was turned back to Souness. The fiery Scot connected with the ball perfectly, but Shilton flung himself full-length to turn the ball round the post. After 71 minutes, Liverpool scored a second goal which gave them the breathing space they needed. Needham handled the ball in trying to prevent Dalglish taking it past the stranded Shilton. As the ball ran free McDermott lobbed the ball into the empty net. The goal did not count, but McDermott scored from the penalty spot.

Clemence had to make only his second save of the game late on from Birtles. Before the end, thousands of Forest supporters streamed out of the ground, having seen their team outplayed by Liverpool. In a last-minute burst Francis fired over the bar and Clemence saved well from a Needham header. After the game, Forest skipper John McGovern said, "This wasn't just a bad result - it was a disaster. We have enjoyed our results against Liverpool in the past couple of years because we have always competed with them. We have never given them an inch. Today we didn't do that. In the dressing room at Derby County, there is a sign that says that giving the ball away is the biggest crime in football. I am afraid we were all guilty."

Ray Kennedy said, "We were all conscious that we had finished in front of them only once in ten games in three years. But we all knew that putting them out of the FA Cup would really hurt them and we wanted to hurt them."

Arsenal beat Brighton 2-0 at home, while West Ham United beat Orient 3-2 away. Chester beat Millwall 2-0 with goals from Trevor Storton - a former Liverpool player - and Ian Rush - soon to be a Liverpool player. The 18-year-old Rush was watched by Manchester City manager Malcolm Allison, who saw the youngster score Chester's second goal after 34

Nottingham Forest: Shilton; Anderson, Gray, McGovern, Lloyd(Burns,46), Needham, O'Neill, Bowyer, Birtles, Francis, Robertson.

Liverpool: Clemence, Neal, A.Kennedy, Thompson, R.Kennedy, Hansen, Dalglish, Case, Johnson, McDermott, Souness.

Referee: Mr C. White (Harrow)

Attendance: 33,277

minutes with a magnificent diving header. Chester boss, Alan Oakes, was tight-lipped about the possible transfer of Rush, saying: "Ian has done remarkably well in a short time, but as for his future that remains to be seen."

Ray Kennedy

February 16, 1980

Liverpool (0) 2

Fairclough 64, 81

Bury (0) 0

BURY - bottom of the Third Division - battled bravely against Liverpool - top of the First Division. Bury sorted out their long list of injuries so that only two regular first-team players were missing, Whitehead and Mullen. Liverpool had their familiar team line-up with David Johnson leading the attack. On a spring-like afternoon, Phil Thompson won the toss and Liverpool attacked the Anfield Road goal in the first half with a strong sun at their backs. The Reds settled into an early rhythm of attacking football. Bury's 9,000 supporters cheered vociferously when Steve Johnson cut off the ball and sent it for a throw-in. The Shakers defended with enthusiasm and commitment and Liverpool found it difficult to create the space and time they needed. The game was played for a long period in the Bury half of the field and Clemence kept himself warm by pacing up and down the lonely Kop penalty area. Liverpool moved forward constantly, but Bury put nine men into defence, closing everything down quickly. Souness was in commanding form in the middle of the park and he initiated several Liverpool attacks with the pinpoint accuracy of his passes, but the moves broke down due to the massed ranks of the Bury defence. With 16 minutes gone, Keith Kennedy produced the best move of the match up to that point. He hit the ball down the left for Johnson to break through and turn it inside to Halford, whose instant shot was inches over the bar. The Liverpool fans began to show their impatience with their team which, despite constant pressure, failed to provide a goal as Bury defended skilfully. Dalglish and McDermott combined well to provide an opportunity for Johnson, but Keith Kennedy tackled well. The bearded Waddington - who was on Liverpool's books as a youngster before going to Blackburn on a free transfer - performed well at the heart of the Bury defence.

After 23 minutes the Liverpool defence was caught square. A long clearance by Waddington reached Hilton, who was unmarked and played onside by Alan Kennedy. Clemence ran out of the penalty area to clear with a flying kick. There were some ironic cheers from the Bury contingent at some of Liverpool's inadequacies to overrun Bury. McIlwraith moved forward from midfield to drive a shot a yard or two wide. The Bury fans began to cheer everything their team produced as they built up their attacks. Neal sent McDermott clear, and the former Newcastle player controlled the ball well but hit his shot too hard across the goal. David Johnson was booked for a challenge on Forrest. In the final minute of the first period, Ray Kennedy hit Liverpool's best effort, a curling 25-yard shot which Forrest touched over the bar.

Fairclough went on for Johnson at the start of the second half. Within two minutes of the restart, Fairclough had the ball in the net, but was clearly offside when the pass from Dalglish reached him. Liverpool increased their pressure and

they began to create more space for themselves. With Liverpool fully committed to attack, they were left exposed at the back, and Bury threatened to capitalise upon this. A centre by Johnson was intercepted by Case, who turned the ball for a corner. A foul by McIlwraith on Case left the Liverpool man on his back and before the free-kick could be taken McIlwraith held up one finger on each hand to indicate that it was all square after what Case had done to him a few minutes earlier.

When Hansen failed to control the ball, it broke well for Hilton, who took it on and only a well-timed challenge by Clemence blocked the shot. A header from Souness went straight to Forrest and then Neal blasted wide. Howard and Wilson blocked a double effort from Fairclough in the six yard box as Liverpool began to penetrate the Bury defence. Keith Kennedy - brother of Liverpool's Alan - performed well at left-back for the visitors.

Fairclough - with four goals in the last two matches - put Liverpool ahead after 64 minutes. A Dalglish corner from the left reached Case on the far side of the goal. He nodded the ball into the goalmouth and Fairclough went high to beat Forrest with a strong header. The goalkeeper got his hand to the ball but was unable to prevent it from hitting the net.

Some of Liverpool's frustration and desperation left them after the goal, and Bury began to look vulnerable. A fine run and centre from Hansen reached Ray Kennedy, whose header was pushed away by Forrest. Hansen - Liverpool's best player on the day - found the time and space to move on to the attack which delighted the crowd. After 75 minutes, Hilton limped off to be replaced by Madden. He took his place up front in an attempt to salvage a goal.

With nine minutes remaining Fairclough struck again. A superb pass by Neal to Dalglish cracked open the Bury defence. The Scot controlled the ball brilliantly to beat Howard and Forrest before turning it into the path of Fairclough, who sidefooted the ball into the net from 12 yards for his sixth goal in a week.

The Bury players received a standing ovation from all round the ground as they left the field. It was a tribute to their courage and defensive capabilities. They were relegated at the end of the season, finishing in 21st place.

Kevin Keegan's link with Southampton reaped its first dividend at Chepstow. *Man On The Run*, a hurdler Keegan owned in a partnership with new club mate Mick Channon, romped home in the £1,486 Clive Graham Trophy Handicap. Channon's first words to Keegan when he signed for Lawrie

McMenemy were: "I've put you £50 on *Man On The Run*." And with a starting price of 15-2, it netted Keegan a £375 profit before betting tax. In the Cup Everton ran out 5-2 winners against Wrexham. Ipswich beat Chester 2-1, Ian Rush failing to score. West Ham beat Swansea 2-0 at Upton Park. Arsenal drew 1-1 with Bolton, winning the replay 3-0.

In the League Manchester United drew 1-1 at Stoke and remained a point behind Liverpool, who had two games in hand. In the Scottish Cup Aberdeen beat Airdrie 8-0.

Liverpool: Clemence; Neal, A.Kennedy, Thompson, R.Kennedy, Hansen, Dalglish, Case, D.Johnson (Fairclough,46), McDermott, Souness.

Bury: Forrest; Ritson, K.Kennedy, McIlwraith, Waddington, Howard, Wilson, Halford, S.Johnson, Hilton (Madden,75), Lugg.

Referee: Mr C. Seel (Carlisle)

Attendance: 43,769

DIVISION 3 (bottom two)						
Wimbledon	27	7	8	12	28	40	22
Bury	29	9	3	17	35	46	21

David Fairclough, scorer of two goals against Bury

March 8, 1980

Tottenham Hotspur (0) 0   Liverpool (1) 1

McDermott 38

THE game began at a fierce pace with both sides being contained in the middle of the park, 20 yards either side of the halfway line. The game was tense and hard with a sustained move almost impossible. The first shot arrived after 10 minutes when Ardiles - Spurs' Argentinian import - swung the ball wide. Alan Kennedy initiated Liverpool's first combined move. The ball went between McDermott and Case, who overran the ball as he tried to shoot. Miller cut out a McDermott centre but deflected the ball to Johnson, whose low drive into the area was met by McDermott sliding in to turn the ball wide.

After 17 minutes Pratt substituted for Villa, who had been hurt in the opening minutes after a tackle by Souness. McDermott complained to the referee that he had been elbowed by Pratt and tempers flared. Yorath complained about Souness and when the Scot attempted to shake hands with Yorath, the Welshman turned his back.

Slowly Liverpool began to get a grip on the game in midfield. Souness and Ray Kennedy played excellently in the middle and the passing of Souness was immaculate at times. With 34 minutes gone, an indifferent pass by McDermott set up Spurs' first real attack. Thompson deflected a shot by Ardiles, and from the flag-kick Falco made a strong header but Clemence dived to hold the ball. Hansen, in trying to control an awkwardly bouncing ball right in front of his goalkeeper, almost put through his own goal but recovered to head away for a corner. Liverpool then conceded three corners in as many minutes.

Under pressure from Case, Ardiles sent the ball 20 yards straight to McDermott. From 25 yards out McDermott spotted Daines off his line and floated a perfect dipping shot over the goalkeeper and into the top corner of the net. The goal stunned the Spurs' fans into silence at a time when they believed their side was beginning to exert some control on the game.

Hansen went on a magnificent 60-yard run as he nearly broke through the Tottenham defence. Then Johnson spurned a glorious opportunity when he was slow to control a fine pass from Dalglish which gave him a clear shooting chance. In the early stages of the second half Spurs again displayed an inability to cope with Liverpool's offside trap with Falco and Armstrong early victims. Liverpool gradually increased their power and control on the game. Alan Kennedy sent Dalglish away with a superb pass down the line, but Perryman cut off the Dalglish centre. The quality of Spurs' passing out of defence was appalling and Liverpool took

almost total control. From a perfect pass by McDermott, Dalglish drove the ball against the knees of Daines. Liverpool were quicker to the ball and they read situations instantly, leaving Spurs floundering.

Liverpool controlled the midfield, where Souness excelled. Dalglish was felled by Miller and though the Liverpool players appealed for a penalty, the referee awarded a goal kick. Spurs pushed Perryman into an attacking rôle as he urged his players forward in an attempt to get back into the game. Whenever Spurs attacked, Liverpool players got behind the ball *en masse*, and in a typical Tottenham attack, Dalglish came back to dispossess Ardiles and turn the ball to Clemence.

With 62 minutes gone, Clemence was forced to make his first real save of the afternoon when he held a shot from Armstrong. Daines pulled off a spectacular save from Johnson after a superb move involving Souness, Dalglish and McDermott. Johnson struck his angled shot with great power but Daines flung himself to his left to turn the ball over. On 68 minutes Hoddle chipped Clemence, but the goalkeeper turned the ball over.

With twenty minutes remaining, Dalglish missed an easy opportunity. Miller, attempting a back-pass, gave the ball to Souness, who beat Hughton and turned the ball to his compatriot. Dalglish scooped it over the bar from just inside the six-yard box. The game was delayed for a minute or two while police removed a Spurs fan from the pitch.

Tottenham put on a period of sustained pressure, but Liverpool remained calm, and Souness eased the pressure when he gave Johnson the chance to run at the Spurs defence before his shot went inches over the bar. With a minute to go, Hughton saved on the line from Ray Kennedy.

In the other ties, Everton beat Ipswich Town 2-1 at Goodison Park; Arsenal beat Watford 2-1 at Vicarage Road, and West Ham beat Aston Villa 1-0 at Upton Park.

Tottenham Hotspur: Daines; Hughton, Miller, Villa(Pratt,17), McAllister, Perryman, Ardiles, Falco, Armstrong, Hoddle, Yorath.

Liverpool: Clemence; Neal, A.Kennedy, Thompson, R.Kennedy, Hansen, Dalglish, Case, Johnson, McDermott, Souness.

Referee: Mr P. Partridge (County Durham)

Attendance: 48,033

April 12, 1980

Arsenal (0) 0

Liverpool (0) 0

WITH Terry McDermott out with an injury he sustained in the previous Tuesday's 3-0 League win over Derby County, Sammy Lee was introduced for his Cup début, along with Colin Irwin, who replaced Alan Kennedy. Arsenal gambled with the fitness of centre-half David O'Leary after his midweek injury, so the Gunners played their Cup-winning team of last season. On a brilliantly sunny afternoon the firm pitch looked immaculate, but there was a strong breeze blowing into the faces of the Liverpool players in the first period.

After just four minutes Kennedy crossed from the left and Dalglish almost won the ball in a tight challenge. It fell to Johnson who, at full stretch, drove it over the bar, hurting his left leg in the process. Liverpool nerves showed in Arsenal's first attack. Thompson followed a long clearance from Young, but when Clemence came to the edge of the area, Thompson kicked the ball almost out of his hands to concede a corner, from which Young fouled Clemence.

Lee had a marvellous opportunity to score after only eight minutes when Johnson did well from a 60-yard through-ball by Souness, beating O'Leary and Young to the ball and turning it wide to Lee, who had followed up intelligently. Lee's first-time swing drove the ball wide from 20 yards. In the firm, fast conditions judging the weight of passes was a problem for both sides. Souness measured one perfectly for Case to chase and he collected the ball on the line but Young headed away the centre.

Nelson was booked for a body check on Case which left the Liverpool midfield man requiring attention to his left shoulder. Although control was a problem, Liverpool had more of the possession and pushed up more persistently on the Arsenal defence. Brady, the Arsenal orchestrator in midfield, brought the ball cleverly between Case and Neal. He attempted to find Stapleton with a measured pass but Hansen, who was in outstanding form, intercepted and broke up the move.

Arsenal fell foul of Liverpool's offside trap on numerous occasions, but they beat it with a clever pass from Brady as the Liverpool defenders pushed up almost to the half-way line. Brady flicked the ball over their heads, with Stapleton charging through, but Clemence raced 20 yards out of the area to clear with a first-time kick.

After 25 minutes Case had a chance of scoring when a long centre from Kennedy - the former Arsenal man - floated over the heads of the Arsenal defenders. Case had time to pick his spot as the ball bounced high. He tried to head it away from Jennings towards the far post, but sent the ball wide. Then Johnson displayed his skill. Lee drove a good pass down the

right flank. Johnson controlled it well and cut inside Nelson and Young before driving the ball a foot wide from an acute angle. Dalglish beat O'Leary and attempted a chip shot to the top corner, but the ball took a deflection and went for a corner. Under a stream of steady Liverpool pressure, Arsenal players passed back to Jennings on several occasions. With 40 minutes gone Stapleton tried a 40-yard drive which Clemence held comfortably. The Gunners continued to hit long passes out of defence towards the front runners of Stapleton and Sunderland, whilst Liverpool employed more controlled, deliberate tactics and built up slowly from the back.

On the restart, Liverpool set up a series of sustained pressure. Lee won a corner off O'Leary and when Arsenal tried to bring the ball away, Lee dispossessed Stapleton and found Johnson with a great pass down the line. Johnson's centre was headed clear by Young. Then Dalglish stepped over the ball to let it run through to Case, who turned one way and then the other before trying to float the ball over Jennings from the edge of the area, but it went high and wide.

Johnson headed on a beautiful pass for Dalglish, with Nelson having to head the ball for a corner. From the flag-kick Kennedy drove inches wide. Kennedy and Dalglish were involved in a fine move before Case hit the ball straight at Jennings. Arsenal had created little from open play. They only threatened in set-piece situations. A free-kick by Rix was hit over the bar by Young. A double substitution occurred after 55 minutes, with Walford going on for Nelson and Fairclough replacing Case. Fairclough's inclusion gave Liverpool a three-man attack as he took up a position down the right. Play continued to be fought around the Arsenal penalty area with Liverpool in almost total control. On the hour Clemence drove a huge kick downfield. The ball bounced on the edge of the Arsenal area, and as Dalglish chased it, O'Leary, who was limping badly, clearly knocked him down, but the referee waved play on.

Arsenal appealed for hand-ball in a penalty area skirmish and eventually Clemence had to dive at the feet of Stapleton before receiving attention from Ronnie Moran. Clemence was a little dazed, but was able to take the free-kick. Dalglish flicked the ball wide to Johnson, who ran in at full pace, but Jennings anticipated the danger and ran off his line to grab the ball. Lee and Souness were in magnificent form, with the Scot judging the strength of his passes better than any other player on the field. Clemence came off his line to save Liverpool on two critical occasions. Fifteen minutes from time, Clemence produced his most vital save. From a good centre by Price, Sunderland charged in but Clemence clutched the ball off his head with Sunderland falling into the back of the net. Jennings came out of his penalty area to clear as Johnson chased a Dalglish pass. Liverpool drove forward and Arsenal defended valiantly. Rice shrugged off his defensive responsibilities temporarily as he took the ball down the right flank and turned it inside to Sunderland, whose shot swung well off target. Rix broke clear down the left but his centre followed behind Stapleton and the opportunity was lost. With just a few minutes to go, Irwin joined the attack and passed to Fairclough, whose shot went straight at Jennings. With four minutes to go Arsenal went within two inches of getting to Wembley for the third year in succession. Liverpool's offside trap failed them and Clemence's dash out of his area looked ominous as Talbot lobbed the ball towards the empty net. As the Liverpool defenders watched in horror, the ball hit the bar and bounced back for Hansen to head clear.

In the other semi-final, West Ham drew 1-1 with Everton at Villa Park. In the League, Manchester United beat Tottenham 4-1 at Old Trafford to move within two points of Liverpool, who had a game in hand. In the Third Division, Chester beat Colchester 2-1 at Sealand Road with two goals from Ian Rush after 9 and 49 minutes. The second goal was Rush's 17th of the season.

Arsenal: Jennings; Rice, Nelson(Walford,55), Talbot, O'Leary, Young, Brady, Sunderland, Stapleton, Price, Rix.

Liverpool: Clemence; Neal, Irwin, Thompson, R.Kennedy, Hansen, Dalglish, Case(Fairclough,55), Johnson, Lee, Souness.

Referee: Mr K.S. Hackett (Sheffield)

Attendance: 50,174 (at Hillsborough)

Terry's appeal

Liverpool's injured star Terry McDermott learned to-day that he has to appear before the F.A. disciplinary committee and faces possible suspension. He reached 20 disciplinary points after being booked against Derby County at Anfield on Tuesday, and faces the committee on April 21.

McDermott is to appeal over his sending-off in the match against Everton, at Anfield, earlier this season, for which he has served the compulsory one-match ban.

Sammy Lee, who made his FA Cup début against Arsenal

April 16, 1980

Arsenal (0) 1
Sunderland 62

Liverpool (0) 1 aet
Fairclough 51

BOTH Liverpool and Arsenal produced a game of rare quality based on total commitment to their own causes and to the dedication of getting to Wembley. The game swayed back and forth, with Liverpool holding the edge due to the powerful midfield performances of Dalglish and Souness. Dalglish operated in space between the front men and the midfield trio, whilst Souness was brilliant throughout, his distribution and winning of the ball were exceptional. Arsenal's Jennings, Brady and Young were in great form. On the general run of play, however, Liverpool were in control.

For the greater part of the first period, Liverpool played in the Arsenal half, and they went close to scoring after 34 minutes when Walford's careless pass across his own penalty area found Johnson facing goal with Jennings out of position. Johnson swung wildly at the ball and ballooned it over the bar.

Arsenal's defence was magnificent. Pat Jennings gave them immense confidence with his calmness and total command at the back. He saved well from Sammy Lee and Dalglish and particularly well from a mis-judged back pass by O'Leary.

O'Leary allowed Fairclough's header to pass him to give Johnson a clear run. Jennings saved Johnson's shot with his out-stretched legs, but was beaten easily by Fairclough's follow-up shot. Six minutes after Fairclough had scored, Stapleton, running on to O'Leary's pass, beat Clemence only to find that Sunderland had been ruled offside.

Five minutes later David Price lobbed the ball over the Liverpool offside wall for Alan Sunderland to stride through unchallenged and chip the ball over the head of Clemence. Television subsequently confirmed that he was offside - but Arsenal were level and they had earned a replay for their unrelenting spirit against a better side. Clemence had rushed off his line but Sunderland scooped the bouncing ball over him and into the net for the equaliser. The relentless pace continued and Jennings was forced to save a shot on the turn from Dalglish, and Price blocked another shot Ray Kennedy.

The tie might have been settled during the first period of extra time when Johnson scrambled the ball away from O'Leary on the left and found Fairclough waiting in a large space with only Jennings in front of him, but Fairclough's shot went wide.

Graeme Souness

Arsenal: Jennings; Rice, Walford, Talbot, O'Leary, Young, Brady, Sunderland, Stapleton, Price, Rix.

Liverpool: Clemence; Neal, Irwin, Thompson, R.Kennedy, Hansen, Dalglish, Fairclough, Johnson, Lee, Souness.

Referee: Mr K.S. Hackett (Sheffield)

Attendance: 40,679 (at Villa Park)

Receipts: £152,904

April 28, 1980

Arsenal (1) 1
Sunderland 16 secs

Liverpool (0) 1 aet
Dalglish 90

ARSENAL scored after only 16 seconds of this game through Alan Sunderland. The kick-off had to be taken twice, and the ball reached Price, the Gunners' captain, who moved forward and lobbed it high towards the Liverpool penalty area. Stapleton and Hansen went up together and the ball broke loose to Sunderland, who brought it under control, moved past a defender and drove it into the net.

Despite their surprising start, Arsenal were unable to seize the initiative, though in the seventh minute Brady ballooned the ball high over the bar. Arsenal defended stubbornly and relied on the skill of Pat Jennings when necessary.

With 23 minutes gone, Jennings hurled himself across the face of the goal to turn a fierce, swerving volley from McDermott round the post.

Liverpool attacked consistently with measured, carefully paced movements, with Souness dominating the midfield. The return of McDermott released Dalglish for a more attacking role, but although the Reds enjoyed the greater share of possession they rarely troubled O'Leary and Young, both of whom had outstanding games at the back.

The second half began as fast and furiously as had the first, and within a few minutes Thompson body-checked O'Leary, and received a booking. Liverpool's attacking forays were relentless, but the Arsenal defence was solid. Liverpool repeatedly surged upfield with Souness, Lee, and often Neal, driving them forward.

With 66 minutes gone, Liverpool pulled off Alan Kennedy and sent on David Fairclough, the "Supersub". Wave after wave of Liverpool attacks were thrown against the Arsenal defence, and in one goalmouth scramble, Johnson was knocked out and taken off the field. Fairclough also needed attention in the same incident.

Arsenal: Jennings; Rice, Devine, Talbot, O'Leary, Young, Brady, Sunderland, Stapleton, Price, Rix.

Liverpool: Clemence; Neal, A.Kennedy (Fairclough,66), Thompson, R.Kennedy, Hansen, Dalglish, Lee, Johnson, McDermott, Souness.

Referee: Mr P. Partridge (County Durham)

Attendance: 42,975 (at Villa Park)

With less than a minute remaining, and the Arsenal supporters whistling for the referee to signal the end of the game, McDermott attempted one final chip into the penalty area.

The ball went from Souness to Fairclough and on to Hansen, who nodded it forward to find Dalglish clear of O'Leary. Dalglish flicked the bouncing ball into the net.

The game moved into extra-time, and Johnson sprinted back on to the pitch with just four minutes gone. Liverpool found from deep within themselves the belief to win the game. Jennings made a succession of saves in the first fifteen minutes to deny a rampant Liverpool. Then Ray Kennedy produced a thunderous left-foot shot which the Arsenal goalkeeper managed to parry before looking back to see the ball bounce on and over the bar. Jennings was then beaten by a shot from Dalglish, but the ball struck O'Leary and bounced wide.

Bob Paisley (far left) and Tommy Smith urge on the Liverpool side as the game approaches its dramatic climax

May 1, 1980

Arsenal (1) 1
Talbot 11

Liverpool (0) 0

LIVERPOOL'S hopes of the double crashed to an eleventh-minute winner from Brian Talbot as Arsenal progressed to their third successive FA Cup final. Liverpool squandered many opportunities at Highfield Road. Avi Cohen was introduced at left-back in place of the injured Alan Kennedy.

Liverpool began sharply but Arsenal broke the deadlock as a direct result of Ray Kennedy's miscued attempt to play the ball out of the side of the penalty area. The clearance went loose to Stapleton, whose centre surprisingly caught the Liverpool defenders clustered together and Talbot was left unmarked to head the ball in.

The Liverpool midfield remained sharp with Souness, McDermott and Johnson creating several glorious moves which deserved better finishing. Early in the match Kennedy rolled the ball beyond the far post from an awkward high ball, and then forced Jennings to catch a second goalbound attempt. McDermott went close with a volley from short range which Jennings safely grasped.

Liverpool's failing was their lack of variation, repeatedly pumping high centres into the Arsenal penalty area, where Young and O'Leary's height was usually unbeatable. Talbot was a constant threat to Liverpool with his prodigious workrate, and hard tackling. In the dying seconds of the first half, Kennedy saw a point blank shot slither away wide of goal after Jennings had deflected the ball to him.

Arsenal's greater application - particularly in defence - won them the game as Liverpool's frustration grew with each receding minute. Avi Cohen played composedly and went forward to help out the attack whenever possible. He was involved in a fine movement with Dalglish, but the Scot shot wide.

Liverpool dominated the second half for long periods, but were unable to break down the resolute Arsenal defence. Hansen out-thought Arsenal's offside trap with a lob that Neal ran on to and slipped to Dalglish, whose shot went between the legs of O'Leary, but struck Jennings. It was symbolic of Liverpool's misfortune.

Brian Talbot

DISAPPOINTED LIVERPOOL ALREADY REBUILDING

Liverpool will make their second signing of the week when Richard Money, 22, a player equally at home in defence or midfield, moves from Fulham to Anfield for £330,000. Terms have been agreed, and Money, who has been in the England Under-21 squad, will arrive at Liverpool at lunchtime to complete the transfer. Earlier this week, Liverpool paid £300,000 for Ian Rush, 18, the Chester striker.

Bob Paisley, the Liverpool manager, promised that his team "will be fully wound up and going well again" when they meet Aston Villa tomorrow and attempt to clinch the League championship. We are down now, but no-one could say that we were beaten tactically. We had more chances, but we didn't take them."

Arsenal: Jennings; Rice, Devine, Talbot, O'Leary, Young, Brady, Sunderland, Stapleton, Price, Rix.

Liverpool: Clemence; Neal, Cohen, Thompson, Kennedy, Hansen, Dalglish, Lee, Johnson(Fairclough,75), McDermott, Souness.

Referee: Mr P. Partridge (Cockfield, County Durham)

Attendance: 35,335 (at Highfield Road)

January 3, 1981

Liverpool (2) 4
McDermott 27,   Dalglish 39, 54,
R.Kennedy 88

Altrincham (0) 1
Heathcote (pen) 71

WITH John Lennon's *Starting Over* at number one in the charts, Liverpool began another Cup campaign against non-League Altrincham. Kenny Dalglish was able to take his place in the side to maintain his one hundred percent record in the FA Cup. David Fairclough, back after a cartilage operation, was substitute. Altrincham's Malcolm Bailey returned despite having treatment all week for an ankle injury. Graham Heathcote came in for Barry Whitbread, who was substitute.

Two early Liverpool attacks broke down because of offside decisions given against Johnson. Altrincham briefly responded before Johnson broke away down the right flank. Case fed McDermott who was running into the area, but he let the ball go too far and Owens cleared. Barrow delighted the visiting section of the crowd when he struck a shot from 25 yards which tested Clemence. A minute later Liverpool almost took the lead when Dalglish was put through by McDermott and the Scot brought a superb save from Connaughton who conceded a corner with the help of his outstretched right leg. Dalglish tested the Robins with his trickery when he turned Owens on a sixpence to get in a shot which was blocked by Bailey, who later required treatment for a knock on the leg. Heathcote tried to set up an attack and feed Rogers, but Alan Kennedy intercepted and passed back to Clemence. Case sent the lively Dalglish racing through again and the wily Scot easily beat Owens to get in a fierce drive that bounced wide of the far post.

Altrincham had a glimmer of hope when Howard threaded his way through the Reds defence to slip the ball to Rogers on the right, but Alan Kennedy's firm challenge broke up the move. Liverpool attacked relentlessly against a defensive wall of white shirts. Dalglish's volley from the edge of the area flew inches over the bar.

The Alliance Premier league leaders displayed spirited resistance against the Reds' onslaught. Eventually the visitors cracked. Dalglish threaded the ball through the crowded area to McDermott and from a difficult angle on the right he struck the ball into the far corner to beat the hapless Connaughton.

Altrincham won a free-kick from just outside the edge of the area which was taken by Heathcote, with their fans maintaining the chant of "*Alty*". The ball bounced off the Liverpool wall and went out for the visitors' first corner, cleared by a powerful Irwin header. Jimmy Case crossed from the right to set up Ray Kennedy, whose powerful header went inches over the bar. Then Altrincham responded when Howard raced through the middle before passing to Heathcote on the right, his first-time effort going inches over the Liverpool crossbar. Six minutes before the interval, Dalglish

put Liverpool further ahead. McDermott crossed into the box and Money headed on to Dalglish, whose close-range header beat the goalkeeper. Rogers brought a fine save from Clemence with a fierce long-range shot from the left which the goalkeeper turned over the bar.

Altrincham began the second half with their substitute Whitbread on for Bailey. A minute into the second period Barrow was booked for a foul on McDermott. The play in the second half was slower than that in the first. Barrow broke through on the right, and Alan Kennedy failed to clear, but Ray Kennedy completed the process. A poor header from Irwin, attempting to clear, nearly went into his own goal, but Money was alert and cleared off the line. A shot from Rogers was saved by Clemence, who dived to his left.

Dalglish added a third goal from just inside the area. A minute later the Robins' goalkeeper tipped Money's header over the bar. McDermott, with a magnificent defence splitting pass, put Money through in front of goal, but the former Fulham captain was off target with his effort.

At the other end, Money headed out a dangerous cross from Rogers, who was put through by Howard. As the visitors struggled to get into the game, Whitbread struck a shot that went narrowly wide of Clemence's right post.

Clemence saved well from a Rogers header and then the Robins won a corner which was cleared at length by Alan Kennedy. Clemence then brought down Whitbread, and Heathcote beat the England goalkeeper with a well-taken penalty into the far corner.

Lee and Case began a fine flowing move which resulted in Barrow clearing the danger from the in-running McDermott. The visitors' Jeff Johnson raced through to face Clemence, but was pulled up for offside. Case put Dalglish through with a crossfield pass which took out the Altrincham defence and went to Dalglish, but the Scot ran out of space. Howard put Barrow through, but he turned and shot straight at Clemence. The lively Rogers evaded Irwin's tackle to break through, but his shot was saved by Clemence. Two minutes from time, Liverpool added a fourth after a magnificent move involving eight players. Dalglish cleverly headed on for Case on the left, and he crossed for Ray Kennedy to score with a powerful header.

Kenny Dalglish won the *Liverpool Football Echo*'s Sports Personality of the Year for 1980 after heading off a strong challenge from boxer Tony Willis, a mere 44 votes behind. The *Echo* reported: "The Scot has missed only two League matches since joining Liverpool, and during a splendid three-year spell at Anfield, has become an integral part of the club and indeed the whole Merseyside scene. Indeed, his example has been superb at a time when the game needs all its best ambassadors. With the news full of temperamental stars seeking transfers or complaining about tactical moves they don't approve of, Dalglish has been a model professional, seeking to do nothing more than get on with the game."

Everton beat last season's runners-up, Arsenal, with two goals in the final four minutes. West Ham, the Cup-holders, drew 1-1 with Wrexham before losing 1-0 in a second replay. Tottenham Hotspur, who were to go on to beat Manchester City 3-2 in the Final replay, drew 0-0 with Queens Park Rangers, winning the replay 3-1 at White Hart Lane. Manchester City beat Crystal Palace 4-0 at Maine Road.

Liverpool: Clemence; Neal, A.Kennedy, Irwin, R.Kennedy, Money, Dalglish, Lee, Johnson, McDermott, Case.

Altrincham: Connaughton; Allan, Davison, Bailey (Whitbread,46), Owens, King, Barrow, Heathcote, J.Johnson, Rogers, Howard.

Referee: Mr T. Farley (County Durham)

Attendance: 37,170

Kenny Dalglish, *the model professional*

January 24, 1981

Everton (1) 2
Eastoe 17, Varadi 60

Liverpool (0) 1
Case 76

IT was a perfect day for football with blue skies and bright sunshine. The new roof on the Gwladys Street end painted a broad band of blue above the blue army of Everton fans. With John Lennon's *Imagine* at number one in the UK 45 charts, the faithful Goodison hordes dreamt of a Cup victory over their illustrious neighbours. All the tickets were sold days in advance of the game, with the club announcing record receipts of £118,000. However, the receipts did not beat the record set when Liverpool played Manchester United in the semi-final two years ago.

Everton manager, Gordon Lee, announced his team half-an-hour before the kick-off, and played Martin Hodge who had been out of the team since the previous April. Hodge replaced Jim McDonagh, whose ankle injury had failed to heal. Liverpool were without the services of the injured Alan Kennedy, and Avi Cohen played for the first time since the previous September. Lyons won the toss and invited Liverpool to attack the Park end, playing into the sun. Fairclough set the game in motion.

Referee Thomas incurred the early wrath of the Everton supporters when he awarded a free-kick just outside the Everton box when he ruled that Lyons had fouled Dalglish. Shortly afterwards he awarded another kick to Liverpool then ran to the dug-out to hand out a lecture to the watching McDonagh for voicing his opinions too strongly.

With five minutes gone, Varadi forced Souness to concede the first corner of the game. Liverpool got the ball away, but a minute later Everton struck back and a shot from Varadi hit the bar. The referee had already blown for a foul by Lee, which provoked angry retaliation by Ross. Everton had marginally the better of the early exchanges, but the game did not settle into any rhythm with the referee blowing for any minor infringement. The pitch was soft and well-sanded in the middle, which did not help the quality of football. After 16 minutes Fairclough crossed from the left and Bailey lunged to head clear with Lee lurking dangerously. Neal, who had moments earlier required treatment for a cut over the left eye, snapped up the clearance but drove his shot narrowly wide.

A minute later, the Blues took the lead, though there was some doubt as to the scorer. Hartford initiated the move when he beat McDermott in midfield and played the ball through to Eastoe. The flag stayed down, despite a suspicion of offside, but the referee waved play on and Eastoe struck his low shot past the advancing Clemence. Neal chased back and turned the ball away on the line but it struck the in-rushing Cohen and hit the back of the net. Everton awarded the goal to Eastoe.

The Everton fans went wild with delight at their team taking the lead.

The Reds struck back and Fairclough won a corner after a moment of indecision between Lyons and Ratcliffe. Then Bailey conceded another corner, but Liverpool failed to utilise the kick to effect. Cohen found Fairclough wide on the left and the striker slipped the ball inside Lyons, but Ratcliffe cleared. Everton had the advantage in midfield with McMahon and Varadi in fine form. From a corner taken by Ross Clemence punched the ball away which fell to McMahon, whose lob just cleared the bar. A wonderful pass by Neal curled invitingly into the path of Dalglish, but the linesman's flag denied the Scot's progress. After 36 minutes McMahon was booked for going over the top on Neal, and the Liverpool defender received attention. Phil Thompson was in excellent form for Liverpool as he intercepted at vital times and tackled with great determination. After 42 minutes Clemence saved well from a Lyons header as Everton retained the initiative.

Liverpool began the second half without Dalglish, who had sustained a cut in his left instep which needed stitching. Case substituted. Eastoe charged down a free-kick by Thompson to leave himself with only the Reds' skipper to beat before facing Clemence, but Thompson recovered well to dispossess the Everton player. As Everton went forward, Clemence dealt with a Varadi cross. Case had a volley charged down before going in hard on Hodge. Players from both sides became involved in a skirmish. Case was booked, while Souness and Lyons were lectured by the referee. The game lacked pure skill but it provided thrills and great entertainment. Liverpool struggled to attack with any great conviction as both McDermott and Fairclough were dispossessed by Hodge and Wright.

Then O'Keefe darted clear of the Liverpool defence when he received the ball from Eastoe and went wide to elude the advancing Clemence. Eastoe sent his cross to the far post where Varadi hammered the ball into the roof of the net after 60 minutes. After the goal, Eastoe's name went into the book for time-wasting.

A minute later a left-foot drive by Case flashed viciously over the bar. With 65 minutes gone, a fierce tackle by Souness grounded McMahon, and the Scot earned a booking. Five minutes later a curling centre by Varadi was nodded behind by Neal. Liverpool continued to challenge every ball and Ross was forced to tackle Souness after Kennedy had won the ball in the air. With 74 minutes gone, Cohen was booked for tugging at Varadi's shirt. On 76 minutes, Case pulled a goal back for Liverpool.

Everton		Liverpool
Hodge	1	Clemence
Ratcliffe	2	Neal
Bailey	3	Cohen
Wright	4	Thompson
Lodge	5	R.Kennedy
Ross	6	Irwin
McMahon	7	Dalglish
Eastoe	8	Lee
Varadi	9	Fairclough
Hartford	10	McDermott
O'Keefe	11	Souness
McBride	12	Case
		on for Dalglish, 46

Referee: Mr C. Thomas (Porthcawl)

Attendance: 53,804

TV SOCCER

ITV tonight: Granada and HTV: Everton v. Liverpool.
ATV: Shrewsbury v. Ipswich Town.

BBC 1 tomorrow: Watford v. Wolverhampton Wanderers;
Manchester City v. Norwich City

F.A. CUP - Fourth Round

Barnsley	1	Enfield	1
Carlisle United	1	Bristol City	1
Coventry City	3	Birmingham City	2
Fulham	1	Charlton Athletic	2
Leicester City	1	Exeter City	1
Manchester City	6	Norwich City	0
Middlesbrough	1	West Bromwich A.	0
Newcastle United	2	Luton Town	1
Nottingham Forest	1	Manchester United	0
Notts County	0	Peterborough United	1
Shrewsbury Town	0	Ipswich Town	0
Southampton	3	Bristol Rovers	1
Tottenham Hotspur	2	Hull City	0
Watford	1	Wolverhampton W.	1
Wrexham	2	Wimbledon	1

Replays

January 27

Ipswich Town	3	Shrewsbury Town	0
Wolverhampton W.	2	Watford	1

January 28

Bristol City	5	Carlisle United	0
Enfield	0	Barnsley	3
Exeter City	3	Leicester City	1

Kennedy initiated the move and Case moved into a crowded goalmouth to smash the ball into the net, to give Liverpool renewed hope of salvaging the game.

The game exploded into a rousing finale. Varadi drove a shot wide and Fairclough won a corner at the opposite end. Everton defended stoutly. Kennedy got in a shot which was deflected for a corner and as Liverpool's onslaught grew in intensity, Fairclough was brought down by Ross just outside the box.

With five minutes to go, Varadi was put through by O'Keefe and Eastoe and he went wide of Clemence before chipping his shot over the angle. Everton eventually reached the Sixth Round where they were beaten by Manchester City in a replay. The highest score of the Fourth round was Manchester City's 6-0 thrashing of Norwich City. Manchester City's manager, John Bond -Manager of the Month for December - was previously the manager of Norwich, taking over from Malcolm Allison on October 13, 1980. In the Alliance Premier League, Altrincham lost 0-1 away to Northwich Victoria.

January 2, 1982

Swansea City (0) 0

Liverpool (2) 4

*Hansen 35, Rush 45, 88,
Lawrenson 73*

NEW skipper Graeme Souness led out a side which made one late tactical change, with Alan Kennedy being recalled at left back, releasing Mark Lawrenson into midfield. Sammy Lee dropped out and was substitute. Terry McDermott was back in action, while Kenny Dalglish returned to the front line in place of the injured Craig Johnston. After Swansea's 1-3 defeat at Southampton, manager John Toshack - formerly of Liverpool - made two changes, Chris Marustik coming in at left-back, and Nigel Stevenson taking the place of Maxwell Thompson - another former Liverpool player - in central defence. Swansea also had a new captain, Ante Rajkovic taking over the rôle from another former Red, Colin Irwin.

With five minutes gone, Liverpool had a fortunate escape when former Evertonian Gary Stanley drove a low free-kick from just outside the box. It took a deflection off Leighton James, but the ball went inches wide of Cup débutant Bruce Grobbelaar's right-hand post.

The visitors hit back and a corner on the left by Dalglish was met by McDermott, but his shot went wide. Davies slipped while collecting a harmless through-ball from Souness, but he recovered before the inrushing McDermott could capitalise on the mistake. Robbie James broke through from midfield, but Phil Thompson intercepted and cleared. As the action flowed from end to end, Rush found Souness in a good position on the left of the box, but the Scot shot wide. Swansea won a free-kick when Hansen climbed on Latchford's back, and Irwin's low shot was blocked by Kennedy. The former Newcastle player moved up to join the attack and found Lawrenson on the left.

Lawrenson - making his Cup début - moved into the box and won a corner. Dalglish took the kick which fell to McDermott, whose first-time shot was blocked by a crowd of players. The Reds attacked down the right and Rush put in a dangerous cross which was met by McDermott on the volley, the ball passing over the bar.

Swansea responded and Latchford let the ball run through his legs, allowing Mahoney to run on and send in a low shot which was saved by Grobbelaar. Marustik was booked for a late challenge on McDermott. Liverpool performed better in the heavy conditions and on the half-hour Dalglish turned sharply to get in a shot which was blocked by Mahoney. Moments later the mercurial Scot displayed another piece of fine skill when he curled a right-foot shot towards the goal, but the ball deflected off Irwin and went over the bar.

With 35 minutes gone, Liverpool's pressure reaped its rewards. Whelan and McDermott linked from a corner on the right, and the cross to the far post saw Hansen race forward to power a close-range header into the net.

Swansea fans appealed for a penalty after Neal's strong challenge on Leighton James, but the referee waved play on. A magnificent pass by Thompson out to the right beat Swansea's offside trap and Whelan's tremendous shot was parried by Davies. Rush was unable to get his header on target from the rebound.

Dalglish found Kennedy overlapping down the left, and his cross led to Liverpool's second goal when Whelan met the ball at the far post, and his header rebounded from an upright, leaving Rush with a simple tap in to score from close range.

In the opening moments of the second half, Liverpool almost added to their score when Whelan evaded several tackles on the edge of the box and slipped the ball inside to Dalglish, where the Scot saw two shots blocked. The second fell to Rush, but the lean Welshman failed to capitalise on the opportunity. Lawrenson broke down the left as the Reds poured forward at every available opportunity, and his low cross found Rush, who shot wide.

The home side battled grimly to get back into the game, and a speculative shot outside the box by Curtis was blocked by Hansen, who was playing immaculately. Robbie James sent a ball forward and the defence hesitated, expecting an offside decision which was not awarded and Grobbelaar was forced to leave his line quickly to prevent Curtis from scoring. A Swansea free-kick into the Liverpool box almost fell to Irwin but the ball skidded off the wet surface and went out.

The home side began to have more attacking opportunities and Grobbelaar fisted away a high cross from Leighton James. Thompson was then forced to concede a free-kick in a dangerous position just outside his own box. Stanley slipped the ball to Leighton James, and Grobbelaar dived to his left but the ball went out to Latchford who blasted over from close range.

As the game moved down the other end, a long range shot by Kennedy flew over the bar. Souness combined with Rush in a fine move down the left, but the ball eventually went out of play. A magnificent through ball from Souness to Rush initiated another fine move. The ball travelled to Lawrenson, who turned it across the goal to McDermott, but his first-time effort was easily stopped by Davies. Swansea then substituted Marustik with Maxwell Thompson.

Liverpool's response was lethal, and they struck a third goal when Souness threaded another superb ball into the Swansea box. Lawrenson raced onto it and slipped it wide of Davies for his first goal in the FA Cup on his début. Two minutes from time, Rush increased the scoreline to four.

Highlights of the match were shown on BBC 1, along with the Barnet v Brighton (0-0) and Leicester v Southampton

(3-1) games. Tottenham, the Cup-holders, beat Arsenal 1-0 at White Hart Lane on their way to a successive Final appearance, this time against Queens Park Rangers, while Rangers drew 1-1 with Middlesbrough in London, winning the replay 3-2 after extra time, having squandered a 2-0 interval lead. Everton were beaten 2-1 at Upton Park. Manchester United lost by a single goal at Watford, while Nottingham Forest surprisingly lost 1-3 at home to Wrexham.

In the Cup tie at Bournemouth spectators were treated for injuries after a section of barrier collapsed as Oxford took a 2-0 lead after 65 minutes. Stretchers were called for and the injured treated by the side of the pitch.

Swansea City: Davies; Stanley, Marustik (M.Thompson,70), Rajkovic, Irwin, Stevenson, Curtis, R.James, L.James, Mahoney, Latchford.

Liverpool: Grobbelaar; Neal, A.Kennedy, Thompson, Lawrenson, Hansen, Dalglish, Whelan, Rush, McDermott, Souness.

Referee: Mr C. White (Harrow)

Attendance: 24,179

Mark Lawrenson, who scored on his FA Cup début

January 23, 1982

Sunderland (0) 0

Liverpool (2) 3
Dalglish 6, 15, Rush 79

MANAGER Bob Paisley celebrated his 62nd birthday on a day of bright sunshine, a change from the recent weeks of snow and ice. Phil Neal recovered from his thigh injury to continue at right-back, while Alan Kennedy returned on the other wing after missing Liverpool's League Cup replay victory over Barnsley (3-1 at Oakwell) in midweek. David Johnson continued on the bench. Liverpool, playing in all-yellow, kicked off, but Sunderland created the first real chance when a long break by Siddall bounced awkwardly in the Liverpool box and Neal was forced to concede a corner. Buckley's kick went into the area but Grobbelaar caught it safely.

With just six minutes gone, Liverpool broke down the right and Dalglish put them ahead. Neal sent the Scot away in the box and he turned inside Clarke before hitting the ball across the body of Siddall into the goal. Moments later Hansen powered forward and slipped the ball to Rush, whose shot from 18 yards was pushed for a corner by the diving Siddall. The home side - lying second-from-bottom of the First Division with just three wins from 19 games - responded when Cummins found himself with space inside the box before shooting high over the bar. Dalglish then sent Rush clear, but the Welshman's shot rebounded off the bar after beating Siddall.

After 15 minutes Liverpool increased their lead. Neal slipped the ball through to Dalglish on the edge of the box and the wily Scot looked up and chose his spot before curling a magnificent shot wide of Siddall. Sunderland tried desperately to respond quickly against eighth-placed Liverpool. McCoist brought out a spectacular save from Grobbelaar with a ferocious shot, and moments later Elliott hit a fierce shot inches wide. McDermott swept a crossfield ball to Whelan and the Irish international drove a tremendous shot towards the roof of the net before Siddall pushed it out for a corner. Liverpool created numerous opportunities for themselves and Whelan sent in another strong effort which Siddall saved well. Sunderland were devoid of attacking ideas, with an over-reliance on the high ball over the top, but Grobbelaar was in commanding form. Sammy Lee, after playing 84 minutes at right back against Barnsley, operated down the right side of midfield. Liverpool were able to build up smoothly down either flank and Lee played an excellent ball into the box before Whelan was ruled offside. Five minutes before the interval, Dalglish struck a powerful shot over the bar after Clarke had given the ball away. Neal then strode forward to join the attack before two quick corners were booted to safety by the home side. Sunderland substituted Brown for Clarke, with Elliott dropping back into defence. Brown sped towards the Liverpool box before being brought down by Kennedy. Cummins took the free-kick but

his shot rebounded clear off the Liverpool wall. Sunderland gained a corner when Nicholl's volley was deflected, but Grobbelaar cleared the flag-kick easily.

On the hour an attempted shot by Cummins was blocked but fell to McCoist on the edge of the six-yard box who shot but produced a magnificent save from Grobbelaar. A long through-ball found Ritchie in a fine position on the edge of the box, but Grobbelaar collected. Liverpool's strength lay in their ability to pass the ball first-time. A swift break down the right by Dalglish and Lee saw McDermott get in a cross that was kicked clear by the defence. Sunderland replied through Elliott, whose perfect pass to Brown enabled the substitute to move forward on the Liverpool goal until Kennedy's timely interception. Stan Cummins was the home side's best player and on one occasion he wriggled his way through the Liverpool defence before Grobbelaar cleared the danger. Rush netted the ball midway through the second period, but was ruled offside by the referee. Alan Kennedy played a more defensive role than normal, and most of Liverpool's approach work came down the right. Dalglish was in fine form, while Lawrenson was commanding at the back. Dalglish headed over from a Lee cross with Liverpool in rampant mood. Souness tackled Cummins in the left-back position as Liverpool maintained their grip on a game which they dominated from the start. The hard-working Lee cut inside a Sunderland defender before shooting high over the bar. A great ball from Souness saw McDermott break into space down the right and his cross enabled Rush to move forward to plant a header wide of Siddall. Liverpool then substituted Johnson for Dalglish and continued to dominate up to the final whistle.

Tottenham beat Leeds 1-0 in London, while Queens Park Rangers drew 0-0 with Blackpool away, before winning the replay 5-1, with Clive Allen scoring four goals. Ipswich, top of the First Division, beat Luton, top of the Second, 3-0 at Kenilworth Road.

Sunderland: Siddall; Nicholl, Pickering, Hindmarch, Clarke(Brown,46), Elliott, Buckley, McCoist, Ritchie, Rowell, Cummins.

Liverpool: Grobbelaar;   Neal,   Lawrenson, A.Kennedy, Whelan, Hansen, Dalglish(Johnson,80), Lee, Rush, McDermott, Souness.

Referee: Mr A.J. Hamil (Wolverhampton)

Attendance: 28,582

February 13, 1982

Chelsea (1) 2
Rhoades-Brown 8, Lee 85

Liverpool (0) 0

WITH Stamford Bridge bathed in sunshine, eighth-placed Chelsea of the Second Division, played hosts to Liverpool, sixth in the First Division. Liverpool were unchanged while Chelsea's midfield player, John Bumstead, failed a fitness test. Mike Fillery returned to the attack. Chelsea forced an early attack when Walker and Colin Lee combined in the middle of the park. After a move involving Hales and Rhoades-Brown, Lee shot wide of the left post. Liverpool responded by breaking quickly down the right through Neal and Sammy Lee, but Rush was clattered to the ground by Droy. From the free-kick McDermott made a good run down the right before sending a cross out of play.

Grobbelaar saved a Droy header with ease, but then Chelsea took an early lead. Colin Lee robbed McDermott just inside the Liverpool half and sent a magnificent through-ball for Peter Rhoades-Brown to race onto in an attempt to beat the out-rushing Grobbelaar. The Chelsea striker drove a low shot into the right-hand corner of the net.

After good approach work from Souness and Sammy Lee, Rush drove a shot inches over the bar. Liverpool began to put some good moves together and Hansen, Souness and McDermott combined well. Whelan initiated a fine attack when he flicked the ball forward for Dalglish to send a diagonal ball over the left for Rush. Whelan then headed wide from McDermott's cross after a Souness pass. Lawrenson was forced to concede a corner after Hales crossed into the area with Rhoades-Brown lurking dangerously on the left. Chelsea's youngsters threw Liverpool out of their normal rhythm and Hansen was forced into an error when Walker robbed him of the ball in midfield to initiate another attack, which Liverpool dealt with. A through-ball from Hansen fed McDermott, whose close-range volley was well saved by teenaged goalkeeper Steve Francis.

Grobbelaar saved a Droy header as the game ebbed and flowed. Kennedy broke swiftly down the left and slipped the ball to Rush, whose shot from a narrow angle flashed across the goal and struck the far post before Chelsea cleared. Then McDermott hit a fine volley that appeared to be looping just under the bar when Francis flung himself at the ball which went out to Rush. The goalkeeper composed himself enough to save Rush's header.

In the 35th minute a Souness free-kick just over the halfway line found Whelan running into space to power a header narrowly wide. Then Hansen stole forward into space through the middle to drive a low left-foot shot inches wide of the right-hand post.

Liverpool were almost presented with a goal in the opening minute of the second half when Hutchings lobbed the ball back for his goalkeeper, but it went over the head of Francis and into the side-netting. The keeper managed to get a hand to a fierce McDermott drive as Liverpool sought an equaliser. Fillery, Pates and Hales combined well to bring Rhoades-Brown into the game on the left, but his cross was cleared by Souness. Walker, whose pace and trickery caused Liverpool several problems, sent Hales through. The youngster attempted a dipping shot from 25 yards which Grobbelaar held comfortably.

Souness initiated a move by feeding Lee on the right. His cross found Whelan, who had run into the penalty area and Neal just failed to connect with Whelan's improvised flick-on. Nutton brought down Dalglish and Liverpool won a free-kick just outside the penalty area. Souness drove the ball towards goal and it cannoned off the Chelsea wall before Walker cleared.

Grobbelaar dived to his left to prevent a 20-yard drive from Pates as Chelsea strove for a second goal. Colin Lee turned Neal and fed Hutchings, but the midfielder drove his shot well wide. Locke took the ball off the toes of Dalglish after the Scot had been put in possession by Whelan. Then Liverpool increased the pressure, winning two corners in quick succession after determined effort from Dalglish, Lee and Souness. From the second corner, Francis saved Whelan's header. With 70 minutes gone, Liverpool sent on Craig Johnston in place of McDermott. The young Australian tried a shot with his first touch of the ball but the shot lacked power and Francis easily handled.

With just five minutes remaining Chelsea finished off Liverpool's threat with a goal from Colin Lee.

Tottenham beat Aston Villa at White Hart Lane, while Queen's Park Rangers beat Grimsby 3-1 at Loftus Road. Chelsea were beaten in the Sixth Round, 2-3 at home to Tottenham after leading 1-0 at the interval with a goal from Fillery.

Chelsea: Francis; Locke, Hutchings, Nutton, Droy, Pates, Rhoades-Brown, Hales, Lee, Walker, Fillery.

Liverpool: Grobbelaar; Neal, Lawrenson, A.Kennedy, Whelan, Hansen, Dalglish, Lee, Rush, McDermott (Johnston,70), Souness.

Referee: Mr S.G. Bates (Bristol)

Attendance: 41,422

January 8, 1983

Blackburn Rovers (1) 1
Garner 25

Liverpool (2) 2
Hodgson 29, Rush 45

BLACKBURN - fourteenth in the Second Division - entertained Liverpool at the top of the First.

Blackburn: Gennoe; Branagan, Rathbone, Randell, Mail, Fazackerley, Miller, Arnott, Bell, Garner, Brotherston.

Liverpool: Grobbelaar; Neal, A.Kennedy, Lawrenson, Johnston, Hansen, Dalglish, Lee, Rush, Hodgson, Souness.

Referee: Mr K.S. Hackett (Sheffield)

Attendance: 21,967

Ian Rush burst through in the first minute but was foiled. Neal sent Lee away down the right and he held off the challenge of two defenders before slipping the ball across the goalmouth to Hodgson, who miskicked. Blackburn hit back at once, and Kennedy cleared from Bell. As the game moved from one end to the other, Souness supplied Dalglish, who took the ball round the goalkeeper only to see his chip towards an open goal headed away. Blackburn broke on the left through their Irish international Noel Brotherston, but Lawrenson anticipated the danger and robbed the Blackburn forward.

Johnston opened up the way forward down the left when he exchanged passes with Rush, but after his own close-range shot had been blocked, the ball fell to Rush, whose snap shot went wide.

Blackburn threw everything at Liverpool and won two corners in quick succession before Grobbelaar came out to save from Garner. Both teams battled strongly in midfield, and after two minor skirmishes, Souness was booked for a challenge on Brotherston. With 25 minutes gone, the home side took the lead when Grobbelaar dropped a right-wing cross from Miller, and scrambled the ball for a corner. Brotherston's kick was knocked on to Garner, and the Rovers' leading scorer quickly turned on it and hammered the ball into the net from ten yards. Shortly afterwards confusion between Hansen and Lawrenson allowed Brotherston an opportunity to increase the scoreline, but he shot wide of the far post. Just before the half-hour Liverpool equalised. Souness won a loose ball in midfield and put Hodgson - making his Cup début for Liverpool - away with a well-timed pass down the middle. Hodgson sped onto the ball and outpaced the defence before taking the ball round Gennoe and hitting the back of the net. A minute later Lee sent Hodgson away on the right, and the forward's tremendous shot was parried by Gennoe out to Rush, who lofted the ball over the bar with an empty goal

beckoning. The game developed into an intriguing Cup-tie, with both sides creating numerous opportunities and great goalmouth incidents. Bell's long shot was saved comfortably by Grobbelaar and then Brotherston almost broke completely clear. From a magnificent Liverpool move, Dalglish's shot hit the post. Just before the interval, Rush hit his 22nd goal of the season. Lee put the ball inside to Dalglish, who dribbled round three defenders before pushing the ball sideways for Rush to score.

Liverpool were content to play a waiting game, gleaned from many years of experience in Europe. On the counter-attack they continued to be dangerous and Rush clipped an upright from Hodgson's pass. With 56 minutes gone, Dalglish seized upon a loose ball and supplied Rush. He took the Welshman's return pass and struck a fierce shot towards Gennoe which the goalkeeper could only parry, and Dalglish snapped at the rebound, but a defender's boot cleared the danger. An error by Lawrenson almost let in Miller down the right, but the defender recovered and initiated an attacking move.

The home side enjoyed the greater share of the possession at this stage of the game. Johnston fought hard in midfield for Liverpool and challenged every ball, although his passing lacked accuracy. Souness was in inspired form, showed great determination and this ran through the whole Liverpool team. Blackburn were stronger in defence in the second half, and Liverpool created fewer chances. A careless pass by Bell enabled Liverpool to counter and Hodgson fed Dalglish, who turned the ball back for Johnston to hit a fierce shot which Gennoe saved.

David Hodgson

January 29, 1983

Liverpool (1) 2

Dalglish 23, Rush 88

Stoke City (0) 0

IAN Rush returned to the Liverpool team after injury, while Stoke were without England winger Mark Chamberlain, whose brother, Neville, was substitute. A foul on Lawrenson gave Liverpool a free-kick. Referee Courtney held up play while he lectured trainer Ronnie Moran, who had come off the bench to protest. With six minutes gone, Rush controlled a long ball down the left and turned it inside to Dalglish, whose left-foot shot was driven wide. The home side challenged for every ball and when Painter went in with a reckless tackle on Lawrenson he was booked. A moment later Lawrenson exacted his revenge on Painter, and was cautioned for his tackle. A foul by Souness brought him a lecture from Mr Courtney and gave Stoke a free-kick just outside the area. Liverpool struggled to pierce the resolute Stoke defence. A foul by Berry gave Liverpool a free-kick just outside the penalty area, but Dalglish's shot was blocked. The ball rebounded to Kennedy, who blasted it wide. Neal joined the Liverpool attack and drove in a powerful shot which was deflected wide. Bracewell tripped Kennedy and received a booking.

With 23 minutes gone, Liverpool scored. Lee helped a long ball on to Dalglish wide on the right. Dalglish cut inside, dribbled round Hampton and curled a left-foot shot just out of Fox's reach and into the corner of the net. It was his 300th goal in all competitions for Celtic and Liverpool.

Stoke responded by going onto the offensive, urged forward by their manager Ritchie Barker, who received a lecture from the referee for his vociferousness. Stoke won a free-kick 10 yards outside the penalty area, but a shot from Thomas passed too high. Dalglish dribbled into the penalty area before being dispossessed. Then a moment later he ran on to a quick pass by Lee and drove a fierce shot inches wide. Thomas fought valiantly in an attempt to enthuse his side, and he won applause for his dribble that brought the ball out of his own penalty area and deep into Liverpool territory before being stopped by a firm Souness tackle. Liverpool combined well and one move involving six passes almost brought a goal for Rush, but Fox anticipated the danger. Liverpool continued to attack at every opportunity and Neal shot over the bar followed by Dalglish shooting narrowly wide.

Stoke came out for the second half with only one man up front and nine in defence. A fine right-wing move involving Neal, Lee and Dalglish gave Rush a half-chance out on the right, but Watson denied the Welshman. Maguire sent a corner kick behind as Stoke spurned the opportunity to cause Liverpool problems at the back. McIlroy's first time shot was deflected for a corner by Lawrenson, and Maguire's kick was collected safely by Grobbelaar. As Liverpool responded, Johnston tested Fox with a great 25-yard shot which almost went under the goalkeeper's body. Moments later Fox tipped over Dalglish's dipping left-foot shot. The Scot was playing magnificently and he helped out in defence, making two quick tackles in short succession. Rush and Hodgson were tightly marked and Dalglish was often forced to operate alone up front. After 63 minutes Hodgson completed a fine attacking movement by hitting the crossbar. Kennedy had a poor game and an error by him allowed Painter to cross into the goalmouth where Neal headed away.

Hodgson's run down the right and cross to Dalglish saw the Scot fire in a low drive which Fox scrambled away. Then Hodgson shot over the bar as Liverpool maintained their incessant pressure. Neal broke up a rare Stoke attack before Dalglish tried to chip Fox from 30 yards. With two minutes remaining, Fox saved from Dalglish, but Rush followed in to score.

Former Liverpool midfield star Jimmy Case gave Brighton a seventh-minute lead at home to Manchester City. Brighton won the game 4-0. Manchester United beat Luton 2-0 at Kenilworth Road.

NEXT MATCHES AT ANFIELD
CENTRAL LEAGUE
LIVERPOOL v. HUDDERSFIELD TOWN
Tuesday, 1st Feb., 1983 Kick-off 7 p.m.

MILK CUP SEMI-FINAL (1st Leg)

LIVERPOOL v. BURNLEY
Tuesday, 8th Feb., 1983 Kick-off 7.30 p.m.

Liverpool: Grobbelaar; Neal, A.Kennedy, Lawrenson, Johnston, Hansen, Dalglish, Lee, Rush, Hodgson, Souness.

Stoke City: Fox; Parkin, Hampton, Bracewell, Watson, Berry, Painter, McIlroy, O'Callaghan, Thomas, Maguire.

Referee: Mr G. Courtney (County Durham)

Linesmen: Mr I.A. Hendrick (Red Flag);
Mr W.A. Flood (Orange Flag)

Attendance: 36,666

February 20, 1983

Liverpool (0) 1   Brighton & Hove Albion (1) 2
Johnston 67   *Ryan 32,   Case 68*

BRIGHTON, at the foot of the First Division, arrived at Anfield to play against the team at the top of the division. Caretaker manager Jimmy Melia - a former Reds' player - and midfielder Jimmy Case - another former Red - masterminded a sensational victory. It was the first time in 25 years that Brighton had reached this stage of the competition, while Liverpool had gone undefeated for 63 games in cup competitions at Anfield.

Gerry Ryan put the visitors into the lead after 32 minutes following good work down the left wing by Michael Robinson. Liverpool embarked on a campaign of relentless pressure following the reversal, and Craig Johnston equalised with 67 minutes gone. Dalglish crossed the ball from the left and the ball was headed on into a crowded goalmouth by Rush. Johnston acrobatically scooped it over his head and into the net. The game was set for a rousing finale, in which the seething mass of Kopites expected a Liverpool victory. Liverpool's celebrations were short lived as a cross from Ryan was only half cleared and the ball fell to the right foot of Case, who struck a 25-yard shot which deflected off Ronnie Whelan before hitting the back of the net.

Liverpool's response was typical - attacking in relentless waves. Within four minutes of Brighton's second goal, Liverpool had a fine opportunity to level the scores once more. Alan Kennedy went down in the box under a challenge from Robinson and the referee awarded a penalty despite Brighton's protestations. Neal was entrusted with the job of taking the kick in front of the Kop goal. Kennedy did not look and faced his own goalkeeper on the halfway line. Neal pulled the shot wide. Still Liverpool continued to attack towards the baying Kop. Dalglish looped the ball over from close range before Lawrenson's goalbound header was cleared off the line by Ramsey. As the game marched towards its conclusion, Whelan's powerfully-struck shot was deflected wide.

Steve Foster was booked after fouling Rush, but generally he had a magnificent game at the heart of the Brighton defence. Liverpool forced twelve corners and as many free-kicks around the box. Former Brighton player Mark Lawrenson was Liverpool's inspiration in the second half, but the visitors defended admirably. Robinson saw a powerful header rebound off the underside of the crossbar and a left-foot shot by Kennedy struck the post. Liverpool manager, Bob Paisley, was left disappointed once again as his team were knocked out of the only competition he had yet to win, either as a player or a manager.

In the Sixth Round Brighton beat Norwich City 1-0 at home with a second-half goal from Jimmy Case, while Manchester United beat Everton 1-0 at Old Trafford, Frank Stapleton scoring. In the semi-finals United beat Arsenal 2-1 at Villa Park, while Brighton beat Sheffield Wednesday 2-1 at Highbury, Case and Robinson scoring. In the final, Brighton drew 2-2 with Manchester United, but in the replay five days later Brighton were overwhelmed 4-0.

Liverpool: Grobbelaar; Neal, A.Kennedy, Lawrenson, Whelan, Hansen, Dalglish, Lee, Rush, Hodgson(Johnston,61), Souness.

Brighton & Hove Albion: Digweed; Ramsey, Gatting, Grealish, Foster, Stevens, Case, Ward, Robinson, Ryan, Smillie.

Referee: Mr A. Grey (Great Yarmouth)

Attendance: 44,868

***Jimmy Case**, the former Liverpool player who scored the winning goal against the Reds*

January 6, 1984

Liverpool (2) 4
Robinson 8, Rush 28, 86,
Johnston 63

Newcastle United (0) 0

THIS was a game of co-incidences. Michael Robinson, who played against Liverpool in their last Cup match against Brighton, now played for the Reds. Former Reds' players Kevin Keegan and Terry McDermott played for Newcastle, McDermott in his second spell for the club. In his first spell he had played against Liverpool in the 1974 Cup Final, losing 0-3.

Kenny Dalglish was recovering in hospital from an injury to his face, and his place in the side was taken by the young Australian, Craig Johnston, who had an outstanding game. He almost scored after just two minutes and played a part in the first goal which arrived after eight minutes. He headed on a Lee corner-kick to Robinson, who smashed the ball into the back of the net. Newcastle fought back bravely, but were restricted to long-range efforts which were usually off target. Lawrenson superbly marshalled the ebullient Keegan which stifled Newcastle's attacking invention. With 28 minutes gone, Rush scored from Johnston's pass to virtually secure the game for the Reds. Liverpool's relentless attack forced Thomas to save from Souness, Nicol and Kennedy. With 63

minutes gone, Johnston squeezed the ball between the goalkeeper and the post to temporarily silence the army of Geordie fans. Phil Neal crashed to the ground, having been hit on the head by a coin. He soon recovered. Four minutes from time Rush chested the ball home to complete the rout.

Mark Lawrenson had a magnificent game in defence for Liverpool, moving forward whenever possible to join the attack. Sammy Lee and Graeme Souness were dominant in midfield, while Johnston skipped and harassed Newcastle throughout the game.

The game was televised on the Friday night, and on the Saturday Bournemouth sensationally beat the Cupholders, Manchester United, 2-0 at Dean Court. Brighton won by the same score at home to John Toshack's Swansea City. In the 2-2 draw between Plymouth Argyle and Newport County, John Aldridge scored both County goals. The eventual Cup winners, Everton, who beat Watford 2-0 in the final, beat Stoke 2-0 away, while Watford drew 2-2 away to Luton, winning the replay 4-3 after extra time, John Barnes scoring Watford's third goal.

Craig Johnston who had an outstanding game against Newcastle when deputising for Kenny Dalglish

Liverpool: Grobbelaar; Neal, Kennedy, Lawrenson, Nicol, Hansen, Robinson, Lee, Rush, Johnston, Souness.

Newcastle United: Thomas; Anderson, Ryan, McCreery, Saunders, Roeder, Keegan, Beardsley, Waddle, McDermott, Wharton (McDonald, 64).

Referee: Mr K.S. Hackett (Sheffield)

Attendance: 33,566

January 29, 1984

Brighton & Hove Albion (0) 2   Liverpool (0) 0

Ryan 57, Connor 58

FOR the second year in succession, Liverpool were forced to meet Brighton on a Sunday, this time to meet with television requirements. The visitors were without Kenny Dalglish and, devoid of his creative influence, struggled up to the interval, though Joe Corrigan made a fine save from Steve Nicol after 16 minutes. As Liverpool fought for the opening goal, Corrigan effected two saves from Michael Robinson. On the half-hour, Liverpool lost the services of Graeme Souness, who pulled a hamstring stretching for an awkward clearance. Ronnie Whelan replaced the Scot, but Liverpool's grip on the midfield was relinquished. Seconds before the interval, Corrigan advanced bravely off his line to thwart Ian Rush, who had been put clean through. The headband-wearing Steve Foster parried Rush's second attempt from the rebound on the goal-line.

Early in the second half Corrigan touched a Rush left-foot shot round an upright and then spread himself to block a tremendous shot from Robinson. But Grealish began to exploit the pace of Smillie and Penney on the flanks. Connor headed down a Penney cross to Ryan, whose first time shot brought a magnificent save from Grobbelaar. Brighton took the lead after 57 minutes when Ryan went through almost unopposed, and a minute later Connor scored a second goal. Liverpool fought valiantly in an attempt to get back into the game, but they lacked the calm direction and leadership usually afforded them by Souness. Johnston and Nicol wasted genuine opportunities with erratic finishing, while Rush did not receive the sort of service he needed.

Everton had drawn 0-0 with Gillingham on the Saturday, before drawing the Priestfield Stadium replay 0-0 on the following Tuesday. On 6 February, the Blues won 3-0 at Priestfield in a second replay, all the goals coming in the first half. Watford won on the Saturday, 2-0 at Charlton. In the final, Everton beat Watford 2-0, Graeme Sharp and Andy Gray scoring.

Joe Corrigan, who played well against Liverpool, saving from Nicol after 16 minutes and Rush and Robinson in the second half

Brighton & Hove Albion: Corrigan; Hutchings, Gatting, Grealish, Foster, E.Young, Wilson, Smillie, Ryan, Connor, Penney.

Liverpool: Grobbelaar; Neal, Kennedy, Lawrenson, Nicol, Hansen, Robinson, Lee, Rush, Johnston, Souness(Whelan,34).

Referee: Mr B. Stevens (Stonehouse, Gloucestershire)

Attendance: 19,057

F.A. CUP - FIFTH ROUND

Watford 3   Brighton & Hove Albion 1

Watford: Sherwood; Bardsley, Rostron, Taylor, Terry, Franklin, Callaghan, Johnston, Reilly(Atkinson), Jackett, Barnes.

Brighton: Corrigan; Hutchings, Gatting, Grealish, Foster, E.Young, Wilson, Smillie, Ryan(Case), Connor, Penney.

Goals: Watford (Reilly, Johnston, Jackett); Brighton (Wilson, pen.)

Attendance: 28,000   **Half-time**: 2-0

January 5, 1985

Liverpool (1) 3

Rush 4, 74,   Wark 49

Aston Villa (0) 0

ENGLAND manager, Bobby Robson, was a spectator at the game. Villa were in sixteenth position and Liverpool in ninth position in the First Division. Everton played on the Friday before the game, winning 2-0 against Leeds at Elland Road.

With only four minutes of the game gone, Ian Rush put Liverpool into the lead. Gibson's attempted back-pass was intercepted by Dalglish, who took the ball round Spink before squaring it into the goalmouth, where Rush tapped it into the net. The goal followed two early narrow escapes for Villa. Kevin MacDonald - making his Liverpool FA Cup début along with John Wark - brought a fine save out of Spink after he anticipated Nicol's precision pass, and then Spink was forced to dive full-length to save from one of his colleagues.

Gibson almost atoned for his early error when he dribbled through and passed to Walters, whose cross was pushed away by Grobbelaar. Dalglish revelled in the space afforded to him and with Liverpool in fine attacking form, the home side put Villa under constant pressure. As Whelan rushed in on goal, Wark's pass went astray. A powerful Rush shot was deflected for a corner and then Nicol almost burst through as the home side moved forward in relentless attacks. Mark Walters - the Villa dangerman - was starved of suitable service.

With 25 minutes gone, Liverpool won a free-kick eight yards outside the area. Dalglish floated the ball into the box and Nicol timed his run to perfection, arriving at the far post to steer a header wide of Spink. The ball went inches wide of the post. With Souness transferred to Sampdoria, it was left to MacDonald to provide accurate through-balls. One such ball fell to Rush, whose low drive hit the side-netting. Moments later a half-volley from Wark went narrowly wide. Walters and Withe combined effectively on the edge of the Liverpool penalty area, but MacDonald cleared the danger with a huge clearance upfield.

As the second half began, Dalglish sent a shot wide of the near post, before he exchanged headers with Nicol as the Reds continued on the attack. Ormsby cleared. With 49 minutes gone, Rush slid the ball through to Wark on the right. The Scot took the ball forward five or six yards before unleashing a ferocious shot which Spink reached but was unable to keep out of the net. It was Wark's fourteenth goal of the season.

As Villa sought a goal which would bring them back into the game, Grobbelaar raced out of his goal to clear. Walters, who had tormented Liverpool in the previous meeting between the clubs on December 15 which finished goalless, was not in the game. He did not receive the service he needed and he was well-marshalled by Phil Neal, who was spoken to for a tackle on Walters. Neal joined the attack to fire a first-time effort narrowly wide. Nicol headed on to Dalglish and the Scot's left-footed drive flew high into the crowd.

Dalglish appeared to lack potency in the box, but his creative influence assisted Liverpool's cause. Whelan, Wark and Dalglish combined effectively to provide MacDonald with a scoring chance, but his shot went wide. The visitors looked dangerous on the break and when they won a free-kick just outside the penalty area McMahon beat the wall with a powerful shot which flew wide.

Wark climbed high to meet a Whelan cross, but Rush failed to make contact with MacDonald's header. After 74 minutes Liverpool increased their lead. Rush picked up a 25-yard pass from Whelan, held off two defenders and rounded the goalkeeper to score.

After the game manager Joe Fagan said, "The Dalglish-Rush combination is a little bit special. He just keeps going, our Kenny. I was a bit apprehensive before the match because of all the changes. But the result said it all. The lads believe in themselves." For Villa, absent skipper Allan Evans was missed in the centre of defence, while Tony Dorigo struggled at full-back and Gordon Cowans failed to justify his recall.

John Wark revelled in the freedom afforded by MacDonald's inclusion in the team. Neal added after the game, "Don't let's get carried away too much. We played well, but that was only one game. There is a long way to go to Wembley and we have got to keep it up if we hope to do anything."

On the Sunday following the game Graeme Souness saved Sampdoria from defeat when he scored the equalising goal against Juventus, who led through a fifth-minute goal by Michel Platini. Souness struck after 75 minutes.

Manchester United, the eventual Cup-winners, beat Bournemouth 3-0 at Old Trafford, while the beaten-finalists, Everton, disposed of Leeds. Leicester City beat Burton Albion 6-1 at the Baseball Ground, with Gary Lineker scoring three, but the match was subsequently ordered to be replayed after the Albion goalkeeper was struck on the head by missiles. Leicester won the re-played match 1-0 behind closed doors at Highfield Road. Hereford drew 1-1 with Arsenal, losing the Highbury replay 2-7.

Liverpool: Grobbelaar; Neal, Kennedy, Lawrenson, Nicol, Hansen, Dalglish, Whelan, Rush, MacDonald, Wark.

Aston Villa: Spink; Gibson, Dorigo, Williams, Ormsby, McMahon, Birch, Rideout, Withe, Cowans, Walters.

Referee: Mr G. Courtney (County Durham)

Attendance: 36,877

January 27, 1985

Liverpool (1) 1   Tottenham Hotspur (0) 0
Rush 17

LIVERPOOL'S undersoil heating ensured that the match took place, despite the threat of snow and inclement conditions. The crowd was reduced by the climatic conditions. With former Anfield star, Ray Clemence, in goal, Tottenham, who beat Charlton 2-1 in a replay in the previous round, were much fancied to win at Anfield. Within ten minutes of the start, Crooks and Grobbelaar both received treatment from the trainers after the goalkeeper dived to save at the feet of the Spurs' striker. A strong wind made control difficult, and the speed of the tackling meant that players had little time to settle on the ball. Roberts, Perryman and Stevens shackled Rush and Wark, while at the other end MacDonald reinforced the centre-back pairing of Hansen and Gillespie in order to cope with the twin-threat of Falco and Crooks. John Chiedozie troubled Liverpool with his speed, but he was well-marshalled by Alan Kennedy, assisted by Whelan and Wark.

After 17 minutes, Rush struck for Liverpool. Clemence's poor goal-kick was mis-headed sideways by Miller. Roberts failed to clear the danger under pressure from Nicol, and Rush pounced to beat Clemence. Tottenham, who had added steel to their usual artistic trademark, fought to the end of this titanic struggle. They rarely threatened Grobbelaar because of the strength of the cover in front of the goalkeeper, though the defence was sometimes beaten in the air.

Dalglish hit the ball into the net, but the score was disallowed for a push by the Scot on Stevens. As the game moved into injury time, Hansen burst through upfield and knocked the ball past Stevens, who fouled him. The long-legged Scot kept going, but was halted by the referee's whistle.

Everton beat Doncaster Rovers 2-0 at Goodison, while Manchester United beat Coventry 2-1 at Old Trafford. The sensational result of the round was Third Division York City's 1-0 home win over Arsenal.

Liverpool: Grobbelaar; Neal, Kennedy, Gillespie, Nicol, Hansen, Dalglish, Whelan, Rush, MacDonald, Wark.

Tottenham Hotspur: Clemence; Stevens, Hughton, Roberts, Miller, Perryman, Chiedozie, Falco, Galvin, Hoddle (Mabbutt,40), Crooks.

Referee: Mr K.S. Hackett (Sheffield)

Attendance: 27,905

Kevin MacDonald

February 16, 1985

York City (0) 1
Sbragia 85

Liverpool (0) 1
Rush 52

YORK City did not risk including Keith Houchen in the side, despite his penalty strike in the previous round against Arsenal. Houchen continued to struggle with a thigh injury and his place was taken by Derek Hood. The groundstaff arrived at the ground early to clear the 30 tons of straw from the pitch which had been used to combat the effects of the frost. The teams kicked off in bright sunshine.

York City: Astbury; Senior, Hay, Sbragia, MacPhail, Haslegrave, Ford, Butler, Walwyn, Hood, Pearce.

Liverpool: Grobbelaar; Neal, Kennedy, Gillespie, Nicol, Hansen, Dalglish, Whelan, Rush, MacDonald, Wark.

Referee: Mr P. Willis (County Durham)

Attendance: 13,485

Butler sent striker Walwyn chasing towards the edge of the Liverpool box but the centre-forward was denied by a firm tackle from Kennedy. Liverpool responded when a precise through-ball from Dalglish presented Wark with an opportunity on the edge of the area which he shot narrowly wide. The 3,000 travelling Merseyside fans were silenced after seven minutes when Butler beat Grobbelaar after Hood, making only his second appearance following a cartilage operation, put Butler in possession. The linesman flagged for offside, and the Liverpool fans packed into the Bootham end cheered again.

The Minstermen settled into their rhythm earlier than the visitors, who did not enjoy the hard surface. York attacked without regard for Liverpool's reputation and Pearce volleyed high over the top from 20 yards. Then Ford beat Kennedy on the right and sent over a cross which was headed out by Hansen. The Scot was outstanding in the heart of the Liverpool defence as the home side maintained their advantage. Walwyn beat Gillespie in the air and Hood volleyed the loose ball over the bar. Walwyn's style was awkward with his use of his arms and legs and in a tussle with Grobbelaar, the goalkeeper was awarded a free-kick. A Pearce cross was met by Walwyn and Sbragia got in a close-range header which went straight to Grobbelaar.

Liverpool had been unable to display the free-flowing football which had given them a 3-0 win in midweek against Arsenal. The testing surface was largely responsible, but the Third Division side played above themselves to frustrate Liverpool. With 52 minutes gone, however, Rush hit his 15th goal of the season. A long free-kick from midway inside his own half by Gillespie was touched on by Dalglish. Rush turned on the edge of the box to power his shot into the net.

The York manager, Denis Smith - the former Stoke star - had built a side which refused to be beaten and it took a solid challenge from Kennedy to deny Ford. Moments later Dalglish twisted and turned his way to the left of the box before sending in a high centre which was headed goalwards by Whelan. The Irishman's effort beat Astbury but was scrambled off the line by MacPhail. With the home side pouring forward Senior crossed from the left and Neal's headed clearance fell to Hood, whose first attempt was charged down before his second shot was saved by Grobbelaar. Liverpool's slender lead meant that they were unable to relax their efforts, and Walwyn headed narrowly wide.

With five minutes remaining, Sbragia hit the bar. Walwyn also struck the post and Sbragia equalised from close range after a desperate scramble.

Everton beat Telford 3-0 at Goodison Park with two goals in the space of three minutes by Gary Stevens and Kevin Sheedy. A further goal by Trevor Steven meant that Everton won a close battle against their non-League opponents. The part-timers were not disgraced and gained a half-share of the 47,000 attendance receipts. Southall saved well to prevent Williams giving Telford a half-time lead.

Manchester United beat Blackburn 2-0 at Ewood Park on the Friday preceding the York Cup-tie.

LIVERPOOL FOOTBALL ECHO

Zola floored in demo

Budd shock as protesters hit Wirral race

International athletic star, Zola Budd, was brought down by black demonstrators at Wirral's Arrowe Park when she was half-way through a first lap of the women's championship event. A group of about 50 demonstrators confronted her as she led more than 400 competitors in the race. She was coming round a bend entering on the last part of the circuit when the protesters leapt over tape barriers to stop her. She was believed to have been felled on icy ground and as police ran to her aid, marshalls escorted her to a first aid tent.

February 20, 1985

Liverpool (2) 7
Whelan 15, 55,   Wark 28, 58, 79,
Neal 72, Walsh 83

York City (0) 0

GOALKEEPER Mike Astbury, who had kept eight clean sheets before the 1-1 draw at Bootham Crescent, was beaten seven times by a rampant Liverpool. The Third Division side began confidently and dominated the opening fifteen minutes, but a goal from Ronnie Whelan changed the complexion of the game.

The Minstermen gambled on the fitness of Keith Houchen, who failed to appear after the interval still feeling the effects of his thigh injury and two-week absence from training.

Kenny Dalglish received the M.B.E. at Buckingham Palace on the Tuesday before the game, and gave a magnificent display in his 750th senior appearance. It was Dalglish who sent Wark chasing into the right of the box. Wark cut back his cross into the path of Whelan, who scored from close range. The goal seemed to take the heart out of York, and after 28 minutes Neal's pass into the box saw Wark and Rush combine before Wark powered a shot beyond the despairing Astbury.

After the interval, Neal and Nicol worked a right-wing corner into the area and Whelan rifled a right-foot shot across the goalkeeper and into the net.

Three minutes later an inch-perfect cross from Dalglish allowed Wark a free header. Liverpool continued to dominate the game, even though Ian Rush limped off after 65 minutes, to be replaced by Paul Walsh, whose presence only served to enthuse Liverpool more. After 72 minutes Walsh worked his way into the box before crossing to Neal, who scored on his 34th birthday.

With 79 minutes gone, a brilliant through-ball from Dalglish found Walsh, whose shot was blocked by Astbury before Wark completed his hat-trick by forcing home the rebound. Seven minutes before the finish Walsh crowned a highly-impressive display with a marvellous goal. Steve Nicol crossed into the area and Walsh's powerful volley hit the back of the net. It was Liverpool's sixth successive home win.

John Wark, a hat-trick hero against York

Liverpool: Grobbelaar; Neal, Kennedy, Gillespie, Nicol, Hansen, Dalglish, Whelan, Rush(Walsh,65), MacDonald, Wark.

York City: Astbury; Senior, Hay, Sbragia, MacPhail, Haslegrave, Ford, Butler, Walwyn, Houchen (Hood,45), Pearce.

Referee: Mr P. Willis (County Durham)

Attendance: 43,010

March 10, 1985

Barnsley (0) 0

Liverpool (0) 4

Rush 55, 80, 84,
Whelan 72

SECOND Division Barnsley, who beat Southampton 2-1 at the Dell in the previous round and beat Brighton 2-1 at Oakwell in the Fourth Round, entertained Liverpool on a damp, dark Sunday with the prize of a place in the semi-finals at stake. Managed by Bobby Collins, the former Leeds United and Everton star, Barnsley had not lost at home in more than five months in any competition. The Tykes played their part in a first half which lacked the usual excitement associated with Cup ties. The game was negative and typically hard throughout the opening period, but Liverpool took advantage of a defensive error after 55 minutes, and the game was virtually over.

Dalglish stole past full-back Wayne Goodison and crossed low into the middle, where goalkeeper Clive Baker appeared to make a clean catch, but the ball inexplicably slipped from his grasp and fell in front of Rush, who shot into goal. Barnsley responded with a determined display of courage and Nicol cleared off the toe of Agnew and Grobbelaar saved well from the same player. Then defender Billy Ronson attempted an unnecessary back-pass to his goalkeeper, and Rush moved in swiftly to round Baker and turn the ball back inside. A defender's boot thwarted John Wark, but the ball carried to Ronnie Whelan who scored Liverpool's second goal.

Liverpool began to play with a high level of skill and great determination and they left Barnsley chasing the game. A marvellous piece of combination involving MacDonald, Nicol, Neal and Dalglish finished with Rush scoring with clinical precision after 80 minutes, and four minutes later the lean Welshman hit his hat-trick after an inch-perfect pass from Dalglish.

After the third goal the floodlights went out, but were restored soon afterwards. A black dog also made two appearances on the playing pitch without disturbing Liverpool's total control. Rush's three goals took his total to 18 in just 25 games. He also struck a post with a superb flying header. Kevin MacDonald worked prodigiously in defence and linked up regularly in attack with Dalglish and Nicol.

In other ties, all played on the preceding Saturday, Luton Town beat Watford 1-0 at Kenilworth Road in the Fifth Round second replay; Everton drew 2-2 with Ipswich Town at Goodison, defender Derek Mountfield scoring an equalising goal after 86 minutes while Ipswich were down to ten men; and Manchester United beat West Ham United 4-2 at Old Trafford, with Norman Whiteside scoring a hat-trick, including one from the penalty spot.

Barnsley: Baker; Joyce, Goodison, Ronson, May, P.Futcher, Owen, Thomas, R.Futcher, Agnew(Gray,74), Campbell.

Liverpool: Grobbelaar; Neal, Kennedy, Lawrenson, Nicol, Hansen, Dalglish, Whelan, Rush, MacDonald, Wark.

Referee: Mr C. Downey (Harlow, Middlesex)

Attendance: 19,838

Ronnie Whelan wheels away in delight after scoring Liverpool's second goal against Barnsley

April 13, 1985

Liverpool (0) 2 Manchester United (0) 2 aet
Whelan 87, Walsh 119   Robson 68, Stapleton 98

STEVE Nicol failed a morning fitness test on a calf strain, and Sammy Lee continued on the right side of midfield with Jim Beglin maintaining his position at left-back in the absence of Alan Kennedy. Liverpool wore their all-yellow change strip and they attacked the Stanley Park End.

Whiteside and Lee were involved in an early altercation, and Lee won a free-kick on the right side of the box. Dalglish's cross enabled Wark to steal between two defenders and head narrowly past the goal. With Liverpool attacking furiously from the kick-off, Dalglish lofted the ball into the United half for Rush to chase. The Welshman was pulled down by Hogg, but the free-kick amounted to little. The game was fought at a fast pace, with heavy tackles from both sides. As Olsen prepared to take one of several corners gained by United, he was struck by an object thrown from the terraces, but he took the kick and his difficult cross swerved over the bar. Following a Gidman throw from the right, the ball fell to Stapleton, who mis-hit his shot. The ball fell to Whiteside, who stretched to reach it before hooking his shot wide. United gained eight corners in the first 25 minutes as they began to dominate. The Manchester side had won six out of their last seven FA Cup ties against Liverpool. Gidman played superbly as he overlapped down the right, and he sent Strachan clear with a fine forward pass. Strachan's cross swerved out for a goal kick. With 34 minutes gone, Hogg was booked when he slid into the back of Rush. Whiteside orchestrated United's determined battle for supremacy, with

Paul Walsh

Olsen and Strachan able generals. The interval arrived with neither goalkeeper having had a vital save to make.

Immediately upon resuming, United established an attack when Strachan played a ball into the box towards Hughes. The Welsh striker's first-time shot was well held by Grobbelaar. Then Strachan found himself clear on the left after taking on a through-ball from Whiteside. The Scot broke into the area, but Grobbelaar twice made instinctive saves to deny the United player. As the ball went back into the area, Olsen's shot passed narrowly wide. Grobbelaar's handling in the first period was suspect due to the swirling wind, but his two-handed save from Hughes, after a pass from Gidman, increased his confidence.

Liverpool's Paul Walsh substituted for John Wark as they sought the opening goal. Dalglish sent Rush racing through the Welshman's progress was halted by Gidman just outside the box. From the free-kick, Dalglish's shot curled round the wall and passed inches wide.

With 68 minutes gone, United took the lead. They gained a corner on the left which was lofted in by Strachan and glanced on by Hogg. The ball fell to England captain Bryan Robson, whose fierce shot from six yards took a deflection on its way into the net.

Liverpool increased their endeavour and with just three minutes left Neal and Lee combined to find Whelan just outside the box. The Eire international curled a tremendous shot from 20 yards over Bailey's head and into the net.

The game moved into extra-time. United continued to maintain their domination of the game and eight minutes into the first period of extra-time Frank Stapleton's shot from just outside the box appeared to take a deflection and flew wide of Grobbelaar, low into the corner of the net.

Liverpool continued to fight until the final whistle. The lessons begun with Shankly and continued by Paisley were maintained under the managership of Joe Fagan and with just one minute remaining Paul Walsh equalised to deny United their victory. Dalglish shook off the attentions of Strachan and hit a ball towards the far post, where Ian Rush rose above Arthur Albiston to get in his header. Gary Bailey was only able to parry the effort and as the ball dropped on the line, Walsh bundled it into the net. The Kop, moved to the Gwladys Street terraces for the game, was ecstatic.

In the other semi-final at Villa Park, Everton beat Luton Town 2-1 in extra-time after trailing at the interval.

Liverpool: Grobbelaar; Neal, Beglin, Lawrenson, Lee, Hansen, Dalglish, Whelan, Rush, MacDonald, Wark(Walsh,58).

Manchester United: Bailey; Gidman, Albiston, Whiteside, McGrath, Hogg, Robson, Strachan, Hughes, Stapleton, Olsen.

Referee: Mr G. Courtney (Spennymoor)

Attendance: 51,690 (at Goodison Park)

April 17, 1985

Liverpool (1) 1
McGrath (o.g.) 39

Manchester United (0) 2
Robson 47, Hughes 60

IAN Rush was unfit and his place taken by Paul Walsh, whose late goal forced this replay. Steve Nicol replaced Sammy Lee.

Liverpool's passing was not up to their usual high standard and with just 17 minutes gone, United almost took the lead. Grobbelaar dropped a Gidman free-kick while under pressure from Whiteside, and Stapleton's fierce shot was blocked on the line by Neal. The game was played at a frenetic pace and the quality of football suffered.

With 39 minutes gone, Walsh and Dalglish combined well and Nicol was set free on the right. Nicol's centre was headed past Bailey by defender Paul McGrath, who attempted to prevent Wark from making contact. It was a fortuitous goal, and very much against the run of play, for United were the better side and showed more composure. With Kenny Dalglish a creator of chances for men like Rush, Liverpool's potency in front of goal was diluted.

Almost immediately upon the resumption, United equalised when Robson burst through from a Hughes pass. The young Welshman was strong, quick and brave and possessed a keen footballing brain. Liverpool responded in their traditional manner and MacDonald tested Bailey from long range with a dipping volley. Dalglish broke through to shoot straight at the goalkeeper. These were rare Liverpool threats. On the hour United took the lead, and it looked to be decisive. Strachan's intelligent pass enabled Hughes to score with a strike of great maturity. Liverpool substituted Dalglish with Gary Gillespie in an attempt to add height and weight to an impotent attack, but it was a defiant gesture rather than a potent one.

Phil Neal played a magnificent captain's rôle, driving his men on throughout the game in an attempt to get his side to Wembley. In the Final, Manchester United beat Everton 1-0 after extra time, with a goal from Norman Whiteside.

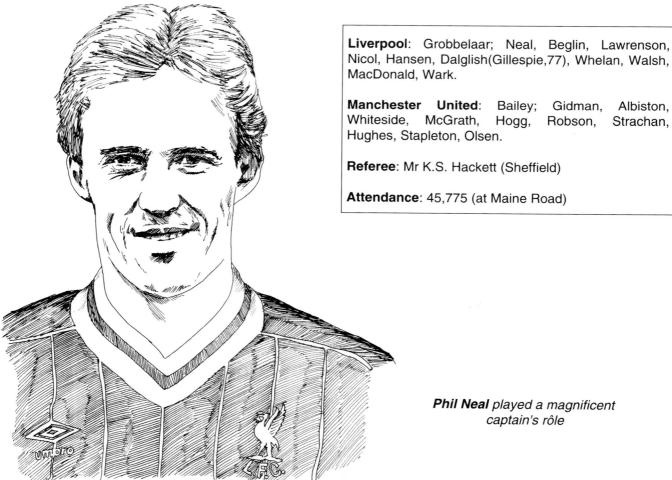

Liverpool: Grobbelaar; Neal, Beglin, Lawrenson, Nicol, Hansen, Dalglish(Gillespie,77), Whelan, Walsh, MacDonald, Wark.

Manchester United: Bailey; Gidman, Albiston, Whiteside, McGrath, Hogg, Robson, Strachan, Hughes, Stapleton, Olsen.

Referee: Mr K.S. Hackett (Sheffield)

Attendance: 45,775 (at Maine Road)

***Phil Neal** played a magnificent captain's rôle*

January 4, 1986

Liverpool (2) 5
*MacDonald 23, Walsh 33,
McMahon 73, Whelan 78, Wark 81*

Norwich City (0) 0

LIVERPOOL players Jan Mølby, a Dane from Kolding and the Dutch club Ajax, and Steve McMahon, formerly of Everton and Aston Villa, made their débuts in the Cup. The leaders of the Second Division, Norwich City, were fancied in many quarters to provide a shock at Anfield. The Canaries had just one defeat in their previous 8 matches, and had seven straight wins in the League. Liverpool were in third place in the First Division, but had not won a league game since December 7, when they beat Aston Villa 3-0 at Anfield. Since then they had lost two and drawn three of their next five fixtures. The dynasty of Shankly, Paisley and Fagan was over, and Kenny Dalglish took over the helm as player-manager, under the astute guidance of Bob Paisley. Dalglish was not available for selection due to injury, and Walsh took his manager's place against the Milk Cup holders. The pitch was soft underneath and extremely slippery on top due to the incessant shower of snow which fell throughout the first half. Norwich were unable to cope with the conditions. As Liverpool settled first, Rush broke clear on the right and found Johnston, whose cross was turned in first-time by Walsh, and Woods saved with his legs. Moments later, Whelan forced his way into the box and Woods saved from point-blank range. Then a forward ball from Lawrenson was headed down by MacDonald and Rush's first-time shot went narrowly wide.

Kevin MacDonald was in fine form for the home side operating on the left side of midfield, and after 23 minutes he began the systematic destruction of the visitors. A neat through-ball from Walsh enabled MacDonald to rifle home the opening goal. MacDonald was used intelligently by the

Liverpool management in a free-running midfield role and his diagonal runs constantly threatened Norwich and left them completely unaware of his movements at times. After 33 minutes, Liverpool won a free-kick. Mølby's accurate kick found Walsh, who headed into goal. Norwich responded by playing close, neat football on a pitch which demanded the early ball sent forward. MacDonald found space at will by cutting infield.

The snow abated as the teams took to the field for the second half. Norwich broke quickly down the right, but Barham wasted his cross. Rush showed great skill when he flicked the ball over the head of Bruce, and as he shaped to shoot on the edge of the box, the Norwich defender recovered to get in a vital tackle.

After 54 minutes, the visitors sent on John Deehan in attack for midfielder David Williams. Norwich put together a fine move and Mendham volleyed towards goal, but Grobbelaar covered the shot. A foul by Watson on Walsh midway inside the Norwich half meant that the striker had to receive attention. Mølby's free-kick was cleared by a packed visiting defence. John Wark replaced Walsh, who had sustained an injury and limped off. Shortly afterwards, Liverpool hit a third goal. With Steve Bruce temporarily out of action and down in the Liverpool half, MacDonald played an excellent through-ball which McMahon ran on to and controlled before slotting it past Woods. Johnston's accurate cross from the right fell to Whelan, whose powerful header from eight yards beat Woods. Liverpool continued to dominate, and when Woods failed to hold a Johnston header from Whelan's corner, Wark slotted home the fifth goal.

In the other ties, Arsenal won 4-3 at Grimsby, Ipswich drew 4-4 at home to Bradford; Tottenham drew 1-1 at Oxford; Peterborough beat Leeds 1-0 at home; and York City beat Wycombe Wanderers 2-0 at home. Everton were scheduled to play on the Sunday after this game. They beat Exeter City 1-0 at Goodison.

Kevin MacDonald

Liverpool: Grobbelaar;   Nicol,   MacDonald, Lawrenson,   Whelan,   Hansen,   Walsh(Wark,65), Johnston, Rush, Mølby, McMahon.

Norwich City: Woods; Culverhouse, Van Wyk, Bruce, Phelan,   Watson,   Barham,   Drinkell,   Biggins, Mendham, Williams(Deehan,54)

Referee: Mr D. Hutchison (Harrogate)

Attendance: 29,082

January 26, 1986

Chelsea (0) 1
Speedie 62

Liverpool (1) 2
Rush 45, Lawrenson 47

CHELSEA suffered the misfortune of seeing their star striker Kerry Dixon stretchered off after six minutes, having fallen awkwardly. From that moment on, the game failed to live up to expectations and both sides struggled to find their true form and created few chances in an uninspiring first half. Defender Colin Lee limped off with a hamstring injury minutes before the interval, and Chelsea, having used their substitute when Canoville went on for Dixon, were reduced to ten men. Liverpool used the opportunity of having an extra man to make the breakthrough. Rush slotted home his nineteenth goal of the season in the three minutes added on for injury time at the end of the first period. Lee failed to appear for the second half.

Two minutes into the second period, Lawrenson added a further goal for the Reds. Nicol and Walsh combined effectively down the right and the rangy Liverpool defender finished off a fine move by slotting his shot under the body of the diving Eddie Niedzwiecki.

Chelsea manager John Hollins had inspired his team, and on the hour the game took off as the home side fought gallantly with ten men. David Speedie, watched by the Scotland team manager, Alex Ferguson, led Chelsea's period of attack and threat. Gillespie's challenge on Doug Rougvie produced strong appeals for a penalty which were waved aside. Two minutes later, Pat Nevin's free-kick curled away from Grobbelaar's reach and Speedie hooked a shot into goal. The prodigious Speedie almost equalised seven minutes from the end when he turned in the box and drove in a low shot that rebounded clear off Grobbelaar's legs. Liverpool held on to the final whistle and progressed through to the Fifth Round.

In the Saturday ties, Arsenal beat Rotherham United 5-1 at Highbury; Aston Villa and Millwall drew 1-1 at Villa Park; Everton beat Blackburn 3-1 at Goodison; Brighton beat Hull City 3-2 on Humberside; Luton won 4-0 at home to Bristol Rovers; Manchester City drew 1-1 at home to Watford; Notts County had a 1-1 home draw against Tottenham; Peterborough United beat Carlisle 1-0 at home; Reading drew 1-1 at home to Burnley; Derby County beat Sheffield United 1-0 away; Sheffield Wednesday beat Orient 5-0 at Hillsborough; Sunderland and Manchester United drew 0-0 on Wearside; Southampton beat Wigan Athletic 3-0 at the Dell; West Ham United and Ipswich drew 0-0 in London; and York City beat Altrincham 2-0 at home. In the replays, Bury beat Reading 3-0; Manchester United beat Sunderland 3-0; Millwall beat Villa 1-0; and Tottenham beat Notts County 5-0. Watford and Manchester City drew 0-0 after extra time, Watford winning the second replay 3-1. Ipswich and West Ham drew 1-1, before the Hammers won a second replay 1-0.

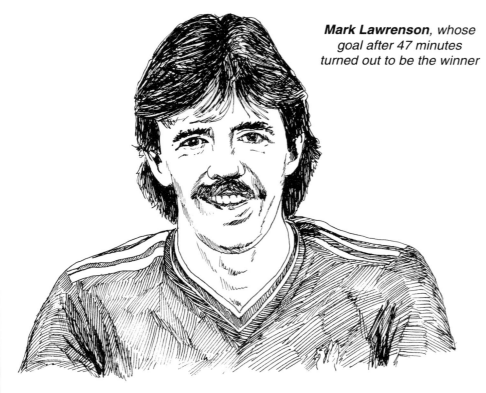

Mark Lawrenson, whose
goal after 47 minutes
turned out to be the winner

Chelsea: Niedzwiecki; Lee, Dublin, Pates, Rougvie, Bumstead, Nevin, Spackman, Dixon(Canoville,8), Speedie, Murphy.

Liverpool: Grobbelaar; Nicol, Beglin, Lawrenson, Whelan, Hansen, Walsh, Johnston, Rush, Mølby, Gillespie.

Referee: Mr A. Robinson (Waterlooville)

Attendance: 33,625

February 15, 1986

York City (0) 1
Ford 60

Liverpool (0) 1
Mølby (pen) 64

RONNIE Whelan was out injured - joining Paul Walsh and Gary Gillespie on the injured list - and player-manager Kenny Dalglish returned for only his second game since New Year's Day. This was the only change to the team which lost 0-1 at Queen's Park Rangers in midweek in the Milk Cup semi-final first leg. Bootle-born Mark Seagraves retained his place. Steve McMahon, who missed the previous seven games with knee ligament trouble, was substitute.

York City - who lay in 13th place in the Third Division - had purchased a £3,000 plastic covering for the pitch earlier in the week to ensure that the game would go ahead. The ground was nevertheless hard, full of holes and ruts, and heavily sanded. The players wore training shoes to suit the conditions.

Tony Canham, who a year ago was playing for non-League Harrogate Railway, tested Grobbelaar early in the game with a fine left-foot shot after a strong run down the left wing. Minutes later Canham again beat Lawrenson and Mølby on the same flank before Johnston conceded a corner. Then Gary Ford put Dale Banton - a £50,000 buy from Aldershot - through and, with the Liverpool players appealing for offside, the York player shot wide with only Grobbelaar to beat.

Liverpool eased the tremendous pressure when Dalglish won a corner through his persistence. Lee's flag-kick on the right was back-headed goalwards by Seagraves before Leaning punched clear. Canham then put Banton through but Mølby, acting as sweeper, produced a fine tackle and Lawrenson cleared the danger.

Good work by Wark put Rush in possession but the Welshman lost his footing on the surface. At this stage, Liverpool's one-touch football was a pleasure to watch, though it lacked real potency.

Dalglish back-heeled the ball to Rush and received the ball back before beating John McPhail and turning quickly to get in a first-time effort which Leaning held by diving to his left. Hood sent through a magnificent ball over the Liverpool midfield and Hansen, under pressure from Banton, turned and put Wark in possession. Moments later a Wark header from Lawrenson's pass was well saved by Leaning.

As York increased the pressure with the interval approaching, Steve Senior's free-kick on the right was headed down by Walwyn. The ball fell to York skipper MacPhail and his fierce volley was brilliantly turned away by Grobbelaar.

Liverpool began the second half in determined mood, and a Beglin long-range shot was turned away for a corner. Lee took the kick and exchanged passes with Lawrenson before crossing into the area where Seagraves climbed high to get in a header which flew inches wide. York City's strength lay in their ability to swiftly counter-attack and they won a free-kick eight yards from the edge of the penalty area after Lawrenson

fouled Mills. Dalglish impeded York's progress when he blocked a Walwyn shot and, after a frantic scramble for possession, the implacable Beglin cleared the danger.

The game was a typical Cup-tie with the football flowing from end to end, and when Rush was sent clear he fell after a challenge from Leaning, who had left his goal. The referee refused to award a penalty, despite Liverpool's strong appeals.

On the hour Walwyn went after a high ball pumped through the middle and turned it to Ford, who scored with a low shot from 14 yards.

Liverpool responded immediately, and put York under great pressure. The ball bobbled awkwardly in the penalty area and Rush and Johnston challenged. McAughtrie handled, and the referee had no hesitation in awarding a penalty. Liverpool's Danish midfielder strode up and slotted the ball home for his 12th goal of the season, six of them from the spot.

Inspired and prompted by Dalglish, Liverpool began to take control of the game. York, though, did not give up and won a free-kick on the edge of the area. Senior's kick almost found the hovering Banton, but Wark cleared the danger.

The replay was scheduled to take place on February 18 with only the stands ticketed. The prices were: Main Stand, Kemlyn Road and Paddock - £5; Main Stand (wing section) - £3.50.

In the only other ties on the day, Arsenal drew 2-2 away to Luton; Brighton drew 2-2 away to Peterborough; and Southampton were held to a 0-0 draw by Millwall at the Dell. In the replays, Arsenal and Luton drew 0-0, Luton winning 3-0 in a second replay; Brighton beat Peterborough 1-0; and Southampton beat Millwall 1-0.

York City: Leaning; Senior, Hood, McAughtrie, MacPhail, Mills, Ford, Banton, Walwyn, Haslegrave, Canham.

Liverpool: Grobbelaar; Lee, Beglin, Lawrenson, Wark, Hansen, Dalglish, Johnston, Rush, Mølby, Seagraves.

Referee: Mr H. Taylor (Leicester)

Attendance: 12,443

February 18, 1986

Liverpool (1) 3
Wark 19, Mølby 94,
Dalglish 98

York City (1) 1 aet
Canham 43

WITH Liverpool Reserves beating Manchester City Reserves 2-1 at Maine Road with two goals from Brian Mooney (65 and 90), the Liverpool first team were struggling to overcome the gallant resistance of York City, the game going into extra time.   Top of the UK charts was Billy Ocean's *When the Going Gets Tough*, and Liverpool's Cup campaign was certainly getting tough.

The visitors played magnificently throughout and harried Liverpool at every opportunity. Driven forward by Sammy Lee and Jan Mølby in midfield, Liverpool took an early lead through the ever-threatening John Wark. Dalglish and Lee combined effectively and put Lawrenson in possession. The rangy defender moved forward down the right and his first-time cross found Wark, who drove the ball fiercely into the net. Liverpool made the mistake of sitting on their lead, and allowed York to gain the initiative for long periods. After 38 minutes Grobbelaar was forced into action and pulled off a marvellous save from MacPhail. Tony Canham equalised for the visitors with just two minutes of the first period remaining.

In the second half, Keith Walwyn had the ball in the net after running through and shrugging off challenges from Gillespie and Beglin. The goal was disallowed because Walwyn was adjudged to have fouled Gillespie.

Just four minutes into the first period of extra-time, Mølby collected a loose ball in midfield and moved forward before hitting a tremendous 20-yard drive which flew past Leaning. Four minutes after that Dalglish hit Liverpool's third when he squeezed the ball into a gap between the goalkeeper and post after a cross from the tireless Lee.

Kenny Dalglish

Liverpool: Grobbelaar; Lee, Beglin, Lawrenson, Whelan, Hansen, Dalglish, Wark (Johnston,74), Rush, Mølby, Gillespie.

York City: Leaning; Senior, Hood, McAughtrie, MacPhail, Mills, Ford, Banton, Walwyn, Haslegrave (Houchen,90), Canham.

Referee: Mr H. Taylor (Leicestershire)

Attendance: 29,362

March 11, 1986

Liverpool (0) 0   Watford (0) 0

LIVERPOOL, in second place in the table, played hosts to Watford, in tenth place. Tony Coton, the former Birmingham goalkeeper whom Watford bought for £300,000, was in inspired form and he thwarted numerous Liverpool attempts on his goal in a game in which the Reds won 16 corners and Watford just 2.

Kenny Dalglish inspired his side as he prompted and probed in his inimitable style. But Watford were well organised and had Steve Terry and John McClelland in the centre of defence, with manager Graham Taylor bringing in an extra defender in Lee Sinnott. The tactic brought its own reward with a replay.

Liverpool enjoyed almost continuous possession, with the brain of Dalglish maintaining the momentum. With 10 minutes gone Dalglish's header from a Whelan cross was saved well by Coton. The visiting 'keeper then saved twice as Rush powered two headers at goal. Then Lawrenson brushed aside Wilf Rostron's challenge before unleashing a fierce shot inside the box which Coton turned wide.

After the interval Watford defended well, and in order to provide themselves with another option and more speed down the right, the home side sent on Craig Johnston in place of Sammy Lee.

Dalglish created a magnificent opening for Jim Beglin, who was denied by Coton for the second time.

Coton had a magnificent game, with his perfect positioning and excellent reaction saves.

Tony Coton, who produced a superlative display in goal for Watford

Liverpool: Grobbelaar; Lee(Johnston,67), Beglin, Lawrenson, Whelan, Hansen, Dalglish, Gillespie, Rush, Mølby, McMahon.

Watford: Coton; Gibbs, Rostron, Talbot, Terry, McClelland, Sterling, Sinnott, West, Jackett, Barnes.

Referee: Mr R.G. Milford (Bristol)

Linesmen: Mr E.J. Parker (Red Flag);
            Mr D. Mansfield (Orange Flag)

Attendance: 36,775

March 17, 1986

Watford (0) 1
Barnes 47

Liverpool (0) 2 aet
Mølby (pen) 86, Rush 108

KENNY Dalglish made two changes for this replay, recalling himself and Steve McMahon after injury in place of John Wark and Sammy Lee, who was named as substitute. It had been a strange week for Wark, having scored on the previous Saturday, been recalled into the Scottish international squad on the Monday, and dropped for this game. Graham Taylor committed the error of relying too much on what Liverpool might do, and defender Lee Sinnott was retained on the left side of midfield in an attempt to prevent the runs of Johnston and Lawrenson.

Watford's John Barnes scored an excellent goal after 47 minutes, swerving his free-kick around the wall and beating Bruce Grobbelaar as it flew into the bottom right-hand corner of the net.

Watford played well, while Liverpool refused to be beaten and with just four minutes remaining, Rush burst through into the box and was brought down by Coton. The hero at Anfield had given Liverpool a lifeline and Mølby despatched the penalty into the bottom left-hand corner of the net.

Watford's negative tactics based on destructive rather than constructive play proved to be their downfall. An over-emphasis on breakaways meant that they created little and Liverpool seized the initiative in extra time. After 108 minutes, Dalglish tested the Watford defence on the edge of the box and found Rush, whose shot into the corner of the net was his 23rd goal of the season.

The Southampton manager, Chris Nicholl, was watching, since his team were to play the winners.

Boxer Steve dies

BOXER Steve Watt has died, three days after collapsing in the ring during a welterweight bout. A British Boxing Board of Control inquiry will be held next week into the fight.

Family and friends of the Scottish welterweight champion (27) were at his bedside in Charing Cross Hospital when he died last night. A hospital spokesman said he had put up "a tremendous battle for life."

He had been stretchered from the ring in the tenth round of his bout with southern area welterweight champion Rockey Kelly.

Paul Walsh congratulates *Ian Rush*, who has scored Liverpool's second goal

Watford: Coton; Gibbs, Rostron, Talbot(Allen,110), Terry, McClelland, Sterling, Sinnott, West, Jackett, Barnes.

Liverpool: Grobbelaar; Gillespie, Beglin, Lawrenson, Whelan, Hansen, Dalglish, Johnston, Rush, Mølby, McMahon.

Referee: Mr R.G. Milford (Bristol)

Attendance: 28,097

April 5, 1986

Liverpool (0) 2
Rush 99, 104

Southampton (0) 0 aet

ON a day when Cliff Richard and The Young Ones were at the top of the UK charts with *Living Doll*, and when West Tip won the Grand National at 15-2, and when Graeme Souness was due to have talks with Sampdoria president Paul Mantovani in an attempt to secure his early release from a three-year contract in order to pursue a management career, and when Kenny Dalglish was named Manager of the Month for March, Liverpool beat Southampton at White Hart Lane.

Mark Lawrenson was unfit and Liverpool named an unchanged side, with John Wark on the bench. The Saints left out Joe Jordan in favour of George Lawrence, although they included fit-again Jimmy Case - the former Red - and Danny Wallace.

Liverpool made a positive start with Mølby crashing a shot against a defender and Johnston having a shot blocked from the rebound. Moments later Mølby put Johnston away on the right and the Australian forced Shilton to make a good save. The Saints produced an early threat when Lawrence went close with a header from Armstrong's free-kick after Hansen had fouled Wallace. As the game flowed, Liverpool went close when Dalglish almost converted a low Rush cross into the goalmouth. With both sides willing to play it hard, Wright received attention and then Case was spoken to by the referee for a tackle on Whelan. The heavy rain made the pitch slippery, but both sides adapted well. Rush and Johnston were in lively form for the Reds. Johnston broke free down the right and Rush just failed to get on top of the ball with his header. As Liverpool gained control, Shilton just managed to tip a dipping Rush volley over the bar. Then Holmes kicked a Whelan header off the line from the corner before Mølby forced a save from the Southampton goalkeeper.

The Saints responded when Cockerill shot inches wide after a free-kick by Case had rebounded to him off a defender. Case was in splendid form, hoping to help his new team beat the side where he began his career. The midfielder held off Mølby's tackle before setting Armstrong free on the left. The cross was too strong and Beglin conceded a corner.

Ten minutes before the interval the Southampton centre-back, Mark Wright, was carried off on a stretcher after a collision with his own goalkeeper and Johnston. Shilton had come out in an attempt to prevent the Liverpool man, but the England goalkeeper caught Wright with both feet. Wright was later found to have broken a small bone in his right leg. From the corner, Rush almost forced the ball home, but the Saints responded with an attack of their own in which Lawrence was denied by Grobbelaar.

Andy Townsend substituted for Wright in the second half. Liverpool continued to hold the initiative, though the Southampton defence coped extremely well. Liverpool won a free-kick 30 yards from goal, and Mølby stepped up to take the kick, but fooled the defence and passed sideways to McMahon, whose powerful drive flew inches wide. Moments later the Reds gained another free-kick in almost an identical position, but Mølby's intelligent lob failed to find a Liverpool player. Johnston was playing magnificently, and he fell over Armstrong when a header by Rush almost set him free. Mølby was thwarted by the determined Holmes in another attack. A Whelan volley from 15 yards was comfortably saved by Shilton. A fine pass from Case threatened danger until the movement broke down through poor play by Moran. With 62 minutes gone, Hansen brought the ball inside and McMahon found Whelan with an inch-perfect forward pass. Whelan's strike beat Shilton, but the ball flew past an upright.

Liverpool could not afford to relax, and a Lawrence header went close but it lacked power. Whelan forced Shilton to produce two fine saves in quick succession. Then Whelan miscued a volley from 15 yards and Rush turned the ball into the goalmouth before a defender cleared for a corner. Wallace won a free-kick after a Hansen foul, and Cockerill's shot went wide. After a tremendous struggle, the game moved into extra time.

Nine minutes into the first period, Rush latched on to a poor back pass and scored. Southampton tried to fight their way back into the game, but a second Rush goal after a fine run by Nicol killed off the Saints.

In the other semi-final at Villa Park in front of 47,711 champions Everton beat Sheffield Wednesday 2-1 after extra time with goals from Alan Harper after 47 minutes and Graeme Sharp, with a volley after 97 minutes. Carl Shutt scored for Wednesday after 48 minutes. The Blues were forced to rule out 33-goal Gary Lineker and suffered a blow after 27 minutes when Trevor Steven limped off, Harper substituting.

Liverpool: Grobbelaar; Gillespie, Beglin, Nicol, Whelan, Hansen, Dalglish, Johnston, Rush, Mølby, McMahon(Wark,80).

Southampton: Shilton; Holmes, Dennis, Case, Wright(Townsend,46), Bond, Lawrence, Cockerill, Moran, Armstrong, Wallace.

Referee: Mr A. Saunders (Newcastle-upon-Tyne)

Attendance: 44,605 (at White Hart Lane)

LIVERPOOL WIN MERSEYSIDE FINAL

RUSH HITS TWO GOALS

LINEKER OPENS SCORING

LIVERPOOL COMPLETE DOUBLE

Everton (1) 1

Lineker 27

Liverpool (0) 3

Rush 57, 84, Johnston 63

GEORGE Michael was top of the UK singles charts with *A Different Corner*; Graeme Souness was manager of Glasgow Rangers; Alan Ball had his Portsmouth managerial contract extended for a further year; Dave Mackay was returning home after managing Al Arabi of Kuwait; Aberdeen beat Hearts 3-0 in the Scottish Cup Final; India declared at 322 for 5 against Gloucester at Cheltenham; Alain Prost snatched pole position ahead of Ayrton Senna in the Monaco Grand Prix; Yorkshire were top of the

county championship in cricket; Kenny Dalglish was named Manager of the Year (taking over from Howard Kendall) and Liverpool Football Club were proclaimed as both the League Champions and FA Cup winners.

Gary Gillespie was unable to play due to a stomach virus and his place was taken by Mark Lawrenson, whose place against Chelsea in the final League match of the season was taken by Gillespie. Lawrenson had a leg injury.

Kevin MacDonald kept the midfield rôle that he had

filled so well during the previous five games of the championship race. The substitute's place went to Steve McMahon, the only Merseyside player in the Liverpool twelve.

In the Everton team Derek Mountfield showed no ill-effects from the knee injury which had bothered him all week. Mountfield had not been able to train normally and was a major doubt, but he was put through a rigorous workout on the morning of the match and came through it without any problems, which meant that Everton fielded their

strongest possible team with the exception of Neville Southall. Adrian Heath was named as substitute. This was Mountfield's third Cup final in succession.

Kenny Dalglish, named manager of the year on the Friday, did not announce his team until after the party had reached Wembley.

He said, "It is very bad luck for Gillespie, but it is bad luck also for Paul Walsh and Sammy Lee. They have all played a part in our championship and Cup successes and it was very difficult to leave those players out."

Dalglish, the first player manager at Wembley, led his team into the sunshine alongside Howard Kendall. The 105th Cup final was, for the first time, an all-Merseyside affair. The players were introduced to Her Royal Highness, The Duchess of Kent, dressed in neutral green. Bruce Grobbelaar sported a bright red cap.

Threaten

Everton had the first chance to threaten danger when Hansen pushed Sharp just outside the box and conceded a free-kick. Stevens took the kick and shot high over the top.

Flowing

Play swept from end to end and the game was flowing smoothly in the opening exchanges. Whelan fouled Reid, and Stevens' free-kick was aimed for the head of Mountfield, but Hansen rose above him to head clear for the Reds. One fan climbed on to the roof of the stadium at the Liverpool end, and perched dangerously in an attempt to see the action.

MacDonald tried to break clear but he was dispossessed with a brilliant tackle by Ratcliffe.

Anxious

The Liverpool fans became anxious when Dalglish needed treatment following a Mountfield challenge. With twenty minutes gone, Everton were denied a penalty when Nicol appeared to push Sharp in the back as the striker tried to meet a cross from Stevens. Sharp ran after the referee, but the official waved away the Everton claims. Everton poured forward and an accurate ball from Reid into the box forced Nicol to dispossess Lineker to concede a corner on the left that was cleared without any trouble.

Goal

Everton were marginally the better side up to this point and Lineker got the first goal after 27 minutes - his 40th of the season.

Reid split the Liverpool defence with a magnificent through ball, and the England striker raced into the box with Hansen in close proximity. Lineker's first shot rebounded off Grobbelaar, and Lineker, goal-poacher supreme, rammed the ball home from close range. Kendall and his coaches, Harvey and Heaton, leapt off the bench in glee at the goal. The fan on the roof did not see the goal as he had been removed by officials for reasons of safety.

Mountfield sent a long ball into the area that Grobbelaar took comfortably despite the presence of Lineker.

Blocked

MacDonald sent a great ball into the box which Rush managed to control, but his shot on the turn was blocked by Ratcliffe.

Mimms rushed off his line to save at the feet of the in-coming Johnston after another fine ball into the box by MacDonald.

With five minutes remaining to the interval, Ratcliffe conceded a corner on the right which Liverpool wasted.

Liverpool then indulged in a series of intricate passes between Mølby, Rush and

Ian Rush *goes round Bobby Mimms to score Liverpool's first goal*

Beglin, which culminated with Mølby getting in a shot which was charged down on the edge of the box by Bracewell, and the referee almost immediately blew the whistle.

A long throw from Stevens almost found Sharp at the near post but Grobbelaar grabbed the loose ball. The game had not seen many shots on goal, but Steven found the space to drive in an angled shot from the right of the penalty area which flew wide of the post.

Struggled

Liverpool struggled to find their championship form at this stage of the game, and although Rush found Dalglish in the area, the player-manager sent his shot high and wide.

Sheedy - formerly at Anfield - broke clear of three defenders before sending a right-foot shot across the goalmouth which passed narrowly wide. Sheedy's season had been dogged by injury, but he showed his shooting power after Johnston conceded a foul for hands on the edge of the area. His shot was aimed at the bottom left-hand corner of the goal, and Grobbelaar fumbled it before turning it wide for a corner.

Angry

Grobbelaar and full-back Beglin exchanged angry words as they struggled to maintain an understanding.

With 57 minutes gone, Rush hit an unexpected equaliser. Stevens gave the ball away to Whelan, who found Mølby. The Dane's immaculate through-ball was picked up by Rush, who rounded the advancing Mimms before slipping the ball into the unguarded net.

In the previous 120 games in which Rush had scored, Liverpool had not lost, and the goal gave the Reds fresh impetus at a time when Everton were clearly on top.

Goal

Just six minutes later, Johnston scored for the Reds. Rush found Mølby on the left of the goal and his cross went to Johnston, six yards out. The Australian midfielder slotted the ball home to the joy of the army of Liverpool fans. Everton replaced Stevens with

Heath, but Liverpool had gained the ascendancy, and scored a clinching third goal with just six minutes remaining.

Beaten

Rush found Mølby, who found Whelan with an inch-perfect pass. The Irishman sent the ball back across to Rush, who rifled home the ball into the right-hand corner with Mimms completely beaten.

After the game, Kenny Dalglish said, "The lads have put in a great effort

this season and have done everything that has been asked of them.

Credit

They deserve as much credit for what they've achieved as anyone. I am delighted as much for them as I am for myself and I am so fortunate and proud to be associated with them. The backroom staff of Bob Paisley, Roy Evans, Ronnie Moran and Tom Saunders have worked so hard and have been a great help to me. All I did was pick the

Craig Johnston has just scored to put Liverpool ahead

Kenny Dalglish *holds aloft the FA Cup*

right team. We did so well to win the League - the Wembley victory is just the icing on the cake for us. There was only John Wark at the club with a cup winners' medal before the game. Now a few more people have got them and I think on the day we deserved to win.

Composed

We were composed in the first half but Gary Lineker took his goal well after a great ball through.

The most important thing for us then was not to go berserk. Fortunately we had Rushie in our side - he always looked likely to score and he popped up with a couple. He's a dream come true.

Superb

Craig Johnston scored a superb second goal and Jan was involved in two. I'm thoroughly delighted we came out on top.

It will be hard to follow this season's success and all we can do is try our best. Apart from me we have a very young side and there's a lot of football left in the lads.

There can't be much wrong with Everton because they finished second in the League and runners-up in the Cup.

Disappointed

Obviously they will be disappointed not to have won anything but we're not going to gloat over Everton's lack of success. We are both from the same city - we've a lot of respect for each other and the teams and fans have produced a memorable season for Merseyside."

Charity Shield

Three months later the teams fought out a 1-1 draw at Wembley in the Charity Shield. Heath (80) and Rush (88) were the scorers.

EURO BLOW FOR SOCCER GIANTS
~~~~~~~~~~~~~~~

THERE will be no European club football for English teams next season. But UEFA's Executive Committee meeting in Zurich has offered the hope that teams could be readmitted for season 1987-88.

They noted "important efforts" by English clubs to improve the conduct of their fans following the Heysel Stadium tragedy of a year ago and added: "If the improvement continues in a way that would guarantee complete security in a future participation, the committee reserves the right to re-consider its position in 1987.

FA secretary Ted Croker said he expected the no-return-yet verdict. but was optimistic about the future.

"Over the last two or three weeks I began to feel reasonably certain we would not get back. I then pressed for some firm assurance to give the hope we really need for the next year. I trust that is what they are saying," said Croker.

"We need an incentive. If we then show the same improvement as we have seen this season, then, on that basis, I feel we should get back."

Croker says this season the record of English fans has been as good as any in Europe.

He will continue to press UEFA to look carefully at England's points allocation for the UEFA Cup when teams are re-admitted.

The number of entries, between one and four, is based on a country's performances in the three European competitions over the previous four seasons.

A two-year ban with no points accruing would probably mean only two English teams eligible on the return.

Croker will ask that England's record over the four years before banishment be taken into account.

RUSH RECORD

IAN RUSH said after the game: "This day matches anything in my career.

To score two in the FA Cup Final is wonderful. We were more determined than ever this season after what happened in Brussels last year."

Rush's goals took his total to 31 this season and meant that he has now scored ten times in games against Everton - a record for a Liverpool player.

Rush, who was watched by Juventus officials, said that he intended to finish his career at 30 - and would like it to be at Liverpool. "I would like to secure myself so that I can finish at 30. If at Liverpool that's great - if not I'll have to think about going abroad.

Gary Lineker said: "I know nothing about Barcelona. Nobody has spoken to me. As far as I am concerned I expect to start next season at Goodison. I'm concentrating only on the World Cup now. We had the game won today but threw it away. One silly mistake did it for us."

Everton: Mimms; Stevens(Heath,72), Van Den Hauwe, Ratcliffe, Mountfield, Reid, Steven, Lineker, Sharp, Bracewell, Sheedy.

Liverpool: Grobbelaar; Lawrenson, Beglin, Nicol, Whelan, Hansen, Dalglish, Johnston, Rush, Mølby, MacDonald.

Referee: Mr A. Robinson (Waterlooville)

Linesmen: Mr A. Gunn (Sussex); Mr R.A. Hart (Durham)

Reserve Linesman: Mr C. Topliss (Dorset)

Attendance: 98,000

Receipts: £1,100,000

A New Era

1987 - 1993

January 11, 1987

Luton Town (0) 0   Liverpool (0) 0

THE Cupholders were forced to contend with swirling snow in their defence of the trophy. With a ban on away supporters introduced by Luton, the crowd was fiercely partisan, though a few Liverpool supporters infiltrated the home side's defences. The game was played on a Sunday and televised. On a plastic pitch which Liverpool manager Kenny Dalglish openly criticised, the visitors were content to survive and created few chances of their own.

Midway through the first half, Mick Harford crashed a 30-yard shot against the Liverpool crossbar, but the Reds' rearguard generally did well against the aerial threat of Harford and Newell, the former Liverpool reserve. Mark Lawrenson superbly marshalled the tricky winger Brian Stein.

Shortly before the interval Liverpool enjoyed a brief spell of domination and Rush hit a shot straight at Les Sealey, and a McMahon shot was headed out by Mal Donachy.

In the second half Craig Johnston cleared off the line after Ricky Hill's cross had gone beyond Liverpool's central defenders. Ronnie Whelan fired high into the stand from a low cross by the tireless Johnston. Long before the end, a goalless draw looked inevitable. Liverpool had scored just three goals in their previous six games, an indication of their goalscoring weakness.

On the previous Saturday, Everton beat Southampton 2-1 at Goodison Park; Manchester United beat Manchester City 1-0 at Old Trafford with a Norman Whiteside goal; Arsenal beat Reading 3-1 away. Also on the Sunday Crystal Palace beat Nottingham Forest 1-0 at home and Leeds United beat non-League Telford 2-1 at West Bromwich's ground.

Luton Town: Sealey; Johnson, Grimes, Nicholas, Foster, Donaghy, Hill, B.Stein, Newell, Harford, Preece.

Liverpool: Grobbelaar; Gillespie, Beglin, Lawrenson, Whelan, Hansen, Walsh, Johnston, Rush, Mølby, McMahon.

Referee: Mr A. Gunn (Burgess Hill)

Attendance: 11,085

Craig Johnston

January 26, 1987

Liverpool (0) 0

Luton Town (0) 0 aet

Barry Venison

LIVERPOOL began slowly and took the whole of the first half as they attacked the Kop to recover. They lacked ideas and their inadequacies in front of goal cost them a replay at Kenilworth Road, Luton forcing a toss for venue, and winning. Barry Venison made his Cup début for Liverpool, in place of Jim Beglin, and John Wark deputised for Steve McMahon. Luton played Tim Breacker at right-back and pushed Ashley Grimes into midfield, David Preece dropping out.

With 70 minutes gone, Ian Rush missed an open goal after Wark's shot had rebounded to him off the goalkeeper. Rush was subjected to a lot of fierce tackling and remained doubtful for the second replay.

For about 15 minutes in the second half, Liverpool enjoyed a period of domination. Wark headed into Sealey's arms, and then left-foot and right-foot shots went wide. Walsh shot fiercely, but Sealey was equal to the task, and Mølby also forced the goalkeeper to make a good save. Later Rush blasted Walsh's pass into the side-netting. Alan Irvine and Gary Ablett limbered up on the touchline for considerable periods of time, but were not used. Liverpool relied exclusively on crosses from the right wing which were dealt with comfortably by Foster and Donaghy.

The only clear chance in extra time came when Mølby hit a post with a curling shot which beat Sealey.

As well as three heavy fouls on Rush, which made him doubtful for the replay, Alan Hansen had to receive repeated attention for a deep cut in his forehead which required stitches.

Walsh partnered Rush up front with a great deal of imagination, but many supporters felt that Alan Irvine, on the substitutes' bench, should have been given a chance, feeling that his height and pace might have created something positive to end the stalemate.

Midway through the second half of normal time Liverpool dominated without being able to finish off their excellent creativity.

Liverpool: Grobbelaar; Gillespie, Venison, Lawrenson, Whelan, Hansen, Walsh, Johnston, Rush, Mølby, Wark.

Luton Town: Sealey; Breacker, Johnson, Nicholas, Foster, Donaghy, Hill, B.Stein, Newell, Harford, Grimes.

Referee: Mr A. Gunn (Burgess Hill)   **Attendance**: 34,822

January 28, 1987

Luton Town (1) 3

B.Stein 33,   Harford (pen) 78,
Newell 81

Liverpool (0) 0

WITH Robbie Nevil at the top of the UK charts with *C'est La Vie*, Liverpool were well beaten by a very good side which once again enjoyed home advantage. The visitors' substitutes had played less than two full first-team matches between them, which showed that Liverpool's playing personnel was stretched to the limit. Both players were used during the course of the game, but their introduction added little to a side which was outplayed for long periods.

Gary Gillespie was penalised for a foul, and from the free-kick Brian Stein crashed the ball home. The Cup-holders struggled to chase the game from then onwards. In the second half Luton added to their score when Jan Mølby fouled Stein, and Mick Harford scored from the spot. Mike Newell completed the rout.

As well as the three goals, Grobbelaar diverted Foster's powerful strike on to the woodwork, and Craig Johnston kicked off the line from a Stein header before Grobbelaar dived acrobatically to deny Newell as the home side were rampant.

Liverpool lacked the power and invention to break down Luton's well-organised defence, in which Foster and Donaghy excelled. Johnston and Walsh worked tirelessly, but Walsh lacked the strength to impose himself on the game, and Johnston's intelligent running was nullified by his erratic final pass. The midfield lacked pace and creativity in the middle and penetration on the wings, and Sealey was hardly tested at all.

In another second replay, Stoke beat Grimsby 6-0. In the Fourth Round Luton drew 1-1 at home to Queens Park Rangers, with Harford scoring from the spot. In the Loftus Road replay, Rangers won 2-1, before losing to Leeds United at Elland Road 2-1 in the Fifth Round.

Right: **Mike Newell**, *scorer of Luton's third goal*

Luton Town: Sealey; Breacker, Johnson, Nicholas, Foster, Donaghy, Hill, B.Stein, Newell, Harford, Grimes.

Liverpool: Grobbelaar; Gillespie, Venison, Lawrenson, Whelan, Hansen, Walsh(Ablett,86), Johnston, Rush, Mølby, Wark(Irvine,73).

Referee: Mr D.S. Vickers (Ilford)

Attendance: 14,687

January 9, 1988

Stoke City (0) 0

Liverpool (0) 0

IMMEDIATELY prior to this cup-tie with Stoke, Liverpool announced that Bruce Grobbelaar would not be able to play due to a leg injury he suffered earlier in the week. The injury was kept secret in the hope that he would be fit to face Stoke, but he failed to recover in time, and Mike Hooper deputised. Hooper made his début at Wembley when Grobbelaar was injured during the Charity Shield against Everton in 1986. Four other players, Peter Beardsley, John Aldridge, Ray Houghton and John Barnes, also made their débuts for Liverpool in the Cup. Full-back Barry Venison was unfit and Mark Lawrenson regained the place at full-back he originally lost through injury. The pitch was extremely soft due to the torrential rain.

Liverpool began in determined mood against their Second Division opponents and Barnes had an early shot blocked before he weaved his way around several defenders and created an opportunity for Beardsley, whose shot took a deflection before being held by Barrett. Both sides struggled to keep their footing in the wet conditions. Stoke began to assert themselves, and Hooper was forced to race off his line to intercept a pass from Cliff Carr. The home side pressed home their advantage, and Lawrenson cleared off Simon Stainrod's boot, before Hooper dived low to save from Steve Parkin. Liverpool responded and Aldridge had a shot blocked at the Stoke end, while at the other end Stainrod almost connected with a dangerous cross. Then Gillespie carelessly delivered a crossfield pass which Stainrod took up before being crowded out by the Liverpool defence. As the game flowed from end to end, Whelan's 25-yard drive tested Barrett, who pushed the ball behind.

With 27 minutes gone, Gillespie headed Barnes's corner into the net, but he pushed a defender in the process. A powerful shot from McMahon rebounded from a defender. An unnecessary foul by Whelan earned Liverpool only their fourth booking of the season. Stoke's endeavour and resilience cancelled out Liverpool's superior skill. Just before the interval Hooper had a moment of uncertainty when he flapped at a Carr corner, but Nicol headed firmly behind as a precautionary measure.

Liverpool began the second half in the same manner as they had started the first. Beardsley and Houghton combined brilliantly and Barnes was fed with an inch-perfect pass just inside the penalty area. He struck the ball with his less-reliable right foot. A flick inside from Aldridge gave Houghton an opportunity, but his right-foot shot went narrowly wide. Stoke countered immediately and Hooper was forced to make an excellent save from Nicky Morgan. Whelan was Liverpool's powerhouse in midfield, though McMahon and Barnes were somewhat subdued. Barnes played quite deep but began to move forward into more threatening positions, though he was well marshalled and given little space to display his skill.

George Berry was booked for a foul on John Barnes, and Barnes took the free-kick himself, finding Beardsley on the edge of the penalty area. Beardsley's accurate shot passed narrowly wide. The home side, roared on by a vociferous crowd, created problems for Liverpool and when McMahon was hustled out of possession, Hansen and Gillespie were forced to save Liverpool.

Beardsley went close when he picked up a ball just outside the box before seeing his shot deflected for a corner by Berry. Stoke replaced Stainrod with Shaw, in an attempt to bolster their defence. Four Liverpool players combined in a move which ended with Beardsley shooting wide with a left-foot shot.

With five minutes to go, Shaw beat Liverpool's offside trap and shot, but Hooper raced off his line and saved.

In the other ties, the Cup-holders, Coventry City, beat Torquay 2-0. Arsenal beat Millwall 2-0 at Highbury; Luton beat Hartlepool 2-1 away; Everton drew 1-1 at Hillsborough; non-League Sutton United held Middlesbrough 0-0 at Gander Green Lane; West Ham beat Charlton 2-0; and Wimbledon beat West Bromwich Albion 4-1 before 7,252 people.

John Wark was "absolutely gutted" at sitting out the Ipswich against Manchester United FA Cup tie at Portman Road because his £100,000 transfer from Liverpool was not completed in time. The televised game, with Wark in the commentary box, finished 2-1 to Manchester United.

Stoke City: Barrett; Dixon, Carr, Talbot, Bould, Berry, Ford, Henry, Morgan, Stainrod(Shaw,75), Parkin.

Liverpool: Hooper; Gillespie, Lawrenson, Nicol, Whelan, Hansen, Beardsley, Aldridge, Houghton, Barnes, McMahon.

Referee: Mr T. Mills (Barnsley)

Attendance: 31,979

Receipts: £111,000 (a record)

January 12, 1988

Liverpool (1) 1

Beardsley 9

Stoke City (0) 0

Peter Beardsley

WITH a high, gusty wind Liverpool attacked in relentless waves from the kick-off and after just nine minutes, Beardsley deceived Scott Barrett with an awkward, bouncing shot from George Berry's hurried clearance from a Barnes corner, one of 13 Liverpool corners. At that stage, Barrett had already saved from Beardsley and had seen a fierce shot by Barnes deflected narrowly wide. The goal inspired Liverpool to further attacking delights, though they lacked the final penetration that their creativity deserved. Before the interval Barrett also saved from Barnes, Aldridge and Whelan, and an Aldridge header which found the net was disallowed for offside, and Gillespie headed against an upright. Numerous other shots went wide or were blocked, and Lee Dixon almost put through his own goal.

Barnes operated down the right, and Houghton down the left. Beardsley linked up intelligently with Whelan and McMahon, and Liverpool's creative genius flourished. The Reds won eight corners in the first period, without conceding one, while they did not concede their first free-kick, for a foul by Houghton on Talbot, until three minutes before the break. Stainrod volleyed high over the bar as a token of Stoke's determined resistance, but otherwise Liverpool enjoyed almost total domination of the game. Barrett was the Stoke hero in the second half as he saved well on many occasions. Beardsley, Barnes, Houghton and Aldridge either sent the ball wide or against defenders as they maintained their onslaught. In one attack Aldridge had a shot parried by Barrett. Barnes hit the rebound against the full-back Dixon and then Barnes saw his second attempt hit the leg of Berry before going over the bar. Hooper was rarely employed but he saved well from Morgan and Graham Shaw, a late substitute. In another replay, Everton drew 1-1 against Sheffield Wednesday after extra time at Goodison, but won the second replay 5-0 - all the goals coming in the first half. Middlesbrough finally beat Sutton United 1-0 with a Paul Kerr goal after 111 minutes.

Liverpool: Hooper; Gillespie, Lawrenson, Nicol, Whelan, Hansen, Beardsley, Aldridge, Houghton(Johnston,82), Barnes, McMahon.

Stoke City: Barrett; Dixon, Carr, Talbot, Bould, Berry, Ford, Henry, Morgan, Stainrod(Shaw,68), Parkin.

Referee: Mr T. Mills (Barnsley)

Attendance: 39,147

January 31, 1988

Aston Villa (0) 0

Liverpool (0) 2
Barnes 53, Beardsley 86

John Barnes

NIGEL Spackman made his Cup début for Liverpool in a televised Sunday game. Manager Kenny Dalglish managed to keep the absence of Gary Gillespie and Ronnie Whelan a secret until about an hour before the kick-off. He did not employ Spackman in central defence but pushed him into midfield, with Nicol switching to partner Hansen and Gary Ablett coming in at left-back. Bruce Grobbelaar returned after a four-match absence. The performance of Nicol was of vital importance due to the threat of Villa's strikers, Gary Thompson and Alan McInally.

Liverpool took a long time to settle down, being content to soak up Aston Villa's pressure. Grobbelaar made a vital save from McInally and Paul Birch sent in three crosses which failed to find a single Villa player.

With 53 minutes gone, Barnes headed powerfully past Spink from a Houghton cross. Tony Daley had a shot blocked by Barry Venison, and a further one by Grobbelaar as Villa sought an equalising goal. Aldridge hit the bar in the first half and repeated that feat in the second half. Beardsley and Barnes forced fine saves from Spink.

With four minutes remaining Beardsley increased Liverpool's lead after a fine Aldridge pass. The Proud Preston record of winning the League without losing a game and winning the Cup without conceding a goal was still a possibility. Second Division Villa, managed by Graham Taylor, were more determined to win promotion.

Wimbledon beat Mansfield Town 2-1 away, while Everton beat Middlesbrough 2-1 in a second replay after 1-1 and 2-2 draws.

Aston Villa: Spink; Gage, Gallacher, A.Gray, Evans, Keown, Birch, Lillis, Thompson, Daley(Aspinall,76), McInally.

Liverpool: Grobbelaar; Ablett, Venison, Nicol, Spackman, Hansen, Beardsley, Aldridge, Houghton, Barnes, McMahon.

Referee: Mr K.S. Hackett (Sheffield)

Attendance: 46,324

February 21, 1988

Everton (0) 0

Liverpool (0) 1
Houghton 76

LIVERPOOL retained the team which defeated Aston Villa in the previous round, while Everton fielded the same personnel as those who beat Middlesbrough. The televised game was tightly contested throughout the first half, with few chances being created by either side, with defences dominating. There were no corners or genuine shots on goal during the first period, and although Everton had the greater share of possession, Liverpool looked the more dangerous, especially with the creative genius of Beardsley and Barnes. With 20 minutes gone, Everton's Peter Reid, their midfield general, limped off, and was replaced by Paul Bracewell, who made a major contribution for the first time in almost two years.

On the hour, a flick by Aldridge almost put Beardsley through. As Liverpool began to threaten, Pointon headed over his own bar and McMahon's 20-yard drive forced Southall to save. The tackling was fierce, though the game was well handled by the referee.

With 76 minutes gone, Beardsley played a return pass behind Gary Stevens for Barnes, and the winger curled a cross just out of the reach of Neville Southall, and Houghton dived to head the winner in his first derby appearance. With Kylie Minogue top of the charts with *I Should Be So Lucky*, Houghton noted his own fortune after the game, saying: "That's my first senior headed goal. The ball just came over John Aldridge's head and fortunately I was there. I just saw it coming and headed it down. The match was the same as the derby I watched and it was as quick as I expected. There was not much time to stand on the ball and the first goal was always going to be crucial."

Ian Rush - playing in Italy with Juventus - saw the game and said, "It was nice to see Liverpool win but I thought Everton gave them a good game. But the longer the score was 0-0 the more you had to favour Liverpool. I didn't think it was a great game, but it was a hard game. In the first half I don't think

Liverpool really had a chance but that's how good they are. They didn't really play well but they beat one of the best teams in the country."

Everton manager Colin Harvey said, "We'll bounce back, I'm quite confident of that. I'm very disappointed. I thought we battled very hard and created a couple more chances, but we defended badly on the cross for the goal. We got caught. When you lose your most influential player it doesn't help. But I'm not making excuses - a good player replaced him."

Liverpool manager Kenny Dalglish added, "Maybe the only bit of football in the match brought the goal. I didn't think the game was as good as the past two matches and that could have been because of the midweek internationals."

In the other Fifth Round ties played on the preceding Saturday, Arsenal beat Manchester United 2-1 at Highbury; Nottingham Forest beat Birmingham 1-0 away; Wimbledon beat Newcastle 3-1 away; Portsmouth beat Bradford City 3-0 at home; Port Vale and Watford drew 0-0, Watford winning the replay 2-0 at Vicarage Road; Luton and Queen's Park Rangers drew 1-1, Luton winning the replay 1-0 at Kenilworth Road; and Manchester City beat Plymouth 3-1, with goals from Scott (7 minutes), Simpson (77), and Moulden (89) before a crowd of 29,206.

Everton: Southall; Stevens, Pointon, Van Den Hauwe, Watson, Reid(Bracewell,20), Steven, Heath, Sharp, Snodin, Power(Harper,77).

Liverpool: Grobbelaar; Ablett, Venison, Nicol, Spackman, Hansen, Beardsley, Aldridge, Houghton, Barnes, McMahon.

Referee: Mr J. Martin (Alton, Hampshire)

Attendance: 48,270

Ray Houghton *wheels away after scoring*

March 13, 1988

Manchester City (0) 0

Liverpool (1) 4

Houghton 32,
Beardsley (pen) 53,
Johnston 77, Barnes 85

WITH Bomb The Bass top of the UK charts with *Beat Dis*, Liverpool performed their own version which they might have called Beat Us. The Reds made two changes from the Everton Cup-tie, with Gary Gillespie replacing Barry Venison, and Craig Johnston coming in for John Aldridge. City played Mike Stowell in goal for Eric Nixon; Ian Brightwell replaced Mark Seagraves - the former Anfield player - who was on the bench; and Paul Lake played instead of Ian Scott.

Liverpool's experienced professionals combined with devastating effect in this televised match to out-think, out-play and out-class City's youngsters in almost every department. Within the first ten minutes Steve Nicol - playing at right-back - raced into the City penalty area before being fouled and Peter Beardsley saw a shot deflected after he pounced onto Houghton's short corner.

With 32 minutes gone, Beardsley's pass sent Barnes away down the left and Houghton volleyed the winger's cross into goal. The City players protested that Barnes had handled and,

although the ball certainly hit his arm, the referee - perfectly placed - ruled that the ball had hit Barnes' hand and allowed the goal to stand.

In the second period, Liverpool overran their opponents. Steve Redmond mis-headed an attempted clearance and Johnston raced away unchallenged. Lake brought him down after he had rounded the goalkeeper. In the absence of Aldridge, Beardsley took the penalty and slotted it past Stowell. Paul Stewart forced a great save from Grobbelaar after an Imre Varadi cross. Johnston then beat the offside trap to round Stowell and neatly slot the ball home as he fell. Five minutes from time Barnes completed the scoring from Beardsley's immaculate pass.

In the other Sixth Round ties - all played on the preceding Saturday - Luton Town beat Portsmouth 3-1 at home; Wimbledon beat Watford 2-1 at Plough Lane before 12,228 spectators; and Nottingham Forest beat Arsenal 2-1 at Highbury.

Ray Houghton receives the congratulations of his delighted team-mates

Manchester City:
Stowell; Gidman, Hinchcliffe, Brightwell, Lake, Redmond, White, Stewart, Varadi, McNab, Simpson.

Liverpool:
Grobbelaar; Gillespie, Ablett, Nicol, Spackman, Hansen, Beardsley, Johnston, Houghton, Barne, McMahon.

Referee: Mr A. Gunn (South Chailey, Sussex)

Attendance: 44,047

April 9, 1988

Liverpool (1) 2
Aldridge (pen) 14, 51

Nottingham Forest (0) 1
Clough 66

LIVERPOOL played the fit-again John Aldridge, who replaced the industrious Craig Johnston, while Forest played the same team which beat Arsenal in the previous round. Unbeaten in the League before the game with Manchester City, Liverpool had won only one of their five previous League encounters before this tie. On April 2, Forest beat Liverpool 2-1 at the City Ground, with an own goal from Alan Hansen and another from Neil Webb. Forest fielded the same side which won that match, while Liverpool played Mølby in place of Beardsley and Johnston in place of Houghton. It was a negative formation which failed to outwit Brian Clough, Forest's manager.

Beardsley was brought back to torment Forest's central defenders with his swift runs and intelligent distribution, while Houghton brought additional strength down the right. The result was that Barnes received appropriate service. Gary Ablett was inadequate against the troublesome Crosby and was assisted by Barnes, a factor in the winger's game which was often overlooked. Hansen and Gillespie gradually came to terms with the threat of Nigel Clough, and Crosby - from non-League Grantham - was denied the service he required and received early on, which prompted Ablett to foul him after only five minutes, for which the Liverpool defender received a yellow card.

Early on Barnes shot wide after exchanging passes with Houghton. With 11 minutes gone, Ablett brought down Crosby again and was fortunate not to be dismissed. Three minutes later Barnes seized on a pass from McMahon before moving threateningly into the penalty, where he was brought down by Steve Chettle. Aldridge dispatched the kick into exactly the bottom right-hand corner as he had done so in the League game seven days earlier.

Until the penalty, Forest had had the upper hand with Clough the inspiration, playing first-time balls at great speed. With 22 minutes gone, Spackman, fed by Barnes, manoeuvred his way through the Forest defence before being thwarted by Sutton, who threw himself at the feet of the

Liverpool player. Fourteen minutes later Beardsley beat Wilson and unleashed a powerful shot which Sutton turned round a post.

Forest began the second half as commandingly as they had done the first and Clough, after Crosby's long throw was flicked on, headed narrowly wide. Five minutes later Foster got his head to a free-kick from the left by Rice, but Grobbelaar was well-positioned to hold the ball. Moments later Liverpool scored a goal of rare brilliance. Beardsley's immaculate pass found Barnes, whose cross from the left curled away from the Forest defence and was volleyed home by the lethal John Aldridge.

John Aldridge is congratulated by John Barnes

Shortly afterwards Barnes and Beardsley linked up again as the diminutive Beardsley was put through before his attempt was blocked by the Forest goalkeeper. After a further long throw by Crosby which was flicked on at the near post by Wilkinson, Clough stabbed the ball home from two yards. The goal gave the Forest team hope, but Liverpool maintained their superiority. Twelve minutes from the end, Liverpool had three attacking players against one defender, but Aldridge moved into an offside position and the thrilling flowing movement broke down. Two minutes later a rapid movement down the left between Houghton and Beardsley ended with Houghton crossing to Barnes, whose shot was saved by Sutton as he dived full-length. Minutes from the end Grobbelaar saved well from a 25-yard drive from Wilson.

In the other semi-final at White Hart Lane, Wimbledon beat Luton Town 2-1. Mick Harford gave the Hatters the lead after 47 minutes before John Fashanu equalised from the penalty spot after 54 minutes. Dennis Wise scored the winner after 80 minutes before 25,963 spectators.

Liverpool: Grobbelaar; Gillespie, Ablett, Nicol, Spackman, Hansen, Beardsley, Aldridge, Houghton, Barnes, McMahon.

Nottingham Forest: Sutton; Chettle, Pearce, Walker, Foster, Wilson, Crosby, Webb, Clough, Wilkinson, Rice.

Referee: Mr G. Courtney (Spennymoor)

Attendance: 51,627 (at Hillsborough)

CHAMPIONS LOSE FINAL

BEARDSLEY'S DISALLOWED GOAL

WIMBLEDON DESERVE VICTORY

Liverpool (0) 0

Wimbledon (1) 1
Sanchez 37

TWO days before the final - in which Liverpool attempted to win their second Double in three seasons - Craig Johnston was urged to reconsider his decision to leave Anfield and return to Australia. Gordon Taylor, secretary of the Professional Footballers' Association, reacted to news that Johnston, who would possibly feature in the FA Cup Final, was to quit Liverpool and football. Mr Taylor told the Anfield management that if the South African-born midfield player gave up football they could not sue him for breach of contract. Liverpool would be left holding his registration papers, as he still had a year of his contract to run. Mr Taylor added, "If he walked out now, he would not be able to play again without the club's permission. He would be saying goodbye to football. I have asked him to have a serious rethink." Mr Taylor planned to speak to Johnston again next week before the player left for Australia with his wife and two daughters.

Mr Taylor added, "As I understand it, Craig's father is ill, and he wants to be closer to him." It was not the sort of preparation that Liverpool wanted as they embarked on an historic course.

A game before the Final featured teams involving a Jimmy Tarbuck XI and David Frost's Dons for the Lord Taverners' Trophy. The game finished 1-1. Boxers Lloyd Honeyghan and Terry Marsh played for the Reds, while rock superstar Rod Stewart and Eddy Grant played for Frost's team. Twelve years before this final, Wimbledon were not even in the Football League. But they had earned the right to grace the Wembley turf with a game based on sheer hard work, determination and courage - allied to a home-spun philosophy. Wimbledon arrived at Wembley in a minibus. Hours before the game, John Barnes was nominated as Footballer of the Year and with Liverpool already crowned as the League champions after a season filled with excellent performances, Liverpool were expected to win handsomely. The President of UEFA, Jacques Georges, was in the Royal Box. Wimbledon, however, were well-known as an extremely fit team. Coach Don Howe drew on his vast experience to cool the team down during the interval with the help of wet towels filled with ice. Skipper Dave Beasant was in mercurial form.

Save

The 6ft 4ins goalkeeper saved well from Houghton after 13 minutes, after Beardsley had put Houghton through. Soon afterwards Beasant desperately grabbed a Beardsley pass destined for the lurking Aldridge. With 27 minutes gone he saved from Aldridge with his legs, then twisted sideways to scoop the loose ball away with his arm.

Immediately before the interval, Beasant saved well from a close-range shot by Hansen.

With 36 minutes gone Beardsley pounced on a long clearance from Gillespie, held off an illegal challenge from Andy Thorn and chipped the ball cleverly into the net before realising that referee Hill - known for his willingness to play the advantage rule - had blown for a free-kick.

Sanchez goal

With Liverpool still smarting from that decision, Wimbledon scored. Nicol fouled Terry Phelan near the byline, and Lawrie Sanchez stole in between Nicol and Gillespie to reach Dennis Wise's free-kick. Manager Kenny Dalglish reflected afterwards, "Just before the Beardsley incident he had let another one go and he did play advantage. Then Wimbledon break away and score and the Cup is won and lost within a minute."

Penalty save

On the hour Clive Goodyear was adjudged to have brought down Aldridge unfairly and the striker, who was about to be substituted, stepped up for his twelfth penalty of the season. Beasant flung himself sideways and Aldridge became the first player in history to miss a penalty in the Final at Wembley.

He was immediately replaced by Johnston. Liverpool did not perform up to their usual high standards in the second half, and the Wimbledon goal appeared to have dejected them.

Ten minutes after Johnston was introduced, Mølby replaced Spackman, but the substitutions made little difference to a Liverpool side which looked lethargic and short of ideas against an uncompromising, tough and industrious side.

Demoralised

When the game was over, the Anfielders looked demoralised. McMahon and Barnes were lying flat out on the Wembley turf, and Ronnie Moran and Roy Evans moved in amongst them to demand that they get their heads up. Dave Beasant became the first goalkeeper to walk up the steps to collect the FA Cup from the Princess of Wales.

Dave Beasant and *Laurie Sanchez* celebrate with the FA Cup

Beaten Liverpool skipper Hansen said after the game, "The referee made a bad decision and he admitted it.

Bad decision

He could see that Beardsley had broken away from the tackle but pulled him back. I told him he had made a bad decision and he told me: 'Fair comment'. I think he accepted that he made a split-second decision that went against him." The referee said, " I suppose there was every opportunity to play advantage, and perhaps in hindsight I should have done." Midfielder Steve McMahon said, "We had our chances to win, and Aldridge has been brilliant from the spot all season."

Tears

Dave Beasant said after the game, "My dad has never seen me play in his life before. He has just not been interested. But he finally agreed to come and watch when I told him I had got him a ticket. When I saw him in the crowd I had tears in my eyes. This was my 351st consecutive appearance in a Wimbledon shirt."

Lawrie Sanchez said, "I don't score many goals. That was only my fifth of the season and my first in the Cup, but they tend to be vital. I also got the goal that put us into the First Division a couple of years ago."

Tribute

Manager Bobby Gould added, "This win is a tribute to Don Howe and his sheer professionalism. He is now enjoying his moment of glory and he deserves it."

Double

In Scotland, Celtic's Centenary Year dream was fulfilled in a 2-1 Scottish Cup final victory against Dundee United to complete a League and Cup double. Frank McAvennie scored twice in the last 15 minutes to leave Dundee United as beaten finalists in nine appearances at Hampden.

John Aldridge has just missed from the penalty spot

Liverpool: Grobbelaar; Gillespie, Ablett, Nicol, Spackman(Mølby,74), Hansen, Beardsley, Aldridge(Johnston,64), Houghton, Barnes, McMahon.

Wimbledon: Beasant; Goodyear, Phelan, Jones, Young, Thorn, Gibson(Scales,63), Cork (Cunningham,57), Fashanu, Sanchez, Wise.

Referee: Mr B. Hill (Kettering)

Linesmen: Mr G.M. Tyson (Sunderland); Mr M.E. Pierce (Portsmouth)

Reserve Linesman: Mr D. Redshaw (Derbyshire)

Attendance: 98,203

January 7, 1989

Carlisle United (0) 0

Liverpool (1) 3

Barnes 33, McMahon 65, 84

LIVERPOOL named an unchanged side, keeping faith with Jan Mølby in the heart of defence. This was Mølby's second senior appearance for the club since his release from prison for a drink-driving offence. Peter Beardsley was a former Carlisle player, making 102 appearances and scoring 22 goals.

Carlisle made three changes from their Fourth Division game against Crewe Alexandra on January 2nd, the sides sharing two goals. James Robertson replaced Butler; Richard Sendall was named as a substitute, Archie Stephens taking his place. Carlisle - with their fans packed into the Warwick Road End - were third from bottom of the Fourth, while Liverpool were in third place in the First Division.

Early in the game Mølby pulled down Hetherington and Carlisle were awarded a free-kick on the left of the box. From Halpin's high centre, Saddington rose on the penalty spot and sent a powerful header straight into the arms of Hooper. Stephens - born in Liverpool - combined well with Robertson as the home side broke down the right. Graham curled a centre towards the six yard box and Hooper collected as Stephens lurked dangerously. After five minutes Beardsley slipped a clever ball to Barnes on the left, whose centre across the face of the goal provided an opportunity for Aldridge, but he failed to make contact from four yards out with an empty net beckoning.

Aldridge sent a short square pass to McMahon just inside the box in a central position and the midfield player's shot dipped over the bar. Then Hooper launched a long kick deep into the Carlisle half and Beardsley gave chase. McKellar raced to the edge of his box, but was beaten to the ball by Beardsley. The goalkeeper was exposed, but the cross was too high for Aldridge.

With 27 minutes gone, the home side forced a corner on the right. Paul Fitzpatrick - once on Liverpool's staff - met Halpin's corner kick and when the ball dropped, Hetherington's first-time effort flew over the top. With 33 minutes gone, Liverpool took the lead. Houghton stretched the home defence on the right-hand side of the box and he found Beardsley, whose shot rebounded clear off the goalkeeper. Barnes smashed the ball into the net from 12 yards. The Reds' travelling army of some 6,000 supporters roared their approval of the goal. Aldridge and McMahon combined well in an effort to capitalise on the lead. McMahon's centre to the far post was headed back across the goal by Aldridge, but Gorman and Jeffels cleared the danger. Whelan and McMahon dominated the game from midfield and they gave valuable service to Beardsley and Aldridge up front. Just before the interval, Nicol, employed in a more natural role on the right, sent in a cross which Aldridge almost met with an attempted diving header.

Liverpool began the second half in determined mood. Barnes sent in a high cross and Aldridge forced McKellar to scramble a save at the far post. Aldridge, McMahon and Houghton were all involved in a magnificent flowing movement before the ball was switched to the right to Nicol, whose powerful run down the wing finished with a high centre which was tipped over the bar by the Carlisle 'keeper. Burrows - making his Cup début for Liverpool - sent a short throw to Beardsley and the ball travelled on to Barnes, whose angled shot was charged down by Jeffels. When the ball broke out of the box, Whelan sent a shot high over the bar. Carlisle responded when Stephens sent Hetherington clear on the right of the box. The finish failed to test Hooper. Beardsley ended a direct run at goal with a powerful 25-yard shot which flew narrowly wide of the left-hand post. Whelan was booked for an over-enthusiastic challenge on Stephens. With 65 minutes gone, Mølby found Beardsley with an inch-perfect crossfield pass and the England player brought his international colleague Barnes into the action on the left of the box. Barnes played a simple ball to McMahon, who rifled home from six yards.

Carlisle lost heart and a back-pass by Jeffels to McKellar passed only inches wide of the left-hand upright for a Liverpool corner. The Carlisle 'keeper saved well from Aldridge, who dived to meet a cross from the right. Fyfe replaced Stephens after 72 minutes, but the home side fought a lost cause. Beardsley found McMahon on the overlap and the midfielder made progress into the box to score with a simple shot past McKellar.

The Cup-holders, Wimbledon, beat Birmingham City 1-0 away with a goal from Gibson; Bradford knocked out Tottenham at home with a first-half goal from Mitchell; Manchester United drew 0-0 at Old Trafford with Queen's Park Rangers; Millwall beat Luton Town 3-2; non-League Welling United lost 0-1 at home to Blackburn Rovers; but the sensation of the round was non-League Sutton United's 2-1 home defeat of First Division Coventry City before a crowd of 8,000.

Carlisle United: McKellar; Graham, Dalziel, Saddington, Jeffels, Fitzpatrick, Robertson (Sendall,60), Gorman, Stephens(Fyfe,72), Hetherington, Halpin.

Liverpool: Hooper; Ablett, Burrows, Nicol, Whelan, Mølby, Beardsley, Aldridge, Houghton, Barnes, McMahon.

Referee: Mr T. Holbrook (Walsall)
Attendance: 18,556

January 29, 1989

Millwall (0) 0

Liverpool (0) 2
Aldridge 57, Rush 63

IN their first-ever visit to the Den Liverpool employed three centre-backs and made their intentions clear that they had not come to lose in front of Millwall's biggest crowd of the decade. Dalglish relegated Beardsley and Houghton to the substitutes' bench and brought in defender Alex Watson to smother the long-ball heavily employed by the London side. During the opening 15 minutes it looked as though their tactics might not work as Jimmy Carter gave David Burrows a testing time. However, Millwall were guilty of losing possession on numerous occasions and Liverpool were allowed to settle into their familiar patient pattern of play. The visitors' display was highly professional and they were used to defusing volatile situations and then turning the game around in their favour.

In a game of high drama and tension, Jan Mølby excelled. His pin-point passes tested the Millwall defence on several occasions, though Liverpool lacked the killer punch in the first period, during which a flowing Millwall move ended with a Terry Hurlock cross and a brave lunge by Briley, whose challenge was immediately halted by McMahon's boot, which made contact with the Millwall captain's face. Teddy Sheringham and Tony Cascarino had little opportunity to impose themselves on the game as Liverpool crowded the man on the ball and prevented Millwall from displaying their own attacking flair, which had taken them to fourth place in the Second Division. The Lions' first shot on goal did not arrive until the 43rd minute when a fierce drive by Hurlock flew ten feet wide of the post.

During the first ten minutes of the second period, a Briley header went just over the bar and then Sheringham had a shot smothered by the agile Grobbelaar.

Liverpool were at their most dangerous when under threat, and two goals in the space of six minutes ended Millwall's dream of Wembley. A Barnes corner-kick to the near post after 57 minutes caught the Lions' defence sleeping and a powerful header from Aldridge found the back of the net. Six minutes later a magnificent flowing movement ended with a second goal. Rush turned Ian Dawes and squared the ball to Aldridge, who dummied and Barnes intelligently back-heeled to the supporting Rush, whose clinical angled shot hit the post before entering the net.

Carter had a glorious opportunity a minute later but he snatched at his chance and the ball flew straight to Grobbelaar. Liverpool sat on their two-goal lead and soaked up everything that Millwall created. The Anfield men displayed no frills in defence and their occasional swift counter-attacks looked capable of adding to their score against an increasingly-anxious Millwall. The Lions struggled to break through against a well-disciplined Liverpool side.

Millwall manager John Docherty said afterwards, "They paid us a lot of respect with their team selection, but they are the cream of English football and nobody beats them too often. We needed a little bit of luck around the box but it did not come." Kenny Dalglish added, "All tribute to the Millwall fans. They applauded us both on and off the pitch and I would never mind coming back after this reception." Jan Mølby said, "The double must still be a possibility for us - anything can happen. The good news is that Rushie and Aldo are now scoring together rather than separately and that's exactly what we've needed. There's a new feeling within the side now, a new confidence again, and I think we showed that in the way we tackled Millwall because The Den is a tough place to leave with a win. We've got to fancy our chances in the Cup with all that going for us and in the League we're going all out to catch Arsenal." Aldridge, commenting on the developing potential of his partnership with Rush said, "Partnerships take a long time to settle. But I've got a feeling we're going to get a few goals between us now. And, touch wood, we haven't lost while we've been playing together." Rush added, "It's taken a bit of time, but things are getting better now."

The other Fourth Round ties were played on the Saturday before this tie. Wimbledon beat Aston Villa 1-0 at Villa Park; Blackburn Rovers beat Sheffield Wednesday 2-1 at Hillsborough; Brentford beat Manchester City 3-1 at Griffen Park; Charlton Athletic beat non-League Kettering 2-1 at home; Grimsby and Reading drew 1-1 at Blundell Park; Hartlepool drew 1-1 at home to Bournemouth; Manchester United beat Oxford United 4-0 at Old Trafford; Nottingham Forest beat Leeds 2-0 on Trentside; Plymouth held Everton to a 1-1 draw in the West Country; Sheffield United drew 3-3 at home to Colchester; Stoke were held at home to a 3-3 draw against Barnsley, who led 3-1 at the interval; Swindon and West Ham drew 0-0 at the County Ground; Watford and Derby drew 1-1 at Vicarage Road; non-League Sutton lost 8-0 at Norwich; and Hull City beat Bradford City 2-1 away.

Millwall: Horne; Thompson, Dawes, Hurlock, Wood, McLeary, Carter, Briley, Sheringham, Cascarino, O'Callaghan.

Liverpool: Grobbelaar; Ablett, Burrows, Nicol, Whelan, Mølby, Watson, Aldridge, Rush, Barnes, McMahon.

Referee: Mr G. Courtney (Spennymoor)

Attendance: 23,615

February 18, 1989

Hull City (2) 2
Whitehurst 34, Edwards 44

Liverpool (1) 3
Barnes 15, Aldridge 52, 53

STEVE Nicol was named captain in the continued absence of Alan Hansen and the usual replacement, Ronnie Whelan. There were three changes compared with the side that beat Millwall in the previous round. Gillespie, Houghton and Beardsley replaced Watson, Whelan and Rush. Mølby operated in midfield for the Reds with Gillespie and Ablett in the centre of the back four. Hull City named the same side which beat Bradford City 2-1 in the previous round.

With only eight minutes gone Gillespie, who had been out of action with knee ligament trouble since early October, collapsed after making a tackle and was replaced by Alex Watson.

In a typical Cup-tie, both sides moved the ball about quickly and Houghton prevented Edwards from scoring with a late challenge. At the other end Barnes broke away and sent a low cross into the goalmouth which was kicked off the line.

After 15 minutes, Beardsley drifted into space on the left and centred perfectly for Barnes to direct his header wide of Hesford. Moments later Beardsley was fouled but advanced on goal before the referee's whistle pulled him back. The free-kick brought no advantage to Liverpool. Then Aldridge intercepted a careless back pass by Jobson before shooting into the side netting.

As Liverpool's domination increased, Hesford pulled off two magnificent saves. Aldridge hit a shot a yard wide of Hesford's goal from a perfect pass by Beardsley. In a rare attacking move by Hull, De Mange - formerly on the books of Liverpool - sent Edwards free before Nicol raced back to dispossess him. Jacobs then headed a chip from Beardsley off the line as Liverpool maintained their pressure. A minute later

Liverpool's over-casual approach cost them dearly. A cross by Askew eluded Ablett, who appeared to slip, and Whitehurst equalised. Liverpool's response was to go back on the offensive, and Aldridge and Nicol both headed wide.

A minute before the interval Aldridge conceded a free-kick in the middle of the field. The ball went to Edwards, who was left almost completely unmarked to put the ball past Grobbelaar.

The Reds went straight on to the attack as the second half began and Beardsley created chances for McMahon and Barnes, though both players failed to capitalise on the opportunities. With 52 minutes gone Liverpool equalised after fine work by Nicol enabled Beardsley to break free on the right and from his accurate centre Aldridge headed his 13th goal of the season.

Just one minute later Beardsley set McMahon free in the penalty area and the former Evertonian gave Aldridge the simple task of stabbing the ball home. Hull replied when Edwards broke clear towards the Liverpool goal and Watson brought him down with a clumsy tackle which earned him a booking. The irrepressible Beardsley covered every inch of the field and constantly tormented Hull with his intelligent running. Burrows, who was the most consistent Liverpool defender, required treatment for a knock in the face.

Liverpool continued to press forward and Beardsley fired in a left-foot shot from near the penalty spot which went wide of a post. Another shot went across the goalmouth from Beardsley and McMahon hit the top of the stand. The home side were presented with several opportunities due to Liverpool's defensive limitations.

John Aldridge

Hull City: Hesford; Brown, Jacobs, De Mange, Jobson, Buckley, Payton(Saville,72), Roberts, Whitehurst, Edwards, Askew.

Liverpool: Grobbelaar; Ablett, Burrows, Nicol, Gillespie (Watson,9), Mølby, Beardsley, Aldridge, Houghton, Barnes, McMahon.

Referee: Mr M.G. Peck (Kendal)

Attendance: 20,058

March 18, 1989

Liverpool (1) 4

McMahon 15, Barnes 62,
Beardsley 79, 82

Brentford (0) 0

LIVERPOOL were unchanged from the side which defeated Luton Town 5-0 in midweek, while Brentford were without defender Ratcliffe - due to an ankle injury - and winger Smillie, who failed a fitness test on his hamstring. Goalkeeper Parks was available after dislocating his thumb and Brentford brought with them 7,000 fans and 2,500 plastic inflatable bees. The visitors were in 12th place in the Third Division, while Liverpool were in fourth place in the First.

Liverpool almost took the lead in the first minute when Nicol initiated a fine move by playing a superb ball forward to McMahon, who found Beardsley on the edge of the area. Beardsley slipped the ball forward to Houghton, whose shot struck the legs of the advancing Parks and the danger was cleared. Moments later Houghton's low right-wing cross was kicked away by the 6ft 4ins Evans. A magnificent ball from Barnes set McMahon free, but Parks raced out of his goal to clear. The former Spurs' goalkeeper played the ball to Nicol, whose high cross towards Aldridge was too strong. With six minutes gone Cadette collected a pass from Sinton and fired wide from a good position. Evans cleared from Aldridge after Barnes had curled in a great cross and moments later Parks dived full length to parry a ferocious shot from Whelan.

Brentford almost went ahead after ten minutes when Grobbelaar beat out a shot from Stanislaus but he recovered

Peter Beardsley

and denied Blissett's follow up. After 15 minutes Beardsley moved on to Staunton's pass on the left before cutting inside the full back and crossing for Whelan, whose volley hit the bar. Then Beardsley's inch-perfect pass allowed Houghton to get behind the Brentford defence and as Parks rushed out, Houghton chipped the ball square over the goalkeeper to McMahon, who stooped near the far post to head his sixth goal of the season.

With 24 minutes gone, a fierce drive from Staunton hit Godfrey and looped over the crossbar for a corner. Good work by Nicol on the right wing caused panic in the Brentford defence, but Evans challenged Aldridge and eliminated the threat. Five minutes before the interval Blissett fired wide.

Two minutes into the second half, Nicol received treatment after fouling Sinton. Watson and Burrows began warming up, but Nicol resumed. Centre-back Millen caused problems for his defence when he misjudged a clearance and allowed Beardsley to run at goal. The England striker raced into the penalty area and hit a low cross, but Evans read the situation and sent the ball for a corner. With 53 minutes gone, Evans headed on a corner to Godfrey, who hooked a shot over the crossbar from 12 yards. The Bees played some good football and caused Liverpool numerous problems with their direct, fluent style. Houghton blasted inches wide on the hour. Three minutes later a fine run by Barnes followed a great dribble by Beardsley. Feeley's tackle conceded a corner. Houghton took the flag-kick, Barnes headed on at the near post and Whelan headed over the bar into the Kop.

Two minutes later Barnes collected the ball midway in the Brentford half and accelerated as he beat three players before clipping a neat left-foot shot past Parks. In the 75th minute the Bees replaced Godfrey with the experienced striker Sealy. Four minutes later Barnes crossed low from the by-line for Aldridge to scramble in a shot which Parks blocked. As the ball broke Gillespie's attempt hit the post. Within seconds Houghton found Beardsley, who embarked on a superb run which took him into the Brentford box and he placed his shot out of the reach of the goalkeeper.

Three minutes later Beardsley collected a pass from Barnes before turning sharply and hitting a fierce left-foot drive which beat Parks.

Liverpool: Grobbelaar; Ablett, Staunton, Nicol, Whelan, Gillespie, Beardsley, Aldridge, Houghton, Barnes, McMahon.

Brentford: Parks; Feeley(Bates,83), Stanislaus, Millen, Evans, Cockram, Jones, Sinton, Cadette, Blissett, Godfrey(Sealy,75).

Referee: Mr T. Holbrooke (Walsall)   **Attendance**: 42,376

April 15, 1989

Liverpool (0) 0   Nottingham Forest (0) 0

match abandoned

ALAN Hansen, who had not featured in the first team since damaging a knee against Atletico Madrid in a pre-season friendly, was not expected to be in contention for this game, even though he travelled in a squad of fifteen players. Barry Venison was due to replace the injured Gary Gillespie in a reshuffled back four, but Hansen was drafted in when Venison was hit by a virus infection overnight. Hansen's last competitive match was the FA Cup final defeat by Wimbledon at Wembley last May, but he proved his recovery in the reserves on the Tuesday before this game, having undergone two knee operations. Apart from Hansen, the League leaders lined up as expected, with striker Ian Rush back on the bench after his absence due to injury. Forest, chasing a unique Wembley treble, relied on the side that last Sunday relieved Luton of the Littlewoods Cup.

There was severe over-crowding behind the Liverpool goal at the Leppings Lane End and after just six minutes the police ordered the referee to take the teams off. At that stage several hundred fans had already clambered over the perimeter fence to escape, but others were not so fortunate. Many casualties were ferried to Sheffield's Royal Hallamshire Hospital. They were carried from the pitch on perimeter advertising boards, supported by fans desperate to assist. Forty-five minutes after the emergency began, some supporters were still being given heart massage.

Liverpool's Kenny Dalglish and Forest's Brian Clough went onto the pitch to talk to police. To make matters worse, sporadic fighting took place among rival fans as hundreds of Liverpool supporters wandered aimlessly around the pitch, shocked and bewildered. More than 50 minutes after the game was stopped, Dalglish made a public announcement appealing for calm, and for help for the emergency services. Liverpool had protested about the Hillsborough ticket allocation immediately the semi-final venue had been announced. They had fewer tickets than Nottingham Forest, despite a much higher average gate. Liverpool chief executive, Peter Robinson, said of the incident, "Apparently a gate was opened, fans got in and the area behind the goal was over-populated."

Twenty-three ambulances were at the ground and medical teams from surrounding areas were called in to help. The injured were rushed to the Royal Hallamshire and the Northern General hospitals. At 4.17pm police announced that the game had been abandoned because of "a serious incident". Fans, officials, and ambulancemen ripped down advertising hoardings to carry the injured fans from the pitch. Some fans were lifted to safety by fans in the stand above the Leppings Lane End. Television pictures showed victims being given the kiss of life and having their chests pumped. A line of policemen was stretched across the pitch to keep rival fans apart as other fans joined police, ambulancemen and officials to tend the casualties. Ambulances were driven onto the pitch and some fans stood in tears as they witnessed the harrowing scenes. Police, firemen and ambulancemen struggled to reach the injured through the chaos on the pitch. There was applause as fans sprinted across the pitch with advertising hoardings to carry the injured away.

BBC commentator Desmond Lynam, who was in the tunnel leading to the pitch, reported: "There are people in tears here. There has been no violence from the Liverpool fans. They say they got the wrong end of the ground, the gates were opened and the tickets were not inspected. They are blaming the authorities for opening the gates." One fan told BBC news: "People just walked in that gate and the police just let them walk in. There are people lying dead there on the floor. It was choc-a-bloc and as people tried to get into the front the police tried to force them back into the ground and this ground was allocated for an FA Cup Semi-Final because it could have dealt with any problems and now it hasn't."

There was doubt as to whether the competition would continue. Peter Robinson said, "My personal view is that it should be abandoned for this year in respect to the dead and injured. I must stress that is my own view and not that of my board. If the competition does continue, which I think is likely, the money taken from both the semi-final and the final should be donated to the disaster fund." Forest Chairman, Maurice Roworth said, "I believe the competition should now be called off. Whoever gets to Wembley, the final would be devalued because of the many fans who have died or been injured. It is the saddest day of my life. I thought it was a nightmare."

Liverpool postponed their match with West Ham on the Wednesday after the semi-final and also their game against Arsenal on the following Sunday. "We appreciate that life has to go on and that we will have to play again some time. But we also believe there must be a proper period of mourning, and that probably ought to last a fortnight, which would mean our first game would be against Everton at Goodison," said Peter Robinson.

Liverpool reacted to the disaster by deciding to approach the police and the licensing authorities for permission to pull down the steel barriers separating the Kop and the visitors' standing area from the pitch. Peter Robinson added, "I have thought for a long time that the introduction of seats is the only way that a crowd can be properly controlled. You can direct fans into areas of terracing but, as we have just seen, it is impossible to be certain you have the right number of people in any given space unless they are sitting down. Obviously it would cost a lot of money, but I think we should be working towards that end."

In the weeks that followed, it was announced that 95 Liverpool fans had died, and since the weeks immediately following the tragedy, Tony Bland became the 96th victim when his life-support machine was switched off.

Everton: Southall, McDonald, Van den Hauwe, Ratcliffe, Watson, Bracewell, Nevin, Steven, Sharp, Cottee, Sheedy.

Norwich City: Gunn; Culverhouse, Bowen, Butterworth, Linighan, Townsend, Gordon, Allen, Rosario, Crook, Putney.

Referee: Mr G. Courtney (Spennymoor)

Attendance: 46,533

Goal: Nevin, 26

In the First Division, Arsenal beat Newcastle United 1-0 at Highbury with a Brian Marwood goal after 69 minutes to stay top, three points clear of Liverpool, who had a game in hand.

Arsenal	33	19	9	5	62	32	66
Liverpool	32	18	9	5	55	24	63

Kenny Dalglish *is comforted by spectators at Hillsborough*

Liverpool: Grobbelaar; Ablett, Staunton, Nicol, Whelan, Hansen, Beardsley, Aldridge, Houghton, Barnes, McMahon.

Nottingham Forest: Sutton; Laws, Pearce, Walker, Wilson, Hodge, Gaynor, Webb, Clough, Chapman, Parker.

Referee: Mr R. Lewis (Great Bookham)

Attendance: 53,000

May 7, 1989

Liverpool (1) 3
Aldridge 3, 58,
Laws (og) 72

Nottingham Forest (1) 1
Webb 33

BOTH Forest and Liverpool announced the same teams which had begun the fateful Hillsborough contest. Since that abandoned game, Forest had beaten Middlesborough 4-3 away in the Barclays League; Everton 4-3 at Wembley in the final of the Simod Cup; and Millwall 4-1 at home in the Barclays League. Liverpool did not play again until May 3rd, when they drew 0-0 at Goodison Park in the League. Forest were going for a unique treble, having won both the Littlewoods and Simod cups.

On a day of glorious sunshine, John Aldridge - the former Kopite now playing for his beloved Reds - broke free of his depression to hit two goals. His first, after John Barnes had seen a fierce shot parried high into the air by goalkeeper Steve Sutton, brought a release to the emotional chains around the Liverpool team. After 33 minutes Grobbelaar dived late to allow a tame shot from Webb to trickle over the line for an equaliser.

In the second period Forest were lethargic and offered little resistance to a Liverpool side which appeared destined for a Wembley appearance. With 58 minutes gone, Barnes broke down the right. Houghton had the time to hook over a cross and Aldridge met it almost unchallenged to head home. Defender Brian Laws put through his own goal after 72 minutes, and the match was Liverpool's. Lee Chapman hit a through ball for the speedy Des Walker to run onto in the 78th minute, but it was not handled with the conviction of a man who truly believed the game was there to be saved. With a wide open goal, Walker prodded the ball clear.

Aldridge said after the game, "We did it for the fans who've died at Hillsborough. Under the circumstances it's a bit sad the way we've got to Wembley. But we've done it for the fans who died, their families and for the magnificent supporters here today. That was in our minds when we went out - it was the only way to motivate ourselves for this game - trying to do it for them. Now it will be a magnificent occasion to play Everton in the final."

Manager Kenny Dalglish added: "If we can ease the burden of the bereaved we will be happier for them than for ourselves today. I don't think you could have written it better when you consider we'll be playing Everton at Wembley.

The lads wanted to get through this one as a mark of respect for the victims and their families and only secondly for themselves. And it's very fitting that we are playing Everton. We are happy about it, if that's the right word in these circumstances. There was only one team that was going to win today. Only one team wanted to win as far as I was concerned - we wanted it more than they did."

Liverpool: Grobbelaar; Ablett, Staunton, Nicol, Whelan, Hansen, Beardsley, Aldridge, Houghton, Barnes, McMahon.

Nottingham Forest: Sutton; Laws, Pearce, Walker, Wilson, Hodge, Gaynor(Starbuck,60), Webb, Clough, Chapman, Parker(Glover,82).

Referee: Mr R. Lewis (Great Bookham)

Attendance: 38,000 (at Old Trafford)

John Aldridge, scored after just three minutes to put Liverpool ahead, and added a second goal with a header after 58 minutes from a Houghton cross

LIVERPOOL WIN MERSEYSIDE FINAL

RUSH HITS WINNING GOAL

McCALL DOUBLE STRIKE

Everton (0) 2
McCall 90, 102

Liverpool (1) 3 aet
Aldridge 4, Rush 95, 104

WILSON was preferred to Clarke on the Everton bench, while Liverpool could find no place for Gary Gillespie. The crowd was put in good humour when Liverpool group The Spinners took centre stage before the kick-off, when Gerry Marsden gave an emotional rendition of You'll Never Walk Alone and Abide With Me. A minute's silence was observed after the teams took to the field in memory of the 95 Liverpool supporters who died five weeks previously. Everton wore their new kit for the first time. The Blues kicked off in bright sunshine attacking the tunnel end of the stadium where the Liverpool fans were massed. Everton won the first corner of the match after 83 seconds when Ablett challenged Cottee in the area. Sheedy bent his kick in from the right and Nicol's misdirected header caused problems for the Liverpool defence. Steve McMahon volleyed off the line to clear the danger. With just four minutes gone, an excellent through-pass from the Scot, Nicol, sent McMahon racing into Everton territory. The England midfielder crossed low from the right and picked out Aldridge, whose first-time effort sent the ball into the top left-hand corner of the Everton goal.

Stung into retaliation, Everton began to challenge heavily for the ball and after ten minutes a late challenge by Sharp on Staunton caused the young defender to receive treatment from Roy Evans just inside his own half. Moments later a good move down the right involving Nevin and Cottee ended with McDonald crossing the ball from the touchline for Sharp to glance on in the area, but Nicol defended well and calmly nodded the ball back to Grobbelaar.

Everton enjoyed more possession and after 16 minutes Sheedy played a left wing corner to Nevin, who was on the angle of the penalty box. The Scot drove a fierce shot towards the goal, only to see the ball swerve narrowly wide of Grobbelaar's far post. Two minutes later, Whelan sent Barnes away down the left wing and his dangerous centre passed over the head of Ratcliffe, where Aldridge was in position. The Liverpool striker's flying header flashed inches wide of the goal.

Good chance

For a brief spell Liverpool played the ball around neatly in the Everton half with time and space and they created a good chance when a cross from Houghton on the right eluded everyone in the area except Barnes, whose header at the far post was directed straight at Southall.

With 27 minutes gone, good combination by Liverpool gave Whelan the chance to slip a glorious ball for Barnes to run onto. The flying winger sped past McDonald and hit a low centre across goal which eluded everyone. Everton relied on Sharp to pressure the Liverpool defence with his height. He rose unchallenged in the box to meet a Van den Hauwe cross, but was unable to direct his powerful header on target. An intelligent pass from Whelan gave Aldridge a shooting opportunity but the Eire international shot over the bar from close range.

Powerful

After 33 minutes, Barnes went on a powerful run which took him into the heart of the Everton half only to be upended by Ratcliffe 25 yards from goal. The winger took the free-kick himself, curling the ball to the left of Southall's goal. A high wayward back-pass from

Ian Rush *celebrates the winning goal against Everton,*
his second in the match

McDonald was seized upon by Aldridge, but Southall timed his advance perfectly and gathered the ball on the edge of his area as Aldridge challenged.

Bicycle kick

Sharp headed forward a free-kick and Watson attempted a bicycle kick in the Reds' box, but connected with Ablett's face. The defender continued after treatment. Seven minutes before the interval, Houghton and Nicol worked a short corner together down the right and after the Everton defence had only partially cleared the danger, Nicol drove a shot wide from 18 yards. Everton relied on Sharp too much, without varying their options. Nevin did not receive much of the ball, despite his reputation for trickery.

Failed

Grobbelaar failed to cut out McDonald's cross-field pass as Sharp went up to challenge. The ball broke free with the Liverpool goalkeeper out of his goal and Sharp passed to Sheedy, whose powerful drive cannoned off Hansen and went out of play.

Determined

The Reds began the second half determined to increase their lead. After only two minutes Barnes forced McDonald into a foul near the Everton goal-line. The winger's free-kick was headed out by Van den Hauwe, only for Houghton to play the ball back in for Beardsley, who was flagged offside.

Another cross from Barnes from the left was aimed at Aldridge's head, but he was put off by a good challenge from Ratcliffe and Southall gathered with ease. Five minutes into the second half, Southall saved a Beardsley shot with his legs after the Liverpool striker had capitalised on a mistake by Bracewell and sprinted clear.

Dispossessed

Some fine passing from Everton ended when Steven broke forward from the centre of midfield and looked as if he would have a clear run on goal before being dispossessed with a great tackle from Staunton.

Skill

After 56 minutes Barnes used his strength, pace and skill to burst over the halfway line and trick his way through the Everton defence before unleashing a shot past Southall's left post from 18 yards. With Liverpool controlling the midfield, McCall was brought on for Bracewell after 58 minutes. The former Bradford skipper had been on the field only for a few seconds when his pass found Sharp in the Liverpool half. The Scot knocked the ball first time into the path of Cottee, who took the ball in his stride before being felled by Hansen 20 yards from goal. Sheedy drove the free-kick into the wall.

Intercepted

After 61 minutes, Staunton saw his back-pass to Grobbelaar intercepted by Ablett, who was unaware that his goalkeeper was behind him and as Steven pounced on the loose ball, he was fouled by Ablett. Sheedy placed the free-kick into the heart of the

Liverpool box and Bruce Grobbelaar punched clear. Sharp headed the ball on for Cottee in the box as Everton enjoyed a spell of enormous pressure, but Hansen remained indefatigable and put in a vital tackle. At the other end Ratcliffe's timely challenge on Houghton cleared a threat.

Dive

Seconds later Beardsley weaved his way through the Everton defence and into the box before being denied with a firm challenge from Watson. Three minutes later a crossfield ball by Houghton picked out Barnes on the left. His left-foot drive was deflected by McDonald and Southall was forced to dive low to his right to palm the ball away for a corner. A firmly-struck shot by Steven was blocked by Ablett.

Substituted

With 72 minutes gone, Aldridge was substituted by Rush, a player needing just one goal to create a new scoring record in Merseyside derbies. Five minutes later, Everton boss Colin Harvey took off Sheedy and replaced him with Wilson, who had scored Everton's winning goal at Derby in an impressive display five days before the final.

Persistence

Everton continued to press forward and in the dying seconds of the game their persistence brought its own rewards when Nevin slipped the ball to Watson in the Liverpool area. The low shot from the centre-half was palmed out by Grobbelaar and McCall met the ball first, and drove the

ball firmly into the net. Liverpool replaced Staunton with Venison at the start of extra-time. Barry Venison operated at right back and Nicol switched to the left in a reshuffle of the back four. Everton, encouraged by their goal, began extra-time brightly and Cottee fired in a low shot which forced Grobbelaar to save. At the other end, Houghton drove straight at Southall.

History

Just four minutes into extra-time, Rush collected the ball from Nicol in the box, swivelled and crashed home a magnificent goal to create derby history and put Liverpool into the lead again. It was Rush's 20th derby goal, breaking the record held by the legendary Dixie Dean of Everton.

Equality

Three minutes before the end of the first period, McCall chested down Hansen's headed clearance to volley from the edge of the box to restore equality. Play flowed from end to end, and two minutes later Barnes crossed from the left and Rush stooped low to glance a header past Southall for Liverpool's third goal.

Saved

Five minutes into the second period of extra-time, a shot from Rush was deflected by Ratcliffe. The ball broke for Houghton, whose shot was saved by the legs of Southall. Three minutes later Southall raced off his line to deny Rush once again with the use of his legs. After 117 minutes Barnes cut in from the left and Southall dived to palm the ball away seconds before turning a Beardsley drive round the right-hand post.

Crossbar

In the final minute of an enthralling match, Steven played a free-kick square to McDonald, whose shot from 20-yards flew narrowly over the crossbar.

After the game Liverpool manager Kenny Dalglish said, "To our credit, our lads came back after Everton had equalised in injury-time. Usually when a team equalises near the end of 90 minutes, as they did, it gives them an incentive to go forward into extra-time with a lot more confidence and enthusiasm. But that's a tribute to these lads.

They've been absolutely magnificent.

Contribution

There were 13 used and there were four or five sitting on the bench who have made a contribution throughout the Cup.

Although they didn't get the medals they have been very, very good to us. The game was a credit to football. I thought both teams showed a tremendous amount of character and will to win. Both worked very hard. Perhaps one or two players were running from memory. I didn't think we'd blown it when they equalised late. We've done that ourselves to teams in the past. We just had to pick ourselves up and carry on as best we could.

Hillsborough

Obviously we'd like to think this win can help people in some way. That's probably why it makes it a little better than some of the other wins. It's better than the last one because of Hillsborough."

Everton manager Colin Harvey said: "I honestly thought we were going to win it after equalising as late as we did. It gave us the impetus to do it, and though they had a bit more possession than us, I thought we looked more dangerous when we built attacks.

Disappointed

I'm disappointed, but I thought we worked hard and got something out of the game. I was pleased with us as a team. It was a difficult occasion for the players. They were under a lot of pressure from the media and from the occasion itself, but they rose to it and added to a brilliant final.

Capable

Stuart McCall did things that I knew he's always been capable of, but that he hasn't been doing generally this season. Neville Southall is disappointed because he's let a couple of goals in which he thought he should have stopped. I thought they were good goals, but that's him. I think it was always going to be a good game.

Even though people invaded the pitch it wasn't a problem as such. They got off quickly enough and in that way they behaved themselves.

We took some good things out of the game and we've got to take them into next season. I told the players afterwards that we've done well in the Cup, but our League form has been poor. I told them to have a good think about themselves over the summer and let's start again next season."

Dixie

Ian Rush said: "I think there was a chance I wasn't going to be sub, although I half expected to be. It's a great honour for me to have

Ronnie Whelan, in his capacity as captain, holds aloft the FA Cup for Liverpool

beaten Dixie Dean's record. He is a legend and it means a lot to me. I was delighted to have scored twice. It makes up for quite a few things.

I have struggled with injury and illness so it is good to come back with goals. People will say it was a perfect end for me, but it was a perfect end for Liverpool."

Unbelievable

Steve Nicol - recently named as Footballer of the Year - said: "I think throughout the game we always felt we had the edge. All we needed to do was step up a gear. It's been an unbelievable season for me but it's not finished yet - hopefully. If we can get the championship it will be a year to remember."

Fated

Kevin Ratcliffe said: "Liverpool were fated to win the Cup."

Alan Hansen: "It was a great game, played by two good sides. John Aldridge and Ian Rush scored the goals, but really it's about 15 or 16 players.

Spoiled

The crowd coming on the pitch spoiled the occasion for me - it took the edge off our lap of honour."

Three days after the final, Liverpool beat West Ham 5-1 at Anfield to set up a championship decider against leaders Arsenal at Anfield three days after that.

Dramatic

In a dramatic game, in which Liverpool needed only a draw or a defeat by a single goal, the Gunners robbed Liverpool of a second double when they won 2-0. In an emotional televised encounter, the Reds played tentatively during the first period, giving nothing away, and playing it tight.

Goals

Gradually in the second half, Arsenal tightened their grip on the game, and came out of their defensive shell. The Gunners' goals came from Alan Smith after 52 minutes when he moved on to a Winterburn free-kick, and Michael Thomas in the last minute, who scored after a perfect pass from Smith. Liverpool would have secured the championship with a single-goal defeat, but that last-gasp winner from Thomas denied them.

Reception

On returning to the city, both teams were given a tremendous welcome by the thousands of fans who turned out to see the open top buses as they weaved their way through the crowded streets.

Ian Rush and *John Aldridge* show off the FA Cup to the Liverpool fans

Everton: Southall; McDonald, Van Den Hauwe, Ratcliffe, Watson, Bracewell(McCall,58), Nevin, Steven, Sharp, Cottee, Sheedy(Wilson,77).

Liverpool: Grobbelaar; Ablett, Staunton(Venison,91), Nicol, Whelan, Hansen, Beardsley, Aldridge(Rush,72), Houghton, Barnes, McMahon.

Referee: Mr J.B. Worrall (Warrington)

Linesmen: Mr M.G. Peck (Kendal); Mr A.W. Smith (Rubery, Birmingham)

Reserve Linesman: Mr J. Winter (Middlesbrough)

Attendance: 82,800 (at Wembley)

January 6, 1990

Swansea City (0) 0   Liverpool (0) 0

LIVERPOOL travelled to Swansea to play the Third Division side, currently lying in mid-table. Lee Bracey, the young Londoner, had been axed earlier in the season after conceding 23 goals in his opening ten games, and had Swansea tempted Chelsea to part with Roger Freestone, the youngster might not have had the opportunity to turn in a magnificent performance which denied Liverpool on numerous occasions. The 21-year-old former West Ham product - who was signed by manager Terry Yorath on a free transfer - held Liverpool at bay almost single-handedly.

The visitors struggled to cope with the heavy conditions in the first period, and Swansea - fired up by veteran Alan Curtis, who created most of Swansea's attacking moves on a clinging, rain-saturated pitch - enjoyed greater possession in the first half. It was not until the 37th minute that Rush had a shot on goal, and Bracey stopped it. Rush's second attempt just before the interval was superbly saved by the goalkeeper.

In the second half, Liverpool increased their pressure and Bracey's performance matched Liverpool's endeavour. He finger-tipped a snap shot from Steve Nicol over the bar before saving bravely from Barnes. Eleven minutes later he dived at full stretch after Beardsley had been put menacingly in the clear and within a minute he saved well from McMahon after the midfielder had combined well with Barnes. The home side were reduced to sporadic raids, and after 76 minutes Keith Walker hit a shot on the turn and his effort flew inches over the bar.

Curtis said after the game: "I could not help but feel that old tingling excitement when we arrived back in town from our Aberystwyth training headquarters 24 hours before the match. The crowds were talking football in the street outside; there was a buzz and a tremendous air of expectation. Throughout the game our supporters were tremendous. It was marvellous to see the ground packed again and I don't think we let them down."

On the Sunday, Manchester United beat Nottingham Forest 1-0 at the City Ground. Crystal Palace beat Portsmouth 2-1 after being a goal behind at the interval, and scoring the winner with a penalty in the 89th minute.

F.A. CUP - THIRD ROUND
(Saturday, January 6, 1990)

Birmingham	1,0	Oldham Athletic	1,1
Blackburn Rovers	2,1	Aston Villa	2,3
Blackpool	1	Burnley	0
Brighton & Hove A.	4	Luton Town	1
Bristol City	2	Swindon Town	1
Cambridge United	0,3	Darlington	0,1
Cardiff City	0,0	Queen's Park Rangers	0,2
Chelsea	1,2	Crewe Alexandra	1,0
Crystal Palace	2	Portsmouth	1
Exeter City	1,0	Norwich City	1,2
Hereford	2	Walsall Town	1
Huddersfield Town	3	Grimsby Town	1
Hull City	0	Newcastle United	1
Leeds United	0	Ipswich Town	1
Leicester City	1	Barnsley	2
Manchester City	0,1	Millwall	0,1
Middlesbrough	0,1	Everton	0,1
Northampton Town	1	Coventry City	0
Plymouth Argyle	0	Oxford United	1
Reading	2	Sunderland	1
Rochdale	1	Whitley Bay	0
Sheffield United	2	Bournemouth	0
Stoke City	0	Arsenal	1
Torquay United	1	West Ham United	0
Tottenham Hotspur	1	Southampton	3
Watford	2	Wigan Athletic	0
West Bromwich A.	2	Wimbledon	0
Wolverhampton W.	1	Sheffield Wednesday	2

Second Replays

Millwall	3	Manchester City	1
Everton	1	Middlesbrough	0

Swansea City: Bracey; Trick, Coleman, Melville, Walker, Thornber, Harris, Curtis, Hughes, Chalmers, Legg.

Liverpool: Grobbelaar; Hysén, Venison, Nicol, Whelan, Hansen, Beardsley, Staunton, Rush, Barnes, McMahon.

Referee: Mr A. Gunn (South Chailey)

Attendance: 16,098

January 9, 1990

Liverpool (3) 8

Barnes 22, 43, Whelan 40,
Rush 53, 77, 83, Beardsley 54,
Nicol 86

Swansea City (0) 0

CUP-HOLDERS Liverpool registered their biggest win in the competition as a League side with this 8-0 rout of Swansea. Lee Bracey, the star of the first game, saved early on from Nicol and caught a dangerous Barnes cross and suggested that he would be a barrier once again. The Swans kept their hosts at bay for 22 minutes before the floodgates opened.

Steve Staunton evaded the challenges of Alan Curtis and Des Trick and sent in a cross which Barnes turned into goal. The Reds kept their options open as Barnes and Nicol regularly changed flanks, and Whelan added a second goal following Beardsley's corner. Two minutes from the interval a magnificent move involving Beardsley released McMahon, whose cross was put into the net by Barnes, who hit his 14th goal of the season.

The home side maintained their pressure after the interval and added two further goals in quick succession. Rush got the final touch after Glenn Hysén headed on Staunton's right-wing corner, and within a minute Beardsley beat Bracey again following a spectacular solo run after Hysén's clearance had put him through. At this point four Swansea fans ran onto the pitch carrying a Welsh flag before being taken away by stewards without the game being halted. After 77 minutes Rush clipped the ball low and accurately past Bracey for Liverpool's sixth goal. The Swans rarely threatened Grobbelaar, but he was beaten when a Swansea fan ran onto the pitch and fired into the net from close range at the Anfield Road end.

Skipper Andrew Melville - a target of Liverpool transfer speculation - drove his team forward and refused to be beaten. John Hughes hit the post with a fierce shot in a breakaway after going past Hysén. Rush headed his hat-trick after an inch-perfect cross from Nicol. Four minutes from time Nicol chipped the goalkeeper to score the eighth goal. The score would have been even greater but for Bracey saving from Nicol, Beardsley and Rush in the final moments of an historic game.

After the game Bracey said: "I've got a bad case of backache after that. I just wanted to keep it below double figures. Kenny Dalglish had said a few things to put the frighteners on me. But he needn't have bothered ... I was frightened to death anyway playing in front of that crowd."

Dalglish added: "The goalkeeper made some good saves in the previous game and he didn't do badly tonight. You couldn't blame him for any of the goals but eight have gone past him." Ian Rush commented: "What really finished Swansea was the running of Steve McMahon. They just didn't know how to cope with that. For the first twenty minutes we were guilty of just standing around but once they tired that was it."

***Ian Rush**, who hit a hat-trick in the rout of Swansea City*

Liverpool: Grobbelaar; Hysén, Venison, Nicol, Whelan, Hansen, Beardsley, Staunton, Rush, Barnes, McMahon.

Swansea City: Bracey; Trick(Hutchison,72), Coleman, Melville, Walker, Thornber, Harris, Curtis (James,46), Hughes, Chalmers, Legg.

Referee: Mr A. Gunn (South Chailey)

Attendance: 29,194

January 28, 1990

Norwich City (0) 0

Liverpool (0) 0

NORWICH were in ninth position and Liverpool were top of the First Division as this game took place. Irish singer Sinéad O'Connor was top of the UK 45 charts with *Nothing Compares 2 U*. International managers Bobby Robson and Andy Roxburgh were in attendance. Unchanged Liverpool settled down quickly and Staunton fired narrowly wide from an angle and Bryan Gunn saved a Rush header after Nicol flicked on Beardsley's corner. McMahon and Whelan controlled the midfield area, while rare Norwich attacks were competently dealt with by the twin centre-backs, Hansen and Hysén. The home side went close to scoring after 24 minutes when Glenn Hysén kicked off the line a Dale Gordon shot. After 34 minutes, from their first corner, Robert Rosario headed against the top of the crossbar. The first half lacked genuine goalscoring opportunities.

The pace of the game increased greatly in the second half. Beardsley released Rush, took a return pass, and shot narrowly wide after 56 minutes. Fleck turned Hysén inside-out but shot wide, and, on the hour Dale Gordon fired over the top before breaking free on the left. His cross was deflected towards the near post by Whelan, and the wrong-footed Grobbelaar changed direction to pull off a magnificent save. In typical cup-tie fashion, the play moved swiftly from end to end, and Beardsley fired weakly at Gunn after seizing upon an error by Andy Linighan in the Norwich penalty area. Good work by Rosario brought Townsend into the game, and the midfielder forced a good save from Grobbelaar, who dived low and to his left.

With nine minutes remaining Beardsley left Linighan behind with a swift turn before sending in a low drive which Gunn held comfortably. Two minutes from time, a shot from Gordon trickled across the face of the goal with Rosario unable to supply the finishing touch. In the dying seconds Barnes broke free from the attention of Ian Culverhouse and produced a magnificent chip which brought an excellent save from Gunn.

Norwich City: Gunn; Culverhouse, Bowen, Butterworth, Linighan, Townsend, Gordon, Fleck, Rosario, Crook, Phillips.

Liverpool: Grobbelaar; Hysén, Venison, Nicol, Whelan, Hansen, Beardsley, Staunton, Rush, Barnes, McMahon.

Referee: Mr K.S. Hackett (Sheffield)

Attendance: 23,152

F.A. CUP
FOURTH ROUND

Saturday 27 January, 1990

Arsenal	0	Queen's Park Rangers	0
Aston Villa	6	Port Vale	0
Barnsley	2	Ipswich Town	0
Blackpool	1	Torquay United	0
Bristol City	3	Chelsea	1
Crystal Palace	4	Huddersfield Town	0
Millwall	1	Cambridge United	1
Oldham Athletic	2	Brighton & Hove A.	1
Reading	3	Newcastle United	3
Rochdale	3	Northampton Town	0
Sheffield United	1	Watford	1
Southampton	1	Oxford United	0
West Bromwich A.	1	Charlton Athletic	0

Sunday 28 January, 1990

Hereford United	0	Manchester United	1
Sheffield Wednesday	1	Everton	2

Replays

Monday 29 January, 1990

Cambridge United	1	Millwall	0
Watford	1	Sheffield United	2

Tuesday 30 January, 1990

Newcastle United	4	Reading	1
Queen's Park Rangers	2	Arsenal	0

January 31, 1990

Liverpool (1) 3

Nicol 17,   Barnes 56,
Beardsley (pen) 64

Norwich City (1) 1

Fleck 20

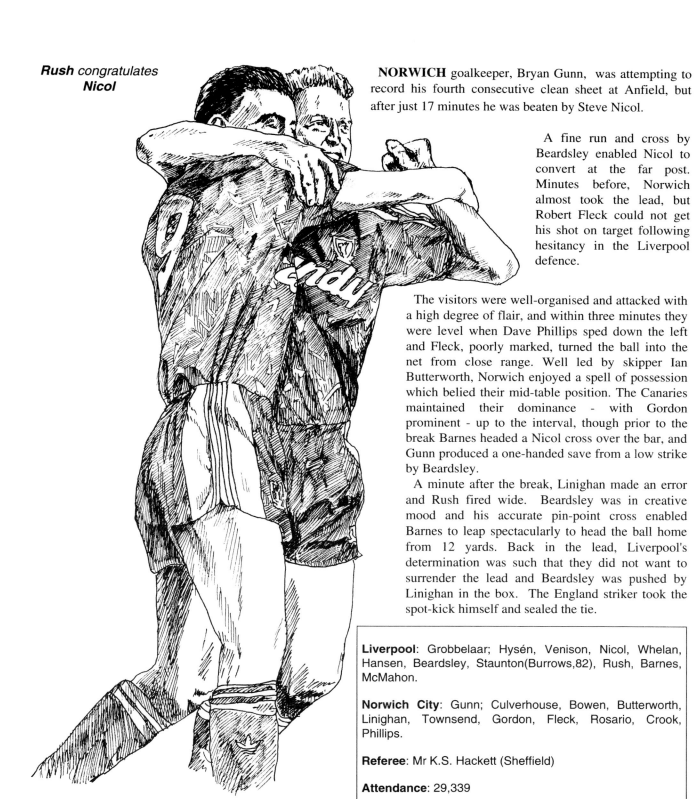

Rush** congratulates* ***Nicol

NORWICH goalkeeper, Bryan Gunn, was attempting to record his fourth consecutive clean sheet at Anfield, but after just 17 minutes he was beaten by Steve Nicol.

A fine run and cross by Beardsley enabled Nicol to convert at the far post. Minutes before, Norwich almost took the lead, but Robert Fleck could not get his shot on target following hesitancy in the Liverpool defence.

The visitors were well-organised and attacked with a high degree of flair, and within three minutes they were level when Dave Phillips sped down the left and Fleck, poorly marked, turned the ball into the net from close range. Well led by skipper Ian Butterworth, Norwich enjoyed a spell of possession which belied their mid-table position. The Canaries maintained their dominance - with Gordon prominent - up to the interval, though prior to the break Barnes headed a Nicol cross over the bar, and Gunn produced a one-handed save from a low strike by Beardsley.

A minute after the break, Linighan made an error and Rush fired wide. Beardsley was in creative mood and his accurate pin-point cross enabled Barnes to leap spectacularly to head the ball home from 12 yards. Back in the lead, Liverpool's determination was such that they did not want to surrender the lead and Beardsley was pushed by Linighan in the box. The England striker took the spot-kick himself and sealed the tie.

Liverpool: Grobbelaar; Hysén, Venison, Nicol, Whelan, Hansen, Beardsley, Staunton(Burrows,82), Rush, Barnes, McMahon.

Norwich City: Gunn; Culverhouse, Bowen, Butterworth, Linighan, Townsend, Gordon, Fleck, Rosario, Crook, Phillips.

Referee: Mr K.S. Hackett (Sheffield)

Attendance: 29,339

February 17, 1990

Liverpool (1) 3
*Rush 39, Beardsley 64,
Nicol 77*

Southampton (0) 0

KENNY Dalglish kept faith with the side which drew at Norwich, but Southampton manager Chris Nicholl was forced to make two significant changes. Central defender Neil Ruddock, who scored in the previous round against Oxford United, was absent through suspension, and his place was taken by Kevin Moore. Jimmy Case - formerly of Liverpool - and Paul Rideout were available after injuries, but Matthew Le Tissier was a late omission with an ankle injury, Ray Wallace taking his place.

Liverpool kicked off attacking the Kop and they were soon on the offensive with Barnes playing a square pass infield for McMahon, whose dipping shot flew over the bar from a central position just outside the box. Nicol, Beardsley and Rush combined well on the right before Case made a timely interception. Whelan sent Beardsley away down the right, and the striker cut into the box before losing out to Russell Osman. Nicol sent in a deep cross from the right and a header from Barnes passed over the bar as Liverpool maintained the edge over their opponents, lying in the middle of the table.

After 19 minutes the Saints' skipper, Case, lobbed the ball into the area and Rod Wallace was presented with a fine opportunity from ten yards, but he was unable to connect and Grobbelaar safely collected. Barnes twisted his way past two defenders before hitting a cross which was headed clear by Moore. Moments later, Barnes took a through ball from Burrows on the angle of the area and only a well-timed tackle by Ray Wallace denied the England winger.

As Liverpool continued to dominate, Venison played a fine ball in behind the Southampton defence which Beardsley collected on the right hand side of the box before slipping a short pass back into the path of Nicol, whose first-time cross was cleared by Osman. The ball fell to Burrows, who elected to shoot from long range and the ball travelled well wide of the target.

Liverpool's strength lay on the wings, and McMahon and Beardsley combined effectively to provide Nicol, on the right, with a genuine chance which he hammered across the face of the goal without a Liverpool player being able to find a touch. With 36 minutes gone, Liverpool gained a corner on the right. Nicol and Beardsley combined to send the ball in and the Southampton defence was troubled before a side-foot shot by Whelan was saved by Flowers, who used his legs.

Following another corner on the right, Liverpool took the lead. Nicol found Beardsley, who centred into the area where Whelan attempted to shoot. The ball worked its way to Rush, who smashed it into the back of the net from eight yards. The visitors finished the half on the offensive, but Liverpool remained in control.

Rod Wallace burst into attack as the second half got underway, but he was brought down by Whelan as he crossed the halfway line in the middle of the park. The free-kick was taken quickly, and Burrows lofted the ball clear as it came into the area. Rod Wallace took the corner kick on the right, and Cockerill's shot was blocked by Hysén in front of the Kop goal. McMahon and Rush combined to present Beardsley with an opportunity, but he shot high over the bar. Nicol moved determinedly down the right before finding Rush and Horne headed clear the Welshman's centre. Hysén dispossessed Rod Wallace with a well-timed tackle just outside the box. When Southampton gained a free-kick 30 yards out, the ball was slipped to Osman, whose powerful shot took a deflection before Grobbelaar gathered safely. A moment of controversy followed when Whelan played a magnificent ball over the top of the visiting defence. Moore was forced to handle to prevent Rush from breaking clear. The inevitable free-kick and booking did not follow as the referee played the advantage, but Nicol fired wide with a shot from just outside the box. The referee played the advantage again when Osman appeared to foul Rush just inside the visitors' half. Barnes broke free down the left but he failed to find the target after cutting inside.

McMahon received treatment from Roy Evans after limping badly. He remained on the field and was instrumental in creating the opening from which Beardsley increased Liverpool's lead. The diminutive England striker chipped the ball over Flowers from 10 yards.

After 66 minutes Barnes limped off with a groin injury and was replaced by Eire international Ray Houghton after a lengthy absence from the first team. The Saints responded minutes later with a double substitution, pulling off Ray Wallace and Alan Shearer, and replacing them with Sammy Lee - formerly of Anfield - and Neil Maddison.

With 77 minutes gone, Nicol lobbed Flowers to seal victory.

Liverpool: Grobbelaar; Hysén, Venison, Nicol, Whelan, Hansen, Beardsley, Burrows, Rush, Barnes (Houghton,66), McMahon.

Southampton: Flowers; Horne, Benali, Case, Moore, Osman, Ray Wallace(Lee,73), Cockerill, Rideout, Shearer(Maddison,73), Rod Wallace.

Referee: Mr N. Midgley (Bolton)

Attendance: 35,961

March 11, 1990

Queen's Park Rangers (1) 2

Wilkins 29, Barker 82

Liverpool (0) 2

Barnes 55, Rush 80

KENNY Dalglish restored Glenn Hysén to the side in place of Gary Gillespie, and Ray Houghton began his first game since 1989. The home side retained the side which beat Blackpool in a second replay. Liverpool opened in confident mood, playing in front of a television audience once again. Barnes and Rush both went close in the first ten minutes, but despite Liverpool's territorial advantage, Ray Wilkins and Simon Barker kept a grip on the game and dictated the home side's pattern of play. Colin Clarke directed two headers wide of the Liverpool goal before Wilkins put the Londoners ahead. Grobbelaar failed to deal with Barker's cross and the ball fell to the feet of Wilkins, who drove the ball high into the unguarded net. A collision with Clarke caused the referee to limp off and he handed the whistle to one of the linesmen, Mr Lynch.

With 53 minutes gone, Dalglish substituted Venison with Gillespie, who took up the right-back position, while Barnes moved into Beardsley's role up front. Two minutes later Liverpool equalised through John Barnes, who curled a tremendous free-kick over the Rangers' four-man wall and past Seaman from 25 yards.

Rangers' fluency and determination temporarily deserted them, and with Barnes swapping places with Beardsley, Rush was given more room in which to manoeuvre. Rush almost found the net after Nicol had crossed from the left, but Danny Maddix blocked the shot. Ten minutes from the end, Gillespie ventured upfield after collecting a ball from Houghton. Gillespie held up play sufficiently for Rush to shout for the pass, and, once delivered, the striker unleashed a powerful left-foot drive from 18 yards which beat Seaman. The Reds ought to have won the game, but Barker's determination took him through several tackles and he powered home an equalising goal between the crossbar and Grobbelaar's near post.

Ray Wilkins

THE INDEPENDENT

~~~~~~~~~

Capriati, 13 is youngest finalist

JENNIFER CAPRIATI made tennis history in Boca Raton, Florida, yesterday as the youngest finalist in a professional tournament, 18 days before her 14th birthday. The American broke the record of her opponent in the final, Gabriela Sabatini (14 years and 11 months).

Sabatini, the top seed and world No. 3, proceeded to put youth in its place by defeating her 6-4, 7-5 in a match that lasted 95 minutes.

In football, Simon Barker earned Queen's Park Rangers a replay seven minutes from the end of their FA Cup quarter-final tie against Liverpool at Loftus Road yesterday. He scored the equaliser in the 2-2 draw. The sides meet again at Anfield on Wednesday, with the winners playing Crystal Palace in the semi-finals.

In the other semi-final, Manchester United, who defeated Sheffield United through a Brian McClair goal at Bramall Lane yesterday, face the winners of Wednesday's Aston Villa-Oldham Athletic tie.

Ayrton Senna, driving a McLaren, won the US Grand Prix, the first of the season, from Jean Alesi in a Tyrell and Thierry Boutsen in a Williams.

Queen's Park Rangers: Seaman; Bardsley, Sansom, Parker, McDonald, Maddix, Wilkins, Barker, Clarke, Wegerle(Falco,78), Sinton.

Liverpool: Grobbelaar; Hysén, Venison(Gillespie,53), Nicol, Whelan, Hansen, Beardsley(Staunton,73), Houghton, Rush, Barnes, McMahon.

Referee: Mr B. Hill (Kettering) sub: Mr K. Lynch (Lincoln, 29 minutes)

Attendance: 21,057

March 14, 1990

Liverpool (1) 1   Queen's Park Rangers (0) 0
Beardsley 4

LIVERPOOL'S midfield lacked determination and subtlety against a strong-tackling and dangerous Rangers side. Ronnie Whelan and Steve McMahon conceded second best to veteran Ray Wilkins and Simon Barker and Liverpool's greater possession lacked potency.

With only four minutes gone, Peter Beardsley scored a magnificent goal from Ray Houghton's inch-perfect inside pass. Venison's long throw was transferred through the defence by Houghton for Beardsley, who scored from 10 yards. He had scored in every round of the Cup this season. After five minutes, Rush - making his 400th Liverpool appearance - was superbly placed to score from a Barnes cross but the ball was deflected over the bar by a defender. A slight deflection from Hysén prevented Colin Clarke from equalising after Rangers broke dangerously down the right. Whelan headed off the line after a corner kick had not been cleared properly by the Liverpool defence. In the 42nd minute he almost scored a copy of the goal but he pulled his shot inches wide. Replacement referee Alan Seville - who came in for the injured Brian Hill - denied John Barnes a penalty when he was brought down by Danny Maddix inside the area on the hour. Barnes' theatrical fall militated against his being awarded the penalty which the foul deserved.

Liverpool had a succession of chances and McMahon twice shot high over the bar. Beardsley, Barnes and Venison all forced David Seaman, Peter Shilton's England understudy, to fine saves. But Rangers refused to be denied and they maintained an air of elegance throughout the game. Their passing was precise and accurate, while the forward line did not allow Hansen and Hysén to settle. Wilkins, despite his lack of height, twice climbed high to make headers which passed narrowly wide. In the second half Clarke pulled his shot wide after being put through by Alan McDonald. Mark Falco substituted for Wegerle near the end as Rangers sought the goal which would take the game into extra-time.

In the Sixth Round tie played between Oldham and Aston Villa, Joe Royle's free-scoring side beat the Villans 3-0 to face Manchester United in the semi-final. In the First Division, Manchester United drew 0-0 with Everton at Old Trafford.

Peter Beardsley, whose goal after just four minutes was enough to settle the tie against a skilful and determined Rangers side

Liverpool: Grobbelaar; Hysén, Venison, Nicol, Whelan, Hansen, Beardsley, Houghton, Rush, Barnes, McMahon.

Queen's Park Rangers: Seaman; Bardsley, Sansom, Parker, McDonald, Maddix, Wilkins, Barker, Clarke, Wegerle(Falco,68), Sinton.

Referee: Mr A. Seville (Birmingham)

Attendance: 38,090

April 8, 1990

Crystal Palace (0) 4
*Bright 47, O'Reilly 70, Gray 88,
Pardew 109*

Liverpool (1) 3 aet
*Rush 14, McMahon 81,
Barnes (pen) 83*

EARLIER in the season, Liverpool beat Palace 9-0 at Anfield and in January the Merseysiders won 2-0 in London. All the odds suggested a Liverpool victory in front of the watching millions who saw it on television prior to the game featuring Oldham and Manchester United, which finished 3-3. Liverpool looked strangely lethargic, and although they took the lead early, they lacked the determination to kill Palace off.

Ian Rush scored his 23rd goal of the season after just 14 minutes, running on to a through ball from Steve McMahon and hitting a wonderful angled shot past goalkeeper Nigel Martyn. The Welsh striker was forced to leave the field after 30 minutes in obvious pain from a rib injury sustained in a collision with Palace defender Gary O'Reilly. Steve Staunton substituted, but with two defenders on the bench manager Kenny Dalglish's wisdom was called into question, since he ignored the claims of the emerging striker Ronnie Rosenthal.

After the goal, the game was played at a slow pace and there was nothing to suggest that the match would explode into action in the manner in which it did. Only seconds into the second half, John Pemberton set off on a powerful run down the right. The Liverpool defence was taken by surprise as he fired in a cross which went to Mark Bright after John Salako had touched it on. Bright cracked the ball past Grobbelaar.

The Eagles seized the initiative, though Liverpool had chances to go back in front before Palace took a surprise lead. FIFA referee George Courtney decided that Alan Hansen had pushed Bright to the ground, and Andy Gray sent his free-kick deep into the Liverpool defence and O'Reilly crashed the ball home. Both managers were off the bench shouting instructions to their teams. Palace survived two near-misses before the Reds equalised. In the 74th minute Geoff Thomas cleared a Barnes shot off the line and then goalkeeper Martyn blocked a David Burrows shot only to see the linesman flag for offside.

With the minutes ticking away, Palace were hit by two goals in two minutes. Venison, who had taken over from Gary Gillespie at half-time, crossed the ball low behind Palace's defence following a free-kick. The ball fell to McMahon, who powered a rising drive out of the reach of Martyn. Then Liverpool were awarded a penalty when Pemberton tripped Staunton as he raced towards goal. Barnes stepped up and shot the Reds back in front.

The Eagles were in no mood to concede the game after their marvellous fighting display, and Gray headed an equaliser with just two minutes left to force extra time. Seconds from the end of normal time, Andy Thorn appeared to have clinched the game for Palace but his header thudded against the bar and out of danger.

Liverpool's greater experience ought to have won them the game in extra time, but Palace scored the winner after 109 minutes. Pardew, who cost the London side a mere £7,000 from non-League Yeovil Town three years previously, put the finishing touch to a corner kick from Gray, which was flicked on by Thorn to Pardew, who crashed his header past a despairing Grobbelaar.

Palace boss, Steve Coppell, said after the game: "It has been a grind and when I took over five years ago, I never dreamed that we would get to an FA Cup Final in such a short period of time. It's also the perfect answer to certain ex-players who said that we were the worst team on earth. I don't think we looked that today! I've got exactly the same feeling as I experienced as a player with Manchester United. I've not lost in a semi-final and this is my fourth. These Palace players all come from the lower divisions and now they can experience what I've been telling them about for so long. I thought that we would nick it 1-0 before the start, but to score four times against the best defence in football is incredible."

Liverpool manager Kenny Dalglish said: "The blame on this defeat rests entirely with the defence." Glenn Hysén, Liverpool's Swedish international defender said: "Three Palace goals came from headers and that's not the way to play if you want to win. It was not just bad luck."

Palace were installed as Cup favourites after the game at odds of 6-5, with Manchester United at 5-4 and Oldham at 4-1. In the semi-final replay at Maine Road, United beat Oldham 2-1 after extra-time.

In the final, Palace and United shared six goals, though United won the replay 1-0.

Crystal Palace: Martyn; Pemberton, Shaw, Gray, O'Reilly, Thorn, Barber, Thomas, Bright, Salako, Pardew.

Liverpool: Grobbelaar; Hysén, Burrows, Gillespie (Venison,46), Whelan, Hansen, Beardsley, Houghton, Rush(Staunton,30), Barnes, McMahon.

Referee: Mr G. Courtney (County Durham)

Attendance: 38,389 (at Villa Park)

January 5, 1991

Blackburn Rovers (0) 1
Garner 46

Liverpool (0) 1
Atkins (og) 90

SECOND Division Blackburn Rovers had lost more home games than anyone else in the League. Fans had staged a terrace sit-down during the previous game against Oxford United (the visitors won 3-1) calling for the resignation of manager Don Mackay and chairman Bill Fox. Liverpool were at the top of the First Division, and a victory was apparently inevitable. In Sydney, Australia took their overnight score from 259-4 to 518 all out and Greg Matthews hit 128 in the Third test. On the Saturday, non-League Woking beat West Bromwich Albion 4-2 after being a goal down at the interval - and at the Hawthorns. In snooker, Steve Davis was beaten 5-1 in the fifth round of the Mercantile Credit Classic in Bournemouth. It was the time of the underdog. Blackburn's current position at the bottom of the Second Division was:

	Pl	W	D	L	F	A	Pts
Blackburn Rovers	**25**	**7**	**5**	**13**	**26**	**41**	**26**
Leicester City	23	7	5	11	32	48	26
Portsmouth	25	6	7	12	31	41	25
Plymouth Argyle	25	5	10	10	29	40	25
Watford	25	5	9	11	22	31	24
Hull City	25	5	7	13	40	63	22

The home side were encouraged by the inclusion of Garner, the club's record goalscorer playing his first game for a month, and the skilful left-sided midfielder, Scott Sellars, both of whom had undergone identical groin operations in the summer.

Blackburn Rovers: Mimms; Atkins, Duxbury, Reid, May, Moran, Gayle(Johnrose,87), Millar, Stapleton, Garner, Sellars (Shepstone,77).

Liverpool: Grobbelaar; Hysén, Burrows, Nicol, Staunton (Mølby,72), Gillespie, Rosenthal, Houghton, Rush, Barnes, McMahon.

Referee: Mr M.G. Peck (Kendal)

Attendance: 18,524

The visitors started in confident mood, though they lacked the penetration their possession play required. Ronnie Rosenthal - making his Cup début - was put clear by Steve McMahon, and the Israeli-international slid a left-foot shot wide of the post with only Bobby Mimms - the £250,000

record signing former Everton goalkeeper - to beat. The signing from Tottenham Hotspur also beat away a close-range header from Rosenthal as the striker sought to make his mark. With 17 minutes gone, Frank Stapleton mis-kicked in front of goal. Grobbelaar saved at the feet of the advancing Garner in the first period, which did not betray the drama about to be served up.

Blackburn's aerial threat caused Liverpool's defence several problems and in the first minute of the second half, David May's high throw-in went past a cluster of red shirts to Garner, whose shot entered the net at the far post. Garner had begun only two games this season and although he played in Blackburn's B team in the previous week, he was not expected to play, but he pleaded with manager Don Mackay to play him. Five minutes later Barnes found the back of the net, but the referee had spotted an infringement by Rush on Mimms. With 62 minutes gone, Moran - the first player to be sent off in an FA Cup final - was shown the red card for an unintentional trip on Rush. Rush said after the game: "I thought Kevin was a bit unfortunate. It wasn't a sending off offence." Eight minutes later Liverpool skipper Glenn Hysén was also sent off for a trip on Garner. Millar, Burrows, Staunton and Reid were also booked, but it was not a dirty game merely an indication of referees acting on the laws of the game to stamp out the professional foul.

With the scoreboard clock showing that the 90 minutes were officially up, Nicol won a throw-in near the right-hand corner flag and the Scot wasted no time in tossing the ball to the feet of Houghton, who looped his centre high into the box over the head of Gillespie, who was impeded by Stapleton. A penalty was not forthcoming, but the ball fell at the feet of Atkins, and the ball entered the net off the defender's ankle. It was a fortunate ending to a game which Liverpool rarely looked like winning.

West Bromwich Albion: Rees; Shakespeare, Harbey(Palmer,74), Roberts, Bradley, Strodder, Ford, West, Bannister, McNally, Robson.

Woking: Read; Mitchell, Cowler, Pratt, Barton, Wye, Brown, Biggins, Frank(Worsfold, 87), Buzaglo, Wye.

Referee: Mr R. Hamer (Bristol)

Attendance: 14,516

Goals: West (34); Buzaglo (58, 64, 73); Worsfold (89); Bradley (90).

January 8, 1991

Liverpool (2) 3

Houghton 15, Rush 24,
Staunton 82

Blackburn Rovers (0) 0

THIS tie was played in atrocious conditions with a swirling, gale-force wind sweeping across Anfield. The Reds brought in the immaculate ball-playing Jan Mølby in place of the tough-tackling David Burrows, a victim of 'flu. Staunton was switched to left-back, while the Dane was drafted into midfield.

Jan Mølby, the Dane who played in midfield and replaced defender David Burrows

Early in the game Mike Duxbury appeared to have handled a Nicol cross, but no penalty was given, and after only fifteen minutes an inviting through-ball from Mølby allowed Houghton to run on to the ball before playing a one-two with Gillespie, receiving the return and rifling a low shot into the corner of the net. Mølby continued to dominate the proceedings and as he ran on to a through-ball from Nicol, he forced Mimms to race off his line and block the Dane. Barnes - wearing gloves to keep out the bitter cold - found Rush in the area after 24 minutes, and the Welshman, with his back to goal, swivelled on the spot and directed a shot high and wide of Mimms' left hand. The goal was Rush's 33rd in the FA Cup. As the Reds maintained their superiority over the Second Division side, McMahon was booked for a 43rd minute foul on the Rovers' skipper, Nicky Reid.

Early in the second half Houghton limped off and was replaced by Ablett. In the 55th minute McMahon became the third England midfield player to be sent off in 29 days, following the dismissals of Neil Webb and Paul Gascoigne. McMahon lunged at the former Anfield winger, Howard Gayle, who crashed heavily to the turf. With ten minutes remaining the Liverpool bench protested so vehemently at a decision that Mr Peck was called over by his linesman and the referee appeared to reprimand Ronnie Moran. Two policemen also added words of caution to the bench.

Two minutes later Rosenthal created a chance for Staunton, who netted to seal the tie beyond all doubt. After the game manager Dalglish said: "This club has had the best disciplinary record in the last three years and has won the Fair Play Trophy to prove it. But, in the last two games, we have had more players sent off than in the past three years. If we are going to try and interpret the letter of the law, then, for the benefit of football, we must sit down and talk about the problems." The Blackburn manager, Don Mackay, suggested it was time for the Football Association to look at the question of appointing different officials for Cup replays. He also suggested that there was an emotional hangover from the original tie at Ewood Park, adding: "Maybe I am asking for them to do the impossible, but anyone who watched the television highlights could see the emotion involved. I don't think anyone would doubt that everyone - including the referee - picked up the thread of that emotion. There could have been a serious situation ... You tell players to forget what has happened before, but they cannot, and you can't expect referees to be anything but human, either. Maybe if someone different had been in charge of the game tonight, things may have been a bit different."

A day earlier, Cup-holders Manchester United beat Queen's Park Rangers 2-1 at Old Trafford. Crystal Palace, last year's losing finalists, had drawn on the Saturday 0-0 at home to Nottingham Forest.

Liverpool: Grobbelaar; Hysén, Mølby, Nicol, Staunton, Gillespie, Rosenthal(McManaman,86), Houghton(Ablett,48), Rush, Barnes, McMahon.

Blackburn Rovers: Mimms; Atkins, Duxbury (Johnrose,71), Reid, May, Moran, Gayle, Millar, Stapleton, Garner, Sellars.

Referee: Mr M.G. Peck (Kendal)

Attendance: 34,175

January 26, 1991

Liverpool (0) 2   Brighton & Hove Albion (0) 2
Rush 48, 50   Small (pen) 73, Byrne 77

WHILE Liverpool forced a late draw at Blackburn in the previous round, the Seagulls beat Scunthorpe United 3-2 before a crowd of 7,785 at the Goldstone Ground. Liverpool manager, Kenny Dalglish, aware that his team had no divine right to victory, had called for an improvement on recent performances, but it was not forthcoming in a lacklustre display. Weakened by injuries and suspensions, Liverpool were unable to find their usual fluency and rhythm against a Second Division side which showed great character, determination and organisation. Staunton went close to opening the scoreline before the interval when he had one shot smothered by Perry Digweed and another which flashed inches wide of the far post. The Brighton custodian also denied the dangerous Rush with a sliding tackle outside the area in a first half which lacked style.

Early in the second period, Rush collected an accurate forward ball from Barnes and slotted home the first goal. Following a right-wing corner, John Crumplin saw Grobbelaar pull off a magnificent reflex save from his fierce angled drive. A minute later Rush shot home Venison's neat pass and it seemed as though Liverpool would cruise into the Fifth Round. Brighton had other ideas. Mike Small cracked home a 73rd-minute penalty awarded after Staunton had fouled Paul McCarthy.

Digweed then clutched a brilliant effort from Rush before Grobbelaar parried Clive Walker's low drive. The giant Small nodded back Crumplin's right-wing centre for John Byrne to power a header into the net from close range. Small had two other chances to win the game for the visitors in the closing minutes but desperate defending by Ablett and Nicol earned a draw after victory for the home side had appeared likely.

Brighton's Gary Chivers said after the game: "They just stopped playing, they stopped coming forward. Liverpool have got quality players. They kept the ball for quite a while - once for 19 passes - but then they stopped playing. It's a mental thing. When you stop coming forward as they did you tend to defend more. Because they were defending we were able to keep our momentum going and that took us forward. Mark Barham had to go off after a bang on the head, the boss (Barry Lloyd) pushed John Byrne up front. It was a brilliant move and I think he might have done it anyway, because we had to go hunting the game. We got a penalty just at the right time and that gave us the boost we needed."

Byrne - who had an operation on his cartilage just four weeks before this game - learned after the game that the grandfather who brought him up had died in a Manchester hospital, aged 91. Byrne had visited him on his way to the match at Anfield.

In other ties, Manchester United beat Bolton Wanderers 1-0 at Old Trafford with a 79th minute goal from Mark Hughes; Millwall and Sheffield Wednesday shared eight goals at The Den; Guy Whittingham scored four of Portsmouth's five against Bournemouth; Shrewsbury - third from bottom in the Third Division - beat seventh in the First Division Wimbledon 1-0 at home.

*Despite two goals from **Ian Rush**, Liverpool failed to win the tie at the first attempt against Second Division Brighton*

Liverpool: Grobbelaar; Venison, Burrows, Nicol, Staunton, Ablett, Carter, Mølby, Rush, Barnes, Rosenthal(Beardsley,68).

Brighton & Hove Albion: Digweed; Crumplin, Gatting, Wilkins, McCarthy, Chivers, Barham (Chapman,68), Wade (McGrath,60), Small, Byrne, Walker.

Referee: Mr B. Hill (Kettering)

Attendance: 32,670

January 30, 1991

Brighton & Hove A. (1) 2 Liverpool (1) 3 aet
Small 37, Byrne 97   *McMahon 10, 114, Rush 107*

BRIGHTON introduced Robert Codner in place of Bryan Wade, while Liverpool had Steve McMahon back after suspension in place of Rosenthal, and Whelan coming in for Mølby, relegated to the substitutes' bench. Brighton made a spirited start, but McMahon deflated their enterprise after just ten minutes when he won a race for possession to force the ball home after Perry Digweed had parried a daisy-cutter from John Barnes.

Grobbelaar's agility prevented Codner from equalising with a lob after 25 minutes, but as a scrappy first half came to a close, Walker's mis-hit shot bobbled through the massed Reds' defence for Mike Small to fire low past the leaden-footed Grobbelaar after a terrible back-pass by skipper Whelan. The goal brought Dalglish, Ronnie Moran and Roy Evans to their feet as it looked palpably offside.

Staunton, Rush and Barnes were all denied by the superb Digweed before the interval, and on resuming, Nicol shot narrowly wide after being put in possession by John Crumplin. Then Digweed executed magnificent finger-tipped saves from McMahon, twice, Barnes and Whelan. After 72 minutes McMahon slid a shot wide from the goalline as the visitors attacked incessantly. Brighton, now subdued, almost took the lead when Dean Wilkins flighted a left-foot free-kick towards the top corner of the net. Grobbelaar pulled off a superb finger-tipped save. In the closing moments Small almost put through his own goal, before Digweed reacted to force extra time.

Seven minutes into the first period of extra-time, Byrne shot Brighton into the lead. Before the change of ends, Venison brought Digweed to his knees with a powerful shot.

After 107 minutes, Digweed was rooted to the spot when Rush slotted home a pass from Beardsley, on as substitute. As the game drew to a close, Grobbelaar saved a low shot from Walker as Brighton fought for a winning goal. Six minutes before the finish McMahon collected a Rush flick to score his second goal and a tie against Everton in the Fifth Round. Liverpool signed David Speedie from Coventry for £675,000 before the tie with Brighton. After the game manager Dalglish said: "I don't think any of the players could have given me any more in commitment and workrate. Every single Liverpool player did themselves, the club and the jerseys they wore proud."

Brighton & Hove Albion: Digweed; Crumplin, Gatting, Wilkins, McCarthy, Chivers, Barham, Byrne, Small, Codner, Walker(Chapman,112).

Liverpool: Grobbelaar; Venison, Burrows, Nicol, Whelan(Beardsley,102), Ablett, Carter (Mølby,91), Staunton, Rush, Barnes, McMahon.

Referee: Mr B. Hill (Kettering)

Attendance: 14,392

Left: ***Steve McMahon***, *who scored twice against Brighton in the extra-time victory*

February 17, 1991

Liverpool (0) 0

Everton (0) 0

EVERTON left out Mike Milligan and Peter Beagrie and switched from a five-man midfield to a five-man defence and recalled Martin Keown and Ray Atteveld in an attempt to inject more toughness and purpose into the side. Liverpool made two changes, although Peter Beardsley was left on the bench. McMahon returned to take over from the injured Whelan, while Rush returned up front in a shuffle which had no room for Venison. Everton, who had beaten Charlton Athletic and non-League Woking in previous rounds, forced a goalless draw at Anfield in a thrilling Merseyside encounter which was televised live. Eight days previously Liverpool had beaten Everton 3-1 at Anfield in a League encounter which was closer than the scoreline suggested. With only 16 minutes gone, Steve McMahon was carried off with an injury and Barry Venison replaced him.

The Blues, in a season of change and with a new manager in Howard Kendall - his second spell in charge - were tactically correct and they might well have won the game but for a penalty appeal turned down by the referee when Pat Nevin was brought down in the area by Gary Ablett. Everton were much the superior team in the first half and looked confident from the first whistle. Grobbelaar saved well from a long-range effort from McDonald and then the home side almost fell behind when skipper Hysén played a back-pass straight to Sharp, but the Scot had his shot blocked by Grobbelaar, who snatched the ball away from the advancing Nevin. Keown's dangerous header was tipped over the top by Grobbelaar, and after the interval Nevin's lob bounced narrowly wide. The visitors were playing to their limit and introduced Tony Cottee into the affair in an attempt to gain the vital winner. Liverpool responded by introducing Beardsley to the accompaniment of a mighty roar from the Kop. Kevin Ratcliffe was forced to make a desperate goal-line clearance from a Staunton shot with the marauding Rush nearby. With just five minutes left, Beardsley's cracking shot passed the wrong side of the upright.

Liverpool: Grobbelaar; Hysén, Burrows, Nicol, Mølby, Ablett, Speedie(Beardsley,71), Staunton, Rush, Barnes, McMahon(Venison,16).

Everton: Southall; McDonald, Ebbrell, Ratcliffe, Watson, Keown, Atteveld, McCall, Sharp, Sheedy (Cottee,56), Nevin.

Referee: Mr N. Midgley (Manchester)

Attendance: 38,323

***Gary Ablett**, who had a good game against Everton*

F.A. CUP
FIFTH ROUND

Saturday, February 16, 1991

Cambridge United	**4**	Sheffield Wednesday	**0**
Notts County	**1**	Manchester City	**0**
Portsmouth	**1**	Tottenham Hotspur	**2**
West Ham United	**1**	Crewe Alexandra	**0**

Monday, February 18, 1991

Norwich City	**2**	Manchester United	**1**

Monday, February 25, 1991

Southampton	**1**	Nottingham Forest	**1**

Wednesday, February 27, 1991

Shrewsbury Town	**0**	Arsenal	**1**

Monday, March 4, 1991

Nottingham Forest	**3**	Southampton	**1**

February 20, 1991

Everton (0) 4
Sharp 47, 73,
Cottee 89, 114

Liverpool (1) 4 aet
Beardsley 32, 71, Rush 77,
Barnes 102

EVERTON manager Howard Kendall dropped Stuart McCall and recalled Andy Hinchcliffe and Mike Newell. Liverpool found a place for Beardsley in place of Speedie, and Venison in place of McMahon. Houghton and Speedie were named as substitutes. The Reds began brightly and played the more controlled football with Mølby allowed the freedom and space of central midfield. With 32 minutes gone, Liverpool took the lead through Beardsley. Ratcliffe hesitated as he moved to make a clearance and Rush stole the ball before racing clear. Hinchcliffe headed off the line but Beardsley - starting a match for Liverpool for the first time in more than two months - hit a snap shot which was deflected wide of Ratcliffe and the diving Southall. The visitors maintained their lead up to the interval, when Kendall replaced the struggling Atteveld with McCall.

Just two minutes after the resumption, Sharp headed the equalising goal via Grobbelaar's hand from a Hinchcliffe cross from the left. Nevin might have put Everton ahead four minutes later but scooped the ball over the bar. The game flowed from end to end and Liverpool began to look less self-assured. Ablett was booked for protesting over the award of a free-kick to Everton. Taking a pass from Nicol and cutting in from the right, Beardsley shot Liverpool back in front with a spectacular left-foot shot after 71 minutes. He drifted away from Nevin before firing high past Southall from twenty yards. The tie took a further twist when Sharp scored his second goal two minutes later after a defensive error between Grobbelaar and Nicol allowed the Everton striker to move in and steer the ball into an empty net. Both sides looked capable of scoring every time they went forward, and Rush put Liverpool ahead after 77 minutes. Mølby was allowed total freedom from a corner and then Rush was completely unmarked to head past Southall. With the game drawing to a conclusion, and a Liverpool victory in sight, Kendall replaced Nevin with Cottee and he had been on the field only four minutes when he scored an equalising goal with just a minute remaining. McDonald and McCall combined well to beat the Liverpool defence and present Cottee with an opportunity from close range.

Extra-time followed, and the previously subdued Barnes curled a right-foot drive from the left wing past Southall from 25 yards to put Liverpool ahead once again, but Everton had refused to lie down, and six minutes before the end Cottee slipped a shot under Grobbelaar's body after a mistake by Hysén, who stepped over Mølby's back-pass, believing it was going to Grobbelaar.

After the game, Everton manager Howard Kendall said: "This was one of the greatest Cup ties certainly Merseyside - if not football - has ever seen. My team were absolutely tremendous. I cannot speak too highly of them for coming back four times. They showed tremendous character." Liverpool central defender Gary Ablett said: "I haven't played in a game like that since I was at school. When you score four goals away from home you expect to win but we were sloppy at the back and got punished for it. We were told about it in the dressing room afterwards."

***Steve Nicol**, who played well in the derby Cup-tie and laid on a goal for Beardsley after 71 minutes*

Everton: Southall; Atteveld(McCall,45), Hinchcliffe, Ratcliffe, Watson, Keown, Nevin(Cottee,85), McDonald, Sharp, Newell, Ebbrell.

Liverpool: Grobbelaar; Hysén, Burrows, Nicol, Mølby, Ablett, Beardsley, Staunton, Rush, Barnes, Venison.

Referee: Mr N. Midgley (Manchester)

Attendance: 37,766

February 27, 1991

Everton (1) 1
Watson 12

Liverpool (0) 0

WITH Kenny Dalglish having resigned five days earlier, coach Ronnie Moran was in charge of the team. He introduced goalkeeper Mike Hooper into the team for the League game four days previously at Luton, which the Reds lost 1-3, after leading at the interval, but for this second replay he brought back Grobbelaar. Burrows was replaced by Venison, while Speedie and Tanner were named as the substitutes. Kendall dropped Nevin in favour of Atteveld, and Nevin and Cottee were on the bench.

Rush turned Keown in the third minute but his low shot was well held by Southall. With only 12 minutes gone Everton scored the goal which proved to be the winner. Atteveld's free-kick was flicked on by Sharp and then by Watson. Nicol attempted to clear but could only glance the ball backwards, where Keown seized the ball and smashed in a shot which Grobbelaar saved with his outstretched left foot. The ball fell at the feet of Mølby, but went through his legs and Watson - the former Anfield reserve - pounced to steer the ball into the net from close range.

Mølby distributed the ball intelligently in the first period and with Houghton working prodigiously, Liverpool caused Everton several problems, despite the frustrations which had beset the club since Dalglish's departure.

Everton, however, closed down swiftly and harried their opponents at every opportunity, riding high on the emotion following their goal. Southall saved expertly from Rush and Nicol as the Reds sought an equaliser and on the hour Kendall substituted Nevin for Atteveld in an attempt to try and wrest a greater share of possession and more penetration. For ten minutes Everton gained the initiative before Liverpool's final flourish.

A tremendous shot by Nicol was well saved by Southall and Rush had a magnificent header which went the wrong side of the post. The introduction of Speedie failed to bring Liverpool a goal their football deserved on the day before Moran's 57th birthday.

Watson said afterwards: "I just saw the ball bouncing in the box and as soon as I struck it, I knew it was going in. They put a lot of pressure on us and I think we defended well and showed we can keep a clean sheet. Neville Southall was magic. He made three absolutely marvellous saves but then you expect that kind of thing from him - he's brilliant."

Ian Rush said: "If it wasn't for the world's best goalkeeper we would have won comfortably. That was the best we have played recently and I felt I could have got a hat-trick. I have always felt Southall is the best in the game and he proved it in this game. He was absolutely brilliant."

Caretaker manager Ronnie Moran said: "I am still smiling. That was the best we have played for weeks."

Everton went on to play West Ham United in the quarter-finals, and although Watson scored again, the Blues lost 2-1 at Upton Park. In the semi-finals, the Hammers were beaten 4-0 by Nottingham Forest, who lost the final to Tottenham Hotspur 2-1, despite leading at the interval.

Neville Southall

Everton: Southall; McDonald, Hinchcliffe, Ratcliffe, Watson, Keown, Atteveld(Nevin,60),McCall, Sharp, Newell,Ebbrell.

Liverpool: Grobbelaar; Hysén, Venison(Speedie,71), Nicol, Mølby, Ablett, Beardsley, Houghton, Rush, Barnes, Staunton.

Referee: Mr J.B. Worrall (Warrington)

Attendance: 40,201

January 6, 1992

Crewe Alexandra (0) 0

Liverpool (3) 4

McManaman 9,
Barnes 26, 28, (pen) 89

WITH former Anfield midfielder Graeme Souness now manager, Liverpool embarked on a Cup campaign at Crewe, where right-back Rob Jones began his career. The home side included former Liverpool reserve Craig Hignett in their ranks. Liverpool took the lead after only nine minutes when Jones overlapped to collect Houghton's pass before centring low for McManaman to score with a first-time shot. The visitors played with great skill and only the excellence of goalkeeper Dean Greygoose kept the Reds at bay.

With just eleven minutes gone the keeper saved well from a Michael Thomas effort. After 26 minutes Mark Wright powered in a header from a Dean Saunders corner which Dave McKearney headed off the line, but as the loose ball was driven into the area, Barnes flicked it home to increase Liverpool's lead. (The England international played a 'B' game against Everton at Melwood on the previous Saturday in an attempt to prove his fitness after injuring his Achilles the previous August. Barnes operated up front in the first half and in midfield for the second. He did not score but had a header saved, fired narrowly wide and had an appeal for a penalty refused when he went down in the box. The game ended 1-1, with Barnes laying on the pass for Liverpool's goal, scored by Robbie Fowler.) Two minutes later Barnes took McManaman's return pass to score with a volley off the side of his foot.

Early in the second half Crewe almost reduced the lead but substitute Colin Rose headed over after Grobbelaar had parried an Edwards drive. Following Darren Carr's flick, Aaron Callaghan fired wide from close range. A minute from time Barnes converted a penalty to complete a thoroughly professional performance.

In the ties played on the preceding Saturday Everton beat Southend 1-0 with a Peter Beardsley goal scored after 15 minutes. Fourth Division Wrexham beat Arsenal 2-1, despite trailing at the interval.

Rob Jones

Crewe Alexandra: Greygoose; Wilson, McKearney, Carr (Sorvell,78), Callaghan, Walters, Hignett, Naylor, Jasper(Rose,28), Gardiner, Edwards.

Liverpool: Grobbelaar; Jones, Mølby, Nicol, Wright, Tanner, Saunders, Houghton(Marsh,46), McManaman, Barnes, Thomas.

Referee: Mr T. Holbrook (Walsall)

Attendance: 7,400

February 5, 1992

Bristol Rovers (0) 1
Saunders 59

Liverpool (1) 1
Saunders 38

ON the day former Anfield favourite Kevin Keegan became manager of Newcastle United, Liverpool struggled to a draw against Second Division Bristol Rovers at Twerton Park. Liverpool brought in David Burrows at left-back, Mike Marsh in midfield, and Mark Walters in place of John Barnes, with Jamie Redknapp and Ronnie Rosenthal on the bench. Rovers brought in Clark instead of Twentyman - son of the former Liverpool player, Cross instead of Maddison, White in place of Browning, and Pounder instead of Stewart, and also found a place for Meyhew.

Bristol Rovers: Parkin; Alexander, Clark, Yates, Cross, Skinner, Meyhew, Reece, White, Saunders, Pounder.

Liverpool: Grobbelaar; Jones, Burrows, Marsh, Wright, Tanner, Saunders, Houghton, Walters, Mølby, McManaman.

Referee: Mr B. Hill (Kettering)

Attendance: 9,464

The home side displayed a good deal of fighting spirit and were disappointed when referee Hill waved away appeals for a penalty when Burrows brought down David Meyhew. Liverpool enjoyed a degree of control in the first half without displaying their finer skills. Jan Mølby was the architect of midfield as Liverpool forced seven corners. From the last of these, Dean Saunders gave the visitors the lead. Marsh's flag-kick was headed down by Wright, and Saunders held off the challenge of Steve Yates to score off an upright and the head of Parkin. The home side responded immediately and Meyhew fired wide when well placed. Two minutes before the interval, Meyhew seized on a back-pass by former Rovers player Nick Tanner but was brought down by Burrows. The denial of Rovers' penalty claim ignited the game and the home side stormed onto the attack as the second half got underway. Grobbelaar fumbled a cross from Pounder before saving well from Meyhew as the Pirates went in search of an equaliser.

Their reward came after 59 minutes when Meyhew moved menacingly down the right wing before providing an opportunity for Carl Saunders - scorer of four goals in the previous round against Plymouth Argyle - to shoot into the goal with a right-foot shot past Grobbelaar.

The home side deserved the goal after a period of intense pressure which the Anfielders struggled to cope with. Walters almost scored with a volley which passed narrowly wide. After the game, manager Souness said: "We are happy to still be in the competition. It was always going to be hard here and so it proved. They worked hard and will be pleased with their performance. I think we can do better than that."

Bristol Rovers manager, Dennis Rofe said: "I was proud of my players. We go to Anfield full of optimism and confident that we can get a result."

***Dean Saunders**, who scored for Liverpool after 38 minutes when he held off the challenge of Steve Yates. The ball rebounded off an upright and the head of Parkin*

February 11, 1992

Liverpool (0) 2
McManaman 50,
Saunders 77

Bristol Rovers (1) 1
Saunders 18

ON a night when former Anfield striker John Aldridge hit his 30th goal of the season for Tranmere in a 1-1 draw at Sunderland, Liverpool struggled to find the net against Rovers, who went in at the interval with a single-goal lead. The Pirates dominated the first period when the Reds failed to find any cohesion and penetration. The visitors created the first opening after just five minutes when Devon White headed into the arms of Grobbelaar following an Andy Reece corner.

Rovers sensed that Liverpool were well below their customary form and their confident opening enabled them to take the lead after 18 minutes. Carl Saunders - a £70,000 purchase - chested down a headed clearance from Burrows before hitting a tremendous right-foot drive which flew into the top corner of the net. It was a goal which only served to increase Liverpool's insecurities, and manager Souness showed his displeasure from the dugout. Liverpool's frustrations grew and Burrows unnecessarily challenged Saunders. The impetuous act earned him a booking and Saunders required prolonged treatment. Four minutes before the break Ian Alexander saved Wright's header off the line.

After a stinging half-time lecture from Souness - who received the Manager of the Month award for January before the match - it was a different Liverpool which came out for the second half. Ian Rush - back after two knee operations - replaced Ronnie Rosenthal up front. McManaman switched from the left flank to the right on instructions from skipper Wright. The Kop increased the volume of its support and just five minutes into the second period McManaman cut across the edge of the penalty area and beat goalkeeper Brian Parkin with a rising 20-yard left-foot shot. It was a marvellous goal - his ninth of the season - scored on McManaman's 20th birthday. The young Liverpool player was in exceptional form after his goal, and his marker, Steve Cross, was replaced by Adrian Boothroyd after 68 minutes. With fifteen minutes remaining the £2.9 million Dean Saunders missed an easy opportunity when Boothroyd turned a ball into the path of the Liverpool striker. Three minutes later, however, Saunders hit the winning goal after excellent approach work by McManaman, who finished a marvellous run after taking a pass from Mike Marsh by drifting past a series of challenges before providing Saunders with his 20th goal of the season. The supporters of the football lodgers at Twerton Park, Bath celebrated a fine performance by their heroes with a rendition of "*Goodnight Irene*".

McManaman said afterwards: "I'll always remember the goal. It's one of my best and a great way to celebrate my birthday." Manager Souness - who gave McManaman a new five-year contract earlier in the season - added: "His performance was exceptional. In the second half we got an extra yard from somewhere and I thought the performances of Rush and McManaman between them were the biggest reason the game turned round. Rush looked as if he had never been away. He's been out so long but his sharpness, alertness and anticipation unsettled their defence. I'm just delighted to be in the next round. All credit to Rovers, they came here, were not overawed, and they worked extremely hard to prevent us from playing."

Liverpool: Grobbelaar; Jones, Burrows, Nicol, Wright, Marsh, Saunders, Houghton, Rosenthal(Rush,46), Redknapp, McManaman.

Bristol Rovers: Parkin; Alexander, Clark, Yates, Cross(Boothroyd,68), Skinner, Meyhew, Reece, White, Saunders, Pounder.

Referee: Mr B. Hill (Kettering)

Attendance: 30,142

F.A. CUP

Bolton Wanderers	2	Brighton & Hove A.	1
Cambridge United	0	Swindon Town	3
Leicester City	1	Bristol City	2
Portsmouth	2	Leyton Orient	0
West Ham United	2,1	Wrexham	2,0
Charlton Athletic	0,1	Sheffield United	0,3
Chelsea	1	Everton	0
Nottingham Forest	2	Hereford United	0
Southampton*	0,2	Manchester United*	0,2
Notts County	2	Blackburn Rovers	1
Sheffield Wednesday	1	Middlesbrough	2
Derby County	3	Aston Villa	4
Ipswich Town	3	Bournemouth	0
Norwich City	2	Millwall	1
Oxford United	2	Sunderland	3

** Southampton won **4-2** on penalties*

Steve McManaman

Bruce Grobbelaar

February 16, 1992

Ipswich Town (0) 0   # Liverpool (0) 0

IPSWICH Town - lying second in the Second Division - played host to fourth in the First Division Liverpool on a freezing day.

Ipswich Town: Forrest, Johnson, Thompson, Stockwell, Wark, Linighan, Milton, Palmer, Whitton, Dozzell, Kiwomya.

Liverpool: Grobbelaar; Jones, Burrows, Nicol, Wright, Marsh, Saunders, Houghton, Rush, Redknapp (Kozma,55), McManaman.

Referee: Mr A. Buksh (Dollis Hill)

Attendance: 26,100

The Blues tested Grobbelaar early on when a Neil Thompson free-kick was parried by the Liverpool goalkeeper before he kicked the ball away with his right leg to safety. The swirling wind and freezing temperatures hindered the quality of the play. The home side collectively cost less than half a million pounds, but they had a fine first half in which their enthusiasm and the devastating speed of Chris Kiwomya caused Liverpool several problems. With ten minutes gone, Gavin Johnson turned Mark Wright but could only head over at the far post from Mick Stockwell's cross. Then Thompson centred from the left following Stockwell's crossfield ball and Kiwomya shot tamely. Liverpool broke away immediately and Saunders weaved his way into the box and, faced only by goalkeeper Craig Forrest, he hesitated before firing wide. A long-range effort from Jamie Redknapp forced Forrest into a finger-tipped save. Ipswich concluded the half in the same manner in which they had begun it. Grobbelaar twice dealt with Steve Whitton's inswinging corners, and John Wark - the 34-year-old former Anfield player - hit the crossbar with a header from Thompson's corner-kick.

In the second period, Wright and Nicol played superbly to counter the twin threat of Kiwomya and Jason Dozzell.

Wright had the ball in the net after 48 minutes but the effort was disallowed for a push on David Linighan and Saunders forced Forrest to make two saves.

A Thompson free-kick bounced off Grobbelaar's chest and the home side attacked strongly down the right with Dozzell collecting Kiwomya's flick in the box before crossing low, and with players from both sides fighting for possession, Houghton struck the foot of his own post before the ball rebounded into the arms of Grobbelaar.

With 55 minutes gone, Liverpool then introduced Istvan Kozma, their recent £300,000 signing from Dunfermline, into the match, becoming the first Hungarian to play for an English League side.

Ipswich manager John Lyall said afterwards: "I don't think I have ever seen a game played in more difficult conditions. The longer the game went on the windier it seemed to get. The ball was doing something all the game and not often what the player wanted it to do."

John Wark added: "I honestly believe that we can win it up there but I am just sick that we didn't do it the first time because we had some excellent chances. We had some young players out there so we have got to be happy with the result. I couldn't stop myself when I headed the ball against the crossbar. I wanted to get it down but it just flew off my head before I could direct it properly."

In other ties played on the preceding Saturday, Chelsea beat Sheffield United 1-0; Norwich City beat Notts County 3-0; Nottingham Forest beat Bristol City 4-1; Portsmouth drew 1-1 with Middlesbrough at Fratton Park; and Sunderland drew 1-1 at home to West Ham United.

In the League's Second Division, Kenny Dalglish's Blackburn Rovers beat Kevin Keegan's Newcastle United 3-1 at Ewood Park, after Kelly gave the visitors the lead after just 12 minutes. However, David Speedie - the former Anfield player - hit a hat-trick.

Saturday, February 15, 1992

Blackburn Rovers: Mimms; Price, A.Wright, Cowans, Hill, Hendry, Wilcox, Atkins, Speedie, Newell, Brown.

Newcastle United: T.Wright; Ranson, Stimson, O'Brien, Bradshaw, Neilson, Watson, Peacock, Kelly, Clark, Brock.

Referee: Mr P. Jones (Loughborough)

Attendance: 19,511

Goals: Newcastle: Kelly (12);
Blackburn Rovers: Speedie (42, 59, 75)

Managers: Kenny Dalglish (Blackburn);
Kevin Keegan (Newcastle)

February 26, 1992

Liverpool (1) 3
Houghton 45, Mølby 98,
McManaman 100

Ipswich Town (0) 2 aet
Johnson 82, Dozzell 95

THE ball-playing, close-passing skills of the visitors threatened to win them the game and a Mick Stockwell drive early on brought a close-range save from Grobbelaar. Chris Kiwomya wasted possession on several occasions, otherwise the East Anglian side would have created further chances for themselves. Stockwell provided Dozzell on one occasion and Rob Jones got in a vital tackle to deny the visitors. Liverpool lacked urgency and determination in the first half, relying mainly on the threat of Walters, whose crosses were too infrequent to threaten Ipswich. With 23 minutes gone, Walters created an opening for Marsh, who combined well with Houghton before having his shot parried by Forrest. As the game went into injury time in the first half Walters crossed from the left and Houghton punished a half-cleared header from Thompson by forcing the ball into the net. During the interval linesman Ken Loach replaced referee Alf Buksh, who sustained a groin injury.

The visitors came out for the second period in determined mood. Simon Milton shot wide before testing Grobbelaar again with an effort from long range which the Liverpool goalkeeper tipped over the bar. The game flowed from end to end and McManaman supplied Walters, who shot straight at Forrest. With eight minutes remaining, Wark intercepted a Walters' pass to Saunders and put Steve Whitton in possession, and his centre to the far post was headed home by Gavin Johnson, taking the tie into extra-time. From a free-kick by Jones, Walters headed inches wide in a late Liverpool rally.

Souness introduced Ronnie Rosenthal late in the game, and his tremendous pace caused Ipswich problems in the extra half-hour. Goddard clipped the crossbar for Ipswich before Dozzell raced clear to beat Grobbelaar at the second attempt after 95 minutes. The visitors' lead was short-lived as Mølby curled home a right-foot free-kick from 18 yards following a Stockwell foul on Saunders. Just two minutes later McManaman took Rosenthal's return pass and chipped

Forrest. Still Ipswich believed they could snatch something from the game and Whitton shot over before Grobbelaar denied Johnson to hold on to victory.

Jan Mølby

Mølby said after the game: "I've been out of action after flaking a bone on a knee. I've not trained for three weeks. I've not even kicked a ball; I've just been swimming. But the manager decided to take a risk with me and three other players - Houghton, Nicol and Jones - and it paid off." Souness added: "I thought Ipswich were very good and their manager must be proud of them."

At Upton Park, Sunderland beat West Ham 3-2 with two goals from John Byrne (6 and 25) and one from David Rush (79 minutes). Martin Allen had pulled the Hammers level with two goals after 39 and 51 minutes.

In other replays, Portsmouth beat Middlesbrough 4-2 away, and Southampton beat Bolton 3-2 at The Dell.

Liverpool: Grobbelaar; Jones, Harkness(Kozma,98), Nicol, Wright, Marsh, Saunders, Houghton, Walters (Rosenthal,82), Mølby, McManaman.

Ipswich Town: Forrest; Johnson, Thompson, Stockwell, Wark(Zondervan,116), Linighan, Milton, Palmer(Goddard,65), Whitton, Dozzell, Kiwomya.

Referee: Mr A. Buksh (Dollis Hill) sub: Mr K. A. Leach (Wolverhampton,46)

Attendance: 27,355

March 8, 1992

Liverpool (0) 1
Thomas 67

Aston Villa (0) 0

LIVERPOOL recalled Whelan, Barnes and Thomas in place of Marsh, Mølby and Walters and replaced Burrows with Venison, while Ron Atkinson brought in Nigel Spink for Les Sealey, and Mark Blake for Darius Kubicki. The Villa side included the former Anfield utility player, Steve Staunton. Whelan had had a series of knee operations and played just two reserve games, while Barnes made his first appearance for seven weeks, and Thomas had only a few days training since his last game five weeks previously. Barnes was Liverpool's main threat in the first half, while Whelan held the midfield together in his usual manner.

With 12 minutes gone, Parker's throw-in was touched on by Paul McGrath to former Evertonian, Kevin Richardson, whose right-foot volley passed narrowly wide. With 25 minutes gone Dalian Atkinson lifted the ball over Wright, before Grobbelaar dived to his left to pull off a fine save. Rob Jones operated on the left flank with Venison on the right, and the former Sunderland skipper constantly denied Dwight Yorke. Through the middle, Cyrille Regis and Dalian Atkinson were frustrated by Wright and Nicol. Villa were unable to link, sustain possession and drive the Liverpool defence to enforced errors.

With 67 minutes gone, Micky Thomas - the villain of the piece after scoring the goal which denied Liverpool the title in 1989 - put the finishing touch to a fine move involving Houghton, Whelan and Barnes, who released Thomas into the final quarter of the field. Thomas took his time and weighed up the options before clipping it beyond the despairing dive of Spink.

The visitors threatened after Steve Froggatt substituted and a 74th-minute free-kick from Richardson was headed away before Parker's right-foot drive was saved by Grobbelaar. Regis released Froggatt, but the youngster drove his cross wildly across goal and Atkinson was unable to stab the ball home.

Thomas said afterwards: "It was a great feeling, especially after I'd missed one a few minutes earlier. I'd hardly done any training since my hamstring injury and I think that showed." Souness praised the 30-year-old Whelan, who had fought back after three knee operations since August 29, when he was injured in a game against Everton. "He epitomises everything about this club. He has been out for the best part of a year, but he showed great character and every good thing there is in football. There was a big doubt about his career. After being out so long he was outstanding. I'm delighted to see him back and so are the Liverpool supporters. We are a different team now. It was an enormous gamble today - win or bust - but hopefully we will have more men back for the semi-final." Whelan added: "All along they said that medically there was nothing wrong with me but I felt there was something wrong and that's when I started to worry about it." Villa manager Ron Atkinson said: "We should have beaten them but my money is now on them to win the Cup."

Michael Thomas

Liverpool: Grobbelaar; Jones, Venison, Nicol, Whelan, Wright, Saunders, Houghton, Thomas (Mølby,85), Barnes, McManaman (Rosenthal,77).

Aston Villa: Spink; Blake(Kubicki,46), Staunton, Teale, McGrath, Richardson, Daley, Parker, Regis, Atkinson, Yorke(Froggatt,73).

Referee: Mr P. Don (Middlesex)

Attendance: 29,109

April 5, 1992

Liverpool (0) 1
Whelan 117

Portsmouth (0) 1 aet
Anderton 110

ON the day when Portsmouth Football Club celebrated the 94th anniversary of their formation, they gained a highly creditable 1-1 draw against Liverpool at Highbury. All the opposition that Pompey had dispatched from the FA Cup had worn red - Exeter, Leyton Orient, Middlesbrough and Nottingham Forest - and they fancied the scalp of Liverpool on their way to Wembley. Reduced to ten men through the injury of Steve McManaman, Liverpool clawed their way back from impending defeat to force a replay at Villa Park. As the teams came out for the kick-off, a sailor paraded a banner declaring "*Play Up Pompey!*" A cloud of ticker-tape flew into the air at the Portsmouth end, accompanied by thousands of blue-and-white balloons. A single red flare lit up the Liverpool end.

Kicking off at one o'clock, Portsmouth forced the early pace and almost scored after only three minutes when Mark Chamberlain shot wide. A tackle from Whelan forced Chamberlain out of the game after only ten minutes. In a thrilling first half McManaman teased the opposition and provided opportunities for Rush, Houghton and Barnes. Alan McLoughlin's fine positional sense almost brought a goal on three occasions. Firstly he hesitated before firing over from a Colin Clarke headed pass. With four minutes to go before the break, he drove a shot towards goal from inside the box but Grobbelaar saved spectacularly. From the resulting corner, McLoughlin's back-heel beat everyone except Ray Houghton, who was wisely covering and his goalline clearance was turned back by Clarke into the arms of Grobbelaar. Earlier Martin Kuhl had squandered a fine opportunity as Pompey belied their Second Division status. As the half-time whistle drew closer, Knight was forced to save from Whelan.

Venison replaced the injured Burrows at the interval. As the second half wore on, Portsmouth increased in confidence and caused Liverpool several problems. Substitute Warren Aspinall brought a great save from Grobbelaar and twice within the next few minutes, Liverpool showed their strength on the counter-attack. Andy Awford denied Rush at the near post from a Barnes cross before Knight blocked at the feet of Thomas after McManaman had surged upfield. The mercurial talent of McManaman was unable to fulfil its rich potential due to the lack of service he received. Thomas and Clarke might have settled the game in normal time, but the match finished goalless at the end of ninety minutes.

Rush headed over and also fired against the crossbar, and a long-range effort from Whelan was saved as Liverpool sought the opening goal. Portsmouth reasserted themselves and when Grobbelaar dropped a cross from Chris Burns, Nicol headed Clarke's header off the line. Portsmouth continued to enjoy the greater share of possession and always looked dangerous. An Anderton volley flew inches over the bar before he raced onto Neill's through-ball to slot the ball home beyond Grobbelaar just ten minutes from time. As the clock ticked way, Liverpool's season appeared to be over, but a late run by Nicol brought a free-kick against Awford. Barnes curled the 20-yard kick against the post. The ball fell to Whelan, who fired home for a dramatic equaliser.

In the other semi-final, Sunderland beat Norwich City 1-0 with a Byrne goal after 35 minutes.

Saturday April 4, 1992
~~~~~

In the middle of a General Election campaign Party Politics won the £125,000 Martell Grand National at Aintree today.

The eight-year-old, purchased only a few days ago for a reputed £80,000 by David Thompson for his wife Patricia, is a giant of a horse, the biggest in the 40-strong field, trained by Nick Gaselee at Upper Lambourn and ridden by Carl Llewellyn.

Party Politics, starting at 14-1, was followed home by the long-time leader, Romany King, who was just two and a half lengths adrift at the finish with the Irish challenger Laura's Beau a further 15 lengths away third and Docklands Express fourth.

1. Party Politics	**14-1**
2. Romany King	**16-1**
3. Laura's Beau	**12-1**
4. Docklands Express	**15-2 fav.**

Liverpool: Grobbelaar; Jones, Burrows(Venison,46), Nicol, Whelan, Wright, McManaman, Houghton (Marsh,88), Rush, Barnes, Thomas.

Portsmouth: Knight; Awford, Beresford, McLoughlin (Whittingham,108), Symons, Burns, Neill, Kuhl, Clarke, Chamberlain(Aspinall,10), Anderton.

Referee: Mr M. Bodenham (Looe, Cornwall)

Linesmen: Mr U.D. Rennie (Sheffield), red trim; Mr B.A. Wiggington (Bristol), yellow trim

Attendance: 41,869

Ronnie Whelan *celebrates his equalising goal against Portsmouth just three minutes from time*

May 13, 1992

Liverpool (0) 0

(Liverpool win 3-1 on penalties)

Portsmouth (0) 0 aet

FOR the first time in FA Cup history, a semi-final was decided on penalty kicks at the end of a gruelling encounter which finished goalless, but which contained several thrills. With manager Graeme Souness in hospital following a heart by-pass operation, the Reds gained a dramatic victory almost a year after Souness was installed as manager.

Portsmouth begun brightly and created the first genuine opportunity in the 12th minute when Darren Anderton raced onto Andy Awford's ball and lobbed narrowly wide of the target with Grobbelaar racing out of goal. Liverpool enjoyed the greater share of possession in the first half with their precision passing and more controlled football. Early on Knight held a Rush header under the crossbar from a Mølby free-kick and after fifteen minutes Thomas slipped the ball through to Saunders in the box, but Knight was alert and slid at the striker's feet, deflecting the shot into the air before Kit Symons cleared the danger. Thomas dived to head a Nicol centre wide of the target as Liverpool responded, and four minutes before the interval excellent covering from Burrows cut out a Beresford cross following a superb pass from Ray Daniel.

In the second half, Portsmouth stood off and allowed Liverpool to enjoy greater possession. After 50 minutes Barnes' short ball to Mølby was powerfully driven goalwards by the Dane, but Knight was equal to it. Portsmouth were restricted to counter-attacks, and Burrows denied the lurking Clarke with a decisive touch on a Beresford cross.

Burrows, in an uncustomary central defensive role, twice prevented substitute Guy Whittingham with fierce tackles before denying Anderton with great defensive work.

With 35 minutes gone, Beresford rescued the ball from the by-line to get in a centre to McLoughlin, whose shot crashed against the crossbar as Liverpool's defence remained flat-footed. In the final minute of normal time, Knight was adjudged to have handled outside his area. Barnes stepped back to take the kick, but he drove the ball at the wall.

In extra-time Saunders had two attempts on goal, the first was easily dealt with by Knight, but the second brought the goalkeeper to his knees. The Pompey keeper saved from Rush and then raced to the edge of his area to collect Beresford's short back-pass with Rush threatening.

Portsmouth began an offensive of their own and with Jones a victim of cramp, he managed to divert a Whittingham cross away from Beresford with Grobbelaar stranded. The game then moved into the drama of penalties.

Martin Kuhl missed the initial penalty, but Barnes, Rush and Saunders converted to earn a place in the final. Symons converted his penalty for Portsmouth.

John Barnes scores from the spot

Liverpool: Grobbelaar; Jones(Walters,117), Burrows, Nicol, Whelan(Venison,69), Wright, Saunders, Mølby, Rush, Barnes, Thomas.

Portsmouth: Knight; Awford, Beresford, McLoughlin (Aspinall,117), Symons, Burns, Neill, Kuhl, Clarke (Whittingham,73), Daniel, Anderton.

Referee: Mr M. Bodenham (Cornwall)

Attendance: 40,077

VICTORY OVER SUNDERLAND

SOUNESS ATTENDS FINAL

RUSH'S HISTORIC GOAL

Liverpool (0) 2 Sunderland (0) 0

Thomas 47,   Rush 67

DEFYING doctors' orders less than a month after a triple by-pass heart operation, Graeme Souness sat on the bench, orchestrating his side, but the 58-year-old coach Ronnie Moran led the Liverpool team out at Wembley against Second Division Sunderland, led by Malcolm Crosby, who was appointed a month before Sunderland's Cup run began. The Metropolitan police mounted a large crowd control operation with 800 London police officers on duty to handle the capacity 80,000 crowd.

The capital's police were assisted by colleagues from Merseyside and from Northumbria, while British Transport Police helped oversee the carriage of the travelling supporters.

Souness sat flanked by club physiotherapist Paul Chadwick, and doctor Bill Reid. The combined bands of the Lifeguards and The Blues and Royals played the National Anthem.

The Duchess of Kent, whose husband was the President of the Football Association, was introduced to the teams. Before taking her seat in the stands, she

moved towards Souness and offered him a few words of encouragement. Prior to the final, Sunderland lost their dependable defender John Kay. Crosby responded by dropping Paul Hardyman, who had played in all of the previous rounds. He moved Anton Rogan to left-back and packed his midfield in an attempt to force Liverpool to miss the power of Whelan.

Peter Davenport touched the ball to John Byrne in a re-taken kick-off. Liverpool opened up the Sunderland defence after just three minutes when Thomas

moved onto Houghton's through-ball but his shot sailed high over the bar. Most of Liverpool's early attacks involved Nicol, who got forward dangerously from left-back and almost made Steve McManaman redundant. A first-time shot by Rush was saved by Tony Norman, but from then on Sunderland began to gradually assert themselves.

The Wearsiders probed at Liverpool's aerial weakness in defence, and added to Liverpool's problems by moving the ball quickly and directly on the floor. A fierce shot from Kevin Ball skimmed dangerously off the wet surface, and Grobbelaar did well to scramble to his near post and turn the ball round. Former Evertonian Paul Bracewell, in an attempt to avoid his fourth losers' medal, worked prodigiously in midfield and calmed events down.

Volley

Byrne - who had scored in every round - miscued a volley from six yards out after Ball had headed a corner back to him, and fired in another shot which was off target.

Mølby became too casual inside his own penalty area and presented Bracewell with the ball, and only a last-second deflection by Wright sent the shot inches wide. Norman saved at full length from Saunders, before McManaman ran down the right in a dangerous manner before being stopped by Bracewell.

Penalty chance

A minute before the interval Bracewell took the legs from under the lively McManaman, and referee Philip Don waved play on, although the television replays later proved that it had been a genuine penalty chance.

McManaman - playing his first senior game since chipping a kneebone during the first semi-final against

Portsmouth - switched to the right flank after the break in the same way he had done in the victory over Bristol Rovers in the Fourth Round replay.

Goal

Two minutes into the second half, McManaman paved the way for Liverpool's opening goal. He threw off the challenge of Brian Atkinson and Gordon Armstrong before clipping a magnificent ball between three defenders for the unmarked Thomas, who let the ball bounce before hooking a right-foot shot into goal from 12 yards which Norman touched on its way into the roof of the net.

Dominate

Liverpool began to dominate as Sunderland lost belief in themselves. The earlier downpour gave way to Wembley sunshine as Liverpool began to flourish. Norman tipped a shot from Mølby over the bar. Saunders headed against the crossbar and the Reds increased the pressure. Thomas played a pass from Saunders into the path of Rush after 67 minutes and the Welshman stroked the ball home with the inside of his right foot for a record fifth goal in FA Cup finals.

A long-range lob from Houghton eluded the net, and Saunders had an effort

Ian Rush and
Steve McManaman
celebrate

Liverpool: Grobbelaar; Jones, Burrows, Nicol, Mølby, Wright, Saunders, Houghton, Rush, McManaman, Thomas.

Sunderland: Norman; Owers, Ball, Bennett, Rogan, Rush(Hardyman,69), Bracewell, Davenport, Armstrong (Hawke,77), Byrne, Atkinson.

Referee: Mr P. Don (Middlesex)

Linesmen: Mr R.J. Harris (Oxford); Mr J. Hilditch (Staffordshire).   **Reserve**: Mr K. Morton (Bury St.Edmunds)

Attendance: 79,544 (at Wembley)

by Norman as Sunderland's Wembley dream evaporated.

In Scotland, Rangers beat Airdrie 2-1 at Hampden Park to clinch the League and Cup double for the first time in fourteen years.

Mix - up

Mark Wright climbed the steps at Wembley to receive the Cup from the Duchess of Kent. There was a mix-up in the presentation of the medals at the end of the game, with Sunderland being presented with the winners' medals.

The medals had been given to the Duke of Kent for presentation by Graham Kelly, the F.A. Chief Executive. Ronnie Moran said after the final: "Our passing wasn't sharp enough in the first half and, give credit to Sunderland, they had a couple of chances to score. I thought they played well."

Cigars

"I even thought they might have had a penalty but then right on half-time we could have had one too, so it evens itself out. Once we got the break in the second half, we were on our game. But we never eased up because you need a third goal before you can get the cigars out."

Opposite:

Liverpool captain **Mark Wright** *holds aloft the FA Cup which he has just received from the* **Duchess of Kent**

January 3, 1993

Bolton Wanderers (2) 2
McGinlay 7, Seagraves 22

Liverpool (0) 2
Winstanley 56 (og), Rush 82

BOLTON, of the Barclays League Second Division, had gone 14 games without defeat and were lying in seventh place in the table. Liverpool were eleventh in the Premier League. The overnight temperature in Greater Manchester was -6.5C, which improved to -3C by kick-off time. The pitch remained half-frozen despite the undersoil heating, which had been in place for twelve years at Burnden Park. Last season, under the management of former Liverpool player, Phil Neal, Bolton went close to putting Southampton out of the cup. The fair-haired Scot, John McGinlay, was signed by present manager Bruce Rioch from Millwall for £100,000 and he formed an incisive partnership with former Celtic striker, Andy Walker.

Bolton's attitude and their first-half performance were of the highest order, and they caused Liverpool enormous problems right from the kick-off, and they went into an early lead after just seven minutes. The former Derby player, Scott Green, beat Stig Bjørnebye, Liverpool's Norwegian import. Green's cross enabled McGinlay to side-foot the ball past the advancing Hooper. McGinlay and Walker were in excellent form, and the Liverpool defence panicked. Torben Piechnik and Mike Hooper did not form an understanding, and with 20 minutes gone, McGinlay's shot struck a post, and David Lee failed to make use of the rebound.

With 22 minutes gone, Seagraves arrived to head home Patterson's corner after Tony Kelly had nodded on. Nine minutes later Hooper blocked at Walker's feet, and later parried the striker's drive.

Liverpool missed the suspended Jamie Redknapp in central midfield, but soon replaced Michael Thomas with Ronnie Rosenthal, the Israeli international, in the second period. Within three minutes, Rosenthal picked up a deflection and ran clear of Bolton's central defenders before hitting the post with his fierce drive, but the ball rebounded to Mark Winstanley and the defender put the ball into his own net.

The goal gave Liverpool fresh hope, and restricted Bolton to a shot from Brown and a close effort from McGinlay. The Reds attacked relentlessly in search of an equalising goal, and Rush had a shot turned aside by Branagan.

Eight minutes from time, Seagraves sliced his back-pass and McManaman seized on the ball. Branagan blocked at the feet of the Liverpool winger, but Rush - the goal poacher supreme - was on hand to slot home the goal which took him closer to Denis Law's record of FA Cup goals.

After the game, Bolton manager Bruce Rioch said, "I enjoyed the game and I think the players did but it is tinged with disappointment. If you play against Liverpool and afterwards you have that feeling, you know you've done well. We started very well. We might have had a third and fourth goal. The first half was excellent for us and at that stage we still felt we had a good chance of winning the game. The goals were unfortunate. We were not able to keep the momentum going in the second half, but we're very pleased with what we've done. It's nice to go back to a big club and we'll look forward to the replay. If we create chances, we've got people who can score. It's obviously more difficult for us now because Liverpool will be on their own pitch."

Graeme Souness said, "When you go two goals down on that sort of tricky pitch you do wonder if you are going out of the Cup."

Ronnie Rosenthal

Bolton Wanderers: Branagan; Brown, Burke, Lee, Seagraves, Winstanley, Green, Kelly, Walker, McGinlay, Patterson.

Liverpool: Hooper; Marsh, R.Jones, Nicol, Piechnik, Bjørnebye, McManaman, Hutchison, Rush, Barnes, Thomas(Rosenthal,53),

Referee: Mr R. Groves (Weston-Super-Mare)

Attendance: 21,502

January 13, 1993

Liverpool (0) 0   Bolton Wanderers (1) 2
McGinlay 3, Walker 78

BOLTON scored after just three minutes and left Liverpool chasing shadows throughout the game. Mike Marsh, the midfield player, was at right-back, Rob Jones, the right-back, was at left-back, and left-back Stig Inge Bjørnebye, was played at centre-half in a team which lacked cohesion and understanding. David Lee, the 25-year-old signed from Southampton last month, gave Marsh a torrid time, and in the second half, Jones was despatched to the right wing in an attempt to contain the threat of Lee.

Lee slipped past Marsh in the third minute to get in a cross which was met by McGinlay, who headed home. With 15 minutes gone, Ronnie Rosenthal almost scored an equaliser, but his shot from close range was blocked by Branagan's legs. Lee was in mercurial form for Bolton, despite being unable to command a regular first-team place. He created havoc down Liverpool's right wing, and Walker's effort was blocked by Hooper.

With 33 minutes gone, Seagraves put Rosenthal in the clear, but the Israeli forward shot wide. Moments later Marsh was booked for another foul as his frustration grew at receiving a drubbing from Lee. Soon afterwards Rosenthal and Tony Kelly also went into the book. With the interval approaching, Lee shot wide.

In the second period, Souness switched Marsh and Jones in an attempt to deny Lee. With 52 minutes gone, Thomas was carried off clutching a damaged Achilles. He was replaced by Don Hutchison.

Twelve minutes from time, McGinlay's cross was headed home by Walker to complete Liverpool's misery.

After the game, Liverpool manager Graeme Souness said, "We were outplayed and outfought by a better team. They deserved to win and they were better than us in all departments. This club's history is based on, and steeped in, passion. The vast majority of players out there played as if they have never been told what passion or Liverpool Football Club is all about." Bolton's manager, Bruce Rioch, said, "It's a great night for the team and all my players. You will never get me saying anything detrimental about anybody at Liverpool Football Club."

F.A. CUP
THIRD ROUND

Cambridge U.	(0)	1	**Sheffield Wed.**	(0)	2
Heathcote 50	*7,754*		*Harkes 55, Bright 57*		
Leicester City	(0)	2	**Barnsley**	(1)	2
Thompson (pen) 66,			*Whitlow (og) 27,*		
Oldfield 78	*19,137*		*Redfearn 62*		
Middlesbrough	(0)	2	**Chelsea**	(0)	1
Wright 72,			*Mohan (og) 70*		
Falconer 82	*16,776*				
Norwich City	(0)	1	**Coventry City**	(0)	0
Beckford 47	*15,301*				
Southend United	(1)	1	**Millwall**	(0)	0
Collymore 6	*8,028*				

Replays

Charlton Athletic	(0)	1	**Leeds United**	(1)	3
Pitcher (pen) 87			*Speed 3, Garland (og) 59,*		
	8,337		*McAllister 89*		
Huddersfield T.	(1)	2	**Gillingham**	(0)	1
Robinson 21,			*Green (pen) 54*		
Dunn 56	*5,144*				
Reading	(0)	0	**Manchester C.**	(2)	4
			Sheron 3, Holden 32,		
	12,065		*Flitcroft 68, Quinn 71*		

Liverpool: Hooper; Marsh, Jones, Stewart, Piechnik, Bjørnebye, Walters, Redknapp, Rosenthal, Barnes, Thomas (Hutchison,52).

Bolton Wanderers: Branagan; Brown, Burke, Lee, Seagraves, Winstanley, Green, Kelly, Walker, McGinlay, Patterson.

Referee: Mr R. Groves (Weston-super-Mare)

Attendance: 34,790

Postscript
by
Alan Robinson
Referee 1986 Final

Postscript
by
Alan Robinson
Referee 1986 Final

ON Cup Final weekend we read and see much of the happenings concerning the players of both teams, but very little of the referee and linesmen.

This is quite right that the concentration should be made on the stars of the game, for they are centre stage, performing their talents to the world. The officials wish to keep a low profile, and allow the heroes of the supporters to do battle for the most coveted club trophy in the history of football.

Having achieved the ambition of a lifetime, many people have enquired how I spent my Wembley weekend, and I thought it might be interesting to relate the sequence of events.

Gwen, my wife, and I left our Waterlooville home during the Friday morning to ensure we would be on time at the hotel to greet the other officials. I knew Allan Gunn (senior linesman) and Chris Topliss (reserve linesman) very well from a long association with both, but had never before come into contact with Robbie Hart, the other linesman.

Since the appointment, I had been in regular telephonic communication with them all, and my feelings were confirmed that once we were all together, everyone gelled as one happy family team.

Reg Paine, the Referees' Officer of the Football Association, called to pay our fee and expenses. Incidentally, the fee was £50, exactly the same as any League match. (The fee is currently £160.) He brought with him the newly designed linesman's flags to be used the next day. These were duly tried out, because I wanted my colleagues to be comfortable with this new invention where a sleeve bearing the flag rotates about the shaft.

On Friday evening, we were honoured at the "Eve of Final" rally. This is a gathering of over 300 referees, who pay tribute to their colleagues so privileged the following day. The evening is hosted by the London Society, and after cabaret and speeches, Peter Willis, the National R.A. President, presented magnificent plaques to mark the occasion.

After the closure proceedings we spent the next hour autographing copies of the official programme.

Following a restless night the morning of May 10th was damp and miserable, but the weather could never dampen our spirits on such a day. Together with our wives we duly reported to the F.A. Offices at Lancaster Gate at 10.45am. Minor formalities were completed and it was off on the drive to Wembley, and as we entered the Stadium there were good wishes from many fans.

After placing our kit in the dressing room, we walked across the VIP restaurant and by now the sun was setting its seal on that magnificent day. It was interesting to note the final preparations, such as brushing the red carpet from the Royal Box to the edge of the pitch, washing down adverts, television cameras being aligned, and stewards gathered together eating packed lunches before reporting to their posts. Naturally I could not eat much, in fact just a fruit cocktail. We then took a look out from the balcony beneath the famous towers. Even with the thousands making their way to the entrances it was amazing to be able to spot some friends and relations.

Next port of call was the actual playing area to inspect virtually every blade of grass and the goal nets. This allowed us to soak up the atmosphere which was so important in settling down the pre-match nerves.

On return to the dressing room, we were delighted to see many telemessages, cards and letters awaiting us. Such kind thoughts really gave one a lift, knowing such support was around you.

After changing, the team captains and managers came in with team sheets, and I explained a few points on law interpretation, especially with respect to goalkeepers parrying the ball down to their advantage. When they had departed I briefly repeated my instructions to the linesmen, which we had dealt with in detail earlier in the day.

At the right time we were summoned to the tunnel and on emerging at the entrance the noise was deafening. As we walked out together, I could hardly hear the words exchanged with Allan Gunn alongside me. A truly wonderful moment to savour. It was essential that we tried to enjoy and remember every detail.

With the formal presentations to the Duchess of Kent over, I set the game in motion. Fortunately, it went very smoothly with only one controversial incident to speak of. During the first half, Sharp of Everton and Nicol of Liverpool clashed in the Reds' penalty area, with both finishing on the ground. The Everton forward claimed a penalty, but I would have none of it. I was close to the action, with a perfect view, and as both appeared to be going for the ball, with absolutely no intent of fouling. I gave my decision honestly, and I wonder if both these players were frank with each other if they discussed the incident when on World Cup duty for Scotland that summer. The rest of the game is now history, with Liverpool exerting their authority to win 3-1 and achieve the 'Double'.

Then it was the climb up those 39 steps to collect my gold medal: words of congratulations from both sets of supporters and dignitaries, including the Duchess. Following normal procedure, the match ball was given to the winning captain, but knowing it was my last game in the top flight, Alan Hansen very kindly presented it to me. With the champagne flowing, suddenly sadness hit me for this was the absolute finish of my career.

Eventually, we changed back into our blazers and flannels and made our way to reunite with our wives and proudly show off our medals. On leaving the Stadium a quick interview was given to the local press, and it was farewell to the Mecca of our game.

The evening was spent being entertained by The Football Association at a top class night club where Jack Jones, the American singer, topped the bill. The mood we were in, nobody was in any rush to get to bed as we reminisced over that memorable day.

After a few hours sleep, the next morning was taken with a casual walk along the Bayswater Road and Green Park, and following lunch we said our farewells. I returned home feeling both mentally and physically tired, but very satisfied in my own mind. The players and spectators had been a credit to the game and that was the thing that really mattered.

SUBSCRIBERS

Presentation Copies

1 Liverpool Football Club
2 Tommy Smith, M.B.E.
3 The Football Association
4 The Association of Football Statisticians

5 Brian Pead	28 Marko Melolinna	51 Elizabeth Pyke
6 Neil Cowland	29 A. C. Jones	52 Siôn Woodward
7 Ian Roberts	30 Bryan Jones	53 Richard Frankcam
8 Jacqui Roberts	31 Steven Kelly	54 Trevor C. Jenkins
9 Ian Walker	32 Keith Stanton	55 Jendrik Gamböck
10 Janet Walker	33 Martin Stewart	56 Paul Martin
11 Alan Robinson	34 Jennifer Morgan	57 John Harris
12 Christopher Wood	35 Jo Bowman	58 Iain Alasdair Watt
13 Mark Hedworth Golledge	36 Ian Tilley / When Sunday Comes	59 T. McKinlay, Liverpool Supporters Club
14 Colin Cameron	37 Bernie Maher	60 G. Strong
15 Torbjørn Flatin	38 Paul Crewe	61 Dave Perks
16 Pål Møller	39 John B. Richardson	62 G.T. Allman
17 Sorrel Pead	40 Cliff Sorrell	63 A.T. Reason
18 Peter Macey	41 Jim Gardiner	64 R. Watson
19 Ray Spiller	42 Elaine Bates	65 G.R. Hughes
20 Sue Burgess	43 Per Knudsen	66 Sue Palin
21 Alan Cowland	44 David R. Moores	67 Robert Crabb
22 Frank Cowland	45 S.G.V. Reakes	68 Brendan Oxlade
23 Janet Cowland	46 Brian R. Phillips	69 Fiona Lumley
24 Lee Gadd	47 Gordon A.E. Williams	70 Jim Veal
25 Douglas J. Pennell	48 Colin Paul Williams	71 Vince Brooks
26 Tony Reidy	49 Barry J. Hugman	72 P. Bland
27 Jonny Stokkeland	50 Elizabeth Pyke	73 John Edward Martin

74	George Harold Gerrard	112	Adam Chamberlain	150	Gerard Scully
75	Nigel John Palmer	113	Ian McGinnigle	151	Filippo Rossi
76	Carlton Strickland Sutton	114	Christopher McCormick, Junior	152	Ronnie Christopher Dewhurst
77	Shaun J.T. Wilde	115	Neil Stephens	153	John J. Pearman
78	Len Font	116	W. Menagh	154	Sverre André Grand
79	R.W. Thompson	117	W. Menagh	155	Nicholas Reynolds
80	D.G. West	118	George Coffey	156	Steve A. Waters
81	Anthony Shaw	119	Stan Henderson	157	David Houlgate
82	Geoff Walker	120	Ola Helgedagsrud	158	J.P. Jackson
83	Robert Walsh	121	F.F. Davies	159	Graham P. Kelly
84	Greg Murphy	122	Martin John Taylor	160	Alex J. Brown
85	Gary Richards	123	Roy Hollister	161	J.J. Morgan
86	Miss J.D. McIntyre	124	Trevor Hollister	162	David Toole
87	George James Smith	125	Joseph Williams	163	Ray Carroll
88	Alan G. Gaskin	126	Anthony Horton	164	Alastair James Byron
89	Peter G. Gaskin	127	F.J. Fazackerley	165	Peter Russell
90	Christopher Scott	128	Joseph A. Snellgrove	166	Ken Russell
91	J. Fisher	129	K.L. Cundle	167	Carl Stephen Shaw
92	E. Sixsmith	130	Einar Kvande	168	M. Davies
93	A.E. Newton	131	K.A. Stewart	169	Donald Keith Graham
94	K.F. Stewart	132	K.A. Stewart	170	J.W. Lawrenson
95	Barry Conway	133	Alan J. Maloney	171	M. Cringle
96	H.A. Johnson	134	Robert Storry	172	Colin Deakin
97	Thomas Hurst, Senior	135	Graham Tyson	173	Brian Bradley
98	Paul Taylor	136	John O. Morgan	174	Roger Clegg
99	Nicholas Robert Lester	137	Anthony Putt	175	Brian Currie
100	Carl van Breemen	138	David Gant	176	Thomas John Evans
101	Sheldon F. Collins	139	Peter Dybell	177	Joseph McCready
102	Trond Shult Ulriksen	140	Stephen Flanagan	178	Adrian William Killen
103	Paul Rooney	141	Caroline Gillian Tasker	179	Ian R. Wilkins
104	Anne McCullough	142	David Saw	180	Eugene A. MacBride
105	Robert John Durham	143	Stephen Murphy	181	D.A. Lambert
106	Maldwyn Owen Jones	144	John F. Rankin	182	Kenneth Sidney Davis
107	J.M. Foulds	145	Ian Clarke	183	John Davies
108	Tom Sheridan	146	B.G. McAndrew	184	Leif Kåre Larsen
109	Jim Cooke	147	John Joseph Coyle	185	J.J. Price
110	Alan Humphreys	148	Martin J. Hearn	186	Alec Kenneth Robinson
111	Paul Garner	149	Cliff Jackson	187	Derek N. Harrison

188	Mark S.H. Smith	226	N.A. Mellish	264	Kjetil Tørring
189	Leslie Stewart Cates	227	Edward Doran	265	Jason & Shaun Pead
190	Gary Dredge	228	John White	266	Arild Hafsås
191	Roy Foster	229	Robert W. Atkinson	267	Sue Pool
192	Sara Ferris	230	William A. Rankin	268	Robin Gowers
193	Jessica Ferris	231	David George Eccleston	269	Torgeir Vindenes
194	F.W. Kearns	232	Fred J. Eccleston	270	Simon Welsh
195	Ralph Quigley	233	Paul A. Eccleston	271	Ben Lawrence
196	Gary Watson	234	John P. Kenny	272	Steve Entwistle
197	Roger H. Fredriksen	235	Sigfús Guttormsson	273	Ian Hoodless
198	Mick Bailey	236	Nigel Howe	274	Geoff Bacon
199	Sandra J. Ireland	237	Cian Malcolm Loftus	275	Maurice & Dave Cox
200	David Plumbley	238	Kjell Haugen	276	Paul Thune
201	Graham Neaves	239	Alan Hindley	277	Ketil Thomassan
202	P.A. Read	240	Paul Whalen	278	Simon Jacobs
203	D. Williams	241	Paul Molyneux	279	Egil Andresen
204	L. Hanlon	242	Les Jackson	280	Colin Mason
205	Donna M.L. Morrison	243	Gerry Furey	281	Bill Belsham
206	Peter White	244	Doug Heggie	282	Graham Bilke
207	Peter Bryson	245	Gavin Shaw	283	Trevor Cook
208	Jon Bryson	246	P. McCombs	284	Graham Dean
209	James Griffiths	247	Charlie Mallia	285	Andrea Pennell
210	Bernie McLachlan	248	Stephen Rose	286	Mike Chubb
211	Robert McCormick	249	Peter J. Traynor	287	Natalie Ide
212	J. Blundell	250	Keith Wilkinson	288	Geir Bratteli
213	G. Kendall	251	John W. Marston	289	John Taylor
214	Stephen James Rose	252	Robert John Roberts	290	Trond Skjærstad
215	Ian Kelly	253	Rónán Barrett	291	André Øien
216	Samantha Hill	254	Chr. Knuth-Winterfeld	292	Peter Arvidsson
217	Roar Strande	255	Robert Duan	293	Jan Borgeraas
218	Geir Kittelsrud	256	Donald V. Adamson	294	Andy Marsden
219	George Thelwell	257	Mark Paul Williams	295	Michael Overton
220	Mike Lijinsky	258	Bjay Green	296	Gerry Packman
221	Steve 'Scouse' Roberts	259	Peter S. Walsh	297	J. Ringrose
222	J. Riding	260	Dominic Winship	298	G. Eric Brown
223	Gary Oyitch	261	D.A. McDowall	299	Johnston Kirkpatrick
224	David M. Andrews	262	Keith & Susan Blayze	300	John Cowland
225	David Humphreys	263	Thomas Kjærland		**Limited Edition Subscribers**

ILLUSTRATIONS

Each illustration in this book is available in a Limited Edition of 500 black and white prints. Each print will be numbered and signed by the artist. The unframed illustrations are available in A5 size at £8.99 each picture, or £80.00 for a set of ten. Some of the illustrations are also available in A4 size at £12.99 each picture, or £120.00 per set of ten. These are indicated in bold type on the following pages.

Further details upon request from

Neil Cowland,
Champion Press, P.O. Box 284, Sidcup, Kent, DA15 8JY

ILLUSTRATIONS

Kevin Keegan		392	Jimmy Melia	366	Alan Robinson	522
Kevin Keegan		396	Arthur Metcalfe	109	Fred Rogers	229
Kevin Keegan		404	John Miller's medal	1	Ronnie Rosenthal	521
Ray Kennedy		424	Tom Miller	148	Ian Ross	352
King George V		131	Gordon Milne	310	James Ross	8
King George VI		273	Jan Mølby	499	Ian Rush & Paul Walsh	458
Billy Lacey		111	**Jan Mølby**	511	Ian Rush	461
Billy Lacey		122	John Molyneux	297	Ian Rush	486
Chris Lawler		318	Bobby Moore	317	Ian Rush & John Aldridge	489
Tommy Lawrence		313	**Phil Neal**	452	**Ian Rush**	491
Mark Lawrenson		438	Ernest Needham	35	**Ian Rush**	500
Mark Lawrenson		454	Mike Newell	468	Ian Rush & Steve McManaman	517
Tommy Lawton		262	**Steve Nicol & Ian Rush**	493	Ian St.John	315
Sammy Lee		429	**Steve Nicol**	503	Ian St.John & Roger Hunt	333
Henry Lewis		138	Berry Nieuwenhuys	217	Bill Salisbury	193
Reg Lewis		274	Ronald Orr	92	Percy Saul	90
Billy Liddell		281	Fred Pagnam	133	**Dean Saunders**	506
Billy Liddell		290	**Bob Paisley**	264	Roy Saunders	292
Alec Lindsay & Kevin Keegan		395	Bob Paisley	271	**Elisha Scott**	135
John Lindsay		195	Bob Paisley	280	Elisha Scott	215
George Livingstone		59	Bob Paisley & Tommy Smith	431	John Shafto	232
Nat Lofthouse		283	Bob Paisley	396	Bill Shankly	248
Ephraim Longworth		100	Jack Parkinson	65	**Bill Shankly**	334
Ephraim Longworth		158	E. Partridge	150	Bill Shankly	386
James McBride		5	Jimmy Payne	277	Bill Sahnkly	395
John McConnell		95	Ernest Peake	107	Jackie Sheldon	140
Kevin MacDonald		447	H.J. Pearce	105	Peter Shilton	358
Kevin MacDonald		453	H. Pearson	155	Peter Shilton	391
James McDougall		203	J.H. Peddie	32	Danny Shone	172
John McKenna		177	David Pratt	184	Cyril Sidlow	260
Donald McKinlay		142	Alex Raisbeck	55	Smith, Huddersfield	146
McLaren		164	Alex Raisbeck	76	Tommy Smith	324
Steve McMahon		501	Archie Rawlings	175	Tommy Smith & McLintock	375
Steve McManaman		508	Bill Rawlings	175	**Tommy Smith**	408
Joe McQue		14	Sam Raybould	61	Graeme Souness	414
Matt McQueen		10	W.G. Richardson	211	Graeme Souness	430

Neville Southall	**504** Peter Thompson	**328** Ronnie Whelan	**488**
Alan Stevenson	**381** Peter Thompson	**338** **Ronnie Whelan**	**514**
Willie Stevenson	**327** Phil Thompson	**383** Thomas Wilkie	**18**
James Stewart	**96** Phil Thompson	**419** Ray Wilkins	**495**
Harry Storer	**34** John Toshack	**389** Charlie Wilson	**144**
Geoff Strong	**360** **John Toshack, Kevin Keegan**	**400** **Mark Wright**	**518**
Albert Stubbins	**253** Barry Venison	**467** Vic Wright	**225**
Albert Stubbins	**257** E.J. Vinall	**228** John Wyllie	**2**
Brian Talbot	**432** James Walsh	**166** Ron Yeats	**322**
Jack Taylor	**53** Paul Walsh	**451** **Ron Yeats**	**334**
Phil Taylor	**237** John Wark	**449**	
Clive Thomas	**407** Alfred West	**68**	
Michael Thomas	**512** Ronnie Whelan	**450**	

CHAMPION PRESS
P.O. BOX 284
SIDCUP
KENT
DA15 8JY

TEL: 081-302-6446